SOCIOLOGY
IN A CHANGING WORLD

HARCOURT BRACE JOVANOVICH, INC.

Forth Worth   Philadelphia   San Diego   New York

Orlando   Austin   San Antonio

Toronto   Montreal   London   Sydney   Tokyo

SOCIOLOGY
IN A CHANGING WORLD

Second Edition

William Kornblum

City University of New York,
Graduate School and University Center

In collaboration with
Carolyn D. Smith

Publisher: Ted Buchholz
Acquisitions Editor: Chris Klein
Developmental Editor: Meera Dash
Project Editor: Mike Hinshaw
Production Manager: Annette Dudley Wiggins
Art & Design Supervisor: Vicki McAlindon Horton
Text Design: Miriam Smith
Cover Design: Vicki McAlindon Horton
Cover Illustration: John Craig

Library of Congress Cataloging-in-Publication Data

Kornblum, William.
    Sociology in a changing world / William Kornblum in collaboration
with Carolyn D. Smith. — 2nd ed.
      p.   cm.
    Includes index.
    ISBN0-03-030993-X
    1. Sociology.   I. Smith, Carolyn D.   II. Title.
HM51.K66   1991
301—dc20   90-5299
                                           CIP

Address for Editorial Correspondence
Harcourt Brace Jovanovich, Inc., 301 Commerce Street, Suite 3700, Fort Worth,
TX 76102

Address for Orders
Harcourt Brace Jovanovich, Inc., 6277 Sea Harbor Drive, Orlando, FL 32887
1-800-782-4479, or 1-800-433-0001 (in Florida)

Printed in the United States of America

2 3 4   061   9 8 7 6 5 4

Harcourt Brace Jovanovich, Inc.
The Dryden Press
Saunders College Publishing

To Susan,
my partner in the Great Adventure,
& Morris Janowitz,
my mentor

PREFACE

The more I study, teach, and do research in sociology, the more I love the subject. No other area of intellectual work overlaps with so many other fields of knowledge; none straddles the sciences and the humanities so squarely or offers such varied insights into the vexing questions of our own time. It is out of this conviction that I undertook the demanding task of creating and revising this book. My greatest hope is that it will convey the excitement of sociological discovery and move its readers to take more advanced courses in the field.

Throughout the world, sociology is taking on new importance in ways that were only beginning to appear when the first edition of *Sociology in a Changing World* was being written. Major, often tumultuous changes are creating an ever-increasing demand for scientific description and analysis of human behavior. The revolutionary changes in Eastern Europe and the Soviet Union, the new awareness of the severity of social problems in our own society, and the growing crisis in the global environment are some of the most dramatic situations that sociology now addresses. There is also growing recognition that information has become a key source of wealth and power. In consequence, sociological concepts and methods are being applied with increasing frequency throughout the major institutions of modern societies. The study of sociology is attracting a far more diverse student population than was true when the field was little more than an academic specialty. *Sociology in a Changing World* therefore is designed not only to meet the requirements of the standard introductory course but also to address recent changes in the discipline, the students, and the work of sociologists.

This book is designed for the basic introductory course, but I hope its emphasis on the frontiers of sociological research and its combination of classic and new research will make it a useful reference source for students to carry with them through more advanced social-science courses. One major way in which *Sociology in a Changing World* differs from other sociology texts is in its consistent focus on issues of social change. Moreover, it is not slanted toward one or another perspective, ideological or methodological; rather, it presents ample evidence of the strengths and weaknesses of the interactionist, functionalist, and conflict approaches to the explanation and prediction of social change. In addition, it has a stronger grounding in demographic, ecological, and historical methods than is found in existing comprehensive texts. And throughout the text an effort is made to strike a balance between the use of comparative and historical material and research based on American culture and the social changes that have occurred and are occurring today in the United States.

While I was writing the first edition, I brought the manuscript to my students at Queens College of the City University of New York. I wanted them to use the book and to criticize the manuscript as I was revising it. Some of the students were young undergraduates, tired of college textbooks whose content and design reminded them of high school books. Others were older adults going back to school after many years in the "real world"; they were distinctly wary of sociological platitudes. All wanted clear information about how sociology could matter in their professional and personal lives. Most were avid critics. They pointed out numerous places where concepts were not presented clearly enough or where their interest flagged. On the other hand, their enthusiasm for the theme of social change and the concept of the sociological imagination was evident. They found that these ideas applied in many concrete ways to their own interests and aspirations. The value of observing a changing world with a sociological eye quickly became real to them.

Later I used the first edition in teaching the introductory course at Queens College and thus had a chance to test the finished text under normal classroom conditions. The students tended to appreciate the comparative material in the text but also indicated a preference for a bit more emphasis on current social issues, a suggestion I have tried to incorporate in this revision. Students did not have any trouble with the separation between the chapters on social stratification and social class. The earlier placement of the chapter on stratification allows for greater emphasis on inequality and life chances in the discussion of deviance and collective behavior. Nevertheless, in this revision I have tried to make these chapters stand alone more solidly so that the instructor can vary the order of presentation as desired.

I hope that both instructors and students will be able to benefit from the strengths of this book. After the first edition appeared, I had the benefit of much criticism from my graduate students and professional colleagues at the City University and elsewhere. I have tried to use their comments and suggestions wherever possible and appropriate. I know, also, that any book can be improved. Like my students and colleagues, you will undoubtedly have ideas about improvements that might be made in future editions. Please feel free to send your ideas or comments to me at the CUNY Graduate School, 33 West 42nd St., New York, NY 10036.

HIGHLIGHTS OF THE SECOND EDITION

I n revising the text I have focused on three broad areas of concern. The first, in keeping with the theme of the book, is social change. This edition contains much material on the revolutionary change occurring in Eastern Europe and the Soviet Union. A new section in the chapter on social change is devoted to the ecological, cultural, and institutional impact of war. The chapter itself has been moved from the end of the book to a location at its center, where it serves to round out the section on social dynamics and introduce some of the concepts that are emphasized in the last two sections of the book. The chapter on population growth and urbanization has also been moved to an earlier location in order to give greater prominence to the importance of these large-scale trends in generating social change.

Another area that has received special attention in this edition is the interactionist perspective in sociology. I have taken a more inclusive view of this perspective, focusing on rational-choice theory as well as on symbolic interactionism. A new section on principles of interaction is included in the chapter on interaction in groups, and interactionist concepts like the free-rider problem and the bystander effect are addressed throughout the text.

Social problems in the United States are not only growing more serious but also attracting much greater public attention and concern. Accordingly, in this edition I have included more material on contemporary social problems such as AIDS, teenage pregnancy, and corporate crime. I have also added a new feature, "Challenges to Contemporary Society," that discusses research and policy with respect to several prominent issues on today's public-policy agenda.

DISTINCTIVE FEATURES

S ociology in a Changing World differs from its competitors primarily in its emphasis on social change. Throughout, the book highlights the tension between attempts to modify social institutions and efforts to maintain traditional modes of behavior. The text also tries to point out the unanswered questions on the frontiers of social-scientific research and the challenges facing American society today. The following are some of the special features that incorporate this teaching philosophy:

- Opening vignettes, some fictional, some based on classic sociological writings, some from recent literature, but all illustrating the questions to be addressed in the chapter.
- Boxes within the chapters: these, like the vignettes, highlight crucial points or feature important studies or research traditions.
- "Visual Sociology," a photo essay in each chapter that shows how sociologists analyze photographs or other visual material as part of their research.
- "Frontiers of Sociology," a major feature that appears in about half of the chapters and discusses current research in subject areas covered in the chapter, relating it to applied research and policy issues.
- "Challenges to Contemporary Society"— a major feature on research and public policy regarding important contemporary issues, including serious social problems in the United States today.
- Chapter summary—a thorough but concise rendering of the critical concepts and relationships presented in the chapter.
- End-of-chapter glossary—students will not have to flip to the end of the book to review important terms and their definitions.
- "Where to Find It," a set of suggested readings that includes not only books and journal articles but also basic references and data sources.
- Key concepts—significant concepts discussed in the chapter are highlighted in the margins.
- A contemporary, mature design, which is a product of close cooperation between the designer (a leading magazine art director) and the author and editors, with the goal of integrating all aspects of the book's design with its content.

ORGANIZATION OF THE TEXT

In organizing the book, I resisted the temptation to perform radical surgery on the standard introductory sociology course. There are traditional approaches to the subject that deserve respect, such as presenting an overview of sociology and its history, introducing the basic research methods, examining the dimensions of social inequality, and including a series of chapters on major social institutions. But I have added to this solid, time-tested framework and in some cases have moved a chapter from its traditional position in an introductory text.

The first eleven chapters of the book set forth most of the concepts that any student needs to know and be able to use. This makes the book easy to adapt to courses of different length. In addition, the first three parts of the book introduce many of the basic sociological explanations of social stability and change. This means that topics such as social stratification and social movements are presented in the first half of the book rather than in later sections. Other fundamental concepts are also presented in these early chapters—community, social class, bureaucracy, urbanization, and many others. I refer repeatedly to these concepts in the second half of the book, rather than introducing them and then going on to entirely new material.

Another nontraditional aspect of the book's organization is the position of chapter 8, "Stratification and Social Mobility." This chapter introduces the concept of social stratification and shows how stratification systems have changed throughout human history. Chapters 9 and 10 deal primarily with reactions to stratification, whether those reactions take the form of deviant behavior and crime or of protests, social movements, and other kinds of collective behavior. The activities of deviant groups and social movements are a major source of change in stratification patterns. Thus the text proceeds from stratification to deviance and collective behavior in order to highlight significant dimensions of social change. A further analysis of stratification and social class is presented in Part IV, "Social Divisions."

SYNOPSIS

The book is divided into five parts. Part I, "Social Science," introduces the "human science" of sociology: Chapter 1 traces the history of sociology and introduces the major perspectives used by sociologists, and chapter 2 describes the methods used by sociologists in conducting their research. The chapters in Part II, "Social Structure," focus on some of sociology's most fundamental concepts. Chapter 3 introduces the elements of social structure; Chapter 4 discusses culture; and Chapter 5 explores the relationships among population growth, urbanization, and community. Part III, "Social Dynamics," covers many of the processes that seem to account for social stability and change. Chapter 6 discusses socialization; Chapter 7 examines the structure of groups and how people behave in groups of different kinds, and Chapter 8 introduces the concept of social stratification. Chapters 9 to 11 move from the structure and function of groups within a society to the processes that change societies. Chapter 9 deals with deviance; Chapter 10 examines collective behavior and social movements, phenomena that often bring about major changes in stratification systems, cultural norms, and social institutions; and Chapter 11 summarizes the ways in which sociologists think about and conduct research on the causes and consequences of social change.

The three chapters in Part IV, "Social Divisions," examine social inequality, particularly in American society. Chapter 12 deals with inequalities of social class, and Chapters 13 and 14 focus on social inequalities due to race, ethnicity, age, and gender. Part V, "Social Institutions," applies the concepts and perspectives discussed earlier in the book to an analysis of several major institutions. Chapter 15 explores the changing nature of the family; Chapter 16 introduces religion and Chapter 17 education and the communications media. Chapter 18 deals with economic institutions and Chapter 19 with political institutions; finally, Chapter 20 analyzes the institutions of science, technology, and medicine.

ANCILLARY PACKAGE

The second edition of *Sociology in A Changing World* is accompanied by an extensive, integrated ancillary package designed to augment students' understanding of sociology and offer instructors additional teaching aids and resources.

- The Annotated Instructor's Edition is the complete student version of the text with teaching hints printed in the margins. The margin annotations include discussion topics, examples, additional resources, keys to sociology overhead transparencies, films referred from the Instructor's Manual, and assignments from the workbook, *Using Your Sociological Imagination*.
- The Instructor's Manual includes lecture outlines, instructional goals, teaching suggestions that explain the distinctive features and central concepts of each chapter, topics for discussion, suggestions for using the charts and tables, a film guide, and sample assignments for the *SocialScene* software.
- The Study Guide provides students with a self-paced review of the text. Each chapter begins with an outline and learning objectives, followed by a fill-in-the-blank review, a matching exercise in which key terms are matched with their definitions, a self-test consisting of 15 multiple-choice and 5 true-false questions, and a short-answer section that requires the student to apply concepts presented in the text. Answers to the matching exercise and self-test are provided.
- The Study Guide for Non-Native Speakers, written by Eileen Roesler of the Intensive English Language Center at Wichita State University, offers assistance to students whose primary language is not English. It includes material from the text's other study guide, with additional vocabulary, reading strategies, cultural idioms, and other helpful units, including a glossary.
- The computerized study guide allows students to personalize their study program. With the publisher's new software, ExamTutor™, the student can answer questions from a single chapter to achieve specific learning objectives or answer randomly selected questions from any number of chapters. It is available in IBM and Macintosh versions.
- The workbook, *Using Your Sociological Imagination*, is designed to prompt students to think carefully about what they have learned in each chapter of the text. Several types of questions are included.

Some require the student to evaluate a recent event in sociological terms; some ask the student to refer to a table or chart; some encourage the student to think critically about concepts discussed in the text. The workbook contains five exercises per chapter, including one question based on the "Visual Sociology" section. The students receive the workbook shrink-wrapped free with a purchase of a new text.

- The Test Bank, prepared by Carol Boggs of the University of North Carolina at Charlotte, includes multiple-choice, true-false, and short-answer questions. Each chapter has approximately 150 questions and is page-referenced to the text.
- Computerized Test Bases are available in IBM, Macintosh, or Apple II format. The publisher's new ExaMaster™ software allows instructors to create tests using fewer keystrokes. Easy-to-follow screen prompts guide instructors step-by-step through test construction. ExaMaster™ provides three ways to create tests:

1. **EasyTest**™ allows users to create a test from a single screen. It compiles a test using the questions chosen from the database, or randomly selects questions based on instructor-specified parameters.
2. **FullTest**™ gives a range of options for test creation. With FullTest™, the instructor may

- □ select questions while previewing them on screen
- □ edit existing questions, or add personalized questions
- □ add or edit graphics (in MS-DOS version)
- □ link related questions, instructions, and graphics
- □ have questions randomly selected from a wider range of criteria
- □ create criteria on two open keys
- □ block specific questions from random selection
- □ print as many as 99 different versions of the same test and answer sheet.

3. **RequesTest**™ is for the instructor without access to a computer. By calling 1(800) 4-HRW-HLP, instructors can order tests that conform to their criteria. The publisher will compile the tests and either mail or fax them to the instructor within 48 hours.

- Gradebook Software is included with the IBM and Macintosh versions of ExaMaster. ExamRecord™, the publisher's gradebook program, allows instructors to record, curve, graph, and print grades. ExamRecord takes raw scores and converts them into grades by criteria set by the instructor. Users can set the curve they want, and can see the distribution of the grades in a bar graph or a plotted graph.
- *SocialScene*™ Software, an interactive software program developed by Stefan Savage and Dean Savage of Queens College, allows students to explore basic procedures of social-scientific data analysis using an actual data set taken from the General Social Survey of the National Opinion Research Center. The program is available for both Apple and IBM-compatible personal computers.

The Holt Software Support Line is open Monday through Friday, 9 A.M. to 4 P.M. Central Standard Time to answer questions about any of its computer programs. The number is 1(800) 4-HRW-HLP.

- Overhead Teaching Transparencies enhance classroom lectures with a collection of 50 full-color transparencies that illustrate sociological concepts. All contain brand-new information to supplement (not duplicate) material contained in the textbook.
- The Script to Accompany the Overhead Transparencies offers suggestions for effective use of the sociology transparencies. This manual includes a master list of the transparencies, suggested use, and an instructor's guide for each transparency.
- Video Modules are new to the second edition. Instructors can select from a variety of Sociology Video Modules developed from the Dallas County Community College

District television course in introductory sociology. The modules are short clips from the actual telecourse highlighting relevant subject matter. The television course is coordinated with the second edition of *Sociology in a Changing World*.

- The Video Instructor's Manual accompanies the new Video Modules and offers teaching goals, descriptions, suggested uses, and other helpful elements for each video segment.

The Sociology Newsletter is a semi-annual newsletter available to instructors using the second edition. The newsletter provides timely information instructors can share with their students and includes articles about issues and research of sociological interest.

ACKNOWLEDGMENTS

Creating the second edition of *Sociology in a Changing World* has been a great challenge and a real pleasure. The responses to the first edition were so favorable that the process of incorporating suggestions for improvement made it possible to revise the book without making drastic changes in the intent or the thematic core of the first edition. Many colleagues, friends, and professional associates who helped me on the first edition also lent their support and expertise to the preparation of the second edition.

Among the many people who continue to influence this project, my greatest debt by far is to my editor and collaborator Carolyn Smith. It was Carolyn who first encouraged me to take on this project, and when my resolve wavered, her faith in our ability to complete it sustained me. Carolyn has untangled my prose, agonized with me over reviewers' comments, and kept track of the endless details that go into creating a scholarly text. There is not one word in this book that she has not thought about; every page bears the stamp of her expertise. Guy Smith also has my gratitude for his supportiveness during the long and demanding revision process.

Another incentive for revising the text was the promise that Miriam Smith would once again create the design and layout. Miriam is the art director of *Newsday*'s Sunday magazine, and a prize-winning design artist. We all wanted a text that would integrate sociological ideas with the design and layout of the book. I hope you will agree that Miriam has helped us achieve an unusual merger of visual and textual material. I also want to thank my dear friends Gary Rogers, Ben Smith, and Margo Smith for helping and encouraging Miriam during the often stressful months of work on design and layout. A special thanks to Margo Smith for her professional camera work on some of the chapter openings.

My colleagues at the City University of New York were unstinting with their suggestions and advice. Although I cannot thank them all, I would be remiss not to publicly thank Vernon Boggs for his faith in my ability and his deep commitment to sociological research and education. Rolf Meyersohn has been heroic in his generosity with books and articles and words of encouragement. My colleague Charles Kadushin's intimate knowledge of the publishing world was invaluable on many occasions, as were Erol Ricketts' mastery of recent demographic and ecological research and the profound knowledge of social movements and class theory shared by Stanley Aronowitz, William DiFazio, and Bogdan Denitch. If I have managed to avoid a natural predisposition toward male bias, much of the credit must go to Susan Kornblum, Cynthia Epstein, Judith Lorber, June Nash, and many other colleagues who shared their insights and knowledge. Finally, let me thank Jane Moore and the staff at the CUNY Graduate School library for putting up with this notorious bibliopath.

A special note of thanks is due to Professor Glenn Currier of El Centro Community College in Dallas, Texas. Glenn was an early adopter and supporter of the text and a source of great inspiration to me in the revision process. Many of the new ideas in the book are a result of discussions with Glenn about his experience using the book with his students. My own students at Queens College continued to offer me insights into possible revisions, but I gained additional perspective from Glenn's fresh and creative reading of the early revision plans. I am also extremely grateful to Glenn for his work on the Dallas County Community College District television course that will use *Sociology in a Changing World* as its basic text.

Over several years of textbook writing I have learned that the comments offered by reviewers are essential to a book's success. No single author can hope to adequately represent a field as complex and large as sociology. One needs dedicated reviewers to correct mistakes of fact, interpretation, and emphasis. I might often disagree with reviewers, but I always find their comments and suggestions helpful. The first edition benefited from the comments of the following reviewers, many of whose ideas continue to inform the second edition:

Dorothy Balancio
Mercy College

Bernard Beck
Northwestern University

Phillip Bosserman
Salisbury State College

Brent T. Bruton
Iowa State University

Chuck Carselowey
Oklahoma City Community College

Robert E. Clark
Midwestern State University

Mary Beth Collins
Central Piedmont Community College

Vasilikie Demos
University of Minnesota

Jack Dison
Arkansas State University

Martin Epstein
Middlesex Community College

Charles E. Faupel
Auburn University

Joseph Galaskiewicz
University of Minnesota

Eric P. Godfrey
Ripon College

Scarlett Hardesty
University of Arizona

Benton Johnson
University of Oregon

Martin L. Levin
Emory University

Jerry L. L. Miller
University of Arizona

James D. Orcutt
The Florida State University

Larry M. Perkins
Oklahoma State University

David L. Preston
San Diego State University

J. D. Robson
University of Arkansas

Jeffrey P. Rosenfeld
Nassau Community College

Wesley Shrum
Louisiana State University

Richard L. Simpson
The University of North Carolina

Kathleen Tiemann
Mercer University

C. Edwin Vaughan
University of Missouri

Theodore C. Wagenaar
Miami University

Eric A. Wagner
Ohio University

Joe Walsh
Bucks County Community College

Chaim I. Waxman
Rutgers, The State University of New Jersey

Steven R. Wilson
Temple University

Thomas J. Yacovone
Los Angeles Valley College

William W. Zellner
Doane College

In producing the second edition we added reviewers who either had direct experience with the first edition in class or had strong opinions about the book and how it could be strengthened. I wish to thank these reviewers for their dedication and insight:

Elizabeth Almquist
University of North Texas

Michele Aronica
Saint Joseph's College

Augustine Aryee
Fitchburg State College

Richard Bales
Illinois Central College

Brent Bruton
Iowa State University of Science and Technology

R. E. Canjar
University of Maryland

Mary Beth Collins
Central Piedmont Community College

Glenn Currier
El Centro College

Ken Elder
Southeastern Oklahoma State University

Laura Kramer
Montclair State College

John Hall
University of California

Denny Hill
Georgia Southern College

Kathryn Kuhn
University of Texas

Theodore Long
Merrimack College

Joseph Marolla
Virginia Commonwealth University

George Martin
Montclair State College

Virginia McKeefery-Reynolds
Northern Illinois University

Ephraim Mizruchi
Syracuse University

John Roman
University of Maine

Gary Spencer
Syracuse University

Paul Stowell
Wenatchee Valley College

Timothy Wickham-Crowley
Georgetown University

Kenneth Wilson
East Carolina University

Steven Vassar
Mankato State University

In preparing the second edition of the text I especially needed a team of professional editors and publishers who would recognize the strengths of the first edition and work with me to make improvements while keeping the basic elements of the original content and design. I found such people in Kirsten Olson, Christopher Klein, Meera Dash, and Ted Buchholz of Holt, Rinehart and Winston. They all encouraged me, and also Carolyn and Miriam, whenever we had good ideas, and they were sensitive in their criticism when our work was in its formative stages; my thanks also go to Vicki McAlindon Horton, Michael Hinshaw, and Annette Wiggins for their skillful and thorough production coordination. We could not have asked for a better team to work with.

Thanks also go to Laurie R. Beck for her research assistance; to Freda Leinwand for her painstaking photo research; and to my students at the City University of New York, both graduates and undergraduates, for keeping me "turned on" to sociology.

William Kornblum

BRIEF CONTENTS

Part One **SOCIAL SCIENCE** 2

Chapter 1 Sociology: An Introduction 4
Chapter 2 The Tools of Sociology 32

Part Two **SOCIAL STRUCTURE** 62

Chapter 3 Societies and Nations 64
Chapter 4 Culture 92
Chapter 5 Population, Urbanization, and Community 122

Part Three **SOCIAL DYNAMICS** 156

Chapter 6 Socialization: Creating the Person 158
Chapter 7 Interaction: From Couples to Corporations 190
Chapter 8 Stratification and Social Mobility 222
Chapter 9 Deviance and Social Control 252
Chapter 10 Collective Behavior and Mass Publics 286
Chapter 11 Social Change 316

Part Four **SOCIAL DIVISIONS** 350

Chapter 12 Social Class 352
Chapter 13 Inequalities of Race and Ethnicity 388
Chapter 14 Inequalities of Gender and Age 424

Part Five **SOCIAL INSTITUTIONS** 458

Chapter 15 The Family 460
Chapter 16 Religion 494
Chapter 17 Education and the Communications Media 524
Chapter 18 Economic Institutions 558
Chapter 19 Political and Military Institutions 592
Chapter 20 Science, Technology, and the Environment 626

CONTENTS

Part One: Social Science 2

CHAPTER 1
Sociology: An Introduction 4

- The Sociological Imagination 6
- Sociology, the Human Science 7
  The Social Environment 8
  Levels of Social Reality 8
- From Social Thought to Social Science 9
  The Age of Enlightenment 10
  The Age of Revolution 11
  The Great European Sociologists 11
  The Rise of Modern Sociology 12
  The Social Surveys 13
  The Chicago School and Human Ecology 13
- Major Sociological Perspectives 16
  Interactionism 16
  Functionalism 18
  Conflict Theory 19
  The Multidimensional View of Society 20
- Summary 23
- Where to Find It 24
- Glossary 25
- Art and the Sociological Eye 26

CHAPTER 2
The Tools of Sociology 32

- Applying the Sociological Imagination 34
  Formulating Research Questions 35
  Reviewing the Literature 37
- The Basic Methods 38
  Observation 38
  Experiments 40
  Survey Research 42
  Research Ethics and the Rights of
    Respondents 48
- Analyzing the Data 49
  Reading Tables 49
  Percent Analysis 50
  Correlations 52
- Theories and Perspectives 53

- Challenges to Contemporary Society:
    Prostitution and AIDS 54
- Summary 57
- Where to Find It 58
- Glossary 59
- Visual Sociology: An Urban "Combat Zone" 60

Part Two: Social Structure 62

CHAPTER 3
Societies and Nations 64

- The Social Order 66
  Society and Social Structure 67
  Elements of Social Structure 67
- Populations and Societies 72
  The First Million Years: Hunting and
    Gathering 74
  The Agrarian Revolution 76
  The Industrial Revolution 78
- Society and the Individual 80
  From Gemeinschaft to Gesellschaft 81
  Role and Status in Modern Societies 81
- Societies and Nation-States 83
  The State 83
  The Nation-State 83
  Conclusion 85
- Frontiers of Sociology: Populations on the
    Move 85
- Summary 87
- Where to Find It 88
- Glossary 89

CHAPTER 4
Culture   92

- **The Meaning of Culture**   94
  Dimensions of Culture   95
  The Normative Order   97
  Social Institutions   100
  Culture and Social Change   100
- **Culture, Evolution, and Human Behavior**   101
  The Social Darwinists   101
  Sociobiology   102
- **Language and Culture**   104
- **Crossing Cultural Lines**   106
  Ethnocentrism and Cultural Relativity   106
  Cultural Universals   106
- **Civilizations and Cultural Change**   107
  Effects of Cultural Contact   108
  Conclusion   113
- **Frontiers of Sociology: Changes in American Culture**   113
- **Summary**   117
- **Where to Find It**   118
- **Glossary**   119
- **Visual Sociology: Urban Indians**   120

CHAPTER 5
Population, Urbanization, and Community   122

- **People, Cities, and Urban Growth**   124
  The Population Explosion   124
  The Growth of Cities   130
- **The Urban Landscape**   135
  Urban Expansion   135
  Metropolitan Areas   137
- **Urban Communities**   139
  The Decline-of-Community Thesis   140
  Subcultural Theory   141
- **Cities and Social Change**   145
  Inequality and Conflict   145
  Conclusion   148
- **Challenges to Contemporary Society: Planning Urban Environments**   149
- **Summary**   151
- **Glossary**   152
- **Where to Find It**   153
- **Visual Sociology: Favelas in Brazil**   154

Part Three: Social Dynamics   156

CHAPTER 6
Socialization: Creating the Person   158

- **The Meaning of Socialization**   160
- **Nature versus Nurture**   162
  Behaviorism   162
  Feral Children   164
  The Need for Love   164
  Changing Group Norms: Robbers Cave   165
- **The Social Construction of Personality**   168
  Freud's Theory of Personality   168
  Interactionist Models of the Self   169
  Erikson's Theory of Development   172
  Theories of Moral Development   173
- **Socialization and Human Environments**   173
  The Micro-Environment   175
  The Larger Social Environment   176
- **Agents of Socialization**   178
  The Family   178
  The Schools   179
  The Community   179
  The Peer Group   179
  The Mass Media   179
- **Gender Socialization**   180
- **Socialization and Social Change**   182
- **Frontiers of Sociology: Emotions—Innate or Learned?**   183
- **Summary**   185
- **Where to Find It**   186
- **Glossary**   187
- **Visual Sociology: Socialization through Interaction**   188

CHAPTER 7
Interaction: From Couples to Corporations   190

- **Groups and the Social Fabric**   192
  Social Categories and Social Groups   193
  Primary and Secondary Groups   193
  Communities   195
  Networks   195
- **Interaction in Groups**   199
  Principles of Interaction   199
  The Economic Person vs. the Social Person   202
  Communication and Behavior in Groups   203
  Interaction and Group Structure   205
- **Formal Organizations and Bureaucracy**   208
  Bureaucracy and Obedience to Authority   210

Commitment to Bureaucratic Groups   212
● **Groups in Complex Societies**   213
● **Frontiers of Sociology: Ordinary People,**
   Extraordinary Groups   215
● **Summary**   217
● **Where to Find It**   218
● **Glossary**   219
● **Visual Sociology: Friendship Groups**   220

CHAPTER 8
Stratification and Social Mobility   222

● **The Meaning of Stratification**   224
   Caste, Class, and Social Mobility   225
   Life Chances   227
● **Stratification and the Means of Existence**   228
   Stratification in Rural Villages   228
   Stratification in Industrial Societies   230
● **Stratification and Culture**   230
   The Role of Ideology   231
   Stratification at the Micro Level   233
● **Power, Authority, and Stratification**   235
● **Stratification in the Modern Era**   237
   The Great Transformation   238
   Class Consciousness and Class Conflict   238
   Social Mobility in Modern Societies: The
      Weberian View   240
● **Theories of Stratification**   241
   Conflict Theories   241
   The Functionalist View   243
   The Interactionist Perspective   244
   Conclusion   244
● **Challenges to Contemporary Society:**
   Stratification and the World Economic
   System   245
● **Where to Find It**   248
● **Glossary**   249
● **Summary**   247
● **Visual Sociology: Stratification in the United**
   States and the Soviet Union   250

CHAPTER 9
Deviance and Social Control   252

● **What Is Deviance?**   254
● **Dimensions of Deviance**   257
   Deviance and Stigma   258
   Deviance and Crime   259
   Deviance and Changing Values   260
   Deviant Subcultures   262
● **Theoretical Perspectives on Social Deviance** 264
   Biological Explanations of Crime   264
   Social-Scientific Explanations of Deviance
      and Crime   265
   The Functionalist Perspective   265
   Conflict Perspectives   266
   The Interactionist Perspective   270
● **Crime and Social Control**   273
   Ecological Dimensions of Crime   273
   Institutions of Coercive Control: Courts and
      Prisons   276
● **Challenges to Contemporary Society:**
   The Gang Phenomenon   279
● **Summary**   281
● **Glossary**   282
● **Where to Find It**   283
● **Visual Sociology: The Hobo**   284

CHAPTER 10
Collective Behavior and Mass
Publics   286

● **The Meanings of Disorder**   288
   The Nature of Collective Behavior   290
   A Typology of Spontaneous Collective
      Behaviors   291
   Dimensions of Social Movements   294
● **Social Movement Theory**   295
   Theories of Revolution   296
   Social Movements and Charisma   297
   Theories of Mass Society   300
● **Social Movements in Everyday Life**   301
   Resource Mobilization Theory   301
● **Mass Publics and Public Opinion**   303
   Mass Publics   303
   Public Opinion   308
● **Frontiers of Sociology: The Study of Leisure** 309
● **Summary**   311
● **Glossary**   312
● **Where to Find It**   313
● **Visual Sociology: The Labor Movement**   314

CHAPTER 11
Social Change 316

- **Meanings of Social Change** 318
- **Two Forces of Social Change** 320
  War and Conquest 320
  Modernization 323
- **Social Change in Everyday Life** 329
  Gender Roles and the Family 330
  Race Relations in a Postindustrial
    Society 330
  Environmental Politics and Policies 332
- **Models of Change** 333
  Evolutionary Models 335
  Cyclical Theories 336
  Conflict Models 337
  Functionalist Models 337
  Conclusion 338
- **Challenges to Contemporary Society:**
    The Impact of Telecommunications 339
- **Summary** 341
- **Glossary** 342
- **Where to Find It** 343
- **Art and Social Change** 345

Part Four: Social Divisions 350

CHAPTER 12
Social Class 352

- **Dimensions of Social Inequality in America** 354
  Measures of Social Inequality 355
  Changing Views of Social Inequality 357
  Class Awareness in America Today 364
- **Social Class and Life Chances in the**
    United States 366
  The Upper Classes 367
  The Middle Classes 368
  The Working Class 369
  The Poor 371
  Farmers and Farm Families 375
- **More Equality?** 376
  Inequality and Mobility 377
  Education and Mobility 378
  Social Mobility and the Two-Paycheck
    Family 379
  Conclusion 380
- **Frontiers of Sociology: Research on Poverty** 380
- **Summary** 383
- **Glossary** 384
- **Where to Find It** 385
- **Visual Sociology: Diet and Social Class** 386

CHAPTER 13
Inequalities of Race and Ethnicity 388

- **The Meaning of Race and Ethnicity** 390
  Race: A Social Concept 391
  Racism 392
  Ethnic Groups and Minorities 393
- **When Worlds Collide: Patterns of**
    Intergroup Relations 394
  Genocide 394
  Expulsion 396
  Slavery 397
  Segregation 398
  Assimilation 399
- **Culture and Intergroup Relations** 404
  Stereotypes 404
  Prejudice and Discrimination 405
  Ethnic and Racial Nationalism 406
  Affirmative Action 408
- **Theories of Racial and Ethnic Inequality** 408
  Social-Psychological Theories 408
  Interactionist Theories 409
  Functionalist Theories 410
  Conflict Theories 410
  Ecological Theories 412
- **A Piece of the Pie** 414
- **Challenges to Contemporary Society:**
    The Growing Hispanic Presence in
    North America 416
- **Summary** 419
- **Glossary** 420
- **Where to Find It** 421
- **Visual Sociology: An End to Apartheid?** 422

CHAPTER 14
Inequalities of Gender and Age 424

- **Gender, Age, and the Life Course** 426
  The Life Course—Society's Age Structure 426
  Sex Ratios and Their Implications 427
  Cohorts and Age Structures 429
- **Gender and Age Stratification** 433
  Gender Roles: A Cultural Phenomenon 434
  Historical Patterns of Gender and Age
    Stratification 436
  Sexism and Ageism 439
- **Perspectives on Gender and Age**
    Stratification 441
  A Functionalist View of Gender and Age
    Roles 442
  Interactionist Views of Gender and Age
    Stratification 443
  Conflict Perspectives on Gender and Age
    Stratification 446

- Gender, Age, and the Changing
  Social Fabric   447
  The Women's Movement 447
  Social Movements Among the Elderly 449
- Frontiers of Sociology: Gender and the Life
  Course in Aging Societies   451
- Summary   453
- Glossary   454
- Where to Find It   455
- Visual Sociology: Keeping Women in
  Their Place

Part Five: Social Institutions   458

CHAPTER 15
The Family   460

- The Nature of Families   462
  The Family as an Institution 462
  Defining the Family 464
  Variations in Family Structure 466
  The Changing Family 467
  The Family Life Cycle 470
- Dynamics of Mate Selection and Marriage   474
  Marriage as Exchange 474
  Norms of Mate Selection 474
  Romantic Love 476
  Marriage and Divorce 477
  Sources of Marital Instability 479
  The Impact of Divorce 480
- Perspectives on the Family   481
  The Interactionist Perspective 481
  Conflict Theory and Alternatives to the
      Family 482
  Functionalist Views of the Family 484
  Conclusion: "Here to Stay" 486
- Challenges to Contemporary Society:
  The Black Family   486
- Summary   489
- Glossary   490
- Where to Find It   491
- Visual Sociology: An Extended Family   492

CHAPTER 16
Religion   494

- Religion in Society   496
  The Power of Faith 497
  Varieties of Religious Belief 501
  Religion and Social Change 505
- Structure and Change in Modern Religions   507
  Forms of Religious Organization 507
  Religious Interaction and Change 509
- Trends in Religion in the United States   511
  Unofficial Religion 513
  Religiosity 513
  Religious Pluralism 514
  Religious Organizations and Free Riders
      514
  Fundamentalism 515
  Conclusion 516
- Challenges to Contemporary Society:
  Religion and Social Change   517
- Summary   519
- Glossary   520
- Where to Find It
- Visual Sociology: Forms of Religious
  Expression   522

CHAPTER 17
Education and the Communications
Media   524

- Education for a Changing World   526
  The Nature of Schools 526
  Who Goes to School? 528
  Schools and Adolescent Society 529
  Education and Citizenship 529
- Attainment, Achievement, and Equality   530
  Educational Attainment 530
  Educational Achievement 533
  Education and Social Mobility 534
  Education for Equality 536
- The Structure of Educational Institutions   538
  Schools as Bureaucracies 539
  Changing the System: Desegregation 541
- The Communications Media   543
  Media Institutions in Modern Societies 544
  Patterns of Media Consumption 545
  Television and Violence 546
  The Differentiation of Media Institutions 547
  Media Power and Its Limits 548
- Challenges to Contemporary Society:
  The Electronic Classroom   551
- Summary   552
- Glossary   554
- Where to Find It   555
- Visual Sociology: Students and
  Social Change   556

CHAPTER 18
Economic Institutions   558

- **Sociology and Economics**   560
- **Markets and the Division of Labor**   562
  The Nature of Markets 562
  Markets and the World Economic System 563
- **Economics and the State**   565
  Political-Economic Ideologies 567
  Political Economics in Practice: After the
    Cold War 571
- **Workers, Managers, and Corporations**   575
  Alienation 578
  Individuals and Corporations 579
  Sociological Perspectives on
    the Workplace 580
  Conclusion 583
- **Frontiers of Sociology: Work and Careers in
  the 1990s**   584
- **Summary**   587
- **Glossary**   588
- **Where to Find It**   589
- **Visual Sociology: Depression in Steeltown**   590

CHAPTER 19
Political and Military Institutions   592

- **The Nature of Politics and Political
  Institutions**   594
  Politics, Power, and Authority 594
  Legitimacy and Authority 596
- **The Political Ecology of States and
  Territories**   598
  States and Borders 600
  Citizenship and Political Participation 601
- **Political Institutions in Modern Societies**   603
  Democratic Political Systems 606
- **Perspectives on Political Institutions**   607
  Structural Prerequisites of Democracy 607
  The Power Elite Model 608
  The Pluralist Model 610
  Politics and Social Interaction 611
- **Military Institutions**   613
  The Economic Role of the Military 614
  Military Socialization 616
  Social Change and Military Institutions 617
- **Frontiers of Sociology: Voting Behavior in
  the United States**   618
- **Summary**   621
- **Glossary**   622
- **Where to Find It**   623
- **Visual Sociology: Elections**   624

CHAPTER 20
Science, Technology, and the
Environment   626

- **The Nature of Science and Technology**   628
- **Scientific Institutions: The Sociological View**   630
  The Sociology of Science 630
  The Norms of Science 633
- **Technology in Modern Societies**   634
  Dimensions of Technology 635
  Technological Dualism 635
  Technology and Social Change 640
  The Quest for Energy 642
  Technology in Everyday Life 643
- **Science, Technology, and Society: The Case
  of Medical Technology**   643
  The Hospital: From Poorhouse to Healing
    Institution 646
  Hyptertrophy in Health Care? 647
  Medical Sociology 647
- **The Impact of Technology**   648
  Technological Systems 648
  Environmental Stress 649
- **Summary**   651
- **Glossary**   652
- **Where to Find It**   653
- **Visual Sociology: Environmental Concern**   654

ABOUT THE AUTHOR

W illiam Kornblum is a professor of sociology at the Graduate School of the City University of New York, where he helps train future instructors and researchers in the social sciences. He also teaches introductory sociology and other undergraduate courses at Queens College of the City University of New York.

A specialist in urban and community studies, Kornblum began his teaching career with the Peace Corps in the early 1960s, when he taught physics and chemistry in French-speaking West Africa (see the introduction to Chapter 11). He received his doctorate in sociology from the University of Chicago in 1971. He has also taught at the University of Washington at Seattle and worked as a research sociologist for the U.S. Department of the Interior. At the CUNY Graduate School he continues to conduct research on urban environmental issues for the Department of the Interior and to direct research on youth and employment and on urban policy. He is currently engaged (with Terry Williams) in a long-term study of life in public housing projects, sponsored by the MacArthur Foundation.

The author's other publications include *Blue Collar Community*, a study of the steel-making community of South Chicago; *Growing Up Poor* (with Terry Williams), a study of teenagers growing up in different low-income communities in the United States; and *Social Problems* (with Joseph Julian), a comprehensive textbook about social problems and social policies in the United States.

SOCIOLOGY

IN A CHANGING WORLD

PART ONE

SOCIAL SCIENCE

Social change is occurring around us all the time. It shapes our day-to-day existence even when we are unconscious of its causes and unaware of its effects. Neighborhoods change as newcomers move in or more housing is built; factories close or open in response to changes in the economies of other continents; wars and natural disasters push people out of their homelands; new technologies alter old life-styles and stimulate people to find new ways of living. Sociology is the science that attempts to make sense of these changes. It is devoted to studying why social change occurs and how it affects people in different societies or within a society.

The first part of this book introduces some basic sociological concepts. Chapter 1 introduces the major perspectives that sociologists use to analyze questions of social stability and change, and Chapter 2 describes the methods that sociologists use in conducting their research.

PART I
CHAPTERS

● Sociology: An Introduction

● The Tools of Sociology

CHAPTER OUTLINE

● **The Sociological Imagination**

● **Sociology, the Human Science**

  - The Social Environment
  - Levels of Social Reality

● **From Social Thought to Social Science**

  - The Age of Enlightenment
  - The Age of Revolution
  - The Great European Sociologists
  - The Rise of Modern Sociology
    - The Social Surveys
    - The Chicago School and Human Ecology

● **Major Sociological Perspectives**

  - Interactionism
    - Rational Choice— The Sociological View
    - Symbolic Interactionism
  - Functionalism
  - Conflict Theory
  - The Multidimensional View of Society

Jim Holland

National Park Service Ranger Glen Livermont, Badlands National Park, South Dakota

CHAPTER 1

SOCIOLOGY: AN INTRODUCTION

"What I would like to do," he says as a wistful expression crosses his broad features, "is set up a summer education institute on my family's ranch. I would have people from the reservation, from the government, and from colleges and universities. We would run courses for students and for ourselves about the conditions of Indians and about the problems of saving the natural environment. Maybe we'd also get a better idea about why the reservation system is so messed up."

The speaker is Glen Livermont, a young man who grew up on the Pine Ridge Sioux Reservation in South Dakota. Glen now works as a National Park Service ranger at Badlands National Park, which adjoins the Pine Ridge Reservation; he has worked there full time since finishing college. His family's ranch shares a boundary with the park, and at times when he is out on patrol he can see his kin herding cattle or mending fence. His dream is to find a way to live on the ranch and at the same time use his education for the good of the tribe and the larger society.

"What would you personally gain from starting such an institute?" I ask him.

Glen barely hesitates; clearly he has given a lot of thought to his dream. "I think it would help me understand myself and my people better. For example, I would like to know how we can achieve more stability in our leadership. Every two years we elect a tribal council, and two years later that group is thrown out and a new one is elected. We can't make any progress that way. We don't get a chance to settle down with one group of leaders and work together to develop the reservation. I want to understand why that is

and how it could change. Some people think we should give up the reservation system altogether, but that might be much worse for many Indian people. After all, the reservations are all we have left from what was ours before the Europeans came.

"Also, you know," he continues, "running an institute on the ranch would be a way for me and my family to stay on the ranch. The way cattle prices are now, we can't all afford to live off ranching alone. That's the biggest thing, I guess: I'm trying to figure out ways we could all stay on the land. How great it would be if people could come to the ranch to study! Young people especially. We could teach them how Indians feel about the land. I'm already doing a lot of this kind of teaching in the park; it's not as far-fetched as it might sound. Sure, it's a romantic idea—I see us riding horses over the Badlands and stopping at the sacred places—but it's also got a very practical side."

I meet many people like Glen Livermont in the course of my travels as a sociologist. Wherever I conduct my research—urban housing projects, grimy union halls, plush corporate headquarters—I hear people talking about their dreams, both for themselves and for their society. And I hear them talking about their troubles and their fears. Some, like Glen, recognize the links between their hopes and fears and the larger social forces that produce change in their families and communities. Sometimes, also, they can imagine how established ways of doing things might be changed or improved. This awareness is often referred to as the sociological imagination. There are times of the year when few tourists show up at the visitors center in

Porcupine, South Dakota. During such times Glen can hone his sociological imagination and dream of a future almost within his grasp.

The sociological imagination is closely intertwined with the work of sociologists. Our job is to stimulate that imagination by helping people understand how society changes and how social change affects them. At times we may even help a dream like Glen's become reality.

THE SOCIOLOGICAL IMAGINATION

Everyone should be able to develop a sociological imagination, although not everyone can do so as easily as Glen Livermont has. It is easier for people who have experienced rapid changes in their way of life to see such changes from a sociological perspective. In the nineteenth century, for example, the Sioux societies that spanned the Great Plains of North America saw their people massacred and their traditional way of life crushed by more numerous and powerful invaders moving westward across the continent. Glen can easily see how social forces affect his life. On his people's reservation, the consequences of social change are inescapable.

Most people need more help in applying their sociological imagination. Often they fail to distinguish between social forces and personal troubles. If they become unemployed, they blame themselves for failing to do better; if they divorce, they blame each other. When they see crime, they blame "human nature"; when they see success, they praise individual achievement. But this tendency to think of life as a series of individual mistakes or successes blinds them to the fact that social conditions also shape individual human lives, often in ways for which individuals can hardly be held accountable. And the habit of seeing events mainly in terms of how they affect individuals blinds people to the possibility of improving the way their society is organized.

Sociologists are concerned with how social conditions influence our lives as individuals. **Social conditions** are the realities of the life we create together as social beings. Conditions such as poverty, or wealth, or crime and drug use, for example, differ from biological facts (facts concerning our behavior and needs as animals) and psychological facts (facts about our patterns of behavior as individuals). Sociologists do not deny that psychological facts are important.

Sociologists are concerned with how social conditions, rather than "human nature" or individual mistakes or successes, influence people's lives.

Differences among individuals help some people cope with stress better than others, sieze opportunities that others allow to slip by, or fail where others succeed. But before saying that the success or failure of an individual or group is due to psychological causes, the sociologist tries to look at how social conditions such as poverty or wealth, war, or changes in the availability of jobs affect the individual's chances of success.

According to sociologist C. Wright Mills, who made famous the term **sociological imagination,** people often believe that their private lives can be explained mainly in terms of their personal successes and failures. They fail to see the links between their own individual biographies and the course of human history. Often they blame themselves for their troubles without grasping the effects of social change on their lives. "The facts of contemporary history," Mills cautions, "are also facts about the success and the failure of individual men and women."

When a society is industrialized, a peasant becomes a worker; a feudal lord is liquidated or becomes a businessman. When classes rise or fall, a man is employed or unemployed; when the rate of investment goes up or down, a man takes new heart or goes broke. When wars happen, an insurance salesman becomes a rocket launcher; a store clerk, a radar man; a wife lives alone; a child grows up without a father. (1959, p. 3)

According to Mills, neither a person's biography nor the history of a society can be understood unless one takes into account the influence of each on the other. The social forces of history—war, depression or recession, increases in population, changes in production and consumption, and many other social conditions—become the forces that influence individuals to behave in new ways. But those new ways of behavior themselves become social forces and, in turn, shape history. The Russian Revolution and the victory of the Allies in World War II enabled the Soviet Union to gain political and economic dominance over Poland, Hungary, East Germany, and other nations of Eastern Europe. The Soviets imposed a dictatorship in those nations and did not allow individuals to form businesses. As a result, individuals learned how to conduct business in secret on the black market. The ideals of Soviet-style socialism, which we discuss in detail later, were not taken very seriously by the more innovative members of Eastern European society. In time the actions of many individuals undermined the Soviet system and led to the revolutions against communism that have dominated the headlines during the past few years.

By applying the sociological imagination to the events in the communist world or life on a reservation or any other situation in which people seek to improve their lives, one can "grasp history and biography and the relations between the two within society" (Mills, 1959, pp. 5–7). One of the main objectives of this book is to help you apply your sociological imagination to an understanding of what social forces are shaping your own biography and those of the people you care about. The sociological imagination can help us avoid needlessly blaming ourselves for the troubles we encounter in life. It can help us understand, for example, why some people are rich and powerful but many others are not; why the benefits of good health care or enriching education are available to some but not to others; or why women may find themselves resenting the men in their lives. The sociological imagination helps us sort out which facts about ourselves are explained by our place in society and which ones are a result of our own actions. Above all, the sociological imagination can suggest ways in which we can realistically bring about change in our lives and in society itself.

SOCIOLOGY, THE HUMAN SCIENCE

Glen Livermont's question about the unstable leadership of the Pine Ridge Reservation is a good example of what sociology attempts to explain. To answer it, one would need more information about how people on the reservation perceive their leaders. One would also need information about relations between the tribal leadership and the U.S. government, which still controls much of what occurs on the reservations. To determine whether the situation Glen describes is unique to the Pine Ridge Sioux or is common to many reservations, we would need comparative information about other reservations and how their leadership has changed over time. Above all, anyone seeking answers to these questions must understand the tragic history of the conquest and domination of Native Americans by white Americans.

Sociology is the scientific study of human societies and human behavior in the many groups that make up a society. Sociologists must ask difficult, sometimes embarrassing, questions about human life in order to explore the consequences of cataclysmic events like those that drove the Native Americans onto reservations. To understand the possibilities of change in the conditions of people like the Sioux, sociologists are continually seeking knowledge about what holds a society together even in the face of conquest, and about the ways in which a society changes in the face of great social forces like war and migration.

The Social Environment

The knowledge sociologists gather covers a vast range. Sociologists study religious behavior; conduct in the military; the behavior of workers and managers in industry; the activities of voluntary associations like parent-teacher groups and political parties; the changing relationships between men and women or between the elderly and their parents; the behavior of groups in neighborhoods; the activities of gangs, criminals, and judges; differences in the behaviors of entire social classes—the rich, the middle classes, the poor, the down-and-out; the way cities grow and change; the fate of entire societies during and after revolutions; and a host of other subjects. But how to make sure the information gathered is reliable and precise, how to use it to build theories of social cohesion and social change—that is the challenge faced by the young science of sociology.

As in any science, there are many debates in sociology about the appropriate ways to study social life and about which theories or types of theories best explain social phenomena. Most sociologists would, however, agree that

Human actions are limited or determined by "environment." Human beings become what they are at any given moment not by their own free decisions, taken rationally and in full knowledge of the conditions, but under the pressure of circumstances which delimit their range of choice and which also fix their objectives and the standards by which they make choices. (Shils, 1985, p. 805)

This statement expresses a core idea of sociology: that individual choice is never entirely free but is always determined to some extent by a person's environment. In sociology, *environment* refers to all the expectations and incentives established by other people in a person's social world. For the sociologist, therefore, the environment within which an individual's biography unfolds is a set of people and groups and organizations, all with their own ways of thinking and acting. Certainly each individual has unique choices to make in life, but the social world into which that person was born—reservation, urban ghetto, comfortable suburb, immigrant enclave in a strange city—determines to varying degrees what those choices will be. Mills was referring to this idea when he spoke of "the intersection of biography and history."

> *A core idea of sociology is that individual choice is determined to some extent by the environment—that is, by expectations and incentives established by others.*

Levels of Social Reality

In their studies of social environments, sociologists look at behaviors ranging from the intimate glances of lovers to the complex coordination of a space shuttle launch. Thus, for purposes of analysis we often speak of social behavior as occurring at three different levels of complexity: micro, middle, and macro. The **micro level** of sociological observation is concerned with the behaviors of the individual and his or her immediate others—that is, with patterns of interaction among a few people. One example is Erving Goffman's studies of the routine behaviors of everyday life. Goffman's research showed how seemingly insignificant ways of acting in public actually carry significant meanings. Thus, in a study titled "Territories of the Self" (1972), Goffman categorized some of the ways in which we use objects as "markers" to claim a personal space:

Markers are of various kinds. There are "central markers," being objects that announce a territorial claim, the territory radiating outward from it, as when sunglasses and lotion claim a beach chair, or a purse a seat in an airliner, or a drink on a bar the stool in front of it. . . . There are "boundary markers," objects that mark the line between two adjacent territories. The bar used in supermarket checkout counters to separate one customer's batch of articles from the next is an example. (pp. 41–42)

The last time you placed your sweater or book on an empty seat on a bus you told yourself that when someone came for the seat you would take up your things. But you hoped that the stranger who was coming along the aisle would get your message and choose another seat; you would defend your extra space as long as possible. You communicated all this by the manner in which you placed your marker and the persistence with which you defended "your" space.

Some sociologists deal almost exclusively with much larger-scale, or **macro**, levels of analysis. The macro level of social life refers to whole societies and the ways in which they are changing—that is, to revolutions, wars, major changes in the production of goods and services, and similar social phenomena that involve very large numbers of people. One example of macrosociological analysis is the study of how the shift from heavy manufacturing to high-tech industries has affected the way workers earn their livings. Another is the study of how the invasion and settlement of the American West in the nineteenth

and early twentieth centuries gave rise to the beliefs and actions that drove Native Americans onto reservations.

Middle-level social phenomena are those that occur in communities or in organizations such as businesses and voluntary associations. Middle-level social forms are smaller than entire societies but larger than the micro-level social forms in which everyone involved knows everyone else or is in close proximity to the others (as in a bus or a classroom). When Glen Livermont talks about how his tribe has been affected by the history of European conquest of the Native Americans, he is thinking about the way a macrosociological phenomenon (the wars of conquest) affected a middle-level social phenomenon (his tribe). But he also seeks to understand those effects at the level of individuals and their families within the tribe— that is, at the micro level.

Figure 1-1 presents the three basic levels of sociological analysis, with some examples of the types of studies conducted at each level. Throughout this book we show how the sociological imagination can be applied at different levels of society. In this chapter we set the stage by describing the basic perspectives from which modern sociologists approach the study of social conditions. In the next chapter we outline the procedures and methods used by sociologists in conducting their research. We begin here with a brief description of the origins and development of the science of sociology.

FROM SOCIAL THOUGHT TO SOCIAL SCIENCE

L ike all the sciences, sociology developed out of prescientific longings to understand and predict. The central questions of sociology have been pondered by the world's great thinkers since the earliest periods of recorded history. The ancient Greek philosophers (particularly Socrates, Plato, and Aristotle) believed that human societies inevitably arose, flourished, and declined. They tended to perceive the past as better than the present, looking back to a "golden age" in which social conditions were presumed to have been better than those of the degraded present. Before the scientific revolution of the seventeenth century, the theologians and

Each of these passengers in a railroad station waiting room has claimed a personal territory. Note that almost every person has taken a separate bench and has chosen to sit at one end of the bench. If another person came to that bench, he or she would probably choose to sit as far away as possible.

© Marc P. Anderson

Figure 1–1: **Levels of Sociological Analysis**

ANALYTICAL LEVEL		SOCIAL BEHAVIORS STUDIED	TYPICAL QUESTIONS
	Macro	Revolutions; intercontinental migrations; emergence of new institutions.	How are entire societies or institutions changing?
	Middle	Relations in bureaucracies; social movements; participation in communities, organizations, tribes.	How does bureaucracy affect personality? Do all social movements go through similar stages?
	Micro	Interaction in small groups; self-image; enactment of roles.	How do people create and take roles in groups? How are group structures created?

philosophers of medieval Europe and the Islamic world also believed that human misery and strife were inevitable. As the Bible put it, "The poor always ye have with you." Mere mortals could do little to correct social conditions, which were viewed as the work of divine Providence.

The Age of Enlightenment

The roots of modern sociology can be found in the work of the philosophers and scientists of the "Great Enlightenment," which had its origins in the scientific discoveries of the seventeenth century. That pivotal century began with Galileo's "heretical" proof that the earth was not the center of the universe and ended with the publication of Isaac Newton's *Principia Mathematica*. Newton is often credited with the founding of modern science. He not only discovered the laws of gravity and motion but, in developing the calculus, also provided later generations with the mathematical tools whereby further discoveries in all the sciences could be made.

Hard on the heels of this unprecedented progress in science and mathematics came a theory of human progress that paved the way for a "science of humanity." Francis Bacon in England, René Descartes and Blaise Pascal in France, and Gottfried Wilhelm Leibniz in Germany were among the philosophers who recognized the social importance of scientific discoveries. Their writings emphasized the idea of progress guided by human reason and opposed the dominant notion that the human condition was ordained by God (Bury, 1932; Nisbet, 1969).

Today we are used to inventions crowding one upon another. Between the childhood of our grandparents and our own adulthood, society has undergone some major transformations: from agrarian to industrial production; from rural settlements and small towns to large cities and expanding metropolitan regions; from reliance on wood and coal as energy sources to dependence on electricity and nuclear power; from typewriters to computers. But in the seventeenth century people were used to far more stability. Ways of life that had existed since the Middle Ages were not expected to change in a generation. The rise of science transformed the social order. As was often said at the time, science "broke the cake of custom." New methods of navigation made it possible to explore and chart the world's oceans and continents. Applied to warfare, scientific knowledge enabled Europeans to conquer the peoples of Africa, Asia, and the Western Hemisphere. In Europe, those conquests opened up new markets and stimulated new patterns of trade that hastened the growth of some regions and cities and the decline of others. The entire human world had entered a period of rapid social change that continues today and shows no signs of ending.

The Age of Revolution

The vehicle of social change was not science itself, since relatively few people at any level of society were practicing scientists. Rather, the modern era of rapid social change is a product of the many new social ideas that captured people's imagination during the eighteenth century. The series of revolutions that took place in the American colonies of Britain, in France, and in England all resulted in part from social movements unleashed by the triumphs of science and reason. The ideas of human rights (that is, the rights of all humans, not just the elite), of democracy versus rule by an absolute monarch, of self-government for colonial peoples, and of applying reason and science to human affairs in general—all are currents of thought that arose during this period.

The revolutions of the eighteenth century loosed a torrent of questions that could not even have been imagined before. The old order of society was breaking down as secular (i.e., nonreligious) knowledge replaced sacred traditions. The study of laws and lawmaking and debates about justice in society began to replace the idea that kings and other leaders had a "divine right" to rule. Communities were breaking apart; courts and palaces and great estates were crumbling as people struggled to be free. What would replace them? Would the rule of the mob replace the rule of the monarch? Would greed and envy replace piety and faith? Would there be enough

During the nineteenth century, sociologists tended to focus on entire societies and how their special characteristics influence human behavior and social change.

opportunities in the New World for all the people who were being driven off the land in the Old World? Would the factory system become the new order of society, and, if so, what did that imply for the future of society?

No longer could the Scriptures or the classics of ancient Greece and Rome be consulted for easy answers to such questions. Rather, it was becoming evident that new answers could be discovered through the **scientific method:** repeated observation, careful description, the formulation of theories based on possible explanations, and the gathering of additional data about the questions that followed from those theories. Why not use the same methods to create a science of human society? This ambitious idea, typical of the new concepts emerging from the social ferment of the eighteenth and early nineteenth centuries, led to the birth of sociology. It is little wonder that the French philosopher Auguste Comte thought of sociology, even in its infancy, as the "queen of sciences," one that would soon take its rightful place beside the reigning science of physics. It was he who coined the term *sociology* to designate the scientific study of society.

The Great European Sociologists

In the nineteenth century an increasing number of philosophers and historians began to see themselves as specializing in the study of social conditions and social change. They developed ambitious global theories of social change based on the essential qualities of societies at different stages of human history, and they devoted much of their attention to comparing existing societies and civilizations, both past and present. As Auguste Comte put it, the age of discovery had revealed such an array of societies that "from the wretched inhabitants of Tierra del Fuego to the most advanced nations of Western Europe," there is such a great diversity of societies that comparisons among them will yield much insight into why they differ and how they change (1971/1854, p. 48).

The nineteenth-century sociologists tended to think in macrosociological terms. Their writing dealt with whole societies and how their special characteristics influence human behavior and social change. Karl Marx, for example, was both highly appreciative and extremely critical of the societies of his day. His analysis of those societies led him to predict major upheavals arising from conflicts between the owners of wealth and the impoverished workers. The great French sociologist Émile Durkheim did not agree with Marx's prediction that violent revolutions would transform society. Durkheim's theories explain social change as resulting from population growth and from changes in the ways in which work and community life are organized. Still another great European theorist, Max Weber, was the first to understand the overwhelming importance of bureaucratic forms of social organization in modern societies and to point out their increasing dominance in the lives of individuals.

Each of these three sociological pioneers based his theories on detailed reviews of the history of entire societies. Marx wrote about the origins of free enterprise and capitalism in the Western nations. Durkheim wrote about the transformations that occur as societies evolve from hunting and gathering to industrial production. Weber produced volumes about the organizations found in precapitalist and capitalist societies. But to become a science rather than a branch of philosophy, sociology had to build on the research of its founders. The twentieth century brought changes of such magnitude at every level of society that sociologists were in increasing demand. Their mission was to gain new information about the scope and meaning of social change.

The Rise of Modern Sociology

We credit the European social thinkers and philosophers with creating sociology, but nowhere did the new science find more fertile ground for development than in North America. By the beginning of the twentieth century, sociology was rapidly acquiring new adherents in the United States and Canada, partly owing to the influence of great European sociologists like Marx and Durkheim, but even more because of the rapid social changes occurring in North America at the turn of the century. Waves of immigrants to cities and towns, the explosive growth of population and industry in the cities, race riots, strikes and

Culver Pictures

Karl Marx (1818–1883) was a German "political economist" who spent most of his life as an exile in London. He is best known for his critique of capitalism and his intense efforts to promote socialism; in fact, in his later years he was an ardent revolutionary as well as a writer on social and economic issues. Marx's belief that conflict over scarce resources leads to social change is at the heart of conflict theory.

labor strife, moral crusades against crime and vice and alcohol, the demand for woman suffrage—these and many other changes caused American sociology to take a new turn. There was increasing demand for knowledge about exactly what changes were occurring and who was affected by them. The field of sociology therefore began to emphasize the quest for facts about changing social conditions, the empirical investigation of social issues.

"Empirical" information refers to carefully gathered, unbiased data regarding social conditions and behavior. In general, modern sociology is distinguished by its relentless and systematic search for empirical data to answer questions about society. Journalists also seek the facts about social conditions, but they must "cover" many different events and situations and present them as "stories" that will attract their readers' interest. Because they usually cannot dwell on one subject very long, journalists frequently must content themselves with citing examples and quoting experts whose opinions may or may not be based on empirical evidence. In contrast, sociologists study a situation or phenomenon in more depth, and when they do not have enough facts they are likely to say, "That is an empirical question. Let's see what the research tells us, and if the answers are inconclusive we will do more research." Evidence based on measurable effects and outcomes thus is required before one can make an informed decision about an issue. To use the sociological imagination to ask relevant questions and to seek answers to those questions backed by evidence that can be verified by others are among the chief goals of modern sociology.

The Social Surveys. The empirical focus of American sociology began largely as an outgrowth of the reform movements of the late nineteenth and early twentieth centuries. During this period the nation had not yet recovered from the havoc created by the Civil War. Southern blacks were migrating to the more industrialized North in ever-increasing numbers, and at the same time millions of European immigrants were finding ill-paid jobs in the larger cities, where cheap labor was in great demand. By the turn of the century, therefore, the nation's cities were crowded with poor families for whom the promise of "gold in America" had become a tarnished dream. In this time of rapid social change, Americans continually debated the merits of social reform and proposed new solutions for pressing social issues. Some called for socialism, others for a return to the free market or a ban on labor organizations or an end to immigration or the removal of black Americans to Africa. But where would the facts to use in judging those ideas come from?

In order to gain empirical information about social conditions, dedicated individuals undertook numerous "social surveys." Jacob Riis's (1890) account of life in New York's Lower East Side; W. E. B. DuBois's (1899) survey of Philadelphia blacks; Emily Balch's depiction of living conditions among Slavic miners and steelworkers in the Pittsburgh area (1910); and Jane Addams's famous *Hull House Maps and Papers* (1895), which described the lives of her neighbors in Chicago's West Side slum area—these and other carefully documented surveys of the living conditions of people experiencing the effects of rapid industrialization and urbanization left an enduring mark on American sociology. DuBois, for example, helped direct sociological research to questions of racism and social conditions in minority communities. Box 1-1 presents an excerpt from the landmark survey conducted by DuBois, the first black sociologist to gain worldwide recognition. DuBois helped direct sociological research to issues of racism and social conditions in minority communities, using empirical data to provide an objective account of the dismal social conditions of northern blacks at the turn of the century.

The Chicago School and Human Ecology. By the late 1920s the United States had become the world leader in sociology. The two great centers of American sociological research were the University of Chicago and Columbia University. At these universities and others influenced by them, two distinct approaches to the study of society evolved. The "Chicago school" emphasized the relationship between the individual and society, whereas the major East Coast universities, which were more strongly influenced by European sociology, tended toward macro-level analyses of social structure and change.

The sociology department at the University of Chicago (the oldest in the nation) extended its influence to many other universities, especially in the Midwest, South, and West. At that time the department was under the leadership of Robert Park and his younger colleague Ernest Burgess. Park in particular is associated with the Chicago school. His main contribution was to develop an agenda for sociological research that used the city as a "social laboratory." Early in his career Park had been a journalist, and he never lost the journalist's love of "getting the facts." He favored an approach in which facts concerning what was actually occurring among people in their local communities (the micro and middle levels) would be collected within a broader theoretical framework. That framework attempted to link macro-level changes in society, such as industrialization and the growth of urban populations, to patterns of settlement in cities and to how people actually lived in cities.

In one of his essays on this subject, Park began with the idea that industrialization causes the breakdown of traditional "primary-group" attachments (those of family members, age-mates, or clans). After stating the "probable" relationship between the effects of industrialization and high rates of crime, Park asked several specific questions:

What is the effect of ownership of property . . . on truancy, on divorce, and on crime?

In what regions and classes are certain kinds of crime endemic?

In what classes does divorce occur most frequently? What is the difference in this respect

Box 1–1: **Occupations of Blacks in Philadelphia, 1896**

W. E. B. DuBois was one of the first American sociologists to publish highly factual and objective descriptions of life in American cities. An American-born black, DuBois earned his doctorate in philosophy at Harvard before the turn of the century, when sociology was still regarded as a subfield of that discipline. But, as can be seen in this excerpt from his account of black life in Philadelphia about a century ago, DuBois was able to sharpen his arguments about the effects of racial discrimination with simple but telling statistics.

For a group of freedmen the question of economic survival is the most pressing of all questions; the problem as to how, under the circumstances of modern life, any group of people can earn a decent living, so as to maintain their standard of life, is not always easy to answer. But when the question is complicated by the fact that the group has a low degree of efficiency on account of previous training; is in competition with well-trained, eager and often ruthless competitors; is more or less handicapped by . . . discrimination; and, finally, is seeking not merely to maintain a standard of living but steadily to raise it to a higher plane—such a situation presents baffling problems to the sociologist. . . .

And yet this is the situation of the Negro in Philadelphia; he is trying to better his condition; is seeking to rise; for this end his first need is work of a character to engage his best talents, and remunerative enough for him to support a home and train up his children well. The competition in a large city is fierce, and it is difficult for any poor people to succeed. The Negro, however, has two especial difficulties: his training as a slave and freedman has not been such as make the average of the race as efficient and reliable workmen

as the average native American or as many foreign immigrants. The Negro is, as a rule, willing, honest and good-natured; but he is also, as a rule, careless, unreliable and unsteady. This is without doubt to be expected in a people who for generations have been trained to shirk work; but an historical excuse counts for little in the whirl and battle of bread-winning. Of course, there are large exceptions to this average rule; there are many Negroes who are as bright, talented and reliable as any class of workmen, and who in untrammeled competition would soon rise high in the economic scale, and thus by the law of the survival of the fittest we should soon have left at the bottom those inefficient and lazy drones who did not deserve a better fate. However, in the realm of social phenomena the law of survival is greatly modified by human choice, wish, whim and prejudice. And consequently one never knows when one sees a social outcast how far this failure to survive is due to the deficiencies of the individual, and how far to the accidents or injustice of his environment. This is especially the case with the Negro. Every one knows that in a city like Philadelphia a Negro does not have the same chance to exercise his ability or secure work according to his talents as a white man. Just how far this is so we shall discuss later; now it is sufficient to say in general that the sorts of work open to Negroes are not only restricted by their own lack of training but also by discrimination against them on account of their race; that their economic rise is not only hindered by their present poverty, but also by a widespread inclination to shut against them many doors of advancement. . . .

What has thus far been the result of this complicated situation? What do the mass of the Negroes of the city at present do for a living, and how successful are they in those lines? And in so far as they are successful, what have they accomplished, and where they are inefficient in their present sphere of work, what is the cause and remedy? These are the

W. E. B. DuBois

Culver Pictures

between farmers and, say, actors?

To what extent in any given [ethnic] group . . . do parents and children live in the same world, speak the same language, and share the same ideas, and how far do the conditions found account for juvenile delinquency in that particular group? (1967/1925, p. 22)

This agenda of research questions, of which those quoted here are a small sample, inspired and shaped the work of hundreds of

sociologists who were influenced by the Chicago school. To this day Chicago remains the most systematically studied city in the United States, although similar research has been carried out in other large cities from Seattle to New York.

As you can see from the types of questions that Park asked, the distinctive orientation of the Chicago school was its emphasis on the relationships among social order, social

questions before us, and we proceed to answer the first in this chapter, taking the occupations of the Negroes of the Seventh Ward first, . . .

Of the 257 boys between the ages of ten and twenty, who were regularly at work in 1896, 39 per cent were porters and errand boys; 25.5 per cent were servants; 16 per cent were common laborers, and 19.5 per cent had miscellaneous employment. The occupations in detail are as follows:

Total population, males 10 to 20	651	
Engaged in gainful occupations	257	
Porters and errand boys	100	39.0%
Servants	66	25.5
Common laborers	40	16.0
Miscellaneous employment		
Teamsters	7	
Apprentices	6	
Bootblacks	6	
Drivers	5	
Newsboys	5	
Peddlers	4	
Typesetters	3	
Actors	2	
Bricklayers	2	51 19.5
Hostlers	2	
Typist	2	
Barber,	1	
Bartender,	1	
Bookbinder,	1	
Factory hand,	1	
Rubber-worker,	1	
Sailor,	1	
Shoemaker	1	
	257	100%

Source: DuBois, 1967/1899.

disorganization, and the distribution of populations in space and time. Park and Burgess called this approach **human ecology**. With many modifications, it remains an important, though not dominant, perspective in contemporary sociology.

Human ecology, as Park and others defined it, is the branch of sociology that is concerned with population growth and change. In particular, it seeks to discover how pop-

ulations organize themselves to survive and prosper. Human ecologists are interested in how groups that are organized in different ways compete and cooperate. They also look for forms of social organization that may emerge as a group adjusts to life in new surroundings.

A key concept for human ecologists is *community*. There are many ways of defining this term, just as there are many ways of defining most of the central concepts of sociology. From the ecological perspective, however, the term *community* usually refers to a population that carries out major life functions (e.g., birth, reproduction, death) within a particular territory. Human ecology does not assume that there will ever be a "steady state" or an end to the process of change in human communities. Instead, it attempts to trace the change and document its consequences for the social environment. What happens when newcomers "invade" a community? In what way are local gangs a response to recent changes in population or in the ability of members of a community to compete for jobs? Not only do populations change, but people's preferences and behaviors also continually change. So do the technologies for producing the goods and services we want. As a result, our ways of getting a living, our modes of transportation, and our choices of leisure activities create constant change not only in communities but in entire societies.

The Chicago school became known for this "ecological" approach, the idea that the study of human society should begin with empirical questions about population size, the distribution of populations over territories, and the like. The human ecologists recognized that there are many other processes by which society is governed, but their most important contribution to the discipline of sociology was to include the processes by which populations change and communities are formed.

MAJOR SOCIOLOGICAL PERSPECTIVES

Sociological *perspectives* are based on different problems of human society, such as the problem of population size, the problem of conflict between populations, the problem of how people become part of a society, and other issues that we will encounter throughout this book. Although human ecology remains an important sociological perspective, it is by no means the only one employed by modern sociologists. Other perspectives, to which we now turn, guide empirical description and help explain social stability and social change.

Interactionism

Interactionism is the sociological perspective that views social order and social change as resulting from all the immense variety of repeated interactions among individuals and groups. Families, committees, corporations, armies, entire societies—indeed, all the social forms we can think of—are a result of interpersonal behavior in which people communicate, give and take, share, compete, and so on. If there were no exchange of goods, information, love, and all the rest—that is, if there were no interaction among people—obviously there would be no social life at all.

The interactionist perspective usually generates analyses of social life at the micro level of interpersonal relationships, but it is not limited to that level of social reality. It also looks at how middle- and macro-level phenomena result from micro-level behaviors or, conversely, how middle- and macro-level influences shape the interactions among individuals. From the interactionist perspective, for example, a family is a product of interactions among a set of individuals who define themselves as family members. But each person's understanding of how a family ought to behave is a product of middle- and macro-level forces: religious teachings about family life, laws dealing with education or child support, and so on. And these are always changing. You may have experienced the consequences of changing values that cause older and younger family members to feel differently about such issues as whether a couple should live together before marrying. In sum, the interactionist perspective insists that we look carefully at how individuals interact, how they interpret their own and other people's actions, and the consequences of those actions for the larger social group (Blumer, 1969; Frank, 1988).

The general framework of interaction-

ism contains at least two major and quite different sets of issues. One set has to do with the problems of exchange and choice: How can social order exist and groups or societies maintain stability when people have selfish motives for being in groups—that is, when they are seeking to gain as much personal advantage as they can? The second major problem is how people actually manage to communicate their values and how they arrive at mutual understandings. Research and explanations of the first problem fall under the heading of "rational choice" (or exchange theory), while the second issue is addressed by the study of "symbolic interaction." (In recent years these two areas of inquiry have emerged as quite different yet increasingly related aspects of the study of interaction. This is a rapidly developing area of sociology for which there is at present no single, agreed-upon method of presentation.)

Rational Choice—The Sociological View.

Adam Smith, whose famous work *The Wealth of Nations* (1910/1776) became the basis for most subsequent economic thought, believed that individuals always seek to maximize their pleasure and minimize their pain. If over time they are allowed to make the best possible choices for themselves, they will also produce an affluent and just society. They will serve others, even when they are unaware that they are doing so, in order to increase their own benefit. They will choose a constitution and a government that protects their property and their right to engage in trade. They will seek the government's protection against those who would infringe on their rights or attempt to dominate them, but the government need do little more than protect them and allow them to make their own choices.

You may have already encountered this theory, often known as *utilitarianism*, in an economics or political science course. In sociology it is applied to a variety of issues. Often this rational-choice view of interaction is referred to as *exchange theory* because it focuses on what people seem to be getting

The ecological approach to sociological research seeks to discover the relationships among social order, social disorganization, and the distribution of populations in space and time.

out of their interactions and what they in turn are contributing to the relationship or to the larger group. In every interaction something is being exchanged. It may be time or attention, friendship, material values (e.g., wages or possessions), or less easily calculated values like esteem or allegiance. The larger the number of interacting members, the more complex the types of exchanges that occur among them. But people do not usually remain long in interactions that are "one-way." Soon they begin to feel that they are being exploited or treated unfairly. They then leave the relationship or quit the group (Homans, 1961). In industry, for example, if workers feel that they are not being paid enough for their work they may form a union, bargain collectively with the bosses, and even go on strike. But in doing so all workers will weigh the potential benefits against the losses they may experience—losses in pay, in esteem, in friendship, and so forth. The choices are not always easy, nor are the motivations always obvious. When many values are involved, the rational calculation of benefits and costs becomes even more difficult.

Rational-choice models of behavior prompt us to look at *patterns* of behavior to see how they conform to and depart from normal expectations of profit and loss. But they do not always tell us the values on which these calculations are based. For that we need more research and different perspectives. How we learn what to value in the first place, how we communicate our choices and intentions, how we learn new values through interaction—all are subjects that require other concepts than are available in rational-choice theories of behavior. Such questions lead us toward research on how human interaction is actually carried out and understood by people in their daily lives.

Symbolic Interactionism. When we make calculated choices in interacting with other people, we may be said to be acting rationally. But there are likely to be other forces shaping our behavior as well. For example, you may select a particular course because the instructor is rumored to be good. But what does "good" mean—clear and well organized? an easy grader? friendly? humorous? The dimensions of a choice can be very complicated, and we may not be aware of

everything that goes into our decisions. For example, you may, without realizing it, choose a course as much to be with certain other people as to be in that particular course. Our choices tell other people about us: what we like, what we may want to become, and so on. Indeed, the way people dress, the way they carry themselves (body language), the way they speak to each other, and the gestures they make (whether they are aware of them or not) convey a great deal of information that is not always intentional or expressed in speech. There are levels of communication that give information without speaking it, or speak one thing and mean another. But words are of great importance, too, and the content of communication is first made explicit in words and sentences. Sociologists refer to all these aspects of behavior as *symbolic interaction*. From the symbolic-interactionist perspective, "society itself tends to be seen as a mosaic of little scenes and dramas in which people make indications to themselves and others, respond to those indications, align their actions, and so build identities and social structures" (Rock, 1985, p. 844; see also Goffman, 1959; Hughes, 1958).

Symbolic interactionists call attention to how social life is "constructed" through the mundane acts of social communication. For example, in all the choices students make—their joining of friendship groups, their learning of the informal rules of the school, their challenging and breaking of those rules—the social order of student society, or "college culture," is actually "constructed." Erving Goffman, whose work was mentioned earlier, is known for his research on these processes. Goffman applied the symbolic-interactionist perspective to the study of everyday interactions like rituals of greeting and departure, to daily life in asylums and gambling houses, and to behavior in streets and public places. His work examines how people behave in social situations and how their "performances" are rated by others.

The power of symbolic interactionism lies in its ability to generate theories about how people learn to play certain roles and how those roles are used in the social construction of groups and organizations. However, if we want to think sociologically about more complex phenomena, such as the rise of bureaucratic organizations or the reasons that some societies experience revolutions, we also need the concepts developed by two other perspectives: functionalism and conflict theory.

Functionalism

Is society simply the sum total of countless micro-level interactions, or do the organizations within a society have properties independent of the actions of individuals? When we speak of the family, the army, the corporation, or the laboratory, we generally have in mind an entity marked by certain specific functions, tasks, and types of behavior. The army requires that its members learn to engage in armed combat, even if that is not what they will be doing most of the time. The family requires that its members behave in nurturant ways toward one another. The farm requires that those who run it know how to plant and harvest. Individual interactions may determine how well a given person performs these various tasks, but the larger organization—the army, the family, the farm—establishes specific ways of behaving, of doing the work of that organization, which the individual must master. In this sense the organization, which exists longer than the life of any of its members, has its own existence.

The **functionalist** perspective in sociology asks how society manages to carry out the functions it must perform in order to maintain social order, feed large masses of people each day, defend itself against attackers, produce the next generation, and so on. From this perspective the many groups and organizations that make up a society form the structure of human society. This social structure is a complex system designed to carry out the essential functions of human life. The function of the family, for example, is to raise and train a new generation to replace the old; the function of the military is to defend the society; the function of schools is to teach the next generation the beliefs and skills they will need to maintain the society in the future; and the function of religion is to develop a shared sense of morality.

When a society is functioning well, all its major parts are said to be "well integrated" and in equilibrium. But periods of rapid social change can throw social structures out of equilibrium. Entire ways of life can lose their purpose or function. When that happens, the various structures of society can become poorly integrated, and what were formerly useful functions can become "dysfunctional."

Consider an example. The family structure in agrarian societies, in which most people work the land, typically includes three generations, with many members in each generation all living close to one another. Labor is in great demand; many hands are needed where there are no machines to perform work in fields and barnyards and granaries. The emphasis on early marriage and large numbers of children that is found in the agrarian family is highly functional for a nonindustrialized, labor-short society. But when such a society industrializes and its agriculture becomes mechanized, families often continue to produce large numbers of children even though the demand for farm labor has decreased. When they grow up, those children may migrate to towns and cities. Often such migrants maintain the value of large family size, but if there are a limited number of jobs in the cities they may join the ranks of the unemployed, and their children, in turn, may grow up in poverty. In this situation the family can be said to be poorly integrated with the needs of the society; the value of large family size has become dysfunctional—it no longer contributes to the well-being of groups or individuals.

Conflict Theory

A major flaw in the functionalist perspective is the fact that we have rarely seen anything approaching equilibrium in human societies. Conflict and strife appear to be as basic to society as harmony, integration, and smooth functioning. In our century alone, two world wars and many civil wars have disrupted the lives of millions of people. Almost as devastating as the wars was the Great Depression of the 1930s, the most severe economic slump in modern history. Worst of all were the nightmares of the Nazi Holocaust and the purges of Stalinist Russia, in which over 20 million people were exterminated.

The world wars, the Depression, and the Holocaust shocked and demoralized the entire world. They also called into question

Sovfoto

These Russian men and women are searching for the bodies of their loved ones in the aftermath of a battle in World War II. As wars become more destructive, the study of social conflict and its solutions takes on even greater urgency.

In Marx's view, the division of people in a society into different classes, defined by how they make a living, always produces conflict.

the optimism of the nineteenth- and early-twentieth-century social philosophers, many of whom believed in the promise of progress through modern science and technology. But between 1914 and the end of World War II there were enough instances of modern ideas and technologies being put to horrible uses to disillusion all but the most ardent optimists. Bewildered intellectuals and political leaders turned to sociology to find some explanation for those horrors.

One explanation was provided by Marxian theory. According to Marx, the cause of conflict in modern times could be found in the rise of capitalism. Under capitalism, forms of exploitation and domination spread. For example, in the early period of industrial capitalism workers were forced to work twelve hours a day, six days a week; in less developed areas of the world large populations were virtually enslaved by the new colonial powers.

At the heart of capitalism, for Marx, is conflict among people in different economic classes, especially between those who control wealth and power and those who do not. Marx believed that the division of people in a society into different classes, defined by how they make a living, always produces conflict. Under capitalism this conflict occurs between the owners of factories and the workers. Marx believed that class conflict would eventually destroy or at least vastly modify capitalism. His theory is at the heart of what has come to be known as the **conflict perspective.**

In the 1960s, when protests against racism and segregation, the Vietnam War, pollution of the environment, and discrimination against women each became the focus of a major social movement, the conflict perspective became more prominent. It clearly was not possible to explain the rapid appearance of major social movements with theories that emphasized how the social system would function if it were in a state of equilibrium. Even Marxian theory did not do a very good job of predicting the protest movements of the 1960s or their effects on American society. The environmental movement and the women's movement, for example, were not based on economic inequalities alone, nor were the people who joined them necessarily exploited workers. Sociologists interested in the role of conflict in social change therefore had to go beyond the Marxian view. Many turned to the writings of the German sociologist Georg Simmel, who argued that conflict is necessary as a basis for the formation of alliances. According to Simmel, conflict is one means whereby a "web of group affiliations" is constructed. The continual shifting of alliances within this web of social groups can help explain who becomes involved in social movements and how much power those movements are able to acquire.

The concept of power holds a central place in conflict theory. From the functionalist perspective, society holds together because its members share the same basic beliefs about how people should behave. Conflict theorists point out that the role of power is just as important as the influence of shared beliefs in explaining why society does not disintegrate into violent chaos. Power in society is the ability of an individual or group to change the behavior of others. A nation's government, as we will see in Chapter 3, usually controls the use of force (a form of power) to maintain social order. For sociologists who study conflict and power, the important questions are who benefits from the exercise of power and who loses. For example, when the government intervenes in a strike and obliges workers to return to their jobs, does the public at large benefit or does the corporation against which the workers were striking? And what about the workers themselves? What do they gain or lose? Such questions are central to conflict theory today (Gramsci, 1971).

The Multidimensional View of Society

Each of the sociological perspectives just described leads to different questions and different kinds of observations about social life. From the ecological perspective come questions about how populations can exist and flourish in various natural and social environ- ments. From the interactionist perspective come questions about how people get along and behave in groups and organizations of all kinds. Functionalism asks questions about how society is structured and how it works as a social system. And the conflict perspective asks how power is used to maintain order and how conflict changes society. These different perspectives developed as sociologists asked different questions about society. In contemporary sociology each continues to stimulate a relatively distinct body of research based on the types of questions being asked. Yet a great deal of research combines the insights of different perspectives in ways that vastly increase the power of the resulting analysis. Figure 1-2 summarizes the major sociological perspectives and the kinds of ques-

> *No single set of theories explains how societies are formed or why they change; often the most useful view of society is a multidimensional view.*

Figure 1–2: **Major Sociological Perspectives**

PERSPECTIVES		DESCRIPTION	GENERATES QUESTIONS ABOUT . . .	APPLICATIONS
	Interactionism	Studies how social structures are created in the course of human interaction.	How people behave in intimate groups; how symbols and communication shape perceptions; how social roles are learned and society "constructed" through interaction.	Educational practice, courtroom procedure, therapy.
	Functionalism	Asks how societies carry out the functions they must perform; views the structures of society as a system designed to carry out those functions.	How society is structured and how social structures work together as a system to perform the major functions of society.	Study of formal organizations, development of social policies, management science.
	Conflict Theory	Holds that power is just as important as shared values in holding society together; conflict is also responsible for social change.	How power affects the distribution of scarce resources and how conflict changes society.	Study of politics, social movements, corporate power structures.

Box 1–2: **Perspectives on the Duel**

Until the early decades of this century, duels were a fairly common way for men of certain social classes to settle their conflicts. In attempting to understand what is happening in this picture (and why such events are now outlawed), one can apply all of the major sociological perspectives. The functionalist perspective highlights the role of each participant. Each combatant has two seconds (grouped at the left). A starter, who is neutral, plays the role of referee and must make a final effort to resolve the dispute before giving the order to fire. In attempting to determine why duels no longer occur with any frequency, the functionalist perspective would look at how laws and law enforcement agencies have evolved to prevent such drastic means of redressing "injuries" to the male sense of honor.

The interactionist perspective might focus on details of the duel as a social ritual. Once each side has defined the situation as calling for mortal combat, the duel is likely to unfold according to traditional rules, much as any other kind of ceremony would. Theorists who favor a rational-choice approach would note that the actual duel, rather than the negotiations that led up to it, represents a failure of rationality in interaction because the stakes are so high for the loser. And this fact would help explain why the duel has disappeared as a form of conflict resolution, to be replaced, for example, by the lawsuit.

Finally, conflict theorists would ask why duels like these were characteristic of interpersonal conflict in the upper classes. They might also question whether such duels actually resolved conflict or instead stirred up feuds that could last for generations. They might also show that behavior similar to duels, such as street fights and boxing matches, continue to be found in different forms in different social classes.

tions they ask, and Box 1-2 presents an example of the multidimensional view of society.

It is important to be aware that there is no single, unifying set of theories explaining how societies are formed or why they change.

The major perspectives and the social scientists who develop them often seek to explain different aspects of social phenomena. Social life encompasses such a vast array of phenomena that it is doubtful whether a single set of theories will ever explain everything we seek to know about social order and change. As sociologist Joseph Gusfield pointed out at a recent national conference, anyone waiting for a social-scientific Einstein not only is waiting for a train that will not arrive but is in the wrong station (Bernstein, 1988, p. A14). Nevertheless, a student who can grasp and apply the major sociological perspectives will be armed with a powerful set of tools with which to deepen his or her understanding of how and why the social world is changing.

Together, the sociological imagination and the basic sociological perspectives can help you see beyond the headlines and gain greater insight into events occurring in the world today. You will also be better equipped to understand their relevance to your own life, both now and in the future. Perhaps you will be motivated to choose a career in sociology. Box 1-3 contains a further discussion of the types of careers pursued by sociologists, and more information about current sociological research is presented in the Frontiers and Challenges sections of later chapters and in the Appendix. Students who look carefully at those special sections will see that the various perspectives are almost never used alone but are combined with ideas from other perspectives to explain social conditions and social change.

Box 1–3: **Careers in Sociology**

What could be more stimulating than to spend a lifetime learning and teaching about human society? But can one really make a living as a sociologist? And what use is a sociology major if one does not go on to do graduate work in sociology?

In attempting to answer these questions, it is helpful to distinguish between careers in sociology itself and applications of sociology in other fields. In North America most sociologists with graduate degrees teach and conduct research in colleges and universities. This has been true since the early decades of this century, but there is a growing trend toward the application of sociology in many fields outside academia. In 1983, of approximately 21,000 M.A. and Ph.D. sociologists in the U.S. labor force, 52 percent worked full time in academia, 17.5 percent were part-time academics, and 30.5 percent had careers in applied fields outside colleges and universities (Manderscheid and Greenwald, 1983).

Of these groups, the third is increasing steadily; the first two seem to have reached a peak in the late 1970s. Although careers in colleges and universities are difficult to secure in almost any field today because of declining student enrollments, there is hope for the future. The 1990s should see renewed growth in college enrollments and more openings for work in higher education for students who complete graduate school with good credentials.

But there is much more to value in a sociology major than the prospect of going to graduate school. The study of sociology beyond the introductory level can lead to advanced skills in computation, data analysis, and statistics. Research experience in the field can greatly increase your ability to understand social situations and to get along with people from different backgrounds. Sociological training can also be applied in organizations of all kinds. Government agencies, political campaigns, law firms, marketing firms, communications corporations—in these and many other organizations a person with sociological skills can fit in well and make important contributions. Medical sociology, for example, leads to research and program development in health-care fields, and the sociology of developing nations is good preparation for a career in government or private work abroad. The list could be made much longer, but the point is that further study in sociology, regardless of whether or not you want to become a sociologist, is an excellent grounding for the world of work after college.

SUMMARY

*S*ociology is the scientific study of human societies and of human behavior in the groups that make up a society. It is concerned with how social conditions influence our lives as individuals. The ability to see the world from this point of view has been described as the *sociological imagination*.

Sociologists study social behavior at three levels of complexity. *Micro-level* sociology deals with behaviors that occur at the level of the individual and immediate others. The *middle level* of sociological observation is concerned with how the social structures in which people participate actually shape their lives. *Macro-level* studies attempt to explain the social processes that influence populations, social classes, and entire societies.

Sociology as a scientific discipline did not develop until the nineteenth and twentieth centuries, although social thought has been part of human existence since the beginning of recorded history. The scientific discoveries of the seventeenth century led to the rise of the idea of progress, as opposed to the notion of human helplessness in the face of divine Providence. In the eighteenth century, revolutions in Europe and North America completely changed the social order and gave rise to new perspectives on human social life.

Out of this period of social and intellectual ferment came the idea of creating a science of human society. Sociology, as the new science was called, developed in Europe in the nineteenth century. During that formative period a number of outstanding sociologists shaped and refined the new discipline. Among them were Karl Marx, Émile Durkheim, and Max Weber.

In the twentieth century, sociology developed most rapidly in North America, spurred by the need for empirical information concerning social conditions. Numerous "social surveys" were conducted around the turn of the century, and by the late 1920s two distinct approaches to the study of society had evolved at American universities. The "Chicago school" focused on the relationship between the individual and society, whereas the major East Coast universities leaned toward macro-level analysis.

Under the leadership of Robert Park and Ernest Burgess, the Chicago school developed the approach known as *human ecology*. This perspective emphasizes the relationships among social order, social disorganization, and the distribution of populations in space and time. A key concept for human ecologists is *community*, meaning a population that carries out major functions within a particular territory.

Modern sociologists employ other basic perspectives besides human ecology. *Interactionism* is a perspective that views social order and social change as resulting from all the repeated interactions among individuals and groups. One version of this approach is *rational-choice* or *exchange theory*, which focuses on what people seem to be getting out of their interactions and what they contribute to them. Another version is the *symbolic-interactionist perspective*, which studies how social structures are actually created in the course of human interaction.

Functionalism, in contrast, is concerned primarily with the large-scale structures of society; it asks how those structures enable society to carry out its basic functions. In the decades since World War II this perspective has been strongly challenged by *conflict theory*, which emphasizes the role of conflict and power in explaining not only why societies change but also why they hold together.

None of the major sociological perspectives is fully independent of the others. Each emphasizes different questions and different observations about social life. Used in combination, they greatly increase our ability to understand and explain almost any aspect of human society.

GLOSSARY

social conditions: the realities of life that we create together as social beings (**p. 6**).

sociological imagination: according to C. Wright Mills, the ability to see how social conditions affect our lives (**p. 7**).

sociology: the scientific study of human societies and human behavior in the groups that make up a society (**p. 8**).

micro-level sociology: an approach to the study of society that focuses on patterns of social interaction at the individual level (**p. 8**).

macro-level sociology: an approach to the study of society that focuses on the major structures and institutions of society (**p. 9**).

middle-level sociology: an approach to the study of society that focuses on relationships between social structures and the individual (**p. 9**).

scientific method: the process by which theories and explanations are constructed through repeated observation and careful description (**p. 11**).

human ecology: a sociological perspective that emphasizes relations among social order, social disorganization, and the distribution of populations in time and space (**p. 15**).

interactionism: a sociological perspective that views social order and social change as resulting from all the repeated interactions among individuals and groups (**p. 16**).

functionalism: a sociological perspective that focuses on the ways in which a complex pattern of social structures and arrangements contributes to social order (**p. 18**).

conflict theory: a sociological perspective that emphasizes the role of conflict and power in society (**p. 19**).

WHERE TO FIND IT

Books

The Sociological Imagination (C. Wright Mills; Oxford University Press, 1959). Still the best and most passionate statement of what the sociological imagination is, by the person who coined the phrase.

Invitation to Sociology: A Humanist Perspective (Peter Berger; Doubleday Anchor, 1963). A lively look at the science and craft of sociology by an author with a predominantly interactionist perspective.

Human Society (Kingsley Davis; Macmillan, 1949). A classic text in sociology that presents a brilliant overview of how functionalist theories are applied to many social phenomena.

Sociology for Pleasure (Marcello Truzzi; Prentice-Hall, 1974). A collection of studies of offbeat social groups and situations—gypsies, cults, nudist-camp visitors, and many others—that reminds the reader that sociology can illuminate little-known social worlds.

Masters of Sociological Thought (Lewis Coser; Harcourt Brace Jovanovich, 1977). An indispensable source for anyone interested in in-depth treatments of the contributions made by the founders of sociology.

The Handbook of Sociology (Neil J. Smelser; Sage Publications, 1988). A collection of "state-of-the-art" reviews of the literature in major sociological fields.

Journals

Contemporary Sociology The official journal of book reviews in sociology.

American Sociological Review (the journal of the American Sociological Association). The articles in this journal are often quite technical and may be somewhat advanced for the beginning student, but they offer a good perspective on current research.

American Journal of Sociology The oldest journal in sociology; a treasure trove of articles going back to the early decades of the century. Consult the index for earlier papers and recent issues for excellent new research.

Other Sources

International Encyclopedia of the Social Sciences A comprehensive collection of essays that define and discuss the concepts and methods of sociology and social science.

Sociological Abstracts A set of reviews of existing literature on a variety of social-scientific subjects. The abstracts are organized by topic and offer brief overviews of original research papers and other articles.

ART AND THE SOCIOLOGICAL EYE

Cave painting from Los Caballos, Spain.

D rawing and painting give us our earliest evidence of human beings' desire to understand social life and to communicate that understanding to others. We cannot know in much detail how the preliterate cave dwellers of southern Europe and northern Africa lived during the late Ice Age, 10,000 years ago. But drawings like this hunting scene can give us glimpses into the way prehistoric humans felt about their lives. How carefully the artist rendered a typical hunting scene, with special attention to the placement of the hunters before the onrushing antelope. In the very choice of the hunting subject, the ancient artist is communicating a message about what was uppermost in the minds of our early ancestors.

The art of any of the world's peoples, past or present, can likewise be "read" for evidence of how people organize their society, for the nature of interpersonal relationships, for what they value as sacred or simply enjoyable, and for what they despise. Thus, in the painted limestone carving of the Egyptian prince Rahotep and his wife Nofret, probably executed by an official artist of the pharaoh in about 2610 B.C., we see striking evidence that the rulers of one of the world's first civilizations could have either dark or light skin. Outward features such as skin color or hair must not have had the meaning they do in many societies today. And look at how the couple's dress reveals differences in what must have been considered proper appearance for men and women of their social standing. Her breasts are covered, but his chest is bare; his only ornaments are a thin necklace and an equally thin mustache, whereas her hair and jewelry are far more elaborate.

In the same manner, the art of people with histories and ways of life that we may think of as far different from our own can show how much experience we actually share. The figures painted on a vase more than 2500 years ago demonstrate that the soldiers of ancient Greece often had time on their hands just as modern soldiers do. Like their modern counterparts, they also enjoyed passing the time by gambling. Similarly, we can "read" the

Amphora by Exekias, about 530 B.C. Black figure amphora with Achilles and Ajax playing dice.

Prince Rahotep and His Wife Nofret, artist unknown, about 2610 B.C. Painted limestone, height 47¼".

Mother and Child, by Ennutsiak of Frobisher Bay, date unknown. Green stone and red paint or ink, 6.4 × 4.4 × 8.3 cm.

National Museum, Tokyo

Portrait of the Actor Sawamura Sojuro, by Katsukawa Shunsho, 1781. Woodcut on paper, $14\frac{1}{2}$ × 10″.

meaning of the soapstone carving by an unknown Eskimo artist as a statement about the universal quality of parental love and nurturing, just as the scene from an eighteenth-century Japanese woodcut can be read as evidence of longstanding traditions of male dominance and female subordination in Japanese society.

One of the goals of this book is to help you train your sociological eye, to help you learn to interpret the events around you and discover what they convey about social organization and social interaction. As in any introductory course, you will be learning to apply many concepts. And because the concepts and theories of sociology pertain almost exclusively to the study of societies and how they change, the visual material in each chapter is used as a way of applying sociological ideas and highlighting major areas of social change.

Consider two more examples. The famous wedding portrait painted by Jan van Eyck in 1434 can be interpreted at a number of levels. On the surface it is simply a painting of a newly married bride and groom, people of obvious wealth and social standing, in their bedroom. But at a deeper level of meaning, the painting is a study in the symbols associated with marriage in Europe during the fifteenth century. The wedding bed was understood as a symbol of marital fidelity, the dog as a symbol of trust; and the couple have removed their shoes to show that they stand on the holy ground of matrimony. These and other symbols in the painting could not be understood, however, without some study of the way people of that time thought about marriage and its relationship to religious belief.

Similarly, if we seek visual evidence about the lives of the peasants who till the soil throughout much of the world, we can

The Marriage of Giovanni and Giovanna Canami, by Jan van Eyck, 1434. Panel, 33 × 22½″.

Peasant Wedding, by Pieter Bruegel the Elder, about 1565. Panel, 45 × 64″.

The Gleaners, by Francois Millet, 1848. Oil on canvas, 21¼ × 26″.

find it in works like Pieter Bruegel's 1565 painting of the rough pleasures at a peasant wedding and François Millet's moving depiction, nearly three centuries later, of women gleaning bits of fallen grain after the harvest. It would be difficult to empathize with the experience of peasants or of people from any social world other than our own without the ability to recognize the sociological implications of paintings, photographs, and the actual scenes we witness at first hand in daily life.

But let us not confuse sociology and fine art. These artists were not sociologists, nor were they necessarily seeking to make points about society and social change. Their goals were to use the forms of everyday life to make something that would please them and their patrons, to capture the nuances of shape and form, to convey the emotional quality of a scene. The task of the sociologist is to read their art for its social meaning without detracting from the magic that makes art beautiful and timeless.

CHAPTER OUTLINE

- **Applying the Sociological Imagination**
  - Formulating Research Questions
  - Reviewing the Literature

- **The Basic Methods**
  - Observation
  - Experiments
  - Survey Research
  - Research Ethics and the Rights of Respondents

- **Analyzing the Data**
  - Reading Tables
  - Percent Analysis
  - Correlations

- **Theories and Perspectives**

Erica Berger

A social worker interviewing a client

CHAPTER 2

THE TOOLS OF SOCIOLOGY

The debate became so heated that the shredded styrofoam cups littering the table were blown first one way, then the other. College-cafeteria debates sometimes get loud and energetic, especially when the subject is welfare. On this occasion one of the contestants, a member of the Young Conservatives Club, claimed that America's welfare policies encourage dependency. His liberal opponent, though an old friend, tended to get hot under the collar and to mix personal attacks with logic. "You stingy bastard," he shouted. "Don't you know that if they are given a chance to work, people who are on welfare try to get off it as soon as possible?" The debate raged on, just as it does in society as a whole. But what were the contestants really asking, and what were they using as data to back up their arguments?

"You're letting your bleeding heart cloud your vision," the young conservative countered. "Haven't you ever noticed how many fancy cars, Cadillacs and Lincolns, there are in ———— [a poor part of town]? Those people collect welfare and watch the soaps until their boyfriends come by to take them for a ride. Would you go out looking for work when you could spend your time watching TV and cruising for burgers?" The liberal answered by asserting that "people on welfare are forever trying to get off it. Every week my uncle has welfare mothers coming into his office and asking for work. If they watch television, it's because they can't work and have nothing else to do."

Both of these "commonsense" sociologists were making inferences from their own observations, which were not necessarily accurate or relevant to the question being asked. Moreover, although they were arguing about "welfare," they had not adequately defined the terms of the debate. At its broadest level, their question was whether welfare—wealth transferred from the society as a whole to certain categories of people—results in increased social and psychological dependency and reduced motivation. In this question, "people on welfare" could include those who receive low-cost student loans, tax breaks for depleting oil wells, low-cost federal flood insurance, disability payments, or any of hundreds of other direct and indirect subsidies available to certain categories of people. Clearly, our debate about welfare does not refer to all of these categories. Rather, it centers on poor people who receive welfare in the form of payments from the government.

We have determined that the debate over welfare policy focuses on poor people, but does the question refer to *all* poor people, including those who are suffering from the effects of plant closings or disabilities or advanced age, or does it refer to an even more specific category of people who receive certain forms of welfare assistance? A researcher must make the question as specific as possible before deciding what methods to use to gather data that will provide an answer. In our debate, the contestants are probably referring to households receiving Aid to Families with Dependent Children (AFDC), the main form of welfare assistance to poor people who are not in the labor force or receiving unemployment benefits.

Given these qualifications of the term *welfare*, the question a researcher might ask would probably be something like: Does the current system of AFDC payments create dependency, which prevents the recipients from seeking employment or other ways of getting off welfare? Thinking about this more specific question leads to other questions: What categories of people are most likely to be included on the welfare rolls? How long do they stay on welfare? What variables best explain why they get off the welfare rolls or stay on? What part does education play in the length of time people stay on welfare? And what is the significance of the types of jobs available in the local labor market? With questions that specify the populations to be studied and the key variables to consider (time on the welfare rolls, education, available jobs, reasons for terminating or continuing welfare, and the like), the social scientist can begin to design research that will go beyond the impressionistic, unscientific data (such as the presence of Cadillacs and Lincolns in poor neighborhoods) that so often enter into discussions of social issues.

APPLYING THE SOCIOLOGICAL IMAGINATION

Most people associate social-scientific research with questionnaires, opinion surveys, and statistical reports. This is unfortunate. True, sociologists throughout the world use these research techniques, but they also use many other methods to explore social conditions. In this chapter we will review many of the most common research tools used by sociologists. We will show how sociological research conforms to the rules of the scientific method and how the findings lead to changes in theories and, in turn, to new research.

Anyone who embarks on scientific research, no matter what the subject or the method used, will go through many intellectual and emotional ups and downs before the work is done. Very often it will appear that the research is easy to define and conduct; soon, however, it will seem far more complicated, and the research questions themselves may appear less well defined than they did at the outset. This can be just as true in biology or chemistry as in sociology or another social science. Nevertheless, in all research projects certain basic steps must be completed.

> *In all research projects certain basic steps must be completed, though not always in the same order.*

1. *Deciding on the problem.* At first this may be simply a subject or topic of interest. Eventually, however, it must be worded in the form of a specific research question or questions in order to provide a focus for the rest of the work.
2. *Reviewing the literature.* Usually others have conducted research on the same topic. Find their reports and use them to determine what you can accomplish through your own research.
3. *Formulating research questions.* The work of others points to questions that have not been answered. Your own interest, time, resources, and available methods help determine what specific questions

within your broad topic you can actually tackle.

4. *Selecting a method.* Different questions require different types of data—which, in turn, suggest different methods of data collection and analysis. Some of those methods are described in detail in this chapter.

5. *Analyzing the data.* Data are analyzed at each stage of the research, not just at the end.

In this chapter we act as if this step-by-step procedure is always followed by researchers in the social sciences. But do not assume that this procedure can be applied to every research question. Science is rarely a matter of smooth progress toward a final analysis. One does not always progress easily from one step to another, and often one must go back and repeat earlier steps. In addition, some research questions require that we devise new ways of conducting research or new combinations of existing research methods.

Formulating Research Questions

A good deal of information is required even to know what situations or events one should study in conducting research on a particular social issue. General questions about societies or social behavior have to be translated into specific questions that can be studied using observations and measures of all kinds. Émile Durkheim's study of suicide provides a good example of the process by which a sociologist converts a broad question about social change into the specific questions to be addressed in an *empirical study*—a study that gathers evidence to describe behavior and to prove or disprove explanations of why that behavior occurs. These explanations are often, but not always, stated in the form of a **hypothesis,** a statement that expresses an informed or "educated" guess regarding the possible relationship between two or more phenomena.

In his study of suicide Durkheim challenged the intellectuals and scientists of his day. Through the presentation of verifiable statistical evidence on suicide rates in different societies, he demonstrated that he could predict where and when suicides would be more numerous. Psychological reasons might account for why a particular individual committed suicide, but Durkheim showed that "social variables" such as religion or fluctuations in economic conditions could explain differences in the number of suicides from one society or region to another.

The question that eventually led Durkheim to his empirical study of suicide actually had nothing to do with suicide. He began by thinking about the consequences of large-scale social change in Western nations. In particular, he believed that industrialization and the rapid growth of cities weakened people's attachment to their local communities. As they became increasingly anonymous and isolated, they were more likely to engage in a variety of self-destructive acts, the most extreme being suicide. In Durkheim's view, the act of suicide could be explained as much by social variables like rates of marriage and divorce as by individual psychological variables like depression or despair. Thus for Durkheim the study of suicide was a way of exploring the larger concept of integration or lack of integration into society: He sought to discover whether people who were less well integrated into society (i.e., more isolated from other people) were more likely to commit suicide.

If this view was correct, Durkheim reasoned, the rates of suicide among various populations should vary along with measures of

Émile Durkheim (1858–1917) was a French philosopher and sociologist who was especially concerned with the question of what causes social order and with explaining the nature and causes of social solidarity and individual alienation from society. He is best known for his thorough use of empirical research methods to study "social facts" such as suicide.

The Bettmann Archive, Inc.

social integration. He therefore formulated these hypotheses, among others:

- Suicide rates should be higher for unmarried people than for married people.
- Suicide rates should be higher for people without children than for people with children.
- Suicide rates should be higher for people with higher levels of education (because education stresses individual achievement, which weakens group ties).
- Suicide rates should be higher in Protestant than in Catholic communities (because Protestantism places more stress on individual achievement than Catholicism does and this, in turn, weakens group ties).

Each of these hypotheses specifies a relationship between two variables that can be tested—that is, proved true or false—through empirical observation. In sociology, **variables** are characteristics of individuals, groups, or entire societies that can vary from one case to another. The suicide rate in the hypotheses just presented is an example of a social variable. Religion, education, marital status, and number of children are other variables in these hypotheses.

The techniques Durkheim used to establish a set of hypotheses became a model for modern social-scientific research. We would use the same techniques in designing a study of the welfare question. For example, we could state at least the following hypotheses about welfare and dependency:

- Welfare dependency, as measured by length of time on the welfare rolls, varies directly (i.e., in the same direction) with rates of unemployment in the recipient's community. In other words, the higher the rate of unemployment in the welfare recipient's community, the longer her stay on welfare will be.
- Welfare dependency varies inversely (i.e., in the opposite direction) with the recipient's education. That is, the higher a welfare recipient's level of education, the shorter her stay on welfare will be.
- Welfare dependency varies inversely with the age of the first child.[1] Because welfare payments are made to mothers with chil-

dren under eighteen, we can expect that stays on welfare will be longer for women with young children. The older the children, then, the less likely the mother is to remain on welfare.

Each of these hypotheses states a relationship between two variables. The **dependent variable** is the one we want to explain (in this case, welfare dependency), and the **independent variable** is a factor the researcher believes causes changes in the dependent variable. It is necessary to be extremely careful in making statements about causality, however. All social phenomena are caused by a number of variables rather than by only one or two. We can say that lack of education is a cause of welfare dependency, for example, but we must immediately qualify that statement because many mothers who lack education are not on welfare. Thus we say that lack of education is one cause of welfare dependency, since women with more education have an easier time finding alternatives to welfare payments.

But, clearly, the story is more complicated than that. For some, welfare becomes a way of life; for others, it is merely a transition to another job or family or both. How can we find out why some mothers become dependent on welfare payments while others soon leave the welfare rolls? Many sociologists have argued that before anyone can develop a set of testable hypotheses about the causes of welfare dependency (or any other complex social situation) it is necessary to know a great deal about the actual experiences of the people involved. Thus, even if the sociologist has never been on welfare, he or she can attempt to see the world from the viewpoint of welfare recipients and to find out what their daily lives are like. If they exist, such studies are usually the first ones consulted when the sociologist begins research on a particular problem.

> *A hypothesis specifies a relationship between two variables that can be tested through empirical observation.*

---

[1] All of these hypotheses have been shown to be correct (Bane and Ellwood, 1983; Ellwood, 1988).

Reviewing the Literature

Perhaps the insights one would need to understand the issues surrounding welfare dependency are already available in the "literature"—in existing books or journal articles, published statistics, photos, or other materials. There is no need to conduct new research if the answers being sought are already available. Most sociological research thus begins in the library with a "review of the literature."

To stimulate our sociological imagination about welfare dependency, we need to look at a variety of studies that deal with this issue. But it takes some imagination just to think of the kinds of studies to look for. The various sociological perspectives described in Chapter 1 can help organize the search, especially when the perspectives are framed as questions.

Most sociological research begins with a review of the literature to determine whether the answers being sought are already available.

Who? How Many? Where? Who are we talking about and where are they found? This is a way of phrasing the ecological perspective, which suggests why that perspective is helpful in beginning research on an issue. In researching almost any subject involving human behavior, it is helpful to ask who is involved and in what numbers, and where the behavior in question occurs. The ecological perspective gives rise to two types of studies: community studies and demographic studies. Community studies are one of the richest research traditions in sociology. They portray the typical day-to-day life of a particular population. An example of a community study of a welfare population is Carol Stack's *All Our Kin* (1974). Stack spent two years in close company with a group of women, most of whom were on welfare. She visited with them in their kitchens and living rooms. She accompanied them to clinics and welfare offices, day-care centers, churches, and local markets. Stack's study shows that the typical welfare budget is inadequate to provide a "decent" life for an American family. Yet welfare becomes a way of life for some women because it takes so much time to deal with the various social-service agencies and to cope with the problems of poverty that they are unable to accumulate the money or skills they need to escape from their situation.

Stack's study is only one of many studies of poor communities. There are community studies of the rural poor, the aged poor, poor teenagers, and many other populations that have high rates of welfare dependency. This is where demographic studies can be very useful, as they provide counts of people in various relevant population categories—in this case, people on welfare, going on welfare, or getting off welfare. For example, the welfare population referred to in the argument at the beginning of the chapter consists of single mothers, a population that is generally thought to consist of black women living in central-city slums. But demographic studies have shown that there are at least twice as many white women as black on welfare and that in some rural areas high proportions of people of all races are on the welfare rolls. Another common assumption is that when women go on welfare they remain on it forever. But demographic studies (which, among other things, measure the ways in which people earn their income) show that 66 percent of women who go on welfare remain on the welfare rolls for periods of two years or less, and most never do so again (Bane and Ellwood, 1983; O'Neill et al., 1984).

What Groups or Organizations Are Involved? This question stems from the functionalist perspective. It asks how society is organized to deal with a social issue or problem. Functionalist sociologists are concerned with how social policies actually function, as opposed to how they are supposed to function. Kirsten A. Grønbjerg (1977), for example, showed that welfare as a system evolved as a result of Americans' demands that the federal government "do something" about poverty. But she found that certain policies demanded by the public (e.g., requiring that there be no adult male in the welfare recipient's household) do little to reduce welfare dependency. We will see later in the chapter that experimental studies have attempted to trace the consequences of changes in the organization and operation of welfare programs (Auletta, 1982).

Who Has the Power? This is a key question arising from the conflict perspective. Studies that take a conflict approach to poverty frequently criticize the operation of the welfare system. They find that the existing organization of welfare grants is a means by which the powerful attempt to control the behavior of the poor, rather than a system designed to offer support to less fortunate members of society. Thus in their book *Regulating the Poor* (1971) Frances Fox Piven and Richard Cloward showed that welfare rolls expand in times of high unemployment and contract when low-paying jobs are more plentiful. They interpreted this finding as indicating that the welfare system is used by policymakers to maintain a "reserve" of unemployed, less-skilled workers who will be forced to take the worst jobs when they become available. When social-welfare programs have been improved, the authors found, it is usually because the poor themselves have forced policymakers to pay attention to their needs (Piven and Cloward, 1971, 1982).

These are only a few of the studies one would find in a review of the literature on welfare and poverty. They are not cataloged according to the basic sociological perspectives. Rather, one needs to know what questions each of these perspectives raises about an issue. For any research subject, if you ask questions about who and where and how people interact, what organizations and policies guide their actions, and who has the power, you will be well on your way toward a thorough review of what is known about the issue.

THE BASIC METHODS

O nce the researcher has specified a question, developed hypotheses, and reviewed the literature, the next step is to decide on the method or methods to be used in conducting the actual research. Sociological research methods are the techniques an investigator uses to systematically gather information, or data, to help answer a question about some aspect of society. The variety of methods that may be used is vast, with the choice of a method depending largely on the type of question being asked. The most frequently used methods are field observation, experiments, and the survey.

Observation

Participant Observation. Much sociological research requires direct observation of the people being studied. Community studies like Stack's study of women on welfare are based on lengthy periods spent observing a particular group. This research method is rarely successful unless the sociologist also participates in the daily life of the people he or she is observing—that is, becomes their friend and a member of their social groups. Therefore, the central method of community studies is known as **participant observation.** The sociologist attempts to be both an objective observer of events and an actual participant in the social milieu under study—not an easy task for even the most experienced researcher. In such situations the observer faithfully records his or her observations and interactions in *field notes*, which supply the descriptive data that will be used in the analysis and writing phases of the study.

An excellent example of a study based on participant observation is Douglas A. Harper's book *Good Company* (1982). (Photographs from this book appear in the Visual Sociology section of Chapter 9.) Harper spent many months riding on freight trains and living in "jungles" with hoboes. His goal was to describe how hoboes, or tramps or bums as they are often called, actually live and how they learn to trust or distrust one another in a world considered deviant by members of "respectable" society. Here is how Harper describes the experience of getting into the world of the hobo:

I'd been in the yards a couple of days, peeking around, asking questions and making plans. Every time I've gone back to the freights I've had to cross an emotional hurdle—they seem too big, too fast, too dangerous, and too illegal—and I get used to the idea by spending a few days in the yards, testing the waters. . . . I was shifting back into a tramp world for the fourth or fifth time. I'd made cross country trips on freights and I'd spent some weeks the winter before living on Boston's skid row. These experiences were trips into a life I ordinarily did not lead. (1982, p. 3)

This kind of research describes the quality of life of the people involved, and for that

> *Much sociological research requires direct observation of the people being studied, often through participant observation.*

reason it is often called *qualitative* research in order to distinguish it from the *quantitative* research methods we will consider shortly. James Coleman observed that in qualitative research "we report a stream of action in which the interlinking of events suggests how the [social] system functions" (1964, p. 222). He supplied an example of this kind of research from his study *The Adolescent Society* (1961), in which he linked the social groups that form in American high schools to different kinds of achievement in school. In this passage a student tells Coleman why he is in the school's "top" clique:

Well, I'll tell you, like when I came over here, I had played football over at ———. I was pretty well known by all the kids before I came over. And when I came there was ——— always picking on kids. He hit this little kid one day, and I told him that if I ever saw him do anything to another little kid that I'd bust him. So one day down in the locker he slammed this kid against the locker, so I went over and hit him a couple of times, knocked him down. And a lot of the kids liked me for doing that, and I got on the good side of two or three teachers. (1964, p. 222)

Qualitative research carried out "in the field" where behavior is actually occurring is the best method for analyzing the processes of human interaction. A shortcoming of this approach, however, is that it is usually based on a single community or social system, which makes it difficult to generalize the findings to other social settings. Thus community studies and other types of qualitative studies are most often used for exploratory research, and the findings serve as a basis for generating hypotheses for further research.

Unobtrusive Measures. Observation can employ numerous other techniques besides direct participation. Among these are **unobtrusive measures**—that is, observational techniques that measure the effects of behavior but intrude as little as possible into actual social settings. Here are some examples:

The floor tiles around the hatching-chick exhibit at Chicago's Museum of Science and Industry must be replaced every six weeks. Tiles in other parts of the museum need not be replaced for years. The selective erosion of tiles, indexed by the replacement rate, is a measure of the relative popularity of exhibits.

One investigator wanted to learn the level of whisky consumption in a town which was officially "dry." He did so by counting empty bottles in ashcans.

Chinese jade dealers have used the pupil dilation of their customers as a measure of the client's interest in particular stones. (Webb et al., 1966, p. 2)

Observations like these can be transformed into useful measures of the variables under study. Their nature is limited only by the researcher's creativity, and they intrude far less into people's lives than do interviews or participant observation.

An increasingly popular set of observational techniques involves the use of photography and videotape, or *visual sociology*. These techniques can be just as obtrusive as interviewing, if not more so, but they can also be used in unobtrusive ways, depending on the questions being asked. An example of the use of photographic data is the research on nonverbal communication conducted by Edward Hall (1959) and Ray Birdwhistell (1970). These studies demonstrated how people in different cultures use different nonverbal signs and align themselves spatially in different ways during their interactions. The photos show, for example, that in Mediterranean cultures people approach one another far more closely than they do in northern European or Asian cultures. These small differences in behavior can become very important in interpersonal relations.

Another example of visual sociology is the use of photographic materials in studies of urban life. In recent years the use of sys-

The United States has spent billions of dollars to improve the access of handicapped people to transportation and public facilities. How effective have these investments been? Studies using relatively simple observational techniques can help in answering questions like this.

tematic observation coupled with photography has become widespread in studies of how people use public places. Probably the most influential sociologist in this field is William H. Whyte, author of *The Social Life of Small Urban Spaces* (1980). Whyte relies on time-lapse photography to describe the nuances of social interaction in public places.

The use of photography in the study of urban spaces is illustrated in the photo essay that accompanies this chapter. Similar essays appear in the Visual Sociology sections of subsequent chapters.

Experiments

Although for both moral and practical reasons sociologists do not have many opportunities to perform experiments, there is a large literature in the social sciences, especially social psychology, an interdisciplinary science that draws ideas and researchers from both sociology and psychology, that is based on experiments. There are two experimental models that social scientists use frequently. The first and most rigorous is the controlled experiment conducted in a laboratory. The second is the field experiment, which is often used to test public policies that are applied to some groups and not others.

Controlled Experiments. The **controlled experiment** allows the researcher to manipulate an independent variable in order to observe and measure changes in a dependent variable. The experimenter forms an **experimental group**, which will experience a change in the independent variable (the "treatment"), and a **control group**, which will not experience the treatment but whose behavior will be compared with that of the experimental group. (The control group is similar to the experimental group in every other way.) This type of experiment is especially characteristic of studies at the micro level of sociological research.

Consider an example. Which line in Figure 2-1b appears to match the line in Figure 2-1a most closely? Could anything persuade you that a line other than the one you have selected is the correct choice? This simple diagram formed the basis of a famous series of experiments conducted by Solomon Asch in the early 1950s. They showed that the opinion of a majority can have an extremely powerful influence on that of an individual.

Asch's control group consisted of subjects who looked at the lines in a room where they were seated together but were allowed to make their judgments independently.[2] In this group the subjects invariably matched the correct lines, just as you no doubt have. But in the experimental group a different result was produced by the introduction of an independent variable: group pressure.

Asch's experimental group consisted of subjects who were asked to announce their decisions aloud in a group setting. Each sub-

> *In a controlled experiment, the experimental group experiences a change in the independent variable (the "treatment") while the control group does not.*

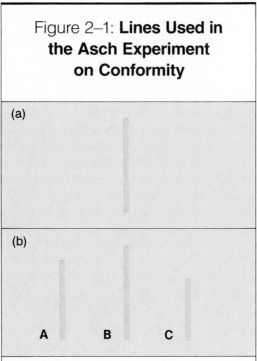

Figure 2–1: **Lines Used in the Asch Experiment on Conformity**

(a)

(b)

A   B   C

Cards like these were used in the Asch experiment. Subjects were asked to judge the lengths of various lines by comparing them with the three lines on the bottom card. The line on the top card quite obviously matches line B on the bottom card; all of the judgements were this simple.

[2]The term *subject* refers to a person who participates in a controlled experiment.

ject was brought into a group of eight people who posed as other subjects but were actually confederates of the experimenter. When the lines were flashed on a screen, those "subjects" all chose a line that was not the matching one. When it was the real subject's turn to choose, he or she was faced with the unanimous opinion of a majority of "subjects" who had picked the wrong line. Thirty-two percent of the real subjects went along with the majority and chose the wrong line as well. And even among the subjects Asch called "independent" (the 68 percent of the real subjects who gave the correct response despite the pressure of the majority) there was a great deal of variation. Some gave the correct response at all times, whereas others gave it only part of the time. This conforming response was less likely when there was at least one other person in the group who also went against the majority. By varying the number of people who said the shorter line was longer Asch was varying the degree of group pressure experienced by the subject. The independent variable (group pressure) thus produced more "errors," or choices of the wrong line (Asch, 1966).

Field Experiments. **Field experiments** are used extensively in evaluating public programs that address specific social problems. In these experiments there is usually a "treatment group" of people who participate in the program and a control group of people who do not participate in it. In one example of this type of experiment, Congress allocated millions of dollars to a study of the effects of after-school jobs on poor teenagers' school attendance. Some members of Congress were concerned that job programs for youth might actually create incentives for teenagers from poor families to drop out of school in favor of work in government-subsidized programs. Accordingly, a team of social scientists was asked to design an experiment that would find out whether jobs could be used as an incentive to remain in school.

In the experiment thousands of teenagers in Baltimore, Denver, rural Missis-

> *Field experiments are often used in evaluating programs designed to address social problems.*

sippi, and other areas were offered jobs after school and during the summer if they agreed to remain in school or to return after having dropped out. An equally large control group consisted of teenagers from similar families in similar (but not the same) communities who were not offered such jobs. This design allowed the researchers to determine what effects the job program had on teenagers' school performance. The results were encouraging: The program produced a 62.5 percent increase in the rate at which dropouts returned to school compared with dropouts in the control group (Manpower Demonstration and Research Corporation, 1980).

Sociologists can conduct "natural experiments" when two similar groups receive differing treatments and the results can be measured. An example of such an experiment that is relevant to debates about welfare dependency concerns teenage pregnancy. Some scholars argue that welfare payments to women with dependent children create an incentive for teenagers to have babies and live on welfare. But in the United States welfare payments are determined by state governments. Some states pay relatively high benefits, while in others the benefits are very low. This situation presents an opportunity to test the hypothesis that rates of teenage pregnancy increase as welfare benefits increase. In fact, when we compare states like California and Pennsylvania (which pay the highest welfare benefits to young mothers) with states like Mississippi and Alabama (which pay the lowest) we find no difference in the rates of pregnancy among poor teenagers. This suggests that welfare benefits alone cannot be used to explain why young unmarried women from low-income households become pregnant (Ellwood and Summers, 1986). These issues are discussed more fully in Chapter 12.

The Hawthorne Effect. A common problem of experimental studies is that just by paying attention to people in an experimental group the researcher may be introducing additional variables. This problem was recognized for the first time in the late 1930s, when a team of researchers led by Elton Mayo conducted a famous series of experiments at Western Electric's Hawthorne plant. The purpose of the study was to determine the effects of var-

The author devotes part of his research to the study of the Times Square area of Manhattan. Here he discusses an upcoming survey with Kathleen McLoughlin, owner of a tavern in the Times Square area and a doctoral candidate in sociology.

ious environmental and social conditions on the workers' productivity. One hypothesis was that improvements in the physical features of the workplace (such as better lighting) and improved social conditions (coffee breaks, different methods of payment, and so on) would result in greater productivity (the dependent variable). But it appeared that *whatever the experimenters did,* the workers' productivity increased. When the experimenters improved the lighting, the workers' productivity increased over that of the control group. When they dimmed the lights, productivity went up again. This was true even when the workers were subjected to somewhat worse conditions or were returned to their original conditions.

At first this series of experiments was considered a failure, and the researchers concluded that the variables they were introducing had little to do with the changes in productivity that resulted. But on further reflection they realized that the real independent variable was not better working conditions but, simply, attention: The workers liked the attention they were getting; it made them feel special, so they worked harder. This led the researchers to design experiments dealing with the effects of attention from supervisors and better communication between workers and managers, and those experiments led to a new philosophy of worker-management relations, described in Chapter 18. Today the term **Hawthorne effect** is used to refer to any unintended effect that results from the attention given to subjects in an experiment.

The Hawthorne effect occurs in a variety of experimental situations. To give just one example, when educators test new textbooks they often obtain better results at first because of the increased attention students receive as observers visit their classrooms. Over time, the effects of extra attention may disappear and the experimenters may conclude that the new books are little better than the ones they replaced. Sophisticated evaluations of educational change anticipate this problem by making sure that the experimental group does not get more attention than the control group.

Survey Research

A sociological survey asks people to give precise information about their behavior, their attitudes, and at times the behavior and attitudes of others (such as other members of their households). There is a world of difference between the modern sociological survey and the "social surveys" conducted around the turn of the century (see Chapter 1). Those surveys attempted to present an unbiased, factual account of the social conditions of a specific community. But their findings could not be applied to other groups. In contrast, today's survey techniques make it possible to generalize from a small sample of respondents to an entire population. Done properly, the modern survey is one of the most powerful tools available to social scientists.

Surveys are the central method used in election polling, market research, opinion polling, television ratings, and a host of other applications. The most ambitious and most heavily used sociological surveys are national censuses. A *national census* is a full enumeration of every member of the society, a regular system for counting its people and determining where and under what conditions they live, how they work and gain income, their patterns of family composition, their age distribution, their levels of educational attainment, and related data. Without these measures, a nation cannot plan intelligently for the needs of its people. The United States conducts a national census every ten years. The 1990 census, the twenty-first in the nation's history, was the largest and most complex ever undertaken; it attempted to enumerate about 250 million people in 106 million housing units.

Once a national census has gathered the basic demographic and ecological facts about a nation's people, it is possible to add more information through the use of smaller and far less costly **sample surveys.** In the United States, this is done regularly through the Census Bureau's Current Population Survey (CPS). From the CPS we get monthly estimates of employment and unemployment, poverty, births, deaths, marriages, divorces, social insurance and welfare, and many other indicators of the social well-being and problems of the American people. Box 2-1 describes the CPS in more detail.

Box 2–1: **The Current Population Survey**

Dan Miller, The New York Times

Rena Tieser

The Current Population Survey (CPS) is a sample survey conducted each month by the Bureau of the Census. Its purpose is to update the decennial national census with monthly data. Each month census enumerators conduct interviews at 58,000 randomly selected American households. These interviews are the nation's only source of information on total employment and unemployment. The CPS is also the most comprehensive source of information on the personal characteristics of the total population, such as age and sex, race, marital and family status, veteran status, educational background, and ethnic origin.

The difficulty of obtaining this kind of information is illustrated by some of the occupational hazards faced by Rena Tieser, a field interviewer for the Census Bureau. In conducting interviews for the Current Population Survey, Tieser has "walked in on seances, marijuana and extracurricular activity" as well as facing the usual difficulties presented by dogs, crime, vacationers, unlisted telephone numbers, and non–English-speakers.

Tieser and her colleagues are assigned about fifty households, which are interviewed in four consecutive months and again in the same months a year later. The first and fifth interviews are conducted face-to-face and referred to as "personals"; the rest are done by telephone. The most difficult people to interview, according to Tieser, are aspiring individuals who have encountered hard times: "They don't want to talk about it" (quoted in Hershey, 1988, p. D1).

In addition to questions about their employment status, respondents to the CPS are asked questions about other characteristics, such as their marital status, living arrangements, money income, educational attainment, and fertility. The data collected in this way are used to create reports that are published annually. These annual series include Series P-20, *Population Characteristics;* Series P-25, *Population Estimates & Projections;* Series P-27, *Farm Population;* and Series P-60, *Consumer Income.*

The Current Population Survey is quite costly (the monthly total is over $2 million), and there are some limitations on the usefulness of the data obtained by this means. For one thing, the data are not useful for describing local and regional populations, since the number of households in any given locality interviewed by the CPS is too small to provide meaningful data. Nevertheless, the survey does provide major social indicators, such as unemployment, on a regular basis, and for this reason it is an extremely valuable tool of macro-level sociological analysis.

Table 2–1: **Attitudes of Americans Toward Environmental Problems**

	Total	North East	North Cent	South	West
When people talk about protecting the "environment" it can mean a lot of different things. *Which* environmental problem do *you* think is most important?					
AIR POLLUTION	16%	13%	19%	15%	17%
WATER POLLUTION	13	18	15	10	11
POLLUTION (GENERAL)	13	13	12	11	18
CHEMICAL/HAZARDOUS WASTE	6	9	5	5	5
GREENHOUSE EFFECT	5	6	4	5	6
ACID RAIN	3	6	2	2	2
SOLID WASTE/LANDFILL	3	5	3	1	1
WILDERNESS/FORESTS	3	1	2	2	6
OCEANS	2	3	—	3	1
PRESERVATION/NATURAL RESOURCES	2	—	1	2	5
RIVER POLLUTION	1	—	1	1	1
WATER CONSERVATION	1	1	—	1	—
NUCLEAR WASTE	1	—	1	1	2
OTHER	7	8	10	7	9
DON'T KNOW	24	17	25	34	16
In the past five years, do you think the problem of toxic and hazardous wastes has gotten better, gotten worse, or stayed about the same?					
GOTTEN BETTER	8%	5%	10%	8%	12%
GOTTEN WORSE	63	71	61	61	60
STAYED SAME	24	21	26	25	25
DON'T KNOW	5	3	3	6	3
Would you be willing or not willing to pay higher taxes of $100 per year for each of the next ten years in order to clean up the toxic and hazardous waste problem in America?					
WILLING	65%	73%	63%	62%	66%
NOT WILLING	28	21	32	31	29
DON'T KNOW	7	6	5	7	5
One way to reduce air pollution is to burn less coal and use more nuclear power to produce electricity. Do you think we should use more nuclear power, or do you think nuclear power has too many problems of its own?					
SHOULD USE MORE NUCLEAR POWER	31%	27%	34%	29%	35%
TOO MANY PROBLEMS	54	59	52	55	51
DEPENDS (VOL)	5	6	5	4	5
DON'T KNOW	10	8	9	12	9

Source: CBS/New York Times Poll, October 31, 1988.

Opinion Polls. Another type of survey research pioneered by sociologists earlier in this century is the *opinion poll*. Today opinion polling is a highly developed industry. Opinion polls are used by marketing firms to help corporations make descisions about their products. Political candidates and their staffs use polls to measure the progress of their campaigns. And elected officials use polls to monitor public opinion on key political and economic issues.

A good example of an opinion survey is the CBS News/New York Times Poll. This poll uses a relatively small sample of respondents, selected at random, whose opinions can be generalized to the entire population of American adults. To get a better idea of how opinion surveys are carried out, let us look at a recent CBS News/New York Times poll on environmental issues.

Table 2-1 presents some of the results of the poll. They show that most of the people interviewed were able to name an environmental problem they considered important. If we look at the bottom line in the response to the first question and compare the percentages of respondents who said "Don't know," we see that on the average (based on the total) more than three-fourths had an opinion. But there were some important differences, with respondents from the southern and North Central states somewhat less able to name the single most important environmental issue.

Poll-takers often wish to confront respondents with the possible consequences of their opinions to see how they will react. Thus in this poll they asked whether respondents thought nuclear power might be used to replace air-polluting sources of energy, such as coal. The results in Table 2-1 show that a clear majority felt that nuclear power entails too many problems to be a viable substitute for energy derived from the burning of coal.

This CBS News/New York Times poll was conducted among a nationwide random sample of 1,606 adults. The term **sample** refers to a set of respondents selected from a specific population. The first step in selecting a sample is to define the population to be sampled; in our example the population consists of adult American citizens. The next step is to establish rules for the *random* selection of respondents. The goal of this procedure is to ensure that within the specified population everyone has an equal chance, or probability, of being selected to answer the survey questions. A sample in which potential respondents do not all have the same probability of being included is called a *biased sample*. To avoid bias, respondents must be selected by some process of random sampling.[3] In other words, any form of "volunteering" to be interviewed must be eliminated. (For example, the researcher cannot intentionally select his or her friends to be part of the sample.) Only a random sample can be considered truly representative of the target population.

The CBS News/New York Times Poll is conducted by telephone, so in order to randomize the selection of respondents the poll designers must produce a list of random phone numbers. They do this by selecting a set of area codes and exchanges that will result in nationwide coverage. They then use a computer program to generate random four-digit numbers that are added to the area codes and exchanges. You may be wondering whether this approach introduces bias by excluding potential respondents who cannot afford telephones. This is indeed the case. But there are techniques that can be used to correct for such bias, which is termed *sample bias*. For example, the pollsters can add extra phone numbers in areas where there are higher proportions of poor residents.

A famous case of sample bias occurred during the 1936 presidential election campaign. The results of a telephone survey conducted by *Literary Digest* magazine indicated that Alfred E. Landon, the Republican candidate, would trounce Franklin D. Roosevelt, his Democratic opponent. At that time many lower-income households did not have telephones. The telephone survey therefore was biased toward upper-income households, whose members were more likely to vote Re-

> **Before selecting a sample, it is necessary to define the population to be sampled and establish rules for the random selection of respondents from that population.**

[3]Random sampling is accomplished by a variety of statistical techniques that are discussed in more advanced courses.

publican. But Roosevelt won the election, and since then political pollsters have been much more alert to the problem of sample bias.

A more recent example of unscientific use of survey methods is Shere Hite's survey of women's attitudes toward their male partners; the results of that survey were published in 1987 in a book entitled *Women and Love*. Since Hite had published other books that attempted to inform readers about how men and women feel about their sex lives and what sexual practices they engage in, her new book was eagerly awaited. However, as soon as it was published it came under intense criticism by social scientists, who attacked it as "the functional equivalent of malpractice for surveys" because it was based on "a convenient sample of the worst sort" (Butterfield, 1987, p. B4).

What the critics were referring to was the fact that the book was based on responses to a questionnaire that had been sent primarily to members of women's groups, hardly a representative sample of the total population of women. Research methods like the mailback survey are often subject to sample bias, since everyone who responds is by definition a volunteer. Moreover, only 4,500 of the 100,000 questionnaires Hite sent out were returned. Mailback surveys generally attempt to obtain high response rates to indicate that they are at least representative of the population that received the questionnaire. Hite's response rate of 4.5 percent was far from adequate to justify the conclusions presented in her book.

Before leaving the subject of opinion polling, we should mention one additional point. The CBS News/New York Times poll described earlier is subject to a *sampling error* of plus or minus three percentage points. This is important information for anyone who reads and interprets poll data. It means that a difference of 3 percent or less between the percentages of American adults expressing certain opinions could be due to chance rather than to a real difference in the distribution of opinions. In other words, it is possible that just by chance a higher percentage of people with a certain opinion was included in the sample than is actually the case in the total population. The possibility of sampling error is more critical when there is a very small difference between two sets of responses— for example, when 51 percent of the sample favors one presidential candidate and 49 percent favors another.

Questionnaire Design. Just as important as careful selection of the sample to be interviewed is the design of the *instrument*, or questionnaire, to be used in the survey. Questionnaire design is both a science and an art. Questions must be worded precisely yet be easily understood. Above all, the questions must be worded so as to avoid biasing the answers (see Box 2-2).

One of the first decisions to make in designing survey questions is whether they should be *open* or *closed*. **Closed questions** require respondents to select from a set of answers, whereas **open questions** allow them to say whatever comes to mind. The items in Box 2-2 are examples of closed questions. An example of an open question would be "Please tell me how you feel about your neighborhood." In answering this type of question the respondent can say that he or she does not like the neighborhood at all or give one or more reasons for liking it. The interviewer attempts to write down the answers in the respondent's own words.

Survey questions must be worded clearly and precisely and in such a way as to avoid biasing the answers.

When researchers wish to include both forced-choice categories and freely given opinions in a single survey, the questionnaire usually begins with open questions and then shifts to closed questions on the same subject. Survey instruments that rely on open questions are often called *interview guides*. They guide the researcher's questions in certain directions and emphasize certain categories of information, but they also allow the interviewer to follow up respondents' comments with further questions.

Surveys and Secondary Analysis. The refinement of sampling techniques in the last fifty years has turned survey research into a major industry. Among the best-known polling organizations today are the Gallup Poll, the Harris Poll, and the CBS News/New York Times Poll. In addition to these commercial polls, there are academic polling organizations at the University of Michigan and the University of Chicago that conduct annual polls on a great many issues of public opinion and policy. We will refer to these polls at many points in this book.

The regular administration of opinion surveys makes it possible to chart changes in public opinion over time. Some examples are presented in Figure 2-2. These comparisons show that there has been a great deal of change in Americans' opinions about women's roles and family size in the past few decades. We discuss these important changes in later chapters; here our interest is in the methods behind the measurements.

A single sample survey, such as the 1938 Gallup poll that provided the first item presented in Figure 2-2, provides a view of the opinions or behavior of a representative *cross section* of a population at one point in time. Responses to the same survey question obtained from comparable samples at other points in time allow the sociologist to make *longitudinal* comparisons, or comparisons that reveal changes in opinions or behavior over time. But we must always be sure that the samples being compared are in fact comparable. In

---

Box 2–2: **Avoiding Bias in Survey Questions**

In *Asking Questions: A Practical Guide to Questionnaire Design* (1982), survey researchers Seymour Sudman and Norman Bradburn of the National Opinion Research Center describe a common abuse of survey methods: the use of biased questions. In a questionnaire mailed to them by a lobbying group the authors noticed questions like these:

1. Do you feel there is too much power concentrated in the hands of labor union officials?

    yes___ no___

2. Are you in favor of forcing state, county, and municipal employees to pay union dues to hold their government jobs?

    yes___ no___

3. Are you in favor of allowing construction union czars the power to shut down an entire construction site because of a dispute with a single contractor, thus forcing even more workers to knuckle under to union agencies?

    yes___ no___

These questions violate even the simplest rules of objectivity in questionnaire design. As the authors point out, they are "loaded with nonneutral words: 'forcing,' 'union czars,' 'knuckle under.'" Such questions are "deceptive and unethical, but they are not illegal" (p. 3). To eliminate bias, one would have to begin by rephrasing the questions. For example, the first question could read

1. Which answer best sums up your feeling about the amount of power held by labor union officials today?
    a.   too much power
    b.   about the right amount of power
    c.   too little power
    d.   don't know

Fair questions avoid nonneutral words and give the respondent an opportunity to answer on either side of the issue or to say that he or she does not know. Whenever you read the results of a survey, ask yourself if the questions are free of obvious bias, if they are specific or general, and if they are threatening or nonthreatening to the respondent. Such an evaluation can make a great difference in how you view the answers.

our example, the populations are comparable because they are similar random samples of American adults.

Another way of obtaining comparable results would have been to go back to the people who answered the question in 1938 and ask the same question again. This technique is called a *panel study* because a randomly selected "panel" of respondents is asked the same question on more than one occasion. It is a valuable technique, especially when we want to find out how people's behavior or attitudes have changed over time. But panel studies are expensive, since the sociologist must find the same respondents even though they may have moved.

In our example, Louis Harris used two comparable polls by his competitor, George Gallup, to make the needed comparisons. This is a common practice. Once polls have been conducted and analyzed for their immediate commercial or scientific value, they are often made available to other researchers, who can use them in comparative studies the way Harris did in this example. This technique of reanalyzing data collected by another social scientist is called *secondary analysis*.

Research Ethics and the Rights of Respondents

In asking any type of question in a survey or other type of sociological study, the researcher must be aware of the rights of respondents. Much sociological research deals with the personal lives and inner thoughts of real human beings. Although most of that research seems relatively innocent, there are many times when the questions asked or the behaviors witnessed may be embarrassing or even more damaging. In one famous example, Laud Humphreys (1970, 1975) studied interactions between men seeking casual sexual encounters in public restrooms. Many of his colleagues attacked him for invading the men's privacy. Others defended him for daring to investigate what had until then been a taboo subject (homosexuality and bisexuality). After all, they reasoned, Humphreys was careful to keep the men's identities secret. But he also followed some of the men home and conducted interviews with them there. They were not aware that he knew about their

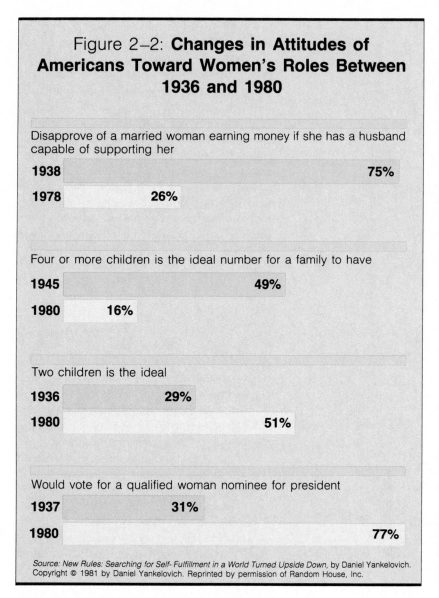

Figure 2–2: **Changes in Attitudes of Americans Toward Women's Roles Between 1936 and 1980**

Disapprove of a married woman earning money if she has a husband capable of supporting her

1938 — 75%
1978 — 26%

Four or more children is the ideal number for a family to have

1945 — 49%
1980 — 16%

Two children is the ideal

1936 — 29%
1980 — 51%

Would vote for a qualified woman nominee for president

1937 — 31%
1980 — 77%

Source: *New Rules: Searching for Self- Fulfillment in a World Turned Upside Down*, by Daniel Yankelovich. Copyright © 1981 by Daniel Yankelovich. Reprinted by permission of Random House, Inc.

homosexual activities, and upon reflection Humphreys himself admitted that he had deceived his subjects.

Sociologists continue to debate the ethical dilemmas raised by Humphreys's research and by studies like the Asch experiment (in which the subject is duped and may feel embarrassed). As a result of such controversies, the federal government now requires that research involving human subjects be monitored by "human subjects review panels" at all research institutions that receive federal funding. A research review must be undertaken before a study can be funded or approved for degree credit. To pass the review, the researcher must provide proof that he or she has taken precautions to protect the fundamental rights of human subjects. Those rights include privacy, informed consent, and confidentiality.

The right of **privacy** can be defined as "the right of the individual to define for himself, with only extraordinary exceptions in the interest of society, when and on what terms his acts should be revealed to the general public" (Westin, 1967, p. 373). **Confidentiality** is closely related to privacy. When a respondent is told that information will remain confidential, the researcher may not pass it on to anyone else in a form that can be traced to that respondent. The information can be pooled with information provided by other respondents, but extreme care must be taken to ensure that none of the responses can be traced to a particular individual.

Informed consent refers to statements made to respondents (usually before any questions are asked) about what they are being asked and how the information they supply will be used. It includes the assurance that their participation is voluntary—that is, that there is no compulsion to answer questions or give information. The respondent should be allowed to judge the degree of personal risk involved in answering questions even when an assurance of confidentiality has been given.

The ethics of social research require careful attention. *Before undertaking research in which you plan to ask people questions of any kind, be sure you have thought out the ethical issues and checked with your instructor about the ethics of your methods of collecting data and presenting them to the public.*

The fundamental rights of human subjects include privacy, informed consent, and confidentiality.

ANALYZING THE DATA

Survey research normally is designed to generate numerical data regarding how certain variables are distributed in the population under study. To understand how such data are presented and analyzed, let us refer to Tables 2-2, 2-3, and 2-4. We will use these tables as a framework for a discussion of some of the basic techniques of quantitative data presentation and analysis. Other types of sociological data and analytical techniques are explained at appropriate points in later chapters and in the Visual Sociology sections.

Reading Tables

In approaching a statistical table, the first step is to read the title carefully. The title should state exactly what information is presented in the table, including the *units of analysis*—that is, the entity (e.g., individual, family, group) to which a measure applies. In Tables 2-2 and 2-3, the units of analysis are households; in Table 2-4, they are married-couple households.

Also check the source of the information presented in the table. This is usually given in a sourcenote at the end of the table. The source both indicates the quality of the data (census data are considered to be of very high quality) and tells the reader where those data can be verified or further information obtained.

As you begin to study the table, make sure you understand what kind of information is being presented. The numbers in Table 2-2 are **frequency distributions.** For each year (1970 and 1986), they show how various types of households were distributed in the U.S. population. Frequency distributions indicate how many observations fall within each category of a variable. Thus, within the category "Household Type," Table 2-2 indicates that there were 63,401,000 households in the United States in 1970 and that the total increased to 88,458,000 by 1986.

Table 2-2 can tell us a great deal about social change in the United States. For example, social scientists use the term *household* to designate all the people residing at a given address, provided that the address is not a hospital, school, jail, army barracks, or other "residential institution." A household is not necessarily a married-couple family, as is evident from the categories listed in Table 2-2. There are also many households in which a male, with or without his own children, or a female, with or without her own children, is the primary reporting adult. There are also millions of nonfamily households, in which the adults reporting to the census-takers are

Table 2–2: **Types of Households in the United States, 1970 and 1986 (in thousands)**

Household Type	1970	1986
All Households	63,401	88,458
Family Households	51,456	63,558
Married-Couple Families	44,728	50,933
No own children under 18	19,196	26,304
With own children under 18	25,532	24,630
1 child	8,163	9,868
2 children	8,045	9,580
3 or more children	9,325	5,182
Male Householder Families	1,228	2,414
No own children under 18	887	1,479
With own children under 18	341	935
1 child	179	600
2 children	87	260
3 or more children	75	75
Female Householder Families	5,500	10,211
No own children under 18	2,642	4,106
With own children under 18	2,858	6,105
1 child	1,008	2,857
2 children	810	2,061
3 or more children	1,040	1,186
Nonfamily Households	11,945	24,900

Source: Census Bureau, 1987

The Census Bureau defines a household as all persons who occupy a "housing unit" (house, apartment, or single room); they may include related family members and all unrelated persons, if any, who share the housing unit. All persons not living in households are classified as living in group quarters. The term *family* refers to a group of two or more persons related by birth, marriage, or adoption and residing together in a household.

not related (24.9 million in 1986). These include people who are roommates, people who are cohabiting, people who are sharing a house or apartment but do not consider themselves roommates, and many other possibilities.

In earlier times it was considered unfortunate and a bit odd for a woman who was not a widow to head a household with children. It was assumed that a true family was composed of a male head, his wife, their children, and anyone related to them by blood who lived on their premises. The numbers in Table 2-2 show, however, that the number of female-headed households almost doubled between 1970 and 1986. The data also show that although there was an increase in the number of married-couple families (from 44.7 million in 1970 to nearly 51 million in 1986), there was a greater jump in the number of nonfamily households (from 11.9 million in 1970 to 24.9 million in 1986).

Percent Analysis

Comparing the numbers for 1970 and 1986 in Table 2-2 can be misleading. Remember that these are absolute numbers. They show that the number of nonfamily households has increased and that the number of female-headed and male-headed households has also increased. However, so has the number of married-couple families. And so has the total number of households. How, then, can we evaluate the importance of these various changes?

To compare categories from one period to another, we need a way of taking into account changes in the overall size of the population. This can be done through **percent analysis.** Consider the following example.

Percent analysis enables the researcher to take into account changes in the size of a population over time.

Table 2-2 shows that between 1970 and 1986 the number of male-headed households with one or more children rose from 341,000 to 935,000—an almost threefold increase. But how important is this increase in view of the increase in the total population between 1970 and 1986? By using the total number of households in each year as the base and calculating the percentage of each household type for that year, we can "hold constant" the effect of the increase in the total number of households. In the case of male-headed households with one or more children, we find that the increase as a percentage of all households (from 0.54 percent in 1970 to 1.1 percent in 1986) is not as important as the increase in absolute numbers would suggest. The calculation is as follows:

$$341,000/63,401 \times 100 = 0.54$$
$$935,000/88,458 \times 100 = 1.1$$

Table 2-3 presents each household type as a percentage of total households in that year. In this way it eliminates the effect of the increase in overall population size between 1970 and 1986.

The percentages in Table 2-3 reveal some significant changes that would not be evident from a comparison of absolute numbers. Although Table 2-2 seems to indicate that there has been an increase in married-couple families, Table 2-3 shows that when we control for the overall increase in households, married couples declined as a proportion of the total, from 70.5 percent in 1970 to 57.6 in 1986. The proportion of female-headed families, especially those with children, increased during the period. So did the proportion of nonfamily households.

But we cannot yet view these "findings" as definite. We must examine them carefully to be sure we are making the right kinds of comparisons. Look again at Table 2-3. In the category of married-couple families it seems that those with no children of their own decreased as a proportion of the total—from 30.3 percent in 1970 to 29.7 percent in 1986. But

Table 2–3: **Types of Households in the United States, 1970 and 1986 (percentage of total households)**

Household Type	1970	1986
All Households	100.0	100.0
Family Households	81.2	71.9
Married-Couple Families	70.5	57.6
No own children under 18	30.3	29.7
With own children under 18	40.3	27.8
1 child	12.9	11.2
2 children	12.7	10.8
3 or more children	14.7	5.8
Male Householder Families	1.9	2.7
No own children under 18	1.4	1.7
With own children under 18	0.5	1.1
1 child	0.3	0.7
2 children	0.1	0.3
3 or more children	0.1	0.1
Female Householder Families	8.7	11.5
No own children under 18	4.2	4.6
With own children under 18	4.5	6.9
1 child	1.6	3.3
2 children	1.3	2.3
3 or more children	1.6	1.3
Nonfamily Households	18.8	28.1

Table 2–4: **Married-Couple Families by Number of Own Children under 18, 1970 and 1986 (percentage of total households)**

	1970	1986
Married Couple Families		
No own children under 18	42.9	51.6
With own children under 18	57.1	48.4
1 child	18.3	19.4
2 children	18.0	18.8
3 or more children	20.8	10.2
Total	100.0	100.0

this apparent decrease is due to the overall increase in other types of households. Indeed, if we take only the married-couple households and compare categories within it, as shown in Table 2-4, we see that *as a proportion of married-couple households*, those without children actually increased from 42.9 percent to 51.6 percent.

This example should convince you to pay close attention to the comparisons made in numerical tables. In this example we see that married couples with children accounted for a smaller percentage of all married-couple households in 1986 than in 1970, but we would not have seen this without making the additional comparison presented in Table 2-4.

Correlations

The term **correlation** refers to a specific relationship between two variables: As one varies in some way, so does the other. Although the calculation of correlation is covered in statistics courses, for our purposes it will be helpful to know that the measure of correlation between two variables, termed the *correlation coefficient*, can vary between +1.0 and −1.0, with 0.0 representing no measured correlation at all. A correlation coefficient of +1 would indicate that the variables are positively and perfectly related—a change in one variable produces an equivalent change in the same direction (increase or decrease) in the other variable. A correlation coefficient of −1 would mean that the variables are perfectly inversely related; that is, a change in one

produces an equivalent change in the opposite direction in the other. In reality most variables are not perfectly correlated, and correlation coefficients usually fall somewhere between these two extremes.

The search for correlations is a common strategy in many kinds of research. In market research, for example, the investigator seeks correlations between the use of certain products and other social variables. (Thus the consumption of beer correlates with the proportion of male consumers in a target population such as baseball fans; the consumption of light beer correlates with the proportion of older, more weight-conscious male consumers; and so on.)

Social scientists who conduct research on the American family have supplied correlations between length of time on welfare (to return to our earlier example) and independent variables like education, income, and race. They have found, for example, that for female single parents, time on welfare is highly correlated with lack of education and income. If you were to take other courses in sociology and statistics, you would learn techniques for calculating the strength of correlations among variables and for sorting out the effects of different variables on the dependent variable you are studying. You would, for example, be able to determine the separate effects of education, income, race, and age on welfare dependency.

A correlation is a specific relationship between two variables; it does not imply causation.

Correlation and Causation. Although correlation can be very useful in the analysis of relationships among variables, it must not be confused with causation. Often a strong correlation that seems to indicate causality is in fact a spurious or misleading relationship. Take the example of storks and babies. The fable that storks bring babies seemed to be based on a statistical reality: In rural Holland until recent decades there was a correlation between storks nesting in chimneys and the presence of babies in those households. The more storks, the more babies. In fact, however, the presence of babies in the home meant more fires in the fireplace and more heat going up the chimney to attract storks with their own babies. Storks do not bring babies; babies, in effect, bring storks. But the real causal variable is heat, something that was not suggested in the original commonsense correlation.

The fact that two variables are correlated proves only that they are associated in such a way that variations in one are accompanied by regular variations in another. We can say, for example, that lack of household income and receipt of AFDC are correlated; as the number of households in poverty increases, so does the number of households receiving AFDC. But this does not mean that lack of household income *causes* receipt of AFDC. In fact, many people who are poor are not eligible for AFDC because they are men or because they do not have children below the age of eighteen. In a sense, then, the laws establishing the AFDC program, not poverty itself, cause welfare recipiency. Correlations may suggest the possibility of causality, but one must be extremely careful in making the leap from correlation (association) to causation.

The basic theoretical perspectives of sociology are interactionism, functionalism, and conflict theory.

THEORIES AND PERSPECTIVES

The material presented in Tables 2-2, 2-3, and 2-4 is valuable because it shows how the nation's most important survey, the census, reveals fundamental changes in the structure of the population. But how do these facts about household composition relate to larger trends and issues? The census reveals trends, but it does not explain those trends unless an investigator armed with a set of hypotheses goes to work on the facts to make them prove or disprove a theoretical point.

A **theory** is a set of interrelated concepts that seeks to explain the causes of an observable phenomenon. Some theories attempt to explain an extremely wide range of phenomena, while others limit their explanations to a narrower range. In physics, for example, Newton's "theory" of gravitation related the force of gravity to the mass and distance between objects, but it did not try to explain why the force of gravity existed in the first place or how this force was related to others, such as electromagnetism, that could be observed in nature. Einstein's theory of relativity, on the other hand, attempted to explain the relationships among all natural forces, and it predicted forces that had not yet been observed, such as those that are released by nuclear fission.

It is often said that sociology lacks great theories like those of the physical sciences. But this is a debatable point. If theories are judged by their ability to explain observable phenomena and predict future events, then sociology has some powerful theories. At the beginning of this century Émile Durkheim used his theory of social integration to predict the conditions that would lead to the rise of totalitarian regimes like that of the Nazis in Germany. Max Weber's theory of bureaucracy is valuable in explaining the experiences we are likely to have in organizations of all kinds. And Karl Marx's theory of class conflict is still the dominant explanation of the revolutions that occurred in feudal and early capitalist societies. No single sociological theory can explain all of the complexities of human social life and social change, but in this respect sociology is not very different from other social and physical sciences. Different economic theories compete for the attention of policymakers, and the theory of relativity has not fully explained the physical forces that produced the universe.

To cope with the many levels of social explanation, sociologists come to their work armed with **theoretical perspectives**: sets of interrelated theories that offer explanations for important aspects of social behavior. Like the methods of observation and analysis discussed in this chapter, theoretical perspectives are tools of sociological research. They provide us with a framework of ideas and explanations that helps us make sense out of the data we gather.

The basic theoretical perspectives are the ones discussed in Chapter 1: interactionism, functionalism, and conflict theory. We also rely on the ecological perspective for descriptive data regarding communities and populations. At times these perspectives offer competing explanations of social life; at other times they seek to explain different aspects of society; and at still other times they are combined in various ways. As we saw earlier in this chapter, the different perspectives tend to rely on different types of observations or data. Moreover, each approaches a major sociological issue by forming hypotheses about certain types of phenomena and not others. The information generated by that research suggests different ideas to people who come to it from differing perspectives. The ideas flow quickly and new hypotheses are suggested, thereby beginning the research process anew.

CHALLENGES TO CONTEMPORARY SOCIETY

Prostitution and AIDS

AIDS researcher Claire Sterk, a sociologist with the U.S. Centers for Disease Control (CDC), has made a disturbing discovery. Among prostitutes in an eastern city (*not* New York), she finds unexpectedly high rates of seropositivity (the presence of AIDS antibodies in the bloodstream). In her sample, reported in the accompanying table, women who are crack and cocaine addicts but are not intravenous drug users have rates of AIDS virus infection that are almost as high as those found among prostitutes who use heroin intravenously.

Sterk's findings, which were published in *The Lancet*, a prestigious medical journal, confirmed what many who follow trends in drug abuse feared: Women who become addicted to crack often trade sexual favors for the drug. Even when they themselves are not intravenous users, the high frequency of their sexual contacts exposes them to men who may be carrying the HIV virus, which causes AIDS. Earlier studies of AIDS infection among males had shown that frequency of sexual contacts with different partners greatly increases the risk of AIDS infection, so this finding is not surprising (Jaffe et al., 1985). But Sterk was the first researcher to combine qualitative and quantitative data on rates of infection among female crack users and to show that women who become involved in prostitution through cocaine and crack use are at high risk of contracting AIDS.

Sterk's sociological research was part of

a national study of AIDS and prostitution conducted by the CDC from 1985 to 1987. Over 1,000 prostitutes in cities throughout the United States were contacted to determine their sexual practices and other characteristics (e.g., condom use, frequency of different types of sexual activity, patterns of drug use, rates of seropositivity). The study was the first major effort to determine the extent to which the heterosexual population might contract AIDS through prostitution. The research relied on interviews conducted by *ethnographers*, sociologists who are trained in the techniques of participant observation and interviewing in streets, brothels, and other "natural settings."

Although most people in the United States associate AIDS with homosexuality and intravenous drug use, evidence from African nations shows that the disease is spreading rapidly among heterosexuals. This of course gives rise to the question of how the HIV virus spreads to heterosexual populations. Male and female prostitution and bisexuality are often mentioned as possible social pathways to infection. However, in the absence of "hard"

sociological evidence about rates of infection and patterns of sexual behavior and drug use among these populations, this labeling of possible carrier populations is highly controversial and prejudiced.

The recent CDC study of prostitution established that the incidence of HIV seropositivity among female prostitutes throughout the nation is rather low—less than 6 percent of the total sample. But in areas of the United States where overall rates of HIV infection are higher, where the proportion of intravenous drug users is higher, and where rates of homosexuality are higher, the proportion of prostitutes who are seropositive is also higher than the national average. In the portion of the eastern metropolitan region in which she conducted her research Sterk found that rates of HIV infection among streetwalkers (as opposed to call girls) were over 30 percent. Similar results were reported in other cities where there is a high incidence of heroin and cocaine use among streetwalkers. Although the large majority of prostitutes report regular use of condoms, fertility rates also are high in this population. Thus in Sterk's research area more than 100 babies are born each month to HIV-positive women; each of these babies also carries the AIDS virus.

Once we know that a certain population—street prostitutes in this instance—is at great risk, what can be done about the situation? A purely biotechnical solution requires the existence of an AIDS vaccine or a cure for the disease. This "magic bullet" could be administered to everyone and the problem would be solved. But no society can afford simply to wait for such a technological breakthrough. Social measures must be taken to stem the rate of infection, especially among populations that are particularly at risk (once they have been located through sound research). Here again, sociological research and its application in practical interventions is of critical importance.

In a review of AIDS and research in the social sciences, Dorothy Nelkin (1987) notes

HIV SEROPREVALENCE AMONG PROSTITUTES

Drug use	No.	HIV seropositive
Intravenous only	35	16 (46%)
Intravenous and nonintravenous	25	19 (76%)
Changed from intravenous to nonintravenous	11	8 (73%)
Nonintravenous (cocaine and crack)	19	16 (84%)
Never used drugs	19	6 (31%)

Source: Sterk, 1988.

that in the absence of an AIDS vaccine, a major issue is how to change the behavior of people who risk contracting the disease themselves as well as that of people who risk passing it along to others. She notes that sociologists have done a great deal of research on ways to communicate information about risk to different populations. Not much of their research has been about AIDS itself, owing to the relatively recent appearance of the disease, but lessons can be drawn from attempts to control self-destructive behaviors like smoking, drug abuse, and poor choice of diet.

Nelkin concludes that education of at-risk populations so that they will practice safe sex or avoid sharing needles with others, for example, can be more effective if special efforts are made to go beyond the media and the schools. Educators need to understand the leadership and reference-group structure of the target population. They need to be aware of cultural factors such as language, ritual, and humor. They need to know in detail where the people they are trying to reach normally go for help and where they typically receive social support. And once well-designed educational programs have been developed, they must be constantly monitored so that they can be continually improved. Sociological research has shown that multidimensional educational programs can be highly successful, but there is no simple formula for success. Certainly, the programs must be based on sound research of the type that Claire Sterk and others do in the neighborhoods and settings where women and men "at risk" actually live and interact. Similar research is required to make treatment interventions more effective and to educate the general public about the realities of the AIDS crisis so that fear does not breed a hysteria that could be even more dangerous than the disease itself.

SUMMARY

In all scientific research certain basic steps must be completed: deciding on the problem, reviewing the literature, formulating research questions, selecting a method, and analyzing the data. Not all researchers follow these steps in the order given, and often one or more steps must be repeated.

The first step in designing social research is formulating the question—that is, asking a question about a social situation that can be answered through the systematic collection and analysis of data. Often the research question is expressed in the form of a hypothesis. A *hypothesis* states a relationship between two variables that can be tested through empirical observation. The variable that is to be explained is the *dependent variable*. The other variable, a factor that the researcher believes causes changes in the dependent variable, is the *independent variable*.

Before collecting new data, a professional researcher reviews as much existing research and other data sources as possible. This "review of the literature" sometimes supplies all the data necessary for a particular study.

The most frequently used research methods in sociology are observation, experiments, and the survey. Observation may take the form of *participant observation*, in which the researcher participates to some degree in the life of the people being observed. It may also take the form of *unobtrusive measures*, or observational techniques that measure behavior but intrude as little as possible into actual social settings. "Visual sociology" involves the use of photography and videotape to observe people in a variety of settings and interpret their behavior.

Sociological experiments can take one of two basic forms: the controlled experiment and the field experiment. In a *controlled experiment* the researcher establishes an *experimental group*, which will experience the "treatment" (a change in the independent variable), and a *control group*, which will not experience the treatment. The effect of the treatment on the dependent variable can be measured by comparing the two groups.

Field experiments take place outside the laboratory and are often used in evaluating public programs designed to remedy specific social problems. The "treatment group" consists of people who experience a particular social program, and the control group consists of comparable people who do not experience the program. A common problem of experimental studies is the *Hawthorne effect*, which refers to any unintended effect resulting from the attention given to subjects in an experiment.

The third basic method of sociological research, the survey, asks people to give precise information about their behavior and attitudes. The most ambitious surveys are national censuses; the data obtained in a census can be supplemented by smaller, less costly *sample surveys*. A *sample* is a selection of respondents drawn from a specific population. If each member of the target population has an equal chance of being included in the sample, it is a *probability sample*. The respondents in such a sample must be selected by some process of *random sampling*.

Questionnaire design is an important aspect of survey research. Questions must be precisely worded, easy to understand, and free of bias. *Closed questions* require the respondent to select from a set of answers, whereas *open questions* allow respondents to say whatever comes to mind.

Sociological researchers must always consider the rights of human subjects. *Privacy* is the right to decide the terms on which one's acts may be revealed to the public. *Confidentiality* means that the researcher cannot use responses in such a way that they can be traced to a particular respondent. *Informed consent* means that respondents must be told how the information they supply will be used and that they must be allowed to judge the degree of personal risk involved in answering questions.

The data gathered in a survey are usually presented in the form of statistical tables. In reading a table it is important to know what the units of analysis are and what kinds of data are being presented. Absolute numbers reveal the actual size of each category of a variable, but to compare the numbers for different years it is necessary to calculate percentages. Data analysis often leads to the discovery of *correlations,* or specific relationships between two variables. Correlation should not be confused with causation.

Once data have been presented and analyzed, they can be used to generate new hypotheses. The types of hypotheses that might be developed depend on the researcher's *theoretical perspective*—a set of interrelated theories that offer explanations for important aspects of social behavior. The functionalist, interactionist, and conflict perspectives give rise to quite different hypotheses. When new hypotheses have been suggested, the research process begins anew.

WHERE TO FIND IT

Books

Handbook of Survey Research (Peter Rossi et al.; Basic Books, 1983). The latest in comprehensive, though rather technical, coverage of issues in the design, administration, and analysis of sociological survey research.

Asking Questions: A Practical Guide to Questionnaire Design (Seymour Sudman and Norman M. Bradburn; Jossey-Bass, 1982). One of the best available sources on the wording and organization of questions for research instruments such as questionnaires and guides to field research.

Unobtrusive Measures: Nonreactive Research in the Social Sciences (Eugene J. Webb et al.; Rand McNally, 1966). A pathbreaking treatise on how to develop scientific techniques for observing social life in nondisruptive ways.

In the Field: Readings on the Field Research Experience (Carolyn D. Smith and William Kornblum, eds.; Praeger, 1989). A selection of personal accounts by a group of noted ethnographic researchers. Designed to give students a sense of what it is actually like to conduct ethnographic research, especially participant observation.

How to Lie with Statistics (Darrell Huff; Norton, 1954). A charming and valuable book about the uses and misuses of quantitative data. To know how to lie with statistics is also to know how to unmask those who would lie and to credit those who use numbers and statistics properly.

Other Sources

Statistical Abstract of the United States (U.S. Bureau of the Census). The first source consulted for quantitative facts about the population of the United States. Published annually.

Census of the United States An invaluable tool for all the social sciences, but one that requires a patient user. Volumes exist for all states and cities in the United States. The tables show population totals and subtotals by sex, age, race, and occupation. Published every ten years on the basis of analysis of the data gathered in the national census.

The American Statistics Index (Congressional Information Service Inc.). The best single source for statistics collected by agencies of the U.S. government. Published monthly and collected into an annual volume, this index offers the most complete list of public statistics available in the United States.

GLOSSARY

hypothesis: a statement that specifies a relationship between two or more variables that can be tested through empirical observation (**p. 35**).

variable: a characteristic of an individual, group, or society that can vary from one case to another (**p. 36**).

dependent variable: the variable that a hypothesis seeks to explain (**p. 36**).

independent variable: a variable that the researcher believes causes a change in another variable (**p. 36**).

participant observation: a form of observation in which the researcher participates to some degree in the lives of the people being observed (**p. 38**).

unobtrusive measures: observational techniques that measure behavior but intrude as little as possible into actual social settings (**p. 39**).

controlled experiment: an experimental situation in which the researcher manipulates an independent variable in order to observe and measure changes in a dependent variable (**p. 40**).

experimental group: in an experiment, the subjects who are exposed to a change in the independent variable (**p. 40**).

control group: in an experiment, the subjects who do not experience a change in the independent variable (**p. 40**).

field experiment: an experimental situation in which the researcher observes and studies subjects in their natural setting (**p. 41**).

Hawthorne effect: the unintended effect that results from the attention given to subjects in an experimental situation (**p. 42**).

sample survey: a survey administered to a selection of respondents drawn from a specific population (**p. 43**).

sample: a set of respondents selected from a specific population (**p. 45**).

closed question: a question that requires the respondent to choose among a predetermined set of answers (**p. 46**).

open question: a question that does not require the respondent to choose from a predetermined set of answers. Instead, the respondent may answer in his or her own words (**p. 46**).

privacy: the right of a respondent to define when and on what terms his or her actions may be revealed to the general public (**p. 49**).

confidentiality: the promise that the information provided to a researcher by a respondent will not appear in any form that can be traced to that respondent (**p. 49**).

informed consent: the right of respondents to be informed of the purpose for which the information they supply will be used and to judge the degree of personal risk involved in answering questions, even when an assurance of confidentiality has been given (**p. 49**).

frequency distribution: a classification of data that describes how many observations fall within each category of a variable (**p. 49**).

percent analysis: a mathematical operation that transforms an absolute number into a proportion as a part of 100 (**p. 50**).

correlation: a specific relationship between two variables (**p. 50**).

theory: a set of interrelated concepts that seeks to explain the causes of an observable phenomenon (**p. 53**).

theoretical perspective: a set of interrelated theories that offers explanations for important aspects of social behavior (**p. 54**).

VISUAL SOCIOLOGY

All photography in this book is "visual sociology" in the sense that we have chosen pictures that highlight social situations, social relationships, and social institutions. But in assembling a group of photos we can communicate more subtle cues about what it feels like to be in a particular situation or relationship. Through photographs we can convey a great deal about the culture, social structure, and patterns of interaction that characterize a particular social setting, at the same time that we leave the reader free to make his or her own judgments. Sociologists routinely use photography to focus on types of behavior, on the way people sort themselves out in space and time, on patterns of inequality, and much more. These are all aspects of visual sociology that appear in this volume.

AN URBAN "COMBAT ZONE"

In this first photo essay we look at some of the characteristic scenes and interactions found on New York's West 42nd Street. These photographs were shot on only two blocks of this Manhattan thoroughfare. One of the nation's most famous city streets, West 42nd Street is actually, as you can readily see from these photos, many different streets for people from different social worlds.

To the police and social reformers and members of the movement against pornography, West 42nd Street is a "combat zone," meaning that it is a place where the norms of conventional society do not hold, where commercial sex and street hustling are tolerated, and where almost "anything goes."

To the street-wise sophisticate, 42nd Street is "The Deuce," a place where thousands of people pass by in a short period and one can sell almost anything because there will always be a buyer or a "mark" to be fleeced. It's a street of chess hustlers, drug peddlers, porn hawkers, religious revivalists, food and jewelry vendors, shoeshine men, and on and on.

To the urban planner, West 42nd Street is not only a moral combat zone but also a site of class struggle where social groups fight to control an extremely valuable piece of the

most costly urban landscape in America. It is also a frontier of decrepit low-rise buildings in the midst of looming office towers. Its inhabitants are acutely aware that the street is one of the communications hubs of the city, the seat of great institutions of learning like the New York Public Library, and a boundary of the nation's greatest urban entertainment zone, Times Square and Broadway.

And to the sociologist, 42nd Street and the Times Square area make up one of the finest social laboratories one could ask for (Boggs and Kornblum, 1985).

PART TWO

SOCIAL STRUCTURE

I n this part of the book we explore major areas of social continuity· and social change. Chapters 3 and 4 focus on two of sociology's most fundamental concepts: society and culture. Chapter 3 introduces the elements of social structure and explains how various kinds of societies have developed. When we talk about culture, in Chapter 4, we refer to the making of human consciousness—how we think and communicate and how these processes make society itself possible. Because these processes differ from one culture to another, cross-cultural research is a vital aspect of modern sociology.

The world is becoming more and more densely populated. Settlements that were small towns two generations ago are huge cities today. The resulting changes in social life are far-reaching in their consequences. Chapter 5 therefore examines the changes in the nature of human settlements that have accompanied the growth of the world's population, focusing on the meaning of urbanization and the future of community attachments in an urban world.

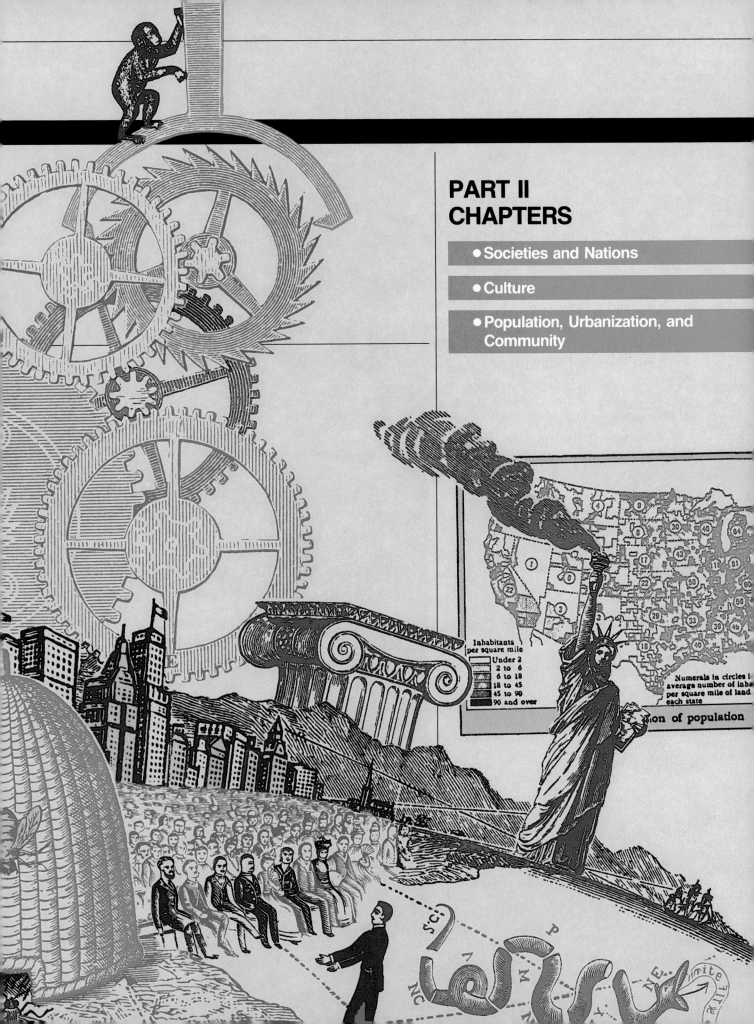

PART II
CHAPTERS

- Societies and Nations
- Culture
- Population, Urbanization, and Community

CHAPTER OUTLINE

● **The Social Order**

- Society and Social Structure
- Elements of Social Structure

● **Populations and Societies**

- The First Million Years: Hunting and Gathering
- The Agrarian Revolution
- The Industrial Revolution

● **Society and the Individual**

- From Gemeinschaft to Gesellschaft
- Role and Status in Modern Societies

● **Societies and Nation-States**

- The State
- The Nation-State
- Conclusion

Erica Berger

Tortilla Flats, a busy, "upscale" restaurant

CHAPTER 3

SOCIETIES AND NATIONS

At the beginning of Sherri's second month on the job things were supposed to be getting easier, but they weren't. If anything, they were getting worse, especially the pressure during the lunch-hour madness. Lunch never seemed to go well. There were always more customers than she could handle. Too many tables to serve, busboys too slow, cooks yelling at her to pick up orders or write more clearly—things were so bad that she dreaded coming in to work. She was falling behind in her studies, too. This part-time waitressing job was turning out to be a disaster. And now that chubby guy at table 14 was leering at her.

"Oh, Miss," he called out as Sherri shot by under a huge tray of burger plates. "Oh, Miss, why are you ignoring me? I haven't even gotten a menu." "Be right there, Sir," she muttered.

She doled out the burger plates as fast as she could and dashed back into the kitchen to get the soups for another table. "Where've you been hiding?" the cook shouted at her from behind his stainless-steel counter. "You better get that soup outta here before I have to heat it up again. Let's go. Move!"

Sherri flew through the swinging doors with the tepid soups. Out of the corner of her eye she saw the chubby guy complaining to Karen, her supervisor, about the slow service. Karen shot her an angry glance. A party of six was waiting to be seated at one of her big tables, which needed to be cleaned off. It was too much. She felt the tears welling up in her eyes. Her makeup would be streaked. She headed for the restroom.

On the way Sherri felt a gentle touch on her shoulder. Betty, the veteran waitress

who had broken her in when she started five weeks ago, smiled at her. "Take it easy, kid! It's not all that bad. My station is under control, so let me help you with the little fat guy and the others."

With her assured efficiency, Betty had Sherri's station under control in a matter of minutes. She made it all look so easy. She never seemed to waste a motion. First she went to the new customers, handed them menus, and told them that things were very busy and their waitress would be right over. She also mentioned some things they might think about ordering (which just happened to be the easiest and quickest ones for a waitress to get). Later, after the rush was over, she took Sherri aside and explained that the pressure on new help often gets worse around the end of the first month because supervisors and cooks no longer think of the newcomers as new. What they always forget when they compare the new waitresses with the old ones, Betty said, is that the veterans have gotten the easier stations because of their seniority. They also know their customers better, including the ones who make trouble, and they get the bigger tips because they have the better tables. She showed Sherri some other tricks that would make the work easier, like warning the busboys when a table was almost ready to be cleaned up and working out a system for letting others know when she was having trouble. "You'll see," Betty assured her. "When you learn to assert yourself somewhat, and take care of emergencies first, and when you learn who you can ask for help, this job will be much easier."

In his extensive research on human relations in the restaurant industry, sociologist

William F. Whyte (1984) found that high-pressure situations like the one Sherri faced often lead less determined, more thin-skinned waitresses to quit. Often the ones who stay are emotionally tougher, better able to cope with the pressure. But he also showed that the intervention of tough yet sensitive pros like Betty often helps newcomers learn how to deal with the pressure, especially by learning the "tricks of the trade." However, not all newcomers are fortunate enough to have caring mentors to help them over the rough spots, and many quit before they can learn how to perform their roles well.

THE SOCIAL ORDER

When our social relations don't seem to be going well—when we experience stress, pressure, or conflict with co-workers or friends—we often jump to the conclusion that we are to blame. We don't stop to look at the powerful influence of social organizations on our lives. Sherri began to think that the cook, the customers, and her supervisor were reacting to her as a person rather than as a waitress. The pressure of her own work made it difficult for her to see that the pressures the cook was experiencing caused him to lash out at her. Their conflict had much more to do with their roles in the social organization of the restaurant than with their individual personalities. One of the main goals of this chapter is to indicate the great diversity of human social structures and to show how they influence individual behavior.

Of course, humans are not the only animals that are capable of social organization. We can learn a lot about life in human societies by comparing ourselves with other social animals. If you look closely at an ant colony or a beehive, for example, you can see a remarkable amount of organization. The nest or hive is a complete social world with workers, warriors, queens, drones, and so on. Each individual ant or bee has something to do and seems to do it quite well. But the differences between human societies and those of social animals like bees are even more important than the similarities. Unlike a human actor, an individual social animal can perform only a certain number of innate (inborn) tasks. The human can learn an infinite number of tasks. The individual bee is born a worker or a queen. Sherri, in contrast, can be a waitress, a college student, a lawyer, a mother, a voter, a taxpayer, and on and on.

We often have difficulty seeing the influence of social organization on our own behavior and that of other people; we take the existence of orderly social relations for granted. We assume that we know how society works and how to steer our way through it. But there will be times (especially when learning to adapt to new social environments) when we will be unsure of what is expected of us and how we should perform. Worse still, there may be times when it seems that society itself is threatened, that its continued existence as we know it is endangered. We catch glimpses of the breakdown of society during riots or wars or severe economic recessions.

At earlier times in human history, plagues and famines were frequent reminders that people had little control over their own destinies. Today plagues and famines still occur, but we are more often faced with real or potential crises of our own making: nuclear war, genocide, environmental disasters, drug addiction, criminal violence. Thus, if we are to continue to exist and thrive as a species, it is vital that we study societies and social structures—how they hold together, how they change, and why they sometimes seem to fall apart.

As in any science, we begin with some basic terms and definitions. The next few pages introduce the principal elements of social structure. The remaining sections of the chapter apply these and related concepts to an analysis of how societies have developed since the beginning of human history and how differences among societies affect the lives of individuals. The chapter concludes with a discussion of the important distinction between societies and nation-states.

Society and Social Structure

The term **society** refers to a population of people (or other social animals) that is organized in a cooperative manner to carry out the major functions of life, including reproduction, sustenance, shelter, defense, and disposal of the dead. This definition distinguishes between societies and populations. The notion of a population implies nothing about the social organization of that population, but the idea of a society stresses the *interrelationships* among the members of the population. In other words, a population can be any set of individuals that we decide to count or otherwise consider, such as the total number of people living between the Rio

> *A society differs from a population in that it is organized in a cooperative manner to carry out the major functions of life.*

Grande and the Arctic Circle, whereas a society is a population that is organized in some way, such as the population of the United States or Canada or the Amish people of Pennsylvania. In the modern world most societies are also (but not always) nation-states.

Social structure refers to the recurring patterns of behavior that people create through their interactions and relationships. We say, for example, that the family has a structure in which there are parents and children and other relatives who interact in specific ways on a regular basis. The larger society usually requires that family members assume certain obligations toward each other. Parents are required to educate their children or send them to schools; children are required to obey their parents until they have reached an age at which they are no longer considered dependent. These requirements contribute to the structure of relationships that is characteristic of the family. (The structure of an extended family is portrayed in the chart in Box 3-1.)

Throughout life individuals maintain relationships in an enormous range of social structures, of which families are only one. There are many others. People may be members of relatively small groups like the friendship or peer group and the work group. They may also be members of larger structures like churches, business organizations, or public agencies. And they may participate in even more broadly based structures, such as political groups and party organizations, or interest groups like the National Rifle Association or Planned Parenthood. All of these social structures are composed of groups with different degrees of complexity and quite different patterns of interaction. A military platoon, for example, is far more complicated than a barbershop quartet, and people behave quite differently in each. But all are different types of social structures. In them our time, our activities, and even our thoughts may be "structured" according to the needs and activities of the group.

Elements of Social Structure

Groups. The "building blocks" of societies are groups. A **group** is any collection of people who interact on the basis of shared expectations regarding one another's behavior.

Box 3–1: **Kinship in a Hunter-Gatherer Band**

Kinship diagrams like the one shown here provide a visual model of one type of social structure, that associated with family statuses extending over more than one generation. Such diagrams are used in both anthropology and sociology to denote lines of descent among people who are related by blood (children and their parents and siblings) and by marriage. To understand the chart one must know the meanings of the symbols used; these are explained in the key to the chart. The chart applies these symbols to show how cross-cousin marriages between members of different bands link the bands together into a larger structure of kinship networks.

The chart illustrates the social structure of a hunter-gatherer group. One individual, Ego, is used as a point of reference, and kinship links are traced from Ego's offspring, parents, grandparents, and more distant relatives.

There are a number of differences between this diagram and that of a typical family in a modern industrial society. The first is the structure of natal bands, in this case bands of individuals who are related through the male lineage (grandfather, father, Ego, Ego's son). Another difference is shown by the striped coloring inside the kinship symbols. In hunter-gatherer societies it is not possible for the entire society to travel and hunt within the same territory. Instead, the society is divided into bands—those formed by the male line of descent in this example. But marriages within the band cannot occur because of the incest taboo, and there are specific rules governing marriage outside the band.

Note that Ego has married his father's sister's daughter, or his first cousin on his father's side. Ego's wife's brother has married a woman from outside their band. This couple has come to live in the husband's natal band. Their daughter has married Ego's son, another cross-cousin marriage. Ego's daughter, on the other hand, will eventually marry someone from

One's immediate family is a group; so are a softball team, a seminar, a caucus, and the workers in Sherri's restaurant. But a collection of people on a busy street—a crowd—is not a group unless for some reason its members begin to interact in a regular fashion. Usually a crowd is composed of many different kinds of groups—couples, families, groups of friends, and so on. They may be molded into a single group in response to an event that affects them all, such as a fire.

Statuses. In every group there are socially defined positions known as **statuses.** Father, mother, son, daughter, teacher, student, and principal are examples of familiar statuses in the family and the school. Human societies include an infinite number of statuses. In a corporation, for example, the statuses range from president and chief executive officer to elevator operator and janitor. Between these two extremes there could be thousands of other statuses.[1] Moreover, the corporation can al-

---

[1] Like many other sociological terms, *status* has more than one meaning. It can refer to a person's rank in a social system and also to a person's prestige or the esteem with which others regard him or her. The fundamental meaning of the term is the one we use here.

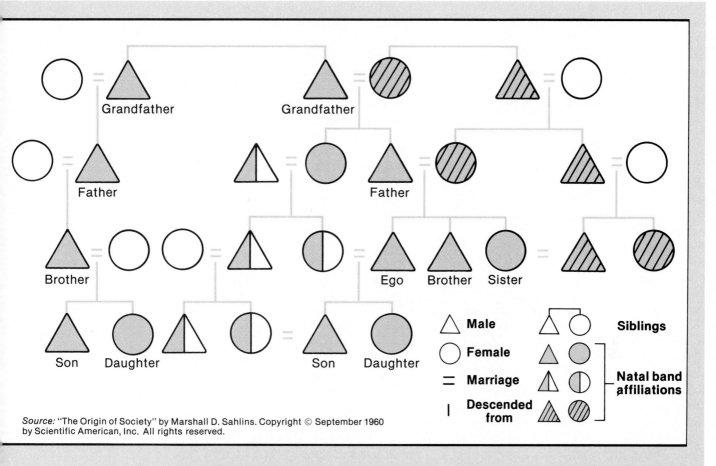

△ Male		
○ Female		
= Marriage		
| Descended from		

Siblings

Natal band affiliations

another band and live outside her natal band. By means of this custom the balance of women coming in and going out of the band is preserved.

Cross-cousin marriages, which are taboo in most Western societies, permit the hunter-gatherer band to develop a strong network of interfamily and inter-band kinship ties. This network widens over the generations and extends the ties of kinship throughout these small mobile societies.

ways create new statuses if the need arises. Thus, in the 1970s, when American society agreed to combat racism and sexism in business and government, many corporations invented the status of affirmative action director to provide equal opportunities for workers of both sexes and all racial and ethnic groups. If the larger society became more deeply concerned about environmental pollution or drug abuse, corporations could create new statuses like pollution control manager or drug counselor. Each of these statuses would then become part of the "corporate structure."

Human societies rely heavily on the creation of statuses to adapt to new conditions like environmental pollution and drug use, and one can often observe this adaptation occurring in daily life. In the family, for example, it is increasingly common—though not universally condoned—for young adults to cohabit before marriage or after divorce. As a large-scale phenomenon, this is a relatively new trend in American society, so new that we have not defined very well the new status of the person who participates in such a relationship. Do we say *boyfriend* or *girlfriend*, *lover*, *mate*, *significant other*, or what? The awkwardness of these terms is due to the fact that this is an emerging status that our society has not yet fully accepted or defined.

This example highlights an essential point about human social structure: It is never fixed or perfectly formed but instead is always changing and adapting to new conditions. Often the process of change involves much conflict and uncertainty, and often there is little consensus about how one should perform in a given status. Should the president of a corporation be an aloof, aggressive leader who directs subordinates with little regard for their feelings? Or should the president show concern for employees' feelings and personal needs and perhaps thereby gain greater loyalty and motivation? This is just one of thousands of dilemmas arising from questions about how we should act in a given social status. To clarify our thinking about statuses in groups and the behaviors associated with those statuses, sociologists make a distinction between a status and a role.

Roles and Role Expectations. The way a society defines how an individual is to behave in a particular status is referred to as a **role.** Sherri was not performing her role as waitress very well, according to the cook and the supervisor (who occupy other statuses within the social structure of the restaurant). Things improved when she got help from someone with more experience at performing the same role. Clearly, the ways in which people actually perform a role may vary widely. They are the product of **role expectations,** the society's expectations about how a role should be performed, together with the individual's perceptions of what is required in performing that role.

To appreciate the importance of role expectations you need only think of the mothers and fathers of your close friends: All hold the same statuses, but how different their behavior is! Part of that difference is due to personality—to psychological variables—but another part is due to how the individual mother and father perceive what is expected of them in the statuses they hold. One mother and father may have been raised to believe that children should work to support the family. They will insist that their children get early job experience. Another couple may have been taught that childhood is too short and should be prolonged if possible. They will not encourage their children to find jobs before they are grown.

Social change makes for even more debate and anxiety about role expectations; we discuss this subject in more detail later in this chapter. For now, consider the example of a mother who is also an attorney (something that was rather rare before women gained greater access to professional training). Because of the demands of her profession, she may be unable to take on a leadership position in the school PTA. However, being active in the PTA may have been one of her role expectations for motherhood before the opportunity for a professional career (and the income it provides) became attractive. Now she may feel harried by the pressure exerted by her conflicting statuses of mother and attorney—to say nothing of her other possible statuses, such as daughter, citizen, consumer, and so on.

This attorney may demand that her spouse perform tasks not traditionally associated with the status of husband, and he may or may not modify his original role expectations about that status; in either case, there is likely to be some conflict in the family as it adjusts to these changes. Another family, in which the mother is also in the labor force but there is no father in the home, has even more adjusting to do. The older children may take on parental roles far sooner than they might have in a two-parent family, but they may also resent this added responsibility and take out their anger on themselves and their siblings. In still another family, one that conforms to the tradition in which the mother is a homemaker and the father works outside the home, the pressures and conflict created by multiple role expectations may not occur in the early years. But what happens when the father retires and gives up his lifelong status of breadwinner? This is a time when traditional families frequently experience strain.

In sum, sociologists do not deny that individual personalities are important in explaining behavior, but they first look for explanations in the ways in which a person's statuses and roles in social structures influence his or her behavior.

Organization in Groups. Groups vary greatly in the extent to which the statuses of their members are well or poorly defined. The family is an example of a group in which statuses are well defined. Although parents carry out their roles in different ways, the law places certain limits on what they can and cannot do and defines many of the obligations of parenthood. Other groups are much more informal. We may form groups for brief periods in buses, hallways, or doctors' offices. There are roles and statuses in these groups also, but they are variable and ill defined. All of the people riding on a bus are passengers, but they do not interact the way the members of a family do. At most, we expect civility and "small talk" from other passengers on a bus, but we demand affection and support from other members of our family.

Social change is constantly making the structure of groups more varied and complex. To continue with our earlier example, the family may seem to have well-defined statuses, but high rates of divorce and remarriage have increased the proportion of families in which one parent is a stepparent (see Chapter 15). Consider the difference in role

expectations for "mother" or "father" in a situation in which each spouse must interact with a new spouse, a new set of children, and a new set of in-laws as well as an ex-spouse and children in the first family, plus the old in-laws, plus his or her own parents. Balancing role expectations among the often-competing demands of these groups can be a daunting task, one that was far less common when divorces were more difficult to obtain.

Groups also vary greatly in the ways in which they are connected with other groups into a larger structure known as an organization. An army platoon, for example, includes the well-defined statuses of private, corporal, and sergeant, each with specific roles to play in training and combat. Platoons are grouped together under the leadership of higher officers to form companies; this pattern is repeated at higher levels to create the battalion and the brigade, as illustrated in Figure 3-1.

Figure 3-1 shows the formal structure

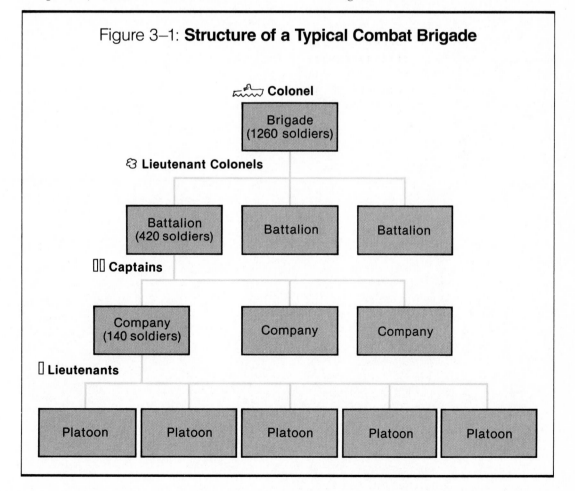

Figure 3–1: **Structure of a Typical Combat Brigade**

Colonel

Brigade
(1260 soldiers)

Lieutenant Colonels

Battalion
(420 soldiers)   Battalion   Battalion

Captains

Company
(140 soldiers)   Company   Company

Lieutenants

Platoon   Platoon   Platoon   Platoon   Platoon

of a typical army combat brigade. It does not show the brigade's informal organization, which consists of the ways in which its members actually relate to one another on the basis of friendships or animosities or mutual obligations of various kinds. (The importance of informal organization is discussed more fully in Chapter 7.)

POPULATIONS AND SOCIETIES

From a biological perspective, the success of any species is measured by how well it meets the broad requirements of population growth and mainte-nance. Every day more than 5 billion people seek and obtain enough food to convert into bodily energy: a minimum of perhaps 1,500 calories a day for survival at starvation levels, 2,500 for body maintenance. Over 70 percent of the world's population is inadequately nourished (that is, obtains fewer than 2,500 calories a day), whereas a smaller proportion, including most (but by no means all) of the North American population, lives comfortably above the daily minimum—perhaps too comfortably for good health (see Figure 3-2). We return to issues of social organization and food production in Chapter 5; for the moment let us concentrate on the human population itself.

The remarkable growth of the world's human population is the great biological success story of the last million years. Through-

Levels of nutritional need are based on average caloric intake per capita. Thus, a level of 120 percent means that the average person takes in 20 percent more calories than are considered necessary for body maintenance.

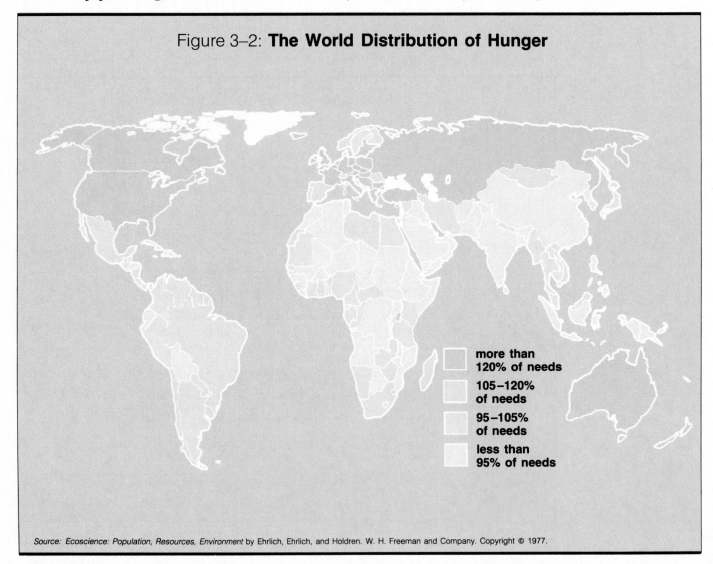

Figure 3–2: **The World Distribution of Hunger**

more than 120% of needs

105–120% of needs

95–105% of needs

less than 95% of needs

Source: Ecoscience: Population, Resources, Environment by Ehrlich, Ehrlich, and Holdren. W. H. Freeman and Company. Copyright © 1977.

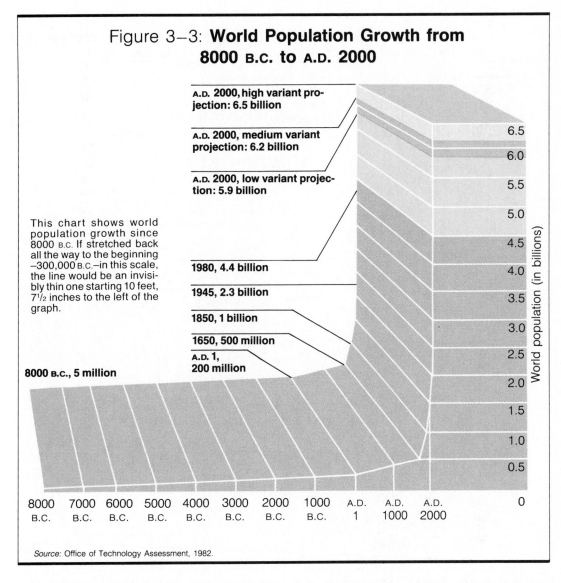

Figure 3–3: **World Population Growth from 8000 B.C. to A.D. 2000**

A.D. 2000, high variant projection: 6.5 billion

A.D. 2000, medium variant projection: 6.2 billion

A.D. 2000, low variant projection: 5.9 billion

This chart shows world population growth since 8000 B.C. If stretched back all the way to the beginning –300,000 B.C.–in this scale, the line would be an invisibly thin one starting 10 feet, 7½ inches to the left of the graph.

1980, 4.4 billion

1945, 2.3 billion

1850, 1 billion

1650, 500 million

A.D. 1, 200 million

8000 B.C., 5 million

World population (in billions)

6.5
6.0
5.5
5.0
4.5
4.0
3.5
3.0
2.5
2.0
1.5
1.0
0.5
0

8000 B.C. 7000 B.C. 6000 B.C. 5000 B.C. 4000 B.C. 3000 B.C. 2000 B.C. 1000 B.C. A.D. 1 A.D. 1000 A.D. 2000

Source: Office of Technology Assessment, 1982.

out most of the evolution of the human species, the world's population remained relatively small and constant. At the end of the Neolithic period, about 8000 B.C., there were an estimated 10 million humans, concentrated mainly in the Middle East, Africa, southern Europe, and a few fertile river basins in India, China, and Latin America. The overall range of human existence was much wider—populations were moving north as the last Ice Age receded about 10,000 years ago—but the human population was nowhere near as widely distributed as it is today. By the time of Jesus Christ there were an estimated 200 million people on the earth, and by the start of the industrial age, about the year 1650, there were an estimated 500 million. By 1945, however, the population had reached about 2.3 billion,

and according to most reliable estimates it will reach about 6 billion by the year 2000. This trend is illustrated in Figure 3-3.

What explains the shape of this population curve, the gradual rise in the world's population during the late Stone Age, the increasing rate of growth in the early millennia of recorded history, the explosive growth after 1650? The answers have to do with the changing production technologies of societies and their ever-increasing ability to sustain their populations, not only those directly involved in acquiring food but the ever-larger numbers of non-food-producers as well. In other words, human population growth is related to the shift from hunting and gathering to agriculture and, later, the shift from agriculture to industrial production as the chief means of

Table 3–1: **History of Major Technological Breakthroughs and Ensuing Population Increases**

Date	World Population in Millions	Most Advanced Economic Type	Limit-raising Technology	Population Increase	Generations Elapsed	Increase per Generation
2 million B.C.		Hunting and gathering	Use of fire, tool making		78,600	
35,000 B.C.	3		Spear-thrower bow and arrow	167%	1,080	0.09%
8000 B.C.	8	Horticultural	Cultivation of plants	975%	160	1.50%
4000 B.C.	86		Metallurgy (bronze)			
3000 B.C.	?	Agrarian	Plow	249%	160	0.78%
1000 B.C.	?		Iron tools			
A.D. 1	300			12%	55.9	0.20%
A.D. 1398	336		Hand firearms	188.4%	16.1	6.80%
A.D. 1800	969	Industrial	Fossil fueled machinery	41.5%	2.6	14.28%
A.D. 1865	1371		Antiseptic surgery, etc.	191.8%	4.4	27.55%
A.D. 1975	4000					

Source: William R. Catton, Jr., *Overshoot: The Ecological Basis of Revolutionary Change*, Urbana: University of Illinois Press, © 1980.

supplying people with the necessities of life (see Table 3-1).

The First Million Years: Hunting and Gathering

A human lifetime is no more than a twinkling in time. What are seventy or eighty years compared with the billions of years of the earth's existence? What is one generation compared with the millions of years of human social evolution? Yet many of us hope to leave some mark on society, perhaps to change it for the better, to ease some suffering, to increase productivity, to fight racism and ig-

norance . . . what vaulting ambitions! And what a radical change from the world view of our ancestors! The idea that people can shape their society—or even enjoy adequate shelter and ample meals—is widely accepted today. But for most of human history mere survival was the primary motivator of human action, and therefore a fatalistic acceptance of human frailty in the face of overwhelming natural forces was the dominant world view.

For most of the first million years of human evolution, human societies were developing out of those of primates. Populations were small because humans, like other primates, lived on wild animals and plants. These sources of food are easily used up and their supply fluctuates greatly, and as a result periods of starvation or gnawing hunger alternated with bouts of gorging on sudden windfalls of game or berries. Thus the hunting-and-gathering life that characterized the earliest human populations could support only extremely small societies; most human societies therefore had no more than sixty members.

Recent archaeological evidence indicates that some hunting-and-gathering societies began to develop permanent settlements long before the advent of agriculture. The emergence of farming was the key change that accelerated human social evolution, but the new evidence shows that in parts of what is now Europe and the Middle East there were stable settlements of hunter-gatherers as early as 30,000 to 20,000 years ago. These rather large and complex societies were most firmly established in the area that is now Israel at the end of the last Ice Age, some 13,000 to 12,000 years ago (Henry, 1989; Stevens, 1988).

Despite the slow pace of human evolution until about 35,000 years ago, some astonishing physical and social changes occurred during that long period, changes that enabled human life to take the forms it does today. Among them were:

- The development of an upright posture (which freed the hands for eventual use of tools) and an enlarged cerebral cortex, making possible vastly increased cognitive abilities and the development of language.

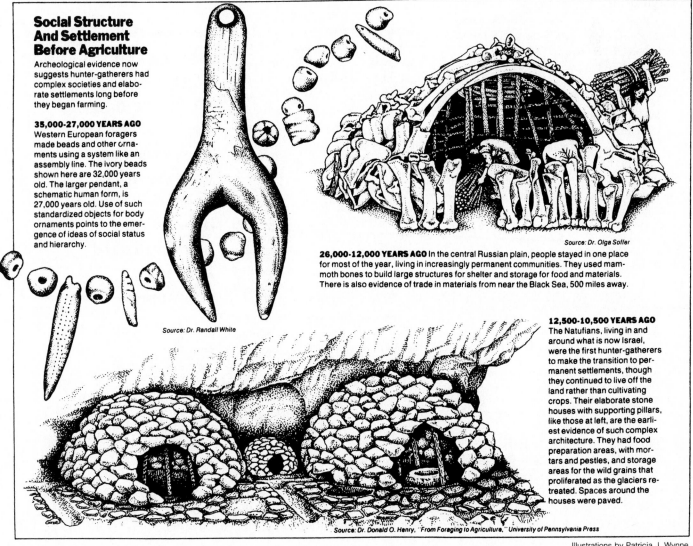

Social Structure And Settlement Before Agriculture

Archeological evidence now suggests hunter-gatherers had complex societies and elaborate settlements long before they began farming.

35,000-27,000 YEARS AGO Western European foragers made beads and other ornaments using a system like an assembly line. The ivory beads shown here are 32,000 years old. The larger pendant, a schematic human form, is 27,000 years old. Use of such standardized objects for body ornaments points to the emergence of ideas of social status and hierarchy.

Source: Dr. Randall White

Source: Dr. Olga Soffer

26,000-12,000 YEARS AGO In the central Russian plain, people stayed in one place for most of the year, living in increasingly permanent communities. They used mammoth bones to build large structures for shelter and storage for food and materials. There is also evidence of trade in materials from near the Black Sea, 500 miles away.

12,500-10,500 YEARS AGO The Natufians, living in and around what is now Israel, were the first hunter-gatherers to make the transition to permanent settlements, though they continued to live off the land rather than cultivating crops. Their elaborate stone houses with supporting pillars, like those at left, are the earliest evidence of such complex architecture. They had food preparation areas, with mortars and pestles, and storage areas for the wild grains that proliferated as the glaciers retreated. Spaces around the houses were paved.

Source: Dr. Donald O. Henry, "From Foraging to Agriculture," University of Pennsylvania Press

Illustrations by Patricia J. Wynne

- Social control of sexuality through the development of the family and other kinship structures and the enforcement of the incest taboo.
- The establishment of the band of hunter-gatherers as the basic territorial unit of human society, coupled with the development of kinship structures that linked bands together into tribes. Within the band, the family became the primary economic unit, organizing the production and distribution of food and other necessities.

The chart in Box 3-1 illustrates how kinship ties link bands together. Anthropologists and sociologists often represent social structures with diagrams of this type. They show how people are related to one another and what their status is in relation to any other person in the structure.

By the end of the last Ice Age, many aspects of this evolutionary process were more or less complete. Human societies had fully developed languages and a social structure based on the family and the band. To be cast out of the band for some wrongdoing (i.e., to be considered a deviant person) usually meant total banishment from the society and eventual death, either by starvation or as a result of aggression by members of another society (Salisbury, 1962). But warfare and violence were not typical of early human societies. As social anthropologist Marshall Sahlins has pointed out,

Warfare is limited among hunters and gatherers. Indeed, many are reported to find the idea of war incomprehensible. A massive military effort would be difficult to sustain for technical and logistic reasons. But war is even further inhibited by the spread of a social relation—kinship—which in primitive society is often a synonym for "peace." Thomas Hobbes' famous fantasy of a war of "all against all" in the natural state could not be further from the truth. War increases in intensity, bloodiness, duration, and significance for social survival through the evolution of culture, reaching its culmination in modern civilization. [1960, p. 82]

On the other hand, one must not romanticize the hunter-gatherers. Their lives were far more subject to the pressures of adaptation to the natural environment than has been true in any subsequent form of society. Individual survival was usually subordinated to that of the group. If there were too many children to feed, some were killed or left to die; when the old became infirm or weak, they chose death so as not to diminish the chances of the others. Thus the frail Eskimo grandfather or grandmother wandered off into the snowy night to "meet the polar bear and the great spirit." It would take additional thousands of years of social evolution before the idea that every person should be allowed to survive, prosper, and die with dignity would occur to our ancestors.

The Agrarian Revolution

One of Karl Marx's many original insights is that the origins of new forms of society are to be found within the old ones, that new social orders do not simply burst upon the scene but are created out of the problems faced by the old order. Thus the often-heard statement that agrarian societies (societies based on the production of surplus food supplies by means of farming) were made possible by the invention of the plow some 3,000 years ago is far from accurate. Indeed, centuries before the plow appears in archaeological records there is evidence that people were experimenting with the domestication of plants and animals and were beginning to conduct regular trade (Stevens, 1986). The plow is just one innovation among many that made it possible for human settlements to exploit the same land year after year, thereby becoming more stable as well as more productive (see Figure 3-4).

Before the invention of the plow, some societies had evolved into pastoral or shepherding societies while others had become horticultural societies.

For some time before the advent of plow-and-harvest agriculture in the Middle East and the Far East, hunting-and-gathering societies were supplementing their diets with foods acquired through the domestication of plants and animals. Some were evolving into nomadic shepherding, or *pastoral*, societies, while others were developing into *horticultural* societies in which the women raised seed crops and the men combed the territory for game and fish. Regarding this momentous

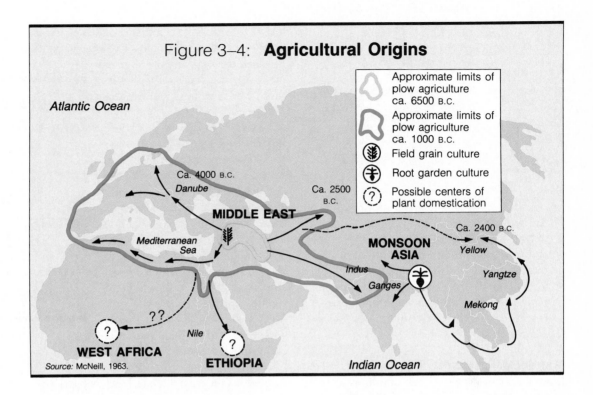

Figure 3–4: **Agricultural Origins**

Source: McNeill, 1963.

change in the material basis of human survival, historian William McNeill has written:

The seed-bearing grasses ancestral to modern cultivated grains probably grew wild eight or nine thousand years ago in the hill country between Anatolia and the Zagros Mountains, as varieties of wheat and barley continue to do today. If so, we can imagine that from time immemorial the women of those regions searched out patches of wheat and barley grasses when the seeds were ripe and gathered the wild harvest by hand or with the help of simple cutting tools. Such women may gradually have discovered methods for assisting the growth of grain, e.g., by pulling out competing plants; and it is likely that primitive sickles were invented to speed the harvest long before agriculture in the stricter sense came to be practiced. (1963, p. 12)

As a result of these and other innovations, agriculture became the productive basis of human societies. Pastoral societies spread quickly throughout the uplands and grasslands of Africa, northern Asia, Europe, and the Western Hemisphere, and grain-producing societies arose in the fertile river valleys of Mesopotamia, India, China, and, somewhat later, Central and South America. Mixed societies of shepherds and marginal farmers wandered over the lands between the upland pastures and the lowland farms.

The First Large-Scale Societies. We have reached the beginning of recorded history (around 4000 B.C.), which was marked by the rise of the ancient civilizations of Sumer, Babylonia, China and Japan, and Benin, and those of the Incas and the Aztecs. The detailed study of these societies is the province of archaeology, history, and classics. But sociologists need to know as much as possible about the earliest large-scale societies because many contemporary social institutions (e.g., government and religion) and most areas of severe social conflict (e.g., class and ethnic conflict) developed sometime in the agrarian epoch—that is, between 3000 B.C. and A.D. 1600.

From the standpoint of social evolution, these dimensions of agrarian societies are the most salient (Braidwood, 1960):

● Agriculture allows humans to escape from dependence on food sources over which they have no control. Agrarian societies produce surpluses that do not merely *permit* but *require* new castes or classes of non-food-producers to exist. An example is the class of warriors, who defend the surplus or add to it through plunder.

- Agriculture requires an ever-larger supply of land, resulting in conflicts over territory and in wars with other agricultural or pastoral societies.
- The need to store and defend food surpluses and to house the nonagrarian classes results in new territorial units: villages and small cities.

New Social Structures: Stratification. Freed from direct dependence on undomesticated species of plants and animals, agrarian societies developed far more complex social structures than were possible in simpler societies. Hunting-and-gathering societies divided labor primarily according to age and sex, but in agricultural societies labor was divided in new ways to perform more specialized tasks. Peoples who had been conquered in war might be enslaved and assigned the most difficult or least desirable work. Priests controlled the society's religious life, and from the priestly class there emerged a class of hereditary rulers who, as the society became larger and more complex, assumed the status of pharaoh or emperor. Artisans with special skills—in the making of armaments or buildings, for example—usually formed another class. And far more numerous than any of these classes were the tillers of the soil, the "common" agricultural workers and their dependents.

The process whereby the members of a society are sorted into different statuses and classes based on differences in wealth, power, and prestige is called **social stratification** and is described in detail in Chapter 8. In general, societies may be **open,** so that a person who was not born into a particular status may gain entry to that status, or **closed,** with each status accessible only by birth. A key charac-

teristic of agrarian societies is that their stratification systems became extremely rigid. Because the majority of the people were needed in the fields, there were few opportunities for people to move from one level of society to another. These therefore were closed societies.

The emergence of agrarian societies was based largely on the development of new, more efficient production technologies. Of these, the plow and irrigation were among the most important. The ancient agrarian empires of Egypt, Rome, and China are examples of societies in which irrigation made possible the production of large food surpluses, which in turn permitted the emergence of central governments led by pharaohs and emperors, priests and soldiers. Indeed, some sociologists have argued that because large-scale irrigation systems required a great deal of coordination, their development led to the evolution of imperial courts and such institutions as slavery, which coerced large numbers of agrarian workers into forced labor (Wittfogel, 1957).

Plow agriculture as practiced in rain-watered lands like Europe and Japan replaced more primitive technologies such as the use of digging sticks to push seeds into the ground. The plow, which turned over the surface soil and enabled seeds to grow more easily, led to the establishment of villages and agricultural manors that could share the oxen and horses required to pull the plows. Thus a few inventions, together with the social arrangements that supported their use, were at the base of the agrarian revolution. In contrast, a rapid increase in the rate of development of new technologies ushered in the industrial revolution of the modern era.

In agrarian societies labor was divided in new ways to perform more specialized tasks, leading to the development of more complex social structures.

The Industrial Revolution

Between about 500 B.C. and about A.D. 1600, new societies formed around cities that controlled limited territories (especially Greece, Phoenicia, and Crete in antiquity, and the city-states of the Italian peninsula and the European riverways in the Middle Ages).

This artist's rendering captures the colossal scale of monument building in the ancient empires, which invariably depended on the work of slaves and their overseers. The slaves were often captive peoples.

The Bettman Archive, Inc.

These societies were to play a major role in bringing about the next revolutionary transition in human social organization: the shift from agriculture to trade and industry.

In 1650, when Holland, Spain, and England were the world's principal trading nations, the population of England was approximately 10 million, of which about 90 percent earned a livelihood through farming of one kind or another. Two hundred years later, in 1850, the English population had soared to over 30 million, with less than 20 percent at work in fields, barns, and granaries. England had become the world's first industrial society and the center of an empire that spanned the world.

In 1860, on the eve of the American Civil War, there were about 30 million people in the United States. Ninety percent of that population, a people considered quite backward by the rapidly industrializing English, were farmers or people who worked in occupations directly related to farming. A mere hundred years later, in 1960, only about 8 percent of Americans were farmers or agricultural workers, yet they were able to produce enough to feed a population of over 200 million. Today less than 3 percent of Americans work on farms and ranches. These dramatic changes in England and America—and in other nations as well—occurred as a result of the industrial revolution.

The industrial revolution is often associated with innovations in energy production, especially the steam engine. But the shift from an agrarian to an industrial society did not happen simply as a result of technological advances. Rather, the industrial revolution was made possible by the rise of a new social order: capitalism. This new way of organizing production originated in nation-states, which engaged in international trade, exploration, and warfare. Above all, the industrial revolution depended on the development of markets that would regulate the supply of and demand for goods and services throughout the world (Polanyi, 1944).

The transition from an agrarian to an industrial society affects every aspect of social life. It changes the structure of society in sev-

The shift from agriculture to trade and industry was made possible by the rise of a new way of organizing production—capitalism.

eral ways, of which these are among the most significant:

- The industrialization of agriculture allows many more people to be supported by each agrarian worker than ever before. Only a relatively small number of people live on the land; increasing numbers live in towns, cities, and suburbs.
- Industrial societies are generally far more receptive to social change than agrarian societies. One result is the emergence of new classes like industrial workers and scientific professionals (engineers, technicians) and new social movements like the women's movement and the movement for racial equality.
- Scientific, technical, and productive institutions produce both unparalleled wealth and unparalleled destructive capacities.
- The world "shrinks" as a result of innovations in transportation and communication; as a result, a "global society" develops, but at the same time the unevenness of industrialization leads to conflicts that threaten world peace.

These are only some of the important features of industrial societies. There are many others, which we analyze throughout this book. We will present research that shows how the types of jobs people find and the ways in which they spend their leisure time change as technology advances and their expectations change. We will also look into the ways in which other major institutions—especially the family— adapt to the changes created by the industrial revolution. In fact, we will continually return to the industrial revolution as a major force in our times. In this regard, a key issue is whether nations that underwent industrial transformations in earlier centuries are now experiencing a "postindustrial" revolution in which the pace of automation accelerates rapidly and service occupations replace manufacturing occupations as the dominant type of employment. Issues like these require us to think about societies as wholes, or at least to think about large parts of societies—entire social institutions and huge populations.

Sociologists are equally concerned with the study of how these changes in the organization of entire societies affect individuals and small groups. The experience of living in different types of societies is also a major field of sociological inquiry, for people create social institutions through their interactions and, in turn, are affected by changes in those institutions. As the world's societies become more and more interdependent, what happens in metropolitan centers like London, Hong Kong, Moscow, or New York affects the lives of villagers in remote parts of the world. Decisions made by the leaders of modern nation-states therefore affect not only the populations of those states but all of the world's people, as we will see in the remaining sections of this chapter and elsewhere in the book (Giddens, 1984; Wolf, 1966, 1984).

SOCIETY AND THE INDIVIDUAL

Unlike all other animal species, human beings have the capacity to live in different kinds of societies. For example, we could adjust to life in a hunting-and-gathering society. It would not be at all easy, of course, but we could do it, especially if our lives depended on it. People have been able to adapt to far worse conditions—even the concentration camps of Nazi Germany and Stalinist Russia. And after all, do we not expect that people who grew up in peasant societies will adjust to the changes that occur as those societies industrialize?

Much research has been done on the subject of individual and group adaptations to new social structures. To note just one example, slavery in the United States, which uprooted large numbers of Africans from smaller tribal societies and thrust them with no preparation into a far larger and more complex society, is a subject of intense study by both historians and sociologists. Despite all the hardships they experienced under slavery and in the decades following emancipation, Africans eventually became an integral part of American society. Like the African-Americans, most major population groups have, at some time in their history, been uprooted and forced to adapt to strange social conditions and institutions. The study of the processes whereby these adaptations occur has become an important area of sociological research.

From Gemeinschaft to Gesellschaft

Imagine that you grew up in an agrarian or slowly industrializing society and then came to live in the United States, as millions of people do each decade. A salient (and probably painful) part of that experience would be getting used to the impersonality of modern American society when compared with the close relationships you had with people you had known all your life in your native society. American society would seem to be composed of masses of strangers organized into highly impersonal categories. You would have to get used to being a shopper, an applicant, a depositor, a fan, a commuter, and so on, and it would be necessary to shift from one to another of these roles several times in a day or even in a half-hour.

Day-to-day life in modern industrial societies is dominated by gesellschaft *social structures and secondary groups.*

Sociologists often describe this experience as a change from **gemeinschaft** (meaning the close, personal relationships of small groups and communities) to **gesellschaft** (meaning the well-organized but impersonal relationships of modern societies). These are German terms taken from the writings of the social theorist Ferdinand Tönnies. Complex industrial societies, Tönnies argued, have developed gesellschaft social structures like factories and office bureaucracies to such a degree that they tend to dominate day-to-day life in the modern world.

A famous application of this distinction to the micro level of society is derived from the American sociologist Charles H. Cooley's discussion of **primary** versus **secondary** groups. "By primary groups," Cooley wrote,

I mean those characterized by intimate face-to-face association and cooperation. They are primary in several senses, but chiefly in that they are fundamental in forming the social nature and ideals of the individual. [Such a group] involves the sort of sympathy and mutual identification for which "we" is the natural expression. (1909, p. 23)

Secondary groups, in contrast, are groups in which we participate for instrumental reasons—that is, in order to accomplish some task or set of tasks. Examples are school classrooms, town committees, and political-party

organizations. We do not have intimate relationships with other members of secondary groups; at least, we do not normally expect to do so and are not concerned about the fact that our relationships in such groups involve only a limited range of emotions.

Of course, when we speak of intimacy in primary groups we do not always refer to love and warm feelings. The intimacy of the members of a family refers to a highly charged set of emotions that can range from love to hate but rarely includes indifference. But in a secondary group, indifference or lack of personal involvement is the norm. We therefore do not usually develop strong feelings toward all the other members of the organizations for which we work or the associations to which we belong, even though we may have one or more close friends among our workmates. The idea that people do not have to form primary attachments in work organizations is also a way of protecting people with less power from those with more. Women in subordinate positions, for example, often need formal protection from men in more powerful positions who make sexual advances. Modern laws on sexual conduct at work classify such behavior as illegal harassment.

Role and Status in Modern Societies

Roles in Conflict. One point all sociological theorists make about the change from gemeinschaft to gesellschaft forms of social organization is that the latter are more complex in terms of the number of statuses people hold and, thus, the number of roles they must perform. One result of this greater complexity is that roles in secondary groups or associations often conflict with roles in primary groups like the family. Much of the stress of life in modern societies is due to the anxiety we experience as we attempt to balance the conflicting demands of our various roles. This anxiety is captured in the terms **role conflict** and **role strain**.

Role conflict occurs when, in order to perform one role well, a person must violate another important role. Parents who are also employees may experience this kind of conflict when their supervisors ask them to put in extra time, which cuts into the time they are able to spend with their children. A recent article in the *Harvard Business Review* (Schwartz, 1989) supporting the idea that corporations should develop a two-track system, one for executives who sacrifice family concerns for the company and another for those who take time off for family needs, has stimulated intense controversy in both business and social-scientific circles. The so-called "mommy track" is attacked as discriminating against women who wish to succeed in business careers while raising their children.

Research on how people behave in disasters also illustrates some of the effects of role conflict. For example, a police officer or firefighter who is on duty during a disaster that affects his or her own family may leave an assigned post to see to the safety of loved ones, thereby violating one role in order to fulfill another (Killian, 1952).

Role strain occurs when people experience conflicting demands in an existing role or cannot meet the expectations of a new one. For example, industrial sociologists (e.g., Whyte and Gardner, 1945) have pointed out that the factory foreman was traditionally a "man in the middle." Caught between the conflicting goals of managers concerned with production quotas and workers concerned with making their workdays bearable, the foreman felt highly stressed. To retreat into the formal role of foreman meant becoming estranged from the workers, but to become "too friendly" with the workers was to court the disapproval of management. Shoshanna Zuboff's research on the impact of computers indicates that the computer regulation of factory work often replaces the supervisor's control, which relieves role strain but may cause the foreman to wonder whether his role has become unnecessary (Zuboff, 1982, 1988).

Role strain in the form of anxiety over poor performance is at least as common as role strain caused by conflicting expectations. For example, the unemployed head of a family feels severe stress as a result of inability to provide for the family's needs (Bakke, 1933; Jahoda, 1982; Jahoda, Lazarsfeld, and Zeisel, 1971). The mother of a newborn baby often feels intense anxiety over how well she can care for a helpless infant, a feeling that is heightened when she herself is young and dependent on others (Mayfield, 1984).

Ascribed Versus Achieved Statuses. Role conflicts may occur in simpler societies, but they are far more common in societies undergoing rapid change. One reason for the relative lack of role conflict in simpler, more stable societies is that in such societies a person's statuses are likely to be determined by birth or tradition rather than by anything the person achieves through his or her own efforts. These **ascribed statuses** (peasant, aristocrat, slave, and so forth) usually cannot be changed and hence are less likely to be subject to different role expectations. Such statuses are found in industrial societies too (statuses based on race or sex are examples), but they tend to become less important in modern institutions than **achieved statuses** like editor, professor, or Nobel Prize winner.

We expect to be able to achieve our occupational status, our marital and family statuses, and other statuses in the community and the larger society. Nevertheless, there is some tension in modern societies between the persistence of ascribed statuses and the ideal of achieved statuses. The empirical study of that tension and of efforts to replace ascribed with achieved statuses (for example, through equality of educational opportunity) is another major area of sociological research. We will show in later chapters that many of the social movements studied by sociologists arose as different groups in a society (e.g., blacks, wage workers, immigrants, and the poor) organized to press for greater access to economic and social institutions like corporations and universities.

> *Simpler, more stable societies tend to be characterized by ascribed statuses, whereas in modern industrial societies most statuses are achieved.*

Master Statuses. One reason so many groups have had to organize to obtain social justice is related to the way statuses operate in many societies. Although any person may fill a variety of statuses, many people find that one of their statuses is more important than all the others. Such a status, which is termed a **master status,** can have very damaging effects (Hughes, 1945). A black man, for example, may be a doctor, a father, and a leader in his church, but he may find that his status as a black American takes precedence over all of those other statuses. The same is often true for women. A woman may be a brilliant scientist and a leader in her community, and fill other statuses as well, but she may find that when she deals with men her status as a woman is more important than any of the others.

The effects of a master status are also felt by people who have been in prison, by members of various racial and ethnic groups, and by members of many other types of groups. For example, people who are particularly beautiful according to the society's prevailing definition of beauty may find that their status as a beautiful or handsome person is a master status that denies them opportunities to be appreciated for their performance in other statuses, such as student or worker.

Patterns of discrimination and prejudice stemming from the problem of master statuses are not easily corrected. We will see at many points in this book that a major source of social change is the efforts of some groups to eliminate those patterns. But when changes are actually made they often take the form of changes in the laws of a nation. This raises the question of the distinction between society and nation.

> *The state has a monopoly over the use of force, a right it gains from the people's belief that it is legitimate for the state to have this power.*

SOCIETIES AND NATION-STATES

We turn now to a discussion of the social entity that, for most people in the world today, represents society itself: the nation-state. The assumed correspondence between society and nation can be seen in the fact that expressions like "the United States" and "American society" are often used interchangeably. Moreover, most people think of their society in terms of national boundaries; thus, if you were asked to name the society of which you are a member, you would be more likely to say "the United States" than "California" or "Chicago" or "the University of Texas." Yet, as we will see shortly, societies and nations are by no means the same thing.

The State

To understand the distinction between society and nation, we need to begin with the concept of the state. "Today," Max Weber (1918) said in a lecture at Munich University, "we have to say that a state is

a human community that (successfully) claims *the monopoly of the legitimate use of physical force* within a given territory. . . . The right to use physical force is ascribed to other institutions or to individuals only to the extent to which the state permits it. The state is considered the sole source of the "right" to use violence. (Gerth and Mills, 1958, p. 78; emphasis in original)

The **state** thus may be defined as a society's set of political structures—that is, the groups and organizations that deal with questions of "who gets what, when, and how" (Lasswell, 1936). The **nation-state** is the largest territory within which those structures can operate without having to face challenges to their sovereignty (their right to govern). Weber was careful to note that the state has a monopoly over the use of force, which under certain circumstances it grants to other agencies (state and municipal governments, for example). But the state gains this right—the source of its power to influence the behavior of citizens—from the people themselves, from their belief that it is *legitimate* for the state to have this power. As we will see in later chapters, the concepts of power and legitimacy are essential to understanding the workings of the modern state; indeed, power is a basic concept at all levels of human social behavior. Here, however, we must examine the idea of a state as it operates in the concept of nation-state or, simply, nation.

The Nation-State

"One nation under God, indivisible, with liberty and justice for all." We can say the words in our sleep. We do not usually give much thought to the significance of what we are doing when we repeat the Pledge of Allegiance. Yet repeating the pledge is a highly significant action: It enhances the legitimacy of the state and thus helps create the nation—in this case, the nation known as the United States of America.

But do all the inhabitants of the United States of America think of themselves as

Figure 3–5: **Tribal Societies Within the Modern State of Nigeria**

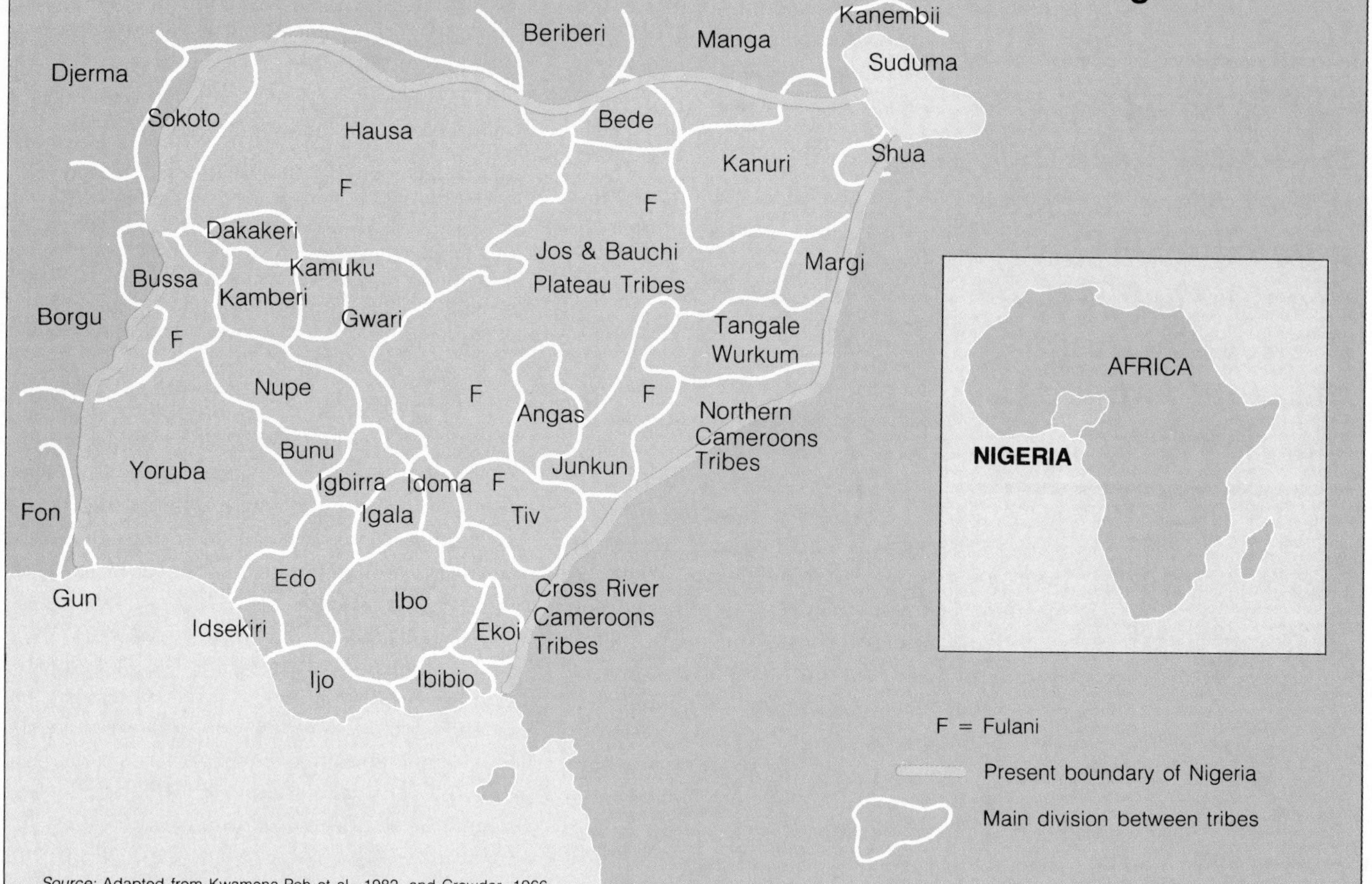

F = Fulani

Present boundary of Nigeria

Main division between tribes

Source: Adapted from Kwamena-Poh et al., 1982, and Crowder, 1966.

members of one nation? To a large extent they do, and this is one of the greatest strengths of that nation. Yet at various times in American history certain groups—blacks, Native Americans, and the Amish, for example—have thought of themselves as separate peoples. And the idea of an "indivisible" nation was fought out in one of the bloodiest wars the world has ever known, the American Civil War of 1861–1865.

In the century since the Civil War the United States has not experienced any real tests of its national solidarity. Countries like Canada, Lebanon, Zimbabwe, South Africa, Iran, Northern Ireland, and many others have been far less fortunate. For them, the issue of creating a national identity that can unite peoples who think of themselves as members of different societies remains a burning question.

Between 1950 and 1970, as peoples all over the world adjusted to the breakup of the European colonial empires, over 100 new states were created, many of them in the poorer regions of Africa and Asia. In these new nations, as in many of the nation-states that existed before the 1950s, the correspondence between national identity and society is often problematic, a situation that frequently produces social upheavals. In Nigeria, for example, a brutal civil war erupted in 1967 over the issue of whether the Ibo, one of several large tribes contained within the nation's boundaries, were free to form a separate nation, the Republic of Biafra. The Ibo rebellion was crushed, but the Ibo still consider themselves a separate people within the Nigerian nation (see Figure 3-5).

The lack of a clear match between society and nation can be seen in the case of entire groups who think of themselves as "a people" (the Ibo, the Jews, Native Americans, and the like) as well as smaller groups. You and your friends are part of "American society," by which we mean the populations and social structures found within the territory claimed by the nation-state known as the United States of America. But you are also part of a local community with smaller structures and more gemeinschaft or primary relationships. Indeed, this community level of society may have greater meaning for you in your daily life than society at the national level.

Conclusion

In this chapter we have looked at social structure from several different viewpoints. We have seen how societies evolved over time as human productive technologies changed; we have discussed various aspects of the relationship between social structure and the individual; and we have distinguished between societies and nations. One of our goals has been to demonstrate that the concept of society is not a simple one. Indeed, sociologists have never agreed on one all-encompassing definition of society, and they probably never will. Perhaps this is a good thing, for it allows flexibility in the analysis of phenomena that are constantly changing.

Another reason for looking at social structure from different angles is to illustrate the point we made in Chapter 1 about different levels of complexity. Whenever we speak of a society, we have in mind a certain level of social organization. The couple, the family, the peer group, the gang, and the team, to cite just a few examples, are micro-level social structures. The community, the firm or company, and the bureaucratic agency are some examples of middle-level structures that often incorporate micro-level ones. The armed forces of a nation, the government of the United States, and multinational corporations like General Motors are national organizations (international in the case of GM) that represent macro-level social structures. These are only some of the more familiar social structures at different levels of society—and new ones are being created all the time. For the individual member of society, the challenge is to fit into the existing structures and yet to try to change them as the conditions of social life change.

FRONTIERS OF SOCIOLOGY

Populations on the Move

Wars, natural disasters, and political repression accelerate the movement of peoples from one place to another. This has been especially true in the twentieth century, even within our own relatively stable society. During World War II, for example, 5 million people of working age left American farms in only four years. The majority found civilian jobs in industry and never returned to the farms. The average net migration from farms to cities was 11,390,000 in the 1940s and 10,130,000 in the 1950s. In other words, more than 20 million people relocated themselves from farms to urban-industrial communities in only twenty years (Bogue, 1969, p. 767).

Think about this for a moment. The transition from an agrarian to an urban-industrial society is not a historical abstraction. It is a reality that has been experienced by millions of Americans who are alive today. In many societies people are moving from farm to factory, from country to city, or, even more difficult, from agrarian life in a third-world nation to life as immigrant workers in an advanced industrial society.

Throughout the world, between the beginning of World War I (1914) and the end of the 1970s an estimated 120 million people were forced to move from one nation to another because of either political violence or severe economic disruption (Beijer, 1969; Zolberg, 1981). Being uprooted in this way means leaving behind old statuses and roles, giving up a way of life, and attempting to recreate these statuses and roles in a new society. It is little wonder, then, that patterns of migration and their social consequences have figured so centrally in the history of sociology.

Studies of human migration attempt to understand the flows of people to and from societies. They also seek to discover why the great movements of people occur and what policies would ease the problems that newcomers to a society experience and create. Can they have a better life in the new society? What is their impact on the people already there who are struggling to achieve higher statuses themselves? What psychic scars does moving from an agrarian to an industrial society leave on immigrants and their children?

The familiar "rags-to-riches" story asserts that through hard work and self-discipline anyone can move up to a higher status. But is the probability of upward movement for new arrivals as great today as it was in America's period of precipitous growth, the so-called Gilded Age (1870–1929)? Edna Bonacich (1972, 1976) is one of a number of contemporary sociologists whose research suggests that moving to a higher economic status will be far more difficult for recent immigrants to the United States than it was for earlier generations. Her research provides

evidence that a dual or "split" labor market has developed in the United States. Some workers obtain jobs in the primary labor market—in industries and corporations where there will be training, promotions, and good pay and benefits. Others are channeled into the secondary labor market, in which jobs are far more menial, unskilled, and low-paying, and lack benefits such as health insurance. Using data on the access of blacks to jobs in the industrial North earlier in this century, Bonacich has shown that unskilled black workers were systematically channeled into the secondary labor market.

Other social scientists (among them Michael Piore, Alejandro Portes, and Saskia Sassen) have demonstrated that recent immigrants to the United States share the fate of earlier migrants from the rural South. Most tend to be shunted into the secondary labor market, where they work as migrant laborers, restaurant workers, mailroom clerks, unskilled factory workers, and hotel chambermaids. These scholars predict, moreover, that as American society becomes even more technologically oriented (that is, as older industries like steel, mining, and heavy manufacturing become more automated) there will be an even wider gap between the primary and secondary labor markets.

As you might suspect, this is a controversial theory. It contradicts one of our society's most precious myths, that anyone who works hard can succeed, and it predicts hard times for more and more workers as automation transforms industrial America into a "postindustrial" society based on automated production technologies. Other sociologists and economists have argued against the "dual labor market" theory. In their view, the failure of some groups to advance economically is caused more by lack of education and similar problems than by structural features of the society itself (Bell, 1973; Sowell, 1983).

Issues like this are likely to remain on the frontiers of sociological research for the foreseeable future. Throughout the world, immigration continues and refugee populations are growing. In every country to which large groups of people migrate, there is bound to be competition between the newcomers and established groups that believe they have a prior claim to whatever benefits the society has to offer.

SUMMARY

A *society* is a population of people or other social animals that is organized in a cooperative manner to carry out the major functions of life. *Social structure* refers to the recurring patterns of behavior that create relationships among individuals and groups within a society. The "building blocks" of human societies are *groups*—collections of people who interact on the basis of shared expectations regarding one another's behavior. In every group there are socially defined positions known as *statuses*. The way a society defines how an individual is to behave in a particular status is called a *role*.

The growth of the world's population is directly related to the evolution of human social structures, which in turn is related to changes in production technologies. The first million years of human social evolution were characterized by a hunting-and-gathering way of life. During that time the family and other kinship structures evolved, and the band became the basic territorial unit of human society. The first "revolution" in production technologies—the agrarian revolution—is commonly linked with the invention of the plow, but for centuries human societies had been acquiring food through the domestication of plants and animals. Some became *pastoral* societies based on the herding of animals while others evolved into *horticultural* societies based on the raising of seed crops. However, the first large-scale agrarian societies evolved after the development of plow-and-harvest agriculture.

Agrarian societies allow people to escape from dependence on food sources over which they have no control. In such societies, people produce surpluses that can be used to feed new classes of non-food-producers such as warriors. At the same time, these societies require increasing amounts of land, and this may lead to conflicts over territory. The need to store and defend food supplies and to house non-food-producers results in the growth of villages and small cities.

The next revolutionary change in hu-man production technologies was the industrial revolution, the shift from agriculture to trade and industry. This began in England around 1650 and spread to the United States and other nations in the next two centuries. Its impetus came not only from technological advances but also from the rise of a new social order: capitalism.

The shift to industrial production affects social structure in several major ways. As a consequence of the industrialization of agriculture, relatively few people live on the land, whereas increasing numbers live in cities and suburbs. Greater openness to change results in the emergence of new classes and social movements. Scientific and technical advances produce tremendous wealth, and the world "shrinks" as a result of innovations in transportation and communication.

For the individual member of a human society, adaptation to new social structures is possible but is likely to be painful. The transition to a more modern society involves a shift from *gemeinschaft* (close, personal relationships) to *gesellschaft* (well-organized but impersonal relationships). *Primary groups* like the family are supplemented, if not replaced, by *secondary groups* (organizations or associations) whose members do not have strong feelings for one another. Roles in secondary groups often conflict with roles in primary groups, a situation known as *role conflict*. *Role strain* occurs when a person experiences conflicting demands within a single role.

Another difference between simpler and more advanced societies is that in the former almost all statuses are *ascribed* (determined by birth or tradition), whereas in the latter there is a tendency to replace ascribed statuses with ones that are *achieved* (determined by a person's own efforts). Ascribed statuses are still found in modern societies, however. Sometimes a particular status takes precedence over all of an individual's other statuses; such a status is referred to as a *master status*.

For most people in the world today, the

word *society* suggests the nation-state, or nation, of which they are members. (A *state* is a society's set of political structures, and a *nation-state* is the territory within which those structures operate.) But although the members of a society often think of themselves as members of a particular nation, this is not always so, and in extreme cases the lack of a clear match between society and nation can result in a civil war.

In sum, there are several levels of social organization, ranging from small groups to entire nations. For the individual the local community, with its primary relationships, may have greater meaning than larger social structures.

WHERE TO FIND IT

Books

Human Society (Kingsley Davis; Macmillan, 1949). A classic text in sociology, valuable for its clear statements and examples of the functionalist perspective, with good definitions of many key sociological concepts.

Ecoscience: Populations, Resources, Environment (Paul R. Ehrlich et al.; W. H. Freeman, 1977). An authoritative text in human ecology with excellent background material on population, societies, and the natural environment.

The Rise of the West (William K. McNeill; University of Chicago Press, 1970). Not as slanted toward Western civilizations as its title may suggest, this masterful history of the world's major civilizations is a valuable source of material on the social structures and ideas that shaped the modern world.

Other Sources

Historical Statistics of the U.S. from Colonial Times to 1970 (U.S. Bureau of the Census, 1975). An invaluable source of tables and charts showing changes in population, national origins, work, place of residence, and many other vital indicators of social change in the United States.

Statistical Yearbook (United Nations Educational, Scientific, and Cultural Organization [UNESCO]). Published annually, this is one of the best sources of comparative information about the world's nations and the trends occurring in them.

GLOSSARY

society: a population that is organized in a cooperative manner to carry out the major functions of life (**p. 67**).

social structure: the recurring patterns of behavior that create relationships among individuals and groups within a society (**p. 67**).

group: a collection of people who interact with one another on the basis of shared expectations regarding one another's behavior (**p. 67**).

status: a socially defined position in a group (**p. 68**).

role: the way a society defines how an individual is to behave in a particular status (**p. 70**).

role expectations: a society's expectations about how a role should be performed, together with the individual's perceptions of what is required in performing that role (**p. 70**).

social stratification: the process whereby the members of a society are sorted into different statuses (**p. 78**).

open society: a society in which social mobility is possible for everyone (**p. 78**).

closed society: a society in which social mobility does not exist (**p. 78**).

gemeinschaft: a term used to refer to the close, personal relationships of small groups and communities (**p. 81**).

gesellschaft: a term used to refer to the well-organized but impersonal relationships among the members of modern societies (**p. 81**).

primary group: a small group characterized by intimate, face-to-face associations (**p. 81**).

secondary group: a social group whose members have a shared goal or purpose but are not bound together by strong emotional ties (**p. 81**).

role conflict: conflict that occurs when in order to perform one role well a person must violate the expectations associated with another role (**p. 81**).

role strain: conflict that occurs when the expectations associated with a single role are contradictory (**p. 81**).

ascribed status: a position or rank that is assigned to an individual at birth and cannot be changed (**p. 82**).

achieved status: a position or rank that is earned through the efforts of the individual (**p. 82**).

master status: a status that takes precedence over all of an individual's other statuses (**p. 82**).

state: a society's set of political structures (**p. 83**).

nation-state: the largest territory within which a society's political structures can operate without having to face challenges to their sovereignty (**p. 83**).

VISUAL SOCIOLOGY

© Eric Kroll, Taurus Photos

Comparing Societies

These pictures can be used to compare three types of societies: hunting-and-gathering, feudal, and modern. They are grouped to show, for each type of society, a typical individual, a typical primary group, and a representative social institution.

Hunting-and-gathering societies are represented by the hunter himself, in this case a !Kung bushman with his hunting bow. Among the bushmen the typical primary group is the extended family, which includes hunters, younger and older family members, and mothers and babies, all living in close proximity and usually traveling long distances together as they follow the game to its seasonal feeding grounds. Hunting-and-gathering societies have no governmental agencies or business firms. Their political and economic life is guided by the leaders of the band or the clan (a closely interacting set of extended families).

© John Marshall

© John Marshall

Courtesy of the American Museum of Natural History

The carefully coiffed woman with the ornate necklace in the second set of pictures is Marguerite of York, a fifteenth-century English noblewoman. In the style of late feudal times, she has created a high forehead by plucking or shaving her hair; her goals are to look well at court and to be accepted in the primary group of courtiers who attend the king and queen, as shown in the group engraving. The medieval guild, represented here in a fifteenth-century French print, was a major institution of feudal societies. It could have been a group of bankers, as in this case, or it could be made up of bakers, armor makers, smiths, coopers, potters, or weavers. Each occupation was organized into a guild, and anyone in it had to start as an apprentice and work his way up to journeyman and then master. Note that most guilds were composed entirely of men.

The worker in a modern society, a welder in this case, is using a technology that was not even dreamed of in an earlier epoch, but that technology often involves the worker in a network of large organizations like the firm, the labor union, the insurance agency, and the government. Such organizations are represented here by the men gathered in a corporate boardroom. Note again the gender of the group. Below this powerful corporate group there may be many women workers, but typically the key decisions are made by men. They will decide whether the firm will hire more workers or lay some off, whether it will move to another place or switch to another form of production, and so on. Such decisions have a major impact not only on the worker but also on his or her nuclear family (that is, the couple and their children).

91

CHAPTER OUTLINE

- **The Meaning of Culture**
  - Dimensions of Culture
  - The Normative Order
  - Social Institutions
  - Culture and Social Change

- **Culture, Evolution, and Human Behavior**
  - The Social Darwinists
  - Sociobiology

- **Language and Culture**

- **Crossing Cultural Lines**
  - Ethnocentrism and Cultural Relativity
  - Cultural Universals

- **Civilizations and Cultural Change**
  - Effects of Cultural Contact
  - Conclusion

Jeffrey Jay Foxx

A Lacandon man and his son, direct descendants of the ancient Mayans

CHAPTER 4
CULTURE

October 2, 1492. Under a moonlit sky the three ships carry full sail as they speed ever westward. "A brave trade wind is blowing and the caravels are rolling, plunging, and throwing spray as they cut down the last invisible barrier between the Old World and the New. Only a few moments now, and an era that began in remotest antiquity will end.

"Rodrigo de Triana, lookout on *Pinta*'s forecastle, sees something like a white sand cliff gleaming in the moonlight on the western horizon, then another, and a dark line of land connecting them. '*Tierra! tierra!*' he shouts, and this time land it is.

"Columbus's ship, the *Santa Maria*, approaches the *Pinta*, and Columbus calls out to the smaller vessel's captain, 'Señor Martín Alonso, you have found land. I give you five thousand *maravedis* as a present!'"

The land they had sighted—the first time Europeans had seen the Western Hemisphere since the vaguely recorded travels of the Northmen about A.D. 1000—was one of the smaller islands of the Bahamas in the Caribbean Sea. When the first boats put ashore, Columbus named the island San Salvador and immediately conducted a ceremony in which he took possession of the land in the name of "the Catholic Sovereigns." The ceremony was witnessed by a gathering of curious inhabitants of the island. These were the first American Indians ever described in writing by a European, as Columbus did in his journal:

In order that we might win good friendship, because I knew that they were a people who could better be freed and converted to our Holy Faith by love than by force, I gave to some of them red caps and to some glass beads, which they hung on their necks, and many other things of slight value, in which they took much pleasure; they remained so much our friends that it was a marvel; and later they came swimming to the ship's boats in which we were, and brought us parrots and cotton thread in skeins and darts and many other things. . . . Finally they swopped and gave everything they had, with good will; but it appeared to us that these people were very poor in everything. They go quite naked as their mothers bore them; and also the women, although I didn't see more than one really young girl. . . . They bear no arms, nor know thereof; for I showed them swords and they grasped them by the blade and cut themselves through ignorance; they have no iron. Their darts are a kind of rod without iron, and some have at the end a fish's tooth and others, other things. . . . They ought to be good servants and of good skill, for I see that they repeat very quickly all that is said to them; and I believe that they would easily be made Christians, because it seemed to me that they belonged to no religion. I, please Our Lord, will carry off six of them at my departure to Your Highness, so that they may learn to speak. [Quoted in Morison, 1942, pp. 229–230]

Even from this brief excerpt it is clear that Columbus was thinking about the possibility of enslaving the Indians. "'These people are very unskilled in arms. . . . With fifty men they could all be subjected and made to do all that one wished.' It is sad but significant that the only Indians of the Caribbean who have survived are those who proved both willing and able to defend themselves. The Tainos, whom Columbus found so gentle and handsome and hospitable, are long since extinct" (Morison, 1942, p. 233).

For persons of Native American heritage, like sociologist Russell Thornton, the five-hundredth anniversary of this landing is no cause for celebration. "Far from it!" Thornton observes.

In the centuries after Columbus these "Indians" suffered a demographic collapse. Numbers declined sharply; entire tribes, often quickly, were "wiped from the face of the earth." This is certainly true of the American Indians on the land that was to become the United States of America. For them the arrival of the Europeans marked the beginning of a long holocaust, although it came not in ovens, as it did for the Jews. The fires that consumed North American Indians were the fevers brought on by newly encountered diseases, the flashes of settlers' and soldiers' guns, the ravages of "firewater," the flames of villages and fields burned by the scorched-earth policy of vengeful Euro-Americans. The effects of this holocaust of North American Indians, like that of the Jews, was millions of deaths. In fact, the holocaust of the North American tribes was, in a way, even more destructive than that of the Jews, since many American Indian peoples became extinct.

It is truly remarkable that during these 500 years somehow—reasons range from chance to adaptation to determination—most North American Indian tribes survived their horrendous history. Even more remarkable, numerous tribes have shown recent population gains. [Thornton, 1987, pp. xv–xvi]

THE MEANING OF CULTURE

At one level, the story of what happened that day in October 1492 concerns what typically happens when people from drastically different cultures come into contact with one another. To the Europeans, the peaceful Taino Indians seemed childlike in their innocence. Looking down on them from the vantage point of their armed ships, the Europeans never doubted that the Indians had no religion of their own or that they could do anything but benefit from learning the language of the invaders. The disdain they felt for these newly discovered "savages" is evident even in their earliest communiqués to their royal sponsors.

For their part, it would be difficult to overestimate the shock and confusion the Indians must have felt as they stared up at the great ships from their suddenly insignificant dugout canoes or when they witnessed the devastating effects of cannon or rifle fire. No wonder that wherever they encountered the Europeans, the Indians began to covet the powerful new killing tools made of iron and steel. No wonder that the Europeans never doubted, even as they learned from the Indians how to survive in their new environment, that their own way of life was the only true civilization. Indeed, so powerful did the notion of European superiority become that even today we celebrate the "discovery" of the New World by the European explorers. Too often we forget that what happened in 1492 was not the discovery of a new world but the establishment of contact between two worlds, both already old (Jennings, 1975; Parry, 1963).

Was the European way of life really superior? Were the Europeans really doing the Indians a service? In fact, the arrival of the "civilized" Spanish and other Europeans among the Taino, even as very infrequent visitors, spelled the doom of the smaller Indian society. But even when cultural contact occurs on a more equal basis, as it does when people from different modern cultures meet, it is difficult to achieve understanding and arrive at mutually beneficial forms of cooperation. Why is this so? Many of the answers may be found in the study of human culture.

In everyday speech the word *culture*

refers to pursuits like literature and music. But these forms of expression are only part of the definition of culture. To the social scientist, "a humble cooking pot is as much a cultural product as is a Beethoven sonata" (Kluckhohn, 1949, quoted in Ross, 1963, p. 96). Like social structure, culture is a basic concept in sociology, because culture is what makes humans unique in the animal kingdom. Human social structures, from the simplest family to the most complex corporation, depend on culture for their existence. But although societies cannot exist without cultures, the two are not the same thing. As we saw in Chapter 3, *societies* are populations that are organized to carry out the major functions of life. A society's *culture* consists of all the ways in which its members think about their society and communicate about it among themselves.

We can define **culture** as all the modes of thought, behavior, and production that are handed down from one generation to the next by means of communicative interaction—through speech, gestures, writing, building, and all other communication among humans—rather than by genetic transmission, or heredity. This definition encompasses a vast array of behaviors, technologies, religions, and so on—in other words, just about everything made or thought by humans. Among all the possible elements of culture that could be studied and analyzed, social scientists are interested primarily in aspects that help explain social organization and behavior. Thus, although they sometimes analyze trends in movies and popular music (since those trends significantly affect behavior in the modern world), they are more likely to study aspects of culture that account for such phenomena as the behavior of people in corporations or the conduct of scientific research.

Dimensions of Culture

The culture of any people on earth, no matter how simple it may seem to us, is a complex set of behaviors and artifacts. A useful framework for thinking about culture was suggested by Robert Bierstedt (1963). Bierstedt views culture as having three major dimensions: **ideas,** or ways of thinking that organize human consciousness; **norms,** or accepted ways of doing or carrying out ideas; and **material culture,** or patterns of possessing and using the products of culture. Figure 4-1 presents

Figure 4–1: **Dimensions of Culture**

IDEAS	NORMS	MATERIAL CULTURE
Scientific knowledge	Scientific methods and standards	Tools, medicines
Values	Laws, rewards, punishments	Law books, jails, courts
Folklore (e.g., ideas about diet)	Folkways (e.g., patterns of food preparation and serving)	Everyday items of consumption (e.g., the meal and the equipment used to serve it)
Ideologies (e.g., capitalism, communism)	Technologies (e.g., computer data processing, auto production)	

some examples of these three dimensions, along with two aspects of culture, *ideologies* and *technologies*, that combine elements from more than one dimension.

Norms. Norms are specific rules of behavior or, as Robert Nisbet (1970) wrote, "the adjustments which human beings make to the surrounding environment. We may think of them as solutions to recurring problems or situations" (p. 225). But norms involve more than behavior. Any given norm is supported by the idea that a particular behavior is correct and proper or incorrect and improper. "The moral order of society is a kind of tissue of 'oughts': negative ones which forbid certain actions and positive ones which [require certain] actions" (Nisbet, 1970, p. 226). If we think about a complex aspect of everyday life like driving a car, it is evident that without norms life would be far more chaotic and dangerous than it already is. When we drive we keep to the right, obey traffic lights and speed limits, and avoid reckless behavior that could cause accidents. These are among the many norms that allow the automobile to be such an essential article of North American culture.

Examples of norms are easy to find. Take the college or high school classroom. The classroom is organized according to norms of educational practice—there should be a textbook or books; there should be class discussion; there should be assignments, exams, grades. Note that these "shoulds" correspond to actual behavior. Norms usually refer to behavior that we either approve or disapprove of. However, members of a culture often disagree about how a particular norm operates. Thus in the example of classroom organization there is considerable debate about what educational practices are most effective.

Values. Values are more abstract than norms; they are the ideas that support or justify norms. **Values** are socially shared ideas about what is right. Thus for most people in North America education is a value; that is, they conceive of it as a proper and good way to achieve social standing. The norms associated with this value vary, however. For some people, the norms of obtaining an education mean attending college; for others, they mean apprenticeship and on-the-job learning.

The tendency for people to decorate themselves is found in practically all human cultures. This Indian dancer is decorated in a traditional and elaborate fashion to celebrate a Hindu holy day.

Changes in values often result in changes in norms. This can be readily seen in the case of smoking. The norms governing smoking are changing rapidly as a result of changing values regarding health. Until recent years the norms of smoking in the United States were very liberal. One could light up almost anywhere, and nonsmokers were expected not to complain. Recently, however, greater emphasis on fitness and health, as well as new knowledge about the dangers of breathing smoke, have increased the value people place on clean air and tipped the balance against the earlier norms. But the change has not occurred without conflict between smokers and nonsmokers and their representatives in courts and legislatures.

In a large and diverse society there is bound to be a good deal of conflict over values. Some people are satisfied with the way wealth and power are distributed, for example, while others are less satisfied with the status quo. Some people feel that it is desirable to attempt to improve one's own well-being and that society as a whole gains when everyone strives to be well off. Others assert that the value of individual gain conflicts with the values of community and social cohesion; too great a gap between the well-off and the not-well-off creates suffering, envy, crime, and other problems, it is said. Such value conflicts result in continual change in the norms governing behavior in a society.

Ideologies. As indicated in Figure 4-1, **ideologies** are sets or systems of ideas and norms. They combine the values and norms that all the members of a society are expected to believe in and act upon without question. A classic study of the emergence of an ideology was Max Weber's (1974/1904) analysis of the link between Protestantism and capitalism (*The Protestant Ethic and the Spirit of Capitalism*). Weber noticed that the rise of Protestantism in Europe coincided with the rise of private enterprise, banking, and other aspects of capitalism. He also noticed that a majority of the most successful early capitalists were Protestants. Weber hypothesized that their religious values taught them that salvation depended not on good deeds or piety but on how they lived their entire lives and particularly on how well they adhered to the norms of their "callings" (occupations). As a result, the Protestants placed a high value on frugality and abstinence. To prove that they were worthy of salvation, they devoted themselves tirelessly to commerce and plowed their profits back into their firms. But Catholics, who did not share these values, were less single-mindedly dedicated to their business ventures. Indeed, they often spent their profits on good deeds rather than investing them in their businesses. Weber attempted to show how a set of religious values and norms combined with economic norms to create the ideology of capitalism.

A contemporary example of an ideology may be found among religious fundamentalists. Christian fundamentalists in the United States generally share a set of ideas and norms of behavior that include the value of prayer, the value of family and children, the negative value of abortion and secular humanism (an ethical system based on scientific knowledge

> **Values are the ideas that support or justify norms.**

rather than on religious teachings), the belief in salvation and redemption for one's sins, and other values.

Technologies. Technologies are another aspect of culture that spans two of Bierstedt's major dimensions. **Technologies** are the things (material culture) and the norms for using them that are found in a given culture (Bierstedt, 1963; Ellul, 1964). Without the norms that govern their use, things are useless. The president of Sony Corporation illustrated this point with the example of a tape recorder that failed in Japanese markets, not because it was a bad product but because the Japanese had not yet developed norms for using it. The same problem plagues the home-computer industry in the United States today. The computer itself appeals to the values of efficiency and learning, but the norms regarding its use in the home have not yet developed fully (Kornblum and Julian, 1989).

Another example of the interaction of norms and material culture in advancing a technology is found in modern telecommunications. The electronic machinery to transmit movies directly into the home via the telephone now exists. But norms have not been developed to sort out how artists, suppliers, and others will be paid for their products and how their work can be protected against resale by the home consumer. Conflict over how the norms will operate is holding up technological change in this case and many others.

The Normative Order

Every culture includes a wide array of norms—its **normative order**—that constitutes a system of social control. **Social control** may be defined as the set of rules and understandings that control the behavior of individuals and groups in that culture. As Park and Burgess (1921) put it, "An examination of the moral code of any given group . . . will disclose many identities with that of any other given group. . . . All groups have such 'commandments' as 'Honor thy father and mother,' 'Thou shalt not kill,' 'Thou shalt not steal' " (p. 787).

Norms are taught as absolutes. The Ten Commandments, for example, are absolutes:

Box 4–1: **Constructing a Typology of Norms**

Typologies are ways of grouping observable phenomena into categories in order to identify the regularities in what may appear to be a great variety of observations. In the chart presented here, the subject is norms of various types. The sociologist constructs the types by comparing various dimensions along which norms may differ. The norms listed in the Ten Commandments, for example, differ in many ways. The norm "Thou shalt not kill" not only is generally believed and passed along from one generation to the next but also is codified in laws. So is the commandment "Thou shalt not steal," which is an important part of the written laws of our society. But the commandment "Remember the sabbath and keep it holy" is not a written law in the United States, at least not in the federal statutes. These differences indicate that norms may differ according to whether they are informally taught to new generations or whether they are formal, written "laws of the land."

Another dimension along which norms may differ is the degree to which they are sanctioned—that is, the degree to which adherence to them is rewarded

and violation of them is punished. The norm that men do not wear hats indoors is relatively weak. On the other hand, the norm that men and women do not casually display (or "flash") their genitals is strongly sanctioned.

Using these two comparative dimensions—mode of development (formal vs. informal) and degree of sanction (weak vs. strong)—we can create four categories: (1) norms that are informal and are weakly sanctioned (for example, table manners, dress fashions), (2) norms that are informal but are strongly sanctioned (such as adultery), (3) norms that are part of the formal legal code but are weakly sanctioned (parking regulations, antismoking laws, and so on), and (4) norms that are formal laws and are strongly sanctioned (for example, capital offenses like murder of a police officer or treason in wartime).

By juxtaposing the two dimensions, each with its two categories, we arrive at a fourfold classification of norms (see chart). But as Max Weber (1949) observed, such a classification is an "ideal-typical" arrangement of observations in a form that accentuates some aspects and neglects

"Thou *shalt not* kill," "Thou *shalt not* steal," and so on. Yet the same explorers who swore to bring the values of Western civilization (including the Ten Commandments) to the "savage" Indians thought little of taking the Indians' land by force. Queen Elizabeth I of England could authorize agents like Sir Walter Raleigh to seize remote "heathen and barbarous" lands without viewing this act as a violation of the strongest norms of her own society (Jennings, 1975). Protests by the Indians often resulted in violent death, but the murder of Indians and the theft of their land was rationalized by the notion that the Indians were an inferior people who would ultimately benefit from European influence. In the ideology of conquest and colonial rule the Ten Commandments did not apply.

In the social sciences, punishments and

rewards for adhering to or violating norms are known as **sanctions**. As these examples show, cultural norms can vary according to the degree of sanction associated with them. Rewards can range from a smile to the Nobel Prize; punishments may vary in strength from a raised eyebrow to the electric chair. During the period of European colonial expansion, the murder of a native was far less strongly sanctioned than the murder of another European.

The most strongly sanctioned norms are called **mores**.[1] They are norms that people consider vital to the continuation of human groups and societies, and therefore they figure prominently in a culture's sense of morality. **Folkways**, on the other hand, are far

[1]This term, pronounced "morays," is the plural of the Latin word *mos*, "custom."

		DEGREE OF SANCTION	
		Relatively Weak	**Relatively Strong**
MODE OF DEVELOPMENT	**Informal**	Folkways, fashions	Taboos, mores
	Formal	Misdemeanor laws, some rules, guidelines, civil rights laws	Capital-offense laws, felony laws

others. These ideal types (folkways, mores and taboos, misdemeanor laws, and felonies or capital offenses) are useful because they establish standards against which to compare the norms of other cultures. For example, not all cultures treat the norm about the sabbath the way Americans do. In parts of Israel or the Islamic lands one could be arrested for violating the sabbath laws. Typologies like this one also help identify areas of social change, as when one compares the way the sabbath was treated in American laws earlier in this century, when stores were obliged to close on Sunday, with the way

it is treated today, when Sunday is often viewed as another shopping day.

But the aspects of society described by ideal types are rarely so uncomplicated in real life. Even the norms that seem most formal and unambiguous, such as the prohibition against murder, become murky under some conditions, as in cases of self-defense or in war, or in arguments about the death penalty and abortion. Study of how actual behavior departs from the ideal-typical version invariably offers insights into how cultures and social structures are changing in the course of daily life.

less strongly sanctioned. People often cannot explain why these norms exist, nor do they feel that they are essential to the continuation of the group or the society. Both terms were first used by William Graham Sumner in his study *Folkways* (1940/1907). Sumner also pointed out that laws are norms that have been enacted through the formal procedures of government. Laws often formalize the mores of a society by putting them into written form and interpreting them. But laws can also formalize folkways, as can be seen, for example, in laws governing the wearing of clothing in public places.

Sumner also pointed out that a person who violates mores is subject to severe moral indignation, whereas one who violates folkways is not. People who violate folkways such as table manners or dress codes may be thought

of as idiosyncratic or "flaky," but those who violate mores are branded as morally reprehensible. Thus among prisoners there are norms for the treatment of other prisoners that depend on the types of crimes they committed "outside." Rapists and child molesters are moral outcasts; their offenses are the most reprehensible. Such offenders are often beaten and tormented by other prisoners.

Box 4-1 presents a typology of norms according to their degree of sanction and their mode of development—that is, whether they are formal or informal. Laws and other norms, such as company regulations or the rules of games and sports, are known as *formal norms*. They differ from *informal norms*, which grow out of everyday behavior and do not usually take the form of written rules, even though they too regulate our behavior. For example, when one waits to enter a movie theater, it is usually permissible to have one member of a small group save a place in line for the others. And in a "pickup" basketball game a player can call a foul and the opposing player usually cannot contest the call. Of course, there are times when such norms are disputed, depending on how the people involved define the situation. In the case of the basketball game, when the player on whom the foul is called disagrees with the call—and the score is extremely close—different definitions of the situation can lead to conflict.

Social Institutions

Before we continue our discussion of culture, it is important to introduce the important concept of social institutions. In popular language the word *institution* generally refers to a large bureaucratic organization like a university or hospital or prison (usually with cafeterias that serve "institutional food"). But although this meaning of the word is important in everyday language, the sociological use of the term should not be confused with this meaning. In sociology, an **institution** is a more or less stable structure of statuses and roles devoted to meeting the basic needs of people in a society. The family is an institution that controls reproduction and the training of new generations. The market is an institution that regulates the production and exchange of goods and services. The military is an institution that defends a society or expands its territory through conquest. Any particular family, corporation, or military unit is a group or organization within one of these institutions.

Within any given institution, norms specify how people in various statuses are to perform their roles. Thus, to be a general or a recruit or a supplier of military hardware is to have a definite status in a military institution. But to carry out one's role in that status is to behave in accordance with a normative system—a set of mores and folkways that distinguishes a particular institution from others. For example, in a well-known paper on becoming a military recruit, Sanford Dornbusch (1955) described how all the signs of a person's status in civilian life, from fashions in dress to the use of free time, are erased in boot camp. The new status of recruit must

be earned by adhering to all the norms of military life. So it is with every social institution: Each has a specific set of norms to govern the behavior of people within that institution.

A dominant feature of human societies is the continual creation of new social institutions. The history of human societies is marked by the emergence of new institutions like the university or the laboratory, a feature that the social theorist Talcott Parsons (1951, 1966) labeled **differentiation**. By this term he meant the processes whereby sets of social activities performed by one social institution are divided among different institutions. In small-scale agrarian societies, for example, the family not only performs reproductive and training functions but is also the primary economic institution. As societies become larger and more complex, the processes of differentiation result in the emergence of new institutions designed to manage economic production (corporations), train new generations (schools), develop new technologies (science), or perform other important social activities. (Many of those institutions are discussed in detail in Part V.)

> *A dominant feature of human societies is the continual creation of new social institutions.*

Culture and Social Change

Figure 4-1 and Box 4-1 present some key aspects of human culture, but they leave out all the social processes whereby elements of culture are produced and changed and diffused from one society to another. An unsuspecting reader might even conclude that a society's norms and values are shared equally by all of its members, which is hardly an accurate view of culture. Useful as our charts may be for defining the principal forms of mental and material culture, they skirt some important questions.

Cultures in all societies change, and much of social science is devoted to trying to understand and predict those changes. Norms and values that once were thought to be odd or criminal may come to be shared by the majority of the society's members. In the 1988 Olympic Games, for example, American women dominated many events in which they had previously been weak performers. Star athletes such as Florence Griffith-Joyner demonstrated to the American public that a woman can be muscular and athletic and still project a "feminine" identity. In the past, American women were often reluctant to lift weights and improve their strength for fear of being considered unfeminine. As the level of world competition increased, Americans found ways to overcome the older values that said women had to be soft in order to be feminine. The Frontiers section of this chapter outlines other fundamental changes that have taken place in our norms and values.

Another important issue in understanding culture and social change is the question of the extent to which human culture is determined by biological factors, if at all. Are there any features that all human cultures share—any norms, for example, that are found in all known societies? And what happens when two cultures exist within the same society or nation? The remainder of this chapter will explore these questions, beginning with one that has long been a subject of lively debate: the connection between culture and biology.

CULTURE, EVOLUTION, AND HUMAN BEHAVIOR

Of all the species of living creatures on this planet, human beings are the most widely distributed. The early European explorers—Columbus, Magellan, Cook, da Gama, and all the others—marveled at the discovery of human life thriving, more or less, in some of the earth's most inhospitable environments. Why is it that, in adapting to so many different climates and environments, humans did not evolve into separate species, as occurred among other animals? Both biologists and social scientists have been fascinated by this question. But it was Darwin's theory of evolution and, in particular, of "natural selection" that began to provide scientific explanations of these phenomena.

The essence of Darwin's theory of evolution is that mutations (unexpected physical changes) in organisms occur more or less randomly from one generation to the next. When those mutations improve individuals' ability to survive in their environment, they are "selected for"; that is, individuals who show the new traits are more likely to survive and have young, and therefore are more likely to pass on their traits to the next generation, than those who lack the new traits. Over a few generations these mutations can become so extensive that two species are created where once there was only one. This process of natural selection accounts for the great diversity of animal and plant life on the earth and for the ability of animals and plants to adapt to new environments.

Darwin's theory of evolution was based on his empirical observations of the natural world, especially those he had made as a scientist aboard the HMS *Beagle* during an extensive voyage of exploration in the early 1830s. On that voyage Darwin had observed over and over again that some species had modified their physical form in ways that seemed to "fit" or "adapt" them to their environment. It took him almost two decades of study and reflection to make sense of his observations. After all, much of what he had observed directly challenged the fundamental beliefs of most of the religious and scientific leaders of his day. But when Darwin considered all the information, and especially his observations of similar species on different islands, it became clear to him that God had not created all the living things on earth at once—instead, they had been evolving over many millions of years. And this theory can be applied to all other species, including humans.

The Social Darwinists

The theory of evolution had a dramatic impact on biological science but an even greater effect on the prevailing views of human society. Among the social thinkers who were most profoundly influenced by Darwin was Herbert Spencer, whose writings in sociology and philosophy were to dominate intellectual life in much of the Western world from 1870 to 1890.

According to Spencer, the fact that humans, unlike other species, have remained similar even on different continents must be explained by the fact that we adapt to changes in our environment through the use of culture rather than through biological adaptation. This process, which can be termed **cultural evolution**, parallels biological evolution in that the most successful adaptations are handed down to the next generation (Geertz, 1973). Spencer had this process in mind when he coined the phrase "survival of the fittest." He meant that the people who are most successful at adapting to the environment in which they find themselves are most likely to survive and to have children who will also be successful.

Spencer believed that it is impossible, by means of intentional action, to improve on the course of cultural evolution. The task of sociology, as Spencer saw it, is to discover that course through empirical observation and analysis. Sociologists should not engage in efforts to change society. To do so would be futile, and it could have the damaging effect of violating the principle of survival of the fittest in favor of "artificial preservation of those least able to take care of themselves" (Spencer, 1874, p. 343).

Spencer's view, which came to be known as **social Darwinism**, claimed to explain why some people prospered during the industrial revolution while others barely scraped by. The people who were being pushed off the land and into the factories and slums of the cities were less well equipped culturally to succeed in an urban environment than people who could innovate and invent. There was not much for government to do, according to Spencer's theory, besides keep the peace and let the most competitive groups in society flourish. In so doing, those groups would give less competitive groups a chance to survive, if not to thrive.

Darwin's theory thus spawned a revolution in social thought. It also produced North America's first prominent sociologist and social philosopher, William Graham Sumner. Like Spencer, Sumner based his theory of society on humans' need to adapt to an environment of scarcity. When resources, especially land, were plentiful, there would be peace, and institutions based on democratic forms of government could flourish. But eventually, when population growth made it necessary to distribute the same amounts of resources among more people, societies would lean toward oligarchy (rule by the most powerful) and greater use of coercion and force.

By the end of the nineteenth century, efforts to apply Darwin's theory of natural selection to human societies had reached their logical extreme. Largely as a result of the work of Sumner and other followers of Spencer, early sociologists in the United States and other Western societies favored the view that Western culture, with its emphasis on competition within the capitalist system, was clearly superior to all others and that the people who were most successful at competing within that system were to be considered superior human beings.

The next generation of social scientists, who became prominent around the turn of the century, rejected this theory. They could point to mounting evidence that wealth itself brings privilege to the children of the wealthy, regardless of whatever innate or learned traits they may possess. Cultural evolution, they argued, is a result of the development of more effective institutions and is not related to the innate qualities of individuals. Successful business firms, for example, are able to prosper in a highly competitive environment because of their superior organization. That is, their success can be explained without recourse to arguments about the genetic fitness of their leaders.

Sociobiology

The tendency to explain social phenomena in terms of biological causes such as physiology or genes is known as *biological reductionism*. For example, explanations of crime that assert that there are genes that produce criminal behavior reduce the explanation of crime to biological causes. Some form of biological reductionism has emerged in every generation since Darwin's time.

The most recent version of biological reductionism is **sociobiology**. This term was coined by the Harvard biologist Edward O. Wilson (1975) to refer to efforts to link genetic factors with the social behavior of animals. When applied to human societies, sociobiology has drawn severe criticism from both social scientists and biologists. Nevertheless, some sociologists support the sociobiological hypothesis that

The sociobiological hypothesis that certain aspects of human behavior are genetically determined is not supported by direct evidence.

genes can explain certain aspects of human society and behavior (Barash, 1977; Caplan, 1978; Quadagno, 1979; Sahlins, 1976; van den Berghe, 1979). Because this hypothesis is so controversial it deserves a closer look.

Let us take as an example the incest taboo, one of the strongest and most widespread norms in human life. The social scientist tends to explain the incest taboo as a cultural norm necessary for the existence of the family as a social institution. The family is an organized group with a need for well-defined statuses and roles. Should the different statuses within the family become confused, as would undoubtedly happen if sexual intimacy were permitted between children and their parents or between brothers and sisters, it would be difficult to maintain the family as a stable institution (Malinowski, 1927; Davis, 1939).

Sociobiology takes a different view. For the sociobiologist, the incest taboo develops from

a deeper, more urgent cause, the heavy physiological penalty imposed by inbreeding. Several studies by human geneticists have demonstrated that even a moderate amount of inbreeding results in children who are diminished in overall body size, muscular coordination, and academic performance. More than 100 recessive genes have been discovered that cause hereditary disease . . . a condition vastly enhanced by inbreeding. [Wilson, 1979, p. 38]

Throughout most of the history of human evolution, sociobiologists point out, humans did not have any knowledge of genetics. Thus "the 'gut feeling' that promotes . . . sanctions against incest is largely unconscious" (Wilson, 1979, p. 40). Individuals with a strong predisposition to avoid incest passed on more of their genes to the next generation because their children were less likely to suffer from the illnesses that result from inbreeding. And over many centuries of natural selection of individuals who did not inbreed, humans developed "an instinct [to avoid inbreeding] which is based on genes" (Wilson, 1979, p. 40).

This leap, from the observation of a strong and persistent norm like the incest taboo to the belief that certain human behaviors are genetically programmed, is an example of the sociobiological hypothesis regarding human nature. Sociobiologists have proposed a hypothesis in which not only the incest taboo but also aggression, homosexuality, and religious feelings are genetically programmed, and they believe that future discoveries by geneticists will prove their hypothesis correct.

Although it is true that genes set limits on human abilities and can be shown to influence many aspects of brain functioning, the hypothesis that genetic programming establishes complex forms of normative behavior is not supported by direct evidence—there is as yet no proof that such genes or sets of genes actually exist (Lewontin, 1977, 1982). Nevertheless, the rules of science require that we not reject the sociobiological hypothesis and that it remain an open area of investigation.

The counterargument to sociobiology is that the human brain and other physical attributes are products of interaction between cultural and biological evolution and that in the past 100,000 years of human evolution there has been relatively little organic change in our species. Instead, the important developments in human life have occurred as a result of social and cultural change. This widely accepted view of culture denies that humans have innate instincts such as an instinct to avoid incest. It argues instead that the great advantage of culture in human evolution is its creation of a basis for natural selection that would not be dependent on genes but would allow humans to adapt relatively quickly to any physical or social environment (Geertz, 1973).

Archaeological evidence shows that humans were using tools for primitive agriculture and making jewelry and personal adornments over 30,000 years ago (Stevens, 1988). No doubt they began using fire even earlier. Once humans could use fire and hand tools and simple weapons, the ability to make and use these items skillfully increased the survival chances of those who possessed these skills. This would create conditions for natural selection in which the traits that were being "selected for" were those that had to do with the manipulation of cultural and social aspects of life. These abilities (dexterity, rationality, leadership, social skills, etc.) would in turn influence the further development of the human brain, again through the process of natural selection.

This view is supported by research showing that the higher primates use simple tools and that they teach this cultural technique to their young (Goodall, 1968; Schaller, 1964). Jane Van Lawick Goodall (1968), for example, described how chimpanzees use sticks to probe for termites and chew leaves to produce a pulp to be used as a sponge to draw water out of tree stumps. These and many other instances of rudimentary culture among animal species demonstrate that culture is not unique to humans; that is, we are not alone in using culture to aid in adaptation. What happened in the case of humans that did not happen (or at least has not happened yet) in any other species is that at a certain stage in human prehistory our ability to alter our cultures in response to changing conditions developed so quickly that the human species entered a new realm of social life. In other words, culture became self-generating. And once it had been freed from genetic constraints, culture had no limits.

LANGUAGE AND CULTURE

Perhaps the most significant of the inventions made possible by culture is language. The learning of culture takes place through language. From our enormous capacity to learn and use language is derived our collective memory (myths, fables, sayings, ballads, and the like), as well as writing, art, and all the other media that shape human consciousness and store and transmit knowledge. Note that although the capacity to learn language appears to be innate (Chomsky, 1965), language does not occur outside a cultural setting and indeed is the most universal dimension of human cultures.

To return to the example at the beginning of this chapter, as savage as they may have appeared to Columbus and his crew, the Taino had language. They could learn Spanish, just as the explorers could have learned their language if they had made an effort to do so. But without a language in which they could communicate with each other, the Taino and the explorers misunderstood each other far more than they would have if they had had this powerful tool at their disposal. And

without language neither side could explain to the other its strange behaviors and different ways of dealing with the physical world. To the Taino the musket was a fascinating mystery, while to the explorers a Taino hunter-fisherman, wearing little clothing and with mysterious markings on his face, was an outlandish sight indeed. The importance of language in overcoming cultural barriers like these can hardly be exaggerated.

What is unique about human language? Primatologists have shown that our closest evolutionary kin, the great apes (especially chimpanzees and pygmy chimpanzees), can learn language to some extent. Although their throats are not capable of producing the sounds that humans mold into language, apes do have the capacity to use language; that is, they can grasp the meanings of words as symbols for things and relationships. Through the use of sign language, or special languages using typewriters and other devices, apes can be taught a limited vocabulary.

The informal record for primate language is held by Koko, a female gorilla who was trained by Dr. Francine Patterson using American Sign Language. Koko learned over 300 words. She also disproved the theory that apes can learn words but cannot invent new concepts. Koko invented sign words for *ring* ("finger bracelet") and *mask* ("eye hat") and was even able to talk in sign language about her feelings of fear, happiness, and shame (Hill, 1978). More recent research using a pygmy chimpanzee named Kanzi has revealed that apes may actually be able to learn language through observation and imitation, the way a child does, rather than through long and difficult training (Eckholm, 1985).

Fascinating as these experiments are, they only confirm the immense difference in communicative ability between humans and the apes. After months of training, an adult ape can use language with no more skill than an average two-and-a-half-year-old human infant (Harris, 1983; Terrace, 1979). And no amount of training can produce the more advanced uses of language found in all normal humans, no matter what their culture. For example, every human language allows its speakers to express an infinite number of thoughts and ideas that can persist even after their originators are gone. This property of human language, which is not shared by any other known species (Eisley, 1970), allows humans to transmit their culture from one generation to the next.

So complete is the human reliance on language that it often seems that language actually *determines* the possibilities for thought and action in any given culture. Perhaps we are actually unable to perceive phenomena for which we have no nouns or to engage in actions for which we have no verbs. This idea is expressed in the **linguistic-relativity hypothesis.** As developed by the American linguists Edward Sapir and Benjamin Whorf in the 1930s, this hypothesis asserts that "a person's thoughts are controlled by inexorable laws or patterns of which he is unconscious. . . . His thinking itself is in a language—in English, in Sanskrit, in Chinese. And every language is a vast pattern-system, different from others" (Whorf, 1961, p. 135).

This observation was based on evidence from the social sciences, especially anthropology. For example, Margaret Mead's field research among the Arapesh of New Guinea had revealed that they had no developed system of numbers. Theirs was a technologically simple society, and therefore complex numbering systems were not much use to them. They counted only "one, two, and one and two, and dog" (*dog* being the equivalent of four and probably based on the dog's four legs). To count seven objects, the Arapesh would say "dog and one and two." Eight would be "two dog," and twenty-four would come out as "two dog, two dog, two dog." It is easy to see that in this small society one would quickly become tired of attempting to count much beyond twenty-four and would simply say "many" (Mead, 1971).

Other cultures have been found to have only a limited number of words for colors, and as a result they do not make some of the fine distinctions between colors that we do. And in a famous example Whorf argued that

many languages have far less developed ways of referring to time than English and other Indo-European languages do. In English we have verb tenses, which allow us to distinguish among past, present, and future time. The language of the Hopi Indians lacks clear tenses, and it seemed to Whorf that this made it unlikely that the Hopi culture could develop the systems of timekeeping that are essential to modern science and technology.

Thus in its most radical form the linguistic-relativity hypothesis asserts that language actually determines the possibilities for a culture's norms, beliefs, and values. But there is little justification for this extreme version of the hypothesis. The Arapesh did not have a developed number system but they could easily learn to count using the Western base-ten system. Once they were exposed to the money economy of the modern world, most isolated cultures formed words for the base-ten number system or else incorporated foreign words into their own vocabularies. They had no difficulty understanding the use of money, and this too became incorporated into so-called primitive cultures.

A more acceptable version of the linguistic-relativity hypothesis recognizes the mutual influences of culture and language. One does not determine the other. For example, someone living in Canada or the northern parts of the United States is likely to have a much larger vocabulary for talking about snow (*loose powder, packed powder, corn snow, slush* . . .) than a person from an area where snow is rare. A person who loves to watch birds will have a much larger vocabulary about bird habitats and bird names than one who cares little about bird life. In each case we realize that in order to share the world of birdwatchers or fans of winter sports we will need to learn new ways of seeing and of talking about what we see. So, although the extreme version of the linguistic-relativity hypothesis is incorrect, it has been a valuable stimulus toward the development of a less biased view of other cultures. We now understand that a culture's language both expresses how the people of that culture perceive and understand the world and, at the same time, influences their perceptions and understandings.

The linguistic-relativity hypothesis asserts that language determines thought and, therefore, culture. In reality language and culture influence each other.

CROSSING CULTURAL LINES

Ethnocentrism and Cultural Relativity

As our discussion of language has shown, until we study other cultures it is extremely difficult to view our own with detachment and objectivity. Unless we can see ourselves as others see us, we take for granted that our cultural traits are natural and proper and that traits that differ from ours are unnatural and somehow wrong. Our ways of behaving in public, our food and dress and sports—all of our cultural traits have become "internalized," so they seem almost instinctive. But once we understand another culture and how its members think and feel, we can look at our own traits from the perspective of that culture. This *cross-cultural perspective* has become an integral part of sociological analysis.

The ability to think in cross-cultural terms allows people to avoid the common tendency to disparage other cultures simply because they are different. However, most people live out their lives in a single culture. Indeed, they may go so far as to consider that culture superior to any other, anywhere in the world. This attitude is termed **ethnocentrism** by social scientists. Ethnocentrism refers to the tendency to judge other cultures as inferior in terms of one's own norms and values. The other culture is weighed against standards derived from the culture with which one is most familiar. Columbus's assumption that the Taino Indians could benefit from the adoption of European cultural traits is an example of ethnocentric behavior. But such obvious ethnocentrism is not limited to historical examples. We encounter it every day, for example, in our own use of the term *American* to refer to citizens of the United States, as if the people of Canada and the Latin American nations were not also Americans. Another example is our tendency to judge other cultures by how well they supply their people with consumer goods rather than by how well they adhere to their own values.

To get along well in other parts of the world, a businessperson or politician or scientist must be able to suspend judgment about other cultures, an approach that is termed **cultural relativity**. Cultural relativity entails the recognition that all cultures develop their own ways of dealing with the specific demands of their environment. This kind of understanding does not come automatically through the experience of living among members of other cultures. It is an acquired skill.

There are limits, however, to the value of cultural relativity. It is an essential attitude to adopt in understanding another culture, but it does not require that one avoid moral judgment entirely. We can, for example, attempt to understand the values and ideologies of the citizens who supported the Nazi regime even though we abhor what that regime stood for. And we can suspend our outrage at racism in our own society long enough to understand the culture that produced racial hatred and fear. But as social scientists it is also our task to evaluate the moral implications of a culture's norms and values and to condemn them when we see that they produce cruelty and suffering.

Cultural Universals

The cross-cultural approach to social research grew in part out of efforts to identify "cultural universals." If we could know, for example, whether the family as a social institution is found in all cultures, and how norms governing family behavior differ from one culture to another, we would be better equipped to understand how families adapt to various kinds of social change. In the United States the family is said to be characterized by the nuclear family unit (mother, father, and children) and by monogamy. But given our high rates of divorce and remarriage, it might be more accurate to describe the American family as tending toward what has been termed *serial monogamy*—that is, more than one spouse but only one at a time (Harris, 1983). Sociologists who study the family seek to discover whether this pattern exists in all industrial societies and whether it is also found in other types of cultures, in which case it could not be viewed as an adaptation to industrial society (Goode, 1971).

When we examine cultures for patterns of family organization that are like ours, we find that the nuclear family unit is the dominant family structure in many hunter-gatherer societies. In fact, the Eskimos have a kinship system so much like ours that the American system of measuring descent through the father's line, organizing families into small nuclear units, and encouraging remarriage after the death or departure of a spouse is sometimes referred to as the "Eskimo kinship system" (Harris, 1983; Murdock, 1967). Thus the nuclear family and serial monogamy are by no means unique to cultures that are adapting to an industrial social order.

In recent years the search for cultural universals has given way to other uses of cross-cultural comparisons. Every subfield of sociology has a literature on such comparisons. In cross-cultural studies of social stratification, for example, we generally try to find out whether the values attached to certain occupational statuses are shared all over the modern world. These studies have shown that in every society with a modern occupational structure (i.e., one dominated by scientific and technical occupations), people have remarkably similar ideas about the prestige of jobs such as engineer, teacher, doctor, and factory worker (Hodge, Treiman, and Rossi, 1966).

> *Civilizations are advanced cultures whose elements are shared by a number of distinct societies.*

Why do cross-cultural similarities exist? In some cases it is because elements of a culture have diffused across national boundaries and become part of a larger culture called a civilization. Because much cultural change occurs within the context of major civilizations, we devote the rest of this chapter to a discussion of civilizations and cultural change.

CIVILIZATIONS AND CULTURAL CHANGE

Civilizations are advanced cultures. They usually have forms of expression in writing and the arts, powerful economic and political institutions, and innovative technologies, all of which strongly influence other cultures with which they come into contact. Some civilizations, like those of ancient Greece and Rome or the Maya of Central America, died thousands of years ago

and exist today only in museums and ruins and in the consciousness of scholars, artists, and scientists. Others are living civilizations with long histories, like those of China and India, that were conquered by other civilizations and are rising again in forms that combine the old with the new. Islamic civilization is an example of such a civilization; much of the unrest in the Islamic world is due to conflicts that pit orthodox leaders like the late Ayatollah Khomeini against Western-influenced leaders like Jordan's King Hussein. Then there are the dominant civilizations of North America, Europe, the Soviet Union, and Japan. They are dominant because they compete on a world scale to "export" their ideas and their technology—in fact, their entire culture, their "blueprint for living."

Like most of the principal concepts in the social sciences, the concept of civilization can be elusive. It is used in many different contexts, in popular language as well as in social-scientific usage. In popular speech the word *civilization* is often used to make negative comparisons between people who adhere to the norms of polite conduct, and are therefore said to be "civilized," and those who are "uncouth" and act like "barbarians" or "savages." This is how the word was understood by the explorers of Columbus's time, and colonial conquest was justified in part as an effort to civilize the barbarians.

In his effort to trace the origins of Western notions of what is civilized and what is barbaric behavior, the German sociologist Norbert Elias (1978/1939) showed that much of what we call "civilized" behavior is derived from the norms of the courts of medieval Europe. Elias based his study on accounts by medieval writers of the spread of "courtesy" (the manners of the court) to other levels of society. The following are some examples from a thirteenth-century poem on courtly table manners:

A man of refinement should not slurp his spoon when in company; that is the way people at court behave who often indulge in unrefined conduct.

It is not polite to drink from the dish, although some who approve of this rude habit insolently pick up the dish and pour it down as if they were mad.

A number of people gnaw a bone and then put it back in the dish—this is a serious offense. [p. 85]

Through his analysis of writings on manners Elias demonstrated that Western norms concerning the control of bodily functions, from eating and sleeping to blowing one's nose, arose in the Middle Ages as the courts consolidated their power over feudal societies and exported the standards of courtly behavior to the countryside. Such behavior became a sign that a person was a member of the upper classes and not a serf or a savage.

In the social sciences, the most common use of the term *civilization* stems from the study of changes in human society at the macro level, which often requires comparisons among major cultures. In this context, a **civilization** is "a cultural complex formed by the identical major cultural features of a number of particular societies. We might, for example, describe Western capitalism as a civilization, in which specific forms of science, technology, religion, art, and so on, are to be found in a number of distinct societies" (Bottomore, 1972, p. 130). Thus Italy, France, Germany, the United States, Sweden, and many other nations that have made great contributions to Western civilization all have private corporations, and their normative orders, laws, and judicial systems are quite similar. Even though each may have a different language and each differs in the way it organizes some aspects of social life (European and North American universities define academic degrees differently, for example), they share similar norms and values and can all be said to represent Western civilization.

Effects of Cultural Contact

Although sociologists do not distinguish among cultures in terms of how "civilized" they are, this standard is often applied by members of different cultures when they come into contact. The contact between Columbus and his crew and the natives of the West Indies is typical of such episodes. The explorers represented the relatively advanced civilization of Europe, while the Indians represented a much simpler culture, one that seemed totally "uncivilized" to the explorers. Throughout the period of world exploration, from the late fifteenth to the early nineteenth century, explorers and traders brought back reports of "savages" living in every part of the globe.

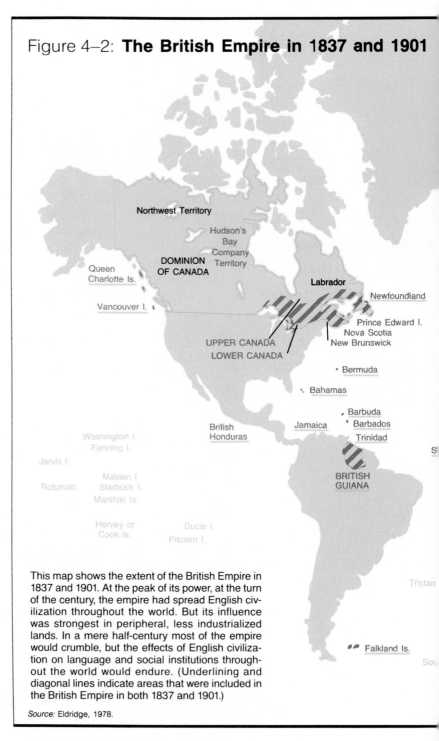

Figure 4–2: **The British Empire in 1837 and 1901**

This map shows the extent of the British Empire in 1837 and 1901. At the peak of its power, at the turn of the century, the empire had spread English civilization throughout the world. But its influence was strongest in peripheral, less industrialized lands. In a mere half-century most of the empire would crumble, but the effects of English civilization on language and social institutions throughout the world would endure. (Underlining and diagonal lines indicate areas that were included in the British Empire in both 1837 and 1901.)

Source: Eldridge, 1978.

These episodes of cultural contact—and often conflict as well—shaped the history of the next two centuries and continue to influence human existence.

Through such processes as exploration and conquest, civilizations invariably spread beyond their original boundaries. Figure 4-2

The British Empire in 1837

The British Empire in 1901

1   British East Africa
2   British Central Africa
3   Transvaal
4   Natal
5   Orange River Colony
6   Cape Colony
7   Somaliland

shows how through much of the nineteenth century England spread its version of Western civilization throughout the world as it conquered tribal peoples and established colonies in Africa and Asia. Along with colonial rule came cultural imperialism, the imposition of a new culture on the conquered peoples. This meant that colonial peoples had to learn the languages of their conquerors, especially English, Spanish, French, Portuguese, and Dutch (or Afrikaans). Along with language came the imposition of ideologies like Christianity in place of older beliefs and religions.

Box 4–2: **Loan Words**

The diffusion of culture from one society to another can be seen in the tendency of languages to "borrow" words from other languages. Traders, missionaries, and colonists all leave their mark in the form of words like *kiplefti* (Swahili for "traffic circle," in which traffic must keep to the left) or the Arabic *combuter* (computer). English is full of loan words. From French we get *reservoir, tête-à-tête, clique, recherché, fait accompli, grotesque, debonair,* and many other words. *Assassin* comes from Arabic, *pizza* from Italian, *trek* from Afrikaans. English, in turn, has left its mark on languages throughout the world: French has picked up *shampooing, drugstore,* and *supermarket; cowboy* has entered Serbo-Croatian as *kovboj; school* and *ski* (itself originally Norwegian) have become the Persian *eskool* and *eski;* Dutch has picked up *trawler;* and Germans look forward to *das Weekend.* Sometimes loan words are translated before they enter the receiving language; thus *skyscraper* has become *gratte-ciel* in French, *rascacielo* in Spanish, and *neboskrjób* in Russian. And sometimes loan words turn up in quite unexpected places, a clear indication of cultural contact. Examples include the *kʰape* of the Arizona Tewa (from the Spanish *café*); *finesteri,* "window," in Sesotho, the language of Lesotho (from the Italian *finestra*); and Arabic *framlah* (strawberry), from the Italian *fragola.*

Source: Courtesy of Gina Doggett, Center for Applied Linguistics.

According to historian Fernand Braudel, "The mark of a living civilization is that it is capable of exporting itself, of spreading its culture to distant places. It is impossible to imagine a true civilization which does not export its people, its ways of thinking and living" (1976/1949, p. 763). In his research on the contacts and clashes between the great civilizations surrounding the Mediterranean Sea during the 1500s, Braudel uses three important sociological concepts to explain the spread of civilizations around the world. Those concepts are acculturation, assimilation, and accommodation.

Acculturation. People from one civilization incorporate norms and values from other cultures into their own through a process called **acculturation**. Most acculturation occurs through intercultural contact and the borrowing or imitation of cultural norms. But there have been many instances of acculturation through cultural imperialism, in which one culture has been forced to adopt the language or other traits of a more dominant one. Thus people in societies that were colonized in the nineteenth century were forced to learn the language of the conquering nation.

Aspects of our culture that we take for granted usually can be shown to have traveled a complicated route through other cultures to become part of our way of life. Braudel's study of the Mediterranean civilizations shows that many of the plants and foods that became part of life around the Mediterranean Sea, and later were imported to the New World, were themselves borrowed from other cultures and incorporated into those of the Mediterranean societies. Box 4-2 gives some examples of another aspect of culture that is frequently incorporated into other cultures and civilizations.

The concept of acculturation can also be applied to how a newcomer people adopts the cultural ways of the host society. But acculturation is rarely a one-way process: At the same time that they are becoming more like their hosts in values and behavior, newcomers teach members of the host society to use and appreciate aspects of their own culture. Indeed, most of the things we think of as part of the American way of life, from hamburgers, pizza, and baseball to

> *Through acculturation, people incorporate norms and values from other cultures into their own.*

democracy and free enterprise, originally were aspects of other cultures. That they have become incorporated into American culture through acculturation, and in the process have become changed from their original forms, does not deny the fact of their "foreign" origin (Linton, 1936).

Assimilation and Subcultures. When culturally distinct groups within a larger civilization adopt the language, values, and norms of the host civilization and their acculturation enables them to assume equal statuses in the social groups and institutions of the host civilization, we refer to that process as **assimilation**. When groups become assimilated into American society, for example, people often say that they have been "Americanized." Assimilation has been a major issue for immigrant groups in North America, as it still is for immigrants all over the world. It is no surprise then that we continually see articles in the press that ask such questions as Will the various Hispanic peoples in America give up their language over time? Will American Jews marry members of other groups and lose their distinct identity? Will Italian-Americans gradually forget their cultural heritage and come to think of themselves as "100 percent Americans"? These are the kinds of questions that form the subject matter of racial and eth-

nic relations in "pluralistic" societies like those of the United States and the Soviet Union. Both of these societies (which are also civilizations) are composed of a multitude of peoples, each of which once had its own culture but is under pressure to become assimilated into the dominant civilization.

When a culturally distinct people within a larger culture fails to assimilate fully or has not yet become fully assimilated, we say that it is a **subculture** within the larger culture. (The term is also applied to groups that have had significantly different experiences from those of most members of the society.) People who maintain their own subculture generally share many of the values and norms of the larger culture, but they retain certain rituals, values, traditions, and norms—and in some cases their own language—that set them apart. Thus we speak of African-American, Latin, Native American, and a host of other subcultures in the United States. As we discuss in Chapter 13, these are also known as *ethnic groups*, since their members have a sense of shared descent, a feeling of being "a people" with a history and a way of life that exists within a larger and more culturally diverse society. The Visual Sociology section of this chapter illustrates how Native Americans may be viewed as an ethnic subculture in North American cities and how their historical ex-

This visual evidence tells us that the Hispanic population is increasingly important in this neighborhood, even though the older firms established by earlier immigrant groups remain. In the future the neighborhood may be largely Hispanic, but it is also possible that the Jewish, Chinese, and Hispanic groups will live together and share the streets and businesses and housing indefinitely. Much will depend on the rate of arrival of new immigrants.

perience as a conquered people continues to shape their ways of thinking about life even in an urban milieu.

Ethnic subcultures are created out of the experience of migration or invasion and subsequent adaptation to a host culture. But subcultures are also created out of the experience of people in complex societies who actively seek to create and maintain a way of life distinct from that of other members of their society (Fischer, 1976; Gans, 1967). For example, there are subcultures in large cities composed of artists and other people whose livelihood depends on the arts: theater people, rock musicians and record producers, visual artists, gallery owners, art critics, curators. The list could be expanded to include media artists and avant-garde artists who band together to find new forms of expression and perhaps poke fun at conventional norms. When a subculture that challenges the accepted norms and values of the larger society establishes an alternative life-style, we call it a **counterculture**. The hippies of the 1960s, along with members of New Left political groups, activists in the women's movement, and environmental activists, formed a counterculture that had a significant influence on American politics and foreign policy during the Vietnam War years (Roszak, 1969).

Frequently subcultures are under intense pressure to conform to the society's most widely accepted norms and values or adapt to new ways, new technologies, or the like. Social scientists often investigate the changing norms and values of such subcultures—the gay subcultures, the subculture of rock musicians and other celebrities, or the subcultures of occupational groups like Appalachian miners, Wall Street lawyers, and doctors—to name only a few of the many that could be listed (Backer, 1982; Bosk, 1979; Caudill, 1976; Erikson, 1976; Millman, 1976; Smigel, 1964). Frequently this research is valuable in predicting trends in such areas as drug use, popular music, or patterns of labor-management conflict and cooperation (Boggs and Meyersohn, 1989; Flores, 1988; Nyden, 1984).

Accommodation and Resistance.

Throughout history many societies have withstood tremendous pressure to become assimilated into larger civilizations. But even greater numbers have been either wiped out or fully assimilated. Only a century ago, for example, there were many hundreds of hunter-gatherer societies still in existence throughout the world. Today there are probably fewer than 100, and these live in the most isolated regions of the earth.

Larger and smaller societies do not usually develop ways of living together without the smaller ones becoming extinct or totally assimilated into the larger ones. But when the smaller, less powerful society is able to preserve the major features of its culture even after prolonged contact, **accommodation** is said to have occurred. In the Islamic civilization of the Middle East, for example, before the creation of Israel in 1948 Jews and other non-Muslims usually found it rather easy to maintain their cultures within the larger Arab societies. Compare this pattern of accommodation with the experience of the Jews in Spain, who were forced to leave in 1492 in one of the largest mass expulsions in history.

Accommodation requires that each side tolerate the existence of the other and even share territory and social institutions. The history of relations between Native Americans and European settlers in the Western Hemisphere is a complex story of resistance and accommodation. Throughout the period of conquest, expansion, and settlement by the Europeans there was continual resistance by the native peoples. This resistance took many forms, including refusal to adopt Christianity, to speak English or Spanish, to sell goods and services to the settlers, and to fight in the Europeans' wars. Resistance did not save Native Americans from death by disease, military conquest, or famine, but it did allow them to maintain their cultures and to borrow from the settlers the cultural customs that were most advantageous to them. For example, the Plains Indians adopted horses from the Spanish explorers, which completely changed their culture, and much later they borrowed trucks from American culture, which helped them adapt to modern ranching.

> *When a less powerful society is able to preserve its culture after prolonged contact with a more powerful society, accommodation has taken place.*

© William Strode, Four by Five, Inc.

The culture of modern industrial societies, with its reliance on gasoline engines and air-conditioned buildings, often coexists with traditional ways of life. In this case a truck eases the task of transporting a camel through the urban environment.

Conclusion

Most cultures in the world today have had to confront the influence of at least one expanding civilization. In some instances the result has been prolonged conflict and the eventual annihilation of the smaller society and its culture. But in most cases acculturation, assimilation, and accommodation have combined to produce significant changes on all sides. Often some aspects of the smaller society's culture have been preserved, but at the same time it has been modified to meet the demands of a changing social and physical environment. As the social sciences assume a greater role in contemporary human affairs there is hope that the probability of accommodation and mutual understanding across cultures will increase. In the meantime, however, older patterns of conflict, intolerance, and exploitation remain dominant.

FRONTIERS OF SOCIOLOGY

Changes in American Culture

We live in a time that some sociologists think is marked by such rapid social change that we may experience what Alvin Toffler (1971) termed *future shock*. The notion of future shock is derived from the social-scientific concept of *culture shock*, the feeling of disorientation and depression one experiences upon encountering a culture with norms and values markedly different from one's own. The Indians who were kidnapped by explorers and brought to the courts of Europe experienced severe culture shock. Many Americans experience culture shock when they first encounter the extreme poverty of some third-world societies. But the popular idea of future shock asserts that social change is so pervasive in our own society that many people are in a continual state of disorientation.

What are the facts? Do you or people close to you experience culture shock when confronted with changes in your lives? And are there really so many significant changes occurring? Some respected social scientists argue that we are becoming a more self-centered or narcissistic culture (Lasch, 1978; Slater, 1976; Yankelovich, 1981). Others point to drastic changes in sexual mores over the past generation or so (Blumstein and Schwartz, 1983). Still others point to the sharp decline in manufacturing employment, the rise of automation, the growth of service industries, and similar changes that are thought to produce changes in American culture. These arguments enliven bankers' and advertisers' din-

Table A: Percentages of White American Teenage Girls Who Have Ever Had Premarital Intercourse, by Age, 1938–1949, 1971, and 1976

Age	1938–1949	1971	1976
14	—	2.1	2.6
15	1.0	4.3	7.0
16	2.0	8.8	16.4
17	8.0	18.1	29.1
18	14.0	28.7	42.2
19	18.0	42.6	55.8

Sources: Kinsey, Pomeroy, and Martin, 1953, p. 286 (the data are taken from a figure, which limits the preciseness of the percentages); Zeinik, Young, and Kantner, 1979. Adapted from *Middletown* by Robert S. Lynd and Helen Merrell Lynd, © 1929 by Harcourt Brace Jovanovich, Inc.; renewed 1957 by Robert S. and Helen M. Lynd. Reproduced by permission of the publisher.

Table B: Out-of-Wedlock Births per 1,000 Live Births, Middletown, 1957–1975

Year	Out-of-Wedlock Births	Total Live Births	Out-of-Wedlock Births per 1,000 Live Births
1957	106	1,838	57.7
1960	104	1,752	59.4
1962	98	1,667	58.8
1964	110	1,671	65.8
1966	132	1,644	80.3
1968	112	1,615	69.3
1970	156	1,733	90.0
1972	174	1,468	118.5
1974	204	1,379	147.9
1975	178	1,221	145.8

Sources: Figures for out-of wedlock births are from U.S. Census data; total live births are from Indiana State Board of Health 1976a, p. 90, and 1966–1975. Adapted from *Middletown* by Robert S. Lynd and Helen Merrell Lynd, © 1929 by Harcourt Brace Jovanovich, Inc.; renewed 1957 by Robert S. and Helen M. Lynd. Reproduced by permission of the publisher.

ners, political contests, and social-policy debates all over America. But how are we to make sense of all the conflicting claims?

A useful technique for studying how people experience social change is to study a community that is considered representative of the larger society. One of the first, and still the best known, of these community studies is the Middletown series. This study was undertaken by Helen and Robert Lynd in the 1920s. Their goal was to gather data on the attitudes and behaviors of Americans in a typ-

ical midwestern manufacturing city—Muncie, Indiana. The results of their research were published in what has become a classic of American sociology: *Middletown* (1929).

During the Great Depression the Lynds returned to Muncie to find out how the traumas of unemployment, mortgage foreclosures, and plant shutdowns had affected the community and its residents. They entitled their second volume *Middletown in Transition* (1937). Forty years later, in the late 1970s, a team of sociologists went back to Muncie to

Table C: Percentage of Middletown Adolescents Reporting Disagreement with Their Parents, by Subject and by Sex, 1924 and 1977

Source of Disagreement	Boys		Girls	
	1924	1977	1924	1977
The hours (1924: hour) you get in at night	45%	46%	43%	42%
The number of times you go out on school nights during the week	45	31	48	35
Your grades at school (1924: grades at school)	40	34	31	28
Your spending money	37	38	29	29
Use of the automobile	36	29	30	22
The people (1924: boys or girls) you choose as friends	25	33	27	36
Home duties (yardwork, cooking, helping around the house, etc.) (1924: . . . [tending furnace, cooking, etc.])	19	45	26	46
Church and attendance at religious services (1924: . . . and Sunday School attendance)	19	11	19	13
The way you dress (including hair style, general grooming) (1924: the way you dress)	16	25	25	19
Going to unchaperoned parties	15	27	28	29
Sunday (or Sabbath) observance, aside from attendance at services (1924: Sunday observance, aside from just going to Church and Sunday School)	14	6	14	3
Clubs or societies you belong to	6	6	10	5
Other causes of disagreement (please explain) (1924: state any other causes of disagreement)	10	16	8	28
Number of Cases (N)	(348)	(442)	(392)	(488)

Sources: Lynd and Lynd, 1929, p. 322: Middletown III high school survey, 1977. Adapted from *Middletown* by Robert S. Lynd and Helen Merrell Lynd, © 1929 by Harcourt Brace Jovanovich, Inc.; renewed 1957 by Robert S. and Helen M. Lynd. Reproduced by permission of the publisher.

find out how people were experiencing changes in American norms and values. Tables A, B, and C compare the results from the Lynds' earlier work with the more recent Middletown survey.

Tables A and B indicate that the norms and behavior of Middletown residents underwent major changes, especially in the area of sexual conduct. Table A presents data from national surveys of sexual activity among unmarried white women. The data suggest that there was a dramatic loosening in the norms governing premarital sexual activity, a change reflected in the data on increases in out-of-wedlock births in Middletown from 1957 to 1975 (Table B).

Other data from the Middletown studies indicate that some elements of American culture are remarkably stable. This can be seen in Table C. When Middletown adolescents were questioned about sources of conflict between themselves and their parents, the results for 1924 and 1977 were not very different. Both in the 1920s and in the late 1970s, parents and teenagers fought about issues related to the teenager's independence, as seen in conflicts over curfew time, grades, spending money, and going out on school nights. Because in American culture the car is a symbol of independence, it is not surprising that Middletown teenagers fought with their parents about using the family car in the Roaring Twenties just as they do today.

The most significant changes in values, as reflected in conflicts between parents and teenagers, appear to center on personal lifestyles. Note that today's teenage boys are more likely to fight with their parents about hair styles and personal grooming than their counterparts in the 1920s were. This finding is reversed for girls, perhaps reflecting the fact that in the 1920s girls had far less freedom than boys did, and for a young woman to assert herself by "bobbing" her hair was shocking in the same way that the idea of a boy wearing a ponytail or a punk haircut is today.

No matter how deeply we probe, the findings from a single community will always leave us wondering whether the same conclusions apply to American culture in general. Fortunately, the data from national surveys can give us at least a partial answer to this question. In *New Rules* (1981) Daniel Yankelovich, one of the nation's leading survey researchers, assembled data from his own and other surveys of public opinion that stress areas of change in American values. These data, summarized in Table D, confirm some of the changes indicated by the Middletown data, especially those pertaining to marriage and the family. The survey data indicate other significant changes as well. For example, in a study of American cultural values in the 1950s Robin Williams (1952) listed as the dominant values achievement and success, hard work and activity, efficiency and practicality, material comfort, equality, freedom, external conformity, science and rationality, and nationalism and patriotism. The Yankelovich data do not directly challenge this list of values, but they do show that there have been significant changes in how we interpret them in our own lives. Thus, although we still value success and material comfort, we increasingly question the value of hard work for its own sake, and we are increasingly anxious about the future. No longer do we trust our government in all it does. We are far more likely to be critical of our society and its institutions than we were in earlier periods. We still value equality of opportunity very highly, but the Yankelovich data show that the women's movement has produced some stunning changes in the way we think about the division of labor both in the home and in the workplace.

How permanent are these changes? Do they really represent fundamental shifts in the most strongly held values of American culture? Or can we expect a shift back toward traditional values and norms? Yankelovich's data indicate that the changes will not be reversed soon, but at the same time we must keep in mind the continuities shown by the Middletown studies. These changes and continuities in our values are something to which sociologists must pay close attention, as they are always on the frontiers of research. Older values and norms coexist with the new, making our society even more culturally diverse. For some this continual change may produce "future shock" in the form of psychological stress, but many other members of this rapidly changing culture will never experience future shock because they have grown up expecting to live with conflicting values and divergent norms.

Table D

Condemn premarital sex as morally wrong

| 1967 | 85% |
| 1979 | 37% |

Favor decision making abortion up to 3 months of pregnancy legal

| 1973 | 52% |
| 1980 | 60% |

Agree that both sexes have the responsibility to care for small children

| 1970 | 33% |
| 1980 | 56% |

Increase in level of anxiety and worry among young Americans 21–39 years of age

| 1957 | 30% |
| 1976 | 49% |

Agree that "the people running the country don't care what happens to people like me"

| 1966 | 26% |
| 1977 | 60% |

Agree that they "can trust the government in Washington to do what's right"

| 1958 | 56% |
| 1978 | 29% |

Experience a "hungering for community"

| 1973 | 32% |
| 1980 | 47% |

Agree that it is morally acceptable to be single and have children

| 1979 | 75% |

Agree that interracial marriages are not morally wrong

| 1977 | 62% |

Agree that it is not morally wrong for couples to live together even if they are not married

| 1978 | 52% |

Agree that they would like to return to standards of the past relating to:
—sexual mores
—"spic and span" housekeeping
—women staying home and only men working outside the home

| 1979 | 21% |

Source: Adapted from *New Rules: Searching for Self-Fulfillment in a World Turned Upside Down*, by Daniel Yankelovich. Copyright © 1981 by Daniel Yankelovich. Reprinted by permission of Random House, Inc.

SUMMARY

In popular speech the word *culture* refers to such pursuits as art, literature, and music. But in the social sciences it refers to all the modes of thought, behavior, and production handed down from one generation to the next by means of communicative interaction. Sociologists are concerned primarily with aspects of culture that help explain social organization and behavior.

Culture can be viewed as consisting of three major dimensions: *ideas, norms,* and *material culture.* Norms are specific rules of behavior, and they are justified by *values,* or socially shared ideas about what is right. *Ideologies* are systems of values and norms that the members of a society are expected to believe in and act upon without question. *Technologies* are the things (material culture), and the norms for using them, found in a given culture.

Every culture includes a wide array of norms, collectively termed the *normative order.* The normative order constitutes a system of *social control,* the set of rules and understandings that controls the behavior of members of that culture. *Sanctions* are rewards and punishments for adhering to or violating norms. Strongly sanctioned norms are called *mores,* and more weakly sanctioned norms are known as *folkways.*

A *social institution* is a more or less stable structure of statuses and roles devoted to meeting the basic needs of people in a society. Within any given institution there are norms that specify how people in various statuses are to perform their roles. New institutions continually emerge through the process of *differentiation.*

One of the most hotly debated questions in the social sciences is how much, if at all, human culture is determined by biological factors. Darwin's theory of evolution set the stage for this debate. According to that theory, the process of "natural selection" favors traits that allow an individual organism to survive and pass on those traits to the next generation. It is this process that permits animals and plants to adapt to new environments.

Herbert Spencer and other social thinkers, who came to be known as *social Darwinists,* attempted to apply Darwin's theory to humans' ability to adapt to social environments. Spencer used the phrase "survival of the fittest" to describe this ability. People who were able to survive in the urban environment created by the industrial revolution were viewed as superior human beings.

A more recent attempt to attribute social phenomena to biological processes is *sociobiology,* which refers to efforts to link genetic factors with the social behavior of animals. According to the sociobiologists, such behaviors as incest avoidance, aggression, and homosexuality may be genetically programmed in human beings. As yet there is no evidence that such genes or sets of genes actually exist, but the sociobiological hypothesis remains an open question.

A more widely accepted view of culture denies that humans have innate instincts and states that at a certain stage in prehistoric times human culture became self-generating. Thus, human evolution is not dependent on genes; instead, cultural techniques allow humans to adapt to any physical or social environment.

The learning of culture is made possible by language. Although apes have been taught to use language to some extent, human language is unique in that it allows its speakers to express an infinite number of thoughts and ideas that can persist even after their originators are gone. According to the *linguistic-relativity hypothesis,* language also determines the possibilities for a culture's norms, beliefs, and values. A less extreme form of that hypothesis recognizes the mutual influences of culture and language.

The notion that one's own culture is superior to any other is called *ethnocentrism.* To understand other cultures it is necessary to suspend judgment about those cultures, an approach termed *cultural relativity*. Cross-cultural research has been used in efforts to find "cultural universals," or cultural traits that are found among humans everywhere. Some cultural universals, such as the family, have been identified, but in recent years the search for cultural universals has given way to cross-cultural comparisons in specific areas of sociological study.

Similarities among cultures have resulted from the processes by which cultures spread across national boundaries and become part of a larger, more advanced culture called a civilization. A *civilization* may be defined as a cultural complex formed by the identical major cultural features of a number of particular societies.

A key feature of civilizations is that they invariably expand beyond their original boundaries. The spread of civilizations can be explained by three processes: acculturation, assimilation, and accommodation. When people from one civilization incorporate norms and values from other cultures into their own, *acculturation* is said to occur. The process by which culturally distinct groups within a larger civilization adopt the language, values, and norms of the host civilization and gain equal statuses in its institutions is termed *assimilation*. (If a distinct people fails to assimilate fully, it is referred to as a *subculture*, but if it challenges the accepted norms and values of the larger society it may become a *counterculture*.) And when a smaller, less powerful society is able to preserve its culture even after prolonged contact with a major civilization, *accommodation* has taken place.

WHERE TO FIND IT

Books

Sociobiology (Edward O. Wilson; Harvard University Press, 1975). This is the book that initiated the most recent version of the nature-nurture controversy. It contains a wealth of information about various types of animal and insect societies, but it fails to account for the influence of culture and social institutions on human societies.

The Interpretation of Cultures (Clifford Geertz; Basic Books, 1973). A set of essays that explores the many meanings of human culture, including a fine essay on the relationship between culture and human social and physical evolution.

Sex and Temperament in Three Primitive Societies (Margaret Mead; Morrow, 1935). A classic study that, on the basis of detailed observations, argues against the theory that the differing behavior of males and females is determined by genetic factors. Instead, Mead provides evidence for the theory that those differences are due to cultural training.

Cultural Anthropology (Marvin Harris; Harper & Row, 1991). A basic textbook that covers in detail the cultures of nonindustrial peoples.

Journals

Technology and Culture A quarterly journal devoted to studies of the interrelationships between cultural and technological change.

Signs A quarterly journal that supplies valuable data on women in various societies and cultures.

Human Organization A quarterly journal that publishes articles dealing with all areas of applied social science, including case studies, comparative studies, and theoretical essays.

GLOSSARY

culture: all the modes of thought, behavior, and production that are handed down from one generation to the next by means of communicative interaction rather than by genetic transmission (**p. 95**).

ideas: the ways of thinking that organize human consciousness (**p. 95**).

norms: specific rules of behavior (**p. 95**).

material culture: patterns of possessing and using the products of culture (**p. 95**).

values: the ideas that support or justify norms (**p. 96**).

ideologies: systems of values and norms that the members of a society are expected to believe in and act upon without question (**p. 97**).

technologies: the products and the norms for using them that are found in a given culture (**p. 97**).

normative order: the array of norms found in a given culture (**p. 97**).

social control: the set of rules and understandings that control the behavior of individuals and groups in a particular culture (**p. 97**).

sanctions: rewards and punishments for abiding by or violating norms (**p. 98**).

mores: strongly sanctioned norms (**p. 98**).

folkways: weakly sanctioned norms (**p. 98**).

institution: a more or less stable structure of statuses and roles devoted to meeting the basic needs of people in a society (**p. 100**).

differentiation: the processes whereby sets of social activities performed by one social institution are divided among different institutions (**p. 100**).

cultural evolution: the process by which successful cultural adaptations are passed down from one generation to the next (**p. 102**).

social Darwinism: the notion that people who are more successful at adapting to their environment are more likely to survive and reproduce (**p. 102**).

sociobiology: the hypothesis that all human behavior is determined by genetic factors (**p. 102**).

linguistic-relativity hypothesis: the belief that language determines the possibilities for thought and action in any given culture (**p. 105**).

ethnocentrism: the tendency to judge other cultures as inferior to one's own (**p. 106**).

cultural relativity: the recognition that all cultures develop their own ways of dealing with the specific demands of their environments (**p. 106**).

civilization: a cultural complex formed by the identical major cultural features of a number of societies (**p. 108**).

acculturation: the process by which the members of a civilization incorporate norms and values from other cultures into their own (**p. 110**).

assimilation: the process by which culturally distinct groups in a larger civilization adopt the norms, values, and language of the host civilization and are able to gain equal statuses in its groups and institutions (**p. 111**).

subculture: a group of people who hold many of the values and norms of the larger culture but also hold certain beliefs, values, or norms that set them apart from that culture (**p. 111**).

counterculture: a subculture that challenges the accepted norms and values of the larger society and establishes an alternative life-style (**p. 112**).

accommodation: the process by which a smaller, less powerful society is able to preserve the major features of its culture even after prolonged contact with a larger, stronger society (**p. 112**).

VISUAL SOCIOLOGY

Urban Indians

In the 1950s the federal government undertook a massive program to relocate Native Americans to Chicago, Denver, Los Angeles, and San Francisco. The Bureau of Indian Affairs supplied free one-way tickets to Indians seeking jobs in these urban centers. It also made a token effort to provide job training. But once it found a job for a relocated person, the government's responsibility ended.

In 1965 San Francisco State University studied the acculturation and adjustment of the relocated Indians. Part of the study was a photographic survey of twenty-four Indian homes by photographer John Collier. As this selection of Collier's photos shows, there was a direct relationship between adjustment to relocation and the "look" of an Indian home. That is, a family's ability to achieve cultural order in the home reflected its ability to cope with urban life.

The federal government defined successful relocation as "terminating" an Indian in the urban industrial wilderness. For the Native Americans, however, successful relocation was a more complex matter. For many, it meant a free trip and some valuable education before returning to settle in their original homelands. For many others, the relocation that was meant to result in assimilation instead created aggressive Red Power activists.

Unpredictably, urban survival required strengthening the "Indianness" of personalities. Without that, people tended toward neurosis or alcoholism. So relocation, a scheme designed to lose Indians in the nation's cities, instead caused a revival of Native American vitality. Their culture did not effectively follow Native Americans into the cities. But their music and writing, created for survival in the city, circulated back to the reservation.

The significant result of the policy of relocation, one that still remains, is a resurgence of Native American culture, not only richly costumed dances and songs, but also an aggressive and sophisticated Red Power movement, the last thing the Bureau of Indian Affairs wanted (Collier, 1981).

An Eskimo family from Alaska. Relocation dropped Arctic hunters into Oakland, California, where they have no friends. They go to movies or sit at home.

A Navajo married to a Walipi living in Palo Alto. Indians must find renewal in the unfamiliar surroundings of urban living.

When I visited this Eskimo family, the wife urged me to photograph her in her Arctic parka, with a wolf-tail ruff and squirrel-skin decorations. Proudly she posed in this Arctic wealth, a symbol of a world left behind.

For the Pomo, relocation means isolation from a supportive ecology and extended family relationships.

Pomos from Clear Lake, California, resettled in Oakland. For the younger generation, quality of education is a major variable in the success or failure of Indian relocation.

Photographs and captions by John Collier

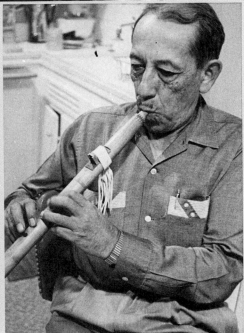

A Sioux family head living in a housing project in Alameda. Alcoholism is the chief threat of relocation.

Like many successful relocatees, this affluent Sioux has retained his Indian allegiances: to Red Power groups in the Bay Area and back home in North Dakota. The flute is a symbol of his identity.

CHAPTER OUTLINE

- **People, Cities, and Urban Growth**
  - The Population Explosion
  - The Growth of Cities

- **The Urban Landscape**
  - Urban Expansion
  - Metropolitan Areas

- **Urban Communities**
  - The Decline-of-Community Thesis
  - Subcultural Theory

- **Cities and Social Change**
  - Inequality and Conflict
  - Conclusion

Margo Smith

Battery Park City, lower Manhattan

CHAPTER 5

POPULATION, URBANIZATION, AND COMMUNITY

In his "Foundation" trilogy of science-fiction novels, Isaac Asimov describes a planet, Trantor, that is the imperial center of a galactic system. All the planets in the system are populated by humans who have long since left their original planet, Earth. Trantor's inhabitants move through an artificial environment that is largely beneath the planet's surface, never catching a glimpse of the sky, for Trantor is a planet of the future, in which people live entirely in environments of their own design. Here is how Asimov describes the planet in his fictional *Encyclopedia Galactica*:

TRANTOR— . . . At the beginning of the thirteenth millennium, this tendency reached its climax. As the center of the Imperial Government for unbroken hundreds of generations and located, as it was, in the central regions of the Galaxy among the most densely populated and industrially advanced worlds of the system, it could scarcely help being the densest and richest clot of humanity the Race had ever seen.

Its urbanization, progressing steadily, had finally reached the ultimate. All the land surface of Trantor, 75,000,000 square miles in extent, was a single city. The population, at its height, was well in excess of forty billion. This enormous population was devoted almost entirely to the administrative necessities of Empire, and found themselves all too few for the complications of the task. . . . Daily, fleets of ships in the tens of thousands brought the produce of twenty agricultural worlds to the dinner tables of Trantor. . . .

Its dependence upon the outer worlds for food and, indeed, for all necessities of life, made Trantor increasingly vulnerable to conquest by siege. In the last millennium of the Empire, the monotonously numerous revolts made Emperor after Emperor conscious of this, and Imperial policy became little more than the protection of Trantor's delicate jugular vein. [1966, pp. 12–13]

In this famous series of novels, Asimov uses trends that are apparent in the world today to create a vision of a future interplanetary empire. At the center of that empire is a planet that is one large city. Its enormous population is dependent on the resources of other planets, just as the major cities of the earth now depend on the surrounding areas for agricultural and industrial products to support their populations.

Is this a realistic vision of the future? Obviously, this question cannot be answered now, but we know that the pressures of population growth and urbanization require us to continue to develop new technologies that can help us control our present environments and explore and colonize new ones. And although we are not there yet, we can readily foresee a time when, if present trends continue, the earth will no longer be able to support its population. So Asimov's vision deserves close attention. It makes us aware that population growth and urbanization may continue until human life is forced to spread beyond the closed environment of our own planet.

Another vision of the future, one that does not see salvation in technological progress, would require us to control population growth and limit the spread of cities. In our own lifetimes this more modest, yet still ambitious, vision is probably the more realistic one. The reasons for this should become evident as we study the effects of population growth and urbanization on the contemporary world. For even if someday we can travel through space on a grand scale, if we have first learned to care adequately for the populations of our own world, we will have gained knowledge that is worthy of being exported throughout the universe.

PEOPLE, CITIES, AND URBAN GROWTH

A simov's vision of the future links population size and density with urban living. People in modern societies typically live in cities or metropolitan areas rather than on farms or in small towns and villages. Indeed, 90 percent of Americans live within twenty-five miles of a city center (Berry, 1978). This means that they live in the human-built environment of cities and suburbs; relatively few live in the "country" environment of rural areas.

Asimov projected two current trends, increasing population and increasing urbanization, into the distant future. Both trends have been typical of human societies throughout recorded history, but they have been especially evident since the industrial revolution made cities the ecological and cultural centers of modern societies. This suggests that we need to study the relationships between population growth and the growth of cities. In this chapter, therefore, we will see how increasing population size and other important changes in populations are connected with the rise of cities and metropolitan areas throughout the world.

The Population Explosion

Before we can study the phenomenon of urbanization, we must understand the impact of population growth on the formation and expansion of cities. In Chapter 3 we describe the extremely rapid growth of the world's population in the past three centuries. If you refer to Figure 3-3, you can readily see that the *rate* of population growth has increased dramatically in this century alone, giving rise to the often-used term *population explosion*. The world's population is currently estimated at 5.2 billion, and according to the Population Reference Bureau (1989) it could reach 8.3 billion by the year 2020. Such rapid population growth cannot continue indefinitely without severe consequences for human survival and well-being.

Unchecked population growth has a number of consequences, of which the most obvious is "increased pressure upon food, space, and other resources and upon the social and community relationships organizing their allocation" (Matras, 1973, p. 5). The pressures of population growth have produced changes in economic and social arrangements throughout history, but never before have those changes occurred as rapidly or on as great a scale as they are occurring today.

Malthusian Population Theory. Is there a danger that the earth will become overpopulated? The debate over population growth is not new. For almost two centuries social scientists have been seeking to determine whether human populations will grow beyond the earth's capacity to support them. The earliest and most forceful theory of overpopulation appeared in Thomas Malthus's *Essay on Population* (1927–1928/1798). Malthus attempted to show that population size normally increases far more rapidly than the food and energy resources needed to keep people alive. Couples will have as many children as they can afford to feed, and their children will do the same. This will cause populations to grow *geometrically* (2, 4, 8, 16, 32, etc.). Meanwhile, available food supplies will increase *arithmetically* (2, 3, 4, 5, 6, etc.) as farms are expanded and crop yields increased. As a result, population growth will always threaten to outstrip food supplies. The resulting poverty, famine, disease, war, and mass migrations will act as natural checks on rapid population growth.

History has proved Malthus wrong on at least two counts. We are not biologically driven to multiply beyond the capacity of the environment to support our offspring, and Malthus himself recognized that people could limit their reproduction through delay of marriage or celibacy. The second fault of Malthusian theory is its failure to recognize that technological and institutional change could expand available resources rapidly enough to keep up with population growth. This has occurred in the more affluent regions of the world, where improvements in the quality of life have tended to outstrip population growth. Improvements in agricultural technology have also increased the yield of crops in some of the less developed parts of the world, such as India. But rates of population growth and exhaustion of environmental resources (firewood, water, grazing land) are highest in the poorest nations. Will reductions in population growth rates and increases in available resources also occur there? Or will the Malthusian theory prove correct in the long run? The theory known as the *demographic transition* provides a framework for studying this question, but before we explore this theory we need to know more about measuring population change.

Rates of Population Change. Populations change as a consequence of births, deaths, out-migration, and in-migration. The relationships of these variables to a society's total population are expressed in the *basic demographic equation*:

$$P_t = P_o + (B - D) + (M_i - M_o)$$

where

P_t = the census count for the later period
P_o = the census count for an earlier period
B = total births between P_o and P_t
D = total deaths between P_o and P_t
M_i = in-migration between P_o and P_t
M_o = out-migration between P_o and P_t

Once they know the absolute values of the terms in this equation, demographers usually convert them into percentages in order to compare populations of different sizes. (We discussed the usefulness of such conversions in Chapter 2.) The most basic measures of population change are *crude rates*, or the number of events of a given type (e.g., births or deaths) that occur in a year divided by the midyear population (Bogue, 1969). Thus the **crude birthrate** (CBR) is the number of births occurring during a year in a given population divided by the midyear population. The **crude death rate** (CDR) is the number of deaths occurring during a year divided by the midyear population. These fractions are usually expressed as a rate per thousand persons. They are "crude" because they compare the total number of births or deaths with the total mid-

> *The rate of reproductive change is a measure of the natural increase of a population (the excess of births over deaths).*

Table 5–1: **Principal Sources of World Population Growth, by Country, 1989**

Country	Population (million)	Annual Growth Rate (%)	Annual Increase (million)
India	835.0	2.2	18.4
China[a]	1103.9	1.4	15.5
Brazil	147.4	2.0	2.9
Bangladesh	114.7	2.8	3.2
Nigeria	115.3	2.9	3.3
Pakistan	110.4	2.9	3.2
Indonesia	184.6	2.0	3.7
Soviet Union	289.0	1.0	2.9
Mexico	86.7	2.4	2.1
United States	248.8	0.7	1.7

[a]China's growth rate estimate is based on a 1982 census by the Chinese government.
Source: Population Reference Bureau, 1989.

year population, when in fact not all members of the population are equally likely to give birth or die.

The **rate of reproductive change** is the difference between the CBR and the CDR for a given population. It is a measure of the *natural increase* of the population; that is, it measures increases due to the excess of births over deaths and disregards in- and out-migration. At present there are several nations in which the rate of reproductive change is zero or less, meaning that there is no natural population growth. West Germany, for example, had a CBR of 11 and a CDR of 11 in 1989, for an annual rate of increase of −0.1 percent. In Austria, the CBR was 12 and the CDR 11, for an annual rate of increase of 0.1 percent. In the United States, the rate of population growth is about 0.7 percent, representing an increase of over 1.5 million people per year. These rates are in dramatic contrast with the annual growth rates of countries like Iraq and Syria, which are over 3 percent. The principal sources of world population growth are listed in Table 5-1.

We can easily see from Table 5-2 that an annual rate of population growth of only 1 percent will lead to an increase of almost 270 percent in a century. And since World War II the world population has been increasing at a rate of over 1.5 percent, which means that by the year 2000 we can expect it to have

passed the projected figure of 6 billion. The processes of population growth and the effects of its control are summarized in the phenomenon known as the demographic transition.

The Demographic Transition. The **demographic transition** is a set of major changes in birth and death rates that has occurred most completely in urban industrial nations in the last 200 years. We saw in Chapter 3 that the rapid increase in the world population in the last century and a half was due in large part to rapid declines in death rates. Beginning in the second half of the eighteenth century and continuing until the first half of the twentieth, there was a marked decline in death rates in the countries of northern and western Europe. Improvements in public-health practices were one factor in that decline. Even more important were higher agricultural yields owing to technological changes in farming methods, as well as improvements in the distribution of food as a result of better transportation, which made cheaper food available to more people (Matras, 1973; Vining, 1985). At the same time, however, birthrates in those countries remained high. The resulting gap between birth and death rates produced huge increases in population. It appeared that the gloomy predictions of Malthus and others would be borne out.

In the second half of the nineteenth cen-

This table shows that an annual increase of only 1 percent in the world's population would lead to approximately 270 percent growth in a century. The world population is currently increasing at a rate of more than 1.5 percent.

Table 5–2:
Relationship of Population Growth per Year and per Century

Population Growth per Year (%)	Population Growth per Century (%)
1	270
2	724
3	1,922

Source: Worldwatch Institute.

tury, birthrates began to decline as couples delayed marriage and childbearing. As a result of lower birthrates, the gap between birth- and death rates narrowed and population growth slowed (see Figure 5-1). This occurred

Figure 5–1: **The Demographic Transition, Sweden, 1691–1963**

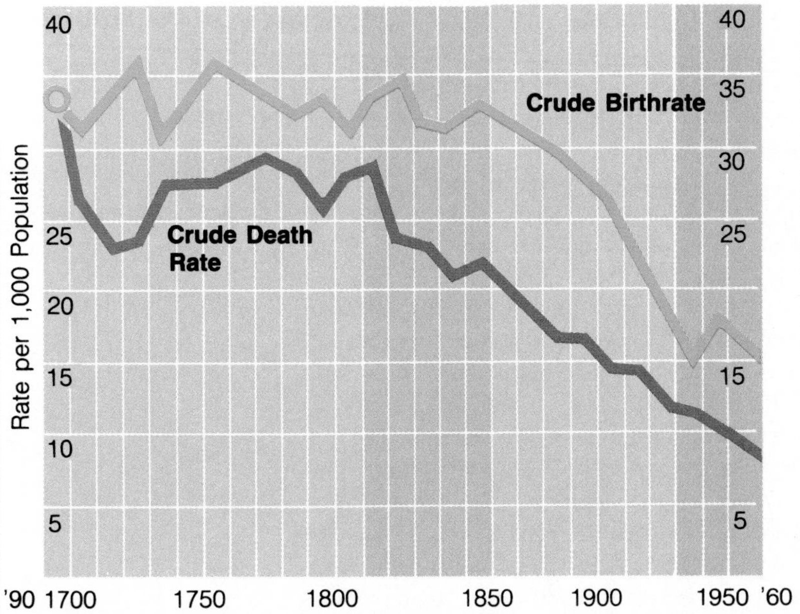

Source: Judah Matras, *Population and Societies*, Englewood Cliffs, N.J., © Prentice-Hall, 1973. Permission of Armand Colin Éditeur.

at different times in different countries, but the general pattern was the same in each case: a stage of high birth- and death rates (the *high growth potential* stage) followed by a stage of declining death rates (the *transitional growth* stage) and, eventually, by a stage of declining birthrates (called the stage of *incipient decline* because it is possible for population growth rates to decrease at this point).

In the second, or transitional growth, stage of the demographic transition, the population not only grows rapidly but undergoes changes in its age composition. Because people now live somewhat longer, there is a slight increase in the proportion of elderly people in the population. And there is a more marked increase in the proportion of people under twenty as a result of significant decreases in infant and child mortality. This is the stage in which many less developed countries find themselves today: Death rates have dropped in the twentieth century because of improved medical care and public-health measures, as well as increased agricultural production. Yet in these societies birthrates have remained high, causing phenomenal increases in population, especially in the younger, more dependent age groups.

No population has entered the third stage of the demographic transition without limiting its birthrate in some way. This can be achieved by encouraging couples to marry later and postpone childbearing or by preventing pregnancies or births through various birth control techniques. In advanced industrial societies, couples use both approaches, making their own decisions about whether and when to have children. In other societies, such as China and India, the state has attempted to limit population growth by promoting birth control through educational programs or by imposing penalties on couples who have more than a prescribed number of children. Such measures have had varying degrees of success, leading some demographers to question whether the less developed countries will be able to complete the demographic transition.

Note that economic and social development is essential if the demographic transition is to occur. Death rates cannot decrease, or food supplies increase, without progress in social institutions like public health, medicine, and transportation. People in more developed societies tend to limit their family size because they seek economic advancement and wish to delay marriage and childbearing until they can support a family.

In many highly industrialized nations, on the other hand, population growth rates have fallen below the rate necessary to maintain the population at the existing level. If a fertility rate of two children or less per couple became the norm for an entire population, the growth rate would slow to zero or even a negative rate. At present the United States, New Zealand, Japan, Australia, and Canada all have total fertility rates of less than 2.0 (Preston, 1986). Similar low rates are appearing in many European nations. This is a highly significant development; if it continued over a generation or more, it would result in negative rates of natural increase and, possibly, other consequences such as slower economic development and labor shortages. Continued low fertility could also result in increased immigration from countries with high birthrates to countries with lower birthrates.

A full exposition of the processes and politics of population control is not possible here. Suffice it to say that most sociologists would agree with the demographer Philip Hauser (1957) that low population growth rates are due primarily to a combination of delay of marriage, celibacy, and the use of modern birth control techniques. This trend is beginning to occur in many less developed nations. Data from Thailand, for example, show that the proportion of married women practicing contraception increased from 14 percent in 1970 to 58 percent in 1981. Similar trends are appearing in much of Latin America and parts of Asia (Brown et al., 1984). We will have occasion to refer to the demographic and ecological processes that affect population patterns at many points in this book.

Population Growth and Urbanization.

Studies of the demographic transition in Europe (Friedlander, 1969; Laslett, 1972, 1983) have concluded that its specific course in any given society depended on a complex combination of factors: higher age at marriage and fewer couples marrying, use of birth control techniques, increased education, migration to other countries, and rural–urban migration. Some of these factors are discussed in Box 5-1. In each case, however, the bulk of

the population growth was absorbed by the cities. Rapid urbanization thus was to some extent an outgrowth of the demographic transition.

Urbanization refers to the proportion of the total population that lives in urban settlements. Although urbanization and the growth of cities have occurred together, it is important to distinguish between the two. Cities can continue to grow even after the majority of the population is urbanized and the society's dominant institutions (government agencies, major markets, newspapers, television networks) are located in its urban centers. Such continued growth and merging of urban populations undoubtedly occurred on Trantor, the entirely urban planet of the future described by Asimov at the beginning of the chapter.

Urbanization contributed to the lower birthrates that are characteristic of the third stage of the demographic transition. As Louis Wirth pointed out, "The decline in the birthrate generally may be regarded as one of the most significant signs of the urbanization of the Western world" (1968, p. 59). In the city a variety of factors lead to the postponement of marriage and childbearing. For one thing, living space is limited. For another, newcomers to the city must find jobs before they can even think about marrying, and often they lack the ties to family and kin groups that might encourage them to marry and have children.

In a study of declines in birthrates in non-Western cities, Warren C. Robinson (1963) found that, contrary to the experience of cities in the West, the populations of some cities in Asia and Africa increased faster than those of rural areas. The reason seems to be that rapid change in rural areas, especially the mechanization of agriculture, pushes rural people to the cities, where they often live in shantytowns and villagelike settlements. (Such settlements are illustrated in the Visual Sociology section of this chapter.) In those settlements the rural tradition of large families is not quickly altered. In addition, because they have greater access to health care during pregnancy and childbirth, the infant death

> *Although urbanization is linked with rapid population growth, life in cities tends to limit the size of urban families.*

Box 5–1: **Rural–Urban Migration**

Along with birth- and death rates, migration is a key factor in population size. People have migrated from one region or country to another throughout history, compelled to seek new homes because they have exhausted their food supplies or have been driven out by invaders or because they believe they will find a better life in the new land. People have also migrated from the country to the city throughout history, but rural–urban migration has become especially pronounced in the last two centuries.

The forces that impel residents of rural areas to migrate to cities are not fully understood. There is continual debate over whether rural people are "pushed" into cities by conditions beyond their control or "pulled" to cities by the attractions of city life. Of course, both push and pull factors affect rural–urban migration, but it is not clear exactly how they interact. It appears, however, that "it is the push of existing rural circumstances which suggests to the rural resident that things might be better in the urban area" (Breese, 1966, p. 80).

Several factors may be responsible for pushing people out of rural areas. Chief among these is overpopulation, which reduces the amount of food and work available per rural resident. Others include lack of opportunities to obtain farm land (e.g., as a result of inheritance norms like *primogeniture*, in which only the oldest son inherits land) and the seasonal nature of employment in agriculture. When rural people who are experiencing these conditions become aware of higher living standards in urban places, they may develop a sense of relative deprivation. "They

view with great interest the reported higher income, access to education, and other rumored facilities of the urban area" (Breese, 1966, pp. 80–81). The feeling of relative deprivation is intensified by improvements in communication and transportation that provide rural people with more "feedback" about the advantages of life in the city.

A significant pull factor is the presence of relatives and friends in the city. These individuals can be called upon for help when the rural migrant arrives in search of a new home and a job. This factor produces what is known as *chain migration*, a pattern in which a network of friends and relatives is transferred from the village to the city over time. The result is the formation of a small, homogeneous community within the city.

Chain migration operates across national boundaries as well as between rural and urban areas in the same country. For example, a large proportion of the immigrants to American cities in the twentieth century have been rural people from European and Asian countries. Once a few hardy souls have established a foothold, their families and friends can join them. In this way small ethnic communities are formed within the city, like the Chinatowns of New York and San Francisco, the Slovenian community in Cleveland, or the Mexican community in Chicago. Recently this pattern has been established in suburban portions of metropolitan areas as well as in central cities. In this way the suburbs of metropolitan areas in the South and West have become home to large numbers of immigrants from Vietnam.

Box 5–2: **Defining Metropolitan Areas**

Formal definitions of urban places have changed considerably in the twentieth century. Traditionally, an urban place was defined as any incorporated area with 2,500 or more inhabitants. But this definition became highly unsatisfactory as cities expanded and their surrounding areas became increasingly urbanized, especially after World War II. As early as 1910 the U.S. Bureau of the Census introduced the concept of the *metropolitan district*, or metropolitan area. In 1950 it began to apply the concept of the *urbanized area*. Such an area includes a central city (or twin cities) with a population of 50,000 or more, plus surrounding areas with a population density of over 1,000 people per square mile.

The concept of an urbanized area was refined in 1970 and given the label *standard metropolitan statistical area* (SMSA). An SMSA is an area with an urban center of 50,000 persons or more, including the county containing that center and neighboring counties closely associated with the central area by daily commuting ties. SMSAs contain not only urban areas, which occupy 10 percent of the land, but also open space, forests, recreation areas, parks, and cropland.

The accompanying chart shows the proportions of the U.S. population living in rural, urban, metropolitan, and nonmetropolitan areas. The organization of data shown in the chart is useful because the curve above the area for each category shows its relative trend in population growth. In order to find out how many millions of people lived in a metropolitan area in 1980, for example, subtract the reading at the bottom of the area for that year from the reading at the top of the area for the same year. For 1980 the line at the bottom of the area falls at about 75 million and the line at the top at about 225 million; thus there were about 150 million residents of metropolitan areas in the United States in that year.

rate may be lower among the migrants than in rural villages. But when these populations become part of the urban economy, they too begin to limit their family size.

In sum, urbanization is closely linked with rapid increases in population, but at the same time the nature of life in cities tends to limit the size of urban families. Cities grow primarily as a result of migration, but new migrants do not find it easy to form families. Thus, in his research on the changing populations of Western industrial cities, Hauser (1957) showed that birthrates were lowest in the areas of the city that had the highest proportions of new migrants. The eventual result of large-scale migration to cities may be a slowdown in population growth: As an increasing proportion of a society's population lives in cities, the rate of growth of the population as a whole tends to drop.

The Growth of Cities

In Chapter 3 we mentioned that cities became possible when agricultural populations began to produce enough extra food to support people who were not directly engaged in agriculture, such as priests, warriors, and artisans. Changes in the technology of food production enabled ever-larger populations to be supported by the same number of agricultural workers. This has been a central factor in the evolution of cities, but as we will see shortly, the most dramatic increases in urban populations have occurred only in the past 150 years.

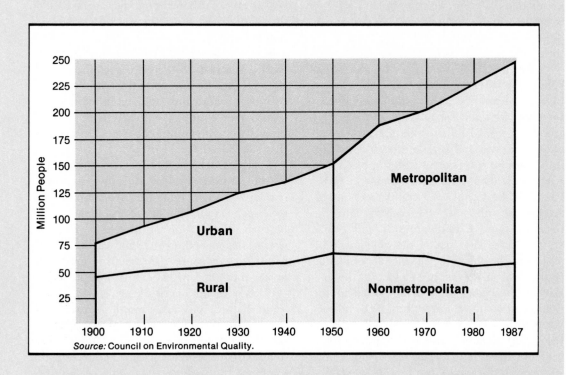

Source: Council on Environmental Quality.

The Urban Revolution. The increasing tendency of people throughout the world to live in cities has been referred to as the *urban revolution*. The extent of this "revolution" can be grasped by comparing a few figures. In 1800, only 3 percent of the world's people lived in cities with populations over 5,000, and of this proportion, a mere 2.4 percent lived in cities with populations over 20,000. Between 1800 and 1970, a period during which the world population increased fourfold, the percentage of people living in cities with 5,000 or more inhabitants increased elevenfold, whereas that of people living in cities with 100,000 or more inhabitants increased almost fourteenfold. By 1970, fully one-third of the world's population lived in cities (Matras, 1973; Vining, 1985).

These data indicate not only that increasing percentages of the world population are living in cities but also that the cities themselves are larger than ever before. The growth of cities in this century has given rise to the concept of the **metropolitan area**, in which a central city is surrounded by a number of smaller cities and suburbs that are closely related to it both socially and economically. Most people in the United States live in large metropolitan areas, as Box 5-2 demonstrates.

Large-scale urbanization is a relatively recent development in human history. As Kingsley Davis (1955) pointed out, "Compared to most other aspects of society—such as language, religion, stratification, or the family—cities appeared only yesterday, and urbanization, meaning that a sizable proportion of the population lives in cities, has developed only in the last few moments of man's existence" (p. 429). Although there were a few cities as early as 4000 B.C., they were very small and were supported by large rural populations. The famous cities of ancient times were minuscule by modern standards: Babylon covered roughly 3.2 square miles, Ur some 220 acres (Davis, 1955).

Preindustrial cities like Ur and Nineveh, early Athens and Rome, and the ancient Mayan Indian cities were vastly different from the cities we know today. They did not grow around a core of office buildings and retail outlets the way industrial cities do. Instead, they were built around temples or other ceremonial buildings (e.g., Notre Dame in Paris). Close by the temple one could find the palaces of the rulers and the courtyards of the royal families. Parade grounds and public shrines made the core of the ancient city a spacious place where the city's population could meet on special occasions. On the outskirts of these ancient cities one found not the rich, as in contemporary cities with well-developed transportation networks, but the poor, who lived in hovels and were often pushed from one location to another according to the whims of those with more wealth and power (Braudel, 1984; Breese, 1966; Sjoberg, 1968). Preindustrial cities are described in more detail in Box 5-3.

A variety of factors limited the size of cities. Among them were farming methods that did not produce enough surplus food to feed many city dwellers, the lack of efficient means of transporting goods over long distances, inadequate technology for transporting water in great quantities, and the lack of scientific medicine (which made urban living, as Davis put it, "deadly"). Not until about 1800 did large-scale urbanization become possible.

The speed with which urbanization has changed the size and layout of cities is remarkable. "Before 1850 no society could be described as predominantly urbanized, and by 1900 only one—Great Britain—could be so regarded. Today . . . all industrial nations are highly urbanized, and in the world as a whole the process of urbanization is accelerating rapidly" (Davis, 1968, p. 33). By 1985, 42 percent of the world population lived in urban areas, and by the year 2000 nearly half of the world population is expected to live in urban areas—40 percent in developing countries and 78 percent in developed countries (Census Bureau, 1986). Africa now has the fastest rate of urbanization, and at the turn of the century about 70 percent of the population of Latin America will live in urban areas, a rate of urbanization comparable to that of North America and Europe. As Figure 5-2 shows, at the beginning of the twentieth century there were only four cities with populations over 2 million; by 1990 there were 87 such cities, with another 85 expected to reach that size by 2000.

Rapid urbanization occurring throughout the world brings together diverse groups of people in cities that often are not prepared to absorb them. The social problems caused by such urbanization are immense. They include housing, educating, and caring for the health of newcomers; preventing gang violence; training newcomers for jobs in industries they never heard of; preventing intergroup hatred; and many more. Moreover, as the world becomes ever more urbanized, populations become increasingly interdependent. Urban populations are supported, for example, by worldwide agricultural production, not just by the produce grown in the surrounding countryside. In the same way, the problems of one major city or one large urbanizing region can no longer be thought of as isolated from the problems of the older, more affluent urbanized regions.

Urban Societies. Urbanization produces urban societies. By this we mean not only that cities are the cultural and institutional centers of a society but also that urban life has a pervasive influence on the entire society (Durkheim, 1964/1893; Weber, 1962/1921; Wirth, 1968/1938). Today the United States is spanned by interstate highways that link the nation's rapidly growing urban and suburban places and carry traffic through rural areas at high speeds. Waterways, forests, hills, and valleys are channeled and cut and bulldozed to make way for expanding settlements. Once considered far from the urban scene, national parks and forests now receive millions of visitors from the metropolitan centers. And in an urban society more and more people, even those

Box 5–3: **Preindustrial Cities**

Preindustrial cities have no central business district. Instead, the city's center is likely to be a cathedral or mosque or a fort or palace (Sjoberg, 1968; Weber, 1962/1921). The rest of the city is divided up into "quarters" or "wards" inhabited by different ethnic and occupational groups. There is little specialization in land use (e.g., no separate areas devoted to factories or businesses or residences). And unlike the upper classes of industrial cities, the elites of the preindustrial city live near the center, with the lower classes inhabiting outlying areas, and "outcast" groups living on the fringes.

The large cities of India provide examples of the ecological patterns typical of preindustrial cities. As Gerald Breese (1966) pointed out, "One of the most noticeable features of large Indian cities is their combination of very high population density in relatively small areas and relatively low population density over other large areas" (p. 56). Also characteristic of Indian cities is the use of many forms of transportation on the same roads and streets: "Animal and vehicular transportation ranges from the sluggish camel and donkey to the speeding truck. . . . Between these are the tonga cart, pedicab, motorcycle rickshaw, bicycle, oxcart, taxi and private automobile, trucks of various kinds, handcart, bus, and streetcar" (pp. 56–57). Similarly, there is a mixture of land uses within the same area and even on a single site. For example, "It is not uncommon to find manufacturing and sale of the same article combined in one establishment" (p. 59).

It is worth noting that this ecological pattern is not limited to ancient cities or to cities in developing nations. The same characteristics (wealthy citizens living near the center of town, artisans living and working in the same place) could be seen in American cities in the midnineteenth century. The modern city began to emerge only after the development of rapid mass transit and the automobile. For this reason, preindustrial cities are sometimes referred to as _pedestrian_ and industrial cities as _mechanized._

© In Stock, Photo Researchers

living in isolated rural communities, share in the mass culture of urban society—the television and radio programs, the movies, the books and magazines, all of which stress themes that appeal to people who are familiar with metropolitan living. In an urban society not everyone lives in the cities, but no one can escape the pervasive influence of the urban centers.

The concept of an urban society may become clearer if we look at a society that has not become fully urbanized, such as India. Until the early twentieth century, the rate of city growth in India was relatively slow. But beginning in the 1920s the populations of India's cities increased dramatically, and by 1960 seven Indian cities had populations of over 1 million. Yet India has not become an urban society. It remains, in the words of Noel P. Gist (1968), "a land of villagers." Because of persistently high birthrates and declining death rates in the villages, India's rural population

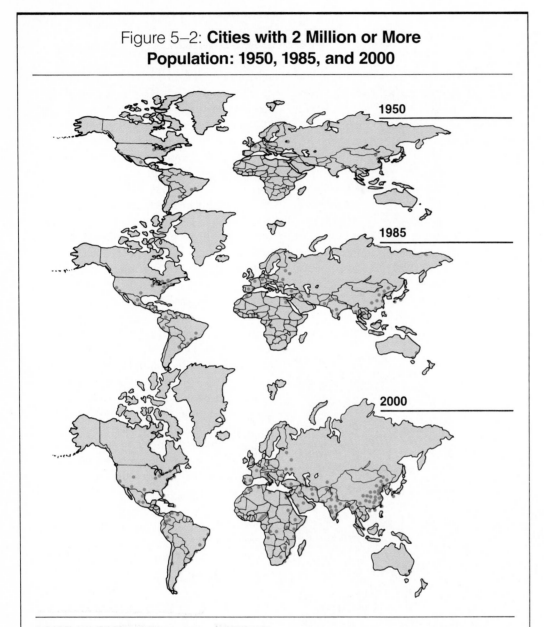

Figure 5–2: **Cities with 2 Million or More Population: 1950, 1985, and 2000**

The cities with the fastest growth rates at the present time are Lagos, Tehran, Bangalore, and Kinshasa with growth rates between 4.0 and 5.0 percent. In recent years, Mexico City's population grew by about 569,000 per year (3.7 percent), and São Paulo and Jakarta each have been growing by more than 3.5 percent annually during the past five years. In contrast, Tokyo's annual increase has been about 1.3 percent.

Source: Census Bureau, 1986.

is growing almost as fast as its urban population. And although the growth of the cities has affected village life, especially through the efforts of city-trained teachers, health officials, administrators, and storekeepers, it has had little effect on the social structure of rural India. Thus, as a whole, Indian society exhibits the extremes of rural isolation and urban dynamism, with all the chaos and poverty that are characteristic of societies undergoing major social change.

Throughout the twentieth century sociologists have devoted considerable study to urbanization and the changes that accompany it. The ways in which the growth of cities and metropolitan regions alters the surface of the planet are part of the sociological study of urbanization. So are questions about how cities change our experience of community and our relationships with others. Finally, sociologists continue to focus on the changing patterns of inequality and conflict that occur in metropolitan regions. The remaining three parts of this chapter explore these issues in greater detail.

THE URBAN LANDSCAPE

Urban Expansion

The effects of urbanization began to be felt in American society after the Civil War. As the population began to push into the West, waves of immigrants from Ireland, Germany, Italy, and many other parts of central and southern Europe streamed into the cities of the East. In the 1840s and 1850s, for example, approximately 1,350,000 Irish immigrants arrived in the United States, and in just twelve years, from 1880 to 1892, more than 1.7 million Germans arrived (Bogue, 1984). In other chapters we have more to say about the im-

pact of the great migrations from China and Korea and Latin America, the importation of slaves from Africa, and the large numbers of people of all races and ethnic groups who continue to arrive in our cities. The point here is that for well over a century North American cities have been a preferred destination for people from all over the world and have experienced numerous waves of newcomers since their period of explosive growth in the nineteenth century.

The science of sociology found early supporters in the United States and Canada partly because the cities in those nations were growing so rapidly. It often appeared that North American cities would be unable to absorb all the newcomers that were arriving in such large numbers. Presociological thinkers like Frederick Law Olmsted, the founder of the parks and recreation movement, and Jacob Riis, an advocate of slum reform, urged the nation's leaders to invest in improving the urban environment, building parks and beaches, and making better housing available to all (Cranz, 1982). As we saw in Chapter 1, these reform efforts were greatly aided by sociologists who conducted empirical research on the social conditions in cities. In the early twentieth century many urban sociologists lived in cities like Chicago that were characterized by rapid population growth and serious social problems. It seemed logical to use empirical research to construct theories about how cities grow and change in response to major social forces as well as more controlled urban planning.

The founders of the Chicago school of sociology, Robert Park and Ernest Burgess, attempted to develop a dynamic model of the city, one that would account not only for the expansion of cities in terms of population and territory but also for the patterns of settlement and land use within cities. They identified several factors that influence the physical form of cities. Among them are "transportation and communication, tramways and telephones, newspapers and advertising, steel construction and elevators—all things, in fact, which tend to bring about at once a greater mobility and a greater concentration of the urban populations" (Park, 1925, p. 2). The role of transportation is described in one of Park's essays:

This lunchtime scene in a downtown business district shows how people often seek opportunities for sociability in places where urban planners did not expect them to. William H. Whyte has shown that successful urban planning anticipates such needs and provides for them.

© Marc P. Anderson

The extent to which . . . an increase of population in one part of the city is reflected in every other depends very largely upon the character of the local transportation system. Every extension and multiplication of the means of transportation connecting the periphery of the city with the center tends to bring more people to the central business district, and to bring them there oftener. This increases the congestion at the center; it increases, eventually, the height of office buildings and the values of the land on which those buildings stand. The influence of land values at the business center radiates from that point to every part of the city. (1967/1926, pp. 57–58)

The Concentric-Zone Model. Park and Burgess based their model of urban growth on the concept of *natural areas*—that is, areas in which the population is relatively homogeneous and land is used in similar ways without deliberate planning. For example, "Every great city has its racial colonies, like the Chinatowns of San Francisco and New York, the Little Sicily of Chicago. . . . Most cities have their segregated vice districts . . . their rendezvous for criminals of various sorts. Every large city has its occupational suburbs, like the Stockyards in Chicago, and its residential enclaves, like Brookline in Boston" (Park, 1925, p. 10). They saw urban expansion as occurring through a series of "invasions" of successive zones or areas surrounding the center of the city. For example, migrants from rural areas and other societies "invaded" areas where housing was cheap. Those areas tended to be close to the places where they worked. In turn, people who could afford better housing and the cost of commuting "invaded" areas farther from the business district, and these became the Brooklines, Gold Coasts, and Greenwich Villages of their respective cities.

Park and Burgess's model, which has come to be known as the *concentric-zone model*, is portrayed in Figure 5-3. (Figure 5-4 applies the model to Chicago.) Because the model was based on studies of Chicago, its center is labeled "Loop," the term that is commonly applied to that city's central zone. Surrounding the central zone is a "zone in transition," an area that is being invaded by business and light manufacturing. The third zone is inhabited by workers who do not want to live in the factory or business district but at the same time need to live reasonably close to where they work. The fourth or residential zone consists of higher-class apartment build-

Figure 5–3: The Concentric-Zone Model

I Loop

Factory zone

II Zone in transition

III Zone of working people's homes

IV Residential zone

V Commuter zone

Source: Park and Burgess, 1925.

ings and single-family homes, and the outermost ring, outside the city limits, is the suburban or commuters' zone; its residents live within a 30- to 60-minute ride of the central business district (Burgess, 1925).

Studies by Park, Burgess, and other Chicago school sociologists showed how new groups of immigrants tended to become concentrated in segregated areas within inner-city zones, where they encountered suspicion, discrimination, and hostility from ethnic groups that had arrived earlier. Over time, however, each group was able to adjust to life in the city and to find a place for itself in the urban economy. Eventually many of the immigrants were assimilated into the institutions of American society and moved to desegregated areas in outer zones; the ghettos they left behind were promptly occupied by new waves of immigrants (Kasarda, 1989).

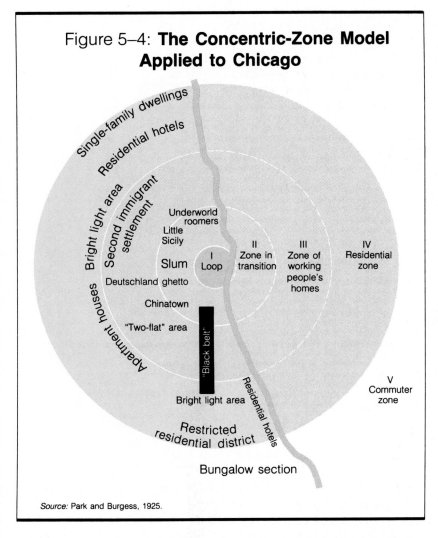

Figure 5–4: **The Concentric-Zone Model Applied to Chicago**

Single-family dwellings

Residential hotels

Bright light area

Second immigrant settlement

Apartment houses

Deutschland ghetto

Chinatown

"Two-flat" area

"Black belt"

Bright light area

Restricted residential district

Bungalow section

Underworld roomers

Little Sicily

Slum

I Loop

II Zone in transition

III Zone of working people's homes

IV Residential zone

V Commuter zone

Residential hotels

Source: Park and Burgess, 1925.

Note that each zone is continually expanding outward. Thus, Burgess wrote, "If this chart is applied to Chicago, all four of these zones were in its early history included in the circumference of the inner zone, the present business district. The present boundaries of the [zone of transition] were not many years ago those of the zone now inhabited by independent wage-earners" (p. 50). Burgess also pointed out that "neither Chicago nor any other city fits perfectly into this [model]. Complications are introduced by the lake front, the Chicago River, railroad lines, historical factors in the location of industry, the relative degree of the resistance of communities to invasion, etc." (pp. 50–51).

The Sector Theory. Although the concentric-zone model seemed to fit Chicago and some other American cities quite well, it was challenged by sociologists who sought to account for patterns of urban development that differed significantly from the model. In 1939, for example, Homer Hoyt proposed the *sector theory* of residential development. His research had shown that the high-income areas of many cities did not form a continuous zone, as Park and Burgess had suggested, but were located in one or more sectors of the city that extended outward along major transportation routes. These sectors tended to resemble wedges and were, Hoyt believed, a result of changes brought about by the increased use of automobiles. In 1964 Hoyt amended his theory. Noting that "the automobile and the resultant belt highways encircling American cities have opened up large regions beyond existing settled areas," he concluded that "future high grade residential growth will probably not be confined entirely to rigidly defined sectors" (p. 229).

The Multiple-Nuclei Model. In 1945 Chauncey Harris and Edward L. Ullman proposed a third model of urban expansion. Their model was based on the idea that modern industrial cities do not have a single center but, rather, have several nuclei around which different kinds of activities tend to cluster. This creates a number of specialized districts devoted to business activity, retailing, manufacturing, and so on. The development of these districts is related to the kinds of facilities available there. For example, retailers prosper in areas that are easily accessible to shoppers, whereas manufacturing requires large blocks of land near rail or water transportation routes and may be better situated in industrial "satellite" towns (such as Oakland, California, or Worcester, Massachusetts) that are on the outskirts of cities.

Metropolitan Areas

The classic Chicago school models of urban expansion failed to anticipate the enormous growth of urban areas since the mid-twentieth century. Although Hoyt revised his sector theory in an effort to take this trend into account, that theory cannot be applied to the rise of suburban communities with their own shopping centers or to the merging of cities and suburbs to form huge metropolitan areas. In addition, the early models of urban ecology were concerned with patterns of growth within a particular city, not with the urbanization of entire societies. This is not to say that the early models are no longer valid. The concentric-zone model remains useful for determining how the continual expansion of the city's commercial core affects land uses in areas farther from the center. The sector model is helpful in predicting the likely directions of growth when new highways or mass transit lines are constructed. The multiple-nuclei model helps in analyzing the growth or decline of particular kinds of urban settlements, such as satellite cities of steel-producing cities.

Megalopolis. After 1920 new metropolitan areas developed largely as a result of the increasing use of automobiles and the construction of a network of highways covering the entire nation. The shift to automobile travel brought former "satellite" cities within commuting distance of the major industrial centers, thereby adding to the size of those metropolitan areas. In the South and Southwest, new metropolitan areas developed. In fact, in recent years these have become the fastest-growing urban areas in the nation.

Since World War II, sociologists have been studying an increasingly important urban phenomenon: the emergence of large multinuclear urban systems. The term **megalopolis** is used to describe these vast complexes, whose total population is over 25 million. Jean Gottmann (1978) pointed out that a megalopolis is not "simply an overgrown metropolitan area"; rather, it is a system of cities distributed along "a major axis of traffic and communication" (p. 56). According to Gottmann, there are six megalopolises in the world today: the American Northeastern Megalopolis, the Great Lakes Megalopolis, the Tokaido Megalopolis in Japan, the megalopolis in England (the London area), the megalopolis of northwestern Europe (extending from Amsterdam to the Ruhr), and the Urban Constellation in China (centered on Shanghai). Three others appear to be developing: the Rio de Janeiro–São Paulo complex in Brazil, the Milan–Turin–Genoa triangle in northern Italy, and the urban swath extending from San Diego to the San Francisco Bay area.

A megalopolis is characterized by an "intertwined web of relationships between a variety of distinct urban centers . . . expressed partly in a physical infrastructure consisting of highways, railways, waterways, telephone lines, pipelines, water supply and sewage systems criss-crossing the whole area, and partly in more fluid networks, such as the flows of traffic, the movement of people and goods, the flows of telephone calls [and] of mail" (Gottmann, 1978, p. 57). Despite their interdependence, however, "the sizes and specializations of the various . . . components [of a megalopolis] are extremely varied, as demonstrated by the diverse characteristics of the cities, towns, villages, suburban and rural areas that form the vast system" (p. 57). Therefore a megalopolis can best be described as a huge social and economic mosaic.

The recent history of Los Angeles provides a good example of the development of a megalopolis (see Figure 5-5). Between 1960 and 1970 the population of Los Angeles increased by over 2 million, double the growth of Chicago and more than that of New York and San Francisco put together (Smith, 1968). Today the Los Angeles metropolitan area continues to grow, although at a somewhat slower rate. As a result of its extraordinary growth, the region must struggle to control the effects of air pollution from more than 3 million automobiles. Not only is smog a serious problem in the region, but Los Angeles must transport its water over long distances at an increasingly high cost, an environmental constraint that may eventually limit the growth of the entire region (Brown and Jacobson, 1987).

> *The term* megalopolis *is applied to large multinuclear urban systems that contain a variety of distinct urban centers.*

Decentralization. One effect of the growth of megalopolitan areas is *decentralization*, in which outlying areas become more important at the expense of the central city. This trend is not new. In the 1960s and 1970s large numbers of middle-income city dwellers moved to suburban areas while the poor remained in the central cities. Business and industry also moved to the suburbs, giving rise to widespread speculation that central cities would become a thing of the past. Recently, however, the central cities of some metropolitan areas, mainly New York, Philadelphia, and Chicago, have shown renewed vitality. Far from decaying, they have become major financial and cultural centers serving the needs of huge populations. On the other hand, medium-sized cities like Gary, Indiana, and Paterson, New Jersey, have suffered, since their central business districts have little to offer suburban dwellers in the way of financial services like banking and insurance or cultural institutions like theaters and symphony orchestras (Kornblum and Williams, 1978).

An important feature of megalopolitan areas is their diversity. These huge urban regions include many different kinds of communities: ethnic communities in both central cities and suburbs, middle-class "bedroom" suburbs, industrial towns, areas devoted to truck gardening or dairy farming, "second-home" communities (e.g., beachfront areas), and others. Each meets the economic and cultural needs of a specific urban population. Sociologists have devoted considerable study to these urban communities, and we discuss their findings in the next section.

URBAN COMMUNITIES

"The city," wrote Robert Park, is more than a set of "social conveniences—streets, buildings, electric lights, tramways, and telephones, etc.; something more, also, than a mere constellation of . . . courts, hospitals, schools, police, and civil functionaries of various sorts. The city is, rather, a state of mind, a body of

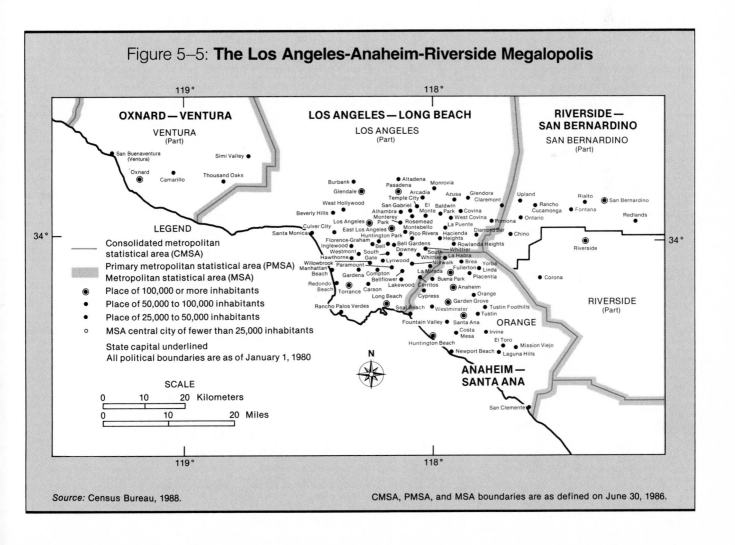

Figure 5–5: **The Los Angeles-Anaheim-Riverside Megalopolis**

Source: Census Bureau, 1988.   CMSA, PMSA, and MSA boundaries are as defined on June 30, 1986.

customs and traditions. . . . It is a product of nature, and particularly of human nature" (1925, p. 1).

The connection between the city and human nature has been a recurrent theme in literature throughout history. Many literary images of the city are negative. In the Bible, for example, the cities of Sodom and Gomorrah are symbols of the worst aspects of human nature. The poet Juvenal complained that Rome produced ulcers and insomnia and that it subjected its residents to burglars and dishonest landlords. American literature also contains many negative images of the city. Thomas Jefferson, for instance, wrote, "I view great American cities as pestilential to the morals, health, and the liberties of man." And Henry David Thoreau escaped from the city to Walden Pond in an effort to "rediscover his soul" (Fischer, 1976).

Social scientists who study cities have devoted a great deal of attention to the tension between "community" and "individualism" as it relates to life in cities. Country dwellers have been thought of as "happily ensconced in warm, humanly rich and supportive social relationships: the family, neighborhood, town," whereas city dwellers are "strangers to all, including themselves. They are lonely, not emotionally touching or being touched by others, and consequently set psychically adrift" (Fischer, 1976, p. 19). On the other hand, country dwellers are sometimes viewed as "stifled by conventionality, repressed by the intrusion and social control of narrow-minded kin, neighbors, and townsmen," whereas city dwellers are "free to develop individual abilities, express personal styles, and satisfy private needs" (p. 20). These views of the city are obviously contradictory, and much research has been devoted to the question of how urban life affects individuals and communities. In this section we look at some of the findings of that research and the theories of urban life that have been proposed on the basis of those findings.

The Decline-of-Community Thesis

Early studies of the nature and effects of urban life were dominated by efforts to evaluate the differences between rural and urban societies. They tended to reach rather gloomy conclusions. We have already noted that Ferdinand Tönnies described the process of urbanization as a shift from gemeinschaft (a community based on kinship ties) to gesellschaft (a society based on common interests). Émile Durkheim reached a similar conclusion: Small rural communities are held together by ties based on shared ideas and common experiences, whereas urban societies are held together by ties based on the interdependence of people who perform specialized tasks. Both Tönnies and Durkheim believed that urban life weakens kinship ties and produces impersonal social relationships.

In a 1905 essay entitled "The Metropolis and Mental Life," Georg Simmel focused on the effects of urban life on the minds and personalities of individuals. According to Simmel, cities bombard their residents with sensory stimuli: "Horns blare, signs flash, solicitors tug at coattails, poll-takers telephone, newspaper headlines try to catch the eye, strange-looking and strange-behaving persons distract attention . . . " (Fischer, 1976, p. 30). The urban dweller is forced to adapt to this profusion of stimuli [which Stanley Milgram (1970) termed *psychic overload*], and the usual way of adapting is to become calculating and emotionally distant. Hence the image of the city dweller as aloof, brusque, and impersonal in his or her dealings with others.

This view of the effects of urban life found further expression in the work of Louis Wirth, especially in his essay "Urbanism as a Way of Life" (1968/1938). Wirth began by defining the city as "a relatively large, dense, and permanent settlement of socially heterogeneous individuals" (p. 28). He then attempted to show how these characteristics of cities produce psychological stress and social disorganization. The primary psychological effect of urban life, according to Wirth, is a weakening of the individual's bonds to other people. Without such bonds the individual must deal with the crises of life alone, and often the result is mental illness. In other cases the city dweller, again because of the absence of close ties to friends or kin, lacks the restraints that

The decline-of-community thesis is based on the belief that urban life weakens kinship ties and produces impersonal social relationships.

might prevent him or her from engaging in antisocial behaviors.

Wirth linked social disorganization to the diversity that is characteristic of cities. Unlike rural residents, city dwellers work in one place, live in another, and relax in yet another. They divide their social lives among coworkers, neighbors, friends, and kin. Their jobs, life-styles, and interests are extremely varied. As a result, no single group, be it the family, the friendship group, or the neighborhood, controls their lives. In Wirth's view, this absence of social control produces *anomie*, or normlessness (see Chapter 9). Urban dwellers frequently do not agree on the norms that should govern their lives, and hence they are likely to either challenge existing norms or ignore them. Consequently, instead of being controlled by the norms of primary groups, the lives of city dwellers are controlled by impersonal agencies like banks and police forces.

One consequence of the impersonality of urban life, some argue, is greater callousness among city dwellers. An often-cited example is the case of Kitty Genovese, discussed in Chapter 7. After that episode, in which a young woman was murdered as thirty-eight residents of nearby apartments who heard her cries did nothing, many commentators called attention to the callous character of city dwellers. But subsequent research on bystander apathy revealed that the presence of many other people tends to diffuse the sense of responsibility. We are less likely to take action if we have reason to believe that someone else will do so (Hunt, 1985; Latané and Darley, 1970). In this sense, the bigger the city and the more one is surrounded by strangers, the more likely it is that such behavior will occur, but this does not mean that city dwellers are alienated from one another when they are among people they know, or that when alone they would not help someone in trouble. The fact that one is likely to feel less responsibility for others when one is surrounded by strangers may be a condition of city life, but it is hardly evidence for the thesis that urban life leads to the decline of community.

Subcultural theory sees the city as a mosaic of communities and intimate social groups.

Subcultural Theory

The idea that urbanization leads to the decline of community has been criticized on a number of grounds. Rural life is nowhere near as pleasant as some urban sociologists have assumed it to be; evidence of this is the almost magical attraction that cities often have for rural people ("How are you gonna keep 'em down on the farm after they've seen New Orleans?"). On the other hand, urban social disorganization is not as extensive as the early urban sociologists believed. Many city dwellers maintain stable, intimate relationships with kin, neighbors, and coworkers. Moreover, urban life is not necessarily stressful or anomic.

Urban Communities. A more recent view of urban life sees the city as a "mosaic of social worlds" or intimate social groups. Numerous studies have shown that the typical urban dweller does not resemble the isolated, anomic individual portrayed by Simmel and Wirth. In fact, communities of all kinds can be found in cities. Many urban dwellers, for example, are members of ethnic communities who have not become fully assimilated into the "melting pot" of American society and are unlikely to do so. They may be the children or grandchildren of immigrants who formed ethnic enclaves within large cities in the late nineteenth and early twentieth centuries, or they may be recent immigrants themselves, trying to build a new life in a strange culture.

But group ties among urban dwellers are not based solely on ethnicity. They may be based on kinship, occupation, life-style, and similar personal attributes (Fischer, 1976; Street et al., 1978; Suttles, 1972). Thus, many cities contain communities of college students, elderly people, homosexuals, artists and musicians, wealthy socialites, and so on. Although the members of any given group do not always live in the same neighborhood, they are in close touch with one another much of the time. Their sense of community is based not so much on place of residence as on the ability to come together by telephone, in special meeting places like churches or synagogues, or even in restaurants and bars (Fischer, 1976; Kornblum and Williams, 1978).

An example of this point of view, known as subcultural theory, is Illsoo Kim's (1981) detailed study of the Korean community in New York City. This growing ethnic community has developed since the passage of the Immigration Act of 1965, which eliminated the nationality quotas established earlier in the century. Largely because of population pressure in South Korea (which has led to overcrowded cities and high rates of unemployment), over 200,000 Koreans have immigrated to the United States since 1965. Most of them have settled in large metropolitan areas, with 80,000 finding new homes in New York City.

Like all immigrants, the Koreans have had to create a new way of life. They have had to find new ways of making a living, and they have had to adapt to a new culture. The first problem has been solved mainly by opening small businesses, the second by establishing neighborhoods where the immigrants can maintain their own culture while they and their children learn the values and norms of Western culture. Kim explains the Koreans' inclination to open small businesses—mainly grocery stores—in this passage:

Old-timers frequently tell newcomers that "running a *jangsa* (commercial business) is the fastest way to get ahead in America." The language barrier partly explains this inclination. . . . This is an insuperable barrier to most Korean immigrants; it deprives them of many opportunities. . . . This fact, combined with differences in both the skills demanded and the system of rewards in the United States, means that occupational status cannot be transferred from the homeland to the new land. A high proportion of Korean immigrants were thus forced to turn to small retail businesses. [1981, pp. 102–103]

Many of the businesses established by Korean immigrants are geared to Korean ethnic tastes and cultural needs. For example, the Koreans are often unwilling to change their diet and will buy most of their food from Korean-owned food stores. Other shops import books, gifts, magazines, and other items from South Korea. Numerous Korean travel agencies satisfy the immigrants' strong desire to visit their homeland. But Korean small businesses are not limited to serving the needs of the immigrant population. A growing number cater to all racial and ethnic groups and supply typically American goods and services.

In summing up the situation of Korean

immigrants in New York, Kim points out that "until they completely master the American language, education, and culture, Koreans will be forced to rely on one another" (p. 319). For this reason they are likely to maintain their own community within the city for at least two generations. However, in time their commitment to education and a better life will cause them to become more fully assimilated into American society, and their ties to the Korean community will be weakened.

The case of the Koreans echoes that of many other immigrant groups, both past and present, as well as that of other groups such as homosexuals and artists. The details may differ, but the tendency to establish ethnic or cultural enclaves in large cities is universal. In a well-known study titled *The Urban Villagers* (1962), Herbert Gans (1967, 1984) de-

In urban societies, where there are large numbers of people who are strangers to one another, sociologists have noted a propensity to wear identifying "uniforms" that indicate the kind of person one wishes to know and interact with.

scribed an Italian neighborhood in Boston. This community was a long-established one with many of the characteristics that are typical of ethnic communities everywhere. But at the time Gans did his research the neighborhood was being destroyed by an urban-renewal project. Its residents were forced to find new homes in other parts of the city, to join new churches, attend new schools, seek out new places to buy food and clothes. For some, the upheaval was so great that it produced depression and anomie (Fried, 1963).

It seems reasonable to conclude that the effects of urban life on communities and individuals are more complex than Durkheim, Simmel, and Wirth suggested. Certainly, social disorganization occurs in cities, but so does social *re*organization. Communities uprooted by urban renewal eventually may be re-formed in other parts of the city or its suburbs. The new community may be less homogeneous than the old one, but it is a community nonetheless.

The Suburbs. Like city dwellers, suburban dwellers have been said to lack the close attachments that are thought to characterize rural communities. In fact, before the late 1960s most social scientists had a rather dismal view of suburban life. Suburbs had grown rapidly after World War II as large numbers of middle-class Americans left the central cities in search of a less crowded, more pleasant life-style. Many suburban dwellers were corporate employees, and in the 1950s and early 1960s they became the subject of a widely held stereotype. The suburbs, it was said, were "breeding a new set of Americans, as mass produced as the houses they lived in, driven into a never ending round of group activity ruled by the strictest conformity. Suburbanites were incapable of real friendships; they were bored and lonely, alienated, atomized, and depersonalized" (Gans, 1967, pp. xxvii–xxviii).

In *The Levittowners*, a study of a new suburban community in New Jersey, Gans (1967) challenged this stereotype. He found that the residents of Levittown lost no time in forming attachments to one another. At first they associated only with their neighbors, but before long they formed more extensive associations based on shared interests and concerns. Moreover, far from being bored and isolated, a majority of the Levittowners were satisfied with their lives and felt that Levittown was a good place to live. Gans concluded that "new towns are merely old social structures on new land" (1967, p. vii). In other words, the contrasts between central-city and suburban life are generally exaggerated.

Other studies have reached similar conclusions, but they do show some differences between the lives of people in suburban and inner-city communities. In a review of research on patterns of interaction among suburban and urban neighbors, Claude Fischer and Robert M. Jackman (1976) found that the frequency of visiting among neighbors increases with distance from the central city. People who live in central-city neighborhoods tend to interact with friends and relatives who do not live in their immediate vicinity, whereas in the suburbs there is a more marked tendency for people to interact with, and then become friends with, their neighbors.

Although friendships with neighbors contribute to people's satisfaction with suburban life, there is evidence that women are less satisfied with suburban residence than men are (Fischer and Jackman, 1976). Men are likely to circulate more freely between city and suburb and to be involved in a greater variety of social worlds. But the women of suburban families are frequently homebound. They often feel cut off from the jobs and cultural life that the central city offers, and they are more dependent on whatever friends they can make and whatever work opportunities they can find in the suburban area.

Some recent research has focused on women who were born in suburban communities after the 1950s and never lived in other types of communities (Stimson, 1980; Wekerle, 1980). For example, Sylvia Fava (1985) found that younger women born in suburban communities do not think of suburban life as stifling or as limiting their opportunities. They may prefer to live in older, more diverse suburban communities within easy commuting distance of the jobs and nightlife of the central cities, but they normally do not feel that their suburban life-style is unsatisfactory. Similar findings are emerging among minority groups and people of working-class origins. These findings indicate that as metropolitan growth continues and the age and density of many suburban communities increase, it becomes increasingly difficult to distinguish between urban and suburban life.

CITIES AND SOCIAL CHANGE

In the preceding section we stressed the presence of a wide variety of communities and subcultures within cities. We saw that contemporary social scientists view the city as a place where many different communities coexist and thrive rather than as a place where people are isolated and do not have a feeling of belonging to a particular social group or community. At the same time, however, there is no escaping the fact that various urban communities are often in conflict. For example, ethnic and racial communities may clash in violent confrontations over such issues as the busing of children to achieve school integration. In this section we examine the origins and implications of such conflicts.

Social change in an urban society is likely to be felt most deeply by city dwellers, for it is in the cities that people are most densely congregated. In recent decades this has been the case in North America as manufacturing jobs have been "exported" to Asia and Latin America. As a result of this shift, American cities are undergoing massive social change. "America's major cities are different places today from what they were in the 1960s," concludes John Kasarda, one of the nation's foremost urban sociologists. New modes of transportation, new communication technologies like satellites and computers, and new industrial technologies (e.g., automation and recycling) are transforming our cities from production and distribution centers to administrative, financial, and information centers. "In the process," writes Kasarda, "many blue-collar jobs that once constituted the economic backbone of cities and provided em-

ployment opportunities for their poorly educated residents have either vanished or moved" (1989, p. 28). Many of these jobs have been replaced by "knowledge-intensive white-collar jobs with educational requirements that exclude many with substandard education." Table 5-3 shows vividly that the demand for individuals with less than a high school education is decreasing steadily in urban job markets.

Inequality and Conflict

As noted earlier, American cities and metropolitan regions have always attracted streams of migrants and immigrants. Migrants arrive from other parts of the nation—blacks from the rural South, Chicanos from the Southwest. Immigrants come from foreign lands—Ireland, Poland, China, Korea, Italy, and many others. Until the 1970s, except during economic depressions or recessions, the new arrivals had no difficulty finding work in the mills and factories that produced textiles, clothing, steel, rubber, glass, cars, and trucks. And much of their education was gained while working. Formal schooling was not as crucial to job success as it is today.

Today, although there are still many manufacturing jobs, it is much more difficult to make a good living at such a job. Within the cities, where the decline in manufacturing jobs has been greatest, the number of low-status jobs, especially in restaurants and other low-paying services, has increased. So has the number of highly paid jobs in management and the professions, positions that require high levels of education. At the same time, about 11 million legal immigrants have entered the country since the 1970s, usually settling in the cities (Steinberg, 1989). The result, often, has been fierce competition between immigrants and older residents.

The net effect of these trends is a growing gap between the "haves" and the "have-nots," especially in large cities (Silk, 1989). The study of *social stratification*—of patterns of inequality and how they produce entire classes of people with differing opportunities to succeed in life—is at the core of sociology and is discussed in detail in later chapters. Certainly the gap between those who enjoy

Table 5–3: **Percentage Distribution of Central-City Jobs, by Education Level of Jobholders, 1970–80**

Central City	Less than High School	High School Graduate	Some College	College Graduate
Baltimore				
1970	48.3	29.2	10.2	12.2
1980	29.6	32.3	19.4	18.6
Boston				
1970	29.4	36.4	16.8	17.5
1980	13/4	28.6	24.7	33.2
Chicago				
1970	37.5	32.3	15.4	14.7
1980	23.4	28.2	23.8	24.7
Cleveland				
1970	35.4	38.0	13.0	13.6
1980	20.7	36.8	22.5	20.1
Detroit				
1970	37.3	36.8	13.9	12.0
1980	21.1	32.8	25.8	20.3
New York				
1970	35.8	33.1	12.7	18.4
1980	22.0	28.8	21.2	28.0
Philadelphia				
1970	39.9	37.0	10.4	12.6
1980	23.2	36.3	18.4	22.0
St. Louis				
1970	43.4	33.0	11.0	12.5
1980	25.4	33.5	22.1	19.0
Washington, D.C.				
1970	22.7	31.9	17.7	27.8
1980	11.3	24.1	24.0	40.6

Source: Kasarda, J. D. "Urban Industrial Transition and the Underclass." *Annals of the American Academy of Political and Social Sciences, 501,* 26-47. Copyright 1989 by Sage Publications, Inc. Reprinted by permission of Sage Publications, Inc.

the good things in life and those who spend their lives simply trying to survive is not unique to cities. Small towns and villages also have affluent and poor residents. But the conflicts and social problems associated with social inequality are most visible in the cities. In many poor neighborhoods, for example, wealthier city dwellers are buying the buildings in which the poor live, forcing them to look elsewhere for homes. In neighborhoods where this occurs, the shops and stores that once catered to lower-income residents cannot afford the higher rents paid by stores that serve the wealthy newcomers. The older stores are often forced out of business. The process whereby poor and dilapidated neighborhoods are renovated by higher-income newcomers while poor residents and merchants are pushed out is known as *gentrification.*

Status Conflict. In the last section we noted that an urban-renewal project had dislocated large numbers of Italian Americans from their Boston neighborhood. Such projects have sometimes been labeled "urban removal" because they remove poor people from decaying neighborhoods and force them to find homes elsewhere. Recently urban renewal has fallen into disfavor, and "redevelopment" has become popular. Redevelopment does not involve the destruction of entire neighborhoods, but it may have similar effects. The planned redevelopment of Times Square in New York City, for example, is intended to restore a sleazy area to its former glory as an entertainment center. The goal is to make the area attractive to "decent" people and to eliminate the "low life"—prostitutes, drug and pornography dealers, and petty criminals—

that has made Times Square a symbol of vice throughout the world (Boggs and Kornblum, 1985; Mollenkopf, 1985).

Not everyone agrees that Times Square should be redeveloped. Owners of legal businesses in the area argue that they are being attacked unfairly, and they have fought the redevelopment plan in the courts. This is a typical instance of *status conflict*, in which different groups vie for territory, occupational advantages, and other benefits. Another example of this type of urban conflict is the Boston busing controversy, in which Polish and Irish residents of South Boston bitterly protested a court order requiring the busing of black schoolchildren into their neighborhood.

Some urban sociologists see the city as divided up into "defended neighborhoods" or territories (Suttles, 1972). This concept was originally developed by Park and Burgess, who viewed such neighborhoods as a type of "natural area" within the city. The defended neighborhood is a territory that a certain group of people consider to be their "turf" or base, which they are willing to defend against "invasion" by outsiders. Neighborhood defense is a common element of urban conflict, although the means used to defend neighborhoods may differ. For example, in wealthy suburban neighborhoods, "defense" takes the form of zoning regulations that establish minimum lot sizes of one acre or more. Such regulations effectively defend the neighborhood against invasion by people who cannot afford the large lots or by developers who would like to erect apartment buildings (Perin, 1977). In less affluent neighborhoods, defense is often conducted by neighborhood improvement groups, which sometimes engage in vigilante action when they fear racial "invasion" (Hamilton, 1969). In poor neighborhoods, defense is very often the province of street-corner gangs.

> *Status conflict, in which different groups compete for territory, jobs, and other benefits, is a frequent type of urban conflict.*

Racial Conflict. Perhaps the most common source of intergroup conflict in American cities has been racial tension. In the belief that the presence of black residents reduces the prestige of a neighborhood and lowers the value of real estate there, whites have resisted efforts by blacks to obtain housing in "their" neighborhoods. This resistance has taken a wide variety of forms, ranging from discrimination by real estate agents to outright violence against black families moving into white neighborhoods. When blacks have succeeded in gaining a foothold in previously all-white neighborhoods, many white families have sold their homes and moved to the suburbs.

Some neighborhoods, however (and their number has increased in recent years) have adapted successfully to the arrival of black residents. Again the reason seems to be the residents' concern for prestige, but in this case their concern is that a violent reaction to integration will give the neighborhood a bad name. According to one recent study, those who accept integration are not worried about "the physical image of the neighborhood, which requires visible contact to be evaluated, but [about] the press- and media-related public image which is transmitted to friends and associates outside the community" (Berry, Goodwin, Lake, and Smith, 1976, p. 260).

Despite the growing acceptance of racial integration in some neighborhoods, blacks remain highly segregated in central cities, which have been deserted by white middle-class families. This phenomenon, known as *white flight*, has traditionally been viewed as indicating that whites are unwilling to live in the same neighborhoods as blacks or to allow their children to attend the same schools. But upon closer analysis it appears that other factors besides intergroup conflict have contributed to the large-scale movement of whites to the suburbs. For example, suburbanization has occurred in cities that do not have large black populations. According to Thomas M. Guterbock (1976), the movement to the suburbs can be explained as much by the desire for less crowded living conditions (and the ability to afford private homes) as by racial tensions in the central cities. This view is supported by census data showing that blacks too are moving to suburban neighborhoods in increasing numbers (Kilson, 1981).

Conflict among groups in urban areas can eventually have beneficial results and lead to major social change. Thus, as the civil rights movement gained legislative victories in the late 1960s, activists turned their attention to problems like residential segregation in cities. Open-occupancy marches in Chicago, St. Louis, Cleveland, and other cities often led to violence, but they also produced interracial commissions to develop policies that would prevent the exclusion of blacks and other minorities from housing markets (Molotch, 1974).

For racial and ethnic minorities, the issue is not so much integration as the ability to establish or maintain a residential community while pursuing opportunities to build a better life. This is among the key findings of recent studies of immigrant groups in South Florida. In looking at the difficulties that Haitian and Cuban refugees encounter in finding jobs in the Miami area, Alejandro Portes and Alex Stepick (1985) found that Cubans could draw upon kin and ethnic networks in Miami neighborhoods in looking for jobs but that the Haitians had no such networks to help them adapt to their new environment.

Conclusion

"In current descriptions of the world," Raymond Williams (1973) writes, "the major industrial societies are often described as 'metropolitan'" (p. 279). By this he means not only that cities have spilled over their boundaries and urbanized vast areas in the suburbs and beyond, but also that at the center or core of these metropolitan regions are institutions that control the lives of people all over the globe. Metropolitan societies obtain food and vital raw materials from all parts of the world. Thus the ecology of the globe and the lives of most of the world's people are increasingly controlled by social processes centered in the metropolitan societies. But does this also mean that Isaac Asimov's vision of an urbanized world, with which we began this chapter, is becoming a reality?

"The city" and "the country" represent two kinds of settlements to us. One is densely populated and complex, with its networks of relationships and institutions. The other is more sparsely settled and marked by more personal attachments. But we also experience many other kinds of social environments: the university or college community, the vacation hideaway, the ethnic enclave within the city, the singles neighborhood, the hospital (which can seem as complex as a city), the suburban bedroom community (which can be as small as a rural village). In an urban environment these and many other types of communities abound. The image of the cement city with its skyscrapers and expressways devouring the rural landscape needs to be revised to reflect a metropolitan ecology marked by many kinds of communities and patterns of settlement.

Moreover, it is not accurate to think of urban society as having eliminated rural communities. Social change is rarely complete, a fact that applies to the transition from rural to urban life as much as it does to any other kind of social change. We speak of the decline of rural populations and of farming as an occupation, yet the idea of living in a semirural community on the outskirts of a metropolitan region has great appeal for many Americans. In fact, the last two censuses have revealed that small communities outside the central cities and older suburbs are the fastest-growing type of settlement in the United States. There gardens supplement income, hunting is a way of stocking the freezer, and fishing is both a popular pastime and a way of enhancing the family's diet. The rural community and its way of life may decline in importance in our culture, but such communities remain important to our economy.

In another sense, however, the urban core does dominate the world. The institutions of the metropolitan center produce and disseminate mass culture. By this means they control the creation of images of life in all kinds of communities. Those images may have their origins in communities outside the central city, as when country singers bring their songs to Nashville or theater people bring their plays or acting talents to urban producers. But even then the culture-producing institutions of the city—its theaters, its television and radio stations, its film and recording companies—transform them into cultural products for mass audiences. Increasingly, then, even the images of the country we see on our television sets are produced in the city. The city becomes the dominant human environment, and its influence pervades every culture.

CHALLENGES TO CONTEMPORARY SOCIETY

Planning Urban Environments

"**C**ities are fantastically dynamic places," comments Jane Jacobs, perhaps the most renowned contemporary writer on cities and urban life. "And this is strikingly true of their successful parts, which offer a fertile ground for the plans of thousands of people." Jacobs, who now lives and works in Toronto, has written extensively about the processes underlying the growth and decline of North American cities. She emphasizes that "people who are interested only in how a city 'ought' to look and uninterested in how it works will be disappointed." As an example, she presents the case of a large inner-city community where

there is a housing project with a conspicuous rectangular lawn which became an object of hatred to the project tenants. A social worker frequently at the project was astonished by how often the subject of the lawn came up . . . and how much the tenants despised it and urged that it be done away with. When she asked why, the usual answer was, "What good is it?" or "Who wants it?" Finally one day a tenant more articulate than the others made this pronouncement: "Nobody cared what we wanted when they built this place. They threw our houses down and pushed us here and pushed our friends somewhere else. We don't have a place around here to get a cup of coffee or a newspaper even, or borrow fifty cents. Nobody cared what we need. But the big men come and look at the grass and say, 'Isn't it wonderful! Now the poor have everything!'" . . .

There is a quality even meaner than outright ugliness or disorder, and this meaner quality is the dishonest mask of pretended order, achieved by ignoring or suppressing the real order that is struggling to exist and to be served. [1961, pp. 14–15]

Failure to learn how to understand and creatively control urban growth, Jacobs believes, is a longstanding problem in this and many other societies. Early in our history many Americans came to hate the congestion and seeming "unnaturalness" of cities and city people. They identified naturalness with the countryside. So as the population grew at an accelerating rate, people attempted to surround themselves with as much "nature" as they could, often in the form of ornamental shrubs and lawns, all separated by fences or other markers of private property. But this is mere toying with nature. It sentimentalizes the power of nature and, according to Jacobs, is dangerous:

Most sentimental ideas imply, at bottom, a deep if unacknowledged disrespect. It is no accident that we Americans, probably the world's champion sentimentalizers about nature, are at one and the same time probably the world's most voracious and disrespectful destroyers of wild and rural countryside. . . . Each day, several thousand more acres of our countryside are eaten by the bulldozers, covered by pavement, dotted with suburbanites who have killed the thing they thought they came to find. . . .

The . . . messes we create in this way become despised by their own inhabitants tomorrow. [They] lack any reasonable degree of innate vitality, staying power, or inherent usefulness as settlements. Few of them, and these only the most expensive as a rule, hold their attraction much longer than a generation; then they begin to decay in the pattern of city gray areas. [p. 445]

These are strong opinions based on sociological reasoning, and not all readers will agree with them. But few social scientists dispute Jacobs's basic point: Cities are natural formations and have a logic of growth that can be understood. Many mistakes in urban planning are made by people with good intentions but limited knowledge of the dynamics of population growth and urban settlement.

This perspective on the organization of urban space has many applications. In Chapter 2, for example, we noted the contribution of research by William H. Whyte to the planning of small public spaces in central-city business districts. Whyte's research asks how people define the spaces they use. In his analysis of the way people use and think about small parks and malls adjacent to high-rise office buildings, Whyte found that some of the most highly rated parks are also the ones that are most heavily used, which "demonstrates how great is the carrying capacity of urban space, given a sensitive design" (1980, p. 75). In this instance the sociologist can show the planner and designer what features and facilities will enhance positive perceptions and increase carrying capacity (the number of people who can use and enjoy an urban space like a small park).

There are also studies of how people actually use urban spaces. These are often highly critical of existing architectural styles. In a study that has influenced a generation of

planners and architects, Jacobs (1961) found that the style of a massive public-housing project or exclusive high-rise apartment building often creates what she terms "all-or-nothing" dilemmas for their residents. Walled off from the neighborhood below, the residents of these vertical ghettos often feel that they must either interact with their immediate neighbors or have little social life at all; the rest of the city is either out of their reach economically or perceived as a fearsome environment.

This and other sociological critiques of large-scale urban-renewal projects have contributed to the emergence of a less grandiose approach to urban planning. This new approach emphasizes community revitalization and reconstruction: It places more value on restoring existing housing and neighborhoods than on razing and rebuilding. In coming years this approach is likely to gain greater support among sociologists and others who study urban change and evaluate the effects of urban policy. Efforts to build affordable housing are already under way in many cities. The challenge faced by urban planners today is to design environments that meet the needs of the people who live and work there.

SUMMARY

Populations change as a consequence of births, deaths, out-migration, and in-migration. The *crude birthrate* is the number of births occurring during a year in a given population divided by the midyear population. The *crude death rate* is the number of deaths occurring during a year divided by the midyear population. The *rate of reproductive change* is the difference between the crude birthrate and the crude death rate for a given population. Since World War II the world population has been increasing at an annual rate of over 1.5 percent, which means that by the year 2000 it will have passed 6 billion.

The *demographic transition* is a set of major changes in birth- and death rates that has occurred most completely in urban industrial nations in the past 200 years. It takes place in three stages: (1) high birth- and death rates, (2) declining death rates, and (3) declining birthrates. These stages are accompanied by changes in the age composition of the population.

Urbanization is closely linked with rapid increases in population, but at the same time the nature of life in cities tends to limit the size of urban families. Cities grow primarily as a result of migration (which is often caused by population increases in rural areas), but new migrants do not find it easy to form families.

The increasing tendency of people throughout the world to live in cities has been referred to as the *urban revolution*. Not only are increasing proportions of the world's population living in cities, but the cities themselves are larger than ever before. The growth of cities in this century has given rise to the concept of the *metropolitan area*, in which a central city is surrounded by a number of smaller cities and suburbs that are closely related to it both socially and economically.

The growth of cities should be distinguished from *urbanization*, which refers to the proportion of the total population concentrated in urban settlements. The end result of urbanization is an "urban society." Not only do cities serve as the cultural and institutional centers of such societies, but urban life has a pervasive influence on the entire society.

Sociologists have devoted a great deal of study to the processes by which cities expand and to patterns of settlement within cities. An early model of urban expansion was the *concentric-zone model* developed by Park and Burgess. In this model a central business district is surrounded by successive zones or rings devoted to light manufacturing, workers' homes, higher-class apartment buildings and single-family homes, and a commuters' zone. To account for patterns of urban development that differed from this model, Homer Hoyt developed the *sector theory*, in which high-income areas are located in sectors extending outward along major transportation routes. A third model, the *multiple-nuclei theory*, was based on the idea that modern industrial cities have several nuclei around which different kinds of activities tend to cluster.

These classic models of urban expansion failed to anticipate the enormous growth of metropolitan areas since the mid-twentieth century. That expansion has occurred largely as a result of the increasing use of automobiles and the construction of a network of highways covering the entire nation. In some areas this growth has created large multinuclear urban systems that are described by the term *megalopolis*. One effect of the development of such areas is decentralization, in which outlying areas become more important at the expense of the central city.

Social scientists who have studied the effects of urban life have been particularly concerned with the tension between community and individualism as it relates to life in cities. Early studies of urban life tended to conclude that it weakens kinship ties and produces impersonal social relationships. Urban life was also thought to produce "psychic overload" and anomie. More recently these conclusions have been criticized by researchers who have found that many city dwellers maintain stable, intimate relationships with kin, neighbors, and coworkers and that urban life is not necessarily stressful or anomic.

Subcultural theory sees the city as a mosaic of social worlds or intimate social groups. Communities of all kinds can be found in cities. Those communities may be based on ethnicity, kinship, occupation, life-style, and similar personal attributes. Suburban dwellers also have been found to be far less bored and isolated than was previously supposed.

Occasionally various communities within cities come into conflict. Such conflict may arise out of different class interests or the conflicting goals of different status groups within the city. Some urban sociologists see the city as divided up into "defended neighborhoods" or territories whose residents attempt to protect them from "invasion" by outsiders.

Today the ecology of the globe and the lives of most of the world's people are increasingly controlled by social processes centered in urban societies. However, urban society has not eliminated rural communities. And urban environments themselves are not uniform; instead, they include many kinds of communities and patterns of settlement.

GLOSSARY

crude birthrate: the number of births occurring during a year in a given population divided by the midyear population (**p. 125**).

crude death rate: the number of deaths occurring during a year in a given population divided by the midyear population (**p. 125**).

rate of reproductive change: the difference between the crude birthrate and the crude death rate for a given population (**p. 126**).

demographic transition: a set of major changes in birth and death rates that has occurred most completely in urban industrial nations in the past 200 years (**p. 126**).

metropolitan area: a central city surrounded by a number of smaller cities and suburbs that are closely related to it both socially and economically (**p. 130**).

urbanization: a process in which an increasing proportion of a total population becomes concentrated in urban settlements (**p. 132**).

megalopolis: a complex of cities distributed along a major axis of traffic and communication (**p. 138**).

WHERE TO FIND IT

Books

The Population of the United States (Donald Bogue; Free Press, 1985). A compendium and discussion of demographic statistics by a leading American demographer and human ecologist.

The Apple Sliced (Vernon Boggs et al.; Bergin and Garvey, 1984). A fascinating collection of sociological studies of New York City by field researchers who know the city well and are able to describe its institutions in vivid terms.

The Social Construction of Communities (Gerald Suttles; University of Chicago Press, 1972). An important theoretical statement; shows how sociology explains phenomena like territoriality and the formation of neighborhoods and communities.

Relations in Public (Erving Goffman; Harper & Row, 1971). Here Goffman's brilliance in analyzing social interaction is applied to the study of street life in urban environments.

The Contested City (John Mollenkopf; Princeton University Press, 1985). Shows how economic transformations and changes in political institutions are affecting urban growth and urban life in the United States.

Journals

Population and Development Review A journal that presents international research on population change and the effects of population variables on other aspects of social and economic development. A valuable source of comparative data and studies of population problems in the third world.

Urban Affairs Quarterly A leading journal of original research on urban social change.

Demography A journal that publishes demographic research and reviews of population studies, including comparative and historical studies.

Other Sources

Urban Affairs Annual Reviews (Sage Publications). Annual volumes on social change in urban regions, focusing on the impact of technologies and changing economic institutions on urban social classes and city governments.

Demographic Yearbook Published annually by the United Nations, Department of International Economic and Social Affairs.. Presents statistics on population, birth and death rates, marriage and divorce, and economic characteristics.

Population Bulletins Four in-depth population reports and two wall charts (world and U.S. population data sheets) are published annually by the Population Reference Bureau.

VISUAL SOCIOLOGY

Favelas in Brazil

These photographs by Janice Perlman provide a fascinating glimpse of life in the squatter settlements and shantytowns that typically surround the rapidly growing cities of Latin America, Asia, and Africa. In Rio de Janeiro, the shantytowns, or *favelas*, are perched on hillsides above the more affluent commercial and residential core of the city. This pattern is both a feature of Rio's hilly landscape and a consequence of the rising cost of land in the city.

The favelas that Perlman studied were subsequently burned by the authorities, the land fenced off and hidden behind advertising signs to await more lucrative urban development. Many of the inhabitants were relocated to the sterile, inadequate row houses shown here.

Many Brazilian social scientists and political and business leaders told Perlman that the inhabitants of the favelas were mainly shiftless men who were marginal to the legitimate institutions of Brazilian society. They had "one foot in the countryside and another in the city," or they were too involved in crime or hustling to settle down to regular employment. Yet Perlman's demographic research showed that somewhat more women than men lived in the favelas and that more than 60 percent of the adult residents were married and living in nuclear-family households. More than 80 percent were recent migrants to the city from the countryside.

In her book, *The Myth of Marginality* (1976), Perlman shows that the very poverty of the favelados made a major contribution to the wealth of those who labeled them as failures. By working "off the books" as servants, unskilled laborers, part-time restaurant workers, and the like, they provided low-cost goods and services to the more secure labor force, thereby helping to keep the cost of living down. Perlman therefore argues for improving life in the favelas by making the land available to their residents rather than wiping them out.

Photographs by Janice Perlman

PART THREE
SOCIAL DYNAMICS

From a helpless, entirely self-centered being, the human infant develops into a person capable of performing roles in a wide variety of social groups. Those groups, in turn, often develop and change—a small business founded by a few close friends, for example, may expand into a complex corporation with a structure far different from that of the original group. Likewise, the structure of an entire society may change as people find new ways of making a living and new ways of organizing to protect their interests. In response to such changes, some people may turn to crime or other socially disvalued behaviors, and others may form protest movements that seek to change the social order.

In this part of the book we cover many of the processes that seem to account for social stability and change. In Chapter 6 we discuss socialization, the process by which individuals become fully participating members of their society. One major outcome of socialization is the ability to function in groups, the subject of Chapter 7. Chapter 8 shows how the members of a society are sorted into social layers or strata and how a society's stratification system changes as its economic and political structure changes. Chapter 9 discusses how and why people deviate from the norms of their culture and how such deviance is related to social stratification. Chapter 10 looks at collective behavior and social movements, phenomena that involve large numbers of people in a society and often bring about major social change, and Chapter 11 summarizes the ways in which sociologists think about and conduct research on the changes that affect the daily lives of people in societies throughout the world.

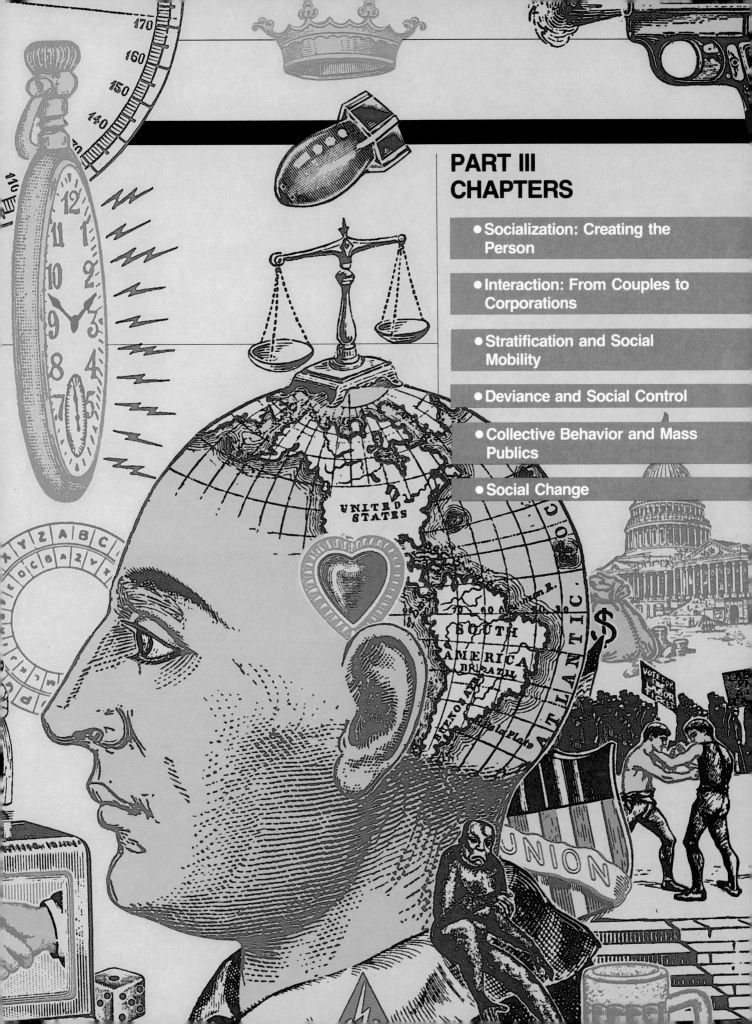

PART III
CHAPTERS

- Socialization: Creating the Person

- Interaction: From Couples to Corporations

- Stratification and Social Mobility

- Deviance and Social Control

- Collective Behavior and Mass Publics

- Social Change

CHAPTER OUTLINE

- **The Meaning of Socialization**

- **Nature Versus Nurture**
  - Behaviorism
  - Feral Children
  - The Need for Love
  - Changing Group Norms: Robbers Cave

- **The Social Construction of Personality**
  - Freud's Theory of Personality
  - Interactionist Models of the Self
  - Erikson's Theory of Development
  - Theories of Moral Development

- **Socialization and Human Environments**
  - The Micro-Environment
  - The Larger Social Environment

- **Agents of Socialization**
  - The Family
  - The Schools
  - The Community
  - The Peer Group
  - The Mass Media

- **Gender Socialization**

- **Socialization and Social Change**

Julia Gaines

Triplets Robert Shafran, David Kellman, and Eddie Galland on the fifth anniversary of their reunion

CHAPTER 6

SOCIALIZATION: CREATING THE PERSON

The cafeteria was crowded when Lisa sat down at her usual table with a cup of coffee. Her friends had not yet arrived from their classes. Lisa could not take her eyes off the young man across from her, who was deep in conversation with a friend. He was round-faced, with a shock of curly hair, twinkling eyes, and a deep, ready laugh. It has to be him, she thought. She had not seen him since their high school graduation two years earlier, but of course it was him.

"Hey, Eddie!" She broke into his conversation, "when did you start school here?"

The friendly-faced youth looked at her blankly, as if she were a complete stranger. "Do I know you?" he asked sheepishly.

Lisa felt her face flush. "Eddie, are you serious? You don't recognize me—Lisa? We went through four years of high school together."

"I'm sorry, Lisa. I didn't go to high school around here at all. But you're not the first person to call me Eddie. My name's Bob, but there must be someone around here named Eddie who looks a lot like me."

Lisa relaxed a bit and laughed. "A lot? Try *exactly*. My friend Eddie not only looks like you but laughs exactly the way you do, drinks coffee the same way, everything. I've got to get you two together."

This encounter in a cafeteria at Sullivan County Community College was the beginning of one of the most unusual episodes in the history of child adoption. Lisa soon arranged to have Eddie and Bob meet. They indeed looked alike. It turned out, in fact, that they were identical siblings who had been separated at birth and raised in different families. Each boy knew he had been adopted, but neither knew about the other. They were delighted to find each other and took to each other instantly. The joy of their meeting was noted in a feature story in the local paper, accompanied by a picture of the brothers.

Then, at another local college, on the other side of the metropolitan area, a visiting friend showed another group of students the story in the paper. The students were stunned when they realized that they knew a third boy, David, who looked exactly like Eddie and Bob. Again a meeting was set up, and amid much weeping and laughter "The Three," as they soon came to be called, were reunited.

The brothers were identical triplets who had been adopted in infancy by three different families. Neither they nor their adoptive parents had any knowledge of the others' existence until these meetings, which occurred when all three boys were in college. And to many people who knew them, first individually and then as brothers, the most uncanny aspect of the story was the degree to which they resembled each other, not only physically but also in their mannerisms, disposition, likes and dislikes, sense of humor, and much more.

"The Three" became celebrities. Overjoyed to have found each other, they moved in together. And since they were all extremely outgoing and humorous, they developed a comedy act, working as performing waiters in a nightclub. Recently they opened a restaurant in Manhattan appropriately named "The Triplets."

THE MEANING OF SOCIALIZATION

The story of the triplets raises the age-old question of whether the most important influence on human beings is their social environment or their innate genetic endowment. In this instance genetics appears far more significant than upbringing in explaining why the triplets were so similar in behavior as well as in appearance. But to better understand this and related issues, it will be helpful first to define some essential terms and concepts.

Socialization is the term sociologists use to describe the ways in which people learn to conform to their society's norms, values, and roles. The processes whereby we learn to behave according to cultural norms—that is, the way we learn our culture—make possible the transmission of culture from one generation to the next. In this way the culture is "reproduced" in the next generation (Danziger, 1971; Parsons and Bales, 1955). Socialization occurs throughout life as we learn new norms in new groups and situations. However, for purposes of analysis, socialization can be divided into three major phases. The first of these is *primary socialization*. It refers to all the ways in which the newborn individual is molded into a social being—that is, into a growing person who can interact with others according to the expectations of society. Primary socialization occurs within the family and other intimate groups in the child's social environment. *Secondary socialization* occurs in later childhood and adolescence, when the child leaves the family for schooling and comes under the influence of adults and peers outside the household and immediate family. *Adult socialization* is a third stage, one in which the person learns the norms associated with new statuses such as wife, husband, journalist, programmer, grandparent, or nursing home patient (Danziger, 1971).

There are a number of unresolved and highly controversial issues in the study of socialization. First, what is the relative strength of biological and social influences in creating the person? Second, how does the person's sense of self become established? Third, how do different social environments, such as the affluent suburban school or the slum neighborhood or the military boot camp, influence socialization? And fourth, what are the limits on what socialization can accomplish, and what are the results of failures of socialization? In this section of the chapter we will explain the significance of these questions and their implications for research on socialization.

Nature Versus Nurture. The nature–nurture debate is about whether what people become—their personalities, their achievements, their ways of interacting with others, and other aspects of their behavior—is influenced primarily by their genetic makeup or by the social environment in which they are raised. In the case of the triplets, the similarity of their personalities and mannerisms, despite their having been raised apart, seems to offer evidence that such traits may have a strong genetic component. This is the "nature" side of the nature–nurture argument, which attributes individual characteristics largely to biological factors. But what about learning in social environments? Are not the influences of parents, other adults, and peers just as important to the formation of the personality as biological factors? In the case of the triplets, because each child was raised in a comfortable home with caring parents, and because each was roly-poly and curly-haired, perhaps the combination of a secure environment and a friendly appearance caused others to expect them to be good-humored and good-natured. This is the "nurture" side of the argument. As we will see shortly, this issue is a source of continuing controversy among social scientists.

The Social Construction of the Self. Another subject that interests sociologists and psychologists is how a person develops a self. When sociologists speak of the self, they are talking about our ability to take roles in human groups and to imagine ourselves in other people's roles. To assume those roles we must be able to hold internal conversations with our "selves." We are forever telling ourselves

> *Socialization is the means by which we learn to behave according to the norms of our culture.*

how to act, how we should have acted, or how we feel someone else should have acted in response to our own actions. The ways in which the self develops through social interaction in childhood and throughout life are captured in the phrase "the social construction of the self."

Consider this example. In a famous study of the influence of peers on individual behavior, William F. Whyte (1943) found that the athletic performance of street-corner boys in Boston reflected the rank they held in their peer group, regardless of their actual ability. A boy who was not considered a leader yet was a good bowler would rarely defeat a boy who had less skill but more prestige in the group. Each member of the group knew how he was expected to perform and would "live up" (or down) to that expectation. In this way the members' shared definitions about what each boy could do tended to become reality in the boy's actual behavior. The peer group thus exerted an immense influence on each boy's conception of himself.

Social Environments and Socialization.

Suppose one of the triplets had been raised in a home in which one of the parents was an alcoholic and there was a great deal of conflict over money. Suppose also that the family eventually broke apart, creating additional conflict over where the child would live. It is likely, though not assured, that these difficult experiences would have caused him to develop personality traits that the other triplets did not share, such as mistrust of others, depression, self-doubt, and pent-up feelings of resentment and anger. Once he had been reunited with his siblings, perhaps this less fortunate triplet would have become more cheerful and self-assured as a result of his experiences in a new, more positive adult environment.

As this hypothetical example shows, the environment in which a person is socialized has a powerful effect on his or her personality and behavior. But because socialization takes place over an entire lifetime, the influences of new social environments can bring out new traits and change patterns of behavior. This means that we must think of socialization as occurring in many different settings, some of which are more desirable than others. For example, although most children receive their primary socialization at home, a significant number do not. Although most elderly people live at home as part of a family, a growing number do not. More than 557,000 Americans are in prisons and about 42,000 are in training schools for juvenile delinquents, 17,000 in juvenile detention centers, and 38,000 in homes for dependent and neglected children (*Statistical Abstract*, 1989). As a result of various changes in American society—such as changes in the stability of marriages, rates of teenage pregnancy, and the ability of people to love and care for their children—the range of social environments is more diverse today than at any time in the past.

She was having a great time with that spaghetti until her father came back into the kitchen. As part of the socialization that will make her a well-functioning adult, this child will soon learn to feel both dirty and silly with food in her hair.

© Reginald Wickham

Agents of Socialization.

Attention to the changing environments in which socialization occurs leads to research on the effects of social institutions like the family, the schools, the military, and the media in creating the kinds of people we observe in our society. We can call these social institutions *agents of socialization* to the extent that their messages, their influences, and the roles they portray influence people to behave in characteristic ways. A term in the Marine Corps, for example, teaches young men to be disciplined fighters with deep loyalty to their peers. A stint as a paratrooper may socialize a young woman to take more daring roles in other areas of her life than she might have before her military experience. Agents of socialization continue to exert their influence long after direct socialization has occurred.

Failures of Socialization. In this chapter we are concerned primarily with the socialization of "normal" members of society—people who are able to perform roles, to feel empathy for others, to express emotions and yet control feelings that are antisocial, to nurture others and raise children who will also be able to nurture, and to take on new roles as they grow older. But the failures of socialization can also tell us a great deal about what is involved in creating the social being. The case of Charles Manson provides an example. Shortly before he was convicted for his part in the Tate–LaBianca murders, one of the bloodiest multiple murders in American history, Manson had been released from prison after serving a ten-year term. In fact, Manson, who was born in a state penitentiary, spent twenty-two of his first thirty-five years in more than a dozen penal institutions. His history is one of complete neglect. He was beaten with a heavy paddle, so he beat others. He was sodomized, so he sodomized others at knifepoint. In fact, he was so undersocialized for life outside prison that before his last release he pleaded to be allowed to stay there.

The issue in cases like Manson's is not whether we should excuse what such individuals have done but whether we can learn from their tragedies so as to prevent others. And scientists, biological and social, still have a good deal to learn. Socialization is an extremely complex process for each individual. Some people who were abused and neglected can nonetheless become good parents, despite the odds. Others who seem to have experienced all the right influences can end up doing evil things, again despite the odds (Wrong, 1961). Even if we could trace all the social influences on a person's development, there would remain many unanswered questions about the combined influences of the person's social experiences and his or her genetic potential. Again the nature–nurture issue looms large and requires that we give it careful consideration.

NATURE VERSUS NURTURE

In the section on sociobiology in Chapter 4 we discuss the debate about cultural versus biological influences on human behavior. Here we will turn again to this debate as it pertains to questions of human potential and development. We examine several areas of research on the relative importance of biological factors and learning in the development of the personality.

Behaviorism

As is noted in Chapter 4, sociobiology is a contemporary form of biological determinism in which it is asserted that human behavior is caused or shaped by biological factors like instincts. The opposing theory, **behaviorism**, asserts that individual behavior is not determined by instincts or any other "hardware" in the individual's brain or glands. Rather, all behavior is learned.

Behaviorism traces its origins to the work of the Russian psychologist Ivan Pavlov (1902). Pavlov's experiments with dogs and humans revealed that behavior that had been thought to be entirely instinctual could in fact be shaped or **conditioned** by learning situations. Pavlov's dog, one of the most famous subjects in the history of psychology, was conditioned to salivate at the sound of a bell. The dog would normally salivate whenever food was presented to him. In his experiment, Pavlov rang a bell whenever the dog was fed. Soon the dog would salivate at the sound of the bell alone, thereby showing that salivation, which had always seemed to be a purely biological reflex, could be a conditioned, or learned, response as well.

The American learning psychologist John B. Watson carried on Pavlov's work with an equally famous series of experiments on "little Albert," an eleven-month-old boy. Watson conditioned Albert to fear baby toys that were thought to be inherently cute and cuddly, such as stuffed white rabbits. By presenting

The nature–nurture debate is about whether human development is influenced primarily by genetic makeup or by the social environment in which one is raised.

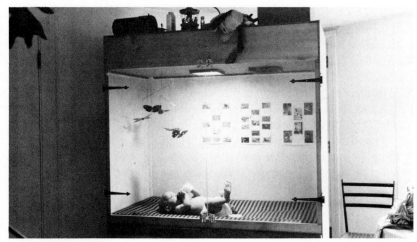

B. F. Skinner and his colleagues developed this crib to enable researchers to control every aspect of an infant's physical and social environment. In this way the researchers could be sure exactly what stimuli the infant was receiving and could measure their effects on learning and development.

these objects to Albert at the same time that he frightened him (i.e., presented a negative stimulus), Watson showed that the baby could be conditioned to fear any fuzzy white object, including Santa Claus's beard. He also showed that through the systematic presentation of white objects accompanied by positive stimuli he could "extinguish" Albert's fear and cause him to like white objects again.

On the basis of his findings Watson wrote, "The cry of the behaviorist is, 'Give me the baby and my world to bring it up in and I'll make it crawl and walk; I'll make it climb and use its hands in constructing buildings of stone or wood; I'll make it a thief, a gunman, or a dope fiend.' The possibility of shaping in any direction is almost endless" (1926, p. 35).

B. F. Skinner carried behaviorism even further by developing more effective techniques of shaping behavior using **operant conditioning**. Any kind of behavior could be an *operant*, a behavior that is shaped in the conditioning process.

For example: An infant is given food; it eats. The food is the stimulus; eating is the response. But the mother wants the infant to sit up straight while eating. She waits until the baby stops squirming for a moment and assumes the desired position. Then she offers the food. Before long the hungry child automatically takes the correct position when seated at the table. The unconditioned response to the food stimulus is eating; the conditioned response is the taking of the desired position. The baby's natural squirming is the operant, a feature of behavior that originally had nothing to do with the stimulus–response

pattern. By waiting until the squirming results momentarily in the desired position before offering the food, the mother *shapes* the stimulus–response pattern.

Skinner and his followers have been quick to point out that conditioning is more complicated than this example suggests and that it is never a one-way process. When the mother rewards the baby with food, she is also likely to show her approval in other ways, such as smiling. Thus, the baby's smiling behavior is also being shaped—or is the baby shaping the mother's smiling behavior? No doubt the child and the mother shape and socialize each other in their respective roles. Recognizing the reciprocal nature of conditioning, many sociologists use variations on Skinner's model to demonstrate how systems of exchange and reward regulate our behavior throughout life.

Behaviorists believe that we are constantly engaging in operant conditioning whether we know it or not. Because scientists believe that almost all human behavior results from learning through various types of conditioning, they think that societies should use conditioning to change the behavior of their members and thereby ensure that socialization has the desired outcomes. This rather radical viewpoint is presented in Skinner's utopian novel, *Walden II* (1948), in which an ideal community eliminates violence, guilt, anxiety, jealousy, and other problems of human life through the careful conditioning of its members.

It is easy to see that behaviorism and sociobiology are at the two extremes of the nature–nurture debate. At one extreme, the sociobiologists assert that there are sets of genes that play a major role in the development of the personality. Homosexuality, aggressiveness, altruism, and other traits have been listed as genetically transmitted, although the specific sets of genes responsible for these traits have not yet been discovered. At the other extreme, the behaviorists deny the need to look any further than the learning process for the mechanisms of socialization. The basic principles of learning seem to explain behavior so well that the behaviorists see no reason to seek any other explanation.

In the history of social science the nature–nurture debate has taken many turns. The claims of the biological determinists have reappeared many times because there is clearly a dimension of individual development that is strongly influenced by biological factors. It is equally clear, however, that biological factors alone are not sufficient for socialization to occur. In this regard it is valuable to review some case studies of infants reared in extreme isolation—that is, infants who had no opportunity whatsoever to learn from humans. These cases demonstrate that to become fully human a person must have caring human attention. We also review some experimental evidence that indicates how changes in a group's norms can produce striking changes in behavior that are completely independent of biological differences between individuals.

Feral Children

The idea that children might be raised apart from society, or that they could be reared by wolves or chimpanzees or some other social animal, has fascinated people since ancient times. Romulus and Remus, the legendary founders of Rome, were said to have been raised by a wolf. The story of Tarzan, a boy of noble birth who was abandoned in Africa and raised by apes, became a worldwide bestseller early in this century and has intrigued readers and movie audiences ever since. However, modern studies of children who have experienced extreme isolation cast doubt on the possibility that a truly unsocialized person can exist.

Until quite recently, the discovery of a **feral child** (literally, "untamed child") always seemed to promise new insights into the relationship between biological capabilities and socialization (Davis, 1947). Each case of a child raised in extreme isolation was looked upon as a natural experiment that would reveal the effects of lack of socialization on child development. Once the child was brought under proper care, studies were undertaken to determine how well he or she functioned. Invariably those studies showed that victims of severe isolation were able to learn but that they did so far more slowly than children who had not been isolated in early childhood (Malson, 1972).

Today it is generally recognized that cases of so-called feral children involve a severe

form of mental retardation or autism that either is induced as a result of the child's rejection by its parents and subsequent isolation or else is present at birth as a result of innate disabilities. In fact, it is likely that early signs of developmental retardation may have led to the child's abandonment in the first place. None of the recorded cases of feral children has allowed investigators to determine which of these possibilities is correct (Bettelheim, 1959). The most we can say about extreme isolation in childhood is that it causes lasting damage to the individual.

The Need for Love

Despite their lack of firm conclusions, studies of children reared in extreme isolation pointed researchers in an important direction: They suggested that lack of parental attention could result in retardation and early death. In studies that compare children reared in orphanages and other group settings with children reared in conventional families, much more is known about the life histories of individual subjects. The researcher therefore can control for the effects of age, race, initial intelligence, and other variables by matching subjects in institutions with comparable subjects in families. If both sets of subjects are the same in terms of the selected variables, any differences observed can be said to have been caused by the experience of being reared in one setting or the other. Such studies have shown over and over again that children reared in orphanages and other residential care facilities are more likely to develop emotional problems, such as depression and passivity, and to be retarded in their cognitive development (e.g., vocabulary) than comparable children reared by their parents (Goldfarb, 1945; Rutter, 1974; Spitz, 1945).

In a series of studies that have become classics in the field of socialization and child development, the primate psychologist Harry Harlow showed that infant monkeys reared apart from other monkeys never learned how to interact with other monkeys (Harlow and

The need for parental attention and love has been demonstrated by studies of primates and of children reared in isolation and in residential care facilities.

In a famous series of experiments, the primate psychologist Harry Harlow showed that an infant monkey would cling to a terrycloth-covered "mother" in preference to a similarly shaped wire "mother." If the surrogate mother could provide some "cuddle comfort" to the baby, Harlow observed, the infant's development would be more normal than that of infants that were deprived of even this minimal degree of warmth and nurturance.

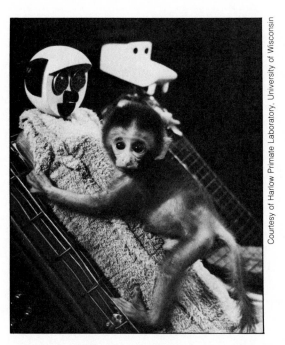

Courtesy of Harlow Primate Laboratory, University of Wisconsin

Harlow, 1962); they could not refrain from aggressive behavior when they were brought into group situations. When females who had been reared apart from their mothers became mothers themselves, they tended to act in what Harlow could only describe as a "ghastly fashion" toward their young. In some cases they even crushed their babies' heads in their teeth before handlers could save them. Although it is risky to generalize from primate behavior to that of humans, these studies of the effects of lack of nurturance bear a striking resemblance to studies of child abuse in humans. This research generally shows that one of the best predictors of abuse is whether the parent was also abused as a child (Kempe and Helfer, 1980; Kempe and Kempe, 1978; Keniston, 1977; Polansky et al., 1981).

These findings confirm our intuitive knowledge that nurturance and parental love play a profound, though still poorly understood, role in the development of the individual. Further evidence of the importance of nurturance can be seen in the life of Helen Keller, the blind, deaf, and mute girl who eventually captured millions of hearts with her moving articles and speeches. The story (told in Box 6-1) of how Keller's teacher rescued her from the prison of her mind is a stunning example of the triumph of loving nurturance over biological limitations. But Keller's story could be interpreted as an ex-

traordinary case in which a unique young woman responded to the love, teaching, and discipline of a gifted teacher. We turn therefore to a landmark experiment dealing with the influence of changing social norms on some very normal children's groups.

Changing Group Norms: Robbers Cave

In a famous demonstration of the influence of social environment on individual behavior, Muzafer Sherif and his colleagues (1961) showed that it is possible to create environments that socialize individuals for competition and intergroup hostility. When the environment is changed so as to promote cooperation and intergroup friendship, *resocialization* takes place and new patterns of intergroup relations emerge. Sherif's study is known as the Robbers Cave experiment because it took place at a Boy Scout camp in Robbers Cave State Park in Oklahoma.

Shortly before the summer of 1954, Sherif and his colleagues recruited twenty-two eleven-year-old boys, all of whom had average IQ scores and came from two-parent, moderate-income, white, Protestant families. This homogeneous group was selected in order to eliminate the possible influences of gender, intelligence, income, religion, race, and family situation. The boys were also rated by their teachers on athletic ability, popularity, other skills such as music and art, and previous camp experience. Using these background data, the experimenters divided the boys into two groups that were matched in terms of size, skills, camp experience, and other characteristics. In evaluating this important research, we need to keep in mind that because of the way the sample was selected, we cannot know how differences in gender or race or social-class background might have affected the outcome. The experimenters made a choice to study only white males, a choice that would be more severely criticized if it were made today.

The boys were told that they would be attending a summer camp, and their parents were informed that the camp, operating under the auspices of the University of Oklahoma, was devoted to the experimental study of interaction within and between teams. Par-

Box 6–1: **From Solitude to Society**

The most important day I remember in all my life is the one on which my teacher, Anne Mansfield Sullivan, came to me. I am filled with wonder when I consider the immeasurable contrast between the two lives which it connects. It was the third of March, 1887, three months before I was seven years old.

The morning after my teacher came she led me into her room and gave me a doll. The little blind children at the Perkins Institution had sent it and Laura Bridgman had dressed it; but I did not know this until afterward. When I had played with it a little while, Miss Sullivan slowly spelled into my hand the word "d-o-l-l." I was at once interested in this finger play and tried to imitate it. When I finally succeeded in making the letters correctly I was flushed with childish pleasure and pride. Running downstairs to my mother I held up my hand and made the letters for doll. I did not know that I was spelling a word or even that words existed; I was simply making my fingers go in monkey-like imitation. In the days that followed I learned to spell in this

uncomprehending way a great many words, among them *pin*, *hat*, *cup* and a few verbs like *sit*, *stand*, and *walk*. But my teacher had been with me several weeks before I understood that everything has a name.

One day, while I was playing with my new doll, Miss Sullivan put my big rag doll into my lap also, spelled "d-o-l-l" and tried to make me understand that "d-o-l-l" applied to both. Earlier in the day we had had a tussle over the words "m-u-g" and "w-a-t-e-r." Miss Sullivan had tried to impress it upon me that "m-u-g" is *mug* and that "w-a-t-e-r" is *water*, but I persisted in confounding the two. In despair she had dropped the subject for the time, only to renew it at the first opportunity. I became impatient at her repeated attempts and, seizing the new doll, I dashed in upon the floor. I was keenly delighted when I felt the fragments of the broken doll at my feet. Neither sorrow nor regret followed my passionate outburst. I had not loved the doll. In the still, dark world in which I lived there was no strong sentiment or ten-

ents and school officials were also told that the experimenters would be looking at "how the boys take it when they win or lose in various activities, when things are not going their way, when they feel others are being good or bad sports or unfair, when situations are felt as more or less frustrating, as well as how the boys pull together and cooperate toward common goals" (1961, p. 55).

The experiment was divided into three phases. In the first phase the members of each group interacted with one another and were unaware of the existence of the other group. The hypothesis for this phase was that in each of the groups a structure of status positions and roles (e.g., leaders and followers in different situations) would emerge as the boys cooperated in preparing meals, pitching tents, keeping the camp clean, and competing in intragroup sports. Indeed, as each group arrived at the camp its members

were already getting to know one another and sorting themselves out into different statuses. Group norms, such as emphasis on courage and not being a sissy, developed rapidly as the boys sought to prove themselves on hikes and in sports. Before long each group had its own name (Eagles and Rattlers), its own song and banner, and its favorite expressions and jokes.

Then the experimenters allowed each group to become aware of the other. Immediately the two groups wanted to compete in every conceivable way. Without any prompting from the counselors, each group began to regard the other (the "out-group") as inferior—a dirty band of sissies and weaklings lacking every trait embodied in the norms of the "in-group." As Sherif described it,

The members of each group began to call their rivals "stinkers," "sneaks," and "cheaters." They refused to have anything more to do with individ-

AP/Wide World Photos

derness. I felt my teacher sweep the fragments to one side of the hearth, and I had a sense of satisfaction that the cause of my discomfort was removed. She brought me my hat, and I knew I was going out into the warm sunshine. This thought, if a wordless sensation may be called a thought, made me hop and skip with pleasure.

We walked down the path to the well-house, attracted by the fragrance of the honeysuckle with which it was covered. Someone was drawing water and my teacher placed my hand under the spout. As the cool stream gushed over one hand she spelled into the other the word *water*, first slowly, then rapidly. I stood still, my whole attention fixed upon the motions of her fingers. Suddenly I felt a misty consciousness as of something forgotten—a thrill of returning thought; and somehow the mystery of language was revealed to me. I knew then that "w-a-t-e-r" meant the wonderful cool something that was flowing over my hand. That living word awakened my soul, gave it light, hope, joy, set it free! There were barriers still, it is true, but barriers that could in time be swept away.

I left the well-house eager to learn. Everything had a name, and each name gave birth to a new thought. As we returned to the house every object which I touched seemed to quiver with life. That was because I saw everything with the strange, new sight that had come to me. On entering the door I remembered the doll I had broken. I felt my way to the hearth and picked up the pieces. I tried vainly to put them together. Then my eyes filled with tears; for I realized what I had done, and for the first time I felt repentance and sorrow.

I learned a great many new words that day. I do not remember what they all were, but I do know that *mother, father, sister, teacher,* were among them—words that were to make the world blossom for me, "like Aaron's rod, with flowers." It would have been difficult to find a happier child than I was as I lay in my crib at the close of that eventful day and lived over the joys it had brought me, and for the first time longed for a new day to come.

Source: Adapted from Keller, 1917.

uals in the opposing group. The boys . . . turned against buddies whom they had chosen as "best friends" when they first arrived at camp. . . . The rival groups made threatening posters and planned raids, collecting secret hoards of green apples for ammunition. . . . In the dining-hall line they shoved each other aside, and the group that lost the contest for the head of the line shouted "Ladies first!" at the winner. They threw paper, food, and vile names at each other at the tables. [1956, pp. 57–58]

The second phase of the experiment began as the Eagles and Rattlers interacted under conditions established by the experimenters. The two groups were encouraged to compete, but under conditions that would prove frustrating because neither group could be expected to win every time. The guiding hypothesis in this phase was that "in the course of competition and frustrating relations between two groups, unfavorable stereotypes will come into use in relation to the outgroup and its members" (p. 42). It was felt that these

negative stereotypes would force the two groups even further apart.

As the two groups competed in a series of baseball games, tug-of-war contests, tent-pitching contests, and other events, the tension and hostility between them increased steadily, and adherence to the norms of good sportsmanship declined. By the end of the second phase, name-calling had become routine and the experimenters often had to intervene in fights among the boys. Within the groups, the boys who did well in the competitions gained increased prestige, while those who failed to help their side win were scorned. Boys who had become leaders because they were known to be good sports were replaced by leaders who were more aggressive and competitive.

In the third phase the experimenters created situations in which members of the two groups would have to cooperate in order to meet goals that went beyond the needs of either group and required concerted action by the two groups. The hypothesis for this phase was that intergroup cooperation for such a purpose would tend to reduce the tensions between the groups. A simulated water shortage brought the two groups into situations in which they had to cooperate in efforts such as starting the water-tank truck. As they worked together, they gradually developed norms that focused on their common goals—norms of cooperation and intergroup peace—which replaced the earler norms that rewarded success in competition. Here is how Sherif described this new situation:

In the end the groups were actively seeking opportunities to mingle, to entertain and "treat" each other. They decided to hold a joint campfire. They took turns presenting skits and songs. Members of both groups requested that they go home together on the same bus, rather than on the separate buses in which they had come. [p. 58]

THE SOCIAL CONSTRUCTION OF PERSONALITY

The Robbers Cave experiment showed how easy it is to change the norms guiding children's behavior when adults are willing and able to do so. Clearly, however, even more powerful socializing forces are brought to bear on the young child in the home. We turn, therefore, to theories of socialization that consider the environments children experience at home.

Both psychologists and sociologists have long been interested in the processes through which the individual personality is formed. In both sociological and psychological theories, the central question is how society's norms and values are incorporated into the individual personality. But as we will see, psychological theories of personality tend to emphasize how the individual's capabilities and limitations affect society, whereas sociological theories look at the influence of groups and social institutions on the formation of individual capabilities. We can illustrate the contributions of each approach by comparing the psychological theory of Freud with the sociological theories of Mead and Cooley.

Freud's Theory of Personality

Sigmund Freud (1921, 1930), the creator of modern psychoanalysis, was the first social scientist to develop a theory of personality and child development that specified how a society's norms are incorporated into the self. His theory leans heavily on the role of interpersonal conflict within the family.

For Freud, the personality or self develops out of the processes of socialization, primarily in the family, whereby the infant is gradually forced to control its bodily urges. These more or less innate urges and sensations are associated with the biological necessities of life: sucking, eating, defecation, genital stimulation, warmth, sleep, and so on. Freud shocked the straitlaced intellectuals of his day by placing sexual urges at the center of his inventory of infant behaviors and showing that these aspects of the self are the primary targets of early socialization—that the infant is taught in many ways to delay physical gratification and to channel its biological urges into socially accepted forms of behavior.

Freud's model of the personality is derived from his view of the socialization process. Freud divided the personality into three functional areas, or interrelated parts, that permit the self to function well in society. They are the id, the ego, and the superego. The part from which the infant's unsocialized drives arise is termed the **id**. The moral codes of adults, especially parents, become incorporated into the part of the personality that Freud called the **superego**. Freud thought of this part of the personality as consisting of all the "internalized" norms, values, and feelings that are taught in the socialization process.

In addition to the id and the superego, the personality as Freud described it has a third vital element, the **ego**. The ego is our conception of ourself in relation to others, in contrast with the id, which represents self-centeredness in its purest form. To have a "strong ego" is to be self-confident in dealing with others and to be able to accept criticism. To have a "weak ego" is to need continual approval from others. The popular expression

Freud divided the personality into three functional areas: id, superego, and ego.

that someone "has a big ego" and demands constant attention actually signals a lack of ego strength in the Freudian sense.

Note that Freud never expected that actual parts of the brain that correspond to the id, ego, and superego would be discovered. Instead, he was referring to aspects of the functioning personality that are observed in the individual.

In the growth of the personality, according to Freud, the formation of the ego or social self is critical, but it does not occur without a great deal of conflict. The conflict between the infant's basic biological urges and society's need for a socialized person becomes evident very early. Freud believed that the individual's major personality traits (security or insecurity, fears and longings, ways of interacting with others) are formed in the conflict that occurs as the parents insist that the infant control its biological urges. This conflict, Freud believed, is most severe between the child and the same-sex parent. The infant wishes to receive pleasure, especially sexual stimulation, from the opposite-sex parent and therefore is competing with the same-sex parent. In order to become more attractive to the opposite-sex parent, the infant attempts to imitate the same-sex parent. Thus for Freud the same-sex parent is the most powerful socializing influence on the growing child.

> **The looking glass self is the reflection of our self we think we see in the behaviors of others.**

Contemporary sociologists who are influenced by Freud's biologically based theories have used his concepts of same-sex attraction and modeling of the same-sex parent's behavior to explain differences between men and women. Alice Rossi (1977), for instance, argues that women's shared experience of menstruation and childbearing creates a strong bond between mothers and daughters. Nancy Chodorow (1974) claims that women's earliest experiences with their mothers tend to convince them that a woman is fulfilled by becoming a mother in her turn; thus women are socialized from a very early age to "reproduce motherhood." Research on socialization has shown that men also are strongly influenced by the same-sex parent. Fathers often serve as models of behavior whom boys will emulate throughout their lives. Remember, how-

ever, that for Freud the child's imitation of the same-sex parent was tinged with conflict, since he believed that the child is in competition with that parent for the affection of the opposite-sex parent.

Freud's theory includes the idea that the conflicts of childhood reappear throughout life in ways that the individual cannot predict. The demands of the superego ("conscience") and the "childish" desires of the id are always threatening to disrupt the functioning of the ego in the individual's daily life, especially in family environments in which normal levels of conflict are either exaggerated or forcefully suppressed. Note, however, that Freud focused on the traditional family consisting of mother, father, and children. The more families depart from this conventional form, the more we need to question the adequacy of Freudian socialization theory.

Interactionist Models of the Self

Freud's theory of socialization and personality development stresses the importance of the parent–child relationship in learning cultural norms and incorporating them into the self. But clearly the individual's interactions with peers and others also play a major role in socialization. In sociology the study of how the self emerges in the context of social interaction is the province of interactionist theories.

The early American sociologist Charles Horton Cooley was a major contributor to the interactionist view of the development of the self. In Cooley's major work on this subject, *Human Nature and the Social Order* (1956/ 1902), we find the concept of the "looking glass self." The looking glass self is the reflection of our self we think we see in the behaviors of others toward us. We are continually attentive to the behavioral cues of others; we wonder whether they think we look good, are expressing ourselves well, are working hard enough, and so on. As we mature, the overall pattern of these reflections of other people's opinions becomes a dominant aspect of our own identities—that is, of how we conceive of ourselves. Cooley believed that through these processes we actually *become* the person we believe others think we are.

Culture and the Self. Cooley's insight into the role of others in defining the self was the foundation for the view of the self proposed by George Herbert Mead. With Cooley, Mead believed strongly that the self is a social product. We are not born with selves that are "brought out" by socialization. Instead, we acquire a self by observing and assimilating the identities of others (Nisbet, 1970). The vehicle for this identification and assimilation is language. As Mead wrote, "There neither can be nor could have been any mind or thought without language; and the early stages of the development of language must have been prior to the development of mind or thought" (1971/1934, p. 272). This view of the emergence of the self clearly places culture (of which, as we have seen, language is an important part) at the center of the formation of the self. The kind of person we become is a cultural construct. Through interaction with people who are Catholic, for example, one takes on the language, the jokes, the style of a person of that religion. If the father is a firefighter and the mother a nurse, certain attitudes about service to society and about illness and danger will carry over to the child. If the same child plays on sports teams with children in the neighborhood, the norms and values of those children and their parents will become part of the child's experience and will be incorporated into his or her personality. Another child, one growing up on a Sioux Indian reservation, will learn some of the same values, such as fair play, reward for achievement, and good citizenship, but will also learn the norms and values of the Sioux (e.g., reverence for one's ancestors and for the natural environment).

As each person learns the norms of his or her culture and its various ways of communicating—whether through language, dress, or gestures—and as each experiences the influences of a particular family and peer group, a unique self is formed. The self, thus, is a product of many influences and experiences; every person emerges with a personality of his or her own, and each has incorporated to varying degrees the values of the larger society and of a particular subculture.

Role Taking: The Significant Other and the Generalized Other. For Mead, two of the most important activities of childhood are play and games. In play, the child practices "taking the roles of others." If you watch preadolescent children play, you will see them continually "trying on" roles: "You be the mommy and I'll be the teacher, and you'll come to school to find out why . . ." or "Pretend I'm Michael Jordan and you're Isaiah Thomas and the score is tied in the fourth quarter. . . ." They are reenacting the dramas of winning and losing, or calling into question the behaviors of the schoolroom, or trying to understand sickness and death. In such games children take the roles of significant others, even though they may not know the "others" personally. **Significant others** are people who loom large in our lives, people who appear to be directly involved in winning and losing, achieving and failing. They tend to be people after whom we model our behavior—or whose behavior we seek to avoid.

To take part in a game, however, a child must have already learned to become, in a symbolic sense, all the other participants in the game. In other words, the person is able to evaluate his or her behavior according to the group's ideas of how a role should be performed. Thus, in a baseball game we shape our own participation according to the roles of the other participants— the pitcher, the batter, the outfielders, and so on. And we judge our own participation by the norms of the game as well as by what we think the other players think of our actions.

> *Play and games are important in the development of the self because they involve taking the roles of others.*

Recently this author watched as two young girls played a game they had invented. It was called "Poor." Both girls came from comfortable homes but were taking the role of the poor, homeless people they often saw in a nearby city. With long, sad faces they whispered to each other "We're poor, so poor. We don't have any place to live." "Yes, we're so poor we have to live in this little closet and take pieces of bread from people." As they huddled in a closet pretending to be poor, the older sister of one of the girls, a junior high school student, overheard their game and came bustling into the room. "Oh, you poor, poor homeless little girls," she declared. "I'm your welfare officer, Miss Biglady. Here are some forms for you to fill out

Box 6–2: "Beehive Soccer"—A Game Without a Generalized Other

Thousands of parents and coaches of Little League teams will want to argue with the following sociological assertion:

Eugene, Ore., July 23—Children under the ages of 8 or 10 should not participate in organized, competitive sports programs, according to a panel of sports medicine experts at the Olympic Scientific Congress here. . . .

In the discussion on children, Dr. Vern Seefeldt, a specialist in motor development at the Youth Sports Institute at Michigan State University, said, "Beginning competition before a child is competent in the skills necessary for the sport can be damaging."

He said "the most obvious reason for children to play sports" was to improve motor

Barton Silverman/The New York Times

skills. But he said inability to develop skills "that promote the success of the team" is the reason most often cited by children for dropping out of sports. . . .

A sociologist, Jay Coakley of the University of Colorado in Colorado Springs, said, "Kids under 10 are incapable of the concept of a team with differing responsibilities shifting to different players depending upon the location and movement of a ball."

"Anyone who has watched a youth soccer game is familiar with what I call 'beehive soccer,' " he said. "Shortly after play starts, all of the players are concentrated around the ball, despite the cries of the adults on the sidelines to stay in position."

He said it would be "better to accept some chaos than to try to impose adult concepts of team play on children."

How much "chaos" should adults accept? The sociology of Little League coaching remains a wide-open field, but it would seem that some youngsters are able to take the role of the generalized other earlier than other children are and that some coaches are better able than their less stoic colleagues to accept normal chaos. As sociologists often say, more research is needed before we can be sure.

Source: New York Times, July 24, 1984, p. C2. Copyright © 1984 by The New York Times Company. Reprinted by permission.

so you can get help." The older girl had joined in the younger girls' game, taking another role that she had been learning about in school.

The **generalized other** is a composite of all the roles of all the participants in the game. According to Mead, a person who participates in a game like "Poor" has developed the capacity for role-taking and now, in his phrase, "takes the role of the generalized other." The capacity for role-taking develops during middle childhood. When little children play team games, they often have a hard time taking specific roles, as can be seen in the example of "beehive soccer" presented in Box 6-2. As children mature, they become increasingly competent at games and team sports.

From the standpoint of personality de-

velopment, the generalized other represents the voice of society, which is internalized as "conscience." For some people, the generalized other demands perfection and strict adherence to every rule. For others, the generalized other may be extremely demanding where sports and other games are concerned but much more relaxed about achievement in school or adherence to the norms of property. For still others, the generalized other may insist on amassing large amounts of money as the primary indicator of success, or it may require community service and not value financial success at all. Within any given culture, such variations will be wide but will tend to follow certain easily recognized patterns.

Erikson's Theory of Development

The difficulty experienced by young children participating in team sports raises the larger issue of whether there are stages in the development of the personality. This question was addressed in the pioneering work of Erik Erikson, which bridges the gap between Freud's psychobiological theory and the interactionist theories of Mead and Cooley. Erikson accepts the Freudian view that early experiences in the home are a key influence on personality development. But he also believes that experiences later in life can change the personality in fundamental ways. Erikson's work incorporates Mead's view of personality formation through interaction with significant others, and his concept of identification is similar to Mead's concepts of role taking and the generalized other. Above all, however, Erikson's theory of human development stresses the continuing socialization of the person throughout the life cycle.

In *Childhood and Society* (1963), Erikson's central work on the formation of the self, the concept of identification takes center stage. **Identification** is the social process whereby the individual chooses adults as models and attempts to imitate their behavior. As just noted, Erikson's concept of identification with the role model is very similar to Mead's view of role taking, but Erikson places more emphasis on the influence of particular individuals than on the influence of particular roles. Thus, a child is influenced by its mother as an individual rather than by the role of mother as she performs it. Moreover, identification with role models occurs throughout life because the personality is continually changing, even though its basic aspects are formed in infancy. The result of this process is the individual's *identity*.

Erikson proposed that a person's identity is shaped by early childhood experiences but that it can change throughout his or her lifetime. He demonstrated, for example, that combat experiences can produce damaged identities because soldiers often feel guilty about not having done enough for their fallen comrades (this is sometimes called "survivor guilt"). For Freud, on the other hand, war-produced mental illness was always related to problems that the soldier had experienced in early childhood.

In his ninth decade Erikson and his wife Joan, his collaborator for forty years, have continued to develop his theory of personality. Armed with new knowledge about aging, they have revised the theory as shown in Table 6-1. The Eriksons' theory, like Freud's, focuses on the conflicts experienced by the developing person. Successful resolution of those conflicts enables the individual to be trusting and caring toward others and prepares him or her for the struggles that will occur in later stages of life. Failure to resolve the conflict experienced in any given stage can produce a person who is immature, unable to engage others in caring and satisfying relationships, and unable to meet the challenges of the next stage.

Table 6–1: Erikson's Stages of Development

Conflict and resolution	Culmination in old age
Old age Integrity vs. despair: wisdom	Existential identity, a sense of integrity strong enough to withstand physical disintegration.
Adulthood Generativity vs. stagnation: care	*Caritas*, caring for others, and *agape*, empathy and concern.
Early Adulthood Intimacy vs. isolation: love	Sense of the complexity of relationships; value of tenderness and loving freely.
Adolescence Identity vs. confusion: fidelity	Sense of complexity of life; merger of sensory, logical, and aesthetic perception.
School Age Industry vs. inferiority: competence	Humility; acceptance of the course of one's life and unfulfilled hopes.
Play Age Initiative vs. guilt: purpose	Humor; empathy; resilience.
Early Childhood Autonomy vs. shame: will	Acceptance of the cycle of life, from integration to disintegration.
Infancy Basic trust vs. mistrust: hope	Appreciation of interdependence and relatedness.

Theories of Moral Development

Throughout life people face a variety of moral dilemmas, and these have a significant effect on their personalities. Social scientists have devoted considerable study to the processes through which people develop concepts of morality. Among the best-known students of moral development are the Swiss child psychologist Jean Piaget and the American social psychologists Lawrence Kohlberg and Carol Gilligan. Piaget stands with Freud and Erikson as one of the most important and original researchers and writers on child development. In the 1920s he became concerned with how children understand their environment, how they view their world, and how they develop their own personal philosophies. To discover the mental processes unique to children he used what was then an equally unique method: He spent long hours with a small number of children simply having conversations with them. These open-ended discussions were devoted to getting at how children actually think. In this way Piaget discovered evidence for the existence of ideas that are quite foreign to the adult mind (Elkind, 1970). For example, the child gives inanimate objects human motives and tends to see everything as existing for human purposes. In this phase of his research Piaget also described the egocentric aspect of the child's mental world, which is illustrated by the tendency to invent words and expect others to understand them.

Kohlberg's theory of moral development consists of three stages: preconventional, conventional, and postconventional.

In the later phases of his research and writing, Piaget devoted his efforts to questions about children's moral reasoning—the way children interpret the rules of games and judge the consequences of their actions. He observed that children form absolute notions of right and wrong very early in life, but that they often cannot understand the ambiguities of adult roles until they approach adolescence. This line of investigation was continued by the American social psychologist Lawrence Kohlberg, whose theory of moral development incorporates Piaget's views on the ways in which notions of morality develop in young children.

Kohlberg's theory of moral development emphasizes the cognitive aspects of moral behavior. In a study of fifty-seven Chicago children that began in 1957 and continued until the children were young adults, Kohlberg presented the children with moral dilemmas like the following: A husband is told that his wife needs a special kind of medicine if she is to survive a severe form of cancer. The medication is extremely expensive, and the husband can raise only half the needed funds. When he begs the inventor of the drug for a reduced price, he is rebuffed because the inventor wants to make a lot of money on his invention. The husband then considers stealing the medicine, and the child is asked whether the man should steal in order to save his wife (Kohlberg and Gilligan, 1971).

By studying children's answers to such dilemmas at different ages, Kohlberg developed a theory of moral development consisting of three stages: (1) *preconventional*, in which the child acts out of the desire for reward and the fear of punishment; (2) *conventional*, in which the child's decisions are based on an understanding of right and wrong as embodied in social rules or laws; and (3) *postconventional*, in which the individual develops a sense of relativity and can distinguish between social laws and moral principles. Very often subjects in the preconventional and conventional stages will immediately assume that stealing is wrong in the situation Kohlberg has posed, but postconventional thinking in older children will cause them to debate the fairness of rules against stealing in the face of the larger moral dilemma involved.

SOCIALIZATION AND HUMAN ENVIRONMENTS

None of the theories of development reviewed so far touches on the many social and natural environments in which human beings are socialized. Children are born into relatively affluent homes in American suburbs, into the squalid slums of Calcutta, the icy wastes of Siberia and the Canadian Arctic, and a myriad other environments, yet in every case those who survive early infancy are socialized to live and perhaps flourish in these diverse settings. Cross-cultural studies attempt to show how socialization processes vary in different societies and how they are affected by demographic trends (trends in population size and composition) within societies. This comparative view of socialization attempts to bring together the often-competing viewpoints of biological, psychological, and sociological explanations of developmental patterns.

Let us take teenage fertility as an example. Most social scientists believe that a child born to a teenage mother is likely to face more difficulties throughout life than a child born to a mother who has herself matured into a young adult. But before considering the social consequences of teenage parenthood, we need some evidence about how the United States rates on this issue compared with other societies with similar levels of economic and social development. Figures 6-1, 6-2, and 6-3 reveal that the United States has significantly higher rates of teenage pregnancy, childbirth, and abortion than other nations with comparable or more permissive laws and medical services. In Canada, for example, there were about 55 births per 1,000 women aged fourteen to nineteen in 1980, compared to almost 90 per 1,000 in the United States.

These comparative data suggest that American teenagers, both white and nonwhite, are less socialized to control the consequences of their sexual behavior than teenagers from the other countries represented in the charts; they also have less information about reproduction and contraception. Additional data on the use of contraceptives in England and the United States offer some empirical support for this hypothesis. In addition, there are cultural contradictions in American patterns of socialization that may play a large role in explaining these differences. In the United States we place a high value on sexuality, judging from our consumption of magazines and television programs that focus on sex and sexual attraction. But we are also a society in which the frank discussion of sexual behavior in the home and school and even among friends is fraught with

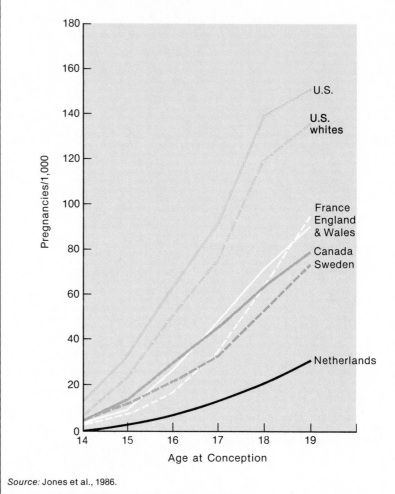

Figure 6–1: **Pregnancies per 1,000 Women, by Single Year of Age, 1980**

Source: Jones et al., 1986.

conflict. It seems that we socialize children to desire sex but not to know much about how to control it. Comparative studies show that one consequence is a higher number of children born to teenage mothers in the United States than in other nations (Jones et al., 1986).

Since teenage mothers are also more likely than nonteenagers to be single mothers and to be living in poverty, a major consequence of the high rate of teenage fertility in the United States is that proportionately more babies are born into homes in which they will not receive the attention and material benefits that will help them realize their full genetic potential (Furstenberg, 1976). In other

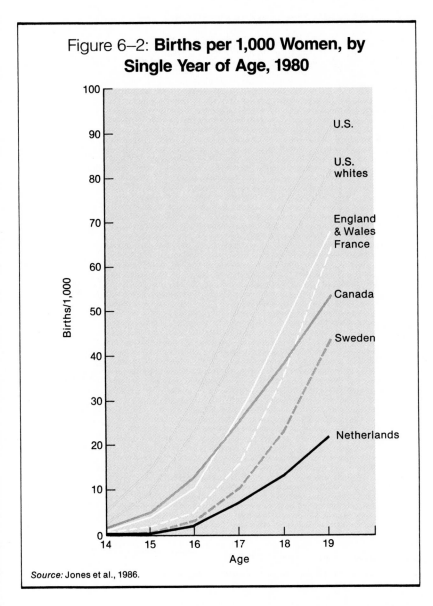

Figure 6–2: **Births per 1,000 Women, by Single Year of Age, 1980**

U.S.

U.S. whites

England & Wales
France

Canada

Sweden

Netherlands

Births/1,000

Age

Source: Jones et al., 1986.

in opportunities to develop the necessary skills. This insight is found in numerous folktales and jokes. "Who was the greatest artist who ever lived?" a newly defunct art critic asked Saint Peter on his way into heaven. "Why, it was Lucius Cadmore," answered Saint Peter without a moment's hesitation. "But I never heard of him," said the sorely perplexed critic. "That's because he never had a chance to paint anything," Saint Peter finished, and turned his attention to the next entrant.

Urie Bronfenbrenner, who has devoted considerable study to the effects of environment on socialization, asks, "What are the environmental conditions necessary for the development of human beings from early childhood on?" He summarizes the conclusions of numerous studies on this question in the form of two propositions:

Proposition 1. In order to develop normally, a child needs the enduring, irrational involvement of one or more adults in care of and joint activity with the child.
Proposition 2. The involvement of one or more adults in care of and joint activity with the child requires public policies that provide opportunity, status, resources, encouragement, example, and, above all, *time* for parenthood, primarily by parents, but also by other adults in the child's environment, both within and outside the home. [1981, p. 39]

The Micro-Environment

Bronfenbrenner's first proposition stresses the internal environment of the home. By the "irrational involvement" of adults, Bronfenbrenner means love. Someone, he explains, must be "crazy about the kid." This conclusion, as noted earlier in the chapter, is implied by the results of various studies of emotional deprivation in childhood. But it also signals the importance of adults' involvement in what ecologists call the child's *microenvironment*. This term refers not only to the family but also to the friends, kin, and others involved in the child's upbringing on a regular and frequent basis. Much contemporary research centers on the effect of different microenvironments on the child's development. For example, Michael Lewis and Candice Feiring's intriguing study of 117 families, "Some

words, these children start off at a disadvantage in that their mothers have not yet reached maturity themselves and are likely to be single parents who may be unable to provide their children with economic security, love, and discipline.

The more general relationship between nature and nurture that is revealed by comparative studies is as follows: A person with lower genetic potential—for math, music, sports, and so on—who has the benefit of an environment that stimulates the full development of those talents can actually achieve more than someone who has greater genetic potential but whose environment is lacking

American Families at Dinner" (1982), shows that a typical three-year-old child interacts regularly with a network of kin, friends, and other adults who also play a significant role in the child's early socialization (see Box 6-3).

Studies of the interactions that socialize children in their micro-environments are looking more and more at the role of adults other than the mother, for in order to determine the effects of growing up in families (or in micro-environments that differ from the traditional family), the social scientist needs far more detailed information about what actually goes on between the child and others outside the immediate parent–child group. One such study (Lindsmith, Strauss, and Denzin, 1978) found that there are at least six categories of significant others in the child's socializing network:

- *Sociolegal others*—parents, guardians, siblings, and other members of the child's kinship system.
- *Socio-others*—people in the family's network of close friends. Often these individuals assume fictional kinship roles, such as "Uncle or Aunt So-and-so." Baby-sitters and neighbors may also fall into this category.
- *Coequals or compeers*—other children, including siblings, who have a strong socializing influence on the child. By the age of three, compeers often rival parents in their impact on the child's sense of self.
- *Child-care experts*—pediatricians, teachers, clergy, psychologists, and other experts who have gained a legitimate influence over the child for any reason. Some researchers argue that the advice of such experts has undermined traditional family socialization practices, but this remains an open question (Lasch, 1984).
- *Media others*—people who join the child's world through television, books, radio, records, and other media. Such characters as Cinderella, the Muppets, Laura Ingalls, Michael Jackson, Alf, and the Simpsons "staff and populate the child's world of fantasy and entertainment." They may have as much contact with some children as any of the other types do.
- *Public place others*—police and fire-fighters, mail carriers, clerks in stores, and

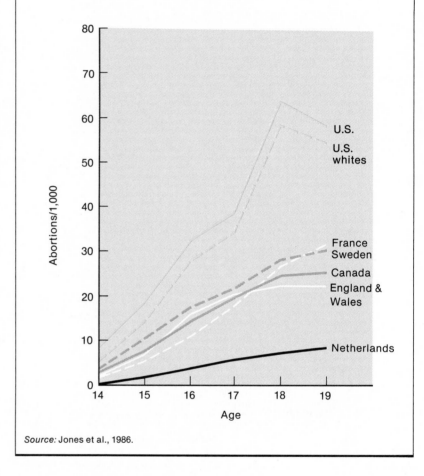

Figure 6–3: **Abortions per 1,000 Women, by Single Year of Age, 1980**

Source: Jones et al., 1986.

strangers encountered in public places are included in a "residual category" of individuals who interact with the child and sociolegal others in specific ways when they are in public.[1]

The Larger Social Environment

Bronfenbrenner's second proposition brings in the larger society's influence on socialization and on the social network in which the child matures. Social policies like support for

[1]These categories are not listed in order of importance; any one of them may occupy a central place in the life of a particular child.

day care and laws dealing with child custody or parental responsibility for children's behavior are an important part of the environment in which socialization takes place. This proposition leads us to look at variations in the social environments of individuals.

Figure 6-4 offers some idea of the diverse social environments in which different people grow up. Some of us were raised on farms, others in cities or suburbs. Some of our families broke up because of divorce or death, and some of us were raised in institutions or by foster parents. When we became adolescents, some of us were involved in delinquent peer groups, while others were members of groups that were carefully channeled toward activities considered favorable to development. Work at paying jobs or at chores in the family business was an everyday routine for some of us, whereas others either lacked opportunities to work or were prevented from doing so by our parents' views

Box 6–3: **Measures of Central Tendency**

The following table, taken from Lewis and Feiring's study of American families, presents information about the social network of the typical three-year-old:

The Three-Year-Old Child's Social Network (n = 117)

	$\bar{X}$	Range
Number of relatives other than parents seen at least once a week	3.20	0–15
Number of child's friends seen at least once a week	4.43	0–13
Number of adults seen at least once a week	4.38	0–24

n refers to the number of subjects in a study.
Source: Lewis and Feiring, 1982, p. 116.

To understand this table you must know something about the common measures of central tendency. The one used in the table is the *mean*, represented by X. To arrive at this number each child's total number of friends, relatives, and other adults seen at least once a week is added to the totals for the other children in the sample. The grand total is then divided by the number of children in the sample. The resulting number can be used to represent the entire sample.

The other common measures of central tendency are the *median* and the *mode*. The median is the number that divides a sample into two equal halves when all the numbers in the sample are arranged from lowest to highest. The mode is simply the score that occurs most frequently in the sample. Sociologists make a point of specifying which of these measures they are using. They try to avoid the term *average* in statistical tables, as it can refer to any one of these measures.

To illustrate all three measures of central tendency, let us use the following data from ten of the children in Lewis and Feiring's sample:

Child	Number of Friends Seen at Least Once a Week
1	2
2	3
3	3
4	7
5	12
6	2
7	3
8	1
9	0
10	5
	38

In this example the mode would be 3 and the median would also be 3, but the mean would be 3.8.

about what is best for children and adolescents. All of these influences, or the lack thereof, contributed in significant ways to our life experiences, which, in turn, shaped our social selves.

As the child matures and begins to leave the micro-environment of the family and related networks, other social structures play a greater part in his or her socialization. And as we will see shortly, the ways in which those structures continue the socialization process throughout a person's lifetime vary greatly from one society to another. In the next and final section of the chapter we turn our attention to these aspects of the larger social environment.

AGENTS OF SOCIALIZATION

Agents of socialization are the social structures that provide the environments and experiences that shape an individual's personality. The most familiar agents of socialization are the family, schools, socializing agencies in the community, the peer group, and the mass media. All of these socializing agents use what sociologists call anticipatory socialization as a technique for instilling norms and developing the person's identity. **Anticipatory socialization** refers to situations in which the individual plays at a role that he or she is likely to assume later in life. Thus, the child who "plays house" is imitating the behavior of adults. The adolescent who attends a senior prom is being socialized in anticipation of a time when he or she will be expected to participate in formal social events.

The Family

The family is the primary agent of socialization. It is the micro-environment into which the child is born and in which his or her earliest experiences with other people occur—experiences that have a lasting influence on the personality. As we saw earlier in the chapter, family environments vary greatly, not only in terms of such key variables as income and education of the parents but also in terms of living arrangements, urban versus rural residence, number of children, relations with

Figure 6–4: **The Different Worlds in Which We Grow Up**

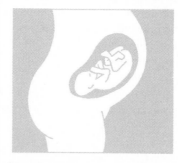

PRENATAL CARE

Seventy-six percent of all pregnant women—79 percent of white women, 62 percent of black women, and 61 percent of Hispanic women—begin prenatal care in their first trimester. A total of 6.8 percent of all babies have a low birthweight.

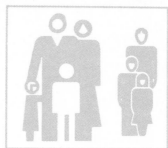

LIVING ARRANGEMENTS

About three-quarters of all children under eighteen live with two parents. Of the 15 million children living with only one parent, 13 million live with their mothers and 2 million live with their fathers.

PLACE OF RESIDENCE

Two-thirds of all children fifteen years old or younger live in metropolitan areas. About 1 million children under fourteen live on farms. Black children are more than twice as likely as white children to live in central cities.

FAMILY INCOME

Twenty percent of all children under eighteen live in poor households. Over 7 million white children and over 4 million black children live in poverty.

OTHER VARIABLES

About one-third of all children aged three to four are enrolled in school. Ninety-four percent of all children aged fourteen to seventeen are enrolled in school. Almost 5 million children between the ages of five and seventeen speak a language other than English at home. In 1987 approximately 3 percent of all children under eighteen were arrested.

kin, and so on. We devote an entire chapter (Chapter 15) to the family, its role in socialization, and the changes it is undergoing. In this section, therefore, we will describe some other major agents of socialization in modern societies. For the sake of comparison, we will look at the way these agents operate in the Soviet Union and the United States.

The Schools

In both the Soviet Union and the United States, the schools are clearly the most important agents of socialization after the family. Studies of Soviet society (Lapidus, 1978; Smith, 1976) indicate that schools exert a more pow-

After the family, the school is the most important agent of socialization for most children.

erful influence on socialization in the Soviet Union than they do in the United States. Children begin attending school for a full day at an earlier age there than they do in the United States or Canada, and day-care and nursery facilities are far more widespread and cost less. Moreover, because Soviet couples have fewer children, it appears to be easier for Soviet parents to monitor their child's school activities. American parents, on the other hand, tend to have more influence on school curricula than Soviet parents do. Conflicts between parents and school personnel over what should be taught and when are not common in Soviet society, in which the schools have an explicit connection with the state and play an important part in political socialization (Attwood, 1985; Bronfenbrenner, 1970).

The Community

In American communities anticipatory socialization is commonplace. Parades on Memorial Day and the Fourth of July reinforce values of citizenship and patriotism. Participation in team sports instills values of fair play, teamwork, and competitive spirit. Shopping trips to suburban malls and downtown department stores prepare children and adolescents for the time when they will be consumers. In Soviet society the experience of shopping and the judgment of a person's social competence on the basis of shopping skills are far less common. Much more developed are organized, politically motivated

youth clubs ("Young Pioneers"), sports clubs, political associations, young workers' associations, and the like. These agents of socialization exist in the United States in the form of scout troops, leagues of all kinds, and church organizations (to name just a few), but they are less overtly political than their Soviet counterparts, and the kind of anticipatory socialization they practice is far more varied than appears to be the case in the Soviet Union.

The Peer Group

In both the United States and the Soviet Union, the peer group tends to be the dominant agent of socialization in middle and late childhood. **Peer groups** are interacting groups of people of about the same age. Among adolescents, peer groups exert a strong influence on their members' attitudes and values. Studies of both societies confirm the high degree of importance adolescents and adults alike attach to their friendship groups, and there do not appear to be any major differences in their impact on socialization in the two societies. Adolescents typically acquire much of their identity from their peers and consequently find it difficult to deviate from the norms of behavior that their peer group establishes (Gans, 1962, 1984; Homans, 1950; McAndrew, 1985; W. F. Whyte, 1943).

Although in both societies the peer group may become even more important than the family in the development of the individual's identity, there is far more diversity in the norms and values of peer groups in the United States than in the Soviet Union. The American teenager is presented with many more life-style choices than the Soviet teenager typically is. And in this relatively greater freedom there are both advantages and disadvantages. American teenagers can try on more adult roles and have more freedom to shift their friendships from one group to another. But that freedom can also lead to confusion and ambivalence, as we saw earlier in the example of sexuality and teenage pregnancy.

The Mass Media

The most controversial agent of socialization in American society is the mass media. (In the Soviet Union the media are a powerful and rapidly changing agent of socialization, but they are controlled by the state.) In debates about the effects of the media on socialization, television comes under the greatest scrutiny because of the number of hours children spend in front of the "electronic baby-sitter." Estimates of how much television children and adults watch vary with the method used to measure viewing time, but in the average American home the set is turned on for over seven hours a day (Kornblum and Julian, 1989).

The effects of all this television viewing on children and adolescents is a subject of intensive research. The major networks employ sociologists who specialize in mass media studies, and a number of government agencies, including the National Institute of Mental Health, sponsor studies of the relationship between the mass media and behavioral disorders ranging from interpersonal violence to depression. During the 1970s social-scientific research on the relationship between televised violence and aggression in children resulted in legislation setting limits on the amount and kind of violence that can be portrayed on daytime and prime-time TV (Reinhold, 1982). But the effects of television on socialization are not by any means all negative. Children, adolescents, and adults in modern American society learn far more about current events, social issues, and the arts, for example, than people did before the advent of television.

GENDER SOCIALIZATION

No discussion of socialization would be complete without some mention of gender socialization. **Gender socialization** refers to the ways in which we learn our gender identity and develop according to cultural norms of "masculinity" or "femininity." Gender is not synonymous with biological sex; "scholars use the word *sex* to refer to attributes of men and women created by their biological characteristics and *gender* to refer to the distinctive qualities of men and women (or masculinity and femininity) that are culturally created" (Epstein, 1988, p. 6). By *gender identity* we mean "an individual's own feeling of whether she or he is a woman or a man, or a girl or a boy" (Kessler and McKenna, 1978, p. 10).

Sigmund Freud (1925) assumed that "biology is destiny" and that children learn their gender by observing whether they have a penis or a vagina. But modern social science has shown that the situation is somewhat more complicated. The development of gender identity occurs during a critical period of every child's socialization. There is a time before which the child is too young to have a gender identity and after which "whatever gender identity has developed cannot be changed" (Kessler and McKenna, 1978, p. 10). Most of the evidence in support of this conclusion comes from studies of children who were assigned to the wrong gender in infancy. In all cases in which adults attempt to change the child's gender identity after the age of three, "the individual either retains her/his original gender identity or becomes extremely confused and ambivalent" (Kessler and Mc-Kenna, 1978, p. 10; Money and Erhardt, 1972).

The strength and pervasiveness of gender socialization is illustrated by the case of Ron Kovic, the author of *Born on the Fourth of July*. Kovic saw himself as a red-blooded American male, a typical product of socialization for boys raised in his community. He was taught to be patriotic, to want to defend his country, to want to prove his manhood in combat and sexual conquest. When he became paralyzed in Vietnam and lost his manhood (in the narrow, conventional sense of that term), he began to doubt everything—including himself, his country, and his friends. His story raises some important issues, not least of which is how we form our ideas of manliness and womanliness and whether those ideas are helpful in meeting the demands of a changing world.

The story of Ron Kovic is a striking example of how powerful gender socialization is and the effects it can have on a person's life. Elsewhere in this book (especially in Chapter 14) we present other examples of the importance of gender in explaining life chances. But here let us take a more mundane example of the results of gender socialization: the way men and women view their own bodies. Men tend to think of their own bodies as "just

Through gender socialization we learn our gender identity and develop according to norms of masculinity or femininity.

about perfect," but women tend to think of themselves as overweight, at least when they compare themselves with a mental image of an attractive woman. These are the findings of a survey of 500 college-age men and women conducted by April Fallon and Paul Rozin of the University of Pennsylvania (Goleman, 1985).

Why do boys grow into men who are happy with their bodies, and why do so many girls become women who are unhappy with theirs? One answer to this question may be found in an analysis of American culture. Men dominate the media—radio, television, newspapers and magazines—that communicate American culture to mass audiences. Girls and women thus are continually exposed to images of women created by men, and those images more often than not portray women as sex objects, to be judged by the shape and size of their breasts, the length of their legs, and the tightness of their skin (Chernin, 1981; Lurie, 1981). It is little wonder, then, that women feel worse about themselves than men—about whom it has been said that it is sexy to be a sagging warrior or a somewhat wrinkled philosopher.

This analysis explains why men are content with their body image but not why women fail to reject male images of their bodies. In her study of gender socialization, Carol Gilligan (1982) identifies some of the wider implications of the socialization patterns that lead men to feel better about their bodies than women do about theirs. Starting with Freud and continuing through the theories of Erikson, Piaget, and Kohlberg, Gilligan argues, male development has been used as a model of "normal" development. Any differences that were seen in women tended to be viewed as variations from the norm. Gilligan notes that all of these theories are based mainly on studies of boys and men and on the assumption that masculine traits are more desirable than feminine traits (so that the goal of the study is to explain why the socialization of women fails to make them "as good as" men). Why not ask what the advantageous qualities of the female gender identity are and why men do not possess those qualities in greater abundance? Here Gilligan points to an empirical study by sociologist Janet Lever (1976, 1978), who focused on primary-school children and their games.

We have seen that Mead, Piaget, and others who follow their lead agree that much social development occurs in the games of childhood as children learn to take the roles of others and see themselves through others' eyes. Lever found important gender differences in children's games and role taking. For example, boys play outdoors more often than girls do. They also play more competitive games that require more complex motor skills (e.g., baseball). Girls, on the other hand, tend to play games that stress sharing, turn taking, and repetition (e.g., jump rope). Most significant, boys often argue in the course of their games, yet rarely does an argument end the game. With girls the opposite is true; arguments are fewer, but when they do occur they usually end the game.

In games, Gilligan contends, women may learn to take the roles of particular others, to feel empathy for a friend and to want to protect the friend's feelings by ending the game and leaving behind the taunts of others. In this way women become adept at the skills of maintaining relationships and expressing emotions, whereas men become more skilled at remaining autonomous while advancing the needs of the group or team. Throughout their lives, as a result, women have difficulty being separate, individual, and assertive; men, conversely, are more likely to be troubled by inability to form intimate relationships, to let go emotionally, and to feel empathy.

Sociologists at the forefront of research on gender are well aware that one can take observations like Gilligan's too far. For example, while men and women may tend to specialize in different styles of feeling and expression, those differences may be more deceptive than real in that they may easily change in different circumstances. (This issue is explored in detail in the Frontiers section of this chapter.) In addition, Cynthia Epstein (1988) points out that men and women often conspire to maintain such differences even when they know they are overdrawn. She argues that women often "protect men and help maintain the myths. For example, they argue that men do not exhibit feelings and will not cry. But men do cry and express emotion, usually in the presence of women who remain mute about it for fear of damaging the male self-image" (p. 236). Men, on the other hand, continue to insist that women need protection, that they need to be excluded from "men's work and men's games" because of their supposed weaknesses. In fact, Epstein and others have shown that these are culturally formed ideas rather than absolute qualities of the sexes. And as men and women confront the consequences of these cultural traits in the form of inequality and blocked opportunities, gender-determined cultural norms are changing rapidly, and so are the processes of gender socialization (Epstein, 1988; Gerson, 1985). We return to this subject at numerous points in later chapters, because among the many momentous changes that are occurring in the world today those affecting gender socialization are among the most profound.

SOCIALIZATION AND SOCIAL CHANGE

In its need to produce new generations of people socialized to function well within its cultural and social environments, a society produces particular traits and characteristics in its members, who in turn create and continually re-create their society. This is true as long as the society is not subject to changes brought about by external forces. "I spent my entire life learning how to hunt," a Kalahari bushman told an anthropologist studying the disappearance of hunter-gatherer societies throughout the world, "but now I want my son to be a farmer or a teacher" (quoted in Eckholm, 1984). Only 200 years ago hunter-gatherer societies that had evolved over thousands of years began to be killed off or pushed out to the least desirable parts of the world. Today such societies are regarded as curiosities. Their forms of socialization no longer produce people equipped to deal with the demands of new social environments. They and their children may mourn the old ways and values, but at least the children know that they must look for socializing agents outside the family and tribe.

Nor are such cultural discontinuities unique to the experience of bushmen and aborigines. To some extent everyone in the modern world experiences discontinuity in socialization. The values and ways of parents are never entirely valid for their children, although the degree to which this is true de-

pends on how much social change is experienced from one generation to the next. Socialization creates the personalities and channels the behaviors of the members of a society, but that socialization is never entirely finished. Thus, in *Manchild in the Promised Land*, his masterpiece about growing up in Harlem during the period of rapid migration of blacks from the South, Claude Brown (1966) wrote that his rural-born parents did not "seem to be ready for urban life." Their rural values and norms of behavior made no sense to their son, who had to survive on Harlem's mean streets:

When I was a little boy, Mama and Dad would beat me and tell me, "You better be good," but I didn't know what being good was. To me it meant that they just wanted me to sit down and fold my hands or something crazy like that. Stay in front of the house, don't go any-place, don't get into trouble. I didn't know what it meant, and I don't think they knew what it meant, because they couldn't ever tell me what they really wanted. The way I saw it, everything I was doing was good. If I stole something and didn't get caught, I was good. If I got into a fight with somebody, I tried to be good enough to beat him. If I broke into a place, I tried to be quiet and steal as much as I could. I was always trying to be good. They kept on beating me and talking about being good. And I just kept on doing what I was doing and kept on trying to do it good. (p. 279)

> *To some extent everyone experiences discontinuity in socialization, because the norms and values of parents are never entirely valid for their children.*

Brown's story is the biography of a young man whose parents were not equipped to socialize him for the demands of a new environment. And so he learned to survive on the streets. He became a thief and a gang fighter. But by his own account, later in his life he was greatly influenced by people who had studied the social sciences and created well-functioning institutions, special schools in particular, that could bring out his talents and socialize him for a more satisfying and constructive life than he had led as a child. In earlier periods of American history he might have been labeled as innately "incorrigible" or beyond redemption and left to a life of violence and self-destruction. The fact that he was not is a tribute to the influence of the social sciences in modern life.

FRONTIERS OF SOCIOLOGY

Emotions—Innate or Learned?

Few human behaviors seem more "natural" than the expression of emotion. People everywhere laugh, cry, grit their teeth, wrinkle their noses in distaste, cover their mouths in embarrassment, clench their fists in anger—the gestures may differ somewhat from one culture to another, but the similarities are far more striking than the differences. No matter what our culture, we all seem to express our emotions in similar ways (Eibl-Eibesfeldt, 1989). Do these almost universal qualities of emotional expression mean that emotions are genetically programmed in humans, as they seem to be in other animals? And if this is so, does it imply that differences in emotional expression between men and women are due to the genetic differences between the sexes rather than to gender socialization?

Some observers of human behavior argue that emotions and emotional expression are innate. Women cry more easily than men, they assert, because over many millennia of human evolution women have tended to specialize in the emotional realm of life, while men have tended to specialize in the rational and cognitive aspects, and these differences have been incorporated into the genetic makeup of the sexes. Most sociologists, on the other hand, would argue that there is much more evidence to support the claim that emotions, like many other aspects of human behavior, are learned through socialization and that differences in emotional behavior between the sexes are yet another example of the results of gender socialization (Fox, 1971; Wilson, 1978).

It seems likely that emotions are determined by both biological and sociological factors. Surely the physical expression of emotion is biologically constrained; we have relatively little choice about how we communicate emotional states. Basic emotions like fear and anger may be innate, the product of millions of years of genetic evolution. More complex feelings such as love and loyalty, on the other hand, must be learned and clearly are shaped by the culture in which the individual is socialized. As for differences between the sexes, comparative evidence from the research of ethologists (scientists who study the evolution of human behavior) shows that men and women in all cultures tend to express emotions in the same ways (see photos). And as yet there is little direct evidence to prove that women are innately more emotional than men.

In recent years sociologists have made significant progress in studying how social structures such as organizational hierarchies bring out and may even require different types of emotional expression. Among the leaders in this field of study is Arlie Hochschild (1979, 1983). In her pathbreaking study of the work of airline flight attendants, she found that the only way women could gain positions on flight crews after World War II was by specializing in making people feel better about flying and helping them feel comfortable while in the air. Hochschild showed that flight attendants (who until recently were almost all female) are trained to follow certain norms of emotional expression or "feeling rules." To be "nice" or "sweet" is defined as a feminine trait in the airlines industry, just as the assertiveness and confidence expressed by the male flight officers are thought to be masculine traits. Hochschild noted that women who feel comfortable with these norms tend to self-select themselves for entry into the occupation, although they may eventually come to resent the stereotyping of their status.

Sociologist Cynthia Epstein points out that in many occupations the way women think about themselves has changed. She observes that in the 1960s, when she began interviewing women lawyers, they often denied that

Examples of the "eyebrow flash": (a) French woman, (b) Yanomami man, (c) Yanomami young woman, (d) !Kung woman (central Kalahari), (e) Huli man (Papua-New Guinea), (f) Balinese man.

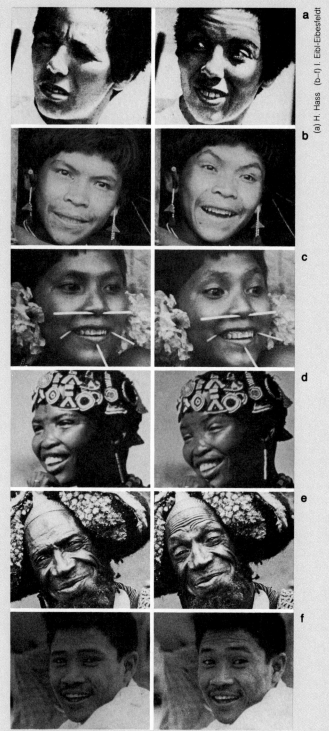

(a) H. Hass (b–f) I. Eibl-Eibesfeldt

Reproduced with permission from: Eibl-Eibesfeldt, HUMAN ETHOLOGY (New York: Aldine de Gruyter) Copyright © 1989 by Irenäus Eibl-Eibesfeldt.

they were working as hard as their male colleagues in order to earn equally high salaries and have the same chances of gaining powerful positions in the firm; "in the 1960s it was unwomanly to concede such attitudes" (1988, p. 88). Ten years later, when she reinterviewed the same women, she found that many felt free to express the desire for wealth and power and had developed strategies that would permit them to compete with men for available judgeships. Changing norms of acceptable aspiration and emotional expression among women have allowed some to shed the stereotype of women as expressive specialists who lack the ability to compete with men in performing rational, technical tasks.

Other researchers have shown that although women and men are capable of the same emotional range and behaviors, socialization tends to create differences that can play an important role in the relationships of adult couples. Francesca Cancian (1987), for example, has studied the ways in which men and women express their love for each other. She finds that men are more likely to act in instrumental ways—that is, to try to attain a goal by using the real and symbolic instruments available to them. Women are more likely to act in expressive ways, by saying what they feel or showing it in their bodily actions. A man may wash his wife's car as a way of showing his affection, but the wife may not recognize this act as an expression of love. The wife may yearn for him to express his love the way she does. Each is likely to misunderstand the other's motives and feelings.

In a recent survey of married couples, Andrew Greeley found that 91 percent of married people say that they can discuss intimate matters with their spouse (cited in Schmidt, 1990). However, close observation

and in-depth interviews like those conducted by Cancian produce quite different results. Research of this nature, which explores one of the most mysterious aspects of human life, is likely to remain an active frontier of sociology for years to come.

SUMMARY

Socialization refers to all the processes whereby we learn to behave according to the norms of our culture. Primary socialization consists of the ways in which the newborn individual is molded into a person who can interact with others according to the expectations of society. Secondary socialization occurs in childhood and adolescence, primarily through schooling, and adult socialization refers to the ways in which a person learns the norms associated with new statuses.

Among the most basic questions in the study of human socialization is that of "nature" versus "nurture": To what extent does the development of the person depend on biological factors, and to what extent does it depend on learning? The two extreme positions on this question are biological determinism, which holds that individual behavior is an outgrowth of the person's genetic makeup, and *behaviorism*, which asserts that all behavior is learned.

Behaviorism originated in the work of Ivan Pavlov, who showed that behavior that was thought to be instinctual could in fact be shaped or *conditioned* by learning situations. This line of research was continued by John B. Watson, whose experiments revealed the ability of conditioning to shape behavior in almost any direction. B. F. Skinner carried behaviorism still further by developing the technique known as *operant conditioning*, in which a behavior that was not originally part of a stimulus–response pattern is shaped into that pattern.

The experiments of the behaviorists seem to indicate that biological factors play a minor role in socialization. On the other hand, biological determinists point to evidence that individual development is strongly influenced by biological factors. However, such factors alone are not sufficient for socialization to occur. This is illustrated by studies of *feral children*, children who have been reared outside human society. Such children are able to learn, but they do so far more slowly than children who have not been isolated in early childhood.

Other studies have found that normal development requires not only the presence of other humans but also the attention and love of adults. Children raised in orphanages and other nonfamily settings are more likely to develop emotional problems and to be retarded in their cognitive development than comparable children who are reared by their parents. The influence of social environment on individual behavior has also been demonstrated in experiments in which social situations are manipulated in such a way as to lead to the creation of new group norms.

Social theories of personality formation focus on the influence of groups and social institutions on the formation of individual capabilities. The earliest of these theories was proposed by Sigmund Freud. Freud believed that the personality develops out of the processes of socialization through which the infant is gradually forced to control its bodily urges. His model of the personality divides the personality into three functional areas: the *id*, from which unsocialized drives arise; the *superego*, which incorporates the moral codes of elders; and the *ego*, or one's conception of oneself in relation to others.

In the growth of the personality, the formation of the ego or social self is critical. According to Freud, this takes place in a series of stages in which the conflict between the demands of the superego and the id is always threatening to disrupt the functioning of the ego.

Interactionist models of socialization stress the development of the social self through interaction with others. One of the earliest interactionist theories was Charles Horton Cooley's concept of the "looking glass self," the reflection of our self we think we see in the behaviors of other people toward us. This concept was carried further by George Herbert Mead, who emphasized the importance of culture in the formation of the self. Mead believed that when children play, they practice "taking the roles of others," especially the *significant others* in their social environment. When they are able to participate in games, they have developed the ability to "take the role of the *generalized other*"—that is, to shape their participation according to the roles of the other participants.

Erik Erikson bridged the gap between Freud's psychological theory and the interactionist theories of Mead and Cooley. His theory of personality formation is based on the concept of *identification*, the social process whereby the individual chooses adults as models and attempts to imitate their behav-

ior. The result of this process is the person's *identity*, the aspect of the ego that conceives of the self in relation to society.

Social scientists have also studied the development of the child's moral reasoning. The leading theory in this area is that of Lawrence Kohlberg, who proposed a three-stage sequence of moral development in which the child's moral reasoning evolves from emphasis on reward and punishment to the ability to distinguish between social laws and moral principles.

Studies of the environments in which socialization occurs have found that normal development requires the involvement of one or more adults in the care of the child, as well

WHERE TO FIND IT

Books

The Child and Society, 4th ed. (Frederick Elkin and Gerald Handel; Random House, 1984). A basic text that offers in-depth coverage of most aspects of childhood socialization.

Not in Our Genes (R. C. Lewontin, Steven Rose, and Leon Kamin; Pantheon, 1984). A strong but fair critique of biological thinking in the field of human development.

In a Different Voice (Carol Gilligan; Harvard University Press, 1982). Argues that the classic theories of human development are biased toward male development and hence neglect important aspects of socialization and personality development.

Journals

Social Psychology Quarterly A journal of the American Sociological Association that is devoted to recent research on "the processes and products of social interaction."

Journal of Health and Social Behavior Another journal of the American Sociological

Association. This one specializes in "sociological approaches to the definition and analysis of problems bearing on human health and illness" and often contains important articles on child welfare, socialization, and problems of health and development through the life cycle.

Other Sources

Basic Handbook of Child Psychiatry (Joseph D. Noshpitz, ed.; Basic Books, 1979). This two-volume series contains many excellent articles about human development. The focus is interdisciplinary, although there is also an emphasis on abnormal socialization and treatment.

Statistical Yearbook Published annually by the United Nations, this is a valuable source of comparative data on infant mortality and other indicators of the health of children, as well as statistical material on education, literacy, and other measures of socialization.

as public policies that promote such involvement. These conclusions indicate the importance of the child's "micro-environment"—that is, the family members, friends, and kin with whom the child interacts on a regular and frequent basis. Also important is the larger social environment, in which other social structures besides the family continue the socialization process throughout a person's lifetime.

After the family, the most important *agents of socialization* are the schools. Other socializing agents in the community include clubs, associations, and churches. But the dominant agent of socialization outside the family is the *peer group*, an interacting group of people of about the same age. Peer groups exert a significant influence on the individual, beginning in adolescence and continuing through childhood. The mass media, especially television, are another significant agent of socialization in American society.

An important aspect of socialization is *gender socialization*, or the ways in which we learn our gender identity and develop according to cultural norms of masculinity and femininity. *Gender identity* is an individual's own feeling of whether he or she is a male or a female. The development of gender identity occurs during a critical period of the child's socialization and cannot be changed after that time.

GLOSSARY

socialization: the processes whereby we learn to behave according to the norms of our culture (**p. 160**).

behaviorism: a theory that states that all behavior is learned and that this learning occurs through the process known as conditioning (**p. 162**).

conditioning: the shaping of behavior through reward and punishment (**p. 162**).

operant conditioning: a conditioning technique in which a behavior that was not originally part of a stimulus–response pattern is shaped into that pattern (**p. 163**).

feral child: a child reared outside human society (**p. 164**).

id: according to Freud, the part of the human personality from which all innate drives arise (**p. 168**).

superego: according to Freud, the part of the human personality that internalizes the moral codes of adults (**p. 168**).

ego: according to Freud, the part of the human personality that is the individual's conception of himself or herself in relation to others (**p. 168**).

significant other: any person who is important to an individual (**p. 170**).

generalized other: a person's internalized conception of the expectations and attitudes held by society (**p. 171**).

identification: the social process whereby an individual chooses role models and attempts to imitate their behavior (**p. 172**).

agent of socialization: an individual, group, or institution that helps teach the beliefs, norms, and values of a society (**p. 178**).

anticipatory socialization: socialization that prepares an individual for a role that he or she is likely to assume later in life (**p. 178**).

peer group: an interacting group of people of about the same age that has a significant influence on the norms and values of its members (**p. 179**).

gender socialization: the ways in which we learn our gender identity and develop according to cultural norms of masculinity and femininity (**p. 180**).

VISUAL SOCIOLOGY

Socialization through Interaction

Socialization occurs throughout society; it is not limited to interactions in families and schools. These pictures demonstrate how easy it is to watch socialization as it occurs if we are aware of some of its more common forms and settings. The next time you are in a hospital waiting room or a department store or walking past a schoolyard or playground, look around you for some of these kinds of socialization.

Much socialization of children takes the form of direct teaching and both intentional and unintentional modeling, in which the child learns by observing an older person. In addition, anticipatory socialization prepares the child for future roles. Such socialization occurs in the seemingly trivial play of a child with a doll; in the "coming out" of a debutante, in which she learns what goes into a successful charity gala or ball; and in the infinite variety of other ways in which we practice the roles that will be ours in later life.

Socialization can also be viewed in terms of who is doing the socializing—that is, the agents of socialization. There is a great deal of difference between what we learn in the classroom or family circle and what we learn from our friends and peers. In the peer group, as an old Arab saying has it, "we become more the people of our time, less the parent's children." That is, we learn the behavior and attitudes that are unique to our generation, although the definition of what is "in" and what is "out" may differ from one group to another.

In the peer group, also, we sometimes learn behaviors that are not approved by the larger society. Among the peer group of construction workers, for example, the older and more experienced members usually teach the "tricks of the trade" to those who are less experienced. They also teach the younger workers how to "take it easy" at appropriate times and even, perhaps, how to ogle passing women. Through the peer group at work, younger workers learn not only the skills required but the entire culture of the workplace, such as the "corporate uniform" and the rules for interacting with corporate colleagues.

© Catherine Ursillo, Photo Researchers

© Peter Arnold, Inc.

© Marc P. Anderson

© Bob Adelman, Magnum

© Rick Kopstein, Monkmeyer

© G. Zimbel, Monkmeyer

© Ray Ellis

© Beth Ullman, Taurus

CHAPTER OUTLINE

● **Groups and the Social Fabric**

- Social Categories and Social Groups
- Primary and Secondary Groups
- Communities
- Networks

● **Interaction in Groups**

- Principles of Interaction
- The Economic Person vs. the Social Person
- Communication and Behavior in Groups
- Interaction and Group Structure

● **Formal Organizations and Bureaucracy**

- Bureaucracy and Obedience to Authority
- Commitment to Bureaucratic Groups

● **Groups in Complex Societies**

Photograph by D. Stevens

Two members of a Los Angeles street gang

CHAPTER 7

INTERACTION: FROM COUPLES TO CORPORATIONS

One warm Saturday evening in late September, more than sixty people were drinking, talking, and listening to the latest soul music and love songs on their portable radios. The Lions were gathered around their bench and the Senior Greeks around theirs. Sally and her friends, like many others, ambled from bench to bench. It was peaceful; there were no rumors of enemy gangs and the only disagreements concerned who would go buy the wine and beer.

At 10:30, Sally and several of her friends headed out of the park to see if they could find someone to buy more pineapple wine. As they passed a bench where several of the Primroses (a female gang from the western side of 32nd Street) were drinking, Sally tripped over a member's foot and a violent struggle ensued. A circle immediately formed around the two young women and when some young men attempted to separate them, the combatants clawed the men. . . .

Blood flowed as they struggled, pulled each other's hair, scratched, punched, bit, and ripped each other's blouses. The crowd was enjoying the scene and began to cheer them on. The women were separated for a few minutes, just enough time to wash their faces and to be encouraged by their friends. One of them grabbed a quart beer bottle and swung it at the other, but the bottle did not break. The fight continued for about another half hour until they were separated. Each side declared a victory and swore that a return engagement was necessary. (Horowitz, 1985, pp. 114–115)

In this account of a fight among members of rival gangs by sociologist Ruth Horowitz, the participants are primarily of Mexican origin and think of themselves as Chicanos and Chicanas. They live in a crowded Chicago neighborhood with a long history of gang activity. In fact, every immigrant group that has settled in the area in the past century has had its gangs of teenagers and young adults. These gangs defend their neighborhood "turf"

and function as social groups that give their adolescent members an identity and in some cases prestige. But in this episode the sociologist is also interested in why the fight broke out when everything seemed so peaceful.

After the fight, Horowitz tells us, "Sally was punished by her mother and had to return home by six o'clock for three weeks, but she swore revenge on the young woman who had come to Sally's park and had 'intentionally' tripped her, an act that demonstrated her disdain of Sally and her friends" (p. 115). Why, we might ask, did Sally immediately define the situation as an intentional trip? To answer this question Horowitz used the concept of *impression management*, which was proposed by one of the best-known analysts of social interaction, Erving Goffman. This phrase refers to behaviors that attempt to "manage" the impressions given to others in order to control their perceptions of a person or event.

When you trip over someone's foot, you can blame the event on crowded conditions or inattention and simply say "Excuse me," thereby placing blame on the situation rather than on the other person's intentions. But to save face for herself and her gang, Sally chose to interpret the trip as intentional. She was then required to defend her honor and that of her gang by acting aggressively. Whether or not she was tripped intentionally, the point is that she did not say "Excuse me" or wait for an apology. She needed to establish her prestige within her gang and in the park, and her impression management depended on fighting. She was not prepared to "be cool" in this situation. "Coolness," Horowitz notes, "is the ability to stand back from certain situations and rationally evaluate others' actions" (p. 88). But in adolescent gangs coolness is of no use when others define the situation as one in which a person's honor is being challenged. Such situations demand an immediate response if one is not to be labeled a "punk" and lose the respect of the other gang members.

GROUPS AND THE SOCIAL FABRIC

As Horowitz's work shows, we judge one another in large part by how well we perform in groups. To be well socialized in a given culture is to be an expert in that culture's norms of social interaction—that is, its rules for behaving in groups. It can be argued, in fact, that one of the functions of education is to socialize the individual in the norms of a far broader array of groups than would be possible through family socialization alone (LeFebvre, 1972).

The "social fabric" of modern societies is composed of millions of groups. Some are as intimate as a pair of lovers. Others, like the modern corporation or university, are extremely large and are composed of many interrelated subgroups. We need to perform well in all of these groups, and to have this ability is to be considered successful by others. But the knowledge needed for success in a group with a formal structure of roles and statuses is quite different from the "smarts" needed for success in intimate groups.

In this chapter we analyze some important aspects of the way people behave in groups. We begin by describing the most common types of groups and showing how they can be linked together by overlapping memberships. This first portion of the chapter illustrates the functionalist view of group interaction. It looks at the structure of groups and the way they operate in society. It also provides typologies of groups and insights into how they are organized. However, simply describing categories of groups and their structure does not explain how groups maintain the commitment of their members or why they change as a consequence of changes in their size and other characteristics. In the middle portions of the chapter we will examine these questions, focusing on the give and take that occurs in groups of different types and on how these interactions produce group norms. This section illustrates interactionist research on behavior in groups.

In the final section of the chapter we will show how formal organization and bureaucracy operate to control conflict and cope with change in groups. The concepts introduced here will be used over and over again in other chapters, for, as we saw in Chapter 3, groups of all kinds are the building blocks of society.

Social Categories and Social Groups

We sometimes group people together artificially in the process of analyzing society (e.g., all the teenagers in a particular community). This results in a **social category**, a collection of individuals grouped together because they share a trait that is deemed by the observer to be socially relevant (e.g., sex, race, or age). But there are also groups in which we actually participate and in which we have distinct roles and statuses. These are **social groups**. A social group is a set of individuals who are recruited according to some membership criterion and are bound together by a set of membership rights and mutual obligations.

The members of a social group have a sense of belonging to the group, which means

The characteristics of social groups include membership criteria, rights and obligations, a sense of belonging, a clear social structure, cohesion, norms and goals, and the possibility of conflict.

that they are aware of their participation in the group and know the identities of the other members of the group. This also implies that group members have a sense of the boundaries of their group—that is, of who belongs and who does not belong. Groups themselves have a social structure that arises from repeated interaction among their members. In those interactions the members form ideas about the status of each and the role each can play in the group (Holy, 1985; Homans, 1950; Merton and Kitt, 1950). A skilled member of a work group, for example, may become the leader while an unskilled member may become recognized as the person others instruct and send on errands.

Through their interactions, group members develop feelings of attachment to each other. Groups whose members have strong positive attachments to each other are said to be highly cohesive, while those whose members are not very strongly attached to each other are said to lack cohesion. Groups also

develop norms governing behavior in the group, and they generally have goals such as performing a task, playing a game, or making public policy. Finally, because groups are composed of interacting human beings we must also recognize that all groups have the potential for conflict among members; the resolution of such conflicts may be vital to continued group cohesion.

Membership criteria, awareness and boundaries, a clear social structure, cohesion, norms and goals, and the possibility of conflict are among the dimensions that define different groups. If we briefly compare two types of groups—say, a computer bulletin board and a married couple—the importance of these dimensions becomes apparent. Membership in the couple is exclusive and cohesion is based on intimacy and trust. If he comes home and says, "Honey, I brought a new woman into our relationship—I think you'll like her," she is likely to throw him out, or worse. Among members of the computer bulletin board, in contrast, the only criterion for membership may be ownership of the proper equipment and payment of dues. Not all the members will know each other, and new members can be added without any sense of reduced cohesion such as would occur in the case of the married couple.

Primary and Secondary Groups

One of the most important distinctions in the study of groups, to which we referred briefly in Chapter 3, is between primary and secondary groups. Here again is Charles Horton Cooley's definition of the **primary group**: "By primary groups I mean those characterized by intimate face-to-face association and cooperation. They are primary in several senses, but chiefly in that they are fundamental in forming the social nature and ideals of the individual" (1909, p. 25). The family is, of course, a primary group. So are friendship groups, the cliques that form within organizations, and many, but not all, teams in sports, business, and the military. For most of us, the primary group of close relatives and friends is the intimate level of our social life; it is the realm of interaction that carries the most emotional content and in which we feel the most affection or love.

Cooley's definition of the primary group requires a few qualifications. First, the idea of face-to-face interaction may be confusing. Some primary groups maintain close feelings of solidarity, or what Cooley called "we feeling," without regular face-to-face interaction. For example, some families can maintain close ties over long distances. Indeed, in a study of family visiting patterns Sheila Klatzky (1971) found that a major reason for long-distance travel in the United States is to maintain family ties. And many relationships that must be considered primary from the standpoint of intimacy have been maintained over long distances for long periods. But there is usually some medium of communication, such as letters or phone calls, that is used to replace proximity in maintaining the bonds of family or friendship.

A second important qualification of Cooley's definition relates to the matter of intimacy itself. Intimacy in primary groups is not always a positive emotion. Indeed, anger, jealousy, and even violence may be just as much features of primary-group intimacy as are love and affection. One way of thinking about this issue is to realize that intimacy in groups allows a person to show any aspect of his or her personality. In a primary group you can usually show your grumpy side or react emotionally without fearing that the other members of the group will withdraw from you.

The concept of a **secondary group** follows from Cooley's definition of primary groups, although he did not actually use the term (Dewey, 1948). Secondary groups are characterized by relationships that involve few aspects of their members' personalities. In such groups the members' reasons for participation are usually limited to a small number of goals. In contrast with the close ties that mark primary groups, the bonds of association in secondary groups are usually based on some form of contract, a written or unwritten agreement that specifies the scope of interaction within the group. All organizations and associations are secondary groups. Your sociology class is a secondary group. Imagine what the response would be if the instructor suddenly asked everyone to hug his or her neighbor or urged students to invest their savings in a stock scheme. Such improbable actions would highlight the unwritten contractual relationship between teacher and student, a relationship that does not allow for such requests.

The Unstable Triad. Primary groups tend to be relatively small because as the number of members increases, the possibility of conflict and coalitions, which split up larger groups, also increases. The strongest social bonds are formed between two people (be they best friends, lovers, or married couples) and are known as **dyads**. If additional people are introduced to the two-person group, problems may arise. Conventional wisdom has much to say about this matter—for example, "Two's a couple, three's a crowd"—and if one observes children's play groups it soon becomes clear that much of the conflict they experience has to do with the desire to have an exclusive relationship with a best friend.

In families, too, the shift from a dyad to a three-person group or **triad** often creates problems. A couple who are experiencing a high level of conflict may believe that a baby will offer them a challenge they can meet together, thereby renewing their love for each other. At first this may seem to be the case, but as the infant makes more demands on the couple's energy and time, the father may feel that the baby is depriving him of attention from his wife and may become jealous of the newcomer. For some couples, the addition of

The people in this photo may appear to be simply a casual assortment of individuals watching an event in a public park. But they include several kinds of social groups. The three friends in the foreground with radios make up a primary group. The couple on the right is a dyad. And in the background can be seen a couple with a baby; they constitute a triad.

© Marc P. Anderson

These children in a school class are dyads in action. Every time the teacher or the camp counselor asks the children to line up in twos, the children are reminded of the conflicts that arise between their loyalty to the intimate group of two or three and the loyalty they may have to larger groups within the classroom.

a child can actually increase the chance of divorce, resulting in a stable mother–child dyad and a single male.

The instability of triads can also be seen among siblings. The third child often has a rough time of it. Not only is the third child "the baby" who imagines it impossible ever to perform as well as the older siblings, but he or she has committed the unintentional sin of breaking the bond between the two older children. Whenever one of the latter becomes intimate and loving toward "the baby," the other will demand attention and remind the third child that he or she is the newcomer. This point should not be exaggerated; sibling triads can be stable and happy. In general, however, the addition of a third child increases the possibility of conflict and coalitions within the family (Caplow, 1969).

Communities

At a level of social organization between the primary group and the larger institutions of the nation-state are communities of all descriptions. **Communities** are sets of primary and secondary groups in which the individual carries out important life functions such as raising a family, gaining a living, finding shelter, and the like. Communities may be either **territorial** or **nonterritorial**. Both include primary and secondary groups, but territorial communities are contained within geographic boundaries, whereas nonterritorial communities are networks of associations that form around shared goals. When people speak of a "professional community," such as the med-

ical or legal community, they are referring to a nonterritorial community. Territorial communities are populations that function within a particular geographic area, and this is by far the more common meaning of the term as it is used both in everyday speech and in social-scientific writing (Bell and Newby, 1974; Suttles, 1972).

Territorial communities are usually composed of one or more neighborhoods. The neighborhood level of group contact includes primary groups (particularly families and peer groups) that form attachments on the basis of proximity—that is, as a result of living near one another. In studies of how people form friendship groups in suburban neighborhoods, both Herbert Gans (1967, 1976) and Bennett Berger (1968) found that proximity tended to explain patterns of primary-group formation better than any other variable except social class. People tend to find friends among others of the same social class who live near enough to allow ease of interaction and casual visiting. In perhaps the most extensive investigation of the effects of proximity, Leon Festinger, Stanley Schachter, and Kurt Back (1950) found that in married-student housing at MIT the rate of friendship choices decreased with the distance between housing units. The closer one person lived to another, the more likely that person was to list the other as a friend.

In simpler societies, in which the rates of urbanization, population growth, and social mobility have not accelerated the way they have in large-scale industrial societies, people are used to living together on the basis of kinship and tribal attachments. As Robert Park noted, it is only under conditions of rapid and persistent social change that proximity helps explain why people form groups (Park, 1967/1926).

Networks

In modern societies people form their deepest friendships in face-to-face groups, but these groups are, in turn, integrated into larger and more impersonal secondary-group structures that may extend well beyond the bounds of territorial communities. In *Street Corner Society* (1943), the study of street-corner peer groups mentioned in the preceding chapter,

William F. Whyte opened with this observation:

The Nortons were Doc's gang. The group was brought together primarily by Doc, and it was built around Doc. When Doc was growing up, there was a kid's gang on Norton Street for every significant difference in age. There was a gang that averaged about three years older than Doc; there was Doc's gang, which included Nutsy, Danny, and a number of others; there was a group about three years younger, which included Joe Dodge and Frank Bonilli; and there was still a younger group, to which Carl and Tommy belonged. [p. 3]

Like the gangs Ruth Horowitz studied in contemporary Chicago, the Nortons were active in a network of neighborhood-level peer groups. They would compete against other groups of boys of roughly the same age in a yearly round of baseball, bowling, and occasional interneighborhood fights (the latter occurring mainly in their younger teenage years). But the Nortons were also integrated into the community through some of its secondary associations. For example, at election time they were recruited by the local political party organization, and some were recruited by the racketeers who controlled their low-income neighborhood. Party organizations and organized-crime groups are examples of secondary associations that extend outside territorial communities.

In-groups and Out-groups. The "corner boys" studied by Whyte tended to be hostile toward similar groups from other street corners and even toward certain boys from their own territory. These distinctions between groups are common and are referred to as *in-group–out-group* distinctions. The **in-group** consists of one's own peers, whereas **out-groups** are those one considers to be outside the bounds of intimacy. Georg Simmel observed that in-group–out-group distinctions can form around almost any quality, even one that outsiders would not consider meaningful at all. Thus, in a study of juvenile groups in a Chicago housing project, Gerald Suttles (1972) found that distinctions were made between boys who lived in lighter or darker brick buildings.

In-group–out-group distinctions are usually based on such qualities as income, race, and religion. In "Cornerville," the community Whyte studied, group boundaries were based on educational background, particularly college versus noncollege education. One of Whyte's informants explained this distinction: "In Cornerville the noncollege man has an inferiority complex. He hasn't had much education, and he has that feeling of inferiority. . . . Now the college man felt that way before he went to college, but when he is in college, he tries to throw it off. . . . Naturally, the noncollege man resents that" (Whyte, 1943, p. 79).

In-group–out-group distinctions often make it difficult for secondary associations to attract members from both groups. We saw in the Robbers Cave experiment (Chapter 6) that each group of boys viewed the other as an out-group and that the only way to merge them into a single cohesive group was to establish goals that required the two groups to cooperate. Similarly, when two ethnic or racial groups in a community make in-group–out-group distinctions, they often find themselves drifting toward different political parties or forming distinct factions within the same party rather than uniting to find solutions to common problems.

Reference Groups. An important area of sociological research is the study of how the decisions we make are influenced by significant or relevant others—that is, by people we admire and whose behavior we try to imitate. The ways in which other people influence our attitudes and behavior are often discussed in terms of the **reference group**, a group that the individual uses as a frame of reference for self-evaluation and attitude formation (Merton, 1968; Secord and Backman, 1974). Some reference groups set and enforce certain values and norms, while others serve as a standard for comparison (Kelly, 1952).

An example of the influence of reference groups can be seen in a study of students at Bennington College conducted by Theodore Newcomb (1958). Newcomb found that conservative students often sought out groups

Some reference groups set and enforce values and norms, while others serve as a standard for comparison.

of like-minded peers who would affirm the values they had brought with them from home. They also tended to go home for visits more often than liberal students. By their senior year, however, they were likely to have shifted their attitudes to match those of a more liberal reference group, since the majority of the students and faculty at Bennington were liberal or radical.

The concept of reference groups has many practical applications. In market research, for example, it is common practice to determine where potential customers tend to seek help in forming their attitudes—which magazines, writers, or television commentators they turn to for guidance. These *opinion leaders*, as they are sometimes called, are the customer's reference group in a particular area of consumption (Katz, 1957).

Note that a reference group is not the same thing as a primary group. The friends with whom you spend much of your time are a primary group and are likely to act as a reference group as well. But we can have numerous reference groups, each of which influences us in different areas. As you choose a profession or career, you will be influenced by the values and norms of reference groups in that field. As you gain new statuses, such as that of parent, voter, or supervisor, you will look to other reference groups: child-care experts, political commentators, and the like. A reference group thus can be quite limited in its relationship to you as an individual: Its influence may act on what you are to become rather than on what you are now.

Social Network Analysis. The study of who people associate with, how those choices are made, and the effects of those choices on social structure and individual personality is known as *social network analysis*. The British social scientist Elizabeth Bott, one of the founders of this branch of sociology, notes that in a social network "each person is, as it were, in touch with a number of people, some of whom are directly in touch with each other and some of whom are not. . . . I find it convenient to talk of a social field of this kind as a network. The image I have is of a set of points, some of which are joined by lines. The points of the image are people, or sometimes

groups, and the lines indicate which people interact with each other" (1977, p. 256).

Social network analysis grew out of studies of the choices people make in becoming members of various social groups. Today network analysis extends beyond this rather narrow subject to studies illustrating how the interconnectedness of certain members of a society can produce interaction patterns that may have a lasting influence on the lives of people both within and outside the network. Sociologist Aubrey Bonnett (1981), for example, studied the "susu's," or rotating credit associations, formed by West Indian ethnic groups in New York and other American cities. These associations are actually networks composed of numerous small groups of neighbors and kin who join with other similar groups, pay an entrance fee, and take turns borrowing funds from the association at far lower interest rates than a bank would charge. Bonnett showed that these associations bring together members of immigrant groups with different histories and values. As one susu organizer told him, "In my susu I have had members from all the islands. . . . You would be amazed to know how it has helped to get ourselves together, yes, this is really a West Indian thing" (p. 67).

Sociologists who study the rich and powerful have described the networks that function in the world of high finance. Figure 7-1, which is taken from a study of the workings of the Rockefeller Financial Group, was used by William Domhoff to show how a network of Rockefeller family members and close business associates in major banks and insurance companies can communicate through the network to decide on huge urban development projects in cities throughout the United States. In other research on social networks, sociologists have demonstrated how the net-

Figure 7–1: **Interlocking Directorates Among the Core Financial Institutions in the Rockefeller Group**

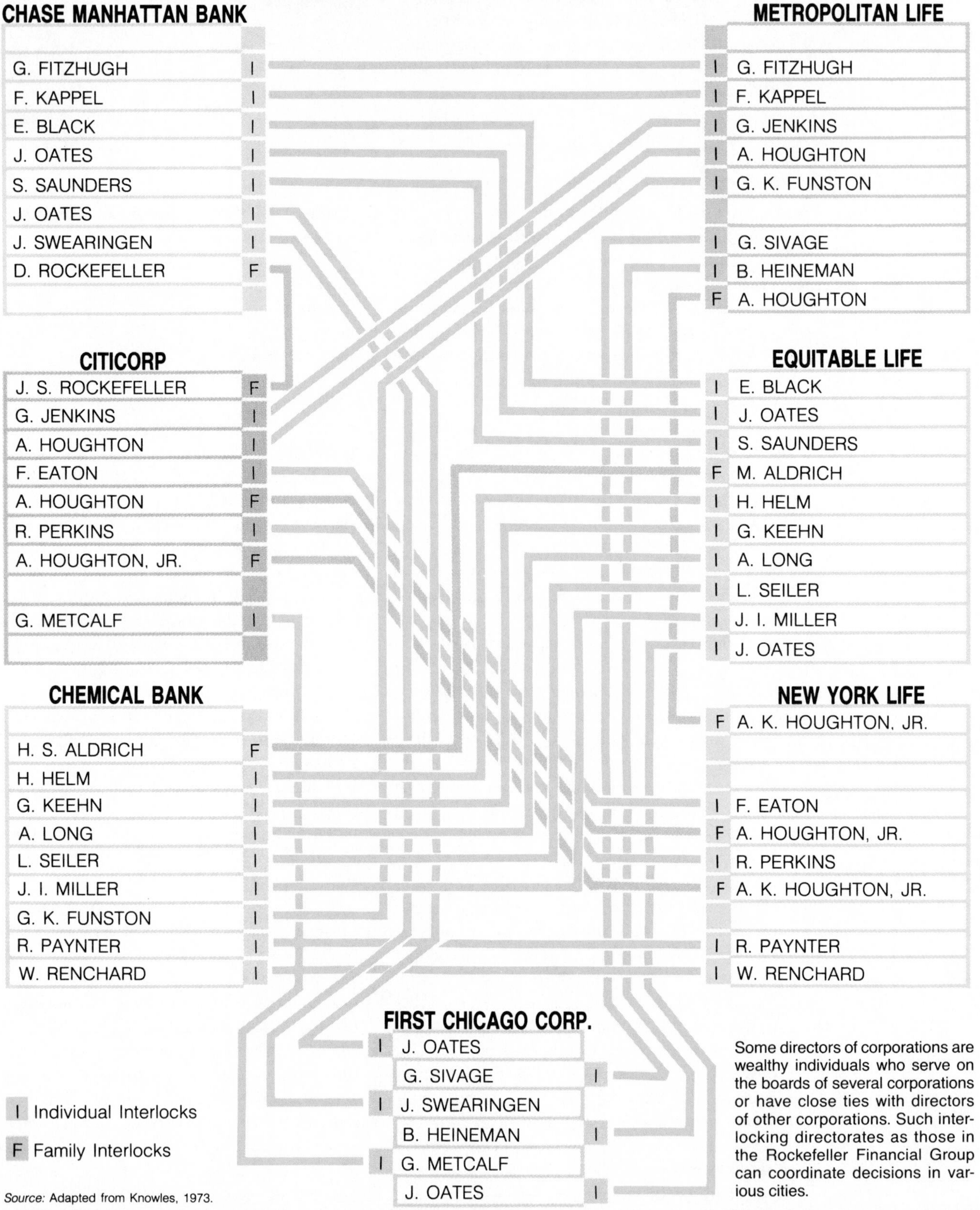

CHASE MANHATTAN BANK

G. FITZHUGH	I
F. KAPPEL	I
E. BLACK	I
J. OATES	I
S. SAUNDERS	I
J. OATES	I
J. SWEARINGEN	I
D. ROCKEFELLER	F

METROPOLITAN LIFE

I	G. FITZHUGH
I	F. KAPPEL
I	G. JENKINS
I	A. HOUGHTON
I	G. K. FUNSTON
I	G. SIVAGE
I	B. HEINEMAN
F	A. HOUGHTON

CITICORP

J. S. ROCKEFELLER	F
G. JENKINS	I
A. HOUGHTON	I
F. EATON	I
A. HOUGHTON	F
R. PERKINS	I
A. HOUGHTON, JR.	F
G. METCALF	I

EQUITABLE LIFE

I	E. BLACK
I	J. OATES
I	S. SAUNDERS
F	M. ALDRICH
I	H. HELM
I	G. KEEHN
I	A. LONG
I	L. SEILER
I	J. I. MILLER
I	J. OATES

CHEMICAL BANK

H. S. ALDRICH	F
H. HELM	I
G. KEEHN	I
A. LONG	I
L. SEILER	I
J. I. MILLER	I
G. K. FUNSTON	I
R. PAYNTER	I
W. RENCHARD	I

NEW YORK LIFE

F	A. K. HOUGHTON. JR.
I	F. EATON
F	A. HOUGHTON, JR.
I	R. PERKINS
F	A. K. HOUGHTON, JR.
I	R. PAYNTER
I	W. RENCHARD

FIRST CHICAGO CORP.

I	J. OATES	
	G. SIVAGE	I
I	J. SWEARINGEN	
	B. HEINEMAN	I
I	G. METCALF	
	J. OATES	I

I Individual Interlocks

F Family Interlocks

Some directors of corporations are wealthy individuals who serve on the boards of several corporations or have close ties with directors of other corporations. Such interlocking directorates as those in the Rockefeller Financial Group can coordinate decisions in various cities.

Source: Adapted from Knowles, 1973.

works of individuals and groups within which people interact provide social support in times of stress or illness. Interestingly, this research often finds that people's social-support networks shrink as they become elderly and infirm and lose the ability to offer support or other resources in exchange (Fischer, 1982).

INTERACTION IN GROUPS

In the preceding section we introduced a wide range of groups and structures of groups. We began with the basic building blocks of social structure, the primary group and the secondary group. We saw that these groups are embedded in more complex structures of groups, such as communities and social networks. We also noted that reference groups act to confirm an individual's values and behavior, and that the distinctions we make between in- and out-groups help us maintain the boundaries of the groups in which we participate. But these descriptions do not tell us what principles of interaction operate to produce cohesion or instability in groups. In this section, therefore, we will take a closer look at interaction in groups.

Simply to observe that a society is a fabric of groups is to neglect two important questions: How can groups stay together in the first place, and how can a fabric of groups produce a cohesive society? Indeed, all around us we see evidence that groups constantly fall apart: Romantic ardor cools; marriages fail; friends argue and seek new friends; successful rock bands split up; businesses go bankrupt; entire nations are fragmented by social and economic upheavals. Certainly new groups are forming all the time, but others are continually breaking up.

When a group disintegrates we often hear explanations like "I felt that I was only giving and not getting"; "We all started to grow in separate directions"; "I no longer shared their values"; or "He [she, they] wanted too much of the [credit, money, power]." In short, when one listens to explanations of why groups fail to stay together it sounds as if people are continually seeking more rewards for themselves or blaming others for taking too much of whatever rewards are available—too much attention, affection, approval, prestige, money, power, or whatever. If this is the case—if people are selfish and take whatever they can get in groups—it does not seem likely that groups could have much cohesiveness or stability or that society could have a recognizable group fabric.

One can imagine even more serious consequences of human greed and self-serving behavior. The seventeenth-century English philosopher Thomas Hobbes was deeply concerned about the relationship between the individual and society. How is society, or any group within it, possible if every individual puts his or her own interests above those of everyone else? Hobbes warned that the sum total of everyone's selfish acts would be a "war of all against all." In *Leviathan*, his great treatise on this problem, he concluded that humanity needs an all-powerful but benevolent dictator to prevent social chaos.

Today people throughout the world reject this notion. We strive to create a social order based on individual freedom, democracy, and the rule of law. Nevertheless, wherever we look we see major threats to such a social order. Often such threats emerge when people feel that the groups they count on, such as political parties and legislatures, are not acting fairly. This brings us back to the question of how, given individual selfishness, humans can achieve order, cooperation, trust, and democracy rather than coercion, terror, and chaos.

The pleasure principle: People seek pleasure and avoid pain.

Principles of Interaction

Social scientists have identified certain principles of interaction that help explain both stability and change in human groups. Among them are the pleasure principle, the rationality principle, the reciprocity principle, and the fairness principle.

The Pleasure Principle. People seek pleasure and avoid pain. This basic principle is easily misunderstood. It implies nothing about what a person considers pleasurable or painful. As we will see shortly, this is a very personal matter that depends on the norms that have been internalized by the individual. In fact, many people seem to find pain or discomfort desirable; examples include athletes and dieters, who seek pain or deprive themselves of pleasure in order to experience the thrill of athletic victory or the satisfaction of wearing a smaller size.

The pleasure principle does not address the question of what people value; all it states is that once one knows what kind of pleasure one wants, one will seek more of it and less of other values that yield less personal pleasure (Bentham, 1789; Homans, 1961). When applied to behavior in groups, the pleasure principle simply means that over time people will continue to interact in a group in which they experience the pleasure of reward but will withdraw from groups in which the pain they experience outweighs their pleasure.

The Rationality Principle. In social life, a gain in pleasure may require some pain as well. For example, when two members of a group of friends become very close and find pleasure in their intimacy, the others may feel left out, and this causes some pain both to the two intimate friends and to those who feel left out. In larger groups, when a rule such as a ban on smoking is made, some members will derive more pleasure than others from the cleaner air. Those whose smoking pleasure is denied will experience an increase in pain. Whether consciously or not, people in groups calculate whether they think they will benefit personally from continued interactions with others in the group. Thus, the smokers in the group may decide that their loss of pleasure outweighs the gains they get by being in the group, and they may decide to withdraw. In the small friendship group, the other friends may feel that the pain of their jealousy outweighs the pleasure of their friendship, and they may exclude the intimate pair from the group.

The rationality principle means that people change their behavior according to whether they think they will be worse or better off as a consequence. In other words, in making decisions about their interactions with others, people tend to make rough calculations of costs and benefits.

Does the idea that people seek a net gain from their interactions mean that they are greedy or self-centered or lacking in motives other than materialism? Not at all. Of course, there are extremes: Hedonists are people who can enjoy only the pleasures of the body. Egotists are people who especially enjoy praise and have little capacity for giving to others. Altruists are people who enjoy giving to others, often at the expense of other pleasures. But most people strive to behave in ways that give them physical pleasure and ego gratification ("boosts" or "strokes") and also give them the satisfaction of helping others. How far they go in either direction depends on what other members of the group are doing (how giving others are, how selfish, how self-sacrificing, etc.)—which brings us to the principle of reciprocity in interaction.

The Reciprocity Principle. In group interactions people usually adhere to a norm stating that what others do for you, you should try to do for others. This is one of the world's most commonly followed rules of interaction; it is known as the norm of reciprocity (Homans, 1950). The Roman statesman Cicero recognized this principle when he wrote "There is no duty more indispensable than that of returning a kindness. All men distrust one forgetful of a benefit" (quoted in Gouldner, 1980, p. 161). But it is not necessary to go back to ancient Rome for evidence that reciprocity is vital to continuing group interaction. Suppose that you and two classmates meet at a local pub. You pick up the check, and the other two agree to do so on future occasions. The next time, one of them pays the check. The third time, the third friend pleads a lack of cash and you each end up paying your own share. You and your second friend will feel that this is an embarrassing lapse on the part of your third friend. If such behavior continues, you will feel that the third friend "takes more than he/she gives" or thinks his/her company is worth the extra money paid by you. It is unlikely that this threesome will stay together very long if such imbalances continue.

Under what conditions could such a group continue in spite of the third friend's breach of the norm of reciprocity? One condition involves a loss of prestige for the third friend. You might ask him or her to make up the debt by doing something else for you. In

> *The reciprocity principle: People expect that others will behave toward them as they behave toward others.*

that case the third friend takes a subordinate position in the group, doing your bidding to make up for the inability to reciprocate on an equal basis (Homans, 1961; Mauss, 1966/1925).

On the other hand, suppose that the nonreciprocator is a movie star or a powerful politician. Then the other two members of the threesome might continue to pay in the hope that the third member would continue to spend his or her valuable time with them and that there would be an even greater reward for them in the future. This kind of relationship is quite common in social life. Social climbers seek ways to flatter and please someone who can confer prestige on them. Power seekers do the same in order to gain positions in which they will have power over others. A suitor may forgo reciprocity for quite a while in the hope of eventual conquest. In these situations and others like them, the participants in the interaction have an intuitive sense of what they are giving and what they are receiving in return or hope to receive in the future.

In the Bible the norm of reciprocity is stated in the form of the Golden Rule. The plea to "do unto others as you would have others do unto you" in effect urges individuals to go beyond expectations of immediate reciprocity and set examples of higher moral behavior in the hope that others will follow them. In real life, however, people tend to prefer that their gains be as immediate as possible.

The Fairness Principle. We see ample evidence that people tend to expect certain kinds of treatment from others and that they tend to become angry when they do not receive it, especially when they themselves feel that they have done what is expected of them in the situation. We want the rules to apply equally to everyone in the game, be it a friendly game of pool or the more complex game of corporate strategy. When we are not rewarded in the same ways as others, we say that we are being treated unfairly.

The unfair condition in which a person or group has come to expect certain rewards for certain efforts, yet does not get them while others do, is called *relative deprivation*. In

> *The fairness principle: People expect to be treated according to the same standards as others and to be rewarded in the same ways.*

times of economic depression, for example, all groups in society must make do with less, and all feel deprived in comparison to their previous condition. If the economy begins to improve and some groups begin to get higher wages or more profits while others experience only limited improvement, members of the less successful group will feel deprived relative to others and will very likely become angry even though their own plight has actually improved somewhat (Merton and Kitt, 1950). The concept of relative deprivation is useful in explaining some aspects of group behavior and appears again in Chapter 10 when we discuss how major social changes like revolutions occur.

People's ideas about what is fair in their interactions with others often conflict with simple calculations of gain and loss. The fact that they might come out ahead in an interaction does not guarantee that they will feel good about it and continue the interaction. This was demonstrated in a series of studies by Daniel Kahneman and his associates (1986). A large number of respondents were asked to judge the fairness of this situation:

A landlord rents out a small house. When the lease is due for renewal, the landlord learns that the tenant has taken a job very close to the house and is therefore unlikely to move. The landlord raises the rent $40 more than he was planning to.

An economist might argue that the tenant should think of the situation in terms of whether the rent increase is offset by the savings in the cost of travel to work (in terms of money, time, convenience, etc.). If the tenant still comes out ahead, it will make sense to sign the new lease. But over 90 percent of the respondents in Kahneman's survey said that the landlord was being unfair. In real life, when people feel that a transaction like this is unfair they often end the interaction, even at some cost to themselves. In this case people intuitively felt that the landlord was unfairly taking advantage of a gain made by the tenant (the new job) without adding anything to the property to earn the right to raise the rent.

The pure-rationality model of behavior predicts that people will act in their own interests so as to maximize their profit. If we were simple profit takers, however, our feelings about fairness would not play such a strong part in explaining group interaction (Frank, 1988). But in fact these feelings are very powerful. Kahneman and his associates examined the strength of these feelings in an experiment in which they asked subjects to divide $20 with another player whom they could not see but were told was in the room. Only two choices were given: to give $10 to each player or to keep $18 and give the other player $2. Out of 161 subjects, 122—76 percent—offered the even split. From this the experimenters concluded that most people are motivated by their own ideas of fairness, presumably as a result of socialization over many years.

In real life, there are many examples of situations in which notions of fairness outweigh the principle of rationality. Barbers and beauticians do not charge more for haircuts on Saturday, nor do ski resorts usually charge more for lift tickets on holidays. Although they might like to profit from the higher demand at those times, they are afraid that people would regard the higher prices as unfair and punish the business by not returning (Frank, 1988). On the other hand, there are many instances in which services are offered at higher rates during "peak seasons," or bargain offers (early-bird specials, off-peak fares, etc.) are used to encourage people to accept services at times other than those they might prefer.

Applications of the fairness principle can be seen in a great many group situations. In the famous study conducted by Elton Mayo and his associates at Western Electric's Hawthorne plant (see Chapter 2), the observers often noticed that workers used various forms of joking and sarcastic teasing to enforce the group's norms. They had a strong sense of what amount of work they should turn out, both individually and as a group, in order to merit their pay: a fair day's work for a fair day's pay. In the Bank Wiring Room, where workers hand-wired electrical circuits, it was common to see the members of a work group gang up and in a joking way hit a fellow worker on the shoulder when he produced more than the other members of the group. This practice was called "binging." A worker was binged by his co-workers if he produced too much in a day or if he did not produce enough, according to their definition of a fair day's work.

The Hawthorne researchers quickly realized that binging was part of the work group's culture. That culture—the group's norms of conduct and the ways in which its members interpreted those norms—was unique to that group and applied only when the group was at work. The culture of this work group had evolved over many years, its norms functioning to control the workers' responses to the demands of the company's managers. Thus, in a later analysis of the Bank Wiring Room observations, George Homans (1951) pointed out that the workers

shared a common body of sentiments. A person should not turn out too much work. If he did, he was a "rate-buster." The theory was that if an excessive amount of work was turned out, the management would lower the piecework rate so that the employees would be in the position of doing more work for approximately the same pay. On the other hand, a person should not turn out too little work. If he did he was a "chiseler"; that is, he was getting paid for work he did not do. [p. 235]

The Economic Person vs. the Social Person

These four basic principles of interaction in groups contain some obvious (and fortunate) contradictions. People calculate their individual gain and loss in interactions, and they act according to their own interests in many situations, but they also have deeply ingrained notions of reciprocity and fairness, which often prompt them to act in favor of the needs of the group or of society as a whole. Most of the time, most people fall somewhere between the extremes of the economic person, whose actions are based on notions of individual gain, and the social person, whose actions are based on ideas of fairness and what the group or society needs. But there are some situations in which the economic person is dominant, while in others the social person takes precedence.

Consider the following example. It's the Friday evening rush hour. The streets downtown are crowded with cars, their drivers eager to get home. Although the light is about to turn red, some drivers move their cars into the intersection. They expect the traffic ahead of them to move up so that they will be clear of oncoming traffic from the cross street. But alas, the traffic ahead does not move and the intersection is blocked. Now the cars on the cross street have a green light, but they cannot move. Fearing that they will miss their first opportunity to move, and amid much horn blowing and gnashing of teeth, some of these drivers also squeeze into the intersection. This chaotic and frustrating situation is known as gridlock. It is the result of a number of drivers acting in what they perceive as their own interests and not thinking about the needs of all the drivers as a group.

Most people fall between the extremes of the economic person (whose actions are based on individual gain) and the social person (whose actions are based on fairness).

Here is another example. The scene is the emergency room of a hospital during the New Year's holiday. The staff is shorthanded, but the waiting room is full of people with injuries, sudden illnesses, and a variety of major and minor complaints. The sympathetic young intern continually tries to take the patients who have been waiting a long time. The veteran emergency room nurse has to remind him that people must be treated according to the severity of their problems. If the limited resources of the staff are distributed evenly, the people in the greatest need will suffer disproportionately. In this situation and others like it, the social good is best served by making the most rational use of scarce resources, that is, by economizing.

In many situations, however, there is serious conflict over what the best use of resources might be. It is not only because of the human tendency toward selfishness that such conflict arises. Often there are disagreements about what different groups or classes of individuals *deserve*. We will come back often to this issue—when we discuss affirmative action, for example, and when we look at the problems involved in increasing equality of opportunity in modern societies.

Communication and Behavior in Groups

"Human interaction," Herbert Blumer observed, "is mediated by the use of symbols, by interpretations, or by ascertaining the meaning of one another's actions" (1962, pp. 179–180). By "mediated" Blumer meant that

we do not normally respond directly to the actions of another person. Instead, we react to our own interpretations of those actions. When we see other drivers moving into an intersection against the light, we begin to feel that everyone is out for themselves and we would be fools to hold back. These interpretations are made in the interval between the stimulus (the other person's action) and the response (our own action). Thus, in the account at the beginning of the chapter, Sally interpreted the tripping incident in a way that demanded that she immediately defend her honor. Her response was indicated by her interpretation and by her need to gain standing in the eyes of her peers.

What factors explain how people decide how to act and whether they should act for their own benefit or according to some notion of what is good for society? This question has been the subject of much research in the social sciences. Let us therefore take a brief look at some research on how people define their needs in social situations.

Definitions of the Situation. In a study of how dying patients are treated by medical groups in hospital emergency rooms, David Sudnow (1967) found that the age of a patient who was brought in with no heartbeat had a great deal to do with what happened next. The arrival of a younger patient who seemed to be dying would produce a frenzy of attempts to restart the heart. At times the entire group of medical personnel would become involved. But an old person with no heartbeat was far more likely to be pronounced dead on arrival, with little or no mobilization of the medical group. The patient's aged appearance caused the members of the group to define the situation as one in which urgent and heroic efforts were not required.

In another study of medical groups, Charles Bosk (1979) found that surgeons developed subtle techniques for covering up the mistakes of residents in training, depending on how a particular situation was defined. They would invoke those techniques when they believed that a mistake was due to lack of knowledge. But mistakes that they believed to be caused by carelessness would often be exposed. The guilty resident would be held up to public scorn, often at a high cost to the new surgeon's status among other doctors.

Both of these studies began by questioning how definitions of the situation account for the ways in which people interact. The emergency room teams that Sudnow observed were performing an unofficial cost-benefit analysis in deciding when to apply heroic measures to heart attack victims. The surgeons were resolving a conflict between their teaching and medical functions. Young surgeons need to learn and practice, and patients need to receive the best possible care. The surgeon in training needs to maintain a good reputation among other doctors and nurses, even if he or she makes mistakes. Such conflicts are resolved by norms that define the legitimacy of mistakes in different situations. The subtle cues that define each situation are communicated through phrases, gestures, and other symbolic behavior, as well as through explicit evaluations of what was good and bad about a particular operation.

The Dramaturgical Approach.
Conscience, the social commentator H. L. Mencken liked to say, is the little voice inside you that says someone may be looking. Many social scientists recognize that people often change their behavior according to who might be looking. Much social interaction depends on how we wish to impress those who may be watching us. For example, Erving Goffman observed that people change their facial expressions just before entering a room in which they expect to find others who will greet them. Couples who are fighting when they are "backstage" often present themselves as models of friendship when they are "frontstage," that is, when they are in the presence of other people. And many social environments, such as hotels, restaurants, and funeral parlors, are explicitly set up with a "front" and a "back" stage so that the public is spared the noisy and sometimes conflicted interaction occurring "behind the scenes." These and other strategies we use to "set a stage" for our own purposes are known as **impression management**.

In a study that applied this "dramaturgical" view of group interaction, James Henslin and Mae Briggs (1971) drew upon Briggs's extensive experience as a gynecological nurse. Their research showed how doctors and nurses play roles that define the situation of a pelvic examination as unem-

Why don't lines like this one at a bus stop dissolve more often into conflicts touched off by cranky or impatient individuals? In general, waiting situations are governed by the norm "first come, first served." However, people on a line may allow this norm to be violated by a person with a baby or a tired elderly woman. Conflicts arise when people disagree over what kinds of violations are permissible.

barrassing and attempt to save each participant's "face" or sense of self-worth. According to Henslin and Briggs, the pelvic examination is carried out in a series of scenes. First, the doctor and the patient discuss the patient's condition. If the doctor decides that the patient needs a pelvic examination, the doctor will leave the room; this is the end of Scene 1. In Scene 2 the nurse enters. Her role is to work with the patient to create a situation in which the body of the patient is hidden behind sheets and her depersonalized pelvic area is exposed for clinical inspection. Through these preparations the patient becomes symbolically distanced from the doctor, allowing the next scene, the pelvic examination itself, to be desexualized. The props, the stage setting (the examining room), and the language used help define the situation as a nonsexual encounter, thereby saving everyone involved from embarrassment.

Altruism and the Bystander Effect.
Intentional efforts to set a stage for purposes of impression management are common in hospitals, restaurants, and many other social settings where patterns of behavior are predictable and regular. But in other public settings, especially streets, parks, and public transportation, people often try to hide behind their anonymity. They shy away from behavior that will be noticed, as can be seen in the example of the bystander effect.

© Marc P. Anderson

Late one night in 1964, Kitty Genovese was returning home from a social gathering when she was attacked by a man who had been following her. He caught up with her in front of a bookstore in the shadow of her apartment building. As she screamed for help, he stabbed her in the chest. Lights went on in some of the apartments, but no one intervened or called the police. One neighbor shouted from a window: "Let that girl alone." The stalker retreated and waited, and when the neighbor no longer seemed to be watching he resumed his attack. He stabbed and raped the young woman in a stairwell of her apartment house, but the police did not receive a call for help from any of her neighbors until thirty minutes after she had first cried out. Interviewed later, the neighbors said things like "I was tired" or "I assumed others were helping" or "Frankly, we were afraid."

This incident, which occurred in New York City, is often cited to illustrate the callousness and indifference of urban dwellers when faced with a victim in distress (Frank, 1988). It might seem from this and similar incidents that when faced with danger and other costs of helping (e.g., time in court, dealing with the police, loss of time from work), people make fairly selfish calculations of gain and loss. But what about all the unselfish acts of heroism one reads about? Victims are dragged from fires and submerged cars and broken ice by self-sacrificing civilians, many of whom die themselves in their efforts to help others. Did Kitty Genovese simply have a bad group of neighbors? Empirical evidence suggests that the situation is more complicated than that.

Social psychologists Irving Piliavin, Judith Rodin, and Jane Piliavin (1969) staged situations on New York City subway trains in which a trained graduate student pretended to collapse. In 62 out of 65 trials someone in the subway car came to the aid of the fallen person. Other studies by Bibb Latané and John Darley (1970) have shown under many experimental conditions that bystanders are likely to offer help to victims. But their research also shows that the presence of other people who do *not* help increases the chances that no one will help. In one simple experiment, a graduate student begins interviewing the subject. The interviewer excuses himself or herself for a moment and enters an adjacent room. Suddenly the waiting subject hears cries for help: "Oh, my God, my foot . . . I . . . I can't get this thing off!" In about 70 percent of the trials, the subject rushes into the room and offers help. But when there is another person in the first room who just sits there and seems to be associated with the experimenter in some way, only 7 percent of the subjects intervene to help the "victim."

In the subway experiment, the helper can see that no one else has offered help. In the Kitty Genovese case, on the other hand, people could conveniently assume that others must be helping. The point is that when responsibility seems to be diffused rather than falling on a particular individual, people are more likely to avoid helping others. But when people cannot avoid defining the situation as involving them, they are likely to throw rationality to the winds and intervene despite the potential costs to themselves. This is so not because they fear that someone may be watching but because, to varying extents, they have been socialized to help others if possible (Rushton, 1980; Schwartz, 1970).

> *People are more likely to avoid helping others when responsibility appears to be diffused.*

Interaction and Group Structure

The preceding examples involve decisions and strategies that individuals use in deciding whether to behave more selfishly or more altruistically in a given situation. But as members of groups, we often explain our actions on the basis of our status in the group rather than on the basis of our individual expectations. "I must do this because I'm expected to lead," we might say, or "I can't decide that without talking to the others and especially to ——— [the group's leader]." These explanations suggest that the structure of groups plays a powerful part in explaining behavior. But the basic principles of interaction—pleasure seeking, rationality, reciprocity, and fairness—can be used to explain the emergence of group structure in the first place.

Six college students of the same sex are hired to participate in a small-group experiment. All are unknown to one another before the experiment. The specific task they are asked to perform is of little importance except that it must involve all the members of the group in a cooperative effort and must not be so difficult that they become frustrated or so easy that they become bored.

Initially the group has no structure. All of the subjects are peers, and all have come for the same reason: to earn some money for participating in the experiment. There are no predetermined statuses or roles. The students listen to a description of what they are to do and then are left alone to get the work under way. Actually they are being observed through a one-way mirror, and all their interactions are being recorded and counted.

Table 7-1 summarizes the data obtained by counting all the interactions—including small utterances like "Oh" and "I see"— occurring in a six-person group meeting for eighteen one-hour sessions. This table shows who initiated each interaction and to whom it was directed, including interactions directed toward the group as a whole. The participants are ranked from high to low on this variable (i.e., initiating an interaction). Thus subject 1 spoke 1,238 times to subject 2, 961 times to subject 3, and so on (Homans, 1961). Subject 1 initiated 3,506 utterances to specific individuals (e.g., "Why don't you . . . ?") and 5,661 utterances to the group as a whole (e.g., "Why don't we . . . ?"), for a total of 9,167 utterances over all the sessions. You can see that subject 6 spoke only about one-ninth as much as subject 1, and that most of what he said was directed to subject 1 (470 utterances). In later interviews the experimenters

Table 7 – 1: Aggregate Matrix for Eighteen Sessions of Six-Man Groups

		Initiated to Individuals						Total to Individuals	To Group as Whole	Total Initiated
		1	2	3	4	5	6			
From Individuals	1		1,238	961	545	445	317	3,506	5,661	9,167
	2	1,748		443	310	175	102	2,778	1,211	3,989
	3	1,371	415		305	125	69	2,285	742	3,027
	4	952	310	282		83	49	1,676	676	2,352
	5	662	224	144	83		28	1,141	443	1,584
	6	470	126	114	65	44		819	373	1,192
Total Received		5,203	2,313	1,944	1,306	872	565	12,205	9,106	21,311

This interaction matrix sums up, or *aggregates*, the number and direction of verbal interactions engaged in by each of six male subjects over eighteen one-hour sessions. It shows how many times each man initiated an interaction with (that is, spoke to) a particular other man. The totals indicate that subject 1 was by far the leader in number of interactions initiated and received, and that subject 6 was the least involved in the group interaction. The matrix shows that people who initiate interactions also tend to receive them: The differences between the number of interactions initiated and the number received are due to the fact that some utterances are answered indirectly by means of utterances directed at the entire group. (The diagonal cells are empty because the experimenters did not count utterances by a subject to himself.)

Source: Social Behavior by George Caspar Homans. Copyright © 1961 by Harcourt Brace Jovanovich, Inc. Reprinted by permission of the publisher.

also found that subject 1 was the most respected member of the group.

What makes the person who initiates and receives the most communications the most respected member of the group? The reasons vary with the specific tasks the group is performing, but if we assume competence at those tasks, usually the person at the center of the communication is spending a lot of time helping others as well as helping the group accomplish its goals. That person not only is concerned with his or her own performance (the rationality principle) but also takes pleasure in helping the others—giving approval, voicing criticism, making suggestions, and so on. In exchange for this help, the other members of the group give approval, respect, and allegiance to the central individual (the reciprocity principle).

Is the person who initiates the most interactions respected simply because he or she talks a lot? Common sense tells us that this is far from true. People who talk a lot but have little to contribute soon find that no one is paying attention to them. Their rate of interaction then drops sharply. Table 7-1 cannot show such changes in interaction patterns, but they are frequently observed in small-group studies. Other patterns have also been identified. Bales and Slater (1955), for example, observed that the person who initiated the most interactions—both in the interest of getting tasks done and in supporting the suggestions of others—often came to be thought of as a leader. The group began to orient itself toward that person and to expect leadership from him or her. A second member of the group, usually the one who initiated the second-highest number of interactions, was often the best-liked person in the group.

Bales and his colleagues concluded that groups often develop both a "task leader" (or instrumental leader) and another leader, whom they called a "socioemotional leader" (or expressive leader). The former tends to adhere quite strictly to group norms and to take the lead in carrying out the tasks undertaken by the group. But this often leaves other members with ruffled feelings. The socioemotional leader is the person who eases the group over rough spots with jokes, encouragement, and attention to the group's emotional climate. Thus, most classes have a class clown whose antics help release the tension of test situations, and most teams have a respected member who can also joke around and get people to relax under pressure. At times these roles are performed by the same person, but generally as the group settles into a given task there is an informal division of labor between the two kinds of leaders.

Recall the Bank Wiring Room observations mentioned earlier. The workers at the equipment wiring tables are an example of small-group structure. Their leader was the person who could turn out the most work in the shortest time and could also help the others do their work. The workers with higher status in the group were those who showed greater competence at their jobs and stronger allegiance to the norms of the group. Newer workers with lesser skills and less shared experience with the others were spoken to less and were less central to the group's interactions. Over time, as these workers were "binged" for producing too little or too much, the other workers would see how they handled the criticism and would form opinions of them accordingly.

One of the most striking aspects of the Hawthorne studies is that they revealed how norms about fairness in the work group are enforced through a particular kind of joking ritual (binging). But why are workers binged when they produce too much? That behavior points to the conflict between the norms of the small work group (which are based on fairness) and those of the larger corporation in which the group is embedded (which are based on rationality). The company would like to obtain greater productivity from the workers, but the workers have their own ideas about what is fair and their own ways of enforcing the group norm. This example brings us to the principle that as group size increases, or as the number of groups in an organization increases, the leaders of the larger organization must invest in ways of controlling the behavior of groups within it (Hechter, 1987). Frequently this investment takes the form of agents of control such as foremen, accountants, inspectors, and the like. These roles become part of the formal structure known as bureaucracy.

> ## In a group, the person who initiates the most interactions often comes to be thought of as a leader.

FORMAL ORGANIZATIONS AND BUREAUCRACY

Informal organizations are groups whose norms and statuses are generally agreed upon but are not set down in writing. The Bank Wiring Room observations are a classic example of the dynamics of informal organizations. The members of the work groups in the wiring room followed group norms that limited their output. Usually such groups have leaders who help create and enforce the group's norms but have no formal leadership position in the company.

Formal organizations have explicit (often written) sets of norms, statuses, and roles that specify each member's relationships to the others and the conditions under which those

---

Box 7–1: "Breakdown in Authority" Breaks Up Town Meeting

Many organizations adopt a formal set of norms for resolving disputes and maintaining order. Often, for example, their members agree to follow *Robert's Rules of Order*, a familiar and widely used set of rules for making decisions in organizations. They become so used to having these rules available—and to the orderliness that results—that only when an event like the one reported here occurs do they realize how important the rules are.

SHERRODSVILLE, OHIO, Feb. 19 (AP)—The Mayor was attacked, the village solicitor was pummeled, the fire station's pool table collapsed, a Village Councilman was charged with assault and the Councilman's father was hospitalized with a heart attack.

"I'm not used to having that kind of breakdown in authority," said the solicitor, Brad Hillyer, on Tuesday, after Monday night's Council meeting in this northeastern Ohio village.

Forty citizens, 10 percent of the population, had gathered at the fire station to hear about a move to disband the two-man Police Department.

Darletta Richardson and her son Richard Richardson Jr., both Council members, were leading the fight to disband the force, saying officers have harassed residents and misused their power. Mayor Joe Stull has ardently opposed their efforts.

As Mr. Stull and the Richardsons heatedly debated the issue, Richard Richardson Sr., watching from the audience, collapsed.

"Are You People Satisfied?"

Emergency medical technicians were called and Mayor Stull promptly adjourned the meeting. Mrs. Richardson rushed to her husband's side, and weeping, said: "Are you people satisfied now? Are you people satisfied now?"

"Don't blame us," the Mayor answered. "If he was in that bad a condition, he shouldn't have been here in the first place."

That, witnesses said, prompted the junior Mr. Richardson to jump onto a table and at Mayor Stull. Both men fell on a pool table, which collapsed.

The two were separated by Mr. Hillyer and by Police Chief Chet Seran and Patrolman John Miley, who make up the disputed police force. Mr. Hillyer was pummeled in the process, but did not require hospitalization.

The senior Mr. Richardson, who is 59 years old, was listed in critical condition today in the intensive care unit at Union Hospital in Dover.

Mayor Stull was treated for a back injury at Union Hospital in Dover.

"This Thing Is Garbage"

The junior Mr. Richardson was charged with assaulting the Mayor.

Before the scuffle, Mayor Stull had refused to read the Richardsons' proposed ordinance to dissolve the police force. "This thing is garbage," Mayor Stull said. "The Police Department will continue here."

Councilman Richardson then made a motion to cut off money to the police, but Mayor Stull rebuffed him.

"I will not accept a motion to cut off funds," the Mayor said. "Take me to court if you wish. Let this be the end of it."

It was then that Mr. Richardson collapsed.

One resident, Virginia Harrington, said, "We pray that not only the heart and body be mended, but that perhaps this tragedy may bind up the wounds of this community."

Source: New York Times, February 20, 1985. Used by permission of The Associated Press.

relationships hold. Organization charts and job descriptions are typical of such organizations. Formal organizations take a wide variety of forms. For example, the New England town meeting is composed of residents of a town who gather to debate and discuss any issues the members wish to raise. The tenants' association of an urban apartment building is also composed of people who reside in a specific place, but its scope of action is usually limited to housing issues. Both of these are formal organizations, since there are rules defining who may participate and the scope and manner of that participation. As is true in many formal organizations, the members of town meetings and tenants' associations try to arrive at decisions through some form of democratic process, that is, by adhering to norms that allow the majority to run the organization but not to infringe on the rights of the minority. Yet we are reminded in Box 7-1 how easily democratic decision-making processes can dissolve into conflict and chaos.

A familiar type of formal organization is the **voluntary association**. People join such groups to pursue interests they share with other members of the group. Voluntary associations are usually democratically run, at least in principle, and have rules and regulations and an administrative staff. Churches, fraternal organizations, political clubs, and neighborhood improvement groups are examples of voluntary associations often found in American communities. Sociologists study these associations in order to understand how well or poorly people are integrated into their society.

The rate of participation in voluntary associations has increased during the past few decades. In his review of research on association membership, Morris Janovitz (1978) concluded that "the long-term trend appears to be one of increasing levels of such participation" (p. 314). Thus, in 1946 Mirra Komarovsky found that over half of her sample of 2,200 urban residents did not belong to any associations. In the 1960s, surveys showed a dramatic increase in association membership. By the 1970s, research results indicated that the majority of household members belonged to a voluntary association. And contrary to the hypothesis that inner-city people are less likely to be active in organizations, Claude Fischer's (1982) studies of organization membership show that city dwellers belong to an average of two groups, while people living on the semirural fringe are, on the average, members of fewer than two groups.

Bureaucracies are another common type of formal organization. A **bureaucracy** is a specific structure of statuses and roles in which the power to influence the actions of others increases as one nears the top of the organization; this is a marked contrast with the democratic procedures used in other kinds of organizations. Voluntary associations, for example, usually have some of the elements of bureaucracies, but they are run as democratic structures in which power is based on majority rule rather than on executive orders, as is the case in pure bureaucracies. We owe much of our understanding of bureaucracies to the work of Max Weber, who identified the following typical aspects of most bureaucratic organizations.

1. *Positions with clearly defined responsibilities:* "The regular activities required for the purposes of the organization are distributed in a fixed way as official duties."
2. *Positions ordered in a hierarchy:* The organization of offices "follows the principle of hierarchy; that is, each lower office is under the control and supervision of a higher one."
3. *Rules and precedents:* The functioning of the bureaucracy is governed "by a consistent system of abstract rules" and the "application of these rules to specific cases."
4. *Impersonality and impartiality:* "The ideal official conducts his office . . . in a spirit of formalistic impersonality . . . without hatred or passion, and hence without affection or enthusiasm."
5. *A career ladder:* Work in a bureaucracy "constitutes a career. There is a system of 'promotions' according to seniority, or to achievement, or both."
6. *The norm of efficiency:* "The purely bureaucratic type of administrative organization . . . is from a purely technical point of view, capable of attaining the highest

Voluntary associations are usually democratically run, whereas in bureaucracies power is based on executive orders.

degree of efficiency" (Weber, 1922, cited in Blau and Meyer, 1971, and Gerth and Mills, 1958).

Weber believed that bureaucracy made human social life more "rational" than it had ever been in the past. Rules, impersonality, and the norm of efficiency are some of the ways in which bureaucracies "rationalize" human societies. By this Weber meant that society becomes dominated by groups organized so that the interactions of their members will maximize the group's efficiency. Once the group's goals have been set, the officials in a bureaucracy can seek the most efficient means of reaching those goals. All the less rational behaviors of human groups, such as magic and ritual, are avoided by groups organized as bureaucracies. But the people in a bureaucracy may not take full responsibility for their actions. For this and other reasons, therefore, Weber had some misgivings about the consequences of the increasing dominance of bureaucratic groups in modern societies.

Bureaucracy and Obedience to Authority

The experiment on conformity conducted by Solomon Asch, discussed in Chapter 2, demonstrated the power of group pressure and raised serious questions about most people's ability to resist such pressure. It also led to many other studies of conformity. None of those studies is more powerful in its implications and disturbing in its methods than the series of experiments on obedience to authority conducted by Stanley Milgram.

Milgram's study was designed to "take a close look at the act of obeying." As Milgram described it:

Two people come to a psychology laboratory to take part in a study of memory and learning. One of them is designated as a "teacher" and the other as a "learner." The experimenter explains that the study is concerned with the effects of punishment on learning. The learner is conducted into a room, seated in a chair, his arms strapped to prevent excessive movement, and an electrode is attached to his wrist. He is told that he is to learn a list of word pairs; whenever he makes an error, he will receive electric shocks of increasing intensity.

The real focus of the experiment is the teacher. After watching the learner being strapped

Culver Pictures

into place, he is taken into the main experimental room and seated before an impressive shock generator. Its main feature is a horizontal line of thirty switches, ranging from 15 volts to 450 volts, in 15-volt increments. There are also verbal designations which range from SLIGHT SHOCK to DANGER—SEVERE SHOCK. The teacher is told that he is to administer the learning test to the man in the other room. When the learner responds correctly, the teacher moves on to the next item; when the other man gives an incorrect answer, the teacher is to give him an electric shock. He is to start at the lowest shock level (15 volts) and to increase the level each time the man makes an error, going through 30 volts, 45 volts, and so on. [1974, pp. 3–4]

In reality, the "learner" is an actor who pretends to suffer pain but receives no actual shock. The experimental subject (the "teacher") is a businessperson or an industrial worker or a student, someone who has been recruited by a want ad offering payment for spare-time work in a university laboratory.

Milgram was dismayed to discover that very large proportions of his subjects were willing to obey any order given by the experimenter. In the basic version of the experiment, in which the "learner" is in one room and the "teacher" in another from which the "learner" is visible but cannot be heard, 65 percent of the subjects administered the highest levels of shock, whereas the other 35 percent were obedient well into the "intense shock" levels.

Milgram used a functionalist argument to explain the high levels of obedience revealed in his experiment: In bureaucratic organizations people seek approval by adhering to the rules, which often absolve them of moral

Max Weber (1864–1920) was a German scholar who made numerous important contributions to sociological thought. He opposed some aspects of Marxian theory, believing that changing values, rather than conflict, are a major source of social change. He also believed that sociology should be "value free"—that political ideas should not enter into social research. Weber was an influential theorist in the areas of religion, bureaucracy, and stratification.

responsibility for their actions. But he also explored the conditions under which conflict will take place—that is, the conditions under which the subject will rebel against the experimenter. He found that when subjects were allowed to speak to one another, they defined the situation in such a way that they could support one another's resolution to defy the experimenter. Moreover, as can be seen in Table 7-2, the situations in which the subject

Table 7–2: **Maximum Shocks Administered in Four Variants of Milgram's Experiment**

Shock Level	Verbal Designation and Voltage Level	1 Remote (*n* = 40)	2 Voice-Feedback (*n* = 40)	3 Proximity (*n* = 40)	4 Touch-Proximity (*n* = 40)
	Slight Shock				
1	15				
2	30				
3	45				
4	60				
	Moderate Shock				
5	75				
6	90				
7	105			1	
8	120				
	Strong Shock				
9	135		1		1
10	150		5	10	16
11	165		1		
12	180		1	2	3
	Very Strong Shock				
13	195				
14	210				1
15	225			1	1
16	240				
	Intense Shock				
17	255				1
18	270			1	
19	285		1		1
20	300	5[a]	1	5	1
	Extreme Intensity Shock				
21	315	4	3	3	2
22	330	2			
23	345	1	1		1
24	360	1	1		
	Danger: Severe Shock				
25	375	1		1	
26	390				
27	405				
28	420				
	XXX				
29	435				
30	450	26	25	16	12
	Mean maximum shock level	27.0	24.53	20.80	17.88
	Obedient subjects (%)	65.0	62.5	40.0	30.0

[a]Indicates that in Experiment 1, five subjects administered a maximum shock of 300 volts.

The four variants of Milgram's experiment differed in terms of proximity between the "teacher" and the "learner." The variants were: (1) Remote (different rooms, in which the learner could be seen but not heard); (2) Voice feedback (different rooms, in which the learner could be seen and heard); (3) Proximity (both in the same room); and (4) Touch proximity (both in the same room, in which the teacher was told to force the learner's hand onto the electrode).

Source: Obedience to Authority by Stanley Milgram. Copyright © 1974 by Stanley Milgram. Reprinted by permission of Harper & Row. Publishers, Inc.

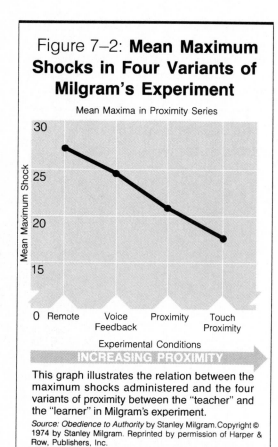

Figure 7–2: **Mean Maximum Shocks in Four Variants of Milgram's Experiment**

Mean Maxima in Proximity Series

INCREASING PROXIMITY

This graph illustrates the relation between the maximum shocks administered and the four variants of proximity between the "teacher" and the "learner" in Milgram's experiment.

Source: Obedience to Authority by Stanley Milgram. Copyright © 1974 by Stanley Milgram. Reprinted by permission of Harper & Row, Publishers, Inc.

is forced to confront the consequences of his or her behavior seem to diminish the ability to rely on "duty" to justify that behavior. This effect is presented in graphic form in Figure 7-2.

When Milgram published the results of these experiments, he was criticized for deceiving his subjects and, in some cases, causing them undue stress. The controversy created by this study was one of the factors leading to the establishment of rules for the protection of human subjects in social-scientific research (see Chapter 2).

Commitment to Bureaucratic Groups

Another question related to the impact of bureaucracy on individuals is how bureaucratic groups, which are based on unemotional and "rational" systems of recruitment, decision making, and reward, can sometimes attract strong commitment from their members. One possible answer is ideology: People believe in the goals and methods of the bureaucracy. Another explanation is that people within a bureaucracy form primary groups that function to maintain their commitment to the larger organization. Perhaps both explanations are valid—both primary-group attachments and ideology may be operating to reinforce people's commitment to the organization. A number of studies have addressed this question.

Primary Groups in Bureaucracies. In one of those studies, Morris Janowitz and Edward Shils were assigned by the U.S. Army to study the attitudes of German soldiers captured during World War II. They were attempting to discover what had made the German army so effective a force that isolated units continued to fight even in the face of certain defeat. As Shils explained it, he and Janowitz "discovered the influence of small, closely knit groups on the conduct of their members in the performance of tasks set them from the outside" (1948, p. 48).

The soldiers of the German army behaved the way they did not because of their ideological commitment to the Nazi cause but because of their loyalty to small combat units whose members had become so devoted to one another that to continue to fight even in the face of defeat, so as not to be dishonored as a group, seemed the only possible course of action. The close primary-group structure of the German army was one of the secrets of its success (a fact that has not gone unnoticed by modern military analysts, as shown in Box 7-2). The army was an extremely efficient organization. Ideology figured very little in its effectiveness.

Ideological Primary Groups. Primary groups would seem to have no place in a "pure" bureaucracy, yet the study just cited, together with the Hawthorne experiments and other empirical studies, shows that there is no bureaucracy that completely eliminates primary groups. In the case of the German army, it appears that the development of primary groups among combat troops increased the effectiveness of the organization as a whole. Another important study of this subject was Philip Selznick's (1952) analysis of what made the Bolsheviks so effective that they won out in the fierce competition for political dominance in Russia. Selznick's data show that the ideologically based primary group was the key element in the Bolsheviks' organization. Small, secret "cells" of devoted communists were organized in neighborhoods, factories, army units, farms, and universities. Through years of tense and often dangerous political activity, the members became extremely devoted to one another and to their revolutionary cause. According to Selznick, this doubling of ideological and primary-group cohesion made the Bolsheviks themselves an "organizational weapon."

GROUPS IN COMPLEX SOCIETIES

"What is the difference between Czechoslovakia and the United States?" asks a joke that was recently popular in Eastern Europe. The answer: "The United States has a Communist party." Among the many reasons for the downfall of Communist party rule in Eastern Europe was the destruction of much of the fabric of group membership in nations where the Communist party held absolute power for so many decades. In the Soviet Union and China and their satellite nations, freedom of association in groups was banned in an effort to prevent the rise of political competition. Ironically, in the United States freedom of association extended to the Communist party,

although not without difficulty. In consequence, the United States has a Communist party, while in the nations of Eastern Europe Communists are changing their name to avoid being associated with past repression. And now that absolute rule by the Communist party has ended, the people of Eastern Europe are creating new political and voluntary groups of all kinds almost daily.

As we saw in Chapter 3, in simpler tribal or peasant societies most social structures are primary groups. The tribal village is usually so small that everyone knows everyone else. The family, the extended family, the age- and sex-segregated peer groups, and even the village itself all allow for everyone to know everyone else and to interact on an almost daily basis. Typically these societies lack a secondary-group level of life. In traditional peasant societies, for example, there often were no associations that brought together soldiers or chicken farmers or artisans in groups that extended beyond the limited bounds of the village. And yet that level of social life is what makes contemporary societies so efficient.

The differences between simpler and more complex societies can also make interactions among members of those societies confusing and frustrating. For example, when they were first assigned to peasant villages in Africa and Asia, American Peace Corps volunteers were unprepared to cope with situ-

---

Box 7–2: **Primary Groups in the Army**

The U.S. Army has recently implemented a major shift in its policy regarding the assignment of combat troops. Under the new policy, soldiers are assigned by unit rather than as individuals and remain in the same unit from the time they are trained through their deployment overseas and afterward. Under the new plan, replacements for soldiers who are discharged will join the unit as a team, not as individuals coming from separate outfits.

The change in policy is a direct reflection of research like that conducted during World War II by Morris Janowitz and Edward Shils, which showed that troops who stay together fight better be-

cause they care more about one another. This concept has been applied not only by the Nazis but also by the British army. In the U.S. Army it was tested during the 1980s in an experiment in which troops in selected companies were kept together for their enlistment term of three years.

It is believed that this approach will lift morale, foster loyalty, and improve fighting ability. According to General Robert Elton, deputy chief of staff for personnel, "I think we have reached a milestone in a very key Army program. We're changing the culture of the Army" (quoted in *The New York Times*, November 7, 1989).

ations in which villagers came to them with requests for money or help with marital and family problems. For the young Americans, such requests were appropriate only among members of primary groups—but the villagers did not know how to engage in interactions that are typical of secondary groups (Luce, 1964).

In his most famous theoretical work, *The Division of Labor in Society* (1893), Émile Durkheim reasoned that as a society becomes larger and more complex there is a vast increase in the interdependence among its members as the tasks required to feed, house, educate, communicate with, transport, care for, and defend them become more complex. Faced with more choices regarding who to interact with and how to live life, the individual gains much more freedom than is available to a member of a simpler society, who (for better or worse) is confined to a narrow set of local primary groups. But Durkheim also saw that the modern person could be overwhelmed by the choices open to him or her and find it difficult to decide what groups to join and what norms to conform to.

Max Weber shared Durkheim's concern about the prospects for human happiness in the modern world. According to Weber, the fundamental paradox of modern society was the rise of bureaucracies, which greatly expanded the efficiency and rationality of society but "disenchanted the world." By this he meant that the modern formal organization, which is so effective in science, the military, the state (government), economic production, and almost every other aspect of modern life, at the same time deprives human life of a sense of magic, spirituality, and mastery over the environment. The individual becomes a tiny cog in a huge set of interlocking organizations. Within those organizations he or she fills specific statuses and enacts clearly defined roles yet feels more and more oppressed. Weber deplored the type of person that he felt was most often produced by the organizations of modern society, "a petty routine creature, lacking in heroism, human spontaneity, and inventiveness" (Gerth and Mills, 1958, p. 50).

In his efforts to understand the behavior of individuals in the groups typical of modern societies, Weber distinguished between *rational* and *traditional* motives. Rational motives are easy to understand and predict because ends and means can be calculated and behavior changed on the basis of experience. Thus Weber proposed that business firms are rationally motivated. The producer uses the measures of costs and benefits to minimize production costs and maximize the market price for a given volume of goods. If buyers begin substituting another type of product, the producer must take immediate action, such as improving its product or producing a new one, to avoid losing money. All the members of the firm will be affected by these decisions. The producer cannot allow other sentiments to affect its actions, for to do so will in the long run only make matters worse for the firm.

At the opposite extreme from rationality is tradition. Traditional norms motivate our actions because we believe them to be right: We have always done things that way. The traditional norms of family life say that parents must care for their children, not because they will reward them later in life or because they will love them for doing so, but because they are parents and child care is what parents do. Religious groups may also require the unquestioning performance of certain rituals, not because they will necessarily help people enter heaven or make them better people, but simply because that is the way those rituals have always been performed.

Weber recognized that there are many possible combinations of motives between these two extremes. We can pursue profit but allow attachments to family members or people in our community to affect the extent to which we pursue economic goals. We can strive for success in the form of a promotion to a better job, but the effort will never entail purely rational behavior. To win a promotion we may need to show that we uphold the less formal traditions of the corporation—its styles of dress, for example—while at the same time demonstrating our ability to act rationally, to bring in more profits or save on costs or enhance the firm's power or prestige. In sum, life in complex organizations requires skill at performing roles in various types of groups within those organizations. It requires that we balance traditional and rational motives and that we understand the interactions between groups and among individuals within those groups.

FRONTIERS OF SOCIOLOGY

Ordinary People, Extraordinary Groups

How can we explain why some people seem to give up their own identity in favor of unquestioning allegiance to groups such as religious cults, extremist political groups, or small groups of murderers like that led by Charles Manson? What does it take to resocialize a person to be a member of a group whose beliefs are in direct opposition to those he or she was taught in childhood? This question is on the frontiers of research in both sociology and social psychology.

We saw in Chapter 2 and in this chapter how this issue was raised in the Asch and Milgram experiments. Studies of conformity in groups point to the powerful pressure that a unified group can exert on the opinions and feelings of its members. Additional evidence for the power of groups to shape individual behavior comes from studies like the "prison" research conducted by social psychologist Philip G. Zimbardo.

Zimbardo and his colleagues at Stanford University were interested in the psychological and sociological processes involved in taking the roles of prisoner and prison guard. They created a simulated prison in the basement of a building at Stanford University and placed an ad in a local newspaper for subjects to take part in a psychological experiment for pay. From the people who responded to the ad, they selected twenty-four "mature, emotionally stable, normal, intelligent white male college students from middle-class homes throughout the United States and Canada." None had a prison record, and all seemed very similar in their values. By the flip of a coin, half were assigned to be prison guards and half to be prisoners.

The "guards" were instructed about their responsibilities and made aware of the potential danger of the situation and their need to protect themselves. The "prisoners" were unexpectedly picked up at their homes by a mock police car, handcuffed, and taken blindfolded to the improvised jail, where they were searched, deloused, fingerprinted, given numbers, and placed in "cells" with two other prisoners.

The subjects had signed up for the sake of the money, and all expected to be in the experiment for about two weeks. But by the end of the sixth day the researchers had to cancel the experiment because the results were too frightening to allow them to continue. As Zimbardo explained:

It was no longer apparent to most of the subjects (or to us) where reality ended and their roles began. The majority had indeed become prisoners or guards, no longer able to clearly differentiate between role playing and self. There were dramatic changes in virtually every aspect of their behavior, thinking, and feeling. In less than a week the experience of imprisonment undid (temporarily) a lifetime of learning; human values were suspended, self-concepts were challenged, and the ugliest, most base, pathological side of human nature surfaced. We were horrified because we saw some boys (guards) treat others as if they were despicable animals, taking pleasure in cruelty, while other boys (prisoners) became servile, dehumanized robots who thought only of escape, of their own individual survival, and of their mounting hatred for the guards. [1972, p. 243]

The researchers found that about a third of the guards became extremely tyrannical and enjoyed their control over the "prisoners." They invented new ways of breaking the prisoners' spirit and group solidarity. Another third performed their roles as "tough but fair" prison guards, and another third were helpful to the prisoners in small ways—but none ever interfered with the actions of the tyrannical guards or openly took the side of the prisoners. Moreover, Zimbardo lamented, "they never even came to me as prison superindendent or experimenter in charge to complain." Far faster and more thoroughly than the researchers thought possible, "the experiment had become a reality."

Zimbardo's dismay was echoed in the research papers published by Milgram, Asch, and many others. Why are people so easily resocialized? Why do they so readily accept radical definitions of the situation? Why don't they rebel? We can see from Zimbardo's research and the other experiments on conformity that some people rebel privately and others insist on "just doing their jobs" as people in authority have defined them. Yet there is a segment of any human population that will quickly take on strange roles and even relish doing harm to others whom the authorities define as the out-group or as people of lesser value.

In the world beyond the experimenters' laboratories, people are continually giving themselves up to "extraordinary groups" such as the Unification church, Hare Krishna, Synanon, the Weathermen, the Church Universal and Triumphant, the People's Temple, the Nazi party, the Ku Klux Klan, communes religious and political, residential therapeutic communities of all kinds—the list could be expanded almost endlessly. There are many variations in the beliefs, goals, and organization of these groups, as we will have occasion to see in later chapters. But all of them are examples of groups or organizations that resocialize recruits within a group of people who are themselves intense believers. The recruit's doubts are erased as need for the group's approval takes over. Such groups are usually led by one or more charismatic leaders, people who seem to have a special gift for influencing others and a special understanding of the group's values (Shils, 1965). And all such groups demand that the recruit reject his or her former values and sever all previous personal ties.

These norms and interaction patterns exert an immensely powerful influence on recruits. There is no lack of evidence that people can go to extraordinary extremes of behavior in such groups—perhaps no more tragically than in the case of the People's Temple, in which several hundred people committed suicide in response to a perceived threat from outside authorities. What kinds of people are recruited into such groups? For the most unusual and criminal groups, the answer is found by looking at the people who are available to join. They are often unattached, on the street, wandering, alienated from family and friends, and looking for the feeling of belonging to a close peer group (Turner, 1969; Wooden, 1976). But do not conclude that extraordinary groups that resocialize people recruit only unattached people who are estranged or alienated from society. Some groups that resocialize their members can produce great individual and social good, as can be seen in the case of Alcoholics Anonymous and other treatment groups that work to save people's lives or get them on a better track.

SUMMARY

The social fabric of modern societies is composed of millions of groups of many types and sizes. The members of true social groups are recruited according to some membership criterion and are bound together by a set of membership rights and mutual obligations. The group itself has a social structure composed of specific statuses and roles.

A *primary group* is characterized by intimate, often face-to-face, association and cooperation. *Secondary groups* are characterized by relationships that involve few aspects of the personality; the members' reasons for participation are usually limited to a small number of goals. The strongest social bonds are formed between two people and are known as *dyads*. The addition of a third person to form a *triad* reduces the stability of the group.

At the level of social organization between the primary group and the institutions of the nation-state are communities. *Territorial communities* are contained within geographic boundaries; *nonterritorial communities* are networks of associations formed around shared goals. Territorial communities are usually composed of one or more neighborhoods in which people form attachments on the basis of proximity.

Groups formed at the neighborhood level are integrated into networks that may extend beyond geographic boundaries. A key factor in the formation of networks is *in-group, out-group* distinctions. Such distinctions can form around almost any quality but are usually based on such qualities as income, race, or religion. Another type of group is the *reference group*, a group the individual uses as a frame of reference for self-evaluation and attitude formation. The study of whom people associate with, how those choices are made, and the effects of those choices is known as *social network analysis*.

Social scientists have identified certain principles of interaction that help explain both stability and change in human groups. Among them are the pleasure principle, the rationality principle, the reciprocity principle, and the fairness principle. The balance among these principles varies from one situation to another, with economic motives dominating in some instances and social needs winning out in others. From an interactionist perspective, an important factor determining how people behave in a given instance is their definition of the situation.

Many social scientists recognize that people often change their behavior according to who might be looking. The *dramaturgical* view of group interaction regards interaction as though it were taking place on a stage and unfolding in scenes. The strategies that people use to set a stage for their own purposes are known as *impression management*.

Research on the bystander effect has shown that when responsibility seems to be diffused, people are more likely to avoid helping others. But when people define the situation as involving them, they will intervene despite the potential costs to themselves.

Research on small groups has shown that they tend to develop two kinds of leaders, a "task leader" who keeps the group focused on its goals and a "socioemotional leader" who creates a positive emotional climate within the group.

Informal organizations are groups with generally agreed-upon but unwritten norms and statuses, whereas *formal organizations* have explicit, often written, sets of norms, statuses, and roles that specify each member's relationships to the others and the conditions under which those relationships hold. A *voluntary association* is a formal organization whose members pursue shared interests and arrive at decisions through some sort of democratic process. A *bureaucracy* is a formal organization characterized by positions with clearly defined responsibilities, the ordering of positions in a hierarchy, governance by rules and precedents, impersonality and impartiality, a career ladder, and efficiency as a basic norm.

One effect of the increasing dominance of bureaucracies in modern societies is the possibility that individuals will not take full responsibility for their actions. A study of obedience to authority conducted by Stanley Milgram raised serious questions about people's ability to resist pressure to carry out orders for which they are not personally responsible. Milgram also found, however, that rebellion against authority is more likely when individuals who rebel have the support of others. Other studies have found that commitment to bureaucratic organizations is greatest when it is supported by ideology or by strong primary-group attachments.

As a society becomes larger and more complex, it tends increasingly to be characterized by secondary groups and organizations. These make the society more efficient, but they can also cause confusion and unhappiness. Durkheim pointed out that members of complex societies have greater freedom to choose what groups to join and what norms to conform to but that they can be overwhelmed by the choices open to them. Weber examined the effects of the rise of bureaucracies in modern societies. In doing so, he distinguished between *rational* motives, which are based on calculations of ends and means, and *traditional* motives, which are based on the belief that certain actions are inherently right.

WHERE TO FIND IT

Books

Complex Organizations: A Critical Essay, 3rd ed. (Charles Perrow; Scott, Foresman, 1984). A comprehensive text on the sociology and politics of formal organizations.

The Presentation of Self in Everyday Life (Erving Goffman; Doubleday, 1959). One of the classics in the sociology of interaction at the micro level. A "must-read" for anyone wanting to gain greater insight into the dramaturgical approach to the analysis of social life.

Studies in Ethnomethodology (Harold Garfinkel; Prentice-Hall, 1967). Also a classic, this brilliant and controversial collection of original papers illustrates what scientific concern for the most micro and subjective aspects of interaction can yield in the way of fresh insights into how people act in society.

Principles of Group Solidarity (Michael Hechter; University of California Press, 1988). A modern and controversial treatment of the ways in which the rationality principle accounts for social structures of various kinds.

The Compassionate Beast: What Science Is Discovering about the Humane Side of Mankind (Morton Hunt; William Morrow, 1990). A review of classic and recent research on prosocial behavior.

Journals

Administrative Science Quarterly One of the principal journals in the field of organizations and behavior. A valuable source for theoretical and empirical studies of bureaucratic organizations like corporations, government agencies, and universities.

Human Organization Another good source of research on the problems and possibilities of efforts to improve human organizations. More diverse in its scope than the *Administrative Science Quarterly* but also oriented toward economic organizations like firms, labor unions, and regulatory agencies.

Urban Life and Culture A journal specializing in articles about human interaction in urban settings. A source of new empirical studies from the interactionist perspective.

GLOSSARY

social category: a collection of individuals grouped together because they share a trait that is deemed by the observer to be socially relevant (**p. 193**).

social group: a group whose members are recruited according to some membership criterion and are bound together by a set of membership rights and mutual obligations (**p. 193**).

primary group: a social group characterized by intimate, face-to-face associations (**p. 193**).

secondary group: a social group whose members have a shared goal or purpose but are not bound together by strong emotional ties (**p. 194**).

dyad: a group consisting of two people (**p. 194**).

triad: a group consisting of three people (**p. 194**).

community: a set of primary and secondary groups in which the individual carries out important life functions (**p. 195**).

territorial community: a population that functions within a particular geographic area (**p. 195**).

nonterritorial community: a network of relationships formed around shared goals (**p. 195**).

in-group: a social group to which an individual has a feeling of allegiance; usually, but not always, a primary group (**p. 196**).

out-group: any social group to which an individual does not have a feeling of allegiance; may be in competition or conflict with the in-group (**p. 196**).

reference group: a group that an individual uses as a frame of reference for self-evaluation and attitude formation (**p. 196**).

impression management: the strategies one uses to "set a stage" for one's own purposes (**p. 204**).

informal organization: a group whose norms and statuses are generally agreed upon but are not set down in writing (**p. 208**).

formal organization: a group that has an explicit, often written, set of norms, statuses, and roles that specify each member's relationships to the others and the conditions under which those relationships hold (**p. 208**).

voluntary association: a formal organization whose members pursue shared interests and arrive at decisions through some sort of democratic process (**p. 209**).

bureaucracy: a formal organization characterized by a clearly defined hierarchy with a commitment to rules, efficiency, and impersonality (**p. 209**).

VISUAL SOCIOLOGY

Friendship Groups

These photos capture some aspects of the universal experience known as friendship. They show friendship groups in societies throughout the world—from a group of wealthy English boarding school students to scenes from African villages. They convey the emotional quality of interaction among friends, but to the sociological observer they also reveal some characteristic features of friendship groups.

First, let us note the size of the groups. None numbers more than six or seven members. As Georg Simmel first pointed out in his writing on friendship and intimacy, the larger the group is, the more opportunities there will be for conflict and schism. Increasing size brings with it a greater likelihood of jealousy, competition for attention, and conflicting values, and these tensions tend to break larger friendship groups into smaller, more intimate ones like those shown here.

A second observation that we can draw from these photos has to do with the gender differences in friendship groups. Children's friendship groups are involved in anticipatory socialization, in taking roles that will later be incorporated into adult statuses. Thus, the girls are seen holding dolls and practicing the

Photographs by Ken Heyman

interactions that occupy so much of their mothers' time. And unlike the typical male friendship group, female groups often have the responsibility of caring for younger siblings, as we see in at least one of these photos. Males more typically engage in activities that involve physical prowess and changes in the environment, such as turning on a hydrant and creating an instant street shower. We also see in these photos that gender segregation is normally the rule in friendship groups, although there may be many exceptions, such as when games are played in school.

Finally, these photos remind us of the emotional complexity of friendship. Friends can fight and make up, but people who are less than friends often cannot fight without ending the relationship. And consider the photo of the men hugging each other. Is this scene likely to occur in American culture? Perhaps today it is, but until quite recently such a show of emotion between men, even between a father and his son, was discouraged in our culture. Today this norm is changing, although in many other cultures it is still far more acceptable for men to hug and kiss each other than it is in North America.

CHAPTER OUTLINE

- **The Meaning of Stratification**
  - Caste, Class, and Social Mobility
  - Life Chances

- **Stratification and the Means of Existence**
  - Stratification in Rural Villages
  - Stratification in Industrial Societies

- **Stratification and Culture**
  - The Role of Ideology
  - Stratification at the Micro Level

- **Power, Authority, and Stratification**

- **Stratification in the Modern Era**
  - The Great Transformation
  - Class Consciousness and Class Conflict
  - Social Mobility in Modern Societies: The Weberian View

- **Theories of Stratification**
  - Conflict Theories
  - The Functionalist View
  - The Interactionist Perspective
  - Conclusion

Robert White/Sygma

A demonstration in the Soviet Union beneath a statue of Lenin

CHAPTER 8
STRATIFICATION AND SOCIAL MOBILITY

Until very recently Soviet authorities suppressed Tatyana Zaslavskaya's sociological studies in Siberia. As she explains it, "Throughout the long decades of the stagnation period, Soviet sociologists kept hoping against hope that their vital school of thought would gain recognition and the right to exist and develop at its own pace. Their hopes failed." Many of the brightest and most skilled sociologists were labeled "slanderers of Soviet reality" and dismissed from their jobs.

"Though the main targets were Moscow and Leningrad scholars," Zaslavskaya explains, "we in remote Siberia did not have an easy life either. We had to fight stubbornly for the right to continue our research, to poll people on the painful issues which affected their immediate interests." Zaslavskaya and her colleagues were accused of being unpatriotic and provocative—meaning that they "were 'suggesting' to people that they were short of housing, that shops didn't have enough food on sale, that public transportation malfunctioned, and so on. As if they couldn't see all that for themselves!

"As for the results of our research, to be honest, nobody wanted them. Reports were sent to the top Party bodies, raising the same issues over and over again." Whenever they showed that people were angry with their government, or that they faced terrible difficulties in their everyday lives, the data were buried in archives. When their findings appeared in the press (a rare occurrence) sociologists were often punished for their efforts.

Zaslavskaya is now president of the Sociological Association of the Soviet Union. "Today," she observes hopefully, "by virtue of the growth of glasnost and democratization, sociology has been given a prominent role in overhauling the entire system of social relations." Her comments on who supports and who opposes glasnost ("openness") offer some insight into why sociology was almost a taboo subject in Russia throughout most of the twentieth century. "The working class," she writes, "constitutes the largest group in socialist society." If glasnost and perestroika (restructuring of Soviet institutions) progress as intended, working-class people will gain more housing, better and more democratic management of firms and factories, "improved rights when fighting against bureaucracies," and more opportunities to gain new skills and be paid fairly for them. At the same time, however, some workers will lose jobs that are considered unnecessary. Others may have to pay higher prices for food and rent and services if these are no longer guaranteed by the government. All this means that while some categories of workers will find it in their interest to support glasnost, others will not.

Within the working class, according to Zaslavskaya, workers in highly technological industries like electronics, computers, and biosynthesis are most likely to be strong supporters of glasnost: "They are interested in decent and equitable remuneration for high-quality and conscientious labor." The same is true for many groups of workers with average skills, for they also wish to be rewarded for their skills with decent wages rather than having their wages set by government bureaucracies with which they are powerless to argue. The workers who oppose the reforms are "that part of the working class which is employed by privileged agencies and departments, and thus traditionally supplied with more comfortable labor conditions, better wages, and larger benefits from the public funds—not because of better performance, but because of the specific employment." Here she cites the example of workers with large "graft incomes—those employed in car maintenance, public catering services, the State trade system, collective farm markets, and so on." These workers and others who profit directly from pilfering or theft have little interest in reforms that may improve the economy but deprive them of their comforts (quoted in Aganbegyan, 1989, pp. 255–257).

No wonder Zaslavskaya's research and writing was controversial. Before glasnost, the authorities did not want to hear empirical facts showing that Soviet society is divided into layers according to who gets material goods and privileges and who does not. Moreover, in talking about the working class and its divisions, the sociologist was committing the sin of publicly stating that social classes, exploitation, and class conflict can be found throughout Soviet society.

THE MEANING OF STRATIFICATION

Tatyana Zaslavskaya's studies of inequality in the Soviet Union were controversial partly because they showed that many skilled workers were critical of the concept of "leveling." This is the idea that workers, regardless of their level of skill, should want to work for the betterment of all and not for their own advancement. If individuals sought to increase their own gain at all times, as they are encouraged to do in capitalist societies, they would never arrive at the egalitarian society envisioned by socialist ideology. Thus, whereas in other societies workers with much-needed skills might "sell" those skills for high wages, in the Soviet Union they had to be content with wages that were "leveled" toward the average wage for all workers.

Soviet sociologists also gathered evidence showing that people with political power were able to gain special privileges. Communist party officials and their appointed managers constituted a privileged class, the *nomenklatura*, that was not officially admitted to exist even though it was there for all to see. For members of the ruling class, meals were more sumptuous than their official salaries would have permitted; housing was more spacious; day-to-day life was free from many of the restrictions imposed on other groups in Soviet society.

Clearly, leveling did not produce equality, and in some ways it led to greater inequality. Many workers no longer believed that extra effort and hard work would be rewarded. Now, recognizing that the gap between the haves and the have-nots was widening despite official claims to the contrary, the Soviets are undertaking a revolutionary restructuring of their society. They will attempt to hold inequality to a minimum while at the same time using higher salaries and other material benefits to reward greater productivity.

Soviet sociologists are not the only ones who have been criticized for pointing out persistent inequalities and great divisions of wealth and power. American sociologists have also come under fire for finding more inequality than many people in authority will admit exists. Thus, when C. Wright Mills (1956) developed the thesis that there is a "power elite" in the United States consisting of millionaires, high-level politicians, and top military leaders, he was roundly attacked in the press and by many of his colleagues. Mills was vindicated when President Eisenhower warned of the existence of a growing "military–industrial complex" that threatened the American Dream of peace, democracy, and equal opportunity.

Numerous social-scientific studies have demonstrated that all human societies produce some form of inequality (Bendix and Lipset, 1966; Fallers, 1977; Harris, 1980; Murdock, 1949). In the simplest societies this inequality may be due to the fact that one family's fields produce more than another's do, that one family has accumulated a greater herd than others have, or that one family has produced a larger number of brave warriors and thus has received more esteem from the other families in the tribe. But as societies become more and more complex, encompassing ever-larger populations and more elaborate divisions of labor, these simple forms of inequality give way to more clearly defined systems for distributing rewards among members of the society. And those systems result in the classification of families and other social groups into rather well-defined layers, or *strata*. In each society the various strata are defined by how much wealth people have, the kinds of work they do, the kinds of people they marry, and many other aspects of life.

> *In every society people are grouped into different layers or strata according to how they earn their living.*

In this chapter we will see how inequality in societies results in systems of social stratification. **Social stratification** is a society's system for ranking people hierarchically (i.e., from high to low) according to various attributes such as income, wealth, power, prestige, age, sex, ethnicity, and religion. Stratification by race, ethnicity, gender, and age is covered in Part IV. In this chapter we deal primarily with stratification by wealth, power, and prestige, and with the concept of social mobility.

Caste, Class, and Social Mobility

In every society people are grouped into different categories according to how they earn their living. This produces an imaginary set of horizontal social layers, or strata, that are more or less closed to entry by people from outside any given layer. Societies that maintain rigid boundaries between social strata are said to have **closed** stratification systems; societies in which the boundaries are easily crossed are said to be **open** societies.

In open societies it is possible for some individuals and their families, and even entire communities, to move from one stratum to another; this movement is termed **social mobility**. A couple whose parents were unskilled workers may become educated, learn advanced job skills, and be able to afford a private house instead of renting a modest apartment as their parents did. Such a couple is said to experience **upward social mobility**. If they have enough wealth to make their parents comfortable and to help other family members, the entire family may enjoy upward mobility. If everyone with the same education and skills and the same occupation experiences greater prosperity and prestige, the entire occupational community is said to be upwardly mobile. But in an open society fortunes can also decline. People with advanced skills—in engineering or higher education, for example—may find that there are too many of them around. They may not be able to afford the kind of housing, medical care, education for their children, and other benefits they have come to expect. When this occurs, they are said to be **downwardly mobile**.

The best examples of closed societies are found in caste societies. **Castes** are social strata into which people are born and in which they remain for life. Membership in a caste is an **ascribed status** (a status acquired at birth) rather than an **achieved status** (one based on the efforts of the individual). Members of a particular caste cannot hope to leave that caste. Slaves and plantation owners formed a caste society in the United States before the Civil War. Much of modern India remains influenced by caste-based inequalities (see Box 8-1), and South Africa with its system of *apartheid*, or strict racial segregation, is a caste society.

Box 8–1: **The Caste System in India Today**

His name was Natwar Singh, and he was the very image of what you could and could not achieve if you were well-born in Chirora. Natwar . . . was a Thakur, the principal landlord caste in central Uttar Pradesh, and he owned 35 *bighas*, or 17½ acres—a very big farm by local standards. The average farmer owned about two acres. After much prodding, he agreed that his annual profit might go as high as $1,500.

Natwar was a passionate adherent of the tenet that physical labor is beneath the dignity of a Thakur, a belief that idled a good many people in the village. I once asked him what he did with himself all day long. He was stumped. Finally, his friend Tripathy, the village merry-andrew, said, "Checking."

Always at the periphery of Natwar's large, cheerful entourage was a character named Guria. He was gloomy and taciturn, with rudely chopped hair and dark, moony eyes. Always he wore the shapeless, grimy pale shirt and baggy white pajamas common throughout northern India.

Guria was a member of one of the "backward" castes, a term used in contrast to the "forward" castes, the Brahmins and Thakurs. He was a Mallah, meaning fisherman—this because his father had been a fisherman, though Guria himself had turned to farming.

Practically everything in the village turned on caste, but not quite in the way I had expected. I had assumed, for example, that the Scheduled Caste[1] farmers were denied sharecropping work out of age-old prejudice, but it turned out to be something far more modern. Landowners, according to Indrapal Singh, were "afraid that the cultivators will claim the farmer's land, and since the Government always comes down on the side of the Scheduled Castes, they may get it." It hadn't happened yet, Indrapal conceded, but you never know.

In Uttar Pradesh, I was told, almost 45 percent of government jobs are reserved for these minorities, and there are preferential loans and scholarships set aside for them. In a magnificent display of ire, Natwar Singh even composed an entire English sentence for me: "All facilities Scheduled Caste, no facilities other caste."

"But what about the Scheduled Caste families in Chirora?" I objected. "They're miserably poor."

"You're right," said Tripathy with a grin. "But they used to be poorer."

The old caste harmony, based on an unquestioned tyranny, is giving way to a modest level of rivalry. The Scheduled Castes have made a tiny bid for power; the upper castes, so accustomed to unquestioned authority, are wildly overreacting. Caste relations have come to resemble class relations as the ritual element of caste has begun to dwindle. Elsewhere in India, especially in areas where powerful landlords exercise feudal control over entire villages, the competition between the landless and the landowning class has led to riots and horrible

[1]Formerly known as Untouchables but now called "Scheduled Castes" because they are scheduled to receive affirmative-action benefits.

Classes, like castes, are social strata, but they are based primarily on economic criteria such as occupation, income, and wealth. Classes are generally open, at least to some extent, to entry by newcomers, and in modern societies there tends to be a good deal of mobility between classes. Moreover, the classes of modern societies are not homogeneous—their members do not all share the same social rank. There are variations in people's material well-being and in how much prestige they are accorded by others. Within any given class, these variations produce groups, known as **status groups**, that are de-

violence. In Chirora, where—more typically—no one owns more than 20 acres, it's just raised the temperature a few degrees.

Perhaps one can gauge the power of new ideas by the impression they have made on Chirora. No one, for example, was embarrassed at the degraded status of their wives and daughters. India's extremely tentative feminist movement had made no inroads at all. Women, especially married women, were invisible. They stayed behind brick walls in their darkened homes, kneading dough, chopping vegetables, nursing fires, spoiling babies. At times as I walked down a dusty lane, I could see clusters of women circling their saris over their heads, alarmed lest a stranger see them and even look them in the eye. The rule of purdah, which Hindu India inherited from its Moslem occupiers, was complete in Chirora.

Certain women did not qualify for modesty, and thus could be seen outside the home—unmarried girls, widows and Scheduled Caste women, who had to work alongside men in the fields. An unmarried girl is a most insignificant thing, a pair of hands and a mouth, if also a giggle. A villager with three boys and two girls will answer, "Three," when asked how many children he has. Nowadays many of the girls graduate from eighth grade at the local school, but with very few exceptions they don't go any further. And once a girl marries at 14 or 15 her life is fixed; her future is her mother's past.

Source: Traub, 1984. Copyright © 1984 by The New York Times Company. Reprinted by permission.

fined by how much honor or prestige they receive from the society in general.

The concept of status groups is illustrated by "high society." In the United States, people with names like Rockefeller, DuPont, Lowell, Roosevelt, Harriman, and many others, who are of Western European, Protestant descent, often have more prestige than people who have the same amount of wealth but are of Italian or Jewish or African-American descent. The society pages of metropolitan newspapers devote most of their gossip to the philanthropic activities and private affairs of these prestigious families. But most of the old wealthy families in North America came from quite modest origins, as is revealed by the underlying meanings of their names. Rockefeller, for example, means "a dweller in rye fields"; DuPont, "one who lives near the bridge"; Harriman, "a manservant"; Roosevelt, "one living near a rose field." Moreover, people with prestigious family names typically enjoy fortunes gained from activities that were once considered too lowly to permit entry into polite society. Thus the Fords were looked down upon by high society because their fortune was linked to "smelly gasoline"; the Whitneys, whose fortune at the turn of the century spread over five states and 36,000 acres of palatial homes, were looked down upon by older millionaire families because their funds were derived from five-cent trolley fares rather than from railroad freight charges. In sum, both money and family prestige—gained by living expensively and engaging in public philanthropy—are required for entry into the highest levels of upper-class society (Amory, 1960; Domhoff, 1983).

Life Chances

Rankings from high to low are only one aspect of social stratification. The way people live (often referred to as their *life-style*), the work they do, the quality of their food and housing, the education they can provide for their children, and the way they use their leisure time all are shaped by their place in the stratification system.

The way people are grouped with respect to access to scarce resources determines their **life chances**—that is, the opportunities they will have or be denied throughout life: the kind of education and health care they will receive, the occupations that will be open to them, how they will spend their retirement years—even where they will be buried. The place in a society's stratification system into which one is born (be it a comfortable home with access to good schools, doctors, and places to relax or a home that suffers from the grinding stress of poverty) has an enormous impact on what one does and becomes throughout life. A poor child may overcome poverty and succeed, but the experience of struggling out of poverty will leave a permanent mark on his or her personality. And most people who are born poor will not attain affluence and leisure even in the most open society.

STRATIFICATION AND THE MEANS OF EXISTENCE

The principal forces that produce stratification are related to the ways in which people earn their living. In the nonindustrial world the majority of the people are small farmers or peasants. When they look up from their toil in the fields, they see members of higher social strata—the landlords, the moneylenders, the military chiefs, the religious leaders. These groups control the peasants' means of existence—that is, the land and the resources needed to make it produce. Even when farmers or peasants are citizens of a modern nation-state with the right to vote and to receive education, health care, and other benefits, when harvests are poor the landowners still take their full share while

the peasants must make do with less. The system of stratification that determines their fate depends on how much the land can yield. In contrast, in the stratification systems of industrial societies, whether capitalist or socialist, most people are urban wage workers whose fates are determined by the managers of productive firms or state planning agencies. If the firms are no longer productive or consumers no longer desire their products, urban workers may lose their jobs and suffer economic hardship.

The stratification systems of the United States and Canada, where less than one-twentieth of the population works the land, are most relevant to understanding people's life chances in modern industrial societies. But to understand the conditions of life for most of the world's population we must study inequalities in rural villages, where well over two-thirds of the earth's people till the soil and fish the rivers and oceans (see Figure 8-1).

Stratification in Rural Villages

In India and China more than a billion people spend their lives coaxing an existence from the soil. Millions of other rural villagers squeeze a modest existence from the land in

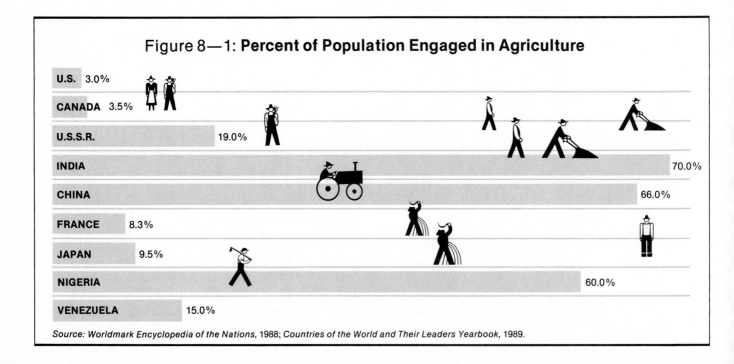

Figure 8—1: **Percent of Population Engaged in Agriculture**

U.S.	3.0%
CANADA	3.5%
U.S.S.R.	19.0%
INDIA	70.0%
CHINA	66.0%
FRANCE	8.3%
JAPAN	9.5%
NIGERIA	60.0%
VENEZUELA	15.0%

Source: Worldmark Encyclopedia of the Nations, 1988; Countries of the World and Their Leaders Yearbook, 1989.

Box 8–2: **Sweetness and Power**

Sugar, tobacco, tea, coffee, cocoa, pepper . . . these and other substances derived from plants that thrive in tropical climates were once unknown in the colder regions of the earth. Of them all, sugar has had perhaps the greatest influence. Sugar can be combined with cocoa to produce chocolate, fermented to produce rum, refined and sold in its pure form, or baked in candy and confections of all kinds. An exotic crop known mainly to European royalty in the fifteenth century, sugar had become an addiction of the masses by the eighteenth century. The craving for sugar and rum stimulated the growth of slavery in the New World and the transformation of entire Caribbean islands into sugar plantations (Mintz, 1985).

Most people do not realize that even today the production of sugar requires extremely dangerous and debilitating labor. This is especially true in Florida, where soft soils prohibit mechanized harvesting of the cane. Let a Jamaican sugar harvester who was brought to Florida as a contract worker continue the description:

In America, we work the roughest way to make a living. Coming over, they ask if you're willing to work seven days a week, willing to wash your own clothes, willing to eat poor, willing to obey, work in all style of weather, eat rice seven days . . .

A lot of accident happen in the cane. When you working, your hand is sweaty, maybe the bill [cane knife] slip and fly up, maybe take your hand or your foot. Maybe take your partner. . . . Your hand become like part of a machine. Look at my palm, the bill rest here—it make a channel for its shape. When you go home, that one hand you have been cutting with you can't use. It's no good for anything else; you got to use the other one until it heal. . . .

We got to watch dangerous things—snake, bobcat, ants climbing up your pants leg to sting you, the cane stalk strike you in the eye, pierce your eardrum. Sometime to make money we got to eat no lunch, we got no time for it, sick and still working. . . . You got to be wise and understand yourself and be quiet, otherwise they send you home. It is very disappointing, the way we are treated. We are slaves. They pay us money, but really they buy us. [Quoted in Wilkinson, 1989, pp. 56–57]

Investigations of working conditions for contract labor in Florida and other cane-producing areas of the United States have spurred sporadic efforts to improve conditions on the plantations. But little has changed. In fact, the officials of the cane-producing companies make free use of arbitrary firings and deportations, and they prefer foreign workers who can be easily controlled and summarily dismissed and sent home. A section of a report published by the Florida Fruit and Vegetable Growers Association, "Why Foreign Workers Are More Productive," explains how raw power maintains the flow of sugar:

The "unique and awesome form of management power" that sugar cane growers exert over their foreign workers provides a super-motivated workforce. As a Vice President of U.S. Sugar once said, "If I had a remedy comparable to breaching"—that is, firing and deporting—"an unsatisfactory worker which I could apply to the American worker, they'd work harder too." [Quoted in Wilkinson, 1989, p. 64]

Central and South America, Africa, and Southeast Asia. Social divisions in these villages are based largely on land ownership and agrarian labor. Yet even in rural villages, inequalities of wealth and power are increasingly affected by world markets for agricultural goods and services, as can be seen in the example presented in Box 8-2.

In peasant societies the farm family, which typically works a small plot of land, is the basic and most common productive group. Such families can be found in the villages of modern India. The Indian village reveals some important dimensions of stratification in third-world societies. For example, women are assigned to hard work in the fields and at the same time are expected to perform almost all of the household duties. This is true even in families that are well off. Men from the higher castes may be innovators, but women of all castes and male members of the "backward castes" do most of the productive work (Myrdal, 1965; Redfield, 1947).

In China before the Communist revolution of the late 1940s and early 1950s, a feudal system of stratification organized the lives of peasants and gentry alike. Among the peasants there were four broad strata (Tawney, 1966/1932). The rich peasants (analogous to Natwar Singh in Box 8-1) had enough land to meet their basic needs and to produce a surplus that could be converted into cash at local markets. They usually had one or more draft animals, and they often hired less fortunate villagers to help in their fields. The "middle peasants" were the second stratum of Chinese village life. They had a small plot of land, barely adequate shelter, and enough food and fuel to get through the winter. A small surplus in good years allowed them to own their own houses and even to have a few animals to provide meat on feast days. Only a very few of these "luxuries" were available to the third stratum, the poor peasants, and virtually none were to be had by the fourth and worst off, the tenants and hired laborers. Most Chinese peasants were in this impoverished stratum.

At the top of the stratification system of prerevolutionary China (i.e., above the rich peasants) were the gentry, the class of landowners whose holdings were large enough to allow them to live in relative comfort and freedom from labor.

What made the lives of the gentry so enviable to the working peasants was the security they enjoyed from hunger and cold. They at least had a roof over their heads. They had warm clothes to wear. They had some silk finery for feast days, wedding celebrations, and funerals. . . . The true landlords among them did no manual labor either in the field or in the home. Hired laborers or tenants tilled the fields. Servant girls and domestic slaves cooked the meals, sewed, washed, and swept up. [Hinton, 1966, p. 37]

As these examples from contemporary India and prerevolutionary China show, in rural villages the facts of daily life are determined largely by one's place in the local system of agricultural production. The poor peasant family, with little or no land, hovers on the edge of economic disaster. Work is endless for adults and children alike. Meals are meager; shelter is skimpy; there is not much time for play. Among the gentry, who have large land holdings and hired help to ease the burdens of work, there are "the finer things of life": education, ample food and shelter, music and games to pass the time. Of course, wealth brings additional responsibilities as well. Participation in village or regional politics takes time away from pleasure, at least for some. So does charity work. But the power that comes with such activities provides opportunities to amass still more wealth. Thus it is that, with few exceptions, the poor remain poor while the rich and powerful usually become richer and more powerful. And between the rich and the poor there are other strata—the middle peasants, the middle castes with skills to sell—whose members look longingly at the pleasures of the rich and console themselves with the fact that at least they are not as unfortunate as the humble poor in the strata below them.

How does this scheme of social stratification compare with that in industrial societies? We will see that there is more mobility in industrial societies but that, just as in rural societies, to be born into the lower strata is to be disadvantaged compared with people who are born into higher strata.

> *Compared to rural societies, industrial societies are characterized by greater spatial and structural mobility.*

Stratification in Industrial Societies

The industrial revolution profoundly altered the stratification systems of rural societies. The mechanization of agriculture greatly decreased the number of people needed to work on the land, thereby largely eliminating the classes of peasants and farm laborers in some societies. This dimension of social change is often called **structural mobility**: An entire class is eliminated as a result of changes in the means of existence. As noted in Chapter 3, the industrial revolution transformed the United States from a nation in which almost 90 percent of the people worked in farming and related occupations into one in which less than 10 percent did so. Today automation and foreign competition are eliminating many of the so-called smokestack industries, thereby creating new patterns of structural mobility.

A second major change brought on by the industrial revolution was a tremendous increase in **spatial mobility** (or geographic mobility). This term refers to the movement of individuals, families, and larger groups from one location or community to another. The increase in spatial mobility resulted from the declining importance of the rural village and the increase in the importance of city-centered institutions like markets, corporations, and governments. Increasingly, one's place of work became separate from one's place of residence; people's allegiance to local communities was weakened by their need to move both within the city and to other parts of the nation; and as a result social strata began to span entire nations. Working-class people created similar communities everywhere, as did the middle classes and the rich (Dahrendorf, 1959; Janowitz, 1978).

Despite these immense changes, our relationship to the means of existence is still the main factor determining our position in our society's stratification system. We continue to define ourselves to one another first and foremost in terms of how we make a living: "I am a professor; she is a doctor; he is a steelworker." Once we have dealt with the essentials of our existence—essentials that say a great deal about the nature and the quality of our daily lives—we go on to talk about the things we like to do with our lives after work or after educating ourselves for future work.

> *To a large extent, people accept their place in a stratification system because the system itself is part of their culture.*

STRATIFICATION AND CULTURE

Why do people accept their "place" in a stratification system, especially when they are at or near the bottom? One answer is that they have no choice; they lack not only wealth and opportunities but also the power to change their situation. But lack of power does not prevent people from rebelling against inequality. Many also believe that their inferior place in the system is justified by their own failures or by the accident of their birth. If people who have good cause to rebel do not do so and instead support the existing stratification system, those who do wish to rebel may feel that their efforts will be fruitless.

Another reason people accept their place in a stratification system is that the system itself is part of their culture. Through socialization we learn the cultural norms that justify our society's system of stratification. The rich learn how to act like rich people; the poor learn how to survive, and in so doing they tacitly accept being poor. Women and men learn to accept the places assigned to them, and so do the young and the old. Yet despite the powerful influence of socialization, at times large numbers of people rebel against their cultural conditioning. To understand their reasons for doing so we need to examine the cultural foundations of stratification systems.

The Role of Ideology

The miners whose strikes threatened to cripple the Soviet economy in 1989 demonstrate the accuracy of Tatyana Zaslavskaya's predictions about the impact of glasnost. The ideology of communism, which the miners had been taught since childhood, stresses the evil of private gain and the value of collective work to build the ideal socialist society. But once they saw some members of their communities becoming wealthy by engaging in private enterprise, while others continued to use political power to maintain their privileged position, the miners used their newfound freedom to lay down their tools in protest. Their action illustrates a crisis in Communist ideology and real confusion about the values of Soviet society.

Unlike Soviet workers, American workers have been taught that employment in private firms and the pursuit of individual gain are commendable. Yet often American workers find it in their interest to unite and go out on strike even when it seems that the majority of Americans do not condone their action. Thus conflicting ideals and values are evident in this nation as well.

Every society appears to have ideologies that justify stratification and socialize new generations to believe that existing patterns of inequality are legitimate. In the United States, for example, people love to hear versions of the "rags to riches" theme as embodied in the stories of Horatio Alger. Following the Civil War Alger wrote numerous books based on this theme. In his first novel, *Ragged Dick*, the central character is a poor but honest boy who comes to the city looking for work. As he walks the streets he sees a runaway carriage; he leaps onto the horses and stops them. In the carriage is a beautiful young woman who turns out to have a rich father. The father takes Dick into his business, where he proves his great motivation and becomes highly successful. A similar theme is repeated endlessly today in stories of poor, hardworking people who win great fortunes in the lottery.

The people of prerevolutionary China were also guided by ideology; they believed in the teachings of Confucius (551–479 B.C.), which emphasized the need to accept one's place in a well-ordered, highly stratified society (McNeill, 1963). Similarly, the castes of Hindu India are supported by religious ideology. The *Rig-Veda* taught that Hindu society was, by divine will, divided into four castes, of which the Brahmins were the highest because they were responsible for religious ceremonies and sacrifices (Majundar, 1951; McNeill, 1963). Over time, other castes with other tasks were added to the system as the division of labor progressed and new occupations developed. Still another powerful ideology had its origins in Europe before the spread of Christianity. Tribal peoples in what is now France and Germany associated their kings with gods, and that association became stronger in the feudal era (Dodgson, 1987).

Religious teachings often serve as the ideologies of civilizations, explaining and jus-

These Soviet miners were striking not only for higher pay and more consumer goods but also for the right to strike itself, which Soviet ideology asserts is unnecessary.

tifying the stratification systems associated with them. But this relationship has not held in every historical period or for every religious movement. Originally, for example, the teachings of Jesus Christ opposed the stratification systems of both the Roman Empire and the Jewish people. "The last shall be first" and "It is easier for a camel to pass through the eye of a needle than for a rich man to enter heaven" were ideas that appealed to the poor and downtrodden and enraged the wealthy and powerful. But over many centuries Christ's teachings were incorporated into church doctrine and organization, and by the Middle Ages Christianity was the ideology underlying the stratification system of kings, lords, merchants, and peasants. The vicars of the church upheld that system by affirming its legitimacy in coronations and royal weddings. They also presided over the execution of heretics who challenged the system, which was viewed as divinely ordained.

Just as Jesus's teachings were used in ancient times to justify social movements for equality, today the black civil rights movement, the movement to end *apartheid* in South Africa, and the struggle of the Northern Irish Catholics for independence from Britain, to name only a few, continually call upon the older imagery of radical Christianity. "We Shall Overcome," the theme song of the civil-rights movement, was borrowed from the African-American Baptist Church version, "I Shall Overcome," and transformed into a moving song of hope and protest with religious overtones that inspired the nonviolent resistance of the movement for racial equality.

> *The connection between culture and stratification can be seen in micro-level interactions such as deference and demeanor.*

Stratification at the Micro Level

These relationships between religious ideologies and the stratification systems of civilizations are macro-level examples of how culture maintains stratification systems from one generation to the next. But we can also see the connection between culture and stratification in the micro-level interactions of daily life. The way we dress—whether we wear expensive designer clothes, "off the rack" apparel, or used clothes from the Salvation Army—says a great deal about our place in the stratification system. So does the way we speak, as anyone knows who has been told to get rid of a southern or Brooklyn accent in order to "get ahead." Our efforts to possess and display **status symbols**—material objects or behaviors that convey prestige—are encouraged by the billion-dollar advertising industry. Many other examples could be given, but here we will concentrate on two important sets of norms that reinforce stratification systems at the micro level: deference and demeanor (Goldhamer and Shils, 1939).

Deference. By **deference** we mean the "appreciation an individual shows of another to that other" (Goffman, 1958, pp. 488–489). In popular speech the word *deference* is often used to indicate how one person should behave in the presence of another who is of higher status. Formulas for showing deference illustrate how our society's stratification system is experienced in everyday life. In the United States, for example, we learn to address judges as "Your Honor" and feel embarrassed for the plaintiff who begins a sentence with "Excuse me, Judge." In most European countries, with their histories of more rigid stratification, people who want to show deference go further and address the judge as "Your Excellence."

Erving Goffman pointed out that deference is not a one-way process. The act of paying deference to someone in a higher status frequently obligates the other person to pay some form of deference in return. For example, "High priests all over the world seem obliged to respond to offerings [of deference] with an equivalent of 'Bless you, my son'" (Goffman, 1958, p. 489). The point here is that deference is often symmetrical, in that both participants defer according to their place in the stratification system. Through deferent behavior and the appropriate response, both parties affirm their acceptance of the stratification system itself. Intuitively we all know this. When we are stopped by a police officer we may become deferential, using the most polite forms of address ("Yes, sir," "No, sir," and the like) in order to avoid punishment. The officer, in turn, may attempt to find out our place in the stratification system and use the appropriate forms of address in speaking to us.

Demeanor. **Demeanor** is the way in which we present ourselves—our body language, dress, speech, and manners. It conveys to others how much deference or respect we believe is due us. Here again the interaction is often symmetrical. The professor must make the first move toward informality in relations with students (an asymmetrical example); but among professors of equal rank there is far more symmetry. The move toward informal demeanor, such as the use of first names, can be initiated by whoever feels most comfortable in his or her status. On the other hand, asymmetry in the use of names can be used to reinforce stratification, as in an office where the secretaries are addressed by their first names while they address their supervisor by his or her last name plus a title such as Mr., Dr., or Professor.

These almost-taken-for-granted aspects of how we carry out social stratification at the micro level can have far-reaching effects. In a prison camp, for example, looking directly into the commandant's eyes could be a sign of defiance, with terrible consequences (Bettelheim, 1943). As is shown in the next chapter that failure to carry out the rules of demeanor—to twitch, to have a runny nose, to encroach on another person's space—can cause a person to be labeled deviant and to be cast out of the "acceptable" strata of society.

POWER, AUTHORITY, AND STRATIFICATION

When the macro dimensions of social stratification change, the changes may be reflected in the behavior of people at the micro level, and those changes, in turn, accelerate change throughout the entire society. Thus, for example, the civil rights and women's movements of recent decades have altered the norms of demeanor for blacks and women. Blacks insist on being referred to as blacks or African-Americans if their ancestors were of African origin, rather than as Negroes. Women increasingly refuse to be called "girls" by men and especially by their supervisors, although some women continue to use the term among themselves. These may seem to be trivial matters, but when people demand respect in everyday interactions, they are also demonstrating their determination to create social change at a more macro level—in other words, to bring about a realignment of social power.

Max Weber defined **power** as "the probability that one actor within a social relationship will be in a position to carry out his own will despite resistance" (1947, p. 152). This is a very general definition; it applies equally well to a mugger with a gun and to a company president ordering an employee to perform a difficult task. But there is a big difference between the types of power used in these examples. In the first, illegitimate power is asserted through physical coercion. In the second, the employee may not want to obey the president's orders yet recognizes that they are legitimate; that is, such orders are understood by everyone in the company to be within the president's power. This kind of power is called **authority**.

> At the macro level, change in stratification systems results from shifts in the groups that command power and authority within a society.

Even when power has been translated into authority, there remains the question of how authority originates and is maintained. This is a basic question in the study of stratification. As we saw earlier, the fact that people in lower strata accept their place in society requires that we study not only the processes of socialization but also how power and authority are used to maintain existing relations among castes or classes. As a case study in the relationship between power and authority on the one hand and stratification on the other, let us briefly review the causes of the French Revolution of 1789.

Why did the French people accept the rule of absolute monarchs for so long before they finally ended that rule in a bloody revolution? In answering this question we can apply all the aspects of stratification discussed so far. We will begin with the feudal stratification system. The major strata of French society, called *estates*, were the nobility, the clergy, the peasantry, and the *bourgeoisie* (merchants, shopkeepers, and artisans). Each estate had its own institutions and culture, causing its members to feel that they were part of a unified community with its own norms and values. The estates were linked together by the time-honored norms of feudalism: vassalage and fealty. A *vassal* was someone who received a grant of land from a lord. In return he swore *fealty*, an oath of service and loyalty, to that lord. The lord, in turn, swore fealty to a more powerful lord, until one reached the highest level of society, the king. (The feudal stratification system is described in detail in Box 8-3.) In such a well-ordered and legitimate system, where were the seeds of revolution? The answer lies in how power, authority, and changing modes of production combined to shake the foundations of feudal France.

In any system of stratification there are likely to be conflicts. Those conflicts may be caused by the ambitions of a particular leader or group, but sometimes the characteristics of the system itself give rise to conflict. Both types of conflict existed in prerevolutionary France. In order to compete with the other major European powers, the king had to raise armies and send fleets abroad, both of which cost huge sums of money and required thousands of men. But the vow of fealty extended only from the king to the highest level of the nobility. The nobles, in turn, were responsible for seeing that their vassals provided more money and men. This system placed severe constraints on the king's power. The king was dependent on the nobles and, through them, on the lesser lords. In return, the lesser lords often demanded more power, thereby challenging the king's authority. In order to reduce the power of the lords, the king went to the clergy and the bourgeoisie for assistance.

As the cities grew and the trading and

Although feudal culture is no longer dominant, its former strength is reflected in monuments like the island cathedral of Mont St. Michel, which symbolizes the combined power of church and state in the French feudal era.

Box 8–3: **Feudal Relations**

Feudalism is a form of social organization that has appeared throughout the world as societies have experienced the so-called agrarian revolution. It took somewhat different forms in China, Africa, Japan, and Europe, but it has always been characterized by a fundamental principle: the subordination of one person to another. As social historian Marc Bloch (1964) wrote, the essence of feudalism is "to be the 'man' of another man. . . . The Count was the 'man' of the king, as the serf was the 'man' of his manorial lord" (p. 145). In this system, known as *vassalage*, it was understood that women shared the loyalties of their male masters.

The swearing of *homage* signified and cemented the relationship of vassalage. As Bloch described it,

Imagine two men face to face; one wishing to serve, the other willing or anxious to be served. The former puts his hands together and places them, thus joined, between the hands of the other man—a plain symbol of submission, the significance of which was sometimes further emphasized by a kneeling posture. At the same time, the person proffering his hands utters a few words—a very short declaration—by which he acknowledges himself to be the "man" of the person facing him. The chief and subordinate kiss each other on the mouth, symbolizing accord and friendship. Such were the gestures—very simple ones, eminently fitted to make an impression on minds so sensitive to visible things—which served to cement one of the strongest bonds known in the feudal era. [1964, pp. 145–146]

The basic relationship of feudalism, signified in the act of homage, is shown in the accompanying diagram. In essence, the vassal exchanges independence for protection, but this relationship can also entail more material exchanges: The lord can give his vassal a manor with the associated land and villagers, and the vassal can provide wealth and soldiers when the lord requires them. Sociologists study feudalism and its relations not only because some institutions derived from feudalism still exist today but also because the exchange of independence for protection continues to appear in modern social institutions. For example, organized-crime "families" often resemble feudal systems, as do many political-party organizations and some business corporations.

manufacturing capacities of the bourgeoisie expanded, the king was increasingly successful at drawing on the wealth of the bourgeoisie and undermining the power of the feudal lords. The court flourished; in fact, it seemed that the king's power had become absolute. But beneath the pomp and display of the court, the feudal stratification system was in ruins. The weakened nobility could no longer hold the fealty of the peasants. Throughout the countryside the peasants groaned under the heavy debts imposed by their feudal masters, and they began to question the right of the nobility to tax them. Meanwhile, in the cities and towns, the rapidly growing bourgeoisie, along with the new social stratum of urban workers, clearly understood that the king's power derived from their productive activities. They felt that they were not adequately rewarded for their support. At the same time, another new stratum, the intellectuals—people who had been educated outside the church and the court—was creating a new ideology and promoting it through new institutions like the press. This new ideology—"liberty, equality, fraternity"—helped spur the revolutionary movement, but the underlying cause of the revolution was a drastic change in the stratification system.

STRATIFICATION IN THE MODERN ERA

We saw in the preceding section that under the leadership of the bourgeoisie a new social order known as capitalism largely destroyed the

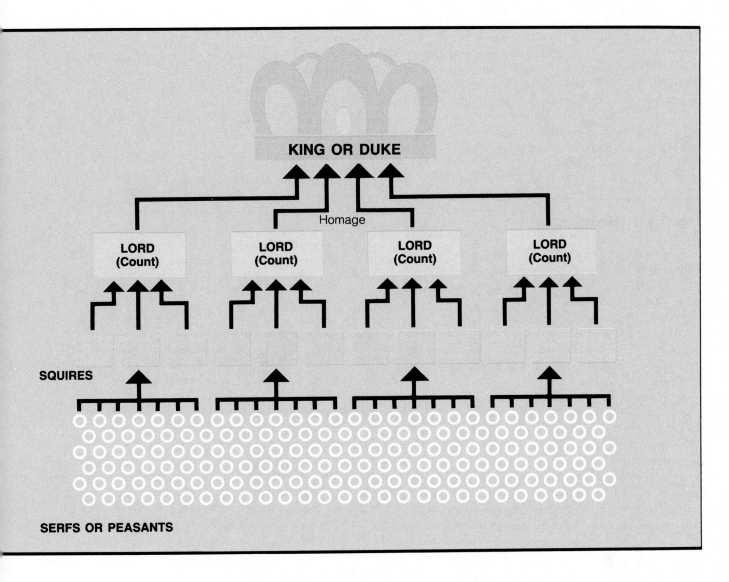

KING OR DUKE

Homage

LORD (Count)   **LORD (Count)**   **LORD (Count)**   **LORD (Count)**

SQUIRES

SERFS OR PEASANTS

feudal system. Capitalism is a form of economic organization based on private ownership and control of the means of production (land, machines, buildings, etc.). Whereas under feudalism land was viewed as belonging to a family as a matter of birthright, under capitalism land can be sold like any other commodity. And whereas feudal labor systems were based on institutions like serfdom, in which peasants were bound to a particular lord, in capitalist systems workers are free to sell their labor to the highest bidder and to endure unemployment when work is unavailable. Capitalism is also an ideology based on the value of individual rights; the ideology of feudalism, in contrast, stressed the reciprocal obligations of different strata of society.

In descriptions by Karl Marx and other observers of nineteenth-century society, cap-

italism seemed almost to explode onto the world scene. Capitalism made possible the dramatic change in production methods that we call the industrial revolution, which transformed England and Europe from a world of towns and villages, courts and cathedrals to a world centered on markets, factories, and crowded cities. A few places where the physical structures of feudalism remain, such as Mont St. Michel in France or Dubrovnik in Yugoslavia, continue to illustrate the contrast between the old order and the new.

The industrial revolution began in England and other parts of Europe in the late seventeenth century. Today it is still occurring in other parts of the world, including China, India, and Africa. The former colonial outposts of England, France, and Germany are only now undergoing the transformation from rural agrarian societies to urban industrial states in which an ever-decreasing portion of the population is engaged in farming. Although not all of these industrializing societies have capitalist economies, they all are developing a class of managers, entrepreneurs, and political power brokers who resemble the bourgeoisie of early capitalism.

The Great Transformation

It is not enough, however, to describe the industrial revolution in terms of the spread of industrial technology and urban settlement. Technological innovations like the steam engine, the railroad, the mechanization of the textile industry, and new processes for making steel and mining coal were accompanied by equally important innovations in social institutions.

In the words of sociologist and historian Karl Polanyi (1944), the industrial revolution was a Great Transformation. For the first time in human history, the market became the dominant institution of society. By *market* we do not mean the places where villagers sold produce or traded handicrafts. Rather, the market created by the industrial revolution was a social network that gradually extended over the entire world and linked buyers and sellers in a system that governed the distribution of goods of every imaginable type, services of all kinds, human labor power, and new forms of energy like coal and fuel oil.

Other key elements of the Great Transformation included the following:

- Goods, land, and labor were transformed into commodities whose value could be calculated and translated into a specific amount of gold or its equivalent—that is, *money* (Marx, 1962/1867; Schumpeter, 1950; Weber, 1958/1922).
- Relationships that had been based on ascribed statuses were replaced with relationships based on *contracts*. A producer hired laborers, for example, rather than relying on kinship obligations or village loyalties to supply workers (Polanyi, 1944; Smith, 1910/1789).

- The business firm or *corporation* replaced the family, the manor, and the guild as the dominant economic institution (Weber, 1958/1922).
- Rural people, displaced from the land, began selling their labor for *wages* in factories and commercial firms in the cities (Davis, 1955).
- In the new industrial order, demands for *full political rights* and *equality of opportunity*, which originated with the bourgeoisie, slowly spread to the new class of wage workers, to the poor, and to women, especially in societies in which revolutions created more open stratification systems (Bendix, 1969; De Tocqueville, 1980/1835; Mannheim, 1941).

The last point deserves some comment. The demand for full political rights originated with the bourgeoisie, who were to become the capitalist class in industrial societies—the owners of the means of production. The bourgeoisie were interested in removing various feudal barriers to economic activity. They therefore called for an end to feudal restrictions on the sale of land, for greater freedom for workers to move from one employer to another, for the elimination of aristocratic privileges like the right to charge tolls for the use of roads and waterways that happened to cross a lord's property, and for an end to voting rights based solely on aristocratic birth. These demands for economic and political rights then spread to the new class of wage workers and to other groups in society. Although the bourgeoisie originally sought rights for itself, it had to form alliances with workers and professionals in order to topple the feudal aristocracy. (Note that these demands originally applied only to men. Similar movements for equal participation by women took many more generations to develop and gain influence, as is shown in Chapter 14.)

Class Consciousness and Class Conflict

The Great Transformation had a profound impact on the stratification systems of modern societies. It produced new and powerful social classes and thereby changed the way people thought about their life chances and the legitimacy of their society's institutions. As Marx wrote in the last chapter of *Capital*, "The owners merely of labor-power, owners of capital, and landowners, whose respective sources of income are wages, profit, and ground rent . . . constitute the three big classes of modern society based upon the capitalist mode of production" (1962/1867, pp. 862–863). Here as elsewhere Marx defined classes in terms of the "modes of production" characteristic of a society in a given historical period. The workers, by far the largest class in modern societies, must sell their labor to the capitalist or the landowner in return for wages. The capitalists and landowners are far less numerous than the workers, but because they own and control the means of existence, they command more of everything of value than the workers do.

Of course, Marx recognized that in societies that had not yet undergone the Great Transformation there were classes that were very different from those of capitalist societies. The peasants of Russia, the slaves of America, and the exploited Indians of Latin America were "precapitalist" classes. Marx predicted that these strata would eventually be transformed into what he termed the *proletariat*, workers who did not own the means of production and had to survive by selling their labor.

Marx believed that the class of wage workers created by capitalism would inevitably rise up against the capitalist class and create a classless socialist society. As noted earlier, this prediction was proved wrong: Proletarian revolutions never occurred in the most industrialized nations. Yet Marx's description of how members of the working class become conscious of their situation as a class remains an important dimension of the study of stratification.

Sources of Class Conflict. "The history of all hitherto existing societies is the history of class struggles," wrote Marx and his collab-

> **Marx believed that the class of wage workers created by capitalism would rise up against the capitalist class and create a classless socialist society.**

orator Friedrich Engels in *The Communist Manifesto* (1969/1848, p. 11). In the modern era, "society as a whole is more and more splitting up into two great hostile camps, into two great classes directly facing each other, bourgeoisie and proletariat" (p. 11). Why did Marx and many other observers of the capitalist system believe that conflict between the bourgeoisie and the proletariat was inevitable? The answer can be found by taking a closer look at Marx's analysis of the evolution of capitalism.

To begin with, Marx observed the misery of industrial workers (many of whom were children) in the smoky factories of industrial England. He saw that however wretched the workers were, there was always a "reserve army" of unemployed people who would be willing to work for lower wages than those who already had jobs. He noticed that the capitalists (and the intellectuals whom they paid to argue in their defense) always blamed the workers themselves for the miserable conditions in which they were forced to exist. If they were hungry, it was because they did not work hard enough or because they spent their pay on too much alcohol or because they could not curb their sexual passions and bore too many children. Thus the capitalists refused to accept blame for the misery of the working class.

Marx also argued that business competition would eliminate less successful firms and result in monopolies, which would control prices and wages and thereby contribute still more to the impoverishment of the workers. Moreover, the capitalists had the power to determine who ran the government and who controlled the police and the army. If the workers were to rebel, the armed forces and police would act as agents of the capitalists. Through these means the workers and the unemployed would be forced to remain a huge, helpless population that could be manipulated by the capitalists. Over time, according to Marx and his followers, these masses of people would become increasingly conscious of their plight and would unite in a revolution that would destroy the power of the capitalists and their allies.

Objective and Subjective Classes. In thinking about how a social class becomes able to take collective action, Marx distinguished between objective and subjective classes. An **objective class** is one that has a visible, specific relationship to the means of production. The workers are an objective class that does not own capital, and the capitalists are an objective class that does. **Subjective class** is more of a cultural concept. Subjective class depends on how the people in a given stratum of society actually perceive their situation as a class. If the workers, for example, are not aware of their situation and do not agree that their fortunes can improve only at the expense of another class (the capitalists), they are not a subjective class. Without this awareness of their situation, the workers are said to lack **class consciousness**. And without class consciousness they cannot form the political associations that will allow them to fight effectively against the capitalists.

In an often-quoted passage, Marx described the peasants of France as an objective class because of their shared experience as agriculturalists with small landholdings, but he was doubtful about their ability to form a subjective class:

A small holding, a peasant and his family; alongside them another small holding, another peasant and another family. A few score of these make up a village, and a few score of villagers make up a Department. In this way, the great mass of the French nation is formed by simple addition of homologous magnitudes, much as potatoes in a sack form a sack of potatoes. . . . In so far as there is merely a local interconnection among these small holding peasants, and the identity of their interests begets no community, no national bond and no political organization among them, they do not form a class. [1963/1869, p. 124]

The working class, Marx believed, would be different from the peasantry because its members would become conscious of their shared interests as a class.

The Classless Society. Marx and other observers of early capitalism believed that the growing conflict between the working class or proletariat and the capitalist class or bourgeoisie would produce revolutions. In those revolutions the proletariat and its allies would depose the bourgeoisie and establish a new social order known as *socialism*. Under socialism the key institutions of capitalism— private ownership of the means of produc- tion, the market as the dominant economic institution, and the nation-state controlled by the bourgeoisie—would be abolished. The new society would be classless because the economic institutions that produced classes would have been eliminated and all the members of society would collectively own the means of production.

Social Mobility in Modern Societies: The Weberian View

Max Weber took issue with Marx's view of social stratification and devoted much of his career to refuting it. Marx had defined social class in economic terms; classes are based on people's relationship to the means of production. Weber challenged this definition of social class. People are stratified, Weber reasoned, not only by their wealth or their situation with respect to the means of production but also by how much honor or prestige they receive from others and how much power they command. A person could be a poor European aristocrat whose lands had been taken away during a revolution, yet his prestige could be such that he would be invited to the homes of wealthy families seeking to use his social status to raise their own. Another person could have little money compared with the wealthy capitalists, and little prestige compared with the European aristocracy, yet could command immense power. The late Mayor Richard S. Daley of Chicago was such a person. He was born into a working-class Irish-American family, and although he was rather well off he was not rich. Yet his positions as mayor and chairman of the Cook County Democratic party organization made him a powerful man. Indeed, Mayor Daley's fame as a politician who led a powerful urban party organization but did not enrich himself in doing so helped his son continue the family tradition of political leadership: In 1989 Richard Daley, Jr., was elected mayor of Chicago.

For Weber and many other sociologists, therefore, wealth or economic position is only one of at least three dimensions that need to be considered in defining social class. Pres-

> *Weber pointed out that people are stratified not only by wealth but also according to their prestige and power.*

tige (or social status) and power are the others. We need to think of modern stratification systems as ranking people on all of these dimensions. A high ranking in terms of wealth does not always guarantee a high ranking in terms of prestige or power, although they often go together.

Other challenges to Marx's view of stratification focus on social mobility in industrial societies. Contrary to Marx's prediction, modern societies have not become polarized into two great classes, the rich and the poor. Instead, there is a large middle class of people who are neither industrial workers nor capitalists (Wright, 1979), and there is considerable social mobility, or movement from one class to another.

Social mobility can be measured either within or between generations. These two kinds of mobility are termed *intragenera-*

tional and *intergenerational* mobility. **Intragenerational mobility** refers to one's chances of rising to or falling from one social class to another within one's own lifetime. **Intergenerational mobility** is usually measured by comparing the social-class position of children with that of their parents. If there is a great deal of stability from one generation to the next, one can conclude that the stratification system is relatively rigid.

Table 8-1 compares social mobility among males in the United States, Germany, and France at midcentury. It shows that aside from the movement away from farming in Germany and the United States, the shift from manual to nonmanual occupations was similar in all three societies. This shift reflected the widespread social change that accompanied the rapid economic development of those societies during the early decades of this cen-

Table 8–1: **Social Mobility in Four Western Populations**

Respondent's Occupation	Father's Occupation		
	Nonmanual	**Manual**	**Farm**
France			
Nonmanual	73%	35%	16%
Manual	18	55	13
Farm	9	10	71
N	(1109)	(625)	(1289)
Germany			
Nonmanual	58%	27%	19%
Manual	38	68	28
Farm	4	5	54
N	(579)	(406)	(321)
United States			
Nonmanual	71%	35%	23%
Manual	25	61	39
Farm	4	4	38
N	(319)	(430)	(404)
Sweden			
Nonmanual	67%	59%	44%
Manual	32	39	44
Farm	1	2	12
N	(57)	(101)	(73)

N = number of respondents.

Intergenerational mobility tables compare people's occupations with those of their parents. Here sons (the respondents) are compared with their fathers. In the United States, for example, 71 percent of sons in nonmanual occupations had fathers who were in nonmanual work. The diagonal cells in the tables represent stability, or no intergenerational mobility. Thus, in France, 55 percent of the respondents in manual occupations had fathers who also did manual work.

Source: Adapted from Lipset and Zetterberg, 1966.

tury. In each society most people had achieved the same social-class position their fathers had. However, some 35 percent of the American and French respondents and 27 percent of the German respondents whose fathers were manual workers had been able to rise into the middle class of nonmanual workers. By this relatively crude measure, about one-third of the younger generation had achieved upward social mobility. One could argue about whether this is a lot or a little, but it is sufficient to indicate that the lines of social class in capitalist societies are far from rigid.

Unfortunately, not all mobility is upward. Downward mobility involves loss of economic and social standing. It is a problem for families and individuals at all levels of the class structure in the United States and elsewhere. In its broadest sense, downward mobility can be defined as "losing one's place in society" (Newman, 1988, p. 7). In fact, the term encompasses many different kinds of experiences. The married woman who works part time and then is divorced, loses the family house, and must move to a small apartment with her children and work full time is experiencing downward mobility. The couple who live with the wife's mother in public housing and then are forced out during a check of official rosters and must seek refuge in a homeless shelter also experience downward mobility. The affluent young couple living in a downtown condominium experience downward mobility when he loses his brokerage job and she must go on maternity leave while he is looking for a new job.

Of course, some proportion of those who experience downward mobility will experience upward mobility again, but once one falls it can be difficult to get back on the upward track, if only because downward mobility affects one's confidence. More important, much downward mobility is due to large-scale changes in the economic structure of modern nations. The shift from manufacturing to information technologies, for example, has caused thousands of blue-collar workers with stable, well-paying jobs to become displaced workers who must undergo retraining and often must accept employment in lower-paid service jobs (Harrison, Tilly, and Bluestone, 1986). The impact of such structural

changes on American society is discussed in more detail in Chapter 18.

THEORIES OF STRATIFICATION

Conflict Theories

As mentioned earlier, Marx's theory of stratification asserts that capitalist societies are divided into two opposing classes, wage workers and capitalists, and that conflict between these two classes will eventually lead to revolutions that will establish classless socialist societies. However, Marx's prediction has not been borne out in any existing socialist society. Deny it as they may, all of those societies have developed well-defined systems of social stratification (Djilas, 1982; Parkin, 1971; Szelenyi, 1983). Each has an elite of high party officials; an upper stratum of higher professionals, scientists, managers of economic enterprises, local party officials, and high police officials; a middle level of well-educated technical workers and lower professionals; a proletariat of industrial and clerical workers and military personnel; and a bottom layer of people who are disabled, criminals, or political outcasts. (These strata are illustrated in the Visual Sociology section of the chapter.)

In capitalist societies there is no persuasive evidence that class conflict is heightening the division between workers and capitalists. Conflict does exist, but the industrial working class is shrinking and the new occupational groups do not always share the concerns of the industrial workers. Moreover, reforms of capitalist institutions have greatly improved the workers' situation, thereby reducing the likelihood that the revolution predicted by Marx will occur.

Modern conflict theorists agree with Marx's claim that class conflict is a primary cause of social change, but they frequently debate both the nature of the class structure and the forms taken by class conflict. Thus Erik Olin Wright (1979) notes that Marxian theorists agree that workers who are directly engaged in the production of goods are part of the working class. However, "there is no such agreement about any other category of wage-earners. Some Marxists have argued that only productive manual workers should be considered part of the proletariat. Others have argued that the working class includes low-level, routinized white-collar workers as well. Still others have argued that virtually all wage-laborers should be considered part of the working class" (p. 31).

This disagreement stems, of course, from the fact that there is far greater diversity within all the classes of modern societies than Marx or his contemporaries imagined there would be. In addition to the bourgeoisie (the owners of large amounts of capital) and the petit bourgeoisie (the owners of small firms and stores), there is a constantly growing professional class, a class of top managers and engineers, another class of lower-level managers, and a class of employees with special skills (e.g., computer specialists, nurses and other medical personnel, and operating engineers). Perhaps many of these people should think of themselves as part of the working class, but they normally do not because they are earning enough to enable them to live in middle-class communities.

In the functionalist view, social stratification occurs because an unequal distribution of rewards is essential in complex societies.

Some conflict theorists focus on other aspects of social stratification besides class conflict. Melvin Tumin (1967), for example, pointed out that stratification systems "limit the possibility of discovery of the full range of talent available in a society"; that they create unfavorable self-images that further limit the expression of people's creative potential; and that they "function to encourage hostility, suspicion, and distrust among the various segments of a society" (p. 58). Problems like wasted talent and poor self-image are among what Richard Sennett and Jonathan Cobb (1972) term "the hidden injuries of class," meaning the ways in which a childhood of poverty or economic insecurity can leave its mark on people even after they have risen out of the lower classes. In Part IV we look more specifically at social stratification in the United States and examine its consequences in human terms.

The Functionalist View

The functionalist view of stratification was originally stated by Talcott Parsons (1937, 1940) and Kingsley Davis and Wilbert Moore (1945). This theory holds that social classes emerge because an unequal distribution of rewards is essential in complex societies. Such societies need to reward talented people and channel them into roles that require advanced training, personal sacrifice, and extreme stress. Thus the unequal distribution of rewards, which allows some people to accumulate wealth and deprives others of that chance, is necessary if the society is to match the most talented individuals with the most challenging positions.

We noted at the beginning of the chapter that skilled workers in the Soviet Union are critical of the concept of "leveling." Tatyana Zaslavskaya's interpretation of this finding is a functionalist one. Zaslavskaya argues that unless there are incentives in the form of high wages and other advantages (such as better housing in areas where good housing is in short supply) engineers and scientists will continue to resent their situation and will not work hard. In the United States the same arguments are used to justify higher salaries for doctors, lawyers, and other professionals. Too much equality, it is said, reduces the incentive to master difficult skills, and as a result the entire society may suffer from a lack of professional expertise.

Critics of the functionalist view of inequality and stratification point to many situations in which people in positions of power or leadership receive what appear to be excessive benefits. In 1984, for example, Michael Jackson earned about $37 million for his record album "Thriller." CBS Records earned over $250 million, which helped pay its stockholders, employees, and contractors, as well as a few executives earning up to $1 million a year. From the point of view of those who are critical of social inequality, these large sums paid to a few people seem wrong, especially when so many others are struggling just to survive. Indeed, the heads of large corporations in the United States often earn more than fifty times as much as the average employee of those corporations. Is such great disparity "functional" when it produces enormous gaps between the very rich and the working classes? Functionalist theory claims that it is, for in a capitalist system of free enterprise top executives will seek the firms that are most willing to reward them for their talents. Those firms will benefit, and so will their workers.

The Interactionist Perspective

Conflict theory explains stratification primarily in economic terms. So does functionalist theory. Both trace the existence of certain classes to the central position of occupation, income, and wealth in modern life. But neither goes very far toward explaining the prestige stratification that occurs within social classes. Among the very rich in America, for example, people who have stables on their property tend to look down on people with somewhat smaller lots on which there is only a swimming pool. And rich families who own sailing yachts look down on equally rich people who own expensive but noisy power boats. The point is that within economic classes people form status groups whose prestige or honor is measured not according to what they produce or how much wealth they own but according to what they buy and what they communicate about themselves through their purchases. Designer jeans and BMW cars are symbols of membership in the youthful upper class. Four-wheel-drive vehicles equipped with gun racks and fishing rods are symbols of the rugged and successful middle- or working-class male. Dress styles that mimic those shown on *Miami Vice* are symbols of urbane professionalism; tweed suits and silk blouses are signs that a woman is a member of the "country club set." All of these symbols of prestige and group membership change as groups with less prestige mimic them, spurring a search for new and less "common" signs of belonging (Dowd, 1985).

Our tendency to divide ourselves up into social categories and then assert claims of greater prestige for one group or another is of major significance in our lives. The interactionist perspective on stratification therefore may not be very useful in explaining the emergence of economic classes, but it is essential to understanding the behaviors of the status groups that form within a given class. Those behaviors, in turn, often define or reinforce or challenge class divisions. The stratification system, in this view, is not a fixed system but is created over and over again through the everyday behaviors of millions of people.

Conclusion

"The first lesson of modern sociology," wrote C. Wright Mills in his study of white-collar workers, "is that the individual cannot understand his own experience or gauge his own fate without locating himself within the trends of his epoch and the life-chances of all the individuals of his social layer" (1951, p. xx). In this chapter we have examined the concepts needed to understand how the phenomenon of "social layering" or stratification arises, how it is related to the means of existence, and how it has changed as human societies have evolved from simpler agrarian forms of production into more complex industrial and even postindustrial societies.

This introduction to social stratification and how it affects life chances has not said much about the class structure of North American society. That is the goal of Chapter 12, in which we will look in more detail at stratification by wealth, power, and prestige in our own society and compare it with stratification in other societies. Concepts of social class will appear in the next three chapters as well. Are criminals rebelling against inequality and their low place in the stratification system? We will see in the next chapter that patterns of deviance are associated with social class and that theories about why people violate social norms often hinge on an analysis of social inequality. What about revolutions, strikes, and social movements that seek equality for oppressed peoples? How do they change a society's stratification system? In Chapter 10 the concept of social class is applied to behavior like rioting and mass violence. We cannot understand how social stratification has shaped human history unless we understand the role of collective behavior and social movements. Finally, in Chapter 11 we consider how large-scale trends in inequality and stratification contribute to social upheaval and social change.

CHALLENGES TO CONTEMPORARY SOCIETY

Stratification and the World Economic System

Today it is no longer possible to think of a society's stratification system separately from those of other societies around the world. More than ever before, the life chances of people in the United States and other highly developed nations are influenced by changes in the structure of industrial employment and the worldwide distribution of jobs. The rapidly growing dependence of the developed nations on markets in the third-world nations, together with the shift of manufacturing jobs to those newer nations, is creating enormous social upheavals, particularly for industrial workers in the United States.

The increase in blue-collar manufacturing work in the third world has been accompanied by an increase in unemployment in regions of the United States that have long been dominated by "smokestack industries." Thus the number of American steelworkers engaged in the actual production of steel has declined from more than 600,000 in 1960 to about 163,000 today. Similar declines have occurred in rubber manufacture, coal mining, glass production, and automobile assembly as these industries have closed many of their plants and raced to increase productivity through automation. After all, robots may be expensive at the outset, but unlike humans they do not have social-class positions to maintain—they do not have to "keep up with the Joneses"—and therefore will not demand higher pay in the future. Nor do robots call in sick or demand vacations.

Harvard sociologist Daniel Bell has been studying these trends since the 1960s. His thesis is that the United States and other advanced societies are becoming "postindustrial" societies. Blue-collar workers are a decreasing segment of the labor force, while professional and technical workers continue to increase in importance (see chart). In Bell's view, the employment gap left by automation and the shift of industrial jobs to the third world will be compensated for by the steady increase in jobs in the service sector. But Bell foresees more than just the expansion of lower-status service occupations:

A post-industrial society is based on services. Hence, it is a game between persons. What counts is not raw muscle power, or energy, but information. The central person is the professional, for he is equipped, by his education and training, to provide the kinds of skills which are increasingly demanded in the post-industrial society. If an industrial society is defined by the quantity of goods as marking a standard of living, the post-industrial society is measured by the services and amenities—health, education, recreation, and the arts—which are now deemed desirable and possible for everyone. [1973, p. 127]

Bell's optimistic predictions are challenged by social scientists who think the transition to a postindustrial society will involve hardships for millions of people and lead to more, not less, inequality. Their research indicates that "mature" industrial societies will not soon solve the problems of loss of skilled jobs, chronic unemployment, and discrimination brought on by these changes in the world's division of labor (Esping-Anderson, 1985; Hopkins and Wallerstein, 1980; Portes and Walton, 1981; Thurow, 1975). These critics contend that the jobs that are now being "exported" to third-world countries like South Korea, Taiwan, the Philippines, and Brazil are near the bottom of the blue-collar prestige ladder. Automation will prevent foreign workers who perform these tasks from ever rising into the higher-paid ranks of the blue-collar labor force. And in developed countries like the United States, Japan, and Australia, the already large populations at the bottom of the stratification ladder are likely to grow still larger.

In the United States, for example, research by William J. Wilson (1978, 1987) shows that in the past the mobility of blacks and others depended on employment in the unionized blue-collar sector of an expanding industrial economy. But as such jobs disappear they tend to be replaced with jobs that require far more education and training or with jobs in low-paying occupations in which there is a good deal of employee turnover and little opportunity for upward mobility. Those who drop out of the highly competitive race for quality education are likely to end up in the lowest-paying service jobs or in a welfare-dependent underclass.

The continued search for evidence to support or disprove this thesis and to evaluate policies that address the problem of growth in the underclass is an important challenge to modern sociology. Will it be possible to develop effective training programs for school dropouts and workers whose factories have been closed? What will be the long-term impact of chronic unemployment of unskilled minority workers? Judging from past experience, the prospects are not bright. In his award-winning analysis of poverty in the United States, William J. Wilson (1987) argues that we need to develop new industrial strategies to bring better jobs to thousands of displaced or redundant workers. Yet he admits that such strategies are unlikely to emerge in the near future.

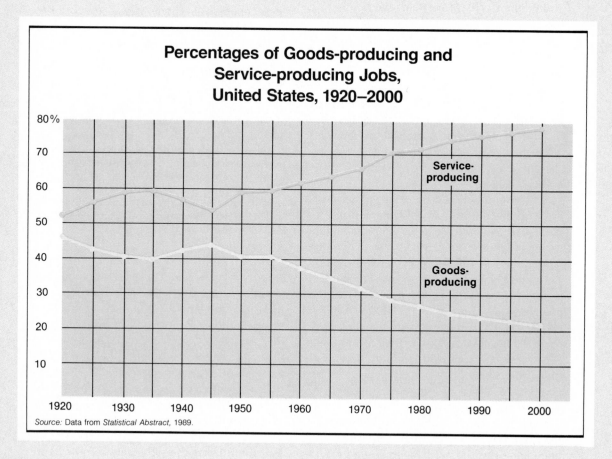

Source: Data from Statistical Abstract, 1989.

SUMMARY

Social stratification refers to a society's system for ranking people hierarchically according to various attributes such as wealth, power, and prestige. Societies in which there are rigid boundaries between social strata are said to be *closed*, whereas those in which the boundaries are easily crossed are said to be *open*. Movement from one stratum to another is known as *social mobility*.

Most closed stratification systems are characterized by *castes*, or social strata into which people are born and in which they remain for life. Membership in a caste is an *ascribed status* (a status acquired at birth), as opposed to an *achieved status* (one based on the efforts of the individual).

Open societies are characterized by *classes*, which are social strata based primarily on economic criteria. The classes of modern societies are not homogeneous; within any given class there are different groups defined by how much honor or prestige they receive from the society in general. Such groups are sometimes referred to as *status groups*. The way people are grouped with respect to their access to scarce resources determines their *life chances*—that is, the opportunities they will have or be denied throughout life.

The principal forces leading to social stratification are created by the means of existence in a given society. Hence, for small farmers or peasants (the majority of the world's population) social strata are based on land ownership and agrarian labor, with the members of the lowest strata doing the hardest work while those at the top of the stratification system are able to live in relative comfort. Modern industrial societies are characterized by *structural mobility* (the elimination of entire classes as a result of changes in the means of existence) and *spatial mobility* (the movement of individuals and groups from one location to another). Yet in modern societies one's relationship to the means of existence remains the basic determinant of one's position in the stratification system.

People accept their place in a stratification system because the system itself is part of their society's culture. The facets of culture that justify the stratification system are learned through the processes of socialization. The system is often justified by an ideology, such as the ideology of communism or Christianity. At the micro level, the norms of everyday interactions serve to reinforce the society's stratification system.

Changes in stratification systems may have as much to do with realignments of social power as with economic or cultural changes. *Power* has been defined as the probability that one actor within a social relationship will be in a position to carry out his or her own will despite resistance. Legitimate power is called *authority* and is a major factor in maintaining existing relationships among castes or classes.

The rise of industrial capitalism had far-reaching effects on stratification systems. According to Karl Marx, capitalism divided societies into classes based on ownership of the means of production. The largest of these classes, the workers, must sell their labor to capitalists or landowners in return for wages. In time, Marx predicted, the workers would become conscious of their shared interests as a class and would rebel against the capitalist class. The outcome of the revolution would be a classless society.

Marx defined social class in economic terms. Max Weber took issue with this definition and pointed out that people are stratified not only by wealth but also by how much honor or prestige they receive from others and how much power they command. Marx's view of stratification is also challenged by studies of social mobility in industrial societies, which have shown that there is considerable movement between classes.

Modern conflict theorists, like Marx, believe that class conflict is a primary cause of social change. They disagree, however, on the nature of the class structure of capitalist societies. Functionalist theorists believe that classes emerge because an unequal distribution of rewards is necessary in order to channel talented people into important roles in society. This view has been criticized because it fails to account for the fact that social rewards in one generation tend to improve the life chances of the next generation. Moreover, the functionalist perspective does not explain why talented people from lower-class families often are unable to obtain highly rewarded positions. From the interactionist perspective, the stratification system is not a fixed system but, rather, one that is created out of everyday behaviors.

WHERE TO FIND IT

Books

Class (Erik O. Wright; Routledge Chapman & Hall, 1985). A modern statement of the materialist approach to social stratification, with emphasis on the diversity of classes in capitalist and noncapitalist societies.

Class, Status, and Power, 2nd ed. (Reinhard Bendix and Seymour Martin Lipset; Free Press, 1966). A collection of influential papers on the study of social stratification.

The Structures of Everyday Life: Civilization and Capitalism, 15th-18th Century (vol. 1), **The Wheels of Commerce** (vol. 2), **The Perspective of the World** (vol. 3) (Fernand Braudel; Harper & Row, 1981). A work of historical and sociological scholarship that is only beginning to influence the social sciences. The great French social historian shows in marvelous detail how social stratification has been largely explained by the way people earn their daily bread, whether in ancient China or medieval Europe or England during the industrial revolution.

The Modern World System (Immanuel Wallerstein; Academic Press, 1974). A sociologist's account of the transformations in social structure and inequality that were brought about by the emergence of two capitalist institutions, the market and the firm.

Other Sources

The Europa Yearbook: A World Summary (Europa Publishers). An annual reference work that provides much detailed information on political, economic, and commercial institutions throughout the world.

GLOSSARY

social stratification: a society's system for ranking people hierarchically according to such attributes as wealth, power, and prestige (**p. 225**).

closed stratification system: a stratification system in which there are rigid boundaries between social strata (**p. 225**).

open stratification system: a stratification system in which the boundaries between social strata are easily crossed (**p. 225**).

social mobility: movement by an individual or group from one social stratum to another (**p. 225**).

upward mobility: movement by an individual or group to a higher social stratum (**p. 225**).

downward mobility: movement by an individual or group to a lower social stratum (**p. 225**).

caste: a social stratum into which people are born and in which they remain for life (**p. 225**).

ascribed status: a position or rank that is assigned to an individual at birth and cannot be changed (**p. 225**).

achieved status: a position or rank that is earned through the efforts of the individual (**p. 225**).

class: a social stratum that is defined primarily by economic criteria such as occupation, income, and wealth (**p. 226**).

status group: a category of people within a social class, defined by how much honor or prestige they receive from the society in general (**p. 226**).

life chances: the opportunities that an individual will have or be denied throughout life as a result of his or her social-class position (**p. 227**).

structural mobility: movement of an individual or group from one social stratum to another that is caused by the elimination of an entire class as a result of changes in the means of existence (**p. 230**).

spatial mobility: movement of an individual or group from one location or community to another (**p. 231**).

status symbols: material objects or behaviors that indicate social status or prestige (**p. 233**).

deference: the respect and esteem shown to an individual (**p. 233**).

demeanor: the way in which individuals present themselves to others through body language, dress, speech, and manners (**p. 234**).

power: the ability to control the behavior of others, even against their will (**p. 235**).

authority: power that is considered legitimate both by those who exercise it and by those who are affected by it (**p. 236**).

objective class: in Marxian theory, a social class that has a visible, specific relationship to the means of production (**p. 240**).

subjective class: in Marxian theory, the way members of a given social class perceive their situation as a class (**p. 240**).

class consciousness: a group's shared subjective awareness of its objective situation as a class (**p. 240**).

intragenerational mobility: a change in the social class of an individual within his or her own lifetime (**p. 241**).

intergenerational mobility: a change in the social class of family members from one generation to the next (**p. 241**).

VISUAL SOCIOLOGY

Stratification in the United States and the Soviet Union

The United States and the Soviet Union, the world's two superpowers, are organized around quite different social institutions and cultures. Yet in many other respects, as these photos demonstrate, the two societies are surprisingly similar. Each, for example, has its class of rich and powerful elites who are insulated from the mass of less advantaged citizens. In both societies these elites are generally made up of executives who manage large industrial or governmental bureaucracies—and their well-to-do families—who live in sheltered communities and are whisked from work to residence in limousines or expensive private cars.

Each society also has a large middle class that is reaping many of the benefits of economic growth and can be seen flocking to the seaside or downtown entertainment districts. Each is a bureaucratic society in which ever-increasing numbers of people work in complex organizations like the military or the national corporations that dominate the economies of both. Each has its class of poor people who eke out marginal livings at work in the lowest-status jobs or in the streets and welfare agencies. All of these classes depend on the farmers, whose numbers in both societies are dwindling as industrialization causes

© H. A. Rockwell, Monkmeyer

TASS from Sovfoto

© Townsend, Monkmeyer

Soviet life from Sovfoto

large farms to be more successful than small ones.

Of course, there are many differences between the class structures of the United States and the Soviet Union, some of which are evident in these photos. In the Soviet Union the commercial middle class—what Marx called the *petit bourgeoisie*, the class of shopkeepers and local businesspeople—is outlawed. Shops and markets are controlled by the state; an individual or small group cannot legally set up a business. In the United States, by contrast, the petit bourgeoisie is an extremely important class. Shopkeepers and local businesspeople have many economic and political links to the elite, and through the activities of chambers of commerce and similar associations the commercial middle class exerts a great deal of influence over local affairs. The Soviet attempt to eliminate private enterprise and the American belief in its vital role in the economy remain at the core of the value conflicts that set apart the two great nations, even though the Soviet Union is undergoing a traumatic transition toward economic competition and free enterprise.

© David Burnett, Woodfin Camp

© Mimi Forsyth, Monkmeyer

CHAPTER OUTLINE

● **What Is Deviance?**

● **Dimensions of Deviance**

- Deviance and Stigma
- Deviance and Crime
- Deviance and Changing Values
- Deviant Subcultures

● **Theoretical Perspectives on Social Deviance**

- Biological Explanations of Crime
- Social-Scientific Explanations of Deviance and Crime
- The Functionalist Perspective
- Conflict Perspectives
- The Interactionist Perspective

● **Crime and Social Control**

- Ecological Dimensions of Crime
- Institutions of Coercive Control: Courts and Prisons

Newsday/Ken Sawchuk

Wall Street broker Michael Milken (center) while facing charges of fraud

CHAPTER 9

DEVIANCE AND SOCIAL CONTROL

House Speaker Thomas S. Foley is angry. So are many other Washington legislators and veteran political journalists. They are angry about the scandal in the U.S. Department of Housing and Urban Development (HUD), which paid about $5.7 million in "consulting fees" to former public officials who helped real estate developers obtain contracts from HUD. They are angry because housing funds that were supposed to benefit poor and working-class residents of urban slums were diverted to aid wealthy developers. With a quick phone call, friends of the President and influential colleagues of the Secretary of Housing and Urban Development could line up millions of dollars' worth of federal funds for their pet projects. Very often the projects they funded were losers that will cost the taxpayers (but not the real estate speculators) additional millions.

Foley is angry because it seems that there is little anyone can do to punish those who misused their public positions and sold their influence. In the words of another Representative, "Congress can't pass a law saying don't be a bum." In fact, Congress has been confronted with problems of ethics among its own members; in 1989 Foley's predecessor was forced to resign because he was accused of abusing the powers of his office for personal gain. A variety of laws governing behavior in public office have been passed in recent years. However, it seems that merely tightening the laws against influence peddling may not be enough to curb the greed of people in positions of power.

Others are angry about the HUD scandal because it points to the great unfairness of law enforcement. In the words of columnist Tom Wicker, "Former Secretary of the Interior James G. Watt is handed $300,000 in public funds for doing nothing but making telephone calls; but as they say in court, 'He's going to walk.' But if some illiterate street kid from a broken family with no hope of a job gets caught knocking over a gas station for $50, he'll do hard time in one of our overcrowded, inhumane prisons." Wicker recommends that the period within which former public officials may not use their influence for private gain, currently only one year, be extended to five or ten years. He adds: "If none of these or any other statutes can be made to apply to the sleazy conduct being documented and the sleazy people being identified, then something is badly wrong— not just at HUD, but in the values and processes of American politics and American justice" (1989, p. A27).

Perhaps this is true. Not only in government but in many business situations, the past few years have seen evidence of rampant greed and corruption. Insider-trading scandals on the Chicago Board of Trade and in major Wall Street financial firms, corruption and cover-ups in the nuclear-power industry, and increasing evidence of scientific fraud at major universities are but a few examples that may represent a dangerous trend. In a notorious case, the owners of one of the nation's largest hotel chains were accused of bilking federal and state tax collectors of millions of dollars by reporting private improvements on their mansion as hotel expenses. "Only the little people pay taxes," one of the owners was quoted as saying to a subordinate. But if the high and mighty flout the bounds of propriety and in some cases flagrantly break the law, why should the less privileged heed the laws?

Indeed, there are equally ominous trends concerning lawbreaking among "the little people." At this writing, drug-related crime is increasing as the crack epidemic sweeps across the nation. Rates of domestic violence and child abuse are on the rise. So is the incidence of gang violence. Crash programs are under way throughout the United States to build more prisons; the dockets of criminal courts are jammed with cases; law enforcement ranks among the top issues in political campaigns everywhere.

Does all this mean that the United States is becoming a nation of deviants and lawbreakers? What actually are the current trends in deviance and crime? And what can be done to alleviate the worst effects of crime and to restore public faith in the courts and the laws? Research on these and related issues is a major field within sociology. No one can offer definitive answers, but sociologists are frequently looked to for research on trends in deviance and criminal behavior as well as explanations of those trends. As with any social condition, before a society can address its crime problems it must be able to distinguish symptoms from causes and to compare recent events with longer-term trends.

WHAT IS DEVIANCE?

Deviance, broadly defined, is behavior that violates the norms of a particular society. But because all of us violate norms to some degree at some time or other, we must distinguish between *deviance* and *deviants*. Deviance can be something as simple as dyeing one's hair purple or wearing outrageous clothing or becoming tipsy at a stuffy party. Or it may be behavior over which the individual has little control, such as being homeless and living on the street, or it may consist of more strongly sanctioned departures from the society's norms—such acts as rape, mugging, and murder. Not all deviance is considered socially wrong, yet it can have negative effects for the individual. For example, "whistle blowers" who publicize illegal or harmful actions by their employers deviate from the norms of bureaucratic organizations, but they benefit the public by calling attention to dangerous or illegal activities. Yet because they deviate from the norm of compliance with authority, whistle blowers are often threatened with the loss of their jobs. This occurred, for example, in the case of the engineers who warned of flaws in the space shuttle's booster rockets before the explosion of the *Challenger* in 1986.

A deviant person, by contrast, is someone who violates or opposes a society's most valued norms, especially those that are valued by elite groups. Through such behavior deviant individuals become disvalued people, and their disvalued behavior provokes hostile reactions (Davis, 1975; Goffman, 1963; Sagarin, 1975; Schur, 1984). *Deviant* may be a label attached to a person or group. Or the word may be used to refer to behavior that brings punishment to a person under certain conditions.

The case of influence peddling by government officials raises an important ques-

Deviance is behavior that violates the norms of a particular society; a deviant person is someone who violates a society's most valued norms.

tion: What are the conditions under which violations of norms are punished? Here is an area of conduct in which there is uncertainty about what is illegal and what is merely sleazy. The confusion over whether crimes were committed in the HUD case shows that deviance is not absolute. As sociologist Kai Erikson explains it, deviance "is not a property inherent in certain forms of behavior; it is a property conferred upon these forms by the audience which directly or indirectly witnesses them" (1962, p. 307). Some of us may believe that influence peddling is deviant, while others may believe that it is acceptable. Which of our views becomes the norm, and which is enforced through rewards and punishments, is just as important as the behavior itself. This point is illustrated in Erikson's study of deviance among the New England Puritans, discussed in Box 9-1.

The study of deviance is central to the science of sociology, not only because deviance results in major social problems like crime, but also because it can bring about social change. Indeed, the Puritans were a deviant group in England at the time of their emigration to the New World. They challenged the authority of the king and many of the central norms that upheld the stratification system of feudal England. In the Massachusetts Bay Colony they created their own society, one in which they were no longer deviant. But as Erikson showed, they also created their own forms of deviance, which reflected their unique problems as a society on a rapidly changing social frontier.

Social control consists of all the ways in which a society establishes and enforces its cultural norms.

The ways in which a society prevents deviance and punishes deviants are known as **social control.** As we saw in Chapter 4, the norms of a culture, the means by which they are instilled in us through socialization, and the ways in which they are enforced in social institutions—the family, the schools, government agencies—establish a society's system of social control. In fact, social control can be thought of as all the ways in which a society establishes and enforces its cultural norms. It is "the capacity of a social group, including a whole society, to regulate itself" (Janowitz, 1978, p. 3).

The means used to prevent deviance and punish deviants are one dimension of social control. They include the police, prisons, mental hospitals, and other institutions responsible for applying social control, keeping order, and enforcing major norms. But if we had to rely entirely on official institutions to enforce norms, social order would probably be impossible to achieve (Chwast, 1965). In fact, the official institutions of social control deal mainly with the deviant individuals and groups the society fears most. Less threatening forms of deviance are controlled through the everyday interactions of individuals, as when parents attempt to prevent their children from wearing their hair in punk styles.

In this chapter we look first at the various meanings of deviance and at how those meanings emerge and change as a society's values change. Then we explore the major sociological perspectives on deviance and social control. The final section deals with the ecology of deviance—its distribution among social classes and subcultures—and with the organization and functioning of institutions of social control.

Box 9–1: **Deviance and Social Cohesion:**
The Salem Witch Hunt

No one knows how the witchcraft hysteria began, but it originated in the home of the Reverend Samuel Parris, minister of the local church. In early 1692, several girls from the neighborhood began to spend their afternoons in the Parris' kitchen with a slave named Tituba, and it was not long before a mysterious sorority of girls, aged between nine and twenty, became regular visitors to the parsonage. We can only speculate about what went on behind the kitchen door, but we know that Tituba had been brought to Massachusetts from Barbados and enjoyed a reputation in the neighborhood for her skills in the magic arts. As the girls grew closer together, a remarkable change seemed to come over them: perhaps it is not true, as someone later reported, that they went out into the forest to celebrate their own version of a black mass, but it is apparent that they began to live in a state of high tension and shared secrets with one another which were hardly becoming to quiet Puritan maidens. [Erikson, 1966, p. 141]

The girls quickly drew the concerned attention of Salem's ministers and its doctor. Unable to understand much about their hysterical state or to deny their claim that they were possessed by the devil, the doctor pronounced the girls bewitched. This gave them the freedom to make accusations regarding the cause of their unfortunate condition.

Tituba was the first to be accused and jailed. She was followed by scores of others as the fear of witches swept through the community. Soon women with too many warts or annoying tics were accused, tried, and jailed for their sins. Then the executions began. In the first and worst of the waves of executions, in August and September 1692, at least twenty people were killed, including one man who was pressed to death under piled rocks for "standing mute at his trial."

For the sociologist, the Salem witch hunt of about 300 years ago is full of meaning in today's world. In an award-winning study, Kai T. Erikson (1966) showed that the crime of witchcraft can be understood as a sign of "social disruption and change." Only a half-century before the devil came to Salem, thousands of accused witches had been burned and hanged during the time when the European states were emerging from feudalism. Backwoods New England also experienced its witch craze during a time of great change. In 1692 the orthodox Puritan way of life was ending: Puritanism was being watered down by rough wilderness ways and urbane city values. The settlements were no longer hemmed in by the wilderness, and the Indians had been pushed away.

In his study of the Salem witch craze, Erikson shows that the punishment of suspected witches served as a defense against the weakening of Puritan society. By casting out the "witches," the Puritans were reaffirming their community values: strict adherence to religious devotion, fear of God, abstinence from the pleasures of secular society (drink, sex, music, dance), and the like. The trial and punishment of the so-called witches illustrates Émile Durkheim's earlier discovery that every society creates its own forms of deviance and in fact *needs* those deviant acts. The punishment of deviant acts reaffirms the commitment of a society's members to its norms and values and thereby reinforces social solidarity. On the surface, Durkheim argued, deviant acts may seem to be harmful to group life, but in fact the punishment of those who commit such acts makes it clear to all exactly what deviations are most intolerable. By Durkheim's reasoning, the stark images of punishment—the guillotine, the electric chair, the syringe, the wretched life behind bars—become opportunities to let the population know that those who threaten the social order will be severely judged.

DIMENSIONS OF DEVIANCE

Deviance is an especially controversial topic: There is usually much disagreement not only about which behaviors are deviant and which are not but also about which behaviors should be strongly punished and which should be condoned or punished only mildly. The debate over whether abortion should be legal is a good example of such disagreements. As Erikson noted, "Behavior which qualifies one man for prison may qualify another for sainthood since the quality of the act itself depends so much on the circumstances under which it was performed and the temper of the audience which witnessed it" (1966, pp. 5–6).

Consider the South African political

leader Nelson Mandela. Mandela was released from a maximum-security prison in 1990 after serving almost thirty years of a life sentence for his leadership of the movement to end *apartheid*, South Africa's racial caste system. The dominant white minority in South Africa regarded Mandela and other opponents of apartheid as criminals. But the black majority viewed him as a hero and a martyr; indeed, black South Africans revere Mandela the way people in the United States revere George Washington. Until the black majority began to mobilize world opinion and other nations began to enforce negative sanctions against South Africa, the white minority was able to define Mandela's opposition to apartheid as a criminal activity.

The power to define which acts are legal and which are illegal is one important di-

AR: See Mandela's earlier book, *No Easy Walk to Freedom.*

Whites in South Africa viewed Nelson Mandela, a leader of the black freedom movement, as a dangerous political deviant. He is shown here with his wife, Winnie Mandela, upon his release after twenty-seven years in the maximum-security prison at Robbins Island.

© A. Tannenbaum, Sygma

mension of deviance. In the case of black protest in South Africa, it is the single most important dimension. In the United States, the power of some groups to define certain acts as deviant helps explain why influence peddling is not a crime but cultivating marijuana is. In this connection it is interesting to note that in the 1960s, when the children of powerful members of society began smoking marijuana, legislators suddenly found themselves under pressure to relax the enforcement of marijuana laws.

The fact that people in power can define what behavior is deviant and determine who is punished fails to explain differences in definitions of deviance in different societies. Behavior regarded as normal in one society may be considered highly deviant in another. For example, in the United States the drinking of alcoholic beverages is considered normal, but in orthodox Islamic culture it is forbidden. Even within a society, members of certain social groups may behave in ways that are considered deviant by others. Clearly, differences in values are another important source of definitions of deviance and of disagreements about those definitions. An example is the controversy over cigarette smoking in restaurants and other public places. Such conflicts can be seen in many other areas as well—abortion, sex education, drug use, date rape, and so on.

Another dimension of deviance has to do with attributes the person cannot control (e.g., race or physical appearance) in contrast to actual behavior, which is usually voluntary. The criminal is deviant in ways that the insane person is not, and it is criminal behavior that is most costly to society. Yet in many situations the insane person is labeled as deviant, and this label may actually drive him or her toward criminality. A related issue is how people who deviate from generally accepted norms manage to survive in societies where they are considered outsiders. In fact, deviant people often form their own communities with their own norms and values, and these deviant subcultures sustain them in their conflicted relations with "normal" members of society.

An important point is that deviant subcultures, which engage in prostitution, gambling, drug use, and other "deviant" behaviors, could not exist were they not performing services and supplying products that people in the larger society secretly demand. It would not be wise, therefore, to draw the distinction between deviant and normal people too sharply. Many people deviate from the norm, and their deviations create opportunities for others whose identities and occupations are deviant.

In sum, three dimensions—power, culture, and voluntary versus involuntary behavior—are the major determinants operating in any society to produce the forms of deviance that are typical of that society.

Deviance and Stigma

To narrow the range of phenomena we must deal with in discussing deviance, let us keep in mind Erving Goffman's (1963) distinction between stigma and deviance. "The term **stigma**," Goffman stated, "refers to an attribute that is deeply discrediting" and that reduces the person "from a whole and usual person to a tainted and discounted one" (p. 3). People may be stigmatized because of mental illness, eccentricity, membership in a disvalued racial or nationality group, and the like. In some instances, their stigma is visible to a stranger, as in the case of a disfigured person like the Elephant Man. Suffering from a disease that grossly distorted his face, the Elephant Man was rejected by society even though he was a highly intelligent person who was treated badly because of the groundless fear that he aroused in others. In other cases stigma is revealed only with growing acquaintance, as in the stigma attached to the children of convicts.

For the stigmatized person, the disqualifying trait defines the person's master status (Becker, 1963; Scull, 1988). (See Chapter 3.) A blind person, for example, may be an excellent musician and a caring parent, but

Although stigmatized people deviate from some norm of "respectable" society, they are not necessarily social deviants who deliberately violate the norms of permissible conduct.

the fact that he or she is blind will outweigh these achieved statuses except in unusual cases like that of Stevie Wonder.

Stigmatized people deviate from some norm of "respectable" society, but they are not necessarily social deviants. The term *deviant*, Goffman argued, should be reserved for people "who are seen as declining voluntarily and openly to accept the social place accorded them, and who act irregularly and somewhat rebelliously in connection with our basic institutions" (1963, p. 143). Among the people Goffman classified as social deviants are "prostitutes, drug addicts, delinquents, criminals, jazz musicians, bohemians, gypsies, carnival workers, hoboes, winos, show people, full time gamblers, beach dwellers, homosexuals, and the urban unrepentant poor." Some people might find Goffman's list controversial; his point, however, is that these are examples of social groups that "are considered to be engaged in some kind of collective denial of the social order. They are perceived as failing to use available opportunity for advancement in the various approved runways of society" (1963, p. 144).

According to the definition of stigma, the population of social deviants is smaller than that of stigmatized individuals; only some stigmatized behaviors are socially deviant. Deviant behaviors are characterized by denial of the social order through violation of the norms of permissible conduct. This point should be kept in mind as we continue our discussion of criminals and other people who are considered social deviants.

Deviance and Crime

Much of the study of social deviance focuses on crime. **Crime** is usually defined as an act, or the omission of an act, for which the state can apply sanctions. Those sanctions are part of the criminal law, a set of written rules that

John Hurt, starring as the pathetically disfigured sideshow attraction in the motion picture "The Elephant Man," manages to escape his sadistic master through the help of the other freaks in the circus.

prohibit certain acts and prescribe punishments to be meted out to violators (Kornblum and Julian, 1989). But the questions of what specific behaviors constitute crime and how the state should deal with them are often controversial.

In every society some behaviors are so extreme that almost everyone will agree they are criminal and should be punished; other behaviors some will consider criminal while others do not. All societies punish murder and theft, for example, but there is far more variation in the treatment of adultery, prostitution, and pornography. Indeed, the largest number of "crimes" committed in the United States each year are so-called public-order crimes, such behaviors as public drunkenness, vagrancy, disorderly conduct, prostitution, gambling, drug addiction, and certain homosexual interactions. Many sociologists claim that these are victimless crimes because they generally cause no physical harm to anyone but the offenders themselves (Schur, 1973; Silberman, 1980). Not all social scientists agree with this view, however. Some point out that crimes like prostitution actually inflict damage on society because they are usually linked with an underworld that engages in far more serious and costly criminal activities (Wilson, 1977).

In the United States, crime is considered one of the nation's most serious social problems. In 1988 the Federal Bureau of Investigation (FBI) reported that one violent crime occurred every twenty-six seconds and one property crime every three seconds. Almost one out of five people have arrest records for nontraffic offenses, and one out of every forty-five adult males is under some form of correctional care, custody, or supervision. The most serious, most frequently occurring, and most likely to be reported crimes are called *index crimes* by the FBI because they are included in its crime index, a commonly used measure of crime rates. These categories of crime are shown in Table 9-1.

For many decades criminologists and other social scientists have criticized the FBI's crime statistics on the ground that they do not reflect differences in effectiveness among crime-reporting agencies. For example, a more professional law enforcement agency in one community could show higher crime rates than an agency in another community that has done a haphazard job of collecting the statistics. Another serious problem is that there is no way of knowing the crime rates for the total population (rather than just for those who actually reported crimes). Since 1973, therefore, the Census Bureau and the Law Enforcement Assistance Administration have conducted semiannual surveys in which respondents are asked whether they or their businesses have been victims of robbery, rape, assault, burglary, or other forms of theft. In general, these "victimization surveys" show that the overall rate of serious crime is between two and three times higher than the reported crime index.

> *Crime includes all forms of social deviance for which the state can apply sanctions.*

Deviance and Changing Values

One of the factors that make it especially difficult to gather and interpret statistics on crime is that definitions of crime and deviance are constantly changing as the society's values change. Almost every week, for example, one hears reports in the media of men who have battered and even killed their wives, often after serving brief prison sentences for previous attacks on their spouses. Why, many ask, are law enforcement agencies unable to prevent and punish spouse abuse and murder? Advocates of new laws and greater investment in prevention point out that until fairly recently a married woman was viewed as the husband's household possession. Although both husband and wife had sworn to "love, honor, and cherish" their partner, these norms were applied far more forcefully to women than to men. This double standard is changing as men and women become more equal before the law, but in the minds of many judges and juries this change is not yet complete, and men who abuse their spouses receive relatively light sentences.

In any society, agreement on particular

Table 9–1: **The Crime Rate 1978 – 1987**

	Estimated Crime 1987		Percent Change Over 1986		Percent Change Over 1983		Percent Change Over 1978	
	No.	Rate per 100,000 Inhabitants	No.	Rate per 100,000 Inhabitants	No.	Rate per 100,000 Inhabitants	No.	Rate per 100,000 Inhabitants
Crime Index total[a]	13,509,000	5,550	+ 2.2	+ 1.4	+ 11.6	+ 7.3	+ 20.5	+ 8.1
Violent	1,484,000	610	− .3	− 1.3	+ 18.0	+ 13.4	+ 36.7	+ 22.5
Property	12,025,000	4,940	+ 2.6	+ 1.6	+ 10.8	+ 6.5	+ 18.8	+ 6.4
Murder	20,000	8.3	− 2.5	− 3.5	+ 4.1	—	+ 2.8	− 7.8
Forcible rape	91,000	37.4	− .4	− 1.3	+ 15.4	+ 11.0	+ 34.8	+ 20.6
Robbery	518,000	213	− 4.6	− 5.5	+ 2.2	− 1.8	+ 21.3	+ 8.6
Aggravated assault	855,000	351	+ 2.5	+ 1.5	+ 30.9	+ 25.8	+ 49.6	+ 34.0
Burglary	3,236,000	1,330	− .2	− 1.1	+ 3.4	− .6	+ 3.4	− 7.3
Larceny— theft	7,500,000	3,081	+ 3.3	+ 2.4	+ 11.7	+ 7.4	+ 25.2	+ 12.2
Motor vehicle theft	1,289,000	529	+ 5.3	+ 4.3	+ 27.9	+ 22.9	+ 28.3	+ 15.0

[a]Because of rounding, offenses may not add to totals.
Source: Statistical Abstract, 1989.

Definitions of deviance are constantly changing as the society's values change.

aspects of crime and deviance can range from weak (in cases in which there is much controversy) to strong (in cases in which there is little disagreement). Negative sanctions, or punishments, can also range from very weak to very strong. Capital punishment is the strongest sanction in the United States, with life imprisonment following close behind. Minor fines or the suggestion that a person undergo treatment for a behavior viewed as deviant are relatively weak sanctions. Nor are all sanctions formal punishments meted out according to law. Some deviance can be punished by means of shunning or the "silent treatment," and milder infractions can be controlled by simply poking

fun at the person in an attempt to change his or her behavior.

Figure 9-1 uses these distinctions to construct a typology of deviance as it is generally viewed in the United States in the late twentieth century. Figure 9-2 suggests what such a typology would have looked like before the Civil War. Together they highlight some of the continuities and changes in patterns of deviance in the United States over the last century. You will probably find points in them to argue with, which is further evidence of the difficulty of classifying deviant behaviors in a rapidly changing society.

Should driving while intoxicated (DWI) be classified as a deviant behavior? We all fear the drunken driver and agree that DWI is dangerous, but because so many of us are social drinkers we have found it difficult not

Figure 9–1: **A Typology of Deviance in the United States**

		STRENGTH OF SANCTION	
		Weak	**Strong**
DEGREE OF CONSENSUS	**Weak**	Recreational drugs Homosexuality Abortion	Sale of whiskey during Prohibition Prostitution Abortion before 1973 Supreme Court ruling
	Strong	Schizophrenia Driving while intoxicated Public drunkenness Corporate crime Wife or child beating	Major crimes (felonies) Treason

to violate this norm, and consequently we have placed relatively mild sanctions on DWI except when the outcome is a fatal accident. In the 1980s, however, DWI became much more controversial and the sanctions against it became stronger. In his study of this issue, Joseph Gusfield (1981) found that the highway death rate has been decreasing since 1945 but that the public's perception of the relationship between highway deaths and drunken driving has sharpened as a result of media coverage and lobbying by citizens' groups.

Our perception and treatment of homosexuality is another example of significant change in Americans' attitudes toward a deviant behavior and the strength of the sanctions invoked. A century ago homosexuality was widely regarded as a serious form of deviance. Homosexuals were persecuted whenever they were exposed. Today there is far less agreement on this subject. To be sure, homosexuality continues to be viewed as deviant by the majority of nonhomosexuals, but it is tolerated to the extent that gay men and women are able to create their own communities and openly fight against such sanctions as discrimination in the labor market. Homosexuals have had some success in gain-

ing passage of laws that would grant homosexual couples the legal standing of de facto married couples. At the same time, however, the perception of AIDS as a "gay disease" has added to the stigma attached to the homosexual identity (Altman, 1987; Bayer, 1988).

Deviant Subcultures

Even when the majority of the population can be said to support a particular set of values, it will contain many subcultures whose life-styles are labeled deviant by the larger population. A deviant subculture includes a system of values, attitudes, behaviors, and life-styles opposed to the dominant culture of the society in which it is found (Brake, 1980). The members of the subculture are also members of the larger society; they have families and friends outside the subculture with whom they share many values and norms. But within the subculture they pursue values that are opposed to those of the larger or "mainstream" culture. Subcultures evolve their own rather insulated social worlds or communities. In the words of one writer on the subject, each of these social worlds has "its own local myths (the county attorney goes easy with us

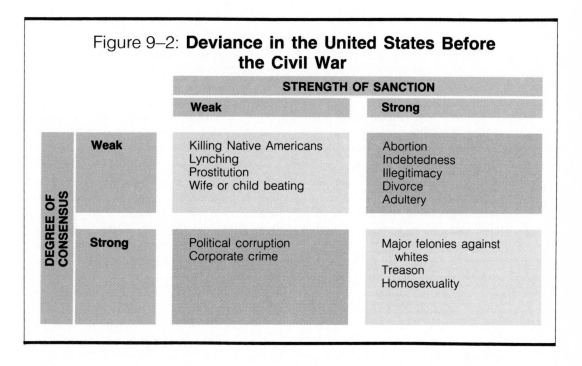

Figure 9–2: **Deviance in the United States Before the Civil War**

		STRENGTH OF SANCTION	
		Weak	**Strong**
DEGREE OF CONSENSUS	**Weak**	Killing Native Americans Lynching Prostitution Wife or child beating	Abortion Indebtedness Illegitimacy Divorce Adultery
	Strong	Political corruption Corporate crime	Major felonies against whites Treason Homosexuality

A deviant subculture includes a system of values, attitudes, behaviors, and life-styles opposed to the society's dominant culture.

'cause he's an old head himself), its own legendary heroes (remember Max—what a crazy one he was), its own honorary members (Blaine the druggist or Sophie at the café), its own scale of reputations (Garth's all right, he's just a little slow about some things), and its own social routine (probably see you at the Totem later on tonight)" (Simmons, 1987, p. 206).

The homosexual subculture provides another illustration. Homosexuals are a deviant subculture because their preference for sexual relations with members of the same sex sets them apart from the majority of the population. Despite the fact that studies of sexual behavior in most modern nations have found homosexual experience to be quite common, involving as many as one in ten men and at least as many women (Kinsey, Pomeroy, and Martin, 1948), homosexuals are often victims of attacks by those who find their behavior threatening or amoral. Indeed, before the Gay Pride movement of the 1960s and 1970s, homosexuals were a "closet" subculture, secretive and highly discreet, with an underground world of clubs and baths and other institutions in large cities that enabled them to remain invisible to members of the larger society. As social acceptance of homosexuality has increased, many homosexuals have "come out of the closet"; that is, they have declared their identity as gay men or lesbians. But the lives of those who differ from the majority are never easy, and many homosexuals still prefer to live in communities that are identified as gay, where their life-style is considered normal.

Many deviant subcultures are harmful to society because they sustain criminal occupations. The outstanding example of such a subculture is organized crime. Professional criminals, including major drug dealers, bookmakers and gamblers, hired killers, and loan sharks, who think of their illegal activities as occupations, often become part of secret crime organizations. The best known of these (but hardly the only one) is the Mafia. Originally a Sicilian crime organization, the Mafia spread to the United States via Sicilian immigration in the late nineteenth century. Today families associated with the Mafia are active in most large cities in North America and elsewhere and often extract millions of dollars from legitimate businesses in exchange for "protection."

The subculture of organized crime is not unique to North America. In Japan, rates of homicide and mugging are small fractions of those in U.S. cities (Buruma, 1984). Yet organized crime thrives there. The Yakuza, as the crime gangs are called, control many illegal businesses, just as they do in other countries, and they often resort to violence to discipline their members. As in the United States, organized crime in Japan is most directly associated with behaviors that are considered deviant, such as prostitution, gambling, and drug use, and a distinct subculture has emerged among those who engage in such behaviors.

In sum, many deviant subcultures flourish because they provide opportunities to engage in behavior that is pleasurable to many people but is considered deviant in "respectable" society. Clearly, therefore, the line between what is normal and what is deviant is not nearly as distinct as one might believe from official descriptions of the norms of good conduct. On the other hand, one must recognize that membership in a deviant subculture, especially for those without money and power, often leads to exploitation and early death. In view of these problematic aspects of deviant subcultures, sociological and other explanations of deviant behavior take on special importance.

THEORETICAL PERSPECTIVES ON SOCIAL DEVIANCE

Biological Explanations of Crime

Early in the twentieth century the Italian criminologist Cesare Lombroso (1911) claimed that his research had proved that criminals were throwbacks to primitive, aggressive human types who could be recognized by physical features such as prominent foreheads, shifty eyes, and red hair. Although Lombroso's theory has been thoroughly refuted by modern researchers, efforts to link body type with crime seem destined to reappear from time to time. In the 1940s, for example, the psychologist and physician William Sheldon announced that body type was correlated with crime. He believed that human beings could be classified into three types: *ectomorphs*, or thin people; *endomorphs*, or soft, fat people; and *mesomorphs*, or people with firm, well-defined muscles. The latter were most prone to crime, according to Sheldon, but he neglected to account for the possibility that mesomorphs simply might have led harder lives than less muscular individuals and were therefore better equipped to commit crimes that require strength (Glueck and Glueck, 1950).

Another biological theory asserts that there may be genetic differences between criminals and noncriminals. During the 1960s researchers discovered that some males have an extra Y chromosome in their cells. It was not at all clear what, if any, effect this extra chromosome has on the individual, but in 1965 geneticist Patricia Jacobs and her coworkers reported that a small but significant proportion of XYY males were to be found among the violent or criminal inmates of a Scottish mental institution. When the mass murderer Richard Speck was erroneously reported to be an XYY male, the idea of the "congenital criminal" became front-page news. But eleven years after the original studies, when over 200 research articles had been published on the XYY phenomenon, medical geneticists had to admit that "the frequency of antisocial behavior of the XYY male is probably not very different from non-XYY persons of similar background and social class" (Ann Arbor Science for the People Editorial Collective, 1977; Borganokar and Shah, 1974; Glaser, 1979). To date, no solid evidence has emerged to link deviance or criminality to biological factors.

To date there is no solid evidence linking deviance or criminality to biological factors.

Social-Scientific Explanations of Deviance and Crime

Early sociological explanations of social deviance were strongly influenced by the biological concept of disease. The earliest of these explanations viewed crime as a form of social pathology, or social disease, that could be attributed to the evils of city life. Corruption, criminality, and depravity were thought to be bred in slums and to infect innocent residents of those grim communities, just as typhoid spread in unclean surroundings and was passed by contact from one victim to another (Queen and Debler, 1940/1925). Thus many early juvenile training schools were built in rural areas where they would be isolated from the "corrupting" influence of cities (Platt, 1977). However, this view of deviance tended to rely on subjective terms and unproved assertions about the spread of crime and deviance. It has been replaced by more objective and verifiable theories derived from the functionalist, interactionist, and conflict perspectives of modern sociology.

The Functionalist Perspective

The functionalist theorist Robert K. Merton (1938) developed a typology of deviance based on how people adapt to the demands of their society. Merton's aim was to discover "how some social structures *exert a definite pressure upon certain persons in society to engage in nonconformist rather than conformist conduct*" (p. 672). "Among the elements of social and cultural structure," Merton continued, "two are important for our purposes. . . . The first consists of culturally defined goals, purposes, and interests. . . . The second . . . defines, regulates, and controls the acceptable modes of achieving these goals" (pp. 672–673).

Merton's explanation of deviance is based on the concept of **anomie**, or normlessness. In his view, anomie results from the frustration and confusion people feel when what they have been taught to desire cannot be achieved by the legitimate means available to them. Merton believes that North America and other modern societies exhibit high levels of anomie because people are socialized to desire success in the form of material well-being and social prestige. For many, however, the means of attaining these culturally defined ends, such as hard work and saving, seem to be out of reach. This is especially true for people who experience rapid social changes, such as the closing of factories, and find themselves deprived of opportunities to attain what they have come to expect from life.

Consider some examples. Possession of money is a culturally defined goal. Work is a socially acceptable mode of achieving that goal; theft is not. Mating is also a culturally defined goal. Courtship and seduction are acceptable means of achieving it; kidnap and rape are not. But if theft and rape are unacceptable means of achieving culturally defined goals, why do they exist? According to Merton, the gap between culturally defined goals and acceptable means of achieving them causes feelings of anomie, which in turn make people more likely to choose deviant strategies of various kinds.

Through socialization we learn the goals and acceptable means of our society. Most of us would love to be rich or powerful or famous. We accept these goals of our culture. We also accept the legitimate means of achieving them: education, work, the electoral process, plastic surgery, acting school, and so on. We are conformists. But not everyone accepts either the cultural goals or the accepted means of achieving them. Some become "innovators" in that they explore (and often step over) the frontiers of acceptable goal-seeking behavior; others (such as hoboes) retreat into a life that rejects both the goals and the accepted means; some rebel and seek to change the goals and the institutions that support them; and still others reject the quest for these precious values while carrying out the rituals of social institutions. (In many bureaucracies, for example, one can find ritualists who have given up the quest for promotion yet insist on receiving deference from people below them in the hierarchy.) Mer-

According to Merton, deviance stems from the anomie, or normlessness, that people feel when culturally approved goals cannot be achieved by the legitimate means available to them.

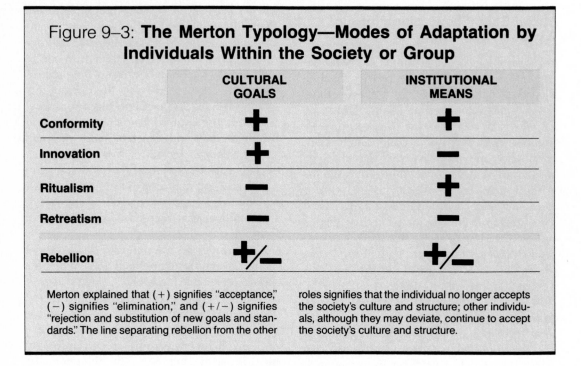

Figure 9–3: **The Merton Typology—Modes of Adaptation by Individuals Within the Society or Group**

	CULTURAL GOALS	INSTITUTIONAL MEANS
Conformity	+	+
Innovation	+	−
Ritualism	−	+
Retreatism	−	−
Rebellion	+/−	+/−

Merton explained that (+) signifies "acceptance," (−) signifies "elimination," and (+/−) signifies "rejection and substitution of new goals and standards." The line separating rebellion from the other roles signifies that the individual no longer accepts the society's culture and structure; other individuals, although they may deviate, continue to accept the society's culture and structure.

ton's typology thus is based on whether people accept either the cultural goals of their society, the acceptable means of achieving them, or neither. Figure 9-3 presents this typology and Figure 9-4 gives examples of all the deviant types in Merton's framework.

You may be wondering what there is in Merton's theory that explains why some poor people resort to crime while so many others do not. The answer lies in the way people who experience anomie gravitate toward criminal subcultures. For example, adolescents who steal to obtain things that their parents cannot afford must learn new norms— they must learn how to steal successfully and must receive some approval from peers for their conduct (Cloward and Ohlin, 1960). As a result, they drift toward deviant peer groups. But this explanation presents a problem for the functionalist perspective: If there are deviant subcultures, the idea that there is a single culture whose goals and means are shared by all members of society is called into question. The presence of different subcultures within a society suggests that another possible cause of deviant behaviors may be conflict between groups.

Conflict Perspectives

Cultural Conflict. In an influential essay entitled "Crime as an American Way of Life," Daniel Bell (1962) observed that at the turn of the twentieth century cultural conflict developed between the "Big City and the small-town conscience. Crime as a growing business was fed by the revenues from prostitution, liquor, and gambling that a wide-open urban society encouraged and that a middle-class Protestant ethos tried to suppress with a ferocity unmatched in any other civilized society" (p. 128). This example of conflict between the official morality of the dominant American culture and the less puritanical outlook of subcultures that do not include moral strictures against gambling, drinking, prostitution, and the like encouraged the growth of criminal organizations. In the United States as in many other societies, such organizations thrive by supplying the needs of millions of

Conflict theorists have pointed out that cultural conflict can result in the definition of some behaviors as deviant.

people in cities, towns, and rural areas who appear to be law-abiding citizens but who nevertheless engage in certain deviant behaviors.

The prohibition of alcoholic beverages in the United States from 1919 to 1932 is an example of how cultural conflict can lead to situations that encourage criminal activity. Prohibition has been interpreted as an effort by the nation's largely Protestant lawmakers to impose their version of morality on immigrant groups for whom the consumption of alcohol was an important part of social life. Once they were passed, however, laws against the production and sale of alcoholic beverages created opportunities for illegal production, smuggling (bootlegging), and illegal drinking establishments (speakeasys). These in turn

supported the rise of organized-crime syndicates. The current laws against drugs like marijuana and cocaine have similar effects in that they lead to the clandestine production and supply of these illegal but widely used substances. Similar opportunities to make illegal profits arise when states pass laws raising the drinking age (Gusfield, 1966; Kornblum and Julian, 1989).

To recognize these effects of cultural conflict is not to condone the sale and use of illegal drugs. Rather, it is to be aware that whenever laws promoted by the powerful in the name of morality impose a set of moral standards on a minority, illegal markets are created that tend to be supplied by criminal organizations. Such organizations often act ruthlessly to control their markets, as can be

Figure 9–4: **Examples of Social Roles Based on the Merton Typology**

MODE OF ADAPTATION	THE POOR	THE MIDDLE CLASS	THE RICH
Conformity	The working poor	The suburban family	The wealthy civic leader
Innovation	The mugger	The embezzler	The stock manipulator
Ritualism	The chronic welfare recipient	The resigned bureaucrat	The hedonist
Retreatism	The wino or junkie	The skidding alcoholic	The bohemian
Rebellion	The bandit	The anarchist	The fascist

These examples are meant to illustrate possible outcomes, not stereotypes. Obviously, not all fascists are rich, nor are all anarchists middle class or all bandits poor. Moreover, perceptions of approved goals and means may vary. In some cases, for example, the very rich, who feel that they could be even richer were it not for legal obstacles in their path, may choose to bend the rules. Also, a number of cultural values besides wealth shape the likelihood that a member of a given class will behave as he or she does.

seen in the murder of Mexican border guards who surprise drug smugglers, the killing of Colombian cocaine traffickers by rival dealers in New York City, or the periodic "wars" that break out between organized-crime families in many large cities.

Marxian Conflict Theory. For Marxian students of social deviance, the cultural-conflict explanation is inadequate because it does not take into account the effects of power and class conflict. Marxian sociologists believe that situations like Prohibition do not occur just because of cultural conflict. They happen because the powerful classes in society (i.e., those who own and control the means of production) wish to control the working class and the poor so that they will produce more. From the Marxian perspective, as criminologist Richard Quinney (1980) points out, "crime is to be understood in terms of the development of capitalism" (p. 41), as it was in Marx's original analysis. From this perspective, most crime is essentially a form of class conflict—either the have-nots taking what they can from the ruling class or the rich and their agents somehow taking what they can from the poor. Box 9-2 shows that precapitalist societies can also be viewed as producing specific forms of crime, such as banditry.

The economic "robber barons"—Jacob Astor; John D. Rockefeller, Sr.; J. P. Morgan; Leland Stanford; Andrew Carnegie; and many others—amassed huge fortunes in the period of booming industrial growth following the Civil War. But they often resorted to illegal means in pursuing the culturally approved goal of great wealth. Among other tactics, they used violence to drive settlers off land they had purchased or to break strikes by workers, and they were not above manipulating prices in order to drive out competitors and monopolize the markets for steel, oil, coal, precious metals, food products, and numerous other goods. In Merton's typology of deviance, their actions would classify them as "innovators" (see Figure 9-4), but from a Marxian viewpoint they were merely carrying out "the logic of capitalism," which was based on the exploitation of the poor by the rich and powerful.

Marxian students of deviance point out that legal definitions of deviant behavior usually depend on the ability of the more powerful members of society to impose their will on the government and to protect their actions from legal sanctions. Thus, the crimes of the robber barons almost always went unpunished. Definitions of what is criminal and who should be punished are generally applied more forcefully to the poor and the working class (Balbus, 1978; Quinney, 1978; Turk, 1978).

Marx and his collaborator Friedrich Engels recognized that the working class (or *proletariat,* as they called it) would resort to individual crimes like robbery when driven to do so by unemployment and poverty, but they believed that the workers would be more likely to form associations aimed at destroying capitalism. The chronic poor, on the other hand, would form a class that Marx called the *lumpenproletariat,* people who were unable to get jobs in the capitalist system or were cast off for not working hard enough or for being injured or sick. Marx did not believe that members of this class would join forces with the proletariat. Instead, they would act as spies, informers, and thugs whose services could be purchased by the rich to be used against the workers. Marx agreed with other thinkers of his time who called the lumpenproletariat the "dangerous class" created by capitalism; from its ranks came thieves, prostitutes, gamblers, pickpockets, con artists, and contract murderers.

It can be helpful to view crime and deviance as symptoms of the class struggles that occur in any society and to show that laws that define and punish criminal behaviors are often imposed by the powerful on those with less power. But to attribute crime as we know it to the workings of capitalism is to suggest that if capitalism were abolished, crime would vanish. This clearly is not the case. In Cuba, for example, homosexuality is considered a serious crime and is severely punished be-

> *Marxian conflict theorists believe that deviance results from the desire of the powerful classes in society to control the working class and the poor.*

Box 9–2: **Bandits**

Bandits, brigands, train robbers, Robin Hoods, bad men and women of the frontiers appear throughout human history. Every society has its myths about great bandits, most of which are loosely based on the actual life histories of criminals who broke away from a life of rural poverty to terrorize the countryside and later become cultural heroes. For the so-

Bonnie Parker

cial historian Eric Hobsbawm (1981), "the crucial fact about the bandit's social situation is its ambiguity. He [or, sometimes, she] is an outsider and a rebel, a poor man who refuses to accept the normal roles of poverty, and establishes his freedom by means of the only resources within reach of the poor: strength, bravery, cunning, and determination. This draws him close to the poor; he is one of them. It sets him in opposition to the hierarchy of power, wealth and influence; he is not one of them" (p. 88).

The more successful the bandit is, however, the more he will be "inevitably drawn into the web of wealth and power, because, unlike other peasants, he acquires wealth and exerts power" (p. 88). Thus under some conditions the bandits of a society may actually form capitalist corporations of sorts, as was the case in the evolution of the Mafia out of the traditions of banditry in Sicily and southern Italy. Under conditions in which there is open class struggle, the bandit can become a revolutionary hero, as in the example of the legendary Mexican bandit Pancho Villa, who became a leader of the Mexican revolution in the early decades of this century.

Jesse James

Pancho Villa

cause the society's leaders think of it as an offense against masculinity and a symbol of a "decadent" culture. And as discussed in Chapter 8, until recently private enterprise was a crime in Soviet society, yet elite factory managers and political leaders often used their influence to amass personal wealth. They were not punished unless they lost their power in the political system (Voslensky, 1980). As these examples indicate, societies with Marxian ideologies are hardly free from their own forms of deviance and crime, and Marxian conflict theory is useful in explaining some aspects of these complex phenomena but not others.

The Interactionist Perspective

Functionalist theories explain deviance as a reaction to social dysfunctions; conflict theories explain it as a product of deviant subcultures or of the type of class struggle that occurs in a society in a particular historical period. Neither of these approaches accounts very well for the issues of recruitment and production. *Recruitment*, in this context, refers to the question of why some people become deviants while others in the same social situation do not. *Production* refers to the creation of new categories of deviance in a society.

Recruitment Through Differential Association.
In 1940 the sociologist and criminologist Edwin H. Sutherland published a paper entitled "White Collar Criminality" in which he argued that official crime statistics do not measure the many forms of crime that are not correlated with poverty. Outstanding among these are *white-collar crimes*—that is, the criminal behavior of people in business and professional positions:

White-collar criminality in business is expressed most frequently in the form of misrepresentation in financial statements of corporations, manipulation in stock exchange, commercial bribery, bribery of public officials directly or indirectly in order to secure favorable contracts and legislation, misrepresentation in advertising and salesmanship, embezzlement and misapplication of funds, short weights and measures and misgrading of commodities, tax frauds, misapplication of funds in receiverships and bankruptcies. These are what Al Capone called "the legitimate rackets." These

and many others are found in abundance in the business world. [1940, pp. 2–3]

Sutherland was pointing out that an accurate statistical comparison of the crimes committed by the rich and the poor was not available. But his paper on white-collar crime also set forth an interactionist theory of crime and deviance:

White collar criminality, just as other systematic criminality . . . is learned in direct or indirect association with those who already practice the behavior; and . . . those who learn this criminal behavior are segregated from frequent and intimate contacts with law-abiding behavior. Whether a person becomes a criminal or not is determined largely by the comparative frequency and intimacy of his contacts with the two types of behavior. This may be called the process of **differential association**. [pp. 10–11; emphasis added]

The concept of differential association offered an answer to some of the weaknesses of functionalist and conflict theories. Not only did it account for the prevalence of deviance in all social classes but it also provided clues to how crime is learned in groups that are culturally distinct from the dominant society. For example, in the 1920s sociologists Clifford Shaw and Henry McKay had observed that some Chicago neighborhoods had consistently higher rates of juvenile delinquency than others. These were immigrant neighborhoods, but their high rates of delinquency persisted regardless of which immigrant groups lived there at any given time. Sutherland's theory explained this pattern by calling attention to the culture of deviance that had become part of the way of life of teenagers in those neighborhoods. According to Sutherland, the teenagers became delinquent because they interacted in groups whose culture legitimated crime. Teenage delinquents did not deviate from conventional norms because the approved means of achieving approved goals were closed to them. Instead, they acted as they did because the culture of their peer group made crime an acceptable means of achieving desired goals.

> *Sutherland's theory of differential association attempts to explain why some people are recruited to deviant groups while others are not.*

In an empirical study that tested Sutherland's theory, Walter Miller (1958) found that delinquency in areas with high rates of juvenile crime was in fact supported by the norms of lower-class teenage peer groups. In three years of careful observation Miller found that delinquent groups had a set of well-defined values: "trouble, toughness, smartness, excitement, fate, and autonomy." Whereas other groups felt that it was important to stay out of trouble, the delinquent groups viewed trouble—meaning fighting, drinking, and sexual adventures—as something to brag about, as long as they didn't get caught. Toughness as shown by physical prowess or fearlessness, smartness as evidenced by the ability to con or outsmart gullible "marks"; the excitement to be found in risking danger successfully; one's fate as demonstrated by luck or good fortune in avoiding capture; and the autonomy that crime seemed to provide in the form of independence from authorities—all were values of delinquent groups that differentiated them from nondelinquent groups in the same neighborhoods.

A study by criminologist Donald R. Cressey (1971/1953) supported the theory of differential association with the finding that embezzlers generally had to learn how to commit their crime by associating with people who could teach them how to commit it with the greatest likelihood of avoiding suspicion. But Cressey also found that people who became embezzlers often had serious personal problems (marital difficulties, gambling, and the like) that directed them toward people who would influence them to commit this form of white-collar crime. When bank officials had problems of this sort, they were vulnerable to suggestions of deviant means of gaining money and solving personal problems while maintaining the outward signs of respectability.

Not all deviants are people whose means of achieving success have been blocked or who are acting out some form of class struggle or have associated with a deviant group. For example, many alcoholics and drug users are not thought of as deviant, either because their behavior is not considered serious or because it is not witnessed by other people. From an interactionist perspective, the key question about such people is how their behavior is understood by others. The central concepts that attempt to answer this question are *labeling* and the idea of the *deviant career*.

Labeling. According to interactionist theory, deviance is produced by a process known as **labeling,** meaning a societal reaction to certain behaviors that labels the offender as a deviant. Most often, labeling is done by official agents of social control like the police, the courts, mental institutions, and schools (Becker, 1963; Erikson, 1962; Gusfield, 1981; Kitsuse, 1962; Lemert, 1967; Schur, 1984). In the labeling process, Howard Becker (1963) stated, "social groups create deviance by making the rules whose infraction constitutes deviance and by applying those rules to particular people and labeling them as outsiders. From this point of view, deviance is *not* a quality of the act the person commits, but rather a consequence of the application by others of rules and sanctions to an 'offender.' The deviant is one to whom that label has been successfully applied; deviant behavior is behavior that people so label" (p. 9).

In a famous experiment that tested the effects of labeling, D. L. Rosenhan (1973) and eight other researchers were admitted to a mental hospital after they pretended that they had been hearing voices. Each of these "pseudopatients" was diagnosed as schizophrenic. Before long many of the patients with whom the pseudopatients associated considered them normal, but the doctors who had made the diagnosis continued to think of them as schizophrenic. As the pseudopatients waited in the lunch line, for example, they were said to be exhibiting "oral-acquisitive behavior." Gradually the researchers were released with the diagnosis of schizophrenia in remission, but none was ever thought to be cured.

Rosenhan and his researchers also observed that not only did the diagnosis of schizophrenia label the patient for life but the label itself became a justification for other

Symbolic interactionists emphasize the importance of labeling in the process by which people define themselves as deviant.

forms of mistreatment. The doctors and hospital staff disregarded the patients' opinions, treated them as incompetent, and often punished them for infractions of minor rules. The hospital's social atmosphere was based on the powerlessness of the people who were labeled as mentally ill.

Rosenhan's study accelerated the movement to reform mental institutions and to deinstitutionalize as many mental patients as possible. But studies of deinstitutionalized mental patients (many of whom are homeless), together with research on the problems of released convicts, have shown that the labels attached to people who have deviated become incorporated into their definitions of themselves as deviant. In this way labeling at some stage of a person's development tends to steer that person into a community of other deviants, where she or he may become trapped in a "deviant career" (Bassuk, 1984).

Deviant Careers. "There is no reason to assume," wrote Becker (1963), "that only those who finally commit a deviant act actually have the impulse to do so. It is much more likely that most people experience deviant impulses frequently. At least in fantasy, people are much more deviant than they appear" (p. 26). Becker suggested that the proper sociological question is not why some people do things that are disapproved of but, rather, why "conventional people do not follow through on the deviant impulses they have" (p. 26). According to Becker and other interactionists, the answers are to be found in the individual's commitment to conventional institutions and behaviors.

Commitment means adherence to and dependence on the norms of a given social institution. The middle-class youth's commitment to school, which has developed over many years of socialization in the family and the community, often prevents him or her from giving in to the impulse to play hooky. "In fact," Becker asserted, "the normal development of people in our society (and probably in any society) can be seen as a series of progressively increasing commitments to conventional norms and institutions" (p. 27).

Travis Hirschi studied how people become committed to conventional norms. Such commitment, he found, emerges out of the interactions that create our social bonds to others. When we are closely tied to people who adhere to conventional norms, we have little chance to deviate. And as we grow older our investment in upholding conventional norms increases because we feel that we have more to protect. This process of lifetime socialization in groups produces a normative system of social control that is internalized in most members of the society (Hirschi and Gottfredson, 1980).

By the same token, a person who once gives in to the impulse to commit a deviant act and is caught, or who becomes a member of a deviant group because it has recruited him or her, gradually develops a commitment to that group and its deviant culture. The reasons for taking the first step toward deviance may be many and varied, but from the interactionist perspective "one of the most crucial steps in the process of building a stable pattern of deviant behavior is likely to be the experience of being caught and publicly labeled as deviant" (Becker, 1963, p. 31).

In a well-known empirical study of youth gangs, William J. Chambliss (1973) applied both the conflict and interactionist perspectives. For two years Chambliss observed the Saints, a gang of upper-class boys, and the Roughnecks, a gang of lower-class boys from the same community. Both gangs engaged in car theft and joyriding, vandalism, dangerous practical jokes, and fighting, and in fact the upper-class Saints were involved in a larger overall number of incidents. But the members of the lower-class gang were more frequently caught, described as "tough young criminals headed for trouble," and sent to reform school. Members of the upper-class gang were rarely caught and were never labeled as delinquent.

Chambliss observed that the upper-class gang members had access to cars and could commit their misdeeds in other communities, where they were not known. The lower-class

> *According to interactionists, a key factor in the development of a deviant career is commitment to the norms of a deviant group.*

boys hung out in their own community and performed many of their antisocial acts there. A far more important explanation, according to Chambliss, pertained to the relative influence of the boys' parents. The parents of the upper-class boys argued that the boys' activities were normal youthful behavior, just the "sowing of wild oats." Their social position enabled them to influence the way their children's behavior was perceived, an influence the lower-class parents of the Roughnecks did not have. Thus the Roughnecks were caught and labeled and became increasingly committed to deviant careers, but the Saints escaped without being subject to serious sanction.

Sociologists often note that members of both gangs engaged in deviant acts, referred to as **primary deviance,** but that only the lower-class boys were labeled as delinquent by the police and the juvenile courts. As a result of that labeling, many of the lower-class boys went on to commit acts that sociologists call **secondary deviance**—that is, behaviors appropriate to someone who has already been labeled as delinquent. (For example, in juvenile detention centers teenage offenders often learn deviant skills such as how to deal in drugs.) The distinction between primary and secondary deviance is useful because it emphasizes that most of us deviate from cultural norms in many ways but that once we are labeled as deviant we tend to commit additional deviant acts in order to fulfill the negative definitions society has attached to us (Lemert, 1951; Schur, 1971).

Reasonable as the labeling perspective appears, it has not always been borne out by empirical research. Some studies have found that people who have been labeled as delinquent after being caught and convicted of serious offenses go on to commit other deviant acts. On the other hand, other studies have found that labeling can lead to decreased deviance and a lower probability of further offenses (Thornberry and Farnworth, 1983; Wilson, 1977).

As societies become larger and more complex, they develop specialized, more or less coercive institutions to deal with deviants.

CRIME AND SOCIAL CONTROL

We have seen that crime as defined by a society's laws is only one aspect of the range of behaviors included in the study of deviance. But the general public and policymakers in government are most concerned with crime and its control. In this final section, therefore, we will touch on some of the most hotly debated issues in the control of crime and the treatment of criminals.

At the beginning of the chapter we presented a very broad definition of social control: "all the ways in which a society establishes and enforces its cultural norms." Certainly it is true that without socialization and the controlling actions of social groups like the family, schools, the military, and corporations there would be much more anomie, crime, and violence. But in considering a society's means of controlling crime, sociologists most often study what might be called "government social control"—that is, the society's legal codes; the operation of its judicial, police, penal, and rehabilitative institutions; and the ways in which its most powerful members promote their views of crime, deviance, and social control (Black, 1984; Scull, 1988).

Ecological Dimensions of Crime

We saw in Table 9-1 that although the voting public may believe that crime is an increasingly serious social problem, crime rates have decreased somewhat in recent years. Table 9-2 shows that the incidence of different types of crime varies from one region of the country to another, with homicides highest in the southern states, rape highest in the western states, and burglary and arson highest in the northeastern states. Ecological data like these are an essential starting point in research on the incidence of crime and provide some insights into why such regional differences exist. In the South, for example, high rates of gun ownership contribute to higher homicide rates. In the West, a larger proportion of the

Table 9–2: **The Crime Rate* and Rates of Violent Crimes, by Region of the United States, 1987**

Offense	Northeast	Midwest	South	West
Crime Index, total	4,839.0	4,908.0	5,893.0	6,460.0
Violent Crime, total	636.0	504.0	607.0	715.0
Murder	6.9	6.7	10.0	8.5
Forcible Rape	29.3	37.1	39.3	42.9
Robbery	284.0	173.0	192.0	223.0
Aggravated Assault	316.0	287.0	366.0	440.0
Property Crime, total	4,204.0	4,403.0	5,286.0	5,746.0
Burglary	1,031.0	1,088.0	1,565.0	1,524.0
Larceny-Theft	2,544.0	2,889.0	3,238.0	3,590.0
M.V. Theft	629.0	426.0	483.0	632.0

*Offenses known to the police per 100,000 population. *Source:* FBI, 1989.

population consists of young, unattached single people, contributing to a higher incidence of rape. And in the Northeast more buildings are old and owned by absentee landlords, making arson for insurance payments a more common crime.

Another contribution of ecological analysis can be seen in data on the relationship between crime and the age composition of a population. Political leaders and social scientists who favor larger police forces and tougher law enforcement argue that these policies are responsible for the decrease in the U.S. crime rate in the past few years. But it is also true that the age composition of the U.S. population is changing rather quickly.

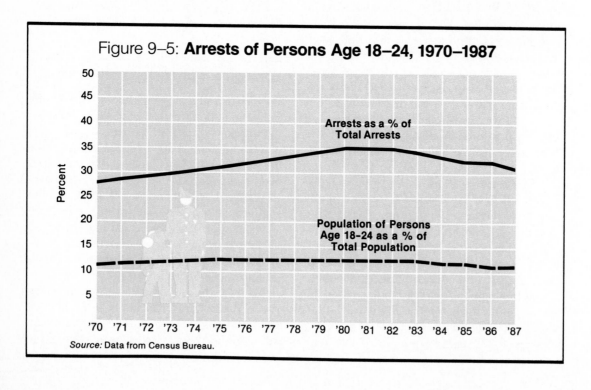

Figure 9–5: **Arrests of Persons Age 18–24, 1970–1987**

Arrests as a % of Total Arrests

Population of Persons Age 18-24 as a % of Total Population

Source: Data from Census Bureau.

Among other things, the "baby boom" generation has moved out of the young-adult years, those in which people are most likely to commit crimes. (About half of all reported violent crimes are committed by males between the ages of fifteen and twenty-four.) And as Figure 9-5 shows, the crime rate is dropping along with the decrease in the portion of the population in this age group. Thus, before taking credit for reducing crime rates, law enforcement agencies and advocates of tough anticrime measures must make certain that lower crime rates are not simply a result of a reduction in the most crime-prone portion of the population.

Still another variable that lends itself to ecological analysis is the effect of possession of firearms on homicide rates. The United States has higher rates of homicide than other Western industrial nations, a fact often thought to reflect a greater overall level of violence. However, in a study comparing rates of violent crime in Denmark and northeastern Ohio, investigators found that rates of assault did not differ in the two areas. What did differ were rates of homicide using firearms; such crimes were much more frequent in Ohio. In Denmark the possession of handguns is banned, whereas in the United States "50 percent of all households have guns and one in five has a handgun" (Mawson, 1989, p. 239).

As mentioned earlier in this chapter, studies of criminal victimization, which ask people about their actual experiences with crime, have provided a major breakthrough in our understanding of crime in complex societies. Thus Figure 9-6 shows that for every 1,000 crimes reported in victimization surveys, only slightly more than half are reported to the police, and only about 6.5 percent result in arrests. The probability that a criminal who is arrested will be sentenced to prison is minuscule, however, although many reported crimes are committed by habitual criminals who do tend to get arrested eventually. Most sociological studies of **recidivism** (the probability that a person who has served a jail term will commit additional crimes and be jailed again) indicate that there is an overall probability of 50 percent that recidivism will occur. Recidivism is most frequent among young minority males from poor backgrounds who are drug and/or alcohol addicts and have been imprisoned on numerous previous occasions for crimes against property (Land, 1989). Given both high crime rates and high rates of recidivism, it is little wonder that the search for solutions to the problem of overcrowded prisons, as well as alternatives to

Figure 9–6: **Attrition of Law Enforcement— 1,000 Committed Index Felonies**

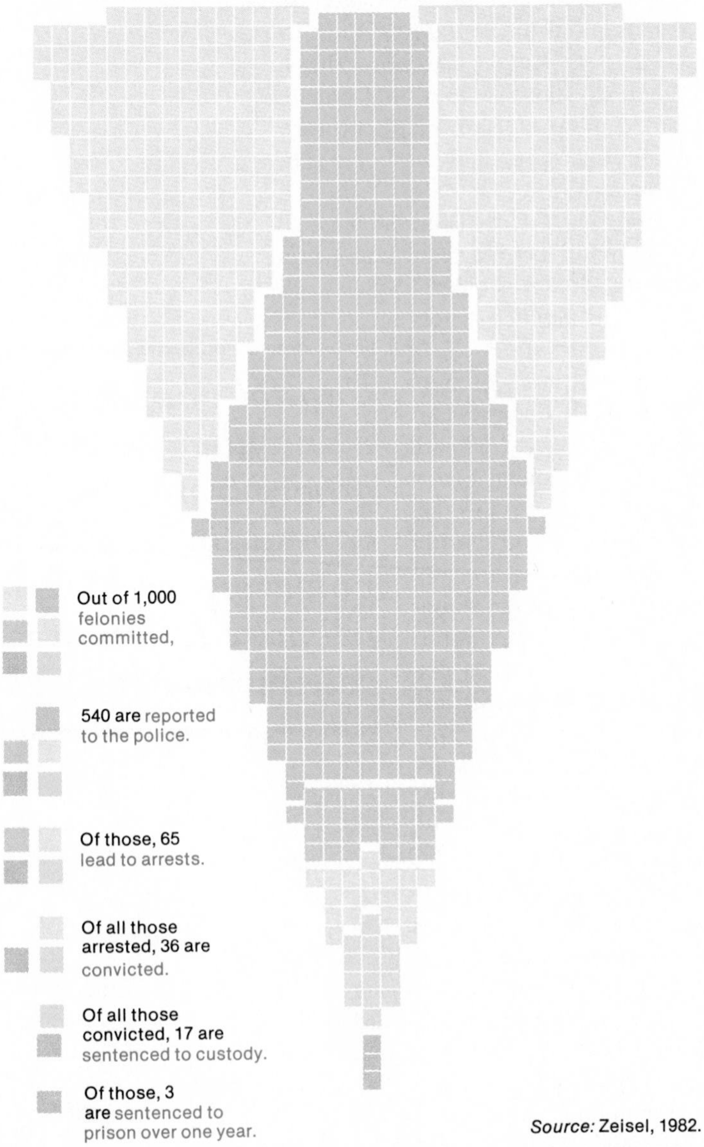

Out of 1,000 felonies committed,

540 are reported to the police.

Of those, 65 lead to arrests.

Of all those arrested, 36 are convicted.

Of all those convicted, 17 are sentenced to custody.

Of those, 3 are sentenced to prison over one year.

Source: Zeisel, 1982.

imprisonment, occupies many researchers at this time.

Institutions of Coercive Control: Courts and Prisons

When the United States consisted mainly of small agrarian communities, social control of deviance and crime was carried out by the local institutions of the family or the church. Parents, for example, were expected to control their children; if they did not, they would lose the respect of other members of the community. But as the size, complexity, and diversity of societies increase, the ability of local institutions to control all of the society's members is diminished (Wirth, 1968/1938). Societies therefore develop specialized, more or less coercive institutions to deal with deviants. Courts, prisons, police forces, and social-welfare agencies grow as the influence of the community on the behavior of its members declines.

Capital Punishment—Cruel and Unusual? Capital punishment provides an illustration of the issues raised by the use of coercive forms of social control. Only recently (during this century in some nations) has the death sentence come to be widely thought of as barbaric. In simpler societies and earlier civilizations, execution was not only a penalty carried out on an individual; it was also an occasion for a public ceremony. People attended beheadings and hangings, and hawkers sold them food and favors as they waited for the bloody pageant. The villain's death reaffirmed their common values, their solidarity as a people who could purge evil elements from their midst.

Today, by contrast, the value of capital punishment is a matter of heated debate. Although many people believe that the death sentence is necessary as a means of discouraging some individuals from committing terrible crimes, others are convinced that there is no justification for putting another person to death, the more so because there is always the possibility that the person did not commit the crime for which he or she was executed.

In one of a series of studies of the equity of capital punishment, criminologists Marvin Wolfgang and Marc Riedel (1973) found that blacks were more likely than whites to be executed for the same crimes and that people who could afford good lawyers were far more likely to escape execution than those who lacked the means to hire the best legal defenders.

In 1972, swayed by research findings and by arguments that capital punishment could be considered "cruel and unusual punishment," the United States Supreme Court ruled in a five-to-four decision that in the absence of clear specifications for when it might be used, the death sentence violated the Eighth Amendment to the Constitution. But Congress has since passed legislation that legalized the death sentence and the Court has not overruled it. As a result, capital punishment has been reinstated in a number of states and is being considered in several others.

But does capital punishment have the effect of deterring people from committing murder, as its advocates claim? Much of the evidence on this subject is negative. As Figure 9-7 shows quite clearly, there is little encouragement to be found in comparisons among states that have the death penalty, states that have had it with interruptions, and states that have never had it. On the other hand, in interviews with criminals charged with robbery James Q. Wilson (1977) found evidence that fear of the death penalty discouraged them from carrying guns. There is still considerable opposition to the death penalty among people who feel that it represents cruel and unusual punishment, but surveys indicate that the tide of public opinion is turning toward support for this most extreme of social sanctions. They also show, for better or worse, that the public's increased concern about crime has led to greater emphasis on use of the death sentence as retribution for murders that have already been committed and less emphasis on the possible deterrent effect of capital punishment.

> *Capital punishment is intended to deter others from committing murder; however, its primary function is retribution.*

Plea Bargaining—A Revolving Door?
Capital punishment addresses a small but sensational part of the crime problem. Many more criminals will commit other types of crimes, and for them too the issue of punishment and rehabilitation is controversial. At present, judges and police officers feel hampered by the relatively limited array of treatments for criminal offenders, as well as the growing backlogs in the courts and the overcrowding of prisons. One means that is often used to reduce the pressure on the judicial system is **plea bargaining,** in which a person who is charged with a crime agrees to plead guilty to a lesser charge and thereby free the courts from having to conduct a lengthy and costly jury trial. The shorter sentences that result from this system diminish somewhat the size of prison populations. Plea bargaining has been criticized as "revolving-door justice"; however, criminologists estimate that increasing the number of offenders who are tried and imprisoned by only 20 percent would place an intolerable burden on the correctional system (Rosett and Cressey, 1976).

Prisons—Schools for Crime? Despite the small proportion of crimes resulting in arrest and imprisonment, prisons remain the social institution with the primary responsibility for dealing with criminals. The arguments used to support this position are functionalist in nature. The functions of prisons are said to be deterrence, rehabilitation, and retribution (i.e., punishment) (Fox, 1952; Hawkins, 1976). As Bruce Jackson, a well-known student of prison life, explains it, a prison is supposed to deter criminals from committing crimes ("its presence is supposed to keep those among us of weak moral strength from actions we might otherwise commit"); it is supposed to rehabilitate those who do commit crimes ("within its walls those who have, for whatever reason, transgressed society's norms are presumably shown the error of their ways and retooled so they can live outside in more acceptable and satisfactory fashion"); and it is supposed to punish criminals, the only function that is clearly fulfilled (1972, p. 248).

Prisons (along with old-age homes, boarding schools, military academies, naval ships, etc.) are an example of **total institutions,** or organizations that assume total responsibility for every facet of the lives of the people who reside within them. As Erving Goffman (1961) explained,

A total institution may be defined as a place of residence and work where a large number of like-situated individuals, cut off from the wider society for an appreciable period of time, together lead an enclosed, formally administered round of life. Prisons serve as a clear example, providing we appreciate that what is prison-like about prisons is found in institutions whose members have broken no laws. [p. 3]

Goffman and others who have written about total institutions have found that new

> *Prisons are intended to serve the functions of deterrence, rehabilitation, and retribution.*

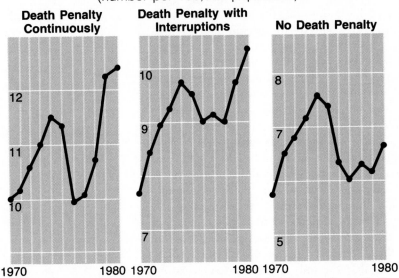

Figure 9–7: **Homicide Rates in States With and Without the Death Penalty, 1970–1980**
(number per 100,000 population)

Death Penalty Continuously · **Death Penalty with Interruptions** · **No Death Penalty**

States that had the death penalty continuously: Arizona, Arkansas, Connecticut, Florida, Georgia, Montana, Nebraska, Nevada, Oklahoma, Texas, Utah, Virginia. States without the death penalty: Alaska, Hawaii, Iowa, Maine, Michigan, Minnesota, New Jersey, North Dakota, West Virginia, Wisconsin, Washington, D.C. All other states had the death penalty with interruptions.
Source: Zeisel, 1982.

members of such organizations usually undergo a period of resocialization during which they are deprived of their former statuses through haircuts, uniforms, and the like. The goal of this process is to socialize the inmates to behave in ways that suit the organization's needs. But in most such organizations there usually also exists a strong inmate culture. This culture consists of norms that specify ways of resisting the officials' control in favor of such values as mutual aid and loyalty among the inmates. Thus in Bruce Jackson's (1972) collection of case histories of criminals and prison inmates, a seasoned convict summed up the world of the total institution: "A penitentiary is like a prisoner-of-war camp. The officials are the enemy and the inmates are captured. They're on one side and we're on the other" (p. 253). But the same prisoner also described another aspect of life in total institutions. Often, as the following passage reveals, the inmates develop "institutional personalities." As they try to conform to the norms of the organization, they become dependent on the routines and constraints of a life with minimal freedom and, hence, minimal responsibility:

I like things to be orderly. You might say I'm a conservative, I like the status quo. If something's going smooth I like that. . . . Some people . . . kind of like it. Get institutionalized. You know, there's a lot of security in a place like this for a person . . . They'll tell you when to get up, they'll tell you when to go to bed, when to eat, when to work. They'll do your laundry for you. You don't have to worry about anything else. (p. 253)

Only relatively recently, mainly in the second half of this century, has the goal of rehabilitation—the effort to return the criminal to society as a law-abiding citizen—been taken seriously as a function of prisons. Critics of the prison system, many of whom argue from a conflict perspective, often claim that far from rehabilitating their inmates, prisons in fact function as "schools for crime." As early as 1864 the great English philosopher and economist Jeremy Bentham wrote that "prisons, with the exception of a small number, include every imaginable means of infecting both body and mind. . . . An ordinary prison is a school in which wickedness is taught by

surer means than can ever be employed for the inculcation of virtue" (pp. 351–352). In the intervening years many studies have attempted to show under what conditions this is true or not and what can be done to increase the deterrent effects of prison and prevent it from becoming a community that socializes criminals.

Yet there is much sociological research that defends prisons as a means of deterrence and a necessary form of retribution. James Q. Wilson (1977) holds to the functionalist position: Societies need the firm moral authority they gain from stigmatizing and punishing crime. He believes that prisoners should receive better forms of rehabilitation in prison and be guaranteed their rights as citizens once they are outside again. But, he states, "to destigmatize crime would be to lift from it the weight of moral judgment and to make crime simply a particular occupation or avocation which society has chosen to reward less (or perhaps more) than other pursuits" (p. 230).

No matter what their sociological perspective, all students of the American prison system agree that by far the least successful aspect of prison life is rehabilitation. In Jackson's extensive interviews with prison inmates, he found that "few people within the walls take seriously the notion of rehabilitation; for most, prison is to punish, restrain, scare. Most other efforts are distant ideals, nice to talk about and consider, but impossible to effect" (p. 248). We cannot do justice to this subject here, but it is important to note that numerous programs intended to rehabilitate prisoners both within and outside prison walls have been undertaken, programs involving therapy, schooling, intensive resocialization, and various forms of occupational training and work experience. But very few have been found to have much effect on recidivism. In the most comprehensive study of these efforts to date, Robert Martinson (1972) found that the only rehabilitation programs that had statistically significant effects on recidivism rates were those that gave inmates job training and work experience that could be used to gain secure employment after their release.

CHALLENGES TO CONTEMPORARY SOCIETY

The Gang Phenomenon

Teenage gang violence has been on the rise throughout the United States since at least the early 1980s. At this writing, gang-related killings, teenage drug addiction, the spread of AIDS through crack use, and the demoralization of neighborhoods are only some of the enormous problems associated with this trend.

Gangs take several forms, including so-called crews, which roam over a wide range of locales, as well as traditional neighborhood-based gangs, which grow out of the perceived need to defend a particular territory. Although gangs are usually formed by teenagers in poor neighborhoods, many gang members come from comfortable suburban homes. Almost everywhere, teenage gang members are involved in the use and sale of drugs. The violence and street crime that accompany drug use have been described as a form of "slow rioting" (Larkin, 1979; Curtis, 1985; Hagedorn, 1988; Macleod, 1987; Williams, 1989).

In Los Angeles, the Crips and the Bloods do battle with automatic rifles and other heavy artillery. In New York, crack crews may resort to gunplay in the streets to enforce discipline, often injuring innocent bystanders. In smaller cities like Milwaukee, gangs may form after a fight between rival boys' groups. As one gang leader explained to researcher John M. Hagedorn, "We had a fight. There was about fifty people coming to fight." When all his friends ran from the police and he stayed, "the police called me a leader so I guess I was" (pp. 97–98). He enjoyed his new reputation, and the fact that the police recog-

nized him and gave his gang a name increased the cohesion of the gang itself.

Wherever teenagers are left largely on their own, usually owing to extreme poverty and neglect, they are likely to form gangs. This phenomenon occurs throughout the world. Homeless children have formed violent gangs in the cities of Colombia, Brazil, and Mexico. In the segregated townships of South Africa, infamous gangs known as Totsis terrorize communities where law enforcement is mainly a matter of protecting white citizens. In major European cities like Naples, Marseilles, London, Liverpool, Berlin, and Moscow teenagers who are bored and feel that their future holds little promise also turn to the thrills offered by gang activity. In most of these cases the adolescent gangs act as a training ground for adult criminal organizations.

It may be reassuring to know that gangs exist in societies other than the United States. But to sociologists who study gangs the steady increase in gang activity, especially drug-related activity, indicates that far more forceful action is needed to stem the resulting tide of violence and death. Sociologist Terry Williams, whose book *The Cocaine Kids* (1989) presents a detailed account of the lives of teenagers in the cocaine industry, is one of many who are attempting to help formulate policies designed to steer teenagers away from drugs. "It's not enough to keep telling the kids 'say no to drugs,'" Williams warns. "We need to be doing far more to provide positive opportunities for growth, especially for kids who need second and third chances to achieve in constructive ways. I'm seeing young men and women in their late teens and early twenties who have been hustling for a few years now. Some of them have made the crazy money and have survived on the streets, but they're looking for ways out of the drug and gang scene. So we have to ask what opportunities are we offering them?"

John Hagedorn agrees that traditional law enforcement alone will not provide a solution because it offers no positive inducements to draw youth away from illegal activities. In Hagedorn's view, there is a need for community-based programs to offer teenagers new opportunities for education and jobs. Moreover, he believes that these programs must be staffed partly by former gang members who are older and can serve as positive role models for the younger gang members. But, he notes, this would only be a first step. "The lack of 'good' jobs is clearly the major factor that has transformed the gang problem in the past decades" (1987, p. 166). Nevertheless, the larger society does not seem willing to invest in the economic development of poor neighborhoods. The President's Commission on the Causes and Prevention of Violence (Curtis, 1985) praised community programs for their success in diverting gang members from violence, but it also pointed out that such efforts must accompany programs aimed at local economic development and job creation.

In sum, the consensus among social scientists is that law enforcement, while clearly important in addressing gang problems, focuses on symptoms and not on causes. Getting at the economic and social roots of gang activity remains a major challenge to American society in the 1990s.

SUMMARY

*D*eviance, broadly defined, is behavior that violates the norms of a particular society. The deviant label is attached to a person who violates or opposes a society's most valued norms. The ways in which a society prevents deviance and punishes deviants are known as *social control*.

There is usually much disagreement not only about which behaviors are deviant but also about which behaviors should be condoned or punished only mildly. An important dimension of deviance is the power of some groups in society to define which acts are legal and which are illegal. Another dimension has to do with attributes the person cannot control, in contrast to actual behavior. In addition, some people are thought of as deviant because of their membership in a group that deviates from the norms of the larger society. To the rest of society they are deviants, but within the group they are not deviant but are conforming to the group's norms.

Deviance should be distinguished from *stigma*. A stigmatized person has some attribute that is deeply discrediting, such as a disfiguring disease, but is not necessarily a social deviant. The study of deviance is concerned with *social deviants*—that is, people who voluntarily violate the norms of their society. In particular, it focuses on criminal deviance—acts or omissions of acts for which the state can apply sanctions.

As a culture's values and norms change, so do its notions of what kinds of behavior are deviant and how they should be sanctioned. The extent to which the members of a society agree on whether or not a particular behavior is deviant can range from weak (in cases in which there is much controversy) to strong (in cases in which there is little disagreement). Negative sanctions, or punishments, can also range from very weak to very strong.

A deviant subculture includes a system of values, attitudes, behaviors, and life-styles that are opposed to the dominant culture of the society in which it is found. Many deviant subcultures are harmful to society because they sustain criminal occupations. Others provide opportunities to engage in behavior that is pleasurable to many people but considered deviant in "respectable" society. The boundaries between what is normal and what is deviant are not distinct.

Biological explanations of deviance relate criminality to physical features, body type, or chromosomal abnormality. These explanations influenced the earliest sociological explanations of deviance, which viewed crime and other forms of social deviance as varieties of "social pathology" that could be attributed to the evils of city life. This view has been replaced by more objective and verifiable theories drawn from the basic perspectives of modern sociology.

Functionalist theories of deviance include Robert Merton's typology based on how people adapt to the demands of their society. In this view, through socialization people learn what goals are approved of in their society and the approved means of achieving those goals. Those who do not accept the approved goals and/or the legitimate means of achieving them are likely to engage in deviant behaviors.

Functionalist theories have been criticized for assuming that there is a single set of values shared by all the members of a society. Conflict theorists stress the relationship between cultural diversity and deviance. The two main types of conflict theories are cultural-conflict theories and Marxian theories. Cultural-conflict theories concentrate on the ways in which conflicting sets of norms result in situations that encourage criminal activity. Marxian theories place more emphasis on class conflict, explaining various types of crime in terms of the social-class position of those who commit them.

Interactionist theories of deviance focus

on the issues of *recruitment* (the question of why some people become deviant whereas others do not) and *production* (the creation of new categories of deviance in a society). Edwin H. Sutherland's theory of *differential association* holds that whether or not a person becomes deviant is determined by the extent of his or her association with criminal subcultures. Interactionists believe that deviance is produced by the process of *labeling*, in which the society's reaction to certain behaviors is to brand or label the offender as a deviant. Once acquired, such a label is likely to become incorporated into the person's self-image and to increase the likelihood that he or she will become committed to a "deviant career."

Studies of the incidence of crime often start from ecological data on crime rates. Studies of criminal victimization, which ask people about their actual experiences with crime, have made a major contribution to the understanding of crime in complex societies like the United States.

The methods used to control crime change as societies become more complex. In larger, more diverse societies the ability of local institutions to control all of the society's members is diminished. Such societies tend to develop standardized, more or less coercive institutions to deal with deviants. Among the most prominent institutions of social control in modern societies are courts and prisons.

The primary functions of prisons are said to be deterrence, rehabilitation, and punishment. However, prisons do not seem to deter crime, and only recently has the goal of rehabilitation been taken seriously. Numerous studies have found that prisons are not successful in rehabilitating their inmates and in fact often serve as "schools for crime." The only rehabilitation programs that appear to be effective are those that give inmates job training and work experience.

GLOSSARY

deviance: behavior that violates the norms of a particular society (**p. 254**).

social control: the ways in which a society encourages conformity to its norms and prevents deviance (**p. 255**).

stigma: an attribute or quality of an individual that is deeply discrediting (**p. 258**).

crime: an act or omission of an act that is prohibited by law (**p. 259**).

anomie: a state of normlessness (**p. 265**).

differential association: a theory that explains deviance as a learned behavior that is determined by the extent of a person's association with individuals who engage in such behavior (**p. 270**).

labeling: a theory that explains deviance as a societal reaction that brands or labels as deviant people who engage in certain behaviors (**p. 271**).

primary deviance: an act that results in the labeling of the offender as deviant (**p. 273**).

secondary deviance: behavior engaged in as a reaction to the experience of being labeled as deviant (**p. 273**).

recidivist: a criminal who is returned to prison after having served at least one term there (**p. 275**).

plea bargaining: a process in which a person charged with a crime agrees to plead guilty to a lesser charge (**p. 277**).

total institution: an organization that assumes total responsibility for every aspect of the lives of the people who live within it (**p. 277**).

WHERE TO FIND IT

Books

The Outsiders: Studies in the Sociology of Deviance (Howard Becker; Free Press, 1963). An original application of the interactionist and labeling perspectives to the study of deviance and crime, using empirical examples.

The Limits of Law Enforcement (Hans Zeisel; University of Chicago Press, 1982). A well-reasoned analysis of the possibilities of and constraints on law enforcement agencies.

Thinking About Crime (James Q. Wilson; Vintage Books, 1977). A more conservative analysis of crime and crime control than that presented by Zeisel and others. Wilson is a major proponent of swifter punishment and more effective enforcement of criminal laws.

Stigma: Notes on the Management of Spoiled Identity (Erving Goffman; Prentice-Hall, 1982). A classic study of how people who differ from the norm are often labeled as deviant. Explores the consequences of such labeling.

The Cocaine Kids (Terry Williams; Addison-Wesley, 1989). A brilliant qualitative study of teenagers enmeshed in a large city's drug industry. Shows successful dealers to be rational entrepreneurs serving the needs of a deviant subculture.

Other Sources

Uniform Crime Reports: Crime in the U.S. An annual report on criminal offenses, arrests, and law enforcement employment. Data are reported by local police departments to the Federal Bureau of Investigation and published by the U.S. Department of Justice.

National Crime Survey A continuing series of reports on the incidence of crime throughout the United States. Published by the U.S. Department of Justice.

Sourcebook of Criminal Justice Statistics A comprehensive annual compilation of statistics on criminal and related matters. Issued by the Bureau of Justice Statistics.

VISUAL SOCIOLOGY

The Hobo

Sociologist Douglas Harper has spent years studying the lives of people on urban skid rows and in hobo jungles. These are deviant populations according to the dominant norms of society. In Merton's typology (see Figure 9-3), the "bums," "hoboes," and "tramps" whom Harper described would be classified as retreatists. But this term itself can become a superficial label, and unless social scientists attempt to discover what the worlds of such people are like, they are all simply lumped together as "deviant" when in fact there are norms and statuses and processes of socialization in these worlds also, which enable the people in them to survive.

In his book *Good Company* (1982), from which these photos are taken, Harper discusses his experiences as a participant observer in the hobo's world. He contrasts the life of hoboes who still ride freight trains and find casual labor in the cities and western fruit farms, with the more sedentary life of skid-row "bums." On his trip West, Harper met Carl, an experienced hobo who became the sociologist's mentor. In this excerpt Harper describes how what he learned was related to his friendship with Carl:

Carl accepted my food because he was down and out, but he knew I was not a regular and he was suspicious of what he'd have to pay. During our first days together he realized I did not really know what to expect from him and he warned: "Some people on this road are helpless. When you start helpin' it's just like having a son. . . . They don't know where it stops! You got to support them—take care of them—you got to provide the hand and I won't do that. If a fella is on this road and he can't learn—then to hell with him." . . .

But even though Carl tried to make our relationship typical, it never was. At first he taught me how to make it on the road and ignored most of my questions. Something changed the chemistry between us and he stepped out of his normal role to tell me about his childhood, his parents, and his life before hitting the road. . . .

Just before I left he said: "I've noticed you change. You've learned that you can make it on the road—now if something overloads it'll always be in the back of your mind. . . . You watch yourself—you'll be reverting back." [pp. 141, 142]

Harper's photos are an important part of the material he collected. They became "a visual inventory of typical behavior in typical spaces—for this group." But the photos could not intrude on his participation in the tramp life, as he relates in the following passage:

As I involved myself more I had to reassess my purpose and methods. I could have continued as I had begun and produced a photographic study from the viewpoint of an outsider, but as I felt myself pulled into the life, my photographic activity changed very much. . . . I made few photographs during my time with Carl. I introduced myself as a writer and photographer and he did not seem to mind my taking pictures until we encountered people he'd known for a long time; then he made it clear that to carry on would be out of the question. . . . The relationship between the photographer and subject in a fieldwork experience is very complicated, but for me the rights and desires of the individuals we choose as subjects are more important than a final purpose that would justify making images when they would not be welcomed. The camera must sometimes be left behind. [pp. 146, 147]

CHAPTER OUTLINE

- **The Meanings of Disorder**
  - The Nature of Collective Behavior
  - A Typology of Spontaneous Collective Behaviors
  - Dimensions of Social Movements

- **Social Movement Theory**
  - Theories of Revolution
  - Social Movements and Charisma
  - Theories of Mass Society

- **Social Movements in Everyday Life**
  - Resource Mobilization Theory

- **Mass Publics and Public Opinion**
  - Mass Publics
  - Public Opinion

Owen Franken/Sygma

Ku Klux Klan cross burning

CHAPTER 10

COLLECTIVE BEHAVIOR AND MASS PUBLICS

On Max Weber's only trip to the United States, in 1904, he made an astute observation. "The Americans are a wonderful people," he wrote. "Only the Negro question and the terrible immigration form a big, black cloud" (Marianne Weber, 1975/1926, p. 315). The great sociologist's comments were prophetic. A few years after his visit, the smoldering tensions between blacks and immigrants erupted in Chicago in a race riot that would change American history.

At the time of Weber's visit, millions of European immigrants were jammed into the slums of northern cities and industrial towns. The bulk of the Asian immigrants were in the West, where they struggled against economic hardships and the terrors of the Oriental-exclusion movement. Most of the black population was concentrated in the rural South, where they were subjected to violent abuse by lynch mobs, brutal public beatings, vigilante raids by the Ku Klux Klan and other extremist groups, and the grinding pressures of poverty. No wonder European social scientists sometimes shook their heads and noted that the "Negro question" was America's most tragic dilemma.

American blacks had gained their legal freedom at the end of the Civil War, but everywhere one looked there was evidence of the racial caste system known as Jim Crow. Usually the inferior and subordinate position of blacks was enforced through the routine norms of daily life. For "uppity niggers" who might get out of hand, violence was a quick solution and one that carried a clear message to other blacks: Retribution would be swift for those who "forgot their place."

Despite the systematic violence aimed at them, African-Americans never gave up their claim to a share of the American Dream. The young sociologist W. E. B. DuBois and other black intellectuals challenged the racial caste system and created the ideology of "the new Negro." There was an accelerating movement of blacks toward the relatively greater freedom and opportunity that could be found in the North. These changes formed the basis of black resistance to the caste system, a resistance marked to this day by outbreaks of severe rioting, on the one hand, and the slower, more painstaking activity of the civil rights movement on the other.

Just fifteen years after Weber's American tour, in 1919, a bloody riot broke out between blacks and whites in Chicago. It began at a public beach when black bathers, who believed that a young black boy who had drowned had been stoned by whites, began stoning the white bathers. The truth or falsehood of the rumors that raged through the city during the ensuing week of violence made little difference to the rioters. They defined the situation as one in which violence was justified both for self-defense and for revenge. As William Tuttle describes it,

Once ignited on July 27, the rioting raged virtually uncontrolled for the greater part of five days. Day and night white toughs assaulted isolated blacks, and teenage black mobsters beat white peddlers and merchants. . . . As rumors of atrocities circulated throughout the city, members of both races craved vengeance. White gunmen in automobiles sped through the black belt shooting indiscriminately as they passed, and black snipers fired back. Roaming mobs shot, beat, and stabbed to death their victims. The undermanned police force was an ineffectual deterrent to the waves of violence which soon overflowed the environs of the black belt and flooded the North and West Sides of the Loop, Chicago's downtown business district. Only several regiments of state militiamen and a cooling rain finally quenched the passions of the rioters, and even then sporadic outbursts punctuated the atmosphere for another week. The toll was awesome. Police officers had fatally wounded seven black men during the riot. Vicious mobs and lone gunmen had brutally murdered an additional sixteen blacks and fifteen whites, and well over 500 Chicagoans of both races had sustained injuries. [1978, pp. 9–10]

THE MEANINGS OF DISORDER

Imagine what it must have been like on that Lake Michigan beach when the riot broke out. Suddenly a peaceful beach scene is transformed into chaos and extreme violence. Most people are panic-stricken. They round up their children, assemble their belongings, and run for safety. Others remain behind and join in the fray. It seems as if the world has been turned upside down. Order is replaced by uncertainty, disorder, danger, rage.

How often such events occur in the modern world! Before you complete this course angry riots may occur in South Africa or the Philippines or Latin America, or perhaps in this country. But these terrifying episodes are not isolated events. They are symptoms of social conflict and forerunners of the social movements that bring about changes of all kinds.

In the aftermath of the bitter Chicago riot, Chicago blacks initiated a new phase in the history of race relations in the United States. In the past, in both the South and the North, blacks had usually been the victims of collective behavior. They had been terrorized by lynch mobs, vigilante groups, and gangs of street toughs, and the violence directed against them had helped maintain their position as a separate caste in American society. But in the Chicago riot and in other race riots that took place at about the same time, blacks stood their ground and fought back. And out of the fighting came a heightened sense of their own power and a determination not to allow themselves to be treated as inferior.

In this chapter we look closely at outbreaks of civil disorder of all kinds, and especially at the great uprisings associated with revolutions and with the birth of new social institutions. Such momentous episodes, in which masses of people rage through the streets, are the most severe form of collective behavior. The race riots that occurred during the civil rights movement in the United States, the huge rallies and demonstrations that ushered in the Nazi regime in pre-World War II Germany, the strikes and picketing that

Caught up in the frenzy of violence that accompanied the infamous Chicago race riot of 1919, these men are stoning a black man.

Chicago Historical Society

spurred the labor movement, the demonstrations that enlivened the women's movement in the 1970s, the riots and demonstrations in Romania and other Eastern European dictatorships in 1989, and the rioting by young blacks in South Africa against apartheid—these are examples of the mass events that have shaped history in our own time.

But there are less extensive and less dangerous incidents of mass behavior in modern societies that are nonetheless important. Think of the panic that occurs when a local bank is rumored to be short of funds, the fear and crankiness of the drivers outside service stations during a gasoline shortage, or the joyful anticipation of the crowds that form outside ticket offices when a popular rock star announces a concert. These events also have economic and social significance: Banks fail when panicked depositors suddenly withdraw their savings; politicians watch their popularity ratings decline; rock promoters wait in gleeful anticipation of full houses as the lines of ticket buyers form.

In fact, during the past fifty years many sectors of the American economy have profited from the behavior of large numbers of people. The fast-food industry, for example, depends on the behavior of the millions of Americans who stop for burgers and fries as they stream home from beaches or concerts or movies. Every year the toy industry produces gimmicks like the Cabbage Patch Kids or Teenage Mutant Ninja Turtles (Heros on the Half Shell), or toys that can be transformed from cars and trucks into killer robots, and fortunes are made and lost on the accuracy of predictions about whether the public will embrace such notions. The computer industry also has profited from fads and crazes: In the early 1980s people rushed to buy personal computers and computer games, partly because many parents believed that without a computer in the home their children would be unable to cope with the new demands of a changing society.

The study of mass or collective behavior encompasses a wide range of phenomena and presents many problems of classification and explanation. Yet this subject deserves our attention here because of its influence on social change. The student occupation of Beijing's Tiananmen Square; the strikes and protests in Poland, Czechoslovakia, Hungary, and Romania that toppled Communist dictatorships; the jubilant crowds that welcomed Nelson Mandela after his release from prison in 1990—all attest to the immense power of people who are moved to collective action for social change.

In our attempt to understand the nature and importance of these behaviors we turn first to the concepts that define their similarities and differences. From there we turn to theories regarding why these episodes occur, how social movements mobilize, and with what consequences. Finally, we discuss the concept of mass publics, especially the leisure and consumption behavior of large populations.

The Nature of Collective Behavior

The term **collective behavior** refers to a continuum of unusual or nonroutine behaviors engaged in by large numbers of people. At one extreme of this continuum is the spontaneous behavior of people who react to situations they perceive as uncertain, threatening, or extremely attractive. The violent rioting of the crowds in the Chicago race riot in 1919 is one example of spontaneous collective behavior. Another is the sudden action of coalminers who decide that conditions in the mines are unsafe and walk off their jobs in a sudden and unplanned wildcat strike. Such behaviors are not governed by the routine norms that control behavior at the beach or on the job (Smelser, 1962).

At the other extreme of the continuum of collective behaviors are rallies, demonstrations, marches, protest meetings, festivals, and similar events. These involve large numbers of people in nonroutine behaviors, but they are organized by leaders and have specific goals. When workers in a union plan a strike, for example, their picketing and rallies are forms of organized collective behavior whose purpose is to demonstrate their solidarity and their determination to obtain their demands. When blacks marched in commemoration of those who died in the 1919 race riot, the event was organized to build solidarity and publicize a new determination to resist racism. In such cases the organization that plans the event and uses collective behavior to make its feelings or demands known is a **social movement**. Social movements are intentional efforts by groups in a society to create new institutions or reform existing ones. Such movements often grow out of more spontaneous episodes of collective behavior, and once they are organized, they continue to plan collective events to promote their causes (Blumer, 1978; Genevie, 1978). Some movements, like the antiabortion (pro-life) movement, resist change; others, like the labor movement, have brought about far-reaching changes in social institutions.

The American labor movement provides many examples of the ways in which spontaneous episodes of collective behavior and the social movements associated with them can change the course of a society's development. During the nation's stormy transition from an agrarian to an industrial society, workers fought against the traditional right of employers to establish individual wage rates and to hire and fire workers as they pleased. They demanded instead the right to organize unions that could negotiate a collective wage rate (collective bargaining) for each category of workers. They also demanded better working conditions and benefits. Mass picketing, sit-down strikes, and pitched battles between workers and company agents or the police were everyday events in the 1890s.

Often the workers joined in walkouts, rioting, or other spontaneous collective actions when faced with mine disasters or intolerable working conditions. From these episodes of bitter conflict emerged the modern labor movement. In the ensuing decades, culminating in the period of New Deal legislation in the 1930s, the workers' demand for collective bargaining was *institutionalized*. By this we mean that the right to join unions and to bargain collectively was incorporated into the nation's laws. Labor unions thereby became recognized organizations and collective

> **Social movements are intentional efforts by groups in a society to create new institutions or reform existing ones.**

This crowd of demonstrators in Hong Kong is protesting the military assault on students in Beijing's Tiananmen Square in the spring of 1989.

© Gina Doggett

bargaining the recognized means of settling labor disputes. The unions, in turn, had to discipline their workers by specifying when collective behavior such as strikes and other actions could be used. In sum, the labor union and collective bargaining had become legitimate social institutions. Strikes were permitted only at certain times (e.g., when labor contracts expired), and the unions themselves discouraged wildcat strikes and other unorganized collective behaviors.

The range of spontaneous collective behaviors is extremely large. Such behaviors extend from the demonstrations and riots that mark major revolutions to the fads, fashions, crazes, and rumors that sweep through modern societies with such rapidity that what is new and shocking one day will be a subject of nostalgia the next. Some of these types of collective behavior become associated with social movements, but many do not. For example, in the early 1970s the craze known as streaking (in which one or more people ran nude in front of a large gathering) called attention to other forms of public nudity. Suddenly the number of beaches, parks, and recreation areas where people were going nude increased dramatically (Douglas and Rasmussen, 1977; Fortin

and Ecker, 1978), and people who believed in the goodness of nude living joined forces with the older naturist movement to sponsor "nude-ins" and other collective events that publicized their beliefs. But the naturist movement has not given rise to organizations dedicated to expressing nudist values; there is no nudist movement comparable to the civil rights movement or the women's movement.

A Typology of Spontaneous Collective Behaviors

Sociologists who study collective behavior try to discover the conditions under which different types of spontaneous collective behavior occur and why these events do or do not become linked to social movements. Typologies that classify these phenomena are an important first step toward understanding why collective behavior assumes particular forms and develops through recognizable stages.

Crowds and Masses. Students of spontaneous forms of collective behavior often begin by examining the structure of such behavior—that is, by discovering whether the people who engage in a particular kind of behavior are in close proximity to one another or whether they are connected in a more indirect way. In this regard it is useful to dis-

Collective behavior can occur in crowds, masses, or both.

© S.P.A.D.E.M.

The title of this famous photograph, "Mordus du cyclisme," means "bitten by cycling." These inhabitants of a Parisian neighborhood give their local heros a sendoff during the cycling craze that swept the country at the turn of the century.

tinguish between crowds and masses. A **crowd** is a large number of people gathered in close proximity, for example at a demonstration or a football game. A **mass** is more diffuse; it does not occur in a physical setting. A mass is a large number of people oriented toward a set of shared symbols or social objects (Lofland, 1981); an example is the audience for a particular television program. Collective behavior can occur in crowds, in masses, or in both at once.

Motivating Emotions. The actual behavior a crowd or mass generates depends largely on the emotions evoked by particular social situations. The Salem witch hunt described in Chapter 9 developed out of fear and hysteria among the mass of Puritan New Englanders. Hostility aroused by anger, desire for revenge, or enraged hatred is another common motivating emotion in episodes of collective behavior. Lynch mobs are one kind of hostile crowd. The crowd of angry strikers that violently opposes "scabs" trying to cross a picket line is another. At the mass level, the outbreak of animosity toward the Exxon Oil Corporation in 1989 following a huge oil spill by one of its tankers in Alaska is an example of collective behavior provoked by hostility.

Joy is a third important emotion that motivates crowds and masses. The Mardi Gras celebrations in Latin America and New Orleans involve large, joyful crowds that create a "moral holiday" in which behaviors are tolerated that would not be acceptable in public at other times. At the mass level, the joy that swept through the American population in 1980 when the hostages who had been held captive in Iran for over a year were finally released is an example of joyful collective behavior.

By cross-classifying the most significant emotions (fear, hostility, and joy) that motivate collective behavior with the structural dimensions of crowd and mass, sociologist John

The emotions that may motivate collective behavior include fear, hostility, and joy.

Lofland created a typology that includes a wide range of spontaneous collective behaviors. This typology is presented in Figure 10-1. Can you think of examples of your own for the various types? Where, for example, would you place the Boston Tea Party, the riots that often occur during spring break in Florida, or the massive party that took place in the Los Angeles Coliseum after the closing ceremonies of the 1984 Summer Olympics?

The Lofland typology is useful as a means of classifying some types of collective behavior, but remember that often there are interactions among these categories: Mass behavior may turn into crowd behavior; spontaneous collective behavior may generate a social movement. For example, when the stock market crashed in 1929, at the beginning of the Great Depression, crowds of panic-stricken investors spilled onto the streets of the financial districts of New York, Chicago, and San Francisco. There, within sight of one another, people found their fears magnified. And those fears quickly spread through the mass of Americans. The panic started among people who had made investments on credit, but it spread to people who merely had savings in local banks. Crowds of terrified savers descended on the banks, which were unable to handle the sudden demand for withdrawals because they themselves had been investing in stocks that were suddenly worthless. As a result, millions of Americans lost all of their savings. In the aftermath of the stock market crash and the resulting mass panic, social movements formed to seek reforms that would protect investors against similar episodes in the future. Nevertheless, local banks still occasionally fail, in part because of panicky "runs" by depositors.

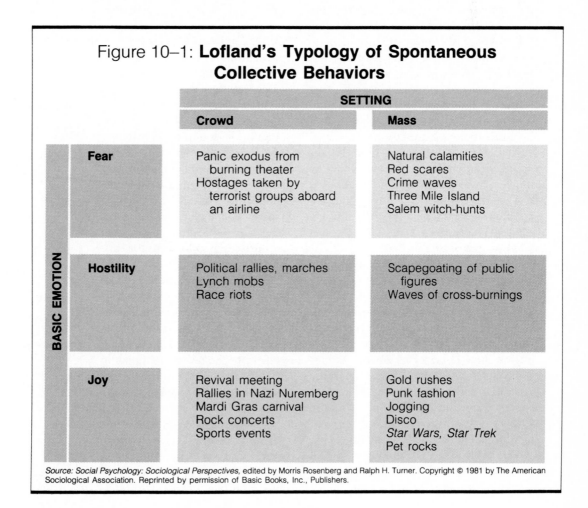

Figure 10–1: **Lofland's Typology of Spontaneous Collective Behaviors**

		SETTING	
BASIC EMOTION		**Crowd**	**Mass**
	Fear	Panic exodus from burning theater Hostages taken by terrorist groups aboard an airline	Natural calamities Red scares Crime waves Three Mile Island Salem witch-hunts
	Hostility	Political rallies, marches Lynch mobs Race riots	Scapegoating of public figures Waves of cross-burnings
	Joy	Revival meeting Rallies in Nazi Nuremberg Mardi Gras carnival Rock concerts Sports events	Gold rushes Punk fashion Jogging Disco *Star Wars, Star Trek* Pet rocks

Source: Social Psychology: Sociological Perspectives, edited by Morris Rosenberg and Ralph H. Turner. Copyright © 1981 by The American Sociological Association. Reprinted by permission of Basic Books, Inc., Publishers.

Dimensions of Social Movements

There are as many types of social movements as there are varieties of spontaneous collective behavior. Just think of how many "causes" can motivate people to take organized action. We have a social-welfare movement, a civil rights movement, a women's movement, an environmental-protection movement, a consumer movement, an animal-rights movement, and on and on. Within each of these movements numerous organizations attempt to speak for everyone who supports the movement's goals.

Classifying Social Movements. Social movements have been classified into four categories based on the goals they seek to achieve:

1. *Revolutionary movements* seek to overthrow existing stratification systems and institutions and replace them with new ones (Hopper, 1950). The Russian Bolsheviks who founded the Communist party were a revolutionary social movement that sought to eliminate the class structure of Russian society. They also believed that the institutions of capitalism—the market and private property—must be replaced with democratic worker groups or *soviets* whose efforts would be directed by a central committee. Meanwhile certain other institutions, especially religion and the family, had to be either eliminated or drastically altered.

2. *Reformist movements* seek partial changes in some institutions and values, usually on behalf of some segments of society rather than all. The labor movement was basically reformist. It sought to alter the institutions of private property by requiring the owners of businesses to bargain collectively with workers concerning wages and working conditions and to reach an agreement that would apply to all the workers in the firm. This would replace the old system of individual contracts between workers and employers, but it would not totally destroy the institution of private property.

3. *Conservative movements* seek to uphold the values and institutions of society and generally resist attempts to change them, unless their goal is to undo undesired changes that have already occurred. The conservative movement in the United States seeks to reinforce the values and functions of capitalist institutions and to support the traditional values of such institutions as the family and the church.

4. *Reactionary movements* seek to return to the institutions and values of the past and, therefore, to do away with some or all existing social institutions and cultural values (Cameron, 1966). The Ku Klux Klan is part of a reactionary social movement that seeks a return to the racial caste system that was supported by American legal institutions (laws, courts, and the police) until the 1954 Supreme Court decision that declared the "separate but equal" doctrine unconstitutional.

Other Types of Movements. Although they cover some of the movements that have had the greatest impact on modern societies, the categories just described do not include all the possible types of movements. Herbert Blumer (1969), for example, identified a fifth category, *expressive social movements*, or movements devoted to the expression of personal beliefs and feelings. Those beliefs and feelings may be religious or ethical or may involve an entire life-style, as in the case of the punk movement of the 1980s. An important aspect of expressive social movements is that their members typically reject the idea that their efforts ought to be directed at changing society or the behavior of people who do not belong to their movement. Their quest is for personal expression, and if others choose to "see the light," that is welcome.

Other social scientists who recognize the diversity of social movements either identify more categories or develop subcategories that combine elements of those outlined earlier. For example, in *The Pursuit of the Millen-*

> *Expressive social movements are devoted to the expression of personal beliefs and feelings; millenarian movements envision a better world to come.*

nium (1961), Norman Cohen analyzed what are known as *messianic* or *millenarian* movements, which are both revolutionary and expressive. Often these begin as small movements with a charismatic leader (someone who seems to possess special powers) and a few devoted followers. These movements envision a perfect society of the future, "a new Paradise on earth, a world purged of suffering and sin, a Kingdom of the Saints" (p. xiii).

An example of a millenarian movement is the People's Temple, whose 900 members committed suicide by drinking cyanide-laced Kool-Aid in Jonestown, Guyana, on November 18, 1979. In his insightful study of the events leading up to the tragedy, sociologist John Hall (1987) demonstrates that popular interpretations of this shocking story are inadequate. The conclusion reached in most previous accounts is that the movement's leader, Jim Jones, was a deranged personality who acted as the Anti-Christ and led his misguided followers to their death. Such accounts, according to Hall, may be comforting expressions of moral outrage, but by exaggerating the influence of an individual personality they lead to wrong ideas about how such tragedies can occur.

In his analysis of the Jonestown tragedy, Hall shows that the members of the People's Temple were part of a cohesive social movement. Many were of modest means, some quite poor; in addition, many were black. They felt alienated from the larger society and saw the Temple as their community and often as their family. It is only by understanding the strength of their attachments to one another and to their belief in Jones's vision of a better world to come that one can make sense of what appears to be a senseless, insane episode of collective behavior. Faced with what they perceived as imminent attacks on the religious community they were building in the jungle, the Temple members worked themselves into a frenzy in which they became convinced that by drinking the poison they were "stepping over" into a better world. Hall's study shows that Jones planned the act of "collective martyrdom" but that the vast majority of the Temple members followed to the end because of their unshaken belief in the goals of their social movement.

SOCIAL MOVEMENT THEORY

Collective behavior and social movements can be placed along a continuum according to how much they change the societies in which they occur. At one end of the continuum are revolutions; at the other are fads or crazes. In this century there have been three revolutions that have had a major impact on world history: the Communist revolutions in Russia and China and the Fascist revolution that brought Hitler to power in 1933. These can be placed at the high end of the continuum. At the low end are fads and crazes that may excite us for a while but usually do not bring about lasting change in the major structures of society (Turner, 1974). Some people become so completely involved in a fad or craze—as occurred, for example, in the case of the game of Trivial Pursuit—that they devote all their energies to the new activity.

Between the two extremes of revolutions and fads are social movements that capture the attention of masses of people and have varying effects on the societies in which they occur. The women's movement, the civil rights movement, and the environmental-protection movement are examples of movements with broad membership in many nations and the continuing power to bring about social change. The antinuclear movement, the antismoking movement, the pro-life movement, the pro-choice movement, the evangelical movement, and the hospice movement (see Chapter 14) are examples of more narrowly focused movements that are concerned with a single issue or set of issues but also exert powerful pressure for change in the United States and other societies. Then there are movements that may involve large numbers of people for a brief time but have limited effects on society. An example is the movement to aid famine victims in Africa. In the United States, concern about hunger in Ethiopia originated among a small number of people, but when rock-music promoters enlisted the help of major artists and the music industry to produce the benefit record "We Are the World" and the Live Aid Concert, millions of Americans took notice of the situation, and by buying records and attending concerts they contributed to famine relief. These more transient social movements serve to "raise consciousness" about a social condition, but they do not usually bring about lasting social change.

Theories of collective behavior and social movements often seek to explain the origins and effects of revolutionary and reform movements (McAdam, McCarthy, and Zald, 1988). In the remainder of this section we discuss several such theories. We begin by examining the nature of revolutions and revolutionary movements. Then we consider three theories that attempt to explain why major revolutions and revolutionary social movements have arisen and what factors have enabled them to succeed. Note that these are macro-level theories: They explain revolutions and the associated social movements as symptoms of even larger-scale social change.

Theories of Revolution

Sociologists often distinguish between "long revolutions," or large-scale changes in the ecological relationships of humans to the earth and to one another (e.g., the rise of capitalism and the industrial revolution), and revolutions that are primarily social or political in nature (Braudel, 1984; Wolf, 1984). The course of world history is shaped by long revolutions, whereas individual societies are transformed by social revolutions like those that occurred in the United States and Russia.

Political and Social Revolutions. Sociologist Theda Skocpol (1979) makes a further distinction between political and social revolutions. **Political revolutions** are transformations in the political structures and leadership of a society that are not accompanied by a full-scale rearrangement of the society's productive capacities, culture, and stratification system. **Social revolutions**, on the other hand, sweep away the old order. They not only change the institutions of government but also bring about basic changes in social stratification. Both political and social revolutions are brought about by revolutionary social movements as well as by external forces like colonialism.

The American Revolution, according to Skocpol's theory, was a political revolution. The minutemen who fought against British troops in the Battle of Concord were a political revolutionary group. They did not at first seek to change American society in radical ways. On the other hand, the revolutions that destroyed the existing social order in Russia and China in this century were social revolutions. Their goal was to transform the class structure and institutions of their societies.

Why do revolutionary social movements arise, and what makes some of them content mainly with seizing power while others call for a complete reorganization of society? For most of this century the answer has been some version of Marxian conflict theory, which we examined in Chapter 8. This theory uses detailed knowledge of existing societies to predict the shape of future ones. According to Marx, the world would become capitalist; then capitalist markets would fall under the control of monopolies; impoverished workers and colonial peoples would rebel in a generation of mass social movements and revolutions; and a new, classless society would be created in which the workers would own the means of production.

> *According to the theory of relative deprivation, revolution arises out of a feeling of deprivation relative to other groups in the society.*

Relative Deprivation. The idea that the increasing misery of the working class would lead workers to join revolutionary social movements was not Marx's only explanation of the causes of revolution. He also believed that under some conditions, "although the enjoyments of the workers have risen," their level of dissatisfaction could rise even faster owing to the much greater increase in the "enjoyments of the capitalists, which are inaccessible to the worker" (Marx and Engels, 1955, vol. 1, p. 94). This is a version of the theory known as **relative deprivation** (Stouffer et al., 1949). According to this theory, the presence of deprivation (i.e., poverty or misery) does not by itself explain why people join revolutionary social movements. Instead, it is the feeling of deprivation relative to others. We tend to measure our own well-being against that of others, and even if we are doing fairly well, if they are doing better we are likely to feel a sense of injustice and, sometimes, extreme anger. It is this feeling of deprivation relative to others that gives rise to revolutionary social movements.

Alexis de Tocqueville came to the same conclusion in his study of the causes and results of the French Revolution. He was struck by the fact that the revolution did not occur in the seventeenth century, when the economic conditions of the French people were in severe decline. Instead, it occurred in the eighteenth century, a period of rapid economic growth. Tocqueville concluded that "revolutions are not always brought about by a gradual decline from bad to worse. Nations that have endured patiently and almost unconsciously the most overwhelming oppression often burst into rebellion against the yoke the moment it begins to grow lighter" (1955/1856, p. 214).

> *Social movements usually go through several stages of development in which they become more broad based and better organized.*

As we can see from the democratic movements that are occurring today in the Soviet Union, China, and the nations of Eastern Europe, the revolutionary changes that Marx sought to explain have not altered societies the way he predicted they would. There is a crisis in modern Marxian theory, a crisis brought on by its failure to predict the emergence of new patterns of stratification in the Soviet Union after the initial stages of the revolution, as well as its failure to predict the impact of reformist movements on the situation of workers in capitalist societies (Sweezy, 1980). Most sociologists would agree that this problem stems in part from lack of attention to the changes in organizational structure that social movements typically go through. This is the central focus of the Weberian approach to the analysis of social movements, to which we will now turn.

Social Movements and Charisma

Social movements of all kinds usually go through several stages of development (Dawson and Gettys, 1935; Lang and Lang, 1961):

1. The movement arises during a period of social unrest, with a prophet or agitator as its leader. (Lenin emerges as the charismatic leader of the Bolsheviks after Russia has been devastated by World War I.)
2. As the movement builds, it creates popular excitement in which the vision of the agitator-prophet spreads to growing numbers of people. (The ideology of communism spreads among supporters of the Bolsheviks.)
3. As the movement gains strength, it enters a stage of formal organization, with the beginnings of a division of labor, formal criteria for membership, bureaucratic rules, and so on. (Lenin argues for the power of the Communist party organization against the Communists of the "left," who believe the masses should have more influence over the party.)
4. In its mature stage the movement is institutionalized; that is, it becomes a bureaucracy led by career officials rather than by prophets or agitators. (After Lenin's death, Stalin creates a bureaucratic organization that evolves into a totalitarian dictatorship.)

The literature on social movements is full of debates about whether these four stages are inevitable and why they occur (Moe, 1980; Oberschall, 1973; Tilly, 1978; Turner, 1981). But on one point there is little argument: Social movements initially tend to form around the personality and ideals of a charismatic leader.

The Institutionalization of Charisma.
Charisma, as Weber (1968) defined it, refers to the special qualities that motivate people to follow a particular leader. The charismatic leader appears to possess extraordinary "gifts of the body and spirit" that mark him or her

as specially chosen to lead. The voices that Joan of Arc heard, which convinced her to take up arms to save France, gave her the inspired commitment to her cause that is a central feature of charisma. Mohandas Gandhi, probably this century's greatest example of a charismatic leader, swayed the Indian masses with his almost supernatural spirituality and courage. Similarly, Martin Luther King Jr.'s extraordinary gifts of oratory, faith, and energy allowed him to emerge as the most influential leader of the American civil rights movement. But all of these charismatic leaders faced the problem of how to motivate their followers to continue the movement after they themselves died.

Scholars who follow Weber's lead in this area of research have termed this problem the *institutionalization of charisma* (Shils, 1970). Every social movement must incorporate the goals and gifts of its leaders into the structure of the movement and eventually into the institutions of society without losing track of the movement's original purpose and values. Weber recognized that the more successful a movement became in taking power and assuming authority, the more difficult it would be for it to retain the zeal and motivation of its charismatic founders. Once the leaders had power and could obtain special privileges for themselves, they would resist continued efforts to do away with inequalities of wealth and power. Perhaps the most instructive example of this problem is the institutionalization of the ideals of Marx and Lenin in the organization of the Bolshevik party in Russia after the revolution of 1917.

"Workers of the world unite," Marx urged in *The Communist Manifesto*; "you have nothing to lose but your chains" (Marx and Engels, 1969/1848). The vision of a society in which poverty, social injustice, repression, war, and all the evils of capitalism would be eliminated formed the core of Marxian socialism. The founders of the Bolshevik party realized, however, that revolutions are not made with slogans and visions alone (Schumpeter, 1950). The unification of the workers required an organization that not only would carry forward the revolution but also would take the lead in mobilizing the Russian masses to work for the ideals of socialism. The char-

ismatic leader who built this organization was Vladimir Ilyich Lenin.

Under the leadership of Lenin—and far more ruthlessly under his successor Josef Stalin—any Bolshevik who challenged party discipline was exiled or killed. Because the goals of the Bolsheviks were so radical and the need for reform so pressing, Lenin and Stalin argued that the party had to exert total control over its members in order to prevent spontaneous protests that might threaten the party's goals. By the same logic, other parties had to be eliminated and dissenters imprisoned. Such efforts by an elite to exert control over all forms of organizational life in a society are known as *totalitarianism*. It is ironic that a movement that was intended to liberate the masses ended by imposing new forms of control. However, this is an extreme case. Not all revolutionary movements become totalitarian, although they all appear to face this danger (Moore, 1968).

Co-optation. The Weberian view predicts that social movements will institutionalize their ideals in a bureaucratic structure. And the more successful they are in gaining the power to change society, the more they will be forced to control the activities of their members. In fact, once a movement is institutionalized, with an administration and bureaucratic rules, its leaders tend to influence new charismatic leaders to become part of their bureaucracy, a process that is known as *co-optation*. In the labor movement, for example, maverick leaders who demand reform and instigate protests in their plants are often given inducements such as jobs in the union administration to keep them under control (Geschwender, 1977; Kornhauser, 1952). In politics, a local party organization may identify a neighborhood leader with great personal appeal as someone who might become an opposition candidate in the future. Party leaders often attempt to recruit such an individual to their party by offering inducements such as support in an election campaign in return for loyalty to the party.

> *Through the process of co-optation, new charismatic leaders are persuaded to become part of an organization's bureaucratic structure.*

Box 10–1: **The Seizure of Power in a German Town**

When Adolf Hitler and the National Socialist (Nazi) party came to power in Germany in 1933, their victory was a result of over a decade of political organization. In less than fifteen years the party had grown from a fringe of right-wing radicals to the dominant organization in the nation. The Nazis won at the polls by playing on the deep fear of unemployment among middle-class Germans and on their distrust of the socialist ideas advanced by the labor movement. Hitler and his associates ignited the imagination of many Germans by appealing to their feelings of nationalism and anti-Semitism. But it was in hundreds of communities throughout Germany that the Nazi revolution became a reality.

In an insightful study of the Nazi seizure of power in one German town, William Allen (1965) described the rise of Nazism in Thalburg, a town of about 12,000 residents with a history extending from medieval times. Allen showed that, like other parties at that time, the local Nazis loved mass rallies and parades. They wanted people to demonstrate their support actively, not just to sympathize with them behind closed doors. But the Nazis

Culver Pictures, Inc.

were different from other parties in that they believed in the use of brute force; for example, they were not above using brass knuckles and knives to break up rival parties' meetings.

This use of force, together with the constant parades, was designed to convince citizens of the Nazis' competence and strength. As Hitler himself said, "Cruelty impresses. Cruelty and raw force. The simple man in the street is impressed only by brutal force and ruthlessness. Terror is the most effective political means" (Rauschning, 1940, p. 81).

Once in power, however, the Nazis of Thalburg used more insidious means to maintain their position. They immediately attacked the town's Jewish families, many of whom had lived there for more than two centuries and thought of themselves as German. The Nazis fired Jews from their jobs, ruined their businesses, and confiscated their property. These attacks were the first step in the "atomization" of the community. In subsequent steps, all the voluntary and civic associations of the community, including parent-teacher groups, sports leagues, and similar organizations, were either disbanded or taken over by the Nazis. As Allen put it,

Thalburg's Jews were simply excluded from the community at large. At the same time the Nazis undertook their most Herculean task: the atomization of the community. . . . Though the methods differed, the result was the same, and by the summer of 1933 individual Thalburgers were as cut off from effective intercourse with one another as the Jews had been from the rest of the townspeople. The total reorganization of the society was the most important result of the Nazi revolution. Eventually no independent social groups were to exist. . . . Ultimately all society, in terms of human relationships, would cease to exist, or rather would exist in a new framework whereby each individual related not to his fellow men but only to the state and to the Nazi leader who became the personal embodiment of the state. [1965, p. 214]

At the national level, in 1988 presidential hopeful Jesse Jackson was promised various positions in a new administration by Democratic party leaders who did not wish to support his bid for the presidential nomination.

Theories of Mass Society

Neither Marxian theories of class conflict nor Weberian explanations of the institutionalization of charisma explain why revolutionary movements have so often resorted to totalitarian methods and, even more important, why they have succeeded in imposing total controls on a seemingly compliant population. Sociologists often address these issues through the analysis of what is known as *mass society*.

The concept of mass society is based on the notion that change is so constant in modern societies that people experience anomie (a state of normlessness, of not knowing how to act in new or confusing situations). In their confusion, anomic individuals are easily drawn into panics, mob hysteria, or radical social movements. These, in turn, can lead to the failure of democratic institutions and the rise of totalitarianism. This hypothesis—that modern industrial societies produce anomic populations that are easily manipulated and led into collective behavior on a mass scale— is one version of what is often called the *theory of mass society*. Box 10-1 shows how, in the years before World War II, the Nazis used terror against Jewish citizens, together with the systematic destruction of community associations, to transform Germany into a mass society.

Conservative nineteenth-century social theorists attributed the normlessness of the masses to the increased participation of ordinary citizens in their society's cultural and political life and to the decline in the control exercised by aristocratic elites (Kornhauser, 1959). For example, the aristocratic social theorist Gustav LeBon described industrial societies as creating "an era of crowds" in which agitators and despots are heroes, "the populace is sovereign, and the tide of barbarism mounts" (1947/1896, pp. 14, 207).

LeBon developed the first modern theory of crowd behavior. In its usual definition, he pointed out, "the word 'crowd' means a gathering of individuals of whatever nationality, profession, or sex, and whatever be the chances that have brought them together." But from the psychological viewpoint a crowd can create conditions in which "the sentiments and ideas of all the persons in the gathering take one and the same direction, and their conscious personality vanishes" (quoted in Genevie, 1978, p. 9).

A similar point of view was expressed by Alexis de Tocqueville in his analysis of American democracy. Tocqueville worried that Americans' emphasis on equality would lead to a "tyranny of the majority." By this he meant that the society's leaders were subject to the will of a fickle majority. As a result, he wrote, "I believe it is easier to establish an absolute and despotic government among a people . . . in which the conditions of society are equal than among any other" (1956/1840, p. 322).

In a more optimistic version of the same theory, social theorist Edward Shils (1961) argues that "mass society has aroused and enhanced individuality. . . . Larger elements of the population have consciously learned to value the pleasures of eye, ear, taste, touch, and conviviality. People make choices more freely in every sphere of life. . . . The value of the experience of personal relationships is more widely appreciated" (p. 3). Shils admits that "a part of the population in mass society lives in a nearly vegetative torpor, reacting dully or aggressively to its environment" (p. 3). But the great promise of mass society, as he interprets it, is that an ever-increasing number can enjoy the cultural and material values once reserved for a small elite. This version of the mass society theory supports the hypothesis that all types of social movements may thrive in a mass society but that totalitarian regimes are bound to fail in the long run as a result of mounting demands for greater equality and political participation.

> *The concept of mass society is based on the notion that social change produces anomie, which in turn leads to collective behavior on a mass scale.*

SOCIAL MOVEMENTS IN EVERYDAY LIFE

Most of us will probably never belong to a revolutionary social movement, at least not one devoted to the violent overthrow of a government or society. Nor will many of us experience the deadening force of totalitarian rule. Most of us therefore will not find ourselves helping to rebuild the voluntary associations and communities, the leagues, the hobby groups, the unions and auxiliaries of our societies, as the people of many Eastern European nations are doing today. But many readers of this book will become members of a social movement, if they have not already done so. Even more readers will be members of associations that may have links to social movements. Membership in the Catholic Church, for example, is by no means the same as membership in the antiabortion movement, but there are similarities. Church resources are used to assist the movement in a variety of ways, including contributions of funds and encouragement of members to join the movement.

The resource mobilization problem refers to the ways in which social movements mobilize existing leaders and organizations to contribute support and resources to the movement.

As noted in Chapter 7, increasing membership in voluntary associations of all kinds appears to be a long-term trend in the United States. National surveys conducted in the 1950s found that about one-third of adult citizens were members of voluntary associations; today almost two-thirds of American adults say that they belong to a voluntary association (NORC, 1987). Between 1970 and the present the number of registered nonprofit associations of all kinds increased from somewhat over 10,000 to over 20,000. While a significant minority of Americans are not members of any voluntary organizations or congregations, the majority are active members (U.S. Census, 1987). From the standpoint of reform movements, the importance of these facts is that many of the activists in social movements are recruited from the ranks of voluntary associations (e.g., through mailing lists or membership meetings).

Even people who never join social movements will surely have their lives changed by them. The social critic H. L. Mencken once said that if three Americans are in a room together for more than an instant, two of them will try to change the morals of the third. Campaigns against smoking, drinking, rock lyrics, violence on television, wearing of furs, abortion, and many other behaviors would seem to confirm this notion. So too would patterns in the growth of different types of voluntary associations. Between 1970 and 1985 the number of nonprofit voluntary associations devoted to issues of education and culture increased by over 100 percent. The number of associations devoted to public issues increased by over 400 percent, while the number of associations devoted to ethnic and fraternal activities decreased by about 30 percent and the number of labor unions increased by only about 10 percent (U.S. Census, 1987).

Resource Mobilization Theory

What is the relationship between the range of organized voluntary associations in a society and the reform movements that seek to bring about social change? In sociology this is known as the *resource mobilization problem*, referring to the ways in which social movements mobilize existing leaders and organizations rather than simply relying on the participation of people who happen to be moved to action (Oberschall, 1973; Tilly, 1978; Walsh, 1981; Zurcher and Snow, 1981). A second, and related, issue is known as the *free-rider problem*. This refers to the tendency of many people not to lend their support and resources—time, money, and leadership—to social movements but to reap the benefits anyway (Marwell and Ames, 1985; Olsen, 1965, 1979).

Are these issues important? One need only think of all the American workers who

Table 10–1: **Telephone Survey Results Among Communities in the Three Mile Island Area**

	Subgroup Free Riders (%)	Total (%)	(*n*)
A. Opposed to TMI-1 restart and/or water dumping[a]			
1. Objective free riders[b]	87	43	(288)
2. Contributors		6	(42)
B. In favor of TMI-1 restart			
1. Objective free riders[b]	98	45	(303)
2. Contributors		1	(7)
C. Undecided		5	(33)
		100	(673)

[a] The primary focus of the Lancaster citizens' group was the prevention of the dumping of radioactive water from TMI-1 into the Susquehanna River.
[b] When those who say they never heard of their local SMOs are dropped from the totals, this reduces the percentages of anti-TMI free riders to 84% (213 of 253), and the pro-TMI percentage of free riders to 86% (42 of 49).
Source: Walsh and Warland, 1983.

have benefited from the gains won by the labor movement without themselves making the effort to form unions. Or consider the rapid growth of the environmental-protection movement in the late 1960s and early 1970s. What explains the speed with which that movement captured a central place in public-policy debates? In studying the growth of the movement for environmental quality, sociologist Carol Kronus (1977) found that out of a sample of 209 existing organizations in a midwestern city, more than half gave material and moral support to the new movement. And she found that the groups that did link up with the movement were ones whose goals were in agreement with those of the movement and whose members believed in taking action to improve the quality of life in their community. Free-rider groups, on the other hand, agreed that "something should be done about pollution" but felt that other groups should take action before they could do so.

The free-rider hypothesis predicts that some proportion of the potential members of a social movement will not lend their energies to the movement (Brubaker, 1975). But how many will withhold their participation? Conversely, what proportion will be active and what variables can be used to predict their membership? The answers to this and related questions are not yet clear.

An example of recent research on these issues is Edward J. Walsh and Rex H. Warland's (1983) study of the social movement that emerged after the near-meltdown of a nuclear reactor on Three Mile Island (TMI) near Middletown, Pennsylvania, in 1979. After the accident, anti-nuclear organizations grew in strength throughout the TMI area. Many opposed efforts to start up another reactor at the site, which had not been damaged in the accident. Walsh and Warland found that of those who opposed the start-up of the undamaged reactor, 87 percent were free riders in that they had not contributed in any

The free-rider hypothesis predicts that some proportion of the potential members of a social movement will not lend their energies to the movement.

way to the organizations that opposed the start-up. And of those in favor of the start-up, 98 percent were free riders. Only a very small percentage—6 percent of those in opposition and 1 percent of those in favor—actually participated. Although this is a small proportion, it does show that there are people who are ready to be mobilized as activists on an important social issue. Not everyone is an apathetic or alienated free rider (see Table 10-1).

In predicting the success of any given social movement, resource mobilization theory points out the need to consider how well a movement enlists or mobilizes the resources available to it—for example, how well the women's movement enlists the support of the larger array of women's organizations, how well it manages to convert members into activists, how well it motivates those activists to raise money and generate other resources (e.g., volunteer time), and how well it addresses the free-rider problem. All of these elements contribute to the overall goal of greater equality. Women may passionately desire the changes sought by the movement and may be ready to demonstrate in support of its goals in a crisis, but if resources are not mobilized well, that passion may be of little value and the lasting changes the movement seeks may never come about.

MASS PUBLICS AND PUBLIC OPINION

Most of the examples of social movements we have discussed in this chapter have had a lasting impact on the societies in which they occurred. In this section we apply the insights gained from earlier sections to some of the less world-shaking, yet still exciting, aspects of collective behavior in American life.

Over the past century North America has been transformed from a continent of wide-open spaces and agrarian pursuits to the earth's technologically most advanced and socially most mobile region. Indeed, for the rest of the world North America is synonymous with both the best and the worst aspects of what has come to be known as "modern" society.

In the United States no issue engenders as much controversy or organized collective activity as abortion. Activists on both sides of the issue have fought for reform of existing laws, and their organizational efforts often mobilize thousands of less active supporters.

© Freda Leinwand

Chicago Historical Society

By the 1890s, large, peaceful crowds like this one were an increasingly common feature of the urban scene in America. This photo shows spectators at the 1894 Columbian Exposition in Chicago. Scenes like this provided convincing evidence of the existence of a mass public that would spend increasing amounts of money on clothes, hats, and all manner of consumer goods as their ideas of fashion dictated.

According to Reinhard Bendix (1969), **modernization** consists of all the political and economic changes that accompany industrialization. Among the indicators of modernity are urbanization, the shift from agricultural to industrial occupations, and increasing literacy as well as the demand for greater political participation by the masses. Bendix is quick to point out that his definition does not necessarily apply everywhere in the world. Modernization may not always mean what it has meant in Western societies. But it is probable that, despite setbacks in some nations, modernization will always involve the extension of rights, values, and opportunities from the elites to the masses in a society.

None of these changes in the organization of societies came about without collective protests and social movements of all kinds.

For every radical movement there was a reactionary one, for every revolution a counterrevolution or at least an attempt at one. And social movements continue to exert pressure for change in our norms and institutions. The extension of voting rights to women and blacks had to be won through political struggle. Nor did the benefits of new technologies come automatically to American workers; they had to be won by the labor movement. Likewise, the rapidly expanding cities of North America became scenes of collective protest as new populations of immigrants and new occupational groups fought for "a piece of the pie" (Lieberson, 1980). It is hardly surprising, there-

Collective protests and social movements play an important part in the modernization of societies.

fore, that so much sociological research is devoted to studying how modern society came about, discovering how much further some groups have to go to gain their share of the benefits of modernity, and analyzing the role of collective behavior in these major social changes.

Consider just one important consequence of the labor movement of the late nineteenth and early twentieth centuries: the change in the length of the workweek. "Our lives shall not be sweated, from day until night closes," went the famous refrain of the Industrial Workers of the World, or Wobblies. "Hearts starve as well as bodies; give us bread but give us roses." Figure 10-2 shows how the demand for enough leisure to enjoy the finer things of life produced dramatic changes in the hours of work. Today we take the eight-hour day and the five-day week as the standard for full-time employment, but in another famous 1919 episode of collective behavior American steelworkers shut down the entire industry in protest against the twelve-hour day and the six-day week (Brody, 1960). The concessions won by them and other workers were an essential part of the extension of the benefits of modernity to working people of all classes. The increased leisure created by these changes in hours and days of work, along with greater social mobility owing to a higher overall level of affluence, contributed to the development of mass publics (see Box 10-2).

Mass Publics

Mass publics are large populations (regional or national) of potential spectators or participants who engage in collective behavior of all kinds. Typically this behavior consists of the formation of crowds, audiences, or streams of buyers and voters, but it can also include

> *Increased leisure and greater social mobility in modern societies have contributed to the development of mass publics.*

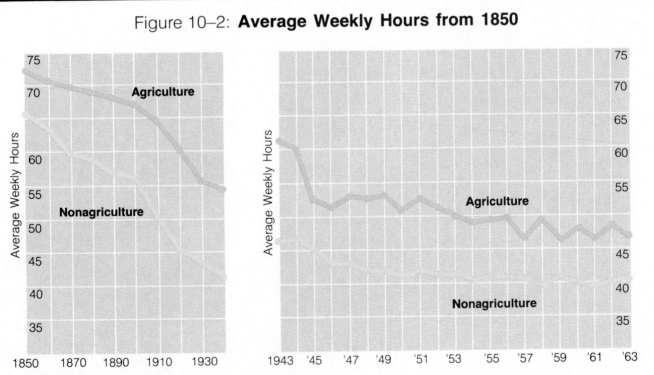

Figure 10–2: **Average Weekly Hours from 1850**

The brief increase in average hours of work between 1940 and 1943 (not shown on the chart) is due to the labor shortages that occurred during World War II.

Source: Data from Bureau of Labor Statistics; adapted from Dankert, Mann, and Northrup, 1965.

Box 10–2: **The Charles Dickens Show**

Do you ever glance at the popular magazines on supermarket racks while waiting in the checkout line? Many of the stories are about celebrities or "stars." What do you suppose it takes for those individuals to become stars?

When people lived in village societies, without roads, railroads, radio, television, or magazines, there was a need for roving entertainers who brought news of the distant royal courts to the people in the villages. Bards recited historical tales and related them to current events; minstrels sang ballads about the lives of the great and the legendary; actors often performed in open-air theaters. Few of these entertainers commanded great prestige, however. For example, Shakespeare's Globe Theatre was simply one of many rowdy places to which local people came for entertainment.

For entertainers like Diana Ross or the Beatles or Michael Jackson or Madonna to become celebrities, there first must be a mass public. Such entertainers must draw audiences from one end of the society to the other, which means that those audiences must share roughly the same values. And if people are going to travel to see a performer, they must be able to hear about the act; there must be media like the press and television that can promote it. There must also be people who concern themselves with scheduling, booking space, selling tickets, advertising, transporting, and otherwise making sure that the event meets people's expectations.

Who was the first celebrity in the modern sense? The English author Charles Dickens is a strong candidate. *A Christmas Carol, David Copperfield, Oliver Twist*, and other novels were serialized in magazines during the 1840s and 1850s and won him a devoted audience throughout the English-speaking world. His books were more widely read than those of any other living author, and he gave public readings from his work. Here is how Raymund FitzSimons (1970) describes Dickens and his audience:

The public readings of Charles Dickens were the greatest one-man show of the nineteenth century. "Dickens is coming!" was the ecstatic shout in towns where he was announced to read. In London the cheers that greeted his appearance on the platform could be heard a block away. In Edinburgh he had to calm a rioting audience. In Glasgow the audience tried to storm the platform and carry him away. In Boston, New York, and Philadelphia people queued for tickets all night in temperatures well below freezing point.

The excesses of his public would today be more associated with a pop star than a writer reading extracts from his own works. Yet, in the true sense of the term, Dickens was a pop star, one of the greatest of all time. . . . The readings appealed, as did the books, to all ages and to all tastes, cultivated and simple. It was this universal appeal that put the readings into a different category from all other entertainments. . . .

For the readings were an entertainment . . . Dickens was a magnificent actor,

Charles Dickens

with a wonderful talent for mimicry. He seemed able to alter not only his voice, his features, and his carriage but also his stature. He disappeared and the audience saw, as the case may be, Fagin, Scrooge, Pickwick, Mrs. Gamp, Squeers, Mrs. Gummidge, Micawber, Bill Sikes, or a host of others. (p. 15)

There were other entertainment stars in the last century, such as P. T. Barnum and Jennie Lind, who with Dickens helped open people's eyes to the fact that there were mass audiences available for the right entertainers. Under these conditions new talent could be discovered and promoted to stardom, and fortunes could be made in the process.

P. T. Barnum and
Commodore Nutt

Culver Pictures, Inc.

crazes, panics, and the spreading of rumors. Thus a massive traffic jam can turn into a dangerous panic; a joyful victory celebration can become a violent riot like the one that occurred after the Detroit Tigers won the World Series in 1984. The panic selling that occurred on Wall Street in October 1987 and resulted in a massive loss of investors' capital is a reminder that mass publics continue to exert important effects even when supposed safeguards are in place. For this reason alone, social scientists, urban planners, and governmental leaders increasingly recognize the need to cooperate in anticipating the behaviors of mass publics.

This recognition has come after some painful experiences. A famous case of failure to anticipate the possible reaction of mass publics was the 1938 radio dramatization of H. G. Wells's novel *The War of the Worlds*. This broadcast, which vividly described an invasion of the earth by Martians, was presented to the radio audience in documentary fashion, beginning with a fictitious news flash and continuing with reports of a spacecraft landing in a New Jersey field and descriptions of the invading Martian army. Before the audience was informed that the broadcast was only a dramatic presentation, hundreds of thousands of Americans began gathering in panicky crowds, while thousands of others jammed telephone lines in efforts to reach loved ones. After this mass panic, broadcasters became far more careful in presenting radio programs (Cantril, 1982/1940).

The availability of more time for leisure pursuits, the development of a mass market for automobiles, and the technological revolution in communications and the mass media have all exerted an immense influence on the life-styles of mass publics, which in turn shape the society in which they live. For example, through their demands for roads, leisure facilities, and services that cater to a highly mobile life-style, Americans have transformed the physical landscape. Rural scenes of farms and small towns still exist, but throughout the nation they are being enveloped by networks of suburbs and shopping malls and pleasure grounds (stadiums, amusement parks, etc.) linked together by a labyrinth of highways (Carter, 1975; Flink, 1975; Thomas, 1956).

Mass publics have also created the conditions that make possible whole new industries. The hot dog was an invention that allowed millions of people to eat while strolling along the boardwalk at Coney Island. But fast food soon became an industry and even, as McDonald's founder Ray Kroc (1977) describes it, an art form:

Consider, for example, the hamburger bun. It requires a certain kind of mind to see beauty in a hamburger bun. Yet, is it any more unusual to find grace in the texture and softly curved silhouette of a bun than to reflect lovingly on the hackles of a favorite fishing fly? Or the arrangement of textures and colors in a butterfly wing? . . . Not if you regard the bun as an essential material in the art of serving a great many meals fast. [p. 99]

The thousands of teenagers and young adults who work in the fast-food industry may not sing rhapsodies to buns and burgers; nevertheless, their industry owes its existence to the behavior of hungry, mobile multitudes—in other words, mass publics.

Public Opinion

The presence of mass publics sets the stage for the emergence of public opinion as a powerful force in modern societies. **Public opinion** refers to the values and attitudes of mass publics. The kinds of behavior that develop out of public opinion include fads, fashions, demands for particular goods and services, voting behavior, and much more. Public opinion is shaped in part by collective behavior, especially social movements. An ex-

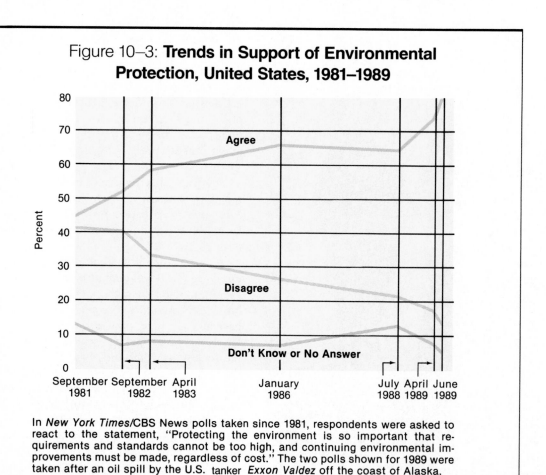

Figure 10–3: **Trends in Support of Environmental Protection, United States, 1981–1989**

In *New York Times*/CBS News polls taken since 1981, respondents were asked to react to the statement, "Protecting the environment is so important that requirements and standards cannot be too high, and continuing environmental improvements must be made, regardless of cost." The two polls shown for 1989 were taken after an oil spill by the U.S. tanker *Exxon Valdez* off the coast of Alaska.

Source: Ruckelshaus, 1989.

ample is the rise of the conservative movement, together with its various submovements (antiabortion, proprayer, antilabor, prodefense, etc.), in the United States in the 1980s. The impact of this movement can be seen in the contrast between the results of the 1964 and 1984 presidential elections. In 1964 Barry Goldwater, who espoused many of the ideals of the current conservative movement, was overwhelmingly defeated by Lyndon Johnson, an outspoken proponent of liberal social-welfare policies. Twenty years later the pendulum of public opinion had swung to the other extreme, and the staunchly conservative Ronald Reagan beat a liberal candidate, Walter Mondale, by an even greater percentage of the popular vote than Johnson had won in 1964. Only a minority, perhaps 25 percent, of those who voted for Reagan thought of themselves as supporters of the conservative movement, but the fact that many of Reagan's conservative ideas could be so widely adopted is an indication of their broader influence throughout American culture.

> *The presence of mass publics leads to the emergence of public opinion as a powerful force in modern societies.*

Public opinion is also shaped by more fleeting shifts in the national mood as citizens respond to experiences that are shared by all, especially through the mass media. For example, no one knows for sure whether the severe droughts that burned crops in the United States and Canada in 1987 and 1988 were a symptom of global warming, but scientists' warnings about this possibility, and their explanations of the "greenhouse effect" caused by high levels of carbon dioxide and other gases in the atmosphere, were made far more vivid by media coverage of the drought. Public support for environmental protection was stimulated still further by coverage of the oil spill by the *Exxon Valdez* in 1989. This effect can be clearly seen in Figure 10-3. What is not clear from this or any other measurement of public opinion is whether what people say they believe is any indication of what they would actually do if they had to devote scarce resources to achieving the desired social change.

FRONTIERS OF SOCIOLOGY

The Study of Leisure

Since the 1940s the pursuit of leisure activities of all kinds has become a passion for those who can afford the time. This is true not only in the United States and Canada but throughout most of the industrial world (Machlis and Tichnell, 1985). People are spending more money on leisure pursuits and engaging in more diverse pleasures than ever before. In ancient Rome and feudal Europe only the nobility had leisure; everyone else toiled ceaselessly in the fields or at their crafts. The limited leisure available to the masses took the form of religious festivals and games. The notion that common people could enjoy leisure in specified blocks of time—weekends, holidays, vacations, retirement—would have been viewed as revolutionary. However, the rise of modern social movements changed the expectations of "common folk" about many values, including leisure.

One consequence of the increase in leisure time in North America has been the steady growth of institutions devoted to leisure and recreation. Today it is estimated that over 350 million visits are paid to national parks in the United States each year and that approximately 700 million visits are made to state parks. Over 45 million tickets to major-league baseball games are sold each year, and about 15 million people attend NFL football games. About 415 million rounds of golf are played each year. There are well over 60 million bowlers, and at least 9 million people own an outboard motor. There are some 1,100 opera companies in the nation; they perform for at least 14 million people a year. This list of facts hardly begins to exhaust the demography of leisure in the United States, but it does indicate the staggering magnitude of the phenomenon. Try maneuvering through the traffic jam caused by a college football game when 60,000 fans are trying to get home for dinner. Imagine the same scene repeated simultaneously at thousands of other locations, some smaller and some larger, and you can begin to grasp the impact of leisure pursuits.

Data like those just presented tell only part of the story of leisure's impact on a modern society. In the United States, people's leisure preferences increasingly shape the landscape itself. Highways extend to beaches and mountain recreation sites. Large portions of states like Florida, Montana, Wyoming, Arizona, and California are managed as leisure and recreation areas by powerful state and national land management agencies. Private vendors of recreation services (motels, tennis courts, restaurants, shops, etc.) crowd the tourist gateways to major attractions like Yellowstone Park or the Great Smokies. In major cities, leisure institutions like theaters, symphony orchestras, museums, sports complexes, and parks are vital to the local economy and culture. Without them the city would become a dark ghost town after business hours. Urban planners and city leaders therefore compete to attract talent and develop such institutions into tourist and cultural centers. Leisure for the millions translates into jobs for hundreds of thousands of people in every region of the country.

Sociologists conduct research on numerous aspects of leisure. A frequent finding of time-budget studies, for example, is that women in the United States have less discretionary time, or time for activities not associated with work and household duties, than the men in their lives. About ten hours a week less free time makes leisure a contested value in many households (Vanek, 1974; Robinson, 1977). The working poor also enjoy less leisure than people in classes above them—but researchers have also found that youthful members of the professions, who can afford leisure pursuits like skiing, often feel too pressed for time to enjoy their affluence and leisure (Lindner, 1970).

Sociological research is also applied to recreation planning and marketing; park and open-space planning; conflict resolution in recreation areas; evaluation of policies to address problems like overcrowding, littering, and crowd control; and much more (Shelby and Heberlein, 1985). An example of work on this research frontier is the research on overnight camping in parks that has been conducted for many years by Donald Field, dean of research at the University of Wisconsin School of Agriculture, and William Burch, a professor of forestry at Yale. Both Field and Burch are sociologists, but each is employed in a professional school that supports research on issues of recreation and resource management. Field, Burch, and their colleagues have helped develop a set of easy-to-administer questionnaires for use in studying patterns of campground and back-country usage. They have taught recreation managers that merely counting visitors is far less meaningful than learning about the social-group membership of campers and park users (Burch, 1971; Field & O'Leary, 1973). To know the proportions of families with children, young couples, young-adult groups, and so on among visitors to campgrounds and parks is to gain far greater power to predict changing activity patterns than is provided by data on total visits alone. A simple point perhaps, but one that has helped establish recreation research as an important frontier of sociological inquiry.

SUMMARY

The term *collective behavior* is used to refer to a continuum of unusual or nonroutine behaviors engaged in by large numbers of people. At one end of the continuum is the spontaneous behavior of people reacting to situations they perceive as uncertain, threatening, or extremely attractive. At the other end are events that involve large numbers of people in nonroutine behaviors but are organized by leaders and have specific goals. The organization that plans such events is a *social movement*.

The study of spontaneous forms of collective behavior often begins by distinguishing between crowds and masses. A *crowd* is a large number of people gathered in close proximity to one another. A *mass* is a large number of people oriented toward a set of shared symbols or social objects. Collective behavior can occur in crowds, in masses, or in both at once. The actual form taken by crowd or mass behavior depends on the emotions elicited by social situations. The most significant categories of emotions that motivate collective behavior are fear, hostility, and joy.

Social movements have been classified into four types based on the goals they seek to achieve. Revolutionary movements aim to overthrow existing stratification systems and social institutions; reformist movements seek partial changes in some institutions and values; conservative movements attempt to uphold the existing values and institutions of society; and reactionary movements seek to return to the institutions and values of the past. In addition, there are expressive social movements, or movements devoted to the expression of personal beliefs and feelings, and millenarian movements, which are both revolutionary and expressive.

Sociologists often distinguish between "long revolutions," or large-scale changes in the ecological relationships of humans to the earth and to one another, and revolutions that are primarily social or political. *Political revolutions* are transformations in the political structures and leadership of a society that are not accompanied by a full-scale rearrangement of the society's productive capacities, culture, and stratification system. *Social revolutions* not only change the institutions of government but also bring about basic changes in social stratification.

According to Marx, revolutions would occur as a result of the spread of capitalism: Impoverished workers and colonial peoples would rebel against the capitalists and create a new classless society. In addition, Marx and Tocqueville pointed to the role of *relative deprivation*, noting that the feeling of deprivation relative to others—not the presence of deprivation itself—may give rise to revolutionary social movements.

Weber and other sociologists have concentrated on the tendency of social movements to develop into bureaucratic organizations led by career officials. In their early stages, according to Weber, movements are led by people with a special quality known as *charisma*. Over time, however, those leaders' goals must be incorporated into the structure of the movement, a process that is termed the institutionalization of charisma. However, the more successful the movement, the more difficult it is to maintain the zeal of its founders. In extreme cases the process can end in *totalitarianism*, or efforts by an elite to control all forms of organizational life in a society.

Another view of collective behavior holds that modern industrial societies produce anomic populations that are easily manipulated and led into collective behavior on a mass scale. Conservative nineteenth-century social theorists attributed the normlessness of the masses to their increased participation in political life, coupled with the loss of control by aristocratic elites. A more contemporary theory of mass society points out that an increasing number of people can enjoy the cultural and material values once reserved for the elite.

Studies of the resource mobilization problem focus on the ways in which social movements mobilize existing leaders and organizations rather than relying on the participation of people who happen to be moved to action. A related issue is the free-rider problem, the tendency of many people not to lend their support and resources to social movements but to reap the benefits anyway. Research on the latter issue has shown that the majority of people who express an opinion on an issue are not active in social movements concerned with that issue.

Mass publics are large populations of potential spectators or participants who engage in collective behavior of all kinds. Such factors as increased leisure time, the almost universal use of automobiles, and the technological revolution in communications and the mass media have had an immense influence on the life-styles of mass publics, which in turn shape the society in which they live. Mass publics have transformed the physical landscape and created the conditions that make possible whole new industries.

The presence of mass publics makes possible the emergence of *public opinion*, or the values and attitudes of mass publics. The behavior that develops out of public opinion can take a variety of forms, including fads, fashions, and demands for particular goods and services. Public opinion is shaped in part by collective behavior, especially social movements. It is also affected by experiences shared by all the members of society through the mass media.

GLOSSARY

collective behavior: nonroutine behavior engaged in by large numbers of people responding to a common stimulus (**p. 290**).

social movement: organized collective behavior aimed at changing or reforming social institutions or the social order itself (**p. 290**).

crowd: a large number of people who are gathered together in close proximity (**p. 292**).

mass: a large number of people who are all oriented toward a set of shared symbols or social objects (**p. 292**).

political revolution: a set of changes in the political structures and leadership of a society (**p. 296**).

social revolution: a complete transformation of the social order, including the institutions of government and the system of stratification (**p. 296**).

relative deprivation: deprivation as determined by comparison with others rather than by some objective measure (**p. 296**).

charisma: a special quality or "gift" that motivates people to follow a particular leader (**p. 297**).

modernization: a term used to describe the changes that societies and individuals experience as a result of industrialization, urbanization, and the development of nation-states (**p. 304**).

mass public: a large population of potential spectators or participants who engage in all kinds of collective behavior (**p. 305**).

public opinion: the values and attitudes held by mass publics (**p. 308**).

WHERE TO FIND IT

Books

The Crowd in History (George Rudé; Wiley, 1964). A fascinating account of the influence of riots, demonstrations, and protests on the history of the industrializing Western world.

Collective Behavior and Social Movements (Louis Genevie; Peacock, 1978). A comprehensive anthology of important papers and research articles in the field of collective behavior and social movements.

A History of Recreation: America Learns to Play, 2nd ed. (Foster Rea Dulles; Appleton, 1965). This history of recreation in America covers the transformation of the nation from one in which religion dominated all leisure to one characterized by differentiated leisure institutions such as theater, popular music, and sports of all kinds.

The Dynamics of Social Movements (Meyer N. Zald and John McCarthy; Winthrop, 1979). A thorough analysis of competing explanations of the evolution of social movements.

The Logic of Collective Action (Mancur Olson; Harvard University Press, 1965). A classic treatise on the costs and benefits of individual choices to engage in collective action; includes a good analysis of free riders.

Freedom Summer (Doug McAdam; Oxford University Press, 1990). An outstanding example of recent research on collective behavior. It shows that people who become involved in social movements like the civil rights movement often remain activists throughout their lives.

Other Sources

The Gallup Poll An annual compilation of polls taken throughout the year by Gallup, Inc. Available in the reference section of most college and university libraries.

Research reports published by the National Opinion Research Center, University of Chicago. The *General Social Survey: Cumulative Codebook* is an annual survey available through the data archives of most colleges and universities. It provides measures of the demographic characteristics and behaviors of a large sample of Americans.

VISUAL SOCIOLOGY

The Labor Movement

In the 1930s, after years of mass protests and efforts to organize unions and ensure the right of workers to belong to unions, the American labor movement finally won the protection of the law. The struggle to gain the rights to organize workers, to bargain collectively for better wages and working conditions, to go out on strike, and to be bound by labor contracts resulted in the creation of a new institution, the labor union.

The acceleration of industrial production after the Civil War brought workers together in larger numbers than ever before. Images of the new industrial masses were presented to the public in the form of engravings like the one shown here, which portrays the battle between steelworkers and Pinkerton agents in Homestead, Pennsylvania, in 1892. During the bitter labor-management disputes of the 1930s, photographers often captured the fervor of working-class solidarity, as can be seen in the photo of workers in Canton, Ohio, proudly displaying the food they are sending to striking miners.

Today the image that many Americans have of unions is of an institution that has matured and perhaps entered a period of decline. The nation's top labor leaders are used to lobbying in the halls and offices of government, but they are also accused of not being forceful enough in organizing workers in new industries, gaining new members, and convincing a new generation of the need for collective bargaining. Yet when sociologists look at the recent history of union organization among farm workers, or at the renewed activity of unions among clerical, technical, and professional workers (e.g., teachers, secretaries, and health-care workers), they caution against concluding that we have seen the demise of collective behavior among workers.

CHAPTER OUTLINE

● **Meanings of Social Change**

● **Two Forces of Social Change**
- War and Conquest
- Modernization

● **Social Change in Everyday Life**
- Gender Roles and the Family
- Race Relations in a Postindustrial Society
- Environmental Politics and Policies

● **Models of Change**
- Evolutionary Models
- Cyclical Theories
- Conflict Models
- Functionalist Models
- Conclusion

Margo Smith

An African newcomer to American urban life

CHAPTER 11

SOCIAL CHANGE

One sultry African night, as the people of Blokosso were sleeping, a band of thieves crept into their houses and ransacked them. They stole radios, jewelry, and expensive articles of ceremonial clothing. But as the villagers assessed the damage early the next morning, they mourned a far greater loss. Never before in anyone's memory had a robbery like this one occurred in the village. It was not the goods themselves they missed, for these could be replaced. It was the loss of a way of life, a social world, that they lamented. "We loved to sleep outside on the very hot nights," said Mr. Joseph, one of the most respected men in the village; "the women by this palm grove in the soft sand along the lagoon, the men under the lamp a bit. We like to talk and sleep with each other. We are not used to sleeping with our things."

Throughout history theirs had been a village society. Blokosso was one of several fishing villages inhabited by the Ebrie tribe. In the nineteenth century the Ebrie's lands and waters became part of French West Africa, but not until the late 1950s and the 1960s did the presence of Europeans significantly change Ebrie culture and daily life. The big changes for the people of Blokosso and the other villagers came when a canal was dug through the barrier island that separated their lagoon from the ocean. The canal allowed the small town established by the French colonists, Abidjan, to become a major commercial center.

Before long the town began to expand rapidly. Rising land prices and higher taxes obliged the Ebrie villagers to sell their land and take up work in the growing colonial city. They were able to keep small plots in the village to use for gardens until the demand for housing in the expanding city was too great even for the gardens. The people of Blokosso built new houses on their remaining land. These ventures into real estate and construction made many families rather wealthy, but they also brought new dimensions of social inequality to the village, and with these came new patterns of envy and conflict.

Gradually, in the time before the robbery occurred, Blokosso had ceased to be a self-sustaining village with its own economy and tribal culture. Instead, it was becoming a "village enclave," a little island of cultural homogeneity in an urban society. The robbery was a blunt statement to the villagers about how much change had occurred in a short time and how much more was likely to come.

For me, the experience of living in Blokosso at that time (during 1962 and 1963) was as much of a revelation as the robbery was to the villagers. I had been trained as a biologist and was living in Blokosso while teaching physics and chemistry in a junior college. During the day I delighted in opening up to students the secrets of matter and energy. In the evenings, however, the villagers taught me lessons about living in a totally different social world, one that was experiencing even more rapid social change than my own.

Mr. Joseph, my best friend in the village, was a middle-level executive in one of Abidjan's insurance agencies. He commuted across the lagoon in a motorized dugout canoe.

During the day his mind was entirely devoted to business. In the evenings he dealt with the problems of a traditional African family. His three wives became more and more jealous of one another as new wealth and their rising expectations led to new opportunities for better health and more leisure and also to new sources of conflict. I watched him and his family deal with the impact of change on their lives. I saw the villagers attempt to invoke their ancestral spirits and to use witchcraft to cope with new phenomena like robberies. The entire colony had become independent from France only two years before, and I saw the villagers, now citizens of a new nation called Ivory Coast, becoming interested in politics and current events.

During that time my own interests shifted from the physical to the social sciences. Nothing has ever interested me more than the villagers' questions about what social change has brought to them and what it has caused them to lose. When I began to study sociology, I discovered that such questions are at the core of this young science. I also found that in order to understand social change, it was necessary to understand how social structures operate and how conflict occurs in all kinds of human interactions. This meant studying populations, social structures and cultures, principles of interaction—indeed, all the subjects discussed in the preceding chapters.

MEANINGS OF SOCIAL CHANGE

Throughout this book we deal with social changes of all kinds. The term **social change** refers to variations over time in the ecological ordering of populations and communities, in patterns of roles and social interactions, in the structure and functioning of institutions, and in the cultures of societies. We have seen that such changes can result from social forces building within societies (**endogenous forces**) as well as from forces for change exerted from the outside (**exogenous forces**). Changes in social organization and culture that result from a society's need to feed a growing population are examples of endogenous social change; the effects of war, conquest, and colonial rule on traditional societies are examples of exogenous social change. Often both types of change occur simultaneously.

As I sat under the palm trees with my Ebrie friends, we endlessly debated issues of social change. In many ways our debates were about the difference between change and progress. "Before the white man came," my friends told me, "we had time but no watches. Now we have watches but no time." The village primary school was known in Ebrie as the "paper house" where children struggled to master the three R's in order to be able to earn money, or "white man's paper." But there was also general agreement that many of the technologies introduced by the Europeans were of immense importance. Health-care innovations that could prevent debilitating diseases like malaria or schistosomiasis were considered a great blessing. Yet the most prestigious Western invention from the villagers' viewpoint was the camera, for with it, they exclaimed, "our children can see their ancestors."

The people of Ivory Coast and other

> *Social change may result from forces building within societies (endogenous forces) or from forces exerted from the outside (exogenous forces).*

F. Willett

This lighthearted sculpture by a traditional African artist shows a missionary or colonial administrator being ferried around in a dugout canoe. Colonial regimes were a major exogenous source of social change.

societies that are undergoing rapid social change do not see the future as a matter of becoming Westernized. Rather, they strive to blend their own culture with certain aspects of Western culture. They are aware of a decline in their sense of community and mourn the weakening of their culture, but they actively embrace the aspects of modernity that will permit more of them to lead longer and perhaps more enjoyable lives. For them there is no question of returning to an earlier state. Change is inevitable. They want to help make the change, however, and to do this they understand that they must compete in modern social institutions like schools and businesses while at the same time they attempt to preserve their village life as best they can.

The Ebrie are experiencing many of the varieties of social change that we have discussed in the preceding chapters. Modern sociology helps us organize our thinking about the complex set of changes that societies have experienced in the course of human history. Thus in Chapter 1 we noted that sociologists think about change at the micro, middle, and macro levels of social life even while recog-

nizing that changes at all of those levels are interrelated. At the micro level, social change is experienced through new patterns of individual and small-group interaction. For example, there are changes in intimate social groups like couples and the family, such as the emergence of new norms guiding sexual behavior and the organization of family roles. And we have seen how urbanization affects the nature of primary groups. In village societies, primary groups are usually based on kinship and gender and age. In urban social environments, such groups are often formed when people become friends within secondary associations like offices, schools, and community organizations. Urbanization also offers the individual more choices in terms of friendships and life-styles. This aspect of urbanization frees people from the conformity of village life. But the great number of choices—choices regarding sexual conduct, values, and manners of all kinds—also creates ambiguity and anxiety. We often do not know how to behave or what groups to join, and this confusion can produce a state of normlessness or anomie.

Rapid social changes at the micro level

provide a fertile field of inquiry for social scientists. Among the subjects of current research at this level are changes in gender roles, in the use of leisure time, and in the process by which recent immigrants become acculturated to the United States and other advanced societies. Many other examples could be added.

At the middle level of social life, change is most often experienced in communities, economic organizations, and governing bodies. There are at least two dominant trends at this level of social experience: the increasing democratization of political life and the rise of complex bureaucratic institutions. For example, much conflict in the world today revolves around questions of who will have the right to participate in a society's basic institutions. Throughout the world, people are demanding (though by no means always gaining) full citizenship rights and equal participation in the "good life" as it is defined in their culture. They no longer accept lack of wealth or prestige, or a particular skin color or religion, as criteria that can exclude them from economic and political opportunities. We could list many examples of this trend, perhaps none as significant as the civil rights movement in the United States and the anti-apartheid movement in South Africa.

Macrosocial change produces the major social forces that shape change throughout a society. Many, perhaps most, of the changes that occur at the middle and micro levels, where we actually experience change in our own lives, are generated by large-scale, even revolutionary, changes at the macro level. These changes do not occur quickly, but they alter the ecological order, the system of stratification, and the social institutions of entire societies. Populations become urbanized; cities expand into metropolitan and even megalopolitan systems; and demands for more energy, food, transportation, recreation, and information create incentives for the development of new technologies and institutions. Entire social classes are shaped by these macro-level changes and attempt to adapt to them. Tribal agriculturalists are absorbed into modern market systems, and many of those who cannot make a living from the land be-

come part of the industrial working class. Others become members of other classes—professionals, managers of business enterprises, clerical workers—and a few will even join the ranks of the very rich or powerful. But these economic classes are only the beginning. People continue to be ranked by age, gender, ethnicity, or race. And the social movements they join express their desire to obtain a larger share of their society's resources. New institutions emerge to educate, employ, inform, transport, shelter, and care for the health of ever-larger populations. And as societies become more complex, the tasks of government become increasingly specialized and subject to greater conflict.

Many other examples of macro-level change in societies throughout the world could be given. In the past 300 years many of the world's societies have changed from agrarian to industrial and then to postindustrial production; from feudal to capitalist (or from capitalist to socialist or from communist to social-democratic) economic organization; and from colonial outpost to independent nation. In studying social change at the macro level, sociologists often seek to chart the effects of great forces like war and conquest on the one hand and, on the other, to predict the consequences of the transformations known as modernization. In the following section we examine these forces in some detail.

TWO FORCES OF SOCIAL CHANGE

War and Conquest

War is among the greatest and certainly the most violent of the forces that produce social change. Ironically, the deadliest forms of warfare are associated with the rise of modern civilizations. As societies have become more advanced in their command of technology and their social organization, the devastation caused by war has increased. The wars fought by so-called primitive societies were frequently ritual affairs; the combatants often withdrew from the field after a single skirmish. Although not all preindustrial warfare was so ritualistic, relatively few combatants were killed because the technologies for killing were so limited compared with those available today.

In the Middle Ages, often viewed as a warlike time owing to the influence of knights and Crusaders, the rate of fatalities among warriors was about 2 percent. In contrast, in World War I the proportion was 40 percent. Moreover, modern warfare is increasingly dangerous not only for the combatants but for civilians as well. In World War I about half of those who died were civilians, but in the Vietnam War the toll rose to more than 75 percent (Galtung, 1985; McNeill, 1982).

Any evaluation of the place of war in social change must consider three broad questions. First, what are the ecological effects of war on human populations? Second, how do wars help shape the consciousness and culture of a people? Third, how does war change the institutions of societies?

The Ecological Impact of War. Casualties and conquest are the major ecological effects of war. Like an epidemic of cholera or bubonic plague, war accounts for extraordinary and rapid declines in population. Pitirim Sorokin (1937) estimated that between A.D. 1100 and 1925 about 35.5 million people died in European wars alone. World War I claimed the lives of about 8.4 million soldiers and about 1.4 million civilians, and in World War II about 17 million military personnel and about 34 million civilians died. It is estimated that the Soviet Union lost about 15 million people during the latter war and that in China about 22 million perished. Germany lost 3.7 million, Japan about 2.2 million, and the United States slightly under 300,000.

When millions of men are killed, entire populations are unbalanced for more than a generation. Many women remain single or become widows and either do not have children or raise children alone. The effect may be to reduce population pressure on food and other resources, but at the same time there are labor shortages and economic disarray due

> *The major ecological effects of war are casualties and conquest.*

to the loss of so many skilled workers (Beer, 1981).

War also results in large-scale shifts in population and rapid acceleration of economic change. For example, the western parts of the United States and Canada experienced their most rapid growth as a result of mobilization for war during the first half of this century. New dams, new electric-power plants, new factories to produce all kinds of goods were built. San Diego, Los Angeles, San Francisco, Portland, Seattle, and Vancouver all experienced massive population growth, as did many inland centers of industry and agriculture. The end of the war saw continued growth in the western states as young families who had come west during the war decided to settle there permanently.

For the losers in war, the ecological consequences of defeat are usually far more dramatic. Population loss, economic subjugation, the imposition of a foreign language and culture, and forced movement to new towns and industrial areas are common. During the genocidal wars waged by whites against Native Americans in the nineteenth and early twentieth centuries the consequences for the losers were death, expulsion, and banishment to reservations. For tribal peoples of Africa, invasion, war, and conquest led to colonial rule and rapid social change, often imposed through taxation, labor gangs, military draft, and similar means.

The Cultural Impact of War. War changes a society's culture by stamping the memories of chaos and cruelty, heroism and camaraderie on entire generations. Years after a major war its effects on values and norms continue to be felt. One need only think of the impact of the American Civil War on the former Confederate states, an impact that remains strong today and can be seen in Civil War memorials, rebel yells, the conduct of interracial relations, and North–South animosities. Recent sociological research shows that even for generations that did not experience war, the memory or threat of warfare is perceived as extremely important. Table 11-1 shows that people will cite specific wars first among "national events or changes that

Table 11–1: **U.S. Respondents' Rank Ordering of Important Events as They Perceive Them (N = 1243)**

Event/Change (N)	Age					
	18–29	30–39	40–49	50–59	60–69	70 plus
World War II (265)	14	16	24	29	30	23
Vietnam (144)	18	18	13	2	4	1
Space exploration (93)	8	6	8	10	6	8
Kennedy assassination (62)	3	8	10	3	1	1
Civil rights (77)	7	7	5	7	6	3
Nuclear war, threat of (55)	6	5	6	4	2	3
Communication/transportation (46)	1	4	4	5	3	9
Depression (43)	3	3	2	5	7	13
Computers (23)	2	1	2	3	2	0
Terrorism (43)	4	2	0	1	1	0
Moral decline (28)	2	2	2	2	4	1
Women's rights (20)	1	2	3	0	2	1
Other event/change (357)	30	26	22	29	33	37
	100	100	100	100	100	100
	(289)	(312)	(200)	(167)	(165)	(110)

Source: Schuman and Scott, 1989.

seem especially important to you"—even if they themselves were not alive during those wars.

The impact of a major war can also be seen in the damage done to the minds and bodies of the survivors. In addition to the thousands who have been maimed and mutilated, thousands more suffer from *post-traumatic shock disorder*, in which the shock of war continues to haunt the victim, or *survivor guilt*, the feeling of shame that many survivors feel because they escaped the fate of their comrades. These effects have been described by the Italian social observer Primo Levi, who was imprisoned at Auschwitz and liberated by Russian soldiers. When the soldiers encountered the piles of dead and the groans of the dying, Levi reports, they felt shame: "They did not greet us, nor smile; they seemed oppressed . . . it was the shame which the just man experiences when confronted by a crime committed by another, and he feels remorse because of its existence" (1989, p. 72).

This kind of shame and guilt pervades a culture that has been torn by war. People feel that those who died were the best, the most valorous of society's members. Levi describes the shame he felt at the death of Chaim, a watchmaker who tried to teach him how to survive in the camp, and Szabo, a tall, silent Hungarian peasant who needed more food than others yet never failed to help his weaker companions. He tells of his guilt over the fact that Robert, a professor at the Sorbonne, died even though he "spread courage and trust all around him," and that Baruch, a longshoreman from Livorno, died on the first day because he hit back when the guards beat him. "These, and innumerable others, died not despite their valor but because of it" (p. 83).

Wars also change national cultures by increasing contacts among different cultures. In the case of modern nations like Japan, Italy, Germany, and Korea, all of which have experienced military occupation by foreign powers, the cultural consequences include the acculturation of new norms and behaviors. For example, baseball was introduced to Japan by U.S. occupation troops after

War affects national cultures by generating shame and guilt and by increasing contacts among different cultures.

World War II and is now that nation's most popular spectator sport. Indeed, the influence of North American culture, conveyed through movies, sports, consumer goods, and language, spread rapidly throughout Southeast Asia as a result of World War II and its lingering political consequences.

War and Social Institutions. The structure of a society, especially its major social institutions, may be drastically changed by war and preparation for war. The mobilization of large numbers of people and the marshalling of new technologies for military purposes have a centralizing effect on social institutions. In the United States, for example, the growth of large research universities in the 1960s was accelerated by huge investments in applied science and technology after Russia became the first nation to launch a space satellite. Universities that were capable of developing new science programs grew rapidly, and their administrations gained greater power. The power and influence of the national government has also grown, often at the expense of local governmental institutions, as a consequence of the two world wars and the continuing arms race. Providing for national defense is extremely expensive and requires that the central government be granted increased taxing powers.

> *The structure of a society may be changed by war and preparation for war.*

The high cost and massive scale of national defense during the past forty years has led to an increase in the power of military institutions. Social scientists have issued frequent warnings about the possible adverse consequences of this trend (Lasswell, 1941; Titmus, 1958). Political scientist Harold Lasswell (1941), for example, warned that modern nations were in danger of becoming what he called "garrison states." The military threatened to become more powerful than the institutions of democratic rule, a trend that often results in military takeovers in nations where democratic institutions and the rule of law are not adequately protected (see Chapter 19).

Military institutions are also affected by social changes occurring on a world scale. An example is the relaxation of the East–West "cold war" in the late 1980s, which resulted in demands that some of the costs of defense be diverted to other uses. As more of the world's leaders and citizens become aware of the dangers facing the natural environment, there is growing pressure to divert military spending to pay for environmental protection and cleanup projects. Major nations are far from a consensus on this reallocation of resources (Table 11-2 indicates the trade-offs involved), but it is certain that environmental protection will compete with military programs for funds in coming decades.

Modernization

A second major source of social change is the set of trends that are collectively known as **modernization**. This term encompasses all the changes that societies and individuals experience as a result of industrialization, urbanization, and the development of nation-states. These processes occurred during a period of two or more centuries in the Western nations and Japan, but they are taking place at a far more rapid rate in the former colonial societies that are today's new nations.

The term *modernization* should be used cautiously, in its sociological sense rather than as a value judgment about different societies. It does not mean that we can judge life in modern societies as better or more satisfactory or more humane than life was for people in societies like the one the Ebrie once knew. We noted earlier that modern societies have developed the capacity to cause more destruction and human suffering than any simpler society could possibly have caused. And we have seen in other chapters that many of the advantages enjoyed by the most modern nations have come at great cost to simpler, less modern societies. Yet the term *modernization* summarizes most of the major changes, for better or worse, that societies throughout the world are experiencing, albeit at differing rates and with different amounts of disruption.

Table 11–2: **Trade-Offs Between Military and Social or Environmental Priorities**

Military Priority	Cost	Social/Environmental Priority
Trident II submarine and F-18 jet fighter programs	$100,000,000,000	Estimated cost of cleaning up the 10,000 worst hazardous waste dumps in the United States
Stealth bomber program	$68,000,000,000	Two thirds of estimated costs to meet U.S. clean water goals by the year 2000
Requested SDI funding fiscal years 1988–92	$38,000,000,000	Disposal of highly radioactive waste in the United States
2 weeks of world military expenditure	$30,000,000,000	Annual cost of the proposed U.N. Water and Sanitation Decade
German outlays for military procurement and R&D, fiscal year 1985	$10,750,000,000	Estimated costs to clean up West German sector of the North Sea
3 days of global military spending	$6,500,000,000	To fund Tropical Forest Action Plan over 5 years
Development cost for Midgetman ICBM	$6,000,000,000	Annual cost to cut sulfur dioxide emissions by 8–12 million tons/year in the United States to combat acid rain
2 days of global military spending	$4,800,000,000	Annual cost of proposed U.N. Action Plan to halt Third World desertification, over 20 years
6 months of U.S. outlays for nuclear warheads, fiscal year 1986	$4,000,000,000	U.S. government spending on energy efficiency, fiscal years 1980–87
SDI research, fiscal year 1987	$3,700,000,000	Enough funds to build a solar power system serving a city of 200,000
10 days of European Economic Community military spending	$2,000,000,000	Annual cost to clean up hazardous waste sites in 10 European Economic Community countries by the year 2000
1 Trident submarine	$1,400,000,000	Global 5-year child immunization program against 6 deadly diseases, preventing 1 million deaths a year
3 B-1B bombers	$680,000,000	U.S. government spending on renewable energy, fiscal years 1983–85
2 months of Ethiopian military spending	$50,000,000	Annual cost of proposed U.N. Anti-Desertification Plan for Ethiopia
1 nuclear weapon test	$12,000,000	Installation of 80,000 hand pumps to give Third World villages access to safe water
1-hour operating cost, B-1B bomber	$21,000	Community-based maternal health care in 10 African villages to reduce maternal deaths by half in one decade

Source: Renner, 1989.

Neil Smelser (1966) associates modernization with these changes:

1. *In the realm of technology*, a developing society is changing from simple and traditionalized techniques toward the application of scientific knowledge.
2. *In agriculture*, the developing society evolves from subsistence farming toward the commercial production of agricultural goods. This means specialization in cash crops, purchase of nonagricultural products in the market, and often agricultural wage labor.
3. *In industry*, the developing society undergoes a transition from the use of human and animal power toward industrialization proper, or men working for wages at power-driven machines, which produce commodities marketed outside the community of production.
4. *In ecological arrangements*, the developing society moves from the farm and village toward urban concentrations. [pp. 110–111; emphasis added]

These processes can take place simultaneously, but this is not always the case. Many societies mechanize their agriculture and begin to produce cash crops for foreign markets before their cities and urban forms of employment have begun to grow rapidly. This was the case, for example, in Sri Lanka (formerly Ceylon), Indonesia, and many of the newer African nations.

Smelser and others who study modernization have shown that "technical, economic, and ecological changes ramify through the whole social and cultural fabric" (1966, p. 111). In the political sphere of life, we see the authority systems of the village giving way to domination by the institutions of nation-states. In the area of education, as societies attempt to produce workers who can meet the needs of new industries, new educational institutions are established. In the area of religion, there is a decrease in the strength of organized religions. Families change as traditional extended families adapt to new economic institutions that demand greater mobility. Stratification systems also change as a result of increased social and spatial mobility. Older patterns of gender inequality are modified (and often replaced by new forms of inequality) as women are in greater demand to fill positions in new economic institutions. And the emergence of a new class, the wage workers, increases the power of the common people, usually adding to their determination to become better educated and to participate more fully in political life. None of these changes is inevitable or irreversible; workers, for example, may see their unions "busted" in times of recession or economic change. But in the long run all of these trends are likely to appear in a modernizing society.

Figure 11-1 contrasts modern and nonmodern societies along eight dimensions of social change. Remember, however, that any particular society will show many variations within these categories. Yet it is also true, as we will see shortly, that differences among societies seem to be reduced by modernization.

Modernization in the Developing Nations.
Social scientists often use the term *third world* to refer to nations that have won independence from colonial dominance in the decades since World War II. If the "first world" is that of the capitalist nation-states and the "second world" that of the communist nations, the third-world nations are those that are not aligned with either of these "worlds" but are united in their need to survive in an environment dominated by more politically or economically powerful nations.

But the term *third world* can be misleading, since in the past twenty-five years

These Chinese teamsters have converted an old tractor for use as a truck, an example of "intermediate technology" in a modernizing nation.

Figure 11–1: **Social Differences Between Modernized and Nonmodernized Societies**

FOCI OF DIFFERENCES BETWEEN SOCIETIES	RELATIVELY MODERNIZED SOCIETY	RELATIVELY NONMODERNIZED SOCIETY
1. Specialization of organizations: specialized orientation to a single aspect of behavior	Vast majority operate continually in such contexts ("compartmentalization")	Relatively few operate in such contexts
2. Interdependency	High (low self-sufficiency)	Low (high self-sufficiency)
3. Relationship emphases (dominant patterns)	Rationality; universalism; functional specificity	Tradition; particularism; functional diffuseness
4. Patterns of centralization	Relatively high degree of centralization necessary and feasible	Relatively low degree of centralization necessary and feasible
5. Generalized media of exchange and markets	Generalization of media of exchange, and use of money in general, are high and increasing; extensive and increasing use of markets	Low generalization and limited use of money; limited use of markets
6. Bureaucracy	Widespread and specialized	Limited
7. Family considerations	Important, but decreasing amounts of social control, education, role preparation, and general orientation occur in a family context	Important; major social control, learning, role preparation, and general orientation occur in family context
8. Town–village interdependencies	Urban, industrial, with main flow of goods and services (and know-how) from urban to rural contexts	**Rural, agricultural, with main flow of goods and services from rural to urban contexts (rents, taxes, interest, profits)**

Source: Richard P. Appelbaum, *Theories of Social Change*, pp. 40–41. Copyright © 1970 by Houghton Mifflin Company. Used by permission.

many of these nations have made strides toward modernity along all or at least some of the dimensions presented in Figure 11-1. For this reason, we prefer to use the term *developing nations* or *modernizing nations*. A **developing nation** is one that is undergoing a set of transformations whose effect is to increase the productivity of its people, their health, their literacy, and their ability to participate in political decision making. These transformations occur at different rates in different nations. Such differences are evident when we compare nations like Mexico and Brazil, which are industrializing rapidly, with nations like Chad and Mali in the interior of Africa, which are having far more trouble achieving the hallmarks of modernization (see Table 11-3).

The theory of modernization as we have described it implies that modernization will occur along all of these dimensions in every society. But the differing experiences of the developing nations call this view into ques-

tion. Not only do we often see the industrialization of agriculture (i.e., the growth of huge mechanized farms) without the rise of industrial cities, or the growth of cities without a decline in the strength of organized religions or the emergence of modern educational institutions, but we also see the rise of antimodernist social movements in some of these nations (Germani, 1973). Events in the Islamic world are a case in point. In Pakistan, Iran, Saudi Arabia, Libya, the Sudan, and other Islamic nations, a fundamentalist religious movement has been gaining strength in

Table 11–3: **Hallmarks of Change in Developing Nations**

	CHILE	CUBA	BOLIVIA	EGYPT	EL SALVADOR	ETHIOPIA	INDIA	MEXICO	PAKISTAN	TURKEY	UNITED STATES	UNITED KINGDOM	JAPAN	SOVIET UNION
Percentage of population living in urban areas	82	69	45	44	39	14	23	66	28	45	74	78	76	64
Percentage of population that is illiterate	11	5	37	62	41	96	66	17	17	31	0.5	0.5	0.5	0.5
Education expenditures as a percentage of gross national product	5.8	6.3	3.1	4.5	3.8	4.1	3.0	3.4	1.9	2.9	6.8	5.7	6.0	6.7
Daily newspaper, estimated circulation per 1,000 inhabitants	87	118	46	78		1	20		14	88	269	421	575	405
Number of radio receivers per 1,000	300	317	571	157	336	92	56	292	75	119	2,133	986	696	504
Number of TV receivers per 1,000	113	164	59	41	64	1.2	2.9	111	11	119	646	457	560	307
Energy consumption, kilograms per capita	910	1,434		618		30	200	1,760	211	789	9,431	4,538	3,503	5,768
Military expenditure per capita as a percentage of gross national product	4.8	5.0		8.2	4.1		3.5	0.5	6.1	5.2	6.4	5.1	1.0	15.0
Percentage of population under age 15	32	29	44	40	45	45	39	42	44	39	22	20	22	25

Source: Population Reference Bureau, 1985; UNESCO, 1984; United Nations, 1984; *Statistical Abstract*, 1985.

the past two decades. This resurgence of traditional Islamic beliefs and practices denies that modernization must be accompanied by the rejection of religious faith, by the separation of religion and government, or by more democratic political participation. These and other aspects of the Western version of modernity are being strongly challenged by the Islamic fundamentalist movement.

The rise of such antimodernist movements is not limited to the Islamic nations. Similar movements can be seen in the United States. The Moral Majority and other conservative groups plead for a return to more traditional values, and some radical groups advocate a return to self-sufficient communities that would engage in farming on a small scale. The effects of such movements on a society's institutions show that modernization does not necessarily follow a single direction or imply a single set of changes (e.g., the decline of religious faith, the rise of science, or the growth of industrial cities).

Another challenge to this view of modernization is posed by the fact that the world's resources of raw materials, water, and energy are far less plentiful than they once were. Today there are serious doubts about whether those resources are adequate to permit the poor nations to become developed to anywhere near the extent that the Western nations have, or whether the rich nations can continue to grow as they have in the past.

Modernization and Dependency. Some sociologists argue that the development of the more advanced modern nations actually impedes development in the newer nations, or at least channels it in directions that are not always beneficial. André Gunder Frank (1966), for example, questions the idea that the less developed societies are merely at an earlier stage of modernization than the advanced nations. He cites the development of one-crop economies in many parts of Central and Latin America as evidence of how social forces in the developed nations actually transform the tropical countryside. According to Frank, when peasants give up subsistence agriculture and trading in local markets because

their land has been absorbed into huge banana or coffee plantations, this produces a form of underdevelopment that did not exist before, one in which the peasantry is transformed into a class of landless rural laborers.

Immanuel Wallerstein (1974) has proposed a more general theory that he calls *world system theory*. In this theory he divides the world into **core states**, **semiperipheral areas**, and **peripheral areas**. The core states include the United States, England, France, the Soviet Union, and Japan, which are the most technologically advanced nations and dominate the banking and financial functions of the world economy. The semiperipheral areas are places like Spain and Portugal, the oil-producing nations of the Middle East, and Brazil and Mexico. In these areas industry and financial institutions are developed to some extent, but they remain dependent on capital and technology provided by the core states. The peripheral areas include much of Africa, Asia, and Latin America. They supply basic resources and labor power to the core states and the semiperipheral areas. This world system, Wallerstein asserts, is based on various forms of economic domination and does not require political repression as well.

Wallerstein's theory has the drawback of suggesting that the so-called core states do not themselves include areas of production that resemble the peripheral, dependent regions more than they do the fully modernized nations. There is evidence that even the most modern nations contain such regions. For example, in a study of sharecropping in California, Miriam J. Wells (1984) showed that large California berry growers have been dividing their land into small plots and renting

This Mexican Indian woman is a descendant of the ancient Mayans. In her village, Amatenango del Valle, the women make pottery for export to nearby towns and cities. Her child stands a far better chance of growing to adulthood as a result of modern public-health and sanitation practices.

them to low-income farm laborers. Wells contends that the growers have adopted this strategy as a means of avoiding the higher costs of unionized farm labor. "The sharecropper is responsible for maintaining the plots, for harvesting and packing the fruit, and for hiring and paying whatever labor is necessary to accomplish these tasks" (p. 17). In return, the sharecropper receives from 50 to 55 percent of the proceeds minus the costs of handling, loading, hauling, and marketing the crop. Wells points out that modernization theory views sharecropping as an obsolete form of production, yet it can reappear even in the most advanced societies under certain conditions—for example, lack of machinery for harvesting. Once again, therefore, we see that modernization is not a unilinear process with inevitable outcomes for every society or nation.

Modernization and the Individual. In a famous study entitled *Becoming Modern*, Alex Inkeles and D. H. Smith (1974) surveyed 6,000 men in six developing nations to find out whether there is a set of distinctive traits that mark the world view or outlook of "modern man." Inkeles replicated this work in subsequent years and used the findings to develop a 500-question Overall Modernity Scale to measure the attitudes that make up the "modern" personality. Among those attitudes are open-mindedness, independence from traditional authorities, a sense of personal efficacy, the desire to be an informed citizen, and a readiness for new experiences (Inkeles, 1983).

These findings regarding modern attitudes are supported by the results of comparative studies of occupational prestige. When adults in different societies are interviewed about how they would rate certain occupations, there is a surprising similarity in their opinions. Although the nations in which such surveys have been conducted vary widely in the extent to which they have industrialized, in the education of

> *The "modern" personality is characterized by open-mindedness, independence from traditional authorities, a sense of personal efficacy, and readiness for new experiences.*

their population, and in their political development, their citizens evaluate the prestige of various occupations in roughly the same way (Hodge, Treiman, and Rossi, 1966). In other words, respondents in nations all over the world tend to assign the same rank to a particular occupation even when that occupation does not employ large numbers of people in their society. These studies are important because they show that even in less technologically advanced societies people have "bought into" the attitudes prevailing in more modern societies. And this implies that they will attempt to find employment in more highly ranked occupations.

Research on modernization throughout the world has shown that over time the developing nations tend to become more like the developed nations. This is true not only for judgments of occupational prestige but also for other aspects of life, such as family roles and political participation. There may be exceptions to these trends in particular nations, and sometimes there is a sense of loss, as we saw in the case of the Ebrie, but for better or worse the fate of people in modernizing nations is increasingly tied to trends and events in the developed nations.

SOCIAL CHANGE IN EVERYDAY LIFE

People often experience social change as highly problematic, and they often blame themselves for not coping with it more effectively. But as we saw in Chapter 1, the sociological imagination requires that we ask how our own troubles are related to larger social forces. And we have seen that modernity brings with it many contradictions. In pursuing new opportunities in education, leisure pursuits, intimate relationships, and political participation, we also create new problems for ourselves. Thus, according to social theorist Ralf Dahrendorf (1981), "anomie has become an element of the lives of many and notably of those who are still on the way to becoming full members of their societies" (p. 42).

Like most social theorists, Dahrendorf does not believe that we can or should attempt to reverse the course of modernization. Instead, he believes, we need "flexible institutions, capable of adjustment without disruption" (p. 163). We are far from achieving such flexibility, however. When we look at the range of problems we encounter in our daily lives, we can readily see how much more change is needed. To appreciate this point more fully, let us briefly review some of the dilemmas of modern life that result from rapid social change. These and related topics are discussed in more detail in Parts IV and V.

Gender Roles and the Family

Clearly, one of the most significant social changes in Western societies in the past quarter-century has been the changing definition of women's roles. The entry of women into the labor force is only one indicator of this aspect of social change. Today well over half of all married women with children are at work in offices, factories, and other workplaces, compared with only about 4 percent in 1890. But it should be noted that there have always been subgroups in the population, especially African-Americans and immigrants, for whom women's wages were necessary to the family's survival. And among women who "kept house" toward the turn of the century, some 20 percent took in lodgers and earned cash in this fashion (Aldous, 1982; Modell and Hareven, 1973).

For both women and men, these changes often produce feelings of guilt and stress. One writer on the subject (Fallows, 1985) urged young mothers to reject career goals so that they could raise their children themselves. On the basis of observations of day care centers, she had concluded that day care is a poorly developed institution that cannot substitute for maternal care. Arguments of this nature are common. But other studies show that high-quality day care does not impede a child's development. Moreover, advocates of gender equality question the assumption that child rearing should remain the primary role of women. This assumption has the effect of depriving women of opportunities to contribute their skills and talents to society. If day care is inadequate, why not improve it through public funding, education of child-care workers, and the like, rather than forcing women to return to their traditional role as homemakers?

These arguments call attention to the need for more research on the future of families and other intimate groups in which children are reared. Some sociologists attempt to show how day care can be improved. Others conduct research on how people actually cope with changes in the household division of labor. Are we moving toward a "symmetrical society" in which men and women share equally in household and occupational pursuits? If so, the evidence suggests that we still have a long way to go. In an analysis of data from 555 couples, Carmi Schooler, Joanne Miller, and their associates (1985) found that typically the husband's sphere of household work "tends to be limited to household repairs, whereas wives are responsible for and actually do a vastly wider range of the household tasks" (p. 112).

Another major issue related to changes in the family is whether welfare recipients should be required to work at paid jobs in order to remain eligible for welfare benefits. This question also involves the matter of day care, since single parents must have adequate care for their children while they gain the skills and experience needed to enter the labor force. Are we willing, as a society, to invest in new social-welfare institutions like day care? The answer to this question awaits further debate and political conflict. So too does the question of what, if anything, we can do about problems like teenage pregnancy, sexually transmitted diseases, or high rates of divorce. Changes in values give us more choices, more opportunities to realize our potential as individuals, but at what cost to society (Bellah et al., 1985)?

Race Relations in a Postindustrial Society

Another significant area of social change is race relations. When we look at the bitter racial strife occurring in South Africa, we often congratulate ourselves on the progress our society has made toward racial equality. Racial discrimination in the United States, which until fairly recently was supported by laws in many parts of the nation and by informal norms elsewhere, has decreased a great deal as a result of the civil rights movement of the 1960s. Since that stormy decade, blacks have made gains in all of our society's major institutions. Voting rights, greater access to education and jobs, achievement in sports, and full civil rights for blacks are often taken for granted. Yet here, too, much remains to be accomplished. In a review of the gains made by blacks and the obstacles still to be overcome, Thomas Morgan (1985) writes:

I still see the sign, "Whites Only," but it is not hanging from some Southern motel. The words "Whites Only" come to mind when I go as a journalist to cocktail parties and other events where crucial contacts and decisions are being made and I am the only black not serving the hors d'oeuvres. I see the sign when I hear racially insensitive comments by white acquaintances who profess a knowledge of black culture . . . and reject the idea of discrimination, but who have no real black friends or who do not socialize with blacks outside professional settings.

[The reality] is that America remains a divided society outside the office. This reality is even more difficult for young, middle-class professional blacks, who came of age in the 1960s and still feel racism of a subtler nature both at work and in recent policy positions taken by the Federal Government. [sec. 6, p. 32]

For poor and working-class blacks, the realities of American race relations are far less subtle than they are for middle-class blacks. As Figure 11-2 shows, the class structure of

Figure 11–2: **Changes in Size of Livelihood Classes in Race-Ethnic Groups, 1972–1982**

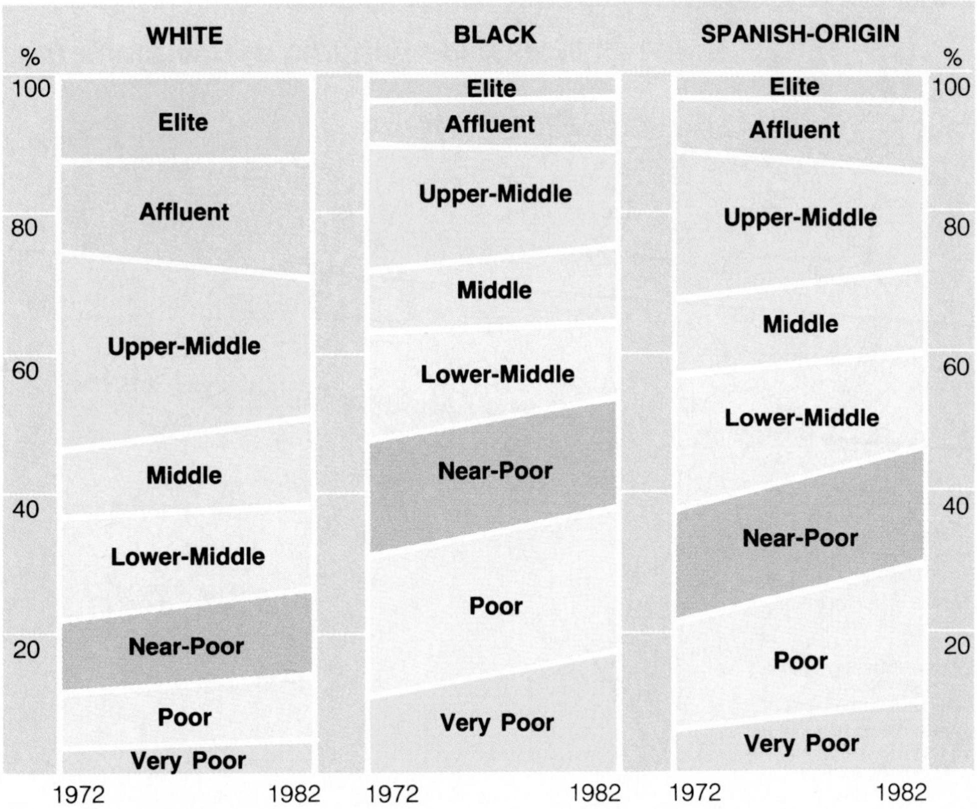

blacks and Hispanics is very different from that of whites. Although the proportion of affluent, upper-middle-class whites has been increasing in recent years and now constitutes more than half the population, among black and Hispanic minorities this proportion is extremely small and has not been growing very fast, if at all. At the same time, the proportion of families and households at the bottom of the class structure has been increasing. Thus, as William J. Wilson and other sociologists who study race relations have pointed out, there are really two worlds of blacks and Hispanics in America: the relatively comfortable and the increasingly impoverished.

Changes in the economic structure of society supply the main explanation for the growing divergence between the haves and the have-nots. Manufacturing jobs and many kinds of blue-collar service jobs are becoming far less numerous, while the number of jobs in white-collar service industries like finance,

insurance, and banking is growing rapidly. Increases in the number of high-technology items like computers have not yet made up for the loss of jobs in heavy industries like steel, autos, glass, and rubber. Blacks and Hispanics are more severely affected by these changes because they have long depended on heavy industry as a source of jobs.

Environmental Politics and Policies

A third area in which social change touches the individual is public policy. What public policies are likely to emerge as the United States is transformed into a postindustrial society? We cannot fully answer this question, as we are living through this period now and in fact are participating in it as voters, as opinion leaders, and in some cases as policymakers. Nor is it ever entirely possible to separate public opinion from how citizens feel about their political leaders. At this writing, for ex-

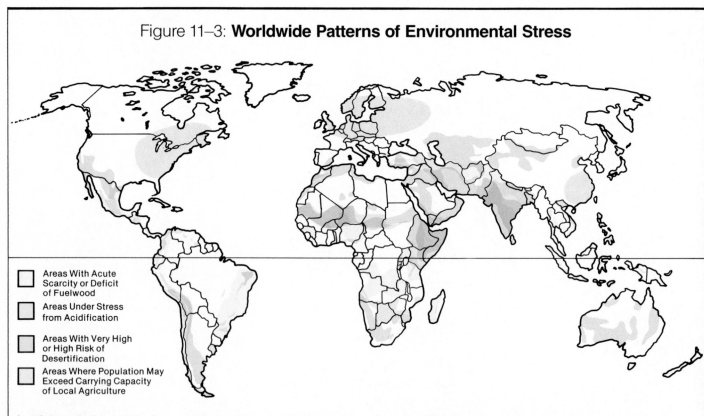

Figure 11–3: **Worldwide Patterns of Environmental Stress**

☐ Areas With Acute Scarcity or Deficit of Fuelwood

☐ Areas Under Stress from Acidification

☐ Areas With Very High or High Risk of Desertification

☐ Areas Where Population May Exceed Carrying Capacity of Local Agriculture

Land degradation results from a variety of human activities. Shown are regions threatened by desertification, overharvesting of firewood, acid rain, and stress induced by efforts to feed more people than the land is actually able to support.

Source: Clark, 1989.

Table 11–4: **Food Insecurity in Selected African Countries, 1986**

Country	Number of People	Share of Population
	(million)	(percent)
Ethiopia	14.7	34
Nigeria	13.7	13
Zaire	12.0	38
Tanzania	6.6	29
Kenya	6.2	29
Uganda	6.1	40
Mozambique	5.9	42
Algeria	4.1	18
Ghana	4.1	31
Sudan	3.4	15
Zambia	2.7	39
Mali	2.5	33
Chad	2.4	47
Morocco	2.4	11
Somalia	2.3	42

Source: Brown et al., 1989.

ample, we do not know whether the conservative ideas espoused by former President Ronald Reagan will remain popular throughout the Bush administration. However, if we consider one of the master trends in world politics we can make some rather safe predictions.

A subject that is likely to produce significant political upheaval around the world is environmental politics. Environmental issues like the exhaustion of food resources, the spread of deserts, the destruction of forests by acid rain, and the denuding of large tracts of land for paper and fuelwood are fast gaining a high place on the agenda of world politics. Figure 11-3 shows that population growth in excess of food-producing capacity is occurring in the Middle East and many parts of Africa; that fuelwood is scarce in India, Africa, and eastern Brazil; and that deserts are expanding on all the continents. Victims of "food insecurity" (people who lack sufficient food for normal health and physical activity) now total over 100 million (Brown et al., 1989). Table 11-4 lists some African nations in which food insecurity is a serious problem, often touching well over a third of the population.

What are the political implications of these physical and social conditions? Gro Harlem Brundtland, chairperson of the World Commission on Environment and Development, answers that "to secure our common future, we need a new international ethic based on the realization that the issues with which we wrestle are globally interconnected." The only way different nations can pursue their own self-interest, she adds, is for the United Nations or a similar world political body to become the institution in which environmental policy is made. And that policy cannot "insult the poor and tell them that they must remain in poverty to 'protect the environment'" (1989, p. 190). Clearly, the wealthy nations must make equal sacrifices to achieve a stable environment. This issue is discussed further in Box 11-1.

As the worldwide environmental crisis worsens, citizens of the United States and Canada will increasingly be faced with the need to regulate their economies and end practices that contribute to pollution. This will be a costly and politically wrenching process, as can be seen in the difficulty of developing policies for solid-waste disposal or the abatement of acid rain. A divided civic culture, in which many people wish to be responsive to the environmental crisis and many others wish not to think about it, is certain to produce conflict for years to come—unless a crisis like flooding due to global warming creates such an obvious threat that unity of purpose is achieved overnight. We cannot wait for a crisis, however. Thus we face a dilemma brought on by great changes in the environment coupled with slower changes in the political culture. This situation points to the need to look more closely at the models that sociologists use in assessing social change and predicting its course.

MODELS OF CHANGE

"We are such stuff as dreams are made on. And our little life is rounded with a sleep." These words from Shakespeare's *The Tempest* capture one of the basic difficulties of studying social change. In one short lifetime we catch glimpses of our ability to create a better world,

Box 11–1: **Carrying Capacity and Environmental Politics**

The term *carrying capacity* refers to the earth's capacity to support life. It is defined as "the *maximum persistently feasible load*—just short of the load that would damage [an] environment's ability to support life of [a particular] kind" (Catton, 1980, p. 4). The load placed by a species on its environment is based on that species's requirements for energy, space, shelter, and so on. It also includes demands on the environment to assimilate wastes. Problems like acid rain, toxic landfills, and pesticide poisoning of fish-breeding areas are among the problems caused by excessive demands on the environment to assimilate wastes produced by the human species.

The burden placed on the environment is more severe in the developing nations than in the developed ones, since those nations have the world's fastest-growing populations but do not have the resources to feed their people adequately or to invest in environmental protection. However, the developed nations also contribute significantly to the problem. The United States, for example, produces five tons of carbon dioxide per person each year and leads all industrial nations except Canada in the amount of energy used per unit of production of goods and services. And fuel consumption is the primary cause of air pollution and global warming.

Among the most serious indications of the earth's reduced carrying capacity is desertification. Lester Brown and his associates (1974) have shown that the process of desertification, or the expansion of deserts, is occurring at many locations in Africa, Asia, and Latin America. Reversal of this dangerous trend will require long-term efforts on an international basis.

Another serious problem related to the environment's carrying capacity is the need to feed rapidly growing populations. In the 1960s, population growth combined with crop failures produced enormous decreases in food production per capita in the developing nations.

During the 1970s, a series of genetic advances launched what became known as the "green revolution." Dwarf varieties of wheat, corn, and rice that could accept high doses of fertilizers, resist tropical heat, and produce up to twice the harvests of previous varieties were developed. But the green revolution turned out to be a mixed blessing. The "miracle" varieties required large amounts of fertilizer, which the developing nations could barely afford, and the larger harvests often drove down grain prices, causing farmers to migrate to already overcrowded cities.

But the green revolution has not been a total failure. The countries in which it has occurred have at least gained some time in which to attempt other forms of economic development, reduce their rates of population growth, and try to solve their environmental problems.

In recent years the developed nations have attempted to lead the global movement for environmental quality, but they have been subjected to strong criticism for their part in creating the problem in the first place. According to President José Sarney of Brazil, industrialized countries like the United States do the most harm to the global environment. "They discharge their wastes into the atmosphere, damaging the ozone layer, and they still stockpile nuclear arms which can destroy humanity two or three times over. They are the worst plunderers." Clearly, as one observer writes, "It is not easy to be a leader in the solution when one is a leader in the problem" (Shabecoff, 1989, p. A22).

but we can never realize all our ambitions, nor can we know what will become of our achievements or the problems we leave to later generations. We may see the return of Selective Service (the draft) if the nation goes to war; prices may shoot up again as inflation rates rise; long lines may form at gasoline pumps during an oil shortage; or we may be faced with new medical problems like AIDS that affect the lives of large numbers of people. To cope with these changes, we may join new social movements and attempt to build new institutions or work to improve the ones we already have. We may also record our desire for a better society in cultural products of all kinds, in poetry and plays and novels, in film and music, and perhaps in social-scientific studies. Yet we know that social change will continue after we are gone, and we wonder whether it is possible to foresee what will happen to our society and civilization in the distant future.

Sociologists have often attempted to develop models of social change that span many generations and predict the future of whole societies or civilizations. Of course, none of these theories can be tested using data from actual experience. As Robert Nisbet (1969) has observed, "None of us has ever seen a civilization die, and it is unimaginable, short of cosmic disaster or thermonuclear holocaust, that anyone ever will." Instead,

we see migrations and wars, dynasties toppled, governments overthrown, economic systems made affluent or poor; revolutions in power, privilege, and wealth. We see human beings born, mating, child-rearing, working, worshipping, playing, educating, writing, philosophizing, governing. We see generation succeeding generation, each new one accepting, modifying, rejecting in different proportions the works of preceding generations. We see, depending upon our moral or esthetic disposition, good and evil, greatness and meanness, tragedy, comedy, and bathos, nobility and baseness, success and failure. [p. 3]

Nisbet's point is that we can trace trends in all of these areas, but it is extremely difficult to develop theories that can explain them all and, more important, predict the decline of existing societies and civilizations or the rise of new ones. Even when we believe we are witnessing the birth of a new society out of the chaos of revolution or war, it takes

many generations to distinguish what is truly new, in terms of culture and social structure, from what has been carried over from the past. Despite these difficulties, models of change that seek to predict the future of entire societies or civilizations can be helpful. They allow us at least to compare new ideas about social change with those that have been in use for many decades. Let us therefore review the most significant models of large-scale social change that have been proposed by sociologists in the past two centuries.

Evolutionary Models

Many of the founders of sociology were strongly influenced by evolutionary views of social change even before Darwin's theory seemed to offer an analogy between biological and social evolution (Nisbet, 1969). The main components of the nineteenth-century evolutionary model are:

1. *Social change is natural and constant.* Social order exists even while change occurs; social change, on the other hand, is the means of attaining higher levels of social order.
2. *Social evolution has a direction.* Societies become increasingly complex. Émile Durkheim, for example, viewed societies as evolving from simpler forms based on similar segments like villages to more complex forms based on division of labor and the resultant interdependence among ever-larger numbers of people.
3. *Social evolution is continuous.* Change occurs as a result of social forces acting within a society, even without exogenous influences like colonialism. This happens through a steady series of stages. Many, but not all, evolutionary theories interpret social change as progress toward better conditions of life.
4. *Change is necessary and proceeds from uniform causes.* Because social change occurs naturally, continuously, and from within, it must be necessary. In other words, whether or not we want change, it will occur because of the logic of social evolution. And social evolution will be similar in all societies because all socie-

ties are similar in their ways of dealing with the dilemmas of human existence.

Two assumptions that are implicit in the nineteenth-century model of social evolution have been strongly criticized by twentieth-century social scientists. The first is that all of the world's societies would eventually resemble those of Western Europe in their institutions and even in their cultural values and ideologies. The second is that social evolution represents progress.

Modern evolutionary theorists refer to earlier models as *unilinear* because they predict that all societies will inevitably come to resemble Western societies. A less ethnocentric version of evolutionary theory is found in *multilinear* models of social change. These models do not assume that large-scale change in a society represents progress, and they attempt to account for the values that are lost as well as for those that are gained. Multilinear models also emphasize that one must study each society separately in order to discover the evolutionary stages that are unique to a particular society as well as those that have been experienced by other societies too (Lenski and Lenski, 1982; Sahlins and Servide, 1960; Steward, 1955). Thus societies like Ivory Coast, where the Ebrie live, have not developed much heavy industry. On the other hand, Ivory Coast has a relatively advanced agricultural base that provides the surpluses needed for modernization to take place in other areas of social life.

Multilinear models can be useful in accounting for the erratic course of modernization in the Islamic world, or in helping the Ebrie in their attempts to understand what aspects of their village culture might remain viable even as their tribe becomes incorporated into a modern African state. But such models do not tell us why societies like Great Britain have declined from the heights of imperial power or why the ancient civilizations of Egypt, Greece, and Rome flourished, declined, and ultimately became material for courses in ancient history and classics. Cyclical theories of social change attempt to explain such phenomena by placing the possibility of decline at the same level as that of growth and "progress."

Cyclical Theories

In 1918, when Europe had been devastated by World War I, Oswald Spengler, a German schoolteacher-turned-historian, published a controversial book, *The Decline of the West*. Spengler's gloomy thesis was that all societies pass through stages roughly equivalent to the life stages of human beings: infancy, youth, adulthood, and old age. The West, he argued, had passed through its maturity in the eighteenth century and was now entering a long period of decline. This process was inevitable and irreversible. There was nothing anyone could do to change its course.

A similar but more positive "rise and fall" theory of social change was developed by the British historian Arnold Toynbee. Toynbee suggested that all societies grow and decline as they respond to the challenges posed by their physical and social environments. In this "challenge and response" model, a society like England must solve basic ecological problems, such as the fact that it is a small island nation with a limited supply of farmland. It responds by emphasizing foreign trade and using its superior naval power to protect its trade routes. When its naval power declines, it must find new ways of meeting these challenges or face further decline. Thus for Toynbee the rise and fall of a society is accounted for by continual innovation in response to changes in its environment. However, although this theory is quite convincing as an explanation of history, it says little about what any particular society may expect in the way of challenges in the future.

Pitirim Sorokin (1937), a Russian immigrant who greatly influenced American social theory in the early twentieth century, also developed a cyclical theory of social change. His theory attempted to account for why a society or civilization might change in a particular way. All societies, he wrote, are continually experiencing social change, and such change originates in their culture. This is because cultures are not unified but are marked by opposing sets of values, norms, and lifestyles. At one extreme of a society's cultural system is its "ideational culture," so named because it stresses spiritual values, hard work, self-denial, and a strong moral code. At the

other extreme is its "sensate culture." This set of cultural traits encourages sensory experiences, self-expression, and gratification of individual desires. Neither of these extremes can produce a stable society. Ideational culture results in benefits that are enjoyed by pleasure seekers in later generations, and the society will decline until this trend is reversed and ideational traits are emphasized once again. At some point in its history a society may combine these two cultural tendencies. Then, according to Sorokin, it has reached its "idealistic point." But such a golden age is not likely to last forever.

Conflict Models

Cyclical theories of social change, with their cycles of rise and fall and their brief golden ages, may seem to confirm the common notion that history repeats itself. This notion is erroneous, however. Societies may experience similar events, such as wars or revolutions, at different times in their history, but the actual populations and issues involved are never exactly the same. More important, cyclical theories fail to deal with changes in social institutions or class structures. This is where conflict models of social change are most useful. They argue that conflict among groups with different amounts of power produces social change, which leads to a new system of social stratification, which in turn leads to further conflict and further change.

"The history of all hitherto existing societies," wrote Karl Marx and Friedrich Engels in *The Communist Manifesto*, "is the history of class struggles" (quoted in Truzzi, 1971, p. 204). These struggles are the source of social change in every period of history. In any society, Marx argued, the main conflicting classes will be the exploiters and the exploited, those who control the means of production and those whose labor power is necessary to make those means of production actually produce. The exploited workers could become a revolutionary class—that is, one that could bring about an entirely new social order. But this can occur only when changes in the means of production—new technologies like the factory system, for example—make older classes obsolete.

In earlier chapters we have discussed the shortcomings of this model of social change, especially the inadequacies of the Marxian concepts of class and class conflict. We know that revolutionary class conflict has not occurred in many capitalist societies, and at the same time we see in the experience of Polish workers today that class conflict can exist in societies that claim to have eliminated worker exploitation. Yet as we look around the world at the struggles between the haves and the have-nots, the rulers and the ruled, the rich nations and the poorer nations, we cannot help but apply Marxian categories and test Marx's theory of social change over and over again.

Some modern conflict theorists depart from the Marxian view of social change, finding conflict among many different kinds of groups and in every social institution. For the German social theorist Ralf Dahrendorf (1959), this conflict produces social change at all times, but the change is not always revolutionary. We cannot change our laws, our bureaucracies, or even our families, for example, without first experiencing conflicts among various group and individual interests. In most cases it is only when the deprivation experienced by whole classes or status groups is extreme that conflict is likely to be violent and to produce the unrest that could end in revolutionary social change.

Functionalist Models

From a functionalist perspective, social change occurs as a result of population growth, changes in technology, inequalities among classes and status groups, and efforts by different groups to meet their needs in a world of scarce resources. There is no prediction of rise and fall or unilinear changes like those we find in early evolutionary theory or even in classical Marxian theory. Instead, the functionalist model sees change as occurring on so many fronts that it seems incredible that society can exist at all.

One of the dominant figures in functionalist social theory, Talcott Parsons, developed a *homeostatic* model of society. As change occurs, he said, a society's institutions attempt to restore it to something approaching equilibrium. Conflict is minimized through the emergence of legitimate governing institutions; decisions are made about who governs and with what form and degree of authority. Adjustments are also made in economic institutions: New occupational roles develop; old ones decline; wages and status rankings such as occupational prestige explain who gets what rewards. Cultural institutions, schools, the arts, the media, and religious institutions maintain the shared values that support our feeling that our government is legitimate, that a certain amount of inequality is required to maintain individual initiative, and that opportunities are distributed as well as can be expected.

Parsons and other functionalist theorists do not contend that efforts to adapt to change, to create an integrated, well-functioning social system, always work. The integrated functioning of social institutions can be disrupted, sometimes quite severely, when some institutions experience rapid change while others are slow to adapt. Technological innovations in health care, for instance, make possible longer lives for some individuals at great expense, but other economic and political institutions have been slow to develop norms for distributing these costly benefits among the members of society and finding ways of paying for them. This type of disparity between technological and institutional change is illustrated by the case of telecommunications, which is discussed in the Challenges section of this chapter.

Conclusion

The last two models of social change we have described—the conflict and functionalist models—clearly reflect two of the theoretical perspectives that are among the basic conceptual tools of sociology. They are most useful at the global or macro level of analysis. But they can also be used, along with the interactionist perspective, to explain social change at the micro and middle levels of social analysis. We can best illustrate this point with a closing example.

How can we use the basic sociological perspectives to understand what is happening to the Ebrie as they become part of a bustling West African city? Starting from an ecological viewpoint, we must ask how the Ebrie are managing to make the transition from rural to urban life. We see them becoming more dependent on a worldwide economy. Changes in the value of their nation's currency, for example, can affect them just as much as the failure of a yam crop might have in an earlier time. The interactionist perspective helps us listen as they speak about how these changes affect them. It lets us see how they are adapting to a life led largely among strangers. Functionalism helps us understand how some of their tribal institutions can survive in a modern society. We see new roles emerging, and at the same time we see old ones declining in the face of new values like those regarding the place of women in society. Finally, the conflict perspective tells us that a good part of the answer to how much of Ebrie culture will persist and how much will be lost depends on the extent to which the Ebrie themselves resist assimilation into the national culture. Their struggle to maintain their language, their forms of worship, and their world view will continue, even if it produces some conflict among themselves.

It is not necessary to travel to the developing nations to witness rapid social change. Change is occurring in every society at all times and at all levels of social life—in the way children are raised and educated, in the way we interact in groups and organizations, in how people who deviate from the norm are treated, in how we address new plagues like AIDS or potent illegal drugs, in patterns of inequality and stratification. Certainly there is stability in societies, but changes, some welcome and some frightening, are everywhere as well. Understanding and predicting social change is a central task of social scientists. The study of social movements reveals much about intentional social change, but sociological research on other aspects of social life, from socialization and interaction to the control of deviance, yields insights into the world's social future. These basic "social dynamics" have been covered in the preceding chapters. Our task now is to expand on this base and explore the ways in which social change occurs and how it affects the major institutions of society.

CHALLENGES TO CONTEMPORARY SOCIETY

The Impact of Telecommunications

If one asks a person born in the early decades of this century what life was like "back then," one is likely to hear accounts of an age before television and before convenient telephone systems, an age of rail travel, of slower cars on two-lane roads, of laborious mental calculation (not calculators and computers) and chancy medical diagnostics (not high-tech CT scans or sonograms). Even this author, not yet old and no longer young, vividly remembers what our society was like before everyone had a television set. We gathered at the radio and imagined the action. Later, when we could see familiar radio stars on TV, it was sometimes a shock to connect the face with the well-known voice.

Almost everyone associates social change with changes in technology. People born only two decades ago will do the same when they talk about all the changes brought about by new computer and telecommunications technologies. Compact disks, camcorders, cable television, digital audio, high-definition video, fiberoptics, microcomputers, faster computer chips, and many other innovations have burst upon the scene in the past few years. These technologies will produce immense social changes in coming decades. Sociologists are already at work trying to understand the speed at which the new technologies will diffuse through the population and the consequences they will have for our lives (Pea and Sheingold, 1987). However, sociologists are less concerned with the inventions themselves than with their social uses and the norms and organizations that govern their use (or nonuse

or misuse). Let us take the consequences of the new telecommunications technology as an example.

Imagine your home only a few years from now. Your living room has an entertainment center connected to the local fiberoptic phone system. You can make video movie selections on your computer screen. Your equipment will record the material (for a modest fee), and you can watch it at your convenience. The same is true for audio selections. Do you want to audition the latest sensations on the music scene? No need to go shopping in a crowded mall. Just order your selection through the computer; it will be automatically recorded on your digital-audio recorder (for another fee) and you will have it in your own collection. Those collections are stored in computer memory—no messy little boxes or records to bother with. The entire history of music—video, movies, text, and voice recordings—is available to you over the computer-phone circuitry. What is your pleasure—R&B, country, disco soul, heavy metal, classic rock, jazz, fusion, pop? You name it and you can dial up a catalog and order the sounds you like (for a modest fee, billed to your credit account; of course, you must have an account).

Health care is just as advanced as entertainment. There's a personal health center in your bathroom. Insert your wrist and it measures your pulse and blood pressure. Insert a finger and it painlessly takes readings of your blood count, blood sugar, cholesterol, and other vital signs. Your lung functioning, muscle tone, brainwaves, and heart function can also be measured. All these data are sent to your doctor's mainframe computer, where your medical records are kept. You can have the equivalent of a visit to a doctor's office every day if you wish (a modest fee is charged for each set of data entered). The monitoring devices help avoid unneeded office and hospital visits and provide (for a fee billed directly to your credit account) a higher quality of daily health monitoring than could have been imagined a few years ago.

We could continue this imaginary visit to the home of the future. The automated home workspace makes visits to the office unnecessary and eliminates much frustrating commuting. An on-line inventory of foods and beverages is delivered automatically to the automated kitchen (and charged electronically to your credit account). But wait. Will these technologies actually be common enough for you to enjoy in this lifetime?

Most of these innovations already exist. The technology is available. But then why are the systems not in place? Why are we not experiencing these changes more quickly? The answers are sociological, not technological.

Ithiel de Sola Pool (1977), the world's most renowned telecommunications researcher until his death in 1987, pointed out that although technologies may be available, society may not be prepared to accept them. This is so for a variety of reasons. First, there are risks for anyone who is an early adopter of a new technology on either the supply or the demand side. On the supply side, the company that chooses to sell a particular invention bets that one type of equipment will win out over others. Many will make the wrong choice and lose vast sums, as occurred in the case of video disk versus video tape. The buyer also takes a risk. Prices are higher at first, and the equipment may quickly become obsolete as new, more efficient systems come on-line. And the "modest" fees mentioned earlier may not be modest at all for the early adopters. So most potential vendors of the systems and most potential users will wait on the sidelines, and change will occur far more slowly than it might if the risks were not so great.

Perhaps the slow pace of adoption of these technologies is reasonable. How well do we understand their social consequences? Will everyone need a credit line to enjoy the benefits of telecommunications? What about the poor? Perhaps they will be even more deprived in the telecommunications-based world of the future. And what about protecting the rights of those who produce entertainment materials? Artists have a right to be paid for sales of their work. How will the usage fees be shared with them, and how will their work be protected against illegal copying? A major challenge of telecommunications lies in developing social systems to cope with the consequences of these innovations. Another challenge is to understand the processes of adoption and risk so that one can know when to plunge ahead and when to wait.

SUMMARY

Social change refers to variations over time in the ecological ordering of populations and communities, in patterns of roles and social interactions, in the structure and functioning of institutions, and in the cultures of societies. Such changes can result from forces building within societies (*endogenous forces*) as well as from forces exerted from the outside (*exogenous forces*). Changes at the micro, middle, and macro levels of social life usually are interrelated.

One of the major forces that produce social change is war. The primary ecological effects of war are casualties and conquest. War also results in large-scale shifts in population and rapid acceleration of economic change. It can affect a society's culture in a variety of ways, and it may drastically change the structure of a society, especially its major social institutions.

A second major source of social change is the set of trends that are collectively known as *modernization*. This term is used to describe a set of social changes that have taken place in societies throughout the world as a result of industrialization, urbanization, and the development of nation-states. These changes include a shift from simple techniques toward the application of scientific knowledge, an evolution from subsistence farming toward the commercial production of agricultural goods; a transition from the use of human and animal power toward the use of power-driven machines; and a movement from the farm and village toward urban concentrations. These processes may or may not take place simultaneously.

Social scientists often use the term *third world* to refer to nations that have won independence from colonial dominance in the decades since World War II. Such nations are also called *developing nations* or *modernizing nations*. They are undergoing a set of transformations in their institutions whose effect is to increase the productivity of their people, their health, their literacy, and their ability to participate in political decision making. Some sociologists argue that the development of the more advanced nations actually impedes development in the newer nations. Wallerstein's world system theory divides the world into *core states*, *semiperipheral areas*, and *peripheral areas*.

Research on the effects of modernization on the individual has found that the "modern" personality is characterized by open-mindedness, independence from traditional authorities, a sense of personal efficacy, the desire to be an informed citizen, and readiness for new experiences. Comparative studies of occupational prestige have found that adults in different societies evaluate the prestige of various occupations in roughly the same way. Research on modernization has also shown that over time the developing nations tend to become more like the developed nations.

People often experience social change as highly problematic. In pursuing new opportunities in education, leisure activities, intimate relationships, and political participation, they may find themselves without a clear set of norms to guide their lives and hence may experience anomie. The entry of large numbers of women into the labor force, for example, has upset the traditional norms of family life. Similarly, the civil rights movement has greatly reduced racial discrimination in the United States, but for a large proportion of the black population these gains have been offset by changes in the structure of the economy. A third area in which social change touches the individual is public policy, which may involve trade-offs between conflicting goals such as eliminating poverty and protecting the environment.

Sociologists have often attempted to develop models of social change that can be used to predict the future of whole societies or civilizations. Many of the founders of sociology favored an evolutionary model in which social change is seen as natural and constant; all societies inevitably become increasingly complex through a steady series of stages. Modern evolutionary theorists refer to such models as *unilinear* because they predict that all societies will undergo the same process of change. *Multilinear* models emphasize that one must study each society separately to discover the evolutionary stages unique to a particular society.

A variety of theories are based on a cyclical view of social change, in which civilizations rise and fall, respond to a series of challenges, or alternate between two opposing sets of cultural values. Conflict theorists argue that conflict among groups with different amounts of power produces social change, which leads to a new system of social stratification, which in turn leads to further conflict and further change. From a functionalist perspective, social change occurs as a result of population growth, changes in technology, inequalities among classes and status groups, and efforts by different groups to meet their needs in a world of scarce resources. The latter two perspectives can be applied to change at the micro and middle levels of social life as well as to changes at the macro or global level.

GLOSSARY

social change: variations over time in the ecological ordering of populations and communities, in patterns of roles and social interactions, in the structure and functioning of institutions, and in the cultures of societies (**p. 318**).

endogenous force: pressure for social change that builds within a society (**p. 318**).

exogenous force: pressure for social change exerted from outside a society (**p. 318**).

modernization: a term used to describe the changes societies and individuals experience as a result of industrialization, urbanization, and the development of nation-states (**p. 318**).

developing nation: a nation that is undergoing a set of transformations in its institutions whose effect is to increase the productivity of its people, their health, their literacy, and their ability to participate in political decision making (**p. 326**).

core state: a technologically advanced nation that has a dominant position in the world economy (**p. 328**).

semiperipheral area: a state or region in which industry and financial institutions are developed to some extent but that remains dependent on capital and technology provided by other states (**p. 328**).

peripheral area: a region that supplies basic resources and labor power to more advanced states (**p. 328**).

WHERE TO FIND IT

Books

The Transition from Capitalism to Socialism (John D. Stephens; University of Illinois Press, 1986). A study that takes seriously Marx's prediction of a transition from capitalism to socialism and examines the prospects for such a transition in the context of the evolution of the welfare state in Scandinavian and other European nations.

Social Change, 2nd ed. (Wilbert Moore; Prentice-Hall, 1974). A summary of theories of social change by a sociologist who contributed to the theory of modernization.

The Wretched of the Earth (Frantz Fanon; Grove Press, 1968). A classic and burning analysis of the psychology of colonial peoples and their yearning for independence even in the face of violence and bloodshed.

Social Change and History (Robert A. Nisbet; Oxford University Press, 1969). A gracefully written history of ideas of social change.

Technology, the Economy, and Society: The American Experience (Joel Colton and Stuart Bruchey, eds.; Columbia University Press, 1987). This collection of eleven articles assesses the role of technology in transforming everything from agriculture, industry, and the structure of corporations to politics, law, the military, education, and religion.

Journals

Politics and Society A critical journal devoted to studies of social change and theories of social change.

Economic Development and Cultural Change A journal of economic and sociological writing about the interrelationships between culture and economics, and their influence on social change in developing nations.

Other Sources

Statistical Yearbook Published annually by the United Nations, Department of International Economic and Social Affairs. Presents general socioeconomic statistics.

Worldwatch Papers A series of research monographs on environmental issues and social change published by the Worldwatch Institute, 1776 Massachusetts Ave. N.W., Washington, D.C. 20036.

The Road to Calvary, by Simone Martini, about 1340. Panel, 10 × 6″.

ART AND SOCIAL CHANGE

Artists are witnesses to social change just as sociologists are, but they use different forms of expression and different media in assessing the consequences of change. The artist's statement is more emotional and aesthetic, whereas the sociologist strives for greater objectivity and more general conclusions. But each attempts to capture the most significant qualities of changing social worlds. In looking at this series of paintings, we can use the sociological eye to see how artists over the centuries have depicted moments of social upheaval and change.

These paintings span a period of six centuries, from 1340 to 1962, although the majority are from our own century. Each conveys an artist's impression of a time of great social change. People's daily lives are being severely disrupted, for better or worse, by great social movements or far-reaching changes in the fate of entire social classes. There is an extraordinary dynamism in these paintings; the people they portray are being swept up in the great events of their time.

Simone Martini's depiction of the road to Calvary portrays a scene in which Christ, the Virgin and saints, and the Roman soldiers and commoners all are caught up in a chaotic and violent event. But the artist sets the scene against the backdrop of a fortified town, suggesting the strains in the medieval social order of Europe that were occurring as a result of the accelerating renaissance in art, science, and commerce. The Renaissance threatened

The Executions of the Third of May, Francisco de Goya, 1808. Oil on canvas, 8'8¾" × 11'3⅞".

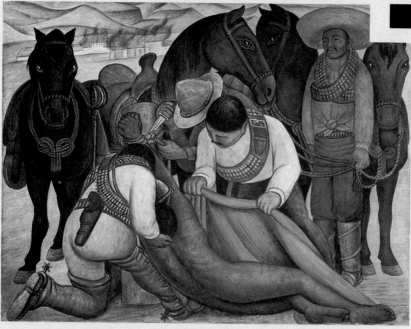

The Liberation of the Peon, by Diego Rivera, 1931. Fresco, 74 × 95″.

the longstanding dominance of the church and the feudal state. Thus the painting makes a strong connection between the changes that occurred in Jesus's time and those that were occurring in Europe during the fourteenth century.

We have seen ample evidence throughout this book that revolutions, civil wars, and invasions of the weak by the powerful are often either consequences or causes of lasting social change. It is no wonder, then, that scenes of war are so often portrayed in paintings. Francisco Goya's painting of an execution is a fierce rendering of the brutality of the Napoleonic conquest of Spain. Firing-squad ex-

Guernica, by Pablo Picasso, 1937. Oil, 11′6″ × 25′8″.

ecutions like these took place in Madrid after the weak Spanish monarchy had refused to resist the invasion. But it is not necessary to know the details of this moment in history. Goya's painting gains its timeless beauty and horror from the way he portrays the behavior of individuals under extreme conditions. The soldiers' faces are hidden. The soldiers are presented as automatons following orders rather than as humans. The dying civilians, in contrast, are all too human in their reactions. Some stare defiantly at their executioners while others cower with their faces covered.

Over a century later another Spanish painter, using an entirely different graphic style and different symbols, captured the terror of war waged against a defenseless population. In one of his greatest paintings Pablo Picasso captured the agony and confusion that the citizens of Guernica, a little farming town, must have felt as German bombers flattened their homes and barns during the Spanish Civil War. And in yet another artistic style the Mexican muralist Diego Rivera combined the artistic traditions of Mexican folk art and Italian Renaissance frescos to symbolize the liberation of the peon from the landowning class, whose property is shown in flames in the background.

Bal au Moulin de la Galette, Pierre-Auguste Renoir, 1876. Oil on canvas, 51½ × 69″

In Auguste Renoir's painting of a gala scene in a nineteenth-century Parisian café, in Reginald Marsh's view of Depression-era Chicago, and in Ben Shahn's stark rendering of life and death in a mining family, we see other modern artists offering insights into their times and the cultures of their societies. The shimmering quality of Renoir's style conveys a vivid impression of France at a time when the rapidly growing bourgeoisie was enjoying new freedoms and new opportunities to enjoy the finer things in life. Women, for example, felt freer to appear in public and interact as equals with men. Marsh, on the other hand, gives us a glimpse into the seedy lives of men without families, set adrift to haunt the skid rows of American cities as a consequence of rapid industrialization and the "boom and bust" cycle of American business. And finally, in *Miners' Wives* Shahn depicts the suffering of women in a poor mining community. Their grief is made more vivid by the distance between the doorway of their home and the mine and its owners, who appear in the background.

Do not let these brief comments prevent you from using your own sociological eye to explore the values and relationships represented in these paintings. One of the goals of this book is to help you develop the ability to "read" the meanings and symbols contained in a variety of human scenes, whether they are the works of artists or the events of your own life.

Tattoo and Haircut, by Reginald Marsh, 1932. Tempera on masonite, 46½ × 48″

Miners' Wives, by Ben Shahn, 1948. Egg tempera on board, 48 × 36″

PART FOUR

SOCIAL DIVISIONS

An American who was born in this half of the twentieth century has lived through events that have dramatically changed the fortunes of many groups in the U.S. population. The economic growth and prosperity of the 1950s brought the promise of relative affluence for all, or almost all, Americans. Blue-collar workers and their families were encouraged to buy houses and cars, to take trips on the new interstate highway system, to send their children to college. Blacks and other minority groups won major advances in civil rights and economic security. Women, too, increasingly rejected their status of cultural and economic inferiority. However, these and other victories are incomplete. Social divisions remain, even though in some instances they are becoming less severe.

The next three chapters look in more detail at social inequality, particularly in American society. Chapter 12 deals with inequalities of social class. After a discussion of how inequalities are defined and measured, the chapter moves to an analysis of how social inequalities due to lack of wealth, education, prestige, and other rewards affect people's chances of achieving success and "the good life." Chapter 13 examines how present patterns of racial and ethnic inequality have evolved from historical patterns of intergroup hostility, conflict, and cooperation. Chapter 14 explains how the roles a culture defines as appropriate for women and men of different ages are related to patterns of inequality in that society.

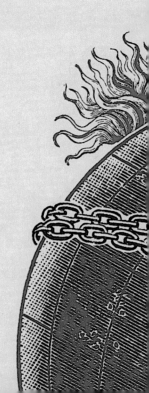

PART IV
CHAPTERS

- Social Class

- Inequalities of Race and Ethnicity

- Inequalities of Gender and Age

CHAPTER OUTLINE

● **Dimensions of Social Inequality in America**

- Measures of Social Inequality
- Changing Views of Social Inequality
- Class Awareness in America Today

● **Social Class and Life Chances in the United States**

- The Upper Classes
- The Middle Classes
- The Working Class
- The Poor
- Farmers and Farm Families

● **More Equality?**

- Inequality and Mobility
- Education and Mobility
- Social Mobility and the Two-Paycheck Family
- Conclusion

José More

Steelworkers' union leader Ed Sadlowski, South Chicago

CHAPTER 12

SOCIAL CLASS

I t takes union leader Ed Sadlowski less than ten minutes to drive to work in the morning. On some days, however, his memories and emotions make the trip seem far longer. The South Chicago neighborhoods he traverses on his way to the union hall, neighborhoods he has known since childhood, echo the history of the American working class and provide ample evidence of its uncertain future.

Soon after Ed leaves his brick bungalow in the neighborhood known as the East Side, where in the bitter strike of 1937 ten steelworkers were gunned down during a union rally, his car winds through the old neighborhoods surrounding U.S. Steel's South Works. Black and Chicano men who were once steelworkers, and still would be if they had the opportunity, form sullen circles at the street corners. Some wave a greeting to Ed as he passes.

Most of the big mills at South Works have been shut down. Only a skeleton crew of fewer than 1,000 workers is still working at the giant plant that once employed more than 12,000. As recently as the mid-1970s South Works was Illinois's largest basic steel mill and the pride of Chicago's South Side. Now only a few mournful whistles blow at the end of each shift. Wind howls through the empty parking lots. Most of the bars at the mill gates are boarded up, and the stores sell used clothing and furniture or the cheapest of new goods.

Steel making was once a decent way of life in South Chicago, just as it was in many other steel towns throughout America's man-

ufacturing belt. Ed's union, the United Steelworkers of America, has seen its membership fall from about 1.3 million in the mid-1970s to fewer than 800,000 at the end of the 1980s. Automation in steel production and competition from developing nations have brought plant closings and layoffs to steel towns all over the Western world. Ed's community of South Chicago is not alone, but this knowledge offers him little comfort.

Marlene Sadlowski, Ed's wife, sees these changes from another angle. She and their youngest daughter, Diane, work as case counselors in the Illinois State Attorney's office. Marlene works on abuse cases, Diane on gang-related crimes. Daily they see and hear stories of alcoholism, violence, neglect, poverty. They can't help wondering whether these problems would be less severe if people at the bottom of society had a brighter future. They know that even when the mills were running full blast there was crime and violence in South Chicago, but now the caseloads have increased and the prospects for the poor seem bleaker.

Soon Diane will marry and probably settle somewhere near her parents in South Chicago, just as her oldest sister Susan has done. Susan and Raul just bought an old house in the neighborhood. Raul and Cricky, Diane's fiancé, are both construction workers. The Sadlowskis' son, Edward Jr., is also handy with tools, but he has chosen to work in the labor movement. He is working for Save Our Jobs, an organization of ex-steelworkers that is trying to win the pay and pensions lost by the workers when their mill went bankrupt. Like his father, Edward may wear a white shirt to work much of the time, but all his thoughts and activities are about blue-collar workers and the conditions of their lives.

As he eases his car into the parking lot at the union hall, Ed misses the spirit of friendly competition that once pervaded the hall during union elections. Many of his old friends have been pensioned off. Some, like Alice Pueralla, the first woman union president, have gone to early graves as a result of cancer and other job-related diseases. But Ed is not nostalgic about the "good old days." He has no romantic ideas about what it was like to pour hot steel. He didn't want that life for his kids. What he is angry about is the loss of opportunities and what he sees as the failure of the steel corporations to share their wealth with the people who created it: the workers.

Ed also disagrees with many of his fellow unionists. "Too many of them spend their time thinking about cooperation with the bosses," he claims. "The only effective unionism is a class-conscious, fighting unionism. For us to make gains, we've got to fight." Among the steelworkers who run the remaining mills, there is little argument with this position. But Ed and other union leaders in communities like South Chicago continue to wonder about the fate of the men on the corners who never had a chance to get steady blue-collar work with decent pay and working conditions.

DIMENSIONS OF SOCIAL INEQUALITY IN AMERICA

Ed Sadlowski's life-style might be described as "middle-class," but he thinks of himself as a member of the working class. The top executives of the corporations that own the mills, whose decisions shape the future of Ed's community, are members of the upper class. Ed's wife and daughter are middle-level managers in a large bureaucracy; their occupations place them in the middle class even if they share the concerns of blue-collar workers. The local banker, whose bank holds the mortgage on the Sadlowskis' house, belongs to an upper-class golf club in a nearby community. The banker's lawn is mowed by a black youth who is striving to move into the more secure working class. The unemployed men who spend their days on the street corners of South Chicago are the poor. Some have been poor for a long time; others are up against hard times because of the chronic depression in heavy industry.

In different regions of the nation the details of social inequality may differ, but the basic patterns of wealth, prestige, and power are the same. As Ed Sadlowski and his family look around them, they see people in other classes, people with more prestigious educational credentials or greater wealth, who seem to be insulated from economic shocks like unemployment. Members of the working class have always had fewer advantages than those in the classes above them, and when the industries on which they depend for a living decline, they face the painful prospect of downward mobility.

This chapter reintroduces many of the terms and concepts defined in Chapter 8 and applies them to the study of inequality and stratification in the United States. First we discuss the ways in which sociologists measure inequality and their changing views of how inequalities result in the formation of social classes. Then we examine social classes and life chances in the United States today and analyze the influence of social-class position on opportunities for upward mobility.

We will see that there is nothing static about social inequality in the United States. As is clear from cases like that of the Sadlowski family, changes in the American class structure are occurring even as this chapter is being written.

Measures of Social Inequality

The basic and most readily available measures of inequality in any society are wealth, income, occupational prestige, and educational attainment. The Nobel Prize-winning economist Paul Samuelson stated that "if we made a pyramid out of a child's blocks, with each layer portraying $1,000 of income, the peak would be far higher than the Eiffel Tower, but almost all of us would be within a yard of the ground" (1973, p. 85). (See Figure 12-1.) An even more skewed distribution applies to wealth in the form of personal assets: Only 5.9 percent of American households have a net worth of $250,000 or more, whereas 26.3 percent have a net worth of less than $5,000 (see Figure 12-2). Remember, too, that inequality expressed in dollars of

> *All societies are characterized by inequalities of wealth, income, occupational prestige, and educational attainment.*

income, or possession of property and stocks, translates into large differences in what people can spend on health care, shelter, clothing, education, books, movies, trips to parks and museums, vacations, and other necessities and comforts.

The distribution of educational attainment and occupational prestige is more nearly equal than the distribution of wealth and income. **Educational attainment,** or number of years of school completed, has become more equal over time in America. The educational attainment of America's black population, for example, has risen dramatically in the past twenty-five years, and today it is not much different from the distribution of educational attainment in the general population, except that the rates of college completion by blacks still lag somewhat. Hispanic Americans have also shown great improvement in their level of educational attainment, but they continue to lag behind blacks and whites (see Figure 12-3).

In a rapidly changing economy like that of the United States, educated people are in increasing demand and education thus becomes a more common route to upward mobility. Improvements in educational achievement—in basic reading, writing, and computational skills—are increasingly vital to

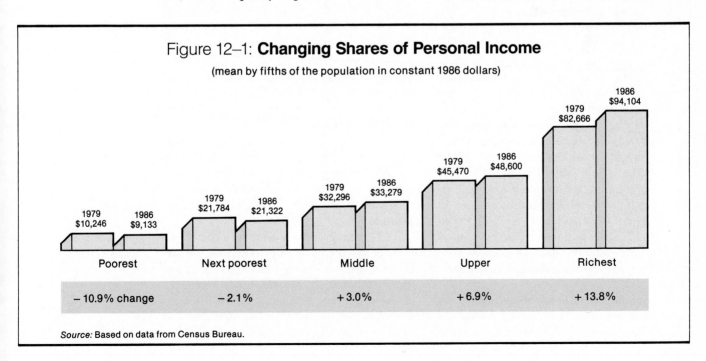

Figure 12–1: **Changing Shares of Personal Income**

(mean by fifths of the population in constant 1986 dollars)

Poorest	Next poorest	Middle	Upper	Richest
1979 $10,246 — 1986 $9,133	1979 $21,784 — 1986 $21,322	1979 $32,296 — 1986 $33,279	1979 $45,470 — 1986 $48,600	1979 $82,666 — 1986 $94,104
− 10.9% change	− 2.1%	+ 3.0%	+ 6.9%	+ 13.8%

Source: Based on data from Census Bureau.

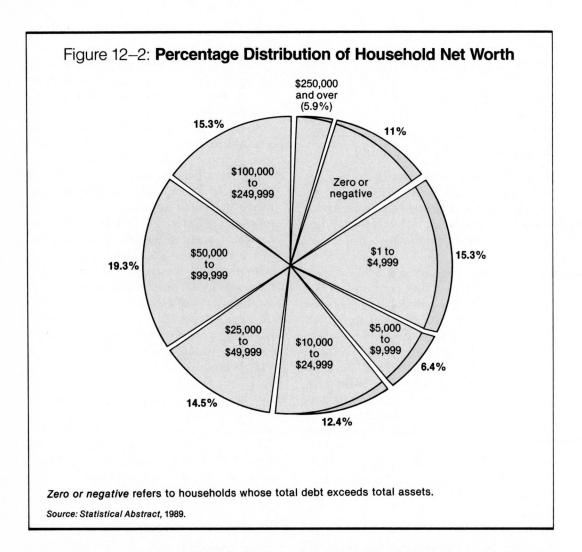

Figure 12–2: **Percentage Distribution of Household Net Worth**

$250,000 and over (5.9%)

11%

15.3%

$100,000 to $249,999

Zero or negative

15.3%

$50,000 to $99,999

$1 to $4,999

19.3%

$25,000 to $49,999

$10,000 to $24,999

$5,000 to $9,999

6.4%

14.5%

12.4%

Zero or negative refers to households whose total debt exceeds total assets.

Source: Statistical Abstract, 1989.

individual careers. For the entire society, improvements in **educational achievement** represent improvements in the nation's "human capital," the wealth-producing capacity of its people (Harbison, 1973). But educational attainment and educational achievement are not always correlated. When people are moved through the school system without meeting certain minimum achievement criteria, attainment figures mask significant gaps in achievement. As a result (as we will see in Chapter 17), large segments of the population are unable to achieve nearly as much as they might, either for themselves or for their society.

Another aspect of social inequality, **occupational prestige,** is measured using surveys of how people throughout a society rate

different jobs. Such surveys find that the prestige people attach to an occupation is heavily influenced by the education required for the job or the authority it offers its holder, as well as by income (Bose and Rossi, 1983; Blau and Duncan, 1967; Hodge, Seigel, and Rossi, 1964). Thus many occupations that do not pay extremely high salaries are highly rated nonetheless. Table 12-1 shows how selected occupations are ranked according to their prestige.

These measures of wealth, income, education, and occupational prestige indicate that not all Americans share equally in "the good life." But what are the larger consequences of these patterns of inequality, both for individuals and for society? Do they combine to form an identifiable system of social-class stratification in the United States? In the rest of this chapter we explore these questions, but before doing so let us look at how views of inequality have changed during the past century and a half as the United States has been transformed from an agrarian society to an urban industrial society and, finally, to a "postindustrial" society.

Changing Views of Social Inequality

The dominant view of American society before the industrial revolution was the Jeffersonian view, which envisioned a society in which the majority of families lived on their own farms or ran small commercial or manufacturing enterprises (Lipset, 1979; Shi, 1985; Stone and Mennell, 1980). This view emphasized the value of economic self-sufficiency through hard work, a value that has persisted to the present time. Yet even in Jefferson's time the pattern of agrarian and small-town

independence was not universal. In the early nineteenth century American society was already developing a rather complex and diverse set of stratification systems. In New England and the Middle Atlantic states, the Jeffersonian ideal of rural farmers and town-dwelling tradesmen, all with similar degrees of power and prestige, was reflected in reality. But in the larger cities a landless wage-earning class was emerging, as was a class of factory owners, bankers, and entrepreneurs. Throughout most of the southern states, by contrast, the major classes were the plantation owners and their families and staffs, the town merchants and tradesmen, and the marginal "poor white" farmers; in addition to these classes, there was a caste—the slaves.

Native Americans were not included in any of these stratification systems. By the 1830s they were already a *pariah group*—they were excluded from the stratification system and considered too different or inferior to be el-

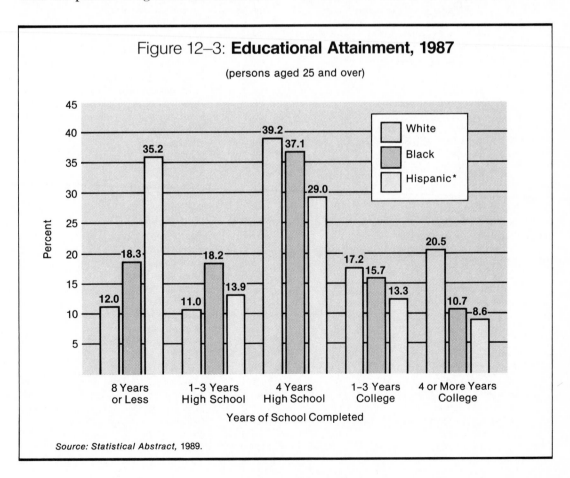

Figure 12–3: **Educational Attainment, 1987**

(persons aged 25 and over)

Source: Statistical Abstract, 1989.

Table 12–1: **Prestige Scores of Selected Occupations**

Occupation	Prestige	Occupation	Prestige
Physician	95.8	Post office clerk	42.3
Mayor	92.2	Beautician	42.1
Lawyer	90.1	Piano tuner	41.0
College professor	90.1	Landscape gardener	40.5
Architect	88.8	Truck driver	40.1
City superintendent of schools	87.8	House painter	39.7
Owner of a factory employing 2,000 people	81.7	Hairdresser	39.4
Stockbroker	81.7	Pastry chef in a restaurant	39.4
Advertising executive	80.8	Butcher in a shop	38.8
Electrical engineer	79.5	Washing-machine repairman	38.8
Building construction contractor	78.9	Automobile refinisher	36.9
Chiropractor	75.3	Someone who sells shoes in a store	35.9
Registered nurse	75.0	Cashier	35.6
Sociologist	74.7	File clerk	34.0
Accountant	71.2	Dress cutter	33.3
High school teacher	70.2	Cattledriver working for own family	33.0
Manager of a factory employing 2,000 people	69.2	Cotton farmer	32.4
Office manager	68.3	Metal-container maker	31.1
Administrative assistant	67.8	Hospital aide	29.5
Grade school teacher	65.4	Fireman in a boiler room	29.2
Power house engineer	64.5	Floor finisher	28.8
Hotel manager	64.1	Assembly-line worker	28.3
Circulation director of a newspaper	63.5	Book binder	28.2
Social worker	63.2	Textile-machine operator	27.9
Hospital lab technician	63.1	Electric-wire winder	27.6
Artist	62.8	Vegetable grader	27.4
Electrician	62.5	Delivery truck driver	26.9
Insurance agent	62.5	Shirt maker in a manufacturing plant	26.6
Private secretary	60.9	Person who repairs shoes	26.0
Floor supervisor in a hospital	60.3	Fruit harvester, working for own family	26.0
Supervisor of telephone operators	60.3	Blacksmith	26.0
Plumber	58.7	Housekeeper	25.3
Police officer	58.3	Flour miller	25.0
Manager of a supermarket	57.1	Stock clerk	24.4
Car dealer	57.1	Coal miner	24.0
Practical nurse	56.4	Boardinghouse keeper	23.7
Dental assistant	54.8	Warehouse clerk	22.4
Warehouse supervisor	54.2	Waitress/waiter	22.1
Assembly-line supervisor in a manufacturing plant	53.8	Short-order cook	21.5
		Baby-sitter	18.3
Carpenter	53.5	Rubber mixer	18.1
Locomotive engineer	52.9	Feed grinder	17.8
Stenographer	52.6	Garbage collector	16.3
Office secretary	51.3	Box packer	15.1
Inspector in a manufacturing plant	51.3	Laundry worker	14.7
Housewife	51.0	Househusband	14.5
Bookkeeper	50.0	Salad maker in a hotel	13.8
Florist	49.7	Janitor	12.5
Tool machinist	48.4	Yarn washer	11.8
Welder	46.8	Maid (F)/household day worker (M)	11.5
Wholesale salesperson	46.2	Bellhop	10.6
Telephone operator	46.2	Hotel chambermaid (F)/hotel bedmaker (M)	10.3
Auto mechanic	44.9	Carhop	8.3
Typist	44.9	Person living on welfare	8.2
Keypunch operator	44.6	Parking lot attendant	8.0
Typesetter	42.6	Rag picker	4.6

Source: Adapted from Bose and Rossi, 1983.

igible for citizenship. As a consequence of their pariah status in many parts of the nation, together with the settlers' desire to inhabit their lands, most Native Americans were steadily pushed into the lands west of the Mississippi.

The Impact of the Depression. A century later, in the mid-1930s, a quite different view of inequality had emerged. In the midst of the most severe economic and social depression in world history, President Franklin D. Roosevelt claimed that "one third of the nation [was] ill-housed, ill-clad, and ill-nourished." Faced with mass poverty and unemployment, with able-bodied workers selling apples on street corners, the grandparents of many of today's college students questioned the reality of the American Dream. Many observers saw heightened conflict between workers and the owners of capital. To many intellectuals it seemed that the dire predictions of Karl Marx were coming true and that only a communist revolution could save millions of people from starvation. Largely as a result of the Depression and fear of social disorder, legislators in the United States passed reform measures like the Social Security Act to alleviate the worst effects of poverty.

Muncie, Indiana, made famous by Helen and Robert Lynd in their study *Middletown*, provided numerous examples of the gap in income and life-style between the working class and the owners or managers of capital. In the decades since 1880, industrialization had transformed Muncie from a sleepy agricultural trade center with 6,000 inhabitants into a bustling city of more than 36,000. According to the Lynds (1937), Muncie's businessmen "lived in a culture built around competition, the private acquisition of property, and the necessity for eternal vigilance in holding on to what one has" (p. 25). Below them was a middle class of managers, teachers, and clergymen who believed in the right of the business class to control wealth and power. In contrast, "Across the railroad tracks from this world of businessmen is the other world of wage earners—constituting a majority of the city's population" (p. 25).

As a result of the Depression, there was more hostility between economic classes in Muncie in the late 1930s than there had been when the Lynds had first studied Muncie's class system, a few years before the Depression. The workers and their families were far less likely to feel that the business class had a right to its wealth, and they were increasingly drawn to social movements, especially the labor movement, that challenged the power of the business class. The business class itself was far less unified because the managers of the large corporations moving into the city did not feel obligated to join the clubs and churches of the established elite. The Lynds' study is described in more detail in Box 12-1.

Yankee City and the Chicago Ghetto. In the mid-twentieth century a number of studies of inequality in American communities refined our knowledge of how income and prestige combine to produce stratification in modern communities. The research of William Lloyd Warner on social class in a New England town and Drake and Cayton's classic study of the caste system in an urban ghetto are important examples because they describe class relations more clearly than earlier studies did.

Warner's study was conducted in the seaside town of Newburyport, Massachusetts. Once famous for its whaling fleet and Yankee sea captains, Newburyport had become a small city with 17,000 inhabitants. It had a number of textile and shoe factories and had managed to hang onto quite a few of its Yankee families, descendants of the hardy seafarers of the nineteenth century. For this reason, Warner dubbed the community Yankee City.

Here is how Warner began his description of the class structure of Yankee City:

Studies of communities in New England clearly demonstrate the presence of a well-defined social-class system. At the top is an aristocracy of birth and wealth. This is the so-called "old family" class. The people of Yankee City say the families who belong to it have been in the community for a long time—for at least three generations and preferably

> **The Depression increased the degree of hostility between different economic classes.**

Box 12–1: **Social Classes in Middletown: 1925–1985**

Muncie, Indiana, or "Middletown," is the most famous community in American sociology. In 1924 and 1925, and again in 1935, Helen and Robert Lynd studied this small midwestern industrial city. They selected Muncie because it "was not extraordinary in any way and so could be taken as a good specimen of American culture, at least of its midwestern variant" (Caplow et al., 1983, p. 3). Their books, *Middletown* (1929) and *Middletown in Transition* (1937), were "the first to describe the total culture of an American community with scientific detachment. They were also the first to replicate a community study in order to trace the velocity and direction of social change" (Caplow et al., 1983, p. vii).

When the Lynds first studied Middletown, they became convinced that social-class divisions, especially those between the working class and the owners of local firms, were reaching a state of crisis. When they returned during the Depression, they continued to find evidence that the business class dominated the city's social institutions. In one famous passage, a local factory worker described the influence of the "X family": "If I'm out of work I go to the X plant; if I need money I go to the X bank, and if they don't like me I don't get it; my children go to the X college; when I get sick I go to the X hospital" (Lynd and Lynd, 1937, p. 74).

The X family (actually the Ball family) owned the large glass works in Middletown. The Ball brothers had built a fortune in glass-jar making and then had expanded into real estate, railways, banking, and retail stores. They worked so

hard that they had little time to enjoy the pleasures their wealth could obtain. But the Lynds found that their children appeared to be creating a distinctive upper class with exclusive country clubs, farms where their horses could be maintained, and private planes.

In the late 1970s Theodore Caplow, Howard Bahr, Bruce Chadwick, and their collaborators returned to Middletown to see how the community had changed over more than forty years. They found that the city's stratification system had changed a great deal since the Depression. The population had increased from about 40,000 to over 80,000. This increase in size had brought new patterns of mobility to the community:

The local dominance of a handful of rich families that looked so threatening in 1935 quietly faded away during the decades of prosperity that followed World War II. Hundreds of fortunes were made in the old ways and new—building subdivisions and shopping centers; trading in real estate; selling insurance, advertising, farm machinery, building materials, fuel oil, trucks and automobiles, furniture. . . . Middletown's new rich . . . lived much less ostentatiously than their industrial predecessors, and much of their money was spent away from Middletown (for yachts in Florida, condominiums in Colorado, boarding schools for their children, and luxury tours to everywhere for themselves). . . . The handful of families whose wealth antedated World War II adopted the same style. The imitation castles of the X, Y, and Z families were torn down or converted for institutional uses. [p. 12]

The distinctive upper class that the Lynds saw emerging in Middletown in the 1930s had vanished by the 1970s.

many generations more than three. "Old family" means not only old to the community but old to the class. [1949, p. 12]

The new families of Yankee City's upper class, who possessed wealth but had not gained "old

family" status, "came up through the new industries—shoes, textiles, silverware—and finance" (p. 12). Below this upper class, people in Yankee City identified an upper-middle class of highly respectable people who "may

Meanwhile, at the lower end of the socioeconomic scale, life-styles were becoming more homogeneous. The residential building boom that began after World War II continued, year after year, to submerge the flat, rich farmlands at the edge of town under curved subdivision streets bordered by neat subdivision houses with various exteriors but nearly identical interiors. They all had central heating, indoor plumbing, telephones, automatic stoves, refrigerators, and washing machines. [Caplow et al., 1983, pp. 12–13]

By the 1970s the factory workers of Middletown were much better off than they had been in 1935. They enjoyed job security, health insurance, and paid vacations, and their incomes were higher than those of many white-collar workers. These changes had come about largely as a result of the activities of labor unions, which had been excluded from Middletown's factories in 1935 but were accepted soon afterward (Caplow et al., 1983). But in the 1980s the tide turned again, and Middletown, like many other industrial cities, began losing manufacturing jobs and gaining more low-paid service jobs.

Today the community of Middletown is far less self-contained than it was in the early decades of the twentieth century. It is subject to the influence of outside forces such as the shift of manufacturing jobs to other regions and even to other countries. Members of all social classes are more dependent on impersonal institutions such as corporations, national unions, and international markets. As a result, the old upper class has less influence, and the class structure is less cohesive and much less clear-cut than it was in the 1930s.

be property owners, such as storekeepers, or highly educated professionals, but they do not have the wealth or family status to be included in the upper class" (p. 13).

Below these classes Warner's respon-

dents identified three "common man" levels. These made up the lower-middle class, which was composed primarily of clerks, skilled tradesmen, other white-collar workers, and some skilled manual workers. Directly below this class, and most difficult for the respondents to separate from those above and below it, was the "upper-lower class," or the people Yankee City residents identified as "poor but honest workers, who more often than not are only semi-skilled or unskilled" (p. 14).

In Yankee City the lowest class, which Warner called the "lower-lower class," was described as the "low-down Yankees [and immigrants] who live in the clam flats" and have a bad reputation among the classes above them. "They are thought to be improvident and unwilling or unable to save money . . . and therefore often dependent on the philanthropy of the private or public agency and on poor relief" (p. 14).

The six "prestige classes" identified by Warner on the basis of the Yankee City interviews are listed in Table 12-2, along with the percentage of the city's population in each class and the proportion of income spent on necessities by members of each class. It is interesting that Warner's terms, such as *upper-middle class* and *lower-middle class*, have become part of our everyday vocabulary.

At about the same time that Warner was conducting his study, other social scientists were attempting to describe stratification in larger, more complex communities. Among those efforts was the first full-scale study of Chicago's African-American community. It was carried out by St. Clair Drake and Horace Cayton in the 1940s and published under the title *Black Metropolis*.

Studies of inequality in southern communities had already documented the existence of a racially based caste system in the South (Dollard, 1937). But did this racial caste system also operate in northern cities like Chicago? At the time of Drake and Cayton's study, Chicago's black population was almost entirely concentrated in a single urban ghetto. A **ghetto** is a section of a city that is segregated either racially or culturally (e.g., by race, religion, or ethnicity). Large numbers of blacks worked outside the ghetto, but even those who could afford housing elsewhere were excluded from other neighborhoods by long-established patterns of residential segregation. In addition, despite the integration of workers in industrial occupations, especially steel and meat packing, Drake and Cayton (1970/1941) showed that Chicago's blacks were barred from more comfortable, better-paying jobs in other fields. They called this pattern of occupational segregation, in which blacks could rise only so far, the *job ceiling*. In their view the job ceiling, together with the segregation of blacks in the ghetto, constituted a northern form of the racial caste system (see Figure 12-4).

Social Classes in Postindustrial Society.
In the decades since these studies were conducted, stratification in the United States has been strongly affected by technological and social changes. One of those changes concerns the position of the working class. At the turn of the century only three out of ten workers were employed in the service sector while seven out of ten were employed in the production of goods, including farm produce (Bell, 1973; Fuchs, 1968). By the 1950s the proportions were roughly equal, and by 1990 three-quarters of all workers were engaged in providing services rather than producing goods of any kind (*Statistical Abstract*, 1990). According to Daniel Bell (1973), this change represents a "revolution taking place in the structure of occupations and, to the extent that occupation determines other modes of behavior . . . it is a revolution in the class structure of society as well" (pp. 125–126). Bell and other sociologists believe that we now live in a postindustrial society in which what counts is not "raw muscle power" but scientific, technical, and financial information. The dominant person in this new order of society is the professional, who is equipped by education and training to supply the skills and information that are in most demand.

Although Marx argued that social-class divisions in industrial societies would become sharper and that class conflict would become more bitter, many American sociologists find evidence to the contrary. They find that changes in the structure of the American

Table 12–2: Prestige Classes in "Yankee City" and Proportion of Income Spent on Necessities of Life, 1941

Prestige Class	Percent of Total Population	Percent Spent on Necessities
Upper-upper	1.4	33
Lower-upper	1.6	35
Upper-middle	10.2	51
Lower-middle	28.1	59
Upper-lower	32.6	66
Lower-lower	25.2	75

"Necessities of life" include food, shelter, and clothing.
Source: *The Social Life of a Modern Community*, by W. Lloyd Warner and Paul S. Lunt, copyright © 1941. Reprinted by permission of Yale University Press.

economy, and especially in the types of jobs it produces, have resulted in a blurring of class lines and an easing of class conflict between industrial workers and the owners and managers of the means of production. More people work in offices, fewer in factories. More people live in metropolitan suburbs, fewer in gritty industrial communities like South Chicago. The union electrician or plumber wears a work shirt but maintains a home in a suburb with neighbors who work in offices. The computer operator wears a white shirt and has graduate training in computer science but may receive an hourly wage. The social-class membership of these two employees and many others appears to be more than a simple matter of worker versus owner of capital. Some sociologists argue, therefore, that the various dimensions of stratification—educational attainment, occupational prestige, income, wealth, and family status—overlap in complicated ways that make it difficult for people to form well-defined ideas about social-class membership (Hodge and Treiman, 1968; Nisbet, 1970). Moreover, such

Although class boundaries have become blurred, social-class divisions in the American population can still be identified.

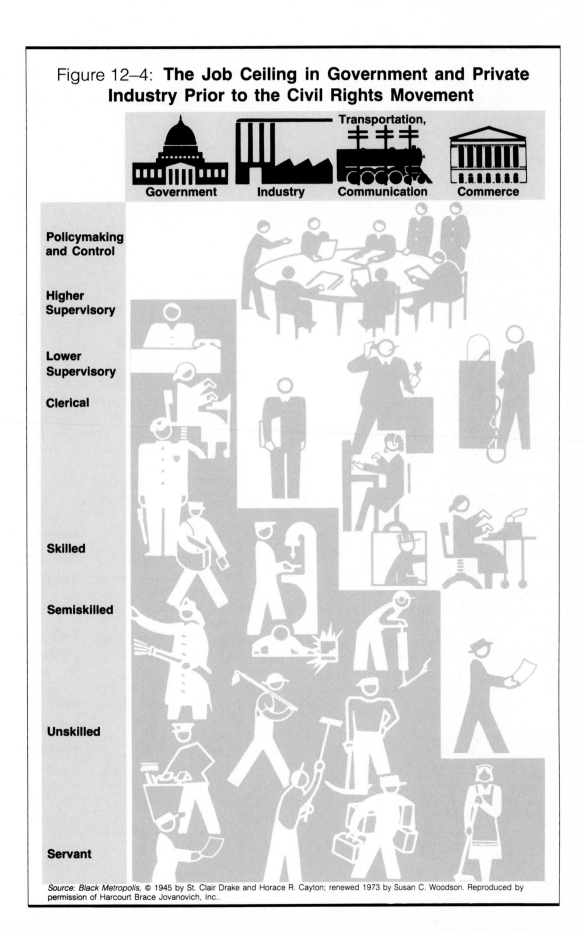

Figure 12–4: **The Job Ceiling in Government and Private Industry Prior to the Civil Rights Movement**

Source: Black Metropolis, © 1945 by St. Clair Drake and Horace R. Cayton; renewed 1973 by Susan C. Woodson. Reproduced by permission of Harcourt Brace Jovanovich, Inc..

factors as race, ethnicity (national origin), religion, and life-style crisscross economic class divisions and further blur what may once have been clearly defined class boundaries (Jackman and Jackman, 1983; Polsby, 1980).

However, other sociologists are convinced that inequalities in income, wealth, and family status still produce clear social-class divisions in the American population. Although it is true that industrial workers are a declining proportion of the labor force, they are still a large segment of the population, as are the poor below them. And these populations continue to demand social-welfare policies like unemployment insurance and medical benefits, in keeping with their interests as less advantaged classes. Members of the more affluent middle and upper classes also recognize the interests that they share; they may demand such benefits as tax reductions or aid to college students (Rossides, 1976; Szymanski and Goertzel, 1979; Wright, 1979). Thus some sociologists contend that the American public does recognize class divisions and that class inequalities do play an important role in determining life chances. Although this debate continues, the empirical evidence presented in the next section shows that people in the United States have a good idea of the social class to which they belong.

Class Awareness in America Today

As we mentioned in Chapter 8, Marx reasoned that social class has both subjective and objective dimensions. In his view, objective social class depends on a person's relationship to the means of production (whether the person owns capital or land, sells his or her labor power, engages in a profession, etc.). Subjective social class is determined by how a person thinks about his or her membership in a social class. In Marx's view, many people who objectively are members of the working class because they sell their labor power and do not own capital in fact identify with the concerns of the owners of capital because they help run the businesses that employ them; in other words, their subjective class is not the same as their objective class. To this day,

research on class awareness distinguishes between these two views of social class.

The subjective method of measuring social-class membership uses interviews in which respondents give their opinions about the class rankings of other members of the community. Because this method of assigning people to classes is based on personal opinions, it is often called the *subjective method*. A second method uses indicators of rank such as occupational prestige, place of residence and type of home, level of education, and income, which are combined to form a composite index. Because these measures are not affected by the respondents' opinions, this way of assigning people to classes is often called the *objective method*. Researchers have found high correlations between the data generated by both methods (Hollingshead, 1949; Kahl, 1965).

Recently a new version of the subjective method has been used to study social-class divisions. It consists of asking people what class they themselves belong to. Thus, in a study of how a random sample of Americans actually think about social class (Jackman and Jackman, 1983), respondents were asked this question: "People talk about social classes such as the poor, the working class, the middle class, the upper-middle class, and the upper class. Which of these classes would you say you belong to?" From Table 12-3 it is clear that very few people had trouble assigning themselves to a social class. The largest proportion, 43.3 percent, thought of themselves as members of the middle class. Blacks and Hispanics were less likely than whites to assign themselves to the middle class and more likely to place themselves in the working class.

The directors of this study, Mary and Robert Jackman, concluded that "at their basis, classes take shape in the public awareness as clusters of people with similar socioeconomic standing" (p. 217). The term *socioeconomic standing* (usually referred to as **socioeconomic status** or **SES**) re-

Socioeconomic status, or SES, is based primarily on occupational prestige, followed by family prestige, education, and earned income.

Table 12–3: **Distribution of Responses to Class-Identification Question**

(for total sample, by race and sex)

	Poor	Working	Middle	Upper-middle	Upper	Other[a]	No Social Classes	Don't Know	Not Ascertained	Total *N*
Total sample	7.6%	36.6%	43.3%	8.2%	1.0%	1.3%	0.5%	1.5%	0.2%	1,914
Whites	4.8	35.8	46.4	9.0	1.0	1.1	0.5	1.3	0.2	1,648
Blacks	27.7	41.5	22.1	1.5	1.5	2.6	0.5	2.6	0.0	195
Other[b]	14.1	39.1	32.8	7.8	0.0	1.6	0.0	3.1	1.6	64
Men	5.4	41.4	40.5	8.5	1.1	1.4	0.9	0.5	0.4	802
Women	9.2	33.1	45.2	8.0	0.9	1.2	0.2	2.2	0.1	1,112

[a] This category includes identification with two classes (for example, "poor and working," "working and middle") and irrelevant responses.
[b] This category includes Asians, Hispanics, and Native Americans.

The Jackmans argued that the best way to ask people how they perceive themselves in a class-stratification hierarchy was by giving them information about how others define class and allowing them to refuse to categorize themselves and even to deny that classes exist at all. Other studies have shown that when people are asked simply, "What social class do you belong to?" the answer "Don't know" can attain response rates of almost 20 percent, and denials that there are classes account for almost 14 percent (Gross, 1953). But when questions are asked in the form preferred by the Jackmans, sociologists find denial rates of only about 1 percent and "don't know" response rates of only about 2 percent.

Source: Jackman and Jackman, 1983.

quires further definition. When people think of social-class divisions in American society, they first assign various occupations to broad class ranks. When there is confusion about how an occupation is ranked, people tend to think of other aspects of social class, such as family prestige, education, and earned income. And as they think about these factors they tend to reach a consensus about what social class they belong to and what classes others should be assigned to.

But that consensus is by no means perfect. Some blue-collar occupations—for example, many skilled trades, such as those of plumber and electrician—are relatively well paid; in fact, they are better paid than many office jobs. This leads people to classify the holders of such jobs as members of the middle class, while at the same time they may assign holders of jobs in offices and stores to the working class. Remember also that the distinction between the "lower-middle" and "upper-lower" classes was the most difficult one for Warner's respondents in Yankee City and the other communities he studied.

In addition to this ambiguity in how people distinguish among social classes, there is the problem of how classes are perceived in rural, as opposed to urban, areas. Most studies of social inequality in America also exclude the farm population, which is relatively small—about 6 million people, or less than 2.4 percent of the total population (Strange, 1988). But since the early years of the nation's history farmers have occupied a special place in American culture and the U.S. economy (Vidich and Bensman, 1960). And although the farm population cannot be considered a single social class, the problems faced by farmers in a society that is steadily eliminating family farms have caused them to develop a strong class identity. Hence, in the following description of America's major social classes we include farmers and people living in rural areas dominated by agriculture, forestry, and mining.

SOCIAL CLASS AND LIFE CHANCES IN THE UNITED STATES

The evidence that Americans make definite social-class distinctions raises questions about what those classes mean, not only in people's consciousness but also in the daily life of American households and in the society's attempts to cope with far-reaching social change. Numerous social-scientific studies have shown that one's social class tells a great deal about how one will behave and the kind of life one is likely to have. Following are some typical examples.

Class and Health. A child born into a rich upper-class family or a comfortable middle-class family is far less likely to be premature or have a low birthweight than one born into a working-class or poor family. And a baby born into a family in which the parents are working at steady jobs is far less likely to be born with a drug addiction or AIDS or fetal alcohol syndrome than a child born to parents who are unemployed and homeless.

Among adults, a salaried member of the upper class who directs the activities of other employees is less likely to be exposed to toxic chemicals or to experience occupational stress and peptic ulcers than wage workers at their machines and video consoles. Those workers, in turn, are more likely to have adequate health insurance and medical care than the *working poor*—dishwashers, migrant laborers, temporary help, low-paid workers, and others whose wages for full-time work do not elevate them above the poverty level (Ellwood, 1988). The working poor are the largest category of poor Americans, and like those who lack steady jobs they often depend on local emergency rooms for medical care and report that they have neither family doctors nor health insurance. The same poor and working-class population is also more likely to smoke, consume alcohol, and be exposed to homicide and accidents—while receiving less police protection—than members of the classes above them.

Education. Children of upper-class families are more likely to be educated in private schools than children from the middle or working classes. Sociologists have shown that education in elite private schools is a means of socializing the rich. A study of socialization in elite American prep schools (Cookson and Persell, 1985) found that "preppies" live in a special kind of total institution (see Chapter 9) in which they are stripped of their usual privileges. In response, they develop close ties to their classmates, ties that often last throughout life and become part of a network they can draw upon as they rise to positions of power and wealth. The segregation of upper-class adolescents in prep schools also serves the purpose of limiting dating and marriage opportunities to members of the same class.

> *Social-class membership has a significant impact on a person's life chances and political outlook.*

Although middle-class parents are more likely than rich parents to send their children to public schools, they tend to select suburban communities where the schools are known to produce successful college applicants. The public schools that serve the middle classes spend more per pupil than the schools attended by working-class and poor children, and they offer a wider array of special services in such areas as music, sports, and extracurricular activities. Children in the middle and upper classes also tend to have parents who insist that they perform well in school and can help them with their schoolwork. Moreover, children from working-class and poor families are more likely to drop out of school than children from upper-class families.

Politics. The poor and members of the working class generally vote for Democratic party candidates, whereas upper- and middle-class voters are more likely to choose Republican candidates. Throughout the industrialized world, voters with less wealth, prestige, and power tend to vote for candidates who promise to reduce inequalities, while voters with higher socioeconomic status tend to choose candidates who support the status quo. Thus, in their studies of social-class identification, the Jackmans found that 48.5 percent of poor respondents and 43 percent of respondents who assign themselves to the working class believe the federal government should be doing more to achieve full employment and job guarantees, as opposed to only 24 percent of upper-middle-class respondents. They also found that about 48 percent of working-class respondents believe that "some difference in levels of income inequality [but less than currently exists] is desirable to sustain people's motives to achieve in the society," whereas almost 50 percent of upper-middle-class respondents feel that a "great difference" is desirable. Members of all classes tend to agree that whatever differences there are ought to be based on individual achievement rather than on advantages inherited at birth. Members of the the working class and the poor, however, are more likely than members of other classes to vote for candidates who propose measures that would increase equality of opportunity.

Many other examples could be presented to illustrate the influence of social class on individuals in American society. But social-class divisions also affect the society as a whole. Let us turn, therefore, to the macro-level consequences of social class.

The Upper Classes

Only 1 percent of the respondents in the Jackman study identified themselves as members of the upper class. Sociologist Daniel Rossides (1976) estimated the size of this class as ranging from 1 to 3 percent of the total population. Warner and his colleagues also estimated the size of the upper class at under 3 percent of the population. The richest members of the upper class, about 0.5 percent of the total population, control over 20 percent of all personal wealth in the United States (Smith and Franklin, 1974; Turner and Starnes, 1976). And according to the Internal Revenue Service, in 1986 the top 1 percent

of taxpayers received 14.7 percent of total reported income.

The upper class may be divided into two subgroups: the richest and most prestigious families, who constitute the elite or "high society" and tend to be white Anglo-Saxon Protestants, and the "newly rich" families, who may be extremely wealthy but have not attained sufficient prestige to be included in the communities and associations of high society. Earlier in this century, families whose wealth came from railroads and banking looked down upon "upstarts" like Rockefeller and Ford, whose money came from oil and automobiles. More recently, the great manufacturing families—the Du Ponts (chemicals), the Rockefellers (oil), the Carnegies and Mellons (steel and coal)—have questioned the upper-class status of families like the Kennedys, whose wealth originally came from merchandising and whose Irish descent marked them off from the rich Protestant families.

Members of the upper class tend to create special places in which to live and relax. They often maintain apartments in exclusive city neighborhoods as well as country estates in secluded communities. They send their children to the most expensive private schools and universities, maintain memberships in the most exclusive social clubs, and fly throughout the world to leisure resorts frequented by members of their own class.

A question that sociologists continually debate is whether the upper class in America is also the society's ruling class. Some, like C. Wright Mills and William Domhoff, argue that the upper class not only holds a controlling share of wealth and prestige, which it can pass along to its children, but also maintains a virtual monopoly over power in the United States. A ruling class, Domhoff states, "is socially cohesive, has its basis in the large corporations and banks, plays a major role in shaping the social and political climate, and dominates the federal government through a variety of organizations and methods" (1983, p. 1). Mills (1956) attempted to show that this ruling class produces a "power elite" composed of its most politically active members plus high-level employees in the government

The upper class accounts for 1 to 3 percent of the population but controls more than 20 percent of all personal wealth.

and the military. The power elite, in other words, is the leadership arm of the ruling class.

Other sociologists and political scientists contend that there is no single, cohesive ruling class with an identifiable power elite that carries out its bidding. This is known as the pluralist concept (Keller, 1963; Parsons, 1965; Polsby, 1980). These researchers agree that there is a readily identifiable upper class in American society. However, its power is not exerted in a unified fashion because there are competing centers of wealth and power within the upper class; moreover, its members' viewpoints on social policy are often opposed to one another. (We return to the debate between the power elite and pluralist theories in Chapter 19.)

The Middle Classes

Unlike the upper classes, in which family status establishes who is included in the highest stratum and who is not, the middle class includes far more varied combinations of wealth and prestige. This makes it more difficult to establish precise boundaries between the upper-middle, middle, and lower-middle classes. Thus, 8.2 percent of the Jackmans' respondents assigned themselves to the upper-middle class while 43.3 percent felt that they belonged in the middle class. However, on the basis of several objective measures of socioeconomic status, Rossides (1976) estimated that the upper-middle class includes from 10 to 15 percent of the American population and that the middle class comprises from 30 to 35 percent.

People who identify themselves as members of the upper-middle class tend to be highly educated professionals. Most often they have attended graduate schools and built successful careers as engineers, lawyers, doctors, dentists, stockbrokers, and corporate managers. But their comfortable incomes, usually more than $75,000 a year, may also be derived from family-owned businesses. Members of this class typically live in the suburbs. They join expensive country clubs, are active in community affairs, and spend a

Photographer Barbara Norfleet was studying the life-styles of the very wealthy in the United States when she caught this patrician gentleman stepping off his yacht on a summer day in Massachusetts.

These passengers enjoying a Caribbean cruise are typical of the upper middle class. Only about 15 percent of the population has enough income to afford this kind of luxury.

good deal of time transporting their children to "enriching" activities.

The upper-middle class also includes a subgroup that is identified in the popular media as yuppies, or young urban professionals. Members of this group have even more education than their parents, are more likely to be single or recently married, and delight in finding old central-city neighborhoods that can be renovated and restored. (The "invasion" of older urban communities by upwardly mobile professionals and managers is termed *gentrification* and is discussed in Chapter 5.)

Another segment of the middle class is composed of people whose income is derived from small businesses, especially stores and community-oriented businesses (in contrast with large corporations that have offices at many locations). Often referred to as the *petit bourgeoisie* or independent small-business owners, the members of this class may be found among the leaders of local chambers of commerce and other business associations that advocate local economic growth. Erik Olin Wright and his colleagues (1982) found that of the 9 percent of Americans who employ other workers, the majority are members of the petit bourgeoisie and employ fewer than ten people.

The middle class is probably the largest single class in American society, but in cultural terms it is highly diverse. The dominant image of the middle class from the end of World War II until the mid-1970s was of a suburban population living in relatively new private homes. The culture of the suburban middle class was thought to be shaped by the experience of frequent changes of residence and long-distance commuting, together with status symbols like "the ranch house with its two car garage, lawn and barbecue, and the nearby church and shopping center" (Schwartz, 1976, p. 327). The suburban middle class was said to be oriented toward family life and suspicious of the offbeat (Fava, 1956; Riesman, 1957; Seeley, Sim, and Loosley, 1956). However, empirical research by a number of sociologists, including Bennett Berger (1961), Herbert Gans (1967), and William Dobriner (1973), has shown that suburban communities are far from homogeneous, that many people who think of themselves as members of the working class can be found in them, and that there is no easily identified middle-class suburban culture.

Another change in the nature of the middle class has to do with education. In the 1950s and 1960s a college diploma was often viewed as a passport to the American middle-class way of life. But we will see later that, although education remains the primary route to upward mobility for people without inherited wealth, the college diploma has lost some of its power to open the door to middle-class prestige. The most general points that sociologists can make about the middle class are that its members tend to be employed in non-manual occupations and that they usually have to work hard to afford the material things that are more easily acquired by the upper-middle class. Identification with the middle class is likely to be highest among teachers, middle- and lower-level office managers and clerical employees, government bureaucrats, and workers in the uniformed services.

> *The middle class is the largest class in American society and consists of professionals, businesspeople, and entrepreneurs.*

The Working Class

The Jackman survey found that 36.6 percent of Americans identify themselves as part of the working class, and Rossides (1976) estimated its number at 40 to 45 percent of the population. This is the class that is undergoing the most rapid and difficult changes in America today. As noted earlier, changing production technologies and the spread of industrialization throughout the world have resulted in plant shutdowns in the United States and a shrinking number of stable, benefits-paying jobs for members of this class.

The most important characteristic of the working class is employment in skilled, semi-skilled, or unskilled manual occupations. Another distinguishing feature of this class is union membership; in fact, labor unions refer to their members as "working people." However, the proportion of workers who are union members is declining. In the mid-1970s approximately 23 percent of the American labor force belonged to labor unions. Today that proportion has declined to about 17 percent, largely as a result of the decline in factory employment. The significance of this trend is that many workers have less protection against arbitrary changes in their working conditions and earnings.

There are two major divisions within the American working class. The first is often known as the industrial working class and consists of blue-collar workers who work in large manufacturing industries and are members of industrial unions. The United Automobile Workers, the United Steel Workers, the International Ladies Garment Workers Union, the United Mineworkers, and the International Brotherhood of Teamsters are examples of such unions (Aronowitz, 1984; Blauner, 1964; Burawoy, 1980; Kornblum, 1974). The second major division of the American working class is composed of workers employed in skilled crafts, especially in the construction trades (Halle, 1984; LeMasters, 1975).

Sociologists have found that the industrial working class is more conscious of its class identity and more prone to believe that its fortunes as a class depend on its ability to win out in labor–management conflicts. Members of the skilled trades, by contrast, are more likely to be uncertain about their class identity and occasionally to think of themselves as members of the middle class. But for both segments of the working class, financial worries are a routine fact of life (Halle, 1984). The situation of women in this class is especially problematic, since they are often the first to suffer the effects of layoffs and plant closings (Rosen, 1987), an issue that is discussed further in Chapter 14.

There is more racial and ethnic diversity in the working class than in other classes. White workers in the working class are far more likely to work alongside black and Hispanic workers, for example, than are white members of other classes. This sit-

> *Members of the working class are employed in skilled, semiskilled, or unskilled manual occupations and are extremely diverse in racial and ethnic terms.*

© Elliot Erwitt, Magnum

These hotel workers, proudly showing off the luxurious accommodations they help maintain, are part of the working class. In fact, there are now far more people employed in restaurants and hotels than in metals, automobile, and textile production combined.

uation often brings workers of different races and ethnic backgrounds into competition with one another when jobs are in short supply or an industry is shrinking as a result of automation. The animosity produced by such competition is due largely to the fear of losing one's job and skidding downward into the ranks of the poor.

The Poor

Studies of socioeconomic standing usually underestimate the poor population because many people in this class think of themselves as working people who are underpaid or "down on their luck." Thus in the Jackman survey only 7.6 percent of the respondents identified with the poor as a social class, a far smaller proportion than is indicated by official statistics, which show that 13.5 percent of Americans are living in poverty. But the poor as a social class are an even larger proportion of the total population. Rossides (1976) calculated that between 20 and 25 percent of Americans are poor, a figure that includes not only people who are officially classified as poor but also the working poor—that is, people who have jobs but whose incomes are too low to allow them to maintain a level of living that most Americans would consider comfortable.

Social scientists often point out that poverty is not an absolute concept. A family of four in the United States that earns $10,000 a year is poor by official standards, yet compared with equivalent families in India or Africa it is doing quite well. The U.S. family probably has permanent shelter, even if it is in a slum or a run-down neighborhood. It probably receives some form of government income supplement, if only in the form of food stamps and federal medical insurance (Medicaid). The poor family in Africa or India, by contrast, may be living without permanent shelter and may be forced to beg and to sift through scraps to obtain enough food to survive. Although there are poor families and individuals in the United States who exist under similar conditions, most of the U.S. poor are not in immediate danger of starvation.

Does this mean that the poor in the United States are better off? In absolute terms—that is, in comparison with the poor in very poor nations—they are not deprived of the necessities of life. In relative terms—that is, in comparison with the more affluent majority in the United States—they are severely deprived. This distinction between absolute and relative deprivation is important in explaining how people feel about any social condition and especially about being poor. It is no comfort to a child in a poor family in the United States whose parents cannot afford fancy sneakers or frequent trips to the ice cream store or a color TV that there are people starving in Africa. In short, people feel poor in comparison with others around them who have more.

According to official government guidelines, the poor are people who live below a certain annual income ceiling, which is currently about $12,500 for a nonfarm family of four. (The ceiling is lower for farm families, because they presumably can supplement their income by growing some of their own food.) From the 1950s through the 1970s, the proportion of officially impoverished individuals and families in the United States declined steadily—from 22.4 percent in 1959 to 11.4 percent (24.5 million people) in 1978. In the early 1980s, however, the proportion of people below the poverty line increased, passing 15 percent in 1984. In the late 1980s poverty increased among African-American and Hispanic minorities and decreased somewhat among whites, as shown in Figure 12-5. All told, 32.5 million people in the United States live in poverty as defined by official statistics. But the reason this number remains so high while unemployment rates decline is a subject of continuing social-scientific research.

The working poor furnish one explanation of this situation. In a recent study of the causes of poverty in the United States, David Ellwood found that among two-parent families who were poor, 44 percent had at least one member who was working full time.

Official statistics show that 13.5 percent of Americans are living in poverty, but the poor actually account for as much as 25 percent of the population.

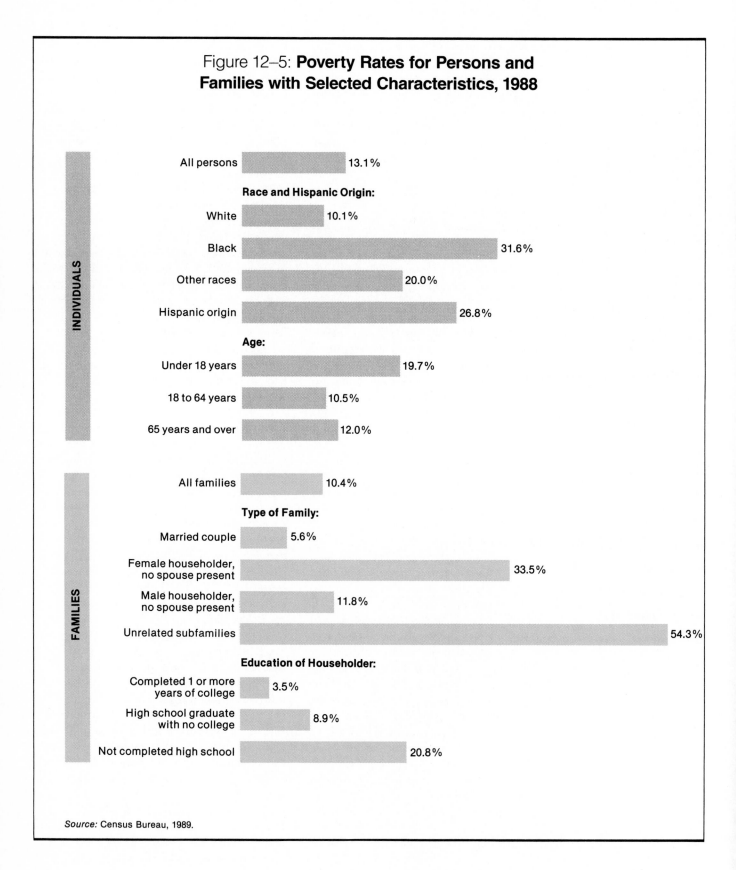

Figure 12–5: **Poverty Rates for Persons and Families with Selected Characteristics, 1988**

INDIVIDUALS

All persons — 13.1%

Race and Hispanic Origin:

White — 10.1%

Black — 31.6%

Other races — 20.0%

Hispanic origin — 26.8%

Age:

Under 18 years — 19.7%

18 to 64 years — 10.5%

65 years and over — 12.0%

FAMILIES

All families — 10.4%

Type of Family:

Married couple — 5.6%

Female householder, no spouse present — 33.5%

Male householder, no spouse present — 11.8%

Unrelated subfamilies — 54.3%

Education of Householder:

Completed 1 or more years of college — 3.5%

High school graduate with no college — 8.9%

Not completed high school — 20.8%

Source: Census Bureau, 1989.

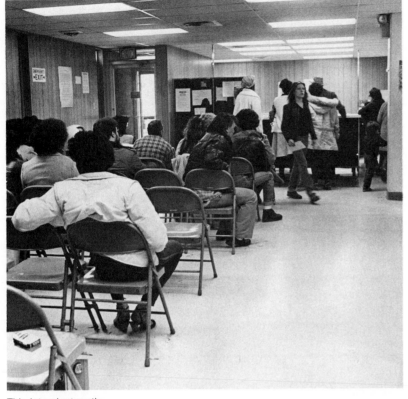

Franken/Sigma

Low wages, Ellwood states, are a major cause of poverty, for "work does not always guarantee a route out of poverty. A full-time minimum-wage job (which pays $4.25 per hour) does not even come close to supporting a family of three at the poverty line. Even one full-time job and one half-time job at the minimum wage will not bring a family of four up to the poverty line" (1988, p. 88). Because so many of the jobs created during the economic expansion of the 1980s were low-wage jobs, the rates of employment and poverty have risen simultaneously.

Another reason we can have increasing poverty amid increasing affluence is that the gap between the rich and the poor is increasing. As shown in Figure 12-1, from 1979 to 1986 the poorest fifth of the population experienced a decrease in income of almost 11 percent and the next poorest suffered a decrease of a little over 2 percent, while the middle fifths experienced a modest increase and the richest fifth an increase of almost 14 percent.

This late-nineteenth-century drawing and modern photograph represent two quite different approaches to aiding the poor. The drawing depicts a well-off mother and her children bringing baskets of food to the poor. This form of individual charity, which the rich often thought of as their responsibility and obligation, frequently engendered hostility rather than gratitude. The modern welfare system replaces the individual gift with "entitlements," that is, payments and other services to poor people who qualify for them. But the modern system also needs improvement, for it is inadequate to provide a dignified quality of life and in many cases fosters dependence on welfare institutions.

New York Public Library Picture Collection

Still a third reason for the increase in poverty is the increase in the number of single-parent, female-headed families. Among the leading causes of poverty is the breakup of marriages or long-term relationships, which leave women alone with the responsibility for raising small children and earning the income to do so. Such families often become poor because it is more difficult for a woman to support a family alone than it is for a man. As we will see in Chapter 15, one result of this trend toward the "feminization" of poverty is that a rising proportion of the nation's children are growing up in poor, female-headed families and are deprived of the advantages enjoyed by children from more affluent homes.

A common stereotype of the poor in the United States is that they are heavily concentrated in inner-city minority ghettos. Ellwood's study of poverty shows this notion to be false, as can be seen in Figure 12-6. The poor in large central cities account for 19 percent of the total poor population, with only 7 percent concentrated in high-poverty neighborhoods. Fully 29 percent of the poor reside in rural and small-town communities, and 19 percent live in the affluent suburbs of large cities. In short, the poor live everywhere and are not concentrated in a single type of community.

One reason for this pattern is that the poor are an extremely diverse population. A large portion of the poor are aged people living on fixed incomes (Social Security or very modest savings or pensions). Other categories of poor people include marginally employed rural workers and part-time miners in

> *A major reason for the increase in poverty is the increase in the number of single-parent, female-headed families.*

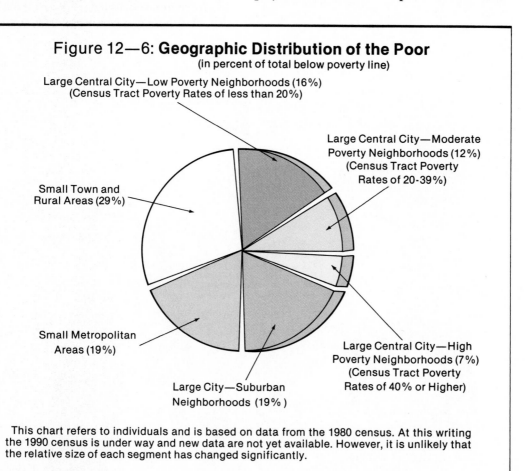

Figure 12—6: Geographic Distribution of the Poor
(in percent of total below poverty line)

Large Central City—Low Poverty Neighborhoods (16%)
(Census Tract Poverty Rates of less than 20%)

Large Central City—Moderate Poverty Neighborhoods (12%)
(Census Tract Poverty Rates of 20-39%)

Small Town and Rural Areas (29%)

Small Metropolitan Areas (19%)

Large City—Suburban Neighborhoods (19%)

Large Central City—High Poverty Neighborhoods (7%)
(Census Tract Poverty Rates of 40% or Higher)

This chart refers to individuals and is based on data from the 1980 census. At this writing the 1990 census is under way and new data are not yet available. However, it is unlikely that the relative size of each segment has changed significantly.

Source: Ellwood, 1988.

communities from Appalachia to Alaska; migrant farm workers in agricultural areas throughout the United States; chronically unemployed manual workers in the industrial cities; disabled workers and their families; and people who have been displaced by catastrophes like hurricanes, drought, or arson. For all of these groups, poverty brings enormous problems of insecurity and instability. Many poor people do not even know where they will be living next month or next year. This problem is especially acute for farm families who have been driven from their land.

Farmers and Farm Families

In analyzing the situation of the poor in America, it is helpful to look at what is occurring in rural areas, where a large proportion of the poor live. Although many rural communities are experiencing renewed economic growth as factories relocate to areas where the costs of energy, space, training, and wages are lower, in communities based on agricultural production poverty rates continue to increase. A survey of 1700 American farmers (Robbins, 1985) indicated that approximately 36 percent of American farmers owed more than 40 percent of their assets (land and equipment, livestock, and crops in the ground) to lending institutions. Within this category of heavily indebted farmers, 15 percent (or over 5 percent of all farmers) owed 70 percent or more of their total assets. It is likely that by the time this book appears many of these farmers will have gone out of business.

This situation repeats a condition that has been part of American social life for more than a hundred years as the nation has been transformed from a rural society to an urban one. Although the dream of owning a family farm, or keeping one in the family, has always been an important part of American culture, the rising cost of farm technology, together with the need for ever-larger amounts of land to make farms profitable, has steadily pushed farm families off the land. Very large farms devoted to the production of a narrow range of crops and farm products now dominate North American agriculture. In the United States, over half of total farm production comes from only about 4 percent of the nation's farms.

In consequence, more farmers are employed by large agribusiness operations, and each decade a smaller percentage own family farms (Strange, 1988).

Larger farms are typically owned by corporations that may also can, freeze, package, or otherwise prepare the crop for sale in supermarkets. These agribusinesses may be highly efficient producers, but they have some negative social consequences for rural counties. Studies by rural sociologists have shown that communities dominated by large farms are characterized by a declining population, a decreasing number of local businesses and civic associations, and an increase in poverty. One study done for the U.S. Congress in 200 of the richest agricultural counties in the United States found that the more farm size increases, the more the poverty rate in the country also increases as people are displaced from the land and must search for marginal employment (Office of Technology Assessment, 1986; Goldschmidt, 1978; MacCannell, n.d.).

As a social class, farmers still take pride in the fact that the United States has the highest level of agricultural production in the world, but this does little to alleviate their difficulties. Moreover, as a class, American farmers are continually at the mercy of a fickle world economy, a condition that they increasingly share with blue-collar workers in industrial communities like South Chicago.

One method farmers have traditionally used to hold onto the land they love is for some family members to find work in a nearby town while others continue to work the land. In fact, about half of all farmers farm part time and work at wage-paying jobs full time. An increasing number of women in farm families work full or part time in rural factories. Many also work at home producing knitwear and other apparel on a piecework basis or performing electronic data processing via computer networks. Still others have service jobs. The strategy of trying to maintain the household's level of living by adding more wage earners is increasingly common in other social classes as well. This is a trend with far-reaching implications, not only for the way Americans think about social class but for all of the society's institutions.

MORE EQUALITY?

The presence of large numbers of poor people in a country as affluent as the United States is a major public-policy issue as well as a subject of extensive social research. However, policy debates on this issue are often clouded by problems of definition. Most Americans will say that they believe in equality, citing the claim of the nation's founders that "all men are created equal." But when pressed to define equality they may stumble over the difference between **equality of opportunity** (equal opportunity to achieve material well-being and prestige) and **equality of result** (actual equality in levels of material well-being and prestige). Americans may believe that opportunities to succeed should be distributed equally and that the rules that determine who succeeds and who fails should be fair. But their commitment to the ideal of equality falters in the face of their belief that hard work and competence should be rewarded and laziness and incompetence punished (Jencks et al., 1972). Thus many Americans believe that poverty is proof of personal failure. They do not stop to ask whether poor Americans have ever been given equality of opportunity, nor do they stop to notice how hard many poor people work (Liebow, 1967).

Sociologists who study inequality in modern societies usually ask how equality of opportunity can be increased and the gaps between the haves and the have-nots decreased. Yet they are also highly aware of how difficult it is to narrow that gap in the United States or any other society. For, as sociologist Herbert Gans (1985) observes somewhat ironically, poverty is so persistent that one can well ask whether it might have some positive functions. Gans goes on to describe a number of "positive" functions of poverty:

- The existence of poverty ensures that society's dirty work will be done. . . . Society can fill these jobs by paying higher wages than for "clean" work, or it can force people who have no other choice to do the dirty work.
- Because the poor are required to work at low wages, they subsidize a variety of economic activities that benefit the affluent. For example,

domestics subsidize the upper middle and upper classes, making life easier for their employers.
- Poverty creates jobs for a number of occupations and professions that serve or "service" the poor, or protect the rest of society from them. . . . Penology would be minuscule without the poor, as would the police.
- The poor can be identified and punished as alleged or real deviants in order to uphold the legitimacy of conventional norms. [pp. 155–161]

These and other hidden functions of poverty, Gans argues, are far outweighed by its dysfunctions—suffering, violence, and waste of human and material resources. And they could be eliminated by "functional alternatives" such as higher pay for doing dirty work, or by the intentional redistribution of income.

The role the government should play in alleviating poverty is a major issue in American society today. It is frequently asserted, both in government and in the social sciences, that government has no business engaging in large-scale redistribution of income in the interests of the lower classes. This viewpoint, represented in the writings of conservative social scientists like Milton Friedman (1962), George Gilder (1982), and Charles Murray (1984), as well as in current social policies, agrees that public funds must be spent to provide the poor a "safety net" of programs to prevent suffering, but it also holds that programs to redistribute wealth infringe on individual freedom and the right of private property.

For much of this century, from the 1930s to the beginning of the 1980s, the dominant policies regarding inequalities of social class were based on a more liberal political philosophy. The policies that established the social security system, unemployment insurance, Aid to Families with Dependent Children, Medicare and Medicaid, disability insurance—in short, the social safety net itself—depended for funding on taxation and were based in part on the idea that the rich should pay proportionately more for these programs through a system of graduated taxation. In the past decade, however, the idea of tax equity (taxation according to one's means) and taxation itself have been subjected to much criticism and alteration. This issue is discussed further in the Frontiers section of this chapter.

Inequality and Mobility

"More equality" means more opportunities for upward mobility. Consider two children, one born to a laborer and a homemaker, neither of whom completed high school, and the other born to parents who are both highly educated businesspeople. If—assuming equal intelligence, motivation, and so forth—both children have the same probability of attaining wealth, power, and prestige, we could argue that equality of opportunity exists. It is evident, however, that full equality of opportunity does not exist in any known society. On the other hand, although the laborer's child has a greater chance of becoming poor and powerless, some children from humble origins will become well educated and have successful careers and may even gain powerful positions in society—that is, experience upward mobility.

In Chapter 8 we noted that there is substantial upward mobility in the United States. But Americans have traditionally hoped for more. They have long cherished the idea of going from rags to riches, the dream that a person of poor or very modest origins and upbringing could achieve great success through his or her own efforts. We noted in Chapter 8 how this theme was expressed in the "rags to riches" stories of Horatio Alger. This highly symbolic form of upward mobility, in which a person rises during his or her own lifetime from low family status to membership in the professional or managerial elite, is known as **long-distance upward mobility.**

In an ambitious study carried out by Peter Blau and Otis Dudley Duncan (1967) with the help of the Current Population Survey, 20,700 respondents representing approximately 45 million men between the ages of twenty and sixty-four were asked a series of questions about their occupations and those of their parents. The responses provided social scientists with the most reliable estimates of social mobility available up to that time. The data confirmed that overall mobility in the United States had not changed much since the end of World War II. But a new and significant finding of the Blau and Duncan study concerned long-distance mobility. The data revealed that "nearly 10 percent of manual sons achieve elite status [high-prestige occupations] in the United States, a higher proportion than in any other country. . . . In respect to mobility from the middle class into the elite, however, the ratio . . . though high, is not outstanding" (p. 436). The researchers concluded that "it is the underprivileged class of manual sons that has exceptional chances for mobility into the elite of this country" (p. 435). Subsequent studies have replicated the Blau and Duncan research (Hauser and Featherman, 1977; Tyree and Treas, 1974).

These findings seem to confirm the image of America as a land of opportunity. Hard work and diligent application to studies are rewarded. But the relatively high rates of long-distance mobility by children of manual workers are misleading. Only 10 percent of all occupations are in the "elite" category, and therefore the proportion of all workers who achieve long-distance mobility is extremely small. Yet the fact that some individuals can "pull themselves up by their own bootstraps" helps to maintain the myth that long-distance mobility is possible for all.

As shown in Chapter 8, people may experience downward as well as upward mobility. Every year many thousands of people face hard times. They lose their jobs; disasters wreck their homes and lives; illnesses sharply curtail their income and exhaust their savings; divorce deprives them of income and security. In her study of downwardly mobile middle-class women and men, Katherine S. Newman (1988) found that most men and women who lose good white-collar jobs spend months searching for new jobs and often must accept jobs that pay less and offer less prestige than the ones they lose. This is especially true for people over the age of forty.

According to Newman, downward mobility "is a hidden dimension of our society's experience because it simply does not fit our cultural universe." We are rich in symbols that celebrate success, such as lavish balls and weddings, but we are poor in myths or ceremonies to help people caught in the grip of downward mobility "make the transition from a higher to a lower status" (1988, p. 9). Moreover, American society has not developed adequate institutions for coping with downward mobility and its effects on individuals and families. Programs for disaster relief and community reconstruction, job retraining, day care, and the like need to be made more effective.

Education and Mobility

For people who are downwardly mobile as well as those who are just entering the labor force, education is the primary route to individual success and upward mobility. In recent decades, as opportunities in the manufacturing sector of the economy have declined, educational attainment has become an ever more important route to a better career. Hundreds of thousands of displaced workers are being urged to move into other careers through special retraining programs or by returning to school. But sociologists have ample evidence that although educational attainment is the most important single route to occupational success, the benefits of education are highly influenced by the society's class system.

In a review of data on educational attainment and social mobility, Christopher Jencks and his colleagues (1972) found that

roughly half the children born into the upper-middle class will end up with what we might call upper-middle-class educational credentials, i.e., with more schooling than 80 percent of their age-mates. Likewise, about half the children born into the lower class will end up with what we might call lower-class credentials, i.e., less schooling than 80 percent of their age-mates. Upper-middle-class children will average 4 years more schooling than lower-class children. [p. 138]

No one is surprised when sociologists find that children from advantaged homes do better in school than those from homes in which the parents are less well educated and less able to help their children with schoolwork, and that children from advantaged backgrounds usually obtain more formal schooling than disadvantaged children—as well as "extras" like tutoring and SAT-preparation courses. But how important is family background compared with other social and individual variables? People often contend that individual intelligence is at least as important

as family background in explaining educational attainment. Others assert that the quality of the schools that children attend is the key variable.

Jencks and other sociologists have found that most of the differences in educational attainment can be explained by the pressure placed on children by upper-middle-class parents (Jencks et al., 1972; Sewall, Haller, and Ohlendorf, 1970). And they have reached the surprising conclusion that intelligence, as measured by early-childhood IQ scores, does not explain nearly as much of the difference in educational attainment as is often thought. "If we compare the most genetically advantaged fifth of the population to the least genetically advantaged fifth, and hold everything else constant [e.g., class, race, sex, and school quality], their educational attainments will probably differ by about two years" (Jencks et al., 1972, p. 145).

What happens, apparently, is that many children with high levels of innate intelligence do not do as well as they might because pressures and models in the home are lacking; conversely, less intelligent children who come from advantaged homes in which they are pressured to excel overcome their innate deficits and do well enough to go on to college. We encountered this idea in Chapter 6, in which we explored the effect of the child's micro-environment on socialization. There we saw that the specific environment in which a person is raised can have a tremendous effect on the extent to which that person is able to fulfill his or her genetic potential.

The effects of social class do not end with formal education. People from upper-middle-class families whose educational attainment is below average still tend to find better jobs than people from lower social-class backgrounds. Upper-class families often help their children find jobs in companies that they own or control. They can also use their networks of influential friends and associates for this purpose. And they socialize their children to behave in ways that are favored by employers. These advantages lend further support to the claim that family background has as great an influence on social mobility as educational attainment.

Social Mobility and the Two-Paycheck Family

Another area in which large-scale social change has affected the possibility of upward mobility pertains to the position of women in American society. For most of American history it was taken for granted that "a woman's place is in the home" (Hayghe, 1982). A married woman was expected to be in charge of the household and her husband was supposed to "bring home the bacon"; women's work in the home was not considered equivalent to men's work. At the turn of the century, therefore, only 4.6 percent of married women were in the labor force.

Women's participation in the labor force increased slowly in the first half of the twentieth century, but in the 1960s a number of factors combined to produce a rush of women into jobs outside the home. Those factors included changing ideas about women's needs and abilities, an increase in the proportion of relatively well-educated young adults in the population, and the beginning of a period of rapid inflation, which eroded men's ability to earn enough to maintain their family's customary level of living. Between 1968 and 1980 approximately 600,000 women entered the labor force each year. Today, as a result, almost 57 percent of all married women in the United States are in the labor force.

The implications of this trend are far-reaching. The trend helps explain the rise of social movements calling for more day-care services, increased enforcement of occupational-safety rules, and comparable pay for work that is of comparable worth. But sociologists are also interested in the impact of women's labor force participation on larger patterns of social stratification and inequality.

The data in Table 12-4 show that in 1987 the median income of dual-earner families was about $14,000 higher than that of families in which only the husband was an earner. This added income may make it easier for such families to pay their bills. But the table also shows that much of the apparent difference disappears when we control for the effects of inflation. Between 1970 and 1987, real household income did not increase by very much. Thus, even dual-earner families are having trouble achieving the American Dream of well-being for all. The addition of a second paycheck does not add enough to the family's income to raise the household to another social class. It usually serves to maintain its existing class position and to add a few extras

Table 12–4: **Median Income, by Type of Family and Relationship, 1970–1987**

(in current and constant 1987 dollars)

Current Dollars	1970	1975	1980	1985	1987
Married-Couple Families	$10,516	$14,867	$23,141	$31,100	$34,700
Wife in Paid Labor Force	12,276	17,237	26,879	36,431	40,422
Wife *Not* in Paid Labor Force	9,304	12,752	18,972	24,556	26,652
Male Householder, no wife present	9,012	12,995	17,519	22,622	24,804
Female Householder, no husband present	5,093	6,844	10,408	13,660	14,620
Constant 1987 Dollars					
Married-Couple Families	30,779	31,394	31,917	32,857	34,700
Wife in Paid Labor Force	35,931	36,399	37,073	38,489	40,422
Wife *Not* in Paid Labor Force	27,232	26,928	26,167	25,943	26,652
Male Householder, no wife present	26,377	27,441	24,163	23,900	24,804
Female Householder, no husband present	14,907	14,452	14,355	14,432	14,620

Source: Statistical Abstract, 1989.

to its quality of life. In more difficult times, when one earner loses a job, the "second" job often becomes the household's primary means of survival.

Conclusion

It is apparent from the research we have described, as well as from official statistics, that there is a large group of Americans—the poor—who are unable to achieve upward mobility. The poor are the most controversial class in American society, since their presence challenges the American ideal of equality of opportunity. Moreover, more than any other social class, the poor depend on public policies directed at easing their plight. And as we have seen, policies that require the use of public funds to aid the poor are controversial because they involve a redistribution of wealth from people with money and other advantages to those with far less (Thurow, 1981).

Rapidly changing societies like the United States, in which economic transformations continually create new occupations and eliminate others, also experience major readjustments in their patterns of class inequality. For Ed Sadlowski and other union leaders, this is a truism. They see the drama of changing economic institutions and new inequalities played out every day in the union halls and on the street corners of their communities. But even areas like Silicon Valley in California are not immune to the booms and busts of changing fortunes and their impact on social inequalities.

In the Frontiers section of this chapter and in the next two chapters, we will look at how sociologists contribute empirical knowledge to these policy debates. However, to know what our chances are of reducing the size of the poor population, we also need to know what is happening to blue-collar workers and their families. In addition, it is necessary to gain greater understanding of the attitudes and behaviors of the rich and the upper-middle class, for the members of these classes have the wealth and power needed to change the conditions of the classes below them.

FRONTIERS OF SOCIOLOGY

Research on Poverty

The poor in America must spend their days in an unending struggle for survival and dignity. That many lose in their attempt to gain self-sufficiency is shown in the statistics on welfare dependency and the growing numbers of homeless people in large American cities. In recent years there has been much debate over what American society should be doing to aid the poor. The Reagan administration and its conservative supporters proposed that society should maintain a "social safety net" of welfare programs such as Social Security, Aid to Families with Dependent Children, unemployment insurance, and disability payments—all programs created by the liberal New Deal administration of the 1930s and 1940s. Moderate conservatives like President Bush believe that these programs are vital but that they should serve smaller populations than they did during the 1970s. They argue that people who receive welfare payments and are in any way able to work should be encouraged and even, in some cases, forced to seek jobs so that society is not forced to transfer an ever-increasing share of its wealth to the poor.

More liberal critics, on the other hand, claim that the conservatives are attempting to return American society to a condition that existed before the Great Depression, when the poor were thought to be simply shirking their responsibilities or, in the case of the elderly and other dependent populations, to be the responsibility of nongovernmental institutions like the family or the church (Piven and Cloward, 1982; Harrington, 1981). Others contend that critics of welfare programs often "blame the victims" of poverty rather than the social conditions that produce it (Ryan, 1971).

Social-scientific evidence tends to support the original goals of welfare institutions. In a study of poverty in the United States, for example, David Ellwood performed a "natural experiment" based on the fact that welfare payments to single parents of dependent children (AFDC) vary greatly among the different states. "If welfare was the cause of changes in the family structure," Ellwood reasoned, "then there ought to be more single-parent families in the states where benefits were the highest. But there were not," as can be seen from the accompanying chart. Mississippi, which pays less than $350 per month to a family of three, has a higher percentage of dependent children than Cal-

ifornia, which pays more than twice that amount.

Many sociologists and political leaders believe that there is a class of Americans that is not only poor but actually trapped in poverty by de facto segregation, lack of education and skills, lack of power to change such institutions as schools and the labor market, and lack of the personality traits needed for success in an increasingly technological society. The name given to this population is the *underclass* (Auletta, 1982; Glasgow, 1981; Myrdal, 1970). But is there really such a class? And if there is, how can we recognize it, and what can be done to reduce its numbers?

Debates about what constitutes an underclass extend back into history. In his classic survey of poverty during the industrial revolution, *London Labour and the London Poor*, Henry Mayhew (1968/1861–1862) identified a large nonworking class that he could divide into three distinct groups: those with physical impairments; those with "intellectual defects" (e.g., the insane and the re-

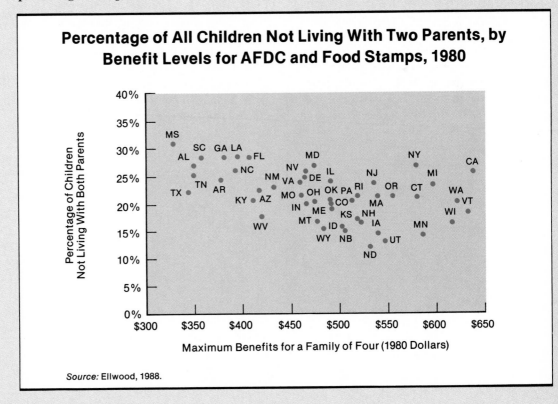

Percentage of All Children Not Living With Two Parents, by Benefit Levels for AFDC and Food Stamps, 1980

Source: Ellwood, 1988.

tarded); and those with "moral defects." In his account of the United States in the 1830s, Alexis de Tocqueville described a dangerous "rabble" of nonworking poor who inhabited and endangered the cities. And Karl Marx referred to the lowest class of capitalist society, the lumpenproletariat, as the "dangerous class."

The so-called underclass of contemporary societies consists of people who have grown up in a world of chronic poverty, especially in central-city ghettos and other areas with extremely high rates of welfare recipiency. According to William J. Wilson (1987, 1989), the existence of this "truly disadvantaged" class is due to a "structural cleavage" that separates ghetto residents from other members of society. Ghetto residents are cut off not only spatially (i.e., by segregation) but also in terms of economic opportunities; they cannot find jobs with decent pay and benefits. This situation, in turn, is a result of "the continuous industrial restructuring of American capitalism" (1989, p. 183).

Wilson's belief that the underclass is a result of structural changes is shared by most social scientists. Conservative critics argue, however, that the underclass is a product of chronic welfare recipiency—that there is, in fact, a "welfare subculture" that perpetuates poverty. For sociologists, this translates into an empirical question: Who are the welfare poor, and how probable is it that once they go on welfare they will become dependent on it? In their major study of this subject, Mary Jo Bane and David Ellwood (1983) found that almost half of all women who go on welfare leave the program within two years but that among those who remain on welfare for more than two years, 60 percent will have spells of welfare dependency lasting at least six years. Young black women from poor urban communities have the greatest risk of becoming chronic welfare recipients, especially when the woman is a high school dropout. Bane and Ellwood estimate, for example, that "a white high school graduate who begins her spell of AFDC when she becomes divorced or separated from her husband would have an average spell length [on welfare] of roughly four years. At the other extreme, we estimate that a nonwhite high school dropout who begins AFDC when she becomes a single parent will average nearly ten years in her [welfare] spell" (1983, pp. iii–iv).

Bane and Ellwood's research confirms that a significant proportion of the poor—currently estimated at 9 million Americans—are part of a large and perhaps growing underclass. This population is characterized by lack of education, segregation in areas with high rates of poverty, and dependence on various forms of welfare. The danger revealed in this and other research on poverty is that the high rates of teenage pregnancy and early school leaving among the poor, especially the minority poor, will contribute to the continued growth of the underclass.

SUMMARY

The basic measures of inequality in any society are wealth, income, occupational prestige, and educational attainment. In American society the distribution of educational attainment and occupational prestige is more nearly equal than the distribution of wealth and income.

Sociological views of inequality in America have changed as the nation has been transformed from an agrarian society to an urban industrial society and then to a postindustrial society. The Jeffersonian view of America envisioned a society in which the majority of families lived on their own farms or ran small commercial or manufacturing enterprises. However, this view did not apply to the larger cities, the southern states, or Native Americans. During the Great Depression, the effects of industrialization tended to increase hostility between the major economic classes in American society, particularly between workers and the owners of businesses. In the mid-twentieth century, several important studies of inequality in American communities revealed the existence of a complex social-class system as well as a racial caste system.

The shift from an economy based on manufacturing to one based on services has resulted in a blurring of class lines and an easing of class conflict between industrial workers and the owners and managers of the means of production. Nevertheless, some sociologists argue that Americans continue to recognize social-class divisions. When people are asked what social class they belong to, the largest proportion say that they are members of the middle class. They base their class assignments on *socioeconomic status*, which is derived primarily from occupation but also takes into account family status, education, and earned income.

Social-class position has important consequences for the daily life of individuals and households. Members of the upper classes tend to have better health and more adequate health care than people in the lower classes. They are also likely to receive more and better education. In politics, the poor and members of the working class generally support the Democratic party while those in the middle and upper classes support the Republican party.

The upper class is estimated at under 3 percent of the U.S. population. The richest among them control over 20 percent of all personal wealth in the United States. This class may be divided into the wealthiest and most prestigious families, who make up the elite or "high society," and families who have acquired their money more recently. Sociologists continually debate whether the upper class in America is also the society's ruling class.

The upper-middle class includes from 10 to 15 percent of the American population, and the middle class comprises from 30 to 35 percent. Members of the upper-middle class tend to be highly educated professionals. The middle class, the largest single class in American society, is culturally extremely diverse. In the past it was thought to be associated with a family-oriented, conservative, suburban life-style, but recent studies have shown that there is no easily identified middle-class suburban culture.

The working class, which accounts for at least one-third of the U.S. population, is undergoing rapid and difficult changes as production technologies change and industrialization spreads throughout the world. Members of this class are employed in skilled, semiskilled, or unskilled manual occupations, and many are union members. The American working class can be divided into industrial workers and those employed in skilled crafts. There is more racial and ethnic diversity in the working class than in other classes.

Estimates of the proportion of the population living in poverty vary widely, depending on the standard used to define poverty. According to official statistics, 13.5 percent of Americans are living in poverty. A significant proportion of the poor have jobs that do not pay enough to support their families. Another large percentage of poor families are single-parent families headed by women. Other categories of poor people include aged people living on fixed incomes, marginally employed rural workers and part-time miners, chronically unemployed manual workers, and disabled workers and their families. Farmers are another group of people in danger of becoming poor.

Policy debates on the issue of poverty are often clouded by problems of definition. Although many Americans believe in *equality of opportunity*, they are less committed to the ideal of *equality of result*. Most sociologists agree that a completely egalitarian society is impossible to achieve; instead, they concentrate on how much present levels of inequality can and should be reduced. This leads to research on the extent of upward mobility in American society.

Research on *long-distance upward mobility* (from low family status to membership in the elite) has revealed relatively high rates of mobility into elite occupations by children of fathers in manual trades. Although this suggests that long-distance mobility is possible for everyone, in reality only a very small number of people are able to achieve this dramatic form of upward mobility.

In recent decades educational attainment has become an ever more important route to a better career. Yet the benefits of education are highly influenced by social class. It has been shown that family background is the most important variable in the extent to which children succeed in school and the amount of education they eventually receive—more important than individual intelligence or the quality of the schools children attend. Another trend that has affected the possibility of social mobility in the United States is the large-scale participation of women in the labor force. It appears, however, that the addition of a second paycheck does not add enough to the family's total income to enable the household to rise to a higher social class.

GLOSSARY

educational attainment: the number of years of school an individual has completed (**p. 355**).

educational achievement: mastery of basic reading, writing, and computational skills (**p. 356**).

occupational prestige: the honor or prestige attributed to specific occupations by adults in a society (**p. 356**).

ghetto: a section of a city that is segregated either racially or culturally (**p. 361**).

socioeconomic status (SES): a broad social-class ranking based on occupational status, family prestige, educational attainment, and earned income (**p. 364**).

equality of opportunity: equal opportunity to achieve desired levels of material well-being and prestige (**p. 376**).

equality of result: equality in the actual outcomes of people's attempts to improve their material well-being and prestige (**p. 376**).

long-distance upward mobility: a form of upward mobility in which a person rises during his or her own lifetime from low family status to membership in a professional or managerial elite (**p. 377**).

WHERE TO FIND IT

Books

The American Class Structure: A New Synthesis (Dennis Gilbert and Joseph A Kahl; Dorsey Press, 1982). A valuable summary of American sociological writing about class, with good reviews of the work of Warner, the Lynds, Mills, and many others, together with clear explanations of modern studies in stratification and mobility.

Class Structure: A Critical Perspective (Albert Szymansky; Praeger, 1983). A well-written text that views inequality and class in the United States from a critical perspective.

Class Awareness in the United States (Mary Jackman and Robert Jackman; University of California Press, 1983). An important original research monograph on the subjective experience of social class in the United States.

Poor Support (David Ellwood; Basic Books, 1989). An influential summary of research and policy analysis dealing with poverty in the United States, with lengthy discussions of the working poor and the theory of the underclass.

Journals

Monthly Review A monthly journal of critical social-scientific writing and research on class and inequality. Most articles are Marxian in orientation.

Monthly Labor Review The U.S. Department of Labor's journal presenting analyses of wages, earnings, changes in employment, and other aspects of economic stratification.

Other Sources

Current Population Reports Published monthly by the Bureau of the Census, U.S. Department of Commerce, these reports present data on income and employment patterns for American households.

Handbook of Economic Statistics Published annually by the U.S. Department of Labor, this volume compares economic statistics for the communist nations, the Common Market, the United States, and selected other nations, permitting measures of relative inequality and stratification.

Handbook of Labor Statistics This annual compilation of statistical data published by the U.S. Department of Labor presents material on labor conditions and labor-force characteristics for the United States and selected foreign countries.

VISUAL SOCIOLOGY

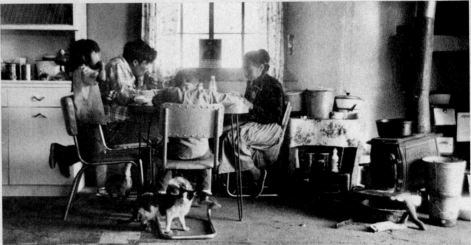

Diet and Social Class

To most Americans, the expression "living high on the hog" refers to people who have enough money and leisure to enjoy the finer things of life, especially good food and drink—in fact, plenty of good food and drink. The original form of this expression, "eating high off the hog," meant that one could afford to eat cuts of meat like pork chops, loin roasts, and smoked hams. Not so high on the hog is the meat used for bacon and sausage, and on the lowest part, the belly, there is little meat; instead, one finds lard and fat for cracklings. To be poor in America, therefore, is to eat low off the hog. But as we see in these photos, the modern meaning of "high on the hog" goes well beyond the literal hog.

A visual sociology of eating immediately makes us aware of a fundamental aspect of social inequality, the food that people can obtain and the settings in which they eat. This collection of pictures starts with the modern equivalent of the hunter-gatherer, a homeless man foraging through garbage for a discarded morsel or something that can be traded for food or alcohol. The indigent elderly woman eats a "no-frills" meal at the senior center, and the mother in the farm worker's family cooks rice and beans over a wood stove.

People who can afford to eat out, even

at Woolworth's modest lunch counter, are on a somewhat higher rung of the social ladder, but a more desirable level is one at which it is possible to fill one's market basket regularly and even choose luxury items such as imported mineral water. And those in the highest ranks of society can enjoy the finest cuts of meat and even the type of feast at which the way the food is presented is as important as its quantity and quality.

CHAPTER OUTLINE

● **The Meaning of Race and Ethnicity**

- Race: A Social Concept
- Racism
- Ethnic Groups and Minorities

● **When Worlds Collide: Patterns of Intergroup Relations**

- Genocide
- Expulsion
- Slavery
- Segregation
- Assimilation

● **Culture and Intergroup Relations**

- Stereotypes
- Prejudice and Discrimination
- Ethnic and Racial Nationalism
- Affirmative Action

● **Theories of Racial and Ethnic Inequality**

- Social-Psychological Theories
- Interactionist Theories
- Functionalist Theories
- Conflict Theories
- Ecological Theories

● **A Piece of the Pie**

Civil rights leader Polly Heidelberg, Meridian, Mississippi

CHAPTER 13

INEQUALITIES OF RACE AND ETHNICITY

"So many people think the civil rights movement began in the 1960s with all that praying and singing and marching. But let me tell you, down here in Mississippi we were in a movement for civil rights long before all that began. I think for many of us in Meridian it began in the 1930s, when we sent the men to see President Roosevelt to ask for the government commodities."

The speaker is Polly Heidelberg, a founder of the civil rights movement in Meridian, Mississippi. Among the events that have burned themselves into her memory are the murders of three young civil rights workers, James Chaney, Michael Schwerner, and Andrew Goodman, who worked together in Mississippi during the "Freedom Summer" of 1964. Chaney was an African-American resident of Meridian; Schwerner and Goodman were volunteers from northern colleges. And Polly Heidelberg was one of the last people the boys saw before they set out for the little village of Philadelphia, Mississippi, where they were murdered and hastily buried in an earthen dam.

"Miz" Heidelberg, as she is known in Meridian, was a neighbor of Chaney's, and she feels responsible for "bringing him into the movement." She knew all three boys, and even now when she thinks of them her eyes cloud over and she prays for their souls. In this interview, however, she is reminiscing about the origins of the civil rights movement, which began much earlier.

"Our folk down here in Mississippi were starving during the thirties," she says. "It wasn't only us blacks, mind you, but we were hit particularly bad. And toward the later years of the Depression, when it began to get a bit better for the whites, we were still sunk in a great misery. There were people who just didn't have enough to eat, and we had done about as much sharing as we could do. I said to my husband, who was in the Brotherhood [of Sleeping Car Porters], 'Listen, you better get up to Washington with the others and tell President Roosevelt that we need food down here. We need some carloads of government food, you know, the commodities, or we are going to have a lot of children die soon.'

"Well, they did go to Washington and they did talk to the President, and sure enough we did begin to get some of the emergency commodities here in Meridian and in other towns in the Black Belt. Now that was when the singing and the real organizing began. People can't sing and get themselves together on empty bellies."

As she speaks, Miz Heidelberg and I are sitting in a white-owned coffee shop in a white neighborhood of Meridian. One of her granddaughters, a child of about four, has finished eating and is playing quietly on the floor. I am scribbling Heidelberg's words on a notepad while attempting to eat an ample southern breakfast. An interview with Miz Heidelberg is fun. She often slips riddles into her speech to gently tease the listener. She is also a deeply religious and patriotic person, and her speech is filled with allusions to God and country.

Miz Heidelberg tells me about the

movement to integrate the armed forces during the war, about the bitterness of racial strife during the 1950s, and about the exhausting, exhilarating years of the 1960s. There is no end to the movement as she sees it. Civil rights was only one aspect of the struggle for true equality of opportunity. Now there must be more progress toward economic equality. There is conflict in Meridian over General Motors' Delco parts plant, which has moved there from "up North." Should blacks side with the United Auto Workers, who are attempting to organize workers at the plant, or should they side with the mayor and the Chamber of Commerce, who fear that if Meridian becomes known as a union town other companies will be discouraged from locating there? Miz Heidelberg thinks the black community will support the union drive as a route toward economic equality.

We have finished our breakfast and the child on the floor is becoming restless. Miz Heidelberg asks me, "Do you know the hymn that goes, 'The great trees are bending / The Good Lord is sending / His people up to higher ground'? What do you think 'higher ground' is?" Stammering a bit, I begin saying something about loftier values, greater spirituality . . . "Sure, you could think about it that way," she interrupts, "but to me 'higher ground' is right where we are now. It's you and me and the child having breakfast in this coffee shop here in Meridian, Mississippi."

THE MEANING OF RACE AND ETHNICITY

Why is it that so many African-Americans like Polly Heidelberg have had to struggle out of poverty and still feel that their people have a long way to go? How can we explain prejudice and racial discrimination, and how can we measure their effects on individuals and social institutions? Many social scientists focus their research on the question of why some groups in a society fare better than others—and, thus, why children born into subordinated racial or ethnic groups find the paths to success so much more difficult than children with similar abilities who are born into more advantaged groups.

The United States is not unique in the extent to which inequality and hostility among its ethnic and racial groups result in severe social problems. In Great Britain, not only does conflict between Catholics and Protestants in Northern Ireland heighten tensions between the Irish and the English, but the Scottish and Welsh subgroups are also highly conscious of their separate identities (Hechter, 1974). In much of Asia and Africa, hostility between groups with different cultural or racial backgrounds often breaks out in riots. In the Soviet Union, glasnost has unleashed ethnic nationalism among peoples who were annexed after World War II, such as the Estonians, Latvians, and Lithuanians, and in the Middle East the animosities between Jewish and Arab populations are continually erupting in episodes of violence and suffering.

Given its importance throughout the world, it is no wonder that the study of racial and ethnic relations has always been a major subfield of sociology. Most societies include *minority groups*, people who are defined as different according to the majority's perceptions of racial or cultural differences. And in many societies, as the ironic song from the musical *South Pacific* goes, "You've got to be taught to be afraid/of people whose eyes are differently made/or people whose skin is a different shade/you've got to be carefully taught." Sociologists try to get at the origins of these fears and groundless distinctions that categorize people as different and influence their life chances.

In this chapter we first look at how race and ethnicity are defined and at the concept of a minority group. We will then analyze patterns of intergroup relations, particularly in American society. This is followed by a presentation of social-scientific theories that seek to explain the phenomena of intergroup conflict and accommodation. Rather than discussing each of the major racial and ethnic groups in American society in turn, throughout the chapter we present examples from the experience of blacks, Hispanic Americans, Native Americans, and other ethnic groups that have played an important part in American history.

Race: A Social Concept

Of the millions of species of animals on earth, ours, *Homo sapiens*, is the most widespread. For the past ten millennia we have been spreading to every corner of the globe. But we have not done so as a single people; rather, throughout our history we have been divided into innumerable societies, each of which maintains its own culture, thinks of itself as "we," and looks upon all others as "they." Through all those millennia of warfare, migration, and expansion, we have been colliding and competing and learning to cooperate. The realization that we are one great people despite our immense diversity has been slow to evolve. We persist in creating arbitrary divisions based on physical differences that are summed up in the term **race.**

In biology, the term *race* refers to an inbreeding population that develops distinctive physical characteristics that are hereditary. Such a population therefore has a shared genetic heritage (Coon, 1962; Garn, 1965). But the choice of which physical characteristics to use in classifying people into races is arbitrary. Skin color, hair form, blood type,

Race is a social concept; the specific physical characteristics used to assign people to different races vary from one society to another.

and facial features such as nose shape and eyefolds have been used by biologists in such efforts. In fact, however, there is a great deal of overlap among the so-called races in the distribution of these traits. Human groups have exchanged their genes through mating to such an extent that any attempt to identify "pure" races is bound to be fruitless (Alland, 1973; Dobzhansky, 1962; Gould, 1981).

Yet doesn't common sense tell us that there are different races? Can't we see that there is a Negro, or "black," race of people with dark skin, tightly curled hair, and broad facial features; a Caucasian, or "white," race of people with pale skin and ample body hair; and a Mongoloid, or "Oriental," race of people with yellowish or reddish skin and deep eyefolds that give their eyes a slanted look? Of course these races exist. But they are not a set of distinct populations based on biological differences. The definitions of race that people use in different societies emerged from the interaction of various populations over long periods of human history. The specific physical characteristics that we use to assign people to different races are relatively meaningless—people from the Indian subcontinent tend to have dark skin and straight hair; Africans from Ethiopia have dark skin and narrow facial features; American blacks have skin colors ranging from extremely dark to extremely light; and whites have facial features and hair forms that include those of all the other supposed races. There is no scientifically valid typology of human races; what counts is what people in a society *define* as meaningful.

In short, race is a social concept that varies from one society to another, depending on how the people of that society feel about the importance of certain physical differences among human beings. In reality, as Edward O. Wilson (1979) has written, human beings are "one great breeding system through which the genes flow and mix in each generation. Because of that flux, mankind viewed over many generations shares a single human nature within which relatively minor hereditary influences recycle through ever-changing patterns, between the sexes and across families and entire populations" (p. 52).

Racism

Throughout human history, numerous individuals and groups have rejected the idea of a single human nature. Tragic mistakes and incalculable suffering have been caused by the application of erroneous ideas about race and racial purity. Some of these are described in Box 13-1. They are among the most extreme consequences of the attitude known as racism.

Racism is an ideology based on the belief that an observable, supposedly inherited trait, such as skin color, is a mark of inferiority that justifies discriminatory treatment of people with that trait. In their classic text on racial and cultural minorities, Simpson and Yinger (1953) highlighted several beliefs that are at the heart of racism. First and most common is the "doctrine of biologically superior and inferior races" (p. 55). Before World War I, for example, many of the foremost social thinkers in the Western world firmly believed that whites are genetically superior to blacks in intelligence. However, when the U.S. Army administered an IQ test to its recruits, the results showed that performance on such tests was linked to social-class background rather than to race. And when investigators controlled for differences in social class among the test takers, the racial differences in IQ disappeared (Kleinberg, 1935). Since that time there have been other attempts to demonstrate innate differences in intelli-

Box 13–1: **The Tragic Quest for Racial Purity**

The desire to achieve "racial purity" has taken a variety of forms throughout human history. It can be seen in the prohibition of marriages between blacks and whites, which could be found until quite recent times in many American states and until 1985 was rigidly enforced in South Africa. Of the thousands of lynchings of blacks that took place in the United States between 1865 and 1954, the majority resulted from accusations that the victims had made sexual advances to white women.

The quest for racial purity took its most terrible form in Hitler's Nazi state, which exterminated millions of Jews, thousands of handicapped people, and over 400,000 gypsies. Ironically, the gypsies were the true descendants of the ancient Aryan tribes from which the Nazis claimed descent—the race they were attempting to purify.

Laws that permit the state to sterilize individuals considered unfit to have children have also been justified by the notion of racial purity. Between 1924 and 1972, for example, over 7,500 men and women who were considered feebleminded or antisocial were sterilized by the state of Virginia, in this case with the goal of removing "impure" stock from the white race. They included unwed mothers, prostitutes, petty criminals, and chronically unruly children.

The unhappy consequences of such laws can be seen in the case of Doris Buck, a supposedly feebleminded woman who would not be considered mentally deficient by today's standards. Doris Buck was not informed that she had been sterilized because, as Justice Oliver Wendell Holmes ruled in a Supreme Court decision concerning her sister Carrie, "three generations of imbeciles are enough" (*Buck v. Bell*, 1928). Doris Buck later married and repeatedly tried to conceive a child. She finally discovered the cause of her inability to have children, but there was nothing she could do about it.

"One might . . . say that Doris Buck's disappointment ranks as nothing compared with millions dead in wars to support the designs of madmen," writes Stephen Jay Gould (1981, p. 336). "But can one measure the pain of a single dream unfulfilled, the hope of a defenseless woman snatched by public power in the name of an ideology advanced to purify a race?"

gence among people of different races. All of these efforts are biased by the use of tests based on the culture of middle-class white Americans, and none has been able to demonstrate that any real differences remain when the effects of social-class differences are eliminated (Gould, 1981).

Racism is an ideology based on the belief that a supposedly inherited trait is a mark of inferiority that justifies discrimination against people with that trait.

The notions that members of different races have different personalities, that there are identifiable "racial cultures," and that ethical standards differ from one race to another are three other racist doctrines that have been debunked by social-scientific studies over the past fifty years. But even though these doctrines have been discredited, we will see shortly that they continue to play a major role in intergroup relations in many nations. And this tendency to denigrate socially defined racial groups extends to members of particular ethnic groups as well.

Ethnic Groups and Minorities

Ethnic groups are populations that have a sense of group identity based on a distinctive cultural pattern and, usually, shared ancestry, whether actual or assumed. Ethnic groups often have a sense of "peoplehood" that is maintained within a larger society (Davis, 1978; Kornblum, 1974). Their members usually have migrated to a new nation or been conquered by an invading population. In the United States and Canada, a large proportion of the population consists of people who either immigrated themselves or are descended from people who immigrated to the New World or were brought there as slaves.

Between 1820 and 1960 approximately 42 million people immigrated to the United States, and Figure 13-1 shows that about 2.5 million people arrived in the United States each decade between 1950 and 1980. (Note that we are referring to legal immigrants, not those who enter illegally or are turned away. Also, we should point out that many immigrants intend to return to their own society, and eventually some 15 to 20 percent will do so.) In recent years there has been a dramatic acceleration of immigration to the United States; between 1981 and 1984 almost 2.7 million legal immigrants arrived, as well as an unknown but large number of illegal immigrants. Figure 13-2 shows that the greatest flows of new immigrants come from Asia and from Central and Latin America.

Ethnic and racial populations are often treated as **minority groups.** Louis Wirth (1945), a pioneer in the study of racial and ethnic relations, defined a minority group as a set of "people who, because of their physical or cultural characteristics, are singled out from the others in the society in which they live for differential and unequal treatment, and who therefore regard themselves as objects of collective discrimination" (p. 347). The existence of a minority group in a society, Wirth explained, "implies the existence of a corresponding dominant group with a higher social status and greater privileges. Minority status carries with it exclusion from full participation in the life of the society" (p. 347).

In the United States the term *minority* often suggests "people of color," meaning African-Americans, American Indians, Mexicans (many of whom have the darker coloring of Amerindian ancestry), and Asians. But the term can also be applied to people with lighter skin coloring. In Great Britain, for example, the Irish were a conquered people who were subjected to economic and social discrimination by the English. It is not surprising, therefore, that when the Irish began immigrating to the United States in the nineteenth century they were treated as an inferior minority by people of English ancestry. This attitude was especially prevalent in cities like Boston and New York, to which the Irish came in large numbers to escape famine and poverty in Ireland.

It should also be noted that the term *minority* does not always imply that the population is numerically inferior to the dominant group. There are counties in some states in the South, and entire cities in the North, in which African-Americans are a numerical majority yet cannot be considered the dominant group because they lack the power, wealth, and prestige enjoyed by the white population.

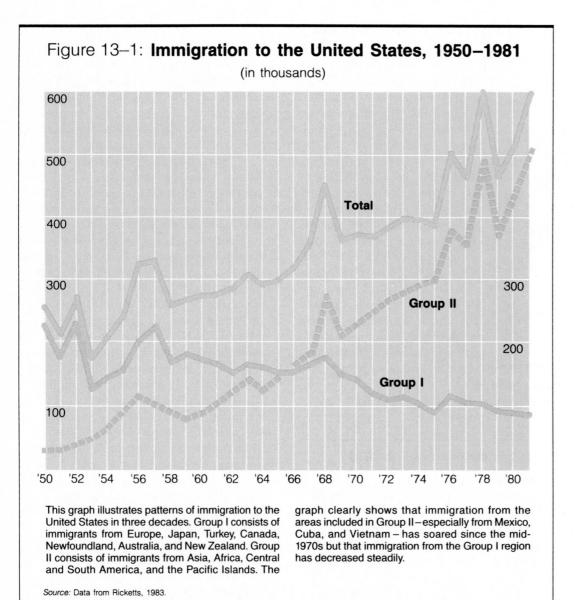

Figure 13–1: **Immigration to the United States, 1950–1981**

(in thousands)

This graph illustrates patterns of immigration to the United States in three decades. Group I consists of immigrants from Europe, Japan, Turkey, Canada, Newfoundland, Australia, and New Zealand. Group II consists of immigrants from Asia, Africa, Central and South America, and the Pacific Islands. The graph clearly shows that immigration from the areas included in Group II—especially from Mexico, Cuba, and Vietnam – has soared since the mid-1970s but that immigration from the Group I region has decreased steadily.

Source: Data from Ricketts, 1983.

WHEN WORLDS COLLIDE: PATTERNS OF INTERGROUP RELATIONS

Throughout history, when different racial and ethnic groups have met and mixed, the most usual outcome has been violence and warfare. In fact, the desire for peaceful and cooperative relations among diverse peoples has emerged only relatively recently. In this section we explore a continuum of relations between dominant and minority groups that extends from complete intolerance to complete tolerance, as shown in Figure 13-3. At one extreme is extermination or genocide; at the other is assimilation.

Genocide

In a study of a New Guinea tribe, the Siane, Richard Salisbury (1962) found that the members of this isolated highland tribe believed that anyone from another tribe wanted to kill them. Therefore, the Siane felt that they must kill any member of another tribe they might encounter. (Fortunately, they excluded the

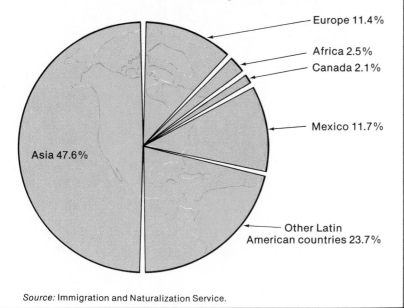

Figure 13–2: **Where Legal Immigrants Come From**

Percent of the 2,864,406 people who immigrated legally from 1981 to 1985. Percentages are rounded.

Europe 11.4%

Africa 2.5%

Canada 2.1%

Mexico 11.7%

Asia 47.6%

Other Latin American countries 23.7%

Source: Immigration and Naturalization Service.

anthropologist from this norm.) We often think of such behavior as primitive, savage, or barbarous. Yet barbarities on a far greater scale have been carried out by supposedly ad-

vanced societies. The most extreme of these is **genocide,** the intentional extermination of one population, defined as a "race" or a "people," by a more dominant population.

There have been numerous instances of genocide in recent history. Those incidents have been characterized by a degree of severity and a level of efficiency unknown to earlier civilizations. Consider the following examples:

● The Native American populations of North, Central, and South America were decimated by European explorers and settlers between the sixteenth and twentieth centuries. Millions of Native Americans were killed in one-sided wars, intentional starvation, forced marches, and executions. The population of Native Americans in North America was reduced from more than 4 million in the eighteenth century to less than 600,000 in the early twentieth century.

● When England, France, Germany, Portugal, and the Netherlands were engaged in fierce competition for colonial dominance of Africa during the nineteenth and early twentieth centuries, millions of native people were exterminated. The introduction of the Gatling machine gun made

Figure 13–3: **A Continuum of Intergroup Relations**

INTOLERANCE   TOLERANCE

GENOCIDE	EXPULSION	SLAVERY	SEGREGATION	ASSIMILATION
The intentional extermination of a population, defined as a "race" or a "people."	The forcible removal of a population from a territory claimed by another population.	Ownership of one population by another, which can buy and sell members of the enslaved population and controls every aspect of their lives.	Ecological and institutional separation of races or ethnic groups.	The process by which a minority group blends into the majority population and eventually disappears as a distinct people within the larger society.

The placement of slavery to the right of expulsion is not meant to imply that slavery is less severe than expulsion. The reason for the placement is that slaves and slave masters are interdependent populations within a single society, whereas expulsion excludes the subordinated population from any form of membership in the society.

it possible for small numbers of troops to slaughter thousands of tribal warriors.

- Six million Jews, 400,000 gypsies, and at least 2 million Russian civilians were killed by the Nazis during World War II; about 1 million Armenians were killed by Turks in the 1930s; thousands of Pakistanis and Indians were slaughtered after the partition of India in 1947; and thousands of Tamils living in Sri Lanka were exterminated by Sinhalese in the 1980s.

Mass executions and other forms of genocide are almost always justified by the belief that the people who are being slaughtered are less than human and in fact are dangerous parasites. Thus the British and Dutch slaughtered members of African tribes like the Hottentots in the belief that they were a lower form of life, a nuisance species unfit even for enslavement. The Nazis justified the extermination of Jews and gypsies by the same twisted reasoning.

Expulsion

In many societies, extended conflicts between racial or ethnic groups have ended in **expulsion,** the forcible removal of one population from territory claimed by the other. Thus, on the earliest map of almost every major American city there appears a double line drawn at the edges where the streets end. This is the Indian Boundary Line, and it symbolizes the expulsion of Native Americans from lands that have been taken from them in order to create a city in which they will be strangers.

Expulsion was the usual fate of North America's native peoples. As white settlement expanded westward, Native Americans were continually expelled from their tribal lands. After the 1848 gold rush and the rapid settlement of the West Coast, the pressure of white settlement pushed the Indian tribes into the high plains of the West and Southwest. Between 1865 and the 1890 massacre of Sioux Indians at Wounded Knee, South Dakota, the remaining free tribes in the West were forced to settle on reservations. In the process the Indians lost more than their an-

AP/Wide World Photos

Japanese immigrants and native-born Americans arriving at a U.S. internment camp after their homes and property had been confiscated.

cestral lands. As the famous Sioux chief and seer Black Elk put it, "A people's dream died" (quoted in Brown, 1970, p. 419).

The forced settlement of Native Americans on reservations is only one example of expulsion. Asian immigrants in the American West also suffered as a result of intermittent attempts at expulsion referred to as the *Oriental exclusion movement*. In an effort to prevent the large-scale importation of Chinese laborers into California and other states, Congress passed the Chinese Exclusion Act of 1882, which excluded Chinese laborers from entry into the United States for ten years. But the exclusion act did little to relieve the hostility between whites and Asians. Riots directed against Chinese workers were common throughout the West during this period, and Chinese immigrants were actually expelled from a number of towns. In 1895, for example, a mob killed twenty-eight Chinese immigrants in Rock Springs, Wyoming, and expelled the remaining Chinese population from the area (Lai, 1980).

The most severe example of expulsion directed against Asians in the United States occurred in 1942 after the Japanese attack on Pearl Harbor and the American entry into

World War II. On orders from the U.S. government, more than 110,000 West Coast Japanese, 64 percent of whom were American citizens, were ordered to leave their homes and their businesses and were transported to temporary assembly centers (Kitano, 1981). They were then assigned to detention camps in remote areas of California, Arizona, Idaho, Colorado, Utah, and Arkansas. When the United States Supreme Court declared unconstitutional the incarceration of an entire ethnic group without hearing or formal charges (*Endo* v. *United States*, 1944), the Japanese were released, but by then many had lost their homes and all their possessions. In 1989 the U.S. Congress finally voted to pay modest reparations to the families of Japanese Americans who had been imprisoned during the war, but at this writing the payments have not yet been made.

Slavery

Somewhat farther along the continuum between genocide and assimilation is slavery. **Slavery** is the ownership of a population, defined by racial or ethnic or political criteria, by another population that not only can buy and sell members of the enslaved population but also has complete control over their lives. Slavery has been called "the peculiar institution" because, ironically, it has existed in some of the world's greatest civilizations. The socioeconomic systems of ancient Greece and Rome, for example, were based on the labor of slaves. And the great trading cities of late medieval Europe, such as Venice, Genoa, and Florence, developed plantation systems in their Mediterranean colonies that were based on slave labor. In fact, the foremost student of slave systems, Orlando Patterson, comments that

there is nothing notably peculiar about the institution of slavery. It has existed from before the dawn of human history right down to the twentieth century, in the most primitive of human societies and in the most civilized. . . . Probably there is no group of people whose ancestors were not at one time slaves or slaveholders. [1982, p. vii]

Figure 13-4 indicates the magnitude of the transatlantic slave trade; the arrows represent the relative size of each portion of that terrible traffic in humanity. The arrows do not show, however, that for the Americas to acquire 11 million slaves who survived the voyage on the slave ships and the violence and diseases of the New World, approximately 24 million Africans had to be captured and enslaved (Patterson, 1982; Fyfe, 1976).

It is evident from the figure that the United States imported a proportionately small number of slaves. Although somewhat less than 10 percent of all slaves were sold in the United States, by 1825 almost 30 percent of the black population in the Western Hemisphere was living in the United States (Patterson, 1982). This was due to the high rate of natural increase among the American slaves. In Brazil, by contrast, the proportion of slave imports was relatively high, but there was also a high mortality rate among the slaves owing to disease and frequent slave rebellions.

At the time of the first U.S. census in 1790, 757,000 blacks were counted in the overall population. By the Civil War the number had increased to 4.4 million, of whom all but about 10 percent were slaves. In the

Extended conflicts may end in expulsion, removal by force of one group from territory claimed by another.

As the property of their masters, slaves could be punished in whatever way their owners and overseers saw fit, as this scene from a Caribbean plantation illustrates. Sociologist Orlando Patterson showed that the slaves' rate of natural increase (i.e., their birthrate) varied inversely with the severity of their treatment.

© John R. Freeman & Co.

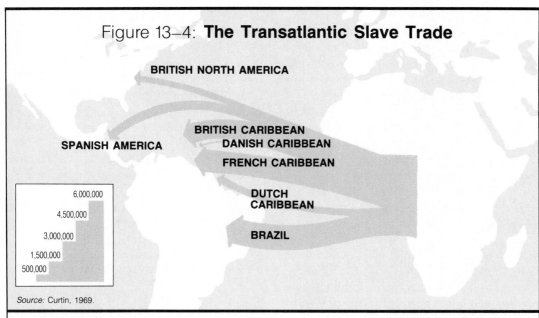

Figure 13–4: **The Transatlantic Slave Trade**

BRITISH NORTH AMERICA

BRITISH CARIBBEAN

DANISH CARIBBEAN

SPANISH AMERICA

FRENCH CARIBBEAN

DUTCH
CARIBBEAN

BRAZIL

6,000,000
4,500,000
3,000,000
1,500,000
500,000

Source: Curtin, 1969.

From the end of the sixteenth century to the early decades of the nineteenth, approximately 11 to 12 million Africans were imported to the New World (Patterson, 1982). The map shows that the largest numbers of slaves were sent to the European colonies in the Caribbean and to Brazil.

southern states that fought in the war, one-third of white families had slaves, the average being nine "chattels" per owner (Farley and Allen, 1987). (The term *chattels* refers to living beings that are considered property, including slaves and, in some instances in other cultures, women.)

It can be inferred from the great increase in the slave population that slaveholders in the United States treated their slaves less badly than slaveholders in other parts of the Western Hemisphere did. This does not mean, however, that the American slaves did not bitterly resent their condition and struggle against it. Patterson points out that the slave has always striven against all odds "for some measure of regularity and predictability in his social life. . . . Because he was considered degraded, he was all the more infused with the yearning for dignity" (1982, p. 337). Patterson concludes that one of the chief ironies of slavery throughout history has been that "without [it] there would have been no freedmen" (p. 342). In other words, the very idea of freedom developed in large part from the longing of slaves to be free.

Segregation

Although African-American slaves gained their freedom during the Civil War and became citizens of the United States, this did not mean that they became fully integrated into American society. A long period of segregation followed. **Segregation** is the ecological and institutional separation of races or ethnic groups. The segregation of racially or ethnically distinct peoples within a society may be voluntary, resulting from the desire of a people to live separately and maintain its own culture and institutions. The Amish, the Hutterites, and the Hasidic Jews are examples of groups that voluntarily segregate themselves. But segregation is often involuntary, resulting from laws or other norms that force one people to be separate from others. Involuntary segregation may be **de jure**—that is, supported by laws that prohibit certain peoples from interacting with others or place limits on such interactions. Or it may be **de facto**—that is, enforced by unwritten norms that result in involuntary segregation, which then exists as if it were "in fact" legally required.

Segregation in South Africa today is supported by a set of laws that "determines a person's rights and privileges on the basis of his or her racial classification" (Crapanzano, 1985, p. 52). The most salient of these laws is the Population Registration Act, which was enacted in 1950 and required that every person in South Africa be assigned to a racial group: white, black, colored (i.e., of mixed white and black ancestry), or Asian. Subsequent acts that required non-whites to live in specific places and to carry passes that must be shown on demand reinforced the South African system of racial segregation, or *apartheid*. Although these laws are being phased out by the white-ruled government, at this writing blacks have not yet gained full citizenship.

In the United States, legally sanctioned segregation no longer exists, but this has been true only in recent years. Before the civil rights movement of the 1960s, de jure segregation was common in the United States, especially in the southern states. The system that enforced segregation was supported by **Jim Crow** laws in many states. This term refers to laws that enforced or condoned segregation, barred blacks and other minorities from the polls, and the like. (Jim Crow was a nineteenth-century white minstrel performer who performed in blackface and thereby reinforced black stereotypes.) This system was in effect for about 100 years, from just after the Civil War until the early 1970s. During that period the so-called color line was applied throughout the United States to limit the places where blacks could live, where they could work and what kinds of jobs they could hold, where they could go to school, and under what conditions they could vote.

At first the color line was an unwritten set of norms that barred or restricted black participation in many social institutions. By the turn of the century, however, segregation had become officially sanctioned through leg-

islation and court rulings. This official segregation was rationalized by the "separate but equal" doctrine set forth by the Supreme Court in *Plessy* v. *Ferguson* (1896). Under this doctrine, separate facilities for people of different races were legal as long as they were of equal quality. In addition, de facto segregation and the existence of a "job ceiling" based on race served to keep blacks in subordinate jobs and segregated ghettos, as we saw in Chapter 12 in the case of Chicago's "black metropolis."

Only after years of struggle by opponents of de jure segregation did the United States Supreme Court finally decide, in the landmark case of *Brown* v. *Board of Education, Topeka* (1954), that "separate but equal" was inherently unequal. The *Brown* ruling put an end to legally sanctioned segregation of schools, hospitals, public accommodations, and the like. But it took frequent, often violent demonstrations and the mobilization of thousands of citizens in support of civil rights to achieve passage of the Civil Rights Act of 1964. That act mandated an end to segregation in private accommodations, made discrimination in the sale of housing illegal, and initiated a major attack on the job ceiling through the strategy known as affirmative action. Despite these judicial and legislative victories, however, de facto segregation remains a fact of life in the United States, especially in large cities (Davis, 1978; Hamilton, 1984; Taeuber and Taeuber, 1965). (See Box 13-2.)

> ## Assimilation

One of the factors that led to Jim Crow was the fear of racial intermarriage, since the ideology of white supremacy held that intermarriage would weaken the white race. As late as 1950, thirty states had laws prohibiting such marriages, and even after racist sentiments began to diminish in the 1950s, nineteen states (seventeen of them in the South) maintained such laws until the Supreme Court declared them unconstitutional in 1967 (Holt, 1980).

Intermarriage between distinct racial and ethnic groups is an important indicator of **as-**

Segregation of racially or ethnically distinct peoples within a society may be voluntary or involuntary; involuntary segregation may be de jure (required by law) or de facto (enforced by unwritten norms).

Box 13–2: **Segregation in American Cities**

Social ecologists Karl and Alma Taeuber (1965) devised a statistical method for measuring racial segregation in cities and towns. Known as the segregation index, it measures the dissimilarity or difference in the distribution of black households in a given city from the distribution that would be expected if there were no segregation. In a city in which blacks make up half the population, for example, one would expect half the households on every block to have black residents. In a city whose population is 10 percent black, one out of ten households on each block would be black. The extent to which each block departs from this expectation is a measure of segregation for that block; averaging this measure over the entire city yields a citywide segregation index. As the Taeubers explain,

The index of residential segregation can assume values between 0 and 100. The higher the value, the higher the degree of residential segregation, and the lower the value, the greater the degree of residential intermixture. The value of the index may be interpreted as showing the minimum percentage of nonwhites who would have to change the block on which they live in order to produce an unsegregated distribution—one in which the percentage of nonwhites living on each block is the same throughout the city (0 on the index). For instance, if some governing council had the power and the inclination to redistribute the population of Birmingham so as to obtain an unsegregated distribution of white and nonwhite residences, they would have to move 92.8 percent [in 1960] of the nonwhites from blocks now containing an above-average proportion of nonwhites to blocks now disproportionately occupied by whites. [p. 30]

The accompanying table presents segregation indexes for twenty-eight American cities with populations over 100,000 from the Taeubers' original 1965 study and a 1983 replication carried out by Conrad Taeuber for the U.S. Civil Rights Commission. The data show that residential segregation in American cities has decreased since the beginning of the civil rights movement in the late 1950s. Although segregation in some cities, such as Oakland, California, and Gary, Indiana, has fallen below the 70 percent level, high segregation indexes remain a fact of American urban life. Taeuber also pointed out that most changes in segregation patterns are due to the movement of blacks into newer suburban communities and older white neighborhoods in the cities. Integration resulting from the movement of whites into black neighborhoods happens very rarely, and when it does it often involves the displacement of lower-income blacks in favor of new housing for more affluent whites.

The Taeubers' ecological research is valuable in providing indicators of change in residential segregation, but it tells us little about the extent of segregation in the institutions of government and the economy. For example, Chicago and Los Angeles, both of which have persistently high rates of residential segregation, have had black mayors. And Philadelphia, one of the few cities that have shown slight increases in racial segregation, also has had a black mayor. None of these mayors could have been elected

similation, the pattern of intergroup relations in which a minority group is forced or encouraged or voluntarily seeks to blend into the majority population and eventually disappears as a distinct people within the larger society. (We saw in Chapter 4 that assimilation refers to the process by which a culturally distinct group adopts the language, values, and norms of a larger society. Here we are using the term in a broader sense, to include social as well as cultural blending.) Needless to say, it makes a great deal of difference in an ethnic or racial group's history whether it has been the victim of forced assimilation or

without a large proportion of white votes. Thus, although patterns of residential segregation provide evidence of the continuing deep division between the races in the United States, one must also consider other indicators, such as occupational segregation and equality of political representation, to come up with a full measure of the extent of segregation in this or any other society.

City	1970	1980
Chicago	93	92
Cleveland	90	91
St. Louis	90	90
Philadelphia	84	88
Baltimore	89	86
Atlanta	92	86
Kansas City	90	86
Memphis	92	85
Birmingham, Ala.	92	85
Dallas	96	83
Pittsburgh	86	83
Indianapolis	90	83
Jacksonville, Fla.	94	82
Houston	93	81
Los Angeles	90	81
Nashville, Tenn.	90	80
Boston	84	80
Milwaukee	88	80
Washington, D.C.	79	79
Richmond, Va.	91	79
Cincinnati	84	79
Newark, N.J.	76	76
New Orleans	84	76
New York City	77	75
Columbus, Ohio	86	75
Detroit	82	73
Gary, Ind.	84	68
Oakland, Calif.	70	59

has been allowed to absorb the majority culture at its own pace.

Many Latin American societies offer examples of peaceful, long-term assimilation of various racial and ethnic groups. For example, as a result of generations of intermarriage, Brazilians distinguish among many shades of skin color and other physical features, but racial discrimination is largely absent. There are some places in Brazil in which there is discrimination against blacks, but these are the exception rather than the rule (Fernandes, 1968).

In the United States, assimilation has had a more troubled history. In an influential treatise on this subject, Milton Gordon (1964) identified three "ideological tendencies" that have affected the treatment of minority groups at various times. These ideologies specify how ethnic or racial groups should change (or resist change) as they seek acceptance in the institutions and culture of American society. They are as follows:

1. Anglo-conformity—the demand that culturally distinct groups give up their own cultures and adopt the norms and values of the dominant Anglo-Saxon culture.
2. The melting pot—the theory that there would be a biological merger of ethnic and racial groups that would result in a "new indigenous American type" (p. 85).
3. Cultural pluralism—the belief that culturally distinct groups can retain their communities and much of their culture while participating in the institutions of the larger society.

Because these ideological tendencies have played an important role in intergroup relations in the United States, we examine them in some detail.

Anglo-conformity. The demand for Anglo-conformity rests on the belief that the persistence of ethnic cultures, ethnic and racial communities, and foreign languages in an English-speaking society should be aggressively discouraged. The catchword of this ideology is *Americanization*, the idea that immigrants and their children must become "100 percent Americans" by losing all traces of their "foreign" accents, abandoning their ethnic cultures, and marrying nonethnic Americans. This demand is reflected in the movement to make English the official language of the United States, along with opposition to bilingual education. In some cases discrimination against members of certain ethnic groups is rationalized by the statement that they are not yet fully American.

The Melting Pot.

In an 1893 paper a young historian named Frederick Jackson Turner challenged the notion that American culture and institutions had been formed by the nation's original Anglo-Saxon settlers. Turner's essay argued that the major influences on American culture were the experiences of the diverse array of people who met and mixed on the western frontier. Turner held that "in the crucible of the frontier the immigrants were Americanized, liberated, and fused into a mixed race" (1920/1893, pp. 22–23).

Turner's "crucible" became widely known as the "melting pot," from a play about a Russian immigrant by Israel Zangwell. As David, the play's hero, explains,

America is God's crucible, the great Melting Pot where all the races of Europe are melting and reforming! Here you stand, good folk . . . in your fifty groups, with your fifty languages and histories, and your fifty blood hatreds and rivalries. . . . Germans and Frenchmen, Irishmen and Englishmen, Jews and Russians—into the Crucible with you all! God is making the American. [1909, p. 37]

The melting-pot view of assimilation attracted many scholars, artists, and social commentators, but sociologists were not convinced that it was an accurate view of what actually happens to ethnic groups in American society. Their research showed that certain ethnic groups have not been fully assimilated, either through intermarriage or through integration into the nation's major institutions. Instead, there remain distinct patterns of **ethnic stratification;** that is, different groups appear to be valued differently depending on how closely they conform to Anglo-Saxon standards of appearance, behavior, and values. People of Scandinavian or northern European descent, for example, are more readily accepted into the top levels of corporate management than people of Mediterranean descent, who in turn are more readily accepted than black, Hispanic, and Asian minorities.

In an early empirical study of assimilation, Ruby Jo Reeves Kennedy (1944) ana-

lyzed rates of ethnic intermarriage in New Haven, Connecticut. She found that intergroup marriages increased in frequency between 1870 and 1940 but that although there was a growing tendency for members of *ethnic* groups to marry outside their group, there remained a very strong tendency for people to marry within their own *religious* group. From this finding Kennedy developed the hypothesis of the "triple melting pot," the idea that assimilation occurs first among groups that share the same religion and later among groups with different religions. More recently, in *Beyond the Melting Pot*, Nathan Glazer and Daniel Patrick Moynihan (1970) also concluded that ethnic and racial assimilation is far from inevitable. Ethnicity does not disappear as a result of assimilation; ethnic subcultures are continually being created and changed. Thus *Beyond the Melting Pot* pointed to the emergence and significance of cultural pluralism in American life.

As new waves of immigrants from all over the world have streamed into the United States in the past decade—Jews fleeing religious intolerance in Russia, Italians and Poles fleeing economic depression in their com-

The young black woman shown in this 1888 engraving from *Harper's Weekly* entitled "Their Pride" is about to go away to a teacher-training college. All newcomers to urban America, be they blacks from the rural South or immigrants from European countries, have recognized that education is the best route to upward social mobility.

munities, Central and Latin Americans fleeing dictatorships and poverty, refugees from Asian countries torn by conflict—all have tended to join other members of their nationality group who settled in the United States in earlier decades. Although the influx of new immigrants has led to conflicts between older and newer residents of some communities, in many cases it has resulted in new growth in those communities— in new ethnic businesses such as restaurants and grocery stores, and new social institutions such as churches and social clubs. It has also reinforced pride in ethnic identity as expressed in language and other aspects of ethnic subcultures. This infusion of new energy into older ethnic neighborhoods and communities confirms Glazer and Moynihan's thesis that the emergence of cultural pluralism is a significant aspect of life in American society.

Cultural Pluralism. The recognition that ethnic groups maintain their own communities and subcultures even while some of their members are assimilated into the larger society gave support to the concept of cultural pluralism. A **pluralistic society** is one in which different ethnic and racial groups are able to maintain their own cultures and life-styles even

The view of American society as a melting pot has been challenged by sociologists who have identified distinct patterns of ethnic stratification.

The end of the American Civil War brought on a wave of egalitarian sentiment, as this 1869 engraving of "Uncle Sam's Thanksgiving Dinner" demonstrates. But in practice the American "melting pot" did not provide an equal opportunity for all groups to become full-fledged Americans.

as they gain equality in the institutions of the larger society. Michael Waltzer's (1980) comparative research on pluralism in the United States and other societies has shown that although white ethnic groups like the Italians, Jews, and Scandinavians may have the option of maintaining their own subcultures and still be accepted in the larger society, blacks and other racial minorities frequently experience attacks on their subcultures (e.g., opposition to bilingual education or African studies courses) and, at the same time, are discriminated against in social institutions. Waltzer concludes that "racism is the great barrier to a fully developed pluralism" (p. 787).

The problems of pluralism are illustrated by the case of the French-speaking Quebecois minority in Canada. The Quebecois account for almost 28 percent of the Canadian population and are the majority in the province of Quebec. This leads to a situation in which a group with its own culture and language seeks protection against pressure to assimilate into the dominant culture, and yet demands equal access to the society's political, economic, and cultural institutions. The resulting tensions and hardships have led to the demand that Canada become a bilingual nation, with English and French given equal status. In the 1970s and again in the 1990s this demand broadened into a social movement calling for the creation of an independent French-speaking nation within a Canadian "federation."

As this example shows, a truly pluralistic society is very difficult to achieve. The various ethnic and racial subgroups within the society feel a strong sense of cultural identity, which they wish to preserve. At the same time, they demand equal access to the society's institutions: access to better schools, opportunities to obtain jobs in every field, opportunities to hold important positions—in short, a fair share of the wealth and power available in the society. These desires sometimes conflict, with the result that some groups may be tempted to "go it alone"—that is, form their own cultural and political institutions (e.g., their own businesses, newspapers and other media, labor unions, etc.)—or else give up their ethnic identity in order to gain greater access to the society's major institutions.

UNCLE SAM'S THANKSGIVING DINNER.

CULTURE AND INTERGROUP RELATIONS

Why do ethnic stratification and inequality persist in societies that are becoming increasingly pluralistic, like those of the United States and Canada? Sociologists have proposed a variety of theories to explain racial and ethnic inequality. Before we explore them, however, we need to understand the cultural basis of ethnic diversity and intergroup hostility—that is, the underlying values and attitudes that shape people's consciousness of other groups and, hence, their behavior toward members of those groups. Chief among these are the tendency to view members of other groups in terms of stereotypes and to use those stereotypes to justify differential attitudes (prejudice) and behaviors (discrimination) toward such individuals.

Stereotypes

People often express the opinion that specific traits of members of certain groups are responsible for their disadvantaged situation. Thus, in South Africa it is common for whites to assert that blacks "are not ready for full citizenship because they remain childlike and simple." In the United States, the fact that Hispanics are more likely to be found in low-paying jobs is explained by the assertion that "they don't want to learn English." And the fact that black unemployment rates are generally twice as high as white unemployment rates is explained by the statement that "they don't want to work; they like sports and music, but not hard work, especially in school." These explanations are **stereotypes,** inflexible images of a racial or cultural group that are held without regard to whether or not they are true.

Sociologist William Helmreich (1982) conducted a study of widely held stereotypes regarding America's major ethnic and racial groups (see Figure 13-5). He found that "every single stereotype discussed turns out to have a reason, or reasons" (p. 242). Those reasons usually stem from earlier patterns of inter-

Figure 13–5: **Some Common Stereotypes**

JEWS

The Jewish mother
Internationalists plotting to take over the world
Shrewd businessmen
Have horns
The chosen people
Killed Jesus Christ
Smarter
Cheap
Control Wall Street and the banks
Rich and ostentatious
Pushy and aggressive
Control the media
Have big noses

ITALIANS

"Mangia! mangia!"
Stupid, ignorant, suspicious of education
Family-oriented, clannish, distrustful of outsiders
Great singers
Talk with their hands
Belong to the Mafia
Cowards in battle
Violent and quick-tempered
Great shoemakers

BLACKS

Hypersensitive
Sexual prowess
Physically powerful, great athletes
Dirty and slovenly
Stupid
Musically gifted, great rhythm, terrific entertainers
Lazy and shiftless
Big Cadillacs and flashy clothes
Violent criminals

JAPANESE

Chauvinistic
Hardworking, ambitious, and competitive
Highly educated and intelligent
Japanese women are servile and obedient
The sneaky Jap
Strong family ties
Great imitators
Law-abiding

CHINESE

Sly, sinister, and deceitful
"No tickee, no washee"
Inscrutable
The best food in the world
Learned and wise
Love to gamble
Cruel
Strong family ties
Quiet, polite, and deferential

IRISH

Heavy drinkers
Good at politics
Sexually repressed
Very religious
Highly nationalistic
Literary, witty, and gregarious
The "fighting Irish"

POLES

Dumb
Dirty
Racists and bigots
Uneducated
Boorish and uncultured, low class

WASPS

Honorable
Hardworking, industrious, and thrifty
Cold and insensitive
Well-mannered, polite, genteel
Snobbish
Wealthy and powerful
Guilt-ridden do-gooders

HISPANICS

Big on machismo
Lazy
Refuse to learn English
Don't care if they're on welfare
Don't value education
Warm, expressive, and emotional
Violent and hot-tempered

Source: Excerpted from *The Things They Say Behind Your Back* by William B. Helmreich. Copyright © 1982 by William B. Helmreich. Reprinted by permission of Doubleday and Company, Inc.

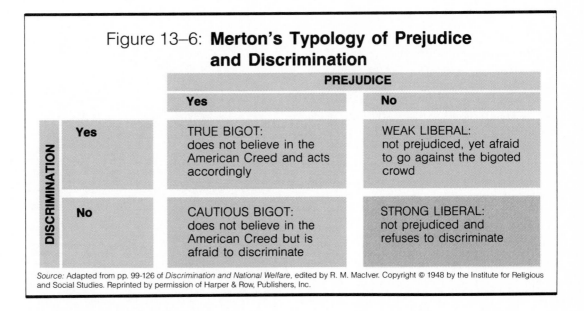

Figure 13–6: **Merton's Typology of Prejudice and Discrimination**

		PREJUDICE	
		Yes	**No**
DISCRIMINATION	**Yes**	TRUE BIGOT: does not believe in the American Creed and acts accordingly	WEAK LIBERAL: not prejudiced, yet afraid to go against the bigoted crowd
	No	CAUTIOUS BIGOT: does not believe in the American Creed but is afraid to discriminate	STRONG LIBERAL: not prejudiced and refuses to discriminate

Source: Adapted from pp. 99-126 of *Discrimination and National Welfare,* edited by R. M. MacIver. Copyright © 1948 by the Institute for Religious and Social Studies. Reprinted by permission of Harper & Row, Publishers, Inc.

group relations. For example, jokes about stupid Poles stem from a period in the nineteenth century when uneducated Polish peasants immigrated to the United States. The idea that blacks are good at music or sports also has some basis in fact, not because blacks are genetically superior in those areas but because when blacks were barred from other avenues to upward mobility they were able to succeed in entertainment and sports; as a result, many young blacks have developed their musical and athletic talents more fully than whites have. Thus, although stereotypes usually have some basis in fact, they never take account of all the facts about a group. As the famous social commentator Walter Lippmann once quipped, "All Indians walk in single file, at least the one I saw did."

> *Racial or cultural stereotypes are inflexible images that are held without regard to their validity.*

Prejudice and Discrimination

The fact that many people hold stereotypical ideas about other groups may be an indication that they are ignorant or prejudiced, but it does not imply that they will actually discriminate against people who are perceived as different. In a classic study of prejudice, the social psychologist Richard LaPiere (1934) traveled throughout the United States with a Chinese couple, stopping at about 250 restaurants and hotels. Only one of the establishments refused them service. Six months later LaPiere wrote to each establishment and requested reservations for a Chinese couple. Over 90 percent of the managers responded that they had a policy of "nonacceptance of Orientals." This field experiment was replicated for blacks in 1952, with very similar results (Kutner et al., 1952; Shibutani and Kwan, 1965).

The purpose of such experiments is to demonstrate the difference between prejudice and discrimination. **Prejudice** is an attitude that prejudges a person, either positively or negatively, on the basis of real or imagined characteristics (stereotypes) of a group of which that person is a member. **Discrimination,** on the other hand, refers to actual unfair treatment of people on the basis of their group membership.

The distinction between attitude and behavior is important. Prejudice is an attitude; discrimination is a behavior. As Robert Merton (1949) pointed out, there are people who are prejudiced and who discriminate against members of particular groups. Others are not prejudiced but discriminate because it is expected of them. With these distinctions in mind, Merton constructed the typology shown in Figure 13-6.

Merton's typology is valuable because it points to the variety of attitudes and behaviors that exist in multicultural and multiracial societies. However, it fails to account for situations in which certain groups are discriminated against regardless of the attitudes and behaviors of individuals. This form of discrimination is part of the "culture" of a social institution; it is practiced by people who are simply conforming to the norms of that institution and hence is known as **institutional discrimination**.

At its simplest, institutional discrimination is the systematic exclusion of people from equal access to and participation in a particular institution because of their race, religion, or ethnicity. But over time this intentional exclusion leads to another type of discrimination, which has been described as "the interaction of the various spheres of social life to maintain an overall pattern of oppression" (Blauner, 1972, p. 185). This form of institutional discrimination can be quite complex. For example, in analyzing the conditions that led to the riot that broke out in the Watts community of Los Angeles in 1965, Robert Blauner (1972) observed that blacks were trapped in a self-perpetuating set of circumstances that almost inevitably resulted in discrimination: Blocked educational opportunities result in low skill levels, which together with job discrimination limit their incomes. Low income forces them to become concentrated in ghettos, which lack adequate public services such as transportation, making the search for work even more difficult. In those neighborhoods, also, the schools do not stimulate achievement, thereby repeating the pattern in the next generation. At the same time, the police patrol ghettos "to the point of harassment," with the result that young blacks are more likely to be arrested—and to be denied jobs because of their arrest records.

All of the institutions involved—the employers, the local governments, the schools, the real estate agencies, the agencies of social control—may claim that they apply consistent standards in making their decisions: They hire the most qualified applicants; they sell to the highest bidder; they apply the law evenhandedly; in short, they do not discrim-

Chicago Historical Society

inate. Yet in adhering to its institutional norms each perpetuates a situation that was created by past discrimination.

Ethnic and Racial Nationalism

The conditions that contributed to the Watts riot are an example of the pervasive and discouraging effects of institutional discrimination. In the face of such discrimination, racial and ethnic groups frequently organize their members into movements to oppose social inequality. Those social movements often appeal to ethnic or racial nationalism—that is, to the "we feeling" or sense of peoplehood shared by the members of a particular group.

Ethnic (or **racial**) **nationalism** is the belief that one's ethnic group constitutes a distinct people whose culture is and should be separate from that of the larger society. Feel-

During and after the 1919 Chicago race riots, many African-Americans were evicted from homes in integrated working-class neighborhoods and forced back into the ghetto. One such incident is shown in this photo taken during the riots.

ings of nationalism among America's ethnic and racial groups have often been strongly affected by nationalist movements outside the United States. American Jews, for example, were deeply influenced by Zionism, a movement that arose in the late nineteenth century with the goal of creating a Jewish homeland in the holy land of Palestine (now Israel). Similarly, Irish Americans have been influenced by the struggle of the Catholic minority in Northern Ireland to gain independence from England, and Polish Americans have been affected by the attempts of the Polish Catholic church and the Solidarity labor movement to win autonomy from the Soviet Union and its allies in the Polish government. Often nationalist movements produce a new or renewed ideology of pluralism that replaces the goal of complete assimilation into the larger society. We can see this very clearly among African-Americans.

In his famous study *An American Dilemma* (1944), the Swedish social scientist Gunnar Myrdal noted that African-Americans were in fact "exaggerated Americans." Myrdal believed that blacks had assimilated American values and norms more than any other ethnic or racial group and that they had no distinctive subculture of their own. This theme was repeated in the influential work of E. Franklin Frazier (1957), the leading black sociologist of his generation. Frazier, like Myrdal, believed that African-Americans had no distinctive culture. They had the same religions, language, and values as white Americans, and the folkways they had developed (e.g., musical forms like jazz and the blues) had become part of the general American culture.

Events of the late 1950s and the 1960s drastically changed these views of black cultural assimilation. Along with the civil rights movement of the 1960s came a wave of nationalism. Black intellectuals and community leaders began calling not merely for integration but for cultural pluralism. Leaders like Stokely Carmichael of the Student Non-Vi-

olent Coordinating Committee and Malcolm X, the charismatic Black Muslim leader, preached that "black is beautiful" and that African-Americans should drop the term *Negro* in favor of *black*. In Carmichael's words, "They oppress us because we are black and we are going to use that blackness. . . . Don't be ashamed of your color" (quoted in Bracey, Meier, and Rudwick, 1970, p. 471). In recent years many black Americans have gone further and adopted the term *African-American* in order to emphasize their common heritage and deemphasize somewhat the racial character of their shared background.

At various times in North American history, ethnic or racial nationalism has strained the social fabric. Entire populations, such as African-Americans, Puerto Ricans, or French Canadians, have yearned to become entirely separate from the larger culture and society. But at other times nationalism has been a creative social force, welding a racial or ethnic group into a more politically conscious community able to struggle more effectively for its rights. As the Native American sociologist Russell Thornton notes, there are some highly positive aspects of nationalism or, in the case of Native Americans, tribalism. "Research shows," he writes, "that American Indians make considerable efforts to reaffirm tribalism in urban areas by living in Indian neighborhoods, by maintaining contacts with reservation areas and extended families, and by creating urban American Indian Centers. Frequent results are a new tribalism for urban American Indians and, sometimes, 'bicultural' individuals, that is, American Indians who live successfully in Indian and non-Indian worlds" (1987, p. 239).

A key to Indian survival, Thornton concludes, is the ability to maintain an Indian identity while interacting with non-Indians in an urban environment. The same point is often made by Hispanic and African-American sociologists. One difficulty in maintaining a bicultural existence is that it requires assertion of the minority group's values, its ways of expression, its history, and its demands for greater equality. Frequently the demand for more equality is expressed in terms of the need for affirmative action.

> *Groups that experience discrimination may organize their members into movements that appeal to feelings of ethnic or racial nationalism.*

Affirmative Action

The quest for racial and ethnic equality is high on the nation's social-policy agenda (U.S. Commission on Civil Rights, 1981). Our society's foremost governmental and economic institutions are besieged with demands for *affirmative action*—that is, for policies designed to correct persistent racial and ethnic inequalities in promotion, hiring, and access to other opportunities. Equally forceful are the demands to do away with affirmative-action "quotas." Conservatives bitterly oppose affirmative action (Glazer, 1975; Sowell, 1972), whereas liberals feel that it is necessary if our society is to undo the effects of past discrimination (Horowitz, 1979).

We saw earlier that the Supreme Court struck down the doctrine that "separate but equal" facilities and institutions did not violate the constitutional rights of African-Americans. It did so largely because social-scientific evidence showed that separate institutions are inherently unequal. Similar arguments have been advanced in affirmative-action cases that have reached the Court. If a fire department in a city whose inhabitants are 30 percent black and Hispanic has no firefighters from those minority groups, it can be demonstrated that there is a pattern of discrimination that can be changed only if the institution is required to hire a certain number of minority applicants—a quota—within a designated time. However, members of the majority may feel that they are victims of "reverse discrimination," in which they are being penalized for the wrongs of earlier generations. Thus, difficult choices remain: Should employers mix or replace decisions based on experience and merit with decisions based on race and ethnicity? In essence, the courts have said that they must, but there are still bitter disputes about the meaning and use of affirmative action.

It should be noted that affirmative action applies to women as well as to racial and ethnic minorities. The effects of institutional discrimination against women are explored in the next chapter.

THEORIES OF RACIAL AND ETHNIC INEQUALITY

For large numbers of people a dominant aspect of life in American society is racial or ethnic inequality and, often, hostility. How can we explain the persistence of these patterns of hostility and inequality? The first thought that comes to mind is that many people are prejudiced against anyone who is different from them in appearance or behavior. This may seem to explain phenomena like segregation and discrimination, but it fails to explain the variety of possible reactions to different groups. Social-psychological theories that focus on prejudice against members of out-groups find the origins of racism and ethnic inequality in individual psychological processes, but there are also theories based on the major sociological perspectives that view prejudice as a symptom of other aspects of intergroup relations.

Social-psychological theories of ethnic and racial inequality see the origins of prejudice in individual psychological orientations toward members of out-groups.

Social-Psychological Theories

The best-known social-psychological theories of ethnic and racial inequality are the frustration-aggression, projection, and authoritarian-personality theories. All of these see the origins of prejudice in individual psychological orientations toward members of out-groups, but they differ in important ways.

Frustration-Aggression. The frustration-aggression hypothesis, which is associated with the research of John Dollard, Neil Miller, and Leonard Doob (1939), holds that the origin of prejudice is a buildup of frustration. When that frustration cannot be vented on the real cause, the individual feels a "free-floating" hostility that may be taken out on a convenient target, or **scapegoat**. For example, in the case of workers who have been laid off

because of a downturn in the economy, the scapegoat is likely to be a racial or ethnic group that is perceived as stealing jobs. To justify the hostility directed at the out-group, the prejudiced individual often grasps at additional reasons, usually in the form of stereotypes, for hating the "others."

Projection. The concept of projection is also used to explain hostility toward particular ethnic and racial groups. **Projection** is the process whereby we attribute to other people behaviors and feelings that we are unwilling to accept in ourselves. John Dollard (1937) and Margaret Halsey (1946) applied the concept of projection to white attitudes toward black sexuality. Observers had noted that southern whites frequently claimed that black males are characterized by an uncontrollable and even vicious sexuality. The theory of projection explains this claim as resulting from the white males' attraction to black females, an attraction that was forbidden by strong norms against interracial sexual contact. Thus the white male projected his own forbidden sexuality onto blacks and developed an attitude that excused his own sexual involvement with black women.

The Authoritarian Personality. The frustration-aggression and projection explanations of prejudice are quite general in that anyone can develop pent-up frustrations that will engender hostility under certain conditions, and anyone can project undesirable traits onto others. A more specific social-psychological explanation of prejudice is the theory of the authoritarian personality, which emerged from attempts to discover whether there is a particular type of person who is likely to display prejudice.

In 1950 a group of social scientists led by Theodor Adorno published an influential study entitled *The Authoritarian Personality.*

Their research had found consistent correlations between prejudice against Jews and other minorities and a set of traits that characterized what they called the authoritarian personality. Authoritarian individuals, they found, were punished frequently as children. Consequently, such individuals feel an intense anger that they fail to examine (Pettigrew, 1980). They submit completely to people in positions of authority, greatly fear self-analysis or introspection, and have a strong tendency to blame their troubles on people or groups that they see as inferior to themselves. Unfortunately for Jews, blacks, and other minorities that have been subordinated in the past, the anger and hostility of the authoritarian personality is often directed against them.

Interactionist Theories

Not far removed from these social-psychological theories of intergroup hostility are theories derived from the interactionist perspective in sociology. But instead of locating the origins of intergroup conflict in individual psychological tendencies, interactionists tend to look at how hostility or sympathy toward other groups, or solidarity within a group, are produced through the norms of interaction and the definitions of the situation that evolve within and between groups. A few examples will serve to illustrate how the interactionist perspective is applied.

From his analyses of interaction in many different kinds of groups, Georg Simmel concluded that groups often find it convenient to think of nonmembers or outsiders as somehow inferior to members of the group. But why does this familiar in-group, out-group distinction develop? Simmel explained it as arising out of the intensity of the interactions within the group, which leads its members to feel that other groups are less important. Once they have identified another group as inferior, it is not a great leap to think of its members as enemies, especially because doing so increases their own sense of group solidarity (Coser, 1966; Simmel, 1904).

These theories were tested in the Rob-

> *From the interactionist perspective, hostility or sympathy toward other groups is produced through the norms of interaction and definitions of the situation that evolve within and between groups.*

bers Cave experiment described in Chapter 6, in which Muzafer Sherif and his associates (1956) demonstrated how conflict and hostility between racial or ethnic groups can be overcome by creating situations that require the groups to cooperate to achieve a common goal. In real life it is not so easy to set up cooperative situations in order to break down the barriers that separate racial and ethnic groups, but such situations do occasionally occur—for example, when people from different ethnic and racial backgrounds compete in sports or when they work side by side in school and in industry. Unfortunately, the integration and friendship found in such settings are not sufficient to overcome the more deepseated prejudices and fears of many people about minority groups. As film director Spike Lee observes, racists place all black people in one of two categories: "entertainers and niggers." By this he means that people with racist sentiments have a way of excluding famous entertainers and sports figures from their negative feelings about blacks as a group, thereby accentuating their failure to see all blacks as individual human beings.

Functionalist Theories

The difficulty of reducing racism and discrimination through interaction leads to the question of whether racial and ethnic inequalities persist because they function to the advantage of certain groups. One answer was provided by the functionalist theorist Talcott Parsons (1968), who wrote that "the primary historic origin of the modern color problem lies in the relation of Europeans to African slavery" (p. 366). Parsons was not denying that racism is produced through interactions. Rather, he was pointing out that the specific form taken by those interactions—oppression, subordination, domination of blacks by whites—is directly related to the perceived need of white colonialists and traders to use blacks for their own purposes. The whites could abduct, enslave, and sell Africans because their societies had developed technologies (e.g., oceangoing ships and navigational

instruments) and institutions (e.g., markets and trading corporations) that made them immensely more powerful than the Africans.

From the functionalist perspective, inequalities among ethnic or racial groups exist because they have served important functions for particular societies. Thus, to return to the example of South Africa, it is functional for the white government to insist on maintaining *apartheid* because to do otherwise would mean that whites would become a minority group in a black-dominated society. But if world opinion continues to condemn the white regime and if blacks continue to build group solidarity and challenge that regime, it will become less and less "functional" for the white government to insist on complete *apartheid*. Indeed, there is much speculation that the nation's white rulers released Nelson Mandela and took steps to legalize the formerly banned African National Congress as a way of showing the world that they were willing to begin negotiations toward some form of shared power. Their move can also be interpreted as an attempt to forestall a full-scale black revolution. The functionalist perspective thus tends to identify patterns of social integration that will return a society to a more or less stable condition with limited loss of power for those in control of the society.

> *From the functionalist perspective, inequalities among ethnic or racial groups exist because they have served important functions for particular societies.*

Conflict Theories

Conflict theories, on the other hand, do a better job of explaining why black South Africans are unlikely to be satisfied with the limited reforms offered by the white government. At this writing, for example, there is severe racial conflict in South Africa. The new white regime has promised reforms but has not promised full democratic rights for black South Africans. There has been some relaxation of the pass laws and some reform of laws

This World Series victory celebration illustrates how the intensity of interaction on a team can help overcome barriers of racial prejudice.

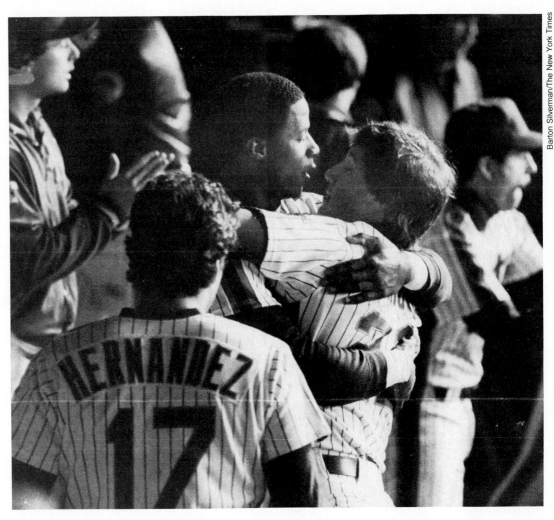

Barton Silverman/The New York Times

regarding interracial marriage, but there has as yet been little real change in the racial caste system. Clearly, if more fundamental changes are to occur and more bloodshed is to be avoided, the institution of *apartheid* must be abolished. If this happens, conflict at both the domestic and international levels will have been the primary cause of change.

Conflict theories trace the origins of racial and ethnic inequality to the conflict between classes in capitalist societies. Marx believed, for example, that American wage earners were unlikely to become highly class conscious because ethnic and racial divisions continually

Conflict theories trace the origins of racial and ethnic inequality to the conflict between classes in capitalist societies.

set them against one another and the resulting strife could be manipulated by the capitalist class. Thus, in American history we see many examples of black and Mexican workers being brought in as strikebreakers by the owners of mines and mills, especially during the 1920s and 1930s. Strikebreakers from different racial and ethnic groups often absorbed the wrath of workers, which might otherwise have been directed at the dominant class. To forge class loyalties despite the divisions created by racial and ethnic differences, Marx believed, it would be necessary for workers to see that they were being manipulated by such strategies.

Internal Colonialism. Conflict perspectives on racial inequality also include the theory of

internal colonialism. According to this theory, many minority groups, especially racial minorities, are essentially colonial peoples within the larger society. Four conditions mark this situation:

1. The "colonial" people did not enter the society voluntarily.
2. The culture of the "colonial" people has been destroyed or transformed into a version of the dominant culture that is considered inferior.
3. The "colonial" population is controlled by the dominant population.
4. Members of the "colonial" people are victims of racism; that is, they are seen as inferior in biological terms and are oppressed both socially and psychologically (Blauner, 1969; Davidson, 1973; Hechter, 1974). In the Soviet Union, for example, groups like the Armenians, the Ukrainians, and many others claim that they are treated as internal colonies in that they get fewer opportunities for advancement and less of the society's resources than Russian citizens do.

These characteristics describe colonial peoples everywhere, but the theory of internal colonialism asserts that they also apply to subordinated ethnic and racial groups in societies like England, the United States, Canada, and the Soviet Union. Michael Hechter (1974) extended the theory to show that societies that have created colonial or "ghettoized" populations within their boundaries also develop a "cultural division of labor" in which the subordinated group is expected to perform types of work that are considered too demeaning to be done by members of the dominant population. The South African institution of *Baaskop* is an example of this phenomenon. It is a set of norms that specifies that lower-status, physically exhausting work is appropriate for blacks and that higher-status work is appropriate for whites; that whites should never accept "black" work or allow themselves to be subordinate to blacks.

Ecological Theories

Are the segregated ghetto communities of black and Hispanic Americans a product of internal colonialism? The answer to this question depends on whether the residents of those communities are able to achieve upward mobility. According to ecological theories of intergroup relations, such mobility should occur naturally in the course of a group's adaptation to the culture and institutions of the larger society. The eventual outcome should be the existence of racially and ethnically integrated communities.

Ecological theories explore the processes by which conflict between racial or ethnic groups develops and is resolved. Along these lines, the early Chicago school sociologist Robert Park (1914) devised a cyclical model to describe intergroup relations in modern cities. That model consisted of the following stages:

Ecological theories explore the processes by which conflict between racial or ethnic groups develops and is resolved.

1. *Invasion*: One or more distinct groups begin to move into the territory of an established population.
2. *Resistance*: The established group attempts to defend its territory and institutions against the newcomers.
3. *Competition*: Unless the newcomers are driven out, the two populations begin to compete for space and for access to social institutions (housing, jobs, schooling, recreational facilities, etc.); this extends to competition for prestige in the community and power in local governmental institutions.
4. *Accommodation and cooperation*: Eventually the two groups develop relatively stable patterns of interaction. For example, they arrive at understandings about segregated and shared territories (Suttles, 1967).
5. *Assimilation*: As accommodation and cooperation replace competition and con-

flict, the groups gradually merge, first in secondary groups and later through cultural assimilation and intermarriage. They become one people. A new group arrives, and the cycle begins again.

Of course, this is an abstract model. It represents what Park and other human ecologists believe are the likely stages in intergroup relations. The Korean-American sociologist Ilsoo Kim (1981) found that Korean merchants in New York City have met resistance both from white merchants and from black residents of ghetto communities when they have purchased stores in those communities, but eventually they have reached

an accommodation with those groups. This finding tends to support the Park model, although the extent to which assimilation will occur remains an open question. On the other hand, critics point out that there is not always a steady progression from one of these stages to the next. Moreover, as Box 13-3 shows, accommodation, cooperation, and assimilation do not occur in every case. The ecological model fails to explain why and how groups compete for power and under what conditions they eventually come to cooperate. Nevertheless, the model presents a general picture of the stages that culturally distinct groups often (but by no means always) go through over time.

As a result of their unsuccessful resistance to the European invasion, Native Americans were segregated on reservations, many of which lacked adequate resources to permit them to share in the American Dream.

© Fujihira, Monkmeyer Press

Box 13–3: **The Case of Eskimo Starvation**

During the 1950s a severe famine struck thousands of Inuit Eskimos in the frozen barrens of northern Canada. Untold numbers died of starvation. Many more survived the famine but became dependent on the government dole. What do intergroup relations have to do with this situation?

Ecological theory demands that we look first at the material basis of Eskimo life and the people's relationship to the land they inhabit. Centuries of conflict between Eskimos and Indians had forced the Inuit to the far north. There they had become "the people of the deer." They were hunters and gatherers who lived by following great herds of caribou, on which they were totally dependent. A seemingly endless supply of deer meat and hides for clothing and tents was the basis of the Eskimos' adaptation to the hardships of life in the Arctic. But interracial contact was to drastically change this situation.

With the coming of white settlers to the more temperate portions of Canada and to the United States, the demand for furs rose. White and silver fox furs were especially valued by the settlers. Well before the end of the nineteenth century the Eskimos were in contact with white traders, who exchanged trinkets for furs and soon exchanged rifles for even more furs. Large numbers of caribou were slaughtered to be used as bait for fox trapping. The "people of the deer" became the "people of the fox" (Mowat, 1975). But this meant that the Eskimos were no longer a people apart. They had become dependent on the world demand for furs. When that demand shifted because of the changing tastes of fur wearers, the Eskimos' way of life was destroyed.

Faced with starvation, the Inuit trekked for hundreds of miles to seek help from white traders, soldiers, and missionaries at the trading posts and army communications bases. They were given grudging handouts, often insufficient to maintain life. The government's policy was to avoid creating dependence, to encourage the native people to live in their traditional ways, even though this was no longer possible. The result was widespread famine and, for the survivors, dependence on the dole. Not until they themselves began to demand entry into the economic and political institutions of the white-dominated society did assimilation and pluralism become possible.

A PIECE OF THE PIE

Up to this point we have explored the patterns of intergroup relations, the cultural basis of those patterns, and some of the theories that have been proposed to explain them. But we have not discussed how groups actually win—or fail to win—a fair share of a society's valued statuses and other rewards, that is, a piece of the social pie. In particular, the persistence of racial inequality in the United States requires more attention. This is a complex problem that is a source of continuing controversy.

How can we explain the fact that so many social problems in the United States today are associated with race? As William Julius Wilson (1984) has stated, "Urban crime, drug addiction, out-of-wedlock births, female-headed families, and welfare dependency have risen dramatically in the last several years and the rates reflect a sharply uneven distribution by race" (p. 75). Wilson and others doubt that racial prejudice and discrimination adequately account for the severity of these problems, for the period since the early 1970s has seen more antidiscrimination efforts than any other period in American history. The answers are to be found, Wilson argues, in how older patterns of racism and discrimination affect the present situation.

In an important study of this issue, sociologist Stanley Lieberson (1980) approached the problem by asking why the European immigrants who arrived in American cities in the late nineteenth and early twentieth centuries have fared so much better, on the whole, than blacks. Lieberson and Wilson agree that the problem of lagging black mobility is a complex one. The situation can be summarized as follows:

1. African-Americans have experienced far more prejudice and discrimination than any immigrant group, partly because they are more easily identified by their physical characteristics. As a result of the legacy of slavery, which labeled blacks as inferior, they have been excluded from full participation in American social institutions far longer than any other group.

2. Black families have higher rates of family breakup than white families. The problems of the black family are not part of the legacy of slavery, however. As Herbert Gutman (1976) has shown, slavery did not destroy black families to the extent that earlier scholars believed it did. Nor did the migration of blacks to the North during industrialization. A comprehensive review of the status of black Americans notes that "there was no significant increase in male-absent households even after the massive migration to the urban North" (Jaynes and Williams, 1989, p. 528). Until the 1960s three-quarters of black households with children under eighteen included both husband and wife. "The dramatic change came only later, and in 1986, 49 percent of black families with children under age eighteen were headed by women" (Jaynes and Wil-

liams, 1989, p. 528). The report reasons that if black two-parent families remained the norm through slavery, the Great Depression, migration, urban disorganization, and ghettoization, it appears unlikely that there is a single cause for the dramatic decline in two-parent families in the last two decades. Recent research by social scientists points to the effects of decreases in manufacturing jobs and the increase in service-sector jobs in causing a sharp decline in the fortunes of black males. (Black females also suffer, but they are more readily recruited into clerical employment.) By 1985 a black male was 2.5 times as likely as a white male to be unemployed. This change, combined with the drug epidemic and other negative trends affecting poor minority communities, is contributing to the difficulty of young couples in forming lasting relationships (Garfinkel and McLanahan, 1986; Wilson, 1987).

It is significant that among Hispanic groups in the United States the Puerto Ricans have experienced northward migration and problems of discrimination that are very similar to those experienced by African-Americans in northern cities. Still a dependent territory of the United States, since World War II Puerto Rico has sent hundreds of thousands of working people to cities like New York, Philadelphia, and Chicago. At present they comprise 14 percent of the Hispanic population in the United States, and their status in the population is very similar to that of blacks. There is a growing Puerto Rican middle class and an even more rapidly growing number of Puerto Ricans among the poor. This situation is due largely to changes in the types of jobs available to unskilled blacks and Puerto Ricans (Sandefur and Tienda, 1988). (The situation of Hispanic subgroups of the American population is discussed more fully in the Challenges section of this chapter.)

3. Structural changes in the American economy—first the shift from work on farms to work in factories and then the shift away from factory work to high-technol-

Among the causes of lagging social mobility among blacks are prejudice and discrimination, high rates of family breakup, and structural changes in the economy.

ogy and service occupations—have continually placed blacks at a disadvantage. No sooner had they begun to establish themselves as workers in these economic sectors than they began to suffer the consequences of structural changes in addition to job discrimination.

It is worth noting that social mobility is more available to blacks today than it was before the civil rights movement. Wilson (1978) noted that by 1970 about 10 percent of employed blacks were in professional or technical occupations or were managers or proprietors. This represented an increase from about 3 percent in 1940, but it was still far below the proportion of whites in those occupations. Thus, although the black middle class is growing, the majority of black workers remain dependent on manual work in industry or lower-level service jobs—types of jobs that are in decreasing supply. As a consequence, although some blacks have been able to achieve a secure middle-class life-style, the majority are in insecure working-class jobs or are unemployed. And chronic unemployment is associated with family breakup, alcohol and drug addiction, and depression. These social problems, in turn, severely hamper the ability of individuals to learn the attitudes and skills they need for entry into available jobs (Wilson, 1987).

You may remember from Chapter 10 that when Max Weber traveled in the United States in 1904 he noted that racial and ethnic inequality was the one great problem that marred the success of the American experiment in democracy. Several decades later, Gunnar Myrdal called the problem of racial inequality the American Dilemma. We have seen that this stain on the American ideals of equality and liberty has not yet been removed. Difficult as it was to achieve, breaking the legal barriers to racial and ethnic equality was insufficient. Progress toward racial equality will require a combination of political organization by the minority group and broad changes in economic and social policy. In any case, with so much remaining to be done, sociological research on these issues is in constant demand.

CHALLENGES TO CONTEMPORARY SOCIETY

The Growing Hispanic Presence in North America

People from Mexico, Puerto Rico, the Dominican Republic, Cuba, and other nations of Central and Latin America constitute the fastest-growing population of newcomers to the United States and Canada. Along with other major nationality groups that have settled in the United States, Spanish-speaking immigrants (and migrants) and their native-born children enrich the society's culture and bring the energies of a youthful and determined new population to many regions of North America.

Like the waves of immigrants who preceded them, the Hispanic newcomers face many challenges. Among them are the following:

The issue of identity. Is there an emerging "Latino" identity that can subsume the separate national identities of Cubans, Mexicans, Puerto Ricans, and others who are defined as Hispanic because of their common language or Spanish surnames?

The problem of equality. How can Hispanic people in the United States counteract their relative poverty in an economy in which they often find themselves in the least desirable jobs and the most precarious economic situations?

To understand these issues it is necessary to have some knowledge of the ecological and historical characteristics of Spanish-speaking people in the United States. By far the largest portion of this population consists of immigrants from Mexico; they account for about 60 percent of the total. U.S. citizens from Puerto Rico comprise another 14 percent, but the 1990 census, which is under way at this writing, will no doubt reveal major changes in the nature of immigration to the United States from Central and Latin America. Political refugees from Central America, especially El Salvador, Guatemala, Cuba, and many nations of Latin America, can be expected to add further to the diversity of the Spanish-speaking population of North America.

As can be seen in Table A, the influx of Spanish-speaking people into the United States began long ago in the case of Mexicans; they were living in parts of the Southwest and California before those regions were incorporated into the United States. In contrast, Cubans and Puerto Ricans began entering the country relatively recently. Like the Mexicans, the Puerto Ricans come mainly in search of low-wage jobs; they differ from the Mexicans in that they are U.S. citizens and can move freely between their island territory and the mainland. Many gravitate to large cities like New York and Chicago. The Cuban immigration is quite different; its origins lie in the Cuban revolution of the late 1950s, and hence it consists largely of middle-class refugees.

The historical facts about each of these groups contribute to the problems experienced by the Hispanic population in attempting to become a more cohesive political force in American society. Leaders of these groups often call for a "Latino" cultural and political identity that would unite the various Hispanic groups. But the emergence of a common Latino identity remains problematic, partly because of the geographic separation of the various Hispanic ethnic groups. Mexicans are heavily concentrated in the Southwest and California, Puerto Ricans in the Northeast, Cubans in Miami and elsewhere in Florida. In each of these areas there may be some members of the other groups, but usually not enough to form a real coalition. As a result, when leaders of the various groups seek support for programs such as bilingual education, they have difficulty speaking with one voice and proposing a unified set of policies.

The outlook for cultural and political unity for Hispanic Americans is further com-

Table A: American Indian, Black, Hispanic, and White Populations, 1492–1980 (in thousands)

Year	American Indian	Black	Mexican origin	Puerto Rican	Cuban origin	White
1492	5,000	0	0	0	0	0
1790	700	800	20	0	0	3,000
1860	400	4,400	28	0	0	27,000
1900	237	8,800	103[a]	0	11	67,000
1950	357	15,000	1,342[a]	301	33	135,000
1960	524	18,900	1,725[a]	893	125	159,000
1970	793	22,600	4,532	1,392	561	178,000
1980	1,418	26,500	8,740	2,014	803	188,000

[a]These population figures refer to individuals born in Mexico or with parents born in Mexico.
Source: Sandefur and Tienda, 1988.

plicated by the prevalence of poverty among these groups. As noted earlier, Cuban immigrants tend to come from middle-class backgrounds, and their major settlements do not include high proportions of poor households. The same cannot be said for Mexicans and Puerto Ricans. Because so many members of these groups work in agriculture and related industries, Mexicans tend to be disproportionately represented among the poor. In the case of Puerto Ricans, the story is more complex. Unlike most other Hispanic groups in the U.S. population, Puerto Ricans have experienced a decline in economic well-being and an increase in poverty. Marta Tienda, one of the nation's foremost authorities on minority poverty, explains that over the past decade "poverty rates soared for Puerto Rican families while they declined for black families" (Tienda and Jensen, 1989, p. 51). This change, she finds, is due largely to the greater success of black women in the labor market and the relative decline in employment of Puerto Rican women in the past twenty-five years. For a variety of reasons, Puerto Rican women have been unable to enter the white-collar labor force in large numbers. Segregated in industrial jobs that do not require high levels of education, Puerto Rican women (as well as men) have suffered disproportionately from the general decline in industrial employment.

Table B shows that Hispanic groups whose populations will increase in coming years will encounter a vastly changed labor market. The number of jobs that require higher education and specialized training will grow, while the number of jobs that do not require a high school diploma (and hence are attractive to immigrants for whom English is a second language) will decrease steadily. This situation affects all minority groups with high proportions of less educated and unskilled members, but it is especially significant for Hispanic groups because they constitute the largest population of newcomers. Clearly, a major challenge for sociologists, educators, and Hispanic Americans themselves is to find ways to increase educational attainment among these groups and to capitalize on the cultural diversity they bring to the nation.

Table B Central City Jobs in Industries, by Mean Education of Employees, 1970 and 1984 (in Thousands)

Average level of education of industrial workers	1970	1984	Change, 1970–1984
New York			
Less than high school	1,445	953	−492
Some higher education	1,002	1,241	239
Philadelphia			
Less than high school	396	224	−172
Some higher education	205	244	39
Boston			
Less than high school	168	124	−44
Some higher education	185	252	67
Baltimore			
Less than high school	187	114	−73
Some higher education	93	105	15
St. Louis			
Less than high school	197	109	−89
Some higher education	98	96	−2
Atlanta			
Less than high school	157	148	−9
Some higher education	92	129	37
Houston			
Less than high school	280	468	188
Some higher education	144	361	217
Denver			
Less than high school	106	111	5
Some higher education	72	131	59
San Francisco			
Less than high school	132	135	3
Some higher education	135	206	71

Source: Sandefur and Tienda, 1988.

SUMMARY

In biology, the term *race* refers to an inbreeding population that develops distinctive physical characteristics that are hereditary. However, the choice of which physical characteristics to consider in classifying people into races is arbitrary. And human groups have exchanged their genes through mating to such an extent that it is impossible to identify "pure" races.

The social concept of race has emerged from the interactions of various populations over long periods of human history. It varies from one society to another, depending on how the people of that society feel about the importance of certain physical differences among human beings. *Racism* is an ideology based on the belief that an observable, supposedly inherited trait is a mark of inferiority that justifies the discriminatory treatment of people with that trait.

Ethnic groups are populations that have a sense of group identity based on a distinctive cultural pattern and shared ancestry. They usually have a sense of "peoplehood" that is maintained within a larger society. Ethnic and racial populations are often treated as *minority groups*—people who, because of their physical or cultural characteristics, are singled out from others in the society for differential and unequal treatment.

Intergroup relations can be placed along a continuum ranging from intolerance to tolerance, or from genocide through assimilation. *Genocide* is the intentional extermination of one population, defined as a "race" or a "people," by a more dominant population. It is almost always justified by the belief that the people who are being slaughtered are less than human.

Expulsion is the forcible removal of one population from territory claimed by another population. It has taken a variety of forms in American history, including the expulsion of Native Americans from their ancestral lands, the Oriental exclusion movement of the nineteenth century, and the detention of Japanese Americans during World War II.

Slavery is the ownership of a population, defined by racial or ethnic or political criteria, by another population that has complete control over the enslaved population. Slavery has been called "the peculiar institution" because it has existed in some of the world's greatest civilizations, including the United States.

Although African-American slaves gained their freedom during the Civil War, a long period of segregation followed. *Segregation* is the ecological and institutional separation of races or ethnic groups. It may be either voluntary or involuntary. Involuntary segregation may be either *de jure* (supported by laws that prohibit certain groups from interacting with others) or *de facto* (enforced by unwritten norms).

Assimilation is the pattern of intergroup relations in which a minority group is forced or encouraged or voluntarily seeks to blend into the majority population and eventually disappears as a distinct people within the larger society. In the United States, three different views of assimilation have prevailed since the early nineteenth century. They are "Anglo-conformity," the demand that culturally distinct groups give up their own culture and adopt the dominant Anglo-Saxon culture; "the melting pot," the theory that there would be a social and biological merger of ethnic and racial groups; and "cultural pluralism," the belief that culturally distinct groups can retain their communities and much of their culture and still be integrated into American society.

Stereotypes are inflexible images of a racial or cultural group that are held without regard to whether or not they are true. They are often associated with *prejudice*, an attitude that prejudges a person, either positively or negatively, on the basis of characteristics of a group of which that person is a member. *Discrimination* refers to actual behavior that treats people unfairly on the basis of their group membership; *institutional discrimination* is the systematic exclusion of people from equal participation in a particular social institution because of their race, religion, or ethnicity. Social movements whose purpose is to oppose institutional discrimi-

GLOSSARY

race: an inbreeding population that develops distinctive physical characteristics that are hereditary (**p. 391**).

racism: an ideology based on the belief that an observable, supposedly inherited trait is a mark of inferiority that justifies the discriminatory treatment of people with that trait (**p. 392**).

ethnic group: a population that has a sense of group identity based on shared ancestry and distinctive cultural patterns (**p. 393**).

minority group: a population that, because of its members' physical or cultural characteristics, is singled out from others in the society for differential and unequal treatment (**p. 393**).

genocide: the intentional extermination of one population by a more dominant population (**p. 395**).

expulsion: the forcible removal of one population from a territory claimed by another population (**p. 396**).

slavery: the ownership of one racial, ethnic, or politically determined group by another group that has complete control over the enslaved group (**p. 397**).

segregation: the ecological and institutional separation of races or ethnic groups (**p. 398**).

de jure segregation: segregation that is supported by formal legal sanctions that prohibit certain groups from interacting with others or place limits on such interactions (**p. 398**).

de facto segregation: segregation that is supported and maintained by unwritten norms (**p. 398**).

Jim Crow: the system of formal and informal segregation that existed in the United States from the late 1860s to the early 1970s (**p. 399**).

assimilation: a pattern of intergroup relations in which a minority group is absorbed into the majority population and eventually disappears as a distinct group (**p. 400**).

ethnic stratification: the ranking of ethnic groups in a social hierarchy on the basis of each group's similarity to the dominant group (**p. 402**).

pluralistic society: a society in which different ethnic and racial groups are able to maintain their own cultures and life-styles while gaining equality in the institutions of the larger society (**p. 403**).

stereotype: an inflexible image of the members of a particular group that is held without regard to whether or not it is true (**p. 404**).

prejudice: an attitude that prejudges a person on the basis of a real or imagined characteristic of a group of which that person is a member (**p. 405**).

discrimination: behavior that treats people unfairly on the basis of their group membership (**p. 405**).

institutional discrimination: the systematic exclusion of people from equal participation in a particular institution because of their group membership (**p. 406**).

ethnic (or racial) nationalism: the belief that one's own ethnic group constitutes a distinct people whose culture is and should be separate from that of the larger society (**p. 406**).

scapegoat: a convenient target for hostility (**p. 408**).

projection: the psychological process whereby we attribute to other people behaviors and attitudes we are unwilling to accept in ourselves (**p. 409**).

internal colonialism: a theory of racial and ethnic inequality that suggests that some minorities are essentially colonial peoples within the larger society (**p. 412**).

nation are often supported by *ethnic nationalism*, the belief that one's ethnic group constitutes a distinct people whose culture is and should be separate from that of the larger society. Policies designed to correct persistent racial and ethnic inequalities in promotion, hiring, and access to other opportunities are referred to as *affirmative action*.

Social-psychological theories of ethnic and racial inequality argue that a society's patterns of discrimination stem from individual psychological orientations toward members of out-groups. Interactionist explanations go beyond the individual level to see how hostility or sympathy toward other groups is produced by the norms of interaction that evolve within and between groups. The functionalist perspective generally seeks patterns of social integration that help maintain stability in a society. Conflict theories trace the origins of racial and ethnic inequality to the conflict between classes in capitalist societies. The conflict perspective includes the theory of *internal colonialism*, which holds that many minority groups are essentially colonial peoples within the larger society. Finally, ecological theories of race relations explore the processes by which conflict between racial or ethnic groups develops and is resolved.

The persistence of racial inequality in the United States is a source of continuing controversy. This complex problem is a result of a number of factors besides racial prejudice and discrimination. Other factors are high rates of family breakup and the effects of structural changes in the American economy. Although social mobility is more available to blacks today than it was before the civil rights movement, the majority of blacks are in insecure working-class jobs or are unemployed.

WHERE TO FIND IT

Books

Divided Opportunities: Minorities, Poverty, and Social Policy (Gary D. Sandefur and Marta Tienda, eds.; Plenum Press, 1988). The chapters in this volume focus on the persistently high rates of poverty among blacks, Hispanics, and Native Americans.

A Piece of the Pie: Blacks and White Immigrants Since 1880 (Stanley Lieberson; University of California Press, 1980). A fine treatment of the comparative mobility of different racial and ethnic groups, especially African-Americans.

The Declining Significance of Race: Blacks and Changing American Institutions, 2nd ed. (William Julius Wilson; University of Chicago Press, 1980). A well-documented study of how changing economic conditions in the United States have altered the fortunes of black Americans.

Race Relations (Harry H. I. Kitano; Prentice-Hall, 1980). An excellent text on race relations, especially in the United States.

The Social Order of the Slum (Gerald Suttles; University of Chicago Press, 1968). A community study based on detailed ethnographic data from a low-income community in the heart of Chicago.

Ethnic America: A History (Thomas Sowell; Basic Books, 1981). A comparative treatise on the success and contributions of the major nationality groups that have made the United States their home.

Other Sources

Harvard Encyclopedia of American Ethnic Groups A valuable collection of essays about ethnic and racial relations in American society. Covers almost every imaginable group in the United States and offers summary essays on sociologically relevant subjects such as slavery, assimilation, ethnic accommodation, and conflict.

VISUAL SOCIOLOGY

An End to Apartheid?

The release of Nelson Mandela, shown here in a triumphant march from prison accompanied by his wife and fellow activist Winnie Mandela, was a signal to the world that apartheid may be ending. South Africa is the world's most infamous "racial state." It is a society in which race, an ascribed rather than an achieved status, determines far more about what a person can become than any other social variable. Can it be that, after years of violent struggle, fundamental reform is coming to South Africa? Can it be that South Africa is about to join the community of democratic nations? At this writing there is great hope; there are signs of real progress; and there is growing recognition that much more needs to be done before majority rule can be established in South Africa.

Scenes like this one at a "whites only" pool are finally giving way to scenes of integration in the giant swimming pool in Cape Town. Increasingly whites and blacks are marching together to end apartheid. These shows of solidarity strengthen the hand of South African President F. W. de Klerk, shown here as he announced the liberation of Mandela in February 1990. De Klerk is striving to bring about reforms that will end the worst and most visible ravages of apartheid. But he is not yet committed to establishing majority rule, a step that would surely make the whites a political as well as a demographic minority.

As signs that say "all races welcome" gradually replace scenes of violent protest, one is reminded of how many years of inexorable struggle, of clandestine social movements, of massacre and brutality were required to get South Africa even this far. It remains to be seen whether South Africa can achieve democracy without experiencing all-out civil war—a dream that is only now beginning to appear possible.

CHAPTER OUTLINE

- **Gender, Age, and the Life Course**
  - The Life Course—Society's Age Structure
  - Sex Ratios and Their Implications
  - Cohorts and Age Structures

- **Gender and Age Stratification**
  - Gender Roles: A Cultural Phenomenon
  - Historical Patterns of Gender and Age Stratification
  - Sexism and Ageism

- **Perspectives on Gender and Age Stratification**
  - A Functionalist View of Gender and Age Roles
  - Interactionist Views of Gender and Age Stratification
  - Conflict Perspectives on Gender and Age Stratification

- **Gender, Age, and the Changing Social Fabric**
  - The Women's Movement
  - Social Movements Among the Elderly

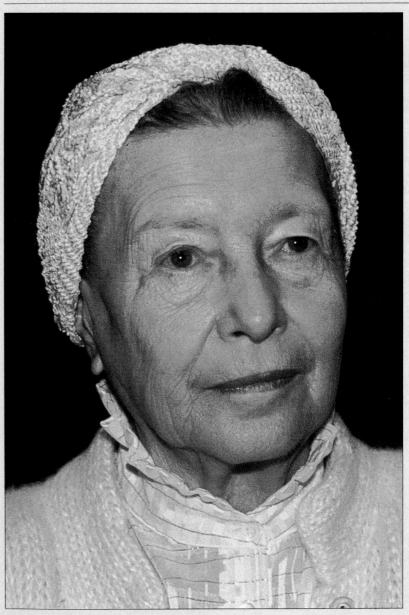

AP/Wide World Photos

Simone de Beauvoir

CHAPTER 14

INEQUALITIES OF GENDER AND AGE

"What a pity Simone wasn't born a boy: she could have gone to the Polytechnique [an elite engineering and science university]!" I had often heard my parents giving vent to this complaint. A student at the Military Academy of Artillery and Engineering, they felt, was already "someone." But my sex debarred them from entertaining such lofty ambitions for me. . . . I made things worse for myself by expressing a desire to become a teacher: [my father] approved my choice on practical grounds, but in his heart of hearts he was far from happy about it. He thought all teachers were low-minded pedagogues. [1959, p. 177]

Simone de Beauvoir, the author of this passage, was too intelligent and courageous to be discouraged. She rebelled against the sexism of her upbringing in the best way she knew, by becoming a brilliant student and a tireless political activist. She was one of the founders of the existentialist movement in modern philosophy and the author of numerous articles and reports on the biology, sociology, and politics of gender and age. Born in Paris in 1908, in her later years she turned her incisive mind to the problems of aging in society. "Too often," she wrote, "the coming of age brings with it the desire to withdraw from the active hubbub of productive work. The unfortunate part of it is that reasons for activity are hard to find again, once former occupations are forbidden" (1973, p. 672).

In her later years de Beauvoir voiced the frustrations and longings that most older people feel in modern societies, but she also attempted to show what it is that allows some people to live life to the fullest while others languish. One of the key factors in how people adapt to aging, it turns out, is gender—that is, the culturally determined traits associated with maleness and femaleness.

Years before the advent of the modern feminist movement, de Beauvoir wrote a highly acclaimed critical study of the position of women in Western societies. As women age, she argued, their waning years are too often wasted in cynicism and feelings of uselessness because they have been denied opportunities to develop their intellectual and creative powers. Writing in 1952, she deplored the fact that women throughout the world were confined to roles in the home and excluded from the more powerful and intellectually creative roles of the wider world. As a result of that prevailing pattern,

not only is [the typical woman] ignorant of what constitutes a true action, capable of changing the face of the world, but she is lost in the midst of the world as if she were at the heart of an immense, vague nebula. She is not familiar with the use of masculine logic. . . . A syllogism is of no help in making a successful mayonnaise, nor in quieting a child in tears; masculine reasoning is quite inadequate to the reality with which she deals. And in the world of men, her thought . . . is indistinguishable from daydreaming. She . . . never comes to grips with anything but words and mental pictures, and that is why the most contradictory assertions give her no uneasiness. . . . She is content, for her purposes, with extremely vague conceptions, confusing parties, opinions, places, people, events; her head is filled with a strange jumble. [1961/1952, p. 564]

GENDER, AGE, AND THE LIFE COURSE

In the decades since Simone de Beauvoir wrote her critique of the position of women in the Western world, there have been far-reaching changes in how we think about gender in daily life. In fact, you may have been shocked by the passage just quoted. College students now take it for granted that women are as intellectually capable as men. After all, by 1986 women had reached numerical parity with men in the professions, where educational achievement is so important. Of the nation's 14 million professionals—doctors, lawyers, accountants, teachers, research scientists, and others—about half are women. Doesn't this indicate that the problems faced by women like Simone de Beauvoir are diminishing? Hardly. In 1986 the weekly earnings of professional women averaged $419, while for male professionals the weekly average was $581 (*Statistical Abstract*, 1989), and the gap between women's and men's earnings is often greater in less prestigious occupations. Moreover, women are more likely to be found in less prestigious professions and men in more prestigious ones. Clearly, men and women are not yet equal, at least in terms of earnings and prestige or, as we will see, in power.

The same issues and questions arise in relation to different age groups. Why are so many children living in poverty? Why have the elderly had to struggle to win economic security after spending so many years working? How are the power and prestige of different age groups changing? Why is it, for example, that the elderly seem to be gaining in political power? Is the same true of young adults?

The first step toward answering these questions is to understand how gender and age contribute to the stratified structure of a society. The population of every society exhibits a particular age and gender distribution, and we devote the first section of the chapter to examining variations in age and gender distributions and their effects on so-

cial institutions. In the chapter's second major section we analyze *gender stratification*—that is, how the roles performed by women and men help create patterns of inequality. We also examine *age stratification*, or how the roles that young people, adults, and the elderly are expected to perform also contribute to inequality. We will see that few aspects of social life are changing as rapidly as gender and age roles, although older patterns of gender and age stratification persist even as these changes are occurring.

In the final section of the chapter we explore various sociological theories that attempt to explain how patterns of gender and age stratification develop and change. We also examine how social movements of various kinds are changing patterns of age and gender stratification.

The Life Course— Society's Age Structure

All societies divide the human life span into "seasons of life" (Hagestad and Neugarten, 1985; Zerubavel, 1981). This is done through cultural norms that define periods of life, such as adulthood and old age, and channel people into age grades— sets of statuses and roles based on age. These systems of age grades "create predictable, socially recognized turning points that provide roadmaps for human lives" (Hagestad and Neugarten, 1985, p. 35). Graduations, communions, weddings, retirements, and funerals are among the ceremonies that are used to mark these turning points.

In all societies cultural norms define periods of life and channel people into age grades— sets of statuses and roles based on age.

Age strata are rough divisions of people into layers according to age-related social roles. We speak of infants, preschoolers, primary school children, teenagers, young adults, and so on; these categories form a series of younger-to-older layers, or strata, in the population. People in different age strata command different amounts of scarce resources like wealth, power, and prestige (Riley, Foner, and Waring, 1988). Thus, numerous laws establish inequalities between youth and adults; they include laws governing the rights to vote, to purchase alcoholic beverages, to incur debt, and the like. In theory, a person who lacks the rights of adult citizenship will be protected by adults, who are responsible for providing him or her with adequate food, shelter, and education (and are presumed to have the resources to do so). In practice, however, hundreds of thousands of children and teenagers do not receive the care that is intended to offset their unequal status under the law.

Cultural norms specify the typical life course in a society; the ceremonies that mark the transition from one phase of the life course to the next are known as rites of passage.

Social scientists often refer to the **life course,** which may be defined as a "pathway along an age-differentiated, socially created sequence of transitions" (Hagestad and Neugarten, 1985, p. 36; see also Cain, 1964; Clausen, 1968; Elder, 1981). The cultural norms that specify the life course and its important transitions create what is thought of as "the normal predictable life cycle" (Neugarten, 1969, p. 121). We expect that we will go to school, find a job, get married, have children, and so on at certain times in our lives, and we consider it somewhat abnormal not to follow this pattern. Social scientists often refer to ceremonies that mark the transition from one phase of life to another as **rites of passage** (Van Gennep, 1960/1908). The confirmation, the bar mitzvah, the graduation, and the retirement party are examples of rites of passage in modern societies.

In the United States and other Western cultures, the life course is constructed from categories like childhood, adolescence, young adulthood, adulthood, mature adulthood, and old age. But our definitions of these categories lack the stability and uniformity of the age grades found in many traditional societies. For example, the French historian Philippe Ariès (1962) showed that in Western civilization the concept of childhood as a phase of life with distinct characteristics and needs did not develop until the late seventeenth century. Before that time children were treated as small adults. They were expected to per-

form chores and to conform to adult norms to the extent possible. When they reached puberty they were usually married, often to spouses to whom they had been promised in infancy.

Norms regarding gender are closely linked to the life course established by a society. Thus, Ariès's study of the emergence of childhood revealed that ideas about the appropriate forms of play and education for boys, and indeed the very concept of boyhood, developed at least a century before the concept of girlhood emerged. In eighteenth-century European societies boyhood was conceived of as a time when male children could play among themselves and receive education in the skills they would need as adults. Girls, in contrast, were treated as miniature women who were expected to work alongside their mothers and sisters. Through these childhood experiences girls and boys learned the norms of gender, the society's definitions of what is "masculine" and "feminine."

Sex Ratios and Their Implications

We can further illustrate the connections between age and gender by showing how age and gender distributions within a population can influence social roles and power. In most societies the numbers of males and females in the population are about equal. Under normal conditions males slightly outnumber females in infancy and childhood, but in adulthood and old age females outnumber males because women tend to live longer than men (Bogue, 1985). Demographers express these relationships in the form of **sex ratios:** The sex ratio of a population is the number of males per 100 females; a sex ratio of 100 means that there are the same number of males as of females in the population. The sex ratio among newborn infants averages between 105 and 106, meaning that there are somewhat more males than females (Bogue, 1969; Hall, 1978; Matras, 1973). But because males tend to be more susceptible to diseases and more prone to homicide and accidents, between the ages of thirty and fifty the proportions of men and women in most populations are nearly equal or are somewhat imbalanced by a shortage of men; by age sixty and beyond, however, females clearly outnumber males.

Figure 14-1 presents trends in sex ratios in the United States from the colonial period to recent years. The figure reveals some striking changes. For most of our history there was an excess of men, but after World War II there was a marked reversal in the gender distribution of the U.S. population. This reversal occurred for a number of reasons. Before World War I men outnumbered women among immigrants to the United States, but the high casualty rates for men during World Wars I and II and the Korean and Vietnam Wars began to reverse the ratio. Also, during the past few decades gains in longevity have been greater for women than for men because of a significant decrease in the number of women who die in childbirth. All of these trends contributed to the rather abrupt reversal in the sex composition of the U.S. population.

But does it really matter that out of a hundred women over the age of fourteen there may be only ninety-six men? Sociologist Marcia Guttentag believes differences like these can have profound consequences. She points out that men tend to seek out women who are, on the average, 2.5 years younger than they are. But in the 1940s and 1950s birthrates were changing drastically. The U.S. birthrate reached its lowest point in history in 1945 and then rose steadily for the next twelve years. This means that when a woman born in, say, 1948 was ready to find a mate, she had to choose from a pool of men two or three years older who had been born at a time when birthrates were lower. In fact, in the early 1970s, for every hundred women aged twenty to

Imbalances in the numbers of men and women and of people of different age groups in a society can have important effects on the lives of people in that society.

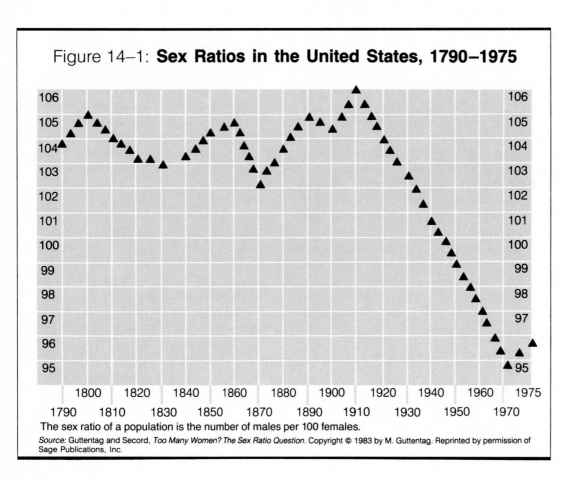

Figure 14–1: **Sex Ratios in the United States, 1790–1975**

The sex ratio of a population is the number of males per 100 females.

Source: Guttentag and Secord, *Too Many Women? The Sex Ratio Question.* Copyright © 1983 by M. Guttentag. Reprinted by permission of Sage Publications, Inc.

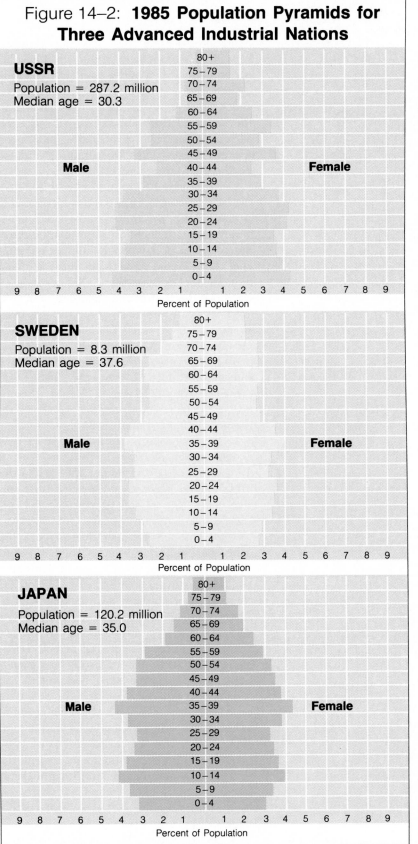

Figure 14–2: **1985 Population Pyramids for Three Advanced Industrial Nations**

USSR

Population = 287.2 million
Median age = 30.3

Male   Female

80+
75–79
70–74
65–69
60–64
55–59
50–54
45–49
40–44
35–39
30–34
25–29
20–24
15–19
10–14
5–9
0–4

9 8 7 6 5 4 3 2 1   1 2 3 4 5 6 7 8 9
Percent of Population

SWEDEN

Population = 8.3 million
Median age = 37.6

Male   Female

80+
75–79
70–74
65–69
60–64
55–59
50–54
45–49
40–44
35–39
30–34
25–29
20–24
15–19
10–14
5–9
0–4

9 8 7 6 5 4 3 2 1   1 2 3 4 5 6 7 8 9
Percent of Population

JAPAN

Population = 120.2 million
Median age = 35.0

Male   Female

80+
75–79
70–74
65–69
60–64
55–59
50–54
45–49
40–44
35–39
30–34
25–29
20–24
15–19
10–14
5–9
0–4

9 8 7 6 5 4 3 2 1   1 2 3 4 5 6 7 8 9
Percent of Population

twenty-four there were only about seventy-five available men. Demographers refer to this phenomenon as the "marriage squeeze." It diminished somewhat in the 1980s, but it continues to have significant effects, particularly among African-Americans (Guttentag and Secord, 1983; Wilson, 1986).

As these examples indicate, an imbalance in the numbers of men and women in a society can have important effects on the lives of members of both sexes. We will see shortly that similar effects can occur with respect to the numbers of people in different age groups within a population.

Cohorts and Age Structures

When we think about age, we tend to think in terms of **age cohorts,** or people of about the same age who are passing through the life course together (Bogue, 1969). We measure our own successes and failures against the standards and experiences of our own cohorts—our schoolmates, our workmates, our senior circle—as we pass through life.

Demographers use the cohort concept in studying how populations change. If we divide populations into five-year cohorts, grouped vertically from zero to 100+ and divided into male and female, we can form a *population pyramid,* a useful way of looking at the influence of age on a society. Figure 14-2 shows population pyramids for three advanced industrial nations; Figure 14-3 presents population pyramids for three third-world nations. Note that high birthrates expand the base of the typical third-world pyramid and that high rates of infant mortality cause the base to decrease rather dramatically within the first ten or fifteen years. High mortality rates in later cohorts bring the pyramid to a sharp point. In the advanced nations, by contrast, the birthrate is far lower and much more constant. There are bulges in the pyramid for particular cohorts, but for the most part the cohorts pass in regular fashion through the stages of life.

The Baby Boom and the Graying of America. When a population experiences marked fluctuations in fertility there are bulges in its

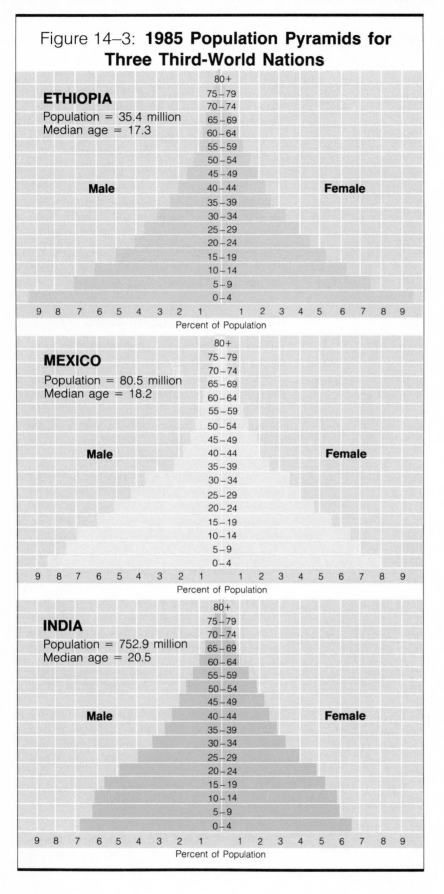

Figure 14–3: **1985 Population Pyramids for Three Third-World Nations**

ETHIOPIA
Population = 35.4 million
Median age = 17.3

Male   Female

Percent of Population

MEXICO
Population = 80.5 million
Median age = 18.2

Male   Female

Percent of Population

INDIA
Population = 752.9 million
Median age = 20.5

Male   Female

Percent of Population

population pyramid that have important effects. Perhaps nowhere in the world has this phenomenon been better studied than in the United States. The "baby-boom" cohorts, which were produced by rapid increases in the birthrate from about 1945 through the early 1960s, have profoundly influenced American society and will continue to do so for the next forty years or more.

Throughout Europe and North America the baby-boom generations did not have nearly as many children as their parents had. A mean family size of 2.1 children per couple is required for a population to remain constant over time (rapid growth requires a mean number of children closer to 3.0 per family). But since the 1970s the mean number of children per family in industrial societies has been about 1.85 (and much lower in nations like Japan and West Germany); as a result, the baby boom has been followed by a relative shortage of children known as the "baby bust" (Keyfitz, 1986). One way to visualize the impact of the baby boom and bust is to compare the population pyramids in Figure 14-4.

As these cohorts mature, they make new demands on the society's institutions. During the 1960s and 1970s, for example, when the baby-boom cohorts passed through their college years, the nation's universities and colleges expanded; the slogan of the day was "Never trust anyone over thirty." Now the baby-boom cohorts are out of college. Faced with declining enrollments and shrinking budgets, institutions of higher education are competing for students and seeking ways to attract members of other cohorts, such as older students who return to school for further training or advanced degrees. The baby boom has also had a tremendous impact on the labor force. Members of the baby-boom cohorts had to compete with one another for access to good jobs after college. The U.S. Department of Labor has estimated that not until the mid-1990s, when the last members of the baby boom are well along in their careers (and the baby-bust generation is entering the labor force), are there likely to be labor shortages, owing to the smaller size of the cohorts that followed the baby boom.

As the baby-boom cohorts move into

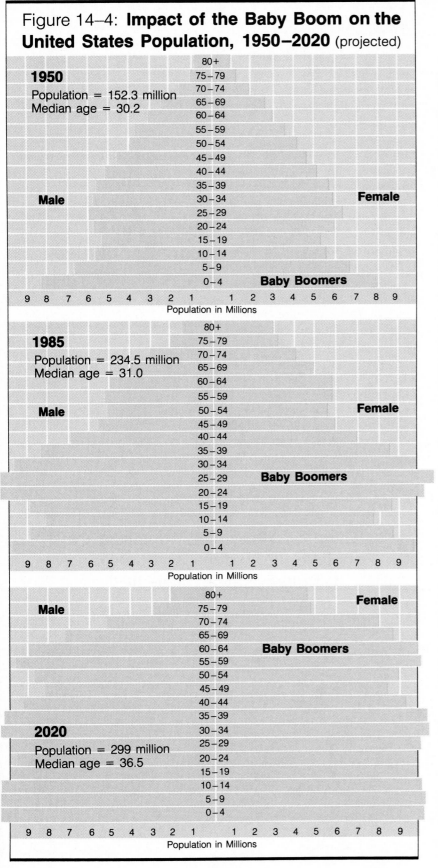

Figure 14–4: **Impact of the Baby Boom on the United States Population, 1950–2020** (projected)

1950
Population = 152.3 million
Median age = 30.2

Male

Female

Baby Boomers

Population in Millions

1985
Population = 234.5 million
Median age = 31.0

Male

Female

Baby Boomers

Population in Millions

Male

Female

Baby Boomers

2020
Population = 299 million
Median age = 36.5

Population in Millions

middle age, the problems of their parents, the aged, take on increasing importance. Table 14-1 shows that the proportion of elderly people in the American population is increasing steadily. This increase—which has been referred to as the graying of America—will result in greater concern about the needs of the elderly and will augment the influence of the aged on American culture and social institutions.

Life Expectancy and Gender. At age sixty-five and beyond, more than 50 percent of North American women are widowed, whereas only 13.6 percent of men have lost their wives. This is because the life expectancy of females is at least seven years longer than that of males. (By **life expectancy** we mean the average number of years that a member of a given population can expect to live beyond his or her present age.) Typically, men die before their wives do. And as noted earlier, they tend to marry women who are younger than they are, making widows the single largest category in the elderly population.

In the future, if male and female roles become more similar and women experience the stresses and risks that are thought to cause earlier death in men, the gap between the life expectancies of the sexes may narrow. Research on sex differences in the causes of death indicates that women may be less vulnerable to death for genetic reasons, but it is extremely difficult to prove this scientifically. The research of Lois M. Verbrugge (1985) on health trends among males and females indicates that the life-styles of men and women in the United States have become more similar; in particular, women's lives are more like men's. This change has unfortunate implications for women's health and longevity. For example, women are now smoking almost as much as men. Smoking among men declined from 53 percent in 1963 to 35 percent in 1985, but throughout the same period the rate for women remained constant at 30 percent. Among older smokers, men were twice as likely to quit the weed as women. Thus it is no surprise that lung cancer now almost equals breast cancer as a leading cause of death for women.

Smoking is only one indicator of the greater stresses women are encountering in their lives today. Many studies of adult women in the labor force show that in addition to bearing the same or greater stress at work (due to lower wages and slower advancement), women still do more work around the home and take on more of the burden of child rearing than the men in their lives. The role conflict created by the responsibilities of home and job affects both women and men, but women continue to feel the stress of this role conflict more heavily. Although there have been some improvements, the situation remains unbalanced and more stressful for women (Rosen, 1987; Epstein, 1988; Hochschild, 1989; Gerson, 1985), a point to which we will return later in the chapter (see Box 14-1).

The preceding discussion assumes that the current trend toward greater gender equality in American society will continue. However, we will see in the next section that this is a problematic assumption.

GENDER AND AGE STRATIFICATION

After class and race, the two most important dimensions of inequality in modern societies are gender and age. As stated earlier, **gender** refers to a set of culturally conditioned traits associated with maleness or femaleness. **Gender roles** are the sets of behaviors that are considered appropriate for individuals of a particular gender. They are directly related to the unequal treatment of men and women in a society. When women's roles are thought to require male direction, as is the case in many households and organizations, the unequal treatment of men and women is directly related to gender roles. Similarly, age is a source of social inequality when people of different ages are treated differently or channeled into statuses and roles that carry differing degrees of prestige or power. All human societies are stratified by age and gender, meaning that males and females and younger and older people are channeled into specific statuses and roles.

As we advance through the life cycle, age and gender roles usually interact in patterning our behavior and consciousness. "Act your age"; "Be a man"; "She's a real lady"—with these familiar expressions we let each other know that our behavior is or is not conforming to the role expectations associated with our particular gender and age. In addition, we often discover that certain roles are not open to us because of our age or our gender—we may be forbidden to drive a car, not allowed to serve our country in military combat, forced to retire from our jobs, and so on.

All societies differentiate among their members on the basis of gender and age in that men and women of different ages are expected to behave in different ways. But the roles assigned to men and women of different ages are accorded differing amounts of income, power, or prestige, and these patterns of inequality contribute to the society's system of stratification. For example, a man who has gained the position of chief executive officer of a *Fortune* 500 firm

> *Gender roles are directly related to the unequal treatment of men and women in a society.*

Table 14–1: Projected Proportions of Population in Various Age Categories, United States, 1980–2080

Year	Percent of Population by Age			
	Total	Under 18 Years	18–64 Years	65+ Years
1980	100.0	28.0	60.7	11.3
1985	100.0	26.3	61.7	12.0
1990	100.0	25.8	61.5	12.7
1995	100.0	25.9	61.1	13.1
2000	100.0	25.1	61.8	13.0
2010	100.0	22.9	63.3	13.8
2020	100.0	22.3	60.4	17.3
2030	100.0	21.6	57.2	21.2
2050	100.0	21.0	57.3	21.8
2080	100.0	20.3	56.2	23.5

Source: Reprinted with permission of The Free Press, a Division of Macmillan, Inc., from *The Population of the United States: Historical Trends and Projections* by Donald J. Bogue. Copyright © 1985 by The Free Press.

Box 14–1: **Hard Choices**

"I remember saying out loud that, if I had been a boy, I would want to go to law school. . . . But I didn't really think at all about the future and a career. I sort of assumed that I would one day get married and have children" (Gerson, 1985, p. 58). The speaker, a law student with no children, is talking to sociologist Kathleen Gerson about how her family created a "baseline" of expectations regarding her future. Another woman, who experienced a similar baseline in her family, explains that under some conditions it is possible for the baseline to change. "My brother's marriage was a very stormy one," she reports. "When he was married, it was my eighth birthday, and there was lots of anger, emotions, screaming, drinking, irregular hours, bad communication. I had a very split image [of marriage], but from about twelve on, I was *very* aware that life was not calico curtains and picking out silver patterns" (pp. 62–63).

For many women, Gerson found, a stable home and family did not necessarily create a desire to lead the same kind of life themselves. Some women from such homes wanted both a career and their own family. A biologist and mother of three says, "I wanted to be a medical doctor from age nine or ten. I also wanted to be a nurse or a scientist." When asked whether she wanted marriage and children, she responds, "I wanted that too. I wanted everything. I did expect to have everything" (pp. 64–65).

These excerpts are from Gerson's book *Hard Choices: How Women Decide About Work, Career, and Motherhood*, which describes the choices and decisions made by a cohort of women who came of age (i.e., college or work age) during the 1970s. These women, Gerson explains, are part of a "subtle revolution." The most salient aspect of that revolution is the rapid rise in the percentage of women in the labor force in recent decades: from 43.3 percent in 1970 to an entirely unexpected 51.2 percent in 1980 and an estimated 70 percent in the early 1990s. For many women, however, the "downside" of the revolution is evidenced in increased childlessness. Choices between career and childbearing are not usually "either/or" propositions, but they often require delay of childbearing or significant career sacrifices for both men and women.

In her interviews Gerson found that no matter how a woman was raised, "the adult life course is neither a predetermined outcome of childhood experiences, nor a series of predictable, orderly steps from one stage to the next" (p. 122). For example, many women who as teenagers expected to pursue occupational careers found that the inequalities and hassles of the work world made childrearing more attractive. A secretary who opted for a second child explains:

I had intended to quit work when I got pregnant with Jenny, to wait until Jenny was in school, and then go back to work. But when I went back, I wanted to go back as other than a secretary. I thought, would I like to be an electrician, a fireman? What is there in the world that I want to spend the rest of my life at? Then it came to me that I really enjoy what I'm doing now more than anything else I've done or anything that I could think of doing. So I decided to have another baby. [pp. 111–112]

Gerson also found many women whose life course veered toward work rather than home. Often the twists and turns in their lives were unplanned and, hence, accompanied by a great deal of confusion and stress. Although the men in their lives shared their dilemmas and frustrations, Gerson's research shows that women continue to bear a disproportionate share of the burden imposed by these hard choices.

will have money and power and great prestige; when he retires, he may still have great wealth, but he will lose the prestige associated with his position. Even greater will be his loss of power upon leaving the corporation. Should he die and leave all his wealth to his wife, the new widow will have the wealth and the prestige that comes with it, but she will have little power unless the fortune is so large that she can become a philanthropist whom others petition for funds.

Gender Roles: A Cultural Phenomenon

Until quite recently it was assumed that there were two spheres of life, one for women and the other for men. "Church, school and family—these chief agents of a child's socialization—worked together to transmit the notion that boys should grow up to be the doers, thinkers, and movers in the world at large. Girls, on the other hand, were expected to grow up to be wives and mothers. Any involvement in the world outside the home would be indirect rather than direct" (Scanzoni and Scanzoni, 1976, pp. 18–19). Out of this gender-based division of labor, which defined the activities that were appropriate for men and women, grew the notion of differences in men's and women's abilities and personalities. These differences were thought to be natural—an outgrowth of biological and psychological differences between males and females (Epstein, 1985). Behaviors that did not fit these patterns were viewed as deviant and in some cases as requiring severe punishment.

In the twentieth century, evidence from the social sciences has called into question the assumption that there are innate biological or psychological reasons for the different roles and temperaments of men and women. Margaret Mead's (1950) famous research in New Guinea directly challenged this assumption. Mead was one of the first social scientists to gather evidence to show that gender-specific behavior is learned rather than innate. In her study of gender roles in three tribes, Mead found that different tribes had

different ways of defining male and female behavior. In one tribe, the Mundugumor, men and women were equally aggressive and warlike, traits that Westerners usually associate only with men. In a second tribe, the Tchambuli, the men spent their time gossiping about women and worrying about their hairdos, while the women shaved their heads and made rude jokes among themselves. In the third tribe, the Arapesh, both men and women behaved in sympathetic, cooperative ways and spent a great deal of time worrying about how the children were getting along, all behaviors that Westerners traditionally associate with women.

Mead's research has been criticized in that she may have been actively looking for gender-role patterns that differed from those that Westerners usually associate with males and females. Nevertheless, her study was highly significant, since it began a line of inquiry that established that gender roles are not innate. Nor are gender roles wholly determined by a society's relationship to its environment. Although hunting-and-gathering societies sent men out to hunt while women cared for the home, in early agrarian societies there was a less rigid division of labor. In early horticultural societies women had more power than they did in hunting-and-gathering societies or in later feudal societies. Women maintained the grain supply and knew the lore of cultivation, and they were priestesses who could communicate with the harvest and fertility gods (Adler, 1979; Balandier, 1971/1890). Table 14-2 illustrates the sexual division of labor in 224 preliterate societies. It shows that as societies evolve from hunting and gathering to agrarian production, the division of labor by sex becomes more varied, although women tend to specialize in household tasks and men in tasks that take them outside the home (d'Andrade, 1966).

The lesson of this cross-cultural research is that gender roles are heavily influenced by culture. Although the relationship of earlier societies to their natural environ-

> *Social-scientific research has shown that gender roles are not innate but are heavily influenced by culture.*

Table 14–2: Cross-Cultural Data from 224 Societies on Subsistence Activities and Division of Labor by Sex

Activity	Number of Societies in Which Activity Is Performed by				
	Men Always	Men Usually	Either Sex	Women Usually	Women Always
Pursuit of sea mammals	34	1	0	0	0
Hunting	166	13	0	0	0
Trapping small animals	128	13	4	1	2
Herding	38	8	4	0	5
Fishing	98	34	19	3	4
Clearing land for agriculture	73	22	17	5	13
Dairy operations	17	4	3	1	13
Preparing and planting soil	31	23	33	20	37
Erecting and dismantling shelter	14	2	5	6	22
Tending fowl and small animals	21	4	8	1	39
Tending and harvesting crops	10	15	35	39	44
Gathering shellfish	9	4	8	7	25
Making and tending fires	18	6	25	22	62
Bearing burdens	12	6	35	20	57
Preparing drinks and narcotics	20	1	13	8	57
Gathering fruits, berries, nuts	12	3	15	13	63
Gathering fuel	22	1	10	19	89
Preservation of meat and fish	8	2	10	14	74
Gathering herbs, roots, seeds	8	1	11	7	74
Cooking	5	1	9	28	158
Carrying water	7	0	5	7	119
Grinding grain	2	4	5	13	114

Source: D'Andrade, 1966. Reprinted from *The Development of Sex Differences,* edited by Eleanor E. Maccoby, with the permission of the publishers, Stanford University Press. © 1966 by the Board of Trustees of the Leland Stanford Junior University.

ment often required that women tend the hearth and home while men went out to hunt for big game, women were also hunting for small game around the encampment and experimenting with new seeds and agricultural techniques. The division of labor by gender was never fixed; it could always be adapted to new conditions. In industrial societies, as the greater strength of males becomes less important as a result of advances in technology, it makes less sense to maintain the ear-

lier divisions of labor. Indeed, modern societies have demanded more involvement of women in a broader range of tasks. Women are now competing with men as military and police officers, engineers, scientists, judges, political leaders, and the like; they may be found in many roles that were assumed to be unsuitable for women earlier in this century.

Table 14-3 shows that women have increased their share of employment in many occupational groups that were formerly male

Table 14–3 **Growth in the Percentage of Women in Major Occupational Groups, 1970–1980**

Major Occupational Group	1970	1980	1970–80 Net Growth
Executives, Managers	18.5%	30.5%	46.9%
Professional Specialty	44.3	49.1	61.2
Technicians	34.4	43.8	57.5
Sales	41.3	48.7	75.4
Administrative Support, Including Clerical	73.2	77.1	89.2
Private Household	96.3	95.3	
Protective Service	6.6	11.8	23.2
Other Service	61.2	63.3	67.5
Farming, Forestry, Fishing	9.1	14.9	
Precision Production, Including Craft	7.3	7.8	10.2
Machine Operators	39.7	40.7	48.5
Transportation Workers	4.1	7.8	23.9
Handlers, Laborers	17.4	19.8	38.8
Total	38.0	42.5	57.5

NOTE: Percentage shown in column 3 is calculated in the following way: the number of women in the occupational group in 1970 is subtracted from the number in 1980 to form the numerator of the fraction; the denominator is the total civilian labor force in the occupational group in 1980 minus the total in 1970; this fraction is multiplied by 100; percentage female is not calculated for occupational groups which declined in size between 1970 and 1980.

Source: Taken from *American Women in Transition,* by Suzanne M. Bianchi and Daphne Spain © 1986, The Russell Sage Foundation. Used with permission of the Russell Sage Foundation.

"turf." The proportions of female executives and managers have increased dramatically, as have those of technicians and professionals. But older barriers and assumptions continue to stand in the way of equal access to male-dominated occupations such as precision production and protective service (e.g., private security). Conversely, women continue to be disproportionately represented in "pink-collar" occupational sectors such as clerical and administrative support and domestic service.

These changes in gender roles have given rise to the demand that women not be excluded from access to any roles, including those that are accorded high levels of power and prestige. The desire for full participation in society also applies to the aged, who, like women, have often been thought of as a subordinate, dependent population. Until recently, for example, the reigning theory in the field of **gerontology** (the study of aging and of older people) stated that people in their later years need to gradually "disengage" from their work and family roles. This means that they should retire from their jobs and find new, less demanding roles with less power and responsibility. But recent research has shown that no single theory can be applied to all aging people. Many have the ability and strength to continue in their earlier roles. Martha Graham, the creator of modern dance in the United States, was actively choreographing and directing well into her 80s. And who would have thought that rock stars like Jerry Garcia and Tina Turner would continue to be teenage idols well into their middle years? Disengagement theory can be, and often is, used as an excuse for unequal treatment based on age (Hochschild, 1975; Maddox and Campbell, 1985).

Historical Patterns of Gender and Age Stratification

In preindustrial societies gender and age often play a greater role in social stratification than do wealth and power. Fewer members of such societies are wealthy or powerful than is true in modern societies, but all are male or female, young or adult or old. Cross-cultural research has provided some insight into the development of gender- and age-based stratification in such societies. Among the main findings of that research are the following:

- Preindustrial societies are usually rigidly age graded and sex segregated. Age cohorts of males and females tend to pass through life in cohesive peer groups. Even after marriage, women and men tend to spend more time with their same-sex peers than they do with their spouses.
- As societies increase in size and complexity, women usually become subordinated to men. There have been few if any societies in which women as a group controlled the distribution of wealth or the exercise of power (Harris, 1980; Leacock, 1978).
- The status of the elderly in preindustrial societies often hinges directly on the importance of traditions and collective memory, or "strategic knowledge" (Demos, 1978; Harlan, 1968; Rosow, 1974). For example, when a society's land-tenure system depends on verbal accounts of who has rights to what land, the knowledge of the elderly about land transfers is a source of power and prestige.

The origins of gender inequality in most modern societies can be traced to the norms of feudal societies.

Larger, more complex societies also exhibit distinct patterns of age- and sex-role stratification, but these are more likely to be part of a multidimensional system of stratification in which class, race, ethnicity, gender, and age are intertwined. In the remainder of this section we focus on two basic questions that pertain to gender- and age-based stratification in modern societies:

1. How was male dominance incorporated into the culture and institutions of modern societies, and what changes in those societies have led women to join social movements for gender equality?
2. What are the current trends in modern societies with regard to the stratification of gender and age roles?

Male Dominance in Feudal Societies. The origins of gender inequality in most modern societies can be traced to their feudal periods. Most industrial societies developed out of feudal societies, either as a result of revolutions (in Europe) or through changes brought about by colonialism (in North and South America, Asia, and parts of Africa). Although they are no longer as easily justified, many of the norms that specify separate spheres of activity for males and females, as well as the subordination of women to men, were carried over into modern societies.

In some feudal societies these norms were far more repressive than those found in modern societies; in others, the subordination of women was disguised as reverence or worship. In European feudal societies, for example, the norms of chivalry and courtly love seemed to elevate women to an exalted status, but in reality they reinforced practices that kept women in undervalued roles. They gave rise to a set of norms that specified that women do not initiate sexual activity, do not engage in warfare or politics but wait for men to resolve conflicts, and do not compete with men in any sphere of life beyond those reserved for women.

The situation of Guinevere in the tales of King Arthur aptly illustrates this point (de Rougemont, 1983; Elias, 1978/1939). Courtly love applied only to women of the nobility. It specified that a woman must be chaste—either a virgin or entirely faithful to her husband at all times. Like Guinevere, she could be worshipped from afar by a noble knight (Lancelot), but she could not be touched or even spoken to without the consent of her male guardian (King Arthur). Figuratively she was set upon a pedestal. In reality, however, she was imprisoned—kept forever separate from the knightly suitor who worshipped her from a distance and engaged in chivalrous acts in her name. Adultery and the subordination of women were common in the lower orders of feudal society, but the women of the nobility were more likely to be constrained by the norms of chastity.

As feudal societies developed and changed, the norms of courtly love were extended to the new middle classes, and in greatly modified forms they still exist today. They can be seen, for example, in the traditions of courtship that persist in Spanish-speaking nations, in which a man serenades a woman (or hires someone to do it on his behalf) and the woman is never without a chaperone. It should be noted that courtly (or romantic) love eventually elevated the status of women from that of property to that of significant other, a change that had far-reaching implications for the position and influence of women in the family, as we will see in the next chapter. At the same time, in many Western cultures norms derived from medieval notions of courtly love continue to justify the notion that there are "good women," whom one reveres and protects, and "bad women," who are available for sexual exploitation. This denial of normal female sexuality and the assertion of the male's sexual needs is associated with a host of psychological and social problems, including the conflict that some women feel about their sexuality and the inability of some men to relate to their wives as sexual partners.

Gender and Age in Industrial Societies.

In modern industrial societies age and gender interact to shape people's views of what role behavior is appropriate at any given time. Before puberty, boys and girls in the United States tend to associate in sex-segregated peer groups. Because they model their behavior on what they see in the home and on television, girls spend more of their time playing at domestic roles than boys do; boys meanwhile play at team sports more than girls do. These patterns are changing at different rates in different social classes, but they remain generally accepted norms of behavior. And they have important consequences: Women are more likely to be socialized into the "feminine" roles of mother, teacher, secretary, and so on, while men are more likely to be socialized into roles that are considered "masculine," such as those of corporate manager or military leader. It is expected that men will concern themselves with earning and investing while women occupy themselves with human relationships (Baron and Bielby, 1980;

New York Public Library Picture Collection

Chodorow, 1974; Rossi, 1980).

Childhood socialization explains some of the inequalities and differences between the roles of men and women, but we also need to recognize the impact of social structures. In the United States, for example, it was assumed until fairly recently that boys and girls needed to be segregated in their games. Boys were thought to be much stronger and rougher than girls, and girls were thought to need protection from unfair competition with boys. This widespread belief translated into school rules that did not permit coeducational sports. Those rules, in turn, reinforced the more general belief that girls' roles needed to be segregated from those of boys. Such patterns have significant long-term effects. As sociologist Cynthia Epstein points out, human beings have an immense capacity "to be guided, manipulated, and coerced into assuming social roles, demonstrating behavior, and expressing thoughts that conform to socially accepted values" (1988, p. 240). Through such means gender roles become so ingrained in many people's consciousness that they feel threatened when women assert their similarities with men and demand equal opportunity and equal treatment in social institutions.

In their adult years men enjoy more

This medieval tapestry depicts the values of chivalry in action. Note the women standing inside their towers, aloof from the fray. Their lot is to watch the combat and hope that their hero will not be skewered by his opponent.

Age and gender interact to shape norms regarding appropriate role behavior in modern societies.

wealth, prestige, and leisure than women do. Working women earn less than men do, and they are frequently channeled into the less prestigious strata of large organizations. Even as executives they are often shunted into middle-level positions in which they must do the bidding of men in more powerful positions. Similar patterns are found in all advanced industrial nations. In her research on gender stratification in Japan, for example, Mary Brinton (1989) has shown that although educated young men and women enter large firms at approximately the same rate, by age forty-five to forty-nine women's participation in those firms is approximately three-fifths that of men while their participation in small firms is one and a half times that of men. These differences are significant because in Japan it is the large firms that provide the best wages, benefits, and job security, whereas in small firms careers are more uncertain. "It is clear," Brinton observes, "that women are not moving up in career ladders in the internal labor markets of large firms" (1989, p. 552).

After their working years are over, men tend to suffer a greater decline in social status than women do because they tend to derive so much of their personal identity from their occupational roles. But although retirement generally presents men with more difficult social and emotional adjustments than those faced by women, most studies of the effects of retirement and loss of occupational roles show that all but a small minority of people adjust to retirement with few lasting negative effects. As the elderly enter their last years, however, the number of men decreases rapidly. Widows often must live in old-age communities and nursing homes (Maddox, 1968; Palmore, 1981), which have extremely low sex ratios. Thus, in old age the issues of gender and age stratification converge: The problems of the elderly are primarily, although not exclusively, the problems of elderly women. This issue will be discussed more fully in the Frontiers section of the chapter.

Sexism and ageism are ideologies that justify prejudice or discrimination based on sex and age.

Sexism and Ageism

Stratification by gender and age is reflected in attitudes that reinforce the subordinated status of women and the elderly. The term **sexism** is used to refer to an ideology that justifies prejudice or discrimination based on sex. It results in the channeling of women into statuses that are considered appropriate for women and their exclusion from statuses that are considered appropriate for men. Sexist attitudes also tend to "objectify" women, meaning that they treat women as objects for adornment or sex rather than as individuals worthy of a full measure of respect and equal treatment in social institutions. This can be seen in the case of beautiful women. Such women receive special treatment from both men and women, but their beauty is a mixed blessing. The beautiful woman is often viewed as nothing more than an object for admiration. Being a woman is a master status (see Chapter 3) in that gender tends to outweigh the person's achieved statuses. This is even more painfully true for beautiful women. Someone like Marilyn Monroe is thought of only in terms of her beauty; the person beneath the surface is ignored.

The objectification of women can be seen in the beauty contest, which came into being in the United States in the summer of 1921 when the first Costume and Beauty Show was held at a bathing beach on the Potomac River. There the women wore tunic bathing suits and hats, but later that year a similar contest was held at Atlantic City, New Jersey, that eventually developed into the Miss America Pageant. In that contest women wore one-piece bathing suits that showed their calves and thighs and created a sensation in the tabloid newspapers. These contests and the publicity they generated made beauty a way for women to gain celebrity and wealth, but they also reflected the dominant male view that the most extraordinary women are those with the most stunning faces and the shapeliest figures (Allen, 1931). Women have been struggling against this view throughout the modern era, a struggle that has frequently been opposed not only by men but also by

This photo from the 1950s shows how explicit sexism was in the American airlines industry at the time. We have not found an equivalent photo for male flight crews. Although female airline employees still must conform to dress codes, they have formed unions and have won more stable careers and greater job security.

women who feel threatened by changes in their traditional statuses.

Sexism is also expressed in violence against women. Two million American women are severely beaten in their homes every year, and 20 percent of visits by women to hospital emergency rooms are caused by battering. (Thousands of men are battered by their wives each year as well, but they are far outnumbered by women victims.) In popular American culture, especially movies and television, violence against women is not condoned, but it is presented as a form of thrilling entertainment. Films like *Nightmare on Elm Street* and *Looking for Mr. Goodbar* suggest that the brightest and most independent women are most likely to be victimized. Examples like these hardly exhaust the overt types of sexism that exist in employment and other aspects of social life in the United States, but they are aspects of American culture that too often go unnoticed. Despite advances in women's rights and changes in women's access to careers, sexism remains commonplace in many areas of American life (Benokraitis and Feagin, 1986).

Ageism is similar to sexism; the term refers to an ideology that justifies prejudice or discrimination based on age. Ageism limits people's lives in many ways, both subtle and direct. It may label the young as incapable of learning. It labels the elderly as mentally incapable or asexual or too frail to get around. But people of all ages increasingly reject these notions. In their everyday lives in families and communities, for example, older people continually struggle against the debilitating effects of ageism. "Just because I need help crossing the street doesn't mean I don't know where I'm going," an elderly woman said to community researcher Jennie Keith (1982, p. 198).

Gerontologist Robert Butler observes that "ageism allows the younger generation to see older people as different from themselves; thus they subtly cease to identify with their elders as human beings" (1989, p. 139). Butler, a physician and social scientist, has found that as the proportion of older people in a society increases, as is occurring in the United States and Europe, the prevalence of ageism also increases. The younger generations, he notes, tend to fear that the older, increasingly frail and dependent generations will deprive them of opportunities for advancement. This fear is expressed in demands for reduced spending on Medicare and other programs that assist the elderly, as well as in the belief that the elderly are affluent and do not need social supports.

PERSPECTIVES ON GENDER AND AGE STRATIFICATION

When scholars ask why people are treated differently because of their gender or age, biological explanations often come up first. To a casual observer it seems obvious that men are stronger than women and are less tied to the home because they do not bear children. And is it not obvious that people in their prime years are mentally and physically superior to the young, who have yet to reach maturity, and to the old, whose bodies and minds are showing signs of decay? We need only to accept these simple biological truths to understand why societies assign different roles to women and the elderly than to men in their prime years. Thus, sociobiologist Desmond Morris (1968) argued that gender roles developed early in human evolution, when apes began hunting. "The females were too busy rearing the young to be able to play a major role in chasing and catching prey," he wrote. They maintained the home base, where the young were reared and the gains of the hunt shared. Once this division of labor was established, it was maintained throughout human evolution.

These biological arguments often anger sociologists, who, as noted earlier, have found that gender and age roles are culturally conditioned rather than biologically determined. For example, the British sociologist Ann Oakley (1974) contends that attempts to explain gender stratification on the basis of analogies to nonhuman societies or early hunting-and-gathering societies are fallacious. Worse still, they are used to justify a view of women in which their confinement to domestic roles is validated by "an image of Mrs. Pregnant-or-Nursing Ape, waiting gratefully with a cooking pot in her hand for the return of Mr. Hunting Ape with his spoil. Mrs. Hunting Ape then kept the home fires burning" (p. 160), just as women are expected or encouraged to do today, long after such a division of roles has ceased to be necessary.

In a thorough review of both biological

and sociological evidence on differences between the sexes, neurophysiologist Ruth Bleier (1984) evaluated research on the question of whether women's hormones establish brain functions that make them more emotional than men, or more intuitive, or less aggressive, or less skilled at mathematics. Even though many biologists and some sociologists suggest that there are clear differences between the sexes in these traits, Bleier found that "whatever characteristic is being measured, the range of variation is far greater among males or among females than between the two sexes" (p. 109). For example, the difference between tennis champion Martina Navratilova and the average woman playing tennis at the country club is much greater than the difference between most male and female tennis players.

But if biological explanations of gender-based stratification are inconclusive or biased, is not the opposite true in the case of age-based stratification? Can anyone deny the biological facts of aging and death? Isn't it only natural for the elderly to perform less important roles as their physical capacities diminish? Again the answer is that it is not obvious at all. In fact, one need only note the influence of some elderly people in modern societies to see the weakness of this argument. The United States and the Soviet Union are both ruled predominantly by older men. In 1985 the Soviet Union brought Mikhail Gorbachev, a man in his fifties, to power after more than thirty years of rule by men in their seventies. And at this writing fully 25 percent of the members of Congress are over the age of sixty.

Sexual behavior among the elderly is another area in which popular notions about the influence of biology on age roles have been disproved. In the late nineteenth century and well into the twentieth it was widely believed that people lose their sexual desire and potency after middle age. In fact, however, a number of studies have shown that the image of the elderly as lacking sexual desire and the ability to enjoy sex is an ageist stereotype. For example, Eric Pfeiffer, Adrian Verwoerdt, and Glenn Davis (1972) gathered data from several samples of elderly people—including individuals as old as ninety-

four—that showed conclusively that although sexual interest and activity tended to decline with age, sex remained an important aspect of the subjects' lives. The researchers also found, however, that elderly men are more interested in sex than women of the same age. The explanations for this difference are cultural rather than biological. Elderly men are in short supply. They tend to be married to women with whom they have had a longstanding relationship that includes an active sex life. If they are not married, they are in so much demand that they have less difficulty than women of the same age in finding a sexually compatible partner (Kornblum and Julian, 1989; Pfeiffer et al., 1972).

Biological explanations of gender- and age-based stratification are inconclusive or biased.

Neurophysiologists and other medical researchers often draw sociological conclusions from their findings. They begin by seeking evidence to challenge or support biological hypotheses and end by pointing to such factors as culture, role behavior, and socialization as the most persuasive explanations for gender and age stratification. In the remainder of this section, therefore, we will look at sociological explanations for the organization of gender and age roles in modern societies.

A Functionalist View of Gender and Age Roles

From a functionalist perspective, society is organized into gender and age roles because specialization on the basis of sex and age made sense from the beginning of human evolution. Women, Kingsley Davis (1949) pointed out, are specialized for reproduction, "whereas the male, with his readier strength but shorter life-span, is specialized for fighting. It is not surprising, then, that the tasks usually associated with womanhood are those most compatible with reproduction. Keeping house, cooking, etc. thus become roles allocated to women, while hunting, herding, fighting, etc., tend to be roles allocated to men" (p. 101).

From a functionalist perspective, gender and age roles developed because specialization on the basis of sex and age was functional in the early stages of human evolution.

This sounds very much like the explanation presented by the sociobiologists, but the functionalist perspective does not imply that the differences between men and women are due to genetic evolution. In fact, it recognizes that although a biologically based division of labor may have had important functions in earlier societies, it has become dysfunctional in modern ones. Clearly, human institutions have developed to a point at which individuals do not attain particular statuses through physical strength or fighting ability. We do not expect the president of the United States to engage in single combat with our enemies, as often occurred in ancient Greece or among Celtic tribes in what is now England. Yet even though the biological advantages of men in terms of strength and stamina have become less important, male dominance of social institutions has continued.

With regard to age stratification, functionalists argue that it depends directly on the roles that people of different ages are expected to perform. For example, elderly people in preliterate societies are culture bearers. They preserve the group's history, its knowledge of crafts and techniques, and its genealogies. The spread of literacy deprives the elderly of their vital role as keepers of cultural knowledge. They are replaced by "knowledge specialists"—lawyers, scientists, teachers, and the like. As a result, their position in the society becomes less important, and they may even come to be seen as burdens (Bengston et al., 1985).

The well-known gerontologists Matilda White Riley and John W. Riley, Jr., believe that there is a growing mismatch between the strengths and capacities of older people and their roles in society. As people live longer, they often find themselves living alone with few constructive roles that demand their time and attention. Neglect of the elderly further reduces their mental and physical strength. The Rileys believe that "increasing numbers of competent older people and diminishing

role opportunities cannot long coexist" (1989, p. 28). In their view, there is an urgent need for many small-scale programs that create work and volunteer opportunities in which older people can use their skills and feel needed.

The functionalist perspective recognizes that shifts in age statuses can have dysfunctional effects. A research project of the Carnegie Foundation attempted to assess the impact of an aging society (i.e., one in which the median age is increasing) on social roles. For example, whose responsibility is it to pay for long-term care of the elderly? A family may have to pay over $25,000 a year to provide nursing home care for a disabled elderly mother or father. Should the sons and daughters take on this responsibility? Most of us would say yes, if we are able to do so. The Carnegie study found, however, that an increasing proportion of people say, in effect, "No sir, that's a public responsibility, let them go on Medicaid." But in that case we would force the elderly to sell all their assets in order to qualify for government aid, since Medicaid is available only to people who have exhausted their own funds before applying to the government for assistance (Pifer and Bronte, 1986).

The question of responsibility for caring for the frail elderly is a controversial policy issue. The conservative position is that family members or close relatives should be required to pay for such care until funds are no longer available. The liberal position is that individuals should not have to be dependent on possibly reluctant family members; moreover, the high costs of long-term care for the elderly are an especially heavy burden for households with low incomes. This issue is discussed further in the Frontiers section of the chapter.

Interactionist Views of Gender and Age Stratification

Changes in age and gender roles do not hinge solely on the way society is organized and how it functions. The way we are socialized to feel about ourselves as people counts heavily as well. In "Growing Up Girlish: The Social Construction of the Second Sex" (1985), Jo

© duomo

Basketball players like Katy Steding of Stanford (no. 23) cannot play the game professionally because there is no professional basketball league for women. One reason for this is that women athletes violate the traditional male preference for weak, submissive women. Indeed, successful female athletes are often accused of taking steroids or of being gay.

Freeman attacked the functionalist perspective on gender roles. She argued that functionalist explanations of gender-based stratification seem to attempt to justify the popular notion that women are by nature more expressive and nurturing and that men are more active and aggressive. In fact, she asserted, it is the process of socialization, in which women and men are encouraged to develop certain personality traits, that makes them assume the roles they do. In this she agrees with Simone de Beauvoir's observation that "the passivity that is the essential characteristic of the 'feminine' woman is a trait that develops in her from the earliest years. . . . It is, in fact, a destiny imposed upon her by her teachers and by society" (quoted in Freeman, 1985, p. 240).

It is one thing to assert that a fact exists, but it is quite another to prove it. What evidence do interactionists provide to support their assertion that gender roles are a product of socialization? First, there is evidence from tests of performance: In the early school grades girls get off to a fast start—they begin speaking, reading, and counting sooner than boys do. Yet by the time they are finishing high school their performance has declined. Although a few may be at the top of their class, the majority have sunk below the performance levels of their male classmates. Apparently it becomes increasingly unrewarding for them to outperform males (Gilligan, 1982; Schechter, 1982).

Interactionists also point to norms specifying that it is unmanly for a male to be defeated in competition with a woman and unfeminine for women to want to compete with men. Jennifer Capriati, the tennis prodigy who was thirteen when she began her professional career in 1990, has learned that men hate to lose to her, but she also knows that she must play against them in order to prepare to compete with the best women players (Finn, 1990). Unlike the tennis star, who describes herself as a fighter, many women who compete against men are made to feel that they will become less feminine as a result.

An example of this effect can be seen in a study of women lawyers conducted by Cynthia Epstein (1981). Self-confidence and assertiveness are vital to success in the legal profession, yet many of Epstein's subjects lacked these traits as a result of their socialization, which had taught them to be submissive. Epstein also observed, however, that women who enter the professions are able to overcome the effects of past socialization. Socialization is not irreversible: Many women professionals have learned to be assertive and to compete for higher-status roles in male-dominated organizations.

The interactionist perspective on gender and age roles emphasizes socialization and the construction of roles through social interaction.

Interactionists have pointed out that throughout history people have learned that males are more highly valued than females, and this thinking casts men as the norm and women as "other," as possessing traits opposite to those attributed to men (de Beauvoir, 1961/1952). Often this definition works in favor of men and to the detriment of women. There are many occasions, however, when the supposed superiority of men subjects them to greater danger and risk of death—in war, for example, or in the mines and factories of the earlier stages of industrialization. However, in the long run such gender-based distinctions usually benefit neither men nor women (Epstein, 1988).

From an interactionist perspective, age roles also are constructed through social interaction rather than being automatically defined by a person's place in various social structures. Our age roles result from the ongoing process of socialization and are intimately connected to our identity, to how we think of ourselves in comparison with others. We learn through interaction how to behave in our age roles—that is, how to behave in ways that our society considers appropriate for people of our age.

Bernice Neugarten pointed out that "there exists what might be called a prescriptive timetable for ordering of major life events; a time in the life span when men and women are expected to marry, a time to raise children, a time to retire" (1969, p. 121). Of course, Neugarten is hardly the first to make this observation—it has appeared in works of literature throughout history. A familiar example occurs in the Bible: "To every thing there is a season, and a time to every purpose under the heaven" (Ecclesiastes 3:1). In most cultures, Neugarten observed, "men and women are aware not only of the social clocks that operate in various areas of their lives, but they are aware also of their own timing and readily describe themselves as 'early,' 'late,' or 'on time' with regard to family and occupational events" (1969, p. 123).

Identity and age-appropriate behavior are also related to social status; an elderly corporate executive, for example, is often treated with far more deference than a retired elderly corporate executive. "Central to any account of adult identity," according to Howard Becker and Anselm Strauss, "is the relation of change in identity to change in social position" (1956, p. 263). The most important such change is the attainment of adulthood, which is marked by entry into such statuses as marriage, military service, and a steady job. Entry into old age, on the other hand, is often marked by retirement from work, which is accompanied by the loss of a significant status and the roles associated with it. In some societies, especially in Africa and Asia, age confers new statuses and roles that are far less ambiguous than those found in the United States. Elderly people in Africa, for example, generally do not attempt to look younger; instead, they accept their age and insist on the respect that is normally given to older people in their culture.

Conflict Perspectives on Gender and Age Stratification

Interactionists often find evidence that the status of an individual within a group is constructed from the small details of everyday behavior. Conflict theorists, on the other hand, ask why entire populations find themselves assigned to certain roles and how they take collective action to change those roles. For Marxian conflict theorists, the origins of contemporary patterns of gender and age stratification are found in the social classes and economic institutions of capitalism. For example, the British social scientist Chris Phillipson (1982) believes that "the logic of capitalism as a productive and social system is irreconcilable with meeting the needs of elderly people" (p. 4). He argues that whenever capitalism is in crisis, as it was in the Great Depression of the 1930s or, on a smaller scale, in the severe recession of the early 1980s, aging working-class people suffer most because their jobs are least secure. They are most likely to become unemployed or forced into early retirement and have to live on small fixed incomes or wages from menial jobs. Elderly members of the lower middle class and the poor suffer as well.

Another Marxian social theorist, Shulamith Firestone (1970), argues that the origins of gender inequality are also found in capitalist institutions. However, she believes that Marx paid too little attention to the gender stratification that occurs within the family in capitalist societies. The model family of England in the mid-eighteenth century, or in America a century or more later, was a highly cohesive "corporate unit": dominant male, submissive and supportive female, obedient children, all organized to do well in a society that prized the accumulation of wealth and its outward trappings. Women in such a society resembled a caste: They had their own world of work and obligations and leisure, but it would always be subordinate to the world of men. Unless women were liberated from the roles that tied them to the kitchen and the nursery, they would never gain equality with men even if economic institutions allowed them to compete on an equal footing.

In the same vein, sociologist Nancy Chodorow (1974) asserts that women must overcome their "pseudo training" if they are to succeed in pursuits outside the home. She observes that in many respects girls are treated the same as boys in that they are urged to do well in school and to develop their skills, yet they are also trained to be "feminine"—that is, to flatter and serve men and not compete with them directly in sports or intellectual pursuits. Being feminine often means accepting lower-status roles later in life. Only social movements that challenge the existing relationships between the sexes will ever liberate women from their inferior roles, according to Chodorow.

Other conflict theorists find evidence of gender and age stratification in all societies, whether capitalist or not. Randall Collins (1975), for example, points out that in traditional agrarian societies a woman was often treated as a form of "sexual property," valued only for her potential as a childbearer and servant; her own property was controlled by her husband or her father or her uncles, and her worth was also calculated on the basis of her family's wealth or prestige. Women in traditional societies continually rebelled against their situation, usually as individuals rather than in organized groups. But they were unable to prevent male dominance from being carried into the institutions of early industrial societies.

Throughout this century, as women have fought for greater equality they have had to overcome a number of obstacles to the unity of their social movement. The feminist social theorist and social historian Nancy Cott (1987) has identified two important areas of continuous struggle: the conflicts between professional and working-class women and between the ideology of professionalism and that of feminism. Professional women often base their demands for equality on their desire for equal treatment in professional training and careers. Working-class women often base their politics less on gender issues and more on issues of class—especially their need to work

> *Marxian conflict theorists believe that contemporary patterns of gender and age stratification are related to the institutions of capitalism.*

under almost any conditions and to participate in labor unions with men who also need to work. Conflicts between women who "want to work" and those who "need to work" have created rifts within the women's movement that continually threaten its solidarity. At the same time, some professional women seek to join with others in organized action to gain advancement within their professions, whereas others claim that one can succeed as a professional only through individual effort; this conflict also continually threatens to divide women who would otherwise be attracted to the women's movement.

Conflicts between age cohorts can also be seen in modern societies. Sociologist Jeffrey Rosenfeld (1979) has found, for example, that people in retirement communities are increasingly likely to leave their money to one another rather than to their children. Another area of conflict between generations is competition for jobs. This competition (along with the fact that older workers tend to be paid more than younger ones) has led to the de-

mand that older workers retire from their jobs—even though the abrupt transition from active work to retirement appears to be harmful to the health and self-image of many older yet still vigorous individuals (Riley and Riley, 1989; Atchley, 1980). As illustrated in the next section, in recent years the elderly have rejected the concept of compulsory retirement.

GENDER, AGE, AND THE CHANGING SOCIAL FABRIC

The Women's Movement

When Simone de Beauvoir wrote *The Second Sex* in 1952, the women's movement was dormant. In the late nineteenth and early twentieth centuries, women had organized social movements to gain full citizenship rights and greater control over reproduction (e.g., through family planning and birth control). In the United States they were known as Suf-

Women in the suffrage movement early in the twentieth century were fighting for the right to vote. Their movement often met with organized resistance from men.

fragettes because they campaigned vigorously for women's suffrage—that is, for the right of women to vote. But in 1920, after the Nineteenth Amendment extended the right of suffrage to women, the movement faded.

The victory of the Suffragettes did not change the patterns of gender stratification, however. For example, in their famous studies of Middletown, Helen and Robert Lynd (1929, 1937) found that women who had worked their way into good factory jobs and professional occupations were severely set back during the Great Depression. Like blacks and members of other minority groups, women were the last to be hired and the first to be fired when times were bad. And although women were hired as factory workers in unprecedented numbers during World War II, they often faced discrimination and harassment and were usually "bumped off" their jobs by returning GIs after the war (Archibald, 1947). Nor did this situation change greatly when women began entering the professions and the corporate world in the 1950s. Women still tended to be limited to roles that were either subordinate to those of men or part of an entirely separate sphere of "women's work."

In her review of the origins of the modern women's movement, Jo Freeman (1973) wrote that even in the mid-1960s the resurgence of the women's movement "caught most social observers by surprise." After all, women were widely believed to have "come a long way" toward equality with men. Their average educational level was rising steadily and they were gaining access to the better professions and even to positions in the top ranks of corporate management. Freeman suggested that the movement developed out of an existing network of women's organizations that made many women aware of the inequality still prevailing in American society and encouraged them to organize to demand equal rights. Influential writing by women activists, such as Betty Friedan's *The Feminine Mystique* (1963), and studies of gender inequality by social scientists like Alice Rossi (1964) and Jessie Bernard (1964), played a major part in this growing awareness.

Meanwhile another, less formal network of women was developing. Women who were experiencing sexism within other social movements—the antiwar movement, the civil rights movement, the environmental-protection movement, and the labor movement—began to form small "consciousness-raising groups" (Morgan, 1970). By questioning traditional assumptions and providing emotional and material support, these groups attempted to develop a sense of "sisterhood." Their members formed a loosely connected network of small groups that could mobilize resources and develop into a larger and better-organized movement.

The women's movement achieved significant victories during the 1970s. The federal Equal Employment Opportunity Commission began to enforce laws barring gender-based discrimination in employment. Lawsuits filed under the Civil Rights Act and other federal laws forced many employers to pay more attention to women's demands for equality in pay and promotion and an end to sexual harassment on the job. Above all, the movement began to change the way men and women think about gender roles. No longer did male assumptions about how work should be divided go unchallenged. In the home, men slowly began to accept roles that had previously been considered "women's work" (Rosen, 1987). And at work they were more likely to have women as supervisors than was true only a decade earlier. Throughout American society the attitudes of both men and women were becoming more favorable toward a more equal allocation of political and economic roles (Yankelovich, 1981).

Despite these changes, gender equality is far from complete. As we saw earlier, studies of the sharing of household tasks reveal that women continue to do more such tasks than men do (Hochschild, 1989). And as Table 14-4 clearly indicates, women in the same

> *The modern women's movement developed out of an existing network of women's organizations, together with consciousness-raising groups that questioned traditional assumptions about sex roles.*

occupational categories as men continue to earn substantially less, even for the same type of work. This persistent pattern of wage inequality, together with the tendency for women to be segregated in such occupations as secretary, bank teller, and primary-school teacher, has led activists in the women's movement to call for new policies designed to reduce inequality (National Academy of Sciences, 1986). Increasingly they have pressed for "comparable worth"—that is, for increases in the salaries paid in traditionally female occupations to levels comparable to those paid in similar, but traditionally male, occupations.

> *As the population continues to age, the political and social influence of older people increases.*

Social Movements Among the Elderly

Although they have been less far-reaching than the women's movement, social movements among the elderly—led by organizations like the Gray Panthers and the American Association of Retired Persons—have had a significant impact on American society. And as the population continues to age, we can expect to see more evidence of the growing power of the elderly. Let us see how changes in the consciousness of elderly people themselves are altering the way sociologists formulate questions about old age.

Until the social movements of the 1960s prompted the elderly to form movements to oppose ageism and fight for their rights as citizens, the most popular social-scientific view of aging was disengagement theory. Numerous empirical studies had shown that old people gradually disengage from involvement in the lives of younger people and from economic and political roles that require responsibility and leadership. In a well-known study of aging people in Kansas City, Elaine Cumming and William Henry (1971) presented evidence that as people grow older, they often gradually withdraw from their earlier roles, and that this process is a mutual one rather than a result of rejection or discrimination by younger people. From a functionalist viewpoint, disengagement is a positive process both for society as a whole (because it opens up roles for younger people) and for the elderly themselves (because it frees them from stressful roles in their waning years).

The trouble with disengagement theory is that, on the one hand, it appears to excuse policymakers' lack of interest in the elderly and, on the other hand, it is only a partial explanation of what occurs in the social lives of elderly people. An alternative view of the elderly is that they need to be *re*engaged in new activities. Known as activity theory, this view states that the elderly suffer a sense of loneliness and loss when they give up their former roles. They need activities that will serve as outlets for their creativity and energy (Palmore, 1981).

Theories of aging are not simply abstract ideas that are taught in schools and universities. The disengagement and activity theories lead to different approaches that often impose definitions of what is appropriate behavior on people who do not wish to conform to those definitions. Today gerontologists tend to reject both theories. They see older people demanding opportunities to lead their lives in a variety of ways based on individual habits and preferences developed earlier in life. Elderly people themselves express doubt that activity alone results in successful adjustment to aging or happiness in old age. For example, in her study of a French retirement community Jennie Keith (1982) found that

Table 14–4 **Median Weekly Earnings of Full-Time Wage and Salary Workers, 1989**

Occupation	Men	Women
Managerial and professional	$695	$485
Technical and sales	466	319
Service occupations	293	216
Precision production	464	325
Operators, laborers	359	257
Farming, forestry, fishing	250	245

Source: Bureau of Labor Statistics, 1989.

the residents . . . seem to offer support to the gerontologists who have tried to mediate the extreme positions, disengagement vs. activity, by introducing the idea of styles of aging. . . . Some people are happy when they are very active, others are happy when they are relatively inactive. From this point of view, life-long patterns of social participation explain the kinds and levels of activity that are satisfying to different individuals. [p. 59]

In sum, for the elderly as well as for women, there is a growing tendency among social scientists to emphasize individual needs and capabilities. The social movements for gender and age equality also advance the needs of individuals, but in a collective manner, by asserting the needs of entire populations and rejecting preconceived notions of what is best for all women, all youth, all men, or all the elderly.

The Hospice Movement. As the large baby-boom generation moves through the adult years and approaches middle age, their parents enter the ranks of the elderly. This demographic change has led to incresed concern about the quality of life of the elderly and about death and the dying process. The questions of how best to prepare to die and whether one can have a "good death" might have seemed strange to Americans of an earlier time, when so many people died as a result of sudden, acute illnesses like pneumonia or tragic accidents in mines and mills. Today, however, about 75 percent of deaths occur among people over age sixty-five, often after a prolonged illness.

People who are dying often experience a period between life and death known as the living–dying interval (Kübler-Ross, 1989). For many dying people and their loved ones, this is a time of extreme importance. During this time there may be reconciliations, clarifications, expressions of love and understanding, and, under the best circumstances, a sense of closure and repose for the dying person. But most people die in hospitals. Nurses, doctors, and orderlies may intrude on these emotional scenes to administer to the patient. The hospital is dedicated to prolonging life, even in a dying patient. As the Rileys express it, "The hospital is geared for treatment and cure, it functions according to standards of effi-

© Marc P. Anderson

ciency and bureaucratic rules, its environment is sterile and unwelcoming to those who would visit patients *in extremis*" (1989, p. 27).

In recent decades, first in Great Britain and later in the United States, a social movement has emerged that is known as the hospice movement. The term *hospice* refers to a place, a set of services, or both; increasingly it refers to a service that can be brought into the dying person's home. The purpose of the hospice is to make the patient as comfortable as possible so that all concerned can use the living–dying interval effectively and humanely. In a hospice the patient and his or her surrounding social group are viewed as the relevant social unit. Medical personnel and other professionals, such as social workers, are available to help everyone involved.

Although many people continue to die in hospitals, hospice care is available in most parts of the United States and is an increasingly popular alternative to hospital death. Dying is never an easy experience, and the hospice movement cannot make it so. Nevertheless, the hospice movement is providing opportunities for new definitions of the last social role in the life course, the dying role, as well as the roles of those who will remain behind to continue their own life course.

She may not be a grand master, but at an advanced age she has developed a powerful chess game. In earlier decades, advocates of disengagement theory might have told her to find a "more suitable" pursuit in keeping with her supposedly declining mental capacities. Activity theorists might have pushed her into activities that she herself did not choose. A modern approach is to help the elderly create environments in which they can decide for themselves how "engaged" or "disengaged" they wish to be.

The hospice movement seeks to make dying patients as comfortable as possible in order to make the final phase of the life course less frightening.

FRONTIERS OF SOCIOLOGY

Gender and the Life Course in Aging Societies

We have seen in this chapter that the United States, like many other industrialized societies, is an aging society. By this we mean that the cohorts of elderly people are almost as large as the cohorts of younger adults and children. This means, in turn, that the proportion of elderly people in the population is increasing. Of course, the proportion of people over sixty-five is increasing steadily in third-world nations as well, but it will not attain the levels reached by the more developed nations until well into the next century. These facts are illustrated in the accompanying table, which shows that there will be dramatic increases in the numbers of people over the age of sixty-five in parts of the world like East and South Asia in the next half-century, and that the proportion of elderly people in populations throughout the world will rise steadily.

The implications of these figures should not be underestimated. Aging as a social phenomenon, together with the needs of the aged in societies all over the world, will receive increasing attention in coming years. And because nations like the United States and the European nations—including the Soviet Union—are leading this demographic trend, we can look to their experiences for indications of what to expect elsewhere in the world.

Matilda White Riley, one of the founders of the field of gerontology and an active researcher for the past fifty years, is associate director of behavioral sciences research at the National Institute on Aging. She thus has an

Population 65 Years of Age and Over, Population Increase, and Percent Aged of Total Population, for World and Major Regions, 1980–2025

	Population (in millions)			Increase (1980 as base = 100)			Percent Aged		
	1980	2000	2025	1980	2000	2025	1980	2000	2025
World	259.4	402.9	760.6	100	155	293	5.8%	6.6%	9.3%
More developed	127.8	166.0	230.3	100	130	180	11.3	13.0	16.7
Less developed	131.7	236.9	530.4	100	180	403	4.0	4.9	7.8
Africa	14.3	27.3	65.9	100	192	462	3.0	3.2	4.3
Latin America	15.5	27.9	61.9	100	179	398	4.3	4.9	7.2
Northern America	26.2	33.1	54.8	100	126	209	10.6	11.1	15.9
East Asia	68.2	116.0	232.4	100	170	340	5.8	7.9	13.6
South Asia	43.8	84.2	195.1	100	192	445	3.1	4.1	6.9
Europe	63.0	74.4	94.9	100	118	155	13.0	14.3	18.2
Oceania	1.8	2.6	4.5	100	147	250	7.9	8.9	12.5
U.S.S.R.	26.6	37.3	51.2	100	140	192	10.0	12.0	14.4

Source: United Nations.

excellent view of the frontiers of sociological research on aging. Two research areas she considers especially important are age stratification and the effects of increasing longevity.

"Longevity," Riley writes, "alters the social structure by increasing structural complexity and hence the options open to individuals as they age" (1985, p. 334). About 60 percent of the increase in the average length of the human life span since prehistoric times has occurred in this century. In the United States, life expectancy at birth has increased from less than fifty years in 1900 to seventy years for men and seventy-eight for women today. But because women's life expectancy has increased more rapidly than men's, it is estimated that by the year 2000 there will be 150 women for every 100 men age sixty-five and over. Among people age eighty-five and over, there will be more than 250 women for every 100 men (Brotman, 1982).

One implication of these facts is that there will be more older people living in more varied family, community, and institutional settings than was true in earlier periods. Kinship structures will become more complex as more households consist of such combinations as father with son, child with great-grandparent, sister with sister-in-law, or ex-husband with ex-wife (Riley, 1985). This is what Riley means by the effects of longevity on the social structure.

If an aging society increases structural complexity, it also alters patterns of stratification, especially in a society that is undergoing rapid economic and technological change. For example, more than 1 million people over the age of sixty are classified by the U.S. Department of Labor as unemployed or as "discouraged workers"—that is, people not in the labor force who want a job but have given up looking. Aging workers experience more and longer periods of unemployment than younger workers do. The causes may be job discrimination, obsolete skills, unwillingness to move, or poor health (Robinson et al., 1985). It is possible that labor shortages will improve the situation of older workers in coming decades. But decreases in the size of the labor force may be offset by the continued loss of jobs as a result of automation.

Increasing longevity also places greater demands on health care and other social-welfare institutions. Never before have so many people lived to such an old age. Over 1 million men and women age seventy-five and over live in nursing homes or other residential-care facilities in the United States. And more than 40 percent of all women age sixty-five and over (i.e., more than 7 million) live alone. For many of these individuals the darker side of aging is loneliness and the fear that failing health will lead to increased dependence on others. Modern societies need to develop social policies directed toward relieving the burdens of the very old, especially those who are alone and cannot call upon family members for support or resources.

SUMMARY

All societies channel people into *age grades*, or sets of statuses and roles based on age. The transitions among these age grades create a *life course* and are often marked by ceremonies known as *rites of passage*. The life course established by a particular society is affected by its norms regarding *gender roles*—that is, the behaviors considered appropriate for males and females.

The distribution of males and females within a population is expressed in terms of the *sex ratio*, the number of men per 100 women. The sex ratio can have a significant effect on the lives of both men and women. Imbalances in the sizes of *age cohorts*, or people of about the same age who are passing through life's stages together, can also affect the distribution of power and opportunity in a society.

All human societies are stratified by age and gender, meaning that males and females and younger and older people are channeled into specific statuses and roles. Throughout life, age and gender roles interact to shape our behavior and consciousness.

Until quite recently it was assumed that there were two separate spheres of life for men and women. Out of this gender-based division of labor grew the notion of differences in men's and women's abilities and personalities. These differences were thought to be based on biological and psychological differences between males and females. In the twentieth century, however, evidence from the social sciences has established that gender roles are not innate, nor are they determined by a society's relationship to its environment. Gender roles are strongly influenced by culture and can change as cultures adapt to new environmental and social conditions.

Preindustrial societies are usually rigidly age graded and sex segregated. As societies increase in size and complexity, women usually become subordinated to men. The status of the elderly in preindustrial societies often hinges on their possession of "strategic knowledge."

The origins of gender inequality in most modern societies can be traced to their feudal periods. In Europe, for example, the norms of courtly love specified that women do not engage in warfare or politics or compete with men in any sphere of life beyond those reserved for women.

In modern industrial societies boys and girls are socialized into "masculine" and "feminine" roles. In their adult years men enjoy more wealth, prestige, and leisure than women do. After their working years are over, men tend to suffer a greater decline in social status than women do. Later, as the number of elderly men decreases rapidly, the largest proportion of the very old are widows.

Gender and age stratification in modern societies is reflected in attitudes that reinforce the subordinate status of women and the elderly. *Sexism* refers to an ideology that justifies prejudice or discrimination based on sex; *ageism* is an ideology that justifies prejudice or discrimination based on age.

It is often claimed that biological factors are enough to explain why people are treated differently on the basis of gender or age. According to sociobiologists, gender roles developed early in human history and were carried through the entire course of human evolution. Critics of this view argue that analogies between human and nonhuman societies, or between modern and preindustrial societies, are fallacious. It has been shown, moreover, that differences among individuals are much greater than differences between the sexes.

The functionalist view of gender and age stratification is similar to the sociobiological explanation, except that the functionalist perspective does not imply that differences between men and women are due to genetic evolution. In fact, it recognizes that a biologically based division of labor has become dysfunctional in modern societies. It also recognizes that shifts in age statuses can have dysfunctional effects.

Interactionists argue that the process of socialization encourages women and men to develop certain personality traits, which cause them to take the roles they do. There is considerable evidence from tests of performance and other social-scientific research to support this claim. Age roles also, according to the interactionist view, are constructed through social interaction rather than being automatically defined by a person's place in various social structures.

Conflict theorists ask why entire categories of people—males, females, the young, the old—are assigned to certain roles. Marxian theorists believe that the origins of gender and age stratification are found in the institutions of capitalism, which benefit from the subordination of women and the elderly. Other conflict theorists find such stratification in all societies and explain it in terms of differences in control over resources such as wealth and jobs.

The modern women's movement arose in the mid-1960s out of an already existing network of women's organizations, together with a less formal network of women in consciousness-raising groups. The movement won significant victories during the 1970s and began to change the way men and women think about gender roles. Attitudes became more favorable toward a more equal allocation of political and economic roles.

As the population as a whole has aged, the impact of the elderly on American society has increased. This is changing the way sociologists view old age. Before the 1970s the most popular social-scientific view of aging was *disengagement theory*, the belief that as people grow older they gradually "disengage"

GLOSSARY

age grade: a set of statuses and roles based on age that is established by the norms of a particular society (**p. 426**).

life course: a pathway along an age-differentiated, socially created sequence of transitions (**p. 427**).

rite of passage: a ceremony marking the transition to a new stage of a culturally defined life course (**p. 427**).

sex ratio: the number of males per 100 females in a population (**p. 427**).

age cohort: a set of people of about the same age who are passing through the life course together (**p. 429**).

life expectancy: the average number of years a member of a given population can expect to live (**p. 431**).

gender: a set of culturally conditioned traits associated with maleness or femaleness (**p. 432**).

gender role: a set of behaviors that are considered appropriate for an individual of a particular gender (**p. 432**).

gerontology: the study of aging and older people (**p. 436**).

sexism: an ideology that justifies prejudice and discrimination based on sex (**p. 439**).

ageism: an ideology that justifies prejudice and discrimination based on age (**p. 441**).

from their earlier roles. An alternative view of the elderly, known as *activity theory*, states that the elderly need activities that will serve as outlets for their creativity and energy. Today gerontologists tend to reject both of these theories, seeing older people demanding opportunities to lead their lives in a variety of ways based on individual preferences.

The growing proportion of elderly people in the population has led to increased concern about the quality of life of the elderly and about death and the dying process. One outcome of this concern is the *hospice* movement, which attempts to provide dying people and their loved ones with a comfortable, dignified alternative to hospital death.

WHERE TO FIND IT

Books

Suburban Youth in Cultural Crisis (Ralph W. Larkin; Oxford University Press, 1979). A study of how youth in a suburban community deal with problems of living, from sex and drugs to getting jobs and dealing with "the establishment." Told from a perspective that is critical of the life chances and experiences of teenagers in America.

Number Our Days (Barbara Myerhoff; Simon & Schuster, 1978). A haunting study of how elderly people struggle to survive and die with dignity. The setting is a senior-citizen center in Venice Beach, California, and the people are elderly Jewish immigrants and refugees from Europe.

Science and Gender: A Critique of Biology and Its Theories on Women (Ruth Bleier; Pergamon Press, 1984). A critical review of the controversial literature on gender and biology.

Deceptive Distinctions: Sex, Gender and the Social Order (Cynthia Fuchs Epstein; Yale University Press, 1989). A critical review of theories and research on gender stratification that presents evidence of the continuing influence of structural factors (e.g., employment channeling and discrimination) on women's unequal position in American society.

Gender Advertisements (Erving Goffman; Harvard University Press, 1979). A subtle treatment of the symbolism of gender and its use in everyday life, with excellent examples of visual material used as sociological data.

Journals

Gender and Society The journal of Sociologists for Women in Society. A rigorous social-scientific journal of theory and research on gender and gender inequality.

Signs A quarterly journal published by the University of Chicago Press that presents new research and theory in gender studies and feminist social science.

Other Sources

Age in America: Trends and Projections. A chartbook that analyzes demographic and socioeconomic trends affecting the United States and its elderly population.

Handbook of Aging and the Social Sciences. A valuable source of interdisciplinary research and policy studies dealing with the condition of the aged in the United States and other Western societies.

VISUAL SOCIOLOGY

Keeping Women In Their Place

Numerous societies have engaged in practices that effectively increased the power of males over females. For example, the practice of binding, and thereby deforming, women's feet limited women to roles that kept them close to the home. This excruciatingly painful process, which began when the child was between four and seven years old, consisted of binding a long strip of cloth around the foot in such a way as to push the toes under the foot and into the sole. In China this practice was common before the twentieth century.

In some African societies today similar practices persist. Some tribes mold the skulls of female children so that the head will become elongated, creating an effect that is thought to be elegant and attractive to potential husbands—despite the limited movement that results for the woman.

Fashions that deform the female body are not limited to non-Western societies. In Europe in the nineteenth century, the use of corsets in an effort to achieve the ideal of an 18-inch waist caused headaches, fainting spells, and spinal disorders among high-status women. Corsets, along with fashions such as hooped skirts and bustles, greatly restricted women's ability to function in societies dominated by men.

It can be argued that dress styles place constraints on men as well as on women—the "uniform" of the gray flannel suit is an example. By and large, however, the clothing worn by men is much less restrictive than that worn by women.

There are, of course, more subtle ways of maintaining dominant and subordinate statuses. As Erving Goffman pointed out in his study of American advertising, "One way in which social weight—power, authority, rank, office, renown—is echoed expressively in social situations is through relative size, especially height" (p. 28). Thus, a male with superior status is usually shown as larger than another male of inferior status, and this vis-

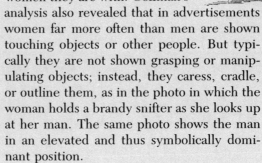

ualization of relative power almost invariably carries over to gender relations. Males are typically shown as larger than the women they are with. Goffman's analysis also revealed that in advertisements women far more often than men are shown touching objects or other people. But typically they are not shown grasping or manipulating objects; instead, they caress, cradle, or outline them, as in the photo in which the woman holds a brandy snifter as she looks up at her man. The same photo shows the man in an elevated and thus symbolically dominant position.

A powerful aspect of advertising photography, Goffman suggests, is its subtlety in conveying images of dependency, of women on men, of children on adults, of inferior on superior. Thus, in the Martini & Rossi ad the woman appears to be a competent pool player, but it is implied that she is dependent on the man standing nearby.

Musée de L'homme, Paris

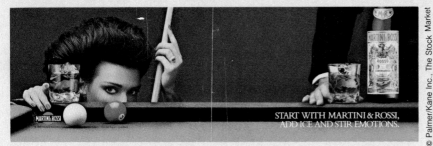

START WITH MARTINI & ROSSI,
ADD ICE AND STIR EMOTIONS.

T-bar
FIELD SERVICE

Calvin Klein Jeans

SAMSUNG
MICROWAVES

SAMSUNG
ELECTRONICS

Museum of the City of New York

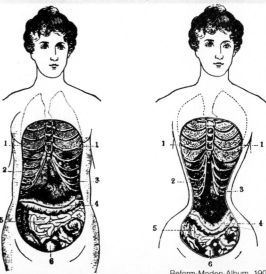

Reform-Moden-Album, 1904

PART FIVE

SOCIAL INSTITUTIONS

C hange is occurring all the time in every major institution of society: High rates of divorce and remarriage change the family as an institution; new products and new methods of production continually create new markets; governments must constantly adjust to pressures from opposing interest groups . . . the list could be made much longer. The processes of institutional change are endless and often complex, but increasingly they can be understood and even predicted through the application of sociological concepts and research.

In Part V, the concepts and perspectives discussed earlier in the book are applied to an analysis of several major social institutions. Chapter 15 explores the changing nature of the family, focusing on research on how family statuses and roles are changing and on the social forces that seem to account for these changes. The other chapters in this section also proceed from an analysis of how the institution is typically organized to a discussion of how it is changing. Chapters 16 and 17 discuss three major cultural institutions—religion, education, and the media—whose role is to transmit and reinforce a society's most cherished values. Chapter 18 deals with the roles and statuses that generate jobs and income. Chapter 19 shows how political institutions determine "who gets what, when, and how." Finally, in Chapter 20 the institutions of science and technology are analyzed, with special attention to their role in health care and environmental issues.

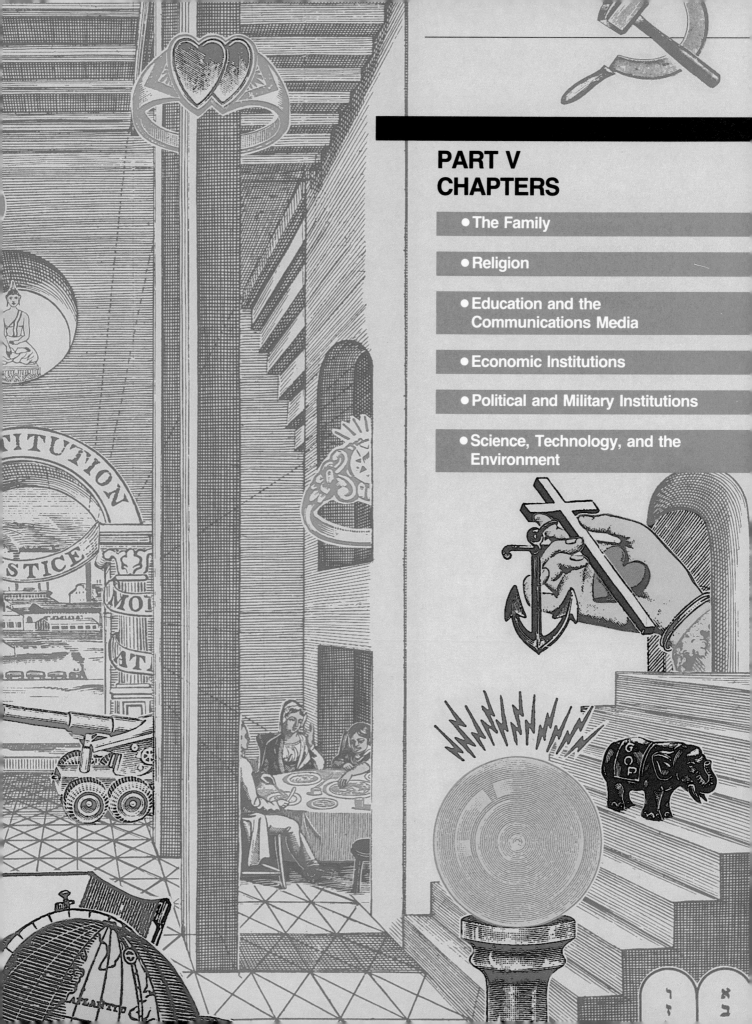

PART V
CHAPTERS

● The Family

● Religion

● Education and the Communications Media

● Economic Institutions

● Political and Military Institutions

● Science, Technology, and the Environment

CHAPTER OUTLINE

- **The Nature of Families**

  - The Family as an Institution
  - Defining the Family
  - Variations in Family Structure
  - The Changing Family
  - The Family Life Cycle

- **Dynamics of Mate Selection and Marriage**

  - Marriage as Exchange
  - Norms of Mate Selection
  - Romantic Love
  - Marriage and Divorce
  - Sources of Marital Instability
  - The Impact of Divorce

- **Perspectives on the Family**

  - The Interactionist Perspective
  - Conflict Theory and Alternatives to the Family
  - Functionalist Views of the Family
  - Conclusion: "Here to Stay"

Margo Smith

Out for the day in Greenwich Village

CHAPTER 15
THE FAMILY

One night, after working the evening shift at a local fried-chicken restaurant, Cedric Smith came home to find that he was locked out of his apartment. Claiming that he was not a legal resident, Housing Authority police prevented him from entering the apartment where he had been living for the past eight years. They pointed out that the apartment was leased only to Marie Woods and her five children (who were also Smith's children). Mr. Smith would be allowed to visit Ms. Woods, but he would have to leave her apartment by midnight or be arrested for trespassing. "I didn't make a fuss, but I didn't want to leave," Mr. Smith told a reporter. "I was thinking, I'm a grown man, and I have kids in this building. I shouldn't have to go."

Instead of remaining a fugitive lover or leaving the scene altogether, Mr. Smith decided to get married. Along with seven other men who were also barred from living with women in the aging public-housing project on Chicago's West Side, Mr. Smith agreed to marry his longtime companion. The couple had been "thinking about marriage" for a long time. It took the Housing Authority's crackdown on nonleaseholder residents to push them into matrimony. Indeed, among the eight couples who were married in a group ceremony, a few said that they were the first members of their families to marry (*New York Times*, November 14, 1988).

At about the same time, Jill S. and Mary R. were picketing the San Francisco headquarters of the American Federation of Teachers. They and other gay couples were demanding that the union negotiate with the city school board to allow same-sex couples to claim the employee health and pension benefits that are normally extended only to married heterosexual partners. Jill and Mary have lived together for almost ten years. Jill, a primary school teacher, receives health benefits; Mary, an artist, does not. Why, they ask, should they be deprived of the spousal benefits that are automatically granted to members of heterosexual married couples simply because they do not fit the conventional stereotype of a married couple?

In yet another part of the nation, in September 1989, family therapist Allison B. is facing a crisis at her practice in Dallas, Texas. After a series of weekly visits, a nine-year-old patient she has been seeing has revealed that her new stepfather is fondling her in a decidedly sexual manner. The girl's natural parents placed her in therapy because she seems withdrawn and depressed. They believe that she is suffering from the effects of their recent separation and divorce. But after the little girl became comfortable in the doctor's office and began talking more openly with her, the bombshell exploded: "Charles, you know, Mommy's new husband, well, he likes to touch me," the girl said innocently. What began as a seemingly easy case of helping a child adjust to a new and more complex family system has become a therapist's nightmare.

Dr. B. now must call the child-protective service and report a case of suspected child sexual abuse. This legal requirement supersedes any notion of privacy or client privilege. Within a few hours a child-protective worker will be calling at the child's mother's home to begin an investigation. Dr. B.

sighs at the thought of the emotional stress that lies ahead for all involved. Eventually she will have to see the parents and stepfather in her office to try to work the situation out, but first the child must be protected.

Each of these three cases illustrates the effects of the enormous changes in family form and function that are occurring in North American society today. They also underline the fact that the family is not just a set of intimate and private interpersonal relationships; society as a whole has a stake in family relationships. Often this means that society, acting through the agencies of government, may intervene in what would otherwise be viewed as private family matters.

The changes occurring in the family are by no means fully understood. We do not yet know, for example, whether the rate at which families dissolve through divorce and are reconstituted through remarriage will continue at the high levels of recent years. We do not know whether efforts to change legal definitions of the family will succeed. We can safely predict, however, that the study of family organization and change will remain an important and lively area of research well into the future.

THE NATURE OF FAMILIES

We continually hear warnings of the "death of the family" in modern societies. As early as 1938, sociologists such as William Fielding Ogburn were writing about the decline of the family. "Prior to modern times," according to Ogburn, "the power and prestige of the family was due to . . . functions it performed. . . . The dilemma of the modern family is caused by the loss of many of these functions in recent times" (p. 139). More recent commentators have pointed to the so-called sexual revolution as a threat to this basic social institution. Others insist that even in the face of trends toward single parenthood, cohabitation without marriage, divorce and remarriage, and smaller family size, the family is nonetheless "here to stay" (Bane, 1976; Goode, 1971).

This chapter shows that there are so many variations in family form even within a single society that it has become increasingly difficult to speak of "the family" as a single set of statuses, roles, and norms. Yet it remains true that in all known societies almost everyone is socialized within a network of family rights and obligations known as *family role relations* (Goode, 1964). In the first section of this chapter, therefore, we examine the family as an institution and show how family role relations have changed during the twentieth century. In the second section we look at issues of family formation, especially mate selection, marriage, divorce, and remarriage. The final section focuses on how the basic sociological perspectives explain changes in family roles and functions and in the interactions between parents and children.

The Family as an Institution

As noted in Chapter 3, all societies, no matter how simple, must meet certain essential needs of their members. Those needs can be outlined as follows (Lenski and Lenski, 1982):

- *Communication among members*, first through language alone and then through specialized institutions devoted to communication.

- *Production of goods and services*, from the basic items required for survival to items designed to satisfy new, more diverse needs created by increasing affluence.
- *Distribution of goods and services*, within societies at first and later, with the rise of trade and markets, among societies as well.
- *Protection and defense*, including protection from the elements and predators and extending to defense against human enemies.
- *Replacement of members*, both the biological replacement of the deceased and the socialization of newcomers to the society.
- *Control of members* to ensure that the society's institutions continue to function and that conflict is reduced or eliminated.

In simple societies many, if not all, of these essential functions are performed by one social institution, the family. However, a look at Figure 15-1 reveals that this is no longer the case. Most of the functions that were traditionally performed by the family are now performed partly or entirely by other social institutions.

Figure 15-1 only begins to illustrate the institutional complexity of modern societies. Not only are there many more separate institutions in modern societies, but basic social functions are often divided among several institutions. Thus the institutions that meet protective and social-control needs include governments at all levels, the military, the judiciary, and the police. Replacement needs

Figure 15–1: **Institutional Differentiation**

		TYPE OF SOCIETY	
		Less Differentiated (gemeinschaft)	**More Differentiated (gesellschaft)**
SOCIAL FUNCTION	**Communication**	Family, kin networks	Mass media
	Production	Family groups	Economic institutions
	Distribution	Extended family, local markets	Markets, transportation institutions
	Protection	Family, village, tribe	Armed forces, police, insurance agencies, health-care institutions
	Replacement	Family	Family, schools, religious institutions
	Social control	Family	Family, religious institutions, government in all forms

are met by the family through mating and reproduction. In addition to the family, religious institutions, education, and other cultural institutions meet the need to socialize new generations.

Like all major social institutions, the family is a set of statuses, roles, norms, and values devoted to achieving important social goals. Those goals include the social control of reproduction, the socialization of new generations, and the "social placement" of children in the institutions of the larger society (colleges, business firms, etc.). But the family's ability to meet these goals is often complicated by rapid social change. When other institutions in a society change, families must adapt to those changes. And when the family changes, other institutions will be affected.

As an example, consider the impact of the "sexual revolution" that began in the 1920s. During that decade, often called the Roaring Twenties, young adults began to upset a moral code that had regulated the behavior of couples for generations, at least among people who considered themselves "respectable." According to this set of norms, women were the guardians of morality. Men were more likely to give in to sexual desire, "but girls of respectable families were supposed to have no such temptations" (Allen, 1931, p. 74). After World War I, however, "respectable" young women began to reject the so-called double standard, which made them adhere to a different and more restrictive moral code than that applied to men. They began smoking cigarettes, wearing short skirts, and drinking bootleg gin in automobiles or at "petting parties." These changes in the behavior of couples produced far-reaching changes in other institutions. Women demanded more education and more opportunities to earn income. This in turn led to demands for new institutions such as coeducational colleges and integrated workplaces, as well as greater access by women to existing institutions such as medicine, law, and science. Although the double standard continues to affect relationships between men and women, today its effects are not nearly as severe as they were before the sexual revolution.

Changes in the institutions in one area of social life can place tremendous pressure on those in other sectors. This is especially true in the case of the family, as will be evident throughout this chapter. Before we examine the ways in which families have changed in this century, however, it is necessary to define some terms that are frequently used in discussing the family.

Defining the Family

The family is a central institution in all human societies, although it may take many different forms. A **family** is a group of people related by blood, marriage, or adoption. The role relations among people who consider themselves to be related in these ways are termed **kinship.** The familiar kinship terms—*father, mother, brother, sister, grandfather, grandmother, uncle, aunt, niece, nephew, cousin*— refer to specific sets of role relations that may vary greatly from one culture to another. In many African societies, for example, "mother's brother" is someone to whom the male child becomes closer and from whom he receives more of his day-to-day socialization than he may from his father. Note that biological or "blood" ties are not necessarily stronger than ties of adoption. Adopted children are usually loved with the same intensity as children raised by their biological parents. And many family units in the United States and other societies include "fictive kin"—that is, people who are so close to members of the family that they are considered kin despite the absence of blood ties (Liebow, 1967; Stack, 1974). Finally, neither blood ties nor marriage nor adoption adequately describes the increasingly common relationship between unmarried people who consider themselves a couple or a family.

The smallest units of family structure are either conjugal or nuclear families. The term **conjugal family** refers to a husband and wife and their children, if any. The term **nuclear family** refers to two or more people related by blood or marriage or adoption who share a household; it does not require that both husband and wife be present in the household or that there be any specific set of

These photos show a conventional nuclear family, with father, mother, and two children, and an extended family, with three generations of family members, including aunts, uncles, and cousins. Although these may once have been the most common forms of traditional and modern family structures, we have seen evidence throughout this book that the number of single-parent families, and of families that share the custody of children after divorce, is increasing.

role relations among the members of the household. Thus all conjugal families are also nuclear families, but the reverse is not true: Two brothers and a nephew living together would be a nuclear family, but they would not be a conjugal family. The conjugal family is the most common type of household in the United States, although, as we saw in Chapter 2, alternative household types have become much more common in the past three decades.

The nuclear family in which one is born and socialized is termed one's **family of orientation.** The nuclear family one forms through marriage or cohabitation is known as one's **family of procreation.** The relationship between the two is shown in Figure 15-2.

Kinship terms are often confusing because families, especially large ones, can be rather complex social structures. It may help to devote a little time to working through Figure 15-2. "Ego" is the person who is taken as the point of reference. You can readily see that ego has both a family of orientation and a family of procreation. So does ego's spouse.

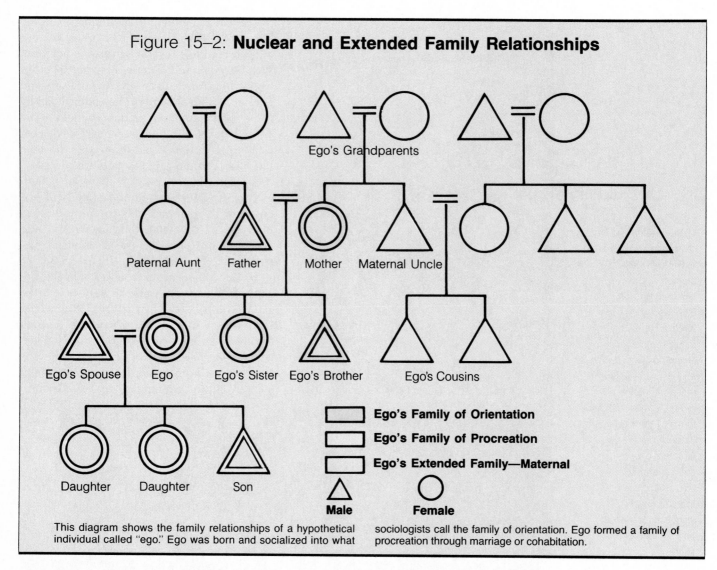

Figure 15–2: **Nuclear and Extended Family Relationships**

Ego's Grandparents

Paternal Aunt   Father   Mother   Maternal Uncle

Ego's Spouse   Ego   Ego's Sister   Ego's Brother   Ego's Cousins

Daughter   Daughter   Son

Ego's Family of Orientation

Ego's Family of Procreation

Ego's Extended Family—Maternal

Male   **Female**

This diagram shows the family relationships of a hypothetical individual called "ego." Ego was born and socialized into what sociologists call the family of orientation. Ego formed a family of procreation through marriage or cohabitation.

Ego's parents become the in-laws of the spouse, and the spouse's parents are ego's in-laws. But like the vast majority of people, ego also has an **extended family** that includes all the nuclear families of ego's blood relatives—that is, all of ego's uncles, aunts, cousins, and grandparents. Ego's spouse also has an extended family, which is not indicated in the figure, nor is it defined as part of ego's extended family. But relationships with the spouse's extended family are likely to occupy plenty of ego's time. Indeed, as the figure shows, the marriage bond brings far more than two individuals together. Most married couples have extensive networks of kin to which they must relate in many ways throughout life.

Variations in Family Structure

For the past several years sociologists have been demonstrating that the traditional household consisting of two parents and their children is no longer the typical American family. In the 1940s an American household was about eight times more likely to be headed by a married couple than by unrelated individuals. By 1980 the ratio had declined to about 2.5. Data from Donald Bogue's (1985) analysis of trends in family composition reveal that the proportion of married-couple families declined from 78.2 percent of all households in 1950 to slightly less than 60 percent in 1983. (In 1988 the proportion stood at 57 percent.) There has been a dramatic increase in female-headed families and nonfamily households. Between 1970 and 1981, the number of female-headed families increased by over 65 percent. There were even greater increases in the numbers of females and males living alone and in the number of unmarried couples and roommates of the same sex. The number of unmarried men and women living together has more than quadrupled since 1970; as of 1987, there were over 2 million such couples.

All of these trends point to a far greater diversity of family types, including far more people living alone and far more women raising children alone, than ever before. There are also more households composed of unrelated single people who live together not just because they are friends but because only by doing so can they afford to live away from their families of orientation. Thus, when they discuss family norms and roles, sociologists must be careful not to represent the traditional nuclear family, or even the married couple, as typical. These considerations become especially important when they discuss low-income and minority families, as we do in the Challenges section of this chapter.

> *Today there is a far greater diversity of family types than ever before.*

The Changing Family

In his pioneering study of changes in the family, William J. Goode (1963) argued that the structure of family units becomes simpler as societies undergo industrialization. Goode was not the first social scientist to make this observation; however, his study was the first to be based on extensive historical and comparative data. After reviewing changes in family structure in Europe and North America over the past seventy-five years, Goode concluded that the smaller family unit composed of a married couple and their children (i.e., the conjugal family) was increasingly dominant in industrial societies. For Goode, the change from the larger extended family to the smaller and more geographically mobile conjugal or nuclear family is part of an even larger worldwide revolution in which people are demanding greater control over the conditions that shape their lives.

From the standpoint of the family, this "revolution" translates into demands for freedom to select one's mate, to decide where to live after marriage, to decide whether to have children and how many to have, and even to terminate the marital relationship. Such choices were impossible in earlier family systems, in which marriages were arranged, the

This etching of a Mormon pioneer family on its way to a social gathering presents one example of variations in family structure. In nineteenth-century Mormon families it was common for the husband to have more than one wife, a practice known as polygamy.

New York Public Library Picture Collection

married couple was expected to live within a larger extended family, and couples were expected to have numerous children.

According to Goode, the driving forces behind the large-scale changes in family structure in this century were economic and technological. The more families had to adapt to an economy in which income was earned outside the family, the more the family had to be mobile and flexible. Families had to be willing to move from one place to another in search of employment. Geographic mobility, in turn, meant that children would not be able to maintain households in which their parents could live—that is, extended families consisting of "three generations under one roof." And because children no longer worked in the home or on the farm, they became less important in economic terms than was the case in earlier epochs; families therefore had fewer children.

In the quarter-century since Goode's study appeared, there has been a wealth of new research that has further developed the idea of a transition from extended to conjugal family systems as a result of industrialization (Huber and Spitz, 1988; Osmond, 1985). More recent studies often focus on issues related to defining the family, studying family history, and distinguishing between ideal and actual family patterns.

Problems of Definition. If one studies who lives in households (i.e., who lives together and eats together more or less regularly), the traditional or "Dick and Jane" family (Mom, Dad, Dick, Jane, and their dog Spot) appears to be the most prevalent family form. However, if one also considers patterns of interaction with others, the family unit might include, say, a grandmother living in a nearby apartment with an unmarried aunt, as well as a divorced uncle in a nearby community. This approach is illustrated in a volume entitled *Beyond the Nuclear Family Model* (Lenero-Otero, 1977), which compares patterns of family structure and interaction in several industrialized societies and finds a wide range of possible patterns. For example, although families may not live with "three generations under one roof," they may live in nuclear

family units in close proximity to one another, a pattern that continues to sustain large extended families. Technologies like the telephone and jet travel allow family members to see one another fairly frequently when they are separated by geographic distance. And when divorce breaks apart a nuclear family and the parents remarry, the reconstituted family may be embedded in a larger set of extended-family relations that may occupy even more of the members' time. None of these and similar patterns that sociologists have often observed were predicted in the theories of Goode and others who studied the revolution in family structure.

Studies of Family History. Studies of family form and patterns of family interaction over time have found a good deal of evidence that challenges the conclusions of Goode's research. For example, demographer Peter Laslett (1972) found that in some parts of England the emergence of the conjugal family seems to have preceded industrialization by many decades. When people migrated to new agricultural regions, they often left behind extended kin groups and became more dependent on the smaller nuclear-family group. Laslett and other researchers have found that modern technologies like the telephone or the automobile enable members of smaller family units, who formerly might have lost touch with their extended families, to maintain their kinship ties (Laslett, 1972).

Similarly, in her research on industrialization in the mill towns of Massachusetts, Tamara Hareven (1978) found evidence that extended families often sent family members whom the land could not support, especially young women, to the towns. There they might marry and form urban families, but often they returned home and married into farm families. In most cases the urban workers managed to maintain close ties with

The traditional two-parent nuclear family is much less prevalent today than in earlier decades, and even families that appear to be conventional nuclear families have extended kinship ties.

their rural kin, especially through letters and visits to friends.

In the case of the black family, research by social historian Herbert Gutman (1976) on the effects of slavery and industrialization has shown that slaves often formed extended families that included strong nuclear units. During the Reconstruction period after the Civil War, many families that had been torn apart by slavery were reunited. Toward the end of the nineteenth century, however, migration caused by the industrialization of agriculture in the South and the demand for unskilled labor in large northern cities created instability in the black family, a pattern that would become prevalent in later decades of the twentieth century. In sum, therefore, the notion that industrialization creates a single dominant family form and predictable patterns of family interaction is no longer widely accepted in the social sciences.

Ideal versus Actual Family Patterns. When politicians and government officials talk about "preserving family values," they often have in mind the traditional two-parent nuclear family. To many people this remains the ideal family form. In reality, however, as Table 15-1 shows, such families are less prevalent today than they were in earlier decades. Increasing numbers of families are headed by a single parent, usually the mother but sometimes the father. Moreover, two-parent families may actually be reconstituted—that is, created by remarriage after divorce or the death of a spouse. Thus what appears to be a conventional nuclear family is really a far more complicated family form with extended ties among parents and siblings in different nuclear families.

Among lower-income people these patterns are especially prevalent—so much so that some researchers have concluded that families without fathers are a direct consequence of poverty. Although they tend to share the same norms of family life as other members of society, poor people bear added burdens that make it difficult, if not impossible, for them to actually meet those norms. In particular, men in such families may not be able to provide their expected share of family income and hence may become demoralized and unable to maintain family relationships. This is especially true when teenagers father children before they are adequately prepared to take economic responsibility for them. Thus in poor families the father often is not a central figure, and female-headed families are

Table 15–1: **Number of Households (in millions) and Percent Change in Household Types, 1960–1988**

Type of Household	Number of Households				Percent Change		
	1960	1970	1980	1988	1960–1970	1970–1980	1980–1988
Total Households	52.8	63.4	80.7	91.0	+20%	+27%	+13%
Family Households	44.9	51.5	59.5	65.1	+15%	+16%	+9%
Married Couple	39.3	44.7	49.1	51.8	+14%	+10%	+5%
Male Householder	1.2	1.2	1.7	2.7	0	+42%	+59%
Female Householder	4.4	5.5	8.7	10.6	+25%	+58%	+22%
Nonfamily Households	7.9	11.9	21.2	25.9	+51%	+78%	+22%
Male Householder	2.7	4.0	8.8	11.3	+48%	+120%	+28%
Female Householder	5.2	7.9	12.4	14.6	+52%	+57%	+18%
One Person	6.9	10.9	18.3	21.9	+58%	+68%	+20%

Despite the absolute increase (1960–1988) from 44.9 to 65.1 million family households, the smallest proportional growth (relative to total households) has been in married-couple families and the greatest has been in single adult householder families, nonfamily households, and one-person households.

Source: Statistical Abstract, 1989.

the dominant family form (Osmond, 1985; Furstenberg and Spanier, 1984).

Contemporary social-scientific research on family structure and interaction increasingly focuses on issues like those just described. At the same time, there is growing recognition that the actual form the family takes may vary greatly at different stages of the life course. For example, as the proportion of elderly people in the population increases, more families must decide whether to care for an aging parent at home. Let us therefore take a closer look at how families change throughout the "family life cycle."

The Family Life Cycle

Sociologist Paul Glick, an innovator in the field of family demography and ecology, first developed the concept of the *family life cycle*, the idea that families pass through a sequence of stages, as follows:

- Family formation: first marriage
- Start of childbearing: birth of first child
- End of childbearing: birth of last child
- "Empty nest": marriage of last child
- "Family dissolution": death of one spouse (Glick and Parke, 1965).

These are "typical" stages in the life cycle of conventional families. Although there are other stages that could be identified within each of these—such as retirement (the years between the time of retirement and the death of one spouse) or the "baby stage" (during which the couple is rearing preschool-age children)—the ones that Glick listed are most useful for comparative purposes.

As the "typical" family structure becomes ever more difficult to identify owing to changes in family norms, the stages of family development also vary. In fact, the stages of the family life cycle have become increasingly useful as indicators of change rather than as stages that all or most families can be expected to experience. The Census Bureau estimates, for example, that there are at least 2.3 million heterosexual couples in the United States who are cohabiting. Although in fact

Table 15–2: **Estimated Median Age at First Marriage: United States, 1890–1985**

	Median Age at First Marriage	
Year	Men	Women
1890	26.1	22.0
1900	25.9	21.9
1910	25.1	21.6
1920	24.6	21.2
1930	24.3	21.3
1940	24.3	21.5
1950	22.8	20.3
1960	22.8	20.3
1970	23.6	21.8
1985	24.8	23.0

Source: Data from *Historical Statistics of the United States*, 1975, and *Statistical Abstract*, 1989.

the majority of these couples will eventually marry, many others will break up or continue to live together without marrying.

When sociologists look at the median age at which people experience the various stages of the family life cycle, significant trends emerge. Consider age at first marriage. In 1890 the median age of Americans at first marriage was 26.1 years for men and 22 years for women; by 1965 it had reached the historic low of 22.8 and 20.6. Then it began rising again slowly, until by 1986 it was 25.5 for men and 23.3 for women, approaching the pattern of a century ago (see Table 15.2). Figure 15-3 shows that age at first marriage tends to be somewhat higher for males than for females and is associated with educational attainment; more educated people are more likely to delay marriage. There is also a tendency for members of minority groups to marry later, as is shown by the curves for blacks and Mexican Americans. This pattern is due to the proportionately lower income levels of these populations. People

Families generally pass through a series of stages known as the family life cycle, but the cycle can vary considerably from one family to another.

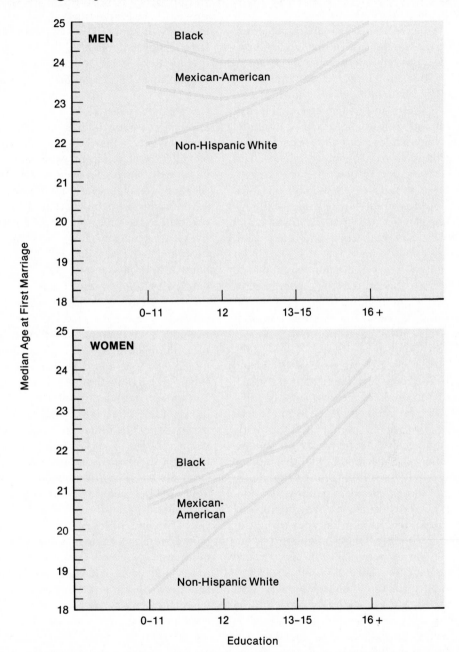

Figure 15–3: **Education Differences in Medium Age at First Marriage, by Race, Ethnicity, and Sex: 1945–59 Birth Cohort**

These figures show that median age at first marriage increases with education for whites and minorities. College-educated men and women tend to marry between the ages of twenty and twenty-five, and the minority–nonminority differences are narrow. Non-Hispanic white women with less than a high school education marry earliest.

Source: Taken from *American Families and Households,* by James A. Sweet and Larry L. Bumpass © 1987, the Russell Sage Foundation. Used with permission of the Russell Sage Foundation.

with lower incomes tend to delay marriage or not to marry because they lack the material means to sustain a marital relationship.

As it passes through the family life cycle, every family experiences changes in its system of role relations. In analyzing these changes, social scientists often modify Glick's stages so as to focus more sharply on interactions within the family. An example is the set of "developmental" stages shown in Figure 15-4. There are major emotional challenges at each of these stages. For example, families with adolescent children must adapt to the children's growing independence. This may involve going through a stage of negotiation over such issues as money, cars, and dating. But researchers who study family life note that parents are often confused about how to interact with their adolescent children. They may assume that it is normal for adolescents to leave the family circle and to become enmeshed in their own peer groups, which often get into trouble. However, as Carol Gilligan (1987) has pointed out, adolescents also want the continuing guidance and involvement of adults.

Earlier research by Erikson (1975) and Bettelheim (1962) also found that too much emphasis on adolescence as a time of separation from the family can be a form of social "cop-out" in which adults fail to provide meaningful goals and activities for adolescents. Many social scientists feel that adolescence is a time for building interdependence as well as independence, meaning that adolescents need to become involved in prosocial interactions such as assistance in caring for elderly or younger family members, or involvement in community agencies or social movements (Coles, 1986; Gottman, 1983).

In later stages of family life the parents must be willing to watch their grown children take on the challenges of family formation while they themselves worry about maintaining their marital roles or caring for their own parents. The latter issue is taking on increasing importance in aging societies like the United States. And since women are still expected to be more nurturing and emotionally caring than men, it often falls to women to worry about the question of "where can Mom live?"

(Hochschild, 1989). According to Elaine Brody, a leading researcher on this issue, "it's going to be primarily women for a long time. Women can go to work as much as they want, but they still see nurturing as their job." Moreover, "with many more very old people, and fewer children per family, almost every woman is going to have to take care of an aging parent or parent-in-law" (quoted in Lewin, 1989, p. A1).

As if these stages were not stressful enough, consider the complications resulting from divorce, remarriage, and the combining of children of different marriages in a new family. It is increasingly common, for example, for teenagers and young adults to have parents who are dating and marrying, and for children to have four parental figures in their lives instead of two. These more complex family systems also pass through the stages of the family life cycle. On television, a wholesome family like the "Brady Bunch" accomplishes this with modest resources and lots of love. In reality, however, such families may experience severe stress. Children in such families often learn to maintain a cheerful demeanor so that adults will not worry about them, but inside they generally experience far more emotional turmoil than children who have not been through the experience of family breakup. The difficulties such children experience—for example, in trying to feel at home in more than one place and having to carry their belongings back and forth—are only now beginning to be understood (Wallerstein and Blakeslee, 1989).

The difficulties faced by children in "intact" as well as troubled families raise the age-old questions of how people decide whom to marry and what makes marriages last. Couples normally do not think they will split up when they marry, nor can they understand the emotional and social consequences of divorce before they have children, but the more people understand some of the reasons for selecting particular individuals as mates and the reasons that some relationships are more lasting than others, the more insight they gain into their own relationships. In the next section, therefore, we examine the sociology of mate selection and marriage.

Figure 15–4: **The Stages of the Family Life Cycle**

Stage	Emotional Process	Required Changes in Family Status
1. Between families: The unattached young adult	Accepting parent–offspring separation	a. Differentiation of self in relation to family of origin b. Development of intimate peer relationships c. Establishment of self in work
2. The joining of families through marriage: The newly married couple	Commitment to new system	a. Formation of marital system b. Realignment of relationships with extended families and friends to include spouse
3. The family with young children	Accepting new generation of members into the system	a. Adjusting marital system to make space for child(ren) b. Taking on parenting roles c. Realignment of relationships with extended family to include parenting and grandparenting roles
4. The family with adolescents	Increasing flexibility of family boundaries to include children's independence	a. Shifting of parent–child relationships to permit adolescents to move in and out of system b. Refocus on midlife marital and career issues c. Beginning shift toward concerns for older generation
5. Launching children and moving on	Accepting a multitude of exits from and entries into the family system	a. Renegotiation of marital system as a dyad b. Development of adult to adult relationships between grown children and their parents c. Realignment of relationships to include in-laws and grandchildren d. Dealing with disabilities and death of parents (grandparents)
6. The family in later life	Accepting the shifting of generational roles	a. Maintaining own and/or couple functioning and interests in face of physiological decline; exploration of new familial and social role options b. Support for a more central role for middle generation c. Making room in the system for the wisdom and experience of the elderly; supporting the older generation without overfunctioning for them d. Dealing with loss of spouse, siblings, and other peers, and preparation for own death. Life review and integration.

Source: McGoldrick and Carter, 1982.

DYNAMICS OF MATE SELECTION AND MARRIAGE

"In the animal kingdom, mating involves only the two partners. For mankind, it is the joining of two enormously complex systems" (McGoldrick and Carter, 1982, p. 179). We may think of mate selection and marriage as matters that affect only the partners themselves, but in reality the concerns of parents and other family members are never very far from either person's consciousness. And as we will see shortly, the values of each partner's extended family often have a significant impact on the mate-selection process.

Marriage as Exchange

People in Western cultures like to think that interpersonal attraction and love are the primary factors in explaining why a couple forms a "serious" relationship and eventually marries. But while attraction and love are clearly important factors in many marriages, social scientists point out that in all cultures the process of mate selection is carried out according to basic rules of bargaining and exchange (Becker, 1973; Goode, 1964; Levitan and Belous, 1981). Sociologists and economists who study mate selection and marriage from this exchange perspective ask who controls the marriage contract, what values each family is attempting to maximize in the contract, and how the exchange process is shaped by the society's stratification system.

Among the upper classes of China and Japan before the twentieth century, marriage transactions were controlled by the male elders of the community—with the older women often making the real decisions behind the scenes. In many societies in the Middle East, Asia, and preindustrial Europe, the man's family negotiated a "bride price" with the woman's family. This price usually consisted of valuable goods like jewelry and clothes, but in some cultures it took the form of land and cattle. Throughout much of Hindu India, in contrast, an upper-class bride's family paid a "groom price" to the man's family. Although such norms appear to be weakening through-out the world, "arranged marriages" remain the customary pattern of mate selection in many societies. The following account describes factors that are often considered in arranging a marriage in modern India:

Every Sunday one can peruse the wedding ads in the classifieds. Many people still arrange an alliance in the traditional manner—through family and friend connections. Caste is becoming less important a factor in the selection of a spouse. Replacing caste are income and type of job. The educational level of the bride-to-be is also a consideration, an asset always worth mentioning in the ad. A faculty member at a college for girls has estimated that 80–90 percent of the students there will enter an arranged marriage upon receiving the B.A. Perhaps 10 percent will continue their studies. In this way, educating a daughter is parental investment toward securing an attractive, prosperous groom. [Smith, 1989]

In all of these transactions the families base their bargaining on considerations of family prestige within the community, the wealth of the two families and their ability to afford or command a given price, the beauty of the bride and the attractiveness of the groom, and so on. Different cultures may evaluate these qualities differently, but in each case the parties involved think of the coming marriage as an exchange between the two families (Goode, 1964). But do not get the idea that only selfish motives are involved in such marriages. Both families are also committing themselves to a longstanding relationship because they are exchanging their most precious products, their beloved young people. Naturally, they want the best for their children (as this is defined in their culture), and they also want a climate of mutual respect and cooperation in their future interfamily relationships.

Norms of Mate Selection

Endogamy/Exogamy. All cultures have norms that specify whether a person brought up in that culture may marry within or outside the cultural group. Marriage within the group is termed **endogamy**; marriage outside the group is termed **exogamy**. In the United States, ethnic and religious groups normally put pressure on their members to remain endogamous—that is, to choose mates from their

Social scientists do not fully understand what causes two people to fall in love or to remain in love. Processes of homogamy, in which people from similar social backgrounds choose each other as mates, are easier to explain.

own group. These rules tend to be especially strong for women. Among Orthodox Jews, for example, an infant is considered to have been born into the religion only if the mother is Jewish. Children of mixed marriages in which the mother is not Jewish are not considered Jewish by birth. The conflict between Orthodox and Reformed Jews over the status of children born to non-Jewish mothers who have converted to Judaism is an example of conflict over endogamy/exogamy norms. Many African tribes have developed norms of exogamy that encourage young men to find brides in specific villages outside the village of their birth. Such marriage systems tend to promote strong bonds of kinship among villages and serve to strengthen the social cohesion of the tribe while breaking down the animosity that sometimes arises between villages within a tribe.

Homogamy. Another norm of mate selection is **homogamy,** or the tendency to marry a person from a similar social background. The parents of a rich young woman, for example, attempt to increase the chances that she will associate with young men of the same or higher social-class standing. She is encouraged to date boys from "good" families. After graduating from high school she will be sent to an elite college or university, where the pool of eligible men is likely to include many who share her social-class background. She may surprise her parents, however, and fall in love with someone whose social-class, religious, or ethnic background is considerably different from

hers. But when this happens she will invariably have based her choice on other values that are considered important in the dating and marriage market, values like outstanding talent, good looks, popularity, or sense of humor. She will argue that these values outweigh social class, especially if it seems apparent that the young man will gain upward mobility through his career. Often the couple will marry and not worry about his lower social-class background. On the other hand, "the untalented, homely, poor man may aspire to a bride with highly desirable qualities, but he cannot offer enough to induce either her or her family to choose him, for they can find a groom with more highly valued qualities" (Goode, 1964, p. 33).

Numerous sociologists have studied the phenomenon of homogamy. In a post-World War II study entitled *Elmtown's Youth,* for example, August Hollingshead (1949) found that 61 percent of the adolescents in a small midwestern city dated within their social class and 35 percent dated members of adjacent classes. In two out of three cases in which a boy crossed class lines, he dated a girl from a lower social-class background. And in two out of three cases in which a girl crossed class lines, she went out with a boy from a higher social class. Those who dated members of a higher class were found to have special qualities in terms of looks, popularity, leadership skills, or athletic ability. Many other studies of dating and mate selection have demonstrated the same patterns of social-class homogamy and the same kinds of departures from that norm (Scanzoni and Scanzoni, 1976). It is reasonable to conclude, therefore, that cultural norms that stress homogamy in dating and marriage also tend to reproduce the society's system of social-class stratification in the next generation.

Homogamy in mate selection generally serves to maintain the separateness of religious groups. Because the Census Bureau does not collect systematic data on religious preferences, it is extremely difficult to obtain accurate data on religious intermarriage. Yet sociologists and religious leaders agree that although parents continue to encourage their children to marry within their religion, there is a trend away from religious homogamy, particularly for Protestants and Catholics (Scanzoni and Scanzoni, 1976).

The norm of homogamy also applies to interracial marriage. Before 1967, when the United States Supreme Court struck them down as unconstitutional, many states had laws prohibiting such marriages. After that decision, marriages between blacks and whites increased by about 26 percent, from about 51,000 in 1960 to about 65,000 in 1970, and their number continues to increase. Yet as a proportion of all marriages, black–white marriages remain less than 3 percent of the total and are less common than other types of interracial marriages. Thus the norm of racial homogamy remains relatively strong in the United States (Heer, 1974).

Romantic Love

Although exchange criteria and homogamy continue to play a significant role in mate selection, for the past century romantic attraction and love have been growing in importance in North American and other Western cultures. Indeed, the conflict between romantic love and the parental requirement of homogamy is one of the great themes of Western civilization. "Let me not to the marriage of true minds admit impediments," wrote Shakespeare in one of his most famous sonnets. The "star-crossed lovers" from feuding families in *Romeo and Juliet*, and the lovers who have forsaken family fortunes to be together in innumerable stories and plays written since Shakespeare's time, attest to the strong value we place on romantic love as an aspect of intimate relationships between men and women.

In his review of worldwide marriage and family patterns, William J. Goode (1964) found that compared with the mate-selection systems of other cultures, that of the United States "has given love greater prominence. Here, as in all Western societies to some lesser degree, the child is socialized to fall in love" (p. 39). Yet although it may be taken for granted that people will form couples on the basis of romantic attachment, important changes in the structure of Western societies had to occur before love as we know it could become such an important value in our lives. In par-

ticular, changes in economic institutions as a result of industrialization required workers with more education and greater maturity. These changes, in turn, lengthened the period of socialization, especially in educational institutions. This made it possible for single men and women to remain unattached long enough to gain the emotional maturity they needed if they were to experience love and make more independent decisions in selecting their mates.

However familiar it may seem to us, love remains a mysterious aspect of human relationships. We do not know very much— from a verifiable, scientific standpoint—about this complex emotional state. We do not know fully what it means to "fall in love" or what couples can do to make their love last. But two promising avenues of research on this subject can be found in Winch's theory of complementarity and Blau's theory of emotional reciprocity.

Complementary Needs and Mutual Attraction Robert F. Winch's (1958) theory of complementary needs, based on work by the psychologist Henry A. Murray, holds that people who fall in love tend to be alike in social characteristics such as family prestige, education, and income but different in their psychological needs. Thus, according to Winch, an outgoing person often falls in love with a quiet, shy person. The one gains an appreciative audience, the other an entertaining spokesperson. A person who needs direction is attracted to one who needs to exercise authority; one who is nurturant is attracted to one who needs nurturance; and so on. Winch and others have found evidence to support this theory, but there are some problems with this research. It is difficult to measure personal needs and the extent to which they are satisfied. Moreover, people also show a variety of other patterns in their choices of mates. There are some people, in fact, who seem to be attracted to each other because of their similarities in looks and behavior rather than because of their differences.

Attraction and Emotional Reciprocity Blau's (1964) theory of emotional reciprocity as a source of love is based on his general theory that relationships usually flourish when people feel satisfied with the exchanges between them. When people feel that they are loved, they are more likely to give love in return. When they feel that they love too much or are not loved enough, they will eventually come to feel exploited or trapped and will seek to end the relationship. In research on 231 dating couples, Zick Rubin (1980) found that among those who felt this equality of love, 77 percent were still together two years later, but only 45 percent of the unequally involved couples were still seeing each other. As Blau explained it, "Only when two lovers' affection for and commitment to one another expand at roughly the same pace do they mutually tend to reinforce their love" (quoted in Rubin, 1980, p. 284).

Blau's exchange approach confirms some popular notions about love—particularly the ideas that we can love someone who loves us and that inequalities in love can lead to separation. And yet we still know little about the complexities of this emotion and how it translates into the formation of the most basic of all social groups, the married couple. This is ironic, because books, movies, and popular songs probably pay more attention to love than to just about any other subject. Nevertheless, psychological and sociological research on love has never been given very high priority. In the late 1970s, in fact, Senator William Proxmire gave one of his "Golden Fleece" awards for waste of government funds to social psychologist Ellen Berscheid for her research on interpersonal attraction between men and women. He commented, "I believe that 200 million Americans want to leave some things in life a mystery, and right at the top of the things we don't want to know is why a man falls in love with a woman and vice versa." Berscheid responded with no hesitation: "I assume the senator has some knowledge of the divorce rate in this country and understands that the absence of love is the basis on which many divorces are instigated. I believe he has been divorced and recently was reconciled with his second wife. He ought to realize better than most people why we should know all we can about the determinants of affection" (quoted in Rubin, 1980, p. 284). (See Box 15-1.)

Marriage and Divorce

More than any other ritual signifying a major change in status, a wedding is a joyous occasion. Two people are legally and symbolically joined before their kin and friends. It is expected that their honeymoon will be pleasant and that they will live happily ever after. But 20 percent of first marriages end in annulment or divorce within the first three years (Bogue, 1985). Of course, divorce can occur at any time in the family life cycle, but the early years of family formation are the most difficult for the couple because each partner experiences new stresses that arise from the need to adjust to a complex set of new relationships. As Monica McGoldrick and Elizabeth A. Carter (1982) point out, "Marriage requires that a couple renegotiate a myriad of personal issues that they have previously defined for themselves or that were defined by their parents, from when to sleep, have sex, or fight, to how to celebrate holidays and where and how to live, work, and spend vacations" (p. 178). For people who were married before, these negotiations can involve former spouses and shared children, resulting in added stress for the new couple.

In the United States and other Western societies, the rate of divorce rose sharply after World War II, accelerated even more dramatically during the 1960s and 1970s, and has decreased only slightly since then (see Figure 15-5). These statistics often lead sociologists to proclaim that there is an "epidemic of divorce" in the United States. But demographer Donald Bogue has concluded that "the divorce epidemic is not being created by today's younger generation. It has been created by today's population aged thirty or more, who married in the 1960s and before" (1985, p. 190). This generation was noted for its search for self-realization, often at the expense of intimate family relationships. It is not yet clear whether subsequent generations, who appear to be somewhat more pragmatic, will continue this trend. If they do, we can expect high divorce rates to continue.

Trial Marriage In the 1980s it was widely believed that the practice of "trial marriage," or cohabitation before marriage, would result

Box 15–1: **Love of a Lifetime?**

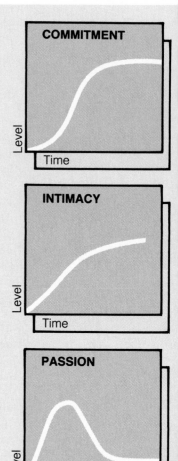

Social psychologists who study love in married and unmarried couples are finding new evidence that confirms what many people have long known intuitively: It is in fact quite difficult for couples to maintain the level of passion they experienced in the early stages of their marriage. "People don't know what they are in for when they fall in love," asserts Yale's Robert Sternberg. "The divorce rate is so high, not because people make foolish choices, but because they are drawn together for reasons that matter less as time goes on" (Goleman, 1985, p. C1).

Sternberg believes that love has three components: intimacy, passion, and commitment. The first is a shared sense that the couple can reveal their innermost feelings to each other even as those feelings change. Passion is largely a matter of physical attraction and sexuality. Commitment is a shared sense that each member of the couple is permanently devoted to the other. Research shows that the fullest love demands all three of these qualities but that over a long relationship passion is the quickest to fade; intimacy develops slowly and steadily as a result

of shared experiences and values; and commitment develops more gradually still (see chart).

In the early stages of a love relationship, the couple may become so caught up in their passion that they do not help each other develop as autonomous individuals. This can produce serious problems in later stages of the relationship. At the same time, commitment alone cannot substitute for the other two qualities of love. "You have to work constantly at rejuvenating a relationship," Sternberg explains, "You can't just count on its being OK, or it will tend toward a hollow commitment, devoid of passion and intimacy. People need to put the kind of energy into it that they put into their children or career" (quoted in Goleman, 1985, p. C6). Studies by Sternberg and many others find that children who have been deprived of parental love, especially by the parent of the opposite sex, often have trouble developing commitment and sharing intimacy. Often they avoid feeling vulnerable and dependent on another person by avoiding strong emotional ties altogether.

in greater marital stability: Couples who lived together before marriage would gain greater mutual understanding and a realistic view of marital commitment, and this would result in a lower divorce rate among such couples after they actually married. However, as the 1990s approached, it became evident that these expectations were unfounded; in fact, the divorce rate among couples who had lived together before marriage was actually higher than the rate for couples who had not done so. Within ten years of the wedding, 38 percent of those who had lived together before marriage had divorced, compared to 27 percent of those who had married without cohabiting beforehand.

On the basis of an analysis of data from a federal government survey of over 13,000 individuals, Larry Bumpass and James Sweet (cited in Barringer, 1989) concluded that couples who cohabit before marriage are generally more willing to accept divorce as a solution to marital problems. They also found that such couples are less likely to be subject to family pressure to continue a marriage that is unhappy or unsatisfactory. In addition, cohabitation has become a predictable part of the family life cycle, not only before marriage but in the interval between divorce and remarriage. Among individuals who remarried between 1980 and 1987, 60 percent lived with a person of the opposite sex beforehand.

Sources of Marital Instability

Because it generally causes a great deal of emotional stress and pain for everyone involved, to say nothing of its financial costs, divorce has received intense study by social scientists. Space does not permit a full treatment of this subject here, but we can discuss some of the major variables associated with divorce.

Age at marriage is one of the leading factors in divorce. It seems that it is best not to marry too young or to wait too long. Women who marry while still in their teens are twice as likely to divorce as are those who tie the knot in their twenties. But those who marry in their thirties are half again as likely to divorce as are those who marry in their twenties. How can we explain these differences?

In a study of age and marital instability, Alan Booth and John N. Edwards (1985) examined data obtained from a national sample of over 1700 couples. Among the younger couples, a pattern that the authors identified as inadequate role performance—especially not being attuned to the other partner's sexual needs and not being comfortable with the role of husband or wife—seemed to explain much of the instability in their relationships. Among those who married at an older age, another pattern appeared. These couples were more likely to engage in bitter disputes over the division of labor within the family—that is, over the definition of gender roles. Women who marry at older ages, for example, are more likely to demand that both partners share equally in the housework.

It appears that earlier in this century, when women were more likely to assume the role of homemaker, marriages had a higher probability of lasting. The demand by women for sharing of household roles—what sociologists often call the demand for the "symmetrical family" in which there is equality of roles as provider and as homemaker—creates new opportunities for both men and women, but it also places more stress on the family in its early stages (Pearson and Hendrix, 1979; Weir and Weir, 1976; Willmott and Young, 1971). (Symmetrical families are not necessarily more dissatisfied with their marriages than nonsymmetrical families, nor do they necessarily encounter more marital problems. However, the greater ability of both partners to be economically independent may allow them to consider divorce sooner than would a couple in which the wife is not in the labor force.)

Besides inadequate role performance, other factors have been found to be correlated with marital instability and divorce. They include the following:

● The couple met "on the rebound" (i.e., after one or both partners had experienced

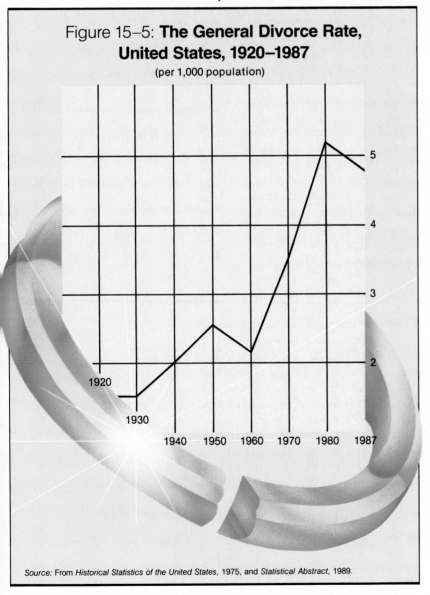

Figure 15–5: **The General Divorce Rate, United States, 1920–1987**
(per 1,000 population)

1920
1930
1940 1950 1960 1970 1980 1987

5
4
3
2

Source: From *Historical Statistics of the United States*, 1975, and *Statistical Abstract*, 1989.

a great loss or hurt) and the new relationship may be flawed as a result.

- One of the partners wants to live at a great distance from his or her family of orientation, suggesting that feelings of hostility toward family members may complicate the relationship.
- The spouses' family backgrounds are markedly different in terms of race, religion, education, or social class, which may result in differences in values that can cause conflict between the spouses.
- The couple is dependent on one of the extended families for income, shelter, or emotional support.
- The couple married after an acquaintanceship of less than six months or after an engagement of more than three years.
- Marital patterns in either spouse's extended family were unstable.
- The wife became pregnant before or within the first year of marriage (McGoldrick and Carter, 1982, based on a survey of research by Becker, 1977; Bumpass and Sweet, 1972; and Goodrich, Ryder, and Rausch, 1968).

These correlates of marital instability do not, of course, necessarily mean that marriages that occur under these conditions are doomed to break up. They merely suggest that on the basis of statistical probabilities such marriages have a higher chance of ending in divorce.

The Impact of Divorce

Today, although divorce has become much more commonplace than it was earlier in the century, it remains a significant event in people's lives—as significant as marriage itself. But unlike a wedding, a divorce is not a happy event. Although some divorces turn out well for both partners, the majority do not. This was a major finding of an extensive study that tracked sixty families with a total of 131 children over a period of ten to fifteen years after divorce (Wallerstein and Blakeslee, 1989). Although some of the adults were happier as a result of the divorce and some of the children fared better than they would have in an un-

happy intact family, more often than not divorce was a wrenching experience for at least one of the former partners. For almost all the children, it had powerful and unanticipated effects.

An important finding of the study (in which parents and children were interviewed individually at regular intervals) was that the turmoil and distress of divorce may continue for a year or more. Many divorced adults continue to feel angry, humiliated, and rejected as much as eighteen months later, and the children of divorced parents tend to exhibit a variety of psychological problems. Moreover, both men and women have a diminished capacity for parenting after divorce. They spend less time with their children, provide less discipline, and are less sensitive to their needs. Even a decade after the divorce, the parents may be chronically disorganized and unable to meet the challenges of parenting. Instead, they come to depend on their children to help them cope with the demands of their own lives, thereby producing an "overburdened child"— one who, in addition to handling the normal stresses of childhood, also must help his or her parent ward off depression (Wallerstein and Blakeslee, 1989).

There is a silver lining to the dark cloud of divorce, however. Since so many adults who are now marrying for the first time come from families that have experienced divorce, they are likely to take more time in selecting their mates in an effort to make sure that their choice is best for both partners; in addition, they try to become economically secure before marrying, thereby eliminating a major source of stress in a new marriage (Blumstein and Schwartz, 1983). If this is true, the recent modest downturn in the divorce rate may be expected to continue in the future. In any case, the data on the effects of divorce on adults and children suggest that societies need to do more to ease the stress experienced by young families—for example, by providing more day care facilities, establishing more flexible work schedules, and offering opportunities for parental leave.

> *The majority of divorces have serious negative effects on at least one of the former partners and on the children.*

PERSPECTIVES ON THE FAMILY

High divorce rates do not indicate that the family is about to disappear as an institution in modern societies. Even though many marriages end in divorce and increasing numbers of young adults postpone marriage or decide not to marry at all, the large majority do marry, and the majority of those who divorce will eventually remarry. Far from disappearing, the family is adapting to new social values and to changes in other institutions, especially economic ones. In the rest of this chapter we review some current research on family roles and relationships from the standpoint of the three basic sociological perspectives.

The Interactionist Perspective

Interactions within the family cover a wide range of emotions and may take very different forms in different families. Families laugh and play together, work together, argue and bicker, and so on. All of these aspects of family interaction are important, but frequently it is the arguing and bickering that drives family members apart. Studies of family interaction therefore often focus on the sources of tension and conflict within the family.

Problems of family interaction can stem from a variety of sources. Often problems arise in connection with critical life stages or events, such as the loss of a job or when adolescent children begin to assert their independence in ways that threaten established family roles and arrangements. And conflicts often occur because of the particular ways in which the family's experiences are shaped by larger social structures. In the armed forces, for example, families often experience severe stress because of frequent moves from one base to another (Shaw, 1979). In many cases such moves draw family members closer together, but in some cases family interactions are marked by tension because of the children's resentment over their inability to maintain stable friendships.

The context within which family life occurs can affect family interactions in other ways as well. At the lower levels of a society's stratification system, for example, money (or the lack of it) is often a source of conflict between parents and between parents and children. But the rich are by no means immune to problems of family interaction. Because they do not have to be concerned about the need to earn a living as adults and because their parents can satisfy any desires they may have, the children of the very rich often develop a sadness that resembles anomie (Wixen, 1979). Their lack of clear goals, which sometimes expresses itself in a compulsion to make extravagant purchases, may give rise to conflict between them and their parents.

In order to study these situations, either to help a family resolve its problems or to understand the nature of family conflict more thoroughly, the social scientist must interact with and observe the family, either at home, in a lab, or in a therapy setting (Minuchin, 1974; Satir, 1972; Walsh, 1982). In one example two family therapists, Augustus Napier and Carl Whitaker (1980), describe a family in which the parents are deeply troubled by the behavior of their seventeen-year-old daughter, the oldest of their three children. The father is a prominent attorney, and the mother is a college-educated woman who has devoted herself to homemaking. The parents' definition of the situation that has brought them into therapy is that they are worried about their daughter. She disobeys, is delinquent, and is depressed enough to make them fear that she might commit suicide. The mother and daughter fight bitterly, but usually the mother retreats. The father often attempts to defend the daughter, but eventually he sides with the mother.

After a few sessions Napier and Whitaker begin to challenge the parents' assumption that it is the daughter who is "the problem." They guess that her depression, anger, and delinquent behavior are symptoms of larger problems in the family. After some gentle probing they identify a triangle of family conflict in which "two parents are emotionally estranged from each other and in their terrible aloneness they overinvolve their children in their emotional distress" (p. 83). The children blame themselves for their parents' problems, or have a low sense of self-worth. The therapists help the couple face the issues that divide them and motivate their children to serve as scapegoats or intermediaries who divert attention from the parents' basic problems.

Families like the one just described need to resolve a contradiction that is inherent in the institution of the family: the need to maintain the individuality of each member while providing love and support for him or her within a set of interdependent relationships. Many families never succeed in developing ways of encouraging each member to realize his or her full potential within the context of family life. And research shows that the core problem is usually the failure of the adult couple to understand and develop their own relationship, even in intact families. Such a couple may become what John F. Cuber and Peggy B. Haroff (1980) termed a "conflict-habituated" or "devitalized" couple. Couples of the first type have evolved ways of expressing their hostility toward each other through elaborate patterns of conflict that persist over many years. In contrast, the devitalized or "empty-shell" marriage may have begun with love and shared interests, but the partners have not grown as a couple and have drifted apart emotionally. Each has the habit of being with the other, a habit that may be strongly supported by the norms of a particular ethnic or religious community. Neither partner is satisfied by the relationship, but neither feels that he or she can do anything to change the situation. Thus the conflicts that might have produced change are reduced to indifference.

Today social scientists who study family interaction must deal with family structures that are more complex than the traditional nuclear family. Divorce and remarriage create many situations in which children have numerous sets of parental figures, parents and stepparents, grandparents and surrogate grandparents, and so on. These changes in family form result in new patterns of family interaction. For example, in a study of 2,000 children conducted over a five-year period, sociologist Frank Furstenberg found that 52 percent of children raised by their mothers do not see their fathers at all, not only because the fathers are absent by choice but because the opportunities for visits decrease as parents remarry or move away (cited in Aspaklaria, 1985). This produces situations in which parents strive to maintain long-distance relationships with their children and occasionally have brief, intense visits with them. Although this type of relationship may not be the most desirable, it appears that when parents and children can express love and affection even when the parents are divorced, the children's ability to feel good about themselves and to love others in their turn may not be impaired.

Box 15-2 discusses another problematic aspect of family interaction that has become a focus of increasing public attention in recent years: child sexual abuse.

Conflict Theory and Alternatives to the Family

From a conflict perspective, none of the changes discussed in this chapter could occur without conflict both within the family and between the family and other institutions. Nor can change occur without ideological and political conflict. In fact, there have been occasions when critics of the family as an institution have called for the complete elimination of the family as we know it.

The Russian Revolution of 1917 challenged the institution of the family as it had never been challenged before. To create a truly classless society, the revolutionary leaders believed, it would be necessary to eliminate marriage and parental roles and all the institutional arrangements that support the traditional nuclear family. Marx and his collaborator Friedrich Engels (1969/1848) believed that the nuclear family structure that had evolved under industrial capitalism was a result of the domination of society by the bourgeois class (see Chapters 8 and 12). Men in bourgeois society were treated as "wage slaves," while women in the bourgeois family were treated as "domestic slaves." Children became "articles of commerce and instruments of labor." To break the influence of

Box 15–2: **Child Sexual Abuse**

No one knows how many children in the United States are sexually abused or molested. It is estimated that there are about 20,000 cases of child sexual abuse each year, most of which do not come to the attention of the authorities. The majority of these incidents are thought to involve family members or close friends of the family. Fewer than 1,000 are thought to occur in day-care centers or early-childhood learning contexts (Finkelhor and Williams, 1988). But we must be extremely wary of estimates like these. They are subject to much error. The reporting systems on which they are based vary greatly in quality and are subject to misinterpretation. This is especially true of estimates about child sexual abuse in day-care centers. There is no doubt that incidents of abuse have occurred in day-care centers, but the extent of the problem has been exaggerated in sensational trials of day-care workers in Los Angeles and New York, threatening the integrity of a much-needed institution.

In addition to strict rules and better protective systems, the public deserves sound data and analysis of such a sensitive problem. Sociologist Richard Gelles, an expert on child abuse, notes that a number of common myths about child abuse (including sexual abuse) also need to be examined, since they "tend to cloud present thinking and confuse future research efforts" (1987, p. 16). Among those myths are the following:

● *Child abuse is rare.* Because of the absense of official statistics before the mid-1960s, most people considered abuse a rare phenomenon. Although experts still disagree about the extent of child abuse, most agree that it affects at least 1 million children per year in the United States.

● *Child maltreatment is confined to mentally ill or disturbed people.* Partly because the most bizarre incidents tend to get the most publicity, the kinds of abuse suffered by many children are thought to be the acts of mentally deranged people. However, research on child abuse has shown that the mental state of the abuser is a relatively unimportant factor in explaining why abuse occurs.

● *Child abuse is confined to families with low socioeconomic status.* Families with low income and limited education are overrepresented in official statistics on child maltreatment. However, middle-class children who are injured are often classified as victims of accidents when in fact they have suffered abuse.

● *Children who have been abused will grow up to be child abusers.* Although there is a higher probability that a person who was abused as a child will abuse his or her own children, the relationship is not a causal one. An abused child will not necessarily grow up to be a child abuser.

● *The problem of child maltreatment is worse today in the United States than at other times or in other countries.* In the past twenty-five years our society has become far more willing to examine child abuse, publicize it, collect statistics, and enact legislation to address the problem. This may give the impression that the problem has become worse when in fact it has not.

Today, although we cannot prove that there is more child abuse, including sexual abuse, than there was in earlier decades, most social scientists believe that the changes that have transformed the family as an institution have contributed to the problem of abuse.

bourgeois values, therefore, traditional family roles would have to be weakened.

The Bolsheviks under Lenin embraced these ideas, and after the revolution they instituted policies that were intended to devalue family life (Buckley, 1985). For example, divorces and abortions were made extremely easy to obtain. Marriages were separated from religious rituals, and couples who lived together were considerd to be married even without legal sanction (this was called de facto marriage). In addition, the inheritance of family property was banned. The theory behind these policies was that the family would "wither away" as the ideal communist society was created. Children would be reared in collective nurseries and schools, and their parents would be free to engage in intimate relations with any partner they chose.

In fact, many of the more radical of these measures failed. For one thing, they appeared to lower the birthrate. This became an especially serious problem after World War II, when the need to replace the millions of industrial workers who had been killed in the war became a top national priority. Also, couples tended to go through the perfunctory communist marriage rituals and then hold larger family weddings, often with religious ceremonies included. Gradually through the postwar years Soviet leaders came to accept the family (Geiger, 1968).

In a study of efforts by Israeli pioneers to create alternatives to the family, Melford Spiro (1970) interviewed a kibbutz's founders and some of its *sabras* (people who were born on the kibbutz). The founders of the kibbutz were opposed to the nuclear family for many of the same reasons as the leaders of the Russian Revolution. They believed that the traditional family structure prevented the development of true gemeinschaft societies in which all would share equally in both wealth and hardships. For this reason, kibbutz children were reared in nurseries, and parents spent only two hours a day playing with them. This proved to be a viable alternative to socialization in the nuclear family, since communal rearing had no adverse effects on the children. But gradually the movement to do away with nuclear families weakened.

Functionalist Views of the Family

From a functionalist perspective, the family evolves in both form and function in response to changes in the larger social environment. As societies undergo such major changes as industrialization and urbanization, the family must adapt to the effects of those changes. Functionalist theorists like Talcott Parsons and William Goode have called attention to the loss of family functions that occurs as other social institutions like schools, corporations, and social-welfare agencies perform functions previously reserved for the family. We have discussed numerous examples of this trend in earlier chapters—the tendency of families to have fewer children as the demand for agricultural labor decreased, the changing composition of households as people were required to seek work away from their families of orientation, the increasing number of two-paycheck households, and so on. The functionalist explanation of these changes in organization is that as the division of labor becomes more complex and as new, more specialized institutions arise, the family, too, must become a more specialized institution. Thus, modern families no longer perform certain functions that used to be within their domain, but they do play an increasingly vital part in early-childhood socialization, in the emotional lives of their members, and in preparing older children for adult roles in the economic institutions of industrial societies (Parsons and Bales, 1955).

A good example of empirical research on the family as it adapts to the requirements of life in modern societies is William H. Whyte's study *The Organization Man* (1957). In the 1950s, when American corporations were expanding rapidly, hundreds of thousands of American men (and a few women) had their first taste of modern corporate life. But because the branches and offices of modern corporations often span the entire continent, corporate managers were required to move from one community to another whenever the company considered it necessary. Whyte conducted in-depth observations of Park Forest, a rather typical middle-class garden-apartment suburb of Chicago. He found

FG: "Joyce at 34."

that unlike families of the working class, which were "putting down roots" in industrial communities, the residents of Park Forest were forced to maintain shallow roots in the community. Their careers in modern corporations and universities required them to keep their families small and to limit their emotional investment in friendships with their neighbors, since this would permit them to leave the community with a minimum of disruption and grief.

Another example of the functionalist perspective on the family can be seen in Mirra Komarovsky's (1980) explanation of her findings in a study of how college men think about the potential careers of their mates. The members of Komarovsky's sample fell into the following categories:

- "Traditionalists" (24 percent) said that they intended to marry women who would find satisfaction in domestic roles without ever seeking outside jobs.
- Men whom Komarovsky termed "pseudo-feminists" (16 percent) claimed that they accepted the idea of a wife's seeking a career outside the home, but they imposed so many conditions that no woman could meet them.
- "Modified traditionalists" (48 percent) favored a pattern in which their wives first would work, then leave their jobs to raise children, and eventually return to work. Although these men were willing to help their wives with the housework, they usually excluded specific tasks: "not the laundry," "not the cleaning," "not the diapers," and so on.
- The "feminist type" was the smallest category, only 7 percent of the total. These men were willing to modify their own roles significantly in order to facilitate their wives' careers. Some recommended a symmetrical allocation of tasks "as long as it is not a complete reversal of roles."
- The remaining 5 percent of the sample felt that marriage was such a remote possibility for them that they could not speculate about it.

From the functionalist perspective, these changes in the way that men expect to perform their roles as husbands are usually explained as resulting from new demands placed on couples. Those demands are generated by changes in economic institutions and the need to adapt to such conditions as inflation, rising standards of living, and the ever-increasing educational requirements of many employers.

Underlying these changes in family functions, of course, are shifts in the society's basic values. An example of such a shift is increased emphasis on individual well-being or self-actualization, as opposed to involvement in communal pursuits or commitment to the goals of a group or organization. This shift in values was the subject of an extensive study by Robert Bellah and associates in the mid-1980s. Among other findings, the researchers concluded that there is a pervasive tension between individualism and commitment in American life, a tension that is often reflected in troubled family role relations. In exploring the feelings of Americans about love, for example, they found that love "creates a dilemma for Americans. In some ways, love is the quintessential expression of individuality and freedom. At the same time, it offers intimacy, mutuality, and sharing. . . . The sharing and commitment in a love relationship can seem, for some, to swallow up the individual, making her (more often than him) lose sight of her own interests, opinions, and desires" (Bellah et al., 1985, p. 93).

This kind of tension is a frequent source of conflict in families. A wife, for instance, may feel smothered by her social status as "Mrs. So-and-So" and by the expectation that she will function as part of a couple rather than as a person who happens to be married. Eventually she may rebel against these constraints (real or imagined) and seek out roles and statuses that reflect her individual needs and desires. She may return to school, take music lessons, change her style of dress, find a job outside the home, and so on, with or without the approval and support of her husband. Such an assertion of individuality by either partner can have a destablizing effect on the family. In the long run, however, when both partners feel more fulfilled as individuals the relationship is often strengthened and conflict diminishes.

Conclusion: "Here to Stay"

When Mark Twain was informed that a British newspaper had printed his obituary, the great humorist cabled the paper to say that "the reports of my death are greatly exaggerated." The same can be said of the family as a central institution of modern societies. Here and in other chapters we have traced the increase in single-parent families, postponement of marriage, and divorce. Certainly these trends present people with more choices regarding family life than were ever available before, but they do not signal an end to traditional family norms and roles. As Mary Jo Bane has noted, the demography of marriage and remarriage, and of childbearing later in life, points to the endurance of the family. As the institution that exerts the strongest influence over primary relationships, courtship, marriage, and socialization, the family is "here to stay" (cited in Skolnick and Skolnick, 1980).

The family is a resilient institution; it adapts to changing economic conditions and changing values. But the strength of the family as an institution does not mean the divorce rate will decrease rapidly or families that experience severe stress due to unemployment, ill health, and the like will have an easier time remaining intact. Indeed, few of the challenges we face in our lives are greater than that of selecting a mate and making family decisions. Thus, social scientists who do research on the family will continue to find that there is a need for the information they provide. Those who work on macrosocial questions—issues of government policy regarding welfare or retirement or home financing, for example—will continue to study the impact of social policies on families. And those who delve into the microsocial world of family interaction will continue to ask how changes in norms and values affect the roles we play in families. As Napier observed,

Every family is a miniature society, a social order with its own rules, structure, leadership, language, style of living . . . The hidden rules, the subtle nuances of language, the private rituals and dances that define every family as a unique microculture may not be easy for an outsider to perceive at first glance, but they are there. [Napier and Whitaker, 1980, p. 78]

CHALLENGES TO CONTEMPORARY SOCIETY

The Black Family

In *A Common Destiny*, a major review of the status of African-Americans in the United States today (Jaynes and Williams, 1989), the authors conclude that "the opportunity for launching a concerted nationwide effort to ameliorate the problems of poverty and underachievement may be greater now than they have been for a long time" (p. 548). This conclusion is based on demographic data indicating a shrinking labor force, research demonstrating that programs in compensatory education and job training can make a difference, and the knowledge that improvements in health care also improve the situation of poor people. But the authors also single out the black family and the situation of black children living in poverty as a major and continuing obstacle to progress in combating severe inequality.

The accompanying charts show that the overall poverty rate for black families is three times higher than that for white families and that illegitimacy rates are more than three times higher for blacks than they are for whites. Half of all black families are headed by single women. What are the implications of these figures?

A 1983 study by the Center for the Study of Social Policy, a nonpartisan research group, noted that increases in the proportion of black single parents and in rates of teenage pregnancy threaten the economic and social gains made by blacks in recent decades. The study

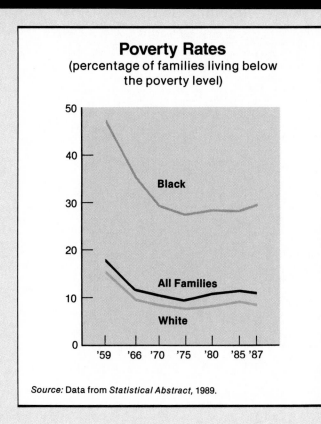

Poverty Rates
(percentage of families living below the poverty level)

Black

All Families

White

Source: Data from *Statistical Abstract*, 1989.

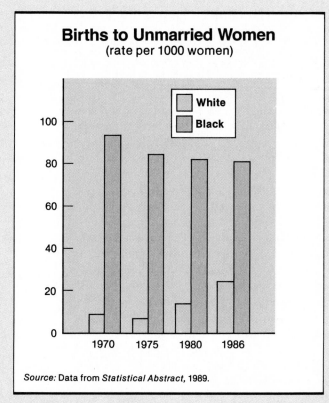

Births to Unmarried Women
(rate per 1000 women)

White
Black

Source: Data from *Statistical Abstract*, 1989.

found that in 1981 the average income of black families with two working parents had reached 84 percent of the average for white families in which both parents worked. But the average for all black families with children was just 56 percent of the average for white families with children, because 47 percent of black families are headed by women (compared with 14 percent of white families) and therefore have, at best, only one wage earner (Cummings, 1983).

These comparisons have contributed to an intense debate about the future of black families in America. Some writers and policymakers have responded to these trends by attacking the social-welfare programs developed since the 1930s and by attempting to replace those programs with incentives to seek wage work. Conservative social theorists argue that because young women become eligible for welfare payments and rent subsidies when they become single mothers, social-welfare programs actually encourage them to have children. They also believe that the availability of welfare further weakens the family as an institution because men are relieved of the responsibility for providing for the women with whom they have fathered children. In George Gilder's words, "Current programs will continue to create a criminal underclass of unlisted male welfare beneficiaries who exploit the welfare trap by living off a series of female recipients" (quoted in Cummings, 1983, p. 56).

Many sociologists dispute this interpretation, however. Harriet Piopes McAdoo, a specialist in the study of disadvantaged women and children, has stated that

the tradition used to be that if a woman got pregnant, they were expected to get married, if not forced to get married, to supply income and a name for the child. But if the man has no job, there's no impetus for them to get married. Her parents would have three people to support instead of just two. The boy would become an additional burden on the family. Parents feel: "Why should I force her to marry him? He'll be a drain." [quoted in Cummings, 1983, p. 56]

Other research on teenage pregnancy indicates that social class, rather than race, explains most of the difference between white and black rates of teenage pregnancy. A study of teenagers from households below the federal poverty standard (Manpower Demonstration and Research Corporation, 1980) showed that there is almost no difference in rates of pregnancy among black, white, and Hispanic teenage girls from poor households: By age nineteen well over half have been pregnant at least once. The major differences are in rates of marriage. Lower-income white teenagers still are more likely to get married than black or Hispanic teenagers are, and this results in far lower rates of illegitimate births among white teenagers than among black and Hispanic teenagers. What is not recognized in these comparisons is that most teenage marriages among lower-income whites end in divorce within five years. By the age of twenty-five, therefore, the proportions of black and white women raised in poor households who are single mothers, on welfare or at work, do not differ significantly.

Even though the data show that the phenomena of teenage pregnancy, female-headed families, and children being raised in poverty are related to social class rather than to race, the fact that more blacks than whites are found in the lower income levels of society means that these problems are proportionally more serious for blacks than they are for whites. Sociologist Joyce Ladner (1973) writes that "life in the black community has been conditioned by poverty, discrimination, and institutional subordination" (p. 425). Under these conditions, she finds, the black family has shown surprising resilience. Although within a given black family there may be households headed by single women, the extended family

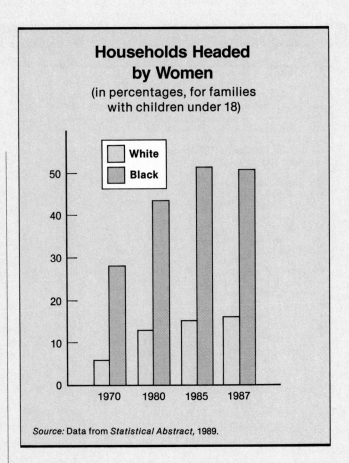

Households Headed by Women
(in percentages, for families with children under 18)

Source: Data from *Statistical Abstract*, 1989.

often provides substantial support for its less fortunate members.

Clearly, there is a need to find ways of helping teenagers of all racial and ethnic groups to avoid becoming parents before they are economically ready to do so. The policy of requiring single mothers to work rather than go on welfare may act as a deterrent to teenage pregnancy, but it will not prevent poor teenagers from being exposed to a culture that tells them that sex is fun and that parenthood is a route to adulthood. Black leaders are urging organizations in their communities, such as churches, schools, and fraternal associations, to provide guidance and support for poor teenagers. By providing teenagers with positive examples as well as jobs and other learning opportunities that compete with early parenthood, black communities may begin to cope with the problems of illegitimacy, teenage pregnancy, and single parenthood, and the lessons learned in this way may be applied in white communities as well. For the data do show that these problems are by no means unique to blacks.

SUMMARY

In all known societies almost everyone is socialized within a network of family rights and obligations that are known as family role relations. In simple societies the family performs a large number of other functions as well, but in modern societies most of the functions that were traditionally performed by the family are performed partly or entirely by other social institutions.

A *family* is a group of people related by blood, marriage, or adoption, and the role relations among family members are known as *kinship* relations. The smallest units of family structure are the *conjugal family*, consisting of a husband and wife and their children, if any, and the *nuclear family*, consisting of two or more people related by blood, marriage, or adoption who share a household. The nuclear family in which one is born and socialized is one's *family of orientation*, and the nuclear family one forms through marriage or cohabitation is one's *family of procreation*. An *extended family* includes an individual's nuclear family plus all the nuclear families of his or her blood relatives.

The traditional household consisting of two parents and their children is no longer the typical American family. Since the 1940s there has been a dramatic increase in female-headed single-parent families and in nonfamily households, as well as in the numbers of females and males living alone and in the number of unmarried couples and roommates of the same sex.

Studies of changes in family structure have shown that family units become simpler as societies undergo industrialization. Economic and technological changes require the family to adapt to an economy in which income is earned outside the family; this means that families must become smaller, more mobile, and more flexible. More recent research has found that nuclear families have not entirely replaced extended families, although extended families do not always live under one roof. Modern technologies like the telephone and the automobile enable members of smaller family units to maintain kinship ties with their extended families.

The typical stages of the family life cycle are family formation, start of childbearing, end of childbearing, "empty nest," and family dissolution (i.e., the death of one spouse). As it passes through this cycle, every family experiences changes in its system of role relations. These changes present major emotional challenges, which are often complicated by divorce, remarriage, and the combining of children of different marriages in a single family.

In all cultures the process of mate selection is carried out according to basic rules of bargaining and exchange. In many societies the customary pattern of mate selection is the "arranged" marriage, in which the families of the bride and groom negotiate the marriage contract. All cultures also have norms that specify whether a person brought up in that culture may marry within or outside the cultural group. Marriage within the group is termed *endogamy*; marriage outside the group is termed *exogamy*. In societies in which marriages are based on attraction and love, individuals tend to marry people similar to themselves in social background, a tendency that is referred to as *homogamy*. Homogamy generally serves to reproduce the society's system of social-class stratification in the next generation and to maintain the separateness of religious and racial groups.

Compared with the mate selection systems of other cultures, that of the United States gives love greater prominence. Yet from a scientific standpoint little is known about this complex emotional state. It appears that people who fall in love tend to be alike in social characteristics but different in their psychological needs; however, this is not always the case. There is also considerable evidence that love relationships are more lasting when the partners' affection for each other is roughly equal.

In the United States and other Western societies, the rate of divorce has risen sharply since World War II. In the 1980s it was widely believed that the practice of cohabitation before marriage would result in greater marital stability, but in fact the divorce rate among couples who had lived together before marriage was actually higher than the rate for couples who had not done so.

Age at marriage has been found to be one of the leading factors in divorce. Marriages that take place when the woman is in her teens or in her thirties are much more likely to end in divorce than marriages that take place when the woman is in her twenties. Among other factors that have been found to be correlated with divorce are marked differences in the family backgrounds of the spouses, dependence on either spouse's extended family, marital instability in either spouse's extended family, and early pregnancy. Studies of the impact of divorce have found that the turmoil and distress of divorce may continue for a year or more. Both men and women have a diminished capacity for parenting after divorce and may come to depend on their children to help them cope with the demands of their own lives.

The structural context within which family life occurs can affect family interactions in a variety of ways. Problems may arise in connection with the demands placed on the family by institutions of the larger society, or as a result of its position in the society's stratification system. A basic contradiction that is inherent in the institution of the family is the need to maintain the individuality of each member while providing love and support for him or her within a set of interdependent relationships.

From a conflict perspective, changes in the family as an institution cannot occur without conflict both within the family and between the family and other institutions. Ideological and political conflict also play a part in changes in the nature of the family.

Functionalist theorists have called attention to the loss of family functions that occurs as other social institutions assume functions that were previously reserved for the family. At the same time, they note that modern families play a vital part in early-childhood socialization, in the emotional lives of their members, and in preparing older children for adult roles.

GLOSSARY

family: a group of people related by blood, marriage, or adoption (**p. 464**).

kinship: the role relations among people who consider themselves related by blood, marriage, or adoption (**p. 464**).

conjugal family: a husband and wife and their children, if any (**p. 464**).

nuclear family: two or more people related by blood, marriage, or adoption who share a household (**p. 464**).

family of orientation: the nuclear family in which a person is born and raised (**p. 465**).

family of procreation: the nuclear family a person forms through marriage or cohabitation (**p. 465**).

extended family: an individual's nuclear family plus the nuclear families of his or her blood relatives (**p. 466**).

endogamy: a norm specifying that a person brought up in a particular culture may marry within the cultural group (**p. 474**).

exogamy: a norm specifying that a person brought up in a particular culture may marry outside the cultural group (**p. 474**).

homogamy: the tendency to marry a person from a similar social background (**p. 475**).

WHERE TO FIND IT

Books

How Americans Use Time (John P. Robinson; Praeger, 1977). An excellent source of comparative data on how much time men and women spend on various activities in their families and households.

Marriage, Divorce, Remarriage (Andrew J. Cherlin; Harvard University Press, 1981). Perhaps the best available source of data and analysis on marriage, divorce, and remarriage and some of the consequences of changes in the family as an institution.

Surviving the Breakup: How Children and Parents Cope with Divorce (Judith S. Wallerstein and Joan Berlin Kelly; Basic Books, 1985). Discusses the psychological and sociological consequences of divorce and family re-formation.

The Family Crucible (Augustus Y. Napier and Carl Whitaker; Bantam, 1980). An introduction to the dynamics of family interaction and family therapy.

Rachel and Her Children: Homeless Families in America (Jonathan Kozol; Crown, 1988). An in-depth study of homeless families. Kozol's purpose is to document the impact of homelessness on children and to pay tribute to the dignity, courage, and strength of many homeless parents.

Journals

Journal of Marriage and the Family Published quarterly by the National Council on Family Relations, Minneapolis, Minnesota. The best journal on family research in the United States.

Sex Roles: A Journal of Research A monthly journal published by Plenum Press.

Adolescence A quarterly journal that publishes divergent points of view on the nature and problems of adolescence.

Other Sources

Current Population Reports A series of special reports on household composition, marriage and divorce, and labor-force participation is available in the census section of your library or from the nearest office of the U.S. Department of Labor or U.S. Publications Office. These reports present detailed demographic and economic data and include comparisons with earlier years.

Vital Statistics of the United States, vol. III: **Marriage and Divorce** An annual compilation that presents a complete count of marriages and divorces in the preceding year. Data are broken down by age, race, previous marital status, and other characteristics.

VISUAL SOCIOLOGY

An Extended Family

The members of the Ivanovich family shown in these photos are gypsies of the Boyash tribe. Only a few of the family's seventy-three members are shown here. A remarkable fact about this gypsy family is that in the midst of poverty and a transient life-style, a highly cohesive extended family thrives from one generation to the next (Kornblum, 1975). All of the family's members, from Alexandre and Marie, the patriarch and matriarch, to the youngest children, live in a single settlement, although of course there are nuclear families within the extended family. The man in the handsome couple shown outside their wagon is the son of Marie and Alexandre Ivanovich. The man training the monkey has married into the family. His name is Cortez, and he is a Boyash whose family had traveled in Spain, which is how he acquired his Spanish name.

During many centuries of wandering through more sedentary societies, the gypsies have become an urban people. They thrive in towns and cities, yet they are constantly moving from one urban base to another. In the case of the Ivanovich family, their occupation keeps them on the road; because the family earns much of its income by training animals for circuses and street shows, they must do a great deal of traveling to buy animals or trade them. Yet wherever they move they keep the extended family together, and with it the gypsy language and culture.

Before the age of radio and television, traveling carnivals and circuses often featured trained bears that danced and climbed a huge ball, as shown here. But today such shows are dying out, as they cannot compete with the thrills offered by television and the movies. And the younger members of the Ivanovich family are more interested in learning

how to repair autos and trucks than in training animals. Only Marie and Alexandre are fully versed in the ancient lore of bear training. Cortez may take over in time, but even so no one is sure who will follow him.

Despite these changes, there is still a demand for the folk entertainment provided by the Boyash gypsies and other carnival people. In this age of electronic entertainment they are a curious throwback to an age of minstrels and bear tamers. And so they draw crowds in the streets of Paris, where these pictures were taken. The trickle of coins from the crowds enables the Ivanovich family to stay together and to socialize new generations into gypsy life in the midst of one of the world's most modern and cosmopolitan cities.

Photographs by Yehuda Yaniv and William Kornblum

CHAPTER OUTLINE

● **Religion in Society**

- The Power of Faith
- Varieties of Religious Belief
- Religion and Social Change

● **Structure and Change in Modern Religions**

- Forms of Religious Organization
- Religious Interaction and Change

● **Trends in Religion in the United States**

- Unofficial Religion
- Religiosity
- Religious Pluralism
- Religious Organizations and Free Riders
- Fundamentalism
- Conclusion

Margo Smith

A Sunday morning television evangelist

CHAPTER 16

RELIGION

The show is called *Thoughts on the Eternal: Sunday Moral Sermon*. It features a fifteen-minute sermon by a guest minister or other spiritual guide. Today's opening homily was given by an Orthodox clergyman in priestly robes who exhorted listeners to "pause and tear yourself away from the conveyor belt of your factory, from the conveyor belt of our streets. Hear the silence that carries healing and creative force."

This televised sermon would not merit much attention were it not that *Thoughts on the Eternal* appears on government-controlled Soviet Television. Ever since the Bolshevik Revolution of 1917, religion and religious practices have been officially banned in the Soviet Union. Russian Orthodox Christianity, the nation's major religion, has declined dramatically: Where once there were more than 50,000 Russian Orthodox churches, there are now fewer than 8,000. Those that have managed to remain in existence have done so under great strain. Their members feared that their attendance at church, if it became known to the authorities, might jeopardize their careers. Like the Orthodox believers, Muslims, Ukrainian Catholics, Protestants, and Jews who wish to worship have done so clandestinely.

According to Leninist and, later, Stalinist thinking, religion had to be suppressed because it led to antirevolutionary attitudes. The Soviet state was to be godless, following Marx's dictum that "religion is the opiate of the masses"—that it deludes people into feeling better and forgetting that they are oppressed by those who exploit their labor. In a true communist society religion would be unnecessary because the old forms of oppression that made it so popular would be ended

In reality, religion never died out in the Soviet Union. Devout people found ways to attend church services. Millions more yearned for spirituality in their lives. Under glasnost the state has reluctantly come to the conclusion that television can meet some of that need, but at this writing none of the sermons on Soviet television has actually mentioned God.

Thousands of miles away, in Tulsa, Oklahoma, the Rev. Oral Roberts not only extols the glory of God on television (before an audience estimated at more than 800,000 households) but has also pioneered techniques for using the power of television to raise millions of dollars in funds for Oral Roberts University and other activities of his evangelical ministry. Long ago Roberts learned what Soviet spiritual leaders will learn if someday the state grants them free access to television. "At this moment in history," Roberts asserts, "the most effective way to reach the masses—in person—is through television." A few years ago Roberts proved this by claiming on television that God had told him to raise $8 million in two months or he would be "called home." The fund-raising drive was successful.

But television preachers can also wilt in the glare of the public spotlight. This happened to the Rev. James Bakker, who was found guilty of defrauding the lucrative evangelical ministry, PTL, that he and his wife Tammy had shaped into an organization with a multimillion-dollar annual budget. Bakker was charged with siphoning off the nonprofit organization's funds to support his lavish lifestyle, and unseemly aspects of his sexual conduct were aired on national television.

Allegiance to television evangelists runs deep in many parts of the United States, especially the South and Southwest, but in the aftermath of this and other scandals among famous television preachers the ambitions of many evangelists have been thwarted. Thus at the same time that the Soviets are learning that television is a proper medium for spirituality, at least in a muted form, Americans are learning to take some televised spirituality with more than a grain of salt.

RELIGION IN SOCIETY

I f televised religion is popular throughout the world, it is not because of the power of television but because of the power of religion. Religion, one of the oldest human institutions, is also among the most changeable and complex. On the one hand, religion expresses our deepest yearnings for spiritual enlightenment and understanding; on the other, conflicts over religious beliefs and practices have given rise to persecution, wars, and much human suffering. Little wonder, therefore, that the founders of sociology, including Émile Durkheim, Karl Marx, and Max Weber, all wrote extensively about the power of religion and the great changes religion has undergone as societies have evolved.

Like other major social institutions, religion is not easy to define. One could begin with a definition that has a concept of God as its core, but many religions do not have a clear concept of God. One could define religion in terms of the emotions of spirituality, oneness with nature, awe, mystery, and many other feelings, but that would not be a very helpful definition because emotions are extremely difficult to capture in words. Taking another tack, one might think in terms of organized religion—churches, congregations, ministers, rabbis, and so on—but clearly the organizational aspect of religion is just one of the institution's many dimensions. It is frustrating to have to work so hard to define something that seems so commonplace, yet without a good working definition of religion it is impossible to compare different religions or refer to particular aspects of religion.

We can approach a working definition of religion by saying that **religion** is any set of coherent answers to the dilemmas of human existence that makes the world meaningful. From this point of view, religion is how human beings express their feelings about such ultimate concerns as sickness or death.

> *Religion may be defined as any set of coherent answers to the dilemmas of human existence that makes the world meaningful.*

Throughout most of human history, until the past century or two, religion dominated all cultural life, as it still does in many societies. This famous engraving of the Four Horsemen of the Apocalypse by Albrecht the end of the earth, which is brought by three riders: Death, War, and Famine. The figure on the white horse represents Christ come to Judgment. Humans still face these threats, but increasingly they view them as caused by their own actions and, with the exception of death in old age, as within their own control.

The Metropolitan Museum of Art; gift of Junius S. Moran, 1919

Almost all religions involve their adherents in a system of beliefs and practices that express devotion to the supernatural and foster deep feelings of spirituality. In this sense, we say that religion functions to meet the spiritual needs of individuals.

But religion has also been defined in terms of its social function: It is a system of beliefs and rituals that serves to bind people together through shared worship, thereby creating a social group. **Rituals** are formal patterns of activity that express symbolically a set of shared meanings; in the case of religious rituals such as baptism or communion, the shared meanings are sacred. The term **sacred** refers to phenomena that are regarded as extraordinary, transcendent, and outside the everyday course of events—that is, as supernatural. The sacred is represented by a wide variety of symbols, which may include a god or set of gods; a holy person such as the Buddha; various revered writings like the Bible, the Torah, and the Koran; holy objects such as the cross or the star of David; holy cities like Jerusalem or Mecca; and much else. The term **profane** refers to all phenomena that are not sacred.

The Power of Faith

Until comparatively recent times religion dominated the cultural life of human societies. Activities that are now performed by other cultural institutions, particularly education, art, and the media, used to be the province of religious leaders and organizations. In hunting-and-gathering bands and in many tribal societies, the holy person, or shaman, was also the teacher and communicator of the society's beliefs and values. In early agrarian societies the priesthood was a powerful force; only the priests were literate and, hence, able to interpret and preserve the society's sacred texts, which represented the culture's most strongly held values and norms. For example, in ancient Egypt, in which the pharaoh was worshipped as a god, his organization of regional and local priests controlled society.

Today religion continues to play an important part in the lives of people throughout the world even though the influence of organized religions is diminishing in many societies. In the United States, for example, the Gallup Poll routinely asks Americans whether they believe in God. In 1944, 96 percent of the population said that they were believers; in the 1980s the proportion of believers remained over 90 percent (Gallup, 1982; Piazza & Glock, 1979). The strength of religious attitudes and the influence of some religions can also be seen in the conflict over abortion, which plays such a prominent role in American politics, and in the controversies generated by Christian fundamentalists who believe in the literal interpretation of the Bible and therefore deny the validity of evolutionary theory. Outside the United States, the Islamic world is torn by religious strife between liberals and fundamentalists, and Lebanon and Northern Ireland remain deeply divided owing largely to conflict between Protestants and Catholics or between Christians and Muslims.

At the same time that religion is a source of division and conflict it can also be a force for healing social problems and moving masses of people toward greater insight into their common humanity. This occurs at the micro level of interaction, for example, in groups like Alcoholics Anonymous, in which spirituality is an essential part of the recovery program. At the macro level, the power of faith can be seen in major social movements like that occurring in Poland, where the Catholic Church has inspired a nonviolent struggle for a more open society.

Secularization and Its Limits. Despite the great power of spirituality, since medieval times the traditional dominance of religion in many spheres of life has been greatly reduced. The process by which this has occurred is termed **secularization**. This process, according to Robert A. Nisbet (1970), "results in . . . respect for values of utility rather than of sacredness alone, control of the environment rather than passive submission to it, and, in some ways most importantly, concern with man's present welfare on this earth rather than his supposed immortal re-

lation to the gods" (p. 388). Secularization usually accompanies the increasing differentiation of cultural institutions—that is, the separation of other institutions from religion. In Europe in the Middle Ages, for example, there were no schools separate from the church. The state, too, was thought of as encompassed by the church or at least as legitimated by the official state religion and church organization. Laws and courts were guided by religious doctrine, and clerical law could often be as important as civil law—indeed, to be tried as a heretic often meant torture and death. Churches engaged in large-scale economic activity, owned much land and property, and often mounted their own armed forces.

The Renaissance, the Enlightenment, and the revolutions of the eighteenth and nineteenth centuries all speeded the process of differentiation in which schools, science, laws, courts, and other institutions gained in-

Box 16–1: **The Huichol Artist**

The conquest of what is now Latin America by Spain and Portugal in the seventeenth century also established the Catholic church as the dominant religious institution in Latin America. Missionary priests enlisted the help of Indians to build churches, missions, and schools as bases from which they would work diligently "to destroy or incorporate religious practices with which the Indians had met their religious needs, relieved their anxieties, and established a moral order" (Stinchcombe, 1968, p. 116). One result of these efforts was that the artistic expressions that represented the Indians' conception of the universe were replaced with expressions of Christian symbolism.

But in remote valleys the ancient cultures still survive. The Huichol Indians, for example, live on communal land in an extremely isolated part of Mexico's Sierra Madre Occidental. There they create pictures by laying brightly colored yarns on boards covered with beeswax. Each picture represents an aspect of the

ancient religious beliefs of the Central American Indians. All of the symbolic and sacred figures on each board are ablaze with color.

In 1985 an art gallery in New York City showed a selection of works by the Huichol artist José Benítez Sánchez. Sophisticated New Yorkers who had read reviews of Sanchez's work crowded the small gallery and marveled at his pictures. At other times the gallery might exhibit more secular art: the "hard-edge" art of the school known as neorealism, or pop art, which uses the imagery of advertising, or abstract-expressionist art, which explores shape, form, and color without using objects or symbols. These forms of art differ dramatically from the work of Indian artists like Sanchez or the art of African wood carvers or Asian calligraphers. In the Indian and African societies art is not differentiated from religion; it is a form of religious expression, and from the viewpoint of the artist the work has less meaning when it decorates

dependence from religious control. However, this process has not occurred at the same rate throughout the world. For example, the removal of education from the control of religious institutions has occurred more slowly in some societies than in others. In Eastern Europe all education was controlled by the state until very recently. In most Western European and American countries there are religious schools, but these are separate from and overshadowed by the state-run educational system (van den Berghe, 1975).

Another example of the increasing differentiation of religion from other institutions is the diminished importance of religion in the arts. "Traditionally," wrote Pierre van den Berghe (1975),

much of music, painting, sculpture, and architecture was devoted to the glorification of God (or his representative, the king). The medieval cathedrals soared loftily from [a] sea of puny houses. . . . In Manhattan, it is St. Patrick's Cathedral that is dwarfed in a forest of skyscrapers. Bach was a church organist: Leonard Bernstein is a jet-set entrepreneur. Van Eyck . . . painted chaste madonnas: Renoir . . . luscious nudes. [p. 213]

Box 16-1 describes a form of artistic expression that has not become secularized, although it is admired in secular societies.

The emergence of new cultural institutions and the weakening of the influence of religion does not result in complete secularization. People who are free to determine their own religious beliefs and practices may attend church less or not at all, but total secularization does not occur (Stark and Bainbridge, 1980). Moreover, in almost every major society one can find examples of conflict over the boundaries between religious and secular institutions (Fenn, 1978).

Religious sentiments and behavior persist even in highly secularized societies like the United States. As sociologist Robert

Tatei Atsinari, José Benitez Sánchez. Photograph by Freda Leinwand.

the home of a well-off couple in a Western capital than it does when it is placed in the home of kin who can appreciate its symbolic meaning.

To fully understand the art of the Huichol artists, one must first try to understand their spiritual or religious world view. When Sanchez explains the symbolism of his art, for example, he begins with the Huichol's perception of their relationship to nature: "Everything is sacrificed on our behalf: the Corn gives us its daughters, Deer its young, the Sun its arrows, and the Sea its plumed-serpent daughters, the rain-filled clouds" (quoted in Negrin, 1985–1986, p. 11). The Huichol are brought up to understand these relationships between humans and nature, and therefore they can feel the spiritual power of the works of Indian artists like Sanchez. People in more secular societies are less able to appreciate this aspect of Huichol art, even though they may be impressed by its bold designs and vivid colors.

Wuthnow (1988) writes, "The assumption that religion in modern societies would gradually diminish in importance or else become less capable of influencing public life was once widely accepted. That assumption has now become a matter of dispute. . . . Modern religion is resilient and yet subject to cultural influences; it does not merely survive or decline, but adapts to its environment in complex ways" (p. 474). We have already seen evidence of this resilience in the way Soviet spirituality is easing into the mass media. In fact, at this writing President Mikhail Gorbachev of the Soviet Union has just met with the Pope—the first meeting between a Soviet Communist leader and the spiritual head of the Roman Catholic church. On the eve of that meeting Gorbachev stated that the Soviet leadership has recognized that "the moral values that religion generated and embodied for centuries can help in the work of renewal in our country, too" (quoted in Haberman, 1989, p. A1).

Major World Religions. In a 1913 essay Max Weber commented that "by 'world religions' we understand the five religions or religiously determined systems of life-regulation which have known how to gather multitudes of confessors around them" (1958/1913, p. 267). Among these Weber included, in addition to Christianity, "the Confucian, Hinduist, Buddhist, and Islamic religious ethics." He added that despite its small population of adherents, Judaism should also be considered a world religion because of its influence on Christianity and Islam as well as on Western ethics and values even outside the religious sphere of life.

In discussing religion sociologists often refer to the "Islamic world" of the Middle East, the "Roman Catholic world" of Latin America and southern Europe, the "Hindu world" of the Indian subcontinent, and the "Buddhist world" of the Far East. The United States, northern Europe, and Australia are among the societies in which Protestantism is strongest. There are also, of course, the nations of Eastern Europe and the Soviet Union, where until recently communism as

These two pictures of cathedrals provide a graphic illustration of secularization. In the medieval town, the cathedral dominated the landscape; it was the highest and symbolically the most important building. In the modern city, even the great cathedral is dwarfed by the greater scale and importance of the commercial buildings surrounding it.

a civil religion was the only legitimate belief system (although millions of people resisted the state's efforts to eradicate traditional religious faiths) (Robertson, 1985). The distribution of the world's major religions is shown in Figure 16-1.

Varieties of Religious Belief

The religions practiced throughout the world today vary from belief in magic and supernatural spirits to complicated ideas of god and saints, as well as secular religions in which there is faith but not God. With such a wide range of religious beliefs and practices to consider, it would be useful to classify them in a systematic way. One often-used system classifies religions according to their central belief. In this scheme the multiplicity of religious forms is reduced to a more manageable list of five major types: simple supernaturalism, animism, theism, abstract ideals, and civil religion. In this section we describe each type briefly. Be warned, though, that not all religions fit neatly into these basic categories.

Simple Supernaturalism. In simpler and rather isolated societies, people may believe in a great force or spirit, but they do not have a well-defined concept of God or a set of rituals involving God. Studies by anthropologists have found that some isolated peoples—

Figure 16–1: **Estimated Religious Membership, by Continent**
(in millions)

NORTH AMERICA (271)

Roman Catholic	142	(52%)
Protestant	113	(42%)
Jewish	8	(3%)
(All Other)	8	(3%)

EUROPE (360)

Roman Catholic	178	(49%)
Protestant	111	(31%)
Eastern Orthodox	45	(13%)
(All Other)	26	(7%)

ASIA (1403)

Hindu	459	(33%)
Moslem	378	(27%)
Buddhist	248	(18%)
Confucian	158	(11%)
(All Other)	160	(11%)

AFRICA (302)

Moslem	153	(51%)
Protestant	81	(27%)
Roman Catholic	58	(19%)
(All Other)	10	(3%)

SOUTH AMERICA (200)

Roman Catholic	187	(94%)
Protestant	11	(5%)
(All Other)	2	(1%)

OCEANIA (19)

Protestant	13	(68%)
Roman Catholic	5	(26%)
(All Other)	1	(5%)

THE WORLD (2,555)

Roman Catholic	628	(25%)
Moslem	554	(22%)
Hindu	461	(18%)
Protestant	373	(15%)
Buddhist	249	(10%)
(All Other)	290	(11%)

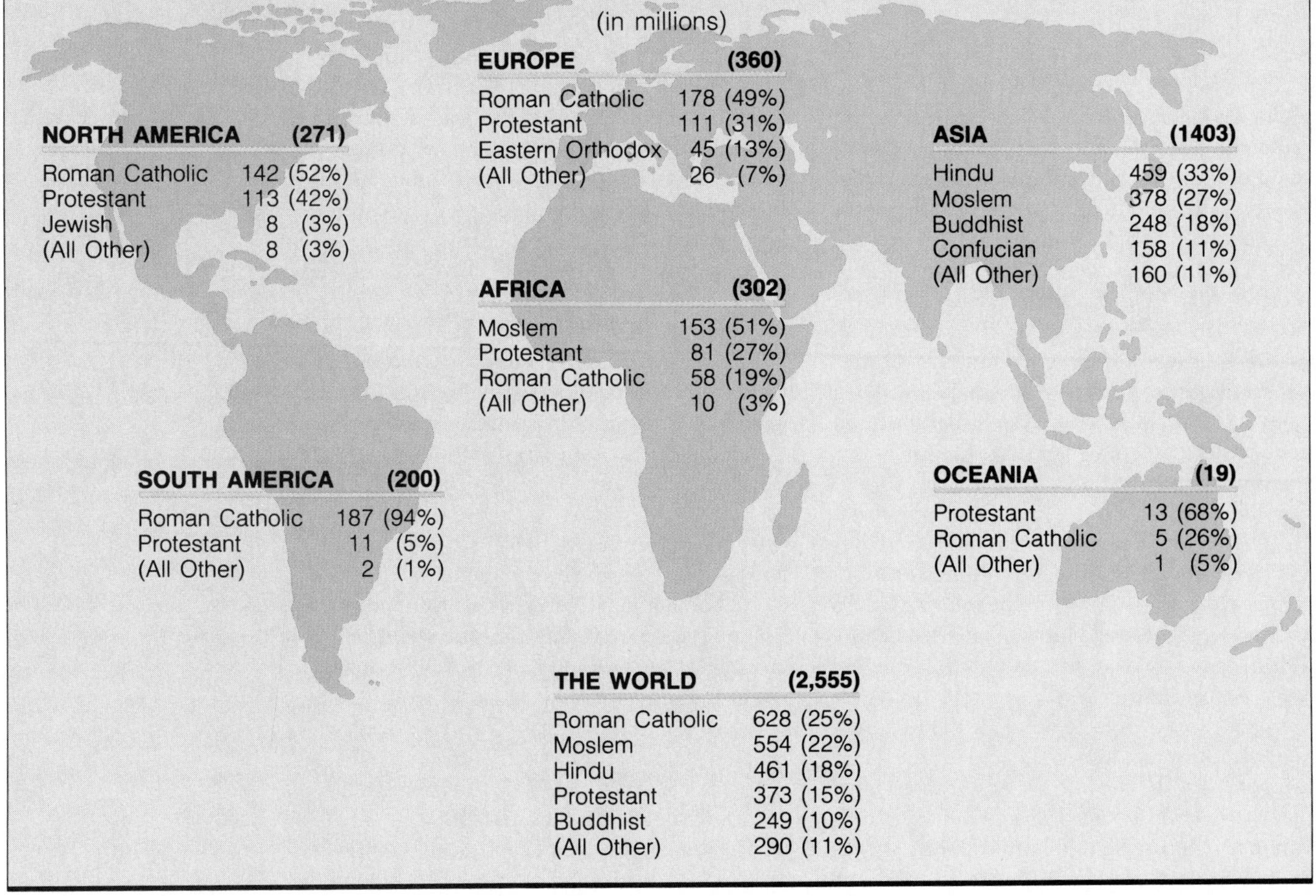

for example, South Pacific island cultures and Eskimo tribes—believe strongly in the power of a supernatural force but do not attempt to embody that force in a visualized conception of God. In this form of religion, called **simple supernaturalism**, there is no discontinuity between the world of the senses and the supernatural; all natural phenomena are part of a single force. This can be seen in the following remarks by an Inuit Eskimo: "When I was small I knew a man who came from the polar bears. He had a low voice and was big. That man knew when he was a cub and his bear mother was bringing him to the land from the ocean. He remembered it" (quoted in Steltzer, 1982, p. 111).

Animism. More common among hunting-and-gathering societies is a form of religion termed **animism**, in which all forms of life and all aspects of the earth are inhabited by gods or supernatural powers. Most of the indigenous peoples of the Western Hemisphere were animists, and so were many of the tribal peoples of Africa before the European conquests. Europeans almost invariably branded American Indians "heathens and barbarians" because, among other things, the Indians believed that "people journeyed into supernatural realms and returned, animals conversed with each other and humans, and the spirits of rocks and trees had to be placated" (Jennings, 1975, p. 48). The same can be said of European attitudes toward African religions. Determined to subjugate nature and make the earth yield more wealth for new populations, the Europeans could not appreciate the meanings of animism for people who lived more closely in touch with nature.

Yet if one takes some time to read about the perceptions of animistic religions, it becomes clear that they contain much wisdom for our beleaguered planet. In one beautifully written account, an Oglala Sioux medicine man, Black Elk, speaks "the story of all life that is holy and is good to tell, and of us two-leggeds sharing in it with the four-leggeds and the wings of the air and all green things; for these are children of one mother and their father is one Spirit" (Neihardt, 1959/1932, p. 1). Black Elk's prayer continues:

Grandfather, Great Spirit, lean close to the earth that you may hear the voice I send. You towards where the sun goes down, behold me; thunder Beings, behold me! You where the White Giant lives in power, behold me! You where the sun shines continually, whence come the day-break star and the day, behold me! You in the depths of the heavens, an eagle of power, behold! And you, Mother Earth, the only Mother, you who have shown mercy to your children! [p. 5]

Traces of animism can also be seen in the religious beliefs of the ancient Egyptians, Greeks, and Romans. The Greeks, for example, spoke of naiads inhabiting rivers and springs, and of dryads inhabiting forests. These varieties of nymphs were believed to be part of the natural environment in which they dwelled, but sometimes they took on semi-human qualities. They thus bridged the gap between a quasi-animastic religion and the more familiar theistic systems that evolved in Greece and Rome.

Theism. **Theistic** belief systems usually conceive of gods as separate from humans and from other living things on the earth, although the gods are in some way responsible for the creation of humans and for their fate. Many ancient religions were **polytheistic**, meaning that they included numerous gods, all of whom occupied themselves with some aspect of the universe and of human life.. In the religion of the ancient Greeks, warfare was the concern of Ares; music, healing, and prophecy were the domain of Apollo; his sister Artemis was concerned with hunting; Poseidon was the god of seafaring; Athena was the goddess of handicrafts and intellectual pursuits; and so on. A similar division of concerns and attributes could be found among the gods of the Romans and, later, among the gods of the Celtic tribes of Gaul and Britain.

The ancient Hebrews were among the first people to evolve a **monotheistic** religion, one centered on belief in a single all-powerful God who determines human fate and can be addressed through prayer. This belief is expressed in the central creed of the Jews: "Hear O Israel, the Lord our God, the Lord is One." Jewish monotheism, based on the central idea of a covenant between God and the Jewish people (as represented in the written laws of

the Ten Commandments, for example), helped stimulate the formal codification of religious law and ritual in writing, so that the Jews became known as "the people of the book." As they traveled and settled throughout the Middle East, the Jews were able to take their religion with them and hold onto the purity of their beliefs and practices (Smith, 1952; Johnson, 1987).

Christianity and Islam are also monotheistic religions. The Roman Catholic version of Christianity envisions God as embodied in a Holy Trinity consisting of God the Father, Christ the Son, and the Holy Spirit of God, which has the ability to inspire the human spirit. But Mary and the saints are angels of God and may at times be worshipped as well, suggesting that the basic monotheism of Christianity can be interpreted in such a way as to include other deities.

The fundamental beliefs of Islam are similar in many respects to those of Judaism and Christianity. Islam is a monotheistic religion centering on the worship of one God, Allah, according to the teachings of the Koran as given by Allah to Mohammed, the great prophet of the Muslim faith. In his early preachings Mohammed appears to have believed that the followers of Jesus and the believers in Judaism would recognize him as God's messenger and realize that Allah was the same as the God they worshipped. The fundamental aim of Islam is to serve God as he requires in the Koran.

> *Polytheistic belief systems include numerous gods; monotheistic systems are centered on belief in a single all-powerful God.*

Another basically monotheistic religion, Hinduism, is difficult to categorize. On the one hand, it incorporates a strong idea of an all-powerful God who is everywhere yet is "unsearchable"; on the other hand, it conceives of a God who can be represented variously as the Creator (Brahma), the Preserver (Vishnu), and the Destroyer (Shiva). Each of these personifications takes a number of forms in Hindu ritual and art. Of all the great world religions, Hinduism teaches most forcefully that all religions are roughly equal "paths to the same summit."

Abstract Ideals. In China, Japan, and other societies of the Far East, religions predominate that are centered not on devotion to a god or gods but on an abstract ideal of spirituality and human behavior. The central belief of Buddhism, perhaps the most important of these religions, is embodied in these thoughts of Gautama Buddha:

Life is a Journey
Death is a return to the Earth
The universe is like an inn
The passing years are like dust

Like all the great religions of the world, Buddhism has many branches. The ideal that unifies them all, however, is the teaching that worship is not a matter of prayer to God but a quest for the experience of godliness within oneself through meditation and awareness.

Another important religion based on abstract ideals is Confucianism, which is derived from the teachings of the philosopher Confucius (551–479 B.C.). The sayings of Confucius are still revered throughout much of the Far East, especially among the Chinese, although the formal study of Confucius's thought has been banned since the Communist Revolution of the early 1950s. The central belief of Confucianism is that one must learn and practice the wisdom of the ancients. "He that is really good," Confucius taught, "can never be unhappy. He that is really wise can never be perplexed. He that is really brave can never be afraid" (quoted in McNeill, 1963, p. 231).

In Confucianism the central goal of the individual is to become a good ruler or a good and loyal follower and thus to carry out the tao of his or her position. *Tao* is an untranslatable word that refers to the practice of virtues that make a person excellent at his or her discipline. As is evident even in this brief description, Confucianism is a set of ideals and sayings that tend toward conservativism and acceptance of the status quo, although the wise ruler should be able to improve society for those in lesser positions. Little wonder that under communism this ancient and highly popular set of moral principles and teachings was banned in favor of what sociologists call a civil religion.

Civil Religion. In recent years some social scientists, notably Robert Bellah (1970), have expanded the definition of religion to include so-called **civil religions**. These are collections of beliefs, and rituals for communicating those beliefs, that exist outside religious institutions. Often, as in socialist societies, they are attached to the institutions of the state. Marxism-Leninism is often said to be a civil religion, symbolized by the reverence paid to Lenin's tomb in the Soviet Union. Central to communism as a civil religion is the idea that private property is evil while property held in common by all members of the society (be it the work group, the community, or the entire nation) is good. The struggle against private property results in the creation of the socialist personality, which values all human lives and devalues excessive emphasis on individual success, especially success measured by the accumulation of property. Although the failure of communist regimes is dramatically apparent at this writing, there are millions of people in the Soviet Union and East-

A gathering in Moscow's Red Square illustrates civil religion in action. The giant photos of secular leaders like Lenin are analogous to statues of saints. The pope, on the other hand, is the sacred leader of a traditional religion, Roman Catholicism.

in which a nonsectarian God is invoked to protect the nation's unity ("One nation under God . . .").

Although there is no doubt that Lenin's tomb and the American flag are viewed as sacred in some contexts, neither communism nor American patriotism can compete with the major world religions in the power of their central ideals and their spirituality. In consequence, sociologists tend to concentrate on religions in the traditional sense—that is, on the enactment of rituals that represent the place of sacred beliefs in human life. In the remainder of this chapter, therefore, we discuss the distribution and structure of religious institutions and the processes by which new ones arise.

Religion and Social Change

Now that the nations behind the former "iron curtain" are enjoying new freedoms, the role of religion in bringing about social change is an important aspect of life in those societies. Indeed, in many parts of the world religion is one of the primary forces opposing or supporting change. However, it is not always a simple matter to predict whether religion will encourage change or hinder it. In Israel, for example, highly orthodox Jews, though they account for a small minority of the electorate, hold the votes necessary to keep the ruling party in power. Because the orthodox political parties favor continued settlement on the West Bank of the Jordan River and oppose the creation of a Palestinian state near Israel's borders, they have used their voting power to produce a stalemate in Middle Eastern politics.

In the United States, the Catholic church plays an active role in seeking social change. The church strongly opposes women's right to obtain abortions legally. Instead, it supports a return to the traditional view of abortion as a crime, which is based on the belief that humans must submit to the will of God and not use their technological skills to achieve power over life and death. In this instance, therefore, although the church is promoting

ern Europe who were socialized to believe in these principles.

In the United States, certain aspects of patriotic feeling are sometimes said to amount to a civil religion: reverence for the flag, the Constitution and the Declaration of Independence, and other symbols of America is cited as an example. Thus most major public events, be they commencements, political rallies, or Super Bowl games, begin with civil-religious rituals like the singing of the national anthem or the recitation of the Pledge of Allegiance,

social change, the change represents a return to an earlier moral standard. Throughout much of Latin America, in contrast, the Catholic church is fighting in support of the masses of urban and rural poor who seek social justice and equitable economic development. In Brazil, for example, the typical Catholic priest or nun favors the political left, which seeks a more egalitarian distribution of wealth and income and is highly critical of the rich.

We could add many other examples of the role played by religion and religious organizations in social change. But in attempting to generalize about the relationship between religion and social change it is useful to return briefly to classic sociological theories. The pioneering European sociologists, particularly Karl Marx and Max Weber, noted the prominent role of religion in social change. But they wondered whether the influence of religious faith is a determining force in social change or whether religious sentiments and the activities of religious organizations are an outgrowth of changes in more basic economic and political institutions.

Marx, as we have seen, believed that economic institutions are fundamental to all societies and that they are the source of social change. In his view, religion and other cultural institutions are shaped by economic and political institutions; they are a "superstructure" that simply reflects the values of those institutions—of markets, firms, the government, the military, and so on. The function of cultural institutions, especially religion, is to instill in the masses the values of the dominant class. In this sense they can be said to shape the consciousness of a people, but they do so in such a way as to justify existing patterns of economic exploitation and the existing class structure. Religion, in Marx's words, is "the opiate of the masses" because it eases suffering through prayer and ritual and deludes the masses into accepting their situation as divinely ordained rather than organizing to change the social system.

For Weber, on the other hand, religion can be the *cause* of major social change rather than the outcome or reflection of changes in other institutions. Weber set forth this thesis in one of his most famous works, *The Prot-*

estant Ethic and the Spirit of Capitalism (1974/ 1904). Noting that the rise of Protestantism in Europe had coincided with the emergence of capitalism, Weber hypothesized that the Protestant Reformation had brought about a significant change in cultural values and that this was responsible for the more successful development of capitalist economic systems in Protestant regions. As Weber explained it, Protestantism instilled in its followers certain values that were conducive to business enterprise, which in turn resulted in the accumulation of wealth. Because the early Protestants believed that wealth was not supposed to be spent on luxuries or "the pleasures of the flesh," the only alternative was to invest it in new or existing business enterprises— in other words, to contribute to the rapid economic growth that is characteristic of capitalist systems (Brown, 1965). This view was reinforced by the belief—also part of the Protestant ethic—that a person who worked hard was likely to be among those predestined for salvation.

Some have questioned the validity of Weber's thesis regarding Protestantism and early capitalism, but religious institutions are undoubtedly capable of assuming a major role in shaping modern societies. Throughout the Islamic world there are currents of orthodoxy and reform that threaten to cause both civil and international wars. And as we have seen, in much of Eastern Europe as well as in the Soviet Union religious groups are in the vanguard of the movement to reform the communist system. So Marx was wrong in his claim that religion functions largely to maintain the existing values of more basic social institutions. On the contrary, they often lead to new ways of organizing societies, to new political and economic institutions as well as whole new lifestyles.

The Marxian view of religion is still relevant to those who are critical of the influence of religious institutions. These critics assert that religion, along with other cultural institutions such as education, serves to reaffirm and perpetuate inequalities of wealth, prestige, and power. When the poor are encouraged to pray for a better life, for example, they are further oppressed by a religion that prevents them from realizing they need to marshal their own power to challenge the status quo. Thus there is still some question as to whether (and how much) religious institutions change society in any fundamental way.

To make informed judgments about this and related issues, we need to have a better understanding of the nature of religious organizations and how they function in modern societies. In the next section, therefore, we describe the main types of religious organizations. In the following section we focus on trends in religious belief and practice in the United States.

This photograph of a religious festival in the province of Chiapas in Mexico clearly shows the social organization of the village church. The male officials of the church (visible in the background) march with banners and candles while the women bear the saint through the village.

Courtesy of Susan Kornblum

STRUCTURE AND CHANGE IN MODERN RELIGIONS

Religion today is a highly structured institution, with numerous statuses and roles within a variety of organizations as well as many kinds of smaller, less bureaucratic groups. This was not always so. The religions of tribal peoples were not highly institutionalized; that is, there were no separate organizations like churches or interfaith councils or youth fellowships. It is true that the occupational status of holy person or priest might exist. Thus most Native American peoples had spiritual leaders who specialized in the rituals and symbols through which the members of the tribe could address the Great Spirit and the sacred spirits of their ancestors. But even in societies that had spiritual leaders or priests, religious practice was intertwined with tribal and family life: There was no concept of the church as a separate institution specializing in religious rituals.

Religion as a fully differentiated institution developed in agrarian societies, and it was in such societies that formal religious organizations first appeared. As we saw in Chapter 3, agrarian societies produce enough surplus food to support a class of priests and other specialists in religious rituals. In those less complex societies religion was incorporated into village and family life; it had not yet become differentiated into a recognized, separate institution with its own statuses and roles (Parsons, 1966). Over time, however, the development of religious institutions resulted in a wide variety of organizations devoted to religious practice. Today those organizations include the church, the sect, and the denomination.

Forms of Religious Organization

Churches and Sects. **A church** may be defined as a religious organization that has strong ties to the larger society. Often in its history it has enjoyed the loyalty of most of the society's members; indeed, it may have been linked with the state itself (Weber, 1963/1922).

An example is the Church of England, or Anglican church. A **sect**, by contrast, is an organization that rejects the religious beliefs or practices of established churches. Whereas the church distributes the benefits of religious participation to anyone who enters the sanctuary and stays to follow the service, the sect limits the benefits of membership (i.e., salvation, fellowship, common prayer) to those who qualify on narrower grounds of membership and belief (Weber, 1963/1922; McGuire, 1987).

Sects require strong commitment from their members and usually are formed when a small group of church members splits off to form a rival organization. The sect may not completely reject the beliefs and rituals of the church from which it arose, but it changes them enough to be considered a separate organization. Most "storefront churches" are actually sects that have developed their own particular interpretations of religious ritual.

An important difference between churches and sects is that churches draw their adherents from a large social environment—that is, from a large pool of possible members—whereas the size of the population from which a sect draws its members tends to be small (Stark and Bainbridge, 1979). Also, churches make relatively limited demands on their members while sects make heavy claims on their members' time, money, and emotional commitment. As Robert Wuthnow (1988) writes, "Churches attempt to regulate or fulfill a few of the activities or needs of large numbers of people; sects attempt to regulate or fulfill many of the activities or needs of small numbers of people" (p. 495).

Denominations. A third type of religious organization is the **denomination**. Unlike a sect, a denomination is on good terms with the religious institution from which it developed, but it must compete with other denominations for members. An example of a denomination is the United Methodist Church, a Protestant denomination that must compete for members with other Protestant denominations, such as Presbyterians, Episcopalians, and Baptists. Denominations sometimes evolve from sects. This occurs when the sect is successful in recruiting new members and grows in both size and organizational complexity. Sociologists who study religion have found that the bureaucratic growth of a sect and its increasing influence over nonreligious matters in the community is associated with a decline in the fervor with which the sect pursues its spiritual ideals and a decrease in its efforts to remain faithful to the claims that originally made it so different. This aspect of religious change is an active area of current research (Welch, 1979; Neibuhr, 1929; Troeltsch, 1931; Pope, 1942).

Cults. Still another type of religious body, the **cult**, differs in significant ways from the organizations just described. Cults are usually entirely new religions whose members hold beliefs and engage in rituals that differ from those of existing religions. A cult may have developed out of an existing religion. This occurred in the case of early Christianity, which began as a cult of Jews who believed that Jesus of Nazareth was the Messiah and who practiced rituals that were often quite different from those of Judaism. Or cults may be developed by people who were not previously involved in a church or sect—for example, people who become active in the various pagan cults found in North America today, such as cults based on ancient forms of witchcraft (Adler, 1979). Most major religions began as seemingly insignificant cults, but new cults are formed every day throughout the world, and very few of them last long enough to become recognized religions. The Jesus People, the Unification Church, and Christian Science are examples of cults that have transformed themselves into sects or churches (McGuire, 1987).

Established religions often absorb cults and sects through the process known as co-optation. This term is not limited to religious institutions; we encountered it in Chapter 10 in connection with social movements. It refers to any process whereby an organization deals with potentially threatening individuals or groups by incorporating them into its own organizational structure (Selznick, 1966). The Roman Catholic church has been particularly

> *Sects and cults are a major source of change in religious organizations.*

successful at co-opting regional Catholic sects by including their leaders in the panoply of lesser saints, thereby allowing people to worship a holy person of their own culture while remaining true to the world church.

Religious Interaction and Change

Sects and cults are a major source of change in religious organizations. People who are not satisfied with more established churches and denominations, or are otherwise alienated from society, often form or join a cult or sect (Nelson, 1984; Smelser, 1984). One of the most convincing explanations of the emergence of sects was suggested by H. Richard Niebuhr (1929), borrowing from Max Weber's (1922) pioneering analysis of churches and sects. According to Weber, churches tend to justify the presence of inequality and stratification because they must appeal to people of all classes. Sects, on the other hand, may be led by charismatic individuals who appeal to people who have felt the sting of inequality. Niebuhr agreed with Weber that class conflict was a primary cause of sect formation. But he observed that as sects become more successful and better organized, they become more like churches and begin to justify existing systems of stratification. This creates the conditions in which new sects may emerge.

New religious movements arise when a "religious innovator" attracts a number of followers whose needs are not met by traditional religions.

Another motivation for the formation of sects or cults is dissatisfaction with the interactions that occur in more established organizations. In church rituals, for example, prayer is often led by a priest or other religious professional and is relatively restrained, whereas in sects and cults communication between God and the individual is more direct and typically allows the individual to express deep emotions. The different styles of interaction in different types of religious organizations can be illustrated by the contrast between the hierarchy of statuses and roles that characterizes the Catholic church, with its pope, cardinals, bishops, priests, and other well-defined statuses—and the seemingly greater equality and looser structure that are typical of a cult like Krishna Consciousness.

Often people who are attracted to cults are influenced by a charismatic leader who inspires them to new and very personal achievements, such as ecstatic experiences, a sense of salvation, or a release from physical or psychological suffering. Some become cult members simply because they are lonely; others are born to cult members and are socialized into the cult.

Some, but by no means all, cults are extremely authoritarian and punitive. Their leaders may demand that members cut themselves off entirely from family and friends and sacrifice everything for the sake of the cult. The leaders may also insist that they themselves are above the moral teachings to which their followers must adhere. Under these conditions of isolation and submission to a dominant authority, cult members may be driven to incredible extremes of behavior—even mass suicide, as occurred in the case of Jim Jones's People's Temple (Hall, 1987). However, not all cults are so dangerous or so easily condemned, and there is an ongoing conflict between norms that protect the right of individuals to belong to cults and efforts to protect people from the harm that can occur when cult leaders place themselves above morality and the law.

G. K. Nelson (1984) draws upon the free and expressive nature of cults in describing how new religious movements are born. Such movements, he writes, "may be seen as the result of religious innovation . . . [which] involves the discovery of new methods by which spiritual needs may be satisfied" (p. 317). According to Nelson, a new cult or movement arises when a "religious innovator" attracts a number of followers. This is particularly likely to occur when traditional religions are failing to meet the needs of their members or when a society is undergoing rapid secularization. Yet it appears that secularization never eliminates people's desire for religious expression. Indeed, some studies of recruitment into cults show that their members often have received a high-quality secular education and a nonreligious upbringing (Stark and Bainbridge, 1985). Such people might be expected to have the most secular views regarding human existence. The fact that they join cults is evidence that secularization itself can lead to religious innovation.

Many of the functions of religion as a fundamental cultural institution—meeting the spiritual needs of individuals, binding together the members of social groups, and sometimes engendering social change—are illustrated by the history of the black church in America, which is summarized in Box 16-2.

Box 16–2: **The Black Church in America**

The respected black sociologist E. Franklin Frazier was a firm believer in the principles of the Chicago school of ecological research and an astute student of race relations. He specialized in two of the most basic social institutions, the family and the church, as they affected and were affected by the situation of black Americans.

Frazier's (1966) study of the history of the black church in America emphasized the role of religion in the social organization of blacks ever since they were imported from Africa to the New World to be sold as slaves. Few aspects of the slaves' African culture were able to survive the experience of abduction and slavery, but one of those that did was dancing, which Frazier referred to as the most primitive form of religious expression. Although the slaves were encouraged to dance, the religious beliefs expressed in their dances were not permitted to flourish in America.

With the coming of Baptist and Methodist missionaries, the slaves found a form of religion in which they could express their most intense feelings. The religious services in which they participated served to bind them into close-knit groups, replacing the bonds of kinship and tribal membership they had lost when they were sold into slavery. However, the freed slaves resented the subordinate status of blacks in the white-dominated churches. They left those churches and established all-black churches.

Out of these black churches, Frazier noted, other forms of black organizational activity emerged. The churches began to play an important role in the organization of the black community in such areas as economic cooperation and the building of educational institutions. The church also became the center of political life for black Americans, the arena in which they learned how to compete for power and position.

The large-scale urbanization of blacks that began in World War I transformed the black church. In particular, the church became more secular, placing less emphasis on salvation and turning its attention to the serious problems of blacks in the here and now. Changes in the class structure of the black community have also been reflected in the black church, with many middle-class blacks shifting to the Presbyterian, Episcopalian, and Congregational churches. A countertrend may be seen in the emergence of "storefront churches" (i.e., sects) that satisfy the spiritual needs of those who prefer a more intimate and expressive form of worship. And some blacks have joined so-called holiness cults that seek to return to an earlier form of expressive Christianity.

At the same time, blacks have become more fully integrated into American society. This has naturally affected the organization of black communities and the black church. Today the church is no longer the central institution it once was. Nevertheless, as Frazier pointed out, the black church has left its imprint on most aspects of black life. And it is clear that the black church (including the Black Muslims and other Islamic sects) provides much of the leadership and many of the rank-and-file supporters of movements for political and economic justice among minority groups in the United States.

Internationally acclaimed singer Aretha Franklin attributes her success to the vitality of the black church in the United States, which sustains an immense market for gospel songs and records.

© Ross-Marino, Sygma

TRENDS IN RELIGION IN THE UNITED STATES

In studying religion in the United States, sociologists are unable to use census data because the Census Bureau does not collect data on religious affiliation. However, some statistics are available from smaller sample surveys such as those conducted by the National Opinion Research Center. The available data indicate that about two-thirds of Americans over age fifteen identify themselves as Protestants, about one-quarter are Roman Catholic, and 2.4 percent identify themselves as Jewish. All other religions combined account for a little over 1 percent of the population. Of the remaining 6.9 percent, two-thirds say that they have no religious affiliation. This latter group of "disbelievers, agnostics, and nonreligious persons" accounts for about one person out of twenty, making it the third-largest category of religious preference in the United States (Bogue, 1985). (See Figure 16-2.)

The religious preferences of Americans have been changing slowly but steadily over the last two generations. The Protestant majority has gradually declined, owing partly to

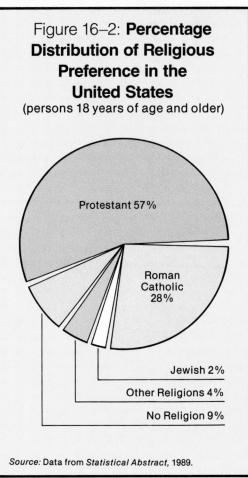

Figure 16–2: **Percentage Distribution of Religious Preference in the United States**
(persons 18 years of age and older)

Protestant 57%

Roman Catholic 28%

Jewish 2%

Other Religions 4%

No Religion 9%

Source: Data from *Statistical Abstract,* 1989.

upward mobility and the tendency of more affluent and educated people to be less active in religious institutions. Meanwhile the proportion of the population who identify themselves as Catholics has been growing, primarily as a result of the large numbers of Hispanic immigrants who have entered the United States in recent years. Also, since the mid-1960s there has been an increase in the percentage of people who express no religious preference. Thus it is possible that by the turn of the century less than half of all Americans will be Protestant (Roozen, 1985).

Membership in a religious organization is quite different from identification with a religious faith, and this is reflected in statistics on church membership in the United States. Because data on membership are obtained from the organizations themselves, there are significant differences in who is included. (Some churches, for example, count all baptized infants, whereas others count only people above a certain age who are formally enrolled as members.) Figure 16-3 illustrates the geographic distribution of reported church membership in the United States. As can readily be seen, different regions of the country are quite different with respect to the church membership of the majority of their residents. Protestants outnumber members

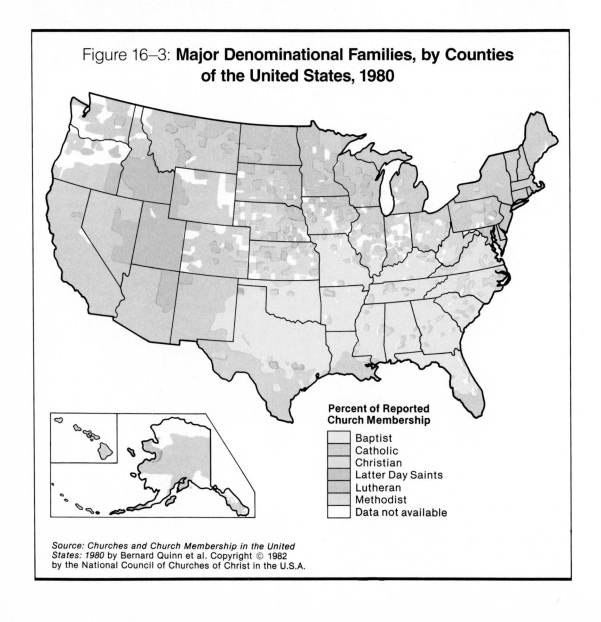

Figure 16–3: **Major Denominational Families, by Counties of the United States, 1980**

Percent of Reported Church Membership

Baptist
Catholic
Christian
Latter Day Saints
Lutheran
Methodist
Data not available

Source: Churches and Church Membership in the United States: 1980 by Bernard Quinn et al. Copyright © 1982 by the National Council of Churches of Christ in the U.S.A.

of all other religions in the South, for example, and in the West and Southwest the Roman Catholic church is dominant. There are also significant differences in church membership by size of place: Protestants are most likely to live in rural places, small cities, and suburbs of smaller cities, while Catholics are found in medium-sized cities and suburbs of larger cities. Jews, who originally migrated to the nation's largest cities, are most numerous in major metropolitan regions such as New York, Los Angeles, Chicago, and Miami (Bogue, 1985).

Unofficial Religion

Religion in the United States is increasingly voluntaristic. People are less likely to practice their religion just because their parents did so. They are more likely than ever to join a religious group that appeals to their desire for membership in a community of like-minded peers and that upholds their particular moral standards (Roof, 1985). People in the United States and Canada are also more likely to engage in what sociologists term *unofficial religion*—a set of beliefs and practices that are "not accepted, recognized, or controlled by official religious groups" (McGuire, 1987, p. 89). Sometimes called folk or popular religion because it is practiced by ordinary people rather than by religious professionals in formal organizations, unofficial religion takes many forms. It is engaged in by people who purchase religious books and magazines, follow religious programs on television, make religious pilgrimages, or practice astrology, faith healing, transcendental meditation, occult arts, and the like—and who may belong to organized churches at the same time. Contrary to older sociological theories, which viewed these practices as holdovers from rural folk cultures, research has shown that urban societies continually produce their own versions of popular religion (Fischer, 1974, 1987).

Americans today are less likely to practice the religion of their parents and more likely to engage in unofficial religion, or beliefs and practices that are not controlled by official religious groups.

Religiosity

Neither church membership figures nor self-reports of religious identification are accurate indicators of the aspect of religious behavior known as **religiosity**. This term refers to the depth of a person's religious feelings and how those feelings are translated into religious behavior. Responses to questions about whether one believes in God and how strongly, whether one believes in a life after death, whether one's religious beliefs provide guidance in making major decisions, and the frequency of one's church or temple attendance all can be used to measure religiosity.

When sociologists study religiosity (as opposed to church membership) some important results emerge. For example, Rodney Stark and William S. Bainbridge (1985) found that about 62 percent of Americans are church members. But church membership varies rather sharply by region. The southwestern states have the highest rate of membership—about 65 percent of adults. Other regions have rates ranging from 53 to 62 percent, but the Pacific states have by far the lowest proportion of adult church members, only 36 percent. Quite different results are obtained on measures of religiosity: 84 percent of Americans believe in the existence of God, and 86 percent express certainty in a life after death. Adults in the Pacific states do not differ greatly on these measures from those in other regions. These figures highlight the difference between church membership and religiosity. The lower rates of church membership on the West Coast are correlated with the greater spatial mobility and lower median age of the populations of those states. People who move frequently tend to sever their attachments not only to churches but to all organizations in the community. Yet people who do not belong to organized churches can nevertheless hold deeply cherished religious beliefs.

Data on church attendance do not support the notion that the United States is becoming an increasingly secular society. In fact, as can be seen in Table 16-1, for some major religions church attendance has been increasing since 1950 (Hout and Greeley, 1987). There are no clear patterns in rates of church attendance between 1939 and 1984. Although

Table 16–1: **Percent of Adults Attending Services Last Week, by Religion and Year, United States, 1939–1984**

Year	Religion				
	Protestant	**Catholic**	**Jewish**	**Other**	**None**
1939	40	64	12	—	1
1950	36	63	32	56	4
1959	39	72	20	49	14
1960	39	70	11	57	12
1969	39	64	8	18	0
1979	40	53	19	40	5
1980	43	47	5	16	6
1984	42	52	13	46	7

Source: Hout and Greeley, 1987.

Catholics have the highest weekly attendance rates and Jews the lowest, those rates can change considerably from one year to the next, for reasons that are not fully understood. Nevertheless, it is clear that the data do not bear out the secularization hypothesis.

Religious Pluralism

Differences in the distribution of religious belief are important; they show how religion helps account for cultural differences among populations within a society. Thus we use the expression "Bible Belt" to refer to the most strongly Protestant areas of the nation—the South and Midwest. The large Catholic populations in some cities make them quite different in cultural terms from the Protestant-dominated suburbs. The large Jewish populations in New York and Miami are reflected in the cultural life of those cities—in joint Hanukkah/Christmas celebrations in offices and schools, for example, and the incorporation of Jewish holidays into the school calendar.

The United States is an example of a society in which the state protects religious pluralism. The First Amendment to the Constitution guarantees freedom of religion, which in turn allows different religions to exist and to compete for adherents if they wish to do so. Religious pluralism is also protected in most European nations today, but before the Protestant Reformation of the sixteenth cen-

tury many European states made Roman Catholicism the official state religion and attempted to force all of their citizens to convert to Catholicism.

In societies in which religious pluralism is protected, one usually can observe the continual formation of new religious organizations. These groups tend to arise either from schisms within existing organizations or as a result of the teaching of charismatic leaders who attract people to new religious movements. But religious pluralism, especially the extensive growth of religion through the mass media, raises the issue of "free riders" discussed in Chapter 10 in connection with the problems faced by social movements.

Religious Organizations and Free Riders

If religions like Protestantism allow for a direct relationship between people and God through individual prayer, won't there be a weakening in the ability of church organizations to enlist people's time and monetary contributions? And if religion comes into the home via television, why should people contribute their time and money to church organizations? This is a version of the classic free-rider problem, the tendency for people to accept the benefits of collective action without contributing to the organization that makes them possible (Olsen, 1971).

In an attempt to solve this problem, most religious organizations in the United States organize their rituals in such a way that individuals cannot obtain the full benefit of prayer without participating in and contributing to the work of the congregation. One must come to church to be considered a "good Christian" or a "good Jew." And, once involved with the congregation, one learns that contributions of time and money are rewarded both in this world and in the hereafter. Such measures cannot entirely solve the free-rider problem, but pressure on individuals to contribute goes a long way. In the case of television evangelism, there is evidence that television audiences respond well to appeals for contributions. At the same time, the availability of free religion on television does not seem to reduce church attendance (Gallup Organization, 1984).

Fundamentalism

Religious *fundamentalists* are believers (and their leaders) who are devoted to the strict observance of ritual and doctrine. They lack tolerance for differences in belief and practice, and they are fiercely opposed to astrology, magic, unorthodox conceptions of religion, and any form of civil religion. In the United States fundamentalist believers may be found in every major religion, but fundamentalism is especially strong among some Protestant churches and sects. Historically, the influence of religious fundamentalism on the culture and politics of American life reached its height in 1919, when the Eighteenth Amendment to the U.S. Constitution prohibited the sale and consumption of alcoholic beverages, regardless of whether one supported the fundamentalist view of alcohol consumption. The repeal of Prohibition represented a defeat for religious fundamentalism in American culture and politics.

Another famous episode involving fundamentalism was the so-called monkey trial of 1925, in which John T. Scopes, a biology

Fundamentalism— strict belief in and observance of ritual and doctrine—may be found in every major religion.

teacher in Tennessee, was charged with teaching the then-forbidden theory of evolution, which many religious fundamentalists oppose because it contradicts the account of creation presented in the Bible. In that trial, Scopes's lawyer, Clarence Darrow, soundly defeated the fundamentalist advocate William Jennings Bryan. The Scopes trial, like the repeal of Prohibition, was widely viewed as a victory for the intellectual opponents of fundamentalism. Although fundamentalism continued to pose a challenge to mainline Baptist, Methodist, and Presbyterian denominations, it remained a minority religious ideology (Simpson, 1983).

Fundamentalism experienced a resurgence during the 1980s, encouraged by conservative social movements against abortion, drug use, divorce, and related issues. Television evangelism attracted many adherents to fundamentalist causes and ways of thinking. The success of the conservative interest group Moral Majority in gaining members and raising funds was based on the development of a national network of fundamentalist believers led by charismatic pastors. But Moral Majority is as much a political organization as a religious one. It opposes abortion, sex education, tolerance for homosexuality, and many other more liberal causes. What, then, is the relationship between fundamentalism and support for Moral Majority?

Empirical data to help answer this question were gathered in an important study conducted in the Dallas–Fort Worth area in the early 1980s. Anson Shupe and William Stacey drew a random sample of 905 respondents and asked them a series of questions about their religious and political views, among other things. The Dallas–Fort Worth area is an important site for such research because it is the largest metropolitan area in a heavily religious region of the United States; in fact, it is often referred to as "the buckle of the Southern Bible Belt" (Shupe and Stacey, 1983). The researchers hypothesized, therefore, that they would find a large number of respondents who had heard of Moral Majority and were favorable toward its views and its political activities.

The results of the survey differed considerably from the researchers' expectations. About 70 percent of the respondents had heard of Moral Majority, but only 16 percent made favorable comments about the organization; 31 percent held unfavorable views. Even more surprising, among religious fundamentalists 29 percent were supporters of Moral Majority, compared to 19 percent among religious conservatives and 14 percent among moderates. In other words, even among fundamentalists only a minority support the political activities of Moral Majority. Thus, although fundamentalism has gained in popularity, there is no evidence that its moral crusades enlist anything like a majority even among fundamentalists.

Conclusion

Earlier in the chapter we discussed the trend toward secularization throughout the world, and we noted the tendency for religion to become increasingly differentiated from other institutions. But we have also seen evidence that secularization is not inevitable, nor is the process of differentiation ever complete. Even in societies in which religion is supposed to be a separate institution, the boundaries between religious and other institutions are far from clear. In West Germany the state collects taxes on behalf of the Catholic and Protestant churches; in Belgium the state pays teachers in both public and Catholic schools; in the United States the tradition of "separation of church and state" is continually under attack, especially when education is concerned (van den Berghe, 1975). And in the early 1980s Bob Jones University in South Carolina claimed the right to engage in discriminatory practices on the basis of religious beliefs. But the Supreme Court ruled against the university, stating that it must conform to antidiscrimination legislation.

Among the world's urban industrial societies, the United States has developed the clearest separation of religion from governmental and educational institutions (Elifson and Hadaway, 1985). Yet in the past twenty-five years there have been three Supreme Court decisions on cases arising out of the reading of prayers or passages from the Bible in public schools (*Engle* v. *Vitale*, 1962; *Abington School District* v. *Schempp*, 1963; *Murray* v. *Curlett*, 1963). Such conflicts over the boundaries between religion and other institutions are of immense interest to sociologists because they indicate whether the process of secularization is proceeding smoothly or meeting with resistance. They show that secularization is not a one-way process and that religion continues to play a highly significant role in human events. Today revivals of religion throughout the world, even in highly modern societies, provide ample evidence that we have yet to fully understand the power of faith in God and the supernatural.

In sum, religion continues to play an important role in the contemporary world. This fact is reflected in the remarks of Robert Ballah, a well-known commentator on American culture. For several centuries, he writes, Americans "have been embarked on a great effort to increase our freedom, wealth, and power. For over a hundred years, a large part of the American people, the middle class, has imagined that the virtual meaning of life lies in the acquisition of ever-increasing status, income, and authority, from which genuine freedom is supposed to come" (Bellah et al., 1985, p. 284). Yet many Americans seem uneasy about their lives despite their material comfort. They seem to yearn for spiritual values without necessarily wanting to return to traditional religious practices. They adhere to the values of individualism, but at the same time they long for the stronger sense of community and commitment that one finds in religious congregations. Bellah predicts that Americans will continue to seek self-actualization as individuals, but that increasingly they will express their desire for community attachments and higher values, either in traditional religions or in civil-religious practice.

> *It is likely that while they continue to seek self-actualization as individuals, Americans will increasingly seek community attachments and higher values both within and outside traditional religious organizations.*

CHALLENGES TO CONTEMPORARY SOCIETY

Religion and Social Change

I t is a striking fact that throughout the world one finds deeply devout individuals involved in movements for social change. Religious workers are killed in El Salvador because they advocate greater democracy and equality. In Poland the Catholic church is a leader in the movement to democratize that nation. American bishops speak out against poverty and inequality in the United States. The civil rights movement has tended to be led by clergymen and bases many of its appeals on biblical principles of justice and equity. Yet on the other hand we could cite many examples of religious intolerance and an apparently high correlation between devotion to religious faith and resistance to social change.

Support for and resistance to social change are relative ideas—relative, that is, to the position of their advocates. If one supports a woman's right to choose whether to have an abortion or not, the social change in question is tolerance for abortion rights (which does not necessarily mean that one favors abortion). If one is opposed to abortion rights, the change one seeks is a return to a situation in which abortion is illegal. As we noted in the chapter, by opposing abortion rights the Catholic church stands for social change in a conservative direction.

In religious life the same institution can stand for conservative social change in one place and for more radical change in another. For example, the conservative Episcopalian

(Anglican) church in Northern Ireland supports the continuation of British colonial rule there, while the Episcopalian church in the United States supports liberal causes such as abortion rights and environmental action. The relationship between the Catholic church and social change is even more complex. In the United States the church is accused by some of its own leaders of having too conservative a view of social change. In Brazil, by contrast, the church is accused of being too liberal. How can a single institution be perceived so differently in two societies?

Part of the answer is that a church that is so large and embraces so many separate organizations can never be free from internal politics. Many Catholic theologians agree with Father Richard P. McBrien of Notre Dame University that "since his election in 1978, Pope John Paul II has been determinedly appointing a certain type of cleric to important archdioceses and dioceses all around the world" (1990, p. A17). According to McBrien and others, these bishops and cardinals tend to be "uncritically loyal to the Pope" and "rigidly authoritarian and solitary" in their leadership style. They are unlikely to take their parishioners' views into account when they differ from those of the pope and his curial associates. For their part, high church officials argue that their function is to keep the church on the right track in defending the sanctity of life while seeking constructive social change where possible. Hence, on many social issues—abortion rights, the rights of homosexuals, treatment of AIDS patients, economic reform—the leadership of the Catholic church (though not always its rank-and-file adherents) tends to act as a conservative force in the United States and other industrial nations.

The opposite is true in Brazil and other Latin American nations, where the Catholic church is identified with movements for radical social reforms. In Brazil, theologian Leonardo Boff and bishop Dom Helder Camara have developed and taught the idea that spiritual salvation is not possible without action to liberate the oppressed. Religion itself could help transform the miserable conditions of the peasantry and the Indians and the impoverished working people (Adriance, 1987; McGuire, 1987). This view has come to be known as "liberation theology."

As liberation theology took hold among many Brazilian Catholics during the 1960s and 1970s, church leaders began to develop what they called "the preferential option for the poor." Recognizing that the so-called miracle of Brazilian economic growth in those decades had not helped most of the nation's poor people, they proposed to correct this situation even at the expense of the spiritual needs of the affluent. Church leaders and lay activists organized thousands of small groups known as Communidade Eclesial de Base, or CEBs. These thirty- to forty-person groups were the building blocks of a powerful social movement to bring both spiritual comfort and economic uplift to the nation's poor masses. Never a very popular strategy in Rome, the CEBs seem nevertheless to have had a real impact in moving Brazil's elite classes toward the realization that if they did not do more to distribute the benefits of economic development they might be swept out of power in the next elections. At this writing it is not clear what the future holds either for liberation theology or for the liberal–conservative dispute among Catholics in the United States. It is clear, however, that like all the major religions of the world, Catholicism will continue to face the challenges of social change.

SUMMARY

*R*eligion is among the oldest and most changeable and complex of human social institutions. It has been defined as any set of coherent answers to the dilemmas of human existence that makes the world meaningful. It has also been defined as a system of beliefs and rituals that serves to bind people together into a social group. *Rituals* are formal patterns of activity that express a set of shared meanings; in the case of religious rituals, the shared meanings are *sacred*, pertaining to phenomena that are regarded as extraordinary, transcendent, and outside the everyday course of events.

Until comparatively recent times religion dominated the cultural life of human societies. Since medieval times, however, the traditional dominance of religion over other institutions has been reduced by a process termed *secularization*. This process is never complete; religion continues to play an important role in the contemporary world.

In simpler and rather isolated societies, people may believe in a great force or spirit, but they do not have a well-defined concept of God or a set of rituals involving God. This form of religion is called *simple supernaturalism*. More common among hunting-and-gathering societies is *animism*, in which all forms of life and all aspects of the earth are inhabited by gods or supernatural powers. *Theistic* belief systems, in contrast, usually conceive of a god or gods as separate from humans and from other living things on the earth. Many ancient religions were *polytheistic*, meaning that they included numerous gods. The ancient Hebrews were among the first of the world's peoples to evolve a *monotheistic* religion, one centered on belief in a single all-powerful God.

In China, Japan, and other societies of the Far East, religions predominate that are centered not on devotion to a god or gods but on an abstract ideal of spirituality and human behavior. In addition, some social scientists have expanded the definition of religion to include *civil religions*, or collections of beliefs and rituals that exist outside religious institutions.

A major controversy in the study of religious institutions has to do with the role they play in social change. Karl Marx believed that cultural institutions like religion are shaped by economic and political institutions and that they function to instill in the masses the values of the dominant class. Max Weber, on the other hand, argued that religion can cause major social change by instilling certain values in the members of a society, which in turn produce changes in other institutions.

Religion today is a highly structured institution, with numerous statuses and roles within a variety of organizations as well as many kinds of smaller, less bureaucratic groups. The main types of religious organizations are the church, the sect, and the denomination. A *church* is a religious organization that has strong ties to the larger society and has at one time or another enjoyed the loyalty of most of the society's members. A *sect* rejects the religious beliefs or practices of an established church and usually is formed when a group of church members splits off to form a rival organization. A third type of religious organization is the *denomination*, which is on good terms with the religious institution from which it developed but must compete with other denominations for members.

A *cult* is an entirely new religion. Along with sects, cults are a major source of change in religious organizations. People who are not satisfied with more established churches and denominations may form or join a cult or sect. New religious movements arise when a "religious innovator" attracts a number of followers. This is particularly likely when traditional religions fail to meet the needs of their members or when a society is undergoing rapid secularization.

Membership in a religious organization is quite different from identification with a religious faith, and this is reflected in trends in religion in the United States. Among those trends are a growing tendency to practice unofficial or "folk" religion and an emphasis on religiosity as opposed to church membership. *Religiosity* refers to the depth of a person's religious feelings and how those feelings are translated into religious behavior. Studies of religiosity find high percentages of Americans believing in the existence of God and in a life after death.

In societies characterized by religious pluralism, one usually can observe the continual formation of new religious organizations. But religious pluralism also gives rise to the "free rider" problem, in which people may enjoy the benefits provided by religious organizations without contributing to those organizations.

Religious fundamentalists are believers who are devoted to the strict observance of ritual and doctrine and lack tolerance for differences in belief and practice. In the United States fundamentalism experienced a resurgence during the 1980s, encouraged by conservative social movements. However, there is no evidence that the moral crusades associated with fundamentalism are supported by a majority of Americans.

GLOSSARY

religion: any set of coherent answers to the dilemmas of human existence that makes the world meaningful; a system of beliefs and rituals that serves to bind people together into a social group (**p. 496**).

ritual: a formal pattern of activity that expresses symbolically a set of shared meanings (**p. 497**).

sacred: a term used to describe phenomena that are regarded as extraordinary, transcendent, and outside the everyday course of events (**p. 498**).

profane: a term used to describe phenomena that are not considered sacred (**p. 497**).

secularization: a process in which the dominance of religion over other institutions is reduced (**p. 498**).

simple supernaturalism: a form of religion in which people may believe in a great force or spirit but do not have a well-defined concept of God or a set of rituals involving God (**p. 502**).

animism: a form of religion in which all forms of life and all aspects of the earth are inhabited by gods or supernatural powers (**p. 502**).

theism: a belief system that conceives of a god or gods as separate from humans and from other living things on the earth (**p. 502**).

polytheistic: a theistic belief system that includes numerous gods (**p. 502**).

monotheistic: a term used to describe a theistic belief system centered on belief in a single all-powerful God (**p. 502**).

civil religion: a collection of beliefs and rituals that exist outside religious institutions (**p. 504**).

church: a religious organization that has strong ties to the larger society (**p. 507**).

sect: a religious organization that rejects the beliefs and practices of existing churches; usually formed when a group leaves the church to form a rival organization (**p. 508**).

denomination: a religious organization that is on good terms with the institution from which it developed but must compete with other denominations for members (**p. 508**).

cult: a new religion (**p. 508**).

religiosity: the depth of a person's religious feelings (**p. 513**).

WHERE TO FIND IT

Books

Religion and Religiosity in America (Jeffrey K. Hadden and Theodore E. Long; Crossroad, 1983). Contains many good empirical papers on religions and religious beliefs.

Radical Departures: Desperate Detours to Growing Up (Saul V. Levine; Harcourt Brace Jovanovich, 1984). A highly readable empirical study of why some middle-class young people join cults.

Religion: The Social Context, 2nd ed. (Meredith B. McGuire; Wadsworth, 1987). An up-to-date, comprehensive text on the sociology of religion with excellent material on religion and social change.

Journals

Journal for the Scientific Study of Religion Available in most college and university libraries, this journal publishes recent research on religious practices, religiosity, and changes in religious institutions.

Other Sources

The Encyclopedia of American Religions (Milton J. Gordon; McGrath, 1978). Contains useful descriptions of religions in America; covers beliefs, organization, distribution in the population, and other aspects.

VISUAL SOCIOLOGY

Forms of Religious Expression

This series of photos reminds us that despite outward differences in religious expression, all religions stimulate a deeply felt spiritual experience in their members. But religious emotions are usually experienced by groups of worshipers who follow the same set of rituals, rituals that have a great deal to do with the quality of the individual's religious experience. For example, in the group of African tribespeople who are dancing and chanting, each member of the community feels transported outside his or her normal consciousness into a realm of ecstasy brought on by the frenzy of the ritual. In the photos of Muslim worshipers at a mosque, of Jews praying at the Wailing Wall in Jerusalem, and of women participating in a Catholic festival in Central America, we see that some sacred rituals are more restrained.

Religious emotions may be deeply felt, and the individual may sometimes feel transported outside his or her normal self, but much of the power of the religious experience comes from being with others of the same faith in a sacred building—a mosque, a synagogue, a church, Outside such places one is in the secular world, but it is nevertheless possible for a person to carry the spirituality of his or her religious faith into everyday life. And we can see in the photos of the street prayer group and the evangelical gospel tent that even in highly secular societies some people seek the greater intensity offered by sect rituals.

These photos may also be viewed in terms of what they tell us about the social organization of religious expression. Notice, for example, the patterns of gender segregation that appear in many of the photos. At

the Wailing Wall we see that, following Orthodox Jewish custom, women and men worship in separate places within the same area. Islamic worship is also strictly segregated by gender. Roman Catholic rituals are often integrated in terms of gender, but there are local variations of the standard rituals in which women and men are separated. In the Episcopal church, both men and women can serve at the altar, but this is a relatively recent development that has resulted from increased demands by women for equal access to church leadership. The modern Protestant sects also display a good deal of gender equality, but as we see in the gospel tent photo, particular rituals often attract more women than men.

CHAPTER OUTLINE

● **Education for a Changing World**

- The Nature of Schools
- Who Goes to School?
- Schools and Adolescent Society
- Education and Citizenship

● **Attainment, Achievement, and Equality**

- Educational Attainment
- Educational Achievement
- Education and Social Mobility
- Education for Equality

● **The Structure of Educational Institutions**

- Schools as Bureaucracies
- Changing the System: Desegregation

● **The Communications Media**

- Media Institutions in Modern Societies
- Patterns of Media Consumption
- Television and Violence
- The Differentiation of Media Institutions
- Media Power and Its Limits

Newsday/Erica Berger

The Japanese Weekend School, Great Neck, New York

CHAPTER 17

EDUCATION AND THE COMMUNICATIONS MEDIA

School children in Prince George's County, Maryland, are taking part in a historic educational experiment. So are their parents, their teachers, and their principals. In Chicago, Miami, New York, and many other school districts throughout the United States, serious efforts at educational reform are under way, but nowhere are their goals quite as ambitious as those of the Prince George's County school district. In that county, one of the nation's largest and most rapidly growing, efforts at educational reform have brought about a dramatic improvement in the county's most troubled schools.

Patricia Green, principal of one of the primary schools involved in the reform effort, says that as a result of the experimental program "teachers can teach and kids can learn." In her school the number of student suspensions has fallen from twenty or thirty per year to about one. And for the first time students in her school and other underachieving schools in the county have scored above the national average on standardized achievement tests (Schorr, 1988).

James P. Comer, a child psychiatrist and educational philosopher, inspires and guides the Prince George's County program. In fact, everyone involved refers to the program as the Comer School Development Program. But Comer first came to national prominence as an educational pioneer in the ghetto schools of New Haven, Connecticut, where he applied his ideas of school management and planning teams to "turn around" that city's most failure-scarred primary schools.

Comer traces his educational innovations to his experiences as an African-American child in East Chicago, Indiana: "My three friends with whom I started elementary school—one died at an early age from alcoholism; one spent most of his life in jail; and one has been in and out of mental institutions all of his life. I was the only one to survive whole." Comer's father, a steelworker, and his mother, a domestic, not only motivated him and his two brothers to learn at home but also they "came to school if there was a problem, and knew how to make sure that people were sensitive and concerned about us. What I've tried to do here in New Haven [and later in Prince George's County] is to shape the system, the school, so that it becomes the advocate and support for the kid, and a believer in the kid in the same way that my parents were" (quoted in Schorr, 1988, p. 232).

Comer's research and experience convinced him that children from neighborhoods that are undergoing severe strain—owing to poverty, racism, unemployment, violence, drug addiction, and related social problems—enter school with major deficits. They are often "underdeveloped in their social, emotional, linguistic, and cognitive growth." As a result, they often withdraw, act up, and do not learn. Of course, not all such students have these problems. Those who do, however, are labeled "slow learners" or "behavior problems" and consequently fall even further behind their classmates. Comer's solution appears very simple on the surface: Change the "climate of demoralized schools by paying much more attention to child development and to basic management of the school" (quoted in Schorr, 1988, p. 233).

Of course, the process of changing school climates and management is much more difficult that this simple formula suggests. The Comer model of institutional change calls for the formation of a School Planning and Management Team in each school; the team is directed by the principal and has from twelve to fourteen members, including teachers, aides, and parents. A second team is made up of helping professionals—the school psychologist, social workers, special-education teachers, and counselors; it acts as an advisory group. The purpose of the teams is to ally the parents with the school so that, in Comer's words, "you reduce the dissonance between home and school and you give the kid a long-term supporter for education at home" (quoted in Schorr, 1988, p. 233; Comer, 1980, 1984, 1985, 1987). Evaluation research on the Comer model and related approaches has identified an additional benefit: Very often the parents are motivated to return to school themselves and train for jobs they previously considered out of reach.

Helping teachers and parents work together to turn around failing schools is exciting, rewarding work. But it is also extremely hard work because old ways and long-established assumptions do not disappear with the mere formation of a committee. It takes time and effort to involve as many teachers and parents in the program as possible. But the results are extremely convincing—so much so that variations of the Comer approach are being implemented to change school systems throughout the United States.

EDUCATION FOR A CHANGING WORLD

Efforts to change the goals and methods of education are not new. One of the most famous trials in history took place in ancient Greece, when Socrates was accused of corrupting the morals of Athenian youth with his innovative ideas and educational methods. Today, the fact that educational reforms like those proposed by James Comer are receiving so much hopeful attention is evidence of the importance of education in modern societies. Education is one of the major institutions that transmit a society's culture, and as such it plays a vital part in the socialization process.

Education may be defined as the process by which a society transmits knowledge, values, norms, and ideologies and in so doing prepares young people for adult roles and adults for new roles. Education thus is a form of socialization that is carried out by specific institutions outside the family, such as schools, colleges, and adult education centers.

Education is a form of socialization carried out by institutions outside the family, especially schools and colleges.

Educational institutions have a huge effect on communities in the United States and other modern societies. Upwardly mobile couples often base their choice of a place to live on the quality of the public schools in the neighborhood. Every neighborhood has at least an elementary school, and every large city has one or more high schools and at least one community college or four-year college. Cities usually also have a variety of school administrations, public and private, and some owe their existence, growth, and development to the presence of a college or university.

The Nature of Schools

Educational institutions affect not only the surroundings but also the daily lives of millions of Americans: children and their par-

This photo of Tibetan refugee children in a classroom in northern India illustrates the similarity of classroom organization in many parts of the world.

ents, college and university students, teachers and professors. Hence, education is a major focus of social-scientific research. To the sociologist, the most common educational institution, the school, is a specialized structure with a special function: preparing children for active participation in adult activities (Katz, 1964). Schools are sometimes compared with total institutions (see Chapter 9), in which a large group of involuntary "clients" is serviced by a smaller group of staff members (Boocock, 1980). The staffs of such institutions tend to emphasize the maintenance of order and control, and this often leads to the development of elaborate sets of rules and monitoring systems. This comparison cannot be taken too literally (schools are not prisons, although some of their "inmates" may think of them as such), but the typical school does tend to be characterized by a clearly defined authority system and set of rules. In fact, so-

ciologists often cite schools as examples of bureaucratic organizations (Parelius and Parelius, 1978).

A more interactionist viewpoint sees the school as a set of behaviors; that is, the central feature of the school is not its bureaucratic structure but the kinds of interactions and patterns of socialization that occur in schools. In the words of Frederick Bates and Virginia Murray (1975), the basic feature of schools is "the behavior of a large number of actors organized into groups that are joined together by an authority structure, and by a network of relationships through which information, resources, and partially finished projects flow from one group to another" (p. 26). In other words, "school-related behavior (e.g., doing homework or grading papers) is part of the school as a social system, whether or not it takes place in the school building" (Boocock, 1980, p. 129). So, too, is the involvement of parents in schools and in the school careers of their children. Students with parents who feel comfortable dealing with teachers, who understand what activities to encourage their children to join, who know where and how to challenge and when to defer to the principal's authority—such children, according to interactionists, have a significant advantage over others.

Conflict theorists, by contrast, view education in modern societies as serving to justify and maintain the status quo (Aronowitz and Giroux, 1985; Bowles and Gintis, 1977). For example, on the basis of his field research on secondary-school students in a working-class community, the British sociologist Paul Willis (1983) concluded that "education was not about equality, but inequality. . . . Education's main purpose . . . could be achieved only by preparing most kids for an unequal future, and by insuring their personal under-development" (p. 110). The group of boys from low-income homes whom Willis observed thought of themselves as "the lads" and delighted in making fun of higher achievers, whom they called "earholes." But in many different ways the "lads" indicated that they believed their teachers were pushing them into low-prestige futures. Willis interpreted the hostility and alienation of these students as a way of resisting the social forces channeling them into working-class careers.

As we will see shortly, this critical perspective challenges the more popular view that education is the main route to social mobility and that it can offset inequalities in family background (Bell, 1973). When sociologists analyze the impact of educational institutions on society, they generally conclude that the benefits of education are unequally distributed and tend to reproduce the existing stratification system (Jencks et al., 1972).

Who Goes to School?

The idea that all children should be educated is a product of the American and French revolutions of the late eighteenth century. In the European monarchies the suggestion that the children of peasants and workers should be educated would have been considered laugh-

able. In those societies children went to work with adults at an early age, and adolescence was not recognized as a distinct stage of development. Formal schooling, generally reserved for the children of the elite, typically lasted three or four years, after which the young person entered a profession.

Even after the creation of republics in France and the United States and the beginning of a movement for universal education, the development of a comprehensive system of schools took many generations. In the early history of the United States, the children of slaves, Native Americans, the poor, and many immigrant groups, as well as almost all female children, were excluded from educational institutions. The norm of segregated education for racial minorities persisted into the twentieth century and was not overturned until 1954 in the Supreme Court's famous ruling on *Brown* v. *Board of Education of Topeka*. Even after that decision, years of civil-rights activism were required to ensure that African-Americans could attend public schools with whites. Thus, although the idea of universal education in a democracy arose early, it took many generations of conflict and struggle to transform it into a strong social norm (Cremin, 1980; Aries, 1962).

In the United States the number of children in school is closely correlated with the birthrate.

Today education is compulsory in the United States. The exact requirements vary from one state to another, but in most states children must attend school until age sixteen. Hence, the rate of attendance at primary school and the first two years of high school is nearly 100 percent. This means that the number of children in school is closely correlated with the birthrate (Bogue, 1985).

The post–World War II baby boom caused a bulge in elementary school enrollments beginning in about 1952 and a massive expansion of the college-age population in the 1960s. During those years there was a parallel boom in employment for elementary-school teachers and then for high school teachers and college professors. But after the boom came the bust: The birthrate fell sharply beginning in the late 1950s, and by the mid-1970s college enrollments also began to decline. These changes had dramatic effects on primary schools, but at the college level they were partially offset by an unprecedented countertrend: the immense increase in the number of older students seeking higher education. Today large numbers of adults are returning to college. Unlike the typical student of earlier years, they are in the labor force, are married and living with their spouses, are going to school part time, and are seeking skills and knowledge to enhance their careers (Bogue, 1985; Silberstein, 1981). The return of so many adults to educational institutions has led many social scientists to describe a future in which education will be a lifelong process in which people of all ages will move in and out of educational institutions (Parelius, 1975). Nevertheless, the most rapidly growing area of education is preschool programs, an important trend that is discussed later in the chapter.

Schools and Adolescent Society

A key feature of education is the fact that schools structure the lives of children and adolescents. This is particularly true at the high school level. A famous study of the effect of schools on adolescents and youth, *The Adolescent Society*, was published by James Coleman in 1961. Its main point was that schools help create a social world for adolescents that is separate from adult society. According to Coleman, this is an almost inevitable result of the growing complexity of industrial societies, in which, as we saw earlier, functions that were formerly performed by the family are increasingly shifted to other institutions, especially educational institutions. Yet schools cannot provide the same kind of support and individual attention that the family can. As a result, according to Coleman, the student is "forced inward toward his own age group, made to carry out his whole social life with others his own age.

In the United States public education is seen as a means of transmitting democratic values, creating equality of opportunity, and preparing new generations of citizens to function in society.

With his fellows, he comes to constitute a small society, one that has most of its important interaction *within* itself, and maintains only a few threads of connection with the outside adult society" (1961, p. 3).

Coleman's research was not unique. Other social scientists have analyzed what has come to be known as the "youth culture" in terms of changes in the structure of American society. Briefly, what has happened is that the rising level of expectations regarding educational attainment has placed more and more demands on the student, resulting in "an almost compulsive independence, a touchiness with respect to any adult expectations and demands; [together with] an equally compulsive conformity and loyalty to the peer group, with very literal observation of group norms and intolerance of deviance" (Boocock, 1980, p. 213).

The risk for society in the development of isolated adolescent cultures is that teenagers will fail to learn how they can become involved in shaping their own society. Great cultural gaps between youth and their parents are often a signal that the older generation has not offered young people enough opportunities to work with adults for social change (Gilligan, 1987; Moscos, 1988).

Education and Citizenship

Another important aspect of education in the United States is the relationship between education and citizenship. Throughout its history this nation has emphasized public education as a means of transmitting democratic values, creating equality of opportunity, and preparing new generations of citizens to function in society. In addition, the schools have been expected to help shape society itself. During the 1950s, for example, efforts to combat racial segregation focused on the schools. Later, when the Soviet Union launched the first orbiting satellite, American schools and colleges came under intense pressure and were offered many incentives to improve their science and mathematics programs so that the nation would not fall behind the Soviet Union in scientific and technological capabilities.

Education is often viewed as a tool for

solving social problems, especially social inequality. The schools, it is thought, can transform young people from vastly different backgrounds into competent, upwardly mobile adults. Yet these goals seem almost impossible to attain. In recent years, in fact, public education has been at the center of numerous controversies arising from the gap between the ideal and the reality. Part of the problem is that different groups in society have different expectations. Some feel that students need better preparation for careers in a technologically advanced society; others believe children should be taught basic job-related skills; still others believe education should not only prepare children to compete in society but also help them maintain their cultural identity (and, in the case of Hispanic children, their language). On the other hand, policymakers concerned with education emphasize the need to increase the level of student achievement and to involve parents in their children's education.

Some reformers and critics have called attention to the need to link formal schooling with programs designed to address social problems. Sociologist Charles Moscos, for example, is a leader in the movement to expand programs like the Peace Corps, Vista, and Outward Bound into a system of voluntary national service. National service, as Moscos defines it, would entail "the full-time undertaking of public duties by young people—whether as citizen soldiers or civilian servers—who are paid subsistence wages" and serve for at least one year (1988, p. 1). In return for this period of service, the volunteers would receive assistance in paying for college or other educational expenses.

Advocates of national service and school-to-work programs believe that education does not have to be confined to formal schooling. In devising strategies to provide opportunities for young people to serve their society, they emphasize the educational value of citizenship experiences gained outside the classroom. At this writing there is little indication that national service will become a new educational institution in the United States, although the concept is steadily gaining support among educators and social critics (Moscos, 1988; Janowitz, 1983; Waltzer, 1983).

ATTAINMENT, ACHIEVEMENT, AND EQUALITY

While some educational reformers focus on the need to expand learning opportunities through nonschool service experiences, by far the majority of scholars and administrators seek improvements in educational institutions themselves. Their efforts often focus on educational attainment, or the number of years of schooling that students receive, and educational achievement, or the amount of learning that actually takes place. Both aspects of education are closely linked to economic inequality and social mobility.

Educational Attainment

In any discussion of education as a major social institution, the concept of **educational attainment** (number of years of school completed) holds a central place. Educational attainment is correlated with income, occupation, prestige, attitudes and opinions, and much else. It is essential, therefore, for social scientists to understand the impact of recent trends in school enrollment on the educational attainment of the population as a whole and of various subgroups of the population.

Table 17-1 shows the median number of years of school completed by the population as a whole in the decades since 1940, and Table 17-2 presents data on educational attainment by race, Hispanic origin, and gender. Both tables apply to the population age twenty-five and older. It is immediately clear that the average American today has much more education than the average American of the early 1940s. It is also clear that whites are more likely to complete high school than blacks, and considerably more likely to attend college. With respect to gender, fewer women than men complete four years of college. At

> *Educational attainment is correlated with income, occupation, prestige, and attitudes and opinions.*

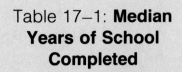

Table 17–1: **Median Years of School Completed**

Year	Median Years of School Completed
1987	12.7
1982	12.6
1980	12.5
1970	12.2
1960	10.6
1950	9.3
1940	8.6

Source: Census Bureau, 1988.

Martin Trow (1966) studied the historical trend toward increasingly higher average levels of educational attainment in the American population, particularly the increase in the proportion of the population completing high school since the late nineteenth century. In his words, the nation now has "universal secondary education . . . through a system of comprehensive high schools, devoted primarily to the education of the great mass of its students for work and life" (p. 448). This is in sharp contrast with the situation in 1870, when there were only 80,000 students enrolled in high schools throughout the country.

Although the public schools were taking in millions of students, in the 1920s they began to use "tracking" systems in which higher-achieving students were placed in accelerated classes while others were shunted into vocational and other types of less challenging classes. Today tracking remains a major problem in public schools. Parents of "gifted" children seek educational challenges for their sons and daughters and do not want them to be held back by slower learners. However, tracking systems can make average students feel less valued, and there is a danger that gifted but alienated students will be labeled as nonachievers.

the high school level, however, the proportions are reversed: More women than men complete high school. With respect to age, the data indicate the increasingly high value placed on education, especially college education. People over seventy-five, who were born in the early decades of the twentieth century, have, on the average, considerably lower levels of educational attainment than their children and grandchildren (Bogue, 1985).

The trend toward increasingly higher levels of educational attainment has had an unexpected effect known as "degree infla-

Table 17–2: **Percent of Persons Age 25 and Older Who Have Completed High School or College, by Race, Hispanic Origin, and Gender: 1947–1987**

	Percent High School Graduate						Percent College Graduate					
	White		Black		Hispanic		White		Black		Hispanic	
Year	M	F	M	F	M	F	M	F	M	F	M	F
1987	77%	77%	63%	64%	52%	50%	25%	17%	11%	10%	10%	8%
1980	71	70	51	51	46	44	22	14	8	8	10	6
1970	57	58	32	35	NA	NA	15	9	5	4	NA	NA
1962	47	50	23	26	NA	NA	12	7	4	4	NA	NA
1947	33	37	13	15	NA	NA	7	5	2	3	NA	NA

NOTE: NA = Data not available
Source: Census Bureau, 1988.

tion." Employers have always paid attention to the educational credentials of potential employees, but today they require much more education than in the past. For example, in earlier decades of this century a person could get a teaching job with a high school diploma; now a bachelor's and often a master's degree is usually required. The same is true of social work. And secretaries, who formerly could get by without a high school diploma, now are often required to have at least some college education and, in some cases, a college degree.

Another problem related to educational attainment is the high rate of functional incompetency among Americans—that is, the large number of people who are unable to read, write, keep a family budget, and the like (see Figure 17-1). Although more and more people are obtaining a college education, many others are being left behind, particularly members of the lower social classes, people for whom English is a second language, and people with learning disabilities. As increasing amounts of education are required for better jobs, this cleavage between educational "haves" and "have-nots" becomes an ever more dangerous trend.

Barriers to Educational Attainment. The educational attainment of various subgroups of the population is virtually identical up to the age of thirteen (Jencks et al., 1972). The picture begins to change in the early secondary-school years, however. Until quite recently the dropout rate for black and Hispanic students in high school was almost twice the rate for white students. In 1970, 10.8 percent of white students dropped out without finishing high school, while among black students the proportion was 22.2 percent. By 1988, the situation had improved remarkably as a result of strenuous efforts by students, parents, and teachers across the United States. In that year 10.3 percent of white students and 12.0 percent of black students dropped out. Table 17-3 shows that graduation rates (the opposite of dropout rates) vary among the states, with the highest in Minnesota at

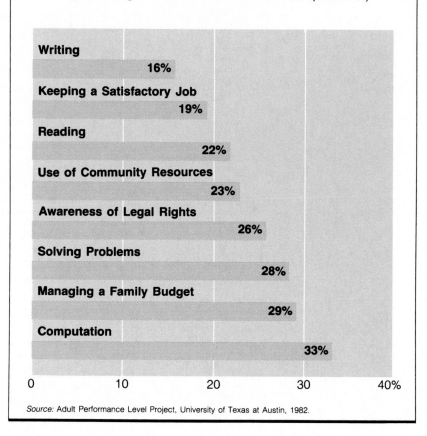

Figure 17–1: **Functional Incompetency Among Americans**

(percentage of all adults who are incompetent in)

Writing	16%
Keeping a Satisfactory Job	19%
Reading	22%
Use of Community Resources	23%
Awareness of Legal Rights	26%
Solving Problems	28%
Managing a Family Budget	29%
Computation	33%

Source: Adult Performance Level Project, University of Texas at Austin, 1982.

90.60 percent and the lowest in Florida at 58.6 percent.

The main reason for dropping out of school is poor academic performance, but there are other reasons as well. Students often drop out because of the demands of work and family roles; many are married, or unmarried and pregnant, and/or working at regular jobs. Whatever the reason, the effects of dropping out can be serious. Dropouts have less chance of joining the labor force than high school graduates; whatever jobs they find tend to be low-paying. In fact, the lifetime earnings of high school graduates average $200,000 more than those of dropouts. Faced with these odds, about 40 percent of dropouts eventually decide to go back to school (Pallas, 1987).

Table 17–3: **Graduation Rate by State For the 1986–87 School Year**

	Rate	Rank		Rate	Rank		Rate	Rank
Ala.	70.2%	34	La.	60.1%	49	Okla.	72.6%	30
Alaska	66.7	41	Maine	79.3	13	Ore.	72.8	28
Ariz.	64.4	45	Mass.	76.5	20	Pa.	78.7	15
Ark.	77.5	18	Md.	74.5	23	R.I.	69.4	36
Calif.	66.1	42	Mich.	62.4	48	S.C.	66.9	40
Colo.	73.7	26	Minn.	90.6	1	S.D.	79.7	12
Conn.	80.5	11	Miss.	64.8	44	Tenn.	67.8	38
D.C.	55.5	51	Mo.	74.4	24	Tex.	65.1	43
Del.	70.1	35	Mont.	86.2	6	Utah	80.6	10
Fla.	58.6	50	N.C.	67.8	37	Va.	74.0	25
Ga.	62.5	47	N.D.	88.4	3	Vt.	78.0	16
Hawaii	70.8	33	N.H.	72.7	29	W.Va.	76.2	21
Idaho	78.8	14	N.J.	77.2	19	Wash.	77.8	17
Ill.	75.7	22	N.M.	71.7	32	Wis.	85.4	7
Ind.	73.7	27	N.Y.	62.9	46	Wyo.	89.3	2
Iowa	86.4	5	Neb.	86.7	4	TOTAL	71.1	—
Kan.	82.1	9	Nev.	72.1	31			
Ky.	67.4	39	Ohio	82.8	8			

Source: U.S. Department of Education.

Educational Achievement

Differences in levels of educational attainment are viewed as a sign that public education is not meeting the expectations of society in terms of the quantity of education provided to citizens. There is also controversy over the *quality* of education, or educational achievement as reflected in scores on standardized tests like the Scholastic Aptitude Test (SAT). **Educational achievement** refers to how much the student actually learns, measured by mastery of reading, writing, and mathematical skills. It is widely believed that the average level of educational achievement has declined drastically in the past two decades. In a 1983 report entitled *A Nation at Risk*, the National Commission on Excellence in Education pointed to the decline in the average test scores of high school students since the mid-1960s and stated that the schools have failed to maintain high educational standards. Other observers attributed the decline to a variety of social conditions such as excessive

television viewing and changing values related to family life.

The mean scores on the SAT did decline significantly between 1965 and 1980—by about 50 points on the verbal section and about 30 points on the mathematical section. Similar declines were recorded in achievement test scores, not only for high school students but also for students in the late elementary-school years. These data were interpreted as indicating that the average educational achievement of American students had decreased. However, on the basis of a thorough analysis of the data, Scott Menard (1981) concluded that there was no significant correlation between the drop in test scores and such factors as changes in educational curricula, automatic promotion, changes in the tests themselves, and nonacademic changes such as increased drug use and the growing number of single-parent families. Instead, he suggested that the decline in test scores might be associated with a complex set of factors linked to the postwar baby boom, including birth order, family size, and child spacing. Some support for this view can be seen in the fact that the decline in test scores seemed to end in the mid-1980s. Nevertheless, there is considerable pressure for higher educational standards and for other reforms; an example is described in Box 17-1.

Education and Social Mobility

Studies by educational sociologists have consistently found a high correlation between social class and educational attainment and achievement, so much so that major efforts to address inequalities in educational opportunities were undertaken during the 1960s and 1970s. Nevertheless, there is evidence that the promise of equal education for all remains far from being fulfilled. Educational institutions have been subjected to considerable criticism by observers who believe that they hinder, rather than enhance, social mobility. Christopher Jencks (1972), for example, argued that schools serve primarily to reproduce the existing stratification system. He asserted that "schools serve primarily as selection and certification agencies, whose job is to measure and label people, and only secondarily as socialization agencies, whose job is to change people" (p. 135).

Jencks noted that the main criterion for granting a diploma or degree (i.e., certification) is usually the amount of time spent in school, not the skills learned. "Imagine," he wrote, "what would happen to high school

Box 17–1: **QUASAR: Reasoning with Numbers**

An example of the kinds of reforms advocated by many educators today is the Ford Foundation's QUASAR project (Quantitative Understanding: Amplifying Student Achievement and Reasoning). The project is designed to teach students a two-step process for solving mathematical problems: performing the numerical calculations and then referring to the problem situation and considering the reasonableness of their answer.

Consider the following problem: An army bus holds 36 soldiers. If 1,128 soldiers are being bused to their training site, how many buses are needed? Most American thirteen-year-olds can perform the necessary calculations to solve this problem. The most frequent answer they give is 31 1/3, which requires that 12 of the soldiers ride in part of a bus. But only 23 percent provide the correct answer, 32, which takes into account the need for a whole number of buses.

The reason relatively few children answer such problems correctly is that the mathematics traditionally taught in school bears little resemblance to mathematics as it is used in the real world. School math is arithmetic, a series of computational tasks that can be solved using rote memory, whereas real-world math is a way of perceiving patterns, analyzing data, and using reasoning to arrive at conclusions. Although students in other countries also have trouble applying thoughtfulness and reflection to quantitative situations, in countries ranging from Canada to Korea significantly higher percentages of thirteen-year-olds are able to solve two-step problems like the one just described (see chart).

Centered in the Houston Independent School District, the QUASAR project focuses on placing traditional math skills in problem-solving contexts that are of everyday interest and usefulness to the student. Calculators and computers are used in ways that encourage experimentation and create new opportunities for developing number sense. The goal is to turn classrooms into environments in which students think as well as memorize and in which teachers stimulate mathematical reasoning as well as transmit facts.

enrollment if states allowed anyone, regardless of age, to take a high school equivalency examination. Most capable students would probably leave high school by the time they were 16" (1972, pp. 135–136). In their study of the relationship between educational certification and inequality, Jencks and his researchers assumed that "the value of any given credential depends solely on how long it takes to acquire" (p. 136). And the chief factor that keeps some students in school and college longer than others, according to Jencks, is family background—in other words, social class. Members of the upper classes often regard college as an important transition to high-status occupations and therefore encourage their children to finish high school and attend college.

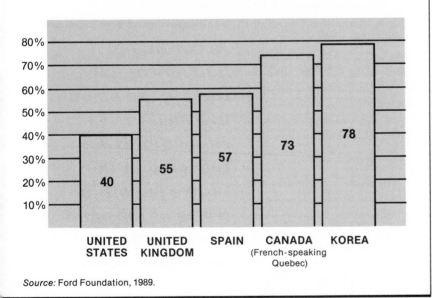

Percentage of 13-Year-Olds Who Can Perform Two-Step Mathematics Problems

Source: Ford Foundation, 1989.

The program also employs new techniques for assessing students' mathematical reasoning abilities, such as observing their problem-solving efforts and asking them open-ended questions (Ford Foundation, 1989).

Inequality in the Classroom. In a book entitled *The Urban School: A Factory for Failure* (1973), Ray C. Rist went even further, bluntly stating that "the system of public education in the United States is specifically designed to aid in the perpetuation of the social and economic inequalities found within the society" (p. 2)—despite the widespread belief that education increases social mobility. In other words,

Schooling has basically served to instill the values of an expanding industrial society and to fit the aspirations and motivations of individuals to the labor market at approximately the same level as that of their parents. Thus it is that some children find themselves slotted toward becoming workers and others toward becoming the managers of those workers. [1973, p. 2]

Rist conducted a landmark study of this issue in which he sought to discover why "the children of the affluent by and large take the best marks and the best jobs" (Katz, 1971, p. xviii). He focused on what actually happens in the classroom, specifically on teachers' expectations regarding their pupils. His hypothesis was that teachers, by expecting a particular level of performance of a particular child, actually cause that child to perform accordingly. In that way the schools create "winners and losers" in the classroom, with the "winners" usually coming from a higher social-class background than the "losers."

Rist observed the interactions between teachers and students in a kindergarten class and a second-grade class at an urban elementary school over a period of about three years. His observations revealed that in the early grades of school there develops "a stratification system, based both on teacher expectations about behavioral and attitudinal characteristics of the child and on a variety of socioeconomic factors related to the child's background" (Rist, 1973, p. 239). By the second grade, children are assigned to groups on the basis of their past performance records, and with few exceptions they have no opportunity to move out of the group to which they have been assigned, regardless of their performance on intelligence or academic tests. For example, one student, unknown to the teacher, had an IQ of 121, but his teacher told Rist that he "will have to go" (i.e., be placed in a special-education class because of low intelligence). The teachers also engaged in more obvious labeling, such as assigning students to groups based on reading ability and calling the groups "Tigers," "Cardinals," and "Clowns."

Inequality in Higher Education. Inequality in higher education is primarily a matter of access—that is, ability to pay. Ability to pay is unequally distributed among various groups in society, and as a result students from poor, working-class, and lower-middle-class families, as well as members of racial minority groups, are most likely to rely on public colleges and universities. Social-scientific evidence indicates that such inequalities are alleviated by federal aid to students from families with low or moderate income. It is likely that without Pell grants, work-study funds, and student loan programs the proportion of students from such families would be far lower than it currently is. Even with such aid, the proportion of low-income students in colleges and universities is lower than that of students from high-income families.

Sandra Baum (1987) examined the educational careers of 2,000 students who were high school seniors in 1980. She found that college attendance rates were higher for students from high-income families than for students from low-income families (60 percent versus 46 percent). However, achievement in school seemed to account for an even larger difference. Students who scored high on achievement tests but came from low-income families had far higher rates of college attendance than low-scoring students from affluent homes. Thus achievement in the primary-school grades seems to be at least as important as family income in explaining a student's success in higher education—but remember that in the lower grades students from more affluent homes tend to achieve more than students from less advantaged homes.

Baum and other researchers have also found that low-income students tend to be concentrated in two-year colleges and that students in such colleges are much more likely to drop out before completing a degree than students who enter four-year colleges. On the basis of findings like these, most educational researchers agree that without college assistance for needy students, class differences in educational attainment and achievement would be much greater. And since public higher-education institutions remain the primary route to college degrees for low-income students, increased support for such institutions also tends to diminish inequality in access to higher education (Baum, 1987; Hansen and Stampen, 1987; Institute for Research on Poverty, 1987).

Education for Equality

The question of whether and in what ways education leads to social mobility remains an open one. Some social scientists view education as an investment like any other: The amount invested is reflected in the future payoff. This is known as human-capital theory. In this view, differences in payoffs (jobs and social position) are justified by differences in investment (hard work in school and investment in a college education). On the other hand, critics of the educational system point out that the resources required to make such "investments" are not equally available to all members of society.

The issue of whether the society as a whole, or only its more affluent members, will invest in its "human capital" through such means as preschool programs and student loans is a major public-policy issue. This is especially true as technological advances coupled with degree inflation increase the demand for educated people (Bell, 1973). Empirical evidence of the effectiveness of such investments may be seen in the results of an innovative study conducted by the High/Scope Educational Research Foundation (Berrueta-Clement et al., 1984).

The subject of the study was a preschool program at the Perry Elementary School, lo-

> *According to human-capital theory, the amount invested in education is reflected in the future payoff in terms of jobs and social position.*

Nursery and preschool programs that focus on enriching the learning environment can have lasting beneficial effects on educational achievement.

cated in a low-income black neighborhood of Ypsilanti, Michigan, a small industrial city on the outskirts of Detroit. The researchers randomly selected 123 three-year-old boys and girls and assigned them either to the preschool group or to another group that would not go to the preschool program. The latter children, like the majority of children at that time, would not be enrolled in school for another two years.

About twice a year for the next twenty years the researchers traced the experiences of the experimental (preschool) and control (nonpreschool) groups. The data in Table 17-4 show that there were important differences between the two groups as a consequence of

the preschool experience. Members of the preschool group achieved more in school, found better jobs, had fewer arrests, and had fewer illegitimate children; in short, they experienced more success and fewer problems than members of the control group. These findings confirm what other, less well-known studies had shown. For example, studies by Benjamin Bloom (1976) and by Piaget and Inhelder (1969) had indicated that as much as 50 percent of variance in intellectual development takes place before the age of four.

The most significant contribution of studies like the High/Scope research is their documentation of the actual improvements that a good preschool program can produce

Table 17–4: **Major Findings at Age 19 in the Perry Preschool Study**

Category	Number[a] Responding	Preschool Group	No-Preschool Group
Employed	121	59%	32%
High school graduation (or its equivalent)	121	67%	49%
College or vocational training	121	38%	21%
Ever detained or arrested	121	31%	51%
Females only: teen pregnancies, per 100[b]	49	64	117
Functional competence (APL Survey: possible score 40)	109	24.6	21.8
% of years in special education	112	16%	28%

[a]Total $N = 123$
[b]Includes all pregnancies
In a longitudinal study at Perry Elementary School, researchers traced the experiences of two groups of people, beginning at 3 years of age. This table shows some results of that study.

Source: Berrueta–Clement et al., 1984.

in disadvantaged children. The High/Scope study was also able to translate its findings into dollar figures. A year in the Perry program cost about $1,350 per child. The researchers showed that the "total social benefit" from the program (measured by higher tax revenues, lower welfare payments, and lower crime costs) was equivalent to $6,866 per person.

Research like the High/Scope study provides ample evidence of the potential value of investments in educational reform. President Bush, wishing to be known as the "education president," has encouraged efforts to institute such reforms. Some of these efforts are occurring at the state level, where there are glaring inequalities in spending per pupil in the public schools. In part, this situation is due to the fact that in most states the bulk of school revenues are derived from local taxes. More affluent communities generate higher revenues and therefore can spend more for education than poor communities. To some extent these disparities are made up for by state and federal funds, but among all sources the federal budget provides the least money for schools (7 percent in 1990). State funds are now more important than federal or municipal funds, and state courts in Montana, Texas, Kentucky, and other states are seeking formulas for spending those funds in ways that will reduce inequalities in educational opportunity (Suro, 1990).

THE STRUCTURE OF EDUCATIONAL INSTITUTIONS

A significant barrier to educational reform is the bureaucratic nature of school systems. We noted earlier that sociologists view the school as a specialized structure with a special socializing function and that it is also a good example of a bureaucratic organization. As any student knows, there is a clearly defined status hierarchy in most schools. At the top of the hierarchy in primary and secondary schools is the principal, followed by the assistant principal and/or administrative assistants, the counselors, the teachers, and the students. Although the principal holds the highest position in the system, his or her influence on students usually is indirect. The teacher, on the other hand, is in daily command of the classroom and therefore has the greatest impact on the students. In this section we discuss several aspects of the structure of educational institutions and attempts to change those institutions.

Schools as Bureaucracies

As the size and complexity of the American educational system have increased, so has the tendency of educational institutions to become bureaucratized (Parelius and Parelius, 1987). The one-room schoolhouse is a thing of the past; today's schools have large administrative staffs and numerous specialists such as guidance counselors and special-education teachers. Teachers themselves specialize in particular subject areas or grade levels. Schools are also characterized by a hierarchy of authority, as shown in Figure 17-2. The number of levels in the hierarchy varies, depending on the nature of the school system. In large cities, for example, there may be as many as seven levels between the superintendent and school personnel, making it difficult for the superintendent to control the way policies are carried out. Similarly, in any given school it may be difficult for the principal to determine what actually happens in the classroom.

The Classroom. In most modern school systems the primary-school student is in the charge of one teacher, who instructs in almost all subjects. But as the student advances through the educational structure the primary-school model, which evolved from the one-room school with a single teacher, is replaced by a "departmental" structure in which the student encounters a number of specialized teachers. The latter structure is derived largely from that of the nineteenth-century English boarding school. But these two basic structures are frequently modified by alternative approaches like the "open" primary-

Sociologists believe that students' experiences in the classroom are of central importance to their later development.

school classroom, in which students are grouped according to their level of achievement in certain basic skills and work in these skill groups at their own pace. The various groups in the open classroom are given small-group or individual instruction by one or more teachers rather than being expected to progress at the same pace in every subject.

Open classrooms have not been found to produce consistent improvements in student performance, but they have improved the school-attendance rates of students from working-class and minority backgrounds. Students in open classrooms tend to express greater satisfaction with school and more commitment to classwork. The less stratified authority structure of the open classroom and the greater amount of cooperation that occurs in such settings may help students enjoy school more and, in the long run, cause them to have a more positive attitude toward learning.

The Teacher's Role. Given the undeniable importance of classroom experience, sociologists have done a considerable amount of research on what goes on in the classroom. Often they start from the premise that, along with the influence of peers, students' experiences in the classroom are of central importance to their later development. One study (Pedersen and Faucher, 1978) examined the impact of a single first-grade teacher on her students' subsequent adult status (see Box 17-2). The surprising results of this study have important implications. It is evident that good teachers can make a big difference in children's lives, a fact that gives increased urgency to the need to improve the quality of primary-school teaching. The reforms carried out by educational leaders like James Comer suggest that when good teaching is combined with high levels of parental involvement the results can be even more dramatic.

Because the role of the teacher is to change the learner in some way, the teacher–student relationship is an important part of education. Sociologists have pointed out that this relationship is asymmetrical or unbalanced, with the teacher being in a position of authority and the student having little choice

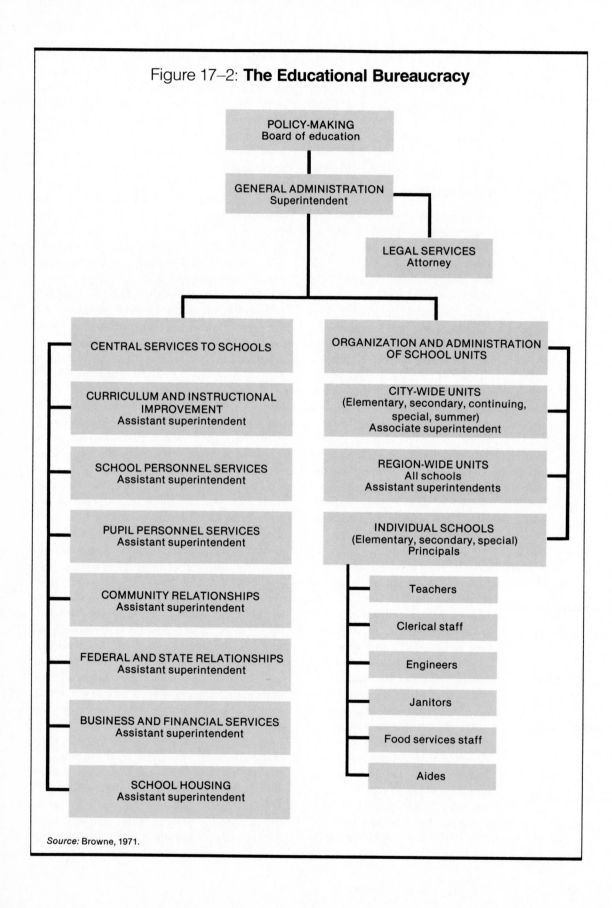

Figure 17–2: **The Educational Bureaucracy**

POLICY-MAKING
Board of education

GENERAL ADMINISTRATION
Superintendent

LEGAL SERVICES
Attorney

CENTRAL SERVICES TO SCHOOLS

CURRICULUM AND INSTRUCTIONAL
IMPROVEMENT
Assistant superintendent

SCHOOL PERSONNEL SERVICES
Assistant superintendent

PUPIL PERSONNEL SERVICES
Assistant superintendent

COMMUNITY RELATIONSHIPS
Assistant superintendent

FEDERAL AND STATE RELATIONSHIPS
Assistant superintendent

BUSINESS AND FINANCIAL SERVICES
Assistant superintendent

SCHOOL HOUSING
Assistant superintendent

ORGANIZATION AND ADMINISTRATION
OF SCHOOL UNITS

CITY-WIDE UNITS
(Elementary, secondary, continuing,
special, summer)
Associate superintendent

REGION-WIDE UNITS
All schools
Assistant superintendents

INDIVIDUAL SCHOOLS
(Elementary, secondary, special)
Principals

Teachers

Clerical staff

Engineers

Janitors

Food services staff

Aides

Source: Browne, 1971.

but to passively absorb the information provided by the teacher. In other words, in conventional classrooms there is little opportunity for the student to become actively involved in the learning process. On the other hand, students often develop strategies for undercutting the teacher's authority: mentally withdrawing, interrupting, and the like (Bayh, 1975; Csikszentmihalyi, Larson, and Prescott, 1977; Holt, 1965, 1967; Ritterband and Silberstein, 1973). Hence, much current research assumes that students and teachers influence each other instead of assuming that the influence is always in a single direction.

Changing the System: Desegregation

The bureaucratic organization of school systems makes them highly resistant to change. The basic classroom unit has remained essentially unchanged since the days of the one-room school, as has the structure in which one teacher is in charge of a roomful of students. Some efforts have been made to apply technological advances, especially closed-circuit television and computerized teaching techniques, to improve instruction in public schools. Although these efforts have had some positive results, including better instructional materials and a greater variety of courses, some teachers oppose such innovations out of fear that they will undermine their authority. (The implications of technological advances in educational methods are discussed further in the Challenges section of this chapter.)

Although legally sanctioned segregation of schools has been eliminated, de facto segregation remains common in many parts of the nation.

Despite the difficulties encountered in changing educational institutions, there are some areas in which they have been forced to change. No doubt the most significant change in educational institutions in the past quarter-century was desegregation. Efforts to desegregate public schools began in 1954 with the Supreme Court's ruling in *Brown* v. *Board of Education of Topeka*; the Court held that segregation had a negative effect on black students even if their school facilities were "separate but equal" to those of white students. In the first few years after this landmark decision, most of the states in which schools had been legally segregated instituted desegregation programs. However, in some states, particularly in the Deep South (or in large urban centers in the North), desegregation orders were resisted, and by 1967 only 26 percent of the nation's school districts were desegregated (Rist, 1979).

Further progress toward desegregated schools was made after the passage of the Civil Rights Act of 1964 and the Elementary and Secondary Education Act of 1965; by 1973, *de jure* (legally sanctioned) segregation had been almost entirely eliminated. However, *de facto* (in-practice) segregation remained common in many parts of the nation. This pattern was created by two factors: school districts' traditional policy of requiring students to attend schools in their own neighborhoods, and "white flight," the tendency of whites to move to the suburbs in order to take advantage of suburban housing opportunities and, in some cases, to avoid sending their children to schools with large percentages of black students. On the basis of an extensive study of the impact of desegregation programs, Coleman (1976) concluded that "policies of school desegregation which focus wholly on within-district segregation . . . are increasing, rather than reducing or reversing, the tendency for our large metropolitan areas to consist of black central cities and white suburbs" (p. 12).

Coleman's findings had a significant influence on the policy debates that took place throughout the 1970s and 1980s over what could be done to increase racial equality in public education, especially the issue of whether schoolchildren should be bused across city lines. Educational policymakers are now seeking ways of promoting racial integration, not only by means of busing plans but also through changes in school curriculums and instructional methods. However, the process of racial integration still has a long way to go. Along with other educational issues, it is likely to occupy a central place on the national policy agenda for the foreseeable future.

Box 17–2: **One Remarkable First-Grade Teacher**

In an unusual study of teacher–student interaction, Eigil Pedersen and Therese Annette Faucher (1978) demonstrated the persisting value of an outstanding primary-school teacher. As debates continue over how much difference good teaching can make and as governments and school systems wonder whether they should do more to reward good teaching, the results of this study bear careful review.

Pedersen and Faucher began their study of IQ and achievement patterns among disadvantaged children at a school that was marked by high rates of failure. A high percentage of the school's graduates failed in their first year of high school and dropped out. The researchers attempted to explain these failure rates in terms of the concept of the "self-fulfilling prophecy," the idea that if teachers expect students to do poorly, the students are likely to perform accordingly. But if the negative prophecy seems to work in

many instances, can we find evidence that a *positive* self-fulfilling prophecy—the belief that students can perform well—will also work? This is what makes the Pederson–Faucher study so interesting.

As they examined the IQ scores of pupils in the school's first-grade classes, the researchers found a clear association between changes in a pupil's IQ and the pupil's family background, first-grade teacher, and self-concept. Further examination of the school's records revealed a startling fact: The IQs of pupils in one particular teacher's first-grade class were significantly more likely to increase in subsequent years than the IQs of pupils in first-grade classes taught by other teachers. And pupils who had been members of that class were more than twice as likely to achieve high status as adults as pupils who had been members of other first-grade classes (see table).

What was so special about Miss A, as the outstanding teacher was labeled?

Adult Status, by First-Grade Teacher

Adult Status	First-Grade Teacher			
	Miss A	Miss B	Miss C	Others
High	64%	31%	10%	39%
Medium	36%	38%	45%	22%
Low	0%	31%	45%	39%
Total	100%	100%	100%	100%
(*N*)	(14)	(16)	(11)	(18)
Mean adult status	7.0	4.8	4.3	4.6

(*N*) = number of students who could be located and interviewed twenty-five years later.

"Adult status" was determined from interviews that included questions on occupational status and work history, highest grade completed, rent paid and number of rooms, and related indicators of social position.

Source: Pederson, Eigil, and Faucher, Therese Annette, "A New Perspective on the Effects of First-Grade Teachers on Children's Subsequent Adult Status," *Harvard Educational Review,* 1978, 48:1, 1–31. Copyright © 1978 by the President and Fellows of Harvard College. All rights reserved.

First, she was still remembered by her students when they were interviewed twenty-five years after they had been in her class. More than three-quarters of those students rated her as very good or excellent as a teacher. They said that "it did not matter what background or abilities the beginning pupil had; there was no way that the pupil was not going to read by the end of grade one." Miss A left her pupils with a "profound impression of the importance of schooling, and how one should stick to it" and "gave extra hours to the children who were slow learners." In nonacademic matters, too, Miss A was unusual. "When children forgot their lunches, she would give them some of her own, and she invariably stayed after hours to help children. Not only did her pupils remember her, but she apparently could remember each former pupil by name even after an interval of twenty years. She adjusted to new math and reading methods, but her success was summarized by a former colleague this way: 'How did she teach? With a lot of love!'" (pp. 19–20).

In summing up their findings, Pedersen and Faucher stated that their data "suggest that an effective first-grade teacher can influence social mobility" (p. 29). Their findings differ from those of Coleman (1976) and Jencks (1972), who believe that there is little correlation between school experiences and adult status. Pedersen and Faucher agree that further research on the relationship between teacher effects and adult status is needed. However, "In the meantime, teachers . . . should not accept too readily the frequent assertion that their efforts make no long-term difference to the future success of their pupils" (p. 30).

THE COMMUNICATIONS MEDIA

We turn now to another major institution of modern societies: the communications media, or mass media. The decade of the 1990s began with a stirring lesson on the importance of communications media in the modern world. Throughout the world people were riveted to their television sets as they learned about the overthrow of a tyrant in Romania. For several weeks they had watched as one after another of the communist states of Eastern Europe faltered and toppled—first Poland, then Hungary, then Czechoslovakia, then East Germany. But the situation in Romania was far more violent—and much more public. In that nation, in fact, television played a dominant role in the revolution that put an end to communist rule.

Shortly before the uprising, the Romanian dictator, Nicolae Ceausescu, had ordered security forces to massacre citizens in the provincial capital of Timisoara. The shootings were ordered over a closed-circuit television network. Following the massacre Ceausescu called for a "spontaneous demonstration" by his supporters in the main square of the capital, Bucharest; the demonstration would be televised and broadcast throughout the nation. However, by giving this order he in effect organized the demonstration that would lead to his downfall.

Students at the University of Bucharest were on their first day of winter vacation when they heard the news of the Timisoara massacre. Many went to the main square, where the university is located. There they encountered the official demonstration in support of the dictator. When Ceausescu tried to defend the killings he had ordered, the students hissed and booed. The dictator reacted with a stunned look and paused in his speech. After a few minutes the television broadcast was stopped. For the first time, viewers throughout the nation became aware not only that a massacre had taken place but also that the dictator who had ordered it was vulnerable himself. In the following days demonstrations against Ceausescu evolved into a full-scale revolution. The revolutionary forces occupied the national television studios, and the world watched the downfall of a notorious tyrant via satellite transmission.

Several months earlier, an equally dramatic rebellion had occurred in China when students and workers held a massive demonstration in Tiananmen Square in Beijing. However, the Chinese dictatorship had been able to maintain its power, partly because it never lost control of the media and, hence, the ability to define the situation for the public. Had the Chinese people, like those of Romania, had the opportunity to watch what was taking place on television, even the entrenched Chinese regime might have fallen.

Media Institutions in Modern Societies

Communications media are institutions that specialize in communicating information, images, and values about ourselves, our communities, and our society. Typical media institutions in modern societies are the print media (newspapers and magazines), movies, radio, and television. In the United States the messages communicated by the media can be political or nonpolitical, religious or secular, educational or purely entertaining, but in every case they use symbols to tell us something about ourselves and our environment.

Many social scientists have been deeply impressed by the media's ability to incorporate people into a society's national life and bring about changes in their traditional values. The media are run by professional communicators, people who are skilled in producing and transmitting news and other communications. These skills can be used to enhance the ability of national leaders to influence and persuade the masses. For this reason, the media are always under pressure to communicate the information and values that people in power want to have communicated.

The influence of the media is a source of continual controversy as different groups strive for greater control over media communications. In many societies the media are subject to strict censorship. The very idea of news and entertainment institutions that are free from censorship by political or religious institutions is a relatively recent development. But even in societies like the United States, which pride themselves on laws that protect the freedom of the press and other media, we can find numerous examples of conflict between norms that establish media freedom and norms that are designed to control the media. When American armed forces invaded Grenada, military officers barred reporters from the field of battle for "security reasons." A reporter who published a story about an organized-crime figure was ordered to reveal the sources of his information to a federal court, but he refused to do so on the ground that the law guaranteed his right to maintain the confidentiality of his informants. We could add many other examples. The point is that the freedom of the press and the other media and their existence as separate institutions can never be taken for granted.

Research on media consumption does not support the theory that the media have produced a mass culture.

In the remainder of this section we look at some typical patterns of media consumption in the United States and at how the media influence individual behavior. We then examine the issue of media differentiation: What is the basic structure of media institutions as we know them, and how has that structure developed in relation to other institutions, especially government and the economy? Finally, we turn to the question of how powerful the media are and whether there are any limits on their power. We will see evidence of the immense influence of the media in American political life, together with other evidence suggesting that the media's ability to determine people's behavior is far from absolute.

Taking full advantage of the presence of TV cameras and reporters, these Romanian protesters remove a statue of Lenin from its pedestal, thereby proclaiming their right to determine their own political destiny.

Patterns of Media Consumption

"Everyone agrees," wrote Harold Wilensky (1964) in an influential paper, "that abundance everywhere brings a rise in mass communications, through radio, television, and press; the development of mass education and the concomitant spread of literacy; and finally, mass entertainment on a grand scale" (p. 173). But he and other sociologists also believe that the media have produced a *mass culture* in which an increasing number of people have similar cultural tastes and political values, which are shaped by the media. At the middle and lower levels of the stratification system, according to this view, people form an increasingly homogeneous mass with similar thoughts and feelings. But those thoughts and feelings are not anchored in spiritual and moral values; they are fluid and can be easily manipulated by those who control media organizations.

But what are the facts? As usual, the first responsibility of the sociologist when faced with claims like these is to try to support or refute them with empirical facts. This effort begins with measures of how much time people actually spend as consumers of different kinds of media communications. For example, in 1988 the average American household had its television sets turned on for almost 50 hours per week. To understand what such numbers signify, it is necessary to compare television viewing with the use of other media and to see how patterns of media consumption change over time. Data from National

Opinion Research Center (NORC) polls taken ten years apart are presented in Table 17-5. They indicate that there has been a decrease in newspaper reading, yet at the same time they show that for the majority of American adults the daily paper remains an important source of news, information, and entertainment. The data also show that contrary to what many people think, television did not make radio obsolete. In fact, radio competes well with television for people's attention, especially at work and in cars, where television generally is not available. Still, television ranks far above all other media in surveys of how people use their leisure time.

The data in Table 17-5 also suggest that there have been small but potentially significant decreases in television watching. Remember that in large populations even small percentage changes can mean large changes in absolute numbers. In fact, the major networks and communications corporations are worried about this trend, for if it continues, it could mean huge losses of advertising revenue. In sum, the data do not lend much support to the mass culture theory. They do show that people consume a great deal of media communication, but their tastes are diverse, and they continue to read as well as to watch and listen. As a result, they are not really homogeneous in their tastes, and the decrease in television viewing time suggests that they are not unduly influenced by media communications.

Television and Violence

Does watching a lot of television lead people to commit violent acts? Few questions about the media have generated as much research and debate as this one. Indeed, this question is a good test of the media's power to influence behavior, as opposed to attitudes and opinions. Each hour of prime-time television programming presents an average of five acts of violence. Various studies have examined the connection between televised violence and violent behavior, especially in children and teenagers. Many of these studies have found a causal relationship between the viewing of violence on television and later aggressive be-

Table 17–5: Media Consumption by American Adults, NORC General Survey, 1975 and 1985

The Press	1975	1985
Read every day	66.9%	53.6%
Once a week	8.5	22.2
Less than once a week	5.4	6.6
Never	4.3	5.8

Radio/hrs./day	1975	1985
None	1.0%	0.0%
1–4 hours	77.0	75.5
5 or more hours	22.0	24.1

Television/hrs./day	1975	1985
None	3.4%	4.5%
1–4 hrs.	78.1	79.0
5 or more hours	18.3	16.7

Total number of respondents in the samples varies between 1.380 and 1.520. Percentages may not add to 100 owing to small number of don't know answers and rounding error.

Source: National Opinion Research Center (NORC), 1986.

havior, but some have concluded that such a relationship cannot be demonstrated (e.g., Kaplan and Singer, 1976; Milavsky, 1977). In 1982, however, the National Institute of Mental Health reported that "there is now 'overwhelming' scientific evidence that 'excessive' violence on television leads directly to aggression and violent behavior among teen-agers" (Reinhold, 1982).

Some researchers believe that the effects of televised violence are indirect. According to Hartnagel, Teevan, and McIntyre (1975), "TV violence influences behavior in an indirect fashion, through its impact on learned values and attitudes. . . . Values and attitudes . . . may be substantially affected by television programming, which may, in turn, influence behavior" (p. 348). Of course, not all viewers are equally likely to be affected by what they see on television. With this in mind, Eli Rubinstein (1981) studied the effects of televised violence on emotionally disturbed children. He found that the children's behaviors were related to what they saw on television: They imitated aggressive behavior and pretended to be characters in their favorite programs.

It is obvious that not every viewer of televised violence is tempted to act out that violence. It is equally clear, however, that there is some not-yet-determined relationship between televised violence and aggressive behavior in some individuals. The relationship appears to depend at least in part on the viewer's emotional condition. Contending that the research findings are inconclusive, the major television networks have resisted efforts to regulate the content of their programming, although the first hour of prime time, from 8:00 to 9:00 P.M., has been labeled the "family hour" and is limited to programs that are deemed appropriate for family viewing.

The Differentiation of Media Institutions

In describing the development of media institutions, a good place to begin is Robert Park's (1967/1925) essay on the development of the newspaper, which was one of the first communication institutions to become differentiated from other institutions. Pointing out that "the power of the press may be roughly measured by the number of people who read it" (p. 80), Park emphasized the role of urbanization in increasing the size of the reading public: "Reading, which was a luxury in the country, has become a necessity in the city" (p. 81). The growth of newspapers thus is closely linked to the growth of cities.

The earliest newspapers, Park observed, were newsletters whose purpose was to keep their readers informed of the latest gossip, whether of the court or of the village. As the number of people to be gossiped about increased, coverage began to be limited to the most prominent individuals among them. When the paper could no longer cover every incident that would interest its readers, it had to choose the ones that were in some way romantic or symbolic and treat them as human-interest stories. Thus, the newspaper became "an impersonal account of manners and life" (p. 84).

As time went by, different kinds of newspapers developed. There were politically oriented papers whose purpose was to report on the doings of government. Such papers tended to come under the control of a particular party, and eventually some rebelled. The rebels—the so-called independent press—included *The New York Times*, which attacked and eventually overthrew the political machine run by Boss Tweed. Over time there also developed a variety of newspapers known as the *yellow press*. The goal of such papers, according to Park, was "to write the news in such a way that it would appeal to the fundamental passions. The formula was: love and romance for the women; sport and politics for the men" (p. 95). Newspapers of this type attracted many more readers than the party papers or the independent press, thereby extending the "newspaper habit" to the mass public.

The outcome of this process of differentiation was what is now known as the press, a cultural institution that is also a business. Newspaper publishers are interested in making a profit by offering news and features that will interest the greatest possible number of readers. However, the press continually struggles to remain independent from other institutions. The freedom of the press is never fully guaranteed. To cite just one example, the outspoken columnist Sidney Schanberg was forced to resign from his position at *The New York Times* after some of his statements provoked an angry outcry from landlords and real estate financiers.

Today the dominant communications institutions in the United States are the electronic media: broadcasting corporations like CBS, NBC, ABC, and Turner Broadcasting, which own television and radio stations of their own and have affiliated local stations throughout the nation. Their growth has been based primarily on the effectiveness of these media as vehicles for advertising, which is their main source of revenue. Can they be depended on to broadcast news that is free from the influence of the advertisers that support them and,

> *The communications media must continually struggle to remain independent from other institutions, especially corporations.*

by extension, the owners and managers of large corporations? This too is an area of much social-scientific research. In one of the best studies of this subject, *Deciding What's News*, Herbert J. Gans (1979) conducted observations and interviews at many of the nation's major newspapers, news magazines, and television networks. He concluded that

since national news is produced commercially, one might imagine that story selectors are under constant pressure to choose news which will attract the most profitable audience. In practice, however, they are not. In the news media I studied, as in most others, editorial and business departments operate independently of each other. Business departments would like to influence editorial decisions in order to increase audience size and attract advertisers, but they can only make proposals. [p. 214]

Media Power and Its Limits

A familiar expression in modern societies is "information is power." And because the media control such a large and diverse flow of information, they have immense power. Questions about the power of the media become especially urgent when one imagines what could happen if control of the media fell into the hands of groups that oppose democratic institutions. In such a case, could the persuasive power of the media be used to destroy individual and political freedom?

George Orwell addressed this issue in his famous book *1984*, which portrays a society in which everyone is constantly watched on two-way television. Not only the actions but also the thoughts of each member of the society are monitored in this way by a powerful central government. Originally published in 1949, *1984* presents a terrifying vision of the potential power of the media when used by a dictator to control the thoughts and behavior of the population. But it is not merely an imaginative fantasy. It is based on the efforts of totalitarian regimes, especially those of Hitler and Stalin, to control the media and use them to control the masses.

In contemporary societies where totalitarian regimes try to control the minds of citizens (e.g., Romania before the 1989 revolution) or in which oppressive regimes attempt to suppress democratic movements (e.g., South Africa), total control over the media is a major goal of the state. In the United States, as noted earlier, media institutions are protected against undue political influence and are governed by professional norms regarding the gathering and broadcasting of information. There is also a wide range of channels to choose among. However, even in the United States and other democratic societies in which freedom of the press is guaranteed, there are still many problems related to access to the media and their power to attract large audiences. For example, the media exert a powerful influence over the conduct of American politics. This is evident in Figure 17-3, which shows the rapid increase in spending on television advertising by political candidates between 1956 and 1980. This trend makes it more difficult for candidates without large budgets to compete effectively in election campaigns. (The role of the media in political processes is discussed more fully in Chapter 19.)

On the other hand, in a democratic society television and other media can be a two-edged sword, conferring power on those in the spotlight but also subjecting them to sometimes embarrassing public scrutiny. Richard Nixon, Jimmy Swaggert, Gary Hart, and Jim and Tammy Bakker are only a few public figures who have risen, and fallen, in front of a national television audience. The public has a stake, therefore, in determining whether the media are adequately and evenhandedly investigating the actions of the powerful and the famous.

> *The media exert a strong influence over the conduct of American politics.*

Technological Limits on Media Power.
When media institutions are well differentiated from political and other institutions, it is actually quite difficult for powerful individuals or groups to manipulate mass audiences. This becomes even more true as changing technologies give people more opportunities to choose the types of messages they receive via the media. Cable television offers the potential for much greater diversity in program content: Viewers can watch everything from

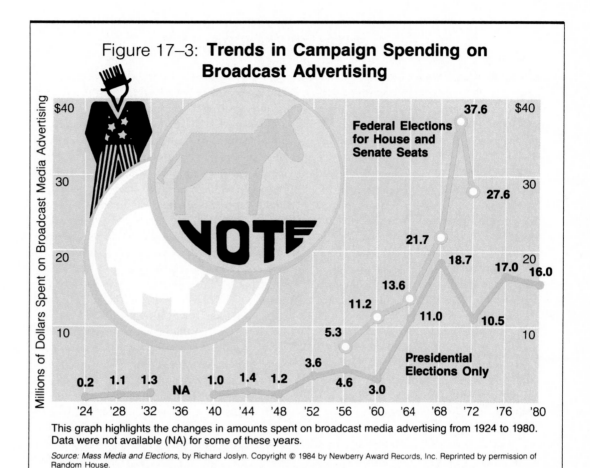

Figure 17–3: **Trends in Campaign Spending on Broadcast Advertising**

Millions of Dollars Spent on Broadcast Media Advertising

$40   30   20   10

Federal Elections for House and Senate Seats

37.6   27.6   21.7   18.7   17.0   20   16.0   13.6   11.2   11.0   10.5   5.3

$40   30   20   10

Presidential Elections Only

0.2   1.1   1.3   NA   1.0   1.4   1.2   3.6   4.6   3.0

'24   '28   '32   '36   '40   '44   '48   '52   '56   '60   '64   '68   '72   '76   '80

This graph highlights the changes in amounts spent on broadcast media advertising from 1924 to 1980. Data were not available (NA) for some of these years.

Source: Mass Media and Elections, by Richard Joslyn. Copyright © 1984 by Newberry Award Records, Inc. Reprinted by permission of Random House.

public affairs to pornography. Videocassette equipment also makes possible a wider range of choices. So although it is entirely likely that the size of the television audiences for special events like the Super Bowl will continue to increase (see Box 17-3), the audience of media consumers is becoming ever more diverse and fickle and, hence, ever more difficult to reach as a mass audience. Even in societies like China, in which the media are agencies of the state and may broadcast only material that has been approved by political leaders, new technologies like VCRs promise to make it even more difficult to control the flow of information.

The Two-Step Flow of Communication.
Another limit on the power of the media is the nature of communication itself. Researchers have not found a direct link between persuasive messages and actual behavior. People do not change their cultural values and norms

just because the media tell them to. Instead, investigators have identified a **two-step flow of communication:** The messages communicated by the media are evaluated by certain respected individuals, who in turn influence the attitudes and behavior of others (Katz, 1966). Such individuals function as **opinion leaders** in matters ranging from voting to the purchase of paper towels, which is one reason that advertisements so often portray a knowledgeable person praising a product to eager, if ignorant, listeners.

The role of influential individuals in the communication process is a reminder that communication via the media has not replaced oral, interpersonal communication, nor is it likely to. On the other hand, the media convey a great deal of information about our cultural environment and cannot help but affect how we perceive that environment. The extent to which they shape our perceptions is a subject of ongoing research and debate.

Box 17–3: **The National Hookup**

It happens every January. After a long season of grueling competition, the two surviving professional football teams face each other in the Super Bowl. The day is now called Super Bowl Sunday. Over 100 million people from coast to coast will watch the game on television. Each minute of advertising time will cost $1,400,000, and America's most successful corporations and their advertising agencies will bid against one another for the time. Truly we have in the Super Bowl an occasion when mass interest in a national sports event creates an audience that crosses all lines of class, race, ethnicity, and religion.

But this level of national attention to one game, and the profits it generates for the team owners, the players, and many others, were not possible before the technology of television made it possible to broadcast events simultaneously across the continent. Television provided football with the national hookup it needed to become a billion-dollar industry. At the same time, football and other professional sports created the media's largest audiences and influenced the scheduling of television time.

In this example two social institutions are intimately connected. Sports is a social institution that is structured in different ways throughout the society. In communities, the most common sports organizations are Little Leagues and school teams. At some large colleges, sports is structured in ways that will generate revenues that can be used to support the college's entire athletic program. The bigger and more competitive a college's football program is, the more it depends on television revenues as well as ticket sales, and the more heavily recruited its players are. Finally, the biggest, fastest, and most talented players are drafted into the business of professional football, which is intimately linked with the nation's most pervasive media institution, television.

Sociologists who conduct research on sports and the media point out that in many societies sports is not conducted as a business that depends on television and advertising. For example, in her study of soccer (the most popular team sport in the world) Janet Lever (1983) found that players may have professional careers but that their teams are not organized as businesses. In Brazil, as in many other nations, sports are engaged in by social clubs in cities and towns. The clubs pay their players, and the clubs with the largest dues-paying membership get the best players. Volunteer directors are elected by councilmen, who in turn are elected by all the shareholders of a club. To qualify as a club director, a man must be a shareholder; making large donations to the club also helps.

Soccer in Brazil, thus, may not be as profitable or as "national" as football in America, but Lever has shown that it also creates a "national hookup." In fact, soccer stars like the famed Pélé are national heroes, as can be seen in the following description:

[Returning from the Mexican World Cup] the team flew to Rio de Janeiro, where they were greeted by close to 2 million ecstatic people waiting in the rain. The secretary of tourism coordinated a special Carnival parade of samba schools. . . . The major clubs from the major cities had contributed players to the winning team. Animosities were suspended for a time of alliance. In a land where communication is problematic, the team's contribution to national unity was of great value. [Lever, 1983, pp. 68–69]

The essential similarity between sports in nations like Brazil and those in which professional sports are a major business is that at the national level, where audiences for championship games are drawn from homes throughout the society, it is television that has enhanced the appeal of sports and given it such a central place in people's identification with their city and their nation.

CHALLENGES TO CONTEMPORARY SOCIETY

The Electronic Classroom

The seventh-graders sit two by two in front of computer monitors, eagerly solving problems in basic arithmatic and simple algebra. Time flies as they watch *The Voyage of the Mimi*, an interactive computer program that looks much like an advanced arcade game with real adventure situations presented in full color and sound. But the action stops as the children on the spaceship *Mimi* use some basic math to figure out how to get themselves out of a jam or plot a new course. They must solve the problem before they can go on. If they need help, they can call up an instructional program keyed to the problem they are trying to solve.

Schools throughout the United States and Canada are experimenting with programs like *The Voyage of the Mimi*. Such programs require access to sophisticated computer equipment, of course, but many schools have already invested in such equipment. And this is only the beginning. Much more software and hardware are being designed for the educational market. In fact, the technology exists to revolutionize the classroom (Becker, 1984; de Sola Pool, 1983). Already many schools send children into classrooms with a microcomputer at each desk. The National Science Foundation and many state economic development agencies are promoting the spread of educational computer networks for interactive learning. The Encyclopaedia Brittanica Company offers one of its encyclopedias on a disk no larger than a compact disk that can be accessed by a CD-ROM player hooked into an appropriate microcomputer.

Students can call up text and photos and do research on any subject without leaving their desks. Typing is no longer taught in the well-equipped junior or senior high school; the course is called keyboarding and encompasses old-fashioned typing and modern word processing. And many more innovations are on the way.

But before getting carried away by the possibilities of the futuristic classroom, consider some of the challenges posed by the new technology. Among the social issues associated with educational technologies are the problem of learning and equity, the problem of diffusion, and the problem of protection of property rights.

Let us assume that we are dealing only with computer-based systems that have been demonstrated to aid learning (this in itself is a major assumption requiring further research). This means that some rather expensive systems are available to aid and accelerate learning. Which children will have access to those systems? More to the point, how will children in ghetto schools with limited budgets or children in remote rural locations or on Indian reservations gain access to them? The issue of equal access to new educational technologies is an example of the broader issue of equity in funding the nation's public schools, referred to in the chapter. There is clearly a danger that the new educational technologies—even those already available in your local computer store—will further widen the gap between the haves and the have-nots in American society (Martinez and Mead, 1980).

The problem of diffusion is also a classic social dilemma; as we saw in Chapter 11, it applies to any new technology. *Diffusion* refers to the spread of a behavior or trait through a population. If we wish a technology to diffuse quickly, we hope that there won't be much conflict about which technology is best (as there was in the case of video disk versus video tape) and that the early adopters will be happy with the innovation and will spread the word to other potential adopters. But new technology is expensive. It may be worthwhile to wait and see what others are doing. Let them make the mistakes and waste their money. Such a policy can delay the formation of a market that can support production of the new technology and reduce its price. This is where applied research and policy come in. Social scientists, in cooperation with innovative school districts, can test new systems and accelerate their diffusion.

At this writing, however, perhaps the thorniest issue related to educational technology is protection. If you as a teacher or student can select books, articles, sheet music, recorded songs, or video tapes from a vast library of such materials, who will pay royalties to the songwriters or novelists or essayists—or their publishers—for those selections? Much information is already in the public domain, meaning that it is no longer owned by anyone and can be freely copied. But much highly desirable material is privately owned. Until a social system is developed for paying the artists and writers and composers and others for their efforts, the existing technology will be stymied and the utopian dreams of the classroom of the future will recede. Here the challenge is not only to devise systems for diffusion and protection but also to get them implemented properly (which may involve some court cases). Clearly, there is a lot of work to be done in this potentially exciting area before the future becomes the present.

SUMMARY

*E*ducation is the process by which a society transmits knowledge, values, norms, and ideologies and in so doing prepares young people for adult roles and adults for new roles. It is accomplished by specific institutions outside the family, especially schools and colleges.

Schools are often cited as examples of bureaucratic organizations, since they tend to be characterized by a clearly defined authority system and set of rules. A more interactionist viewpoint sees the school as a distinctive set of interactions and patterns of socialization. Conflict theorists view schools as institutions whose purpose is to maintain social-class divisions and reproduce the society's existing stratification system.

Education is compulsory in the United States, although the exact requirements vary from one state to another. The post-World War II baby boom caused a bulge in elementary-school enrollments beginning in 1952 and an expansion of the college-age population in the 1960s. These trends were reversed in the 1960s and 1970s, but at the same time increasing numbers of adults have sought additional education.

A key feature of education is the fact that schools structure the lives of children and adolescents. They help create a social world for adolescents that is separate from adult society. Another important aspect of education in the United States is the relationship between education and citizenship. Education is also viewed as a tool for solving social problems, especially social inequality.

Educational attainment refers to the number of years of school a person has completed. It is correlated with income, occupation, prestige, and attitudes and opinions. The average American today has much more education than the average American of the early 1940s. One effect of higher levels of educational attainment is "degree inflation," in which employers require more education of potential employees. Another problem related to educational attainment is the high rate of functional incompetency among Americans.

Educational achievement refers to how much the student actually learns, measured by mastery of reading, writing, and mathematical skills. The steady decline in mean SAT scores in the 1970s and 1980s has been viewed as a sign that average levels of educational achievement have declined. Many experts argue that the decline in test scores is not significant, but many others have called for higher academic standards and major reforms in the educational system.

Educational institutions have been criticized by observers who believe that they hinder, rather than enhance, social mobility. Schools have been accused of serving as "selection and certification agencies" and thereby legitimizing inequality. Higher levels of educational attainment provide the credentials required for better jobs, and students who are able to obtain those credentials usually come from the middle and upper classes. A factor that has been shown to affect students' school careers is teacher expectations regarding students, which are influenced by the teacher's knowledge of the student's family background.

Inequality in higher education is primarily a matter of access—that is, ability to pay. Students from poor, working-class, and lower-middle-class families, as well as members of racial minority groups, are most likely to rely on public colleges and universities. Most educational researchers agree that without college assistance for needy students, differences in educational attainment and achievement would be much greater.

The American educational system is highly bureaucratized, a fact that acts as a major barrier to educational change. Nevertheless, when they have been required to change—as in the case of desegregation—schools have often proved to be very adaptable.

Communications media are institutions that specialize in communicating information, images, and values about a society and its members. The media are run by professional communicators who are skilled in producing and transmitting news and other communications. In some societies the media are subject to strict censorship, and even in societies in which the freedom of the press and other media is protected, that freedom is often threatened by attempts to control the nature of the information communicated by the media.

Some sociologists have criticized the media for producing a "mass culture" in which an increasing number of people have similar cultural traits and values and can be easily manipulated by those who control media institutions. However, data on media consumption do not support the mass culture theory. They show that listeners and viewers are not homogeneous in their tastes and are not unduly influenced by the media. Other research has shown that there is a complex relationship between the viewing of violent acts on television and subsequent aggressive behavior in some subgroups of the population.

The differentiation of the communications media from other institutions is illustrated by the development of newspapers. Over time "the press" became an independent cultural institution that is also a business whose goal is to make a profit. The same can be said of the electronic media, the dominant communications media today.

Because the media in modern societies control such a large and diverse flow of information, they have immense power. In the United States, they exert a strong influence over the conduct of politics. Political candidates without large budgets to spend on media advertising cannot compete effectively in election campaigns, and presidents and other powerful leaders must be able to perform well on television. On the other hand, changing technologies have given media consumers a wider range of choices, thereby limiting the power of the media to influence mass audiences.

GLOSSARY

education: the process by which a society transmits knowledge, values, norms, and ideologies and in so doing prepares young people for adult roles and adults for new roles (**p. 526**).

educational attainment: the number of years of school an individual has completed (**p. 530**).

educational achievement: how much the student actually learns, measured by mastery of reading, writing, and mathematical skills (**p. 533**).

communications media: institutions that specialize in communicating information, images, and values about ourselves, our communities, and our society (**p. 544**).

two-step flow of communication: the process in which messages communicated by the media are evaluated by certain respected individuals, who in turn influence the attitudes and behavior of others (**p. 549**).

opinion leader: an individual who consistently influences the attitudes and behavior of others (**p. 549**).

WHERE TO FIND IT

Books

Growing Minds: On Becoming a Teacher (Herbert Kohl; Harper & Row, 1984). A compelling account of what it is like to become a teacher and to devote one's professional life to teaching.

Culture as History: The Transformation of American Society in the Twentieth Century (Warren I. Sussman; Pantheon, 1984). A brilliant social history dealing with the transformation of American culture in this century. Contains excellent material on the role of fairs, communications, fashions, and much more.

The TV Establishment: Programming for Power and Profit (Gaye Tuchman, ed.; Prentice-Hall, 1974). A collection of critical essays about American television.

Deciding What's News (Herbert Gans; Pantheon, 1979). The best sociological study of how the news we see on television is processed by the media institutions.

Journals

Social Problems A sociological journal devoted to research and policy analysis related to major social problems.

Sociology of Education A quarterly journal published by the American Sociological Association. Presents recent research on education and human social development.

Variety The weekly magazine of the entertainment business. Offers fascinating insights into the power of media institutions.

Other Sources

The Condition of Education An annual publication by the National Center for Education Statistics, U.S. Department of Education. Presents selected statistical information in the form of education "indicators"— key data that measure the "health" of education or its trends.

VISUAL SOCIOLOGY

Students and Social Change

The common theme running through all of these photos is that high school and university students can often be found at the core of movements for social change. In our own society some observers complain that students are complacent and do not become involved enough in the issues of the day. But this is the age group that swells the ranks of the environmental movement, as can be seen in the Earth First demonstration. And during the past few years, students and other college-age youth have been the most active segment of the U.S. population in demanding sanctions against South Africa for its policy of apartheid. To be sure, young people are not alone in these movements, but they are among the most active participants.

Throughout the world, wherever there are demonstrations for social change large numbers of young people are likely to be in the forefront—with the news media nearby, scrambling to cover the story. People around the world were thrilled by the photos of students and others breaking through the wall between East and West Germany in 1989.

The global audience watched in amazement as the movement for democracy and political freedom spread into China and focused on the massive sit-in in Tiananmen Square. But their hopes were dashed as young lives were taken when the army moved in. The photo of the violence in Tiananmen Square also captures the limits of student protest, its vulnerability to armed repression.

In *The Communist Manifesto*, one of the documents that inspired the Chinese Communist Revolution, Marx wrote, "Workers of the world unite; you have nothing to lose but your chains." Should he have written, "Students of the world unite"? Was Marx missing a great force for social change by not considering student movements? These photos remind us that student protest may be a necessary but insufficient force in bringing about large-scale social change. The students in China directed attention to that nation's desire for greater democracy, but without the support of more urban workers and rural peasants there was not quite enough mass sentiment to swing the army over to the cause of freedom, and the movement failed. Without the students nothing might have happened, but their efforts alone were not enough.

© A. Tannenbaum, Sygma

© R. Bossu, Sygma

CHAPTER OUTLINE

● **Sociology and Economics**

● **Markets and the Division of Labor**

- ● The Nature of Markets
- ● Markets and the World Economic System

● **Economics and the State**

- ● Political-Economic Ideologies
- ● Political Economics in Practice: After the Cold War

● **Workers, Managers, and Corporations**

- ● Alienation
- ● Individuals and Corporations
- ● Sociological Perspectives on the Workplace
- ● Conclusion

Margo Smith

It took many hours of skill and patience to weave this basket.

CHAPTER 18
ECONOMIC INSTITUTIONS

E. L. Winthrop, an American businessman from a major city north of the Rio Grande, was on a vacation trip to Mexico. While there he traveled to a remote and rather quaint village somewhere in the province of Oaxaca. While wandering through the dusty streets of that little pueblo, which had neither electricity nor running water, he came upon an Indian man squatting on the earthen-floored porch of his palm hut. The Indian was weaving baskets.

These were not ordinary baskets. Winthrop had never seen such colors and such fine detail as the Indian was weaving into the little containers, using only natural fibers and dyes from the nearby jungle. Into each basket he wove beautiful and fantastic decorations. After staring at the Indian for an embarrassingly long time, Winthrop felt that he must at least buy one of the beautiful baskets, no matter what the price.

When Winthrop learned that the Indian was selling his wares for only fifty centavos, perhaps ten times less than what he had expected to pay, the entrepreneur could not help thinking that here was a fine opportunity to start a thriving business. He knew a confectioner back home who would be overjoyed to obtain these baskets at three or four times the price the Indian was asking. They would make ideal containers for gift candy. And even counting shipping costs and other expenses, both Winthrop and the Indian would surely make out very well.

"I've got big business for you, my friend," he announced to the surprised Indian. "Do you think you can make me one thousand of those little baskets?"

"Why not, patroncito? If I can make sixteen, which is how many I usually take to the market each week, I can certainly make one thousand."

"Good. And what would be the price of each?"

Winthrop imagined that the Indian would enlist the help of his family and kin in the project, and at the prices he could pay they all stood to gain tremendously.

That might be true enough, the Indian admitted, but who then would look after the corn and beans and goats? And if they should have no corn for tortillas and beans for frijoles, how would they live? Yes, the Indian could see that he and his kin would have plenty of money to buy these things as well as many other items that they did not yet possess, but, he explained, it was only the corn he grew himself that he and his family could be sure of. "Of the corn that others may or may not grow," he added respectfully, "I cannot be sure to feast upon."

Not easily discouraged, Winthrop proceeded to show the Indian how wealthy he and his entire village could become even if they continued to sell the baskets for only fifty centavos. The Indian seemed interested, which spurred Winthrop on to more detailed descriptions of the basket assembly line they could begin together in the dusty little town. But after it was all explained, the Indian was still unmoved. The thousands of pesos that could be earned in this way were more than he could reckon with, since he had always used the few pesos from his basket selling only to supplement the modest needs of his family. And besides, as he finally explained to a decidedly frustrated Winthrop,

Besides, señor, there's still another thing which perhaps you don't know. You see, my good lordy and caballero, I've to make these canastitas my own way and with my song in them and with bits of my soul woven into them. If I were to make them in great numbers there would no longer be my soul in each, or my songs. Each would look like the other with no difference whatever and such a thing would slowly eat up my heart. Each has to be another song which I hear in the morning when the sun rises and when the birds begin to chirp and the butterflies come and sit down on my baskets so that I may see a new beauty, because, you see, the butterflies like my baskets and the pretty colors on them, that's why they come and sit down, and I can make my canastitas after them. And now, señor jefecito, if you will kindly excuse me, I have wasted much time already, although it was a pleasure and a great honor to hear the talk of such a distinguished caballero like you. But I'm afraid I've to attend to my work now, for day after tomorrow is market day in town and I got to take my baskets there. Thank you, señor, for your visit. Adios. [Traven, 1968, p. 72]

SOCIOLOGY AND ECONOMICS

This episode is not simply a failure to communicate, nor is it merely an example of ethnocentrism. It goes to the heart of the difference between the subsistence economy of a folk society and the market economy of an industrial society. Winthrop's world is one in which economic institutions like markets and corporations guide his thoughts and actions even when he is on vacation. The Indian's actions and thoughts are also influenced by social institutions, but they are less likely to be economic institutions. Chief among them are the family and the male peer group or *cofradía*. Thus the story of Winthrop's attempt to form a basket assembly line catches the essence of what Max Weber meant when he observed that as societies grow in size, complexity, and rationality there is less enchantment in human life. The Indian could never imagine himself as a captain of industry, the manager of a work force of Indians who would buy their corn in a store with a portion of their wages. But neither could Winthrop appreciate the full meaning of the Indian's refusal and the metaphor of his song.

In this chapter we turn to an analysis of the major economic institutions of modern industrial societies. As we do so, it will be well to keep in mind examples from nonindustrial societies like that of the basket weaver in order to appreciate the enormous changes brought about by economic and social change in the past two centuries. Such examples will also show that there is not just one path toward economic modernization, or only one blueprint for how the economic institutions of a modern society should work.

In any society economic institutions specialize in the production of goods and services. How we survive in modern societies depends on whether we have jobs and income, on the nature of markets, on the public policies that involve governments in economic affairs, on worker–management relations, and so on. Thus it is little wonder that

Both economists and sociologists study how individuals and societies make choices involving scarce resources, but sociologists are concerned with showing how cultural norms affect those choices.

sociologists have dedicated much research to these questions. But if that is true, what distinguishes sociology from economics? In our review of the sociology of economic institutions we begin by distinguishing between these two social-scientific fields.

The well-known economist Paul Samuelson has defined economics as "the study of how people and society end up choosing, with or without the use of money, to employ scarce productive resources that could have alternative uses—to produce various commodities and distribute them for consumption, now or in the future, among various persons and groups in society" (1980, p. 2). Sociologists are also concerned with how individuals and societies make choices involving scarce resources like time and money. But sociologists do not assume that scarcity or supply and demand are the only reasons for making such choices. Sociologists are deeply concerned with showing how the norms of different cultures affect economic choices. For example, we cannot assume that people with equal amounts of money or talent are free to choose the same values or activities. We often find that women who might have chosen to pursue careers in business management have been channeled into such occupations as teaching or social work. Until quite recently, American culture defined the latter occupations as appropriate for women, whereas managerial roles were viewed as appropriate for men. Women therefore did not have the same choices open to them even when they had equal amounts of scarce resources like talent.

It would not be accurate to stress only the differences between sociology and economics, however. Increasingly there are sociologists (and economists) who use the central theory of economics to study all situations in which people choose to "allocate scarce resources to satisfy competing ends" (Coleman, 1986; Hechter, 1983). By "central theory" we mean the central assumption of economics: that people will attempt to maximize their pleasure or profit in any situation, and that they will also try to minimize their loss or pain. Applying this idea to nonbusiness situations, the influential economist Gary S. Becker has conducted research on racial discrimination, marriage, and household choices. In this research he applies an economic approach to the study of the behavior of people in groups and organizations that do not produce goods or services. Becker points out that even the choice of a mate or the decision to have a child can be looked upon as an economic decision because people who make these decisions intuitively calculate the "price" of their actions in terms of opportunities gained or lost. Having a child means giving up other scarce resources, such as free time or income that could be used in other ways. And Chapter 15 explains how intuitive calculations enter into the rational choice of a marriage partner.

Following the lead of rational-choice theorists like Becker, sociologist Michael Hechter (1987) has studied the larger social consequences of the individual's propensity to maximize pleasure and avoid pain. He concludes, among other things, that the larger the number of people in an organization, the more the organization will be required to invest in inspectors, managers, security personnel, and the like in order to control its members' propensity to "do their own thing." The same point was made over a century ago by Karl Marx: "All combined labour on a large scale requires . . . a directing authority. . . . A single violin player is his own conductor, an orchestra requires a separate one" (1962/1867, pp. 330–331).

Although it is tempting to apply principles of rational choice or exchange theory to noneconomic institutions like the family and the church, in this chapter we focus specifically on behavior in economic institutions such as businesses and markets and on the social implications of changes in these institutions. We will see that sociologists are continually comparing the ways in which businesses and other strictly economic institutions are organized in different societies. The comparative study of how these differences relate to other features of a society's culture and social structure are very much a part of the sociological perspective on economic institutions.

Sociologists who study economic institutions are also interested in how markets for goods and services evolve as people learn to use new technologies and to divide up their labor in increasingly specialized ways. They also look at how competition for profits may lead to illegal activities and cause governments to try to regulate economic institutions. In addition, sociologists attempt to show how the labor market is organized and how professions develop. Thus markets and the division of labor, the interactions between government and economic institutions, and the nature of jobs and professions are the major subjects of sociological research on economic institutions. In the rest of this chapter we discuss each of these subjects in turn.

MARKETS AND THE DIVISION OF LABOR

A hallmark of an industrial society is the production of commodities and services and information to be exchanged in markets. In London, Hong Kong, New York, and other major cities throughout the world there are markets for gold, national currencies, stocks and bonds, and commodities ranging from pork bellies to concentrated frozen orange juice. Socialist economies dominated by communist dictatorships did not permit all these different kinds of markets; they tended to limit the number of goods and services that may be traded in markets in order to prevent certain groups from gaining wealth and power. We compare capitalist and communist economies in more detail later in the chapter; in this section we focus on what markets are and what they do.

The Nature of Markets

Markets are economic institutions that regulate exchange behavior. In a market, different values or prices are established for particular goods and services, values that vary according to changing levels of supply and demand and are usually expressed in terms of a common measure of exchange, or *currency*. A market is not the same thing as a marketplace. As an economic institution, a market governs exchanges of particular goods and services throughout a society. This is what we mean when we speak of the "housing market," for example. A marketplace, on the other hand, is an actual location where buyers and sellers make exchanges. Buyers and sellers of jewelry, for instance, like to be able to gather in a single place to examine the goods to be exchanged. The same is true for many other goods, such as clothing and automobiles.

Market transactions are governed by agreements or *contracts* in which a seller agrees to supply a particular item and a buyer agrees to pay for it. Exchanges based on contracts are a significant factor in the development of modern societies. As social theorist Niklas Luhmann (1982) observed, the use of contracts "makes 'impersonal' relations possible: It neutralizes the relevance of the other roles of the participants" (p. 199), such as kinship and other personal relationships, that govern exchanges in nonmarket situations. In contractual relations, for example, the fact that people are friends or kin does not, in principle, change the terms of their agreement and the need to repay debts.

Among hunting-and-gathering peoples and in relatively isolated agrarian societies before this century, markets in the modern sense of the term did not exist. Think of the Indian basket weaver who could not imagine buying corn and other foods. He was used to growing foodstuffs himself and exchanging them as needed with members of his extended family. The idea of buying them with currency was foreign to him. In social-scientific terms, a society cannot be said to have a fully developed market economy if many of the commodities that it produces are not ex-

> *In a market, values are established for goods and services on the basis of supply and demand and are expressed in terms of a common measure of exchange, or currency.*

In colonial America there were many forms of currency, including cowrie shells (used by the Indians) and gold pieces (prized by merchants). An early effort to create a single medium of exchange—money—is shown in this photo of one-third of a dollar.

changed for a common currency at prices determined by supply and demand.

The spread of markets into nonmarket societies has been accelerated by political conquest and colonialism as well as by the desire among tribal and peasant peoples to obtain the goods produced by industrial societies. To illustrate this point and to show what happens as a smaller-scale society becomes integrated into world markets, consider the case of the Tiv, a tribal society living in what is now Nigeria. The story of the Tiv is told in Box 18-1.

Markets and the World Economic System

In the late fifteenth and early sixteenth centuries, according to sociologist Immanuel Wallerstein (1974), "there came into existence what we may call a European world-economy. . . . It was not an empire yet it was as spacious as a grand empire and shared some features with it. But it was different, and new. It was a kind of social system the world had not really known before." The new system was based on economic relationships, not on political empires; in fact, it encompassed "empires, city-states, and the emerging 'nation-states'" (p. 15).

Great empires had been a feature of the world scene for at least 5,000 years before the dawn of the modern era. But the empires of China, India, Africa, the Mediterranean, and the Middle East were primarily political rather than economic systems. Wallerstein argues that because the great empires dominated vast areas inhabited by peoples that lacked military and political power, they were able to establish a flow of economic resources from the outlying regions to the imperial centers. The means used were taxation, tribute (payments for protection by the imperial army), and trade policies in which the outlying societies were forced to produce certain goods for the imperial merchants.

But this system—exemplified most clearly in the case of the Roman Empire—required a huge military and civil bureaucracy, which absorbed much of the imperial profit. Local rebellions and wars continually increased the expense of maintaining impe-

Box 18–1: **The Tiv: Markets in a Subsistence Economy**

In precolonial times the Tiv, a small West African tribal society, were a good example of a *subsistence economy*, one in which producers try to meet the needs of their immediate and extended families and do not produce goods or services for export beyond the family, village, or tribe. Among the Tiv the land was divided up into garden plots on which each family grew its own food. When the harvest was completed, the remaining vegetation was slashed and burned. The ashes served to fertilize the soil, but sometimes a plot was allowed to lie fallow for a few seasons. This meant that there was always a lot of discussion about which plots were to be used by which families in any given season. Never was a garden plot bought or sold—the idea that land could be bought and sold was not part of Tiv culture. The land belonged to the tribe as a whole. Individual families were granted the right to use the land, but there was no such thing as private property in the form of land that could be bought and sold.

Nor was the product of the land thought to be the property of the grower. Food was distributed according to need, and a person who accepted food was ex-

pected to return the gift at some future time. Only a few goods, mainly items of dress worn on ceremonial occasions, were traded for currency—in this case, short brass bars. The Tiv also accepted brass bars from foreign traders in exchange for carvings or woven cloths. But they would have laughed at the idea of trading the bars for food. They would have shared their food with strangers without any expectation of payment.

The conquest of Tivland by the British in the early twentieth century brought immense changes to this nonmarket society. The British colonial administrators were shocked when they observed Tiv weddings, in which it appeared to them that young women were being traded for ceremonial goods. In reality, these exchanges were not market transactions; the items that were given in exchange for a bride were a symbol of respect for the bride's family.

The British also noted that the Tiv seemed always to be at war, either with neighboring tribes or among themselves. To them this was a further sign that they needed to "civilize" the Tiv; in fact, however, the warfare was an outcome of the

rial rule. Political empires thus can be viewed as a primitive means of economic domination. "It is the social achievement of the modern world," Wallerstein comments, "to have invented the technology that makes it possible to increase the flow of the surplus from the lower strata to the upper strata, from the periphery to the center, from the majority to the minority" (p. 16) without the need for military conquest.

What technologies made the new world system possible? They were not limited to tools of trade, such as the compass or the oceangoing sailing vessel, or to tools of domination like the Gatling machine gun. They also included organizational techniques for

bringing land, labor, and local currencies into the larger market economy: ways of enclosing and dividing up land in order to charge rent for its use; financial and accounting systems that led to the creation of new economic institutions like banks; and many others. We discuss the role of science and technology in social change more thoroughly in Chapter 20, but it is important to note here that the term **technology** refers not only to tools but also to the procedures and forms of social organization that increase human productive capacity (Polanyi, 1944).

Although the European colonial powers (and the United States) often used political and military force to bring isolated societies

colonial system of taxation. Each tribal chief was required to pay a certain sum, either in British currency or in a commodity such as pigs. Because the Tiv had no currency and had to struggle to produce the required commodities, they were forced to cultivate more land. Their conflicts with neighboring clans or tribes were caused by the need to acquire more land. Thus the wars that the British observed were an almost immediate result of their own policies.

When the British succeeded in ending the warfare that had broken out among the Tiv, the only remaining source of cash to pay the taxes was wage labor on the colonial plantations. The Tiv therefore sent their sons and daughters to work for the British, and on their own land they began to grow crops that they could sell. Before long they were part of the British market economy, selling their crops and labor for cash with which they could buy manufactured goods. Eventually, like many other small tribal societies, they were engulfed by the larger market system of the more powerful European nations (Bohannon and Bohannon, 1953, 1962).

into their markets, in this century they allowed their former colonies to gain independence yet still maintained economic control over them. This occurred because the economies of the colonial societies had become dependent on the technologies and markets controlled by the Western powers. Today some former colonies are beginning to develop independent economic systems, but their ability to compete effectively in world markets is limited by the increasing power of **multinational corporations**, or "multinationals." These are economic enterprises that have headquarters in one country and conduct business activities in one or more other countries (Barnet, 1980).

Multinationals are not a new phenomenon. Trading firms like the Hudson's Bay Company and the Dutch East India Company were chartered by the major colonial powers and granted monopolies over the right to trade with native populations for furs, spices, metals, gems, and other valued commodities. Thus, exploitation of the resources of colonial territories has been directed by multinational corporations for over two centuries. Modern multinationals do not generally have monopolies granted by the state, yet these powerful firms, based primarily in the United States, Europe, and Japan, are transforming the world economy by "exporting" manufacturing jobs from nations in which workers earn high wages to nations in which they earn far less. This process, which is particularly evident in the shoe, garment, electronics, textile, and automobile industries, has accelerated the growth of industrial working classes in the former colonies while greatly reducing the number of industrial jobs in the developed nations.

Recent changes in worldwide production patterns challenge Wallerstein's thesis that there is a world economic order dominated by the former colonial powers. In particular, industrial nations like the United States and Japan are increasingly losing manufacturing jobs while newly industrializing nations like Brazil and Korea are gaining them. But as Box 18-2 shows, the economic survival of millions of rural workers continues to be heavily influenced by changing markets in the highly developed nations.

ECONOMICS AND THE STATE

The earliest social scientists were deeply interested in understanding the full importance of modern economic institutions. In fact, since the eighteenth century almost all attempts to understand large-scale social change have dealt with the question of how economic institutions operate. But the age-old effort to understand economic institutions has not been merely an academic exercise. The fate of societies throughout the world has been and continues to be strongly

Box 18–2: **Addictive Substances and World Markets**

In 1983, when sociologist Edmundo Morales returned to his birthplace in northern Peru to conduct research on land reform, he found that the peasants of the Andes villages had become dependent on the worldwide traffic in cocaine. Their efforts to gain cooperative ownership of the land they farmed had faded. Instead, most of the able-bodied men in the villages were busy packing for the long trip down the eastern face of the Andes. Most of them would work for months in coca-processing laboratories hidden in the jungle. Some would earn cash income by selling food, especially pork and beef, to the managers of the

cocaine factories. The worldwide demand for cocaine had changed their lives.

Morales was dismayed to see so much urgently needed food being shipped from the impoverished highlands to the jungles. He felt that the enormous growth of the cocaine market had led his people down a false path. They were gaining cash income, perhaps, but in the bargain they were becoming increasingly addicted to cocaine and were neglecting the need for more basic economic progress in their own villages (Morales, 1986, 1989).

But Morales also knew that cocaine was simply another in a long line of substances for which huge markets had

© Edmundo Morales

emerged in the richer nations, with drastic results for the less-developed world. Foremost among those substances was sugar. In the thirteenth century, sugar was a luxury available only to royalty. But as its use as a source of energy and as a basis for alcoholic beverages—especially rum—became more widespread, the demand for sugar production became one of the main causes of European expansion into the tropical regions of the world. Moreover, sugar production required that huge amounts of land be devoted to growing sugar cane, and many cane cutters were needed to harvest the crop. Thus, along with the expansion of sugar production went slavery, first in parts of North Africa and the Azores and later in the Caribbean islands and Latin America (Bennett, 1954; Mintz, 1985). And sugar was only the beginning. The cultivation of wheat, tea, and coffee, the extraction of iron, tin, gold, silver, and copper, and the widespread cutting of primeval forests all were spurred by the emergence of mass markets in the developed nations of the West. Andean coca for cocaine and Indochinese poppies for heroin were latecomers in a series of crops that had changed the earth and all its peoples.

Some scholars argue that economic development in the world's commercial capitals actually produced *underdevelopment*—dependency and poverty and overpopulation—in huge parts of Africa, Asia, and Latin America. But Morales questions the notion of "development of underdevelopment." He believes that despite their tendency to become addicted to cocaine, the villagers of northern Peru are becoming more sophisticated in their market dealings and their understanding of politics. When they turn their attention once again to land reform, as eventually they must, their experiences in recent years will have made them less culturally isolated and more politically effective.

influenced by theories about how economic institutions operate, or fail to do so, in nation-states with different types of political institutions. The major economic ideologies thus are also political ideologies, and economics is often called *political economics*. In this section we review three economic ideologies—mercantilism, capitalism, and socialism—and some variations of them.

Political-Economic Ideologies

Mercantilism. The economic philosophy known as **mercantilism**, which was prevalent in the sixteenth and seventeenth centuries, held that a nation's wealth could be measured by the amount of gold or other precious metals held by the royal court. The best economic system, therefore, was one that increased the nation's exports and thereby increased the court's holdings of gold. The mercantilist theory had important consequences for economic institutions. For example, the guilds, or associations of tradespeople, that had arisen in medieval times were protected by the monarch, to whom they paid tribute. The guilds controlled their members and determined what they produced. In this way they were able to produce goods cheaply, and those goods were better able to compete in world markets, thereby increasing exports and bringing in more wealth for the court. But the workers were not free to seek the best jobs and wages available. Rather, the guilds required them to work at assigned tasks for assigned wages, and the guildmasters fixed the price of work (wages), entry into jobs, and all working conditions. Land in mercantilist systems was not subject to market norms either. As in feudalism, land was thought of not as a commodity that can be bought and sold—that is, a commodity subject to the market forces of supply and demand—but as a hereditary right derived from feudal grants.

Laissez-faire Capitalism. The ideology of **laissez-faire capitalism** attacked the mercantilist view that the wealth of nations could be measured in gold and that the state should dominate trade and production in order to amass more wealth. The laissez-faire economists believed that a society's real wealth could be measured only by its capacity to produce goods and services—that is, by its resources of land, labor, and machinery. And those resources, including land itself, could best be regulated by free trade in world markets (Halevy, 1955; Smith, 1910/1776).

The ideology of laissez-faire capitalism also sought to free workers from the restrictions that had been imposed by the feudal system and maintained under mercantilism. Thus it is no coincidence that the first statement of modern economic principles, Adam Smith's *The Wealth of Nations*, was published in 1776. Revolution was in the air—not only political revolution but the industrial revolution as well. And some of the most revolutionary ideas came from the pens of people such as Adam Smith, Jeremy Bentham, and John Stuart Mill, who understood the potential for social change contained in the new capitalist institutions of private property and free markets.

Private property (as opposed to communal ownership such as existed among the Tiv), is not merely the possession of objects but a set of rights and obligations that specify what their owner can and cannot do with them. The laissez-faire economists believed that the owners of property should be free to do almost anything they liked with their property in order to gain profit. Indeed, the quest for profit would provide the best incentive to produce new and cheaper products. This, in turn, required free markets in which producers would compete to provide better products at lower prices.

These economic institutions are familiar to us today, but the founders of laissez-faire capitalism had to struggle to win acceptance for them. No wonder they thought of themselves as radicals. In fact, their economic and political beliefs were so opposed to the rule of monarchs and to feudal institutions like guilds that they could readily be seen as revolutionary. They believed that the state should leave economic institutions alone (which is what *laissez faire* means). In their view, there is a natural economic order, a system of private property and competitive enterprise that functions best when individuals are free to

pursue their own interests through free trade and unregulated production. As Smith put it, "Every individual . . . intends only his own gain, and he is in this, as in many other cases, led by an invisible hand to promote an end which was no part of his intention" (quoted in Halevy, 1955, p. 90). One of the most famous images in the history of the social sciences, Smith's "invisible hand" refers to the pervasive influence of the forces of supply and demand operating in markets for goods and services. Laissez-faire economists believe that in the long run these forces will improve the lives of people everywhere.

Socialism. Socialism as an economic and political philosophy began as an attack on the concepts of private property and personal profit. These aspects of capitalism, socialists believed, should be replaced by public ownership of property and sharing of profits. As we have noted in earlier chapters, this attack on capitalism was motivated largely by horror at the atrocious living conditions caused by the industrial revolution. The early socialists (Robert Owen in England and Henri de Saint Simon in France) thought of economics as the "dismal science" because it seemed to excuse a system in which a few people were made rich at the expense of the masses of workers. They detested the laissez-faire economists' defense of low wages and wondered how workers could benefit from the industrial revolution instead of becoming "wage slaves." They proposed the creation of smaller-scale, more self-sufficient communities that would produce modern goods but would do so within a cooperative framework.

Later in the nineteenth century, Karl Marx viewed these ideas as utopian dreams. He taught that the socialist state must be controlled by the working class, led by their own trade unions and political parties, which would do away with markets, wage labor, land rent, and private ownership of the means of pro-

> *Socialism is based on the belief that markets and private industry must be eliminated and replaced by state-controlled economic planning, collective farms, and worker control over industrial decisions.*

These photos of children in mines and textile mills by a famous photographer of American labor, Lewis Hine, helped motivate the social movement for "protective legislation," or laws that would protect children and women against exploitation in industry. In many parts of Asia and Africa today, children still constitute over 10 percent of the industrial labor force.

duction. These aspects of capitalism would be replaced by socialist economic institutions in which the workers themselves would determine what should be produced and how it should be distributed.

Marx never completed his blueprint of how an actual socialist society might function. That chore was left to the political and intellectual leaders of the communist revolutions—Lenin, Leon Trotsky, Rosa Luxemburg—and, finally, to authoritarian leaders like Josef Stalin, Mao Zedong, and Fidel Castro. They believed that all markets and all private industry must be eliminated and replaced by state-controlled economic planning, collective farms, and worker control over

industrial decision making. Unless capitalist economic institutions were completely rooted out, they believed, small-scale production and market dealings would give rise to a new bourgeois class.

In the socialist system as it evolved under the communist regimes of the Soviet Union and China, centralized planning agencies and the single legal party, the communists, would have the authority to set goals and organize the activities of the worker collectives, or soviets. Party members and state planners would also devise wage plans that would balance the need to reward skilled workers against the need to prevent the huge income inequalities found in capitalist societies. In Soviet-style societies markets were not permitted to regulate demand and supply; this vital economic function was supposedly performed by government agencies. In the Soviet Union and China, therefore, a large corps of trained planners forecast the demand for basic goods like coal, steel, glass, and so on, as well as for finished consumer products, and set official prices and production quotas. Societies that are managed in this fashion are said to have *command economies*. The state commands economic institutions to supply a specific amount—a quota—of each product and to sell it at a particular price. (Note that not all command economies are dominated by communist parties. Germany under the Nazis and Italy under the fascists were also command economies.)

The Soviet system was notorious for the inefficiency of its economic planning and industrial production. Under the command system factory managers must continually hoard supplies, or raid supplies destined for similar factories in other regions, in order to meet their production quotas. Or they must trade favors with other factory managers to obtain supplies, a system that creates a hidden level of exchange based on bribes and favoritism. And because there are no free markets, goods that are desired by the public often are not available simply because the planners have not ordered them. In fact, in the Soviet-style economies there were always clandestine markets that operated outside the control of the authorities and supplied goods and services to those with the means to pay for them. These "underground" markets increased inequality in those societies and generated greater public disillusionment with command economies and one-party communist rule. Until the massive social upheavals of 1989–1990 the authorities in many Soviet-style regimes seemed to believe that the command system could eventually be made to work, but at the turn of the decade popular revolt and mass dissatisfaction with the lack of economic progress dashed any hope for the revival of traditional planned economies (Charlton, 1985; Harrington, 1989; Prybyla, 1990).

Democratic Socialism. A far less radical version of socialism than that attempted in the Soviet bloc is known as **democratic socialism**. This economic philosophy is practiced in the Scandinavian nations, especially Sweden, Denmark, and Norway, as well as in Holland and to a lesser extent in Germany, France, and Italy. It holds that the institution of private property must continue to exist because people want it to, and that competitive markets are needed because they are efficient ways of regulating production and distribution. But large corporations should be owned by the nation or, if they are in private hands, required to be run for the benefit of all citizens, not just for the benefit of their stockholders. In addition, economic decisions should be made democratically.

Democratic socialists look to societies like Sweden and Yugoslavia for examples of their economic philosophy in practice (Denitch, 1989; Harrington, 1973). In Yugoslav factories and firms, democratically elected workers' councils make basic managerial decisions, including those that determine who should be hired to manage the firm and how its profits should be invested. In Sweden, workers can invest their pension benefits in their firm and thereby gain a controlling interest in it. This process is intended to result in socialist ownership of major economic organizations.

Welfare Capitalism. Welfare capitalism was to some extent a response to the challenge posed by the Russian Revolution, which called attention to many of the excesses of uncontrolled or laissez-faire capitalism. But even more, it was a new way of looking at relationships between governmental and economic institutions. Welfare capitalism affirms the role of markets in determining what goods and services will be produced and how, but it also affirms the role of government in regulating economic competition (e.g., by attempting to prevent the control of markets by one or a few firms).

Welfare capitalism also stresses the role that governments have always played in building the roads, bridges, canals, ports, and other facilities that make trade and industry possible. Expanding on this role, the theory of welfare capitalism asserts that the state should also invest in the society's human resources—that is, in the education of new generations and the provision of a minimum level of health care. Welfare capitalism also guarantees the right of workers to form unions in order to reach collective agreements with the owners and managers of firms regarding wages and working conditions. It creates social-welfare institutions like social security and unemployment insurance. And in order to stimulate production and build confidence in times of economic depression, welfare capitalism asserts that governments must borrow funds to finance large-scale public works projects like the construction of the American interstate highway system in the United States during the 1950s.

The theory of welfare capitalism is associated with the writings of John Maynard Keynes, Joan Robinson, John Kenneth Galbraith, and James Tobin, all of whom contributed to the revision of laissez-faire economic theory. Welfare capitalism dominated American economic policy from World War II until the 1970s, when a succession of economic crises— inflation, energy shortages, and unemploy-

> *Democratic socialism holds that private property and competitive markets are needed but that large corporations should be owned by the nation or run for the benefit of all citizens.*

ment—turned the thoughts of many Americans once again toward laissez-faire capitalism. Today, however, the increasingly evident gap between the haves and the have-nots in American society has given rise to renewed interest in enhancing the institutions of the welfare state—unemployment insurance, health insurance, low-income housing, public education, and others. At the same time, there is no evident desire to pay higher taxes to fund such programs. But the economic and political crisis in the communist nations has created the possibility of an unprecedented investment in welfare institutions, a possibility that reveals a good deal about the relationships between economic and political institutions in the United States.

> *Welfare capitalism affirms the role of markets in determining what goods and services will be produced, but it also affirms the role of government in regulating economic competition.*

Political Economics in Practice: After the Cold War

The Cold War lasted from about 1949 to 1989. It cost the United States, the Soviet Union, and the nations of Europe untold billions of dollars. It also fostered not-so-cold wars in Korea, Vietnam, Afghanistan, and Central America. At the beginning of the 1990s this long, drawn-out political conflict between the superpowers appeared to be over. The fall of dictatorships in Hungary, Romania, Czechoslovakia, Poland, and East Germany; the tearing down of the wall separating East and West Berlin; the passage of laws permitting individual ownership of businesses and property in the Soviet Union—these and related changes have already had a major impact throughout the world, but their full effect remains to be felt.

The end of the Cold War raises some important issues for the sociological study of economic institutions. Among them are the following: How will the transition from command economies to entrepreneurial-style market economies unfold in socialist nations? What are the implications for economic institutions in the United States? Will there be a "peace dividend," and if so, how will it be used? In the rest of this section we take a closer look at these issues.

From Commissars to Entrepreneurs. As the cumbersome and inefficient bureaucracies of state planning are stripped of their power, the commissar (planning bureaucrat) will be replaced by the entrepreneur (Ash, 1989). This process is currently under way in the former socialist nations. In early 1990 the Soviet Union passed legislation allowing citizens to own the means of production (the terms *private property* and *capital* were avoided). New businesses soon appeared throughout the nation. But it is not so easy to transform command economies into market economies. There have been many incidents of conflict between state planners and the owners or managers of the new business cooperatives. Meanwhile the black market has continued to flourish as officials attempt to formulate economic policy.

The closing of noncompetitive factories, layoffs of unneeded workers in factories that remain open, uncertainty about the status of government-issued currency, and confusion over economic policy are contributing to the economic crisis in the Soviet Union and its former satellites. To make a difficult situation worse, the government must find ways to regulate and tax the goods and services traded in the huge black market. In fact, the black market must be merged into the overall market economy. At this writing these problems are creating extreme shortages in Soviet shops and factories. And although Western corporations are investing in new production facilities in Hungary and Czechoslovakia, they are fearful of losing money in the Soviet Union and some of the other former communist societies because of the uncertain economic conditions there. In sum, all of the former socialist nations are groping toward a system that would operate like the social-democratic societies of Europe, but in the meantime they retain elements of the older command system and the unregulated black market.

The United States: A Postindustrial Society? Although many people in the United States see the failure of socialism in the Soviet bloc as a victory for capitalism, sociologists and poll takers have called attention to a growing sense of unease about the U.S. economy. According to veteran economic observer Peter Passell, "Signs of decline are evident to those who care to see them. And many young Americans do not need a doctorate to understand that it is hard to live as well on two incomes as their parents live on one" (1990, p. 4-4). Part *a* of Figure 18-1 shows that between 1980 and 1989 average hourly wages decreased from $9.84 to $9.66 (in constant 1989 dollars), and that although people had more disposable income at the end of the decade than at the beginning, most of the increase came from dividends and interest, which means that lower-income people, who generally do not own stocks and other investments, did not benefit. This observation is reinforced by the trends shown in part *b*, which indicate that when one controls for family size, inflation, government benefits, and taxes, families in the lowest fifth of the income distribution averaged 9.2 percent less income in the period from 1979 to 1987 while those in the upper fifth gained 18.7 percent.

In addition to problems in the domestic economy that tend to widen the gap between the haves and the have-nots, there are indications that the U.S. economy is becoming less competitive in international markets. For example, the United States is lagging in the development of high-technology exports. Although compared with Japan and Western Europe the United States continues to spend more on research and development (see part *c* of Figure 18-1), in the vital markets for computers, communications equipment, and scientific instruments Japan is exporting far more than it imports while the United States is not doing nearly as well. This "technology gap" helps explain why the United States averaged an annual trade imbalance (i.e., more imports than exports) of $97 billion from 1981 to 1990 (Figure 18-1, part *d*). These figures raise the question of how well the United States is doing in making its own transition from an industrial to a postindustrial society.

Figure 18–1: **Some Key U.S. and International Economic Trends**

(a)

THE AMERICAN ECONOMY, IN 1989 DOLLARS		
	1980	**1989**
Disposable income per person	$9,722.00	$11,681.00
Average hourly wages	9.84	9.66
Dividend and interest income per person	2,146.00	3,096.00
Percent of population working	59.6%	63.3%

(b)

CHANGE IN U.S. AVERAGE FAMILY INCOME, 1979–1987; ADJUSTED FOR FAMILY SIZE, GOVERNMENT BENEFITS, TAXES, AND INFLATION		
	Lowest fifth of families	**Highest fifth of families**
All families	−9.2%	18.7%
Families with children	−13.8	18.7
Family head under age 35	−23.3	12.2
Family head over age 65	22.8	19.9

(c)

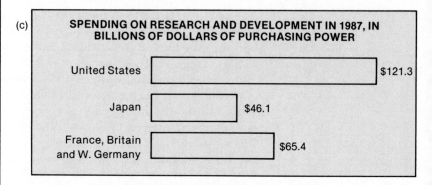

SPENDING ON RESEARCH AND DEVELOPMENT IN 1987, IN BILLIONS OF DOLLARS OF PURCHASING POWER

United States $121.3
Japan $46.1
France, Britain and W. Germany $65.4

(d)

AVERAGE RATE OF GROWTH IN TRADE					
	1965–1980		**1980–1987**		**1981–1988**
	Exports	**Imports**	**Exports**	**Imports**	**Avg. trade balance**
Japan	11.4%	4.9%	5.8%	3.6%	$52 billion
United States	6.4%	5.5%	−0.5%	9.7%	−$97 billion

Source: Data from U.S. Council of Economic Advisers, House Ways and Means Committee, Organization for Economic Cooperation and Development, and the World Bank.

In an influential study entitled *The Coming of Post Industrial Society*, sociologist Daniel Bell (1973) reviewed changes in American economic institutions that indicate that we are undergoing a transition from an industrial to a postindustrial society. A postindustrial society "emphasizes the centrality of theoretical knowledge as the axis around which new technology, economic growth, and the stratification of society will be organized" (p. 116). As societies undergo the transition to postindustrial economic institutions, an "intellectual technology" based on information arises alongside of machine technology. Industrial production does not disappear, but it becomes less important. New industries devoted to providing knowledge and information become the primary sources of economic growth (Etzioni, 1968; Fuchs, 1968; Montagna, 1977; Piore and Sabel, 1985).

Changes in the distribution of jobs in the goods-producing and service-producing sectors of the American economy clearly show the growing importance of services, especially those employing professional and technical workers (see Table 18-1). For Bell, this change is inevitable. Industries decline, but new ones appear. At the turn of the century, for example, over 70 percent of Americans were employed in agriculture and related occupations. Now this figure is a mere 2 percent. Similar transformations are taking place in manufacturing today, and they can be made less painful if the society is willing to invest in education and the retraining of workers in declining industries like mining and steel production.

Other social scientists view these changes less optimistically. Some note that declines in industrial production have pushed thousands of skilled workers into lower-paid jobs in the service sector—for example, in the fast-

> **As societies undergo the transition to postindustrial economic institutions, industries devoted to providing knowledge and information become the primary sources of economic growth.**

Table 18–1: Changes in Goods- and Service-Producing Employment, 1947–1986, and Projections for 2000 (in millions)

	1947	1970	1980	1986	2000	1947–70	1970–80	1980–86	1986–2000
Total	51.8	81.7	102.0	111.6	133.0	+58%	+25%	9%	+19%
Goods-Producing (Total)	26.4	23.6	25.7	24.7	24.7	−1%	+1%	0	0
Agriculture	1.0	.6	1.0	.8	.7	−40%	+40%	−20%	−13%
Mining	2.0	3.6	4.3	4.9	5.8	+80%	+19%	+14%	+18%
Construction	15.5	19.4	20.3	19.0	18.2	+25%	+5%	−6%	−4%
Manufacturing	8.4	11.2	12.2	11.2	10.7	+33%	+9%	−8%	−4%
Durable	7.1	8.2	8.1	7.8	7.4	+15%	0	−4%	−5%
Nondurable	25.4	47.1	64.4	74.4	94.5	+85%	+37%	+15%	+27%
Service-Producing (Total)	4.2	4.5	5.1	5.2	5.7	+7%	+13%	+2%	+10%
Transportation & Utilities	9.0	15.0	20.3	23.5	30.0	+67%	+35%	+16%	+28%
Trade (Wholesale & Retail)	1.8	3.6	5.2	6.3	7.9	+100%	+44%	+21%	+25%
Finance, Insurance, Real Estate	5.1	11.4	17.5	22.5	32.5	+124%	+54%	+29%	+31%
Services	5.5	12.6	16.2	16.7	18.3	+129%	+29%	+3%	+10%
Government	7.9	3.5	3.4	3.3	2.9	−56%	−3%	−3%	−12%

food industry or as janitors or security guards—which helps explain the decline in average hourly wages shown in Figure 18-1 (Aronowitz, 1984; Fallows, 1985; Harrison, Tilly, and Bluestone, 1986). Others are concerned that the gains made by blacks and women in access to better-paying industrial jobs since World War II are being erased. William Julius Wilson (1978) has commented that "access to the means of production is increasingly based on educational criteria . . . and thus threatens to solidify the position of the black underclass" (p. 151). European sociologists have criticized the theory of postindustrial society on even broader grounds, saying that it is likely to produce an increasingly impoverished working class with even more reason to demand a more equal distribution of wealth (Touraine, 1971).

A Peace Dividend? The end of the Cold War could result in large reductions in troops and military equipment in Western Europe as well as large reductions in the military budgets of the United States and the Soviet Union. Nevertheless, major crises like the invasion of Kuwait by Iraq in 1990 could dash any hope for large-scale reductions in military budgets. The world political situation remains far too unstable to automatically assume drastic cuts in military forces.

If there is a peace dividend, it could create other problems, problems in planning how to convert military production and employment to peacetime employment, and conflicts over how to allocate the savings resulting from shrinking military budgets. Thus while political leaders argue over how large the peace dividend will (or should) be during the 1990s, survey research shows that U.S. citizens believe that there will be a peace dividend and that it should be spent to reduce the federal debt and to address social problems like drugs and homelessness. These findings are illustrated in Table 18-2.

It is important to note that a large majority of those who answered the poll believe that military and defense spending should be increased or kept the same. A majority, however, also believe that the United States will

© Susan McCartney, Photo Researchers

This balloon seller in a public square in Krakow, Poland, symbolizes all the many ways in which private enterprise is reappearing in the former Soviet satellite nations

be able to save money as the Cold War winds down, an opinion that is inconsistent with the belief that military spending should not be decreased. From a sociological perspective, the major issue related to the potential peace dividend is who will benefit from it. Will it be used in ways that benefit the public—for example, to improve roads, schools, hospitals, and the environment—or will it be used to increase private wealth through such means as tax reductions (Heilbroner, 1990)? Box 18-3 presents an autoworkers union member's view of the peace dividend.

WORKERS, MANAGERS, AND CORPORATIONS

When Soviet leaders think about the problems of their economy they often look to the United States for comparisons. Our standard of living is among the highest in the world; theirs remains rather low except for members of the elite. North Americans seem to have a lot of incentive to work; Russians frequently seem not to be so

Table 18–2: **Views on Spending and Peace**

	Views of all adults	**Views of those who say the cold war is over**	**Views of those who say the cold war is not over**
Federal spending on military and defense should be:			
Increased	13%	10%	14%
decreased	36	46	31
kept the same	48	43	52
If relations between the U.S. and the U.S.S.R. continue to improve, how much money will the U.S. will be able to save by reducing military spending?			
a lot of money	36	44	31
some	38	37	39
not very much	13	11	15
none at all	9	7	12
If the United States is able to save a lot of money on defense in the next few years, the money should be used to:			
reduce the Federal budget deficit	21	21	21
cut taxes	10	9	10
fight problems like drugs and homelessness	62	64	61
Should the United States increase aid to Eastern European countries that are becoming more independent of the Soviet Union?			
should	33	39	31
should not	59	56	62
Federal spending on the environment should be:			
increased	57	60	58
decreased	4	5	4
kept the same	35	33	35

These data are based on telephone interviews with 1,557 adults conducted January 13, 14, and 15. Of all adults surveyed, 37 percent said the cold war is over; 54 percent said it is not over. Those with no opinion are not shown.

Source: CBS/New York Times Poll, January 25, 1990.

Box 18–3: **Who's Afraid of the Peace Dividend?**

"This story—" said Cousin Jack, slapping the newspaper article he had been reading. "It says that the Cold War is over. We're going to be buddies with the Russkies."

"It's high time that we settled our differences, if you ask me," said Bill.

"Are you nuts, Bill? Everybody knows that this country wouldn't last a minute without the military to spread the tax dollars around. Think about it. If we don't have somebody to fight we'll have to close military bases. What will all our boys and girls in uniform do for a living— lead Boy Scout troops? Bureaucrats will be out of work too. Why, government will be only a shadow of its former self."

"Sounds good so far," said Bill.

"And what about all the factories that build guns and tanks and stealth bombers?" said Cousin Jack, warming to his cause. "They'll have to close along with all the places that make bullets and bombs. Why, the whole country will be in chaos with all those people out of work. It'll be nothin' but soup kitchens and bread lines—coast to coast."

"How about converting those factories to civilian uses?"

"Can't be done!"

"But we converted civilian factories to wartime production at the start of World War II. Change them back!"

"To do what—make Monopoly sets?"

"No, but low-cost housing could be factory-built. And how about high-speed ground transportation, or commercial aircraft? All of those areas have been neglected," said Bill.

"Humph!" snorted Cousin Jack. "So what if factories could be converted? There

are all those ex-GIs with nothing to do. And what about all the high-rankers? I can't think of a sorrier sight than a general with his hand out."

"You have a point. People accustomed to paying $400 for hammers and toilet seats might have a hard time adjusting to the real world. But this country needs people to tackle problems in education and health care, not to mention all the highways, bridges, and airports that need rebuilding to keep us competitive. There seems to be plenty of work for anybody willing to do it."

"I hate to admit this, Bill, but you're starting to make sense."

Source: Adapted from "Bottoms Up!" by Jim Ehlinger [UAW Local 94 (Dubuque) member], *Solidarity*, November 1989, p. 10. The cartoon was drawn by Ehlinger.

motivated. "If all 270 million people in the Soviet Union worked as hard as people work in America," a high Soviet official told a reporter, "we would be so rich that we would have a monkey dancing for you here on the table" (quoted in Maydans, 1985, p. A14).

But when American business managers and sociologists compare the U.S. economy with others, they most often choose Japan as the standard. This is hardly surprising. Japanese firms not only produce steel and automobiles and other industrial products more cheaply and often better than U.S. manufacturers, but also compete aggressively in world markets for products like computer components and office machines, important symbols of the postindustrial age. A major factor in Japan's phenomenal success is the attitudes of its workers and managers. Let us therefore look at how work is typically organized in the United States and Japan.

Japanese Factories. In the typical Japanese factory the workers bargain collectively with managers over wages and working conditions, just as they do in unionized factories in the United States. And in both societies workers expect similar pay and other benefits. However, in the Western nations workers and managers are viewed as natural adversaries. Whatever rights workers and their unions possess have been "gained by continuous inch-by-inch pressure against dogged managerial resistance" (Dore, 1973, p. 115). In Japan, by contrast, the typical worker feels that he or she "belongs to the company" as opposed to merely working for the company (Dore, 1982). During the years following Japan's defeat in World War II, the Japanese developed new forms of labor–management cooperation based on the idea that workers and management have a shared interest in what is good for the company as a whole. Wage inequalities between workers and managers were decreased; time clocks and separate cafeterias were eliminated; and most important, a system of "lifetime commitment" or permanent tenure for workers who entered the plant at a young age was established in large corporations (Abegglen, 1955). Because they know they are in the corporation for life, the workers are committed to the corporation's goals. And because of their commitment to the company, they devote their full energy to improving their productivity, much of which comes through high-quality work.

It should be noted, however, that not all Japanese workers enjoy the advantages of permanent tenure. An increasing amount of work in Japanese firms is "outsourced" to smaller factories in which only a few of the workers have tenure. Even within the large firms, a decreasing proportion of employees are guaranteed jobs with the firm. Lifetime employment, for which the Japanese economy is famous, covers only about 35 percent of the labor force. Younger men and women thus form a secondary class of less advantaged, and perhaps less loyal, employees. Forty percent of Japanese workers are women, and about 25 percent of them (some 5 million women) are called part-time workers although they work up to forty-eight hours a week for an average of $2.40 per hour and few benefits. (Japan has no law requiring equal pay for equal work.) Thus, although Japanese workers are said to be more productive than workers in the United States or Europe, a large part of this productivity stems from the fact that they work far longer hours for lower pay (Clarke, 1989, personal communication). As the level of affluence in Japan increases, sociologists are finding evidence that, as in other nations, workers are demanding more leisure and benefits (Dore, 1982; Kamata, 1982).

U.S. Industry. In the United States, workers appear to be far less committed to the goals of the company, a point that was illustrated in a study of a modern oil refinery by David Halle (1984). Halle reported that 52 percent of the workers declined opportunities for promotion to top positions in their work crews because they did not want to exercise authority. "Nor do they wish to take responsibility for production—they do not want to be concerned about whether the chemical reactions are occurring in the right way. They prefer to take a detached attitude to their jobs, treating work as an intrusion into their social life both inside and outside the plant. They will do their jobs, but they also enjoy the various social activities that go on in the workplace" (p. 155). These attitudes were held by a minority of the workers Halle studied, but their numbers are greater than one would expect in a Japanese firm, in which the organization's goals appear to be more widely

The Western view of workers and managers as natural adversaries is often contrasted with the Japanese idea that workers and managers have a shared interest in what is good for the company.

shared by managers and workers. Other evidence shows that many American workers want to produce high-quality products but feel an organizational and cultural gap separating them from managers even when they share the same goals (Edwards, 1979; HHS, 1973).

Alienation

Many sociologists use the concept of **alienation** to explain the gap between workers and managers. Karl Marx first applied the term to the situation of workers under early capitalism. The worker in a factory performed only a fraction of the work that went into a product and therefore could feel little sense of ownership of the final product. And because the worker typically could not control the work process very much, he or she came to feel like a mere cog in a giant machine, a feeling that produced a sense of not being able to control one's own actions on the job (Fromm, 1961; Marx, 1961/1844). Today the term *alienation* is often used to describe the feeling of being powerless to control one's own destiny (Blauner, 1964; Seeman, 1959). At work, people may feel alienated because their labor is divided up into activities that are meaningless to them. Robert Blauner (1964), for example, found that workers who perform highly repetitive tasks on an assembly line are more alienated than workers in groups whose tasks involve teamwork.

In a study of organizational techniques that have been used successfully in Japan, Ezra Vogel (1979) pointed out that Japanese firms tend to avoid worker alienation by strengthening the role of the small group:

The essential building block of a company is not a man with a particular role assignment and his secretary and assistants. The essential building block of the organization is the section. . . . The lowly section, within its sphere, does not await executive orders but takes the initiative. . . . For this system to work effectively leading section personnel need to know and to identify with company purposes to a higher degree than persons in an American firm. They achieve this through long experience and years of discussion with others at all levels. [pp. 143–145]

The irony of this finding and others like

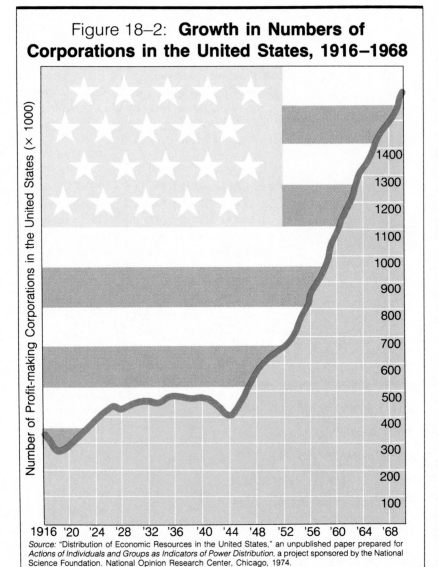

Figure 18–2: **Growth in Numbers of Corporations in the United States, 1916–1968**

Source: "Distribution of Economic Resources in the United States," an unpublished paper prepared for *Actions of Individuals and Groups as Indicators of Power Distribution,* a project sponsored by the National Science Foundation. National Opinion Research Center, Chicago, 1974.

it is that even before World War II American and European industrial sociologists had demonstrated the benefits of team approaches to work. The famous studies by Elton Mayo, discussed in Chapter 2, were designed to find out how workers at any level of an organization could be made to feel less alienation and a greater sense of ownership of their jobs. This research demonstrated the importance of primary-group relationships at work. But the function of the manager is to motivate employees to work more efficiently and at higher levels, a goal that is not easily achieved.

Individuals and Corporations

One possible source of worker alienation is the increasing power of the corporation relative to the individual. In the United States and other industrialized societies, the corporation has gained ever-greater dominance over other economic institutions. Although they may have been established by entrepreneurs like Andrew Carnegie or John D. Rockefeller, who took great risks to build personal empires, modern corporations are bureaucratic organizations whose executive leadership may, at least in principle, be replaced. Sociologists like James S. Coleman (1982) point out that the idea of the *corporate actor* was essential to the development of the modern

corporation. "As economic enterprise outgrew the family," Coleman writes, "it became useful for several persons to join together to carry out the enterprise. They were able to do this only if they were protected [as individuals] from the liabilities that the joint enterprise might incur" (p. 8). This was accomplished by the creation of a new class of "persons"—corporations—that could incur debts and liabilities on their own account. The liability of any individual member of the corporation was limited to the amount that he or she had invested in it.

The emergence of the concept of the corporate actor had far-reaching effects. By the beginning of our own century, the importance of corporate actors (most of which are bureaucratic organizations) had begun to outweigh the importance of individuals in most of the institutional sectors of society. These trends are illustrated in Figures 18-2 and 18-3, which show the dramatic rise in the number of corporations over the past half-century and the changing balance in the attention given to individuals versus corporate actors in one of the nation's most important daily newspapers. "What these changes suggest," Coleman concludes, "is a structural change in society over the past hundred years in which corporate actors play an increasing role and natural persons play a decreasing role" (1982, p. 15).

A further effect of the dominance of corporate actors is that the individual is at a disadvantage in dealings with such actors. Today, corporate actors generally have access to much more information, derived from surveys, advertising, credit ratings, and the like. In conflicts that reach the courts, although the corporate actor and the individual are equal parties in the eyes of the law, in fact the corporate actor usually has the upper hand as it is backed up by numerous specialists, whereas the individual, even with the best legal aid, usually can draw upon only limited resources.

Social movements like the labor movement and the consumer and environmental-protection movements attempt to reduce the asymmetry or imbalance in these relationships (for example, they seek to regulate corporations by making them reveal informa-

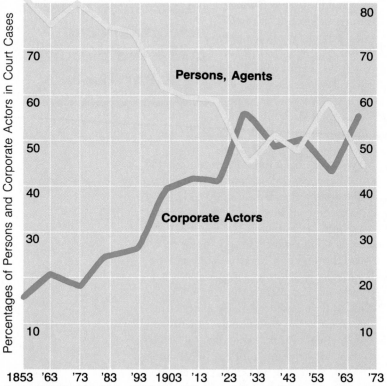

Figure 18–3: **Participation of Persons and Corporate Actors in Court Cases, New York State Court of Appeals, 1853–1973**

Persons, Agents

Corporate Actors

Percentages of Persons and Corporate Actors in Court Cases

Source: "A Study of the Relative Participation of Persons and Corporate Actors in Court Cases," an unpublished paper prepared for *Actions of Individuals and Groups as Indicators of Power Distribution,* a project sponsored by the National Science Foundation. National Opinion Research Center, Chicago, 1974.

tion). Countermovements try to restore the rights of corporate actors; an example is the movement to deregulate business and industry. Such movements are one consequence of the imbalance between the individual and the corporate actor. Another consequence may be an increase in the number of deviant acts directed against corporations of all kinds. People may cheat or steal from corporate actors—for example, they may take out their frustrations by destroying public telephones, scrawling graffiti on mass-transit facilities, or illegally tapping into cable-television boxes—without feeling nearly as guilty as they might if their actions were directed against individuals. Sociological perspectives on work and workers can offer some leads to further progress in dealing with such problems in the future.

Sociological Perspectives on the Workplace

Industrial sociology is concerned with the social organization of work and the types of interactions that occur in the workplace. Like sociologists in other fields, industrial sociologists use the functionalist, conflict, and interactionist perspectives in their research. The results of that research have been used to support various approaches to labor–management relations, as will become clear in the following discussion.

Human Relations in Industry: A Functionalist Perspective. The *human relations* perspective on management is associated with the research of Elton Mayo and his colleagues at Western Electric's Hawthorne plant and in aircraft and metal production plants. Their goal was to use experimental methods and observation of workers and managers on the job in an attempt to understand how the factory's formal organization and goals are affected by patterns of informal organization within the workplace. This was in sharp contrast with earlier approaches to labor–management relations, especially the *scientific management* approach developed early in this century by Frederick W. Taylor.

Scientific management—or Taylorism, as it is often called—was one of the earliest attempts to apply objective standards to management practices. After rising through the ranks from laborer to chief engineer in a large steel company, Taylor turned his attention to the study of worker productivity. He noticed that workers tend to adhere to informal norms that require them to limit their output. For example, he found that the rate of production in a machine shop was only about one-third of what might normally be expected. Taylor decided to use the authority of management to speed up the workers. He fired stubborn men, hired "green hands" who did not know the norms of the experienced workers, and experimented with ways of breaking down the labor of each worker into its components. Every job, he claimed, could be scientifically studied to determine how it could be performed most efficiently. Such "time and motion studies," combined with piecework payment systems that induced workers to produce more because they were paid for each unit produced above a set number, became the hallmarks of scientific management (Miller and Form, 1964). Taylor's principles were quickly incorporated into the managerial practices of American businesses, but they were often resisted by workers and their unions (Braverman, 1974).

Scientific management emphasized efficient performance of tasks and piecework payment systems.

Mayo's experiments were intended to determine what conditions would foster the highest rates of worker productivity. His observations convinced him that increased productivity could be obtained by emphasizing teamwork among workers and managers, rather than through pay incentives or changes in such variables as lighting, temperature, and rest periods (Bendix, 1974). We saw in Chapter 2 that Mayo's research showed that the attention given to the workers was what mattered, not the various experimental conditions. But Mayo drew another, more important conclusion from the Hawthorne experiments:

The major experimental change was introduced when those in charge sought to hold the situation humanly steady . . . by getting the cooperation of the workers. What actually happened was that six individuals became a team and the team gave itself wholeheartedly and spontaneously to cooperating in the experiment. [1945, pp. 72–73]

Although Mayo's research focused on the interactions between workers and managers, the human relations approach that grew out of that research can be said to represent the functionalist perspective on the workplace because it stresses the function of managerial efforts in increasing worker productivity. The functionalist perspective is also illustrated by William F. Whyte's classic study of the restaurant industry, which we encountered in Chapter 3. In a small restaurant, the organization's structure is simple. "There is little division of labor. The owner and employees serve together as cooks, countermen, and dishwashers." But when the restaurant expands, a number of supervisory and production occupations are added to its role structure. According to Whyte, this magnifies old problems and gives rise to new ones:

In a large and busy restaurant a waitress may take orders from fifty to one hundred customers a day (and perhaps several times at each meal) in addition to the orders (much less frequent) she receives from her supervisor. When we add to this the problem of adjusting to service pantry workers, bartenders, and perhaps checkers, we can readily see the possibilities of emotional tension—and, in our study, we did see a number of girls break down and cry under the strain. [p. 304]

Whyte discovered that tension and stress could be reduced, and customers served more happily, if the restaurant was organized in such a way that lower-status employees were not required to give orders directly to higher-status ones. For example, waiters and waitresses should not give orders directly to cooks but should place their orders with a pantry worker or use a system of written orders. By changing the organization of statuses and roles in the restaurant (and, thus, the way they functioned as a social system) it would be possible to increase work satisfaction and output.

The human-relations approach to management emphasized teamwork among workers and managers.

Conflict at Work. The human relations approach seeks to improve cooperation between workers and managers in order to achieve the organization's goals. Industrial sociologists who take a conflict perspective feel that this approach automatically condones the goals of managers and fails to consider more basic causes of worker-management conflict such as class conflict. This results in continual "fine-tuning" of organizational structures rather than in more thorough reforms.

In a study of a midwestern metal products factory, Michael Burawoy (1980) found that even after changes were made on the basis of the human relations approach, the workers continued to limit their output. The workers called this "making out" and saw it as a way of maximizing two conflicting values: their pay and their enjoyment of social relations at work. But instead of wondering why the workers refused to produce more, Burawoy asked why they worked as hard as they did. He concluded that the workers were actually playing into the hands of the managers and owners because neither they nor the unions ever questioned management's authority to control basic production decisions. The norms of the shop-floor culture, of which "making out" is an example, caused the workers to feel that they were resisting the managers' control. As a result, they did not feel a need to engage in more direct challenges to the capitalist system itself.

Conflict-oriented industrial sociologists also study how class and status relations outside the workplace influence shop-floor cultures. For example, in an analysis of work relations in a large midwestern steel mill, William Kornblum (1974) described how ethnic and racial conflicts among whites, blacks, and Chicanos are carried into the plant itself. These conflicts diminish as the steelworkers work together in teams over periods of many years, but the basic class differences that divide workers from managers remain and are institutionalized in the norms of union-management bargaining.

A fundamental problem for conflict sociologists is that class conflict must be shown to exist; it cannot be assumed to exist simply because Marxian theory defines workers and business owners as opposing classes. In fact, there is considerable evidence that despite their misfortunes, workers do not view their interests as opposing those of owners and managers. For example, the severe depression in basic industries like autos and steel has produced high rates of unemployment in the industrial communities of the Midwest and Northeast. Between 1970 and 1987 the number of workers employed in the production of basic steel products fell from 627,000 to 269,000 (*Statistical Abstract*, 1989). Since 1980 about 21,000 steel production jobs have been lost in South Chicago alone. (The data in Table 18-3 show the earnings and health-insurance losses of steelworkers in that community.) But these conditions have not resulted in increased class conflict. Instead, industrial workers who have lost their jobs experience periods of depression. Their anguish is isolated and seems hardly to affect the class consciousness of more fortunate workers. It may be popularized in the lyrics of a Bruce Springsteen song—"They're closing down the textile mill across the railroad track / Foreman says these jobs are going boys / and they ain't coming back to your hometown"—but it has not produced much overt class conflict or new social movements (Bensman and Lynch, 1987).

Professions: An Interactionist Perspective. Factory workers and other low-status employees are not the only subjects of research by sociologists who study work and employment. Because they are a growing segment of modern economic institutions, professionals have also been studied extensively. A **profession** is an occupation with "a body of knowledge and a developed intellectual technique . . . transmitted by a formal educational process and testing procedures. A code of professional ethics governs each profession and regulates relations with colleagues, clients, and the public [and] most professions are licensed by the state" (Montagna, 1977, p. 197). This definition could be applied to a variety of occupations. For example, doctors and attorneys have long been considered professionals, but what about

---

Table 18–3: **Changes in Steelworkers' Incomes, 1979–1983, and Losses in Health-Insurance Coverage**

1979 Income (*n*=525)	Percent of Steelworkers with 1983 Income of		
	Under $10,000	$10,000–20,000	Over $20,000
$10,000 or less	88	6	6
$10,000–20,000	62	25	13
$20,000	36	30	34

Health Insurance	Percentage	
Health insurance dropped owing to layoff	81	(*n* = 633)
Health care put off owing to lost insurance	76	(*n* = 543)
Currently have health insurance	56	(*n* = 655)
No health insurance	44	(*n* = 655)
Medicaid	23	(*n* = 553)
Medicare	4	(*n* = 553)

Source: Adapted from Steelworkers Research Project, 1985.

Figure 18–4: **Degree of Professionalization of Various Occupations**

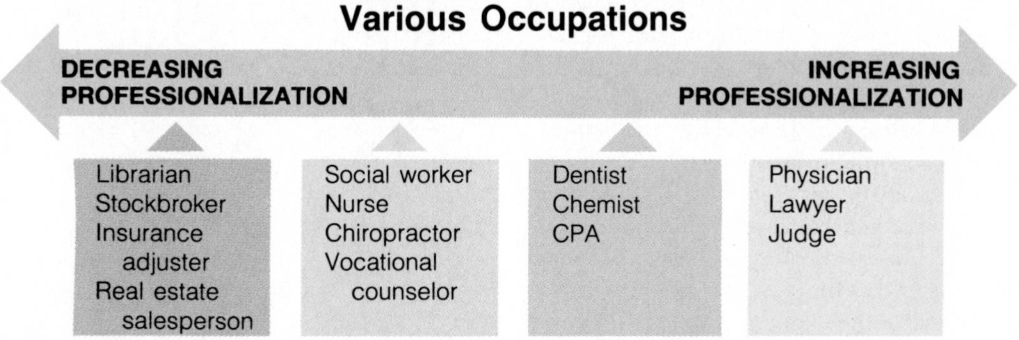

DECREASING PROFESSIONALIZATION			INCREASING PROFESSIONALIZATION
Librarian Stockbroker Insurance adjuster Real estate salesperson	Social worker Nurse Chiropractor Vocational counselor	Dentist Chemist CPA	Physician Lawyer Judge

Source: Reprinted with permission of Macmillan Publishing Company from *Occupations and Society* by Paul D. Montagna, originally published by John Wiley and Sons (New York: Macmillan, 1977).

nurses and stockbrokers? Sociologists have addressed this question in their research on the "professionalization" of occupations—that is, on the way different occupations attempt to achieve the status of professions (see Figure 18-4).

According to Everett C. Hughes (1959), a profession is a set of role relationships between "experts" and "clients," in which the professional is an expert who offers knowledge and judgments to clients. Often the professional must assume the burden of the client's "guilty knowledge": The lawyer must keep secret the client's transgressions, and the physician must hide any knowledge of the sexual behavior or drug use of famous and not-so-famous patients. Professions thus "rest on some bargain about receiving, guarding, and giving out communications" (Hughes, 1959, p. 449).

Interactionist sociologists pay special attention to the role relationships that develop in various professions. They are particularly interested in the processes of professional socialization—learning the profession's formal and informal norms. For example, in a well-known study of professional socialization in medical schools, Howard Becker and his colleagues (1961) found that in the later years

> *In studying professionalization, interactionist sociologists focus on the role relationships in various professions and on the processes of professional socialization.*

of their training medical students' attention is devoted more and more to learning the informal norms of medical practice. The formal science that they learn in class is supplemented by the practical knowledge of the working doctor, and the student's skill at interacting with higher-status colleagues becomes extremely important to achieving the status of a professional physician. In a more recent study on the same subject, Charles Bosk (1979) showed that resident surgeons in a teaching hospital are forgiven if they make mistakes that the older surgeons believe to be "normal" aspects of the learning process, but not when their mistakes are repeated or are thought to be due to carelessness. The point of these and similar studies is that role performance is learned through interaction. Role expectations vary from one profession to another, as do the ways in which these expectations are experienced by members of the profession.

Conclusion

Our discussion of professions can serve as a reminder of a basic characteristic of economic institutions, one that we noted early in the chapter: Economic institutions are concerned with "allocating scarce resources to satisfy competing ends." Thus, just as the guilds of feudal societies controlled access to skilled trades in medieval times, professional associations like the American Medical Association attempt to control access to the professions. Efforts by nation-states to regulate markets and trade, and efforts by managers to increase the productivity of workers, all are concerned with achieving the most advantageous use of scarce resources. This fundamental fact is at the heart of the sociological study of economic institutions.

Sociologists are continually providing evidence that markets are regulated by the state in the interests of certain classes or status groups or that they are controlled by large corporations at the expense of workers or consumers. When sociologists study the activities of large corporations in world markets, for example, they find that a relatively small number of multinational corporations dominate the world economy. Such corporations can have a major impact on the economic systems of nation-states in less developed regions, as well as on the situation of workers in those nations.

In the area of economic theory, we have seen that sociologists are consulted for studies and evaluations of economic institutions in different societies. American managers are particularly interested in comparisons between the United States and its closest competitor, Japan. However, comparisons between capitalist economies and the former socialist economies are also valuable for the insights they provide with respect to the importance of basic economic institutions like markets and the private ownership of capital.

In the area of labor–management relations, we have shown that sociologists play a significant role in the development of managerial philosophies. Of course, much more needs to be done in this area. We still do not fully understand why the participatory system of Japanese firms has proved so successful and if it should be transplanted to other nations. Nor have sociologists done enough research on the changing role of labor unions in a society whose economy is undergoing a transformation from one based on heavy industrial production to one based on the production of sophisticated, high-technology goods and services. Some current research on this subject is discussed in the Frontiers section of the chapter.

FRONTIERS OF SOCIOLOGY

Work and Careers in the 1990s

Structural changes that are taking place in the economy of North America will affect all of us. As new forms of production replace older ones, the demand for different types of skills and careers changes dramatically. This is especially true for people preparing to enter the labor force, since decisions about what educational paths to pursue need to be based not only on personal talents and preferences but also on information about the kinds of employment opportunities that are likely to be available in the future. Sociologists, along with labor economists and manpower researchers in other fields, are continually called upon to conduct research on these questions.

Compared with those of other Western nations, the economy of the United States can be said to be "an astounding job machine" (*New York Times*, June 17, 1984). As the accompanying chart shows, despite the decreases in manufacturing employment referred to in this chapter, the number of jobs in the economy has risen rapidly and the unemployment rate has decreased significantly. And although the United States lost about 2.3 million manufacturing jobs in the severe recession that lasted from 1978 to 1981, there are still at least 25 million Americans employed in such jobs. Although it may be a declining proportion of the overall labor force,

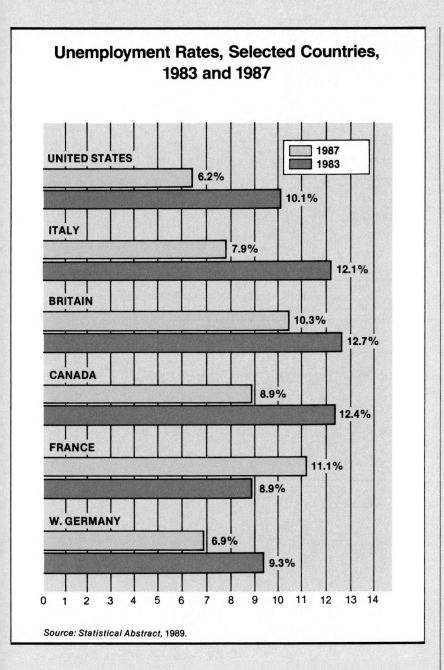

Unemployment Rates, Selected Countries, 1983 and 1987

- 1987
- 1983

UNITED STATES
6.2%
10.1%

ITALY
7.9%
12.1%

BRITAIN
10.3%
12.7%

CANADA
8.9%
12.4%

FRANCE
11.1%
8.9%

W. GERMANY
6.9%
9.3%

0 1 2 3 4 5 6 7 8 9 10 11 12 13 14

Source: Statistical Abstract, 1989.

in industrial sectors using technologically advanced equipment and processes.

What is less easy to estimate, however, is the continuing impact of automation on employment of all kinds. The computer revolution has yet to make itself as fully felt in all sectors of the economy as it has in manufacturing, in which applications of computer control have speeded the development of robot machines to replace human workers. But the Nobel Prize-winning economist Wassily W. Leontief believes that in coming years computers will begin to decrease the rate of growth of many service occupations, especially in clerical fields.

Other research indicates that these decreases will be matched by decreases in the size of the labor force. For example, Robert E. Kennedy's (1986) analysis of the impact of shrinking birth cohorts during the 1960s and 1970s shows that in the 1990s people between the ages of twenty and forty-five "will have little choice about working—they will be under great social pressures to be employed" (p. 67). This pressure will stem in part from their need for income and benefits, but increased pressure to work will also be produced by labor shortages caused by the smaller size of their birth cohorts. This in turn will create a greater demand for women to enter and remain in the labor force and a greater demand for workers with advanced education and skills. If we examine the projected population pyramid for 1995, Kennedy suggests, we can see that women and men will very likely share more equally in the responsibilities and benefits of employment.

Throughout the 1990s there will also be increasing pressure on teenagers to become part of the labor force. As the unemployment rate decreases, teenagers find it easier to find jobs that pay more than the minimum wage. The majority of these jobs are in retail services, especially eating and drinking establishments and supermarkets. Employers, on the other hand, have greater difficulty finding

this is a large number in absolute terms and is likely to remain large for the foreseeable future. In fact, for the decade ahead, forecasters estimate that one out of six new jobs will be created in manufacturing, especially

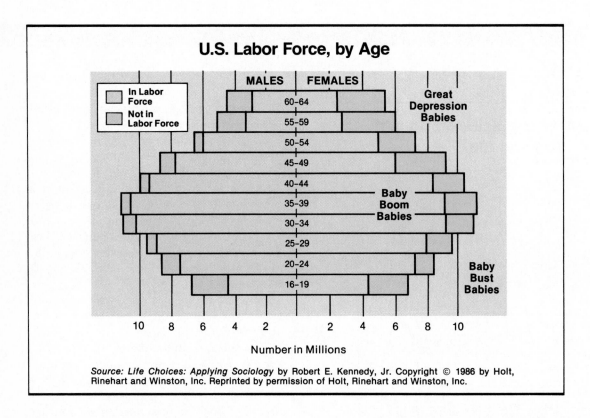

U.S. Labor Force, by Age

MALES | FEMALES

- In Labor Force
- Not in Labor Force

Great Depression Babies

60-64
55-59
50-54
45-49
40-44
35-39
30-34
25-29
20-24
16-19

Baby Boom Babies

Baby Bust Babies

10 8 6 4 2   2 4 6 8 10

Number in Millions

Source: Life Choices: Applying Sociology by Robert E. Kennedy, Jr. Copyright © 1986 by Holt, Rinehart and Winston, Inc. Reprinted by permission of Holt, Rinehart and Winston, Inc.

young workers willing to work at low wages. Already the effects of this situation can be seen in a rapid increase in the number of violations of child labor laws (Joselow, 1989).

On this research frontier, social scientists will continue to monitor how the effects of automation and the structural transformation of the economy interact with decreases in the size of the American labor force. The optimistic prediction is that these changes will diminish the amount of less desirable work and increase the number of jobs in fields devoted to helping others realize their potential or improve their health and well-being. A more pessimistic prediction is that transformations in the economy will continue to produce large-scale displacement of workers and increases in less well-paid service-sector jobs.

Violations of Child Labor Laws
(in thousands)

20

15

10

5

1982 1983 1984 1985 1986 1987 1988

Source: U.S. Department of Labor.

SUMMARY

*E*conomics is the study of how individuals and societies choose to employ scarce resources to produce various commodities and distribute them among various groups in the society. Sociologists are also concerned with how individuals and societies make such choices, but much of their research focuses on how cultural norms affect those choices. The main subjects of sociological research in this area are markets and the division of labor, the interactions between government and economic institutions, and the nature of jobs and professions.

A hallmark of an industrial society is the production of commodities and services to be exchanged in markets. A *market* is an economic institution that regulates exchange behavior. In a market, different values are established for particular goods and services; those values are usually expressed in terms of a common measure of exchange, or currency. Market transactions are governed by agreements, or *contracts*, in which a seller agrees to supply a particular item and a buyer agrees to pay for it. The spread of markets throughout the world began in the late fifteenth century as a result of the development of new technologies that facilitated trade. Today world markets are dominated by *multinational corporations*, economic enterprises that have headquarters in one country and conduct business activities in one or more other countries.

The fate of societies throughout the world has been strongly influenced by the economic ideologies of mercantilism, capitalism, and socialism. *Mercantilism* held that the wealth of a nation could be measured by its holdings of gold, so the best economic system was one that increased the nation's exports and thereby increased its holdings of gold. *Laissez-faire capitalism,* on the other hand, argued that a society's wealth could be measured only by its capacity to produce goods and services—

that is, its resources of land, labor, and machinery. The major institutions of capitalism are private property and free markets.

Socialism arose out of the belief that private property and personal profit should be replaced by public ownership of property and sharing of profits. According to Marx, the socialist state would be controlled by the workers, who would determine what should be produced and how it should be distributed. Soviet-style socialist societies were characterized until recently by command economies, in which the state commands economic institutions to supply a specific amount of each product and to sell it at a particular price. *Democratic socialism* holds that private property must continue to exist but that large corporations should be owned by the nation or, if they are in private hands, required to be run for the benefit of all citizens.

In *welfare capitalism*, markets determine what goods and services will be produced and how, but the government regulates economic competition. Welfare capitalism also asserts that the state should invest in the society's human resources through policies promoting education, health care, and social welfare.

The end of the Cold War has raised the question of how the transition from command economies to entrepreneurial-style market economies will be carried out in socialist nations. Those nations are groping toward social-democratic economic systems, but in the meantime they retain elements of the older command system and the unregulated black market. In the United States, the transition from an economy based on the production of goods to one based on the provision of services has resulted in the displacement of thousands of skilled workers into lower-paid jobs in the service sector. Although the end of the Cold War could produce a "peace dividend," it remains to be seen whether reduced spending on defense will translate into greater investment in society's human capital.

American workers feel an organizational and cultural gap separating them from managers even when they share the same goals. Many sociologists use the concept of *alienation* to explain this gap. This term refers to the feeling of being powerless to control one's own destiny. At work, people may feel alienated because their labor is divided up into activities that are meaningless to them.

In the United States and other industrialized societies, the corporation has gained ever-greater dominance over other economic institutions. Corporations are "fictional persons" that can incur debts and liabilities on their own account. In this century the importance of corporations has come to outweigh that of individuals in most of the institutional sectors of society, and the individual is often at a disadvantage in dealings with corporations.

The scientific management approach to labor–management relations attempted to in-crease productivity by determining how each job could be performed most efficiently and by using piecework payment systems to induce workers to produce more. Efforts to determine what conditions would result in the highest rates of worker productivity led to the recognition that cooperation between workers and managers is an important ingredient in worker satisfaction and output. This gave rise to the "human relations" approach to management, which seeks to improve cooperation between workers and managers.

Conflict theorists feel that the human relations approach fails to consider the basic causes of worker–management conflict. They study how social class and status both at work and outside the workplace influence relations between workers and managers. Interactionist theorists have devoted considerable study to professionalization, or the way in which occupations attempt to gain the status of professions, and to the processes of professional socialization (i.e., learning the formal and informal norms of the profession).

GLOSSARY

market: an economic institution that regulates exchange behavior through the establishment of different values for particular goods and services (**p. 562**).

technology: tools, procedures, and forms of social organization that increase human productive capacity (**p. 564**).

multinational corporation: an economic enterprise that has headquarters in one country and conducts business activities in one or more other countries (**p. 565**).

mercantilism: an economic philosophy based on the belief that the wealth of a nation can be measured by its holdings of gold or other precious metals and that the state should control trade (**p. 567**).

laissez-faire capitalism: an economic philosophy based on the belief that the wealth of a nation can be measured by its capacity to produce goods and services (i.e., its resources of land, labor, and machinery) and that these can be maximized by free trade (**p. 567**).

socialism: an economic philosophy based on the concept of public ownership of property and sharing of profits, together with the belief that economic decisions should be controlled by the workers (**p. 568**).

democratic socialism: an economic philosophy based on the belief that private property may exist at the same time that large corporations are owned by the state and run for the benefit of all citizens (**p. 570**).

welfare capitalism: an economic philosophy in which markets determine what goods will be produced and how, but the government regulates economic competition (**p. 570**).

alienation: the feeling of being powerless to control one's own destiny; a worker's feeling of powerlessness owing to inability to control the work process (**p. 578**).

profession: an occupation with a body of knowledge and a developed intellectual technique that are transmitted by a formal educational process and testing procedures (**p. 582**).

WHERE TO FIND IT

Books

The Coming of Post Industrial Society (Daniel Bell; Basic Books, 1973). The best source of ideas and background on the changes occurring in modern societies like the United States since the rise of computer technology and related electronic or information systems.

English Factory, Japanese Factory (Ronald Dore; University of California Press, 1973). A comparative study of the Japanese and English economies with emphasis on the sociology of labor–management relations. A good treatment of the history of Japan's industrial organization.

The De-Industrialization of America (Barry Bluestone and Bennett Harrison; Basic Books, 1982). A fact-filled study of the causes and consequences of plant closings, community abandonment, and the dismantling of basic industry in the United States.

Out to Work (Alice Kessler Harris; Oxford University Press, 1982). A history of wage-earning women in the United States with much insight into the impact of changing economic institutions on women and their careers.

Capitalism and Freedom (Milton Friedman; University of Chicago Press, 1962). A lucid statement of the laissez-faire perspective on economic and governmental institutions.

Life in Organizations: Workplaces as People Experience Them (Rosabeth Moss Kanter and Barry A. Stein, eds.; Basic Books, 1979). A collection of empirical research studies and thoughtful essays on many aspects of life in organizations, including gender relations, struggles for power, and mobility within the organization.

Life Choices: Applying Sociology (Robert E. Kennedy, Jr.; Holt, Rinehart and Winston, 1986). Several chapters demonstrate how changes in population and economic institutions will affect readers of this book in their lifetime.

Journals

Monthly Labor Review Published by the U.S. Department of Labor. An excellent source of data on employment and unemployment, plant closings and openings, and other economic trends. Also contains analytical articles that interpret major economic trends and changes in the labor market.

The Labor Relations Reporter This publication generally is available only in law, business, or other specialized libraries. It is a valuable tool for anyone interested in research on labor–management issues. Consult bound volumes for weekly news and trend analysis and longer articles on important economic events, which are cited in the weekly summaries.

Other Sources

Current Population Reports: Economic Characteristics of Households in the United States A quarterly report published by the Bureau of the Census. Presents monthly averages of household income and participation in cash and noncash transfer programs.

Handbook of Economic Statistics Published annually by the Central Intelligence Agency. Compares economic statistics for communist, OECD, and selected other countries.

Handbook of Labor Statistics Published annually by the Bureau of Labor Statistics. A compilation of statistical data on labor conditions and labor force characteristics in the United States and selected foreign countries.

Employment and Earnings A monthly report that presents current statistics on U.S. employment, unemployment, hours worked, and earnings. Published by the Bureau of Labor Statistics.

VISUAL SOCIOLOGY

Depression in Steeltown

From the early 1900s to the 1970s, the Mahoning Valley in Ohio was one of America's most important centers of heavy industrial production. The Youngstown area in particular was known for its steel mills. But in the 1970s and 1980s many of the mills in the valley shut down as steel corporations responded to increased competition by closing their older mills. These photos from Dale Maharidge and Michael Williamson's photographic study, *Journey to Nowhere* (1985), capture some of the social consequences of the mill closings.

When the mills on the Ohio River, like the one at Mingo Junction shown here, were operating, steelworkers had the means to raise their children well and even to make the payments on a second mortgage for a backyard swimming pool. But when the mills closed, the steelworkers suddenly found themselves unemployed, with little hope of finding well-paid jobs in the area. The experience of the couple pictured here, the Horvaths, is typical.

"We had a lot of fun here [Luella Horvath reminisced]. I thought I would die here. . . . I'm going from a $60,000 house to a $6,000 trailer. But we're not unhappy. A lot of people are worse off. At least we have a place." . . .

As the couple waits for the moving vans to come for their possessions, Tom sighs, "At least I'll have something to remember it by. Hell, I've got to start from scratch at forty-three years old." [p. 43]

The problem for the Horvaths and so many others who depended on employment in mills and factories is not only that their

Photographs by Michael Williamson

industries are contracting but that in order to find comparable jobs, they must be willing to move wherever work may be available. In theory, labor is mobile; that is, workers move to regional labor markets in search of new jobs or better wages. But in fact, workers who are employed in a community develop deep attachments to their kin and friends. They usually do not give up their way of life without first making an effort to find ways to make ends meet and remain in the community. Often they cannot afford to move and must accept greatly reduced wages and benefits.

These photos also show some of the other consequences of sudden depression in a community. One of these is reduced property values. When workers are forced to sell their homes in order to move on, they face large personal losses. They also find themselves spending long hours on unemployment lines and even more frustrating hours on employment lines when hundreds of workers show up to apply for a small number of industrial jobs. Finally, incidents of arson increase dramatically as desperate people burn their houses to claim insurance payments, or when vandals burn vacant buildings.

CHAPTER OUTLINE

● **The Nature of Politics and Political Institutions**

- Politics, Power, and Authority
- Legitimacy and Authority

● **The Political Ecology of States and Territories**

- States and Borders
- Citizenship and Political Participation

● **Political Institutions in Modern Societies**

- Democratic Political Systems

● **Perspectives on Political Institutions**

- Structural Prerequisites of Democracy
- The Power Elite Model
- The Pluralist Model
- Politics and Social Interaction

● **Military Institutions**

- The Economic Role of the Military
- Military Socialization
- Social Change and Military Institutions

AP/Wide World Photos

Vaclav Havel, Wenceslas Square, Prague, Czechoslovakia

CHAPTER 19

POLITICAL AND MILITARY INSTITUTIONS

On February 21, 1990, President Vaclav Havel of Czechoslovakia addressed the U.S. Congress, speaking to a standing-room-only crowd in the Capitol Rotunda. An essayist and playwright, Havel had written his speech himself in an afternoon. It was greeted by five standing ovations and repeated shouts of "Bravo!" Among the highlights of the speech were these passages:

The last time they arrested me, on October 27 of last year, I didn't know whether it was for two days or for two years. Exactly one month later, when the rock musician Mikhail Koscak told me that I would be probably proposed as a presidential candidate, I thought it was one of his usual jokes. On the tenth of December 1989, when my actor friend Jiri Bardoska, in the name of the Civic Forum, nominated me as a candidate for the office of President of the Republic, I thought it was out of the question that the Parliament we had inherited from the previous regime would elect me.

Nineteen days later, when I was unanimously elected President of my country, I had no idea that in two months I would be speaking in front of this famous and powerful assembly, and that what I say would be heard by millions of people who have never heard of me. . . .

When they arrested me on October 27, I was living in a country ruled by the most conservative Communist government in Europe, and our society slumbered beneath the pall of a totalitarian system. Today, less than four months later, I am speaking to you as the representative of a country that has set out on the road to democracy, a country where there is complete freedom of speech, which is getting ready for free elections and which wants to create a prosperous market economy and its own foreign policy. It is all very extraordinary. . . .

The totalitarian system in the Soviet Union, and in most of its satellites, is breaking down and our nations are looking for a way to democracy and independence. . . .

This is, I am firmly convinced, a historically irreversible process, and as a result, Europe will begin again to seek its own identity without being compelled to be a divided armory any longer. Perhaps this will create the hope that sooner or later your voice will no longer have to stand on guard for freedom in Europe or come to our rescue because Europe will at last be able to stand guard over itself.

But that is still not the most important thing. The main thing is, it seems to me, that these revolutionary changes will enable us to escape from the rather antiquated straitjacket of this bipolar view of the world, and to enter at last into an era of multipolarity; that is, into an era in which all of us, large and small, former slaves and former masters, will be able to create what your great President Lincoln called the family of man. . . .

Without a global revolution in the sphere of human consciousness, nothing will change for the better in the sphere of our being.

It is also true, however, that if there is to be a great change in our understanding of human life we will see it in the leaders we freely select. The lesson of our century is that we all bear the responsibility for our political life and for the actions of our leaders.

THE NATURE OF POLITICS AND POLITICAL INSTITUTIONS

"Politics," Max Weber liked to tell his students, "is the slow boring of hard boards." By this he meant that political change is almost never achieved easily. Creating new political institutions or changing old ones, even just changing the leadership of existing institutions, usually requires years of effort. There will be endless meetings, ideological debates, fund-raising, negotiations, and campaigning. At times, however, especially during revolutions, the pace of political change is fast and furious. Nowhere has this been more true (at least in recent decades) than in the case of Czechoslovakia, in which a playwright, Vaclav Havel, was catapulted to the national presidency. And "students started it" (Ash, 1990, p. 42).

While Czechoslovakia remained a dictatorship under the control of the Soviet Communist party, behind the scenes in Prague and other cities students worked day and night. They edited clandestine newspapers, organized debate and discussion groups, and infiltrated the Communist party and its official youth organizations. On November 17, 1989, to commemorate the death of a Czech student at the hands of the Nazi occupiers fifty years earlier, they staged a demonstration with the blessing of the Communists. But the demonstration quickly turned against the Communists and the ruling dictators. In Wenceslas Square in the heart of Prague, the students began chanting freedom slogans. They called for the release of political prisoners and sang the Czech version of "We Shall Overcome." Those in the front lines tried to hand flowers to the soldiers and police who confronted them. They "raised their arms, chanting, 'We have bare hands.' But the police . . . beat men, women, and children with their truncheons. This was the spark that set Czechoslovakia alight" (Ash, 1990, p. 42).

Within five days after the "massacre," as the students called it, the revolution was well under way. Hundreds of thousands of Czech citizens demonstrated for a new government and an end to the dictatorship. The Magic Lantern, a darkened theater in central Prague, became the headquarters of the revolution. There Havel and scores of former journalists, writers, musicians, political scientists, trade unionists, and student leaders hashed out the outlines of a new government and a transition from communist dictatorship to free elections and a new constitution.

The Czech revolution has been called "the laughing revolution" because it came about swiftly and without the grinding economic crisis experienced by Hungary and Poland. But no one in this revolutionary nation or any of its neighbors has any illusions that rebuilding a new and democratic political order will be easy. "It would be fabulous if it could be so," says Havel; "revolution is too exhausting" (quoted in Ash, 1990, p. 42).

We can gain much insight into what the Czechs, the Romanians, the blacks in South Africa, and others who are trying to bring about political change are experiencing by looking more carefully at politics and political institutions and the place they occupy in national life. Armed with some key concepts and a view of what politics accomplishes for societies, we will then analyze the political ecology of societies. By this we mean the ways in which political institutions organize the world's people into societies and nation-states. Then we examine the political institutions that are most typical of modern nations and the major theories that have been proposed to explain why they operate as they do as well as how they change or resist change. We end with a discussion of the role of politics and the military in human social interaction.

Power is the ability to control the behavior of others; authority is institutionalized power.

Politics, Power, and Authority

In any society, Harold Lasswell (1936) argued, politics determines "who gets what, when, and how." Different societies develop their own political institutions, but everywhere the basis of politics is competition for power. **Power** is the ability to control the behavior of others, even against their will. To be powerful is to be able to have your way even when others resist (Mills, 1959). The criminal's power may come through a gun and the threat of injury. But many people wield power over others without any threat of violence but merely through the agreement of the governed. We call such power authority. **Authority** is institutionalized power—that is, power whose exercise is governed by the norms and statuses of organizations. These norms and statuses specify who can have authority, how much authority is attached to different

statuses, and the conditions under which that authority can be exercised.

Political institutions are sets of norms and statuses that specialize in the exercise of power and authority. The complex set of political institutions—judicial, executive, and legislative—that operate throughout a society form the **state** (see Figure 19-1). In this chapter we concentrate primarily on these explicitly political institutions, but we should keep in mind that in modern societies many institutions that are active in politics are not part of the state. Labor unions, for example, are economic institutions because they represent their members in bargaining with business

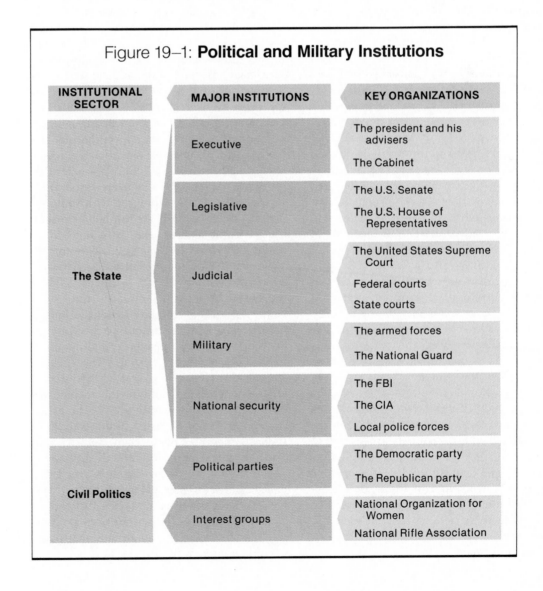

Figure 19–1: **Political and Military Institutions**

INSTITUTIONAL SECTOR	MAJOR INSTITUTIONS	KEY ORGANIZATIONS
The State	Executive	The president and his advisers
		The Cabinet
	Legislative	The U.S. Senate
		The U.S. House of Representatives
	Judicial	The United States Supreme Court
		Federal courts
		State courts
	Military	The armed forces
		The National Guard
	National security	The FBI
		The CIA
		Local police forces
Civil Politics	Political parties	The Democratic party
		The Republican party
	Interest groups	National Organization for Women
		National Rifle Association

owners and managers, but they play an active role in politics when they support particular political candidates or lobby for government-funded benefits for workers and their families.

When we look at the way in which conflicts over scarce resources like wealth, power, and prestige occur, we are looking at politics. From this perspective there can be a politics of the family, in which its members vie for attention, respect, use of the family car, and so on. There can be a politics of the school, in which teachers compete for benefits such as smaller class size or better students. And of course the politics of government at all levels of society determines how the society's resources are allocated among various groups or classes. This broad view of politics, which looks at competition for power and at conflict over the use of power in a variety of settings, was reflected in the work of Karl Marx. According to Marx, the way power is distributed in a society's institutions is a feature of its system of stratification: People and groups that have power in economic institutions, for example, are most likely to have power in political institutions as well (Washburn, 1982). This viewpoint leads logically to the "power elite" thesis—that is, the theory that the most powerful members of a society's major institutions form a tightly knit network of decision makers who control the fate of the mass of citizens. (We say more about the power elite thesis later in the chapter.)

A narrower view of politics centers on the behavior of people in institutions devoted to exercising governmental authority or influencing government decisions. This view is derived primarily from the work of Max Weber and is concerned especially with processes like the competition for power in political parties and electoral campaigns (Janowitz, 1968). This view of politics stresses the role of political institutions in developing policies intended to decrease the strains caused by economic and other inequalities. It thus is a more functionalist view than the broader perspective, which finds political conflict occurring throughout all social institutions. We will need to apply both of these perspectives to our analysis of how political institutions function and change.

Legitimacy and Authority

A basic dilemma that every political institution must solve is how to exercise legitimate authority—that is, how to govern with the consent and goodwill of the governed. "You can't sit on bayonets," goes an old political expression. This is a way of saying that although a state can exercise its power through the use of police force or coercion, eventually this will not be sufficient to govern a society. As the case of Czechoslovakia shows, without the consent of the governed, force will always be necessary, yet its use will ultimately lead to chaos and revolution rather than to a smoothly functioning society.

But why do people consent to be governed without the use of force? For political sociologists since Weber's time, the answer to this question begins with the concept of legitimacy. As defined by political sociologist Seymour Martin Lipset (1981), **legitimacy** is the capacity of a society "to engender and maintain the belief that the existing political institutions are the most appropriate for the society" (p. 64). In other words, legitimacy results from citizens' belief in the norms that specify how power is to be exercised in their society. Even if they disagree with some aspects of their political institutions or dislike their current leaders, they still hold to an underlying belief in their political system.

Legitimacy is often challenged by individuals or groups within a society. When the Soviet leadership renounced the use of force to keep their satellite nations in line, it soon became clear that none of the communist regimes were considered legitimate by the majority of their citizens. The demonstrations in Czechoslovakia described earlier are only one example of how this feeling was communicated to the authorities. The assassination of Prime Minister Indira Gandhi of India by members of the Sikh minority who considered her authority to be illegitimate is another example of how disputes over legitimacy can lead to political instability and violence. On the other hand, as Box 19-1 shows, failure to question the authority of political leaders can create the conditions that make possible abuses of power.

This drawing by the great American political cartoonist Thomas Nast was one of a series that helped destroy the corrupt political machine headed by William Marcy Tweed in the 1870s, but not before Tweed and his cronies had defrauded the people of New York City of over $30 million.

WHO STOLE THE PEOPLE'S MONEY? — DO TELL. N.Y.TIMES.   'TWAS HIM.

Political Culture. Because the stability of political institutions depends so directly on the beliefs of citizens, we can readily see that political institutions are supported by cultural norms, values, and symbols like the Statue of Liberty. These are commonly referred to as the society's *political culture.* When we look at other societies, it is clear that their political cultures differ quite markedly from ours. Americans justify a political system based on competitive elections by invoking the values of citizen participation in politics and equality of political opportunity. Russians and Chinese justify single-party political systems by downplaying the value of citizen participation in politics and asserting the need for firm leaders and a centralized state that will hold the society together and reduce inequalities (Feldmesser, 1968; Moore, 1968; Smith, 1976).

> *Political institutions are supported by a set of cultural norms, values, and symbols known as the political culture.*

Crises of Legitimacy. Societies occasionally undergo political upheavals like those that are occurring at this writing in South Africa, Lebanon, and Central America. When these periods of unrest and instability involve enough of the citizens to such a degree that they challenge the legitimacy of the nation's political institutions, sociologists call the situation a *crisis of legitimacy.* For example, the Declaration of Independence was written during a crisis in which the American colonists challenged the legitimacy of British rule. In modern South Africa, where the black majority lacks the political rights granted to the white citizens, a crisis of legitimacy is forcing the white minority to consider major alterations in the nation's political institutions. Not to do so is to invite a civil war (see Box 19-2).

In sum, as we scan the globe today, it is evident that the world's political ecology includes many states that are extremely stable and many others in which political instability threatens to develop into a crisis of legitimacy.

Box 19–1: **The Kamikaze Mentality**

Kensuke Fukae, the president of a New Jersey corporation, recently recalled his youth in wartime Japan in an editorial published by *The New York Times* (December 7, 1985, p. A27). He focused especially on the Japanese tradition of submissiveness toward people in positions of authority. In the years before World War II this tradition was exploited by the military establishment and used to create a "kamikaze mentality" among the citizens, an attitude that was reinforced by a ban on protests of any kind.

The Japanese group mentality and the "samurai" spirit strengthened the cause of those who urged military spending and strength. Our traditions, after all, taught us not to question leadership and authority. Anyone who questioned the military budget was considered "hikoku-min," or "noncitizen," and as such was thought to be endangering our sacred national security. The more aggressive the military became, the more it was able to win concessions from the moderate elements in the Government who feared being condemned as un-Japanese. . . .

Along with the virtual annexation of Manchuria in 1933 came the establishment of an actual "Thought Police." The military establishment now controlled not only the administration, but also the media. Censorship of news was sanctioned for "national security reasons." Anyone—editor, professor,

politician—expressing a dissenting opinion could be arrested as a Communist sympathizer or similar undesirable. Patriotism ran high in our isolated land, and the administration defined all of its actions in terms of national security.

Within a few years, the media were being used to exhort the people to fight to the glorious end. The kamikaze mentality flourished as citizens of all ages literally sharpened bamboo spears to ward off invaders. Firebombs rained destruction on every major city except the old capital, Kyoto. On March 10, 1945, 200 B–29 bombers incinerated more than 50 percent of metropolitan Tokyo and 80,000 residents. On Aug. 6 and 9, the United States dropped atomic bombs on Hiroshima and Nagasaki. . . .

In the next several days, many officers committed hara-kiri, in keeping with the samurai code. Some young men organized partisan groups to fight to the death rather than be captive. But for most of us, the Emperor's order was absolute. We were and are a deeply patriotic nation.

America, unlike Japan, has a strong tradition of dissent. This country was built on the right to challenge authority. Such a tradition was tragically absent in my homeland as I grew up; Americans should cherish it, for it is such rights that most merit their patriotic devotion. Our loyalty was to our leaders—America's must be to the Constitution.

Source: Copyright © 1985 by The New York Times Company. Reprinted by permission.

THE POLITICAL ECOLOGY OF STATES AND TERRITORIES

The term *political ecology* refers to the distribution of populations among territories and to the kinds of political institutions that operate within those territories. For example, everyone in the United States (with the exception of Washington, D.C. residents) lives simultaneously in a nation, a state, a county, and a municipality. The political ecology of any modern society can be represented by a map of political territories

or jurisdictions, each with its own institutions with specific authority to tax and spend or to enforce laws or maintain public welfare.

The most important political territory in world affairs is the **nation-state**. As noted in Chapter 3, nation-states claim a legitimate monopoly over the use of force within their borders. By this we mean that within a nation-state's borders, only organizations designated by the state (i.e., the government) may use force. But if the citizens believe that their government is legitimate, why is force necessary at all? The answer is that even when citizens believe their government to be legitimate, force (or, more often, the threat of force) may be needed to maintain order and

Box 19–2: **A South African Journal**

In 1990 author Anthony Sampson returned to South Africa for a brief visit, his first in several years. Sampson, an old friend of Nelson Mandela, had been the editor of *Drum* magazine in South Africa from 1951 to 1955. During his recent visit he kept a journal, from which the following passages are excerpted. It is clear from these excerpts that although Mandela and his allies believe that much struggle lies ahead, world opinion will be a key ingredient of change in the South African regime.

We have dinner with Dr. Motlana, who is worried about the strain on his friend Mandela. In the small house in Soweto, Motlana says, surrounded by his comrades and visitors, Mandela has nowhere to relax or exercise.

We discuss again whether the Afrikaners have really lost the will to rule, whether the sheer pressure of the masses will prevail as it did in Eastern Europe. The police and the army, in spite of their large black components, are unlikely to change sides here as they did in Romania. Motlana has spent enough time in jail himself to know the full ferocity of the police. He thinks there's a good deal of violence to come before a peaceful solution is reached. . . .

[Mandela] read a succession of American law books that helped him get a postgraduate degree while in jail. He encouraged other political prisoners to take up the law. I

begin to realize how much of Mandela's optimism depends on his respect for the law, and his trust in the integrity of another lawyer, President de Klerk. He appreciates de Klerk's understanding of politics. De Klerk, as he carefully puts it, "seems to be fully aware of the danger to a public figure of making undertakings which he fails to honor."

He also feels grateful to the news media that kept his cause alive. He talks about the vital role of the press, particularly the alternative press which has pushed the conventional press into taking note of black views. "We've been criticized by some of the alternative press. And that is very healthy," he says, "because a vigorous political movement amongst blacks will arise and be maintained if the press looks at problems objectively." Mandela seems more articulate and more economical with his words now than he was in the 1950s and early 1960s.

I'm still fascinated by the paradox that the international bankers, whom the A.N.C. [African National Congress] had seen as the allies of apartheid during the 1960s and 1970s, should have played a key role in undermining Pretoria when they pulled out their loans in 1985.

I ask Mandela whether he was surprised by that. "I must be frank," he says. "I did not expect such massive support from bankers. But when it did come, it pleased me very much. Because it was an indication of the impact which the A.N.C. and other political organizations had made on the international community."

He stresses, more emphatically than before, the need to reassure whites. "Some sort of structural guarantees may be required in order to allay the fears of the whites, and in order to stem the backlash that comes from the right." But he also repeats that the A.N.C. might simply ignore him. "They may say, 'Well, you are a man of 71. You require a pension.' Or they might say, 'Look, we don't like your face. Please go.' I will obey them." . . .

The names that were unmentionable a few months ago are now commonplace in the headlines. And most people agree about the main cause of the change: the relentless pressure of world opinion, which at last made the Nationalists realize that apartheid is unworkable.

Source: © 1990 by the New York Times Company. Reprinted by permission.

© Alain Nogues, Sygma

ensure compliance with the law. For example, citizens may agree in principle that some of their income should be taken by the state through taxes to cover its expenses, but some individuals may attempt to avoid paying taxes. In fact, it is estimated that the U.S. government lost $64 billion in tax revenues in 1987 because of various kinds of tax evasion (Goleman, 1988). The state may use the threat of imprisonment to enforce compliance with tax laws, but it cannot catch all tax evaders. One of the main reasons even more income does not go untaxed is that most citizens believe the government has the legitimate right to collect taxes.

People who feel that the state uses its power in an illegitimate manner are not allowed to form private armies to resist the state. They may challenge the legitimacy of a particular law in the courts, where rational arguments and interpretations of law replace violent conflict. Nevertheless, all the institutions of the state, including the courts, are ultimately based on the state's monopoly over the use of force (Goode, 1972). In societies in which the state is weak or in which its legitimacy is denied by particular groups, it is common to find bandits, guerrilla armies, or terrorist groups.

States and Borders

The borders that mark off one nation-state from another do not always correspond to what people believe the rightful boundaries of their societies to be. In the United States and Canada we are accustomed to thinking of American or Canadian society as existing within the borders of those two nation-states. In fact, the U.S.–Canadian border is the longest peaceful and uncontested national boundary in the world. In the Middle East and Africa, however, the territories claimed by nation-states and societies do not overlap nearly as well. A good example of this situation is the case of Israel and the Palestinians.

For at least 5,000 years the territory that is now Israel has been fought over by a succession of societies and states. The creation of the state of Israel in 1948 was a victory for the Zionist movement, which had sought a homeland for Jews who did not feel welcome or safe in other societies. But the creation of a Jewish state in the area known as Palestine simultaneously deprived many Palestinians of their territory. The Palestinians thus became a society without a homeland, and many of its members were dispersed to refugee settlements in Jordan and elsewhere, much as the Jews had been dispersed when they were expelled from the same region centuries earlier.

Many other examples of conflict over the borders of societies and states can be found in Africa. During the eighteenth and nineteenth centuries, when several European nations established colonies in Africa, many tribal societies found their territory divided into English and French or German colonies. In other cases different societies were combined within a single colony. Thus, in Nigeria the Ibo, the Yoruba, and the Hausa (among many others), each a separate society with its own territory and culture, were combined into a single colony. The struggle for independence from colonial rule united these peoples, but after Nigeria gained its independence in the early 1960s, jealousy and competition again divided them and weakened the Nigerian state. When oil was discovered in Iboland, the Ibo attempted to establish a separate nation and the result was a civil war. The Ibo were defeated and Nigeria's boundaries remained intact, but thousands of people lost their lives.

The borders of nation-states do not always correspond to what people believe are the rightful boundaries of their societies.

In 1945, at the end of the most devastating war the world had ever experienced, the United Nations was founded in an effort to reduce the frequency and severity of conflicts among states. The UN has gradually become recognized by almost all the nations in the world. Yet for many reasons, including competition among nations for power and influence, the UN has not been very effective as an international peacekeeping organization. Nevertheless, it remains the only world forum and meeting place of nations. The very fact that it continues to exist offers some hope that we may someday develop a system of world citizenship. In the meantime we will continue to live within a political ecology in which each nation defends and controls its own borders (Goodrich, 1974; Wainhouse, 1973).

Citizenship and Political Participation

If you travel abroad, you must obtain a passport. The passport serves as official proof of citizenship; without it you would not be allowed to return to the nation of which you are a citizen. The international system of passports, visas, and border checks is how nation-states control the movement of people across their borders. Migration from less affluent to more affluent nations is held in check by these techniques. Within many nations, also, citizens must carry passports or identity cards as proof of citizenship. But citizenship is far more than a technique for controlling the movement of populations; it is a central feature of political life in modern societies (Janowitz, 1978; Shils, 1962).

Rights of Citizenship. **Citizenship** is the status of membership in a nation-state, and like all statuses it is associated with a specific set of rights and obligations (Bendix, 1969; Weber, 1968). As political sociologist Reinhard Bendix put it, "A core element of nation-building is the codification of the rights and duties of all adults who are classified as citi-

zens" (1969, p. 89). In other words, the roles of citizens in the society's political life must be made clear to all.

In feudal societies most of the members of the society did not participate in political life. The needs of various groups in the population were represented, if at all, by the edicts of powerful landholders, generals, and clergymen. But in modern nation-states as a result of major social movements this form of representation has been replaced by a form based on citizen participation, in which representatives elected by the citizens are entitled to vote on important public issues. But as societies adopted the principle of citizen participation, conflicts arose over the question of who would be included among a society's citizens. This is illustrated by the struggle over citizenship and political participation for blacks that is taking place in South Africa today.

The rights of citizenship include much more than the right to vote. T. H. Marshall (1964) defined those rights as follows:

- *Civil rights* such as "liberty of person, freedom of speech, thought and faith, the right to own property and to conclude valid contracts, and the right to justice."
- *Political rights* such as the right to vote and the right of access to public office.
- *Social rights* ranging from "the right to a modicum of economic welfare and security

These new citizens at a swearing-in ceremony have had to demonstrate knowledge of basic English and awareness of the rights and responsibilities of United States citizens.

to the right to share to the full in the social heritage and to live the life of a civilized being according to the standards prevailing in the society" (pp. 71–72).

This list does not necessarily imply that these rights actually exist in a given society or that they are shared equally by all of the society's citizens. In the United States, for example, before 1920 women were considered citizens but were denied the right to vote.

According to Marshall, four sets of institutions have developed (although not to the same extent in every society) to deliver or protect the rights of citizenship. These are the courts, whose task is to safeguard civil rights; the local and national representative bodies, which are responsible for public decision making and legislation; the social services, which provide some degree of protection against poverty, sickness, and other misfortunes; and the schools.[1] These institutions do not develop simply because they are needed to protect the rights of citizens. As we have seen in earlier chapters, they emerge partly as a result of social movements in which members of groups with less wealth and power struggle to win full participation in the political community. These institutions have also been influenced by people with wealth and power who seek the creation or expansion of social-welfare programs as a means of preventing social unrest (Galbraith, 1984).

Participation in Local Politics. The question of who is entitled to full participation in politics is a key issue at the local level as well as at the national level. At the national level, participation is vital to a group's position in society, as can be seen in the struggles by women and blacks to win the right to vote. But in the cities and towns and communities in which daily life is lived, the same guarantee of full participation plays a role in social mobility. W. E. B. DuBois' study, *The Philadelphia Negro* (discussed in Chapter 1), in-

cludes the following poignant petition by black community leaders to the city's mayor:

We are here to state to your excellency that the colored citizens of Philadelphia are penetrated with feelings of inexpressible grief at the manner in which they have thus far been overlooked and ignored by the Republican party in this city. . . . We are therefore here, sir, to earnestly beseech of you as a faithful Republican and our worthy chief executive, to use your potent influence as well as the good offices of your municipal government, if not inconsistent with the public weal, to procure for the colored people of this city a share at least, of the public work and the recognition which they now ask for and feel to be justly due to them. [1967/1899, p. 374]

At the turn of the century Philadelphia, like most American cities, was dominated by the leaders of the local Republican party organization, who were among the town's richest and most powerful citizens. Immigrant workers and the poor were effectively excluded from political participation. The party that represented their interests, the Democratic party, was unable to gain power in the city. But the Great Depression drastically altered this pattern. Fearing that the misery created by the Depression would lead to unrest among the lower classes that could result in social disorder and even revolution, upper- and middle-class Americans began to look more favorably on the Democrats' call for the creation of new social-welfare institutions. Such institutions would ease the plight of the poor and the unemployed without fundamentally changing capitalist economic institutions. At the same time, the poor and the working class began to exercise the right to vote in increasing numbers. The result was the political turnabout that brought the Democratic candidate, Franklin D. Roosevelt, to the presidency in 1932. As Table 19-1 shows, there was an equally marked turnabout in the political leadership of American cities.

In recent decades research on who participates in local political life has grown in importance, and numerous community studies by contemporary sociologists have explored this issue (Baltzell, 1968; Bernard, 1973; Katznelson, 1981; Kornblum, 1974). We will say more about community politics later in the chapter.

---

[1]Schools are cultural institutions (see Chapter 17), but public schools are created by the state and perform the political function of teaching the norms of citizenship to the next generation.

Table 19–1: **Party of Mayors in Cities of Over 100,000 Population, Selected Years, 1929–1942**

	1929		1932		1935		1938		1942	
	N	%	*N*	%	*N*	%	*N*	%	*N*	%
Republican	45	48.9	21	22.8	17	18.4	14	15.2	16	17.4
Democratic	28	30.4	43	46.7	45	48.9	42	45.7	41	44.5
Third	2	2.2	1	1.1	4	4.4	3	3.3	2	2.2
Nonpartisan and city manager	14	15.2	23	25.0	23	25.0	33	35.8	30	32.6
No information	3	3.3	4	4.4	3	3.3	0	0	3	3.3
Total	92	100.0	92	100.0	92	100.0	92	100.0	92	100.0

Source: Socialism and the Cities by Bruce Stave, Kennikat Press. Reprinted by permission of Associated Faculty Press.

POLITICAL INSTITUTIONS IN MODERN SOCIETIES

T he central problem of modern politics, according to Seymour Martin Lipset, is: "How can a society incorporate continuous conflict among its members and social groups and yet maintain social cohesion and legitimacy of state authority?" (1959, p. 108). This question has taken on particular urgency since World War II, when the colonial empires of Europe crumbled in the face of nationalistic movements throughout the world and dozens of new nations were created (see Table 19-2). Writing in 1963, Edward Shils wondered how modern political institutions could emerge in societies in which most of the citizens lived in traditional communities. "All the founders of the new states," he commented, "face the problems of establishing an effective government and staffing it" (p. 3). Moreover, they face the problems of creating "a rationally conducted administration, a cadre of leaders grouped in the public form of a party system . . . and a machinery of public order" (p. 3). Because these are the political institutions one expects to find in any modern state, let us examine in greater detail

> *Most nations are governed by elected and appointed officials whose authority is defined by laws.*

their structure and the problems associated with their development.

A Rational Administration. Modern nations are governed by elected and appointed officials whose authority is defined by laws. To the extent possible, they are expected to use their authority for the good of all citizens rather than for their own benefit or for that of particular groups. They are forbidden to use their authority in illegitimate ways—that is, in ways that violate the rights of the citizens.

Modern political institutions usually specify some form of separation of powers. The authors of the United States Constitution, for example, were careful to create a system of checks and balances among the nation's legislative, executive, and judicial institutions so that abuses of authority by one could be remedied by the others. Thus, when agents of the Nixon campaign organization were caught breaking into the Democratic party headquarters during the 1972 presidential election campaign and the President and some of his advisers were found to have covered up their role in this and other illegal activities, the impeachment proceedings carried out by the legislative and judicial branches of the government led to the President's resignation.

In many other nations abuses of state authority are far more common. The power of rulers is unchecked by other political institutions, and although citizens may question

Table 19–2: **Chronological Checklist of the 97 Newly Independent Nations**
(since 1943)

Year	Date	No.	Country	Year	Date	No.	Country
1943	Nov. 22	1	Lebanon	1963	Dec. 12	51	Kenya
1944	Jan. 1	2	Syria	1964	July 6	52	Malawi
	June 17	3	Iceland		Sept. 21	53	Malta
1946	Mar. 22	4	Jordan		Oct. 24	54	Zambia
	July 4	5	Philippines	1965	Feb. 18	55	Gambia, The
1947	Aug. 14	6	Pakistan		July 26	56	Maldives
	Aug. 15	7	India		Aug. 9	57	Singapore
1948	Jan. 4	8	Burma	1966	May 26	58	Guyana
	Feb. 4	9	Sri Lanka		Sept. 30	59	Botswana
	May 15	10	Israel		Oct. 4	60	Lesotho
	Aug. 15	11	Korea		Nov. 30	61	Barbados
1949	Mar. 8	12	Vietnam	1967	Nov. 30	62	Yemen (Aden)
	July 19	13	Laos	1968	Jan. 31	63	Nauru
	Nov. 8	14	Cambodia (Kampuchea)		Mar. 12	64	Mauritius
	Dec. 28	15	Indonesia		Sept. 6	65	Swaziland
1951	Dec. 24	16	Libya		Oct. 12	66	Equatorial Guinea
1956	Jan. 1	17	Sudan	1970	June 4	67	Tonga
	Mar. 2	18	Morocco		Oct. 10	68	Fiji
	Mar. 20	19	Tunisia	1971	Aug. 14	69	Bahrain
1957	Mar. 6	20	Ghana		Sept. 3	70	Qatar
	Aug. 31	21	Malaysia		Dec. 2	71	United Arab Emirates
1958	Oct. 2	22	Guinea	1972	Apr. 4	72	Bangladesh
1960	Jan. 1	23	Cameroon	1973	July 10	73	Bahamas, The
	Apr. 27	24	Togo	1974	Feb. 7	74	Grenada
	June 27	25	Madagascar		Sept. 10	75	Guinea-Bissau
	June 30	26	Zaire	1975	June 25	76	Mozambique
	July 1	27	Somalia		July 5	77	Cape Verde
	Aug. 1	28	Benin		July 12	78	Sao Tome and Principe
	Aug. 3	29	Niger		Sept. 16	79	Papua New Guinea
	Aug. 5	30	Burkina Faso (was Upper Volta)		Nov. 11	80	Angola
	Aug. 7	31	Ivory Coast		Nov. 25	81	Suriname
	Aug. 11	32	Chad		Dec. 31	82	Comoros
	Aug. 13	33	Central African Republic	1976	June 28	83	Seychelles
	Aug. 15	34	Congo	1977	June 27	84	Djibouti
	Aug. 16	35	Cyprus	1978	July 7	85	Solomon Islands
	Aug. 17	36	Gabon		Oct. 1	86	Tuvalu
	Aug. 20	37	Senegal		Nov. 3	87	Dominica
	Sept. 22	38	Mali	1979	Feb. 22	88	Saint Lucia
	Oct. 1	39	Nigeria		July 12	89	Kiribati
	Nov. 28	40	Mauritania		Oct. 27	90	Saint Vincent and the Grenadines
1961	Apr. 27	41	Sierra Leone	1980	Apr. 18	91	Zimbabwe
	June 19	42	Kuwait		July 30	92	Vanuatu
	Dec. 9	43	Tanzania	1981	Sept. 21	93	Belize
1962	Jan. 1	44	Western Samoa		Nov. 1	94	Antigua and Barbuda
	July 1	45	Burundi	1983	Sept. 19	95	Saint Kitts and Nevis
	July 1	46	Rwanda	1984	Jan. 1	96	Brunei
	July 5	47	Algeria	1990	Mar. 21	97	Namibia
	Aug. 6	48	Jamaica				
	Aug. 31	49	Trinidad and Tobago				
	Oct. 9	50	Uganda				

Source: Countries of the World and Their Leaders Yearbook: 1989, edited by Frank E. Blair (copyright © 1989 by Gale Research Company; reprinted by permission of the publisher), Gale Research, 1989, p. 166.

the legitimacy of their rule, they are powerless to prevent the rulers' use of coercion in violation of their rights. Such states are often ruled by **demagogues**, or leaders who use personal charisma and political symbols to manipulate public opinion. Demagogues appeal to the fears of citizens and essentially trick them into giving up their rights of political participation. Hitler's ability to sway the suffering German masses made him the outstanding example of demagoguery in this century.

A Party System. Political parties are organizations of people who join together in order to gain legitimate control of state authority—that is, of the government. Parties may be based on ideologies, or they may simply represent competing groups with the same basic values. Many American political sociologists assert that nations must make certain that other political parties are able to compete with the ruling party (Janowitz, 1968, Lipset, 1981; Oberschall, 1973). Failure to protect the existence of an opposition party or parties leads to **oligarchy**—rule by a few people who seek to stay in office indefinitely rather than for limited terms of office.

> *Political parties may be based on ideologies or may represent competing groups with the same basic values.*

Parties that seek legitimate power and accept the rule of other legitimate parties form a "loyal opposition" that monitors the actions of the ruling party, prevents official corruption, and sustains the hopes of people whose needs are not adequately met by the ruling party. Revolutionary political parties, it should be noted, do not view the state as legitimate. They therefore do not agree to seek authority through legitimate procedures like elections. For this reason they tend to be banned by most governments. On the other hand, many modern nations, including the United States, have banned or repressed nonrevolutionary communist parties, largely because of their opposition to private property and their sympathy for the communist-dominated regimes of the Soviet Union and its allies.

Institutions for Maintaining Order. We have seen that states control the use of force within their borders. They also seek to protect their territories against attacks by other states. For these purposes most states maintain police forces and armies. But sometimes the state's leaders have difficulty controlling these institutions, and quite often military factions seize power in what is called a *coup d'état* (or simply *coup*).

A coup usually results in the establishment of an oligarchy in which the state is ruled by a small elite that includes powerful members of the military. The Latin American *junta* is a special type of oligarchy in which military generals rule, usually with the consent of the most powerful members of the nation's nonmilitary elite. Their rule is commonly opposed by members of the intellectual professions, especially journalists, professors, writers, and artists. The dissent expressed by these individuals often leads to censorship and further repression of nonmilitary political institutions.

Regimes that accept no limits to their power and seek to exert their rule at all levels of society, including the neighborhood and the family, are known as **totalitarian regimes**; Nazi Germany and the Soviet Union under Stalin are examples. Such regimes cannot exercise total power without the cooperation of the military. It would be incorrect, however, to attribute the existence of oligarchies and totalitarian regimes to the power of the military alone. On many occasions military leaders have led coups that deposed the state's existing rulers and then turned over state power to nonmilitary institutions.

Nevertheless, in modern societies military institutions have become extremely powerful. Even before the end of World War II Harold Lasswell (1941) warned that nations might be moving toward a system of "garrison states—a world in which the specialists in violence are the most powerful group in society" (p. 457). This theme was echoed by Dwight D. Eisenhower, one of the nation's most celebrated soldier-presidents. As he was leaving office, Eisenhower warned that the worldwide arms buildup, together with the increasing sophistication of modern weapons, was producing an "industrial-military complex." By this he meant that the military and suppliers of military equipment were gaining undue influence over other institutions of the state. (We discuss military institutions more fully in the final section of the chapter.)

Democratic Political Systems

In contrast to oligarchies and totalitarian regimes, democratic societies offer all of their citizens the right to participate in public decision making. Broadly defined, **democracy** means rule by the nation's citizens (the Greek *demos*, from which *democracy* is derived, means "people"). In practice, democratic political institutions can take many different forms as long as the following conditions are met: (1) The political culture legitimizes the democratic system and its institutions; (2) one set of political leaders holds office; and (3) one or more sets of leaders who do not hold office act as a legitimate opposition (Lipset, 1981).

The two most familiar forms of democratic political rule are the British and American systems. In the British *parliamentary* system, elections are held in which the party that wins a majority of the seats in the legislature "forms a government," meaning that the leader of the party becomes the head of the government and appoints other party members to major offices. Once formed, the government generally serves for a specified length of time. If no party gains a majority of the legislative seats, a coalition may be formed in which smaller parties with only a few seats can bargain for positions in the government. Such a system encourages the formation of smaller parties.

In the American *representative* system, political parties attempt to win elections at the local, state, and national levels of government. In this system the president is elected directly, and the party whose candidate is elected president need not have a majority of the seats in the legislature. Success therefore depends on the election of candidates to national office. In the United States two political parties, the Republicans and the Democrats, have developed the resources and

support necessary to achieve this. It is difficult for smaller parties to gain power at the national level because voters do not believe they have much chance of electing national leaders, and even if they do win a few legislative seats they will not be asked to form coalitions, as they would in a parliamentary system.

One-Party Systems. Suppose that a nation has only one political party. Does this mean that it is undemocratic? Not in principle. A one-party state or region can be democratic as long as the citizens are free to form other parties, as long as the party's leaders can be replaced through democratic processes, and as long as the leaders do not violate the rights of citizens. But how likely are these conditions to be met if there are no opposing parties? The evidence suggests that the odds are against democracy in one-party states and regions. For example, David Apter's (1980) study of one-party rule in Ghana showed that a charismatic leader, Kwame Nkrumah, used his power as party leader to perpetuate his own rule. When opposition groups attempted to pursue legitimate political ends, their leaders were imprisoned and Nkrumah dissolved the supreme court. Nkrumah was eventually deposed by a military coup, the fate of many leaders who assume dictatorial power through one-party rule (Zolberg, 1974).

> **Although one-party states can be democratic, in such states political leaders often assume dictatorial power through one-party rule.**

Studies of local politics in the United States have also shown that in cities or counties in which the majority of voters traditionally vote for candidates of only one party an oligarchical political system may develop. Such systems have been dubbed "machines." Usually headed by a dominant party leader or "boss," the machine trades favors and **patronage**—jobs and economic benefits of various kinds—for votes and political influence. Mayor Richard J. Daley of Chicago was considered America's strongest party boss until his death in 1976. His rule over the Cook County Democratic party machine enabled

him to control thousands of patronage jobs, to stifle opponents, and to influence the Democratic party's presidential nominations. After his death there was widespread speculation that the Cook County machine would decline, but in a study of Chicago politics Thomas Guterbock (1980) found that the party machine continues to operate (with many exceptions) at the community level under the leadership of a ward or district boss. To a large extent, however, urban party machines like the one in Chicago are a carryover from America's political past. Social-welfare legislation enacted since the 1930s has decreased people's need for the favors offered by local politicians, and decreasing party identification by voters has weakened local party organizations.

PERSPECTIVES ON POLITICAL INSTITUTIONS

Our description of democratic political institutions leaves open the question we posed earlier: "How can a society incorporate continuous conflict among its members and social groups and yet maintain social cohesion and legitimacy of state authority?" One answer to this question is that a society can resolve conflicts through democratic processes. But this leads us to ask what conditions allow democratic institutions to form and, once formed, what ensures that they actually function to reduce the inequalities that engender conflict. The broadest test of democratic institutions is not whether they are embodied in formal organizations like legislatures and courts but whether they are able to address the problems of inequality and injustice in a society.

There are at least three schools of sociological thought regarding these questions. The first, derived from the functionalist perspective, asserts that democratic political institutions can develop and operate only when certain "structural prerequisites," such as a large middle class, exist in a society. The second school of thought, often referred to as the **power elite model**, is based on the conflict

perspective. It is highly critical of the functionalist view, supporting its criticism with evidence on the ways in which so-called democratic political institutions actually operate to favor the affluent. A third position, known as the **pluralist model**, asserts that the existence of ruling elites does not mean that a society is undemocratic, as long as there are divisions within the elite and new groups are able to seek power and bargain for policies that favor their interests. We explore all of these points of view in the next section.

Structural Prerequisites of Democracy

Seymour Martin Lipset (1981) argues that democratic political institutions are relatively rare because if they are to exist and function well, the society must have attained a high level of economic and cultural development. To prove his theory, Lipset surveyed data on elections, civil rights, freedom of the press, and party systems in forty-eight nation-states. He found that the presence of these institutions was correlated with a nation's level of economic development, its degree of urbanization, the literacy of its citizens, and the degree to which its culture values equality and tolerates dissent. Table 19-3 and Figure 19-2 present these findings in more detail.

In this cross-cultural research and in his research on democracy in the United States, Lipset attempted to show that the growth of a large middle class is essential to democracy. The middle-class population tends to be highly literate and, hence, able to make decisions about complex political and social issues. Moreover, middle-class citizens feel that they have a stake in their society and its political institutions. Accordingly, they often support policies that would reduce the class and status cleavages—the distinctions between the haves and the have-nots—that produce social conflict.

Sociologists who study voting behavior tend to support Lipset's thesis that the stability of democratic institutions rests on structural features that diminish conflict in a society. But their research has revealed something less than complete stability. "Since 1952," Morris Janowitz (1978) noted, "there has been an increase in the magnitude of shifts in voting patterns from one national election to the next. . . . Increasingly important segments of the electorate are prepared to change their preference for president and also to engage in ticket splitting [voting for candidates of different parties]" (p. 102). These shifts in voting behavior may represent new alignments of voters that could lead to major changes in the nation's public policies. The important point, however, is that these realignments, which influence which parties and political leaders gain or lose power, do not affect the process of democratic competition itself.

The Power Elite Model

However important elections are to the functioning of democratic institutions, there are strong arguments against the idea that they significantly affect the way a society is governed. Some social scientists find, for example, that political decisions are controlled by an elite of rich and powerful individuals. This "power elite" tolerates the formal organizations and procedures of democracy (elections, legislatures, courts, etc.) because it essentially owns them and can make sure that they act in its interests no matter what the out-

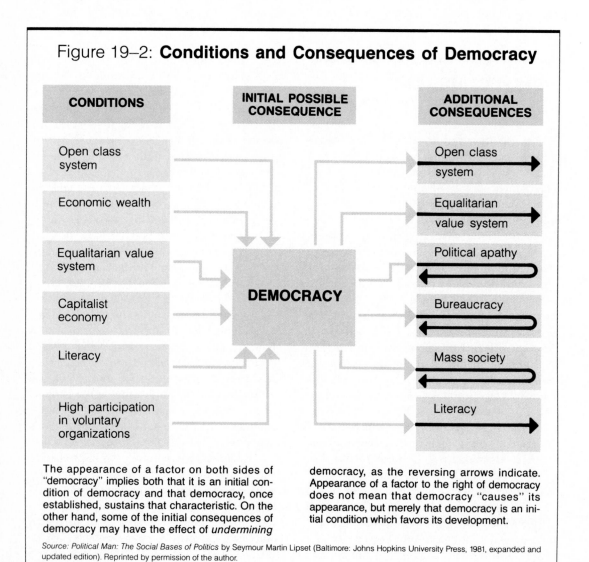

Figure 19–2: **Conditions and Consequences of Democracy**

The appearance of a factor on both sides of "democracy" implies both that it is an initial condition of democracy and that democracy, once established, sustains that characteristic. On the other hand, some of the initial consequences of democracy may have the effect of *undermining* democracy, as the reversing arrows indicate. Appearance of a factor to the right of democracy does not mean that democracy "causes" its appearance, but merely that democracy is an initial condition which favors its development.

Source: *Political Man: The Social Bases of Politics* by Seymour Martin Lipset (Baltimore: Johns Hopkins University Press, 1981, expanded and updated edition). Reprinted by permission of the author.

Table 19–3: **A Comparison of European and Latin American Democracies and Dictatorships, by Wealth, Industrialization, Education, and Urbanization**

A. Indices of Wealth

	Per Capita Income in $	Thousands of Persons per Doctor	Persons per Motor Vehicle	Telephones per 1,000 Persons	Radios per 1,000 Persons	Newspaper Copies per 1,000 Persons
European and English-speaking stable democracies	695	.86	17	205	350	341
European and English-speaking unstable democracies and dictatorships	308	1.4	143	58	160	167
Latin American democracies and unstable dictatorships	171	2.1	99	25	85	102
Latin American stable dictatorships	119	4.4	274	10	43	43

B. Indices of Industrialization

	Percentage of Males in Agriculture	Per Capita Energy Consumed
European stable democracies	21	3.6
European dictatorships	41	1.4
Latin American democracies	52	0.6
Latin American stable dictatorships	67	0.25

C. Indices of Education

	Percentage Literate	Primary Education Enrollment per 1,000 Persons	Post-Primary Enrollment per 1,000 Persons	Higher Education Enrollment per 1,000 Persons
European stable democracies	96	134	44	4.2
European dictatorships	85	121	22	3.5
Latin American democracies	74	101	13	2.0
Latin American dictatorships	46	72	8	1.3

D. Indices of Urbanization

	Percent in Cities Over 20,000	Percent in Cities Over 100,000	Percent in Metropolitan Areas
European stable democracies	43	28	38
European dictatorships	24	16	23
Latin American democracies	28	22	26
Latin American stable dictatorships	17	12	15

Source: Political Man: The Social Bases of Politics by Seymour Martin Lipset (Baltimore: Johns Hopkins University Press, 1981, expanded and updated edition). Reprinted by permission of the author.

come of elections may be. C. Wright Mills, the chief proponent of this point of view, has described the power elite as follows:

The power elite is composed of men whose positions enable them to transcend the ordinary environments of ordinary men and women. They are in positions to make decisions having major consequences. . . . They are in command of the major hierarchies and organizations of modern society. They rule the big corporations. They run the machinery of the state. . . . They direct the military establishment. They occupy the strategic command posts of the social structure. . . .

The power elite are not solitary rulers. . . . Immediately below the elite are the professional politicians of the middle levels of power, in the Congress and in the pressure groups, as well as among the new and old upper classes of town and city and regions. Mingling with them in curious ways . . . are those professional celebrities who live by being continually displayed. [1956, p. 4]

When it was first published, Mills's *The Power Elite* created a stir among sociologists. Mills challenged the assumption that societies that have democratic political institutions are in fact democratic. He asserted instead that party politics and elections are little more than rituals. Power is exercised by a ruling elite of immensely powerful military, business, and political leaders that can put its members into positions of authority whenever it wishes to do so. Mills's thesis was significant for another reason as well: Although Mills appreciated Marx's views on the role of class conflict in social change, he did not believe that the working class could win power without joining forces with the middle class. He therefore attempted to demonstrate the existence of a ruling elite to an educated public, which would then, he hoped, be able to see through the rituals of political life and make changes through legitimate means.

Other sociologists have questioned the power elite thesis on methodological grounds. For example, Talcott Parsons (1960) noted that the power elite was supposed to act behind the scenes rather than publicly. Therefore its actions could not be observed, and the power elite thesis could not be either proved or disproved. The power elite thesis therefore was not scientifically sound, according to Parsons.

Numerous adherents of the power elite thesis have attempted to show that a ruling elite does indeed exist and that its activities can be observed. One of the best known of these researchers is Floyd Hunter (1953), whose classic studies of Atlanta's "community power structure" attempted to show that no more than forty powerful men were considered to have the ability to make decisions on important issues facing the city and its people. Most of these men were conservative, cost-conscious business leaders. The Hunter study stimulated many attempts to find similar power structures in other cities and in the nation as a whole (Domhoff, 1978, 1983). But although the term *power structure* has found its way into the language of politics, these studies have been strongly criticized for basing their conclusions on what people say about who has power rather than on observations of what people with power actually do (Walton, 1970).

The Pluralist Model

The power elite thesis has not gone unchallenged. In another famous study of politics—this one in New Haven, Connecticut—Robert Dahl (1961) found that different individuals played key roles in different types of decisions. No single group was responsible for all of the decisions that might affect the city's future. No power elite ruled the city, Dahl argued. Instead, there were a number of elites that interacted in various ways on decisions that affected them. In situations in which the interests of numerous groups were involved, a plurality of decision makers engaged in a process of coalition building and bargaining.

Interest groups are specialized organizations that attempt to influence public officials on specific issues.

The pluralist model calls attention to the activities of **interest groups** at all levels of society. Interest groups are not political parties; they are specialized organizations that attempt to influence elected and appointed officials on specific issues. These attempts range from **lobbying**—the process whereby interest groups seek to persuade legislators to vote in their favor on particular bills—to making contributions to parties and candidates who will support their goals. Trade unions seeking legislation that would limit imports, organizations for the handicapped seeking regulations that would give them access to public buildings, and ethnic groups seeking to influence the United States' policies toward their country of origin are among the many kinds of interest groups that are active in the United States today.

In recent decades, as the number of organized interest groups has grown, so has the complexity of the bargaining that takes place between them and the officials they want to influence. Social scientists who study politics from the pluralist perspective frequently wonder whether the activities of these groups threaten the ability of elected officials to govern effectively. Thus, a study of a federal economic development project in Oakland, California, found that the personnel in the agency responsible for such projects had to learn to deal with supporting and opposing interest group leaders and elected officials throughout the life of the project. It took six years of constant negotiation on many unanticipated issues—affirmative action in employment, environmental concerns, design specifications—before a firm could win a contract to build an airplane hangar (Pressman and Wildavsky, 1984).

Politics and Social Interaction

From the interactionist perspective, political institutions, like all others, are "socially constructed" in the course of human interaction. They do not simply come into being as structures of norms, statuses, and roles and then continue to function without change. Instead, they are continually being shaped and reshaped through interaction. This view closely parallels the popular notion that democratic political institutions must be continually challenged if they are to live up to their ideals. Otherwise they will become oligarchies that

From the interactionist perspective, political institutions are socially constructed in the course of human interaction.

rule for the benefit of small cliques rather than for the mass of citizens.

The question of how social interaction affects a society's political institutions was a central concern of the leading philosophers of ancient Greece. In his *Politics*, for example, Aristotle "held that humans were made for life in society just as bees were made for life in the hive" (Bernard, 1983, p. 30). Because humans are "political animals," Aristotle wrote, their constant discussions of political issues and their ability to form coalitions allow them to arrive at a consensus regarding what a good society is and how it should be governed. Unfortunately, he concluded, existing political systems were flawed. The divisions and gaps in interaction created by wealth prevented consensus and gave rise to conflict. Moreover, people in occupations like farming did not have enough time to examine all the sides of an issue and work toward agreement with their fellow citizens. In a good society, therefore, all the citizens must be free to devote their full attention to political affairs. (In practice, of course, this required an economy based on the labor of slaves.)

Nearly 2,000 years later the Italian political adviser Niccolò Machiavelli (1469–1527) again took up the relationship between human interaction and political institutions. Machiavelli believed that political institutions had to be based on the recognition that all human beings are capable of evil as well as good. In his *Discourses* he observed that "all those who have written upon civil institutions demonstrate . . . that whosoever desires to found a state and give it laws, must start by assuming that all men are bad and ever ready to display their vicious nature, whenever they may find an occasion for it" (1950/1513, vol. I, p. 3). Some people, he admitted, are merciful, faithful, humane, and sincere, but even though there are virtuous people in every society, political leaders must anticipate the worst possible behavior. In his most famous work, *The Prince*, Machiavelli suggested that the wise ruler or prince would be a master of astuteness—the ability to "read" the intentions of allies and opponents in the tiniest of gestures and reactions—and would also have mastered the skills of diplomacy. At all times, Machiavelli wrote,

a prince . . . must imitate the fox and the lion, for the lion cannot protect himself from the traps, and the fox cannot defend himself from wolves. One must therefore be a fox to recognize traps, and a lion to frighten wolves. Those that wish to be only lions do not understand this. [1950/1513, p. 66]

In the five centuries since they were originally formulated, these ideas have had a powerful influence on political thinkers. The authors of the American Constitution, for example, attempted to avoid situations in which "foxes" or "lions" could take advantage of the weaknesses of others. They anticipated the more self-serving aspects of political interaction rather than simply assuming that a new society would bring about cooperation among citizens: "If men were angels, no government would be necessary" (*The Federalist*, no. 51). It is for this reason, as we noted earlier in the chapter, that they planned a government in which each of the major branches would be able to check any abuse of power by the other branches.

Political Interaction in a Young Democracy.
When Alexis de Tocqueville visited the still-new American democracy in the 1830s, the young French aristocrat was stunned by the "tumult" of American political interactions, which "must be seen in order to be understood." In America, he wrote,

a confused clamor is heard on every side; and a thousand simultaneous voices demand the immediate satisfaction of their social wants. Everything is in motion around you; here, the people of one quarter of a town are met to decide upon the building of a church; there, the election of a representative is going on; a little further, the delegates of a district are traveling in a hurry to the town in order to consult upon some local improvements; or, in another place, the laborers of a village quit their plows to deliberate upon the project of a road or a public school. [1980/1835, p. 78]

Tocqueville expressed surprise at the fact that although they were denied the vote, in the United States "even the women frequently attend public meetings, and listen to political harangues as recreation after their household labors" (p. 79). In fact, the culture of America was so suffused with political issues that he believed Americans could not converse except to discuss issues. The typical American, he observed, "speaks to you as if he were addressing a meeting" (p. 79).

Tocqueville was concerned that democratic societies might encourage the rise of demagogues who could manipulate the masses. But his observations persuaded him that the immense number of competing groups in the American political system would prevent this from happening. And although he worried about the possibility of political conflict tearing the young nation apart, he became convinced that Americans' love of liberty and belief in the legitimacy of their political institutions would carry them through any crisis that might arise.

Political Communication Today.
For those out of power as well as those in power, political communication and the ability to gain the attention of the mass media are major concerns. Sociologist Todd Gitlin (1980) reminds us how important this aspect of politics was to the student radicals who challenged U.S. policies in Vietnam in the 1960s and 1970s. They were only one among many social movements of that period that discovered the great power of television in a society with mass publics (see Chapter 10). Through skillful use of television coverage of staged confrontations, sit-ins, and demonstrations, it was possible for a relatively small group of activists to mobilize larger numbers of supporters. The labor movement had used similar tactics in earlier decades, but by the 1960s it had become easier to communicate to mass audiences and sway public opinion—at least in a society in which the press, including the television news, is relatively free from governmental interference.

> *Tocqueville believed that the immense number of competing groups in the American political system would prevent the rise of demagogues who could manipulate the masses.*

In a world in which the techniques of communication are increasingly sophisticated, it becomes ever more important to analyze political communications and to "read between the lines" of political rhetoric. Often political jargon masks deeds that leaders would rather not admit to. George Orwell, a master of political commentary, made this point in his essay "Politics and the English Language," part of which is presented in Box 19-3.

MILITARY INSTITUTIONS

The problem of civilian control of the military remains the most important issue in many of the world's nation-states. At this writing, for example, the newly elected government of Violeta Barrios de Chamorra in Nicaragua is seeking assurances of allegiance from the nation's military forces,

Box 19–3: **Politics and the English Language**

George Orwell, the author of *Animal Farm* and *1984*, addressed the abuse of language for political purposes in his 1946 essay "Politics and the English Language":

Political speech and writing are largely the defense of the indefensible. Things like the continuance of British rule in India, the Russian purges and deportations, the dropping of the atom bombs on Japan, can indeed be defended, but only by arguments which are too brutal for most people to face, and which do not square with the professed aims of political parties. Thus political language has to consist largely of euphemism, question-begging, and sheer cloudy vagueness. Defenceless villages are bombarded from the air, the inhabitants driven out into the countryside, the cattle machine-gunned, the huts set on fire with incendiary bullets: this is called *pacification*. Millions of peasants are robbed of their farms and sent trudging along the roads with no more than they can carry: this is called *transfer of population* or *rectification of frontiers*. People are imprisoned for years without trial, or shot in the back of the neck or sent to die of scurvy in Arctic lumber camps: this is called *elimination of unreliable elements*. Such phraseology is needed if one wants to name things without calling up mental pictures of them. Consider for instance some comfortable English professor defending Russian totalitarianism. He cannot say outright, "I believe in killing off your opponents when you can get good results by doing so." Probably, therefore, he will say something like this:

While freely conceding that the Soviet regime exhibits certain features which the humanitarian may be inclined to deplore, we must, I think, agree that a certain curtailment of the right to political opposition is an unavoidable concomitant of transitional periods, and that the rigours which the Russian people have been called upon to undergo have been amply justified in the sphere of concrete achievement. [p. 136]

If Orwell sounds highly pessimistic about the conduct of politics, remember that he was writing in a time of even greater political cruelty and chaos than our own. In his lifetime he had seen nations with the most advanced constitutions commit the most brutal acts of war and repression. The point of his essay is that to be politically objective, to seek the true meanings of political acts and the consequences of political beliefs, we must "start at the verbal end":

The great enemy of clear language is insincerity. When there is a gap getween one's real and one's declared aims, one turns as it were instinctively to long words and exhausted idioms, like a cuttlefish squirting out ink. . . . If you simplify your English . . . when you make a stupid remark its stupidity will be obvious, even to yourself. Political language . . . is designed to make lies sound truthful and murder respectable, and to give an appearance of solidity to pure wind. One cannot change this all in a moment, but one can at least change one's own habits, and from time to time one can even, if one jeers loudly enough, send some worn-out and useless phrase . . . into the dustbin where it belongs. [p. 140]

which are still controlled by the former ruling party, the Sandinistas. The democratically elected government in Chile is proving incapable of controlling the military in that nation, which is still controlled by the former dictator, Augustus Pinochet. Throughout the world the problem of how to maintain the allegiance of the military often looms as the largest threat to democracy and to the legitimacy of governments. These situations raise a major question in political sociology: How can states control their military institutions? Answers are to be found in knowledge about the nature of the modern military as a social institution as well as in the political culture of different nations.

A key question about military institutions in all societies, and especially in democracies, is how the military can be made to submit to the guidance of civilian political institutions. A democratic society cannot remain democratic for very long if the military usurps the authority granted to it by the civilian institutions of the nation-state. This is a common occurrence—taking the form of coups led by military "strongmen"—in nations in which the military is not adequately controlled by other institutions.

The problem of civilian control of the military was recognized by Tocqueville, who noted that in aristocratic nations the military could be controlled by the government because the military leaders were aristocrats and therefore were part of the court. "The officer is noble, the soldier is a serf," Tocqueville observed. "The one is naturally called upon to command, the other to obey" (1980/1835, p. 128). Tocqueville formed the hypothesis that greater equality would make a nation less likely to go to war, since its citizens would have more to lose in wars and more power to prevent them. Yet he also feared the ambitions of military leaders in democratic nations. "In democratic armies," he wrote, "all the soldiers may become officers, which . . . immeasurably extends the bounds of military ambition" (p. 129).

Morris Janowitz (1960) responded to Tocqueville's concerns in his analysis of the history of military institutions in democratic nations. He argued that the military has often played a crucial role in establishing and protecting democratic institutions. In the Greek city-states and the Roman republic, as well as the democracies that emerged from the revolutions of the late eighteenth century, citizens were obligated to serve in the armed forces. The military institution could function only through the enlistment of "citizen soldiers." Because the citizen soldier was committed to democratic institutions and was serving because such service was a requirement of citizenship, the military would be unlikely to take over the functions of democratic political institutions. Soldiers would presumably place the values of their society above the demands of the military.

When Janowitz reviewed the impact of new methods of warfare on the military, he concluded that because of the increasing sophistication of military technology, the military in many modern nations has become staffed by "professional soldiers" for whom service in the armed forces is a career. In addition, the shift to a volunteer military, rather than one that depends on citizen soldiers, may threaten the control of civilian institutions over the military.

> *A key question in all societies is how the military can be made to submit to the guidance of civilian political institutions.*

The Economic Role of the Military

Even in the United States, where the threat of military coups is not considered great, the military has so much influence on the economy that social control of the military becomes difficult. The function of the military is, of course, the defense of the nation-state. However, in the United States the military also serves an important economic function as a producer of jobs and revenue. Table 19-4 shows the proportion of defense contracts awarded to firms in each state. These numbers demonstrate the important place of the military in states like Alaska, Connecticut, Maryland, Massachusetts, and Virginia, all of which depend heavily on military production or defense contracts. Note that states like California and New York receive large amounts

Table 19–4: **Department of Defense Contract Awards, by State, 1987**

State	Contract Awards[a] (million dollar)	Amount per Capita
Total	133,262	—
Alabama	1,661	407
Alaska	555	1,057
Arizona	3,211	948
Arkansas	738	309
California	24,515	886
Colorado	2,716	824
Connecticut	5,031	1,567
Delaware	198	307
Florida	5,797	482
Georgia	3,512	564
Hawaii	461	426
Idaho	74	74
Illinois	1,924	166
Indiana	2,231	403
Iowa	600	212
Kansas	1,245	503
Kentucky	462	124
Louisiana	1,685	377
Maine	830	699
Maryland	4,752	1,048
Massachusetts	8,685	1,483
Michigan	1,866	196
Minnesota	2,426	571
Mississippi	1,474	562
Missouri	5,997	1,175
Montana	93	115
Nebraska	257	161
Nevada	232	230
New Hampshire	469	444
New Jersey	3,283	428
New Mexico	584	584
New York	9,625	540
North Carolina	1,247	194
North Dakota	158	235
Ohio	4,550	422
Oklahoma	608	186
Oregon	287	105
Pennsylvania	3,845	322
Rhode Island	478	484
South Carolina	571	167
South Dakota	58	82
Tennessee	986	203
Texas	8,654	515
Utah	1,183	704
Vermont	193	352
Virginia	7,807	1,322
Washington	3,112	686
West Virginia	150	79
Wisconsin	951	198
Wyoming	47	96

— Represents zero

[a]Military awards for supplies, services, and construction. Net value of contracts of more than $10,000 for work in each state and D.C. Figures reflect impact of prime contracting on state distribution of defense work. Often the state in which a prime contractor is located is not the state in which the subcontracted work is done.

Source: Adapted from *Statistical Abstract,* 1989.

of defense-contract funds but that on a per capita basis military spending is less important in those states than in others.

One explanation for these figures is the relationship between political and military institutions. States like Virginia, Maryland, and Alaska have powerful representatives in Congress who can ensure that military contracts are assigned to their state. Another institution that interacts with the military (though in ways that are often marked by conflict) is organized labor. Military contractors can sometimes avoid the unionization of their workers by locating in southern states whose antiunion sentiments are favorable to their interests. Throughout the United States the influence of the military "pork barrel"—federal spending on defense contracts and the resulting employment—often makes it difficult for legislators to oppose increases in military budgets.

Military Socialization

Social control of the military is partially explained by the professional socialization of military personnel. This point was vividly illustrated by Tom Wolfe in *The Right Stuff* (1980). "There were many pilots in their thirties," Wolfe wrote, "who to the consternation of their wives, children, mothers, fathers, and employers, volunteered to go active in the reserves and fly in combat in the Korean War." This was in vivid contrast with the attitude of the footsoldiers in that war, whose morale during some periods of the prolonged conflict "was so bad it actually reached the point where officers were prodding men forward with gun barrels and bayonets" (p. 32).

This contrast between the "fighter jocks," socialized to want to prove they had "the right stuff," and thus win promotion to higher ranks, and the far more cautious draftees and recruits on the ground, raises a series of questions: What motivates a person to face death in war? Is it desire for glory and advancement? Is it fear of punishment? Is it the pressure of collective action? From an interactionist perspective, this contrast results from the ways in which people are socialized in

military institutions, coupled with their definitions of the situation. The fighter jocks define the situation as one in which they *must* act as they do—it is the job for which they have volunteered. The draftees do not define the situation in the same way; they are more interested in their own survival and in adhering to group norms like "Never volunteer."

In his classic study of socialization in a military academy, Sanford Dornbusch (1955) showed that traditional military socialization is designed to develop a high level of motivation and commitment to the institution. Those processes include the following:

- Suppression of previous statuses—through haircuts, uniforms, and the like, the recruit is deprived of visible clues to his or her previous social status.
- Learning of new norms and rules—at the official level, the recruit is taught obedience to the rules of the military; through informal socialization, he or she is taught the culture of the military institution.
- Development of solidarity—both informal socialization and harsh discipline build solidarity and lasting friendships among recruits; they learn to depend on one another.
- The bureaucratic spirit—the recruit is taught unquestioning acceptance of tradition and custom; orders are taken and given from morning to night.

These socialization processes are not always completely effective. One reason for this is that draftees are also subject to peer socialization. They are led to see the military as a total institution and to concentrate on ways of ensuring their own survival within it. They also learn to place loyalty to their buddies above heroic actions like those of the fighter jocks. Even so, as noted in Chapter 7 in the case of German army units that continued to fight even when their situation appeared to be hopeless, the solidarity of military peer groups can lead to extraordinary feats of valor.

Control of the military becomes difficult when the military has a significant influence on the economy.

The woman in this West Point graduation scene has a special reason to celebrate: She is among the first female graduates of the U.S. Army's officer training program.

© Jim Anderson, Woodfin Camp

Social Change and Military Institutions

Like all major social institutions, the military has undergone many changes, some of which can be seen in the transformation of American military institutions in the past two centuries. In the era of the citizen soldier, people expected to be called into service only in emer-

gency situations and to be trained by a small cadre of professional officers. Today, by contrast, the permanent armed forces have more than 3 million members, and the annual military budget amounts to hundreds of billions of dollars (Beer, 1981; Janowitz, 1960).

At this writing, the requirements of highly technological warfare and the need to maintain a complex set of military organizations throughout the world have changed our concept of a military career. The military as a modern social institution requires professionally trained officers who commit themselves to spending much of their working lives in the military. Thus, as the military has evolved, so has its need to recruit and train career officers in specialized military academies.

Over time, the institutions that train professional soldiers have had to adapt to certain changes. For example, as the larger society has accepted the demand for gender equality and women have gained access to occupations that were previously reserved for men, the military has had to redefine its historical perception that women soldiers are better equipped for desk duty than for service in combat. Although to date few women have fought in ground warfare, women in the military are now being trained for combat roles. The idea of women engaging in combat remains controversial, however, as is illustrated by the conflict that arose when a female military officer was suspected of having fought in Panama in 1989.

At least in the United States, the military tends to be rather responsive to civilian demands. Yet cuts in military budgets as a result of the end of the Cold War will offer the U.S. military one of its greatest challenges since the end of World War II: how to remain an effective fighting force, adapted to new forms of conflict (e.g., antiterrorism, small wars, and peacekeeping interventions), while it is scaled down in an era of increasing demand for "peace dividends."

FRONTIERS OF SOCIOLOGY

Voting Behavior in the United States

Sociology has had a profound influence on the conduct of political campaigns and the analysis of election results in the United States. Political polling and studies of voting behavior were pioneered by sociologists. Today such polls and studies are considered essential by any major campaign organization. They indicate to candidates and their staffs where their support is strongest and weakest and how they can use their scarce resources to win the most votes.

Exit polls are a particularly effective means of assessing how the electorate actually voted. They are conducted by interviewers who stop voters at random outside polling places and ask how they voted. They also ask for other information, such as age, education, or religion. Such polls are controversial because if the results are released to the public before all the polls are closed, they may influence the way those who have not yet voted cast their ballots—or whether they come to the polls at all. For example, voters in California who learn from exit polls that voters in the eastern states are not supporting their preferred candidate may not bother to vote. Pending legislation seeks to prohibit the early release of results of exit polls for this reason. Nevertheless, such polls provide highly useful information about the behavior of the elec-

Portrait of the Electorate

% of 1988 total		VOTE IN 1980			VOTE IN 1984		VOTE IN 1988	
		Reagan	Carter	Anderson	Reagan	Mondale	Bush	Dukakis
—	TOTAL	51%	41%	7%	59%	40%	53%	45%
48	Men	55	38	7	62	37	57	41
52	Women	47	45	7	56	44	50	49
85	Whites	55	36	7	64	35	59	40
10	Blacks	11	85	3	9	89	12	86
3	Hispanics	35	56	8	37	61	30	69
20	18–29 years old	43	44	11	59	40	52	47
35	30–44 years old	54	36	8	57	42	54	45
22	45–59 years old	55	39	5	59	39	57	42
22	60 and older	54	41	4	60	39	50	49
8	Not a high school graduate	46	51	2	49	50	43	56
27	High school graduate	51	43	4	60	39	50	49
30	Some college education	55	35	8	61	37	57	42
35	College graduate or more	52	35	11	58	41	56	43
19	College graduate	—	—	—	—	—	62	37
16	Post graduate education	—	—	—	—	—	50	48
25	Union household	43	48	6	46	53	42	57
12	Family income under $12,500	42	51	6	45	54	37	62
20	$12,500–$24,999	44	46	7	57	42	49	50
20	$25,000–$34,999	52	39	7	59	40	56	44
20	$35,000–49,999	59	32	8	66	33	56	42
24	$50,000 and over	63	26	9	89	30	62	37
19	$50,000–$100,000	—	—	—	—	—	61	38
5	Over $100,000	—	—	—	—	—	65	32
25	From the East	47	42	9	52	47	50	49
28	From the Midwest	51	40	7	58	40	52	47
28	From the South	52	44	3	64	36	58	41
19	From the West	53	34	10	61	38	52	46
35	Republicans	86	8	4	93	6	91	8
37	Democrats	26	67	6	24	75	17	82
26	Independents	55	30	12	63	35	55	42

Source: Adapted from CBS News/New York Times Poll, November 8, 1988.

torate. They help social scientists and political analysts predict how the electorate will divide itself in coming elections.

During the 1988 presidential election campaign, polls of potential voters told the candidates where they stood with the electorate at any given time. Michael Dukakis knew he was beaten before a single vote was cast, and George Bush knew that the voters wanted him to become President (CBS/New York Times Poll, September 24, 1988). But the polls could not assure Bush of a "mandate" to continue Ronald Reagan's conservative policies. Polls aid in the analysis of voter preferences during a campaign, but they do not reveal longer-term trends in the political outlook of the electorate. The analysis of such trends is a frontier of research in political sociology.

The strongest mandate a president has received in this century was given to Franklin Roosevelt in 1932 and 1936. As noted in this chapter, by 1936 the Republicans "had been humbled and tossed aside, a thoroughly beaten and confused minority" (Ladd, 1985, p. 11). The Democrats were the majority party in every sense. They controlled Congress, the presidency, many state legislatures, and the urban party machines. The Reagan victories of 1980 and 1984 were not accompanied by a similar turnabout in party strength. The Democrats still controlled the House of Representatives and many state and local governments, and there still were more registered Democrats than Republicans. But the Reagan victories did indicate some significant trends or realignments in the electorate.

The first of these electoral realignments could actually be called a "dealignment." The Reagan victories continued a trend that has been evident for about two decades: an increase in the proportion of nonparty or "independent" voters. Measures of *partisanship*—the tendency of voters to identify with a particular party and to vote for candidates endorsed by that party—show the proportion of partisan voters decreasing from 75 percent in 1964 to 63 percent in 1976, when the num-

ber of independents equaled the number of Democrats. Since 1976 the proportion of partisan voters has continued to decline, so although an important segment of the electorate still identifies with one major party or the other, more people are willing to vote for whichever candidate appeals to them most (Converse, 1976; Norpoth and Rusk, 1982; Wolfinger and Rosenstone, 1980).

The accompanying table shows that this trend continued into the late 1980s. Thirty-six percent of the electorate identified with the Republican party and 37 percent called themselves Democrats, but 26 percent said they were independents.

A second major realignment in the U.S. electorate that has been occurring since the 1970s pertains to voters' feelings about the major parties' economic policies. Traditionally, American voters support whichever "side" seems to offer the most effective program for promoting real economic growth. From the 1870s to the 1920s it seemed that private business and its preferred party, the Republicans, had the best answers. As we have seen, the Depression completely altered that perception. But during the 1970s the Democrats lost their credibility as the "party of prosperity," and at this point in American electoral history the Republicans have more voter support on matters of economic policy.

A third set of realignments in the electorate has to do with the demographic characteristics of party members. As the accompanying table shows, the once solidly Democratic South is no longer a Democratic stronghold. Blacks remain firm supporters of the Democratic party, and Jewish voters are the least partisan of any religious group. Women are more partisan and more likely to be Democrats than men are. Finally, the figures on partisanship by income level show a strong correlation between affluence and identification with the Republican party—which works in the Republicans' favor when economic times are good. But if economic fortunes decline sharply we can expect to see new realignments in the voting public.

SUMMARY

Politics determines "who gets what, when, and how." The basis of politics is competition for *power*, or the ability to control the behavior of others, even against their will. *Authority* is institutionalized power, or power whose exercise is governed by the norms and statuses of organizations. Sets of norms and statuses that specialize in the exercise of power and authority are *political institutions*, and the set of political institutions that operate in a particular society forms the *state*.

Although a state can exercise its power through the use of force, eventually this will not be enough to govern a society. When people consent to be governed without the use of force, the state is said to be legitimate. *Legitimacy* is a society's ability to engender and maintain the belief that the existing political institutions are the most appropriate for that society. It is the basis of a society's political culture—the cultural norms, values, and symbols that support and justify its political institutions.

The most important political territory in world affairs is the *nation-state*, the largest territory within which a society's political institutions can operate without having to face challenges to their sovereignty. The borders that mark off one nation-state from others do not always correspond to what people believe to be the rightful boundaries of their societies. Conflicts over the borders of states and societies have been a fact of political life throughout human history.

Citizenship is the status of membership in a nation-state. The rights of citizenship include civil rights (e.g., freedom of speech, thought, and faith), political rights (e.g., the right to vote), and social rights (e.g., the right to a certain level of economic welfare and security). The institutions that have developed to deliver or protect these rights include the courts, local and national representative bodies, social services, and schools. The question of who is entitled to full participation in politics is a key issue at the local level as well as at the national level.

Modern nations are governed by elected and appointed officials whose authority is defined by laws. To prevent abuses of authority, modern political institutions usually specify some form of separation of powers in which abuses by one institution can be remedied by others. *Political parties* are organizations of people who join together to gain legitimate control of state authority. Parties that accept the rule of other legitimate parties form a "loyal opposition" that monitors the actions of the ruling party and prevents the emergence of *oligarchy*, or rule by a few people who stay in office indefinitely. Regimes that accept no limits to their power and seek to exert their rule at all levels of society are known as *totalitarian* regimes.

Democracy means rule by the nation's citizens: Citizens have the right to participate in public decision making, and those who govern do so with the explicit consent of the governed. In the British *parliamentary* system, elections are held in which the party that wins a majority of the seats in the legislature "forms a government": The leader of the party becomes the head of government and appoints other party members to major offices. In the American *representative* system, the party whose candidate is elected president need not have a majority of the seats in the legislature. In nations or regions in which a single party is dominant, oligarchical political systems are more likely to develop.

Functionalist theorists assert that certain "structural prerequisites" must exist in a society for democratic political institutions to develop and operate. Among these are high levels of economic development, urbanization, and literacy, as well as a culture that tolerates dissent. The *power elite model* holds that the presence of democratic institutions does not mean that a society is democratic; political decisions are actually controlled by an elite of rich and powerful individuals. This view is challenged by the *pluralist model*, which holds that political decisions are influenced by a variety of interest groups through a process of coalition building and bargaining.

Many political thinkers have been concerned with the relationship between social interaction and political institutions. Among the most influential was Machiavelli, who argued that political institutions must be based on the recognition that human beings are capable of evil as well as good. This recognition played a major part in the planning of the government of the United States, in which each branch of the government is able to check abuses of power by the other branches.

In modern nation-states political communication is a major concern for those out of power as well as those in power. It is im-

GLOSSARY

power: the ability to control the behavior of others, even against their will (**p. 595**).

authority: power whose exercise is governed by the norms and statuses of organizations (**p. 595**).

political institution: a set of norms and statuses pertaining to the exercise of power and authority (**p. 595**).

state: the set of political institutions operating in a particular society (**p. 595**).

legitimacy: the ability of a society to engender and maintain the belief that the existing political institutions are the most appropriate for that society (**p. 596**).

nation-state: the largest territory within which a society's political institutions can operate without having to face challenges to their sovereignty (**p. 598**).

citizenship: the status of membership in a nation-state (**p. 601**).

demagogue: a leader who uses personal charisma and political symbols to manipulate public opinion (**p. 605**).

political party: an organization of people who join together to gain legitimate control of state authority (**p. 605**).

oligarchy: rule by a few people who stay in office indefinitely rather than for limited terms (**p. 605**).

totalitarian regime: a regime that accepts no limits to its power and seeks to exert its rule at all levels of society (**p. 605**).

democracy: a political system in which all citizens have the right to participate in public decision making (**p. 606**).

patronage: jobs and economic benefits that party leaders can exchange for votes and political influence (**p. 606**).

power elite model: a theory stating that political decisions are controlled by an elite of rich and powerful individuals even in societies with democratic political institutions (**p. 607**).

pluralist model: a theory stating that no single group controls political decisions; instead, a plurality of interest groups influence those decisions through a process of coalition building and bargaining (**p. 610**).

interest group: an organization that attempts to influence elected and appointed officials regarding a specific issue or set of issues (**p. 610**).

lobbying: the process whereby interest groups seek to persuade legislators to vote in their favor on particular bills (**p. 610**).

portant to analyze political communications and to "read between the lines" of political rhetoric. This is particularly true in societies characterized by mass publics and sophisticated communication techniques.

A major question in political sociology is how states can control their military institutions. A society cannot remain democratic very long if the military usurps the authority granted to it by civilian institutions. One factor that contributes to this problem is the fact that the military is staffed by professional soldiers for whom service in the armed forces is a career. Another factor is the immense influence of the military on the economy. On the other hand, military socialization instills norms and values that may contribute to social control of the military.

WHERE TO FIND IT

Books

From Max Weber (Hans Gerth and C. W. Mills, eds.; Oxford University Press, 1946). See "Politics as a Vocation," a fascinating sociological statement about what it takes to live the life of a professional politician and what kinds of people and professions are best suited to that life.

Politics: Who Gets What, When and How (Harold Lasswell; McGraw-Hill, 1936). Another classic treatment of the meaning of politics and political life. Contains some exceptional insights into political interaction and the personalities of politicians.

Who Votes? (Raymond E. Wolfinger and Steven J. Rosenstone; Yale University Press, 1980). A review of voting studies and recent empirical work on voter turnout.

Politics Against Markets (Gosta Esping-Anderson; Princeton University Press, 1985). Describes the politics of welfare states and the emergence of social-democratic institutions that place limits on the capitalist economies of the Scandinavian nations.

The Last Half Century (Morris Janowitz; University of Chicago Press, 1978). An analysis of the major dimensions of change in American institutions to the present, by one of the nation's foremost sociologists.

The Professional Soldier (Morris Janowitz; Free Press, 1960). A fine example of sociological analysis of a major social institution, the military, and especially the development of its professional cadres of officers and enlisted recruits.

Political Man (Seymour Martin Lipset; Johns Hopkins University Press, 1981). A revision of a classic of political sociology. Traces the rise of democratic political institutions to other changes in a nation's stratification system and economic institutions.

Shooting an Elephant and Other Essays (George Orwell; Harcourt Brace Jovanovich, 1945). Especially important are Orwell's essay on "Politics and the English Language" and his writing on colonialism and class politics.

Journals

Political Science Quarterly A leading journal in the field of political science. Publishes good articles on voting behavior and change in political institutions.

Public Opinion Quarterly A journal of public-opinion studies. Often presents recent research on how Americans and other publics view recent political and economic events.

American Journal of Political Science A general journal of political science with emphasis on American politics.

Other Sources

World Almanac and Book of Facts Published annually by the Newspaper Enterprise Association, New York, New York.

VISUAL
SOCIOLOGY

Elections

Few political institutions are more important than free, contested elections. But how difficult it is to protect this vital institution! We need only think of the Philippines, where for more than twenty years, until the victory of Corazón Aquino in 1986, the regime led by Ferdinand Marcos was able to manipulate elections in order to control state power. Nor is the right of citizens to participate in elections ever fully guaranteed; rather, it must be protected by laws and by the vigilance of an educated citizenry.

Images of our own political campaigns and elections serve to remind us that the right to vote has had to be won by certain groups in the course of American history. Here we see women and blacks voting for the first time after long struggles to win this fundamental right of citizenship.

The existence of elections is not in itself a measure of democracy. There must also be a contest, and it must make a difference who wins. In China, national elections are considered important events, and most people vote. But these elections are usually mere rituals in which citizens are expected to vote for a single slate of candidates and thus affirm their support of the government. Access to state authority is not changed by the election itself.

Wherever there are single-party states, elections are usually either uncontested or rigged. Latin American states are often characterized by such elections, in which citizens are eager to vote yet have little hope that the outcome will change their lives. Even so, the existence of elections holds out the promise that a time may come when an election will be free from coercion and the outcome will make a difference in how the state is governed. But for this to happen there must be other institutions too, such as an independent

legal system that protects the rights of citizens who support opposition candidates. And the elections themselves must be protected so that ballots are secret and are counted fairly. Although these conditions are extremely difficult to establish, we have seen time and again that given an opportunity, people will press for a free, competitive electoral system.

CHAPTER OUTLINE

- **The Nature of Science and Technology**

- **Scientific Institutions: The Sociological View**
  - The Sociology of Science
  - The Norms of Science

- **Technology in Modern Societies**
  - Dimensions of Technology
  - Technological Dualism
  - Technology and Social Change
  - The Quest for Energy
  - Technology in Everyday Life

- **Science, Technology, and Society: The Case of Medical Technology**
  - The Hospital: From Poorhouse to Healing Institution
  - Hyptertrophy in Health Care?
  - Medical Sociology

- **The Impact of Technology**
  - Technological Systems
  - Environmental Stress

AP/Wide World Photos

Los Angeles, California

CHAPTER 20

SCIENCE, TECHNOLOGY, AND THE ENVIRONMENT

I magine a society in which it is illegal to grill hamburgers on an outdoor barbecue, or in which underarm sprays are contraband goods, or in which there are strict limits on the times when one may drive a car. It may sound like a science fiction nightmare, but the possibility of such controls is not imaginary.

In Los Angeles urban planners and social scientists warn that such drastic measures may soon be necessary. Air pollution reaches such alarming levels in the slow-moving air of the Los Angeles Basin that health warnings and "smog alerts" are routine. Unless alternatives to the private car, fluorocarbon sprays, and many industrial solvents are found and put to use soon, the quality of life in Los Angeles is likely to deteriorate rapidly.

About one in twenty residents of the United States live in the Los Angeles region. Within the Los Angeles Basin there are about 14 million people "who speak 85 languages, partition themselves into 168 separate cities, drive nearly 100 million vehicle-miles *per day*, and live in a state that consumes more gasoline than anywhere save the rest of the United States and all of Russia" (Weisman, 1989, p. 16). The area constitutes the sixth-largest economy in the world, and it is estimated that by 2010 it will be home to 18 million people, an increase of about 4 million from the 1990 figure and equal to the combined populations of Chicago and Detroit. Known for its labyrinth of freeways, the vital arteries of social life and commerce in the region, the Los Angeles Basin is only beginning to invest in bus and rail transport. The private car still reigns supreme.

Planners and scientists at California's South Coast Air Quality Management District (AQMD) estimate that it will cost at least $3 billion during the next twenty years to reduce air pollution by the 80 percent scientists believe is necessary. James M. Lents, director of the massive AQMD plan, estimates that this figure translates into 13 percent less pollution emission per person. "We can't do that without touching all aspects of life," he comments, "but this will be *evolution*, not *revolution*—technology will help by developing cleaner versions of today's products. People often won't even realize the difference."

Los Angeles is not alone in facing the daunting problem of air quality. New York, Boston, New Orleans, and many other cities will also face severe challenges in meeting air-quality goals in coming years. At this writing there are 382 counties in the United States, accounting for over half of the population, where federal air pollution standards are exceeded (French, 1990). Residents of the United States are probably going to have to pay more to drive their cars as governments at all levels use gasoline taxes to raise revenues and curb pollution. Similar controls will be necessary in many other nations if the damaging effects of pollution on the planet are to be curbed.

THE NATURE OF SCIENCE AND TECHNOLOGY

"Our ability to look back on ourselves from outer space symbolizes the unique perspective we have on our environment and on where we are headed as a species. With this knowledge comes a responsibility . . . the responsibility to manage the human use of planet ‚earth" (Clarke, 1989, p. 47). Management of the earth includes wise government of its human populations. It also includes the application of scientific knowledge to management and government—by no means a simple task. In this chapter we explore the ways in which science and technologies develop and are controlled and how they can be used to meet the challenges of our future existence on the earth.

Science is a major institutional sector of modern societies: A hallmark of the modern social order is the conduct of scientific research in universities and other research organizations. As shown in Chapter 18, the control of information, especially scientific and technical information, is a source of prestige and power in postindustrial societies. The study of science and technology, therefore, is an increasingly important sociological specialty.

Science is, essentially, knowledge. (The Latin word *scientia*, from which our word *science* is derived, means "knowledge.") But science is a particular kind of knowledge, knowledge that has been obtained through the scientific method (see Chapter 2)—that is, as a result of the process of developing and testing hypotheses. Even so, science encompasses an extremely diverse array of subjects—"from subatomic reactions to mental processes; from mathematical laws of thermodynamics to the economics of race relations; from the births and deaths of stars to the migration of birds; from the study of ultramicroscopic viruses to that of extragalactic nebulas; from the rise and dissolution of cultures and crystals to the rise and dissolution of atoms and universes" (*Encyclopaedia Britannica*, 1967, vol. 20, p. 7). These diverse topics are grouped together under the label *science* because they all involve systematic and repeated observations.

Science is customarily divided into "pure" and "applied" branches. *Pure science* is scientific investigation that is devoted exclusively to the pursuit of knowledge for its own sake, with no immediate concern for using that knowledge to solve practical problems. For example, for over thirty years Barbara McClintock did research on genetics in corn plants, which had no immediate application to agricultural technology but eventually was recognized as having applications in molecular biology. *Applied science*, in contrast, is the application of known scientific principles to a practical problem; the outcome in many cases is new technologies. And as Los Angeles's air-pollution problems illustrate, those technologies can have a tremendous impact on the quality of human life.

As shown in Chapter 4, **technology** is an aspect of culture. It can be defined as theuse of tools and knowledge to manipulate the physical environment in order to achieve desired practical goals. Although modern technologies are often based on scientific discoveries, technology is much older than science; it has its roots in the tool-making and fire-building skills of the earliest human groups. People have always needed to find better ways of doing things or ways of making their lives more comfortable. Technological innovations have met those needs for thousands of years. In fact, technological change proceeded without the benefit of scientific knowledge for the bulk of human history.

Science as we know it today is a relatively recent development. Although its origins may be traced to the mathematicians and philosophers of the ancient world, its emergence as a separate sphere of knowledge, with its own norms and values, dates from the late sixteenth century. From that time on, science "mathematicized and mechanized nature, tested and experimented on nature, pushed and pressed far beyond what nature spontaneously had ever revealed; and . . . not only mastered, but also learned to transform, na-

> *Science—knowledge obtained through the scientific method—is customarily divided into "pure" and "applied" branches.*

Box 20–1: **The Gaia Hypothesis**

Lewis Thomas, a writer and research physician and former chancellor of Memorial Sloan–Kettering Cancer Center, has provided these speculations about the relationship between human beings and the earth:

The notion that life on Earth resembles, in detail, the sort of coherent, connected life we attribute to an organism is now something more than a notion. Thanks in large part to the studies begun in the 1970s by James Lovelock, Lynn Margulis, and their associates, we now know that planetary life, the "biosphere," regulates itself.

It maintains in precision the salinity and acid-base balance of its oceans, holds constant over millions of years the exactly equilibrated components of its atmosphere with the levels of oxygen and carbon dioxide at just the optimal levels for respiration and photosynthesis. It lives off the sun, taking in the energy it requires for its life and reflecting away the rest into the unfillable sink of space. This is the "Gaia hypothesis," the new idea that the Earth itself is alive.

The one biological function the Earth does not yet perform to qualify for the formal definition of an organism is reproduction. But wait around, and keep an eye on it. In real life, this may turn out to be what it started to do twenty years ago [on the occasion of the first moon walk].

Given enough time, and given our long survival as working parts of the great creature (a chancy assumption for the moment), the Earth may be entering the first stages of replication, scattering seeds of itself, perhaps in the form of microorganisms similar to those dominating the planet's own first life for the first two billion years of its Precambrian period. Atmospheres similar to ours may emerge over planets or moons now uninhabitable somewhere in our solar system, and then, with enough time and luck, out in the galaxy, even beyond.

So the first moon walk brought forth two new possibilities of viewing ourselves and our home. First, the Gaia idea of a living Earth, not at all the mystical notion that it would have seemed a few years back (but still carrying the same idea of "oneness" that has long preoccupied the mystics among us), is now becoming the most practical, down-to-earth thought ever thought. And second is the idea of the Earth reproducing itself, and the possible role we might be playing, consciously or unconsciously, in the huge process.

Finally, as something to think about, there is the strangest of all paradoxes: the notion that an organism so immense and complex, with so many interconnected and communicating central nervous systems at work, from crickets and fireflies to philosophers, should be itself mindless. I cannot believe it. [1989, p. 25]

Source: © 1989 by the New York Times Company. Reprinted by permission.

> **Technology is the use of tools and knowledge to manipulate the physical environment in order to achieve practical goals.**

ture" (Cohen, 1982, p. 62). Accelerated by the discoveries of modern science, technology rapidly expanded the human capacity to live in and exploit different habitats. Indeed, in the past two centuries it has changed the face of the earth (Gutkind, 1956). Airports, skyscrapers, housing developments, oil refineries, superhighways, the Panama Canal, the rocket-launching pad at Cape Canaveral are all products of technology that have transformed the surroundings in which human beings live and work. It is this interrelationship between science and technology that is responsible for the breathtaking speed of technological change in our century. (Box 20-1 introduces the Gaia hypothesis, the idea that humans and their cultures and technologies are also part of the living earth and must act accordingly.)

Because technology has had such an enormous impact on modern life, we devote a large portion of this chapter to the ways in which new technologies arise, how they affect social life, and how they lead to social change. As an especially revealing example of how technological change can shape the values and institutions of a society, we will examine the evolution and social impact of medical technology. But first we need to explore the nature of scientific institutions, since they generate the knowledge on which much technological change is based.

SCIENTIFIC INSTITUTIONS: THE SOCIOLOGICAL VIEW

The Sociology of Science

Sociologists who study scientific institutions generally follow one of two basic approaches, described as interactionist and institutional (Ben-David, 1984). Those who use the interactionist approach observe how scientists interact among themselves—for example, how they divide and coordinate work in laboratories and how they approach scientific problems. Those who use the institutional approach study the role of the scientist in different countries, the structure of scientific organizations, and the culture of scientific institutions (i.e., the norms and values of science). This distinction is not total, however; there is a great deal of overlap between the two approaches.

The Interactionist Approach. Studies using the interactionist approach have focused on the scientific community—that is, on "the network of communication and social relationships between scientists working in given fields or in all fields" (Ben-David, 1984, p. 3). The questions asked by sociologists who take this approach pertain to how scientists go about the daily work of research and why scientific "revolutions" sometimes occur. In a well-known study entitled *The Structure of Scientific Revolutions*, Thomas Kuhn (1962) explored the nature of the scientific community. He found that the rules of the scientific method are not adequate to describe what scientists do. Rather than spending their time testing and refuting existing hypotheses in order to establish new, more valid ones, they often take it for granted that existing theories are valid and use them in their efforts to solve specific problems. In other words, the researcher uses existing theories and methods as a **paradigm**, or model, to guide future research.

This view of the scientific community (or, rather, communities of specialized researchers) implies that science is insulated from the rest of society. Scientists are guided by the tradition of research in their field, which is passed along from one generation of scientists to the next. The problems they choose to solve are determined by that tradition, as are the methods they use in trying to solve them. This process continues, according to Kuhn, until the paradigm is no longer useful—that is, until enough members of the scientific community believe a particular set of observations can no longer be explained by existing theories and procedures. Then the community becomes more open to outside influences. Its members explore a variety of ideas not directly related to the dominant paradigm in their field, ideas that in some cases lead to a scientific revolution. When this occurs, the old paradigm is set aside in favor of a new one that will henceforth guide the work of the members of a particular scientific community. Some of the most famous scientific revolutions have occurred in physics—for example, in the shift from Newtonian physics to Einstein's theory of relativity and quantum theory and most recently in the discovery of the existence of subatomic particles.

The Institutional Approach. The institutional approach to the study of science does not contradict the interactionist view. Instead, it asks why science develops differently in different societies, and with what consequences. In this approach, certain conditions encourage the development of scientific institutions. Those conditions include the recognition of empirical research as a legitimate way of gaining new knowledge. In addition, science must be independent from other fields, such as theology or philosophy. Under such conditions separate institutions devoted to scientific research, such as graduate schools and institutes of technology, can develop. This has been the case in the United States, where the introduction of graduate training in the sciences, together with research related to professional training (as occurs, for example, in medical schools), led to the establishment

> *Researchers use existing theories and methods as a paradigm, or model, to guide future research.*

The Oriental Institute, University of Chicago

These two photos, one of an ancient irrigation system in Iran (c A.D.) 900) and one of the Grand Coulee Dam on the Colorado River, show the impact of human technology on the earth's surface. Today there is hardly a part of the globe that does not bear the traces and scars of human technology.

Water and Power Resources Service, U.S. Department of the Interior

of fully equipped research institutes at major colleges and universities. One effect of the presence of such institutes is a large proportion of Americans among the winners of Nobel prizes in the sciences (see Table 20-1).

The institutionalization of science in the United States has had dramatic and far-reaching effects. "In agriculture, education, sociology, and eventually in nuclear research the universities pioneered research on a scale that far exceeded the needs of training students

and was, from the very outset, an operation distinct from teaching" (Ben-David, 1984, p. 146). Attempts have been made to establish similar research organizations in Europe, but these were hampered by the rigid structure of European universities. European universities have a closed system of professorships that cannot accommodate scientists who want to conduct research. A number of specialized research institutes have been established outside the universities, but none is as extensive or as influential as the research institutes associated with American universities.

In the 1950s, during the Cold War, there was widespread recognition that the United States needed to improve its scientific research capacity. As a result, government and universities began cooperating even more closely than they had before. As Daniel Bell (1973) points out, the rush to invest in science produced

the expansion of the universities as research institutions, the creation of large scientific laboratories at universities supported by government (the jet propulsion lab at Cal Tech, the Argonne atomic lab at the University of Chicago, MITRE and Lincoln Lab at MIT, the Riverside electronics lab at Columbia, and the like), [and] the growth of "consortiums" such as the Brookhaven lab on Long Island managed by a half-dozen universities. After these have come the large government health-research centers such as those at the National In-

Table 20–1: **The Nationality of Nobel Prize Winners in the Sciences, 1901–1984**

	1901–1930	1931–1950	1951–1966	1967–1984
United States	5	24	44	66
Belgium	1	1	—	2
Canada	1	—	—	2
France	14	2	4	2
Germany	26	12	7	4
Japan	—	1	1	2
Netherlands	7	1	1	1
Great Britain	16	13	18	18
U.S.S.R.	2	—	7	1
Other Countries	22	17	—	20

This table shows that nations experience changes in the quality of their science as measured by an international standard, the Nobel Prize. However, wealthier nations can devote more funds to scientific institutions, a fact that helps explain patterns in the distribution of prizes. The size of the nation's population is also important, but it does not explain why wealthy nations with large populations (such as Japan) are not significantly increasing their share of Nobel Prizes.

Source: Encyclopaedia Britannica.

stitutes of Health, the major National Science Foundation-supported laboratories, the creation of a vast number of nonprofit research "think tanks" such as Rand, the Institute of Defense Analysis, the Aerospace Corporation, and so on. [p. 248]

One consequence of this unplanned growth of scientific organizations in universities, government, the military, and the private sector, Bell concludes, is that it became impossible to create a single set of policies for the support of science. The various organizations must compete for resources and are vulnerable to changing national needs as well as new demands for scientific knowledge by business and industry. This adds to the complexity and competitiveness of scientific institutions.

These aspects of scientific institutions may also explain their continuing differentiation in the United States and other Western nations. For example, the departmental structure of American colleges and universities has been shown to encourage the growth of new disciplines (Ben-David, 1984). Interdisciplinary programs and new fields of study can be sponsored by existing departments un- til they can compete for support as independent disciplines. An example is the development of statistics as a separate field of study. Originally a branch of mathematics, statistics has been studied and taught by mathematicians and physicists in Europe and Great Britain since the seventeenth century. In the United States, however, departments of biology, education, psychology, economics, and other fields (e.g., demography) developed specialties in statistics. Eventually separate departments of statistics were established.

In sum, since its origins in the independent and often secretive experiments of philosophers and clerics, scientific research has become institutionalized in complex organizations. Yet we will see at many points in this chapter that the process of differentiation through which science becomes an institution separate from

Since its origins in the independent experiments of philosophers and clerics, scientific research has become institutionalized in complex organizations.

others is never complete. The work of scientists must be paid for, and the more their research is "pure" (in that it has no apparent uses that generate profits), the more it must be supported by other institutions like government or industry. This dependence of science on other institutions continually subjects scientists to pressure to make their work relevant to the needs of business or the military. Conflict between scientists and their sponsors thus has been a feature of science since its origins. To understand that conflict more fully, we will take a more detailed look at the norms of scientific institutions.

The Norms of Science

We saw in Chapter 4 that every social institution develops norms that specify how its special functions are to be carried out. This is readily illustrated by the institutions of science. The function of those institutions is to extend knowledge by means of a specific set of procedures (i.e., the scientific method). The norms of science are derived from that function (Merton, 1973).

Universalism. One of the basic norms of scientific institutions is *universalism*: The truth of scientific knowledge must be determined by the impersonal criteria of the scientific method, not by criteria related to race, nationality, religion, social class, or political ideology. This would seem to be self-evident until one remembers that international rivalries have been part of the history of science since the Renaissance. And consider the case of the Russian geneticist Trofim D. Lysenko, who, on the basis of some extremely unscientific research on plant genetics, claimed that acquired characteristics of plants could be inherited by the next generation (Bell, 1973). This claim seemed to offer hope for improvement of the Soviet Union's faltering agricultural production. It also fit well with Soviet ideology, which held that better human beings could be created through adherence to the ideals of the revolution. To Stalin and his advisers, science seemed to have proved the value of the Soviet culture and social system.

Lysenko was granted a virtual dictatorship over biological research in the Soviet Union, and hundreds of geneticists lost their jobs (Joravsky, 1971; Medvedev, 1971). Lysenko was deposed during the Khrushchev era, but the damage done to Soviet agriculture and biological research in the name of ideology lasted many years longer.

Common Ownership. Another norm of science is *common ownership of scientific findings*. Those findings are a result of collaboration and hence are not the property of any individual, although in some cases they may bear the name of the person who first published them, as in "Darwin's theory of evolution" or "Einstein's theory of relativity." One outcome of this norm is frequent conflicts over scientific priority—that is, over who was the first to discover or publish a particular item of scientific knowledge. Thus there is continual controversy over who discovered the differential calculus, Newton or Leibniz, but there are no limitations on the use of that calculus. A further consequence of the norm of common ownership is the norm of *publication*—the requirement of full and open communication of scientific findings in journals accessible to all. Secrecy is out of place in science.

However, because scientific research is so often conducted in the interests of national defense or under the sponsorship of private firms that hope to profit from applications of the findings, the norms of common ownership and publication are often suspended. Such situations have led to innumerable conflicts in scientific circles. An outstanding example is the case of J. Robert Oppenheimer, one of the leaders in the development of the atomic bomb during World War II. Although Oppenheimer's sympathy for certain radical causes was well known, he was given a full security clearance both during and after the war, when he continued his pioneering research on the applications of nuclear physics. But when he publicly stated his support of international sharing of findings in nuclear physics—and opposed the development of a nuclear bomb—his opponents brought up the old charge that he was a subversive and could not be trusted with scientific secrets. In 1953 President Dwight D. Eisenhower ruled that Oppenheimer was to be denied access to secret scientific information, which meant that he would also be denied access to the laboratories where the most important research in nuclear physics was being conducted (Lakoff, 1970; Rieff, 1969).

Disinterestedness. A further norm of scientific institutions is *disinterestedness*. The scientist does not allow the desire for personal gain to influence the reporting and evaluation of results; fraud and irresponsible claims are outlawed. In fact, more than most other activities, scientific research is subject to the scrutiny of others. This is part of the nature of that research, which involves the search for results that can be verified; in other words, science is, in a sense, self-policing. The norm of disinterestedness does not imply that scientists cannot hope to profit from their findings, and there are many instances in which scientists have held lucrative patents for their discoveries. But it does imply that related norms of scientific research, such as unbiased observation and thoroughness in reporting findings, must take precedence over any selfish motives.

Sociologists are concerned that the pressure on scientists to make discoveries that will earn large sums of money will damage the credibility of scientific institutions. The trend toward partnerships between private corporations and scientific institutions may also put pressure on scientists to violate scientific norms. Recently, for example, the Monsanto Chemical Corporation gave $23.5 million to Washington University for biological research and a West German pharmaceutical company invested $40 million in research at Harvard Medical School. Dorothy Nelkin, one of the nation's leading experts on scientific policy, warns that when businesses form alliances with universities to conduct research in such areas as biological technologies, the scientists involved must keep their findings secret until patents have been applied for. Nelkin concludes that such secrecy "violates the social nature of science, the idea that science is

shared, that it's a cumulative activity" (quoted in Broad, 1988, p. C1).

Similarly, when chemists at universities in Utah and Great Britain announced in 1989 that their collaboration had achieved "cold fusion," the production of energy through the fusion of hydrogen atoms at low temperatures (a reaction that scientists believe requires extremely high temperatures), it appeared that a new era of low-cost energy might be on the horizon. But other scientists were highly skeptical. The so-called discoveries had not been published in scientific journals prior to their announcement to the press—a violation of the norm of publication. The cold-fusion apparatus was also kept secret for a time so that the scientists and their universities could apply for patents and enlist the support of major corporations for further research. These actions made scientists suspicious. Before too long the results were found to be incorrect, an outcome perhaps of too much hope for profit and not enough careful measurement (Wilford, 1989).

The norms we have just described are well-established aspects of modern science, which is increasingly differentiated from other institutions, particularly religion and the state. But science was not always viewed as a legitimate institution or a respectable occupation. In fact, early in its history science was often regarded as a dangerous activity with the potential to threaten the existing social order. This can be seen quite clearly in the repression of Galileo by the Inquisition, which is described in Box 20-2.

TECHNOLOGY IN MODERN SOCIETIES

We noted earlier that a significant aspect of modern science is its contribution to the rapid pace of technological change. The technologies produced by scientific research are applied to all aspects of human life and hence are a major force in shaping and changing other institutions in addition to scientific institutions themselves. An example is the impact of technological change on the institutions of mass communication. As discussed in Chapter 17, the advent of radio and then television dramatically changed the ways in which social and cultural values are transmitted to various groups in society. We note other examples of the impact of technology in the following pages. But first it is necessary to enlarge our understanding of what is meant by the term *technology*.

Dimensions of Technology

In Chapter 18 we explain that technology is more than tools and skills, that ways of organizing work are also part of technology. Technology has three dimensions, which may be summarized as follows:

1. Technological tools, instruments, machines, gadgets, which are used in accomplishing a variety of tasks. These material objects are best referred to as *apparatus*, the physical devices of technical performance.
2. The body of technical skills, procedures, routines—all *activities* or behaviors that employ a purposive, step-by-step, rational method of doing things.
3. The *organizational networks* associated with activities and apparatus (Winner, 1977, pp. 11–12).

The last of these dimensions may be clarified by an example. Organizational networks are sets of statuses and roles. All technologies establish or modify such networks. Thus the automobile owner is part of a network that includes dealers, mechanics, parts suppliers, insurers, licensing agents, and junkyard owners. Our great-great-grandparents were probably part of a network of horse dealers, harness makers, buggy suppliers, and blacksmiths, a network that has been largely eliminated by the advent of motorized vehicles.

Technological change can occur in any or all of the dimensions just listed. The most far-reaching changes involve all three, especially the third. For example, the industrial revolution completely changed the organization of economic institutions and also had significant effects on other institutions, such as the family. Likewise, the internal-combustion engine, which made possible the development of the automobile, has completely transformed the ecology of North America (Flink, 1975). On the other hand, some technological changes are limited to modifications in the apparatus or technical skills needed for a particular task (the surgical stapler is an example) and do not affect large numbers of people or have major social impacts.

Not only do technological changes affect various groups and institutions within a society, and sometimes transform a society, but technology itself is affected by the social conditions prevailing at any given time. The acceptance of a particular technological innovation may depend on prior changes in other aspects of a society. Thus, television might not have had as great an impact if it had been invented in the nineteenth century, when working people had far less leisure time than they do today. Other innovations have failed to gain acceptance because they appeared too soon. An example is the Sony Corporation's unsuccessful attempt to introduce tape recorders in Japan in 1950. Japanese consumers did not perceive a need or use for them, and they went unsold. Much the same thing is happening today in the case of home computers. Once the thrill of computer games wears off, the computer often stands idle because the average household has no other uses for it. In consequence, the home computer industry is continually searching for new software to extend the applications of home computers, as has already been done in the case of computers for office use (Sanger, 1984).

Technological Dualism

It should be noted that the effects of new technologies are not always positive. The phrase *technological dualism* is sometimes used to refer to the fact that technological changes often have both positive and negative effects. The introduction of diesel locomotives, for

Technology has three dimensions: apparatus, activities, and organizational networks.

Box 20–2: **Galileo and the Inquisition**

The first person to use a telescope to study the skies was Galileo Galilei, an Italian mathematician who lived from 1564 to 1642. His observations convinced him that the earth revolved around the sun. Up to that time it had been taken for granted that the earth was the center of the universe, and this belief was strongly entrenched in the doctrines of the Catholic church. Galileo's views were so radical that he was tried by the Inquisition, ordered to deny what he knew to be the truth, and forced to spend the last eight years of his life under house arrest.

Galileo's fate illustrates a principle we have mentioned at numerous points in this book: As societies become more complex, the process termed *differentiation* removes various functions from existing institutions and creates new institutions to perform them. Galileo was tried by the Inquisition because in his time science had not yet become differentiated from philosophy and religion. A scientist must on no account discover anything that contradicted the doctrines of the church.

In his play *Galileo*, Bertolt Brecht painted a vivid picture of the constraints placed on Galileo by the situation of science in his day. An assistant has delivered a gift from the Court of Naples—a model of the sky according to the wise men of ancient Greece—and has asked him to explain it. "You see the fixed ball in the middle?" says Galileo. "That's the earth. For two thousand years man has chosen to believe that the sun and all the host of stars revolve about him. Well. The Pope, the cardinals, the princes, the scholars, captains, merchants, housewives, have pictured themselves squatting in the middle of an affair like that." Galileo goes on to predict that before long people "will be learning that the earth rolls round the sun, and that their mothers, the captains, the scholars, the princes, and the Pope are rolling with it."

The assistant is not convinced, but he admits that he has mentioned Galileo's ideas to his mother, Galileo's housekeeper. The housekeeper says to Galileo, "Last night my son tried to tell me that the earth goes round the sun. You'll soon have him saying that two times two is five." Later Galileo says to the assistant, "Andrea, I wouldn't talk about our ideas outside." "Why not?" asks Andrea. "Certain of the authorities won't like it," replies Galileo. His statement is confirmed by a friend: "How can people in power leave a man at large who tells the truth,

example, greatly increased the efficiency of railroad operations, but it also led to the decline and eventual abandonment of railroad towns whose economies were based on the servicing of steam locomotives (Cottrell, 1951). Another example is the automation of industrial production. Automation has greatly improved manufacturing processes in many industries. It has increased the safety of certain production tasks and led to improved product quality in many cases. But it has also replaced thousands of manual workers with machines, and significant numbers of those workers find themselves unemployed and lacking the skills required by the high-tech occupations of post-industrial society (see Box 20-3).

Some observers go so far as to say that technology is a danger to the modern world. They feel that it has become an autonomous force, that it is out of control. This is a recurrent theme in movies and science fiction—HAL, the computer that takes over the ship in *2001: A Space Odyssey*, is a good example. But it is also claimed that technology is increasingly independent from human control in the real world. Events like the accident at the Three Mile Island nuclear-power plant in 1979; the toxic-gas leak that killed more

even if it be the truth about the distant stars?"

Today scientists are studying subatomic particles called quarks. They have proposed that dinosaurs had feathers rather than scales, and they have suggested that the universe began with a big bang and that stars eventually become black holes. They have discovered the process by which the continents were formed and the structure of human genes. In none of these cases have the findings been challenged by "the authorities," religious or otherwise. Rather, they have been judged by the standards of scientific investigation, one of the functions of the institution that we call science.

But the process of differentiation is never complete. In recent years the ancient tension between science and religion has taken a new turn: The scientific theory of evolution has been challenged by fundamentalist religious groups because it contradicts statements in the Bible. These groups have pressured publishers to delete discussions of evolution from textbooks, or at least to mention "creation science" as well as evolution. Although their efforts have had limited success, they have not been ignored.

than 2,000 people in Bhopal, India, in 1984; and the disaster at the Chernobyl nuclear-power plant in the Soviet Union in 1986 seem to indicate that human beings cannot control the technologies they have created.

Sociologists who have studied this issue point out that the problem is not one of humans being dominated by machines but, rather, one of depending on technology to meet a wide and growing range of human needs. The Three Mile Island power plant provided electricity for thousands of homes and businesses; the Bhopal facility produced a pesticide that made possible larger harvests of much-needed grain. The result of our dependence on the benefits of complex technologies is an increasingly complex set of organizations and procedures for putting those technologies to work. This requires more human effort and skill, and the chances of error and breakdown are greater. The point is not that technology is out of control but that often there is a lag between the introduction of new technologies and the development of adequate controls over the application of those technologies.

One of the main issues that concerns social scientists in this regard is why such lags

Box 20–3: **Worker Responses to High Technology**

The rapid growth of employment in industrial regions like California's "Silicon Valley," Route 128 outside Boston, and the "Silicon Prairie" in the Dallas–Fort Worth area, as well as in hundreds of industrial parks throughout the United States, is viewed as one of the benefits of investment in high-technology industries. The term *high technology* is associated with computers, advanced electronics, genetic engineering, and other frontiers of technological change, but it is rarely well defined. And without a clear definition of this term it is almost impossible to assess its impact on society.

As the term is used by academics, policymakers, and journalists, high technology refers to at least one of the following features of technology:

- An extensive degree of technological sophistication embodied in a product.
- A rapid rate of employment growth associated with an innovative product.
- A large research and development effort associated with production (Markson and Bloch, 1985).

One implication of this definition is that it includes job-creating processes like research and development as well as technologies like computers, which also have created new growth in employment. Yet the employment-producing features of high technology can be problematic. Many high technologies, such as robotics and computer-aided design, are intended to reduce employment by substituting the work of machines guided by computers for human production of all kinds. Early machine technologies tended to replace human labor power, but high technology tends to reduce the need for human brain power. Employment in occupations like drafting and industrial drawing in engineering and architecture, for example, is threatened by the accelerating use of computer design and graphics programs (Shaiken, 1985).

During the industrial revolution in England, workers sometimes rioted and wrecked the machinery that was replacing their labor. Such violence against machines was termed *Luddism* after an English stocking maker, Ned Ludlam, who smashed his employer's knitting frame with a sledgehammer and thereby touched off the famous Luddite riots of 1811 and 1812 (Hobsbawm, 1975, Rudé, 1964). Outbursts of collective behavior directed against automation have been relatively rare, however. Instead, workers have generally accepted their fate and looked for other sources of employment.

Nevertheless, the effects of high technology are so threatening to so many workers that unions have taken a number of initiatives designed to alleviate those effects. An example occurred at Britain's Lucas Aerospace, a maker of landing gear and electronic equipment, in the mid-1970s. Automation had reduced the Lucas work force from 18,000 to 13,000. At that point the employees and their union leaders conducted an ambitious study that showed that highly skilled workers were losing their jobs at the same time that many of the society's needs remained unmet. The study suggested hundreds of ways in which the company could employ its skilled work force to meet those needs and still earn profits. Although the plan was rejected, it has served as a model for other worker strategies.

Here is a vivid example of the risks and unintended effects of technology. This bizarre accident that occurred in France early in this century proved to some skeptics that humans could not control the power of their technology. As technology advances, the risks generally increase in proportion to the benefits.

occur. Consider the problem known as wind shear. In recent years numerous major plane crashes have been caused by sudden downdrafts associated with severe thunderstorms on the approaches to airport runways. These downdrafts literally slam large aircraft to the ground. Industry and government officials have known about the wind-shear problem since at least 1975, when an Eastern Airlines jet crashed at New York's Kennedy Airport under such conditions. But not until a similar crash occurred in New Orleans in 1984 were airports ordered to install instruments that could predict such conditions. Why the delay? Some sociologists have argued that the pressure on corporations to show a profit causes them to neglect spending on safety measures. Others, taking a more functionalist view, tend to explain such lags in terms of the time required for organizations to recognize the causes of the problem and develop new statuses and roles to cope with them (Perrow, 1984).

Technology and Social Change

In Chapter 4 we refer to the intimate relationship between the earliest technologies and the subsequent evolution of culture. The obvious importance of technology to human cultural and social evolution has led some sociologists to view technology as a basic principle of social change. The classic statement of this view is that of William Fielding Ogburn (1942). Ogburn hypothesized that inventions affect the size of populations, which in turn influences the course of history. (For example, overpopulation often leads to wars and migrations.) Some inventions affect population directly: Improvements in sanitation, the development of cures for fatal illnesses, and more effective contraceptive techniques are examples. But inventions can also have indirect effects on population. For example, techniques that improve crop yields or permit long-term storage of food surpluses make it possible to support a larger population with a given amount of farm land. And improvements in military technology (e.g., the use of horses in warfare, the invention of gunpowder, and the development of the armored tank) have had dramatic effects on the conduct of war and hence on population size.

Ogburn also proposed the theory known as **cultural lag**. In his words, "A cultural lag occurs when one of two parts of culture which are correlated changes before or in greater degree than the other part does, thereby causing less adjustment between the two parts than existed previously" (1957, p. 167). This theory is most often applied to the adaptation of social institutions to changing technologies. For example, the industrial revolution gave birth to many kinds of machines, often with moving parts that made them dangerous to

In these two photos one can observe the differences between two town centers, which are due largely to the replacement of horses with automobiles. The modern view shows more traffic, more stores, more commerce, and more congestion, among other effects. No wonder many sociologists consider technology to be a major source of social change.

use. The rates of injury and death resulting from industrial accidents climbed rapidly in the decades following the introduction of the new machines to the United States around 1870. Such accidents spelled disaster for workers and their families, since it was hard to prove that the employer was responsible for the accident. It was not until around 1910 that the concepts of employer liability and worker's compensation were adopted, a lag of about forty years.

One problem with the cultural-lag theory is that it fails to account for the effects of social power. For example, workers who sought compensation for the costs of industrial accidents did not have nearly as much power to influence lawmakers as the owners of the machines did. When this power imbalance changed as a result of the labor movement, it became possible to enact legislation that would protect the workers.

The lags described by Ogburn can be at least partially reduced by the process of **technology assessment**, or efforts to anticipate the consequences of particular technologies for individuals and for society as a whole. The massive plan to reduce air pollution in the Los Angeles Basin described at the beginning of the chapter requires careful assessment. According to the National Environmental Policy Act of 1972 and related state laws, any major action by a public agency that affects the environment must be assessed for its impact on the environment and on the citizens involved. Laws that require technology assessment—especially those that require corporations to abide by the findings of such assessments—tend to increase the power of citizens in communities affected by technological change. They are therefore a source both of conflict and of movements for social reform. In the Los Angeles case, a number of small, inadequately funded environmental organizations were able to force the California Environmental Policy Administration to fund the air pollution plan (Weisman, 1989).

Theories that view technological innovations as a source of social change must also recognize that technological changes do not occur at an even pace. Some analysts, particularly the Soviet economist N. D. Kondratieff, believe that technological innovation follows a cyclical pattern. They have shown that the growth of particular industries produces a "long boom," a period of economic expansion and prosperity that lasts about twenty-five years and is followed by a period of decline and depression of about the same duration. This pattern is illustrated in Table 20-2, which shows the cycles of industrial development in Britain since the late 1700s.

It may be that the new technologies of computers and automation will begin another long boom or wave of economic growth in the next decade, as many people in advanced industrial societies hope. But it is clear that in the late 1970s the previous long boom, stimulated in part by the availability of cheap energy, was over. A new economic boom therefore may depend on new developments in energy technologies.

Table 20–2: Long Booms and Associated Industries

Dates	Industry	
1790–1815	Cotton	Mechanization of spinning
1848–1873	Textiles	Mechanization of spinning and weaving
	Engineering	Production by machine of textile machinery, steam engines and locomotives
1896–1921	Engineering	Batch production; semiautomatic machinery; marine engineering; automobiles
	Electrical	
	Chemical	Rise of science-based industries
	Steel	Bulk production
1945–1974	Automobiles	
	Mechanical and electrical consumer durables	Assembly-line mass production
	Petrochemicals	Continuous-flow process production

Source: CSE Microelectronics Group, 1980. Reprinted with permission from CSE Books, London.

The Quest for Energy

Throughout human history a central aspect of technological change has been the quest for new sources of energy to meet the needs of growing populations. That quest has given rise to a succession of energy technologies, each more sophisticated than the last. Animal power gave way to steam-driven machinery, which in turn was replaced by the internal-combustion engine. Reliance on oil and its derivatives, especially gasoline, encouraged the growth of powerful energy corporations, which often lobby government agencies for assistance in developing new technologies like nuclear energy. And today the technologically advanced nations are attempting to control the fusion reaction, in which hydrogen atoms are fused into helium, thereby producing an enormous release of energy. The implications of this energy technology, if it can be achieved, are staggering. Fusion promises to bring about a major revolution in human existence. It could make possible the colonization and exploration of space, the rapid development of the less-developed nations, the elimination of energy technologies based on oil and coal (which pollute the environment), and much else. But the effort to develop fusion power is also indicative of a fundamental crisis in modern life: the dwindling supply of energy resources.

The problem of oil depletion is only the most recent in a series of energy crises that began with the depletion of the supply of game animals through hunting in Paleolithic times. The shortage of meat created conditions that spurred the development of agriculture. Later, in the waning years of the Roman Empire, a shortage of labor power to grind flour encouraged the use of water power. The industrial revolution had its origins in the depletion of the supply of wood during the Renaissance. Coal was plentiful, and experiments with its use as an energy source led to the development of new techniques for producing energy—and new machinery and processes for manufacturing goods. Today, as supplies of oil and coal diminish, the search for new energy sources continues (Hardy, 1973).

It would seem from what we have said so far that the quest for energy is a positive force that results in new, sometimes revolutionary technologies that greatly improve the quality of human life. Many people believe that societies can meet their growing energy needs by continually investing in more sophisticated technologies. This approach has led to the development of huge nuclear-power plants to replace oil-fueled generators, and it is widely hoped that investment in fusion, an even more complex technology, will eliminate the dangers posed by nuclear power.

This view is subject to considerable criticism, however. Amory Lovins (1977), for example, distinguishes between "hard" and "soft" energy paths. The former "relies on rapid expansion of centralized high technologies to increase supplies of energy, especially in the form of electricity." The latter "combines a prompt and serious commitment to efficient use of energy [and] rapid development of renewable energy sources" (p. 25). Present and proposed energy policies favor the "hard" path, which involves intensive use of available coal, oil, and natural gas plus heavy investment in nuclear power. These are "capital-intensive" technologies because they rely heavily on sophisticated equipment (capital) rather than labor power.

"Soft" energy technologies depend on renewable sources like sun and wind and tend to be labor-intensive in that larger numbers of people are needed to produce a given amount of energy. They are more diverse than "hard" energy technologies and are more directly matched to energy needs. (Solar energy, for example, can be used to heat water without first being converted into electricity.) But the major difference between the two paths, according to Lovins, is that whereas the soft path depends on "pluralistic consumer choice in deploying a myriad of small devices and refinements, the hard path depends on difficult, large-scale projects [e.g., nuclear-power plants and fusion reactors] re-

Throughout history the quest for new sources of energy has been a major stimulus for technological change.

quiring a major social commitment under centralized management" (p. 54). Such projects are characterized by a "remote and . . . uncontrollable technology run by a faraway, bureaucratized, technical elite who have probably never heard of you" (p. 55).

Whether or not one accepts Lovins's thesis, the trend toward greater use of nuclear power to generate electricity has become a major social and political issue, which is shown in the discussion of Three Mile Island in Chapter 10. Underlying the conflict over the safety of nuclear-power plants is the issue of control. In the ancient world those who controlled the irrigation systems were the ruling elite; in the United States the "robber barons" of the late nineteenth century often gained both wealth and political influence from their control of oil and coal supplies. Thus, much of the opposition to nuclear-power plants stems from the recognition that control over energy supplies is a key source of economic and political power.

Technology in Everyday Life

In a review of research on the impact of new technologies on the daily lives of Americans, Claude S. Fischer (1985) found that such research has not kept pace with technological innovation. Even revolutionary innovations like the automobile and the telephone remain poorly understood. Conflicting claims abound. For example, in 1936 Helen and Robert Lynd were told by residents of Middletown that automobile use seemed to be decreasing church attendance and generating conflict within the family. But other studies suggested that the automobile was increasing church attendance, especially among more isolated people who found it easier to get to church on Sunday (Flink, 1980).

Given such gaps in our understanding of the impact of technology on social life, Fischer argued that sociologists should avoid assuming that the effects of innovations are experienced by everyone in more or less the same way. Instead, he and others (e.g., de Sola Pool, 1977; Westrum, 1983) believe that

technologies should be thought of as facilitators of human action rather than as forces that dictate what we do. Often, for example, our uses of technologies do not conform with what their innovators believed possible or desirable. A case in point is the growing incidence of computer crimes and the use of home antenna dishes to tap into satellite video transmissions.

The place of technology in modern societies is a subject of continuing controversy. Key issues include not only the impact of technology on daily life but also the need to control the development and uses of technological innovations so that they benefit all sectors of society. The complex interactions between technology and other aspects of the social order can be seen in the case of medical technology.

SCIENCE, TECHNOLOGY, AND SOCIETY: THE CASE OF MEDICAL TECHNOLOGY

Throughout most of human history, limitations on food production, together with lack of medical knowledge, have placed limits on the size of populations. Dreadful diseases like the bubonic plague have actually reduced populations. In England the plague, known as the Black Death, was responsible for a drastic drop in the population in 1348 and for the lack of population growth in the seventeenth century (see Figure 20-1). In 1625 more than 35,000 residents of London died of the plague. Smallpox and dysentery have had similar, though less dramatic, effects (Wrigley, 1969).

Until relatively recently physicians were powerless either to check the progress of disease or to prolong life. In fact, they often did more harm than good—their remedies were more harmful than the illnesses they were intended to cure. As Lewis Thomas (1979) has stated, "Bleeding, purging, cupping, the administration of infusions of every known plant, solutions of every known metal, every conceivable diet including total fasting, most of these based on the weirdest imaginings about the cause of the disease, concocted out of nothing but thin air—this was the heritage of medicine up until a little over a century ago" (p. 133).

Thomas's point is that before the nineteenth century, when scientists finally began to understand the nature of disease, physicians based their treatments on folklore and superstition. In fact, with few exceptions the practice of healing, like many other aspects of science, was closely linked to religion. In ancient Greece people who suffered from chronic illnesses and physical impairments would journey to the temple of Asclepius, the god of healing, in search of a cure. Even today pilgrims still travel to the cathedral at Lourdes in France in the belief that they may be cured of blindness, paralysis, or leprosy. Not until Louis Pasteur, Robert Koch, and other researchers developed the germ theory of disease did medicine become fully differentiated from religion. Their discoveries, together with progress in internal medicine, pathology, the use of anesthesia, and surgical techniques, led to the twentieth-century concept of medicine as a scientific discipline (Cockerham, 1986).

During the nineteenth century scientific research resulted in the discovery of the causes of many diseases, but at first this progress led physicians to do less for their patients rather than more: They began to allow the body's natural healing processes to work and ceased to engage in damaging procedures like bloodletting. At the same time, they made major strides toward improving public-health practices. They learned about hygiene, sterilization, and other basic principles of public health, especially the need to separate drinking water from waste water. These innovations, which occurred before the development of more sophisticated drugs and medical technologies, contributed to a demographic revolution that is still under way in some parts of the world. Suddenly rates of infant mortality decreased dramatically, births began to outnumber deaths, and life expectancy increased. As discussed in Chapter 5, this change resulted not from the highly sophisticated techniques of modern medicine but largely

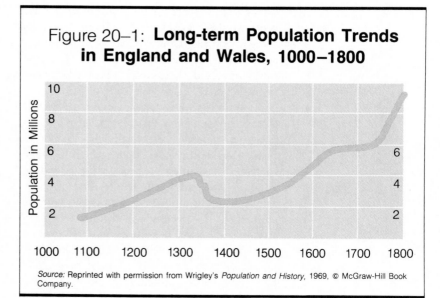

Figure 20–1: **Long-term Population Trends in England and Wales, 1000–1800**

Source: Reprinted with permission from Wrigley's *Population and History*, 1969, © McGraw-Hill Book Company.

from the application of simple sanitation techniques and sterilization procedures (McKinlay and McKinlay, 1977). In fact, these simple technologies have had such a marked effect on infant survival that the rate of infant mortality in a society is often used as a quick measure of its social and economic development (see Figure 20-2).

In sum, as medical science progressed toward greater understanding of the nature of disease and its prevention, new public-health and maternal-care practices contributed to rapid population growth. In the second half of the nineteenth century, such discoveries as antiseptics and anesthesia made possible other life-prolonging medical treatments. In analyzing the effects of these technologies, sociologists ask how people in different social classes gain access to them and how they can be more equitably distributed among the members of a society. The ways in which medical technologies have been institutionalized in hospitals and the medical profession are a central focus of sociological research on these questions.

Improved sanitation techniques and sterilization procedures are largely responsible for the dramatic decreases in infant mortality and increases in life expectancy in the modern era.

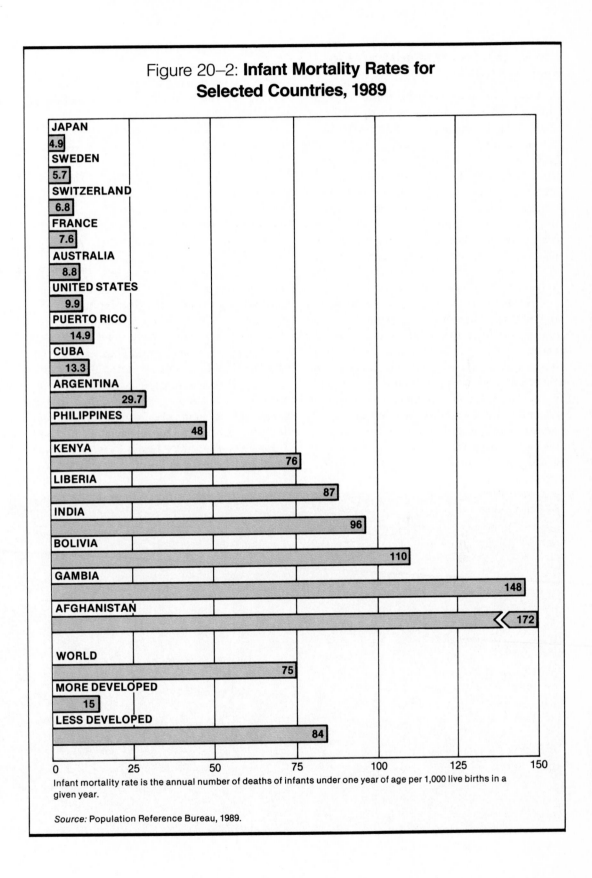

Figure 20–2: **Infant Mortality Rates for Selected Countries, 1989**

JAPAN 4.9
SWEDEN 5.7
SWITZERLAND 6.8
FRANCE 7.6
AUSTRALIA 8.8
UNITED STATES 9.9
PUERTO RICO 14.9
CUBA 13.3
ARGENTINA 29.7
PHILIPPINES 48
KENYA 76
LIBERIA 87
INDIA 96
BOLIVIA 110
GAMBIA 148
AFGHANISTAN 172

WORLD 75
MORE DEVELOPED 15
LESS DEVELOPED 84

Infant mortality rate is the annual number of deaths of infants under one year of age per 1,000 live births in a given year.

Source: Population Reference Bureau, 1989.

The Hospital: From Poorhouse to Healing Institution

In the twentieth century the nature of medicine has changed dramatically as scientific investigation has expanded our knowledge of the causes and cures of disease. That knowledge has led to the development of a vast array of technologies for the prevention and cure of many known illnesses, as well as the long-term care of terminally ill patients. Because the more complex of these technologies are applied in a hospital setting, it is worthwhile to consider the development of the hospital as the major social institution for the delivery of health care.

Historically, hospitals evolved through several stages, beginning as religious centers and eventually developing into centers of medical technology (Cockerham, 1986). The first hospitals were associated with the rise of Christianity; they were community centers for the care of the sick and the poor, providing not only limited medical care but also food, shelter, and prayer. During the Renaissance, hospitals were removed from the jurisdiction of the church and became public facilities.

Because they offered food and shelter to the poor regardless of their health, they soon became crowded with invalids, the aged, orphans, and the mentally ill. The third phase in the development of hospitals began in the seventeenth century, when physicians gained influence over the care of patients in hospitals. Gradually the nonmedical tasks of hospitals disappeared and the hospital took on its present role as an institution for medical care and research.

The modern hospital began to emerge at the end of the nineteenth century as a result of the development of the science of medicine. Especially important were advances in bacteriology and increased knowledge of human physiology, along with the use of ether as an anesthetic. Because the new medical technologies were more complex and often more expensive than earlier forms of treatment, they were centralized in hospitals so that many physicians could use them. Physicians also began to refer patients of all social classes to hospitals, and those pa-

> *Hospitals began as religious centers and eventually developed into centers of medical technology.*

This painting by Jan Beerblock (1739–1806) depicts the sick wards in Sint-Janshospitaal in Bruges, Belgium, a bleak forerunner of modern hospital organization.

tients paid for the services provided to them there.

In the United States the number of hospitals grew rapidly in the twentieth century—from a few hundred at the turn of the century to well over 7,000 in the 1980s. Today hospitals play an important role in the control of medical practice and access to medical care. For example, doctors who want to practice in a particular hospital must be accepted by the hospital's medical board. Patients who want high-quality care in private hospitals must be able to pay the fees charged by those hospitals or have the necessary insurance coverage. And hospitals have a monopoly on advanced medical technologies, a fact that has had a major impact on the American health-care system.

Hypertrophy in Health Care?

Today the technologies available for the diagnosis and treatment of serious illnesses are often described as "miracles of modern medicine." The CT scan, for example, allows hospital technicians to observe a patient's internal organs without the use of X-rays; renal dialysis is used to prevent patients from dying of kidney failure; open-heart surgery is practically a routine operation, with the patient kept alive during the process by an external heart/lung machine; other surgical procedures involve the use of laser beams and fiberoptics to perform delicate operations. All of these technologies require the use of extremely expensive equipment and highly trained personnel.

The development of increasingly sophisticated and costly medical technologies, together with the practice of requiring patients (or their insurance companies) to pay for hospital services, has led to a crisis in American medical care. The high and continually rising cost of medical care has become a major public issue, as has the fact that some groups in the population are unable

The current problems of the health-care system can be traced to the development of narrow medical specialties and a high level of interdependence between physicians and hospitals.

to obtain adequate care. Some critics claim that the American health-care system is suffering from *hypertrophy*, by which they mean that it has developed to a point at which it has become dysfunctional. In their view, excessive emphasis on technological progress has created a situation in which the needs of the patient are subordinated to those of the providers of health care.

According to Paul Starr (1982), the problems of the American health-care system stem from the way in which medical institutions evolved. As medical knowledge increased and technological advances were made, physicians developed narrow specialties and hospitals invested in specialized equipment. The physicians referred their patients to the hospitals for sophisticated medical testing and treatment. At the same time, the institution of health insurance emerged in response to demands for a more equitable distribution of health care. Insurance companies or the government began to pay for the services provided by hospitals. Physicians and hospitals became highly interdependent, so much so that they began to "assert their long-run collective interests over their short-run individual interests" (Starr, 1982, p. 230). Their collective interests involve continued investment in complex technologies, with the result that medical care is becoming more and more expensive. The rising cost of medical care makes it more difficult for the poor, the elderly, and other groups to afford high-quality care and heroic life-preserving measures. But efforts to make health care less costly and more efficient often encounter strong resistance from the medical profession.

Medical Sociology

Starr's study of the evolution of health-care institutions is an example of *medical sociology*. This relatively new field of study has emerged in response to the development of medicine as a major institution of modern societies. Many sociologists are employed by health-care institutions, and some medical schools have established faculty positions for sociologists. These trends are further evidence of the increasing role of sociology in assessing the effects of technological change on other aspects of society.

Medical sociologists use all of the major perspectives that we have discussed in this book. Starr's study shows how conflict over access to medical care influences public policies in the United States. William Goode's (1957, 1960) research on how the structure of the medical profession influences the practice of medicine draws upon the functionalist perspective, and a number of interactionist studies have dealt with the role behavior of physicians and patients. Marcia Millman (1977), for example, found that many doctors are willing to point out colleagues' errors in small-group discussions but will not do so at official meetings because of "a recognition of common interests."

In recent years medical sociologists have faced a new and serious challenge: helping society cope with the ethical issues that arise as it becomes increasingly possible to prolong human life by artificial means. Procedures such as heart transplants are extremely expensive and cannot possibly be made available to all patients who need them. Are they to be limited to those who can pay for them? If not, how should the patients who will benefit from such procedures be chosen? Medical sociologists are frequently asked to conduct research that will affect decisions of this nature—a form of technology assessment.

Another issue that has arisen as a result of advances in medical technology is what exactly constitutes death. Should a person whose brain has stopped functioning be considered dead even if other life functions can be maintained by artifical means? Do patients have a "right to die"—that is, to request that life-sustaining equipment be disconnected if the brain has ceased to function? These are extremely difficult questions, and health-care institutions, whose function is to strive to maintain life whatever the cost, are ill equipped to deal with them. Critics charge that medical technologies simply prolong the dying process, but courts and legislatures have been reluctant to accept the notion of a right to die—a good example of what Ogburn meant by the phrase *cultural lag*.

THE IMPACT OF TECHNOLOGY

Technological Systems

The case of medical technology illustrates once again that technology can be both a blessing and a curse. In recent decades we have become increasingly aware that the problems of human life cannot always be solved by technological means. The "technological fix" can have adverse consequences. In the case of medical technology, vital ethical issues must be addressed. Other technologies, such as nuclear power and chemical plants, can directly threaten human life. As Charles Perrow (1984) writes, "Human-made catastrophes appear to have increased with industrialization as we built devices that could crash, sink, burn, or explode" (p. 11). Perrow also points out that the increasing complexity of modern technology has led to a new kind of catastrophe: the failure of whole systems (i.e., activities and organizational networks as well as apparatus), as in the case of the Three Mile Island accident or the Challenger disaster.

The enormous risks associated with complex technologies have led many observers to call for a more thorough assessment of the potential impact of new technologies before they are put into operation. According to Perrow, it is important to study technological systems in their entirety rather than focusing on individual components of those systems. For example, in the case of Three Mile Island the accident was not a simple matter of a faulty valve but the consequence of a combination of factors—an overworked maintenance staff, equipment failures, ineffective safety precautions, inadequate training, and the unwillingness of scientists and bureaucrats to admit that they might be mistaken. Similar conditions led to

Because of the complexity and danger associated with modern technological systems, it is important to study those systems in their entirety.

the explosion of the Challenger space shuttle in 1986. Once again we are reminded that technology consists not just of apparatus that can malfunction but also of knowledge and skills that may be deficient and of organizational networks that occasionally break down.

Environmental Stress

New technologies often cause new forms of pollution and environmental stress. *Pollution* may be defined as the addition to the environment of agents that are potentially damaging to the welfare of humans or other organisms (Ehrlich, Ehrlich, and Holdren, 1977). *Environmental stress* is a more general term that refers to the effects of society on the natural environment. Pollution is the most common form of environmental stress, but it is not the only one.

One example of environmental stress resulting from technology is the surprising finding that winter fish kills in Wisconsin lakes were caused by snowmobiles. Heavy snowmobile use on a lake compacts the snow, thereby reducing the amount of sunlight filtering through the ice and interfering with photosynthesis by aquatic plants. As the plant life dies, its decomposition further reduces the amount of oxygen in the water. The fish then die of asphyxiation.

The fish–plant–oxygen relationship is a natural ecological system. The snowmobile is a technological innovation with a variety of potential uses. The production, marketing, and use of snowmobiles are elements of a social system. It is this social system that is responsible for the environmental stress resulting from snowmobile use. The land available for snowmobiling is increasingly scarce in an urban society like the United States. Frozen lakes near urban centers thus seem ideal for this purpose, but snowmobiles cause environmental stress in the form of fish kills and thereby create the need for new social controls over the uses of this technology.

Often the need for such controls does

New technologies often result in environmental stress, especially pollution.

not become apparent until a great deal of damage has been done. Nor is it ever entirely clear that new social controls or new technologies can solve the problem at hand. For example, we know how to solve the problem of sulfur emissions from burning coal (which cause the acid rain that destroys forests and lakes), but these solutions are costly and hence are politically controversial. Opinion polls have shown that Americans think not enough is being done to improve and protect the environment. A large majority believe environmental quality is declining. But when faced with the higher tax bills and energy rates required to pay the costs of cleaning up the environment, they often protest (CBS News/New York Times Poll, October 31, 1988).

Studies of the impact and social control of technologies are an increasingly active frontier of sociological research. The Environmental Sociology section of the American Sociological Association routinely publishes research reports that assess the polluting and environmentally stressful impacts of technology. Many such studies have shown that the people who bear the heaviest burden of pollution are most often those who are least able to escape its effects. The poor, minorities, and workers and their families in industrial regions are exposed to higher levels of air, water, and solid-waste pollution than more affluent people (McCaull, 1978). But these studies have also shown that the effects of pollution frequently either are not perceived or are denied by the people who feel them most. For example, a random sample survey on perceptions of pollution in two highly polluted mining and lumbering towns in central Canada (Boldt, Frideres, and Stephens, 1978) found that "half of the total number of respondents interviewed either did not perceive a pollution problem at all, or else regarded it as being of very little importance" (p. 159). The study also found that even among those who did perceive the effects of pollution in the air and water and on the landscape, a huge majority (83–89 percent) were "not prepared to do anything about it" (p. 161).

This is not a surprising finding. People whose livelihoods depend on polluting industries generally learn to tolerate and even ignore the pollution associated with those industries. In fact, when environmental activists protest against the polluting effects of mines and smelters, they often find that their most vocal opponents are those who are most negatively affected by the pollution. In the past twenty years, however, there has been a significant change in attitudes, especially on the part of trade union leaders in polluting industries; such leaders are more likely to press for pollution controls than they were in the past.

In sum, although scientific discoveries and technological advances have produced tremendous improvements in the quality of human life, they have often had negative consequences as well. The risk of cancer caused by the inhalation of asbestos particles, the possibility of large-scale industrial accidents, the ethical issues raised by the use of life-prolonging technologies, and the ever-present danger of nuclear holocaust are as much a part of the modern era as space travel, miracle drugs, and computers that can operate whole factories. Although technology is not "out of control," there is clearly a need for improved procedures for anticipating and preventing the negative consequences of new technologies. Sociologists therefore will increasingly be called upon to participate in efforts to understand and control technological change.

Sulfurous gases and other by-products of industrial production create acidic moisture that pollutes the atmosphere and can be carried far from the source to degrade lakes and forests.

SUMMARY

A hallmark of the modern social order is the conduct of scientific research in universities and other research organizations. *Science* is knowledge obtained as a result of the process of developing and testing hypotheses. Pure science is scientific investigation devoted to the pursuit of knowledge for its own sake. Applied science is the application of known scientific principles to a practical problem.

Technology involves the use of tools and knowledge to manipulate the physical environment to achieve desired practical goals. Technology is much older than science, but the discoveries of modern science are creating new technologies at a rapid rate and have greatly expanded the human capacity to live in and exploit different habitats.

The interactionist approach to the study of scientific institutions focuses on the scientific community or communities, the network of communication and social relationships among scientists. A well-known study based on this perspective found that in many cases scientific researchers do not test and refute existing theories but, rather, assume that they are valid and use them as a *paradigm* for future research. This view of the scientific community implies that science is insulated from the rest of society and that the problems scientists choose to solve are determined by the tradition of research in their field.

The institutional approach to the study of science asks why science develops differently in different societies. In this view, certain conditions encourage the development of scientific institutions. They include recognition of empirical research as a legitimate way of acquiring new knowledge. In addition, science must be independent from other fields. However, scientific institutions are never entirely separate from other institutions because scientific research is often supported by government or industry, a situation that puts pressure on scientists to meet the practical needs of those institutions.

One of the most basic norms of scientific institutions is universalism: The truth of scientific knowledge must be determined by the impersonal criteria of the scientific method. Another norm of science is the common ownership of scientific findings, although such findings sometimes bear the name of the person who first published them. A third norm of scientific institutions is disinterestedness, meaning that scientists do not allow the desire for personal gain to influence the reporting and evaluation of results.

The technologies produced by scientific research are a major force in shaping and changing other institutions. The basic dimensions of technology are physical devices or apparatus, the activities associated with their use, and the organizational networks within which those activities are carried out. The phrase *technological dualism* is sometimes used to refer to the fact that technological changes often have both positive and negative effects.

The importance of technology to human cultural and social evolution has led some sociologists to view technology as a basic principle of social change. They recognize, however, that social institutions are often slow to adapt to changing technologies. This recognition forms the basis of the theory known as *cultural lag*. The time required for social institutions to adapt to technological change can be reduced by the process of *technology assessment*, or efforts to anticipate the consequences of particular technologies for individuals and for society as a whole.

The complex interactions between technology and other aspects of the social order are illustrated by the case of medical technology. Until relatively recently, physicians were powerless either to check the progress of disease or to prolong life. Scientific research led to the discovery of the causes of many diseases during the nineteenth century, but in the twentieth century a vast array of technologies have been developed both for the prevention and cure of illnesses and for the long-term care of terminally ill patients.

The technologies used in the diagnosis and treatment of serious illnesses require extremely expensive equipment and highly trained personnel. This has caused health care to become very expensive, and as a result some groups in the population are unable to obtain adequate care. Some critics claim that extreme emphasis on technological progress has created a situation in which the needs of the patient are subordinated to those of the providers of health care. In recent years medical sociologists have been faced with the challenge of helping society cope with the ethical issues that arise as it becomes increasingly possible to prolong human life by artificial means.

The increasing complexity of modern technology has led to a new kind of catastrophe: the failure of whole systems. The enormous risks associated with complex technologies have led many observers to call for a more thorough assessment of the potential impact of new technologies before they are put into operation. This is especially important from the standpoint of protection of the environment.

GLOSSARY

science: knowledge obtained as a result of the process of developing and testing hypotheses (**p. 628**).

technology: the use of tools and knowledge to manipulate the physical environment in order to achieve desired practical goals (**p. 628**).

paradigm: a general way of seeing the world that dictates what kind of scientific work should be done and what kinds of theory are acceptable (**p. 630**).

cultural lag: the time required for social institutions to adapt to a major technological change (**p. 640**).

technology assessment: efforts to anticipate the consequences of particular technologies for individuals and for society (**p. 641**).

WHERE TO FIND IT

Books

Autonomous Technology (L. Winner; MIT Press, 1977). A fine review of the control-of-technology debate.

The Social Transformation of American Medicine (Paul Starr; Basic Books, 1982). A sociological history that shows why American medical institutions have become increasingly cumbersome and costly.

Jetport (Dorothy Nelkin; Transaction Books, 1974). A good example of a study based on technology assessment and attempts to mitigate the impact of technology on a community.

The Sociology of Science (Robert K. Merton; University of Chicago Press, 1973). An original work by one of the founders of the sociology of science. Extremely useful for concepts and theoretical frameworks.

False Prophets (Alexander Kohn; Basil Blackwell, 1986). A study of dishonesty in the natural sciences and medicine that includes a separate chapter on Lysenko. Raises the question of how widespread scientific fraud may be.

Playing God In Yellowstone (Alston Chase; Atlantic Monthly Press, 1986). A fine analysis of ecological relationships among social institutions and the natural world in a great national park.

Journals

Scientific American This well-known monthly magazine usually includes at least one important article dealing with the impact of new technologies on society.

Bulletin of the Atomic Scientists This famous journal, founded by a coalition of physicists and social scientists, focuses on the control of nuclear energy and weapons.

Journal of Health and Social Behavior A quarterly journal that presents sociological research on problems of human health and illness. Also features articles on change in social institutions and organizations as a consequence of new technologies.

Other Sources

Health, United States, 1988 The thirteenth annual report of the health status of the nation, submitted to Congress by the Secretary of Health and Human Services.

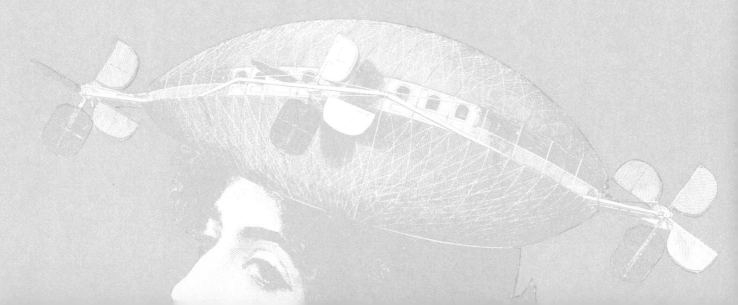

VISUAL SOCIOLOGY

Environimental Concern

These photos illustrate the recent resurgence of environmental concern in North America. They also indicate the importance of collective behavior and social movements in the cause of environmental protection. But what else can one glean from these photos? What does a close look convey to the critical observer?

If one projects oneself into the future and pretends that these photos have been found years later in a box in a closet, what might one say about each image? Take the worker in the yellow protective gear, for example. What is it about this photo that conveys its power? It is a familiar image now, but in the future one might ask why it had such an impact. The juxtaposition of symbols and feelings has a lot to do with what a photo conveys. The yellow garb contrasts starkly with the more natural surroundings. The yellow issues a warning. As the yellow suit becomes associated with environmental damage and the risks of handling hazardous waste, it conveys an ominous feeling. Will it do so in the future? No doubt much depends on the effects of current efforts to control pollution and reverse environmental degradation. The yellow garb, like the ominous and highly symbolic stacks of the nuclear-power plant at Three Mile Island, could fade from memory and lose their symbolic significance, or they could become even more powerful symbols of protest and loss.

The messages conveyed by the written signs in the photos are, at least on the surface, more obvious. They protest pollution or convey a warning: Danger, keep out, we have dangerous pollution here. But are the messages really so obvious? Why, for example, do protestors have to plead, "Give us the warm power of the sun"? Isn't that power given by nature? The implication of the sign is that rather than supporting nuclear energy technology, government and public utilities should invest in solar energy technology. The parents against Diablo—a nuclear-power plant in California—are also emphasizing a symbolic aspect of the environmental movement, the feeling that parents are responsible for protecting the environment in which their children will live.

Interpretations like these may seem obvious, but it is worthwhile to stop and consider what they reveal about the sentiments of participants in a social movement.

JUST GIVE U.S. The WARM POWER Of The SUN

APPENDIX

CAREERS IN SOCIOLOGY

What do you do with a major in sociology? Until fairly recently, the most common career in sociology was that of professor or teacher of sociology. Today there are still more than 15,000 sociologists in academic careers, but other types of careers are also possible. In fact, there has been a dramatic increase in available jobs in what is known as applied sociology. People with sociological training are increasingly being hired by government agencies at all levels, by private firms, and by not-for-profit organizations to apply their knowledge to the practical problems of life in an advanced industrial society. But sociological training does not have to lead to a sociological career. It can be valuable preparation for careers in a wide variety of other professions, including law, business, education, architecture, medicine, social work, politics, and public administration. Whatever the specific occupation, the emphasis will be on understanding human behavior and relationships in different kinds of social settings.

For most careers in sociology, a graduate degree is necessary—a Ph.D. in the case of academic sociology, and an M.A. or Ph.D. for most jobs in applied fields. However, a B.A. in sociology can often be of value in occupations outside of sociology. In addition, at any educational level a sociologist is likely to specialize in a particular area, such as the family, education, health, environmental issues, sex roles, the military, or law enforcement.

Academic Careers

Colleges and universities may place differing amounts of emphasis on teaching and on conducting research. At major universities professors of sociology are expected to devote a significant portion of their time to original research and writing for publication, while at smaller colleges there is more emphasis on teaching. This is not to say that sociologists in the latter institutions do not do research, just that more importance is attached to their teaching.

A professor of sociology at a large university must have a Ph.D. He or she may teach four or five courses a year, including advanced seminars for graduate students. But research and writing are likely to play a greater role in his or her career development. Research projects may be financed by grants from federal or other research agencies, and graduate students may be hired as research assistants using funds from the grant. The professor then can use the project as a means of teaching at the graduate level, while concentrating on publishing scholarly articles and, sometimes, books. The latter are an important element in the university's decision regarding *tenure,* or guaranteed employment, which is generally made during the individual's fifth or sixth year on the faculty.

A sociology instructor in a community college may have an M.A., although many institutions now require a Ph.D. He or she typically does a great deal of teaching, perhaps five courses a semester. Although this teaching load becomes less demanding as courses are repeated, the instructor must continually seek out up-to-date materials and be alert to innovations in teaching techniques. In addition to preparing for courses, he or she is expected to serve on academic and research committees, meet with individual students, and keep abreast of new developments in sociology and related fields.

Another important consideration is that sociologists at colleges and universities not only teach sociology to graduate and undergraduate sociology majors, but also teach students in other disciplines, such as law, education, medicine, social work, and nursing. Almost eight out of ten practicing sociologists are teaching in universities, colleges, and high schools.

Careers in Applied Sociology

Opportunities for sociologists in government, business, and not-for-profit organizations are extremely varied and can be categorized in a number of ways. One approach (Rossi and Whyte, 1983) is to divide applied sociology into three main branches: applied social research, social engineering, and clinical sociology. *Applied social research* is similar in many ways to the basic research conducted at universities, except that it is conducted in order to obtain empirically based knowledge of applied issues. It may take the form of descriptive studies such as victimization surveys, analytical research such as studies of voter preferences, or evaluation research— that is, systematic attempts to estimate the potential effects of a proposed social program or a new approach to management in a business firm. *Social engineering* goes a step further and attempts to use sociological knowledge to design social policies or institutions with a specific purpose. An example is the federally funded preschool program known as Head Start. *Clinical sociology* refers to the use of sociological knowledge in providing assistance to individuals and organizations. A clinical sociologist might, for example, work with a large corporation to find ways of improving employee morale.

To get an idea of the variety of job opportunities in applied sociology, consider the following examples (ASA, 1984a):

Research director in a health center. Sociologists employed by a state-supported health science center teach future physicians, nurses, and other health-care professionals about the sociological aspects of health care. Among other things, they provide data about the population groups served by the center and the distribution of disease and health-care needs in those groups.

Staff researcher in a federal agency. Many sociologists are employed in varied positions by federal agencies. An example is a staff member of a program that administers grants to researchers at universities throughout the country. This involves discussing research plans with applicants and monitoring grants that have been awarded.

Member of the planning staff in a state department of transportation. Opportunities for sociologists in state agencies are also varied. An example is performing long-range forecasting for the transportation department, which entails projecting population shifts in major urban and suburban areas. The sociologist must keep informed about relevant research and prepare frequent reports and analyses based on recent studies.

Staff administrator in a public assistance agency. In local government, a sociologist might serve as program coordinator for a city social-service department. This job would include processing reports and legal forms as well as direct contact with clients of the agency, particularly individuals who are poor, disabled, aged, or members of minority groups. In addition, it would involve helping clients solve personal problems by referring them to other public and private agencies that provide assistance of various kinds.

Staff member of a research institute. A sociologist employed by a private research institute might help carry out studies of specific problems at the request of government agencies, businesses, or political organizations. This could involve developing new research projects (including writing grant proposals) as well as supervising existing ones.

Careers in Other Fields

People with sociological training can be found in occupations that use their training even if they are not specifically referred to as sociologists. For example, a personnel manager in a small manufacturing firm would be considered a business executive rather than a sociologist. But training in industrial sociology and social psychology can be immensely valuable in carrying out the responsibilities of a personnel manager—for instance, in setting strategies and programs for hiring, training, supervising, and promoting employees. Many businesses and other organizations have come to recognize that sociological training is worthwhile for administrators and executives.

Kenneth Donow, a senior adviser to the Public Service Satellite Consortium in Washington, D.C., is an example of a sociologist who has made a successful transition from an academic career to a career in business. Although his training was geared toward a university position, Donow's interest in communications and information policy steered him toward the business world. He was hired by a consulting firm to analyze the worldwide semiconductor industry. It soon became clear to him that business analysis involves the study of formal organizations and social networks, something for which sociologists are ideally suited. He was able to convince other business clients to incorporate sociological approaches into their operations and notes that today "sociological practice has become fully integrated into the largest U.S. corporations" (1990, p. 6). Donow believes that people with sociological training will be increasingly sought by American businesses during the next few decades.

There are many other areas in which sociological training is viewed as appropriate preparation for employment. A publication of the American Sociological Association (1984b) lists the following positions among those that can be obtained with an undergraduate degree in sociology: interviewer, research assistant, recreation worker, group worker, teacher (if certified), administrative assistant, probation and parole worker, career counselor, community planner, editorial assistant, social worker (not certified), and statistical assistant. A graduate degree can also be useful outside of sociology. For example, if you seek a career in a particular industry or field—such as transportation—participating in original research in that field as part of a graduate degree program can provide a means of entering the field with the help of individuals who notice and respect your work.

Employment Prospects for the 1990s

As noted earlier, the majority of practicing sociologists are in teaching positions, and in the 1990s the demand for teachers is expected to increase somewhat. At the same time, there will be more career opportunities in industry and government. Data collected by Ronald Manderscheid and Matthew Greenwald (1983) indicate that in the 1990s approximately 15,000 sociologists will be employed in academic settings, only slightly above the 1980 level. Meanwhile, there will be more than 3000 positions in applied sociology in the public sector, compared to 1,806 in 1980; the greatest growth in this sector is expected to occur in state government. In the private sector, employment in medical and health-care services is expected to increase by more than 400 positions, or 50 percent greater than the 1980 level.

A study of the specific types of jobs held by recipients of M.A. and Ph.D. degrees in sociology (Huber, 1984) found that close to half the M.A.s and one-third of the Ph.D.s are employed by government agencies. About one-third of the Ph.D.s are employed by not-for-profit organizations, as are about one-fourth of the M.A.s. About one-fifth of each group is employed in the private sector. The study also revealed some differences between the work settings of M.A.s and Ph.D.s. In not-for-profit organizations, Ph.D.s predominate in research institutes and M.A.s in health-care services and community welfare programs. In the federal government, Ph.D.s are more frequently employed by divisions of the Public Health Service, while M.A.s are relatively more numerous in the Department of Defense.

Preparing for a Career in Sociology

A bachelor's degree in sociology provides excellent preparation for either graduate study or employment. However, few employers look specifically for sociology B.A.s in preference to other liberal arts degrees. To enhance the value of a B.A. in sociology relative to degrees in other fields, it is advisable to emphasize courses in research methods and statistics.

A graduate degree is necessary to become a practicing sociologist. It is required for any career in academic sociology and for most careers in applied sociology. An M.A. or M.S. is sufficient for teaching in high schools or two-year colleges or for employment in public agencies and private firms. A Ph.D. is usually necessary for teaching and research in universities and for high level positions in research institutes, private industry, and government agencies.

The Ph.D. generally requires four or five years of study, often including the completion of an M.A. In many graduate schools, work is available as part of the learning experience; the graduate student may be employed as a teaching assistant (TA) or research assistant (RA). A TA typically grades exams, meets with students who need extra help, and leads discussion sections. As noted earlier, RAs are generally hired by faculty members who have received grants for specific research projects.

Most graduate degree programs begin with courses on basic theoretical issues, research methods, and statistics. After a year of such courses the student may take an examination and perhaps be awarded the Master's degree. Subsequently the emphasis shifts from course work to actual research. In this phase the student is exposed to a wide variety of research methods, including computer skills, in-depth interviewing, participant observation, and use of census materials, questionnaires, and surveys. This is followed by a set of Ph.D. examinations, which may be written or oral, and then by the writing of a dissertation. The dissertation must be an original piece of scholarship. Usually it entails submitting a formal proposal to a committee of faculty advisers, who also preside over the student's oral defense of the dissertation when it is completed.

More than 130 universities in the United States offer a Ph.D. in sociology, and most of them also offer an M.A. or M.S. More than 150 other schools offer only an M.A. Some graduate programs are designed specifically to prepare students for nonacademic careers in business or government. They may, for example, substitute internships in agency offices for the traditional TA or RA experience.

Applicants to graduate sociology programs do not have to have an undergraduate major in sociology, but the requirements of graduate departments differ considerably in such areas as foreign-language skills and statistics courses. Many departments require applicants to take the Graduate Record Examinations (GRE) and have scores available by the beginning of the calendar year. This is particularly important for financial-aid decisions. Letters of recommendation can greatly influence the decisions of graduate admissions committees.

The reputation of the institution from which an individual receives a graduate degree can have a significant effect on career opportunities. In addition, graduate departments differ in the quality of their programs in various specialties, such as criminology, demography, the study of the family, and so on. The prospective degree candidate should pay careful attention to the department's reputation in specific areas as well as the reputation of the college or university itself. And, of course, it is a good idea to apply to several graduate programs.

To aid students in choosing a graduate program in sociology, the American Sociological Association issues an annual publication entitled *Guide to Graduate Departments of Sociology*. This guide contains information about more than 200 degree programs in the United States and Canada, including degrees awarded, names and specialties of faculty members, special programs, tuition and fees, availability of fellowships and assistantships, deadlines for applications, and how to obtain further information and application forms. The guide is available in college libraries or can be ordered from the American Sociological Association, 1722 N Street N.W., Washington, D.C. 20036.

REFERENCES

American Sociological Association (1984a). *Careers in Sociology*. Washington, D.C.

———— (1984b). *Majoring in Sociology: A Guide for Students*. Washington, D.C.

Donow, Kenneth R. (1990, April). On the transition from the academy to a career in business. *Footnotes* (American Sociological Association), p. 6.

Huber, Bettina J. (1984). *Career Possibilities for Sociology Graduates*. Washington, D.C.: American Sociological Association.

Manderscheid, Ronald W., and Greenwald, Matthew (1983). Trends in Employment of Sociologists. In Howard E. Freeman, Russell R. Dynes, Peter H. Rossi, and William Foote Whyte (eds.), *Applied Sociology*. San Francisco: Jossey-Bass.

    Rossi, Peter H., and Whyte, William Foote (1983). The Applied Side of Sociology. In Howard E. Freeman, Russell R. Dynes, Peter H. Rossi, and William Foote Whyte (eds.), *Applied Sociology*. San Francisco: Jossey-Bass.

REFERENCES

Abbeglen, J. C. (1955). *The Japanese factory*. New York: Free Press.

Addams, J. (1895). *Hull House maps and papers*. New York: Crowell.

Adler, M. (1979). *Drawing down the moon: Witches, druids, goddess-worshippers, and other pagans in America today*. Boston: Beacon.

Adriance, M. (1985). Opting for the poor: A social-historical analysis of the changing Brazilian Catholic church. *Sociological Analysis, 46*, 131–146.

Aganbegyan, A. (1989). *Perestroika 1989*. New York: Scribner's.

Aldous, J. (1982). From dual-earner to dual-career families and back again. In J. Aldous (ed.), *Two paychecks: Life in dual-career families*. Newbury Park, CA: Sage.

Alland, A. (1973). *Human diversity*. Garden City, NY: Doubleday.

Allen, F. L. (1931). *Only yesterday: An informal history of the 1920s*. New York: Harper.

Allen, W. S. (1965). *The Nazi seizure of power: The experience of a single German town*. London: Eyre and Spottiswoode.

Altman, D. (1987). *AIDS in the mind of America*. Garden City, NY: Doubleday.

Amory, C. (1960). *Who killed society?* New York: Harper.

Ann Arbor Science for the People Editorial Collective (1977). *Biology as a social weapon*. Minneapolis: Burgess.

Appelbaum, R. P. (1970). *Theories of social change*. Chicago: Rand McNally.

Apter, D. (1980). *Ghana in transition* (rev. ed.). Princeton, NJ: Princeton University Press.

Archibald, K. (1947). *Wartime shipyard*. Berkeley: University of California Press.

Ariès, P. (1962). *Centuries of childhood*. New York: Vintage.

Aronowitz, S. (1984). *Working class hero*. New York: Schocken.

Aronowitz, S., & Giroux, H. A. (1985). *Education under siege*. South Hadley, MA: Bergin and Garvey.

Asch, S. E. (1966). Effects of group pressure under the modification and distortion of judgments. In H. Proshansky & B. Seidenberg (eds.), *Basic studies in social psychology*. Fort Worth, TX: Holt, Rinehart and Winston.

Ash, T. G. (1989). *The uses of adversity*. New York: Random House.

Ash, T. G. (1990, January 18). The revolution of the Magic Lantern. *New York Review of Books*, p. 42.

Asimov, I. (1966). *Foundation*. New York: Avon Books.

Aspaklaria, S. (1985, September 12). A divorced father, a child, and a summer visit together. *New York Times*, p. C1.

Atchley, R. (1980). *The social forces in later life: An introduction to social gerontology* (3rd ed.). Belmont, CA: Wadsworth.

Attwood, L. (1985). The new Soviet man and woman—Soviet views on psychological sex differences. In B. Holland (ed.), *Soviet sisterhood*. Bloomington: Indiana University Press.

Auletta, K. (1982). *The underclass*. New York: Random House.

Backer, B. (1982). *Death and dying: Individuals and institutions*. New York: Wiley.

Bakke, E. W. (1933). *The unemployed man*. London: Nisbet.

Balandier, A. (1971/1890). *The delight makers*. Orlando: Harcourt Brace Jovanovich.

Balbus, I. (1978). Commodity form and legal form: An essay on the relative autonomy of the law. In C. E. Reasons & R. M. Rich (eds.), *Sociology of law: A conflict perspective*. Toronto: Butterworths.

Balch, E. G. (1910). *Our Slavic fellow citizens*. New York: Charities Publication Committee.

Bales, R. F., & Slater, P. E. (1955). Role differentiation in small decision-making groups. In T. Parsons & R. F. Bales (eds.), *Family, socialization, and interaction process*. New York: Free Press.

Baltzell, D. (ed.) (1968). *The search for community in urban America*. New York: Harper.

Bane, M. J. (1976). *Here to stay: American families in the twentieth century*. New York: Basic Books.

Bane, M. J., & Ellwood, D. (1983). *The dynamics of dependence: The routes to self sufficiency*. Report to the U.S. Department of Health and Human Services. Washington, DC: U.S. Government Printing Office.

Barash, D. P. (1977). *Sociobiology and behavior*. New York: Elsevier.

Barnet, R. J. (1980). *The lean years*. New York: Simon & Schuster.

Baron, J. N., & Bielby, W. T. (1980). Bringing the firms back in: Stratification, segmentation and the organization of work. *American Sociological Review, 45*, 737–765.

Barringer, F. (1989, June 9). Divorce data stir doubt on trial marriage. *New York Times*, pp. A1, A28.

Bassuk, E. L. (1984, July). The homelessness problem. *Scientific American*, 40–45.

Bates, F. L., & Murray, V. K. (1975). The school as a behavior system. *Journal of Research and Development in Education, 2*, 23–33.

Baum, S. (1987). *Financial aid to low-income college students: Its history and prospects*. Institute for Research on Poverty discussion paper no. 846-87. Madison: University of Wisconsin.

Bayer, R. (1988). *Private acts, social consequences:*

AIDS and the politics of public health. New York: Free Press.

Bayh, B. (1975). *Our nation's schools—A report card: "A" in school violence and vandalism*. Washington, DC: U.S. Government Printing Office.

Becker, G. S. (1973). A theory of marriage. In T. W. Schultz (ed.), *Economics of the family: Marriage, children, and human capital*. Chicago: University of Chicago Press.

Becker, G. S. (1977). The economics of marital instability. *Journal of Political Economy, 84,* 1141–1187.

Becker, H. J. (1984, June). *School uses of microcomputers*. Baltimore: Johns Hopkins University, Center for Social Organization of Schools.

Becker, H. S. (1961). *Boys in white: Student culture in medical school*. Chicago: University of Chicago Press.

Becker, H. S. (1963). *The outsiders: Studies in the sociology of deviance*. New York: Free Press.

Becker, H. S., & Strauss, A. L. (1956). Careers, personality, and adult socialization. *American Journal of Sociology, 62,* 253–263.

Beer, F. A. (1981). *Peace against war: The ecology of international violence*. San Francisco: Freeman.

Beijer, G. J. (1969). Modern patterns of international migratory movement. In J. Jackson (ed.), *Migration*. Cambridge, England: Cambridge University Press.

Bell, C., & Newby, H. (1974). *Community studies*. New York: Praeger.

Bell, D. (1962). *The end of ideology*. New York: Free Press.

Bell, D. (1973). *The coming of post industrial society: A venture in social forecasting*. New York: Basic Books.

Bellah, R. N. (1970). *Beyond belief*. New York: Harper.

Bellah, R. N., Madison, R., Sullivan, W. M., Swidler, A., & Tipton, S. M. (1985). *Habits of the heart: Individualism and commitment in American life*. Berkeley: University of California Press.

Ben-David, J. (1984). *The scientist's role in society: A comparative study*. Chicago: University of Chicago Press.

Bendix, R. (1969). *Nation-building and citizenship*. Garden City, NY: Doubleday.

Bendix, R. (1974). *Work and authority in industry*. Berkeley: University of California Press.

Bendix, R., & Lipset, S. M. (1966). *Class, status, and power: Social stratification in comparative perspective* (2nd ed.). New York: Free Press.

Bengston, V. L., Cutler, N. E., Mangen, D. J., & Marshall, V. W. (1985). Generations, cohorts, and relations between age groups. In R. H. Binstock & E. Shanas (eds.), *Handbook of aging and the social sciences* (2nd ed.). New York: Van Nostrand Reinhold.

Bennett, M. K. (1954). *The world's food*. New York: Harper.

Benokraitis, N. V., & Feagin, J. R. (1986). *Modern sexism: Blatant, subtle, and covert discrimination*. Englewood Cliffs, NJ: Prentice-Hall.

Bensman, D., & Lynch, R. (1987). *Rusted dreams: Hard times in a steel community*. New York: McGraw-Hill.

Bentham, J. (1789). *An introduction to the principles of morals and legislation*. London: T. Payne.

Bentham, J. (1864). *Theory of legislation*. London: Trubner.

Berger, B. (1961). The myth of suburbia. *Journal of Social Issues, 17,* 38–48.

Berger, G. (1968). *Working class suburb: A study of auto workers in suburbia*. Berkeley: University of California Press.

Bernard, J. (1964). *Academic women*. University Park: Pennsylvania State University Press.

Bernard, J. (1973). *The sociology of community*. Glenview, IL: Scott, Foresman.

Bernstein, R. (1988, August 30). Sociology branches out but is left in splinters. *New York Times*, p. A14.

Berrueta-Clement, J. R., Schweinhart, L. J., Barnett, W. S., Epstein, A. S., & Weikart, D. P. (1984). *Changed lives: The effects of the Perry preschool program on youths through age 19*. Ypsilanti, MI: High/Scope Press.

Berry, B. (1978). Latent structure of urban systems: Research methods and findings. In L. S. Bourne & J. W. Simmons (eds.), *Systems of cities: Readings on structure, growth, and policy*. New York: Oxford University Press.

Bettelheim, B. (1943). Individual and mass behavior in extreme situations. *Journal of Abnormal and Social Psychology, 38,* 417–452.

Bettelheim, B. (1959). Feral children and autistic children. *American Journal of Sociology, 64,* 455–467.

Bettelheim, B. (1962, Winter). The problem of generations. *Daedalus*, pp. 68–96.

Bianchi, S. M., & Spain, D. (1986). *American women in transition*. New York: Russell Sage.

Bierstedt, R. (1963). *The social order*. New York: McGraw-Hill.

Birdwhistell, R. (1970). *Kinesics and context: Essays on body motion and communication*. Philadelphia: University of Pennsylvania Press.

Black, D. (ed.) (1984). *Toward a general theory of social control*. Orlando: Academic Press.

Blair, F. E. (ed.) (1989). *Countries of the world and their leaders yearbook 1989*. Detroit: Gale.

Blau, P. (1964). *Exchange and power in social life*. New York: Wiley.

Blau, P., & Duncan, O. D. (1967). *The American occupational structure*. New York: Wiley.

Blau, P., & Meyer, M. (1971). *Bureaucracy in modern society*. New York: Random House.

Blauner, R. (1964). *Alienation and freedom*. Chicago: University of Chicago Press.

Blauner, R. (1969). Internal colonialism and ghetto revolt. *Social Problems, 16,* 393–408.

Blauner, R. (1972). *Racial oppression in America*. New York: Harper.

Bleier, R. (1984). *Science and gender: A critique of biology and its theories on women*. New York: Pergamon.

Bloch, M. (1964). *Feudal society* (Vol. 1). Chicago: University of Chicago Press.

Bloom, B. S. (1976). *Human characteristics and school learning*. New York: McGraw-Hill.

Blumer, H. (1969). Elementary collective groupings. In A. M. Lee (ed.), *Principles of sociology* (3rd ed.). New York: Barnes & Noble.

Blumer, H. (1969). *Symbolic interactionism*. Englewood Cliffs, NJ: Prentice-Hall.

Blumer, H. (1978). Elementary collective behavior. In L. E. Genevie (ed.), *Collective behavior and social movements*. Itasca, IL: Peacock.

Blumstein, P., & Schwartz, P. (1983). *American couples: Money, work, sex*. New York: Morrow.

Boggs, V., & Kornblum, W. (1985, January–

February). Symbiosis in the city: The human ecology of Times Square. *The Sciences*, pp. 24–30.

Boggs, V. W., & Meyersohn, R. (1988). The profile of a Bronx salsero: Salsa's still alive! *Journal of Popular Music and Society, 11*, 7–14.

Bogue, D. J. (1969). *Principles of demography*. New York: Wiley.

Bogue, D. J. (1985). *The population of the United States: Historical trends and future projections*. New York: Free Press.

Bohannon, L., & Bohannon, P. (1953). *The Tiv of central Nigeria*. London: International African Institute.

Bohannon, L., & Bohannon, P. (1962). *Markets in Africa*. Evanston, IL: Northwestern University Press.

Boldt, E. D., Frideres, J. S., & Stephens, J. J. (1978). Perception of pollution and willingness to act. In W. R. Burch (ed.), *Readings in ecology, energy, and human society*. New York: Harper.

Bonacich, E. (1972). A theory of ethnic antagonism: The split labor market. *American Sociological Review, 37*, 547–559.

Bonacich, E. (1976). Advanced capitalism and black/white race relations in the United States: A split labor market interpretation. *American Sociological Review, 41*, 34–51.

Bonnett, A. W. (1981). *Institutional adaptation of West Indian immigrants to America*. Lanham, MD: University Press of America.

Boocock, S. S. (1980). *Sociology of education: An introduction* (2nd ed.). Boston: Houghton Mifflin.

Booth, A., & Edwards, J. N. (1985, February). Age at marriage and marital instability. *Journal of Marriage and the Family*, pp. 67–75.

Borganokar, D., & Shah, S. (1974). *The XYY chromosome male. Progress in Medical Genetics, 10*, 135–222.

Bose, C. E., & Rossi, P. H. (1983). Gender and jobs. *American Sociological Review, 48*, 316–330.

Bosk, C. (1979). *Forgive and remember: Managing medical failure*. Chicago: University of Chicago Press.

Bott, E. (1977). Urban families: Conjugal roles and social networks. In S. Leinhardt (ed.), *Social networks: A developing paradigm*. Orlando: Academic Press.

Bowles, S., & Gintis, H. (1977). *Schooling in capitalist America*. New York: Basic Books.

Bracey, J. H., Meier, A., & Rudwick, E. (1970). *Black nationalism in America*. Indianapolis: Bobbs-Merrill.

Brake, M. (1980). *The sociology of youth cultures and youth subcultures*. London: Routledge and Kegan Paul.

Braudel, F. (1976). *The Mediterranean and the Mediterranean world in the age of Philip II*. New York: Harper.

Braudel, F. (1984). *The perspective of the world: Vol. 3. Civilizations and capitalism: 15th–18th century*. New York: Harper.

Braverman, H. (1974). *Labor and monopoly capital*. New York: Monthly Review Press.

Breese, G. (1966). *Urbanization in newly developing countries*. Englewood Cliffs, NJ: Prentice-Hall.

Brinton, M. (1989). Gender stratification in contemporary urban Japan. *American Sociological Review, 54*, 549–565.

Broad, W. J. (1988, May 24). As science moves into commerce, openness is lost. *New York Times*, pp. C1, C6.

Brody, D. (1960). *Steelworkers in America: The non-union era*. Cambridge, MA: Harvard University Press.

Bronfenbrenner, U. (1970). *Two worlds of childhood, U.S. and U.S.S.R.* New York: Russell Sage.

Bronfenbrenner, U. (1981). Children and families. *Society, 18*, 38–41.

Brotman, H. B. (1982). *Every ninth American*. Washington, DC: U.S. Government Printing Office.

Brown, C. (1966). *Manchild in the promised land*. New York: Macmillan.

Brown, D. (1970). *Bury my heart at Wounded Knee*. New York: Washington Square Press.

Brown, L. R., Durning, A., Flavin, C., Heise, L., Jacobson, J., Postel, S., Renner, M., Shea, C. P., & Starke, L. (1989). *State of the world 1989: A Worldwatch Institute report on progress toward a sustainable society*. New York: Norton.

Brown, L. R., & Jacobson, J. (1987). Assessing the future of urbanization. In L. R. Brown et al. (eds.), *State of the world 1987: A Worldwatch Institute report on progress toward a sustainable society*. New York: Norton.

Brown, L. R., Wolf, E., Starke, L., Chandler, W. U., Flavin, C., & Postel, S. (1984). *State of the world 1984: A Worldwatch Institute report on progress toward a sustainable society*. New York: Norton.

Brown, R. (1965). *Social psychology*. New York: Free Press.

Browne, S. (1971). *Encyclopedia of education* (Vol. 8). New York: Macmillan.

Brubaker, E. R. (1975). Free ride, free revelation, or golden rule? *Journal of Law and Economics, 18*, 147–161.

Brundtland, G. H. (1989, September). How to secure our common future. *Scientific American*, p. 190.

Buckley, M. (1985). Soviet interpretation of the woman question. In B. Holland (ed.), *Soviet sisterhood*. Bloomington: Indiana University Press.

Bumpass, L., & Sweet, J. (1972). Differentials in marital instability: 1970. *American Sociological Review, 37*, 754–766.

Burch, W. (1971). *Daydreams and nightmares: A sociological essay on the American environment*. New York: Harper.

Burgess, E. W. (1925). The growth of the city: An introduction to a research project. In R. E. Park & E. W. Burgess, *The city*. Chicago: University of Chicago Press.

Burawoy, M. (1980). *Manufacturing consent*. Chicago: University of Chicago Press.

Buruma, I. (1984). *Behind the mask: On sexual demons, sacred mothers, transvestites, gangsters, drifters and other Japanese cultural heroes*. New York: Pantheon.

Bury, J. B. (1932). *The idea of progress: An inquiry into its origin and growth*. New York: Dover.

Butler, R. (1989). Dispelling ageism: The cross-cutting intervention. *Annals of the American Academy of Political and Social Science, 503*, 138–148.

Butterfield, F. (1987, November 13). Hite's new book is under rising attack. *New York Times*, p. B4.

Cain, L. D. (1964). Life course and social structure. In R. F. Faris (ed.), *Handbook of modern sociology*. Chicago: Rand McNally.

Cameron, W. B. (1966). *Modern social movements: A sociological outline*. New York: Random House.

Cancian, F. (1987). *Love in America: Gender and self*

development. New York: Cambridge University Press.

Cantril, H., with Gaudet, H., & Herzog, J. (1982). *The invasion from Mars*. Princeton, NJ: Princeton University Press.

Caplan, A. L. (1978). *The sociobiology debate: Readings on ethical and scientific issues*. New York: Harper.

Caplow, T. (1969). *Two against one: Coalition in triads*. Englewood Cliffs, NJ: Prentice-Hall.

Caplow, T., Bahr, H. M., Chadwick, B. A., Hill, R., & Williamson, M. H. (1983). *Middletown families: Fifty years of change and continuity*. New York: Bantam.

Carter, L. J. (1975). *The Florida experience*. Baltimore: Johns Hopkins University Press.

Catton, W. R., Jr. (1980). *Overshoot: The ecological basis of revolutionary change*. Urbana: University of Illinois Press.

Caudill, H. M. (1976). *The watches of the night*. Boston: Little, Brown.

Census Bureau, U.S. Department of Commerce (1986, October). *World Population Profile: 1985*. Washington, DC: U.S. Government Printing Office.

Census Bureau, U.S. Department of Commerce (1987, November). Household and family characteristics, March 1986. *Current Population Reports* (Series P-20, No. 419). Washington, DC: U.S. Government Printing Office.

Census Bureau, U.S. Department of Commerce (1988). Educational attainment in the United States: March 1987 and 1986. *Current Population Reports* (Series P-20, No. 428). Washington, D.C.: U.S. Government Printing Office.

Census Bureau, U.S. Department of Commerce (1989). Money income and poverty status in the United States: 1988. *Current Population Reports* (Series P-60, No. 166). Washington, D.C.: U.S. Government Printing Office.

Chambliss, W. J. (1973, December). The Saints and the Roughnecks. *Society*, pp. 23–31.

Charlton, M. (1985). *The eagle and the small birds: Crisis in the Soviet empire from Yalta to Solidarity*. Chicago: University of Chicago Press.

Chernin, K. (1981). *The obsession: Reflections on the tyranny of slenderness*. New York: Harper.

Chodorow, N. (1974). *The reproduction of mothering: Psychoanalysis and the sociology of gender*. Berkeley: University of California Press.

Chomsky, N. (1965). *Aspects of the theory of syntax*. Cambridge, MA: M.I.T. Press.

Chwast, J. (1965). Value conflicts in law enforcement. *Crime and Delinquency*, 2, 151–161.

Clark, W. C. (1989, September). Managing planet Earth. *Scientific American*, pp. 46–54.

Clarke, L. (1989). *Acceptable risk? Making decisions in a toxic environment*. Berkeley: University of California Press.

Clausen, J. A. (1968). *Socialization and society*. Boston: Little, Brown.

Clemmer, D. (1958). *The prison community*. Fort Worth, TX: Holt, Rinehart and Winston.

Cloward, R., & Ohlin, L. (1960). *Delinquency and opportunity: A theory of delinquent gangs*. New York: Free Press.

Cockerham, W. C. (1986). *Medical sociology* (3rd ed.). Englewood Cliffs, NJ: Prentice-Hall.

Cohen, N. (1961). *The pursuit of the millennium*. New York: Harper.

Cohen, R. S. (1982). Science and technology in global perspective. *International Social Sciences Journal*, 34, 61–70.

Colby, A., & Damon, W. (1983). Listening to a different voice: A review of Gilligan's "In a different voice." *Merrill-Palmer Quarterly*, 29, 473–481.

Coleman, J. S. (1961). *The adolescent society*. New York: Free Press.

Coleman, J. S. (1964). Research chronicle: The adolescent society. In P. E. Hammond (ed.), *Sociologists at work*. Garden City, NY: Doubleday.

Coleman, J. S. (1976). Liberty and equality in school desegregation. *School Policy*, 6, 9–13.

Coleman, J. S. (1982). *The asymmetric society*. Syracuse, NY: Syracuse University Press.

Coleman, J. S. (1986, May). Social theory, social research, and a theory of action. *American Journal of Sociology*, 91, 1309–1335.

Coles, R. (1986). *The moral life of children*. Boston: Atlantic Monthly Press.

Collins, R. (1975). *Conflict sociology: Toward an explanatory science*. Orlando: Academic Press.

Comer, J. P. (1980). *School power*. New York: Free Press.

Comer, J. P. (1984). Home-school relationships as they affect the academic success of children. *Education and Urban Society*, 16, 323–327.

Comer, J. P. (1985). *Investing in our children*. New York: Committee for Economic Development.

Comer, J. P. (1987). *Children in need: Investment strategies for the educationally disadvantaged*. New York: Committee for Economic Development.

Comte, A. (1971). The positive philosophy. In M. Truzzi (ed.), *Sociology: The classic statements*. New York: Random House.

Cookson, P. W., & Persell, C. H. (1985). *Preparing for power: America's elite boarding schools*. New York: Basic Books.

Cooley, C. H. (1909). *Social organization: A study of the large mind*. New York: Scribner.

Cooley, C. H. (1956/1902). *Human nature and the social order*. New York: Free Press.

Coon, C. (1962). *The origin of races*. New York: Knopf.

Coser, L. A. (1966). *The functions of social conflict*. New York: Free Press.

Cott, N. F. (1987). *The grounding of modern feminism*. New Haven, CT: Yale University Press.

Cottrell, W. F. (1951). Death by dieselization: A case study in the reaction to technological change. *American Sociological Review*, 16, 358–365.

Cranz, G. (1982). *The politics of park design: A history of urban parks in America*. Cambridge, MA: M.I.T. Press.

Crapanzano, V. (1985, March 25). A reporter at large: South Africa II. *New Yorker*, pp. 52–97.

Cremin, L. A. (1980). *American education: The national experience 1783–1876*. New York: Harper.

Cressey, D. R. (1971/1953). *Other people's money: A study in the social psychology of embezzlement*. Belmont, CA: Wadsworth.

Crowder, M. (1966). *A short history of Nigeria* (rev. ed.). New York: Praeger.

Cuber, J. F., & Haroff, P. B. (1980). Five types of marriage. In A. Skolnick & J. Skolnick (eds.), *Family in transition*. Boston: Little, Brown.

Cumming, E., & Henry, W. (1971). *Growing old: The process of disengagement*. New York: Basic Books.

Cummings, J. (1983, November 20). Breakup of black family imperils gains of decades. *New York Times*, p. 56.

Curtis, L. A. (ed.) (1985). *American violence and public policy*. New Haven, CT: Yale University Press.

Czikszentmihalyi, M., Larson, R., & Prescott, S. (1977). The ecology of adolescent activity and experience. *Journal of Youth and Adolescence, 6,* 281–294.

Dahl, R. (1961). *Who governs?* New Haven, CT: Yale University Press.

Dahrendorf, R. (1959). *Class and class conflict in industrial society*. Stanford, CA: Stanford University Press.

Dahrendorf, R. (1981). *Life chances*. Chicago: University of Chicago Press/Phoenix.

D'Andrade, R. G. (1966). Sex differences and cultural institutions. In E. E. Maccoby (ed.), *The development of sex differences*. Stanford, CA: Stanford University Press.

Dankert, C. E., Mann, F. C., & Northrup, H. R. (eds.) (1965). *Hours of work*. New York: Harper.

Danziger, K. (1971). *Socialization*. Harmondsworth, England: Penguin.

Davidson, D. (1973). The furious passage of the black graduate student. In J. Ladner (ed.), *The death of white sociology*. New York: Vintage.

Davis, F. J. (1978). *Minority-dominant relations: A sociological analysis*. Arlington Heights, IL: AHM.

Davis, K. (1939). Illegitimacy and the social structures. *American Journal of Sociology, 45,* 215–233.

Davis, K. (1947). Final note on a case of extreme isolation. *American Journal of Sociology, 45,* 215–233.

Davis, K. (1949). *Human society*. New York: Macmillan.

Davis, K. (1955). The origin and growth of urbanization in the world. *American Journal of Sociology, 60,* 429–437.

Davis, K. (1968). The urbanization of the human population. In S. F. Fava (ed.), *Urbanism in world perspective: A reader*. New York: Crowell.

Davis, K., & Moore, W. E. (1945). Some principles of stratification. *American Sociological Review, 10,* 242–249.

Davis, N. J. (1975). *Deviance: Perspectives and issues in the field*. Dubuque, IA: William C. Brown.

Dawson, C. A., & Gettys, W. E. (1935). *Introduction to sociology*. New York: Ronald.

de Beauvoir, S. (1959). *Memoirs of a dutiful daughter*. New York: Harper.

de Beauvoir, S. (1961). *The second sex*. New York: Bantam.

de Beauvoir, S. (1973). *The coming of age*. New York: Warner.

Demos, J. (1978). Old age in early New England. *American Journal of Sociology, 84,* s248–s287.

Denitch, B. (1989). *The end of the cold war*. Minneapolis: University of Minnesota Press.

de Rougemont, D. (1983). *Love in the western world*. Princeton, NJ: Princeton University Press.

de Sola Pool, I. (ed.) (1977). *The social impact of the telephone*. Cambridge, MA: M.I.T. Press.

de Sola Pool, I. (1983). *Technologies of freedom*. Cambridge, MA: Belknap Press.

de Tocqueville, A. (1955/1856). *The old regime and the French revolution* (Stuart Gilbert, trans.). Garden City, NY: Doubleday.

de Tocqueville, A. (1956/1840). *Democracy in America*. New York: Vintage.

de Tocqueville, A. (1980/1835). *On democracy, revolution, and society* (J. Stone & S. Mennell, trans.). Chicago: University of Chicago Press.

Dewey, R. (1948). Charles Horton Cooley: Pioneer in psychosociology. In H. F. Barnes (ed.), *An introduction to the history of sociology*. Chicago: University of Chicago Press.

Djilas, M. (1982). *The new class: An analysis of the communist system*. Orlando: Harcourt Brace Jovanovich.

Dobriner, W. M. (1973). The natural history of a reluctant suburb. In J. Kramer (ed.), *North American suburbs: Politics, diversity and change*. Berkeley, CA: Glendessary Press.

Dobzhansky, T. (1962). *Mankind evolving*. New Haven, CT: Yale University Press.

Dodgson, R. A. (1987). *The European past: Social evolution and spatial order*. London: Macmillan Education.

Dollard, J. (1937). *Caste and class in a southern town*. New Haven, CT: Yale University Press.

Dollard, J., Miller, N., & Doob, L. (1939). *Frustration and aggression*. New Haven, CT: Yale University Press.

Domhoff, G. W. (1978). *The powers that be*. New York: Random House.

Domhoff, G. W. (1983). *Who rules America now?* New York: Simon & Schuster.

Dore, R. (1973). *British factory-Japanese factory: The origins of national diversity in industrial relations*. Berkeley: University of California Press.

Dore, R. (1982). Introduction. In S. Kamata, *Japan in the passing lane: An outsider's account of life in a Japanese auto factory*. New York: Pantheon.

Dornbusch, S. (1955). The military as an assimilating institution. *Social Forces, 33,* 316–321.

Douglas, J. D., & Rasmussen, P. K. (1977). *The nude beach*. Newbury Park, CA: Sage.

Dowd, M. (1985, November 17). Youth, art, hype: A different bohemia. *New York Times Magazine*, pp. 26ff.

Drake, S. C., & Cayton, H. (1970/1945). *Black metropolis: Vol. I. A study of Negro life in a northern city* (rev. ed.). Orlando: Harcourt Brace Jovanovich.

DuBois, W. E. B. (1897). The strivings of the Negro people. *Atlantic Monthly, 80,* 194–195.

DuBois, W. E. B. (1967/1899). *The Philadelphia Negro: A social study*. New York: Schocken.

Durkheim, E. (1964/1893). *The division of labor in society* (2nd ed.). New York: Free Press.

Eckholm, E. (1984, October 9). As ancient ways slide into oblivion, hunter tribes face painful choices. *New York Times*, pp. C1, C9.

Eckholm, E. (1985, June 25). Kanzi the chimp: A life in science. *New York Times*, pp. C1, C3.

Edwards, R. (1979). *Contested terrain: The transformation of the workplace in the twentieth century*. New York: Basic Books.

Ehrlich, P. R., Ehrlich, A. H., & Holdren, J. P. (1977). *Ecoscience: Population, resources, environment*. New York: Freeman.

Eibl-Eibesfeldt, I. (1989). *Human ethology*. Hawthorne, NY: Aldine de Gruyter.

Eisley, L. (1970). *The invisible pyramid*. New York: Scribner.

Elder, G. H. (1981). History and the life course. In D. Berteaux (ed.), *Biography and society: The life history approach to the social sciences*. Newbury Park, CA: Sage.

Eldridge, C. C. *Victorian imperialism*. Atlantic Highlands, NJ: Humanities Press.

Elias, N. (1978/1939). The civilizing process. In N. Elias (ed.), *The development of manners*. New York: Urizen.

Elifson, K. W., & Hadaway, C. K. (1985). Prayer in public schools: When church and state collide. *Public Opinion Quarterly, 49,* 317–329.

Elkind, D. (1970). *Children and adolescents: Interpretative essays on Jean Piaget*. New York: Oxford University Press.

Ellul, J. (1964). *The technological society*. New York: Vintage.

Ellwood, D. T. (1988). *Poor support: Poverty in the American family*. New York: Basic Books.

Ellwood, D. T., & Summers, L. H. (1986). Poverty in America: Is welfare the answer or the problem? In S. H. Danziger & D. H. Weinberg (eds.), *Poverty: What works and what doesn't?* Cambridge, MA: Harvard University Press.

Epstein, C. F. (1981). *Women in law*. New York: Basic Books.

Epstein, C. F. (1985). Ideal roles and real roles. *Research in Social Stratification and Mobility, 4,* 29–51.

Epstein, C. F. (1988). *Deceptive distinctions: Sex, gender, and the social order*. New Haven, CT: Yale University Press.

Erikson, E. (1963). *Childhood and society*. New York: Norton.

Erikson, E. (1975). Reflections on the dissent of humanist youth. In E. Erikson (ed.), *Life history and the historical moment*. New York: Norton.

Erikson, K. T. (1962). Notes on the sociology of deviance. *Social Problems, 9,* 307–314.

Erikson, K. T. (1966). *Wayward puritans: A study in the sociology of deviance*. New York: Wiley.

Erikson, K. T. (1976). *Everything in its path*. New York: Simon & Schuster.

Esping-Anderson, G. (1985). *Politics against markets*. Princeton, NJ: Princeton University Press.

Etzioni, A. (1968). *The active society: A theory of societal and political processes*. New York: Free Press.

Fallers, L. (1977). Equality and inequality in human societies. In S. Tax & L. Freeman (eds.), *Horizons of anthropology*. Hawthorne, NY: Aldine.

Fallows, D. (1985). *A mother's work*. Boston: Houghton Mifflin.

Farley, R., & Allen, W. R. (1987). *The color line and the quality of life in America*. New York: Russell Sage.

Fava, S. (1956). Suburbanism as a way of life. *American Sociological Review, 21,* 34–38.

Fava, S. (1985). Residential preferences in the suburban era: A new look? *Sociological Focus, 18,* 109–117.

Feldmesser, R. A. (1968). Function and ideology in Soviet social stratification. In K. London (ed.), *The Soviet Union: A half century of communism*. Baltimore: Johns Hopkins University Press.

Fenn, R. (1978). *Toward a theory of secularization* (Monograph series 1). Storrs, CT: Society for the Scientific Study of Religion.

Fernandes, F. (1968). The weight of the past. In J. H. Franklin (ed.), *Color and race*. Boston: Beacon.

Festinger, L., Schachter, S., & Back, K. (1950). *Social pressure in informal groups*. New York: Harper.

Field, D., & O'Leary, J. T. (1973). Social groups as a basis for assessing participation in selected water activities. *Journal of Leisure Research, 5,* 16–25.

Finkelhor, D., & Williams, L. M. (1988). *Nursery crimes: Sexual abuse in day care*. Newbury Park, CA: Sage.

Finn, R. (1990, March 5). At 13 Capriati wonders, Why the fuss? *New York Times*, p. C1.

Firestone, S. (1970). *The dialectics of sex*. New York: Bantam.

Fischer, C. S. (1974). Astrology and French society: The dialectic of anarchism and modernity. In E. Tiryakian (ed.), *On the margin of the visible*. New York: Wiley.

Fischer, C. S. (1976, 1987). *The urban experience*. Orlando: Harcourt Brace Jovanovich.

Fischer, C. S. (1982). *To dwell among friends: Personal networks in town and city*. Chicago: University of Chicago Press.

Fischer, C. S. (1985). Studying technology and social life. In M. Castells (ed.), *High technology, space, and society*. Newbury Park, CA: Sage.

Fischer, C. S., & Jackman, R. M. (1976). Suburbs, networks, and attitudes. In B. Schwartz (ed.), *The changing face of the suburbs*. Chicago: University of Chicago Press.

FitzSimons, R. (1970). *The Charles Dickens show: An account of his public readings 1858–1870*. London: Bles.

Flink, J. J. (1975). *The car culture*. Cambridge, MA: M.I.T. Press.

Flink, J. J. (1980–1981). The car culture revisited: Some comments on the recent historiography of automotive history. *Michigan Quarterly Review, 19–20,* 772–781.

Flores, J. (1988, Fall). Rappin', writin', and breakin': Black and Puerto Rican street culture in New York. In *In search of New York, Dissent* special issue, pp. 580–585.

Ford Foundation (1989, November). *The Ford Foundation letter, 20,* 1–3.

Fortin, N., & Ecker, M. (1978). *Social problems at Cape Cod National Seashore*. Unpublished report to U.S. Department of the Interior, National Park Service.

Fox, L. (1952). *The English prison and borstal system*. London: Routledge and Kegan Paul.

Fox, R. (1971). *The imperial animal*. New York: Dell.

Frank, A. G. (1966). The development of underdevelopment. *Monthly Review, 18,* 3–17.

Frank, R. H. (1988). *Passions within reason: The strategic role of the emotions*. New York: Norton.

Frazier, E. F. (1966). *The Negro church in America*. New York: Schocken.

Frazier, E. F. (1957). *The Negro in the United States* (rev. ed.). New York: Macmillan.

Freeman, J. (1973). The origins of the women's liberation movement. In J. Huber (ed.), *Changing women in a changing society*. Chicago: University of Chicago Press.

Freeman, J. (1985). Growing up girlish: The social construction of the second sex. In W. Feigelman (ed.), *Sociology: Full circle* (4th ed.). Fort Worth, TX: Holt, Rinehart and Winston.

French, H. F. (1990, January). *Clearing the air: A global agenda*. Worldwatch Paper No. 94.

Freud, S. (1925). Some psychical consequences of the anatomical distinctions between the sexes. *The standard edition of the complete psychological works of Sigmund Freud* (vol. 19). London: Hogarth.

Freud, S. (1960/1921). *Group psychology and the analysis of the ego*. New York: Standard Editions.

Freud, S. (1961/1930). *Civilization and its discontents*. New York: Norton.

Fried, M. (1963). Grieving for a lost home. In L. J. Duhl (ed.), *The urban condition*. New York: Basic Books.

Friedan, B. (1963). *The feminine mystique*. New York: Dell.

Friedlander, D. (1969). Demographic responses and population change. *Demography, 6*, 359–381.

Friedman, M. (1962). *Capitalism and freedom*. Chicago: University of Chicago Press.

Fromm, E. (1961). *Marx's concept of man*. New York: Ungar.

Fuchs, V. (1968). *The service economy*. New York: National Bureau of Economic Research.

Furstenberg, F. (1976). *Unplanned parenthood: The social consequences of unplanned childbearing*. New York: Free Press.

Furstenberg, F., & Spanier, G. (1984). *Recycling the family*. Newbury Park, CA: Sage.

Fyfe, C. (1976). The dynamics of African dispersal. In M. L. Kilson & R. I. Rothberg (eds.), *The African diaspora*. Cambridge, MA: Harvard University Press.

Galbraith, J. K. (1984, September 2). The heartless society. *New York Times Magazine*, pp. 20ff.

Gallup, G. (1982). *Adventures in immortality*. New York: McGraw-Hill.

Gallup Organization (1984). *Religious television in America*. Princeton, NJ: Gallup Organization.

Galtung, J. (1985). War. In A. Kuper & J. Kuper (eds.), *The social science encyclopedia*. London: Routledge and Kegan Paul.

Gans, H. (1962, 1984). *The urban villagers*. New York: Free Press.

Gans, H. (1967, 1976). *The Levittowners: Way of life and politics in a new suburban community*. New York: Pantheon.

Gans, H. (1979). *Deciding what's news*. New York: Pantheon.

Gans, H. (1985). The uses of poverty: The poor pay all. In W. Feigelman (ed.), *Sociology: Full circle* (4th ed.). Fort Worth, TX: Holt, Rinehart and Winston.

Garfinkel, I., & McLanahan, S. S. (1986). *Single mothers and their children: A new American dilemma*. Washington, DC: Urban Institute.

Garn, S. (1965). *Human races* (2nd ed.). Springfield, IL: Thomas.

Geertz, C. (1973). The growth of culture and the evolution of mind. In C. Geertz, *The interpretation of culture*. New York: Basic Books.

Geiger, K. (1968). *The family in Soviet Russia*. Cambridge, MA: Harvard University Press.

Gelles, R. J., & Lancaster, J. B. (eds.) (1987). *Child abuse and neglect: Biosocial dimensions*. Hawthorne, NY: Social Science Research Council/Aldine de Gruyter.

Genevie, L. E. (ed.) (1978). *Collective behavior and social movements*. Itasca, IL: Peacock.

Germani, G. (1973). *Modernization, urbanization, and the urban crisis*. Boston: Little, Brown.

Gerson, K. (1985). *Hard choices: How women decide about work, career, and motherhood*. Berkeley: University of California Press, 1985.

Gerth, H., & Mills, C. W. (1958). *From Max Weber: Essays in sociology*. New York: Oxford University Press.

Geschwender, J. A. (1977). *Class, race and worker insurgency*. New York: Cambridge University Press.

Giddens, A. (1984). *The constitution of society*. Berkeley: University of California Press.

Gilder, G. (1982). *Wealth and poverty*. New York: Basic Books.

Gilligan, C. (1982). *In a different voice: Psychological theory and women's development*. Cambridge, MA: Harvard University Press.

Gilligan, C. (1987). Adolescent development reconsidered. In C. E. Irwin, Jr. (ed.), *New directions for child development*: No. 37, *Adolescent social behavior and health*. San Francisco: Jossey-Bass.

Gilligan, C., Archer, J., & Lloyd, B. (1985). *Sex and gender* (rev. ed.). Cambridge, England: Cambridge University Press.

Gist, N. P. (1968). Urbanism in India. In S. F. Fava (ed.), *Urbanism in world perspective: A reader*. New York: Crowell.

Gitlin, T. (1980). *The whole world is watching: Mass media in the making and unmaking of the New Left*. Berkeley: University of California Press.

Glaser, D. (1979). A review of crime causation theory and its application. In N. Morris & M. Tonry (eds.), *Crime and justice: An annual review of research*. Chicago: University of Chicago Press.

Glasgow, D. (1981). *The black underclass: Poverty, unemployment and entrapment of ghetto youth*. New York: Vintage.

Glazer, N. (1975). *Affirmative discrimination: Ethnic inequality and public policy*. New York: Basic Books.

Glazer, N., & Moynihan, D. P. (1970). *Beyond the melting pot: The Negroes, Puerto Ricans, Jews, Italians, and Irish of New York City* (2nd rev. ed.). Cambridge, MA: M.I.T. Press.

Glick, P. C., & Parke, R., Jr. (1965). New approaches in studying the life cycle of the family. *Demography, 2*, 187–202.

Glueck, S., & Glueck, E. T. (1950). *Unraveling juvenile delinquency*. New York: Commonwealth Fund.

Goffman, E. (1958). Deference and demeanor. *American Anthropologist, 58*, 488–489.

Goffman, E. (1959). The presentation of self in everyday life. Garden City, NY: Doubleday.

Goffman, E. (1963). *Stigma: Notes on the management of spoiled identity*. Englewood Cliffs, NJ: Prentice-Hall.

Goffman, E. (1972). Territories of the self. In E. Goffman (ed.), *Relations in public*. New York: Harper.

Goldfarb, W. (1945). Psychological privation in infancy and subsequent adjustment. *American Journal of Orthopsychiatry, 15*, 247–253.

Goldhamer, H., & Shils, E. (1939). Types of power and status. *American Journal of Sociology, 45*, 171–182.

Goldschmidt, W. (1978). *As you sow: Three studies in the social consequences of agribusiness*. Montclair, NJ: Allanheld, Osmun.

Goleman, D. (1985, March 19). Dislike of own body found common among women. *New York Times*, pp. C1, C5.

Goleman, D. (1985, September 10). Patterns of love charted in studies. *New York Times*, pp. C1, C5.

Goleman, D. (1988, April 11). The tax cheats: Selfish to the bottom line. *New York Times*, pp. A1, D2.

Goleman, D. (1988, June 14). Erikson, in his own old age, expands his view of life. *New York Times*, p. C1.

Goodall, J. V. L. (1968). A preliminary report on

expressive movements and communications in Gombe Stream chimpanzees. In P. Jay (ed.), *Primates: Studies in adaptation and variability*. Fort Worth, TX: Holt, Rinehart and Winston.

Goode, W. J. (1957). Community within a community. *American Sociological Review, 22,* 194–200.

Goode, W. J. (1960). Encroachment, charlatanism, and the emerging profession: Psychology, sociology, and medicine. *American Sociological Review, 25,* 902–914.

Goode, W. J. (1963). *World revolution and family patterns*. New York: Free Press.

Goode, W. J. (1964). *The family*. Englewood Cliffs, NJ: Prentice-Hall.

Goode, W. J. (1971, November). World revolution and family patterns. *Journal of Marriage and the Family*, pp. 624–635.

Goode, W. J. (1972). The place of force in human society. *American Sociological Review, 37,* 507–519.

Goodrich, D. W., Ryder, R. G., & Rausch, H. L. (1968). Patterns of newly wed marriage. *Journal of Marriage and the Family, 30,* 383–390.

Goodrich, L. M. (1974). *The United Nations in a changing world*. New York: Columbia University Press.

Gordon, M. (1964). *Assimilation in American life*. New York: Oxford University Press.

Gottman, J. M. (1983). How children become friends. *Society for Research in Child Development Monograph, 48,* 1–86.

Gottmann, J. (1978). Megalopolitan systems around the world. In L. S. Bourne & J. W. Simmons (eds.), *Systems of cities: Readings on structure, growth, and policy*. New York: Oxford University Press.

Gould, S. J. (1981). *The mismeasure of man*. New York: Norton.

Gouldner, A. (1960). The norm of reciprocity: A preliminary statement. *American Sociological Review, 25,* 161–178.

Gramsci, A. (1971). Selections from prison notebooks. London: Routledge and Kegan Paul.

Grønbjerg, K. A. (1977). *Mass society and the extension of welfare 1960–1970*. Chicago: University of Chicago Press.

Gusfield, J. (1966). *Symbolic crusade: Status politics and the American temperance movement*. Urbana: University of Illinois Press.

Gusfield, J. (1981). *The culture of public problems: Drinking, driving and the symbolic order*. Chicago: University of Chicago Press.

Guterbock, T. M. (1980). *Machine politics in transition: Party and community in Chicago*. Chicago: University of Chicago Press.

Gutkind, E. A. (1956). Our world from the air: Conflict and adaptation. In W. L. Thomas (ed.), *Man's role in changing the face of the earth*. Chicago: University of Chicago Press.

Gutman, H. (1976). *The black family in slavery*. New York: Pantheon.

Guttentag, M., & Secord, P. F. (1983). *Too many women? The sex ratio question*. Newbury Park, CA: Sage.

Haberman, C. (1989, December 1). Gorbachev lauds religion on eve of meeting pope. *New York Times*, pp. A1, A22.

Hagedorn, J. M. (1987). *People and folks: Gangs, crime and the underclass in a rustbelt city*. Chicago: Lakeview Press.

Hagestad, G. O., & Neugarten, B. L. (1985). Age and the life course. In R. H. Binstock & E. Shanas (eds.), *Handbook of aging and the social sciences* (2nd ed.). New York: Van Nostrand Reinhold.

Halevy, E. (1955). The growth of philosophic radicalism (M. Morris, trans.). Boston: Beacon.

Hall, E. (1959). *The silent language*. Greenwich, CT: Fawcett.

Hall, J. R. (1978). *The ways out: Utopian communal groups in an age of Babylon*. London: Routledge and Kegan Paul.

Hall, J. (1987). *Gone from the promised land*. New Brunswick, NJ: Transaction.

Halle, D. (1984). *America's working man: Work, home and politics among blue-collar property owners*. Chicago: University of Chicago Press.

Halsey, M. (1946). *Color blind*. New York: Simon & Schuster.

Hamilton, C. V. (1969). The politics of race relations. In C. U. Daley (ed.), *The minority report*. New York: Pantheon.

Hamilton, C. V. (1984). Political access, minority participation and the new normalcy. In L. W. Dunbar (ed.), *The minority report*. New York: Pantheon.

Hansen, W. L., & Stampen, J. O. (1987, April). *Economics and financing of higher education: The tension between quality and equity*. Paper presented at the annual meeting of the Association for the Study of Higher Education, San Diego.

Harbison, F. H. (1973). *Human resources as the wealth of nations*. New York: Oxford University Press.

Hardy, A. (1973, October). Man's age-old struggle for power. *Natural History*.

Hareven, T. K. (1978). *Transitions: The family and the life course in historical perspective*. Orlando: Academic Press.

Harlan, W. H. (1968). Social status of the aged in three Indian villages. In B. L. Neugarten (ed.), *Middle age and aging*. Chicago: University of Chicago Press.

Harlow, H. F., & Harlow, M. K. (1962, November). Social deprivation in monkeys. *Scientific American*, pp. 137–147.

Harper, D. A. (1982). *Good company*. Chicago: University of Chicago Press.

Harrington, M. (1973). *Socialism*. New York: Bantam.

Harrington, M. (1981). *The other America* (2nd ed.). New York: Penguin.

Harrington, M. (1989). *Socialism: Past and future*. New York: Arcade.

Harris, C. D., & Ullman, E. L. (1945). The nature of cities. *Annals of the American Academy of Political and Social Science, 242,* 7–11.

Harris, M. (1980). *Culture, people, nature: An introduction to general anthropology*. New York: Harper.

Harris, M. (1983). *Cultural anthropology*. New York: Harper.

Harrison, B. B., Tilly, C., and Bluestone, B. (1986, March–April). Wage inequality takes a great U-turn. *Challenge*, pp. 26–32.

Hauser, P. M. (1957). The changing population pattern of the modern city. In P. K. Hatt & A. J. Reiss (eds.), *Cities and society*. New York: Free Press.

Hauser, R. M., & Featherman, D. I. (1977). *The process of stratification*. Orlando: Academic Press.

Hawkins, G. (1976). *The prison: Policy and practice*. Chicago: University of Chicago Press.

Hayghe, H. (1982). Dual earner families: Their

economic and demographic characteristics. In J. Aldous (ed.), *Two paychecks*. Newbury Park, CA: Sage.

Hechter, M. (1974). *Internal colonialism*. Berkeley: University of California Press.

Hechter, M. (1983). *The microfoundations of macrosociology*. Philadelphia: Temple University Press.

Hechter, M. (1987). *Principles of group solidarity*. Berkeley: University of California Press.

Heer, D. (1974). The prevalence of black-white marriages in the United States. *Journal of Marriage and the Family, 36*, 246–258.

Heilbroner, R. (1990, February 15). Seize the day. *New York Review of Books*, pp. 30–31.

Helmreich, W. B. (1982). *The things they say behind your back*. Garden City, NY: Doubleday.

Henry, D. O. (1989). *From foraging to agriculture*. Philadelphia: University of Pennsylvania Press.

Henslin, J., & Briggs, M. (1971). Dramaturgical desexualization: The sociology of the vaginal examination. In J. Henslin (ed.), *Studies in the sociology of sex*. New York: Appleton-Century-Crofts.

Hershey, R. D. (1988, November 4). Counting the jobless a job in itself. *New York Times*, pp. D1, D4.

HHS (U.S. Department of Health and Human Services) (1973). *Work in America*. Washington, DC: U.S. Government Printing Office.

Hill, J. (1978). Apes and language. *Annual Review of Anthropology, 7*, 89–112.

Hinton, W. (1966). *Fanshen: A documentary of revolution in a Chinese village*. New York: Vintage.

Hirschi, T., & Gottfredson, M. R. (1980). *Understanding crime: Current theory and research*. Newbury Park, CA: Sage.

Historical Statistics of the United States, Colonial Times to 1970 (Bicentennial ed.), Part 2. (1975). Washington, DC: U.S. Bureau of the Census.

Hobsbawm, E. (1975). *The age of capital*. New York: Scribner.

Hobsbawm, E. (1981). *Bandits* (rev. ed.). New York: Pantheon.

Hochschild, A. (1975). Disengagement theory: A critique and a proposal. *American Sociological Review, 40*, 553–569.

Hochschild, A. (1979). Emotion work, feeling rules, and social structure. *American Journal of Sociology, 85*, 551–575.

Hochschild, A. (1983). *The managed heart: Commercialization of human feeling*. Berkeley: University of California Press.

Hochschild, A. (1989). *The second shift*. New York: Viking.

Hodge, R. W., Siegel, P. M., & Rossi, P. H. (1964). Occupational prestige in the United States, 1925–1965. *American Journal of Sociology, 70*, 186–302.

Hodge, R. W., & Treiman, D. J. (1968). Class identification in the United States. *American Journal of Sociology, 73*, 535–547.

Hodge, R. W., Treiman, D. J., & Rossi, P. H. (1966). A comparative study of occupational prestige. In R. Bendix & S. M. Lipset (eds.), *Class, status, and power*. New York: Free Press.

Hollingshead, A. (1949). *Elmtown's youth*. New York: Wiley.

Holt, J. (1965). *How children fail*. New York: Dell.

Holt, J. (1967). *How children learn*. New York: Pitman.

Holt, T. C. (1980). Afro-Americans. In *Harvard encyclopedia of American ethnic groups*. Cambridge, MA: Belknap Press.

Holy, L. (1985). Groups. In A. Kuper & J. Kuper (eds.), *The Social Science Encyclopedia*. London: Routledge and Kegan Paul.

Homans, G. (1950). *The human group*. Orlando: Harcourt Brace Jovanovich.

Homans, G. (1951). The Western Electric researches. In S. D. Hoslett (ed.), *Human factors in management*. New York: Harper.

Homans, G. (1961). *Social behavior: Its elementary forms*. Orlando: Harcourt Brace Jovanovich.

Hopkins, T. K., & Wallerstein, I. (eds.) (1980). *Processes of the world-system*. Newbury Park, CA: Sage.

Hopper, R. D. (1950). The revolutionary process: A frame of reference for the study of revolutionary movements. *Social Forces, 25*, 270–279.

Horner, M. (1968). *Sex differences in achievement motivation and performance in competitive and non-competitive situations*. Unpublished doctoral dissertation, University of Michigan, Ann Arbor.

Horowitz, M. (1979). The jurisprudence of Brown and the dilemmas of liberalism. *Harvard Civil Rights–Civil Liberties Review, 14*, 599–610.

Horowitz, R. (1985). *Honor and the American dream: Culture and identity in a Chicago neighborhood*. New Brunswick, NJ: Rutgers University Press.

Hout, M., & Greeley, A. M. (1987). The center doesn't hold: Church attendance in the United States, 1940–1984. *American Sociological Review, 52*, 325–345.

Hoyt, H. (1939). *The structure and growth of residential neighborhoods in American cities*. Washington, DC: Federal Housing Administration.

Hoyt, H. (1964). Recent distortions of the classical models of urban structure. *Land Economics, 40*, 199–212.

Huber, J., & Spitz, G. (1988). Trends in family sociology. In N. J. Smelser (ed.), *The handbook of sociology*. Newbury Park, CA: Sage.

Hughes, E. (1945). The dilemmas and contradictions of status. *American Journal of Sociology, 50*, 353–359.

Hughes, E. (1958). *Men and their work*. New York: Free Press.

Hughes, E. (1959). The study of occupations. In R. K. Merton, L. Broom, & L. S. Cottrell, Jr. (eds.), *Sociology today: Problems and prospects*. New York: Basic Books.

Humphreys, L. (1970, 1975). *Tearoom trade: Impersonal sex in public places*. Hawthorne, NY: Aldine.

Hunt, M. (1985). *Profiles of social research: The scientific study of human interactions*. New York: Russell Sage.

Inkeles, A. (1983). *Exploring individual modernity*. New York: Columbia University Press.

Inkeles, A., & Smith, D. H. (1974). *Becoming modern*. Cambridge, MA: Harvard University Press.

Institute for Research on Poverty, University of Wisconsin/Madison (1987, Fall). *Focus, 10*.

Jackman, M. R., & Jackman, R. W. (1983). *Class awareness in the United States*. Berkeley: University of California Press.

Jackson, B. (1972). *In the life: Versions of the criminal experience*. New York: NAL.

Jacobs, J. (1961). *The death and life of great American cities*. New York: Vintage Books.

Jaffe, H. W., Darrow, W. W., Echenberg, D. G., et al. (1985). The acquired immuno-deficiency syndrome in a cohort of homosexual men. *Annals of Internal Medicine 103*, 210–214.

Jahoda, M. (1982). *Employment and unemployment: A social-psychological analysis*. London: Cambridge University Press.

Jahoda, M., Lazarsfeld, P., & Zeisel, H. (1971). *Marienthal: A study of an unemployed community*. Hawthorne, NY: Aldine.

Janowitz, M. (1960). *The professional soldier: A social and political portrait*. New York: Free Press.

Janowitz, M. (1968). Political sociology. In D. Sills (ed.), *The international encyclopedia of the social sciences*. New York: Free Press.

Janowitz, M. (1978). *The last half century: Societal change and politics in America*. Chicago: University of Chicago Press.

Janowitz, M. (1983). *The reconstruction of patriotism*. Chicago: University of Chicago Press.

Janowitz, M., & Shils, E. A. (1948). The cohesion and disintegration of the Wehrmacht in World War II. *Public Opinion Quarterly, 12*, 280–315.

Jaynes, G. D., & Williams, R. M., Jr. (1989). *A common destiny: Blacks and American society*. Washington, DC: National Academy Press.

Jencks, C., Smith, M., Acland, H., Bane, M. J., Cohen, D., Gintis, H., Heyns, B., & Michelson, S. (1972). *Inequality: A reassessment of the effect of family and schooling in America*. New York: Basic Books.

Jennings, F. (1975). *The invasion of America: Indians, colonialism and the cant of conquest*. New York: Norton.

Johnson, P. (1987). *A history of the Jews*. New York: Harper.

Jones, E. F., et al. (1986). *Teenage pregnancy in industrialized countries*. New Haven, CT: Yale University Press.

Joravsky, D. (1971). *The Lysenko affair*. Cambridge, MA: Harvard University Press.

Joselow, F. (1989, March 26). Why business turns to teen-agers. *New York Times*, pp. 3–1, 3–6.

Joslyn, R. (1984). *Mass media and elections*. Reading, MA: Addison-Wesley.

Kahl, J. A. (1965). *The American class structure*. Fort Worth, TX: Holt, Rinehart and Winston.

Kahneman, D., Knetsch, J., & Thaler, R. (1986). Fairness and the assumptions of economics. *Journal of Business, 59*, S285–S300.

Kamata, S. (1982). *Japan in the passing lane: An outsider's account of life in a Japanese auto factory*. New York: Pantheon.

Kaplan, R. M., & Singer, R. D. (1976). Television violence and viewer aggression: A reexamination of the evidence. *Journal of Social Issues, 32*, 35–70.

Kasarda, J. D. (1989). Urban industrial transition and the underclass. *Annals of the American Academy of Political and Social Science, 501*, 26–47.

Katz, E. (1957). The two step flow of communication: An up-to-date report on an hypothesis. *Public Opinion Quarterly, 21*, 61–78.

Katz, E. (1966). Communication research and the image of society: Convergence of two traditions. In A. G. Smith (ed.), *Communication and culture: Readings in the codes of human interaction*. Fort Worth, TX: Holt, Rinehart and Winston.

Katz, F. E. (1964). The school as a complex social organization. *Harvard Educational Review, 34*, 428–455.

Katz, M. (1971). *Class, bureaucracy, and schools: The illusion of educational change in America*. New York: Praeger.

Katznelson, I. (1981). *City trenches: Urban politics and the patterning of class in the United States*. Chicago: University of Chicago Press.

Keith, J. (1982). *Old people, new lives: Community creation in a retirement residence* (2nd ed.). Chicago: University of Chicago Press.

Keller, H. (1917). *The story of my life*. Garden City, NY: Doubleday.

Keller, S. (1963). *Beyond the ruling class: Strategic elites in modern society*. New York: Random House.

Kelly, H. H. (1952). Two functions of reference groups. In G. E. Swanson et al. (eds.), *Readings in social psychology*. Fort Worth, TX: Holt, Rinehart and Winston.

Kempe, H., & Helfer, R. E. (eds.) (1980). *The battered child* (3rd ed.) Chicago: University of Chicago Press.

Kempe, R., & Kempe, H. (1978). *Child abuse*. Cambridge, MA: Harvard University Press.

Keniston, K. (1977). *All our children*. Orlando: Harcourt Brace Jovanovich.

Kennedy, R. E., Jr. (1986). *Life choices: Applying sociology*. Fort Worth, TX: Holt, Rinehart and Winston.

Kennedy, R. J. R. (1944). Single or triple melting pot? *American Journal of Sociology, 49*, 331–339.

Kessler, S. J., & McKenna, W. (1978). *Gender: An ethnomethodological approach*. Chicago: University of Chicago Press.

Keyfitz, N. (1986). The population that does not reproduce itself. In K. Davis et al. (eds.), *Below replacement fertility in industrial societies: Causes, consequences, policies. Population and Development Review, 12*, supp., 139–145.

Killian, L. (1952). Group membership in disaster. *American Journal of Sociology, 57*, 309–314.

Kilson, M. (1981). Black social classes and integrational poverty. *The Public Interest, 64*, 58–78.

Kim, I. (1981). *New urban immigrants: The Korean community in New York*. Princeton, NJ: Princeton University Press.

Kinsey, A. C., Pomeroy, W. B., & Martin, C. E. (1948). *Sexual behavior in the human male*. Philadelphia: Saunders.

Kitsuse, J. I. (1962). Societal reaction to deviant behavior; problems of theory and method. *Social Problems, 9*, 247–257.

Klatzky, S. (1971). *Patterns of contact with relatives*. Washington, DC: American Sociological Review.

Kleinberg, O. (1935). *Race differences*. New York: Harper.

Knowles, J. C. (1973). *The Rockefeller financial group*. Andover, MA: Warner Modular Pub.

Kohlberg, L., & Gilligan, C. (1971). The adolescent as a philosopher: The discovery of the self in a post-conventional world. *Daedalus, 100*, 1051–1086.

Komarovsky, M. (1946). The voluntary associations of urban dwellers. *American Sociological Review, 11*, 686–698.

Komarovsky, M. (1980). Cultural contradictions and sex roles: The masculine case. In A. Skolnick & J.

Skolnick (eds.), *Family in transition*. Boston: Little, Brown.

Kornblum, W. (1974). *Blue collar community*. Chicago: University of Chicago Press.

Kornblum, W., & Julian, J. (1989). *Social problems*. Englewood Cliffs, NJ: Prentice Hall.

Kornblum, W., & Williams, T. M. (1978). Life-style, leisure, and community life. In D. Street and Associates, *Handbook of contemporary urban life*. San Francisco: Jossey–Bass.

Kornhauser, W. (1952). The Negro union official: A study of sponsorship and control. *American Journal of Sociology, 57*, 443–452.

Kornhauser, W. (1959). *The politics of mass society*. New York: Free Press.

Kroc, R. (1977). *Grinding it out: The making of McDonald's*. Chicago: Henry Regnery.

Kronus, C. L. (1977). Mobilizing voluntary associations into a social movement: The case of environmental quality. *Sociological Quarterly, 18*, 267–283.

Kübler-Ross, E. (1989). *Death: The final stage of growth*. Englewood Cliffs, NJ: Prentice–Hall.

Kuhn, T. (1962). *The structure of scientific revolutions*. Chicago: University of Chicago Press.

Kutner, B., Wilkins, C., & Yarrow, P. R. (1952). Verbal attitudes and overt behavior involving racial prejudice. *Journal of Abnormal and Social Psychology, 47*, 649–652.

Kwamena-Poh, M., Tosh, J., Waller, R., & Tidy, M. (1982). *African history in maps*. Burnt Hill, England: Longman.

Ladner, J. (ed.) (1973). *The death of white sociology*. New York: Vintage.

Lai, H. M. (1980). The Chinese. In S. Thornstrom (ed.), *Harvard encyclopedia of ethnic groups*. Cambridge, MA: Harvard University Press.

Lakoff, S. (1970, Autumn). Science and conscience. *National Journal of Sociology*, pp. 754–765.

Land, K. C. (1989). Review of *Predicting Recidivism Using Survival Models*, by Peter Schmidt and Ann Dryden Witte. *Contemporary Sociology, 18*, 245–246.

Lang, K., & Lang, G. E. (1961). *Collective dynamics*. New York: Crowell.

Lapidus, G. (1978). *Women in Soviet society*. Berkeley: University of California Press.

LaPiere, R. (1934). Attitudes vs. actions. *Social Forces, 13*, 230–237.

Larkin, R. W. (1979). *Suburban youth in cultural crisis*. New York: Oxford University Press.

Lasch, C. (1978). *The culture of narcissism: American life in the age of diminishing expectations*. New York: Norton.

Lasch, C. (1984). *The minimal self*. New York: Norton.

Laslett, P. (1972). Introduction. In P. Laslett & R. Wall (eds.), *Household and family in past time*. Cambridge, England: Cambridge University Press.

Laslett, P. (1983). *The world we have lost* (3rd ed.). London: Methuen.

Lasswell, H. (1936). *Politics: Who gets what, when and how*. New York: McGraw–Hill.

Lasswell, H. D. (1941). The garrison state. *American Journal of Sociology, 46*, 455–468.

Latané, B., & Darley, J. (1970). *The unresponsive bystander: Why doesn't he help?* New York: Meredith.

Leacock, E. (1978). Women's status in egalitarian society: Implications for social evolution. *Current Anthropology, 19*, 247–275.

LeBon, G. (1947/1896). *The crowd*. London: Ernest Bonn.

LeFebvre, H. (1972). *Le droit et la ville*. Paris: Editions Anthropos.

LeMasters, E. E. (1975). *Blue collar aristocrats*. Madison: University of Wisconsin Press.

Lemert, E. M. (1951). *Social pathology: A systematic approach to the theory of sociopathic behavior*. New York: McGraw–Hill.

Lemert, E. M. (1967). *Human deviance, social problems and social control*. Englewood Cliffs, NJ: Prentice–Hall.

Lenero-Otero, L. (ed.) (1977). *Beyond the nuclear family model*. Newbury Park, CA: Sage.

Lenski, G., & Lenski, J. (1982). *Human societies* (4th ed.). New York: McGraw-Hill.

Lever, J. (1976). Sex differences in the games children play. *Social Problems, 23*, 478–487.

Lever, J. (1978). Sex differences in the complexity of children's play and games. *American Sociological Review, 43*, 471–483.

Lever, J. (1983). *Soccer madness*. Chicago: University of Chicago Press.

Levi, P. (1989). *The drowned and the saved*. New York: Vintage.

Levitan, S., & Belous, R. S. (1981). *What's happening to the American family?* Baltimore: Johns Hopkins University Press.

Lewin, T. (1989, November 14). Aging parents: Women's burden grows. *New York Times*, pp. A1, B12.

Lewis, M., & Feiring, C. (1982). Some American families at dinner. In L. M. Laosa & I. E. Sigel (eds.), *Families as learning environments for children*. New York: Plenum.

Lewontin, R. C. (1977). Biological determinism as a social weapon. In Ann Arbor Science for the People Editorial Collective, *Biology as a social weapon*. Minneapolis: Burgess.

Lewontin, R. C. (1982). *Human diversity*. New York: Scientific American Library.

Lieberson, S. (1980). *A piece of the pie: Blacks and white immigrants since 1880*. Berkeley: University of California Press.

Liebow, E. (1967). *Tally's corner: A study of Negro streetcorner men*. Boston: Little, Brown.

Lindner, S. (1970). *The harried leisure class*. New York: Columbia University Press.

Lindsmith, A., Strauss, A. L., & Denzin, N. (1978). *Social psychology* (5th ed.). Fort Worth, TX: Holt, Rinehart and Winston.

Linton, R. (1936). *The study of man*. New York: Appleton.

Lipset, S. M. (1979). *The first new nation*. New York: Norton.

Lipset, S. M. (1981). *Political man*. Baltimore: Johns Hopkins University Press.

Lipset, S. M., & Zetterberg, H. L. (1966). A theory of social mobility. In R. Bendix & S. M. Lipset (eds.), *Class, status, and power: Social stratification in comparative perspective* (2nd ed.). New York: Free Press.

Lofland, J. F. (1981). Collective behavior: The elementary forms. In N. Rosenberg & R. H. Turner (eds.), *Social psychology: Sociological perspectives*. New York: Basic Books.

Lombroso, C. (1911). *Crime: Its cause and remedies*. Boston: Little, Brown.

Lovins, A. B. (1977). *Soft energy paths: Toward a durable peace*. Cambridge, MA: Ballinger.

Luce, I. (1964). *Letters from the Peace Corps*. Washington, DC: Robert B. Luce.

Luhmann, N. (1982). *The differentiation of society*. New York: Columbia University Press.

Lurie, A. (1981). *The language of clothes*. New York: Random House.

Lynd, R. S., & Lynd, H. M. (1929). *Middletown: A study in American culture*. Orlando: Harcourt Brace Jovanovich.

Lynd, R. S., & Lynd, H. M. (1937). *Middletown in transition: A study in cultural conflicts*. Orlando: Harcourt Brace Jovanovich.

MacCannell, D. (n.d.). *Agribusiness and the small community* (manuscript). University of California, Davis.

Machiavelli, N. (1950/1513). *The prince* and *The discourses*. New York: Modern Library.

Machlis, G., & D. L. Tichnell (1985). *State of the world's parks: An international assessment*. Boulder, CO: Westview Press.

Macleod, J. (1987). *Ain't no makin' it: Leveled aspirations in a low-income neighborhood*. Boulder, CO: Westview Press.

Maddox, G. L. (1968). Retirement as a social event in the United States. In B. L. Neugarten (ed.), *Middle age and aging*. Chicago: University of Chicago Press.

Maddox, G. L., & Campbell, R. T. (1985). Scope, concepts, and methods in the study of aging. In R. H. Binstock & E. Shanas (eds.), *Handbook of aging and the social sciences*. New York: Van Nostrand Reinhold.

Majundar, R. C. (ed.) (1951). *The history and culture of the Indian people*. London: Allen and Unwin.

Malinowski, B. (1927). *Sex and repression in savage society*. London: Harcourt Brace.

Malson, L. (1972). *Wolf children and the problem of human nature* (E. Fawcett, P. Aryton, & J. White, trans.). New York: Monthly Review Press.

Malthus, T. (1927–1928/1798). *An essay on population*. New York: Dutton.

Manderscheid, R. W., and Greenwald, M. (1983). Trends in employment of sociologists. In H. E. Freeman, R. R. Dynes, P. H. Rossi, and W. F. Whyte (eds.), *Applied sociology*. San Francisco: Jossey-Bass.

Mannheim, K. (1941). *Man and society in an age of reconstruction*. Orlando: Harcourt Brace Jovanovich.

Manpower Demonstration and Research Corp. (1980). *The youth entitlement demonstration*. New York: Manpower Demonstration and Research Corp.

Markson, A. R., & Bloch, R. (1985). Defensive cities: Military spending, high technology, and human settlements. In M. Castells (ed.), *High technology, space, and society*. Newbury Park, CA: Sage.

Marshall, T. H. (1964). *Class, citizenship and social development*. Garden City, NY: Doubleday.

Martinez, M. E., & Mead, N. E. (1988). *Computer competence: The first national assessment*. Princeton, NJ: Educational Testing Service.

Martinson, R. (1972, April 29). Planning for public safety. *New Republic*, pp. 21–23.

Marwell, G., & Ames, R. E. (1985). Experiments on the provision of public goods II: Provision points, stakes, experience, and the free-rider problem. *American Journal of Sociology*, 90, 926–937.

Marx, K. (1961/1844). *Economic and philosophical manuscripts of 1844*. Moscow: Foreign Languages Publishing House.

Marx, K. (1962/1867). *Capital: A critique of political economy*. Moscow: Foreign Languages Publishing House.

Marx, K. (1963/1869). *The eighteenth Brumaire of Louis Bonaparte*. New York: International Publishers.

Marx, K., & Engels, F. (1955). Wage labor and capital. In *Selected works in two volumes*. Moscow: Foreign Languages Publishing House.

Marx, K., & Engels, F. (1969/1848). *The communist manifesto*. New York: Penguin.

Matras, J. (1973). *Populations and societies*. Englewood Cliffs, NJ: Prentice–Hall.

Mauss, M. (1966/1925). *The gift*. New York: Free Press.

Mawson, A. R. (1989). Review of *Homicide*, by Martin Daly and Margo Wilson. *Contemporary Sociology*, 18, 238–240.

Maydans, S. (1985, August 18). Genial Siberian party leader a man in Gorbachev's mold. *New York Times*, pp. A1, A14.

Mayfield, L. (1984). *Teenage pregnancy*. Unpublished doctoral dissertation, City University of New York.

Mayhew, H. (1968/1861–1862). *London labour and the London poor*. New York: Dover.

Mayo, E. (1945). *The social problems of an industrial civilization*. Boston: Harvard University, Graduate School of Business Administration.

McAdam, D., McCarthy, J. D., & Zald, N. (1988). Social movements. In N. J. Smelser (ed.), *The Handbook of sociology*. Newbury Park, CA: Sage.

McAndrew, M. (1985). Women's magazines in the Soviet Union. In B. Holland (ed.), *Soviet sisterhood*. Bloomington: Indiana University Press.

McBrien, R. P. (1990, March 12). A papal attack on Vatican II. *New York Times*, p. A17.

McCaull, J. (1978). Discriminatory air pollution. In W. R. Burch (ed.), *Readings in ecology, energy, and human society*. New York: Harper.

McGoldrick, M., & Carter, E. A. (1982). *The family life cycle in normal family processes*. London: Guilford Press.

McGuire, M. B. (1987). *Religion: The social context* (2nd ed.). Belmont, CA: Wadsworth.

McKinlay, J. B., & McKinlay, S. M. (1977). The questionable contribution of medical measures to the decline of mortality in the United States in the twentieth century. *Health and Society*, 53, 405.

McNeill, W. (1963). *The rise of the West: A history of the human community*. Chicago: University of Chicago Press.

McNeill, W. H. (1982). *The pursuit of power: Technology, armed force, and society since A.D. 1000*. Chicago: University of Chicago Press.

Mead, G. H. (1971/1934). Mind, self, and society. In M. Truzzi (ed.), *Sociology: The classic statements*. New York: Random House.

Mead, M. (1950). *Sex and temperament in three primitive societies*. New York: New American Library.

Mead, M. (1971). Comment. In J. Tanner & B. Inhelder (eds.), *Discussions on child development*. New York: International Universities Press.

Medvedev, Z. (1971). *The Medvedev papers*. New York: Macmillan.

Menard, S. (1981). The test score decline: An analysis of available data. In B. E. Mercer & S. C. Hey, *People in schools*. Cambridge, MA: Schenkman.

Merton, R. K. (1938). Social structure and anomie. *American Sociological Review, 3*, 672–682.

Merton, R. K. (1948). Discrimination and the American creed. In R. M. MacIver (ed.), *Discrimination and national welfare*. New York: Institute for Religious and Social Studies.

Merton, R. K. (1968). *Social theory and social structure* (3rd ed.). New York: Free Press.

Merton, R. K. (1973). *The sociology of science: Theoretical and empirical investigations*. Chicago: University of Chicago Press.

Merton, R. K., & Kitt, A. (1950). Contributions to the theory of reference group behavior. In R. K. Merton & P. Lazarsfeld, *Continuities in social research*. New York: Free Press.

Milavsky, W. R. (1977, August 19). *TV and aggressive behavior of elementary school boys*. Paper delivered at meeting of American Psychological Association, San Francisco.

Milgram, S. (1970). The experience of living in cities. *Science, 167*, 1461–1468.

Milgram, S. (1974). *Obedience to authority: An experimental view*. New York: Harper.

Miller, D. C., & Form, W. H. (1964). *Industrial sociology* (2nd ed.). New York: Harper.

Miller, W. B. (1958). Lower class culture as a generating milieu of gang delinquency. *Journal of Social Issues, 14*, 5–19.

Millman, M. (1976). *The unkindest cut: Life in the backrooms of medicine*. New York: Morrow Quill.

Mills, C. W. (1951). *White collar*. New York: Oxford University Press.

Mills, C. W. (1956). *The power elite*. New York: Oxford University Press.

Mills, C. W. (1959). *The sociological imagination*. New York: Oxford University Press.

Mintz, S. (1985). *Sweetness and power: The place of sugar in modern history*. New York: Viking.

Minuchin, S. (1974). *Families and family therapy*. Cambridge, MA: Harvard University Press.

Modell, J., & Hareven, T. K. (1973). Urbanization and the malleable household: An examination of boarding and lodging in American families. *Journal of Marriage and the Family, 35*, 466–479.

Moe, T. M. (1980). *The organization of interests*. Chicago: University of Chicago Press.

Mollenkopf, J. (1985). *The contested city*. Princeton, NJ: Princeton University Press.

Money, J., & Erhardt, A. (1972). *Man and woman/Boy and girl*. Baltimore: Johns Hopkins University Press.

Montagna, P. D. (1977). *Occupations and society*. New York: Wiley.

Moore, B. (1968). *The social origins of dictatorship and democracy: Lord and peasant in the making of the modern world*. Boston: Beacon Press.

Morales, E. (1986). Coca and the cocaine economy and social change in the Andes of Peru. *Economic Development and Cultural Change, 35*, 143–161.

Morales, E. (1989). *Cocaine: White gold rush in Peru*. Tucson: University of Arizona Press.

Morgan, R. (ed.) (1970). *Sisterhood is powerful: An anthology of writings from the women's liberation movement*. New York: Random House.

Morgan, T. (1985, October 27). World ahead: Black parents prepare their children for pride and prejudice. *New York Times Magazine*, pp. 32ff.

Morison, S. E. (1942). *Admiral of the ocean sea: A life of Christopher Columbus*. Boston: Little, Brown.

Morris, D. (1968). *The naked ape*. New York: McGraw-Hill.

Moscos, C. A. (1988). *Call to civic service*. New York: Free Press.

Mowat, F. (1975). *The desperate people* (rev. ed.). Toronto: Seal Books.

Murdock, G. P. (1949). *Social structure*. New York: Macmillan.

Murdock, G. P. (1967). *Ethnographic atlas*. Pittsburgh: University of Pittsburgh Press.

Murray, C. (1984). *Losing ground*. New York: Basic Books.

Myrdal, G. (1944). *An American dilemma*. New York: Harper.

Myrdal, G. (1970). *The challenge of world poverty*. New York: Vintage.

Myrdal, J. (1965). *Report from a Chinese village*. New York: Random House.

Napier, A. Y., & Whitaker, C. (1980). *The family crucible*. New York: Bantam.

National Academy of Sciences (1986). *Women's work, men's work: Sex segregation in the workplace* (B. F. Reskin & H. I. Hartmann, eds.). Washington, DC: National Academy Press.

National Commission on Excellence in Education. *A nation at risk: The imperative for educational reform*. Washington, DC: U.S. Government Printing Office.

Negrin, J. (1985–1986, Winter). The Huichol: A pre-Columbian culture in Mexico today. *The Free Spirit*, pp. 10–11.

Neihardt, J. G. (1959/1932). *Black Elk speaks: Being the life story of a holy man of the Oglala Sioux*. New York: Washington Square Press.

Nelkin, D. (1987). AIDS and the social sciences: Review of useful knowledge and research needs. *Reviews of Infectious Disease, 9*, 980–986.

Nelson, G. K. (1984). Cults and new religions: Towards a sociology of religious creativity. *Sociology and Social Research, 68*, 301–325.

Neugarten, B. L. (1969). Continuities and discontinuities of psychological issues into adult life. *Human Development, 12*, 121–130.

Newcomb, T. (1958). Attitude development as a function of reference groups: The Bennington study. In E. Maccoby, T. M. Newcomb, & E. L. Hartley (eds.), *Readings in social psychology* (3rd ed.). Fort Worth, TX: Holt, Rinehart and Winston.

Newman, K. S. (1988). *Falling from grace*. New York: Free Press.

Niebuhr, H. R. (1929). *The social sources of denominationalism*. New York: Meridian.

Nisbet, R. A. (1969). *Social change and history*. New York: Oxford University Press.

Nisbet, R. A. (1970). *The social bond*. New York: Knopf.

NORC (National Opinion Research Center) (1987). *General social survey*. Chicago: University of Chicago.

Nyden, P. (1984). *Steelworkers rank and file*. New York: Praeger.

Oakley, A. (1974). *Women's work: The housewife, past and present*. New York: Vintage.

Oberschall, A. (1973). *Social conflict and social movements*. Englewood Cliffs, NJ: Prentice-Hall.

Office of Technology Assessment, U.S. Congress (1986). *Technology, public policy, and the changing structure of agriculture: Vol. 2. Background papers: Part D. Rural communities*. Washington, DC.

Ogburn, W. F. (1942). Inventions, population and history. In American Council of Learned Societies, *Studies in the history of culture*. Freeport, NY: Books for Libraries Press.

Olsen, M. (1965). *The logic of collective action: Public goods and the theory of groups*. New York: Schocken.

Olsen, M. (1971). *The logic of collective action*. Cambridge, MA: Harvard University Press.

Olsen, M. (1979). Published letter. In L. Krisberg (ed.), *Research in social movements, conflicts and change* (Vol. 2). Greenwich, CT: JAI Press.

O'Neill, J. A., et al. (1984). *An analysis of time on welfare*. Report to the U.S. Department of Health and Human Services. Washington, DC: U.S. Government Printing Office.

Orwell, G. (1945). *Shooting an elephant and other essays*. Orlando: Harcourt Brace Jovanovich.

Orwell, G. (1949). *1984*. New York: New American Library.

Osmond, M. W. (1985). Comparative marriage and the family. In B. C. Miller & D. H. Olson (eds.), *Family studies review yearbook*, Vol. 3. Newbury Park, CA: Sage.

Pallas, A. M. (1987). *School dropouts in the United States*. Washington, DC: U.S. Department of Education, Office of Educational Research and Improvement.

Palmore, E. (1981). *Social patterns in normal aging*. Durham, NC: Duke University Press.

Parelius, A. P. (1975). Lifelong education and age stratification: Some unexplored relationships. *American Behavioral Scientist, 19*, 206–223.

Parelius, A. P., & Parelius, R. J. (1978/1887). *The sociology of education*. Englewood Cliffs, NJ: Prentice Hall.

Park, R. E. (1914). Racial assimilation in secondary groups. *Publications of the American Sociological Society, 8*, 66–72.

Park, R. E. (1967/1925). The natural history of the newspaper. In R. E. Park & E. W. Burgess (eds.), *The city*. Chicago: University of Chicago Press.

Park, R. E. (1967/1925). The city: Suggestions for the investigation of human behavior in the urban environment. In R. E. Park & E. W. Burgess (eds.), *The city*. Chicago: University of Chicago Press.

Park, R. E. (1967/1926). The urban community as a spatial pattern and a moral order. In R. H. Turner (ed.), *Robert E. Park on social control and collective behavior*. Chicago: University of Chicago Press.

Park, R. E., & Burgess, E. W. (1921). *Introduction to the science of sociology* (rev. ed.). Chicago: University of Chicago Press.

Parkin, F. (1971). *Class inequality and political order*. New York: Praeger.

Parry, J. H. (1963). *The age of reconnaissance*. Cleveland: World.

Parsons, T. (1937). *The structure of social action*. New York: McGraw-Hill.

Parsons, T. (1940). An analytic approach to the theory of social stratification. *American Journal of Sociology, 45*, 841–862.

Parsons, T. (1951). *The social system*. New York: Free Press.

Parsons, T. (1960). *Structure and process in modern societies*. New York: Free Press.

Parsons, T. (1965). The concept of political power. In S. M. Lipset & R. Bendix (eds.), *Class, status, and power* (2nd ed.). New York: Free Press.

Parsons, T. (1966). *Societies: Evolutionary and comparative*. Englewood Cliffs, NJ: Prentice–Hall.

Parsons, T. (1968). The problem of polarization along the axis of color. In J. H. Franklin (ed.), *Color and race*. Boston: Beacon Press.

Parsons, T., & Bales, R. F. (1955). *Family, socialization, and interaction process*. New York: Free Press.

Passell, P. (1990, March 4). America's position in the economic race: What the numbers show and conceal. *New York Times*, p. 4–4.

Patterson, O. (1982). *Slavery and social death*. Cambridge, MA: Harvard University Press.

Pavlov, I. (1927). *Conditioned reflexes: An investigation of the physiological activity of the cerebral cortex* (G. V. Anrep, trans. & ed.). London: Oxford University Press.

Pea, R. D., and Sheingold, K. (eds.) (1987). *Mirrors of Minds: Patterns of experience in educational computers*. Norwood, NJ: Ablex.

Pearson, W., & Hendrix, L. (1979). Divorce and the status of women. *Journal of Marriage and the Family, 41*, 375–386.

Pedersen, E., & Faucher, T. A., with Eaton, W. W. (1978). A new perspective on the effects of first-grade teachers on children's subsequent adult status. *Harvard Educational Review, 48*, 1–31.

Perin, C. (1977). *Everything in its place: Social order and land use in America*. Princeton, NY: Princeton University Press.

Perrow, C. (1984). *Normal accidents: Living with high-risk technologies*. New York: Basic Books.

Pettigrew, T. F. (1980). Prejudice. In *Harvard encyclopedia of American ethnic groups*. Cambridge, MA: Belknap Press.

Pfeiffer, E., Verwoerdt, A., & Davis, G. (1972). Sexual behavior in middle life. *American Journal of Psychiatry, 128*, 1262–1267.

Phillipson, C. (1982). *Capitalism and the construction of old age*. London: Macmillan.

Piaget, J., & Inhelder, B. (1969). *The psychology of the child*. New York: Basic Books.

Piazza, T., & Glock, C. Y. (1979). Images of God and their social meaning. In R. Wuthnow (ed.), *The religious dimension: New directions in quantitative research*. Orlando: Academic Press.

Pifer, A., & Bronte, L. (eds.) (1986, Winter). The aging society. *Daedalus*.

Piliavin, I., Rodin, J., & Piliavin, J. (1969). "Good Samaritanism": An underground phenomenon? *Journal of Personality and Social Psychology, 13*, 289–299.

Piore, M. J., & Sabel, C. F. (1985). *The second industrial divide: Possibilities for prosperity*. New York: Basic Books.

Piven, F. F., & Cloward, R. (1971). *Regulating the poor: The functions of public welfare*. New York: Vintage.

Piven, F. F., & Cloward, R. (1982). *The new class war: Reagan's attack on the welfare state and its consequences*. New York: Pantheon.

Platt, A. M. (1977). *The child savers* (2nd ed.). Chicago: University of Chicago Press.

Polansky, N. A., Chalmers, M. A., Buttenweiser, E., & Williams, D. P. (1981). *Damaged parents, an anatomy of child neglect*. Chicago: University of Chicago Press.

Polanyi, K. (1944). *The great transformation*. Boston: Beacon Press.

Polsby, N. (1980). *Community power and political theory* (2nd ed.). New Haven, CT: Yale University Press.

Pope, L. (1942). *Millhands and preachers*. New Haven, CT: Yale University Press.

Population Reference Bureau (1985). *1985 world population data sheet*. Washington, DC: U.S. Government Printing Office.

Portes, A., & Stepick, A. (1985). Unwelcome immigrants. *American Sociological Review, 50*, 493–514.

Portes, A., & Walton, J. (1981). *Labor, class, and the international system*. Orlando: Academic Press.

Pressman, J. L., & Wildavsky, A. (1984). *Implementation* (3rd ed.). Berkeley: University of California Press.

Preston, S. H. (1986). The decline of fertility in non-European industrialized countries. *Population and Development Review, 12*, supp., 26–47.

Prybyla, J. S. (ed.) (1990). Privatizing and marketizing socialism. *Annals of the American Academy of Political and Social Science, 507*.

Queen, S., & Debler, M. M. (1940/1925). *Social pathology*. New York: Crowell.

Quinn, B., Anderson, B., Bradley, M., Goetting, P., & Shriver, P. (1981). *Churches and church membership in the United States 1980: An enumeration by region, state and county based on data reported by 111 church bodies*. Atlanta: Glenmary Research Center.

Quinney, R. (1978). The ideology of law: Notes for a radical alternative to legal oppression. In C. E. Reasons & R. M. Rich (eds.), *Sociology of law: A conflict perspective*. Toronto: Butterworths.

Quinney, R. (1980). *Class, state, and crime*. White Plains, NY: Longman.

Rauschning, H. (1940). *The voice of destruction*. New York: Putnam.

Redfield, R. (1947). The folk society. *American Journal of Sociology, 52*, 293–308.

Reinhold, R. (1982, May 6). An "overwhelming" violence–TV tie. *New York Times*, p. C27.

Renner, M. (1989). Enhancing global security. In L. R. Brown et al., *State of the world 1989: A Worldwatch Institute report on progress toward a sustainable society*. New York: Norton.

Rieff, P. (1969). *On intellectuals: Theoretical studies, case studies*. Garden City, NY: Doubleday.

Riesman, D. (1957). The suburban dislocation. *Annals of the American Academy of Political and Social Science, 314*, 123–146.

Riis, J. A. (1890). *How the other half lives: Studies among the tenements of New York*. New York: Scribner's.

Riley, M. W. (1985). Age strata in social systems. In R. Binstock & E. Shanas (eds.), *Handbook of aging and the social sciences* (2nd ed.). New York: Van Nostrand Reinhold.

Riley, M. W., Foner, A., & Waring, J. (1988). The sociology of age. In N. E. Smelser (ed.), *The Handbook of Sociology*. Newbury Park, CA: Sage.

Riley, M. W., & Riley, J. R., Jr. (1989). The lives of older people and changing social roles. *Annals of the American Academy of Political and Social Sciences, 503*, 14–28.

Rist, R. C. (1973). *The urban school: A factory for failure*. Cambridge, MA: M.I.T. Press.

Rist, R. C. (1979). *Desegregated schools*. Orlando: Academic Press.

Ritterband, P., & Silberstein, R. (1973). Group disorders in the public schools. *American Sociological Review, 38*, 461–437.

Robbins, W. (1985, February 10). Despair wrenches farmers' lives as debts mount and land is lost. *New York Times*, pp. 1, 30.

Robertson, R. (1985). The sacred and the world system. In P. Hammond (ed.), *The sacred in a secular age*. Berkeley: University of California Press.

Robinson, J. P. (1977). *How Americans used time in 1965*. Ann Arbor: University of Michigan, Institute for Social Research.

Robinson, P. K., Coberly, S., & Paul, C. E. (1985). Work and retirement. In R. H. Binstock & E. Shanas (eds.), *Handbook of aging and the social sciences* (2nd ed.). New York: Van Nostrand Reinhold.

Robinson, W. C. (1963). Urbanization and fertility: The non-Western experience. *Millbank Memorial Fund Quarterly, 4*, 291–308.

Rock, P. (1985). Symbolic interactionism. In A. Kuper & J. Kuper (eds.). *The social science encyclopedia*. London: Routledge and Kegan Paul.

Roof, W. C. (1985). *Religion in America today* (Annals of the American Academy of Political and Social Science, Vol. 480). Newbury Park, CA: Sage.

Roozen, D. A. (1985). What hath the 1970s wrought? Religion in America. In C. H. Jacquet (ed.), *Yearbook of American and Canadian churches 1984*. Nashville, TN: Abingdon.

Rosen, E. I. (1987). *Bitter choices: Blue-collar women in and out of work*. Chicago: University of Chicago Press.

Rosenberg, M., & Turner, R. H. (eds.). *Social psychology: Sociological perspectives*. New York: Basic Books.

Rosenfeld, J. (1979). *The legacy of aging: Inheritance and disinheritance in social perspective*. Norwood, NJ: Ablex.

Rosenhan, D. L. (1973). On being sane in insane places. *Science, 179*, 250–258.

Rosett, A., & Cressey, D. R. (1976). *Justice by consent: Plea bargains in the American courthouse*. Philadelphia: Lippincott.

Rosow, I. (1974). *Socialization to old age*. Berkeley: University of California Press.

Ross, H. L. (1963). *Perspectives on the social order*. New York: McGraw-Hill.

Rossi, A. (1964). Equality between the sexes: An immodest proposal. In R. J. Lifton (ed.), *The woman in America*. Boston: Beacon Press.

Rossi, A. (1977). The biosocial basis of parenting. *Daedalus, 106*, 1–31.

Rossi, A. (1980). Aging and parenthood in the middle years. In P. B. Baltes & O. G. Brim, Jr. (eds.), *Life-span development and behavior* (vol. 3). Orlando: Academic Press.

Rossides, D. W. (1976). *The American class system: An introduction to social stratification*. Boston: Houghton Mifflin.

Roszak, T. (1969). *The making of a counterculture*. Garden City, NY: Doubleday.

Rubin, Z. (1980). The love research. In A. Skolnick &

J. H. Skolnick (eds.), *Family in transition*. Boston: Little, Brown.

Rubinstein, E. (1981). Effects of television on violent behavior. In J. R. Hays, T. K. Roberts, & K. S. Solway (eds.), *Violence and the violent individual: Proceedings of the twelfth annual symposium, Texas Research Institute of Mental Sciences*. New York: ⌐P Medical & Scientific Books.

Ruckelshaus, W. D. (1989). Toward a sustainable world. *Scientific American, 261*, 166–174.

Rudé, G. (1964). *The crowd in history*. New York: Wiley.

Rushton, J. P. (1980). *Altruism, socialization and society*. Englewood Cliffs, NJ: Prentice-Hall.

Rutter, M. (1974). *The qualities of mothering: Maternal deprivation reassessed*. New York: Jason Aronson.

Ryan, W. (1971). *Blaming the victim*. New York: Random House.

Sagarin, E. (1975). *Deviants and deviance: A study of disvalued people and behavior*. New York: Praeger.

Sahlins, M. D. (1960, September). The origin of society. *Scientific American*, pp. 76–87.

Sahlins, M. D. (1976). *The use and abuse of biology: An anthropological critique of sociobiology*. Ann Arbor: University of Michigan Press.

Sahlins, M. D., & Servide, E. R. (1960). *Evolution and culture*. Ann Arbor: University of Michigan Press.

Salisbury, R. F. (1962). *From stone to steel*. Parkville, Australia: Melbourne University Press.

Sampson, A. (1990, March 18). 18 days: A South African journal. *New York Times Magazine*, pp. 38ff.

Samuelson, P. (1973, 1980). *Economics*. New York: McGraw–Hill.

Sandefur, G. D., & Tienda, M. (eds.) (1988). *Divided opportunities: Minorities, poverty, and social policy*. New York: Plenum.

Sanger, D. E. (1984, June 4). The expected boom in home computers fails to materialize. *New York Times*, p. A1.

Satir, V. (1972). *Peoplemaking*. Palo Alto, CA: Science and Behavior Books.

Scanzoni, L., & Scanzoni, J. (1976). *Men, women and change*. New York: McGraw–Hill.

Schaller, G. B. (1964). *The year of the gorilla*. Chicago: University of Chicago Press.

Schechter, S. (1982). *Women and male violence*. Boston: South End Press.

Schmidt, W. E. (1990, February 12). Valentine in a survey: Marital fidelity. *New York Times*, p. A18.

Schooler, C., & Miller, J. (1985). Work for the household: Its nature and consequences for husbands and wives. *American Journal of Sociology, 90*, 97–124.

Schorr, L. B. (1988). *Within our reach: Breaking the cycle of disadvantage*. Garden City, NY: Doubleday Anchor.

Schuman, H., & Scott, J. (1989). Generations and collective memories. *American Sociological Review, 54*, 359–381.

Schumpeter, J. A. (1950). *Capitalism, socialism, and democracy* (3rd ed.). New York: Harper.

Schur, E. M. (1971). *Labeling deviant behavior: Its sociological implications*. New York: Harper.

Schur, E. M. (1973). *Radical nonintervention: Rethinking the delinquency problem*. Englewood Cliffs, NJ: Prentice-Hall.

Schur, E. M. (1984). *Labeling women deviant: Gender, stigma, and social control*. New York: Random House.

Schwartz, B. (1976). Images of suburbia: Some revisionist commentary and conclusions. In B. Schwartz (ed.), *The changing face of the suburbs*. Chicago: University of Chicago Press.

Schwartz, F. (1989, January–February). Management women and the new facts of life. *Harvard Business Review*.

Schwartz, S. (1970). Elicitation of moral obligation and self-sacrificing behavior: An experimental study of volunteering to be a bone marrow donor. *Journal of Personality and Social Psychology, 15*, 67–84.

Scull, A. T. (1988). Deviance and social control. In N. Smelser (ed.), *The Handbook of sociology*. Newbury Park, CA: Sage.

Secord, P. F., & Backman, C. W. (1974). *Social psychology* (2nd ed.). New York: McGraw-Hill.

Seeley, J. R., Sim, R. A., & Loosley, E. W. (1955). *Crestwood Heights: A study of the culture of suburban life*. New York: Basic Books.

Seeman, M. (1959). On the meaning of alienation. *American Sociological Review, 24*, 783–791.

Selznick, P. (1952). *The organizational weapon: A study of Bolshevik strategy and tactics*. New York: McGraw-Hill.

Sennett, R., & Cobb, J. (1972). *The hidden injuries of class*. New York: Random House.

Sewall, W., Haller, A., & Ohlendorf, G. (1970). The educational and early occupational status attainment process: Replication and revision. *American Sociological Review, 35*, 1014–1027.

Shabecoff, P. (1989, June 2). Bush's call for leadership in a world cleanup puts the focus on the mess in America's backyard. *New York Times*, p. A22.

Shaiken, H. (1985). *Work transformed: Automation and labor in the computer age*. Fort Worth, TX: Holt, Rinehart and Winston.

Shaw, J. A. (1979). The child in the military community. In J. D. Hall et al. (eds.), *Handbook of child psychiatry*. New York: Basic Books.

Shelby, B., & Heberlein, T. A. (1985). *Carrying capacity in recreation settings*. Corvallis: Oregon State University Press.

Sherif, M., et al. (1956). Experiments in group conflicts. *Scientific American, 195*, 54–58.

Sherif, M., Harvey, O. J., White, B. J., Wood, W. R., & Sherif, C. W. (1988/1961). *The Robbers Cave experiment: Intergroup conflict and cooperation*. Middletown, CT: Wesleyan University Press.

Shi, D. E. (1985). *The simple life: Plain living and high thinking in American culture*. New York: Oxford University Press.

Shibutani, T., & Kwan, K. M. (1965). *Ethnic stratification*. New York: Macmillan.

Shils, E. (1961). Mass society and its culture. In N. Jacobs (ed.), *Culture for the millions*. New York: Van Nostrand Reinhold.

Shils, E. (1962). The theory of mass society. *Diogenes, 39*, 45–66.

Shils, E. (1963). On the contemporary study of the new states. In C. Geertz (ed.), *New societies and old states: The quest for modernity in Asia and Africa*. New York: Free Press.

Shils, E. (1965). Charisma, order, and status. *American Sociological Review, 30*, 199–213.

Shils, E. (1970). Tradition, ecology and institution in the history of sociology. *Daedalus, 99*, 760–825.

Shils, E. (1985). Sociology. In A. Kuper & J. Kuper

(eds.), *The social science encyclopedia*. London: Routledge and Kegan Paul.

Shrag, C. (1971). Leadership among prison inmates. In L. Radzinowics & M. Wolfgang (eds.), *The criminal in confinement*. New York: Basic Books.

Shupe, A., & Stacey, W. (1983). The Moral Majority constituency. In R. C. Liebman and R. Wuthnow (eds.), *The new Christian right: Mobilization and legitimation*. Hawthorne, NY: Aldine.

Silberman, C. (1980). *Criminal violence, criminal justice*. New York: Random House.

Silberstein, R. D. (1981). *Right versus privilege*. New York: Free Press.

Silk, L. (1989, May 12). Rich and poor: The gap widens. *New York Times*, p. D2.

Simmel, G. (1904). The sociology of conflict. *American Journal of Sociology, 9*, 490ff.

Simmons, J. L. (1985). The nature of deviant subcultures. In E. Rubington & M. S. Weinberg, *Deviance: The interactionist perspective*. New York: Macmillan.

Simpson, C. E., & Yinger, J. M. (1953). *Racial and cultural minorities: An analysis of prejudice and discrimination*. New York: Harper.

Simpson, J. H. (1983). Moral issues and status politics. In R. C. Liebman & R. Wuthnow (eds.), *The new Christian right: Mobilization and legitimation*. Hawthorne, NY: Aldine.

Sjoberg, G. (1968). The preindustrial city. In S. Fava (ed.), *Urbanism in world perspective: A reader*. New York: Crowell.

Skocpol, T. (1979). *States and social revolutions*. New York: Cambridge University Press.

Skolnick, A., & Skolnick, J. (eds.) (1980). *Families in transition*. Boston: Little, Brown.

Slater, P. (1976). *The pursuit of loneliness*. Boston: Beacon.

Smelser, N. J. (1962). *Theory of collective behavior* New York: Free Press.

Smelser, N. J. (1966). The modernization of social relations. In M. Weiner (ed.), *Modernization*. New York: Basic Books.

Smelser, N. J. (1984). *Sociology*. Englewood Cliffs, NJ: Prentice-Hall.

Smigel, E. O. (1964). *The Wall Street lawyer: Professional organizational man*. New York: Free Press.

Smith, A. (1910/1776). *The wealth of nations*. London: University Paperbacks.

Smith, C., & Freedman, A. (1972). *Voluntary associations: Perspectives on the literature*. Cambridge, MA: Harvard University Press.

Smith, D. (1989). *Promises* (letter from Madurai). Oberlin, OH: Oberlin Shansi Memorial Association.

Smith, Hedrick. (1976). *The Russians*. New York: Ballantine.

Smith, Huston. (1952). *The religions of man*. New York: Mentor.

Smith, J. D., & Franklin, S. D. (1974, May). Concentration of personal wealth, 1922–1969. *American Economic Review: Papers and Proceedings, 64*, 162–167.

Smith, R. A. (1968). Los Angeles, prototype of supercity. In S. F. Fava (ed.), *Urbanism in world perspective: A reader*. New York: Crowell.

Smith, S. B. (1985, October 9). New TV technologies alter viewing habits. *New York Times*, p. C22.

Sorokin, P. (1937). *Social and cultural dynamics: Vol. 3. Fluctuation of social relationships, war, and revolution*. New York: American Book.

Sowell, T. (1972). *Black education: Myths and tragedies*. New York: McKay.

Sowell, T. (1983). *Ethnic America: A history*. New York: Basic Books.

Spencer, H. (1874). *The study of sociology*. New York: Appleton.

Spengler, O. (1965/1918). *The decline of the West*. New York: Modern Library.

Spiro, M. (1970). *Kibbutz*. New York: Schocken.

Spitz, R. A. (1945). Hospitalism: An inquiry into the genesis of psychiatric conditions in early childhood. In A. Freud (ed.), *The psychoanalytic study of the child*. New York: International Universities Press.

Stack, C. (1974). *All our kin*. New York: Harper.

Stark, R., & Bainbridge, W. S. (1979). Of churches, sects, and cults: Preliminary concepts for a theory of religious movements. *Journal for the Scientific Study of Religion, 18*, 117–133.

Stark, R., & Bainbridge, W. S. (1980). Toward a theory of religion: Religious commitment. *Journal for the Scientific Study of Religion, 19*, 114–128.

Stark, R., & Bainbridge, W. S. (1985). *The future of religion: Secularization, revival and cult formation*. Berkeley: University of California Press.

Starr, P. (1982). *The social transformation of American medicine*. New York: Basic Books.

Statistical abstract of the United States, 1985. Washington, DC: U.S. Bureau of the Census.

Statistical abstract of the United States, 1989. Washington, DC: U.S. Bureau of the Census.

Statistical abstract of the United States, 1990. Washington, DC: U.S. Bureau of the Census.

Stave, B. M. (ed.). (1975). *Socialism and the cities*. Port Washington, NY: Kennikut Press.

Steelworkers Research Project (1985). *Chicago steelworkers: The cost of unemployment*. Chicago: Hull House Assoc.

Steinberg, S. (1989). *The ethnic myth* (2nd ed.). Boston: Beacon.

Steltzer, U. (1982). *Inuit: The north in transition*. Chicago: University of Chicago Press.

Sterk, C. (1988, May 7). Cocaine and HIV positivity. *The Lancet*, pp. 1052–1053.

Stevens, W. K. (1986, December 16). Prehistoric society: A new picture emerges. *New York Times*, pp. C1, C15.

Stevens, W. K. (1988, December 20). Life in the Stone Age: New findings point to complex societies. *New York Times*, pp. C1, C15.

Steward, J. H. (1955). *The theory of culture change: The methodology of multilinear evolution*. Urbana: University of Illinois Press.

Stimson, C. (1980). Women and the American city. *Signs, 5* (supp.).

Stinchcombe, A. L. (1968). *Constructing social theories*. Orlando: Harcourt Brace Jovanovich.

Stone, J., & Mennell, S. (1980). *Alexis de Tocqueville on democracy, revolution, and society*. Chicago: University of Chicago Press.

Stouffer, S. A., Suchman, E. A., DeVinney, L. C., Star, S. A., & Williams, R. A., Jr. (1949). *Studies in social psychology in World War II. Vol. 1. The American soldier: Adjustment during army life*. Princeton, NJ: Princeton University Press.

Strange, M. (1988). *Family farming: A new economic vision*. Lincoln: University of Nebraska Press.

Street, D., & Associates (1978). *Handbook of contemporary urban life*. San Francisco: Jossey–Bass.

Sudman, S., & Bradburn, N. (1982). *Asking questions:*

A practical guide to questionnaire design. San Francisco: Jossey-Bass.

Sumner, W. G. (1940). *Folkways*. Boston: Ginn.

Suro, R. (1990, March 11). Courts ordering financing changes in public schools. *New York Times*, p. A1.

Sutherland, E. H. (1940). White collar criminality. *American Sociological Review, 5*, 1–12.

Suttles, G. (1967). *The social order of the slum*. Chicago: University of Chicago Press.

Suttles, G. (1972). *The social construction of communities*. Chicago: University of Chicago Press.

Sweet, J. A., & Bumpass, L. (1987). *American families and households*. New York: Russell Sage.

Sweezy, P. M. (1980). *Post revolutionary society*. New York: Monthly Review Press.

Sykes, G. M., & Messinger, S. L. (1960). The inmate social system. In R. A. Cloward, D. R. Cressey, G. H. Grosser, R. McCleery, L. E. Ohlin, G. M. Sykes, & S. L. Messinger (eds.), *Theoretical studies in the social organization of the prison*. New York: Social Science Research Council.

Szelenyi, I. (1983). *Urban inequalities under state socialism*. New York: Oxford University Press.

Szymanski, A. J., & Goertzel, T. G. (1979). *Sociology: Class, consciousness, and contradictions*. New York: Van Nostrand Reinhold.

Taeuber, K. E., & Taeuber, A. F. (1965). *Negroes in cities*. Hawthorne, NY: Aldine.

Terrace, H. S. (1979). *Nim*. New York: Knopf.

Thomas, L. (1979). *The medusa and the snail*. New York: Bantam.

Thomas, L. (1989, July 15). Beyond the moon's horizon—Our home. *New York Times*, p. 25.

Thomas, W. L. (1956). *Man's role in changing the face of the earth*. Chicago: University of Chicago Press.

Thornberry, T. P., & Farnworth, M. (1983). Social correlates of criminal involvement. Further evidence on the relationship between social status and criminal behavior. *American Sociological Review, 47*, 211–227.

Thornton, R. (1987). *American Indian holocaust and survival: A population history since 1492*. Norman: University of Oklahoma Press.

Thurow, L. (1975). *Generating inequality: Mechanisms of distribution in the U.S. economy*. New York: Basic Books.

Thurow, L. C. (1981). *The zero sum society*. New York: Penguin.

Tienda, M., & Jensen, L. (1988). Poverty and minorities: A quarter-century profile of color and socioeconomic disadvantage. In G. D. Sandefur & M. Tienda (eds.), *Divided opportunities: Minorities, poverty, and social policy*. New York: Plenum.

Tilly, C. (1978). *From mobilization to revolution*. Reading, MA: Addison-Wesley.

Titmus, R. (1958). *War and social policy: Essays on the welfare state*. London: Allen and Unwin.

Toffler, A. (1971). *Future shock*. New York: Bantam.

Touraine, A. (1971). *The post industrial society: Tomorrow's social history: Classes, conflicts and culture in the programmed society*. New York: Random House.

Traub, J. (1984, September 9). A village in India: Reluctant progress. *New York Times Magazine*, pp. 106ff.

Traven, B. (1966). Assembly line. In *The night visitor, and other stories*. New York: Hill & Wang.

Troltsch, E. (1931). *The social teachings of the Christian churches* (O. Wyon, trans.). New York: Macmillan.

Trow, M. (1966). The second transformation of American secondary education. In R. Bendix & S. M. Lipset (eds.), *Class, status, and power* (2nd ed.). New York: Free Press.

Truzzi, M. (1971). *Sociology: The classic statements*. New York: McGraw-Hill.

Tumin, M. M. (1967). *Social stratification: The forms and functions of inequality*. Englewood Cliffs, NJ: Prentice-Hall.

Turk, A. T. (1978). Law as a weapon in social conflict. In C. E. Reasons & R. M. Rich (eds.), *Sociology of law: A conflict perspective*. Toronto: Butterworths.

Turner, F. J. (1920/1893). *The frontier in American history*. Fort Worth, TX: Holt, Rinehart and Winston.

Turner, R. H. (1974). The theme of contemporary social movements. In R. E. L. Faris (ed.), *Handbook of modern sociology*. Chicago: Rand McNally.

Turner, R. H. (1981). Collective behavior and resource mobilization as approaches to social movements: Issues and continuities. In L. Krisberg (ed.), *Research in social movements* (Vol. 4). Greenwich, CT: JAI Press.

Turner, V. W. (1969). *The ritual process: Structure and anti-structure*. Hawthorne, NY: Aldine.

Tuttle, W. R. (1978). *Race riot*. New York: Atheneum.

Tyree, A., & Treas, J. (1974). The occupational and marital mobility of women. *American Sociological Review, 39*, 293–302.

UNESCO (United Nations Educational, Scientific, and Cultural Organization) (1984). *Statistical yearbook, 1984*. Paris: UNESCO.

United Nations (1984). *World population chart*. New York: United Nations.

U.S. Commission on Civil Rights (1981). *Affirmative action in the 1980's: Dismantling the process of discrimination*. Washington, DC: U.S. Government Printing Office.

Van den Berghe, P. L. (1975). *Man in society: A biosocial view*. New York: Elsevier.

Van den Berghe, P. L. (1979). *Human family systems: An evolutionary view*. New York: Elsevier.

Van Gennep, A. (1960/1908). *The rites of passage*. Chicago: University of Chicago Press.

Vanek, J. (1974). Time spent in housework. *Scientific American, 231*, 116–120.

Verbrugge, L. M. (1985). Gender and health: An update on hypotheses and evidence. *Journal of Health and Social Behavior, 26*, 156–182.

Vidich, A., & Bensman, J. (1960). *Small town in mass society*. Garden City, NY: Doubleday.

Vining, D. R., Jr. (1985, April). The growth of core regions in the third world. *Scientific American*, pp. 42–49.

Vogel, E. (1979). *Japan as number one: Lessons for America*. Cambridge, MA: Harvard University Press.

Voslensky, M. (1980). *La nomenklatura*. Paris: Pierre Belfond.

Wainhouse, D. W. (1973). *International peacekeeping at the crossroads: National support—Experience and prospects*. Baltimore: Johns Hopkins University Press.

Wallerstein, I. (1974). *The modern world system: Capitalist agriculture and the origins of the European world-economy in the sixteenth century*. Orlando: Academic Press.

Wallerstein, J., & Blakeslee, S. (1989). *Second chances: Men, women and children a decade after divorce*. New York: Ticknor & Fields.

Walsh, E. J. (1981). Resource mobilization and citizen protest in communities around Three Mile Island. *Social Problems, 29*, 1–21.

Walsh, E. J., & Warland, R. H. (1983). Social movement involvement in the wake of a nuclear accident: Activists and free riders in the TMI area. *American Sociological Review, 48*, 764–780.

Walsh, F. (1982). Conceptualization of normal family functioning. In F. Walsh (ed.), *Normal family processes*. London: Guilford Press.

Walton, J. (1970). A systematic survey of community power research. In M. Aiken & P. Mott (eds.), *The structure of community power*. New York: Random House.

Waltzer, M. (1983). *Spheres of justice*. New York: Basic Books.

Waltzer, M. (1983). Pluralism. In *Harvard encyclopedia of American ethnic groups*. Cambridge, MA: Belknap Press.

Warner, W. L., & Lunt, P. S. (1941). *The social life of a modern community*. New Haven, CT: Yale University Press.

Warner, W. L., et al. (1949). *Social class in America: A manual of procedure for the measurement of social status*. Chicago: Science Research Associates.

Washburn, P. C. (1982). *Political sociology*. Englewood Cliffs, NJ: Prentice-Hall.

Webb, E., Campbell, D. T., Schwarz, R. D., & Sechrest, L. (1966). *Unobtrusive measures: Nonreactive research in the social sciences*. Chicago: Rand McNally.

Weber, Marianne (1975/1926). *Max Weber: A biography* (H. Zohn, trans. & ed.). New York: Wiley.

Weber, Max (1922). *Gesammelte aufsatze zur Religionssoziologie*. Tübingen, Germany: Mohr.

Weber, Max (1947). *The theory of social and economic organization* (A. M. Henderson & T. Parsons, trans.). New York: Free Press.

Weber, Max (1949). *The methodology of the social sciences* (E. A. Shils & H. A. Finch, ed. & trans.). New York: Free Press.

Weber, Max (1958/1922). Economy and society. In H. Gerth & C. W. Mills (trans. & eds.), *From Max Weber: Essays in sociology*. New York: Oxford University Press.

Weber, Max (1958/1913). World religion. In H. Gerth & C. W. Mills (trans. & eds.), *From Max Weber: Essays in sociology*. New York: Oxford University Press.

Weber, Max (1962). *The city*. New York: Collier.

Weber, Max (1963/1922). *The sociology of religion* (E. Fischoff, trans.). Boston: Beacon Press.

Weber, Max (1968). The concept of citizenship. In S. N. Eisenstadt (Ed.), *Max Weber on charisma and institution building*. Chicago: University of Chicago Press.

Weber, Max (1974/1904). *The Protestant ethic and the spirit of capitalism* (T. Parsons, trans.). New York: Scribner's.

Weir, B. R. J., & Weir, T. (1976). The relationships of wives' employment to husband, wife, and pair satisfaction. *Journal of Marriage and the Family, 2*, 279–287.

Weisman, A. (1989, July 30). L.A. fights for breath. *New York Times Magazine*, pp. 14ff.

Wekerle, G. (ed.) (1980). *New space for women*. Boulder, CO: Westview Press.

Welch, M. R. (1979). Quantitative approaches to sect classification and the study of sect development. In R. Wuthnow (ed.), *The religious dimension: New directions in quantitative research*. Orlando: Academic Press.

Wells, M. J. (1984). The resurgence of sharecropping: Historical anomaly or political strategy? *American Journal of Sociology, 90*, 1–30.

Westin, A. (1967). *Privacy and freedom*. New York: Atheneum.

Westrum, R. (1983). *What happened to the old sociology of technology?* Paper presented to the Society for the Sociological Study of Science, Blacksburg, VA.

Whorf, B. L. (1961). The relation of habitual thought and behavior to language. In J. B. Carroll (ed.), *Language, thought, and reality: Selected writings of Benjamin Lee Whorf*. Cambridge, MA: M.I.T. Press.

Whyte, W. F. (1943). *Street corner society*. Chicago: University of Chicago Press.

Whyte, W. F. (1949). The social structure of the restaurant. *American Journal of Sociology, 54*, 302–310.

Whyte, W. F. (1984). *Learning from the field*. Newbury Park, CA: Sage.

Whyte, W. F., & Gardner, B. B. (1945). Facing the foreman's problems. *Applied Anthropology, 4*, 1–28.

Whyte, W. H. (1957). *The organization man*. Garden City, NY: Doubleday.

Whyte, W. H. (1980). *The social life of small urban spaces*. Washington, DC: Conservation Foundation.

Wicker, T. (1989, August 4). Sleazy but legal. *New York Times*, p. A27.

Wilensky, H. (1964). Mass society and mass culture: Interdependence or independence. *American Sociological Review, 29*, 173–193.

Wilford, J. N. (1989, April 24). Fusion furor: Science's human face. *New York Times*, pp. A1, B6.

Wilkinson, A. (1989, July 24). Sugarcane. *New Yorker*, pp. 56–57.

Williams, R. (1952). *American society*. New York: Knopf.

Williams, R. (1973). *The country and the city*. New York: Oxford University Press.

Williams, T. (1989). *The cocaine kids*. Reading, MA: Addison-Wesley.

Willis, P. (1983). Cultural production and theories of reproduction. In L. Barton & S. Walker (eds.), *Race, class and education*. London: Croom-Helm.

Willmott, P., & Young, M. (1971). *Family and class in a London suburb*. London: New American Library.

Wilson, E. O. (1975). *Sociobiology*. Cambridge, MA: Belknap Press.

Wilson, E. O. (1979). *On human nature*. New York: Bantam.

Wilson, J. Q. (1977). *Thinking about crime*. New York: Vintage.

Wilson, W. J. (1978). *The declining significance of race: Blacks and changing American institutions*. Chicago: University of Chicago Press.

Wilson, W. J. (1984). The urban underclass. In L. W. Dunbar (ed.), *The minority report*. New York: Pantheon.

Wilson, W. J. (1986). *Black poverty and the underclass*. Unpublished proposal to the Ford Foundation.

Wilson, W. J. (1987). *The truly disadvantaged: The inner city, the underclass, and public policy*. Chicago: University of Chicago Press.

Wilson, W. J. (1989). The underclass: Issues,

perspectives, and public policy. *Annals of the American Academy of Political and Social Science, 501,* 182–192.

Winch, R. F. (1958). *Mate selection.* New York: Harper.

Winner, L. (1977). *Autonomous technology: Technics-out-of-control as a theme in political thought.* Cambridge, MA: M.I.T. Press.

Wirth, L. (1945). The problem of minority groups. In R. Linton (ed.), *The science of man in the world crisis.* New York: Columbia University Press.

Wirth, L. (1968/1938). Urbanism as a way of life. In S. F. Fava (ed.), *Urbanism in world perspective: A reader.* New York: Crowell.

Witing, J. (1969). Effects of climate on certain cultural practices. In A. P. Vayda (ed.), *Environment and cultural behavior: Ecological studies in cultural anthropology.* Garden City, NY: Natural History Press.

Wittfogel, K. (1957). *Oriental despotism: A comparative study of total power.* New Haven, CT: Yale University Press.

Wixen, B. N. (1979). Children of the rich. In J. D. Hall et al. (eds.), *Handbook of child psychiatry.* New York: Basic Books.

Wolf, E. R. (1966). *Peasants.* Englewood Cliffs, NJ: Prentice–Hall.

Wolf, E. R. (1984, November 4). The perspective of the world. *New York Times Book Review,* pp. 13–14.

Wolf, E. R. (1984, November 4). Unifying the vision. *New York Times Book Review,* p. 11.

Wolfe, T. (1980). *The right stuff.* New York: Bantam.

Wolfgang, M. E., & Riedel, M. (1973). Race, judicial discretion and the death penalty. *Annals of the American Academy of Political and Social Science, 407,* 119–133.

Wooden, K. (1976). *Weeping in the playtime of others: America's incarcerated children.* New York: McGraw-Hill.

Wright, E. O. (1979). *Class structure and economic determination.* Orlando: Academic Press.

Wright, E. O., Costello, C., Hachen, D., & Sprague, J. (1982). The American class structure. *American Sociological Review, 47,* 702–726.

Wrigley, E. A. (1969). *Population and history.* New York: McGraw-Hill.

Wrong, D. H. (1961). The oversocialized conception of man in modern sociology. *American Sociological Review, 24,* 772–782.

Wuthnow, R. (1988). Sociology of religion. In N. E. Smelser (ed.), *The handbook of sociology.* Newbury Park, CA: Sage.

Yankelovich, D. (1981). *New rules: Searching for self-fulfillment in a world turned upside down.* New York: Random House.

Zangwell, I. (1909). *The melting pot.* New York: Macmillan.

Zeisel, H. (1982). *The limits of law enforcement.* Chicago: University of Chicago Press.

Zelizer, V. A. (1985). *Pricing the priceless child: The changing social value of children.* New York: Basic Books.

Zerubavel, E. (1986). *Hidden rhythms: Schedules and calendars in social life.* Chicago: University of Chicago Press.

Zimbardo, P. G. (1972). Pathology of imprisonment. *Society, 9,* 4–8.

Zolberg, A. (1974). *Creating political order.* Chicago: University of Chicago Press.

Zolberg, A. (1981). International migrations in political perspective. In M. M. Kritz, C. B. Keely, & S. M. Tomasi (eds.), *Global trends in migration: Theory and research on international population movements.* New York: Center for Migration Studies.

Zuboff, S. (1982, Winter). Problems of symbolic toil. *Dissent,* pp. 51–52.

Zuboff, S. (1988). *In the age of the smart machine.* New York: Harper.

Zurcher, L. A., & Snow, D. A. (1981). Collective behavior and social movements. In M. Rosenberg & R. Turner (eds.), *Social psychology: Sociological perspectives.* New York: Basic Books.

GLOSSARY

accommodation: the process by which a smaller, less powerful society is able to preserve the major features of its culture even after prolonged contact with a larger, stronger society.

acculturation: the process by which the members of a civilization incorporate norms and values from other cultures into their own.

achieved status: a position or rank that is earned through the efforts of the individual.

age cohort: a set of people of about the same age who are passing through the life course together.

age grade: a set of statuses and roles based on age that is established by the norms of a particular society.

ageism: an ideology that justifies prejudice and discrimination based on age.

agent of socialization: an individual, group, or institution that helps teach the beliefs, norms, and values of a society.

alienation: the feeling of being powerless to control one's own destiny; a worker's feeling of powerlessness owing to inability to control the work process.

animism: a form of religion in which all forms of life and all aspects of the earth are inhabited by gods or supernatural powers.

anomie: a state of normlessness.

anticipatory socialization: socialization that prepares an individual for a role that he or she is likely to assume later in life.

ascribed status: a, position or rank that is assigned to an individual at birth and cannot be changed.

assimilation: the process by which culturally distinct groups in a larger civilization adopt the norms, values, and language of the host civilization and are able to gain equal statuses in its groups and institutions.

authority: power that is considered legitimate both by those who exercise it and by those who are affected by it.

behaviorism: a theory that states that all behavior is learned and that this learning occurs through the process known as conditioning.

bureaucracy: a formal organization characterized by a clearly defined hierarchy with a commitment to rules, efficiency, and impersonality.

caste: a social stratum into which people are born and in which they remain for life.

charisma: a special quality or "gift" that motivates people to follow a particular leader.

church: a religious organization that has strong ties to the larger society.

citizenship: the status of membership in a nation-state.

civilization: a cultural complex formed by the identical major cultural features of a number of societies.

civil religion: a collection of beliefs and rituals that exist outside religious institutions.

class: a social stratum that is defined primarily by economic criteria such as occupation, income, and wealth.

class consciousness: a group's shared subjective awareness of its objective situation as a class.

closed stratification system: a stratification system in which there are rigid boundaries between social strata.

closed question: a question that requires the respondent to choose among a predetermined set of answers.

collective behavior: nonroutine behavior engaged in by large numbers of people responding to a common stimulus.

communications media: institutions that specialize in communicating information, images, and values about ourselves, our communities, and our society.

community: a set of primary and secondary groups in which the individual carries out important life functions.

conditioning: the shaping of behavior through reward and punishment.

confidentiality: the promise that the information provided to a researcher by a respondent will not appear in any form that can be traced to that respondent.

conflict theory: a sociological perspective that emphasizes the role of conflict and power in society.

conjugal family: a husband and wife and their children, if any.

control group: in an experiment, the subjects who do not experience a change in the independent variable.

controlled experiment: an experimental situation in which the researcher manipulates an independent variable in order to observe and measure changes in a dependent variable.

core state: a technologically advanced nation that has a dominant position in the world economy.

correlation: a specific relationship between two variables.

counterculture: a subculture that challenges the accepted norms and values of the larger society and establishes an alternative life-style.

crime: an act or omission of an act that is prohibited by law.

crowd: a large number of people who are gathered together in close proximity.

crude birthrate: the number of births occurring during a year in a given population divided by the midyear population.

crude death rate: the number of deaths occurring during a year in a given population divided by the midyear population.

cult: a new religion.

cultural evolution: the process by which successful cultural adaptations are passed down from one generation to the next.

cultural lag: the time required for social institutions to adapt to a major technological change.

cultural relativity: the recognition that all cultures develop their own ways of dealing with the specific demands of their environments.

culture: all the modes of thought, behavior, and production that are handed down from one generation to the next by means of communicative interaction rather than by genetic transmission.

de facto segregation: segregation that is supported and maintained by unwritten norms.

deference: the respect and esteem shown to an individual.

de jure segregation: segregation that is supported by formal legal sanctions that prohibit certain groups from interacting with others or place limits on such interactions.

demagogue: a leader who uses personal charisma and political symbols to manipulate public opinion.

demeanor: the way in which individuals present themselves to others through body language, dress, speech, and manners.

democracy: a political system in which all citizens have the right to participate in public decision making.

democratic socialism: an economic philosophy based on the belief that private property may exist at the same time that large corporations are owned by the state and run for the benefit of all citizens.

demographic transition: a set of major changes in birth and death rates that has occurred most completely in urban industrial nations in the past 200 years.

denomination: a religious organization that is on good terms with the institution from which it developed but must compete with other denominations for members.

dependent variable: the variable that a hypothesis seeks to explain.

developing nation: a nation that is undergoing a set of transformations in its institutions whose effect is to increase the productivity of its people, their health, their literacy, and their ability to participate in political decision making.

deviance: behavior that violates the norms of a particular society.

differential association: a theory that explains deviance as a learned behavior that is determined by the extent of a person's association with individuals who engage in such behavior.

differentiation: the processes whereby sets of social activities performed by one social institution are divided among different institutions.

discrimination: behavior that treats people unfairly on the basis of their group membership.

downward mobility: movement by an individual or group to a lower social stratum.

dyad: a group consisting of two people.

education: the process by which a society transmits knowledge, values, norms, and ideologies and in so doing prepares young people for adult roles and adults for new roles.

educational achievement: how much the student actually learns, measured by mastery of reading, writing, and mathematical skills.

educational attainment: the number of years of school an individual has completed.

ego: according to Freud, the part of the human personality that is the individual's conception of himself or herself in relation to others.

endogamy: a norm specifying that a person brought up in a particular culture may marry within the cultural group.

endogenous force: pressure for social change that builds within a society.

equality of opportunity: equal opportunity to achieve desired levels of material well-being and prestige.

equality of result: equality in the actual outcomes of people's attempts to improve their material well-being and prestige.

ethnic group: a population that has a sense of group identity based on shared ancestry and distinctive cultural patterns.

ethnic (or racial) nationalism: the belief that one's own ethnic group constitutes a distinct people whose culture is and should be separate from that of the larger society.

ethnic stratification: the ranking of ethnic groups in a social hierarchy on the basis of each group's similarity to the dominant group.

ethnocentrism: the tendency to judge other cultures as inferior to one's own.

exogamy: a norm specifying that a person brought up in a particular culture may marry outside the cultural group.

exogenous force: pressure for social change exerted from outside a society.

experimental group: in an experiment, the subjects who are exposed to a change in the independent variable.

expulsion: the forcible removal of one population from a territory claimed by another population.

extended family: an individual's nuclear family plus the nuclear families of his or her blood relatives.

family: a group of people related by blood, marriage, or adoption.

family of orientation: the nuclear family in which a person is born and raised.

family of procreation: the nuclear family a person forms through marriage or cohabitation.

feral child: a child reared outside human society.

field experiment: an experimental situation in which the researcher observes and studies subjects in their natural setting.

folkways: weakly sanctioned norms.

formal organization: a group that has an explicit, often written, set of norms, statuses, and roles that specify each member's relationships to the others and the conditions under which those relationships hold.

frequency distribution: a classification of data that describes how many observations fall within each category of a variable.

functionalism: a sociological perspective that focuses on the ways in which a complex pattern of social structures and arrangements contributes to social order.

gender: a set of culturally conditioned traits associated with maleness or femaleness.

gender role: a set of behaviors that are considered appropriate for an individual of a particular gender.

gender socialization: the ways in which we learn our gender identity and develop according to cultural norms of masculinity and femininity.

generalized other: a person's internalized conception of the expectations and attitudes held by society.

genocide: the intentional extermination of one population by a more dominant population.

gerontology: the study of aging and older people.

ghetto: a section of a city that is segregated either racially or culturally.

Hawthorne effect: the unintended effect that results from the attention given to subjects in an experimental situation.

homogamy: the tendency to marry a person who is similar to oneself in social background.

human ecology: a sociological perspective that emphasizes the relationships among social order, social disorganization, and the distribution of populations in time and space.

hypothesis: a statement that specifies a relationship between two or more variables that can be tested through empirical observation.

id: according to Freud, the part of the human personality from which all innate drives arise.

ideas: the ways of thinking that organize human consciousness.

identification: the social process whereby an individual chooses role models and attempts to imitate their behavior.

ideologies: systems of values and norms that the members of a society are expected to believe in and act upon without question.

impression management: the strategies one uses to "set a stage" for one's own purposes.

independent variable: a variable that the researcher believes causes a change in another variable (the dependent variable).

informal organization: a group whose norms and statuses are generally agreed upon but are not set down in writing.

informed consent: the right of respondents to be informed of the purpose for which the information they supply will be used and to judge the degree of personal risk involved in answering questions even when an assurance of confidentiality has been given.

in-group: a social group to which an individual has a feeling of allegiance; usually, but not always, a primary group.

institution: a more or less stable structure of statuses and roles devoted to meeting the basic needs of people in a society.

institutional discrimination: the systematic exclusion of people from equal participation in a particular institution because of their group membership.

interactionism: a sociological perspective that views social order and social change as resulting from all the repeated interactions among individuals and groups.

interest group: an organization that attempts to influence elected and appointed officials regarding a specific issue or set of issues.

intergenerational mobility: a change in the social class of family members from one generation to the next.

internal colonialism: a theory of racial and ethnic inequality that suggests that some minorities are essentially colonial peoples within the larger society.

Jim Crow: the system of formal and informal segregation that existed in the United States from the late 1860s to the early 1970s.

kinship: the role relations among people who consider themselves related by blood, marriage, or adoption.

labeling: a theory that explains deviance as a societal reaction that brands or labels as deviant people who engage in certain behaviors.

laissez-faire capitalism: an economic philosophy based on the belief that the wealth of a nation can be measured by its capacity to produce goods and services (i.e., its resources of land, labor, and machinery) and that these can be maximized by free trade.

legitimacy: the ability of a society to engender and maintain the belief that the existing political institutions are the most appropriate for that society.

life chances: the opportunities that an individual will have or be denied throughout life as a result of his or her social-class position.

life course: a pathway along an age-differentiated, socially created sequence of transitions.

life expectancy: the average number of years a member of a given population can expect to live.

linguistic-relativity hypothesis: the belief that language determines the possibilities for thought and action in any given culture.

lobbying: the process whereby interest groups seek to persuade legislators to vote in their favor on particular bills.

long-distance upward mobility: a form of upward mobility in which a person rises during his or her own lifetime from low family status to membership in a professional or managerial elite.

macro-level sociology: an approach to the study of society that focuses on the major structures and institutions of society.

market: an economic institution that regulates exchange behavior through the establishment of different values for particular goods and services.

mass: a large number of people who are all oriented toward a set of shared symbols or social objects.

mass public: a large population of potential spectators or participants who engage in all kinds of collective behavior.

material culture: patterns of possessing and using the products of culture.

megalopolis: a complex of cities distributed along a major axis of traffic and communication.

mercantilism: an economic philosophy based on the belief that the wealth of a nation can be measured by its holdings of gold or other precious metals and that the state should control trade.

metropolitan area: a central city surrounded by a number of smaller cities and suburbs that are closely related to it both socially and economically.

micro-level sociology: an approach to the study of society that focuses on patterns of social interaction at the individual level.

middle-level sociology: an approach to the study of society that focuses on relationships between social structures and the individual.

minority group: a population that, because of its members' physical or cultural characteristics, is singled out from others in the society for differential and unequal treatment.

modernization: a term used to describe the changes societies and individuals experience as a result of industrialization, urbanization, and the development of nation-states.

monotheistic: a term used to describe a theistic belief system centered on belief in a single all-powerful God.

mores: strongly sanctioned norms.

multinational corporation: an economic enterprise that has headquarters in one country and conducts business activities in one or more other countries.

nation-state: the largest territory within which a society's political institutions can operate without having to face challenges to their sovereignty.

nonterritorial community: a network of relationships formed around shared goals.

normative order: the array of norms found in a given culture.

norms: specific rules of behavior.

nuclear family: two or more people related by blood, marriage, or adoption who share a household.

objective class: in Marxian theory, a social class that has a visible, specific relationship to the means of production.

occupational prestige: the honor or prestige attributed to specific occupations by adults in a society.

oligarchy: rule by a few people who stay in office indefinitely rather than for limited terms.

open question: a question that does not require the respondent to choose from a predetermined set of answers. Instead, the respondent may answer in his or her own words.

open stratification system: a stratification system in which the boundaries between social strata are easily crossed.

operant conditioning: a conditioning technique in which a behavior that was not originally part of a stimulus-response pattern is shaped into that pattern.

opinion leader: an individual who consistently influences the attitudes and behavior of others.

out-group: any social group to which an individual does not have a feeling of allegiance; may be in competition or conflict with the in-group.

paradigm: a general way of seeing the world that dictates what kind of scientific work should be done and what kinds of theory are acceptable.

participant observation: a form of observation in which the researcher participates to some degree in the lives of the people being observed.

patronage: jobs and economic benefits that party leaders can exchange for votes and political influence.

peer group: an interacting group of people of about the same age that has a significant influence on the norms and values of its members.

percent analysis: a mathematical operation that transforms an absolute number into a proportion as a part of 100.

peripheral area: a region that supplies basic resources and labor power to more advanced states.

plea bargaining: a process in which a person charged with a crime agrees to plead guilty to a lesser charge.

pluralistic society: a society in which different ethnic and racial groups are able to maintain their own cultures and life-styles while gaining equality in the institutions of the larger society.

pluralist model: a theory stating that no single group controls political decisions; instead, a plurality of interest groups influence those decisions through a process of coalition building and bargaining.

political institution: a set of norms and statuses pertaining to the exercise of power and authority.

political party: an organization of people who join together to gain legitimate control of state authority.

political revolution: a set of changes in the political structures and leadership of a society.

polytheistic: a term used to describe a theistic belief system that includes numerous gods.

power: the ability to control the behavior of others, even against their will.

power elite model: a theory stating that political decisions are controlled by an elite of rich and powerful individuals even in societies with democratic political institutions.

prejudice: an attitude that prejudges a person on the basis of a real or imagined characteristic of a group of which that person is a member.

primary deviance: an act that results in the labeling of the offender as deviant.

primary group: a social group characterized by intimate, face-to-face associations.

privacy: the right of a respondent to define when and on what terms his or her actions may be revealed to the general public.

profane: a term used to describe phenomena that are not considered sacred.

profession: an occupation with a body of knowledge and a developed intellectual technique that are transmitted by a formal educational process and testing procedures.

projection: the psychological process whereby we attribute to other people behaviors and attitudes we are unwilling to accept in ourselves.

public opinion: the values and attitudes held by mass publics.

race: an inbreeding population that develops distinctive physical characteristics that are hereditary.

racism: an ideology based on the belief that an observable, supposedly inherited trait is a mark of inferiority that justifies the discriminatory treatment of people with that trait.

rate of reproductive change: the difference between the crude birthrate and the crude death rate for a given population.

recidivist: a criminal who is returned to prison after having served at least one term there.

reference group: a group that an individual uses as a frame of reference for self-evaluation and attitude formation.

relative deprivation: deprivation as determined by comparison with others rather than by some objective measure.

religion: any set of coherent answers to the dilemmas of human existence that makes the world meaningful; a system of beliefs and rituals that serves to bind people together into a social group.

religiosity: the depth of a person's religious feelings.

rite of passage: a ceremony marking the transition to a new stage of a culturally defined life course.

ritual: a formal pattern of activity that expresses symbolically a set of shared meanings.

sacred: a term used to describe phenomena that are regarded as extraordinary, transcendent, and outside the everyday course of events.

sample: a set of respondents selected from a specific population.

sample survey: a survey administered to a selection of respondents drawn from a specific population.

sanctions: rewards and punishments for abiding by or violating norms.

scapegoat: a convenient target for hostility.

science: knowledge obtained as a result of the process of developing and testing hypotheses.

scientific method: the process by which theories and explanations are constructed through repeated observation and careful description.

secondary deviance: behavior engaged in as a reaction to the experience of being labeled as deviant.

secondary group: a social group whose members have a shared goal or purpose but are not bound together by strong emotional ties.

sect: a religious organization that rejects the beliefs and practices of existing churches; usually formed when a group leaves the church to form a rival organization.

secularization: a process in which the dominance of religion over other institutions is reduced.

segregation: the ecological and institutional separation of races or ethnic groups.

semiperipheral area: a state or region in which industry and financial institutions are developed to some extent but that remains dependent on capital and technology provided by other states.

sexism: an ideology that justifies prejudice and discrimination based on sex.

sex ratio: the number of males per 100 females in a population.

significant other: any person who is important to an individual.

simple supernaturalism: a form of religion in which people may believe in a great force or spirit but do not have a well-defined concept of God or a set of rituals involving God.

slavery: the ownership of one racial, ethnic, or politically determined group by another group that has complete control over the enslaved group.

social category: a collection of individuals grouped together because they share a trait that is deemed by the observer to be socially relevant.

social change: variations over time in the ecological ordering of populations and communities, in patterns of roles and social interactions, in the structure and functioning of institutions, and in the cultures of societies.

social conditions: the realities of life that we create together as social beings.

social control: the ways in which a society encourages conformity to its norms and prevents deviance.

social Darwinism: the notion that people who are more successful at adapting to their environment are more likely to survive and reproduce.

social group: a group whose members are recruited according to some membership criterion and are bound together by a set of membership rights and mutual obligations.

socialism: an economic philosophy based on the concept of public ownership of property and sharing of profits, together with the belief that economic decisions should be controlled by the workers.

socialization: the processes whereby we learn to behave according to the norms of our culture.

social mobility: movement by an individual or group from one social stratum to another.

social movement: organized collective behavior aimed at changing or reforming social institutions or the social order itself.

social revolution: a complete transformation of the social order, including the institutions of government and the system of stratification.

social stratification: a society's system for ranking people hierarchically according to such attributes as wealth, power, and prestige.

sociobiology: the hypothesis that all human behavior is determined by genetic factors.

socioeconomic status (SES): a broad social-class ranking based on occupational status, family prestige, educational attainment, and earned income.

sociological imagination: according to C. Wright Mills, the ability to see how social conditions affect our lives.

sociology: the scientific study of human societies and human behavior in the groups that make up a society.

spatial mobility: movement of an individual or group from one location or community to another.

state: the set of political institutions operating in a particular society.

status group: a category of people within a social class, defined by how much honor or prestige they receive from the society in general.

status symbols: material objects or behaviors that indicate social status or prestige.

stereotype: an inflexible image of the members of a particular group that is held without regard to whether it is true.

stigma: an attribute or quality of an individual that is deeply discrediting.

structural mobility: movement of an individual or group from one social stratum to another that is caused by the elimination of an entire class as a result of changes in the means of existence.

subculture: a group of people who hold many of the values and norms of the larger culture but also hold certain beliefs, values, or norms that set them apart from that culture.

subjective class: in Marxian theory, the way members of a given social class perceive their situation as a class.

superego: according to Freud, the part of the human personality that internalizes the moral codes of adults.

technologies: the products and the norms for using them that are found in a given culture.

technology: tools, procedures, and forms of social organization that increase human productive capacity; the use of tools and knowledge to manipulate the physical environment in order to achieve desired practical goals.

technology assessment: efforts to anticipate the consequences of particular technologies for individuals and for society as a whole.

territorial community: a population that functions within a particular geographic area.

theism: a belief system that conceives of a god or gods as separate from humans and from other living things on the earth.

theoretical perspective: a set of interrelated theories that offers explanations for important aspects of social behavior.

theory: a set of interrelated concepts that seeks to explain the causes of an observable phenomenon.

total institution: an organization that assumes total responsibility for every aspect of the lives of the people who live within it.

totalitarian regime: a regime that accepts no limits to its power and seeks to exert its rule at all levels of society.

triad: a group consisting of three people.

two-step flow of communication: the process in which messages communicated by the media are evaluated by certain respected individuals, who in turn influence the attitudes and behavior of others.

unobtrusive measures: observational techniques that measure behavior but intrude as little as possible into actual social settings.

upward mobility: movement by an individual or group to a higher social stratum.

urbanization: a process in which an increasing proportion of a total population becomes concentrated in urban settlements.

values: the ideas that support or justify norms.

variable: a characteristic of an individual, group, or society that can vary from one case to another.

voluntary association: a formal organization whose members pursue shared interests and arrive at decisions through some sort of democratic process.

welfare capitalism: an economic philosophy in which markets determine what goods will be produced and how, but the government regulates economic competition.

NAME INDEX

Addams, Jane, 13
Adler, M., 434, 508
Adorno, T., 408
Adriance, M., 518
Aldous, J., 330
Alger, Horatio, 232, 377
Alland, A., 391
Allen, W., 299, 398, 439, 464
Altman, D., 262
Ames, R. E., 301
Amory, C., 227
Ann Arbor Science for the People
    Editorial Collective, 264
Apter, D., 606
Aquino, Corazón, 624
Archibald, K., 448
Ariès, P., 427, 528
Aristotle, 611
Aronowitz, S., 370, 528, 574
Asch, S., 40–41
Ash, T. G., 571, 594
Asimov, I., 123
Aspaklaria, S., 482
Astor, Jacob, 268
Atchley, R., 447
Attwood, L., 179
Auletta, K., 37, 381

Back, K., 195
Backer, B., 112
Backman, C. W., 196
Bacon, Francis, 10
Bahr, H., 360
Bainbridge, W. S., 499, 508, 509, 513
Bakke, E. W., 82
Bakker, James, 495–496, 548
Bakker, Tammy, 495, 548
Balandier, A., 434
Balbus, I., 268
Bales, R. F., 160, 207, 484
Baltzell, D., 602
Bane, M. J., 37, 382, 462, 486
Barash, D. P., 103
Barnet, R. J., 565
Barnum, P. T., 307
Baron, J. N., 438

Barringer, F., 478
Bassuk, E. L., 272
Bates, F., 527
Baum, S., 536
Bayer, R., 262
Bayh, B., 541
Beatles, 306
Becker, G. S., 474, 480, 561
Becker, H. J., 551
Becker, H. S., 258, 271, 272, 445, 583
Beer, F. A., 321, 617
Beijer, G. J., 85
Bell, C., 195
Bell, D., 86, 245, 266, 362, 528, 536,
    573, 631–632, 633
Bellah, R., 330, 485, 504, 516
Belous, R. S., 474
Ben-David, J., 630, 631, 632
Bendix, R., 225, 238, 304, 580, 601
Bengston, V. L., 443
Bennett, M. K., 567
Benokraitis, N. V., 441
Bensman, D., 582
Bensman, J., 365
Bentham, J., 200, 278, 568
Berger, B., 195, 369
Bernard, J., 448, 602, 611
Bernstein, R., 22
Berrueta-Clement, J. R., 536
Berry, B., 124, 147
Berscheid, E., 477
Bettelheim, B., 164, 234, 472
Bielby, W. T., 438
Bierstedt, R., 95, 96
Birdwhistell, R., 39
Black, D., 273
Black Elk, 396, 502
Blakeslee, S., 472, 480
Blau, P., 210, 356, 377, 476–477
Blauner, R., 370, 406, 412, 578
Bleier, R., 442
Bloch, M., 234
Bloch, R., 638
Bloom, B., 537
Bluestone, B., 241, 574
Blumer, H., 16, 203, 290, 294

Blumstein, P., 113, 480
Boff, Leonardo, 518
Boggs, V., 60, 112, 147
Bogue, D., 85, 125, 135, 427, 429, 466,
    477, 511, 513, 528, 529, 531
Bohannon, L., 565
Bohannon, P., 565
Boldt, E. D., 649
Bonacich, E., 86
Bonnett, A., 197
Boocock, S. S., 527, 529
Booth, A., 479
Borganokar, D., 264
Bose, C. E., 356
Bosk, C., 112, 203, 583
Bott, E., 197
Bottomore, T., 108
Bowles, S., 528
Bracey, J. H., 407
Bradburn, N., 47
Braidwood, R., 77
Braudel, F., 110, 132, 296
Braverman, H., 580
Brecht, Bertolt, 636
Breese, G., 129, 132, 133
Briggs, M., 204
Brinton, M., 439
Broad, W. J., 634
Brody, D., 205
Brody, E., 472
Bronfenbrenner, U., 175, 176, 179
Bronte, L., 443
Brotman, H. B., 452
Brown, C., 182
Brown, D., 396
Brown, L., 128, 138, 333, 334
Brown, R., 506
Brubaker, E. R., 302
Bruegel, Pieter, 31
Brundtland, G. H., 333
Bryan, William Jennings, 515
Buck, Doris, 392
Buckley, M., 484
Bumpass, L., 478, 480
Burawoy, M., 370
Burch, W., 310

Burgess, E., 13, 15, 97, 135, 136, 137, 147
Buruma, I., 264
Bury, J. B., 10
Bush, George, 620
Butler, R., 441
Butterfield, F., 46

Cain, L. D., 427
Camara, Dom Helder, 518
Cameron, W. B., 294
Campbell, R. T., 436
Cancian, F., 184
Cantril, H., 307
Caplan, A. L., 103
Caplow, T., 195, 360, 361
Capriati, J., 445
Carmichael, Stokely, 407
Carnegie, Andrew, 268, 579
Carnegie family, 367
Carter, E. A., 474, 477, 480
Carter, L. J., 308
Castro, Fidel, 569
Catton, W. R., Jr., 334
Caudill, H. M., 112
Cayton, H., 359, 361-362
Ceausescu, Nicolae, 543
Census Bureau, U.S., 132, 260, 301
Chadwick, B., 360
Chambliss, W. J., 272-273
Chamorra, Violeta Barrios de, 613-614
Chaney, James, 389
Charlton, M., 570
Chernin, K., 181
Chodorow, N., 169, 438, 446
Chomsky, N., 104
Chwast, J., 255
Clarke, L., 577, 628
Clausen, J. A., 427
Cloward, R., 38, 266, 381
Cobb, J., 243
Cockerham, W. C., 644, 646
Cohen, N., 295
Cohen, R. S., 629
Coleman, J. S., 39, 529, 541, 543, 561, 579
Coles, R., 472
Collier, J., 120
Collins, R., 446
Columbus, Christopher, 93-94
Comer, J. P., 525-526, 539
Comte, A., 11
Confucius, 232, 503
Converse, P., 620
Cookson, P. W., 366
Cooley, C. H., 81, 169, 172, 193-194
Coon, C., 391
Coser, L. A., 408
Cott, N., 446
Cottrell, W. F., 636
Cranz, G., 135
Crapanzano, V., 399
Cremin, L. A., 528
Cressey, D. R., 271, 277
Csikszentmihalyi, M., 541
Cuber, J. F., 482
Cumming, E., 449

Cummings, J., 487
Curtis, L. A., 279, 280

Dahl, R., 610
Dahrendorf, R., 231, 329-330, 337
Daley, Richard, 240, 606-607
Daley, Richard, Jr., 240
D'Andrade, R. G., 434
Danziger, K., 160
Darley, J., 141, 205
Darrow, Clarence, 515
Darwin, C., 101, 102, 633
Davidson, D., 412
Davis, F. J., 393, 399
Davis, Glenn, 442
Davis, K., 103, 131-132, 164, 238, 243, 442
Davis, N. J., 254
Dawson, C. A., 297
de Beauvoir, S., 425-426, 444, 445, 447
De Klerk, F. W., 422
de Rougemont, D., 437
de Saint Simon, H., 568
de Sola Pool, I., 340, 551, 643
de Tocqueville, A., 238, 297, 300, 382, 612, 614
Debler, M. M., 265
Demos, J., 437
Denitch, B., 570
Denzin, N., 176
Descartes, René, 10
Dewey, R., 194
Dickens, Charles, 306-307
Djilas, M., 242
Dobriner, W., 369
Dobzhansky, T., 391
Dodgson, R. A., 232
Dollard, J., 361, 408, 409
Domhoff, G. W., 197, 227, 367, 610
Doob, L., 408
Dore, R., 577
Dornbusch, S., 100, 616, 617
Douglas, J. D., 291
Dowd, M., 244
Drake, S., 359, 361-362
Du Pont family, 227, 367
DuBois, W. E. B., 13, 14, 287, 602
Dukakis, Michael, 620
Duncan, O. D., 356, 377
Durkheim, É., 12, 35-36, 53, 132, 140, 214, 256, 496

Ecker, M., 291
Eckholm, E., 104, 182
Edwards, J. N., 479
Edwards, R., 578
Ehlinger, J., 576
Ehrlich, A. H., 649
Ehrlich, P. R., 649
Eibl-Eibesfeldt, I., 183
Einstein, A., 633
Eisenhower, D. D., 225, 605-606, 634
Eisley, L., 105
Elder, G. H., 427
Elias, N., 107-108, 437
Elifson, K. W., 516
Elkind, D., 173

Ellul, J., 97
Ellwood, D., 37, 41, 366, 371, 373, 381, 382
Elton, R., 213
Engels, F., 239, 268, 296, 298, 337, 482
Epstein, C., 181, 182, 183-184, 438, 445
Epstein, C. F., 432, 434
Erhardt, A., 180
Erikson, E., 172, 181, 472
Erikson, J., 172
Erikson, K. T., 112, 255, 256, 257, 271
Esping-Anderson, G., 245
Etzioni, A., 573
Eyck, Jan van, 28

Fallers, L., 225
Fallon, A., 181
Fallows, D., 330, 574
Farley, R., 398
Farnworth, M., 273
Faucher, T. A., 539, 542-543
Fava, S., 144, 369
Feagin, J. R., 441
Featherman, D. I., 377
Federal Bureau of Investigation (FBI), 260
Feiring, C., 175-176, 177
Feldmesser, R. A., 597
Fenn, R., 499
Fernandes, F., 401
Festinger, L., 195
Field, D., 310
Finkelhor, D., 483
Finn, R., 445
Firestone, S., 446
Fischer, C. S., 112, 140, 141, 144, 199, 209, 513, 643
FitzSimons, R., 306-307
Flink, J. J., 308, 635, 643
Flores, J., 112
Foley, Thomas S., 253
Foner, A., 426
Ford, Henry, 367
Form, W. H., 580
Fortin, N., 291
Fox, L., 277
Fox, R., 183
Frank, A. G., 328
Frank, R. H., 202, 205
Franklin, S. D., 367
Frazier, E. F., 407, 510
Freeman, J., 444, 448
French, H. F., 627
Freud, S., 168-169, 172, 180, 181
Frideres, J. S., 649
Fried, M., 144
Friedan, B., 448
Friedlander, D., 128
Friedman, M., 376
Fromm, E., 578
Fuchs, V., 362, 573
Fukae, K., 598
Furstenberg, F., 174, 470, 482
Fyfe, C., 397

Galbraith, J. K., 570, 602

Galileo, 10, 634, 636
Gallup Organization, 497, 515
Galtung, J., 321
Gandhi, Mohandas, 298
Gans, H., 112, 142, 144, 179, 195, 369, 376, 548
Garcia, Jerry, 436
Gardner, B. B., 82
Garfinkel, I., 415
Garn, S., 391
Gattentag, M., 428, 429
Geertz, C., 102, 103
Geiger, K., 484
Gelles, R., 483
Genevie, L. E., 290, 300
Genovese, Kitty, 141, 204-205
Germani, G., 327
Gerson, K., 182, 432, 433
Gerth, H., 210, 214
Geschwender, J. A., 298
Gettys, W. E., 297
Giddens, A., 80
Gilder, G., 487
Gilder, George, 376
Gilligan, C., 173, 181, 444, 472, 529
Gintis, H., 528
Giroux, H. A., 528
Gist, N. P., 133
Gitlin, T., 612
Glaser, D., 264
Glasgow, D., 381
Glazer, N., 402, 403, 408
Glick, P., 470, 472
Glock, C. Y., 497
Glueck, E. T., 264
Glueck, S., 264
Goertzel, T. G., 364
Goffman, E., 8-9, 17, 191, 204, 233, 254, 258, 259, 277, 278, 456
Goldfarb, W., 164
Goldhammer, H., 233
Goldschmidt, W., 375
Goldwater, Barry, 309
Goleman, D., 478
Goodall, J. V. L., 104
Goode, W. J., 106, 462, 467-468, 474, 475, 476, 484, 600, 648
Goodman, Andrew, 389
Goodrich, D. W., 480
Goodrich, L. M., 601
Goodwin, C., 147
Gorbachev, Mikhail, 442, 500
Gordon, M., 401
Gottfredson, M. R., 272
Gottman, J. M., 472
Gottmann, J., 138
Gould, S. J., 391, 392-393
Gouldner, A., 200
Goya, Francisco, 346-347
Graham, Martha, 436
Gramsci, A., 20
Greeley, A., 184, 513
Greenwald, M., 22
Grønbjerg, K. A., 37
Gusfield, J., 22, 262, 267, 271
Guterbock, T. M., 147, 607
Gutkind, E. A., 629

Gutman, H., 415, 469

Haberman, C., 500
Hadaway, C. K., 516
Hagedorn, J. M., 279, 280
Hagestad, G. O., 426, 427
Halevy, E., 568
Hall, E., 39
Hall, J., 295, 427, 509
Halle, D., 370, 577
Haller, A., 378
Halsey, M., 408
Hamilton, C. V., 147, 399
Hansen, W. L., 536
Harbison, F. H., 356
Hardy, A., 642
Hareven, T., 330, 468
Harlan, W. H., 437
Harlow, H., 164-165
Harlow, M. K., 165
Haroff, P. B., 482
Harper, D., 38, 284
Harriman family, 227
Harrington, M., 381, 570
Harris, C., 137
Harris, L., 48
Harris, M., 104, 107, 225, 437
Harrison, B. B., 241, 574
Hart, Gary, 548
Hartnagel, T., 546
Hauser, P., 128, 130
Hauser, R. M., 377
Havel, Vaclav, 593
Hawkins, G., 277
Hayghe, H., 379
Heberlein, T. A., 310
Hechter, M., 207, 390, 412, 561
Heer, D., 476
Heidelberg, Polly, 389-390
Heilbroner, R., 575
Helfer, R. E., 165
Helmreich, W., 404
Hendrix, L., 479
Henry, D. O., 75
Henry, W., 449
Henslin, J., 204
Hershey, R. D., 43
Hill, J., 104
Hinton, W., 230
Hirschi, T., 272
Hite, S., 46
Hitler, Adolf, 295, 299, 392, 548, 605
Hobbes, T., 199
Hobsbawm, E., 269, 638
Hochschild, A., 183, 432, 436, 448, 472
Hodge, R. W., 107, 329, 356, 362
Holdren, J. P., 649
Hollingshead, A., 364, 475
Holmes, Oliver Wendell, 392
Holt, J., 541
Holt, T. C., 399
Holy, L., 193
Homans, G., 17, 179, 193, 200, 201, 202, 206
Hopkins, T. K., 245
Hopper, R. D., 294
Horowitz, M., 408

Horowitz, R., 191-192, 196
Hout, M., 513
Hoyt, H., 137
Huber, J., 468
Hughes, E., 17, 82, 583
Humphreys, L., 48
Hunt, M., 141
Hunter, F., 610

Inhelder, B., 537
Inkeles, A., 329
Institute for Research on Poverty, 536

Jackman, M., 364, 368, 369, 371
Jackman, R., 144, 364, 368, 369, 371
Jackson, B., 277
Jackson, Jesse, 300
Jackson, Michael, 243, 306
Jacobs, J., 149, 150
Jacobs, P., 264
Jacobson, J., 138
Jahoda, M., 82
Janowitz, M., 209, 212, 213, 231, 255, 530, 596, 601, 605, 607-608, 614
Jaynes, G. D., 415, 486
Jefferson, Thomas, 357
Jencks, C., 376, 378, 528, 532, 534-535, 543
Jennings, F., 94, 98, 502
Jensen, L., 418
Jesus Christ, 233, 508
John Paul II, Pope, 500, 517
Johnson, Lyndon, 309
Johnson, P., 503
Jones, E. F., 174
Jones, Jim, 295, 509
Joravsky, D., 633
Joselow, F., 586
Julian, J., 97, 180, 260, 267, 442

Kahl, J. A., 364
Kahneman, D., 201-202
Kamata, S., 577
Kaplan, R. M., 546
Kasarda, J., 136, 145
Katz, E., 197, 549
Katz, F. E., 527
Katz, M., 535
Katznelson, I., 602
Kaynes, M., 570
Keith, J., 441, 449-450
Keller, Helen, 165, 166-167
Keller, S., 368
Kelly, H. H., 196
Kempe, H., 165
Kempe, R., 165
Keniston, K., 165
Kennedy family, 367
Kennedy, R. E., 585
Kennedy, R. J. R., 402
Kessler, S. J., 180
Keyfitz, N., 430
Khrushchev, Nikita, 633
Killian, L., 82
Kilson, M., 147
Kim, I., 141-142, 413
King, Martin Luther, Jr., 298

Kinsey, A. C., 263
Kitano, 397
Kitsuse, J. I., 271
Kitt, A., 193
Klatzky, S., 194
Kleinberg, O., 392
Kluckhohn, C., 95
Koch, Robert, 644
Kohlberg, L., 173, 181
Komarovsky, M., 209, 485
Kondratieff, N. D., 641
Kornblum, W., 60, 97, 139, 141, 147,
    180, 260, 267, 370, 393, 442, 492,
    581, 602
Kornhauser, W., 298, 300
Kovic, R., 180
Kroc, R., 308
Kronus, C., 302
Kübler-Ross, E., 450
Kuhn, T., 630
Kutner, B., 405
Kwan, K. M., 405

Ladd, E., 620
Ladner, Joyce, 488
Lai, H. M., 396
Lake, R., 147
Lakoff, S., 634
Land, K. C., 275
Landon, Alfred E., 45
Lang, G. E., 297
Lang, K., 297
Lapidus, G., 179
LaPiere, R., 405
Larkin, R. W., 279
Larson, R., 541
Lasch, C., 113, 176
Laslett, P., 128, 468
Lasswell, H., 83, 323, 594, 605
Latané, B., 141, 205
Law Enforcement Assistance
    Administration, 260
Lazarsfeld, P., 82
Leacock, E., 437
LeBon, G., 300
Lee, Spike, 410
LeFebvre, H., 192
Leibnez, Gottfried Wilhelm, 10, 633
LeMasters, E. E., 370
Lemert, E. M., 271, 273
Lenero-Otero, L., 468
Lenin, Vladimir Ilyich, 298, 504, 505,
    569
Lenski, G., 336, 462-463
Lenski, J., 336, 462-463
Lents, J. M., 627
Leontief, W. W., 585
Lever, J., 181, 550
Levi, P., 322
Levitan, S., 474
Lewis, M., 175-176, 177, 472
Lewontin, R. C., 103
Lieberson, S., 304, 415
Liebow, E., 464
Lind, Jennie, 307
Lindner, S., 310
Lindsmith, A., 176

Lippman, Walter, 405
Lipset, S. M., 225, 357, 596, 603, 605,
    606, 607
Lofland, J. F., 292-293
Lombroso, C., 264
Loosley, E. W., 369
Lovins, A., 642-643
Lowell family, 227
Luce, I., 214
Ludlam, Ned, 638
Luhmann, N., 562
Lurie, A., 181
Luxemburg, Rosa, 569
Lynch, R., 582
Lynd, H., 114-115, 359, 360, 448, 643
Lynd, R., 114-115, 359, 360, 448, 643
Lysenko, Trofim D., 633

MacCannell, D., 375
Machiavelli, N., 611-612
Machlis, G., 309
Macleod, J., 279
Maddox, G. L., 436, 439
Madonna, 306
Maharidge, D., 590
Majundar, R. C., 232
Malcolm X, 407
Malinowski, B., 103
Malson, L., 164
Malthus, T., 125
Mandela, Nelson, 257, 422, 599
Manderscheid, R. W., 22
Mannheim, K., 238
Manpower Demonstration and Research
    Corporation, 41, 488
Manson, Charles, 162, 215
Mao Zedong, 569
Marcos, Ferdinand, 624
Markson, A. R., 638
Marsh, Reginald, 348
Marshall, T. H., 601-602
Martin, C. E., 263
Martini, Simone, 345
Martinson, R., 278
Marwell, G., 301
Marx, K., 11-12, 19, 53, 76, 237, 238,
    239-240, 241- 243, 251, 268, 270,
    296, 297, 298, 337, 359, 362, 364,
    382, 446, 482, 495, 496, 506, 556,
    561, 568- 569, 578, 596
Matras, J., 125, 126, 131, 427
Mauss, M., 201
Mawson, A. R., 275
Maydans, S., 576
Mayfield, L., 82
Mayhew, H., 381
Mayo, E., 41-42, 578, 580-581
McAdam, D., 296
McAdoo, H. P., 487-488
McAndrew, M., 179
McBrien, Richard P., 517
McCarthy, J. D., 296
McCaull, J., 649
McGoldrick, M., 474, 477, 480
McGuire, M. B., 508, 513, 518
McIntyre, J., 546
McKay, H., 270

McKenna, W., 180
McKinlay, J. B., 644
McKinlay, S. M., 644
McLanahan, S. S., 415
McNeill, W., 77, 232, 321, 503
Mead, G. H., 170, 172, 181
Mead, M., 105, 434
Medvedev, Z., 633
Meier, A., 407
Mellon family, 367
Menard, S., 533
Mencken, H. L., 204, 301
Mennell, S., 357
Merton, R. K., 193, 196, 265-266, 268,
    284, 405-406, 633
Meyer, M., 210
Meyersohn, R., 112
Milavsky, W. R., 546
Milgram, S., 140, 210-212
Mill, S. J., 568
Miller, D. C., 580
Miller, J., 330
Miller, N., 408
Miller, W., 271
Millet, François, 31
Millman, M., 112, 648
Mills, C. W., 7, 210, 214, 225, 244,
    367, 595, 610
Mintz, S., 229, 567
Minuchin, S., 481
Modell, J., 330
Moe, T. M., 297
Mollenkopf, J., 147
Molotch, H., 148
Mondale, Walter, 309
Money, J., 180
Monroe, Marilyn, 439
Montagna, P. D., 573, 582
Moore, B., 298, 597
Moore, W., 243
Morales, E., 566-567
Morgan, J. P., 268
Morgan, R., 448
Morgan, T., 331
Morison, S. E., 93
Morris, D., 441
Moscos, C., 529, 530
Mowat, F., 414
Moynihan, D. P., 402, 403
Murdock, G. P., 107, 225
Murray, C., 376
Murray, H. A., 476
Murray, V., 527
Myrdal, G., 381, 407, 416
Myrdal, J., 230

Napier, A., 481, 486
National Academy of Sciences, 449
National Commission on Excellence in
    Education, 533
National Opinion Research Center
    (NORC), 301, 545-546
Natwar Singh, 226
Navratilova, Martina, 442
Negrin, J., 499
Neihardt, J. G., 502
Nelkin, D., 55-56, 634

Nelson, G. K., 509
Neugarten, B., 426, 427, 445
Newby, H., 195
Newcomb, T., 196-197
Newman, K. S., 241, 377
Newton, Isaac, 10, 633
Niebuhr, H. R., 508, 509
Nisbet, R., 10, 96, 170, 335-336, 362, 498
Nixon, Richard, 548, 603
Nkrumah, Kwame, 606
Norpoth, H., 620
Nyden, P., 112

Oakley, A., 441
Oberschall, A., 297, 301, 605
Office of Technology Assessment, U.S. Congress, 375
Ogburn, W. F., 462, 640-641, 648
Ohlendorf, G., 378
Ohlin, L., 266
O'Leary, J. T., 310
Olmsted, F. L., 135
Olsen, M., 301, 514
O'Neill, J. A., 37
Oppenheimer, J. R., 633-634
Orwell, George, 548, 613
Osmond, M. W., 468, 470
Owen, R., 568

Pallas, A. M., 532
Palmore, E., 439, 449
Parelius, A. P., 527, 529, 539
Parelius, R. J., 527, 539
Park, R., 13-15, 97, 135-136, 139-140, 147, 195, 412- 413, 547
Parke, R., Jr., 470
Parkin, F., 242
Parry, J. H., 94
Parsons, T., 100, 160, 243, 337-338, 368, 410, 484, 507, 610
Pascal, Blaise, 10
Passell, P., 572
Pasteur, Louis, 644
Patterson, F., 104
Patterson, O., 397, 398
Pavlov, I., 162
Pea, R. D., 339
Pearson, W., 479
Pedersen, E., 539, 542-543
Pélé, 550
Perin, C., 147
Perlman, J., 154
Perrow, C., 639, 648
Persell, C. H., 366
Pettigrew, T. F., 408
Pfeiffer, E., 442
Phillipson, C., 446
Piaget, J., 173, 181, 537
Piazza, T., 497
Picasso, Pablo, 347
Pifer, A., 443
Piliavin, I., 205
Piliavin, J., 205
Pinochet, Augustus, 614
Piore, M., 86, 573
Piven, F., 38, 381

Platt, A. M., 265
Polansky, N. A., 165
Polanyi, K., 79, 238, 564
Polsby, N., 364, 368
Pomeroy, W. B., 263
Pope, L., 508
Population Reference Bureau, 124
Portes, A., 86, 148, 245
Prescott, S., 541
Pressman, J. L., 611
Preston, S. H., 128
Proxmire, William, 477
Prybyla, J. S., 570

Quadagno, J., 103
Queen, S., 265
Quinney, R., 268

Rasmussen, P. K., 291
Rausch, H., 480
Rauschning, H., 299
Reagan, Ronald, 309, 333, 620
Redfield, R., 230
Reinhold, R., 180, 546
Renoir, Auguste, 348
Riedel, M., 276
Rieff, P., 634
Riesman, D., 369
Riis, J., 13, 135
Riley, J. W., Jr., 443, 447
Riley, M. W., 426, 443, 447, 451-452
Rist, R. C., 535-536, 541
Ritterband, P., 541
Rivera, Diego, 347
Robbins, W., 375
Roberts, Oral, 495
Robertson, R., 501
Robinson, J., 310, 570
Robinson, P. K., 452
Robinson, W. C., 128
Rock, P., 17
Rockefeller family, 197-199, 227, 367
Rockefeller, John D., 268, 367, 579
Rodin, J., 205
Roof, W. C., 513
Roosevelt, F. D., 45-46, 359, 602, 620
Roosevelt family, 227
Roozen, D. A., 512
Rosen, E. I., 370, 432, 448
Rosenfeld, J., 447
Rosenhan, D. L., 271-72
Rosenstone, S., 620
Rosett, A., 277
Rosow, I., 437
Ross, Diana, 306
Ross, H. L., 95
Rossi, A., 169, 438, 448
Rossi, P. H., 107, 329, 356
Rossides, D., 364, 367, 368, 369, 371
Roszak, T., 112
Rozin, P., 181
Rubin, Z., 477
Rubinstein, E., 546
Rudé, G., 638
Rudwick, E., 407
Rushton, J. P., 205
Rusk, J., 620

Rutter, M., 164
Ryan, W., 381
Ryder, R., 480

Sabel, C. F., 573
Sagarin, E., 254
Sahlins, M., 76, 103, 336
Salisbury, R, 394
Salisbury, R., 76
Sampson, A., 599
Samuelson, P., 355, 561
Sánchez, José Benitez, 498-49ɡ
Sandefur, G. D., 415
Sanger, D. E., 635
Sapir, E., 105
Sarney, José, 334
Sassen, S., 86
Satir, V., 481
Scanzoni, J., 434, 475-476
Scanzoni, L., 434, 475-476
Schachter, S., 195
Schaller, G. B., 104
Schechter, S., 444
Schmidt, W. E., 184
Schooler, C., 330
Schorr, L. B., 525, 526
Schumpeter, J. A., 238, 298
Schur, E. M., 254, 260, 271, 273
Schwartz, B., 369
Schwartz, F., 82
Schwartz, P., 113, 480
Schwartz, S., 205
Schwerner, Michael, 389
Scopes, John T., 515
Scull, A. T., 258, 273
Secord, P. F., 196, 429
Seeley, J. R., 369
Seeman, M., 578
Seigel, P., 356
Selznick, P., 212, 508
Sennett, R., 243
Servide, E. R., 336
Sewall, W., 378
Shabecoff, P., 334
Shah, S., 264
Shahn, Ben, 348
Shaiken, H., 638
Shakespeare, William, 306, 333, 476
Shaw, C., 270
Shaw, J. A., 481
Sheingold, K., 339
Shelby, B., 310
Sheldon, W., 264
Sherif, M., 165-168, 410
Shi, D. E., 357
Shibutani, T., 405
Shils, E., 8, 212, 213, 216, 233, 298, 300, 601, 603
Shupe, A., 515
Silberman, C., 260
Silberstein, R., 529, 541
Silk, L., 145
Sim, R. A., 369
Simmel, G., 19, 140, 141, 196, 220, 408
Simmons, J. L., 263
Simpson, C. E., 392
Simpson, J. H., 515

Singer, R. D., 546
Sjoberg, G., 132, 133
Skinner, B. F., 163
Skocpol, T., 296
Skolnick, A., 486
Skolnick, J., 486
Slater, P., 113, 207
Smelser, N., 290, 324-325, 509
Smigel, E. O., 112
Smith, 147
Smith, A., 16, 238, 568
Smith, D., 329, 474
Smith, Hedrick, 179, 597
Smith, Huston, 503
Smith, J. D., 367
Smith, R. A., 138
Snow, D., 301
Sorokin, P., 321, 336-337
Sowell, T., 86, 408
Spanier, G., 470
Speck, Richard, 264
Spencer, H., 101-102
Spengler, O., 336
Spiro, M., 484
Spitz, G., 468
Spitz, R. A., 164
Stacey, W., 515
Stack, C., 37, 464
Stalin, Josef, 298, 548, 569, 633
Stampen, J. O., 536
Stanford, Leland, 268
Stark, R., 499, 508, 509, 513
Starnes, C., 367
Starr, P., 647
Steinberg, S., 145
Steltzer, U., 502
Stephens, J. J., 649
Stepick, A., 148
Sterk, C., 54-55, 56
Sternberg, R., 478
Stevens, W. K., 75, 76, 103
Steward, J. H., 336
Stimson, C., 144
Stinchcombe, A. L., 498
Stone, J., 357
Stouffer, S. A., 296
Strange, M., 365, 375
Strauss, A., 176, 445
Street, D., 141
Sudman, S., 47
Sudnow, D., 203-204
Sullivan, Anne Mansfield, 166-167
Summers, L. H., 41
Sumner, W. G., 99, 102
Suro, R., 538
Sutherland, E. H., 270
Suttles, G., 141, 147, 195, 196, 412
Swaggert, Jimmy, 548
Sweet, J., 478, 480
Sweezy, P. M., 297
Szelenyi, I., 242
Szymanski, A. J., 364

Taeuber, A., 399, 400
Taeuber, K., 399, 400

Tawney, R., 230
Taylor, F. W., 580
Teevan, J., 546
Terrace, H. S., 104
Thomas, L., 629, 643-644
Thomas, W. L., 308
Thornberry, T. P., 273
Thornton, R., 93-94, 407
Thurow, L., 245, 380
Tichnell, D. L., 309
Tienda, M., 415, 418
Tieser, R., 43
Tilly, C., 241, 297, 301, 574
Titmus, R., 323
Tobin, J., 570
Toffler, A., 113
Tönnies, F., 140
Touraine, A., 574
Toynbee, A., 336
Traven, B., 560
Treas, J., 377
Treiman, D. J., 107, 329, 362
Troeltsch, E., 508
Trotsky, Leon, 569
Trow, M., 531
Truzzi, M., 337
Tumin, M., 243
Turk, A. T., 268
Turner, 367
Turner, F. J., 402
Turner, R. H., 295, 297
Turner, Tina, 436
Turner, V. W., 216
Tuttle, W., 287-288
Twain, Mark, 486
Tyree, A., 377

U.S. Commission on Civil Rights, 408
Ullman, E. L., 137

Van den Berghe, P. L., 103, 499, 516
Van Gennep, A., 427
Vanek, J., 310
Verbrugge, L. M., 431
Verwoerdt, A., 442
Vidich, A., 365
Villa, Pancho, 269
Vining, D. R., Jr., 131
Vogel, E., 578
Voslensky, M., 270

Wainhouse, D. W., 601
Wallerstein, I., 245, 328, 563-564
Wallerstein, J., 472, 480
Walsh, E. J., 301, 302
Walsh, F., 481
Walton, J., 245, 610
Waltzer, M., 403, 530
Waring, J., 426
Warland, R. H., 302
Warner, W. L., 359-361, 365, 367
Washington, George, 257
Watson, J. B., 162-163
Watt, James G., 253

Weber, M., 12, 53, 83, 97, 98, 132,
    209-210, 214, 235, 238, 240, 287,
    297-298, 416, 496, 500, 506, 507-
    508, 509, 560, 594, 596, 601
Weber, Marianne, 287
Weir, B. R. J., 479
Weir, T., 479
Weisman, A., 627, 641
Wekerle, G., 144
Welch, M. R., 508
Wells, H. G., 307
Wells, M. J., 328-329
Westin, A., 49
Westrum, R., 643
Whitaker, C., 481, 486
Whorf, B., 105
Whyte, W. F., 66, 82, 161, 179,
    195-196, 581
Whyte, W. H., 40, 150, 484-485
Wicker, Tom, 253
Wildavsky, A., 611
Wilensky, H., 545
Wilford, J. N., 634
Wilkinson, A., 229
Williams, L. M., 483
Williams, R., 116, 148
Williams, R. M., Jr., 415, 486
Williams, T., 279-280
Williams, T. M., 139, 141
Williamson, M., 590
Willis, P., 528
Willmott, P., 479
Wilson, E. O., 102, 103, 391
Wilson, J. Q., 260, 273, 276, 278
Wilson, W. J., 183, 246, 332, 382, 414,
    415, 416, 429, 574
Winch, R. F., 476
Winner, L., 635
Wirth, L., 128, 132, 140-141, 276, 393
Wittfogel, K., 78
Wixen, B. N., 481
Wolf, E. R., 80, 296
Wolfe, T., 616
Wolfgang, M., 276
Wolfinger, R., 620
Wooden, K., 216
Wright, E. O., 241, 242, 364, 369
Wrigley, E. A., 643
Wrong, D. H., 162
Wuthnow, R., 500, 508

Yankelovich, D., 113, 115-116, 448
Yinger, J. M., 392
Young, M., 479

Zald, N., 296
Zangwell, I., 402
Zaslavskaya, T., 223-224, 231, 243
Zeisel, H., 82
Zerubavel, E., 426
Zimbardo, P. G., 215-216
Zolberg, A., 85, 606
Zuboff, S., 82
Zurcher, L. A., 301

SUBJECT INDEX

Abington School District v. *Schempp*, 516

Abortion, 97, 505, 517

Accommodation, 112

Acculturation, 110–111

Achieved statuses, 82, 225

Acquired immune deficiency syndrome. *See* AIDS

Addictive substances. *See* Drugs, illegal

Adolescent Society, The (Coleman), 39, 529

Adolescents
conflicts with parents, 115
delinquency of, 270–271
drug use by, 279–280
employment of, 41, 585–586
family's response to, 472
gangs, 191–192, 272–273, 279–280
pregnancy of, 41, 174–175, 486–488
premarital intercourse of, 114
schools and, 529
television and violence, 546–547

Adult socialization, 160

Advertising, 456–457, 548, 549, 550

Affirmative action, 399, 408

Africa
apartheid in South Africa, 225, 399, 410, 411, 422–423, 566, 599
Baaskop in South Africa, 412
black protest in South Africa, 257–258, 599
conflict over borders within, 600
Ebrie tribe in, 317–318, 319, 338
elderly in, 445
food insecurity in, 333
genocide in, 395–396
Ibo in Nigeria, 84, 600
kinship relations in, 464
!Kung bushmen, 90
molding of skulls of female children, 456
one-party system in Ghana, 606
religion of, 502
social change in, 317–318, 319
Tiv society in West Africa, 546–565

African-Americans. *See* Blacks

Age and aging
age cohorts, 429–431
age structure and the life course, 426–427
disengagement theory and, 449
gender and the life course in aging societies, 451–452
graying of America, 431
life expectancy and gender, 431–432
sexuality and, 442
social movements among the elderly, 449–450

Age cohorts, 429–431

Age grades, 426

Age of Enlightenment, 10–11

Age of Revolution, 11

Age strata, 426

Age stratification
ageism and, 441
conflict perspectives on, 446–447
de Beauvoir's perspective on, 425
functionalist view of, 443
historical patterns of, 436–439
in industrial societies, 438–439
interactionist views of, 445
perspectives on, 441–447

Ageism, 441

Agents of socialization, 161–162, 178–180, 188

Aging societies, 451–452

Agrarian revolution, 76–77

Agrarian societies, 77–78, 562–563

Agriculture
class awareness and, 365, 375
"green revolution," 334
modernization and, 324
in peasant societies, 228–230
percent of population engaged in, 228
sharecropping and, 328–329
sugar production, 229

Aid to Families with Dependent Children (AFDC), 33–34, 53, 376, 380–382

AIDS, 54–56, 262, 517

Air pollution. *See* Pollution

Alcohol use, 258, 261–262, 267, 515, 567

Alcoholics Anonymous, 498

All Our Kin (Stack), 37

Altruism and the bystander effect, 204–205

American Association of Retired Persons, 449

American Dilemma, An (Myrdal), 407

American Indians. *See* Native Americans

American Revolution, 296

Americanization, 401

Anglo-conformity, 401–402

Animal Farm (Orwell), 613

Animism, 502

Anomie, 141, 265

Anticipatory socialization, 178, 188

Apartheid, 225, 257–258, 399, 410, 411, 422–423, 556, 599

Apes, language of, 104–105

Apparatus, 635

Applied science, 628

Armenians, 396

Army. *See* Military institutions

Arranged marriage, 474

Art, 26–31, 345–349, 498–499

Ascribed statuses, 82, 225

Asian Americans, 396–397, 404, 413

Assimilation, 111–112, 399–401

Athletics. *See* Sports

Attraction and emotional reciprocity, 476–477

Authoritarian personality, 409

Authority
bureaucracy and, 210–212
definition of, 234
politics and, 595, 596
social stratification and, 236–237

Authoritarian Personality, The (Adorno), 409

Automation. *See* Technology

Average, 177

Baby boom, 429–431

"Baby bust," 430

Bandits, 269

Basic demographic equation, 125
Battering. *See* Spouse abuse
Becoming Modern (Inkeles and Smith), 329
Behaviorism, 162-164
Beyond the Melting Pot (Glazer and Moynihan), 402
Beyond the Nuclear Family Model (Lenero-Otero), 468
Biafra, Republic of, 84
Bias in survey questions, 47
Biased sample, 45-46
Biological reductionism, 102
Birthrate, crude, 125-126
Black Death, 643
Black Metropolis (Drake and Cayton), 361-362
Blacks. *See also* Africa
  age at first marriage, 470-472
  assimilation of, 407
  black church in America, 510
  in Chicago ghetto, 361-362
  Chicago riot of 1919, 287-288
  civil rights movement, 389-390, 407
  class structure of, 331-332
  compard with European immigrants, 414-416
  DuBois's survey of Philadelphia blacks, 13, 14, 602
  education of, 530-532, 536-538, 541
  employment of, 246, 362, 416
  families of, 469, 486-488
  in ghettos, 361-362
  Jim Crow laws and, 399
  lynchings of, 392
  political behavior of, 620
  population of, 417
  poverty of, 486-488
  rural-urban migration, 182
  segregation of, 147-148, 399
  slavery of, 397-398
  social mobility of, 416
  stereotypes of, 404, 405, 409
  terminology in referring to, 234
Body image, 180-181
Bolsheviks, 212-213, 298, 484, 495
Borders of states, 600-601
Born on the Fourth of July (Kovic), 180
Bourgeoisie, 239-240, 243, 251
Brazil, 154-155, 550
Bride price, 474
British Empire, 108-109
Brown v. Board of Education of Topeka, 399, 528, 541
Buddhism, 500-501, 503
Bureaucracy
  characteristics of, 209-210
  commitment to, 212-213
  definition of, 209
  ideological primary groups in, 212-213
  obedience to authority and, 210-212
  primary groups in bureaucracies, 212-213
  schools as, 539-541
Business. *See* Corporations
Bystander effect, 204-205

Cable television, 548-549
Canada, 403, 600
Capital, 571
Capital (Marx), 239
Capital punishment, 276, 277
Capitalism, 19, 97, 237, 268, 446, 506
Capitalism, laissez-faire, 567-568
Capitalism, welfare, 570-571
Careers
  deviant careers, 272-273
  in 1990s, 584-586
  professions, 203-204, 583, 582-583, 648
  in sociology, 22
Carrying capacity, 334
Castes, 225-226
Catastrophes, 302-303, 636, 637, 643, 648-649
Catholic church, 97, 498, 500, 501, 505-506, 508-509, 511-513, 514, 517-518, 522-523
Causation, and correlations, 53
CBR. *See* Crude birthrate (CBR)
CDR. *See* Crude death rate (CDR)
Censorship, 544
Census, national, 42-43
Central tendency, measures of, 177
Chain migration, 129
Change. *See* Social change
Charisma
  charismatic leaders, 295
  co-optation and, 298, 300
  cults and, 509
  definition of, 297-298
  institutionalization of, 297-298
  social movements and, 297-298, 300
Chattels, 398
Chernobyl nuclear accident, 637
Chicago school of sociology, 13-15, 135-136
Child abuse, 483
Child labor laws, 586
Child sexual abuse, 483
Childhood and Society (Erikson), 172
Children. *See also* Education
  agents of socialization of, 178-180
  competition in sports, 171
  day care for, 330
  Erikson's theory of development, 172
  family environment of, 175-176, 177
  feral children, 164
  Freud's theory of personality, 169
  gender socialization of, 180-181, 438
  impact of divorce on, 480
  infant mortality rates, 645
  mean number per family, 430
  need for love, 164-167
  play and games of, 170-171, 181
  Robbers Cave experiment, 165-168
  role taking and, 170-171
  sexual abuse of, 483
  in single-parent families, 482
  socialization of, 160-161, 188-189
  society's influence on, 176-178
  television and, 180, 546
China
  Communist party in, 213

demonstration in Tiananmen Square, 544, 566
  economics of, 569
  elections in, 624
  fatalities from World War II, 321
  footbinding of female children, 456
  ideology of, 232
  marriage in, 474
  rural villages in, 230
  stratification in, 230
Chinese Americans, 404
Christian fundamentalism, 97, 328, 497, 515-516
Christian Science, 508
Christianity, 233, 495, 500-501, 503, 508.
  See also Catholic church; Christian fundamentalism; Protestantism; Religion
Church Universal and Triumphant, 216
Churches, definition of, 507-508.
  See also Catholic church; Protestantism; Religion
Cigarette smoking, 96, 200, 431-432
Cities. *See also* Urbanization
  concentric-zone model, 136-137
  decentralization of, 138-139
  decline-of-community thesis, 140-141
  definition of metropolitan areas, 130-131
  ethnic groups in, 141-142, 144
  ghettos in, 361-362, 382
  growth of, 130-135
  historical development of, 131-132
  inequality and conflict, 145-148
  megalopolis, 138-139
  metropolitan areas, 137-139
  multiple-nuclei model, 137
  planning urban environments, 149-150
  pollution in, 627, 641
  preindustrial cities, 132, 133
  racial conflict in, 147-148
  relocation of Native Americans to, 120-121
  rural-urban migration, 85, 129
  sector theory, 137
  segregation in, 400-401
  social change and, 145-148
  status conflict in, 146-147
  subcultural theory of, 141-145
  suburbs, 144-145, 369
  urban "combat zone," 60-61
  urban communities, 139-145
  urban expansion, 135-137
  urban revolution, 131-132
  urban societies, 132-135
  violence in, 141, 204-205
Citizenship, 529-530, 601-602
Civil religion, 504-505
Civil Rights Act, 399, 541
Civil rights movement, 389-390, 407, 448
Civilizations. *See also* Societies
  cultural change and, 107-113
  definitions of, 107-108
  effects of cultural contact, 108-110

Class consciousness, 240, 364-365
Classes. *See also* Inequality
  changing views of social inequality,
    357, 359
  Chicago ghetto, 361-362
  class conflict, 238-243
  class consciousness, 238-240,
    364-365
  class structure of black and Hispanics,
    331-332
  classless society, 240
  definition of, 226-227
  diet and, 386-387
  education and, 366
  farmers and farm families, 375
  health and, 366
  impact of the Depression, 359
  life chances and, 366-375
  measurement of, 364-365
  measures of social inequality, 355-358
  middle classes, 368-369
  in Middletown, 359, 360-361
  objective and subjective classes,
    239-240
  politics and, 366-367
  in postindustrial society, 362, 364
  upper classes, 367-368
  working class, 369-371
  Yankee City, 359-361, 362
Classless society, 240
Closed questions, 46
Closed societies, 78, 225
Co-optation, 298, 300
Coal, 642
Cocaine Kids, The (Williams), 279
Cold War, 323, 571, 631-632
Collective bargaining, 290-291
Collective behavior. *See also* Groups;
    Social movements
  Chicago riot of 1919, 287-288
  crowds and masses, 291-292
  dimensions of social movements,
    294-295
  disorder, 288-295
  motivating emotions, 292-293
  nature of, 290-291
  typology of spontaneous collective
    behaviors, 291-293
Colleges. *See* Higher education
Colonization, 108-109, 564-565
Coming of Post Industrial Society, The
    (Bell), 573
Commitment, 272
Common Destiny, A (Jaynes and
    Williams), 486
Common ownership of science, 633-634
Communication
  in groups, 203-205
  two step flow of, 549
Communications media. *See also*
    Newspapers; Radio; Television
  as agent of socialization, 179-180
  censorship of, 544
  definition of, 544
  differentiation of media institutions,
    547-548
  media power and its limits, 548-549

in modern societies, 544
  patterns of media consumption,
    545-546
  political coverage in, 612-613
  significance of, 543-544
  technological limits on media power,
    548-549
  television and violence, 546-547
  two-step flow of communication, 549
Communist Manifesto, The (Marx and
    Engels), 239, 298, 337, 566
Communist party, 213, 569, 593
Communities
  as agent of socialization, 179
  decline-of-community thesis, 140-141
  definition of, 195
  for human ecology perspective, 15
  subcultural theory of urban
    community, 141-145
  territorial versus nonterritorial, 195
  urban communities, 139-145
Community studies
  Middletown series, 114-115, 359,
    360-361, 448
  of poverty, 37
Competition, 165-168, 171
Complementary needs and mutual
    attraction, 476
Computers, 97, 551-552, 585, 635
Concentric-zone model of urban growth,
    136-137
Conditioning, 162-163
Confidentiality, right of, 49
Conflict theory
  alternatives to the family and, 482,
    484
  class conflict, 238-243
  conflict at work, 581-582
  conflict in cities, 145-148
  description of, 18-20
  deviance and, 266-270
  education and, 527
  gender and age stratification and,
    446-447
  inequality and, 145-148
  Marxian conflict theory, 268, 270
  racial inequality and, 410-412
  social change models, 337
  social stratification and, 241-243
Confucianism, 500-501, 503
Conjugal family, 464-465
Conservative movements, 294
Contracts, 562
Control group, 40
Controlled experiments, 40-41
Core states, 328
Corporate actors, 579
Corporations
  individuals and, 579-580
  in Japan, 577
  multinational, 565
Correlation coefficient, 52
Correlations, 52-53
Counterculture, 112
Coup d'état, 605
Courts, 276-277

CPS. *See* Current Population Survey
    (CPS)
Crime. *See also* Prisons
  bandits, 269
  biological explanations of, 264
  conflict perspectives on, 266-270
  cultural conflict and, 266-268
  definition of, 259-260
  deviance and, 259-260
  deviant careers, 272-273
  ecological dimensions of, 273-275
  functionalist perspective on, 265-266
  index crimes, 260, 261
  interactionist perspective on, 270-273
  juvenile delinquency, 270-271
  labeling, 271-272
  Marxian conflict theory, 268, 270
  organized crime, 263-264, 267-268
  recruitment through differential
    association, 270-271
  social control and, 273-280
  social-scientific explanations of, 265
  socialization and, 161, 162
  white collar crime, 270, 271
"Crime as an American Way of Life"
    (Bell), 266
Criminal justice system, 276-278
Crisis of legitimacy, 597
Cross section of population, 47
Cross-cultural perspective, 106
Crowds, 291-292
Crude birthrate (CBR), 125-126
Crude death rate (CDR), 125-126
Cuban Americans, 148, 417-418
Cults, 508-509
Cultural conflict and deviance, 266-268
Cultural evolution, 102
Cultural lag, 640-641, 648
Cultural pluralism, 403
Cultural relativity, 106
Cultural universals, 106-107
Culture
  accommodation and resistance, 112
  acculturation, 110-111
  assimilation and subcultures, 111-112
  changes in American culture, 113-116
  civilizations and cultural change,
    107-113
  cross-cultural perspective, 106
  cultural universals, 106-107
  definition of, 94-95
  dimensions of, 95-97
  effects of cultural contact on
    civilizations, 108-110
  ethnocentrism and cultural relativity,
    106
  evolution and human behavior,
    101-104
  ideas as dimension of, 95
  ideologies as dimension of, 97
  intergroup relations and, 404-408
  language and, 104-105, 110
  mass culture, 545
  material culture, 95
  normative order, 97-100
  norms as dimension of, 95-96
  personality and, 170

Culture, *continued*
  social change and, 100-101
  social institutions, 100
  social stratification and, 231-235
  technologies as dimension of, 97
  values as dimension of, 95, 96-97
Culture shock, 113
Currency, 562
Current Population Survey (CPS), 43
Cyclical theories of social change,
    336-337

Data analysis
  correlations, 52-53
  percent analysis, 50-52
  reading tables, 49-50
De facto segregation, 398-399
De jure segregation, 398-399
Death and dying, 450, 648
Death penalty, 276, 277
Death rate, crude, 125-126
Decentralization of cities, 138-139
Deciding What's News (Gans), 548
Decline of the West, The (Spengler), 336
Decline-of-community thesis, 140-141
Defense. *See* Military institutions
Deference, 233-234
Delinquency. *See* Juvenile delinquency
Demagogues, 605
Demeanor, 234
Democracy
  comparison of European and Latin
    American democracies, 609
  definition of, 606
  pluralist model of, 607, 610-611
  power elite model of, 607, 608-610
  structural perspectives of, 607-608
Democratic party, 366-367, 602, 603,
    603, 606, 619, 620
Democratic political systems, 606-607
Democratic socialism, 570
Demographic equation, basic, 125
Demographic studies, of poverty, 37
Demographic transition, 126-128
Demographic transition theory, 125
Denominations, 508
Dependency, 328-329
Dependent variables, 36
Depression
  Great Depression, 359, 448, 602
  in steel mill communities, 590-591
Desegregation. *See* Integration;
    Segregation
Developing nations, 325-328
Deviance. *See also* Crime
  biological explanations of crime, 264
  changing values and, 260-262
  conflict perspectives on, 266-270
  crime and, 259-260
  cultural conflict and, 266-268
  definition of, 254-255
  deviant careers, 272-273
  deviant subcultures, 262-264
  dimensions of, 257-264
  functionalist perspective on, 265-266
  interactionist perspective on, 270-273
  labeling, 271-272

Marxian conflict theory, 268, 270
primary deviance, 273
recruitment through differential
    association, 270-271
secondary deviance, 273
social-scientific explanations of, 265
stigma and, 258-259
typology of, 261-262
Deviant careers, 272-273
Deviant subcultures, 262-264
Dictatorships, 609
Diet and social class, 386-387
Differential association, 270-271
Differentiation, 100
Diffusion, 551-552
Disabilities, 166-167, 258-259
Discourses (Machiavelli), 611
Discrimination, 82, 148, 405-406. *See
    also* Inequality
Disease. *See* Medical technology
Disengagement theory, 449
Disinterestedness of science, 634
Disorder, meanings of, 288-295
Division of labor, 562-565
Division of Labor in Society, The
    (Durkheim), 214
Divorce, 472, 477, 478, 479, 480
Downward mobility, 225, 241, 377-378
Dress styles, 456-457
Driving while intoxicated (DWI),
    261-262
Dropouts, 41, 366, 532
Drugs, illegal, 267-268, 279-280,
    566-567
"Dual labor market" theory, 86
Duels, 21
DWI. *See* Driving while intoxicated
    (DWI)
Dyads, 194

Eastern Europe, 213, 297, 504-505,
    506, 543-544, 548, 566, 571, 593,
    594, 596
Ebrie tribe, 317-318, 319, 338
Ecological theories of racial inequality,
    412-413
Ecology. *See* Human ecology
Economic person versus social person,
    202-203
Economics. *See also* Employment;
    Workplace
  characteristics of economic
    institutions, 583-584
  after Cold War, 571-575
  colonialism and, 564-565
  definition of, 561
  democratic socialism, 570
  laissez-faire capitalism, 567-568
  markets and the division of labor,
    562-565
  markets and the world economic
    system, 563-565
  mercantilism, 567
  "peace dividend," 574-575, 576
  political parties and, 620
  role of military institutions in,
    614-616

socialism, 568-570
sociology and, 560-562
state and, 565, 567-575
stratification and, 245-246
technology and, 641
United States as postindustrial
    society, 572-574
welfare capitalism, 570-571
Ectomorphs, 264
Education
  adolescents and, 529
  barriers to educational attainment,
    532
  citizenship and, 529-530
  classroom structure, 539
  college attendance, 528-529, 530-532
  conflict theory approach to, 527
  definition of, 526
  desegregation of, 399, 541
  dropouts, 41, 366, 532
  educational achievement, 533-534
  educational attainment, 530-532, 533
  electronic classroom, 551-552
  employment and, 145, 146, 418
  for equality, 536-538
  inequality and, 355-356, 357,
    535-536
  interactionist approach to, 527-528
  modernization and, 325
  nature of schools, 526-528
  preschool education, 536-538
  reforms in, 525-526, 534-535
  school attendance, 528-529
  schools as agent of socialization, 179
  schools as bureaucracies, 539-541
  separation of religion from, 516
  social classes and, 366, 369
  social mobility and, 378, 534-535
  structure of educational institutions,
    538-543
  students and social change, 556-557
  teacher's role in, 539, 541, 542-543
  type of government and, 609
Educational achievement, 356, 533-534
Educational attainment, 355-356, 137,
    530-532, 533
Educational technology, 551-552
Ego, 168-169
Elderly. *See* Age and aging; Age
    stratification
Elections, 618-620, 624-625
Electronic classroom, 551-552
Elementary and Secondary Education
    Act, 541
Elmtown's Youth (Hollingshead), 475
Emotions
  attraction and emotional reciprocity,
    476-477
  of collective behavior, 292-293
  friendship groups, 220-221
  love, 164-167, 184, 476-477, 478,
    485
  romantic love and, 476-477
  war and, 322
Empirical information, 12-13
Employment. *See also* Careers; Labor
    movement; Workplace

of adolescents, 41
age of labor force, 586
alienation and, 578
average work week, 305
of blacks, 246, 416
class awareness and, 364-365
conflict at work, 581-582
discrimination in, 82, 148, 362, 363
"dual labor market" theory and, 86
education and, 145, 146, 418, 532
Hawthorne experiment and, 202, 207
human relations in industry, 580-581
of immigrants, 148
individuals and corporations, 579-580
Japanese factories, 577
job ceiling, 362, 363, 399
median weekly earnings of wage and
    salary workers, 449
in modern society, 91
modernization and, 325, 326
"mommy track" in, 82
occupational prestige, 356, 358
of older people, 452
professions, 582-583
restaurant industry, 65-66
sociological perspectives on the
    workplace, 580-583
unemployment in industry, 582,
    590-591
unemployment rates worldwide, 585
United States industry, 577-578
of women, 82, 91, 183-184, 379, 426,
    433, 436, 439, 446-447, 448
work and careers in the 1990s,
    584-586
worker responses to high technology,
    638
Encyclopedia Galactica (Asimov), 123
Endo v. *United States*, 397
Endogamy, 474-475
Endogenous forces, 318
Endomorphs, 264
Energy, quest for, 642-643
Engle v. *Vitale*, 516
Enlightenment, Age of, 10-11
Entertainment, 306-307
Environment
    carrying capacity and, 334
    environmental stress, 649-650
    politics and policies on, 332-334
    pollution, 627, 641, 649-650, 653-654
    public opinion concerning, 309
    technology and, 636-637, 639, 641
Equality of opportunity, 376
Equality of result, 376
Erikson's theory of development, 172
Eskimos
    kinship system of, 107
    religion of, 502
    starvation of, 414
Essay on Population (Malthus), 125
Ethics of social research, 48-49
Ethiopia, 430
Ethnic and racial nationalism, 406-407
Ethnic groups, definition of, 393. *See
    also* Racial and ethnic groups; and
    names of specific groups

Ethnic stratification, 402
Ethnocentrism, 106
Ethnographers, 55
European democracies and
    dictatorships, 609
Evolution, 101-102, 515
Evolutionary models of social change,
    335-336
Exchange theory, 16-17
Exogamy, 474-475
Exogenous forces, 318
Experimental group, 40
Experiments, 40-42
Expressive social movements, 294-295
Expulsion, 396-397
Extended family, 68, 466, 492-493

Fairness principle in group interaction,
    201-202
Families. *See also* Kinship; Marriage
    as agent of socialization, 178-179
    black family, 469, 486-488
    changing family, 467-470
    conflict theory and alternatives to,
        482, 484
    conjugal family, 464-465
    definition of, 464-466
    extended family, 68, 466, 492-493
    family life cycle, 470-473
    family of orientation, 465-466
    family of procreation, 465-466
    farm families, 375
    functionalist view of, 484-485
    gender roles and, 330
    ideal versus actual family patterns,
        469-470
    impact of divorce on, 480
    as institution, 462-464
    interactionist perspective on, 481-482
    in Israel, 484
    Marxian perspectives on, 482, 484
    mean number of children per family,
        430
    modernization and, 325, 326
    nuclear family, 106-107, 464-465
    perspectives on, 481-486
    problems of definition of, 468
    resilience of, 486
    single-parent family, 374, 469-470,
        482, 486-488
    socialization and, 175-176, 177
    studies of family history, 468-469
    two-paycheck family, 379-380
    unstable triad, 194-195
    variations in family structure, 466-467
Family life cycle, 470-473
Family of orientation, 465-466
Family of procreation, 465-466
Family role relations, 462
Farming. *See* Agriculture
Fashion, 456-457
Fast-food industry, 308
Favelas in Brazil, 154-155
Females. *See* Women
Feminine Mystique, The (Friedan), 448
Feminization of poverty, 374
Feral children, 164

Feudalism, 91, 234, 237, 437-438, 567
Field experiments, 41
Folkways, 98-99
Folkways (Sumner), 99
Food supply, 333, 334
Formal norms, 98-100
Formal organizations, 208-209 . *See
    also* Bureaucracy
"Foundation" trilogy (Asimov), 123
France, 241, 242
Free-rider problem, 301-303, 514-515
French Canadians, 403, 407
French Revolution, 234-235, 297
Frequency distributions, 49
Freud's theory of personality, 168-169
Friendship groups, 220-221
Frustration-aggression hypothesis of
    racial inequality, 408-409
Functionalism, 18
Functionalist models
    of family, 484-485
    of gender and age stratification,
        442-443
    of racial inequality, 410
    of social change, 337-338
    of social stratification, 243-244
Fundamentalism. *See* Christian
    fundamentalism
Future shock, 113

Gaia hypothesis, 629
Galileo (Brecht), 636-637
Games, of children, 170-171, 181
Gangs, 191-192, 272-273, 279-280
Garrison states, 323
"Garrison states, " 323
Gay Pride movement, 263
Gemeinschaft, 81
Gender. *See also* Men; Women
    in aging societies, 451-452
    definition of, 180
    life course and, 427, 451-452
    life expectancy and, 431-432
    sex ratios and, 427-429
Gender identity, 180
Gender roles, 330, 432-436
Gender socialization, 180-184
Gender stratification
    conflict perspectives on, 446-447
    cultural perspectives on, 434-436
    de Beauvoir's perspective on, 425
    education and, 530-531
    in feudal societies, 437-438
    functionalist view of, 442-443
    gender roles, 432-436
    historical patterns of, 436-439
    in industrial societies, 438-439
    interactionist views of, 443-445
    in Japan, 439
    perspectives on, 441-447
    sexism and, 439-441, 456-457
    women's movement and, 447-449
Generalized others, 171
Genocide, 394-396
Gentrification, 146, 369
Germany
    fatalities from World War II, 321

Germany, *continued*
    Nazis, 212, 213, 216, 288, 299, 392, 396, 605
    social mobility in, 241, 242
Gerontology, 436
Gesellschaft, 81
Ghettos, 361–362, 382
Glasnost, 223–224, 231
God. *See* Religion; and names of specific religions
Good Company (Harper), 38, 284
Gray Panthers, 449
Graying of America, 431
"Green revolution, " 334
Groom price, 474
Groups. *See also* Collective behavior; Intergroup relations; Social movements
    altruism and the bystander effect, 204–205
    in armies, 212, 213
    communication in, 203–205
    communities, 195
    in complex societies, 213–214
    definition of, 67–68
    definitions of the situation in, 203–204
    dramaturgical approach, 204
    dyads, 194
    economic person versus social person, 202–203
    as element of social structure, 67–68
    "extraordinary" groups, 215–216
    fairness principle in, 201–202
    formal organizations and bureaucracy, 208–213
    friendship groups, 220–221
    in-groups and out-groups, 196
    interaction in groups, 199–207
    intergroup hostility, 165–168
    networks, 195–196
    pleasure principle in, 199–200
    primary and secondary groups, 81, 193–194
    "prison" research and, 215–216
    rational and traditional motives in, 214
    rationality principle in, 200
    reciprocity principle in, 200–201
    reference groups, 196–197
    social categories and, 193
    social network analysis, 197–199
    structure of, 70–72, 205–207
    triads, 194–195
"Growing Up Girlish" (Freeman), 443–444
Gypsies, 492–493

Haitian refugees, 148
Handicaps. *See* Disabilities
Hard Choices (Gerson), 433
Hare Krishna, 216
Hawthorne effect, 41–42
Hawthorne experiment, 41–42, 202, 207
Health, 366, 431–432. *See also* Medical profession; Medical technology
Health insurance, 647

High technology, 638. *See also* Computers
Higher education
    college attendance, 528–529, 530–532
    inequality in, 536
    scientific research and, 631–632, 634
    students and social change, 556–557
Hinduism, 500–501, 503
Hispanics, 331–332, 404, 415, 416–418, 470–472, 512, 530–532
HIV infection, 54–56. *See also* AIDS
Hoboes, 38, 284–285
Homeostatic model of society, 337–338
Homogamy, 475–476
Homosexuality, 262, 263, 268, 270, 515, 517
Horticultural societies, 76
Hospice movement, 450
Hospitals, 646–647
Housing and Urban Development, U.S. Department of, 253, 255
Huichol Indians, 498–499
Hull House Maps and Papers (Addams), 13
Human ecology, 15
Human Nature and the Social Order (Cooley), 169
Human relations in industry, 580–581
Humanism. *See* Secular humanism
Hunting and gathering societies, 68, 74–76, 90, 106–107, 182
Hypertrophy in health care, 647
Hypothesis, 35–36

Ibo, 84, 600
Id, 168–169
Ideas, as dimension of culture, 95
Identification, 172
Identity, 172
Ideologies, 97, 231–233. *See also* specific ideologies
Immigrants
    chain migration and, 129
    Chicago riot of 1919, 287–288
    "dual labor market" and, 86
    employment of, 148
    European immigrants compard with blacks, 414–416
    melting pot and, 402–403
    nineteenth century, 135
    twentieth-century, 393, 394, 395
    in urban communities, 142, 144
Impression management, 191, 204
In-groups, 196
Incest taboo, 103
Income, 355–356, 379–380, 449, 532, 582, 609
Independent variables, 36
Index crimes, 260, 261
India
    caste system in, 226, 232
    cities in, 133–134
    genocide in, 396
    marriage in, 474
    population of, 430
    rural villages in, 229–230
    toxic gas leak in, 636–637

    women in, 227
Indians. *See* Native Americans
Individuals. *See also* Personality
    bureaucracy and, 210–212
    corporations and, 579–580
    social person versus economic person, 202–203
    society and, 80–83
Industrial Revolution, 78–80, 230–231, 237–238, 381–382
Industrial society, 78–80
Industrial Workers of the World, 305
Industrial-military complex, 606
Industry
    accidents and, 641
    depression in steel mill communities, 590–591
    human relations in, 580–581
    in Japan, 577
    modernization and, 324
    type of government and, 609
    unemployment in, 582, 590–591
    in United States, 577–578
Inequality. *See also* Classes; Racial and ethnic groups
    changing views of, 357, 359
    Chicago ghetto, 361–362
    class awareness in American today, 364–365
    conflict theories of racial inequality, 410–412
    ecological theories of racial inequality, 412–413
    in education, 535–536
    educational attainment and, 355–356, 357
    functionalist theories of racial inequality, 410
    of gender and age, 425
    in higher education, 536
    historical perspectives on, 357, 359
    impact of the Depression, 359
    interactionist theories of racial inequality, 409–410
    measures of, 355–357
    mobility and, 377–378
    occupational prestige, 356, 358
    social classes in postindustrial society, 362, 364
    social-psychological theories of racial inequality, 408–409
    theories of racial and ethnic inequality, 408–414
    Yankee City, 359–362, 362
Infant mortality rates, 645
Informal norms, 98–100
Informal organizations, 208
"Information power, " 548
Informed consent, 49
Inquisition, 636
Institutional approach to science, 630–633
Institutional discrimination, 406
Institutionalization of charisma, 297–298

Institutions. *See also* Economics; Education; Families; Military institutions; Politics and political institutions; Religion; Science; Technology
  as agents of socialization, 161–162, 178–180
  definition of, 100
  of social control, 255, 276–278
  total institutions, 277–278, 527
  war and, 323, 324
Instrument, 46
Integration, 147–148, 399, 541
Intelligence and race, 392–393
Interactionism, 16
Interactionist models
  deviance, 270–273
  education, 527–528
  family, 481–482
  gender and age stratification, 443–445
  racial inequality, 409–410
  science, 630
  self, 169–171
  social stratification, 244
Interest groups, 610
Intergenerational mobility, 241
Intergroup relations
  culture and, 404–408
  patterns of, 394–403
Intermarriage, 399–400, 402, 476
Internal colonialism, 411–412
Interview guides, 46
Intragenerational mobility, 241
Islam, 327–328, 500–501, 503
Israel, 484, 600
Italian Americans, 144, 404

Japan
  crime in, 264
  economy of, 572
  factories in, 577
  fatalities from World War II, 321
  gender stratification in, 439
  "kamikaze mentality" in, 598
  market for tape recorders, 635
  marriage in, 474
  population of, 429, 430
  worker alienation and, 578
Japanese Americans, 396–397
Jesus People, 508
Jews, 112, 392, 396, 404, 407, 409, 475, 500–501, 502–503, 511, 513, 514, 522–523, 600, 620
Jim Crow laws, 399
Job ceiling, 362, 363, 399
Jobs. *See* Employment; Workplace
Jonestown tragedy, 295
Journey to Nowhere (Maharidge and Williamson), 590
Junta, 605
Juvenile delinquency, 161, 270–271, 272–273
Juvenile detention centers, 161, 273

"Kamikaze mentality", 598
Kibbutz, 484
Kinship. *See also* Families

definition of, 464
Eskimo kinship system, 107
in hunter-gatherer band, 68
Korean Americans, 142, 413
Ku Klux Klan, 216, 294
!Kung bushmen, 90

Labeling, 271–272, 273
Labor, division of, 562–565
Labor movement, 290–291, 292, 302, 305, 314–315, 353–354, 370, 595–596
Labor-management relations. *See* Employment; Labor movement; Workplace
Laissez-faire capitalism, 567–568
Language, 104–105, 110
Latin America
  Catholic Church in, 498, 506, 517–518
  elections in, 624
  governments of, 609
  Huichol Indians in, 498–499
  illegal drugs and, 566–567
  military institutions in, 613–614
  oligarchy in, 605
Latinos. *See* Hispanics
Leadership
  charismatic leaders, 295
  in groups, 207
  opinion leaders, 197, 549
Legal system, 276–278
Legitimacy, 596
Legitimacy, crisis of, 597
Leisure, 306–310
Levittowners, The (Gans), 144
Liberation theology, 518
Life chances, 227–228, 366–375
Life course, 427, 451–452
Life expectancy, 431–432
Life-style, 227
Linguistic-relativity hyphothesis, 105
Loan words, 110
Lobbying, 610–611
Local politics, 602–603, 606–607
Long-distance upward mobility, 377
Love, 164–167, 184, 476–477, 478, 485
Lower classes. *See* Poverty; Working class
Luddism, 638
Lumpenproletariat, 268

Macro-level of social change, 320
Macro-level of sociology, 9, 10
Mafia, 263–264, 269
Males. *See* Men
Malthusian population theory, 125
Manchild in the Promised Land (Brown), 182
Market research, 197
Markets
  for addictive substances, 566–567
  definition of, 562
  division of labor and, 562–565
  world economic system and, 563–565
Marriage. *See also* Families
  age at first marriage, 470–472

arranged marriage, 474
divorce and, 477–478, 479
endogamy/exogamy, 474–475
ethnic intermarriage, 402
as exchange, 474
gender differences in, 184
homogamy, 475–476
impact of divorce and, 480
norms of mate selection, 474–476
racial intermarriage, 399–400, 476
romantic love and, 476–477, 478
serial monogamy, 106
sources of marital instability, 479–480
trial marriage, 477–478
Mass culture, 545
Mass media. *See* Communications media; Newspapers; Radio; Television
Mass publics, 305, 307–308
Mass society, theories of, 300
Masses, 292
Master statuses, 82–83
Mate selection. *See also* Marriage
  endogamy/exogamy, 474–475
  homogamy, 475–476
  norms of, 474–476
  romantic love and, 476–477
Material culture, 95
Mean, 177
Mechanized cities, 133
Media. *See* Communications media; Newspapers; Radio; Television
Median, 177
Medical profession, 203–204, 583, 648
Medical sociology, 647–648
Medical technology. *See also* Health
  health insurance and, 647
  history of, 643–644
  hospitals, 646–647
  hypertrophy in health care, 647
  infant mortality rates, 645
  medical sociology, 647–648
Megalopolis, 138–139
Melting pot, 402–403
Men. *See also* Gender stratification
  body image of, 180–181
  education of, 530–531
  emotions of, 183–184
  in feudal societies, 437–438
  friendship groups, 220–221
  gender roles of, 432–436
  gender socialization of, 180–182
  in industrial societies, 438–439
  leisure and, 310
  role in the family, 330
  sex ratios and, 427–429
Mental illness, 271–272
Mercantilism, 567
Mesomorphs, 264
"Metropolis and Mental Life" (Simmel), 140
Metropolitan areas, 131, 137–139. *See also* Cities; Standard metropolitan statistical area (SMSA)
Metropolitan district, 130
Mexican Americans. *See* Hispanics
Mexico, 430, 559–560

Micro-level of social change, 319-320
Micro-level sociology, 8-9, 10
Middle classes, 366, 367, 368-369, 607-608
Middle-level of social change, 320
Middle-level sociology, 9, 10
Middletown community studies, 114-115, 359, 360-361, 448
Middletown in Transition, 114-115
Middletown, (Lynd and Lynd), 114, 359, 360-361
Migration of populations, 85-86, 129, 182
Military institutions. *See also* War; names of specific wars
  civilian control of, 614
  after Cold War, 574-575, 576
  communications media and, 544
  defense costs, 323, 324
  economic role of, 614-616
  history of, 614
  industrial-military complex, 606
  in Latin America, 613-614
  military socialization, 616
  primary groups in the Army, 213
  social change and, 617-618
  war and social institutions, 323
  women in, 617, 618
Millenarian movement, 295
Minority groups, definition of, 393. *See also* Racial and ethnic groups
Mobility. *See* Social mobility
Mode, 177
Modernization
  changes associated with, 324-325
  compared with nonmodernized societies, 325, 326
  definition of, 304, 323
  dependency and, 328-329
  in developing nations, 325-328
  individual and, 329
  religion and, 327-328
Modernizing nations. *See* Developing nations
"Mommy track," 82
Monogamy, serial, 106
Monotheism, 502-503
Moral development, theories of, 173
Moral Majority, 328, 515-516
Mores, 98
Multidimensional view of society, 20-22
Multinational corporations, 565
Multiple-nuclei model of urban growth, 137
Murray v. *Curlett*, 516
Mutual attraction and complementary needs, 476
Myth of Marginality, The (Perlman), 154

Nation at Risk, A (National Commission on Excellence in Education), 533
Nation-states, 83-85, 598, 604
National census, 42-43
National Environmental Policy Act, 641
Native Americans
  accommodation and, 112

and Columbus's discovery of America, 93-94, 104, 106, 108
  expulsion of, 396
  genocide of, 395
  Huichol Indians, 498-499
  lanuage of Hopi Indians, 105
  as pariah group, 357, 359
  personal accounts of, 5-6
  population of, 417
  Red Power movement, 120
  religion of, 498-499, 502
  tribalism of, 407
  urban Indians, 120-121
Nature versus nurture
  behaviorism, 162-164
  emotions and, 183-184
  feral children, 164
  need for love, 164-167
  Robbers Cave experiment, 165-168
  socialization and, 160
Nazis, 212, 213, 216, 288, 299, 392, 396, 605
Networks, 195-196
New Guinea tribe, 394-395
New Rules (Yankelovich), 115-116
News media. *See* Communications media; Newspapers; Radio; Television
Newspapers, 546, 547-548. *See also* Communications media
Nigeria, Ibo in, 84
1984 (Orwell), 548
Nobel prize, 631, 632
Nonterritorial community, 195
Normative order, 97-100
Norms
  definition of, 96
  as dimension of culture, 95-96
  of science, 633-634
  traditioanl norms, 214
Nuclear accidents, 302-303, 636, 637, 643, 648
Nuclear energy, 642-643, 653-654
Nuclear family, 106-107, 464-465
Nudity, 291

Objective classes, 240
Objective method, 364
Observation methods of research, 38-40
Occupational prestige, 356, 358
Occupations. *See* Careers; Employment; Professions
Oil resources, 642
Oil spills, 309
Older people. *See* Age and aging; Age stratification
Oligarchy, 605
Olympics, 100-101
One-party systems, 606-607
Open questions, 46
Open societies, 78, 225
Operant conditioning, 163
Opinion leaders, 197, 549
Opinion polls, 44-48
Organization, in groups, 70-72
Organization Man, The (Whyte), 484
Organizations. *See also* Corporations

  formal organizations, 208-209
  informal organizations, 208
  voluntary associations, 209, 301
Organized crime, 263-264, 267-268, 269
Oriental exclusion movement, 396-397
Out-groups, 196

Panel study, 48
Paradigm, 630
Pariah groups, 357, 359
Parliamentary system, 606
Participant observation, 38-39
Partisanship, 620
Pastoral societies, 76
Patronage, 606-607
Peace Corps, 213-214
"Peace dividend," 574-575, 576
Pedestrian cities, 133
Peer groups, as agent of socialization, 179, 188
People's Temple, 216, 295, 509
Percent analysis of data, 50-52
Peripheral areas, 328
Perry preschool study, 536-538
Personality. *See also* Individuals
  culture and the self, 170
  Erikson's theory of development, 172
  Freud's theory of, 168-169
  interactionist models of the self, 169-171
  moral development and, 173
  role taking, 170-171
  social person versus economic person, 202-203
  socialization and, 168-173
Petit bourgeoisie, 251, 369
Philadelphia Negro, The (DuBois), 602
Plague, 643
Plea bargaining, 277
Pleasure principle in group interaction, 199-200
Plessy v. *Ferguson*, 399
Pluralist model, of democracy, 607, 610-611
Pluralistic society, 403
Poles, 404, 405, 407
Political advertising, 548, 549
Political culture, 597
Political ecology of states and territories, 598, 600-602
Political machines, 606-607
Political participation, 602
Political parties, 605. *See also* names of specific parties
Political revolutions, 296
Political-economic ideologies
  after Cold War, 571-575
  democratic socialism, 570
  laissez-faire capitalism, 567-568
  mercantilism, 567
  socialism, 568-570
  welfare capitalism, 570-571
Politics and political institutions
  chronology of newly independent nations, 604

citizenship and political participation, 601–603
communications media and, 548, 549, 612–613
crisis of legitimacy, 597
definition of political institutions, 595
democratic political systems, 606–607
institutions for maintaining order, 605–606
legitimacy and authority, 596
in modern societies, 603–607
nature of, 594–599
one-party systems, 606–607
participation in local politics, 602–603
perspectives on, 607–613
pluralist model, 607, 610–611
political culture, 597
political ecology of states and territories, 598, 600–602
power, authority and, 594–596
power elite model, 607, 608–610
rational administration of nations, 603, 605
social class and, 366–367
social interaction and, 611–613
states and borders, 600–601
structural perspectives of democracy, 607–608
voting behavior in the United States, 618–620
Politics (Aristotle), 611
Polls, opinion, 44–48
Pollution, 627, 649–650
Polytheism, 502
Poor. *See* Poverty
Population
decline due to disease, 643
decline due to war, 321
demographic transition, 126–128
growth of, 72–74, 128, 130
long-term trends in England and Wales, 644
Malthusian population theory, 125
migration of, 85–86, 129, 182
population explosion, 124–130
rates of population change, 125–126
urbanization and, 128, 130
Population explosion, 124–130
Population pyramids, 429–431
Populations and societies. *See* Societies
Post-traumatic shock disorder, 322
Postindustrial society, 572–574
Poverty
of black families, 486–488
community studies of, 37
correlations involving, 53
demographic studies of, 37
favelas in Brazil, 154–155
feminization of, 374
gangs and, 279
geographic distribution of, 374
health and, 366
politics and, 366–367
"positive" functions of, 376
power structure and, 38
research on, 380–382
single-parent family and, 469–470

social class and, 371–375
welfare recipients, 33–34
working poor, 366, 371, 373
Power
conflict theory and, 19–20
definition of, 235–236
politics and, 595
social stratification and, 235–237
welfare system and, 38
Power elite, 367–368
Power elite model, of democracy, 607, 608–610
Power Elite, The (Mills), 610
Power structure, 610
Pregnancy. *See* Teenage pregnancy
Preindustrial cities, 132, 133
Prejudice, 405–406
Premarital intercourse, 114
Presidential elections, 618–620
Primary deviance, 273
Primary groups, 81, 193–194, 212–213
Primary socialization, 160
Primate language, 104–105
Primogeniture, 129
Prince, The (Machiavelli), 611–612
"Prison" research, 215–216
Prisons, 161, 255, 277–278
Privacy, right of, 49
Private property, 568, 571
Profane, 497
Professions, 203–204, 582–583, 583, 648
Prohibition of alcoholic beverages, 267, 515
Projection, 409
Proletariat, 239, 268
Prostitution, AIDS and, 54–56
Protestant Ethic and the Spirit of Capitalism, The (Weber), 97, 506
Protestantism, 97, 500–501, 506, 510, 511–513, 514, 522–523
Psychic overload, 140
Public opinion, 308–309
Publication of scientific findings, 633
Puerto Ricans, 407, 415, 417
Pure science, 628
Pursuit of the Millenium, The (Cohen), 294–295

QUASAR project, 534–535
Quebecois, 403
Questionnaires, 46

Race, as social concept, 391
Racial and ethnic groups. *See also* Blacks; Hispanics; Jews; Native Americans; and names of other ethnic and racial groups
affirmative action and, 408
Anglo-conformity and, 401–402
assimilation and, 111–112, 399–401
authoritarian personality and, 409
conflict theories of racial inequality, 410–412
cultural pluralism, 403
culture and intergroup relations, 404–408

ecological theories of racial inequality, 412–413
education of, 528
equality for, 330–332
ethnic and racial nationalism, 406–407
European immigrants compared with blacks, 414–416
expulsion of, 396–397
frustration-aggression hypothesis of racial inequality, 408–409
functionalist theories of racial inequality, 410
genocide of, 394–396
interactionist theories of racial inequality, 409–410
intergroup relations and, 394–403
internal colonialism of, 411–412
meaning of race and ethnicity, 390–393
melting pot and, 402–403
prejudice and discrimination against, 405–406
projection and, 409
race as social concept, 391
segregation of, 398–399
slavery of, 397–398
social-psychological theories of racial inequality, 408–409
stereotypes of, 404–405
theories of racial and ethnic inequality, 408–414
in urban communities, 141–142, 144, 147–148
in working class, 370–371
Racial conflict, in cities, 147–148
Racial nationalism, 406–407
Racial purity, 392
Racism, 392–393, 403
Radio, 307, 546. *See also* Communications media
Ragged Dick (Alger), 232
Random sampling, 45
Rate of reproductive change, 126
Rational choice model, 16–17
Rational motives, 214
Rationality principle in group interaction, 200
Reactionary movements, 294
Recidivism, 275
Reciprocity principle in group interaction, 200–201
Recreation. *See* Leisure
Recruitment through differential association, 270–271
Red Power movement, 120
Redevelopment, 146–147
Reference groups, 196–197
Reformist movements, 294
Regulating the Poor (Piven and Cloward), 38
Relative deprivation, 201, 296–297
Religion
abstract ideals, 503
animism, 502
automobiles and, 643
black church in America, 510
change in, 509–510

Religion, *continued*
church attendance and, 513–514
churches and sects, 507–508
civil religion, 504–505
cults, 508–509
definition of, 496–497
denominations, 508
forms of religious expression, 522–523
fundamentalism, 97, 328, 497, 515–516
ideology and, 232–233
major world religions, 500–501
Marxian view of, 495, 504–505, 506
modernization and, 327–328
of Native Americans, 498–499
power of faith, 497–498
religiosity, 513–514
religious organizations and free riders, 514–515
religious pluralsim, 514
rituals and, 497
secularization and its limits, 498–500
"separation of church and state," 516
simple supernaturalism, 501–502
social change and, 505–507, 517–518
in Soviet Union, 495, 500–501, 506
structure of, 507–509
television preachers, 495–496
theism, 502–503
trends in the United States, 511–516
unofficial religion, 513
varieties of religious belief, 501–505
Weber's view of, 506
Religiosity, 513–514
Representative system, 606
Republican party, 367, 602, 603, 606, 619, 620
Research
analysis of data, 49–53
ethics in, 48–49
experiments, 40–42
hypothesis in, 35–36
methods of, 38–49
observation methods, 38–40
social-class membership, 364–365
steps in, 34–38
survey research, 42–49
theories and perspectives, 53–54
variables in, 36
Resistance, 112
Resource mobilization theory, 301–303
Restaurants, 65–66, 308, 386–387
Retirement, 439, 445, 449–450
Revolution, Age of, 11
Revolution, theories of, 296–297
Revolutionary movements, 294
Right Stuff, The (Wolfe), 616
Right to die, 648
Rights of citizenship, 601–602
Riots, 287–288
Rites of passage, 427
Rituals, 497, 522–523
Robbers Cave experiment, 165–168, 410
Robert's Rules of Order, 208
Role conflict, 81–82
Role expectations, 70
Role strain, 81, 82

Role taking, 170–171, 181
Roles
in conflict, 81–82
definition of, 70
as element in social structure, 70
Romantic love, 476–477, 478
Romeo and Juliet (Shakespeare), 476
Rural areas, 148, 228–230, 375
Rural-urban migration, 85, 129, 182
Russian Revolution, 482, 484, 495, 570. *See also* Bolsheviks; Soviet Union

Sacred, 497
Salem witch hunt, 256, 292
Sample, 45
Sample bias, 45–46
Sample surveys, 43
Sampling error, 46
Sanctions, 98
Scandals in government, 253–254, 255
Scapegoat, 408–409
Schools. *See* Education
Science. *See also* Technology
applied science, 628
common ownership of, 633–634
definition of, 628
disinterestedness of, 634
Gaia hypothesis, 629
history of, 11, 636–637
institutional approach to, 630–633
interactionist approach to, 630
nature of, 628–629
Nobel prize in, 631, 632
norms of, 633–634
publication of findings, 633
pure science, 628
sociology of, 630–633
universalism of, 633
Scientific management, 580
Scientific method, 11
Scientific revolutions, 630
Second Sex, The (de Beauvoir), 447
Secondary analysis, 46–48
Secondary deviance, 273
Secondary groups, 81, 194
Secondary socialization, 160
Sector theory of urban growth, 137
Sects, 508, 509
Secular humanism, 97
Secularization, 498–500, 516
Segregation, 147–148, 362, 363, 398–399, 400–401, 541
Self. *See* Personality
Semiperipheral areas, 328
"Separate but equal" doctrine, 399, 408
"Separation of church and state, " 516
Serial monogamy, 106
SES. *See* Socioeconomic status (SES)
Sex, definition of, 180
Sex ratios, 427–429
Sex roles. *See* Gender roles; Gender socialization; Gender stratification
Sexism, 439–441, 456–457
Sexual abuse of children, 483
Sexual mores, 114, 116, 174–175, 442, 464
Sharecropping, 328–329

Siane tribe, 394–395
Significant others, 170–171
Simple supernaturalism, 501–502
Single-parent family, 469–470, 482, 486–488
Sinhalese, 396
Sir Lanka, 396
Slavery, 397–398
Smoking. *See* Cigarette smoking
Social category, 193
Social change
in Africa, 317–318, 319
art and, 345–349
changes in American culture, 113–116
cities and, 145–148
civilizations and cultural change, 107–113
conflict models of, 337
culture and, 100–101
cyclical theories of, 336–337
definition of, 318
endogenous forces for, 318
environmental politics and policies, 332–334
in everyday life, 329–333
evolutionary models of, 335–336
exogenous forces for, 318
functionalist models of, 337–338
gender roles and the family, 330
macro level of, 320
meanings of, 318–320
micro level of, 319–320
middle level of, 320
military institutions and, 617–618
models of change, 333, 335–338
modernization and, 323–329
race relations, 330–332
religion and, 505–507, 517–518
socialization and, 182
students and, 556–557
technology and, 640–641
telecommunications and, 339–340
war and conquest, 320–323
Social classes. *See* Classes
Social conditions, 6–7
Social construction of the self, 160–161
Social control, 97, 255, 273–280
Social Darwinism, 101–102
Social environment, 8
Social evolution, 335–336
Social groups, 193. *See also* Groups
Social inequality. *See* Inequality
Social institutions. *See* Institutions
Social interaction and politics, 611–613
Social Life of Small Urban Spaces, The (Whyte), 40
Social mobility
among males in Western countries, 241, 242
of blacks, 416
caste and class and, 225–227
education and, 378, 534–535
inequality and, 377–378
intergenerational mobility, 241
intragenerational mobility, 241
spatial mobility, 231
structural mobility, 230–231

two-paycheck family and, 379–380
Weberian view of, 240–241
Social movements. *See also* Collective
    behavior
  charisma and, 297–298, 300
  civil rights movement, 389–390, 407,
    448
  conservative movements, 294
  corporations and, 579–580
  definition of, 290
  dimensions of, 294–295
  among the elderly, 449–450
  in everyday life, 301–303
  expressive social movements, 294–295
  reactionary movements, 294
  reformist movements, 294
  resource mobilization theory, 301–303
  revolutionary movements, 294
  social movement theory, 295–303
  student protest movement, 544,
    566–567
  theories of mass society, 300
  theories of revolution, 296–297
  women's movement, 447–449
Social network analysis, 197–199
Social order, 66–72
Social person versus economic person,
  202–203
Social research. *See* Research
Social revolutions, 296
Social stratification
  caste, class, and social mobility,
    225–227
  class consciousness and class conflict,
    238–240
  conflict theories of, 241–243
  culture and, 231–234
  deference and, 233–234
  definition of, 78, 145–146, 225
  demeanor and, 234–235
  ethnic stratification, 402
  French Revolution and, 234–236
  functionalist view of, 243–244
  historical development of, 78
  Industrial Revolution and, 237–238
  in industrial societies, 230–231
  interactionist perspective of, 244
  life chances, 227–228
  and means of existence, 228–231
  micro level of, 233–234
  in modern era, 237–241
  power and authority and, 234–236
  role of ideology in, 231–233
  in rural villages, 228–230
  social mobility and, 240–241
  in Soviet Union, 223–224, 250–251
  theories of, 241–244
  in United States, 225
  world economic system and, 245–246
Social structure
  definition of, 67
  elements of, 67–72
  of extended family, 68
  groups, 67–68
  organization in groups, 70–72
  roles and role expectations, 70
  society and, 67

statuses, 68–70
Social surveys, 13, 14
Social-psychological theories of racial
  inequality, 408–409
Socialism, 240, 298, 568–570
Socialism, democratic, 570
Socialization
  adult socialization, 160
  agents of, 161–162, 178–180, 188
  anticipatory socialization, 178, 188
  behaviorism and, 162–164
  community and, 179
  culture and the self, 170
  definition of, 160
  emotions and, 183–184
  Erikson's theory of development, 172
  failures of, 162
  family and, 178–179
  feral children, 164
  Freud's theory of personality,
    168–169
  gender socialization, 180–184
  human evironments and, 173–178
  interactionist models of the self,
    169–171
  mass media and, 179–180
  micro-environment of, 175–176, 177
  military socialization, 616
  moral development and, 173
  nature versus nurture, 160, 162–168
  need for love, 164–165
  peer groups and, 179, 188
  personality and, 168–173
  primary socialization, 160
  Robbers Cave experiment, 165–168
  role taking, 170–171
  schools and, 179
  secondary socialization, 160
  social change and, 182
  social construction of the self,
    160–161
  social environments and, 161
  television and, 180
  through interaction, 188–189
Societies
  aging societies, 451–452
  agrarian revolution, 76–77
  agrarian societies, 562–563
  definition of, 67, 95
  feudal societies, 91, 234, 237,
    437–438, 567
  first-large-scale societies, 77–78
  groups in complex societies, 213–214
  growth of population, 72–74
  history of, 72–80
  hunting-gathering societies, 68,
    74–76, 90, 106–107, 182, 562–563
  individuals and, 81–82
  Industrial Revolution, 78–80
  modernized compared with
    nonmodernized societies, 228–231,
    325, 326
  and nation-states, 83–85
  open versus closed societies, 78, 225
  postindustrial society, 572–574
  social structure and, 67
  stratification of, 78, 228–231

urban societies, 132–135
Sociobiology, 102–104
Socioeconomic status (SES), 364–365
Sociological imagination, 6–7
Sociology. *See also* Research; Visual
  sociology
  careers in, 22
  conflict theory perspective of, 18–20
  definition of, 8
  functionalist perspective of, 18
  historical development of, 9–15
  interactionist perspective of, 16
  levels of social reality, 8–9, 10
  macro level of, 9, 10
  major sociological perspectives, 15–22
  micro level of, 8–9, 10
  middle level of, 9, 10
  multidimensional view of society,
    20–22
  rational choice perspective of, 16–17
  social environment, 8
  symbolic interactionist perspective of,
    17–18
Solar energy, 642
"Some American Families at Dinner"
  (Lewis and Feiring), 175–176, 177
South Africa
  apartheid in, 225, 399, 410, 411,
    422–423, 556, 599
  Baaskop in, 412
  protest in, 257–258, 599
Soviet Union. *See also* Russia
  age stratification in, 442
  civil religion of, 504–505
  Communist party in, 213
  economics of, 569–570, 571
  education in, 179
  fatalities from World War II, 321
  glasnost in, 223–224, 231
  miners' strikes in, 231
  population of, 429
  religion in, 495, 500–501, 506
  science in, 633
  social stratification in, 223–224, 243,
    250–251
  Stalinist regime in, 605
  technological achievements of, 529
Spatial mobility, 231
Sports, 101, 171, 309–310, 322–323,
  445, 550
Spouse abuse, 260, 440–441
Standard metropolitan statistical area
  (SMSA), 130–131
State, definition of, 83
Statistics, 177, 632
Status conflict, in cities, 146–147
Status groups, 226–227
Status symbols, 233
Statuses
  achieved status, 82, 225
  ascribed status, 82, 225
  as element of social structure, 68–70
  master statuses, 82–83
Steel industry, 353–354
Stereotypes, 404–405, 409
Sterilization, 392
Stigma, 258–259

Stratification. *See* Social stratification
Street Corner Society (Whyte), 195-196
Strikes, 291, 292
Structural mobility, 230-231
Structural perspectives of democracy, 607-608
Structure of Scientific Revolutions, The (Kuhn), 630
Student protest movement, 544, 566-567
Students. *See* Education
Subcultures. *See also* Racial and ethnic groups
  assimilation and, 111-112
  deviant subcultures, 262-264
  of urban community, 141-145
Subjective classes, 240
Subjective method, 364
Suburbs, 144-145, 147, 369
Sugar production, 229
Suicide, 35-36
Superego, 168-169
Supernaturalism, simple, 501-502
Survey research
  bias in survey questions, 47
  closed versus open questions, 46
  national census, 42-43
  opinion polls, 44-48
  questionnaire design for, 46, 47
  sample bias in, 45-46
  sampling error in, 46
  sampling techniques, 45-46
  secondary analysis of, 46-48
Survivor guilt, 322
Sweden, 242, 429
Symbolic interactionism, 17-18
Synanon, 216

Tables, reading of, 49-50
Tamils, 396
Taxation, 600
Taylorism, 580
Technological dualism, 635-637, 639
Technology. *See also* Science
  definition of, 97, 628
  diffusion of, 551-552
  as dimension of culture, 97
  dimensions of, 635
  economic booms and, 641
  electronic classroom, 551-552
  environmental stress, 649-650
  in everyday life, 643
  high technology, 638
  history of, 74
  impact of, 648-650
  mass communications technology, 549-550
  medical technology, 643-648
  modernization and, 324
  nature of, 628-629
  quest for energy, 642-643
  social change and, 640-641
  technological dualism, 635-637, 639
  technological systems, 648-649
  telecommunications, 339-340
  worker responses to high technology, 638

world economic system and, 564
Technology assessment, 641
Teenage pregnancy, 41, 174-175, 486-488
Telecommunications, 97, 339-340. *See also* Communications media
Television. *See also* Communications media
  as agent of socialization, 180
  cable television, 548-549
  hours per week of viewing, 545-546
  political advertising on, 548, 549
  political coverage on, 612-613
  religious programs on, 495-496
  sports on, 550
  violence and, 546-547
Tempest, The (Shakespeare), 333
Territorial community, 195
"Territories of the Self" (Goffman), 8-9, 10
Theism, 502-503
Theoretical perspectives, 54
Theories, 53-54
Third world, 325-326. *See also* Developing nations
Three Mile Island accident, 302-303, 636, 637, 643, 648
Tiv society, 546-565
Tobacco. *See* Cigarette smoking
Total institutions, 277-278, 527
Totalitarianism, 298, 605
Traditional motives, 214
Triads, 194-195
Trial marriage, 477-478
Turks, 396
Two-step flow of communication, 549
Typologies, definition of, 98
Typology of norms, 98-99

Underdevelopment, 567
Unemployment. *See* Employment
Unification church, 216, 508
Unions. *See* Labor movement
United Nations, 600-601
Universalism of science, 633
Universities. *See* Higher education
Unobtrusive measures, 39-40
Unofficial religion, 513
Upper classes, 366, 367-368
Upward mobility, 225, 241, 242, 377
Urban communities, 139-145
Urban planning, 149-150
Urban renewal, 146
Urban revolution, 131-132
Urban Villagers, The (Gans), 142, 144
"Urbanism as a Way of Life" (Wirth), 140
Urbanization. *See also* Cities
  definition of, 128
  definition of metropolitan areas, 130-131
  growth of cities, 130-135
  modernization and, 324
  population growth and, 128, 130
  rural-urban migration, 85, 129
  type of government and, 609
  urban revolution, 131-132

urban societies, 132-135
Urbanized area, 130
Utilitarianism, 16

Values
  definition of, 96
  deviance and changing values, 260-262
  as dimension of culture, 95, 96-97
Variables, 36
Victimization, 275
Videocassette equipment, 549
Vietnam War, 321
Villages. *See* Rural areas
Violence
  against women, 260, 440-441
  in cities, 141, 204-205
  crimes of, 260, 261
  on television, 546-547
Visual sociology
  art, 26-31, 345-349
  depression in steel mill communities, 590-591
  diet and social class, 386-387
  elections, 624-625
  environmental concern, 653-654
  extended family, 492-493
  favelas in Brazil, 154-155
  forms of religious expression, 522-523
  friendship groups, 220-221
  hobos, 284-285
  as research method, 39-40
  sexism, 456-457
  socialization through interaction, 188-189
  stratification in the United States and Soviet Union, 250-251
  students and social change, 556-557
  urban "combat zone," 60-61
  urban Indians, 120-121
Voluntary associations, 209, 301
Voting behavior in the United States, 618-620

Walden II (Skinner), 163
War. *See also* Military institutions; and names of specific wars
  cultural impact of, 321-323
  ecological impact of, 321
  fatalities from, 321
  social change and, 320-323
  social institutions and, 323, 324
War of the Worlds, The (Wells), 307
WASPs, 404
Wealth of Nations, The (Smith), 568
Weathermen, 216
Welfare, 33-34, 37, 38, 41, 53, 330, 380-382, 487-488
Welfare capitalism, 570-571
West Africa, 546-565
White collar crime, 270, 271
"White Collar Criminality" (Sutherland), 270
White flight, 147, 541
Witch hunt, 256, 292
Wobblies, 305

Women. *See also* Gender stratification;
  Single-parent family
  as athletes, 101, 445
  body image of, 180-181
  education of, 530-531
  emotions and, 183-184
  employment of, 82, 91, 183-184, 379,
    433, 436, 439, 446-447, 448
  in feudal societies, 437-438
  friendship groups, 220-221
  gender roles of, 432-436
  gender socialization of, 180-182
  health of, 431-432
  in India, 227
  in industrial societies, 438-439
  leisure and, 310
  in the military, 617, 618
  professional versus working-class
    women, 446-447
  role in the family, 330
  sex ratios and, 427-429
  sexism against, 439-441, 456-457
  terminology in referring to, 235
  violence against, 260, 440-441
Women and Love (Hite), 46
Women-headed families. *See* Single-
  parent family
Women's movement, 447-449
Work. *See* Employment; Workplace
Working class
  health and, 366
  Marxian view of, 238-243, 268
  politics and, 366-367
  women in, 446-447
Working poor, 366, 371, 373
Workplace. *See also* Employment
  alienation in, 578
  conflict in, 581-582
  Hawthorne experiment in, 41-42,
    202, 207
  human relations in industry, 580-581
  individuals and corporations, 579-580
  Japanese factories, 577
  in modern society, 91
  "mommy track" in, 82
  professions, 582-583
  restaurant industry, 65-66
  sociological perspectives on, 580-583
  United States industry, 577-578
  work and careers in the 1990s,
    584-586
  worker responses to high technology,
    638
World economic system, 563-565
World system theory, 328
World War I, 321
World War II, 321, 323, 396, 397, 448,
  598, 633

Yankee City, 359-361, 362

Zionism, 407, 600